HANDBOOK OF RESEARCH ON NEW LITERACIES

HANDBOOK OF RESEARCH ON NEW LITERACIES

EDITED BY

JULIE COIRO
MICHELE KNOBEL
COLIN LANKSHEAR
DONALD J. LEU

 Lawrence Erlbaum Associates
Taylor & Francis Group

New York   London

Lawrence Erlbaum Associates
Taylor & Francis Group
270 Madison Avenue
New York, NY 10016

Lawrence Erlbaum Associates
Taylor & Francis Group
2 Park Square
Milton Park, Abingdon
Oxon OX14 4RN

Printed in the United States of America on acid-free paper
10 9 8 7 6 5 4 3 2 1

International Standard Book Number-13: 978-0-8058-5652-1 (Softcover) 978-0-8058-5651-4 (Hardcover)

Library of Congress Cataloging-in-Publication Data

Handbook of research on new literacies / editors, Julie Coiro ... [et al.].
      p. cm.
   ISBN 978-0-8058-5651-4 (alk. paper) -- ISBN 9780805856521 (pbk.)
   1. Media literacy. 2. Information literacy. 3. Computer literacy. 4. Mass media in education. 5.
Internet in education. 6. Communication in education. I. Coiro, Julie.

LB1043.H328 2008
302.2'244--dc22   2007017594

Visit the Taylor & Francis Web site at
http://www.taylorandfrancis.com

and the LEA and Routledge Web site at
http://www.routledge.com

Contents

Preface

Purpose

During a period when the Internet has deeply altered our literacy lives, the *Handbook of Research on New Literacies* provides a central resource to support the emergence of new literacies research. It brings together leading scholars from around the world to review research in their area, from the perspectives they find to provide the greatest insight, as they study how the Internet and other digital technologies profoundly redefine what it means to be literate. We expect the *Handbook of Research on New Literacies* to provide the central leadership for this newly emerging field, directing scholars to the major issues, theoretical perspectives, and interdisciplinary research on new literacies. The *Handbook* helps us to begin the bold new thinking required to reconceptualize literacy research.

Students of the history of literacy research will recall that reading research attracted a broad collection of researchers, from many disciplines, during the final decades of the 20th century. That intensive, interdisciplinary effort prompted a richer and more complex understanding about the nature of reading and it moved literacy research forward in important new directions. A similar phenomenon may be taking place today with new literacies. As literacy and technology converge on the Internet, many scholars from many different disciplines are moving their research into this arena. They find that the constructs emerging in new literacies research inform their own work in productive ways. At the same time, it is increasingly clear that new literacies research also impacts societies, education systems, and public policies in powerful ways. As a result, educators, policy makers, employers, and the public at large all recognize that these new literacies of the Internet will be central to the most important literacy and learning issues of our generation. We believe it is time to capture the emergence of this new area of research, to inform others, and to begin the construction of an important new area of inquiry. We seek to accomplish all of this with *The Handbook of Research on New Literacies*.

This first volume of the *Handbook* is much more about raising questions than it is about providing answers, though both will be found in abundance within these pages. The *Handbook of Research on New Literacies* provides a single location for reviewing wide-ranging, interdisciplinary research through multiple lenses, and in multiple areas of inquiry, in order to determine the most important issues, problems, and questions that must be studied as the Internet becomes this generation's defining technology for literacy and learning. Such a volume is integral to developing the multifaceted perspective necessary to improve our understanding of literacy in online and other digital spaces.

The ethos of the *Handbook* is to provide conceptual, theoretical, and methodological shape for an emerging field without unduly foreclosing on potentially valuable perspectives and epistemological approaches. Our approach has been to allow leading researchers to collectively define central constructs and central issues through their individual work, not to force a single perspective upon a newly emerging field. We are confident that this is the only sensible approach during the emergence of this important area of inquiry, and it is one that takes full advantage of all perspectives about what new literacies are and how we might best study them.

Finally, the irony of a volume on new literacies research that appears within the pages of a 500-year-old technology is not lost on us. Nor is the irony that changes to literacy happen so quickly that some elements of this change will appear, and go unreported in this handbook, during the time required to publish a hard copy volume of this nature. We expect that economic, technology, and research pressures will eventually remove these revealing ironies; the nature of literacy is changing far faster than some elements of our society can respond, especially those so intrinsically connected to printing-press technologies. Like nearly everything else in literacy, this, too, will change.

Audience

The audience for this volume includes members of the international literacy research community, broadly conceived. This includes scholars from the traditional reading and writing research communities, as well as scholars from information science, library and media studies, cognitive science, educational psychology, psychology, sociolinguistics, linguistics, computer-mediated communication (CMC), computer science, and other related areas that find new online literacies to be an important area of investigation. Graduate students in these disciplines will also find the collection of research reviews to be useful. The final section, where we provide reprints of central studies in this area along with commentaries by leading scholars, reflects a special commitment to our readers who are graduate students. We believe these commentaries will demonstrate the benefit of bringing multiple perspectives to bear on the interpretation of research and show students how leading scholars analyze research methods, results, and interpretations. Finally, given recent interest in data-driven public policies around the world, another important audience for this volume will be policy makers and school administrators who seek summaries of the latest research to inform their own important decisions. We believe the research reviews in this volume will be especially useful to their work.

Authors and Structure

Authors have been selected on the basis of their leadership and/or innovative research in their special area of investigation. Each has a clearly established reputation in his or her research area. We include leaders from around the world in the areas of social semiotics and multimodality, online research methodology, ethnographies of new literacies, multimedia studies, cognition and instruction, blogging research, instant messaging (IM) research, gaming, information science, computer-mediated communication, e-learning and learning management, cultural influences on learning technologies, online navigation, reading comprehension research, child and adolescent literacy studies, qualitative methods, experimental methods, and many other important areas of inquiry that are taking place today.

It is far too early to neatly categorize new literacies research into orthogonal topics, each with clearly defined constructs. As with any newly emerging field, the work can be conceptually messy and inchoate. Thus, we are convinced that the structure of this volume will change in subsequent editions as topics, constructs, and perspectives become much more precisely defined. In this volume, we have tried to permit current work to logically cluster itself into categories.

After an initial chapter by the editors, the next five sections represent the principal areas in which significant developments are occurring at the present time. Part I, *Methodologies*, addresses issues introduced by the broad range of methodologies with which research on new literacies is currently taking place. The sweep of these chapters demonstrates the extensive range of current work, from ethnographic approaches to experimental studies. In Part II, *Knowledge and Inquiry*, the authors introduce a number of different perspectives central to understanding how best to use the informational potential of the Internet and other digital contexts to acquire knowledge. Contributors to Part III, *Communication*, review the latest research occurring in new communication contexts such as blogs, instant messaging, and other social networking tools. Articles in this section also explore the roles that gender and language play during new online literacy practices. Part IV, *Popular Culture, Community, and Citizenship: Everyday Literacies*, addresses research in new literacy spaces such as the online and offline worlds of gaming, anime, manga, and fan fiction, as well as the range of challenges

Acknowledgments

We want to acknowledge the generosity of all our contributing authors. We know the extent to which producing invited work adds to already demanding workloads. It is rarely, if ever, convenient to receive such invitations, let alone to accept and meet their deadlines. For this generosity, we are deeply appreciative. We also want to acknowledge the leadership they provide to this emerging field. Their research, insights, and reviews of the work being conducted in their areas are the driving force behind the rapidly emerging area of new literacies research.

In addition, we wish to thank Naomi Silverman from Lawrence Erlbaum Associates for her unstinting moral and practical support for this project. Naomi encouraged this handbook from the outset, when it first began with Erlbaum, and helped keep us on track at crucial points along the long road to its final production. We also thank Naomi's assistant at Erlbaum, Erika Kika. She made our lives much easier with her careful work. In addition our appreciation goes to Project Editor Michele Dimont and Editorial Assistant Mary Hillemeir at Taylor & Francis for their work at the main stages of production.

Finally, we wish to thank the colleagues commissioned by Erlbaum who each reviewed a focus article in the final section of this volume: James Paul Gee, Susan Goldman, Jim Pellegrino, Peggy N. Van Meter, Carla Firetto, Bob Bleicher, David Reinking, Donna Alvermann, Richard Duran, Catherine Beavis, Colin Harrison, and Jackie Marsh. Their analytic insights and commentaries are excellent models of academic inquiry and scholarship.

The Editors

Julie Coiro, University of Rhode Island, USA
Michele Knobel, Montclair State University, USA
Colin Lankshear, James Cook University, Australia
Donald J. Leu, University of Connecticut, USA

CHAPTER 1

Central Issues in New Literacies and New Literacies Research

JULIE COIRO

UNIVERSITY OF RHODE ISLAND, USA

MICHELE KNOBEL

MONTCLAIR STATE UNIVERSITY, USA

COLIN LANKSHEAR

JAMES COOK UNIVERSITY, AUSTRALIA

DONALD J. LEU

UNIVERSITY OF CONNECTICUT, USA

The Handbook of Research in New Literacies explores an increasingly urgent question for educational research: How do the Internet and other information and communication technologies (ICTs) alter the nature of literacy? The answers are likely to provide some of the most important insights about our literacy lives that we may acquire during this century. The answers will also be some of the hardest to obtain, largely because we currently lack adequate theories, constructs, and methods to match the complexity of the question. This volume begins the important work required to integrate the many insights found in multiple lines of research so that we might explore this question in all of the richness and complexity that it deserves.

We seek to advance the study of new literacies by bringing together, for the first time, research taking place around the world in widely diverse disciplines, with even more diverse theoretical frameworks and still more diverse epistemological approaches. Some might see this diversity as a limitation in establishing a common research base; we see it as a powerful advantage. The richness of these multiple perspectives provides us with the best opportunity to understand fully the many issues associated with the changing nature of literacy. We also see in this understanding the best opportunity to help individuals fully realize their potential as global citizens in the 21st century. Our goal with this volume is to begin constructing a foundation on which to begin the important development of the theories, constructs, and methods that will allow us to more thoughtfully study the new literacies emerging with the Internet and other ICTs.

At the beginning, it is essential to acknowledge that the question framing this volume has not suddenly appeared, independent of previous work. As with any good question, this one has an important evolutionary history that should be recognized to understand both where we started and where we are headed. An early version of the question first emerged when precursors to personal computers forced us to confront the possibility that digital technologies might be as much about literacy as they are about technology (e.g., Atkinson & Hansen, 1966–1967).

Following this initial work, a subsequent explosion of personal computing technologies quickly attracted the interest of scholars and researchers with interests in language and literacy. Philosophers, literary scholars, linguists, educational theorists, and educational researchers, among others, pondered the implications of the shift from page to screen for text composition and comprehension (e.g., Bolter, 1991; Heim, 1987; Landow, 1992). They also considered the potential for linguistic theory and literacy education (e.g., Bruce & Michaels, 1987; Reinking, 1988). Questions were raised about the extent to which new technologies altered certain fundamentals of language and literacy and, if so, in what ways and with what consequences. At the same time, some questioned whether there was really anything new to the literacies required by digital technologies or whether digital technologies had simply become the latest tools to accomplish social practices common through the centuries, including reading and writing (Cohen, 1987; Cuban, 1986; Hodas, 1993). Was there really anything new to literacy when the tools change and we simply read and write text on a screen instead of on paper?

The Internet: Unprecedented Dimensions to Both the Speed
and Scale of Change in the Technologies of Literacy

The Internet, however, has brought unprecedented dimensions to both the speed and the scale of change in the technologies for literacy, forcing us to directly confront the issue of new literacies. No previous technology for literacy has been adopted by so many, in so many different places, in such a short period, and with such profound consequences. No previous technology

Table 1.1 World Internet Usage and Population Statistics Adapted from Internet World Stats (2007)

World Regions	Population (2007 Est.)	Population % of World	Internet Usage, Latest Data	% Population (Penetration)	Usage % of World	Usage Growth 2000–2007
Africa	941,249,130	14.2%	44,234,240	4.7%	3.5%	879.8%
Asia	3,735,439,436	56.5%	461,703,143	12.4%	36.7%	303.9%
Europe	801,821,187	12.1%	343,787,434	42.9%	27.4%	227.1%
Middle East	192,755,045	2.7%	33,510,500	17.4%	2.7%	920.2%
North America	334,659,631	5.1%	237,168,545	70.9%	18.9%	119.4%
Latin America/ Caribbean	569,133,474	8.6%	116,847,600	20.5%	9.3%	546.7%
Oceania/ Australia	33,568,225	0.5%	19,243,921	57.3%	1.5%	152.6%
WORLD TOTAL	6,608,626,128	100.0%	1,256,495,383	19.0%	100.0%	248.1%

for literacy permits the immediate dissemination of even newer technologies of literacy to every person on the Internet by connecting to a single link on a screen. Finally, no previous technology for literacy has provided access to so much information that is so useful, to so many people, in the history of the world. The sudden appearance of a new technology for literacy as powerful as the Internet has required us to look at the issue of new literacies with fresh lenses. The speed and scale of this change has been breathtaking.

Consider, for example, the speed with which usage of the Internet increases. In late 2005, an important global milestone was reached—the one-billionth individual began reading, writing, viewing, and communicating online (de Argaez, 2006; Internet World Stats, 2006). Approximately one sixth of the world's population now accesses the Internet. The growth rate has been exponential, most of it having taken place in just the past 5 years (Internet World Stats, 2006; ClickZ, 2006). If this rate continues, almost half of the world's population will be online by 2012, and Internet access will be nearly ubiquitous sometime thereafter. You can see some of these changes in Table 1.1, which summarizes worldwide Internet usage statistics as of November 30, 2007.[1]

The usage statistics in Table 1.1 are far from evenly distributed by age. In countries for which reliable data are available, regardless of the number

---

[1] These data also perfectly illustrate an important challenge to traditional print technologies thrown down by the Internet: The data in Table 1.1 will have profoundly changed by the time that traditional print technologies, used to produce this handbook, make them available to you. In a world of continual change, speed counts in important ways, and the Internet provides access to the latest data far faster than traditional print technologies could ever hope to accomplish. It is an important advantage that the Internet possesses and one of the reasons that access rates, around the world, increase on an exponential basis and why traditional print technologies are under such pressure.

access to the Internet; defining what might be new about literacy within this technology; and public policy responses. Perhaps the most critical issue, however, is how research should be conceived to advance our understanding of the changes taking place in ways that are most productive.

What is going on in the current conjuncture around changes in technologies, communications, institutions and relationships, economic life, and diverse everyday practices—including education—has clearly generated a massive amount of research in diverse fields interfacing with the changing social practices of literacy brought about by the Internet. As with any newly emerging area of research, multiple theoretical perspectives have begun to appear—some more clearly formulated and others more inchoate. Scholars from numerous disciplines, including cognitive science (Mayer, 2001), socio-linguistics (Cope & Kalantzis, 1999; Gee, 2003; Kress, 2003; Lemke, 1998), cultural anthropology (Markham, 1998; Hine, 2000; Miller & Slater, 2000; Wakeford, 1998), information science (Bilal, 2000; Hirsch, 1999), law (Lessig, 2004), and rhetorical studies (D. Andrews & W. Andrews, 2004; Kastman Breuch, 2002; Starke-Meyerring, 2005), among others, have identified changes to literacy as they explore phenomena in daily life in relation to new technologies relevant to their respective areas of study. As many new heuristics appear, informing this multidisciplinary work, we are gradually seeing a new literacies perspective beginning to emerge. This perspective, meaning many different things to many different people, is still in its initial stages, but it has the potential to become a powerful one, redefining what it means to be literate in the 21st century (e.g., Bruce, 2003; Coiro & Dobler, in press; Kellner, 2000; Kist, 2004; Lankshear & Knobel, 2003, 2006; Leu et al., 2004).

A number of variations of different kinds are readily discerned within the terrain covered by the expansive concept of new literacies addressed in this book. Some of these variations are terminological. Different terms, such as *21st century literacies, Internet literacies, digital literacies, new media literacies, multiliteracies, information literacy, ICT literacies, computer literacy,* and so forth, are used to refer to phenomena we would see as falling broadly under a new literacies umbrella.

Other variations are more substantially conceptual and theoretical in nature. The space of new literacies is highly contested. Some authors conceive new literacies as new social practices and conceptions of reading and writing (Street, 1998) emerging with new technologies. Some see new literacies as important new strategies and dispositions required by the Internet (Leu et al., 2004). Others see new literacies as new discourses (Gee, 2003) or in terms of new semiotic contexts (Kress, 2003; Lemke, 2002) made possible by new technologies. Still others see literacy as differentiating into multiliteracies (The New London Group, 1996) or multimodal contexts (Hull & Schultz, 2002), and some see a construct that juxtaposes several of these orientations (Lankshear & Knobel, 2003, 2006).

At the level of definitions, these differences support significantly different conceptions of new literacies. Some stress epistemic values concerned with producing and evaluating knowledge and information pertinent to our personal, civic, and professional lives. In this vein, Leu et. al. (2004) conceived of new literacies as allowing individuals to "use the Internet and other ICTs to identify important questions, locate information, critically evaluate the usefulness of that information, synthesize information to answer those questions, and then communicate the answers to others" (p. 1570), along with 10 principles that define acquisition and developmental processes. Varis' (2000) account of new literacies comprised the integration of several specific literacies: technology and information literacy, media creativity, global literacy, and literacy with responsibility. This account endorses the epistemic values, emphasizes capacity for successful, cross-cultural interaction and collaboration, and manages the social consequences of media with respect to safety, privacy, and so forth.

Other definitions attend more to producing and exchanging meanings by means of encoding and decoding symbols mediated by some technology. Gee (2007), for example, identified video gaming as a new literacy in virtue of the ways game design involves a multimodal code comprising images, actions, words, sounds, and movements that players interpret according to gaming conventions. Since players of real-time strategy games read a map as signifying a land mass that they can build on in recognized ways in competition with other builders, they can participate in the game as a form of social practice, build identities as particular kinds of strategists, and so forth. Video games use new and evolving digital technologies to generate the symbols used in encoding and decoding the meanings that constitute the game.

Some definitions foreground political aspects of representations and discourses in addition to epistemic and meaning-oriented aspects. Kellner (2000), for example, construed new literacies as involving new forms of media literacy, computer literacy, and multimedia literacies whose dimensions include means for enabling "students, teachers, and citizens to discern the nature and effects of media culture," for analyzing media culture "as products of social … struggle," and for stressing "the importance of learning to use the media as modes of self-expression and social activism" (pp. 250–251).

Approaches to new literacies reflect a wide range of specific theoretical preferences and, more generally, theoretical perspectives. For example, research focusing on multimodality as a key feature of new media texts draws heavily on theory from systemic functional linguistics (a variant of sociolinguistics) and discourse theory to develop a social semiotics for analyzing meanings. Approaches concerned with the politics of new literacies—including issues of digital divides or access and equity—often invoke variants of critical theory, but may cast their nets more widely into quite specialized domains such as branches of mathematics concerned with power law distributions (Shirky, 2003). Other foci involve recourse to sociotechnical theory, theories of the social construction of space and time, various kinds of network theories, elements of postcolonial theory, feminist theory, theories of media, informatics, communications theories, hermeneutics, and theories of culture, among many others.

Such variations reflect in turn different emphases at the level of ideals, values, purposes, and projects or "agendas." Priorities and purposes that are evident in work across the spectrum covered by "new literacies" range across such diverse areas as promoting social justice and equity, enhancing cross cultural efficacy, lifting economic productivity, improving formal instruction, building active and informed citizenship, encouraging Internet safety and respect for property rights, and equipping Internet users to discern the quality of information and to use new technologies to present their point of view.

Notwithstanding the conceptual and theoretical richness and diversity that characterizes the field of new literacies theory and research as it has developed to date, and the important insights this work affords, we believe that there are two important limitations in extant approaches to developing a new literacies perspective. First, they do not make Internet technologies, and the social practices that they enable, central to their perspective and build out from there. Rather, they bring theoretical perspectives that have been developed previously from other contexts, and they import them to the new technologies and new literacies landscape. We believe that the new literacies of the Internet are sufficiently distinctive that they require their own theoretical framework—one that is grounded in the social practices of the new literacies of the Internet and other ICT and the contexts and conditions under which these social practices occur, develop, and evolve—in order to adequately understand them. Rather than imposing theoretical perspectives grounded in other contexts, the Internet needs to be respected as a unique context for literacy and used to build its own theoretical foundation. The fact that these new literacies are continuously changing adds further support to this argument.

Second, theoretical orientations toward new literacies typically reflect a single tradition of inquiry: for example, sociolinguistics, psycholinguistics, cognitive theory, sociocultural theory, and sometimes even a single theoretical perspective within that tradition. So far as developing viable approaches to teaching and learning issues within formal settings are concerned, we believe that any adequate theory of new literacies, and the research approaches that collectively contribute to theory development, must bring multiple perspectives to bear on framing the universe of new literacies. Research questions on the new literacies of the Internet and other digital technologies take place in contexts that are far too complex and rich for any single perspective to account for all that is taking place. We believe that to understand these new literacies will collectively require us to bring multiple sets of perspectives to research on new literacies. Multiple realities (Labbo & Reinking, 1999) will need to be recognized before we are fully able to understand what new literacies are, how they come to be, and how they evolve and develop.

Where do we begin? Looking across the tremendously varied terrain in new literacies research, in work as diverse as ethnographies of cyberspace (e.g., Wittel, 2000), computer-mediated communication (e.g., Kelsey & St. Amant, in press), second language research (e.g., Blake, 2000), reading research (e.g., Coiro & Dobler, in press), communications studies (e.g., Castells, 1996; Snyder, 2001), media literacy (e.g., Livingstone, 2002; Livingstone & Bober, 2005), studies of hypertext (e.g., Burbules, 1997; Mayer, 2001; Kellner, 2000), philosophy of technology (e.g., Hickman, 2001), language learning studies (e.g., Lam, 2004), literacy research (e.g., R. Andrews, 2004), informatics (e.g., Levy et al., 2003), educational technology (e.g., Jonassen, 2003), problem-based learning (e.g., Lee & Kim, 2005) and many others, suggests that a narrow definition of new literacies will likely close us off to much of the energy and the rich and complex insights beginning to take place. On the other hand, failing to define, at least in general terms, what we mean by "new literacies research" will perpetuate unconnected lines of research and a far less productive approach. Similar to what has taken place in the open source development movement, we believe that we should seek an approach similar to what von Hippel and von Krogh (2003) referred to as the private-collective model, where everyone benefits. We need to invite everyone to the conversation in order to both define and study the construct of new literacies, while establishing broad parameters so that people can connect their work to something specific. In this way, researchers in disparate fields can push their own understanding forward while also helping to build a common central construct, as we inform current work by other scholars, in other areas, and on other issues. This volume is an attempt to begin this important task of open source development, taking advantage of the richness that defines current research in a manner that enriches our understanding of new literacies and new literacies research.

This is not some wishy-washy policy of "everyone in" for its own sake. It is a policy aimed at progressively pursuing depth, rigor, and sophistication in interdisciplinary research by forging connections where connections have yet to exist and by constructing a platform together for debate and conversation about essential issues in new literacies research and especially to create a space for exchanging ideas across traditional disciplinary borders, research communities, methodological divides, and cultural experiences from around the world.

To pursue the best views and understandings, it is important for diverse options and resources to be on the table at the outset, and for critical opinion to be brought to bear on these so that productive lines of development can be nurtured in accordance with appropriate scholarly criteria and standards. These lines of development may be multiple, so long as they are robust from scholarly standpoints.

This is the philosophy we have adopted here: the pursuit of rigor rather than closure, from a position of openness to views and perspectives that share in common the wish to understand better how people encode, receive, and negotiate meanings in the current technological conjuncture.

Taking such considerations into account, the need to provide both an open context for research in new literacies and some sense of an initial definition that we might all agree to, we see at least four characteristics of an emerging new literacies perspective.

First, new technologies for information and communication and new visions for their use require us to bring new potentials to literacy tasks that take place within these technologies. While they may differ on the label of the construct they use, each set of scholars would probably agree that the Internet and other new ICTs require new social practices, skills, strategies, and dispositions for their effective use.

Second, new literacies are central to full civic, economic, and personal participation in a world community. As a result, they become important to study so that we might provide a more appropriate education for all of our students, in all nations. Moreover, attention to digital divide issues, whether defined in terms of access to the technologies themselves, in terms of instructional equity, or in terms of access to new, democratic tools, become especially important for societies that profess themselves egalitarian.

Third, new literacies are deictic; they rapidly change as defining technologies change. The new literacies of the Internet and other ICTs are not just new today, they will be newer tomorrow and even newer next week, and they will be continuously renewed on a schedule that is limited by only the human capacity to keep up. New technologies for literacy regularly appear, requiring even newer literacies to be able to use them effectively. Of course, literacy has always changed as technologies for literacy have changed (Manguel, 1994). What is historically distinctive is that by definition, the Internet permits the immediate exchange of even newer technologies of literacy. This speeds up the already rapid rate with which new technologies and new literacies appear. The process by which new literacies emerge and evolve is a transactional process (Bruce, 1997; Leu et al., 2004). New technologies invite experimentation to see what they can do. They get pushed into interesting places. Their limits encourage people to try and overcome these limits by modifying the technologies, and so on through endless iterations of kinds that Castells (1996) referred to in terms of a "virtuous circle" (p. 67).

Finally, new literacies are multiple, multimodal, and multifaceted. Thus, they benefit from analysis that brings multiple points of view to understanding them. In a world of exploding technologies and literacy practices, it becomes increasingly difficult to think of literacy as a singular construct that applies across all contexts. This suggests that it is likely to benefit from research that draws upon the complexity that multiple perspectives provide to studying the issue (Labbo & Reinking, 1999). It may also suggest that the area is best studied in interdisciplinary teams as questions become far too complex for the traditional single investigator model.

This volume seeks to provide initial direction for reviewing and undertaking new literacies research from the standpoint of openness that we have described. It provides a beginning base from which to encounter and approach research in this field as consumers and producers through multiple lenses and in multiple areas of investigation.

What, then, are some of the different kinds of lenses—theoretical, methodological, or issues-related—offered to readers in the rest of the book? Multiple theoretical perspectives and disciplines converge in these chapters to help us enrich our individual understandings of new literacies research. Typically, each chapter reviews research from multiple theoretical perspectives, ranging across several areas, including sociocultural theories, games studies, psycholinguistic theories, sociotechnical theories, cognitive science, sociolinguistics, cultural studies, media studies, social constructivism, social presence theory, transactional distance theory, social affordance theory, multiliteracies, multimodal design theory, radical democracy, political economy perspectives, new literacy studies, hypertext theory, intertextuality, new literacies of online reading comprehension, information literacy, media literacy, critical literacy, critical pedagogy, cognitive science, measurement science, feminist theory, gender theory, performativity theory, activity theory, narrative theory, ethnology, diffusion theory, and evidence-centered design theory. In addition, you will find a nearly equally diverse range of methodological perspectives integrated throughout the volume, covering issues in ethnographic, phenomenological, quasi-experimental, experimental, large scale surveys, mixed methods, discourse analysis, and a host of various qualitative methodologies. Perhaps the greatest range, though, is covered in the topics that are addressed. There are too many to list here in their entirety, but separate sections cover a range of important topics in research methodologies, knowledge and inquiry, communication, popular culture, community, and citizenship, and instructional practices and assessment.

Illustrating Principles of Open Development in Our Final Section

Our final section, *Multiple Perspectives on New Literacies Research,* seeks to show the benefits that accrue when scholars from different theoretical and methodological persuasions contribute their different analyses to a peer-reviewed, research study, itself representing different theoretical, methodological, and issues-related perspectives. Five different studies are reprinted in this section and at least two scholars, from different research traditions, share their thoughts about each study. The result helps us to appreciate the gains we can each make by thinking a bit more broadly about issues that concern us, seeing how multiple perspectives enrich our understanding of the emerging construct of new literacies as well as how these different perspectives also enrich our own individual line of research. Much can be gained by developing a better understanding of the many lenses that can be brought to bear on new literacies research. We seek to illustrate this in our final section.

doors to a more thoughtful world that takes greater advantage of the diversity that defines us—for research, for public policy, and most importantly, for our children.

References

Andrews, D., & Andrews, W. (2004). *Management communication: A guide*. Boston: Houghton-Mifflin.

Andrews, R. (Ed.). (2004). *The impact of ICT on literacy education*. London: Routledge Falmer.

Atkinson, R., & Hansen, D. (1966–1967). Computer-assisted instruction in initial reading: The Stanford project. *Reading Research Quarterly, 2*, 5–26.

Bell, D. (1973). *The coming of post-industrial society: A venture in social forecasting*. New York: Basic Books.

Bilal, D. (2000). Children's use of the Yahooligans! Web search engine: Cognitive, physical, and affective behaviors on fact-based search tasks. *Journal of the American Society for Information Science, 51*, 646–665.

Blake, R. (2000). Computer mediated communication: A window on L2 Spanish interlanguage. *Language Learning and Technology, 4*, 120–136. Retrieved December 15, 2006, from http://llt.msu.edu/vol4num1/blake/

Bolter, J. (1991). *Writing space: The computer, hypertext, and the history of writing*. Mahwah, NJ: Lawrence Erlbaum Associates.

Borzekowski, D., Fobil, J., & Asante, K. (2006). Online access by adolescents in Accra: Ghanaian teens' use of the Internet for health information [Electronic version]. *Developmental Psychology, 42*, 450–458.

Bruce, B. (1997). Literacy technologies: What stance should we take? *Journal of Literacy Research, 29*, 289–309.

Bruce, B. (Ed.). (2003). *Literacy in the information age: Inquiries into meaning making with new technologies*. Newark, DE: International Reading Association.

Bruce, B., & Michaels, S. (1987). *Microcomputers and literacy project: Final report*. Cambridge, MA: Harvard University.

Burbules, N. C. (1997). Rhetorics of the Web: Hyperreading and critical literacy in page to screen. In I. Snyder (Ed.), *Taking literacy into the electronic era* (pp. 102–122). New South Wales, Australia: Allen and Unwin.

Castells, M. (1996). *The rise of the network society*. Oxford, U.K.: Blackwell.

Cavanagh, S. (2004). North America. *Education Week*. Retrieved December 11, 2006, from http://counts.edweek.org/sreports/tc04/article.cfm?slug=35n_america.h23

ClickZ Stats (2006). *Population explosion*. Retrieved December 15, 2006, from http://www.clickz.com/showPage.html?page=151151

Cohen, D. K. (1987). Educational technology, policy, and practice. *Educational Evaluation and Policy Analysis, 9*, 153–170.

Coiro, J. L. (2007). *Exploring changes to reading comprehension on the Internet: Paradoxes and possibilities for diverse adolescent readers*. Unpublished doctoral dissertation. The University of Connecticut.

Coiro, J., & Dobler, E. (in press). Exploring the online reading comprehension strategies used by sixth-grade skilled readers to search for and locate information on the Internet. *Reading Research Quarterly*.

Cope, B., & Kalantzis, M. (Eds.). (1999). *Multiliteracies: Literacy learning and the design of social futures*. New York: Routledge.

Cuban, L. (1986). *Teachers and machines: The classroom use of technology since 1920*. New York: Teachers College Press.

Cuban, L. (2001). *Oversold and underused: Computers in the classroom*. Cambridge, MA: Harvard University Press.

de Argaez, E. (2006). *Internet world stats: Usage and population statistics.* Retrieved December 15, 2006, from http://www.internetworldstats.com/stats.htm

Demunter, C. (2005). *Statistics in focus: Internet activities in the European Union* (Vol. 40). Luxemburg: Eurostat/European Commission.

Facer, K., Joiner, R., Stanton, D., Reid, J., Hull, R., & Kirk D. (2004). Savannah: Mobile gaming and learning? *Journal of Computer Assisted Learning. 20,* 399–409.

Gee, J. (2003). *What video games have to teach us about learning and literacy.* New York: Palgrave.

Gee, J. (2007). *Good video games and good learning: Collected essays on video games, learning and literacy.* New York: Peter Lang.

Hargittai, E. (2002). Second-level digital divide: Differences in people's online skills. *First Monday. 7*(4). Retrieved December 15, 2006, from http://firstmonday.org/issues/issue7_4/hargittai

Heim, M. (1987). *Electric language: A philosophical study of word processing.* New Haven, CT: Yale University Press.

Hickman, L. A. (2001). *Philosophical tools for technological culture: Putting pragmatism to work.* Bloomington, IN: University Press.

Hine, C. (2000). *Virtual ethnography.* London: Sage Publications.

Hirsh, S. G. (1999). Children's relevance criteria and information seeking on electronic resources. *Journal of the American Society for Information Science, 50,* 1265–1283.

Hodas, S. (1993, September 14). Technology refusal and the organizational culture of schools. *Education Policy Analysis Archives, 1*(10). Retrieved December 11, 2006, from http://epaa.asu.edu/epaa/v1n10.html

Hoffman, D. L., & Novak, T. P. (1998). Information access: Bridging the racial divide on the Internet. *Science, 280,* 390–391.

Hoffman, J., Wu, H.-K., Krajcik, J. S., & Soloway, E. (2003). The nature of middle school learners' science content understandings with the use of on-line resources. *Journal of Research in Science Teaching, 40,* 323–346.

Hull, G., & Schultz, K. (Eds.). (2002). *School's out! Bridging out-of-school literacies with classroom practice.* New York: Teachers College Press.

INEP-EDUDATABRASIL. (2005). *Sistema de estatisticas educacionais [System of Education Statistics].* Retrieved December 27, 2006, from http://www.edudatabrasil.inep.gov.br

Internet World Stats (2006). *Internet usage statistics—The big picture: World Internet users and population stats.* Retrieved December 27, 2006, from http://www.internetworldstats.com/stats.htm

Jonassen, D. H. (Ed.). (2003). *Handbook of research on educational communications and technology.* Mahwah, NJ: Lawrence Erlbaum, Inc.

Karchmer, R. (2001). The journey ahead: Thirteen teachers report how the Internet influences literacy and literacy instruction in their K–12 classrooms. *Reading Research Quarterly, 36*(4), 442–466.

Kastman Breuch, L.-A. (2002). Thinking critically about technological literacy: Developing a framework to guide computer pedagogy in technical communication. *Technical Communication Quarterly, 11,* 267–288.

Kellner, D. (2000). New technologies/new literacies: Reconstructing education for the new millennium. *Teaching Education, 11*(3), 245–265.

Kelsey, A., & St. Amant, K. (Eds.). (in press). *Handbook of research in computer mediated communication.* Hershey, PA: Idea Group Reference.

Kist, W. (2004). *New literacies in action: Teaching and learning in multiple media.* New York: Teachers College Press.

Korte, W. B., & Hüsing, T. (2006, November 22–25). *Benchmarking access and use of ICT in European schools 2006: Results from head teacher and A classroom teacher surveys in 27 European countries.* Paper presented at the Fourth International Conference on Multimedia and Information and Communication Technologies in Education. Seville, Spain. Retrieved December 15, 2006, from http://www.formatex.org/micte2006/Down-loadable-files/oral/Benchmarking%20Access.pdf

PART I
Methodologies

Introduction to Part I

The chapters in this section approach new literacies research methodology from different angles. Most define their focus by reference to a particular kind of methodological approach or research method. Ron Anderson (Chapter 3) addresses large scale quantitative research on new technology in teaching and learning, Jonna Kulikowich (Chapter 7) reviews experimental and quasi-experimental approaches to new literacies research, Kevin Leander (Chapter 2) discusses research and theory contributing to the development of a connective ethnography of online/offline literacy networks, and Lori Kendall (Chapter 5) addresses the conduct of qualitative interviews. The two remaining chapters define their focus in terms of some area or dimension of new literacies. Sonia Livingstone, Elizabeth Van Couvering, and Nancy Thumim (Chapter 4) address disciplinary, critical, and methodological issues pertaining to what they identify as a trend toward convergence between traditions of research on media and information literacy, respectively. Andrew Burn (Chapter 6) focuses on an approach to researching multimodal texts that pursues a synthesis between semiotic analysis of media texts and investigation of the cultures of those who produce multimodal media texts and those who receive and interact with them.

Themes

Five organizing themes in particular emerge from these chapters as a whole: (a) attention to aspects of research design, (b) concern for methodological matters germane to research quality, (c) the significance of multiple methods and theoretical perspectives for researching new literacies, (d) ideas about methodological innovation in new literacies research, and (e) views concerning future directions and priorities for research in this field. Each helps us to better understand methodological issues in new literacies research.

Adequacy and integrity of the research design for achieving research purposes is a recurrent theme—albeit one that is treated with varying degrees of emphasis and explicitness—throughout the chapters. Design considerations are especially foregrounded in the chapters by Anderson (Chapter 3) and Kulikowich (Chapter 7), which treat large-scale quantitative and experimental research, respectively. These chapters closely attend to matters like the formal characteristics of experiments and control factors and the multiple levels of concern with design in different kinds of studies—including statistical designs, sampling designs, survey and test designs—and how they are informed by appropriate conceptual and theoretical frameworks consonant with the questions being asked, resources available, and the study purposes.

Attention to design considerations is present, albeit less explicitly, in the predominantly qualitative chapters. As will emerge in detail later, Kendall's (Chapter 5) concerns about the nature, role, and conduct of in-depth qualitative interviews and about how the science in qualitative interviews is so often compromised when they are hitched to quantitative surveys can be seen as concerns about research design. Similarly, Leander's (Chapter 2) question about how to develop a connective ethnography around the need to conceptualize our way past binary constructions like online/offline that negate the ways human practices travel seamlessly across "spaces" is very much a question about how to configure data collection methods and procedures sufficient for ethnographic purposes. Andrew Burn's (Chapter 6) contribution can be read as a sustained account of an attempt to develop and realize a research design adequate for investigating meaning in relation to multimodal texts. Similarly, Livingstone and colleagues (Chapter 4) raise methodological questions about how to conduct research that takes due account of the complexity of literacy as a social phenomenon that are, precisely, questions about design.

The chapters, likewise, attend to issues of research quality. Here again, this is most explicit in the chapters dealing with quantitative studies of new literacies. At a detailed level, this is evident in Kulikowich's (Chapter 7) suggestions for how experimental researchers who have effective designs but small sample sizes can strengthen the credibility of their statements by replicating studies and/or by collecting multiple effect sizes from each study and subjecting them to meta-analysis. Similarly, Anderson's (Chapter 3) account is replete with examples of quality enhancement procedures such as estimating sampling errors and applying measurement analysis to data to check if indicators have validated constructs. Elsewhere, Livingstone et al. (Chapter 4) endorse practices of methodological triangulation to maximize quality, such as using observation to cross-check claims from self-reported data. Kendall (Chapter 5) addresses complications for interpretation of data contingent upon the fact that in-depth interviews are "meaning-making situations" (p. 136) that are not well suited to questions seeking "objective" snapshots of things that existed prior to the research.

Several authors address the theme of multimethods research and multidisciplinary approaches to the design and conduct of research in the area of new literacies. Different versions of multimethods approaches can be distinguished. One is where "multimethods" entails "mixed methods" in the sense of investigators collecting and analyzing data, integrating findings, and drawing inferences "using both qualitative and quantitative approaches or methods in a single study or a program of inquiry" (Tashakkori & Creswell, 2007, p. 4).

This involves integrating methods and theories from paradigms that in the past have often been treated as being in tension, if not incompatible. A second version is where the multiple methods and theories used in a study are internal to a research paradigm (e.g., an appropriate mix of either qualitative methods or quantitative methods) or where they are drawn from traditions of research and theory generally seen as compatible with one another rather than in tension or antithetical (e.g., hermeneutic methods from philosophy employed in qualitative research).

While they explicitly refrain from talk of mixed methods, adopting the terminology of multimethods instead, Livingstone, Van Couvering, and Thumim (Chapter 4) endorse the informed use of quantitative and qualitative methods within studies in which research purposes benefit from designs that allow for methodological triangulation using both quantitative and qualitative methods. They note that all individual research methods have limitations and that advocates of multimethod designs and multidisciplinary research approaches aim to overcome or compensate for the limitations and disadvantages of some methods over others. At the same time, they caution against assuming that multidisciplinary or multimethod research will be easy to conceptualize and conduct, and emphasize that the "how" of research must always be answerable to the "what" and "why" of research. Similarly, Anderson (Chapter 3) claims that while large-scale empirical research is largely quantitative, when such studies involve cross-national components, it will often be necessary to employ a combination of qualitative and quantitative approaches to address highly diverse cultural contexts.

An example of multimethods research that does not mix quantitative and qualitative components is found in Burn's (Chapter 6) account of discourse analysis research approaches that do not confine "discourse" to "a language model" alone. Burn describes using a combination of text analysis informed by social semiotic and multimodal theory and analysis of interview data informed by theories of discourse to investigate meaning in the context of computer game texts. Leander's (Chapter 2) survey of researchers working toward developing "connective" ethnography reports investigators using diverse complementary qualitative methods for collecting and analyzing data and, in doing so, drawing on multiple theoretical positions. Leander describes how Miller and Slater (2000), for example, undertook comparative ethnography by extending data collection across household surveys; informal, community-based inquiries; face-to-face interviews; participant observation; and e-mail and chat communications. Comparative analysis employed four "dynamics"—(a) objectification, (b) mediation, (c) normative freedom, and (d) positioning—reflecting theoretical perspectives ranging over poststructuralist, postcolonial, network and media technology theories, among others. At another level, research undertaken by Eva Lam (2000, 2004) and Rod Jones (2004, 2005) and reported by Leander grew from initial grounding in the

& Wellman, 2002), and in the new literacy studies, in school versus out of school (Hull & Schultz, 2001).

How do we work toward building knowledge that might take Internet practices out of the exotic and assert their everydayness and their qualities of the *quotidian?* Perhaps one of the best ways to be confronted is to attempt to research these practices as lived experiences in the everyday lives of youth. This chapter addresses the digital divide of research on literacy, a divide that brackets "digital literacies" and "Internet spaces" in special conference sessions, special journals, and special handbooks such as this. I hope to work the tension between, on the one hand, asserting that digital literacy practices are fascinating, worthy of study, and in many ways unique, and on the other hand, moving toward a methodology for understanding digital literacies as flowing with and interconnected to streams of other literacy practices, material culture, traditional media, movements of people, identity practices, and the social construction of technologies.

As indexed in my use of the phrase "lived experiences," this chapter discusses the development of an ethnographic approach for studying digital literacies as social practices. Ethnography is traditionally recognized as a practice of spending time observing and participating in a particular environment and using a range of data collection techniques to describe human practices in that environment. Baszanger & Dodier (1997, pp. 8–11), considering new developments in ethnography, offer three productively broad characteristics of the goals of ethnography. First, ethnography insists that understanding phenomena requires empirical observation. While it may appear unnecessary to state this characteristic, it is a helpful way of distinguishing ethnographic practice, as social science, from approaches in the humanities that work through deduction, introspection, philosophic inquiry, textual interpretation, and other means. Second, ethnography seeks to remain open to new data and to new codes for interpreting data. This characteristic sets ethnography apart from research methods that establish a priori codes, items to collect, and schedules for data collection. Ethnography works with "sensitizing" concepts, "suggest[ing] directions along which to look" rather than with "definitive" constructs "provid[ing] prescriptions of what to see" (Blumer, 1969, p. 148). This characteristic of openness has long conflicted with the need for methodological structure in research and even more so today given the politics of knowledge production, in some parts of the world, that increasingly favor standardized research structures and reproducibility over endogenous, contingent approaches. Third, ethnography seeks to satisfy the requirement to connect or *ground* observations and interpretations with a specific field that is limited in time and space. This characteristic is important for separating ethnography from some social science methods that dissociate data from its relevant context in order to universalize interpretations. Moreover, this traditional requirement of ethnography is particularly important for the present discussion as the specific context of activity becomes fuzzy or tends to fracture when we follow online practices. This discussion of initial characteristics of ethnography is by necessity limited and is intended merely as a means of orientation; a richer discussion of ethnography with particular utility for research in social linguistics has been recently drafted by the Coordinating Committee of the U.K. Linguistic Ethnography Forum (2004).

My own interests and commitments to understanding social practices through ethnography have been historically shaped in two key ways. A first important influence has been the work of Bruce (1999; Bruce & Leander, 1997; Bruce & Rubin, 1993) on the "situated evaluation" of technology in use. In his empirical work and theory building, Bruce argued that the problems—and possibilities—of technologies in education are a result of the complex interaction of any technological innovation with the particulars of a social situation: "How the features of the technology interact with human needs, expectations, beliefs, prior practices, and alternative tools far outweighs the properties of the technology itself" (Bruce & Rubin, 1993, p. 215). Situated evaluation is a critique of technocentrism (Papert, 1987) and techno-myopia, pushing us to shift our focus from technical tools to the social practices through which the possibilities of such tools are realized. The reasons why technologies do not work according to the ideals of developers, or do work in radically unanticipated ways, often has little to do with the tools themselves and much more to do with the relations of technologies to what we might consider the surround. My perspectives on ethnography were also initially formed by my own ethnographic studies of everyday (nondigital) literacy practices in school settings. In this work, I became invested in understanding student interaction in routine classroom discussions and the ways in which such discussions construct student identities (e.g., Leander, 2002a). In this research, I was also interested in how literacy practices in school relate to those outside of school, which I studied indirectly by considering activities located on the "fringe" of school, such as construction projects and extended fieldtrips (Leander, 2001, 2002b). These early research experiences that complicated the relationship of the school "setting" to other social spaces, along with my earlier training that complicated the relationship of technology to the social world, continue to shape my vision—and desire—to delve into messy discussions of online ethnography.

Ethnography Moves Online: Adaptation and Connective Paradigms

Early work on computer-mediated communication and media studies tended to emphasize the uniqueness of the Internet as a site; the Internet was a place where one could shape relationships, identities, and social projects in a world apart (Mitchell, 1996) from the material world, even if the caffeinated body might suffer in supporting such a life (e.g., Markham, 1998). One of the dominant conversations concerning online research, since its inception, is

The movement of the chapter is from slightly earlier key studies (to around the year 2000) to newer work that is underway or only beginning to appear in print. My own method has been to draw from the literature to review earlier studies and largely from interviews with researchers to review recent and ongoing work. Following a discussion of several connective ethnographic projects, the chapter closes with commentary on future directions for continuing to build connective ethnographic methodology in literacy research.

Early Connective Ethnographies of Internet Practices

The notion of building relations between offline bodies and Internet practices is nearly as old as the popular use of the Internet itself. An early example of this approach is the psychological work of Turkle (1995). Turkle contrasted the real and virtual lives of people who regularly use multiuser domains (MUDs), or virtual worlds that permit participants to interact with text-based objects and spaces. Turkle's methodology was based upon an insistence of observing her key informants face-to-face. She documented multiple relations: MUD enthusiasts seeking emotional support either act out problems from their offline lives or seek to escape from their offline lives. Ironically, for those who seek to escape emotionally, Turkle found that the MUDs often deepen offline anxiety. Other early work that largely built upon traditional ethnographic practices as they were applied to the Internet includes studies by Baym (1995a, 1995b), Correll (1995), and Paccagnella (1997). In these studies, online discussions, as they developed in real time over longer periods, were combined with face-to-face and electronic interviewing, posing of questions to the discussion group, two-way interactions, and other means of triangulating data to get a deeper sense of how communities became meaningful to the participants. While these and other early studies used offline data to support interpretations of online personal or community development, however, they tended to overemphasize the distinctions between online and offline social life (Hine, 2000, p. 27). Offline interpretations were used to build cases for online analysis—the online world or practice was still bracketed at the center of the project.

Building upon this earlier work, the following studies begin to more deliberately and self-consciously develop methodologies and findings that traverse offline and online social life in new ways. The following is a selective and not exclusive discussion of important methodological and empirical connective ethnographies of the Internet (see also Bennett, 2004; Kendall, 1999; Mann & Stewart, 2002; Sade-Beck, 2004). I have drawn from studies taking different forms, including two book-length treatments in the first cases and research articles in the others.

Daniel Miller and Don Slater

The Internet: An Ethnographic Approach reports on Daniel Miller and Don Slater's (2000) study of uses of the Internet and meanings of Internet culture embedded in Trinidad as a place and related to the Trinidadian Diaspora. One the key conclusions of the study is that Trinidadians have a seeming natural affinity for the Internet in its various manifestations. Miller and Slater did not assume a separation of the Internet from other aspects of daily life, and they argued to the contrary that, in Trinidad, there were very few places where commerce or e-commerce, chat on playgrounds or in ICQ, or religious instruction as carried out face-to-face or by e-mail were treated in terms of clear distinctions between the "real" and the "virtual" (p. 6). While some relationships, forms of commerce, and other activities may exist uniquely online, the key issue is that participants weave these social spaces and relations into their lives in such a way that the online is experienced as real and as common place and that transitions between online and offline social spaces and identities may be less marked than researchers assume.

Miller and Slater (2000) called their approach "comparative ethnography" (p. 9), and part of the key to understanding their methodology is to consider their own scholarly histories. Miller studied culture in Trinidad for over a decade, including work on business, consumption, kinship, and identity. In contrast, Slater's expertise was online environments and practices and especially forms of chat. The comparative ethnography proceeded by considering Miller's funds of knowledge of Trinidadian culture in relation to the examination of Internet culture and practice, guided by Slater. For example, the pair posited that in Trinidad, the Internet is associated with the "vanguard of style" (p. 33), through practices such as playing MP3s, remixing music, and searching for fashion information. They interpreted this valuing of the Internet in relation to a more general and historical Trinidadian belief that style—including participating in international fashion—has profound value, as researched by Miller in the mid-1990s. Thus, an important meaning of comparative ethnography for the team involved interpreting current Internet practices in relation to the history of other Trinidadian cultural practices and meanings. Miller and Slater were critical of ethnographic projects that were ahistorical or that bracketed one form of social practice, such as Internet practice, from other aspects of social life: "In most ethnographic reportage of quality, the length and breadth of the study allows one topic to be understood as also an idiom for something else" (p. 22).

Miller and Slater (2000) used a house-to-house survey as a broad means of understanding the extent of the infusion of the Internet into Trinidadian life, conducting this survey within the same diverse housing districts that Miller (1994) used in his earlier research, chosen to represent a "very ordinary section" of the society as a whole, including residential areas, public housing, and a district of squatters (p. 196). The researchers argued that the house-to-house survey gave them a very different kind of information than they would have gleaned from means that are more formal and especially information concerning how Trinidadians often connect to the Internet in highly informal and resourceful ways. Data collection in the surveyed areas also included in-depth individual household interviews and informal inquiries in the four districts (p. 197).

Methodologically, long-standing relationships with Trinidadian families from Miller's earlier research were critically important to developing the project during their 5 intensive weeks of data collection while in Trinidad (Miller & Slater, 2000). Another meaning of *comparative* during data collection involved comparisons across multiple online and offline sites. During the key data collection period, the researchers often engaged in face-to-face interviews in the mornings around broader Internet-culture relations and then spent the afternoons and evenings "lyming" or hanging out in cybercafés, watching people go online or chatting with them online (p. 22). Following their work in Trinidad, the researchers collected Internet data for months following, remaining in touch with some informants for as long as 15 months through chat and e-mail. The pair also made use of their own embodied circulations to interview Trinidadians in London and New York.

In developing an approach to connective ethnography by drawing on insights from Miller and Slater (2000), the most important contribution of their comparative ethnography might be the analytic dimensions they developed for approaching comparative analysis. While the researchers recognized that these dimensions, as "dynamics," are gleaned from the case of Trinidad, they also invited others to take up these four dynamics and to develop them in relation to other ethnographic settings (p. 9). First, "dynamics of objectification" refers to how people recognize or realize themselves through a domain of material culture, including Internet practices and resources (p. 10). This dimension may be one of the most familiar to Internet researchers, as it involves considering how the Internet is used as a means of identification. Second, dynamics of mediation refers to how people make use of the various "features, potentials, and dangers" of the Internet as media (p. 10). With respect to this dimension, Miller and Slater argued that it is essential not to consider the Internet merely as a monolith but to tease out the particulars of the range of practices and media that become collected under the heading of "the Internet." Third, particularly interesting for cross-site analysis, Miller and Slater discussed dynamics of normative freedom, which describes how people engage freedom as it is opened up through Internet practices. The term *normative freedom* used here is intended to capture a paradox: Any notion of freedom also takes the form of a social order (p. 16). As such, at issue is not so much a grand conflict between freedom and constraint but, rather, the particulars of how different forms and discourses of social order come into contact (p. 18). A fourth and final dimension, dynamics of positioning, describes how people engage with networks that transcend their immediate locations, including the flows of cultural, political, and financial resources (p. 10). "Positioning is about strategies for surviving or succeeding in these new flows and spaces" (p. 20).

A fascinating example of drawing on one of these four dimensions for analysis involves Miller and Slater's (2000) discussion of how some Trinidadian teens attribute specific Internet practices to stages of development and identity. In this case, we see the dynamics of objectification traversing online and offline identities. For example, Trinidadian teens describe how a prepersonal Web site phase or pre-ICQ phase is followed by a phase of heavy involvement in cybersex and Internet porn and then a later phase in which Internet sex and pornographic activity is considered uncool. Along with these phases of activity come naming practices: While earlier and less-experienced adolescents might call one another by their ICQ nicknames, this practice is considered uncool by older adolescents (p. 76). The researcher's analysis suggested how other identity categories (e.g., adolescence, man, woman, lesbian, poor, or academic) might also be materially stitched together with particular Internet practices.

A further example of the potential comparative value of the dynamics for analysis, which especially draws out the dynamics of objectification and dynamics of positioning, involves how Trinidadians use Internet practices for the performance of national identity. Trinidadians enter and practice the network "as a people who [feel] themselves encountering it from a place" (Miller & Slater, 2000, p. 105). Despite the broad dispersal of the Trinidadian Diaspora, and despite the global commodification of culture, Trinidadians continually practice their national identities online and consume the Internet as a source of nationalism. For example, the home pages of Trinidadians are often replete with core nationalistic symbols, such as flags, crests, maps, and national statistics. Web pages, online chat, and news groups are also used to practice cultural identities through language play ("lyming"), Trini-style jokes, and even explanations for outsiders to help them learn about Trinidadian culture. Miller and Slater comparatively interpreted this nationalism and practice of cultural identity as related to a historical ethos of resistance to forces such as slavery and colonialism but at the same time as indexing the fragile state of Trinidad as a nation state (p. 115; British and American nationalism was also evident in Hine's, 2000, study, p. 114; see also Mitra, 1997). Instances of national identification practices as documented in ethnography run counter to the rhetoric of replacement or substitution (e.g., Castells, 1996), where global processes of identification somehow overtake forms of identification associated with nation-states and other places.

While Miller and Slater (2000) drew on a strong sense of place and situatedness to understand the Internet in Trinidad, an important relational principle of their larger project was to move beyond the dualism of the local and the global. They worked to build a perspective that did not abstract the global Internet from the local place of Trinidad and "Trininess" as cultural practice but, rather, considered the dialectics and circulations of the general and specific. The ethnography is not about how a global form "out there" is appropriated by a local social space that is set apart, but about "how Trinidadians put themselves into this global arena and become part of a force that constitutes it, but do so quite specifically as Trinidadians" (p. 7).

Christine Hine

Hine's (2000) *Virtual Ethnography* is a rich and influential text for developing ethnographic approaches to researching complex connections among myriad social sites, both online and offline. The topic of Hine's ethnography reported in this text was the event around Louise Woodward, a teenage British nanny tried in Boston, in 1997, for the murder of a child for whom she had been caring. Hine's purpose was to use the events around Woodward as a way of thinking about the social construction of the Internet, a purpose that emerged when the judge for the trial announced that he would release his ruling on the case via the Internet. At the beginning of her study, Hine did not plan the types and forms of data she would collect, but rather, followed leads as the multimediated event around the Woodward case developed. She described a dizzying sense of excitement and engagement with an "ongoing and living event" (p. 71) in trying to capture Web sites that were dynamically developed to report on the case, temporally tracking changes in these Web sites and studying the incoming and outgoing links among them. Hine and an assistant also recorded and archived media reports on the Woodward case from television, radio, and print news media. Following the verdict on the case, Hine's data collection slowed and narrowed; she focused her Web site analysis to support sites for either side in the case, contacted site developers and carried out online interviews with them, and studied some newsgroup interactions around the case. Thus, Hine's connective or virtual ethnography of Internet practice involved data seemingly entirely collected online, and yet articulated these data with accounts from other news media about the case. Traditional news media function as offline data in unbounding the online from social practice.

While Hine's (2000) research and study offered many valuable insights for the development of connective ethnography, including a list of methodological principles (pp. 63–65), in the following, I highlight just a few key issues. The first of these, perhaps most characteristic and unique in Hine's approach, involves understanding the Internet as culture and cultural artifact. The culture/cultural artifact relation is not intended as a dichotomous approach but as an heuristic that captures how everyday Internet practices shape the Internet as a social object and how a broad range of reifications and representations of the Internet also socially shape it as being a particular kind of object. "Treating the Internet as a cultural artifact interrogates the assumptions which viewing the Internet as a site for culture entails, and highlights the status of the Internet as itself a cultural achievement based on particular understandings of the technology" (p. 39). Drawing on science and technology studies, as well as situated studies of other media use, Hine argued that the meaning of the Internet is socially and culturally indeterminate, distributed across a wide and varied range of actors.

Hine (2000) saw events, such as the Louise Woodward case, as active in organizing and recruiting meaningful connections between Internet practices and Internet representations and circumstances of use or the Internet as a cultural artifact. She related the development of Internet-media accounts and discussions of the Woodward case to how television, radio, and print journalism concurrently reported the case and its relationship to the Internet. As with other analyses informed by science and technology studies, Hine's account is somewhat organized around technology trouble: Technical problems force the judge's announcement of his verdict to be delayed, a delay that other media outlets picked up on and used to cast the Internet in a negative light relative to their own superior timing and reliability. Most people learned first of the verdict through television or radio. Yet, even before the trial outcome, Hine documented how the newspapers and television news, who anticipated the Internet-mediated trial news, took on the task of explaining what the Internet was for and what was sensible to do with it, agreeing with or harshly critiquing the judge's decision to use the Internet. Television footage appeared to struggle to figure out how to represent the Internet as a location, showing people seated in front of computers and then zooming in on Web pages.

Less central to Hine's (2000) overall project, but nevertheless an important set of insights, were her analyses of the spatial and temporal dimensions of Internet practice as lived experience. Like others (e.g., Miller & Slater, 2000), Hine critiqued the technocentrism of Castells (1996), who celebrated the Internet-induced temporal collage and reconfiguration of social space. Hine, in contrast, traced how information and advocacy Web sites in the Louise Woodward trial became arranged as more or less central or marginal. Even while the Internet is hypertextually structured and potentially an entirely connected space, Web developers who she studied in the Woodward case had an intense awareness of the territoriality of their own Web sites or the "spatiality which stems from the differential connectedness of sites" (p. 105). This territory-construction by linking is of course also connected to the digital-material realities of Web server space that Web developers struggled for and were allocated. While the number of Web sites associated with the case grew very rapidly (from 165 to over 700 in a week), and some of these sites deemed themselves as official and authoritative, Hine analyzed how the official Louise Campaign for Justice Web site became the key site. The centrality of this site—its flow across the entire network—is analyzed by considering not only the number of hits to the site but also how the more peripheral and amateur sites repeatedly featured prominent links to it. Other circulation-related practices could include a broad range of ways of constructing extensibility and getting attention through media, including the practices of registering Web sites with search engines, paying for registration services, and even handing out business

The event complex is just one instance and example of the importance of gathering and interpreting data from multiple sites. The following passage from my interview with Jones (personal communication, May 30, 2005) is quoted at length as a robust description of the need for online/offline flow in ethnography:

> The difference is that if you just took either [online or offline] side of it, you wouldn't understand what's going on. For instance, you can't hang out with these kids, in the physical world, without having some understanding of what they're doing online, because you wouldn't understand their relationships, you wouldn't understand a lot of the things that they say even because they are contingent upon things that they say online, or certain expressions that develop online and seep into the normal conversation in the physical world. So, not knowing what they're doing online, you'd be pretty much in the same position that their parents are in (laughs). They'd have a lot of secrets from you. At the same time, just looking at what they're doing online—for me this is a really important point—I think would completely miss the point of studying online behavior. Because it would set up this kind of idea that what they do online is somehow separate from what they do offline, that there's this kind of "cyberspace," where they go and do all sorts of these special things, and there's a clear boundary that's drawn, and, that's not what's happening at all. What they're doing online has a lot to do with what they're doing in the real world.

As an everyday example of these traversals, Jones noted how youth routinely remarked that they would not have their particular set of offline friends without the opportunities to meet and develop relationships online.

For data analysis in such a large-scale project, Jones described his central challenge as organizing the data such that a "polychronic orientation" (personal communication, May 30, 2005) can develop around the multiple engagements of any one participant in one particular period. Jones wanted to understand how school assignments, online gaming, life happenings, friendships, romances, and other areas of youth lives are interconnected or bounded at particular moments. "Over the course of six months of someone's life, everything is connected, in one way or another, and so the trick is trying to be able to trace those connections" (personal communication, May 30, 2005). In data collection and analysis, he saw a connective, relational perspective as essential to his project (personal communication, May 30, 2005). Jones and colleagues were using Atlas, a qualitative archiving and analysis tool, to organize, analyze, and search through their data.

Jones (personal communication, May 30, 2005) noted two key ethical issues in his research, the first of which was also discussed by Lam (personal communication, June 5, 2005): How should screen captures of participants' online activity be handled when such data also include the communications of many who have not given informed consent (personal communication, May 30, 2005)? A general approach that Jones and colleagues took to mitigate this dilemma at the outset of the study was to have participants send a message to all of the people on their buddy lists, noting that they were in the study and would sometimes be recorded when interacting. Jones noted, however, that the problem of not being able to control who will "stumble into" (personal communication, May 30, 2005) an online study is still something he did not solve. Another ethical issue in the study concerned one of the participants who was a gay youth and was involved in a number of forms of online activity that may well have concerned his parents had they been aware of them. In the case of this boy, what he was doing and the identity he was projecting online was quite distinct from his offline life in his family; Jones described the boy as engaging in forms of activity that were a likely "rehearsal" (personal communication, May 30, 2005) for activity in the future.

Further Reading

Jones, R. (2004). The problem of context in computer mediated communication. In P. LeVine & R. Scollon (Eds.), *Discourse and technology: Multimodal discourse analysis* (pp. 20–23). Washington, DC: Georgetown University Press.

Jones, R. (in press). Sites of engagement as sites of attention: Time, space and culture in electronic discourse. In S. Norris & R. Jones (Eds.), *Discourse in action: Introducing mediated discourse analysis* (pp. 141–154). London: Routledge.

Brian Wilson: Youth Culture, Global Flows, and Political Activism

On the one hand, Brian Wilson's work was less directly related to literacy than some of the other research discussed in this section, while on the other hand, his work is highly related to a number of research directions concerning literacy, social justice, and youth culture. Wilson was concerned with how media of different types—and in particular Web sites and related online media—are used by youth in different forms of political activism. Wilson's approach to looking across online and offline contexts to understand youth culture developed in part through an earlier ethnography (1995–1998) in which he examined the rave subculture in Southern Ontario, Canada (personal communication, June 7, 2005). The cultural practices of the ravers studied by Wilson included organizing local raves, or all-night dance parties, but also connecting with other ravers around the world online and sharing music. As with other work discussed previously, including Lam's research, Wilson did not set out originally to examine Internet-related practices; rather, he got "pulled into" them after it was clear that the Internet was a "central meeting place, a space of organization, and a cultural reference point for young ravers" (personal communication, June 7, 2005).

Wilson's second major study was an analysis of activist youth organizations/networks and how these networks are tapping into the potential of the Internet to further their causes and voices (personal communication, June 7, 2005).

Leander, K. M. (2003). Writing travelers' tales on new literacyscapes [New directions in research]. *Reading Research Quarterly, 38*(3), 392–397.

Leander, K. M., & Aplin, B. (2005). *Digital literacies as practices of space-time.* Paper presented at the AERA Annual Meeting, Montreal, Canada.

Leander, K. M., & Lovvorn, J. (2006). Literacy networks. *Cognition & Instruction.*

Leander, K. M., & McKim, K. K. (2003). Tracing the everyday "sitings" of adolescents on the Internet: A strategic adaptation of ethnography across online and offline spaces. *Education, Communication, & Information 3*(2), 211–240.

Toward a Connective Ethnography: Future Directions and Possible Resources

In researching online literacies, how do we move from "roots to routes," as the formulation goes—how do we trace and map the texts and contexts articulated in the space-times of literacy practice? How do we reimagine and study the event, the text, the classroom, the school and global relations as a nexus—a "field of relations" (Olwig & Hastrup, 1997)—rather than as a container? If the Internet is not a single thing, but a heterogeneous assemblage of practices, texts, and cultures, then how are online territories performed through semiotic practices (Dodge & Kitchin, 2001)? Further, what form does ethnography take when it is no longer necessarily about physically displacing oneself, but about experiential displacement, a process of following connections?

If literacy research is to build on the connective approach informed by Miller and Slater (2000), Hine (2000), and others, one area of work that could lead in productive directions is actor network theory (ANT), historically associated with science and technology studies. In fact, part of what is striking in both Miller and Slater and Hine is more or less implicit critiques of the work of Castells (1996), with responses to these critiques offered by ANT, and especially the work of Latour (1987, 1988a). Separations of the real and the virtual, and the Internet and the self in Castells (1996) are problematized as dualisms that are overcome through the analysis of circulations and translations as described in ANT. From this vantage point, Miller and Slater conceived of the Internet and of what it meant to feel Trinidadian, as a conclusion rather than a starting point—as an effect of networking as a process.

In Latour's (1987, 1988a) work, space and time are less important than "spacing" and "timing" are (Bingham & Thrift, 2000). Uniquely Latourian is the way in which objects of all sorts—actants—are brought into circulation, including people but also, in his analysis of Einstein's work, trains, clouds, men with rigid rods, lifts, marble tables, mulluscs, clocks, and rulers (Latour, 1988a). The material world is given its due; ANT offers a strong critique of transcendent notions of social life and power (e.g., micro- and macrorelations) and pushes rather to the analysis of the movements, alignments, and translations of everyday things, people, and texts. Historically, Latour (1988b) has had a keen interest in the function of texts in scientific and technical work, and the manner in which texts are immutable, or fix particular facts and forms of knowledge, and yet at the same time are mobile and combinable. Literacy and texts, then, have a pivotal role in knowledge making and in translating the interests of other circulating actants. Use of ANT to conceptualize literacy practices and flows is work that is just beginning (e.g., Brandt & Clinton, 2002; Clarke, 2002; Leander & Lovvorn, 2006) and could be a highly promising resource for the development of connective ethnographic methodologies.

To study circulations—to move researcher bodies to trace traversals at spatial scales beyond the school yard—however, will require teams of researchers and/or novel solutions such as Jones' "big brother" approach described previously (personal communication, May 30, 2005). Jay Lemke (2000), revoicing Hillary Clinton, reminded us that it "takes a village" to study a village. Our current methodologies and studies are not realizations of ideal conceptual models, but rather pragmatic solutions to inquiry that are constrained by location, physical energy, the limits of attention, money, and ready-to-hand resources. Classroom-based research, or research bracketed to a single online Web source, does not happen incidentally, but rather, it is supported by the blocked and cut networks of academic life, isolated bodies, and an individualistic research culture.

While much of this chapter has emphasized connections, part of the promise of a developing connective ethnography will be to map how separations are produced as social achievements. Rather than presuming separations between school and out-of-school literacy practices, for example, such separations can be considered empirically, as forms of identity building, or producing communities, social groups, and institutions. As with connective work that has documented how spatially dispersed people create forms of nationalistic identification online (Miller & Slater, 2000), other forms of separation and identification, as mediated by texts and literacy practices will become evident empirically. Lam's (2004) work pointed to how the hybrid language practices of Romanized Cantonese, associated with a chat room, functions as a community and language-building social space that is somewhat unique and bracketed from other social spaces, but that this bracketing is producing a space of possibility over and against forms of segregation and isolation in school. In my own research, I have begun to document a social-spatial overlay between online social networks, the positions of student bodies in the school building, and the positions of these students' homes in their respective neighborhoods. Being in or out of the network may be reproduced along laminated social spaces.

Another key area of study regarding separations and boundary-making practices in online/offline networks regards how public and private texts and subjectivities are being coconstituted. Jones commented from his work in Hong Kong that young people were talking about "very private things" in online diaries and weblogs, yet posting these "private" messages on the World Wide Web at the same time (personal communication, May 30, 2005). Within this social practice, however, it seems clear that some texts are not intended for a public (e.g., parents), but by certain kinds of friends, as well as certain others reading from certain positions. Jones gave the example of how a poem, written by a girl about breaking up with her boyfriend, could be read by the boyfriend, but also by other friends, who could comment on the boyfriend and on the relationship. We have recorded very similar kinds of interactions, which appear to operate at multiple levels and with different forms of address (Ellsworth, 1997), in the Synchrony study.

Closely related to both circulation and bounding practices, another important area of development, particularly for literacy studies, is to continue to consider how the Internet is reified through various texts and discourses—to trace not only traveling practices, but also how the Internet is objectified as a cultural artifact (Hine, 2000). Drawing on Pauly (1991), Jones (1999) discussed the closely related notion of "commentary," which might include how we talk about the Internet as a realization of the "global village," how we make claims about "Internet addiction," the metaphor of the "information superhighway," and so forth (p. 15). Jones reminded us that this commentary is not merely something to study that is outside of the researcher, but something that informs the researcher's work as well. Critical discourse analysis (Fairclough, 1995; Gee, 1999), which has been so central to the development of the new literacy studies, could continue to be a highly important resource for examining digital practices, but understanding the Internet as a malleable social object demands an analysis of discourses on technology and not just discursive production through technology. In other terms, we may well need to turn our focus partially from the texts that youth are producing on the Internet to read these texts in relationship to the Internet, or to particular Internet practices, as a discursively constituted object. An even greater challenge will be to articulate this type of critical discursive work with the mapping of circulations, over and against assumptions about presumed micro- and macrorelations. In Hine's (2000) imagination, "We could design ethnographic studies to track the ways in which conceptions of the Internet user were embedded into particular access points, advertisements, or pieces of hardware" (p. 35). Hine argues persuasively that we should take an ambivalent stance regarding appropriate sites to study for examining the cultural/discursive production and consumption of the Internet. Many of these sites will surely be offline, including film, print texts of all sorts, fashion, television, school computer labs (as texts), and, reflexively, the means and metaphors researchers use to describe online literacy practices.

References

Abu-Lughod, L. (1991). Writing against culture. In R. Fox (Ed.), *Recapturing anthropology: Working in the present* (pp. 137–162). Santa Fe, NM: School of American Research Press.

Appadurai, A. (1996). *Modernity at large*. Minneapolis: University of Minnesota Press.

Baszanger, I., & Dodier, N. (1997). Ethnography: Relating the part to the whole. In D. Silverman (Ed.), *Qualitative research: Theory, method, and practice* (pp. 8–23). Thousand Oaks, CA: Sage.

Blumer, H. (1969). *Symbolic interactionism*. Berkeley: University of California Press.

Baym, N. (1995a). The emergence of community in computer-mediated communication. In S. Jones (Ed.), *CyberSociety* (pp. 138–163). Newbury Park, CA: Sage.

Baym, N. (1995b). The performance of humor in computer-mediated communication. *Journal of Computer-Mediated Communication, 1*(2), retrieved 6-15-07 from http://jcmc. indiana.edu/vol1/issue2/baym.html.

Baym, N. (1998). The emergence of on-line community. In S. G. Jones (Ed.), *Cybersociety2.0: Revisiting computer-mediated communication and community* (pp. 35–68). Thousand Oaks, CA: Sage.

Bennett, A. (2004). Virtual subculture? Youth identity and the Internet. In A. Bennett & K. Khan-Harris (Eds.), *After subculture: Critical studies in contemporary youth culture* (pp. 162–172). New York: Palgrave.

Bingham, N., & Thrift, N. (2000). Some new instructions for travellers: The geography of Bruno Latour and Michel Serres. In M. Crang & N. Thrift (Eds.), *Thinking space* (pp. 281–301). New York: Routledge.

Brandt, D., & Clinton, K. (2002). Limits of the local: Expanding perspectives on literacy as a social practice. *Journal of Literacy Research, 34*(3), 337–356.

Bruce, B. C. (1999). Challenges for the evaluation of new information and communication technologies. *Journal of adult and adolescent literacy, 42*(6), 435–442.

Bruce, B. C., & Leander, K. M. (1997). Searching for libraries in education: Why computers cannot tell the story. *Library Trends, 45*(4), 746–770.

Bruce, B. C., & Rubin, A. (1993). *Electronic quills: A situated evaluation of using computers for writing in classrooms*. Hillsdale, NJ: Lawrence Erlbaum.

Castells, M. (1996). *The rise of the network society*. Cambridge, MA: Blackwell.

Clarke, J. (2002). A new kind of symmetry: Actor-network theories and the new literacy studies. *Studies in the Education of Adults, 34*(2), 107–122.

Clifford, J. (1992). Traveling cultures. In L. Grossberg, C. Nelson, & P. A. Treichler (Eds.), *Cultural studies* (pp. 96–116). London: Routledge.

Correll, S. (1995). The ethnography of an electronic bar; The lesbian cafe. *Journal of Contemporary Ethnography, 24*(3), 270.

Crang, M., Crang, P., & May, J. (Eds.). (1999). *Virtual geographies: Bodies, space, and relations*. London: Routledge.

Dodge, M., & Kitchin, R. (2001). *Mapping cyberspace*. New York: Routledge.

Ellsworth, E. (1997). *Teaching positions: Difference, pedagogy, and the power of address*. New York: Teachers College Press.

Fairclough, N. (1995). *Critical discourse analysis: The critical study of language*. New York: London.

Gee, J. P. (1999). *An introduction to discourse analysis: Theory and method*. London: Routledge.

Gee, J. P., Hull, G., & Lankshear, C. (1996). *The new work order: Behind the language of the new capitalism*. Boulder, CO: Westview.

Gupta, A., & Ferguson, J. (1997). Discipline and practice: 'The field' as site, method, and location in anthropology. In J. Ferguson & A. Gupta (Eds.), *Anthropological locations: Boundaries and grounds of a field science* (pp. 1–29) . Berkeley: University of California Press.

Hannerz, U. (1996). *Transnational connections: Culture, people, places*. New York: Routledge.

Haythornthwaite, C., & Wellman, B. (2002). The Internet in everyday life: An introduction. In B. Wellman & C. Haythornthwaite (Eds.), *The Internet in everyday life* (pp. 3–42). Malden, MA: Blackwell.

Hine, C. (2000). *Virtual ethnography*. London: Sage Publications.

Holloway, S., & Valentine, G. (2001). 'It's only as stupid as you are': Children's and adults' negotiation of ICT competence at home and at school. *Social and Cultural Geography, 2*(1), 25–42.

Holloway, S, Valentine, G., & Bingham, N. (2000). Institutionalising technologies: Masculinities, femininities, and the heterosexual economy of the IT classroom. *Environment and Planning A, 32*, 617–633.

Hull, G., & Schultz, K. (2001). Literacy and learning out of school: A review of theory and research. *Review of Educational Research, 71*(4), 575–611.

Jones, S. (1999). Studying the Net: Intricacies and issues. In S. Jones (Ed.), *Doing Internet research: Critical issues and methods for examining the Net* (pp. 1–28). Thousand Oaks, CA: Sage.

Kendall, L. (1999). Recontextualizing "cyberspace": Methodical considerations for online research. In S. Jones (Ed.), *Doing Internet research: Critical issues and methods for examining the Net* (pp. 57–74). Thousand Oaks, CA: Sage.

Latour, B. (1983). Give me a laboratory and I will raise the world. In K. Knorr-Cetina & M. Mulkay (Eds.), *Science observed: Perspectives on the social study of science* (pp. 141–170). London: Sage.

Latour, B. (1987). *Science in action.* Cambridge, MA: Harvard University Press.

Latour, B. (1988a). *The pasteurization of France (with irreductions).* Cambridge, MA: Harvard University Press.

Latour, B. (1988b). Drawing things together. In M. Lynch & S. Woolgar (Eds.), *Representation in scientific practice* (pp. 19–68). Cambridge, MA: MIT Press.

Leander, K. M. (2001). "This is our freedom bus going home right now": Producing and hybridizing space-time contexts in pedagogical discourse. *Journal of Literacy Research, 33*, 637–679.

Leander, K. M. (2002a). Locating Latanya: The situated production of identity artifacts in classroom interaction. *Research in the Teaching of English, 37*, 198–250.

Leander, K. M. (2002b). Polycontextual construction zones: Mapping the expansion of schooled space and identity. *Mind, Culture, and Activity, 9*, 211–237.

Leander, K. M., & Loworn, J. (2006). Literacy networks: Following the circulation of texts, bodies and objects in the schooling and online gaming of one youth. *Cognition and Instruction 24*(3), 291–340.

Lemke, J. L. (2000). Across the scales of time: Artifacts, activities, and meanings in ecosocial systems. *Mind, Culture, and Activity, 7*, 273–292.

Mann, C., & Stewart, F. (2002). *Internet communication and qualitative research.* Thousand Oaks, CA: Sage.

Marcus, G. E. (1995). Ethnography in/of the world system: The emergence of multi-sited ethnography. *Annual Review of Anthropology, 24*, 95–117.

Markham, A. N. (1998). *Life online: Researching real experience in virtual space.* Walnut Creek, CA: AltaMira Press.

McCarthy, C., Giardina, M., Harewood, S., & Park, J. K. (2003). Contesting culture: Identity and curriculum developments in the age of globalization, postcolonialism, and multiplicity. *Harvard Educational Review, 73*(3), 449–465.

Miller, D., & Slater, D. (2000). *The Internet: An ethnographic approach.* New York: Berg.

Mitchell, W. J. (1996). *City of bits: Space, place, and the Infobahn.* Cambridge, MA: MIT Press.

Mitra, A. (1997). Virtual commonality: Looking for India on the Internet. In S. Jones (Ed.), *Virtual culture.* London: Sage.

New London Group, T. (1996). A pedagogy of multiliteracies: Designing social futures. *Harvard Educational Review, 66*(1), 60–92.

Olwig, K. F., & Hastrup, K. (Eds.). (1997). *Siting Culture: The shifting anthropological object.* London: Routledge.

Oswell, D. (1998). The place of 'childhood' in Internet content regulation: A case study of policy in the UK. *International Journal of Cultural Studies, 1*, 131–151.

Paccagnella, L. (1997). Getting the seat of your pants dirty: Strategies for ethnographic research on virtual communities. *Journal of Computer Mediated Communication, 3*(1), retrieved 6-15-07 from http://jcmc.indiana.edu/vol3/issue1/paccagnella.html.

Papert, S. (1987). Computer criticism vs. technocentric thinking. *Educational Researcher, 16*, 22–30.

Robins, K. (1996). Cyberspace and the world we live in. In J. Dovey (Ed.), *Fractal dreams: New media in social context* (pp. 1–30). London: Lawrence and Wishard.

Saco, D. (2002). *Cybering democracy: Public space and the Internet.* Minneapolis: University of Minnesota Press.

Sade-Beck, L. (2004). Internet ethnography: Online and offline. *International Journal of Qualitative Methods, 3*(2), retrieved 6-15-07 from http://www.ualberta.ca/~iiqm/back-issues/3_2/html/sadebeck.html.

Skelton, T., & Valentine, G. (Eds.). (1998). *Cool places: Geographies of youth cultures.* London: Routledge.

Spradley, J. P. (1980). *Participant observation.* New York: Holy, Rinehart, & Winston.

Turkle, S. (1995). *Life on the screen: Identity in the age of the Internet.* New York: Simon & Schuster.

U.K. Linguistic Ethnography Forum Coordinating Committee. (2004). *UK linguistic ethnography: A discussion paper.* Unpublished manuscript.

Valentine, G., Holloway, S. L., & Bingham, N. (2000). Transforming cyberspace: Children's interventions in the new public sphere. In S. L. Holloway & G. Valentine (Eds.), *Children's geographies: Playing, living, learning* (pp. 156–173). New York: Routledge.

Valentine, G., Holloway, S., & Bingham, N. (2002). The digital generation?: Children, ICT and the everyday nature of social exclusion. *Antipode, 34*(2), 296–315.

Wakeford, N. (1998). Urban culture for virtual bodies: Comments on lesbian 'identity' and 'community' in San Francisco Bay Area cyberspace. In R. Ainley (Ed.), *New frontiers of space, bodies, and gender* (pp. 176–190). London: Routledge.

Wakeford, N. (1999). Gender and the landscapes of computing in an Internet cafe. In M. Crang, P. Crang, & J. May (Eds.), *Virtual Geographies: Bodies, space and relations* (pp. 178–201). London: Routledge.

CHAPTER 3

Large-Scale Quantitative Research on New Technology in Teaching and Learning

RONALD E. ANDERSON
UNIVERSITY OF MINNESOTA, USA

Introduction

Large-scale empirical studies, especially in cross-national contexts, offer great payoff for the understanding of new literacies and new media, especially those related to teaching and learning. Without scientific sample and standardized measurement, generalization to larger populations is impossible or weak at best. Statistical designs with random-sampling techniques make it possible to generalize to huge populations of learners with relatively small samples and known estimates of error. Standardization of assessment instruments and coordination of procedures for collecting data make it possible to compare national and regional education systems, as well as demographic groups. Longitudinal and panel designs make trend analyses possible, because measures are repeated and statistical variations can be minimized. Experimental designs make it possible to isolate causal processes, because predictive conditions can be controlled and isolated to determine if they affect one or more student outcomes.

These methods, however, tend to be demanding in terms of cost, time, and collaboration. In addition, these types of research on new media issues face unique problems such as rapidly changing technologies. This chapter will review theoretical frameworks; describe the national and international large-scale studies of new media that have been conducted; review some major findings from these studies; discuss methodological issues and options; and discuss challenges and opportunities for such research in the future.

The scope of the studies discussed in this chapter encompasses both student assessments and surveys of utilization of new media, including pedagogical practices of teachers using information and communication technology (ICT). With regard to assessment, we include both studies that assess ICT-related new literacies and selected studies that provide for investigation of the impact of ICT utilization on learning in other subjects, such as mathematics or science.

One evident change during the past three decades has been the terminology for the technology that delivers the new media. Whereas during the 1980s, the principal new media was called "computers," "information technology," or "IT," by the late 1990s, educators in most countries began to refer to it as "ICT" for "information and communication technology." The integration of the Internet and multimedia with computer technology made many feel more comfortable with calling it "ICT." In some countries, however, most notably in the United States, educators refer to it as "information technology," "IT," or simply as "technology." In this chapter, the acronyms *ICT* and the word *technology* will be used synonymously.

This chapter is divided into four main parts or sections. The first section discusses theoretical issues, highlighting conceptualizations in relevant, large-scale studies. The second part describes some key features of each relevant study, ending with one or two illustrative findings from the study. The third section points out common methodological solutions in these types of studies. In the final section, speculations are made about the future and the research that will be needed.

Conceptual and Theoretical Approaches

Many of the chapters of this volume ask the theoretical question, "What are the new literacies?" In this chapter the theoretical question asked is "What should be the priorities when planning large-scale studies of new literacy?"

Relevant conceptual and theoretical work focuses on two areas: one is a measurement or assessment and the other is contextual and causal frameworks. The former is generally concerned with criterion or predicted variables, typically test scores but sometimes attitudinal and behavioral factors. The latter focuses on the interrelation of the predictor variables and their relation with the criterion or predicted variables. Within the discussion of each of these two conceptual tasks the approaches taken in relevant, major studies will be outlined. First, however, a theoretical approach will be outlined for addressing the assessment requirements of a broad spectrum of new literacies.

Toward a Theory for Assessing New Literacies

A project to systematically assess new literacies, particularly large-scale studies, must narrow, or delimit, the scope of the assessment in various ways. If one is interested in a very new and novel media, the choices are likely to be very limited. However, if one is interested in a broad scope of ICTs, then it is necessary to prioritize components and dimensions of the full range of potential content, knowledge, and skills that could be assessed.

In order to delimit the new literacies assessment domain the following dimensions of digital tools, and their associated skills, are proposed:

1. Difficulty/Level: the amount of time and requisite skills required to learn the subject matter or performance. It is assumed that grade level and age are strongly associated with difficulty.
2. Does the content require hands-on or performance assessment or are other forms of assessment feasible?
3. Complexity of problem solving required.
4. The extent to which the information and/or knowledge ranges from highly concrete, explicit information to subjective or tacit knowledge.
5. The length of time that the media or technology has persisted. Has it been in place for a long time, avoiding obsolescence or is it new and novel?
6. Does the task for the student outcomes being assessed require a particular media or ICT or can it be completed manually in a reasonably comparable amount of time without the media or ICT?

Dimensions 2, 5, and 6 are defined in terms of two states or conditions; however, one should assume that these states define polar opposites and a wide range of intermediate states fall in between.

Another assessment condition will be treated as a design factor rather than as a planning dimension and that is the role for which the new literacy is considered relevant or critical. The principal roles that underlie new literacy tasks are productivity or employment roles; learning or student roles; and civic or citizenship roles. Of course, there are other roles such as social roles and leadership roles for which new literacies are relevant, but these roles are generally not salient enough for large-scale assessments. The researcher will initially select one or more roles and then determine what knowledge and skills pertaining to new literacy are relevant to that role or roles.

Given resource constraints, it is not feasible for any one research project to include assessment items for each point along each of these six dimensions or their underlying continua. With respect to difficulty, the researcher will typically select one to three age groups and then target tasks toward the large majority of those within the age group(s). With respect to the other dimensions, decisions are too often made implicitly or without sufficient planning. There are good reasons for choosing a specific decision point on some of the dimensions. However, before discussing this possibility, the major projects defining and measuring computer or ICT literacy will be described first.

Assessment Framework Projects

Comparative assessments typically begin with an assessment framework, which is intended to define the content universe from which test items will be sampled. It also identifies the specific facets or domains and subdomains of the content to be assessed. Key elements of the assessment frameworks will be summarized for each of the large-scale projects that attempted to define aspects of computer or ICT literacies. Many, but not all, of these projects actually attempted to measure technology-related literacies in the field. Empirical details of those studies will be described in the next section of this chapter.

The Minnesota Computer Literacy Assessment (MCLA). In preparation for the 1979 MCLA, the investigators developed the first conceptual framework for the measurement of skills, knowledge, and attitudes relevant to computer utilization by students (Johnson, Anderson, Hansen, & Klassen, 1980). Both the knowledge domain of this framework and the paper-and-pencil test were divided into three subdomains: (a) knowing basic computer concepts; (b) knowing applications and their impact; and (c) understanding and reading simple algorithms (Anderson & Klassen, 1981). While the definition of computer literacy was hotly debated, the attitude and knowledge measures from this study provided the foundation for most of the hundreds of studies on computer attitudes or computer literacy during the decade that followed (Anderson, Klassen, & Johnson, 1981).

The ETS computer competence study. In the early 1980s, the most hotly contested technology issue in education was whether or not computer literacy should include and emphasize computer programming. The programming proponents won out, and in 1986 the Educational Testing Service (ETS) conducted a national assessment of computer programming, calling it "computer competence" (Martinez & Mead, 1988). The study was done under the auspices of NAEP (National Assessment of Educational Progress). While their domains were defined in terms of (a) knowledge and attitudes, (b) computer applications, and (c) computer programming, the principle emphasis was on programming.

The IEA computers in education (CompEd) study. The IEA CompEd study was the first international, technology-related large-scale survey and assessment. Nearly 20 different countries were involved in one or more segments of the student survey between 1988 and 1993 (Pelgrum & Plomp, 1991). For the main student assessment in 1992, the project developed an instrument called the FITT (Functional Information Technology Test). The conceptual domains defined for this test were three-fold: (a) knowing basic computer concepts; (b) knowing applications and their impact; and (c) understanding and reading simple algorithms. An optional, short, and separate computer programming test was developed as well. It is noteworthy that even though this assessment framework was developed more than 10 years after the framework of the MCLA, the categories were quite similar. Micro and personal computers had emerged during that time, but most of the categories and priorities of information technology and information science remained the same.

The NETS (National Educational Technology Standards) project. Because of the demands from schools and teachers, the NETS (National Educational Technology Standards) project was organized by ISTE (International Society for Technology in Education) in the mid-1990s. The resulting standards were published by ISTE (1998), and they remain widely used by teachers, schools, districts, states, and professional associations. The student NETS are embedded within ISTE's NETS-T (standards for teachers) and NETS-A (standards for school administrators). In principle, all teachers and administrators are supposed to meet the student standards as well. NETS is used by NCATE (National Council for Accreditation of Teacher Education) for alignment of standards for technology facilitators and technology leaders. Many assessments have used NETS as guides. For example, North Carolina requires that all 8th-grade students pass a test that is somewhat based on NETS.

The scope of the standards is suggested by the six topics in Table 3.1. Associated with each standard are several criteria for how the standard should be used. The rightmost column gives an illustrative criteria for each standard.

In addition to the standards in Table 3.1, the NETS standards manual includes (a) performance indicators, e.g., "choose an appropriate tool and tech resources for a given task"; and (b) curriculum scenarios with learning activities, e.g., in social studies unit for 9 to 12, students are to create a Web site on population growth after conducting various types of research; and (c) assessment guidelines, e.g., sample rubrics might be provided for a given criterion or standard.

NETS was not designed to be a measurement framework for a research project or assessment, so by themselves the NETS does not constitute a complete conceptual framework. It is not even always explicit about what students

Table 3.1 ISTE'S NETS Foundation (ICT) Standards for Students

No.	Standard topics	Sample criteria
1	Basic operations and concepts	E.g., Students are proficient in the use of technology.
2	Social, ethical, and human issues	Students practice responsible use.
3	Technology productivity tools	Students use technology tools to enhance learning.
4	Technology communications tools	Students use a variety of media and formats to communicate effectively to multiple audiences.
5	Technology research tools	Students use technology to locate, evaluate, and collect information from a variety of sources.
6	Technology problem-solving and decision-making tools	Students employ technology in the development of strategies for solving problems in the real world.

Adapted from ISTE (1998).

The ETS ICT literacy project. ICT Literacy standards were defined by the ICT Literacy Project at the Educational Testing Service (International ICT Panel, 2002). The core construct in its framework of standards was called ICT Proficiency. This was defined in terms of five information management skills: (a) access, (b) manage, (c) integrate, (d) evaluate, and (e) create information. While these five types of information management skills are at the core of their conceptualization, they also claim that ICT Literacy necessarily encompasses Cognitive Proficiency and Technical Proficiency as well. The cognitive domain consists of foundational skills of general literacy and problem solving. The technical domain parallels what is often called *technological literacy*, and subsumes considerable knowledge of hardware, software, and networking.

The Educational Testing Service had hoped for funding to use its framework in an international assessment. Even though the funding was not forthcoming, their framework has been used in the design of instructional modules.

The PISA ICT literacy project. The ETS ICT Literacy framework was adopted by PISA planning groups; however they added "communication" to the five knowledge-management skills. Presently, PISA has not determined if this will be the final conceptual framework to be used in its 2009 assessment.

Summary of assessment frameworks. Developing conceptual models for what should be taught and tested related to the new media has been very challenging. Perhaps the main reason is that the new media are still rather novel and their capabilities change quite rapidly. Yet, the assessment frameworks changed very little for 20 years, up until 2000 and later. Probably this stability occurred because ICT functions remained fairly constant.

In the nearly 30 years since new media literacy studies began, editing and composing text arguably remains the highest priority ICT-based task for the educated citizenry. At the same time, electronic networks and e-mail have been emerging and have yielded new functions that students and others should become familiar with.

During the last 3 decades, the science of both text and graphical processing has made major strides. These strides combined with the Internet have greatly increased the salience of information and knowledge management. Recent assessment frameworks for new media reflect this salience.

The history of the assessment frameworks reviewed in this section so far hint that future framework development must continue to balance change with continuity. It is a delicate balance, which perhaps can be resolved by concentrating on the goals of the endeavor.

Contextual and Causal Frameworks

The other conceptual issue most challenging for large-scale assessment-related studies is a contextual or structural one: what are the relevant contextual factors for understanding or predicting teaching and learning processes and how are these contextual factors best structured? If the project is conceived as a qualitative one, the challenge is likely to be defined in contextual terms; whereas if it is quantitative, then the framework is likely to be defined structurally, especially in terms of how the contextual factors are interrelated in predicting performance on the main outcomes of interest.

Contextual frameworks. These conceptual questions generally cannot typically be answered succinctly. The substantial complexity of the categories and variables involved are often summarized graphically or given a visual representation. Figure 3.1 is a concentric circle diagram typically used to show expanding contexts of influence. Cole (1996) provided the inspiration for this framework, which was used in the early planning phases of the qualitatively oriented SITES case-studies project. In this type of model, each larger circle is assumed to influence the circles within it. The slices represent factors like the curriculum that impinge on or across all contextual levels. The framework (or model) is not intended to be precise in that any given outer circle might have direct influence on more than one concentric circle within it. The labels in the

Figure 3.1 Sample conceptual framework: Contextual aspects in the SITES case-studies project.

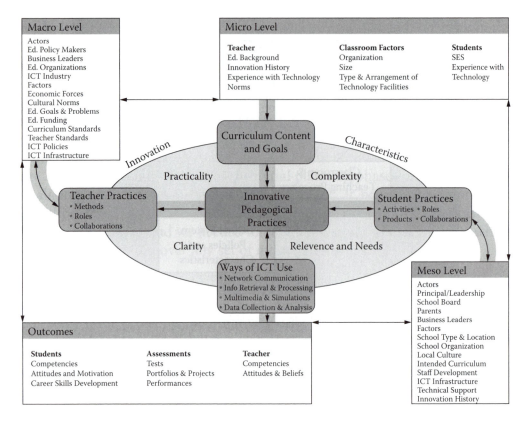

Figure 3.3 Conceptual framework for the SITES module 2 project.

a qualitative study such as a case-studies project. Furthermore, having given some thought to the causal linkages by constructing a blended framework, it may be easier to produce a variety of causal models each dealing with a more narrow scope of the full domain.

Relevant Large-Scale Empirical Studies

The Minnesota Computer Literacy Assessment (MCLA)

Nearly 30 years ago, the first large-scale study of new literacies was conducted in Minnesota. The Minnesota Computer Literacy Assessment, conducted by Anderson, Klassen, Krohn, and Smith-Cunnien (1982) at the Minnesota Educational Computing Consortium (MECC), in which 3,600 randomly selected 8th- and 11th-grade students in Minnesota schools were surveyed and assessed. Anderson, Klassen, and Hansen, (1981) also surveyed 1,000 randomly selected mathematics and science teachers for the 8th and 11th grades and identified some of the factors that facilitated and curtailed the adoption of computers in their classrooms.

At the end of the 1970s, punch cards were still a popular medium for computer utilization. One might be tempted to exclude these early studies from new media (or new literacies) research because of the primitive technology in use then; however, at that time timesharing terminals and microcomputers were already being used extensively to deliver computer assisted (CAI) and computer managed instruction (CMI). During the 1960s and early 1970s, CAI and CMI were largely limited to what was called "drill-and-practice" instruction, but many tutorials, some of which used graphical displays, were utilized by the end of the 1970s in secondary and postsecondary schools. By that time, databases and word processors also were commonly used in education and their use was taught in a number of classrooms. Microcomputers had even been acquired for a few schools and some households.

To provide a glimpse of the MCLA test, here is one of the representative test items in the MCLA:

A Newspaper publisher has the following information about subscribers stored in the computer. They are name, address, and renewal date. How would you arrange the information to be most useful to the delivery person?

  a. ordered listing by address
  b. ordered listing by renewal dates
  c. alphabetical listing of streets
  d. ordered listing by zip code
  e. I don't know

Only 30% of eighth graders and 35% of eleventh graders answered this test item correctly. The poor performance on this item reflects the fact that most students at that time had not been exposed to either the use of a database program or the principles of algorithmic logic.

What is noteworthy about this item, and others like it, is that it is a measure of information literacy, specifically the ability to organize information in such a way as to make it readily accessible and analyzable. Most of the literature on information literacy and new literacies did not begin to appear until the late 1980s and early 1990s (cf., Spitzer, Eisenberg, & Lowe, 1998; Hawisher & Selfe, 2000). New literacies may be deictic, but some elements have been highly persistent. Text editing and organizing information by sorting are technologies that have been critically important for the past 30 years. Yet, because they are "old" technologies, researchers may neglect them.

The test item is additionally interesting because girls were 5% more likely than boys to answer it correctly. The same pattern occurred across some other items associated directly or indirectly to programming logic. This is indicative of how women sometimes have an advantage over men in tests of information literacy. This is especially true with test items requiring procedural logic and skill and/or familiarity with general productivity tools (Anderson, 1987).

The ETS Computer Competence Study

The 1986 study of "computer competence" by the Educational Testing Service (ETS) was mentioned earlier, and it was noted that the assessment domain was divided into three sections: (a) knowledge and attitudes, (b) computer applications, and (c) computer programming. The principle emphasis was on programming.

The study was a massive undertaking. A total of 632 test items were administered in a block design to well over 25,000 students in grades 3, 7, and 11 (Martinez & Mead, 1988). From this study, we know that 90% of the students in those grades had used computers and about 50% were getting some kind of instruction about computers in school. Over a third of the students had a computer at home, even though the home computer was then only a few years old. One of the principal findings of the study was that the exposure to computers at home was equally as significant in predicting students' computer competence as what they were learning in school. A major digital gap was evident in that they found a major advantage in computer competence for students who had a high SES and parents with a college education, who were not racial minorities.

By the late 1980s, packaged productivity software such as word processors, spreadsheet programs, and database programs had become available for all the major microcomputers or personal computers, as they came to be called. This undercut the validity of arguments for universal instruction in computer programming. Meanwhile the term "computer literacy" had come to be used to refer to the skills needed for using computers effectively with productivity-software tools. By the time the results of the study were released, computer programming was no longer given much attention, which accounts for the study having had relatively little impact on education. Ironically, with the introduction of the Internet, the need for people to learn computer programming has arisen again. Some now argue that students should be introduced to, and tested in, HTML and XLM, which are similar to traditional programming languages.

The IEA Computers in Education (CompEd) Study

In 1995 the first large-scale, international study of technology in education was proposed by Tjeerd Plomp and associates at the University of Twente in the Netherlands and approved by the IEA (International Association for the Evaluation of Educational Achievement). The study had two separate stages—one collecting data in 1989, and the second collecting data in 1992. Twenty-two countries participated in the first stage, and 12 countries completed the second stage.

During the 1989 (Stage 1) study, surveys were conducted in each of three types of schools: (a) elementary schools, (b) lower secondary, and (c) upper secondary (Janssen Reinen & Pelgrum, 1993). Within each school sample, questionnaires were completed by the principal, computer coordinator, and several teachers. Sample surveys were completed in each of the 22 participating national systems: Austria, Belgium (Flemish), Belgium (French), Canada (BC), China, France, Germany (Federal Republic), Greece, Hungary, India, Israel, Italy, Japan, Luxembourg, Netherlands, New Zealand, Poland, Portugal, Slovenia, Spain, Switzerland, and the United States (Pelgrum & Plomp, 1993).

During the second stage in 1992, the surveys of school principals and computer coordinators were repeated, but focused on the added component of student assessment. The student questionnaire included attitude and background questions, as well as test items, and was administered to students in one randomly selected classroom within each sampled school. The countries participating in the 1992 study were Austria, Bulgaria, Germany, Greece, Italy, India, Israel, Japan, Latvia, Netherlands, Slovenia, Thailand, and the United States.

In 1992, the CompEd study collected data from over 75,000 students, 5,000 schools, and 10,000 teachers (Pelgrum, Janssen, Reinen, & Plomp, 1993). Each country surveyed a scientifically selected, representative sample of schools and a representative sample of students and selected teachers within schools. With the exception of India and South Africa, where only one region of the country was surveyed, and Greece, where only computer-using schools were sampled, the countries obtained samples representing all of the schools, both academic and vocational. The only excluded schools were those offering only special education or those not serving the targeted grades. The three targeted grades (student populations) were (a) the grade in which the modal age of students was 10 years, (b) the grade in which the modal age of students was 13 years, and (c) the next-to-the-final year of upper-secondary school. In most countries, this resulted in the selection of grades 5, 8, and 11.

This FITT test that was mentioned in the first part of the chapter was bundled with the student questionnaire and administered as a paper-and-pencil task. The study yielded many indicators of the quality of the role of technology across educational systems. At the school level, the indicators included hardware and software availability, location of equipment, and organization of computer support. At the teacher level were measures of teacher training, experience, and classroom practice. At the student level were indicators of knowledge, attitudes, exposure to different learning applications, and the use of home computers for educational purposes. Here are samples of the findings:

1. The number of computers in most countries rose rapidly during the 1980s and early 1990s, but by 1992 the number of computers in typical schools was only enough to allow one class at a time to use computers. Many of the computers were quite primitive. Over 50% of the computers in U.S. schools were Apple II computers (Anderson, 1993).

Table 3.3 Percent Correct on FITT (Practical Computer Knowledge) by Country and Grade Level

Educational system	8th Grade	11th Grade
Austria	69	86%
Germany	69	—
Netherlands	67	—
United States	61	65
Bulgaria	51	62
Japan	49	65
Latvia		70
Slovenia		70

2. The most common use of computers in learning at that time was occurring in conjunction with courses on informatics or other courses for students to learn how to use computers (Pelgrum & Schipper, 1993). However, this was not the case in the United States where science, math, and language-arts teachers were expected to teach ICT skills as students needed them.

3. On the FITT test, which is best viewed as a test of practical computer knowledge, the Western European students in Austria, Germany, and the Netherlands had the highest scores. (See Table 3.3.) Eleventh-grade students in Latvia and Slovenia were also relatively high. On the other hand, students from Bulgaria and 8th-grade Japanese students had the lowest scores. In between these two extremes were students in the United States (Plomp, Anderson, & Kontogiannopoulou-Polydorides, 1996).

The relatively poor performance of Japanese and American students was a surprise to many due to the emphasis on technology in these countries. Japan was historically slow to put computers in their classrooms until a few years after this assessment. Schools and educators in the United States had been emphasizing the integration of computers into education for several years, but the teaching of computing skills had generally been neglected.

American educators tended to believe that students learned IT skills at home and that it was better for teachers of all subjects to be responsible for teaching IT skills only as needed. Most European schools, however, started introducing computer-related (informatics) courses, often on a required basis, in the late 1980s (Brummelhuis, A.C.A. t., 1993; Collis et al., 1996). Ironically, the emphasis on technology integration within American education has resulted in the relative absence of opportunities for elementary and secondary students to obtain instruction in ICT skills.

Teaching, Learning, and Computing (TLC)

The Teaching, Learning, and Computing (TLC) study in 1998 surveyed principals, technology coordinators, and teachers from a national probability sample of all elementary and secondary schools in the United States and from two large targeted or purposive samples of schools: (a) high-end technology-using schools and (b) schools participating national and regional educational reform programs. Results were obtained for about 650 schools in the probability sample and 470 in the purposive samples. From almost all of these schools, questionnaires were received from the principal, the technology coordinator, and three to five teachers. Further details on the study methodology can be obtained from Becker and Anderson, 1998.

While the study was not designed to investigate new literacies, some questions were included regarding teachers' skills with using technology. Their technological prowess was interrelated with beliefs about teaching and several other factors, such as the quality of technology support, were found to be closely correlated (Dexter, Anderson, & Ronnkvist, 2002).

Perhaps the most important findings of this study pertain to teachers and their participation in communities of practice (CoP). Participation in CoPs made it much more likely for teachers to successfully implement improvements in the quality of their instruction, especially if the school culture was in other ways supportive of their attempts to improve teaching (Becker & Riel, 1999).

ICT can play an important role in such instruction. The CoPs, sometimes called "professional communities," operate effectively when teachers share ideas and feedback around their main goals in teaching. This is especially true when teachers' goals are complex and not well understood. Two goals of this type examined in the TLC study were constructivist philosophy and belief in the importance of new literacies in teaching. Implementing effective innovations tend to be rare because of the many demands on teachers' time and attention, but teachers with constructivist beliefs are more likely to use new media in their teaching and to innovate in implementing them.

The IEA SITES Study

The SITES (the Second International Technology in Education Study) study was initiated in 1997 by the IEA to investigate the role of ICT in education. The design of SITES followed the earlier CompEd model in some ways. Both studies had surveys at the school level of principals and of school-technology coordinators. The CompEd study had both a student assessment and a teacher survey and the proposed third module of SITES was to have a student assessment. The SITES study consists of three modules as summarized in Table 3.4.

Table 3.4 SITES Three Modules

Module	Time frame	No. of countries	Issue	Data
1 (SITES-M1)	1997–1999	26	What are the main trends?	Surveys of schools (principals and technology coordinators)
2 (SITES-M2)	1999–2003	28	What innovative teaching uses technology and what does it take?	In-depth case studies of innovative teaching in schools
3 (SITES-2006)	2002–2007	20 (est.)	What are teachers able to do with ICT to improve their learning?	Surveys of schools and teachers

The overall study design was approved by the IEA in 1997, and the survey data of module 1 were collected in 1998. The module 2 case study visits to the school sites were conducted during 2000 and 2001 and the report was released in 2003 (Kozma, 2003). Module 2006 scheduled their data collection for 2006 with the results to be released in late 2007. Each of the three modules will be described briefly in turn.

SITES-module 1. In 1998 data were collected using a questionnaire survey of principals and one of technology coordinators or their equivalents. Twenty-six countries participated by conducting these surveys in one or more of these three school levels: (a) primary, (b) lower secondary, and (c) upper secondary. As reported in Pelgrum and Anderson (1999), SITES-Module 1 produced findings on the extent to which ICT is used (and by whom) in education systems across the globe. These findings include,

- the extent to which education systems have adopted, implemented, and realized the results from objectives that are considered important for education in a knowledge society;
- teaching practices that principals consider to be innovative, important, effective, and satisfying;
- existing differences in ICT-related practices both within and between education systems and what lessons can be learned from this.

The findings on school Internet access were representative of the heterogeneous pattern of cross-national adoption of new ICT. Figure 3.4 shows that while 100% of the schools in Singapore and Iceland had access, some countries had only about a fourth of their schools connected. Most of the other countries had connected over 50% of their schools. What is so remarkable about this pattern is that even in countries that do not speak the dominant language of the Internet, English, most of their schools had been connected and many of the students were using the Internet in school. This rapid connection of schools to the Internet occurred within only about 5 years or less.

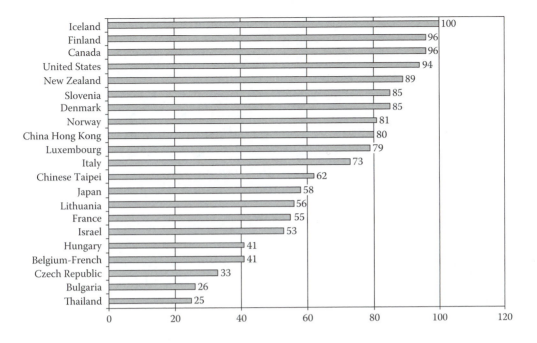

Figure 3.4 Average percent of lower secondary schools with Internet access, 1998 IEA SITES.

On the other hand, Figure 3.4 shows the dismal nature of new media in education—a huge digital divide between the wealthier nations and the poorer ones. Except for Thailand and Bulgaria, developing countries were not included in this study. The Internet has largely passed over many of the countries in the world where electricity is a luxury. Even within wealthier countries like the United States where the digital divide has shrunk, there are still huge (and growing) disparities in the degree and quality of exposure to ICT both inside and outside of school.

SITES-module 2 (case studies). Nearly 30 countries conducted in-depth case studies during 2000 and 2001. The focus of this qualitative research is innovative pedagogical practices that use technology (IPPUT). Typical IPPUTs were classes that did large, group projects; participation in electronic field trips; art classes that switched to the use of painting software; and schools that used data-driven, teacher-based decision making. Each country was given the latitude of selecting its own criteria for case selection, but this had to be what was considered innovative in that country.

The main purposes of this qualitative study were to understand the essential characteristics of these practices, what sustains them, and what outcomes are produced. To accomplish this investigation, each case study describes and analyzes classroom-based processes and their contexts. These case studies were intended to provide policy analysts and teachers with examples of "model" classroom practices and offer policymakers findings regarding the contextual factors that are critical to successful implementation and sustainability of these exemplary teaching practices using ICT.

The 28 countries participating in this module of SITES were Australia, Canada, Chile, China-Hong Kong, Chinese Taipei, Czech Republic, Denmark, England, Finland, France, Germany, Israel, Italy, Japan, Korea, Latvia, Lithuania, Netherlands, Norway, Philippines, Portugal, Russia, Singapore, Slovak Republic, South Africa, Spain, Thailand, and the United States. Each country conducted 4 to 12 case studies, and the total number of cases for analysis was 172. Some results and conclusions of this module can be found on the Web site: http://sitesm2.org . The final report of the project was published as a book by ISTE (Kozma, 2003).

One noteworthy finding was that the students used the Internet as part of nearly every innovative practice selected. Another finding of perhaps greater importance is that the students involved in these innovative pedagogical practices often engaged in activities that could be considered "knowledge management," especially knowledge construction. Typically, such activities were called projects and included the tasks of searching, organizing, and evaluating knowledge. For instance, Germany's first case study found that students "turned into providers of knowledge." Portugal reported a case where the teachers wanted their students to be "constructors rather than receptors of mathematical knowledge." In Norway, Australia, and the United States, to name a few such countries, cases were found where students worked collaboratively with ICT tools to complete large projects yielding diverse types of knowledge. Some of these projects involved shared activity and regular communication with students in other schools and countries.

Not all of the cases included collaboration, constructivism, or creativity in student activities. Imagine the traditional classroom that has received a donation of two laptops that sit in the back of the room to be used only by students who finish their assignments first. If you took a picture of the classroom from where the teacher stands, you would capture mostly children bending over their books at individual desks.

Now contrast that image with the students in the following photograph. These students were using MicroWorlds software to design and represent shape rotations in "Maths." Here the teacher was acting as a facilitator or coach by asking questions. In this classroom, the students were working on their problems in collaborative groups.

The differences in these two types of classrooms were uncovered and elucidated in the IEA SITES study by using qualitative methods, especially classroom observation and interviews.

Survey indicators that captures such subtle contrasts can be constructed but not without extensive experience in the field settings and expertise in survey measurement. This study demonstrates the feasibility and value of using qualitative methods and case studies in an international context and on a fairly large scale.

Figure 3.5 Students using MicroWorlds software in groups with the teacher acting as a facilitator or coach by asking questions.

SITES-2006. SITES-2006 was designed to build on these case study findings from the leading-edge classrooms of SITES-Module 2 (http://www.sites2006.net). Specifically, the school survey and the teacher survey questionnaires include indicators to identify the difference between innovative and typical learning contexts. The study was intended to determine the readiness of schools and teachers to provide a learning environment where students can participate in enriched pedagogical practices.

SITES-2006 also was originally designed to include an assessment of students, which was described in the previous section of this chapter. Sufficient funding, however, was not forthcoming for a student assessment, and it was dropped completely. The surveys of teachers and of schools (principals and technology leaders) went ahead as planned. Data collection proceeded in 2006 and the results are expected in 2007.

Countries participating in SITES-2006 sampled a minimum of 400 schools with the grade in which the majority of 14-year-old students were enrolled, which in most countries was the eighth grade. From each of the sampled and participating schools, attempts were made to obtain completed questionnaires from two mathematics teachers and two science teachers of students in the grade with the most students at age 14.

Despite highly diverse national educational systems around the world, almost every country has established policies regarding ICT in education (cf., Plomp et al., 1996; Plomp, Anderson, Law, & Quales, 2003). SITES in its various modules found many different approaches across countries in the way they take up the ICT challenge in education. Yet, there are common threads such as widespread and rapidly growing access to the Internet. It is particularly noteworthy that in so many countries the majority of educators believe in reform-like teaching practices, e.g., inquiry, project-based learning, and even

Table 3.6 The Intersection of Major Goals and Methods Used in Large-Scale Assessment-Related Research: Illustrative Approaches

	GOALS			
	Exploration	Theory/ hypothesis generation	Assessment and monitoring	Impact studies and evaluations
		Methods		
Qualitative Research: Observation and Interviewing	Case studies	Grounded theory	Constructed response coding	Formative evaluation
Quantitative Research: Surveying and Assessment	Pilot or field testing	Causal theory building	Traditional and online assessment	Summative evaluation

At the time of this chapter writing, OECD PISA is making a decision as to whether or not in 2009 the main assessment will be reading or ICT literacy. The original plan was that the subject would be reading and that plan will probably prevail.

Other studies. While both national and international school-based assessments of ICT knowledge and skill appear to be waning, ICT familiarity surveys of older populations are becoming more commonplace. One organization conducting many such studies is the Pew Internet & American Life Project (http://www.pewinternet.org/about.asp). Another is the World Internet Project (http://www.worldinternetproject.net/) involving 23 countries. The latter is the brainchild of Jeffrey Cole of the University of Southern California, and the project makes it possible for countries to conduct comparable surveys. Their goal is to conduct an annual survey but many, if not most, of the countries are unable to participate in any given year.

The greatest limitation of these types of studies is that all of their indicators of new literacy and use of new media are self-report measures. In that sense, they are more superficial than the studies given major attention in this chapter. Typically, their samples are taken of adult populations, which means that the results cannot be compared directly to school-age populations but sometimes allow for comparison of various adult age groups. Like opinion polling in general, the methodologies of these studies must be carefully evaluated. Whenever methodological details are impossible or difficult to obtain, it signifies that the study's methodological foundation may be weak.

Methodological Issues

Issues pertaining to research methodology are best organized in terms of the goals that are intended and the methods selected to achieve those goals. This structure is represented in Table 3.6, which shows four goals as columns and two types of methods as rows. The cells give illustrative approaches, e.g., grounded theory, that are typical of a given approach when it is used in the pursuit of a given goal category.

This table contrasts both qualitative and quantitative approaches by listing them as methods. While large-scale empirical research tends to be largely quantitative, qualitative approaches are needed for problems that are not well understood and for which indicators have not been refined. Often a combination of qualitative and quantitative approaches is needed in cross-national research due to the highly diverse cultural contexts to be studied (Creswell, 1998; Yin, 1994).

The prior section highlights the major, large-scale empirical studies that relate to new media and new literacies. In the remainder of this section, the discussion reviews the methodological decisions that are largely unique but critical to quantitatively oriented, international comparative assessments. The first methodological issue addressed is that of survey and test design, including item and test construction. Other issues addressed include sampling design, data collection, and data analysis. The discussion suggests criteria that can be used in evaluating existing studies and in planning future ones. These issues are given time and attention here because they are largely neglected in textbooks and the scholarly literature in general.

Survey and Test Design

The first step that needs to be completed after a conceptual framework is the refinement of research questions. Some core or foundational questions underlying all hunches and hypotheses should be derived to serve as orienting devices for priority setting in the project. Research questions also serve a second function of communicating the essence of the study to persons outside the project.

In the course of specifying the research questions, the key units of analysis will become clear. This is important because the units of sampling will be based on them. Most of the studies considered here use several units for sampling and analysis—student, teacher, school are the typical units selected.

In order to answer the research questions formulated, survey instruments will be needed within which are draft items for measuring the required indicators. Quite possibly these questionnaires will need to be revised for different grade levels if multiple grades are targeted. Some questionnaire instruments required for a typical study are listed in Table 3.7. Each instrument and its codebook must be prepared for each population or grade; however, often the manuals can be combined for all populations or grades.

The construction of the survey questionnaires will necessarily be guided by the indicators and constructs to be measured, and the constructs will be identified and elaborated by an analytical framework. A challenging aspect of such an analytical framework is the multilevel structure involving constructs and variables not only for students but also for teachers and schools. Once an

Table 3.7 Instruments and Manuals Required for a Typical Study

	Population 1 (Grade 4)	Population 2 (Grade 8)	Combined
Instruments			
Principal Quest.	x	x	
Tech. Quest.	x	x	
Teacher Quest.	x	x	
Student Quest.	x	x	
Performance Test	x	x	
Manuals*			
Design Plan			X
Curriculum Analysis			X
Sampling			X
Administration			X
Data Entry and Coding**	x	x	
Codebook	x	x	

* Some of these manuals may be combined. The instruments (tests and questionnaires) should be included in one of these manuals or published separately.
** Data Entry and Coding Manual includes cleaning as well as entry and coding. It also should include scoring for assessment items and rules for deriving composite scores or indicators

analytical framework is specified, attention must be devoted to operationalizing the various constructs and factors desired as variables for the analysis.

Sampling Design

The first design step after a conceptual framework and research questions is the delineation of the populations (or universes) to be investigated. From the standpoint of international, comparative assessment in education, generally this means choosing among the alternatives of selecting a grade, an age, or students with a specific number of years of schooling completed. Initially, the IEA studies selected grades but PISA selected an age, 15. Now the IEA studies use a combination of these criteria. A grade is selected by looking in each country for the grade with the most students who are age x. Alternatively it may be the grade with the most students who have completed y years of schooling. This type of population definition is necessary to standardize the bases of comparison across countries.

Whether a grade or an age is the basis for selecting sampling units, the selection is called a *population*. (See Table 3.6.) Often a single grade will be selected from the primary grade level and one from the lower secondary levels. These levels are called populations 1 and 2, because they will not necessarily be the same grades in each country due to differences across education systems, especially in the age that the students first start school.

In SITES-M1, a *target grade range* was also defined for purposes of comparing school resources across educational systems where the grade groupings vary greatly by country. The concept of target grade range was needed for asking questions about the accessible infrastructure and common experiences of students in a meaningful- but-comparable grade grouping. The definition of target grade range was especially significant because not only were many questions worded to refer to these target grades, but the number of students in the grade range was used as the measure of size (MOS) for purposes of sampling and weighting. The target grade range was defined as the three grades containing the most students of age 10 and 14, respectively, for populations 1 and 2. Thus, the target grade would generally, but not always, be the middle of each of these three grades. The biggest technical difficulty with the target-grade-range specification is that in some systems a school-level boundary falls somewhere within the grade range. A guideline for such situations can be to take the school level with the two grades with the most age-eligible students and define those two grades as the target grade range. In such situations, a sampling expert is needed to help adjudicate the choice, taking both the interests of the international coordination and that of the national study into account.

With respect to population coverage, each study must set standards, and especially critical is the maximum exclusion level. In any sampling at the national level, there will be schools that are extremely difficult to include, e.g., prison schools, special-education schools, or even schools that are located in extremely remote areas. An international study will typically allow exclusion of such schools but only up to a total of 3%, 5%, or a similar threshold.

Sampling design is one of the most crucial elements in the methodological quality of these studies. Most large-scale school surveys or assessments use stratified PPS (probability proportionate to size) random sampling. When a random class or classroom is selected for an assessment, cluster sampling is being used as well. Stratified sampling reduces sampling error when the stratification variables define groups that are homogeneous with respect to the dependent variables. Sometimes the biggest challenge is to find a database of all schools with good stratification variables like school type, SES, and region. PPS requires a meaningful MOS (measure of size) variable, which in most school surveys is the size of school as measured by school enrollment. Using PPS makes it possible to adjust the probabilities of selecting any school proportionate to its size. Without such an adjustment, small schools, or students in small schools, have much too high a chance of being included in the final sample.

Nonresponse is perhaps the most difficult and challenging sampling problem. If the nonresponse rate is lower than 50%, it implies that there may be a systematic bias introduced into the sample. Studies set completion rates as standards that have to be met. For example, the minimum completion rate set for SITES-2006 was 85% for schools and 85% for teachers, which means any nonresponse rate greater than 15% is unacceptable. Some projects or researchers set lower minimum completion rates. Others allow for replacement samples, that is, completely separate samples drawn to be used for sampling individual cases if a case from the first sample does not respond after a certain number of tries.

International studies utilize the threat of exclusion of a country's data from publication if the minimum completion rate is not reached. Generally, a compromise is implemented. If the minimum completion percentage is not achieved, the country's data should be flagged or placed "below the line," which means it is placed at the bottom of the table in order to warn readers that those data are more subject to systematic or sampling error.

Sampling classrooms, teachers, and/or students randomly within schools poses another challenge. Once a principal has agreed that the school will participate, then the best procedure is to get from the principal's office a list of classes, teachers, and/or students from which the researcher will randomly select the units to be approached for participation. Producing such lists may be demanding for the school, so some researchers attempt other procedures, e.g., the principal may be asked to distribute the questionnaires randomly to teachers. Such procedures may not produce good random samples, so they should not be used unless there is a validation study done to demonstrate that it works effectively.

Data Collection

Alternative modes or delivery mechanisms for the survey and assessment instruments are of major interest to researchers doing large-scale projects. While standard paper-and-pencil forms of the survey instruments may be provided, electronic-response options also should be considered when feasible and appropriate. Providing the questionnaires on a disc or CD should also be considered.

The novelty of Web-surveys already has worn off in many countries and completion rates are typically very low when questionnaires are long. Thus, multimode surveys should probably be used. The most important way to avoid bias due to electronic modes of questionnaire administration is to make the Web-delivered questionnaire as isomorphic or similar to the paper version as possible (Dillman, 2000). Other potential sources of bias include differences in respondents with respect to familiarity with and feelings toward the technologies involved. These factors need to be measured, so that they can be statistically investigated and used as controls in the analysis.

With a Web-delivery option available, small improvements in response rates should be possible. The costs of Web delivery of questionnaires in many different languages have been high in the past, but technology for this is improving. A number of technical and logistical issues need to be solved, such as developing online questionnaires that can run on most browsers and providing privacy space between students as they are taking the surveys online.

The chief challenges of using the Web for delivering performance assessments are largely technical. One of these challenges is security, which includes the maintenance of the integrity of each student's responses as well as guaranteeing fairness by eliminating opportunities for cheating or in other ways benefiting from the work of other students. Another major challenge is understanding the comparability of Web-based performance assessments. For some purposes, it is important to be comparable to other forms of assessment. However, comparability across subjects and testing occasions is the most critical. Without such comparability, the performance assessment may give certain types of students or types of situations an unfair advantage. International projects have a number of demands that are mostly unique to that environment: translation comparability, comparability of hemispheres, scheduling conflicts with other international studies, and data quality control across countries.

The translation challenge is mainly that of ensuring that words and phrases have essentially the same meanings in each country after translation from a master document. Questionnaires and tests are the biggest translation tasks but any instructions related to the administration of the surveys must also be translated. To ensure comparability, back-translations are needed where an independent translator translates the document back to the original language. When there are disagreements, then a third party should be called in to help resolve the discrepancies. Some projects use a third-party organization to do all or most of the translation, which can be extremely expensive.

The hemispheric challenge is that schools in the northern and southern hemispheres begin their school year at different times of the year. This means that if the assessments are given at the same time of the year in both hemispheres, the schools in one hemisphere will have a half-year advantage. One issue when assessments are given at two different times is that a decision must be made as to whether or not the North goes first or the South. Since most of the countries typically participating in IEA or OECD surveys are in the North, countries in the North probably get more influence over such decisions.

Surveys and assessments require that some school staff be devoted to the study for a time, and student time becomes an issue with assessments. When there are many surveys going on in any given year, these demands become a serious burden for the schools, and it produces noticeable, if not serious, increases in nonresponse rates. When international studies are being planned, the planners always try to take the schedule of other studies using the same population(s) into account.

In order to ensure the highest possible quality control within realistic financial constraints, various structures for quality monitoring should be considered. In a large-scale, international study, a critical element will be one or more consultants hired to be data quality monitors. The data quality monitor would help to work out issues between the national and international staffs regarding the collection and processing of data. The main function of the data

OECD has been able to raise the funds needed to do the ICT-related assessments proposed by either organization during the early part of the 21st century. Even the much less costly surveys of schools and teachers related to new media and new literacies are at risk for adequate funding in the near future.

Global Vision

Besides learning from other educational systems, international studies of innovative or exemplary schools and teaching practices offer the possibility of an overall, global view. It may be that every country's educational system is so different that little can be generalized. However, it is more likely that a common, international vision is emerging on how information technology can best be incorporated into teaching and learning. Actually, there may be several international visions emerging, but we do not know much about these leading-edge commonalities. Unless we know such things, we cannot plan very well for the future, which inevitably will be more global in terms of economic, communication, social, and educational systems.

Because of complexities and costs, very little research on the role of technology in education is conducted comparatively or internationally. However, when sustainability and transferability of innovative, high-impact learning practices are significant objectives, then an international context is critical to understanding the essential ingredients. Cultural traditions such as parental participation in students' computer-based homework, and national policies such as teacher technology certification, may be essential to the success of an educational intervention and have profound implications for its maintenance and transfer. This applies to transport of exemplary practices both within and across national boundaries.

New Technologies and New Media

An analysis of the newly emerging technologies reveals some startling ICTs and new media that will inevitably radically change social relations and raise major new social and ethical issues (Anderson, 2001). In this concluding consideration, three types of new technology (RFID, paintable computers, and artificial cells) are evaluated in terms of their implications for new literacies.

Finding everything with RFIDs. RFID stands for Radio Frequency Identification and consists of an electronic tagging technology that allows an object, place, or person to be automatically identified at a distance. Tags come in various sizes and shapes and can contain antennas, GPS chips, computer chips, and memory chips. Already many items in stores possess these tags. Tags can keep track of location histories, which raises privacy concerns because tags from stores could be sending back information from one's household to all kinds of companies and persons.

The future will likely bring us inexpensive, personal RFID systems to help us keep track of every object in an office or a home. Think of keeping track of everything in your home from your desktop computer. How much easier it would be to write chapters like this! You and everything relevant to you will exist as nodes in many overlapping networks. Personal networking in concert with object networking will create the need for new literacies in much the same way that the Internet meant that new literacies were needed to deal with it.

Wearable, paintable computers. Wearable computers started with clumsy head-gear but have evolved into nearly invisible components of sunglasses and regular glasses wherein small computer monitors are mounted. Printable/paintable computers will help make personal networking a reality because using an ink-jet printer you will be able to print an RFID (computer) tag on every document you view on your computer.

Eventually, more complex computer chips might be painted on specific surfaces. Artists can be creative both in making chip designs and then in painting them on surfaces with other computer chips. In the same way that multimedia literacy emerged as a new literacy in the age of color computer screens, paintings of malleable computer components will require a new dimension of aesthetic appreciation as well as language for creating flexible, powerful, practical, and even beautiful computer logic configurations.

Genetic engineering of "human" cells. Increasingly, computer scientists are predicting that genetic engineering in concert with nanotechnology and advanced robotics in 10 to 20 years will be producing molecular processors and memory devices the size of human cells. One implication of this is that it should be possible to implant these cells in a corner of the brain, interfacing them to our natural, biological brain cells. Once that is perfected, it should be relatively straightforward to build wireless interfaces to the brain such that software routines and data are downloaded to the brain. Furthermore, it would seem that brain cells could be copied and uploaded to the Internet and then shared with one's friends or colleagues, for truly virtual meetings, among other applications.

To build in safeguards for a person to protect his or her "self" probably will require a set of interaction scripts that are unlike any we use today. The uniqueness would be a consequence of the fact that the self consists not only of thought patterns but also of emotional patterns and spiritual routines that are built up over time from a long history of thoughts and emotions. One's spiritual side might be thought of as network of computer logic boards that combine thoughts and feelings around one's deeper beliefs about what is most meaningful in life.

As we come to understand our personal emotional and spiritual life better, we almost certainly will realize that its portrayal and communication will require even newer multimedia than we have now. Consequently, new literacies will be needed to participate in these advances.

Implications for survival of the species. While it is not possible to promise that any of these future scenarios will emerge during our lifetime, we can be sure that if they do, there will be major moral and ethic issues that will have to be confronted. In fact, the survival of humanity will depend on how well we do that. Today's teachers have a grave responsibility: the character education of tomorrow's human beings. To get a healthy glimpse of what it will take to get the next generation ready for the era of even newer media and literacies, we would do well to project ourselves into the future and look back to the present to see what needs to be done to ensure that the human race survives.

References

Anderson, R. E. (1987). Females surpass males in computer problem solving: Findings from the Minnesota Computer Literacy Assessment. *Journal of Educational Computing Research, 3*(1), 39–51.

Anderson, R. E. (Ed.). (1993). *Computers in American schools, 1992: An overview.* Minneapolis: University of Minnesota.

Anderson, R. E. (2001). Youth and information technology. In J. Mortimer, & R. Larson (Eds.), *The future of adolescent experience: Societal trends and the transition to adulthood.* New York: Cambridge University Press.

Anderson, R. E., & Klassen, D. A. (1981). Conceptual framework for developing computer literacy instruction. *AEDS Journal, 14*(3), 128–150.

Anderson, R. E., Klassen, D., & Hansen, T. P. (1981). The affective and cognitive effects of microcomputer based science instruction. *Journal of Educational Technology Systems, 9*(4), 329–355.

Anderson, R. E., Klassen, D., & Johnson, D. (1981). In defense of a comprehensive view of computer literacy. *The Mathematics Teacher, 74*(9), 687–690.

Anderson, R. E., Klassen, D., Krohn, K., & Smith-Cunnien, P. (1982). *Assessing computer literacy.* St. Paul: Minnesota Educational Computing Consortium.

Anderson, R. E., & Plomp, T. (2002). *Proposal for IEA SITES module 3.* Amsterdam: IEA.

Becker, H. J., & Anderson, R. E. (1998) *Survey questions from the teaching, learning and computing: A national survey of schools and teachers.* Irvine: University of California. Retrieved June 7, 2006, from http://www.crito.uci.edu/tlc/html/questionnaires.html

Becker, H. J., & Riel, M. (1999). *Teacher professionalism and the emergence of constructivist-compatible pedagogies.* Paper presented at 1999 Annual Meeting of the AERA, Montreal, Canada. Retrieved June 7, 2006, from http://www.crito.uci.edu/tlc/html/conference-presentations.html

Bielefeldt, T. (2005). Computers and student learning: Interpreting the multivariate analysis of PISA 2000. *Journal of Research on Technology in Education, 37*(4), 339–347.

Brummelhuis, A. C. A. T., (1993, April 13). *Large scale assessment of word processing skills, results from an international option to the core instruments of the COMPED-study.* Paper presented at the Annual Meeting of the AERA, Atlanta, GA.

Cole, M. (1996). *Cultural psychology.* Cambridge, MA: Harvard University Press.

Collis, B., Knezek, G. A., Lai, K. W., Miyasiki, K. T., Pelgrum, W. J., Plomp, T., et al. (1996). *Children and computers in school.* New York: Lawrence Erlbaum.

Creswell, J. (1998). *Qualitative inquiry and research design: Choosing among five traditions.* Thousand Oaks, CA: Sage.

Dexter, S., Anderson, R. E., & Ronnkvist, A. (2002). Quality technology support: What is it? Who has it? And what difference does it make? *Journal of Educational Computing Research, 26*(3), 287–307.

Dillman, D. A. (2000). *Mail and Internet surveys: The tailored design method, second edition.* New York: John Wiley & Sons.

Fuchs, T., & Woessmann, L. (2004). *Computers & student learning: Bivariate and multivariate evidence on the availability and use of computers at home and at school* (CESifo Working Paper 1321). Munich, Germany: CESifo. Retrieved July 7, 2007, from http://www.cesifo-group.de/pls/guest/download/Ifo%20Working%20Papers%20(seit%202005)/IfoWorkingPaper-8.pdf

Hawisher, G. E., & Selfe, C. L. (Eds.). (2000). *Global literacies and the World-Wide Web.* London: Routledge.

International ICT Literacy Panel. (2002, May). *Digital transformation: A framework for ICT literacy.* Retrieved May 1, 2007, from Educational Testing Service website: http://www.ets.org/Media/Tests/Information_and_Communication_Technology_Literacy/ictreport.pdf

ISTE. (1998). *National educational technology standards for students—Connecting curriculum and technology.* Eugene, OR: ISTE.

Janssen Reinen, I. A. M., & Plomp, T. (1993). Staff development as condition for computer integration. *Studies in Educational Evaluation, 19*(2), 149–166.

Johnson, D. C., Anderson, R. E., Hansen, T. P., & Klassen, D. (1980). Computer Literary—What is it? *The Mathematics Teacher, 73,* 91–96.

Jonassen, D. H. (2000). *Computers as mindtools for schools: Engaging critical thinking* (2nd ed.). Upper Saddle River, NJ: Merrill.

Kozma, R. B. (2003). *Design document: Qualitative studies of innovative pedagogical practices using technology.* Menlo Park, CA: SRI International.

Kozma, R. B. (Ed.). (2003). *Technology, innovation, and educational change: A global perspective.* Eugene, OR: ISTE.

Martinez, M. E., & Mead, N. A. (1988). *Computer competence: The first national assessment.* Princeton, NJ: Educational Testing Service.

National Research Council (NRC). (1999). *Being fluent with information technology.* Washington, DC: National Academy Press.

Newmann, F. M., & Associates. (1996). *Authentic achievement: Restructuring schools for intellectual quality.* San Francisco: Jossey-Bass Publishers.

Pelgrum, W. J., & Anderson, R. E. (Eds.). (1999). *ICT and the emerging paradigm for life long learning.* Amsterdam: International Association for the Evaluation of Educational Achievement.

Pelgrum, W. J., Janssen Reinen, I. A. J., & Plomp, T. (1993). *Schools, teachers, students and computers: A cross-national perspective.* Amsterdam: International Association for the Educational Evaluation of Educational Achievement (IEA).

Pelgrum, W. J., & Plomp, T. (1991) *The use of computers in education world-wide.* Oxford, U.K.: Pergamon Press.

Pelgrum, W. J., & Schipper, A. T. (1993). Indicators of computer integration in education. *Computers & Education, 21*(1/2), 141–149.

Plomp, T., Anderson, R. E., & Kontogiannopoulou-Polydorides, G. (1996). *Cross national policies and practices on computers in education.* Dordrecht, The Netherlands: Kluwer Academic Publishers.

Plomp, T., Anderson, R. E., Law, N., & Quale, A. (Eds.). (2003). *Cross national policies and practices on information and communication technology in education.* Greenwich, CT: Information Age Publishing.

Spitzer, K. L., Eisenberg, M. B., & Lowe, C. A. (1998). *Information literacy: Essential skills for the information age.* Syracuse, NY: Eric Clearinghouse on Information and Technology (IR-104).

on unmediated experience in order to critique the media. This suggests the need for a more complex approach to critical literacy. The tool metaphor receives criticism for its instrumentalism, tending to reduce questions of *how* people gain information to the simpler questions of *whether* they have access to information and *how well* they have understood it. It is also problematic that both metaphors are pitched at the level of the individual (or aggregate of individuals), making it difficult to encompass the macrolevel of analysis (the literate society, the critical public sphere, the literacy requirements of democracy, etc.). Part of the promise of rethinking these traditions of research in a converging communications environment is to respond to these critiques in moving forward.

Not surprisingly, following these different theoretical foci, the research questions typically asked within the two traditions also differ. Information literacy research has attended more to questions of access, while media literacy research has paid more attention to questions of understanding. One reason for this is that the media literacy agenda was developed primarily in relation to media for which access, hitherto, has not been a significant problem (terrestrial television and radio). Indeed, it was precisely the widespread accessibility of broadcasting that led to concerns over the power of the media to dominate, since television tells "most of the stories to most of the people most of the time" (Gerbner, Gross, Morgan, & Signorielli, 1986, p. 18). The consequence was a framing of literacy as critical distance from mediated messages. However, as the media and information environment diversifies, additional conceptions of literacy—especially concerned with access and inequality—now come to the fore (Murdock, Hartmann, & Gray, 1995).

The information literacy tradition, on the other hand, has developed primarily in relation to media that have been far from accessible, both because they are unequally distributed and because typically they are complex to find or use. Questions of barriers and enablers to access, therefore, have been foregrounded, spawning initiatives to increase diffusion and enhance equality of distribution. While important, this has distracted attention from critiquing the information sought. These different research questions have led to different methodological choices, a point we develop in the following section.

The Origins of Media Literacy and Information Literacy

First, we consider the disciplinary origins of these two literacy research traditions in more detail, for the empirical findings and methods we discuss next flow from these origins. Work on media literacy comes from the field of media studies, although much of the work has been applied and evaluated within an education research context, often focusing on children. However, the very notion of a *field* of media studies is problematic since it draws on two distinct traditions: the humanities and the social sciences (Levy & Gurevitch, 1994). Corner (1995) identified "the knowledge problem" facing media studies as,

The arts and social science combination in media studies is essentially one which brings together "criticism" and "sociology" as modes of academic knowing. Criticism is a mode privileging individual percipience, in which knowledge is the product of sustained academic attention and intellection … Sociology, on the other hand, in its classic and defining empirical project, is essentially a mode privileging method. (pp. 148–149)

This knowledge problem continues to challenge media studies because of the (laudably) interdisciplinary nature of the field (Schroeder, Drotner, Kline, & Murray, 2003). In relation to media literacy, the knowledge problem takes a particular form. Those more influenced by the arts and humanities see media literacy as a route to enhancing the public's appreciation of, and ability to contribute creatively to, the best that the cultural and audiovisual arts have to offer. The focus is on pleasure and interpretation, creativity and diversity, and originality and quality (Bazalgette, 1999; Buckingham, 2005; Kress, 2003; Sefton-Green, 1999). By contrast, the social science approach sees media literacy as a form of defense against the normative messages of the big media corporations, whose commercialized, stereotyped, unimaginative, and parochial worldview dominates mass culture in capitalist societies (Hobbs, 1998; Kubey, 2004; Potter, 2004). The focus is therefore on uses and gratifications, influences and cultivation effects, and everyday cognitive and social mediations of mass culture. Clearly, different evaluations of the media themselves are at stake, with the media being seen as having the potential to enhance cultural value but also as having the potential to undermine social values (Buckingham, 1989; Hobbs, 1998).

Our second tradition, information literacy, has been hailed as "a major focus and purpose of librarianship, an achievement that took a decade of work" (Marcum, 2002, p. 1). Its conceptual foundations lie in information processing—on how symbols become information and how information, in turn, becomes knowledge (Bawden, 2001; Marcum, 2002). Drawing on cognitive psychology, this approach has spawned a range of experimental studies in which tasks are performed and user reactions tested and tracked (Church, 1999; Hölscher & Strube, 2000). It also investigates users' attitudes and beliefs, and has developed psychological instruments to measure literacy (Richter, Naumann, & Groeben, 2001; Turner, Sweany, & Husman, 2000).

Information literacy is linked historically to computer skills and computer literacy, and so research also examines people's (generally, adults') ability to manipulate hardware and software in order to find information efficiently and effectively. The related field of human-computer interaction (HCI), although it may not mention the concept of information literacy explicitly, treats literacy as an interaction between skilled users and well-designed interfaces. Other kinds of influences, however, are in information literacy, particularly from educationists and librarians who have been instrumental in distinguishing technical skills from information skills (Brown, 1999). Some discuss people's motivation and the appropriateness of content as a key barrier, rather than technical skills. Still others focus on problems of comprehension, understanding, and weighing information (Britt & Gabrys, 2002; Tuathail & McCormack, 1998).

These different areas of information literacy studies overlap in practice. One common feature is that most studies are couched in a context of work and competitiveness, either personal or national (Bruce, 1999; Clausen, 1997). The information-literate person is able to participate in the world of work, for example by being an information worker or a knowledge worker. Conversely, the person who lacks information literacy risks being undervalued by or excluded from an increasingly competitive, information-oriented labor market. In this respect, information literacy research differs from that of media literacy although, recently, arguments for media literacy begin to stress the economic value to a nation of a skilled creative workforce for its cultural industries.

Research and Social Critique

It is clear from these short characterizations that, while they broadly address the same theme, media literacy and information literacy do so from different standpoints. The language of skills and abilities, to be found everywhere in information literacy discussions, is rarely present in media studies, being considered psychologically reductionist, neglecting the important ways in which actions are culturally and historically conditioned. As Hartley (2002) argued,

> Literacy is not and never has been a personal attribute or ideologically inert "skill" simply to be "acquired" by individual persons … It is ideologically and politically charged—it can be used as a means of social control or regulation, but also as a progressive weapon in the struggle for emancipation. (p. 136)

Similarly for McChesney (1996), the risk is that a focus on literacy distracts cultural critics from questions of power for, as he put it, the question is less what people do with the technology than "who will control the technology and for what purpose" (p. 100). In contrast to the strong focus in information literacy research on the individual, this critical perspective directs research toward an integrated analysis of production, text (or technology) and audiences (or users; Livingstone, 1998). In media literacy research, all actions are seen as contextually dependent, and there is little attempt to discern levels of competence underlying observable performance, something that is a priority in information literacy research. Reflecting not only the importance of contextualism but also the discursively constructed nature of cultural contexts, Agre (2004) attacked the information sciences:

The great naiveté of computer science ... [is that it imagines itself] to operate on domains rather than on discourses about domains, it renders itself incapable of seeing the discourses themselves, or the social controversies that pull those discourses in contradictory directions. (p. 28)

In short, the disciplinary origins of media studies and information studies result in different approaches to social critique. In the early days of mass communication research, Lazarsfeld (1941) distinguished the approaches of positivist or liberal scholars from those in the Marxist tradition by labeling the former "administrative research," which "is carried out in the service of some kind of administrative agency of public or private character" (pp. 158–159). This he contrasted with "critical research," which "is posed against the practice of administrative research, requiring that ... the general role of our media of communication in the present social system should be studied" (pp. 159–160). His purpose was to distinguish research that takes its agenda from and produces recommendations useful for public policy or commercial gain from research that maintains a critical independence from established institutions. The former takes on the responsibility of actively shaping social and technological change; the latter seeks to produce independent knowledge that critiques the strategic activities of the establishment.

While Lazarsfeld (1941), in mapping out the future options for then new research domain, attempted an even-handed approach, these two positions have been hotly contested in subsequent decades (Levy & Gurevitch, 1994). For example, in asserting the critical over the administrative, Morrow and Brown (1994) rejected the way that "the logic of statistical generalizations has more of an affinity with the interests of social engineering, rather than social theorizing" (p. 218). For them, social theorizing must, unlike social engineering, analyze critically the "structural relations within and between mediations—relations that turn on the dialectic between human agency and social structure" (p. 218). For their detractors, however, passing up the opportunity to influence public policy for the good is too great a price to pay for independence, even if setting goals for media and information literacy initiatives does seem like social engineering.

Research within media literacy and information literacy divides on this issue. Some work in the field of media literacy embodies the administrative approach, seeking directly to contribute to and influence policy on media literacy (e.g., tracking ICT diffusion and access via government or commercial surveys). Other work takes a critical approach, exploring how people use media for their own sometimes nonnormative or counternormative purposes (Bird, 2003; Gillespie, 1995; Hoover, Clark, & Alters, 2004). In the informational domain, research on the search engine illustrates a similar bifurcation. In the administrative tradition, survey-based studies examine access to and familiarity with search engines (Fox, 2002), the skills of different types of

lack of explanatory context, the rapidly shifting news agenda, and mismatches between visual and verbal information. More generally, when the media challenge their values, audiences are faced with a conflictual negotiation over meanings—as in the case of prolife women watching proabortion drama (Press, 1991) or men watching male violence against women (Schlesinger et al., 1998). Gender, class, ethnicity, and religion also emerge as key differentiators of audience understanding (Christiansen, 2004; Gillespie, 1995; Hoover et al., 2004; Michalski et al., 2002).

So, just as media literacy research should incorporate the study of access, convergence also means that the study of critical understanding should be incorporated into research on information literacy. This also has methodological implications, for much critical literacy research takes a more in-depth qualitative approach than is typical of research on information literacy. One example is the elaboration of the focus group method, extending the time taken and the complexity of the tasks, games or dilemmas presented to respondents, in order to draw out more subtle responses to specific media texts and technologies than simple opinion statements (Barbour & Kitzinger, 1999; Eldridge, 1993; Lunt & Livingstone, 1996; Schlesinger et al., 1998). For example, in studying audiences' critical understanding of television news, focus group participants may be asked not only about their understanding of a particular conflict and the information sources they draw upon but also to imagine that they are journalists and write a news story using series of photographs from television news coverage of the conflict (Philo, 1993).

Another trend is the turn to ethnography, a tradition much better established in media than in information studies (Press & Livingstone, 2006). For example, qualitative research on family dynamics within households seeks to understand the domestic context of access and use of broadcast media, uncovering the issues of gender, generation, and class (Gillespie, 1995; Livingstone, 2002; Morley, 1992; Silverstone & Hirsch, 1992). Such methods permit the researcher to observe behavior in its physical and social context, to integrate and sometimes contrast talk and action, and to analyze relations among different groups (e.g., pupils and teachers, parents and children, or those who visit and those who work in online centers; Bird, 2003; Ginsburg, Abu-Lughod, & Larkin, 2002; Hoover et al., 2004). In relation to information literacy, ethnographic research is conspicuous by its absence; although contexts of usage are clearly important in Internet and mobile phone practice (Ling, 2004). Looking to the emergent Internet studies traditions, however, we find ethnographic studies which highlight cultural and personal context and motivations as key elements of the development of sophisticated practice (Bakardjieva & Smith, 2001; Miller & Slater, 2000); these studies could be expanded to explore the uses, meanings and contradictions of literacy in diverse social contexts.

Creation

By contrast with print literacy research, which has always balanced the study of reading with the study of writing, both media and information literacy research have paid more attention to questions of access, selection and understanding than they have to the creation of content. Both risk positioning the audience or user, therefore, as recipient rather than producer. Moreover, both must address this bias as it becomes ever easier for members of the public to create and disseminate messages in the new media and information environment. Both information and media literacy traditions are now turning their attention to the study of content creation, though this research so far tends mainly to ask who creates content. Their purposes in so doing, the conditions that hinder or facilitate, and the skills and competences involved remain relatively unknown. For example, if we look at video or audio production by members of the public, one study found that 17% of participants in the study owned a camcorder but reported little on how this was used (Gauntlett & Hill, 1999). It may be that the published literature underestimates the extent of amateur audiovisual production. Anecdotal evidence on the use of home video, combined with the sales of camcorders, Webcams, and scanners, suggests that such activity may be widespread, as suggested, for example, by research on fan cultures, where "fan art is important as a means of commenting on the original program, as a form of cultural creation with its own aesthetic principles and traditions" (Jenkins, 1992, p. 248). It is often argued in relation to children that the experience of content production facilitates the development of media literacy (Buckingham, 2005; Sefton-Green, 1999) and, possibly, the provision of opportunities to create content could enable media literacy for adults.

Also by contrast with print literacy, where some grand expectations for democratic participation have been pinned to the rise of literacy, both historically and cross-nationally, neither the fields of media nor information literacy have elaborated such grand hopes, though in a complex media and information environment, the literacies necessary to participate are undoubtedly vital. Arguably, for these hopes to be realized, the public must be sufficiently media and information literate, and sufficiently connected to civil society, not only to receive but also to produce and distribute content. Producing content may be minimally conceived—sending e-mails, visiting chat rooms, creating a Web page—but even this, if used for civic or cultural goals is of significance. Producing content may also be conceived more ambitiously, in a manner generally not possible for audiovisual media, precisely because in relation to the Internet the limitations on volume and accessibility of content, and on the tools to produce content, are modest. The World Wide Web includes many sites constructed by ordinary members of the public, both as individuals and as part of their local or community roles.

Some innovative work is emerging from initiatives to establish resource-rich sites in which people can create media content. Analyses of interviews, observations, and user-generated contents reveal the enablers of content creation and people's implicit understanding of the media more generally (Gauntlett, 1997). Some research concerns community-based creative projects (e.g., Phipps, 2000; Travers, 2002). Although this case study approach is vulnerable to differences across projects, for these are indeed diverse, it can also be sensitive to the contextual factors that influence how and why adults use the technologies, what content they make (Thumim, 2004; Yin, 2003).

Measurement, Standards, and Progression

Literacy has never been easy to measure. This is evident in relation to print in the critical debates surrounding the OECD reports on literacy and the OECD PISA reports on young people's literacy in education (Hamilton & Barton, 2000; OECD, 2004; Roberts, 2000). Theories of media literacy, especially in relation to adults, are notably silent on the question of levels, standards, and progression, being wary even of dividing skills into the basic and the advanced. In many countries, despite the existence of a media education curriculum for children, a national standard for adults has yet to be formulated. What skills, in short, are required, by whom and at what level, if media literacy is to contribute to the goals of citizenship, cultural choice, identity and expression or a vibrant cultural sector?

In its general statement on media literacy, the U.K. Department for Culture Media and Sport (DCMS, 2001) stressed the importance of critical viewing skills and technological competences as a foundation of media literacy, including the (a) ability to distinguish fact from fiction; (b) understand mechanisms of production and distribution; (c) distinguish reportage from advocacy; (d) recognize and assess commercial messages in programs; (e) recognize the economic, cultural, and presentational imperatives in news management; (f) explain and justify media choices in order to inform choice and sustain appropriate degrees of critical distance; and (g) develop technical competence toward information and communication tools, including navigation skills and the ability to create Internet content.

While this is helpful, the lack of agreed standards of media literacy makes the evaluation of pedagogic and policy initiatives particularly challenging. By contrast, practitioners in information science have worked to develop literacy standards to help assess the levels of competence, typically for adult learners. For example, the Association of College and Research Libraries (ACRL) in the United States developed a series of standards, performance indicators, and outcomes for information literacy in higher education. Each level is associated with performance indicators and outcomes and specifies that the information literate student should be able to (a) determine the nature and extent of the information needed (level 1); (b) access needed information effectively and efficiently (level 2); (c) evaluate information and its sources critically and incorporate selected information into his or her knowledge base and value system (level 3); (d) use information effectively, individually or as a member of a group, to accomplish a specific purpose (level 4); and (e) understand many of the economic, legal, and social issues surrounding the use of information and accesses and uses information ethically and legally (level 5).

In the United Kingdom, the Society of College, National, and University Libraries (SCONUL) Advisory Committee on Information Literacy (1999) formulated an alternative model based on seven pillars of information literacy. In this model, information literacy consists of the following skills, in each of which performance can be graded at levels from novice to advanced beginner, competent, proficient or expert: (a) recognize information needs; (b) distinguish ways of addressing gaps; (c) construct strategies for locating information; (d) locate and access information; (e) compare and evaluate information; (f) organize, apply, and communicate information; and (g) synthesize and create information. This model differs from the ACRL model by including basic library skills and IT skills as foundational elements and by stressing strategies for the location of information and the creative dimension of information literacy.

This specification of standards is clearly crucial if education, skills, and training programs are to be developed and evaluated (see National Institute of Adult Continuing Education, 2004; J. Williams, Clemens, Oleinikova, & Tarvin, 2003). While several standardized measures of computer literacy have been proposed (Bradlow, Hoch, & Hutchinson, 2002; Richter et al., 2001; Turner et al., 2000), basic library skills—the other set of foundational skills in the SCONUL model—have not been adequately assessed in the adult population. Nonetheless, the application of such approaches from the study of information literacy to that of media literacy may be beneficial, especially in relation to adults, inviting a broader consideration of how media and information literacy standards can be developed and measured in a converged environment.

For children, more developed media education programs specify age-appropriate skills, progression across levels, and methods for evaluating the delivery of a formal curriculum according to age-graded levels of achievement. For adults, such work remains to be undertaken. One path forward might be to follow the model of the public understanding of science, where survey methods are used to measure aspects of public understanding and knowledge in the scientific domain (e.g., Bauer & Gaskell, 2002). In relation to print literacy, measurement is based on educational testing (OECD, 2004), while the effectiveness of public health communication campaigns is evaluated through opinion surveys based on self-reported health practices and health literacy (Livingstone & Thumim, 2003).

Buckingham (2005), however, noted, "It remains very difficult to provide any definitive evidence about the *effectiveness* of media education, despite the evident enthusiasm and commitment of its advocates" (p. 51). Furthermore, the application of levels and standards in children's media education relies on psychological models of development which have been criticized on a number of counts: (a) they do not distinguish between competence and performance; (b) they neglect the role of social and familial context; and (c) as Buckingham observed, "a third, more radical, critique suggests that developmental models are implicitly normative, and involve the imposition of particular preferred definitions of 'adult' behaviour" (p. 26). This last point takes us back to the critical/administrative distinction in research discussed earlier: An enterprise based on establishing a curriculum, standards, models of progression, criteria for evaluation, and so forth, falls firmly within the administrative camp, and critical scholars raise many methodological, epistemological, and political concerns regarding such an effort.

Although work on information literacy in relation to standards is undoubtedly more developed, it is not that media literacy research has simply overlooked this question, for there has been a long-standing struggle to get media education onto the school curriculum, albeit with only sporadic success (Christ & Potter, 1998). Buckingham (1998) noted that teaching critical literacy has meant teaching literary or aesthetic criticism (training students in discrimination so as to preserve the literary heritage and to inoculate them against mass media manipulation), rather than enhancing employment-related skills to promote the competitive skill base required by the creative and cultural industries. The often implicit purposes underlying media education (following from an equally implicit disagreement regarding the cultural value of media texts), however, have often threatened to derail the media education movement entirely, a tension that continues to shape contemporary discussions over the appropriate uses of newly gained ICT literacy (Hobbs, 1998). By contrast, information literacy is primarily promoted and supported for its benefits to the training of a highly skilled workforce, thereby advancing employment and economic competitiveness. While funding is plentiful for this work, how people critically understand texts, crucial to the ideal of the "informed citizen" (prominent in media literacy research), receives a low priority in relation to information literacy initiatives.

Key questions remain, notably—how can the emphasis on skills, important to employers and policymakers, be reconciled with the attempt to understand critically the symbolic and cultural value of media practices? For example, critical research on the social construction of the child as computer expert (e.g., Facer, J. Furlong, R. Furlong, & Sutherland, 2001) does not examine whether the child really is the expert—in other words, whether the construction is veridical. Conversely, attempts to measure the actual levels of Internet skills among the public show little interest in how this expertise affects social relations within the home or workplace.

Methodological Convergence and Its Challenges

The existence of some fruitful complementarities between media and information literacy traditions does not mean that multidisciplinary or multimethod research will be easy to conduct, not least because literacy—being concerned with people's implicit, complex, and subtle understandings of symbolic representations—is intrinsically difficult to research (Livingstone, 2004). Literacy concerns things people cannot do or may not have recognized the importance of and, when asked, social desirability may lead people to claim greater knowledge than is warranted. Put simply, how do you ask people if they are aware of advertising on Web sites or bias in the news, without introducing the idea or even the expectation that they should recognize such a phenomenon in the first place? Specific kinds of knowledge may be tested, following the model of formal education, but this may say little about awareness or, indeed, actual practices in everyday contexts.

Partly in response to these and other difficulties, a wide range of research methods are employed in media, communication, and information studies, and these have been applied to the study of media and information literacies across diverse populations and across multiple media and information channels and sources. Broad trends in media and communications research, as elsewhere in the social sciences, lean toward the elaboration of existing methods rather than their replacement with wholly new methods, and toward the triangulation of qualitative and quantitative methods rather than the prioritization of any one approach (Alasuutari, 1995; Bertrand & Hughes, 2005; Deacon, Pickering, Golding, & Murdock, 1999; Schroeder et al., 2003).

In adopting multimethod research designs, the aim is to overcome, or compensate for, the disadvantages of certain methods over others. For example, even with good design and a range of checks to limit biases and social desirability factors, surveys still rely on self-reported attitudes and practices, inviting observational methods to complement them. Similarly, qualitative methods sacrifice the advantages of surveys in terms of the diversity and representativeness of the population surveyed; they gain in the ability to pursue issues in greater depth, to contextualize findings, to capture ambivalences and uncertainties, and to crosscheck claims against observational data. Thus, many researchers seek to lay to rest the old battles between qualitative and quantitative research, though some continue to argue for one side or the other. In seeking to bridge the epistemological/ideological battleground that has long existed between proponents of quantitative and qualitative methodologies in the field of media and communications, Jensen (2002) wrote,

> A first step in bridging the apparent abyss between the two paradigms is to ask whether some division of labour can be sustained. At least in principle, most contemporary research would recognize that its choice of methods must depend on what aspect of mediated communication is

Table 4.1 Comparison of Media Literacy and Information Literacy Research Traditions

	Information literacy tradition	**Media literacy tradition**
Technological focus	• Telecommunications • Computing • Information systems	• Broadcasting • Audiovisual media • Print
	Comment: As digital/mobile/online media and information technologies converge, both traditions will increasingly share an overlapping focus.	
Definition of literacy	"Knowledge of one's information concerns and needs, and the ability to identify, locate, evaluate, organize and effectively create, use and communicate information" (Information Literacy Meeting of Experts, 2003).	"The ability to access, analyze, evaluate, and communicate messages in a variety of forms" (Aufderheide, 1993).
	Comment: If a converged unified approach rather than proliferation of literacies is favored, the similarities between these definitions are promising.	
Main research focus and gaps	• Barriers/enablers to access and use • Evaluation of skills and abilities	• Understanding • Critical literacy • Creative/productive literacies
	Comment: The information literacy tradition could benefit from more critical analysis of information; the media literacy tradition could benefit from a more complex account of access. Both approaches lack a sustained analysis of content creation, construing people more as receivers than as producers of information/texts.	
Disciplinary origins	• Engineering/computer science • Library science and education • Design, especially human/computer interaction	• Arts and humanities, especially film studies and cultural studies • Social sciences, especially sociology and social psychology
	Comment: Both approaches are internally divided in their relation to social critique (here theorized in terms of administrative vs. critical research).	
Strengths	• Models of standards, levels and progression • Separation of competence from performance • Complex analysis of access • Measures of the effectiveness of information literacy education • Accessibility guidelines	• Models of content understanding, for example, encoding/decoding, uses and gratifications • Integrated analysis of production/text/audience • Analysis of literacy at meso- and macrolevels (not just as an individual attribute)
	Comment: Research has yet to consider how far the strengths of each approach can benefit the other.	
Preferred methods	Quantitative orientation (surveys, experiments, measurement, evaluation)	Qualitative orientation (interviews, focus groups, ethnographic observation)
	Comment: Both approaches are developing some innovative ways forward in meeting new empirical challenges, thus furthering triangulation of methods in literacies research.	
Justification/ purpose	Employability and competitiveness in the labor market	Critical appreciation, cultural participation, and resistance to dominant media
	Comment: A converged approach to media and information literacies must explicate and debate these and other justifications for the promotion of literacies, recognizing their underlying epistemological and political differences.	

tices in managing and regulating their children's access to and use of different forms of electronic communication, together with children's experiences of being regulated and their growing skills in self-regulation (Livingstone & Bober, 2006).

The balance of research reverses in relation to the dimension of literacy concerned with understanding. Here, most research has been conducted on broadcast media; yet, very little exists for new media (Internet, digital television, mobile communications, and other converged or new electronic information services). The priority here is to develop a subtle and detailed account of how people understand, trust, and critically evaluate information and communication contents delivered on new platforms and disseminated and regulated in unfamiliar ways that can match the analysis already developed for an audience's understanding of (mass, broadcast) television content. Specifically, more research is needed into how people understand online news and political information, including what they define as news in the online environment. The question of trust is central but undertheorized, so findings are often contradictory or unreliable. Survey research here should be complemented by qualitative work, leading to the development of a subtle account of critical literacy in this domain.

Although viewers are well aware of advertising when they are confronted with commercial messages on television (Sancho & Wilson, 2001), the changing conditions of advertising, including sponsorship, branding, merchandising, paid for content, and other forms of promotion through broadcasting, the Internet, and mobile phones, set new literacy requirements. Little research exists on adults' critical awareness of such promotional practices and on how better to support parental mediation of promotion to children (Kunkel & Wilcox, 2001; Montgomery & Pasnik, 1996). Perhaps here, research can learn from advertising literacy research on children and television, now applied to new information and communication environments (Oates, Blades, & Gunter, 2002).

Research is also needed into the degree of content legibility as a complement to levels of public literacy: If a book is badly written or typeset, we do not call the reader illiterate; if the news provides no accessible information about its sources, journalist conventions, or editorial policy, the viewer is not at fault in struggling to evaluate the message; and if a search engine appears to offer unbiased access to information resources while operating with commercial priorities invisible to the user, this limits how the user can critically evaluate the information accessed. This suggests that literacy should be conceived in relational terms, as in usability research, where good understanding is seen to depend on both a usable Web site and a skilled user.

Problematically, in discussions of literacy and, especially, of the population's failure to achieve certain levels of literacy, it is often implicitly assumed that interfaces are well-designed, that the resources are clearly available and merely await appropriate use. But interfaces also obscure, impede, and undermine, this being especially significant in the new media and information environment where conventions of representation are not yet familiar, cues to interpretation are inconsistent or confusing, and a cultural critique of the available information (beyond the crucial but simple questions, e.g., "Can you trust it?" and "Who put it there?") is not widespread. Isaacs and Walendowski (2002) argued that widely used, supposedly user friendly software regularly flouts standard conventions for face-to-face conversation—offering inappropriate or unnecessary information, performing in an unpredictable way, requesting irrelevant information or providing misleading information, and offering confusing or even rude messages. Transgressions of these everyday rules include requiring users to make unnecessarily clicks, failing to retain preferences, breaking the user's flow with pop-ups, asking daft or confusing questions, presenting users with muddled and overfull Web pages, failing to give feedback on whether a process worked or how long it might take, and, lastly, blaming the user by using phrases such as 'fatal error,' 'illegal' or 'invalid.'

A similar focus, on the relation between texts and readers, has been prominent in audience reception studies, inviting lessons to be transferred across from this field to that of new media and information literacies (Press & Livingstone, 2006). On this view, media literacy depends on an effective interaction between the public and the media, with literacy being thought of as a dynamic process rather than a property of individuals. This process may be both enabled and impeded by individual or societal factors as well as by the institutional, textual, and technological factors that shape the interface with the user or audience (Kress, 2003; Snyder, 1998). For example, Burbules (1998) invited a critical semiotics of the online environment to match a critical literacy analysis, arguing that "a thoughtful hyperreader asks why links are made from certain points and not others; where those links lead; and what values are entailed in such decisions" (p. 110).

As noted earlier, by comparison with research on access and understanding, neither tradition has fully explored the core literacy issue of content creation by the public, although a glance at doctoral research topics in media studies departments reveals that this is a burgeoning area of study. What is the range of emerging creative and productive literacies among the population, and what are the barriers and enables in operation? Such questions are pressing, since the changing media environment potentially serves to democratize content creation and dissemination in hitherto unprecedented ways. Never before have the tools to make content been so widely available.

Research priorities include charting the emerging range of experiences with content creation: How many people have created content, what content have they made, and how far do they achieve their ambitions? We also need to know more about the social benefits of apparently mundane content creation (e.g., sending text messages to friends) as well as about the conditions to enable self-evidently significant content creation (artistic content or democratic participation). We also need to understand the barriers and enablers—the skills people need and the difficulties they face, for encouraging content creation and interactivity seems more difficult than commonly supposed (Sparkler, 2004). We note also that although it is widely believed that creating content results in an increased critical understanding of media production processes, little research has examined, still less established, that this is the case (Kunkel et al., 2004). Does making content really improve a critical reading of professionally produced contents? What are the benefits and, possibly, the disadvantages of increasing the ways in which the public not only receives but also responds to, interacts with, and creates its own content?

Finally, having recently conducted a wide-ranging literature review for both media and information literacy (Livingstone et al., 2005), we were struck by how little attention has been paid to the relations among the various dimensions of literacy. Can people be high on media literacy, say in relation to access-related skills and competences but low in terms of critical understanding? It is widely assumed that skills of access precede the more advanced skills of content creation and that experience of content creation enhances critical literacy. The coherence and interdependence of the dimensions of media literacy nonetheless has received little research attention.

On the Importance of Media and Information Literacies

In the introduction to this chapter we asked what is the purpose of media literacy, information literacy, and all the other literacies, and why do they matter? We highlighted three purposes to which literacies are expected to contribute: (a) democratic participation and active citizenship, (b) knowledge economy, competition, and choice, and (c) lifelong learning, cultural expression, and personal fulfillment. After looking at the field in relation to these undoubtedly ambitious aims, clearly, much more research must be done, and many more literacy initiatives must be developed and supported.

This is most evident in the more active, participatory, and creative aspects of engaging with new forms of media. For example, while there are many hopes for the potential for members of the public to participate in online debate, the actual levels of participation are often very low (Jankowski, 2006; Schneider, 1997). For another example, in 2003, researchers conducting a Pew Internet phone survey in the United States found that "44% of Internet users have created content for the online world through building or posting to Web sites, creating blogs, and sharing files;" however, only "13% maintain their own website, and between 2% and 7% of internet users publish a web-log [*sic*]" (Lenhart, Horrigan, & Fallows, 2004, p. 5). Research also repeatedly shows that those who are more literate in these various ways tend to be those who are already privileged, according to traditional measures of inclusion and participation (Doring, 2002; Gunnell, 2002; Livingstone, Bober, et al., 2005). Thus it seems as though largely the same issues which shape who gets involved in the creation of old media are also shaping who gets involved in the creation of digital media and who does not. As Mansell (2004) pointed out,

> Despite the growth in the numbers of internet users, a rather small minority of these users has the capability to use the internet in ways that are creative and that augment their ability to participate effectively in today's knowledge societies. (p. 179)

In this chapter we have mapped some ways forward for media and information literacies research, identifying model studies and fruitful ways of converging two hitherto distinct traditions, as well as identifying some methodological challenges. In the end, we return to theory and urge an ambitious framework for research on new literacies. Media and information literacies do not simply concern the ability to access the electronic program guide for digital television or to complete one's income tax return online. Nor are the purposes restricted to becoming a more informed consumer or getting a higher paying job, though in methodological terms, these may be more readily evaluated against tangible outcomes. For literacy concerns the historically and culturally conditioned relationship among three processes: (a) the symbolic and material representation of knowledge, culture and values; (b) the diffusion of interpretative skills and abilities across a heterogeneous population; and (c) the institutional management (by public and private sector bodies) of the power that access to and skilled use of knowledge brings to those who are literate.

This relationship is grounded in a centuries-old struggle between enlightenment and critical scholarship, setting those who see literacy as democratizing and so as empowering of ordinary people against those who see it as a source of inequality and so as elitist and divisive (Kellner, 2002; Livingstone, 2004; Luke, 1989). Debates over literacy are, in short, debates about the manner and purposes of public participation in society. Without a democratic and critical approach to media and information literacy, the public will be positioned merely as selective receivers, consumers of online information and communication. The promise of literacy, surely, is that it can form part of a strategy to reposition the media user—from passive to active, from recipient to participant, and from consumer to citizen.

References

Agre, P. (2004). Internet research: For and against. In M. Consalvo et al. (Eds.), *Internet research annual* (Vol. 1, pp. 25–36). New York: Peter Lang.

Alasuutari, P. (1995). *Researching culture: Qualitative methods and cultural studies*. London: Sage.

Anderson, B., Brynin, M., Raban, Y., Vicario, L., Ling, R., Nokolov, R., et al. (2004). *E-living: Life in a digital Europe: Waves 1–2, 2001–2002*. Retrieved October 14, 2004, from http://www.eurescom.de/e-living/index.htm

Aufderheide, P. (1993). *Media Literacy: A report of the national leadership conference on media literacy*. Aspen, CO: Aspen Institute.

Bakardjieva, M., & Smith, R. (2001). The Internet in everyday life: Computer networking from the standpoint of the domestic user. *New Media and Society, 3*(1), 67–83.

Barbour, R. S., & Kitzinger, J. (Eds.). (1999). *Developing focus group research: Politics, theory and practice*. London: Sage.

Bauer, M. W., & Gaskell, G. (Eds.). (2002). *Biotechnology—The making of a global controversy*. Cambridge, U.K.: Cambridge University Press.

Bawden, D. (2001). Information and digital literacies: A review of concepts. *Journal of Documentation, 57*(2), 218–259.

Baym, N. (2006). Interpersonal life online. In L. Lievrouw & S. Livingstone (Eds.), *The handbook of new media: Updated student edition* (pp. 35–54). London: Sage.

Bazalgette, C. (1999). *Making movies matter*. London: British Film Institute. Retrieved date, from http://www.bfi.org.uk

Bertrand, I., & Hughes, P. (2005). *Media research methods: Audiences, institutions, texts*. Basingstoke, U.K.: Palgrave Macmillan.

Bird, S. E. (2003). *The audience in everyday life: Living in a media world*. New York: Routledge.

Bolter, J. D., & Grusin, R. (1999). *Remediation: Understanding new media*. Cambridge, MA: MIT Press.

Bradlow, E. T., Hoch, S. J., & Hutchinson, J. W. (2002). An assessment of basic computer proficiency among active Internet users. *Journal of Educational and Behavioral Statistics, 27*(3), 237–253.

Britt, M. A., & Gabrys, G. (2002). Implications of document-level literacy skills for Web site design. *Behavior Research Methods Instruments & Computers, 34*(2), 170–176.

Bromley, C. (2004). Can Britain close the digital divide? In A. Park, J. Curtice, K. Thomson, C. Bromley, & M. Philips (Eds.), *British social attitudes—The 21st report* (pp. 73–98). London: Sage.

Brown, C. M. (1999). Information literacy of physical science graduate students in the information age. *College & Research Libraries, 60*(5), 426–438.

Bruce, C. S. (1999). Workplace experiences of information literacy. *International Journal of Information Management, 19*(1), 33–47.

Buckingham, D. (1989). Television literacy: A critique. *Radical Philosophy, 51*, 12–25.

Buckingham, D. (1998). Media education in the UK: Moving beyond protectionism. *Journal of Communication, 48*(1), 33–42.

Buckingham, D. (2005). *The media literacy of children and young people: A review of the research literature*. London: Ofcom.

Burbules, N. C. (1998). Rhetorics on the Web: Hyperreading and critical literacy. In I. Snyder (Ed.), *Page to screen: Taking literacy into the electronic era* (pp. 102–122). New York: Routledge.

Christ, W. G., & Potter, W. J. (1998). Media literacy: Symposium. *Journal of Communication, 48*(1).

Christiansen, C. C. (2004). News media consumption among immigrants in Europe: The relevance of diaspora. *Ethnicities, 4*(2), 185–207.

Church, G. M. (1999). The human-computer interface and information literacy: Some basics and beyond. *Information Technology and Libraries, 18*(1), 3–21.

Clausen, H. (1997). Internet information literacy: Some basic considerations. *Libri, 47*(1), 25–34.

Corner, J. (1995). Media studies and the "knowledge problem". *Screen, 36*(2), 147–155.

Council of Europe. (2005, March10–11). *Integration and diversity: The new frontiers of European media and communications policy: Draft action plan and draft resolution no. 2*. Retrieved April 25, 2005, from http://www.coe.int/T/E/Com/Files/Ministerial-Conferences/2005-kiev/texte_adopte.asp

Deacon, D., Pickering, M., Golding, P., & Murdock, G. (1999). *Researching communications: A practical guide to methods in media and cultural analysis*. London: Arnold.

Livingstone, S., Bober, M., & Helsper, E. J. (2005) Active participation or just more information? Young people's take up of opportunities to act and interact on the Internet. *Information, Communication and Society, 8*(3), 287–314.

Livingstone, S., & Thumim, N. (2003). *Assessing the media literacy on UK adults: A review of the academic literature: Report commissioned by BSC/ITC/BFI/NIACE.* Retrieved October 10, 2005, from http://www.ofcom.org.uk/static/archive/bsc/pdfs/research/litass.pdf

Livingstone, S., Van Couvering, E. J., & Thumim, N. (2005). *Adult media literacy: A review of the literature.* London: Ofcom. Retrieved October 10, 2005, from http://www.ofcom.org.uk/advice/media_literacy/medlitpub/medlitpubrss/aml

Luke, C. (1989). *Pedagogy, printing and protestantism: The discourse of childhood.* Albany: State University of New York Press.

Lunt, P., & Livingstone, S. (1996). Rethinking the focus group in media and communications research. *Journal of Communication, 46*(2), 79–98.

Lyman, P., & Wakeford, N. (1999). Going into the (virtual) field. *American Behavioral Scientist, 43*(3), 359–376.

Machill, M., Neuberger, C., Schweiger, W., & Wirth, W. (2004). Navigating the Internet: A study of German-language search engines. *European Journal of Communication, 19*(3), 321–347.

Mansell, R. (2004). Political economy, power and new media. *New Media and Society, 6*(1), 96–105.

Marcum, J. W. (2002). Rethinking information literacy. *Library Quarterly, 72*(1), 1–26.

McChesney, R. W. (1996). The Internet and U.S. Communication policy-making in historical and critical perspective. *Journal of Communication, 46*(1), 98–124.

Michalski, M., Preston, A., Gillespie, M., & Cheesman, T. (2002). *After September 11: TV news and transnational audiences.* London: Report to the ESRC/Open University/BFI/BSC/ITC.

Miller, D., & Slater, D. (2000). *The Internet: An ethnographic approach.* London: Berg.

Montgomery, K., & Pasnik, S. (1996). *Web of deception: Threats to children from online marketing.* Washington, DC: Centre for Media Education.

Morley, D. (1992). *Television, audiences and cultural studies.* London: Routledge.

Morrow, R. A., & Brown, D. D. (1994). *Critical theory and methodology* (Vol. 3). Thousand Oaks, CA: Sage.

Murdock, G., Hartmann, P., & Gray, P. (1995). Contextualizing home computers: Resources and practices. In N. Heap, R. Thomas, G. Einon, R. Mason, & H. Mackay (Eds.), *Information technology and society: A reader* (pp. 269–283). London: Sage.

National Institute of Adult Continuing Education. (2004). *ICT skill for life report.* London: Author and Department for Education and Skills.

Oates, C., Blades, M., & Gunter, B. (2002). Children and television advertising: When do they understand persuasive intent? *Journal of Consumer Behavior, 1*(3), 238–245.

Organisation for Economic Co-operation and Development. (2004). *Learning for tomorrow's world: First results from Pisa 2003.* Paris: Author.

Ofcom. (2004a). *The communications market.* London: Author.

Ofcom. (2004b). *Ofcom's strategy and priorities for the promotion of media literacy: A statement.* London: Author.

Ofcom. (2006). *Ofcom Media Literacy Audit: report on adult media literacy.* London: Author.

Office of the e-Envoy. (2004). *UK online annual report.* London: Author.

Pew Internet and American Life (2005, January). *Search engine users: Internet searchers are confident, satisfied and trusting—But they are also unaware and naïve.* Washington, DC: Author. Retrieved date, from www.pewinternet.org

Philo, G. (1993). Getting the message: Audience research in the Glasgow University Media Group. In J. Eldridge (Ed.), *Getting the message: News, truth and power* (pp. 92–113). London: Routledge.

Phipps, L. (2000). New communications technologies: A conduit for social inclusion. *Information, Communication and Society, 3*(1), 39–68.

Potter, W. J. (2004). *Theory of media literacy: A cognitive approach.* Thousand Oaks, CA: Sage.

Press, A. L. (1991). *Women watching television.* Philadelphia: University of Pennsylvania Press.

Press, A., & Livingstone, S. (2006). Taking audience research into the age of new media: Old problems and new challenges. In M. White, & J. Schwoch (Eds.), *The question of method in cultural studies.* (pp. 92–113). Oxford, U.K.: Blackwell.

Rice, R., & Haythornthwaite, C. (2005). New media access, use and equity. In L. Lievrouw & S. Livingstone (Eds.), *Handbook of new media: Updated student edition* (pp. xx–xx). London: Sage.

Richter, T., Naumann, J., & Groeben, N. (2001). The computer literacy inventory (incobi): An instrument for the assessment of computer literacy and attitudes toward the computer in university students of the humanities and the social sciences. *Psychologie in Erziehung Und Unterricht, 48*(1), 1–13.

Roberts, P. (2000). Literacy in the age of information—Knowledge, power or domination? An assessment of the international adult literacy survey. *International Review of Education, 46*(5), 433–454.

Sancho, J., & Wilson, A. (2001). *Boxed in: Offence from negative stereotyping in television advertising.* London: ITC.

Saranjit, S., & Lennard, L. (2004). *Health literacy: Being able to make the most of health.* London: National Consumer Council on behalf of the Department of Health.

Schlesinger, P., Haynes, R., Boyle, R., McNair, B., Dobash, R. E., & Dobash, R. P. (1998). *Men viewing violence.* London: Broadcasting Standards Commission.

Schneider, S. (1997). *Expanding the public sphere through computer-mediated communication: Political discussion about abortion in a usenet news group.* Cambridge: Massachusetts Institute of Technology.

Schroeder, K., Drotner, K., Kline, S., & Murray, C. (2003). *Researching audiences.* London: Arnold.

Sefton-Green, J. (Ed.). (1999). *Young people, creativity and new technologies: The challenge of digital arts.* London: Routledge.

Selwyn, N. (2004). Reconsidering political and popular understandings of the digital divide. *New Media & Society, 6*(3), 341–362.

Sillence, E., Briggs, P., & Fishwick, L. (2004, 24–29 April). *Trust and mistrust of online health sites.* Paper presented at the CHI 2004 Conference, Vienna, Austria.

Silverstone, R., & Hirsch, E. (Eds.). (1992). *Consuming technologies: Media and information in domestic spaces.* London: Routledge.

Slater, D. (2002). Social relationships and identity online and offline. In L. Lievrouw & S. Livingstone (Eds.), *The handbook of new media* (pp. 534–547). London: Sage.

Snyder, I. (Ed.). (1998). *Page to screen: Taking literacy into the electronic era.* London: Routledge.

Society of College, National, and University Libraries (SCONUL) Advisory Committee on Information Literacy. (1999). *Information skills in higher education.* Publisher location: Author.

Sparkler. (2004). *Harnessing the magic of the BBC's community based creative projects: Qualitative research debrief.* London: BBC.

Spink, A., Wolfram, D., Jansen, M. B. J., & Saracevic, T. (2001). Searching the Web: The public and their queries. *Journal of the American Society for Information Science and Technology, 52*(3), 226–234.

Thumim, N. (2004). *Mediation and self-representation in public culture: Two cases from contemporary Britain.* Unpublished doctoral thesis, London School of Economics and Political Science, London.

Towler, R. (2001). *The public's view 2001.* London: ITC/BSC research publication.

Travers, A. (2002). Postmodern research, postmodern practice: Studying the barriers to cyber-literacy among mentally disabled women. *Sociological Practice: A Journal of Clinical and Applied Sociology, 4*(4), 279–291.

Tuathail, G. O., & McCormack, D. (1998). The technoliteracy challenge: Teaching globalisation using the Internet. *Journal of Geography in Higher Education, 22*(3), 347–361.

Turner, G. M., Sweany, N. W., & Husman, J. (2000). Development of the computer interface literacy measure. *Journal of Educational Computing Research, 22*(1), 37–54.

Tyner, K. (1998). *Literacy in a digital world: Teaching and learning in the age of information.* Mahwah, NJ: Lawrence Erlbaum Associates.

Van Couvering, E. (2004, July, 24–30). *New media? A political economy of search engines.* Paper presented at the International Association of Media and Communications Researchers, Porto Alegre, Brazil.

Walton, M., & Archer, A. (2004). The Web and information literacy: Scaffolding the use of Web sources in a project-based curriculum. *British Journal of Educational Technology, 35*(2), 173–186.

Warnick, B. (2002). *Critical literacy in a digital era: Technology, rhetoric and the public interest.* Mahwah, NJ: Lawrence Erlbaum Associates.

Warnick, B. (2004). Online ethos: Source credibility in an "authorless" environment. *American Behavioral Scientist, 48*(2), 256–265.

Williams, J., Clemens, S., Oleinikova, K., & Tarvin, K. (2003). *The skills for life survey: A national needs and impact survey of literacy, numeracy and ICT skills.* Norwich, U.K.: The Department for Education and Skills.

Williams, R. (1983). *Keywords: A vocabulary of culture and society.* London: Fontana.

Yin, R. K. (2003). *Case study research design and methods* (3rd ed.). Thousand Oaks, CA: Sage.

CHAPTER 5

The Conduct of Qualitative Interviews
Research Questions, Methodological Issues, and Researching Online

LORI KENDALL

UNIVERSITY OF ILLINOIS AT URBANA-CHAMPAIGN, USA

This chapter addresses qualitative interviews as a technique for doing research on new literacies. I use the term *qualitative interviews* to differentiate this technique from what sociologists call "structured interviews," for example, survey questionnaires that are administered by an interviewer but stick to a strict and consistent form. In contrast, qualitative interviews include (a) semi-structured interviews, which have a planned list of questions but allow room for dialogue, follow-up questions, and other changes, and (b) unstructured interviews, for which a researcher goes into the interview with only a topic or theme and allows the questions to emerge in dialogue with the interviewee.

In what follows, I first discuss some of the general features of in-depth interviewing focusing in particular on the research questions that match best with interviewing and the questions that interviewing cannot answer. I next discuss the pairing of interviews with other research methods, including an extended critique of the use of in-depth interviews as a follow-up to survey research. Finally, I consider the conduct of in-depth interviews online, discussing some of the advantages and disadvantages of this practice.

Interviews and the Investigation of Meaning

More than any other method, qualitative interviews allow for the exploration of meaning, especially as meaning is constructed by the research participants regarding a topic or setting of interest. The flexibility and ability to probe with follow-up questions along with the dialogic nature of the interview enables the researcher to attempt to see issues from the perspective of the interviewee and to achieve a degree of empathy and understanding with research participants. For this reason, interview research projects often engage with theoretical perspectives such as symbolic interactionism, ethnomethodology, and feminist theory that also focus on meaning and/or on participant perspectives.

Topics of interview research projects also reflect this emphasis on meaning. In particular, interview projects related to new media and new literacies often use interviews to investigate user conceptions of technology. For instance, Savolainen and Kari (2004) interviewed adults in Finland regarding their conceptions of the Internet. Similarly, interviews can be subjected to discourse analysis to illuminate dominant ideologies. In this vein, Clark, Demont-Heinrich, and Webber (2004) interviewed adults in the United States concerning their understanding of the digital divide. Interviews can also be used to analyze accounts of experiences that are difficult to observe such as "flow experiences of Web users" (Pace, 2004, p. 1).

Given that interviews seek disclosure of opinions, conceptions, and other internal states or characteristics and given the dialogic nature of the interview process, interviewers need to develop a special set of interpersonal skills. For instance, Denzin (1989) discussed the problem of "demand characteristics," or the tendency of research participants to anticipate the goals of the researcher and attempt to satisfy those goals. Interviewers must often proceed carefully when inquiring about particular concepts in order to not assume the knowledge or opinions of the interviewee. Clark et al. (2004) provided a particularly useful example of this issue in an extended interview excerpt regarding the digital divide (only part of which I reproduce here):

Interviewer: Have you heard the term "digital divide?"

Tina: No. What is it?

Interviewer: There is another phrase, "computer haves and have-nots." Essentially, for some people, digital divide means that some people have access to computers and other people don't … .

Tina: So the people that aren't wired are thinking that that's unfair that they are … .

Interviewer: It will even be people who all are wired or saying that everyone should be wired.

Tina: Right, like why are you permitting this? Why are you doing this to yourself? (p. 537)

After further navigation of the concept, the interviewer finally elicits an extended reflection from the interviewee regarding her opinions about the importance of obtaining a computer and about the economic constraints in her own life. This excerpt provides an excellent example of the careful introduction and clarification of a concept within the dialogue of a qualitative interview and illustrates the kinds of skills necessary to probe for information without overly influencing the interviewee.

The problem of "demand characteristics" arises in all research, regardless of method. A problem more particular to interviewing involves negotiating a balance between empathy and neutrality. Interviewers often find that self-disclosure can be important to encourage openness from respondents (see, e.g., Madge & O'Connor, 2002, p. 97). Such disclosures, however, must be undertaken carefully to avoid the impression that the interviewer might negatively judge the interviewee in the case of disagreement or differences in opinion or experience. The interviewer also wants to avoid eliciting mere agreement without elaboration.

Although interviews lend themselves to investigations of meaning, ideologies, thoughts, feelings, and so forth, they do not work well by themselves to investigate behavior, as I found in my study of an online group (Kendall, 2002). People in interviews often describe what they do in ways that do not match observations of their behavior (see, e.g., discussion in ibid, pp. 163–164). Commentators often present this question of self-reporting of behavior in interviews as a problem of veracity and may suggest methods for detecting fabrications or ferreting out truthful information (Denzin, 1989). This, however, runs the risk of creating an adversarial atmosphere, at odds with the overarching goal of empathy and understanding. As in other qualitative methods, there is a tension between the researcher's need to immerse himself or herself in the worldview of those studied and the need to retain a critical and analytical attitude toward that worldview. While this tension remains, regardless of the topic of the interview, it can be mitigated by not using interviews to measure behavior. If the research question includes the need to examine behavior, interviews can be paired with other methods such as observation.

This does not mean that behavior ought not to be discussed in interviews. Descriptions of behavior in interviews can give insight into participant beliefs about behavior and can reveal dominant discourses with which the interviewee is familiar. For instance, assertions that I encountered in interviews, such as "everyone is anonymous on the Internet" or "the Internet allows me to meet people I never would have met face-to-face," provide insight into the meaning people give to their online participation and their recognition of how such participation is viewed by others. Hardin (2003) suggested that such accounts be analyzed in the context of their production through asking questions such as "What function is served by the way this account is told?" or "Where do people learn to talk about their life in this way?" (p. 544)

Madge and O'Connor (2002) also benefited from shared status and experience with their interviewees. They, too, were parents and had made use of the parent information Web site they were researching. These factors allowed them to enter the research situation with considerable background information. In many cases, however, more in-depth preparation may be necessary for the researcher in order to bridge potential gaps in understanding during the interview. Denzin (1989) noted that the commitment to reach true understanding with interviewees "moves researchers into a multiple-methods approach to research" (p. 118).

In-Depth Interviews as Follow-Up to Survey Research

Studies of new media that rely solely on interview data are relatively rare. Interviewing is often paired with other research methods. I have already mentioned the possibility of pairing interviews with observations of behavior, and many ethnographic studies with a primary research method of participant observation also include in-depth interviewing. This combination of methods allows the researcher to check interpretations, investigate the meaning of observed behaviors, and acquire biographical and historical information about the interviewee's participation in the group or on the research site.

Interviews often also complement analyses of posted messages, such as those on listservs or bulletin board services. The latter provide examples of relatively public assertions and sometimes of interpersonal interactions. The interviews then provide insight into the private thoughts accompanying those discussions, as well as provide an additional means of assessing participants' presentation of self.

Unfortunately, one of the most common methodological pairings involves the use of interviews as a qualitative follow-up to a quantitative survey. Such a pairing is often undertaken in the interest of methodological "triangulation," presumably so that each method will compensate for the weaknesses of the other. Yet the deductive, hypothesis-driven logic of most quantitative surveys does not make for a good fit with the underlying inductive logic of qualitative interviews. Such studies often give short shrift to the real benefits of in-depth interviewing. In addition to the poor logical fit, the combination of qualitative interviews with surveys has five significant problems:

1. It treats interviewees much like survey respondents: as homogeneous research subjects with whom the achievement of understanding is unproblematic.
2. It violates the research logic of qualitative interviews by deriving categories of analysis from the survey and eliciting further "illustration" of analytical points from interviewees, rather than approaching the interviews inductively and allowing categories of analysis to emerge from interview data.

3. The constraints imposed by the necessity of reporting two different kinds of data within the report, usually an article in a peer-reviewed journal, results in interview data that are inadequately discussed, contextualized, and analyzed.

4. This results in the use of interview excerpts merely to add anecdotal color, treating them as window dressing for the quantitative analysis.

5. Because of these factors, far from strengthening research results through triangulation, the use of qualitative interview data tends to hide and exacerbate weaknesses of the primary survey method.

The combination of large-scale survey data with a smaller subsample of follow-up qualitative interviews is so popular and, I argue, so problematic that in the remainder of this section, I consider in great detail the problems just outlined, using examples from existing studies.

Large-scale surveys seek generalizable findings and usually test causal hypotheses. As such, they work best with large representative samples. For example, studies looking at various aspects of Internet participation usually target a general population of adults (or sometimes, of both adults and children). Status differences such as gender, class, age, and race are considered variables to be controlled for in the analytical model, and therefore, a heterogeneous sample is desirable. The subsequent selection of interview subjects from the survey sample population resembles theoretical sampling (Glaser & Strauss, 1967), in which interviewee (or other case) selection is guided by the research question, with an eye toward varying characteristics that might make a difference to the phenomena of interest; however, this resemblance to theoretical sampling is superficial. The process of theoretical sampling is grounded in the ongoing emergence of meaning through the course of the interviews (or observations). In contrast, the selection of interview subjects in a survey/interview study is generally determined by findings already analyzed from the survey data. Often, a typology is developed based on survey results, dividing respondents into several categories. Participants are then selected from these categories for follow-up interviews (see, e.g., Van Rompaey, Roe, & Struys, 2002; Selwyn, Gorard, & Furlong, 2005). This precludes the use of in-depth interviews to elicit meaningful categories as those categories have already been imposed upon the interviewee. The interview questions thus assume much of what ought to be discovered and attempt to merely elicit illustrative "depth."

For instance, Selwyn et al. (2005) conducted a survey regarding Internet use of 1,001 adults over the age of 21 in the United Kingdom. The quantitative analysis of their data resulted in the development of a typology of four different types of users (and nonusers): (a) broad frequent users, (b) narrow frequent users, (c) occasional users, and (d) nonusers. Respondents were then selected from each of these categories for the purpose of conducting 100 follow-up interviews. As in similar studies, the stated aim of the researchers was to provide "depth" to the survey data: "While these survey data are useful in highlighting the differentiated nature of adults' engagement with the Internet they can tell us only a limited amount about the factors underlying these differences" (p. 12). The researchers sought in particular to "develop 'more nuanced understanding of the reasons for different usage patterns'" (Anderson & Tracey, 2001, as cited in Selwyn et al., 2005, pp. 12–13). As these and other researchers acknowledge, surveys can illuminate patterns of behavior and attitudes, but they cannot tell much about the meaning of those patterns for respondents or the reason for their existence. In short, surveys cannot generally answer the question, "Why?"

In this study, as in most such studies, the survey is discussed first, with a full analysis of the questionnaire data. The subsequent presentation of interview data in this article is also typical. Interviewees are identified only by gender and age, with this information usually appended to quotes from the interviews. (Race is not mentioned, but the sample was relatively homogeneous with regard to race, with only 8% of the survey respondents classified as "non-White British.") We get very little of the social context of these respondents other than some discussion of socioeconomic factors, which were deemed significant to the usage differences uncovered by the study.

Several of the more interesting interview findings are mentioned in the discussion section of the article, with very little elaboration, but no illustrative quotes from the interviews are included. For instance, the authors asserted,

> Our interview data suggest that the *quality* and *nature* of ... access and use remains heavily gendered ... . For some of our less-engaged female interviewees, we saw how any good intentions or expectations which women may have about using computers "ultimately collide with the gendered constraints built into the pre-established territories of the home." (Cassidy, 2001, as cited in Selwyn et al., 2005, p. 20)

Although they earlier quoted a woman whose family members often fought over access, causing her to hold back and merely watch their Internet use, there is very little discussion of this quote, and it is not clear whether this is intended to illustrate their point regarding gendered constraints. In sum, the limitations of this style of reporting survey and interviewee data result in the researchers merely *telling* us what they found through interviews without adequately *showing* us.

An article published as part of the HomeNet study, conducted by researchers at Carnegie Mellon University in Pittsburgh, provides an example of a similar research strategy with regard to survey and interview methods. Boneva, Kraut, and Frohlich, (2001) analyzed gender differences in the use of e-mail through surveys and follow-up interviews. In the article, the researchers provided a methodological discussion of the conduct interviews first, presenting them as the primary data source. Yet in the results section, they discussed the questionnaire data first "to place the interview data findings in context"

(p. 535). Like Selwyn et al. (2005), they suggested that the interviews are needed to provide depth and explanation:

> The survey data analyses describe gender-related patterns of sustaining personal relationships using computers, but they provide no *detail* [italics added] about differences in communication between friends and family or *why* [italics added] women use the Internet more than men for distant partners but not for local ones. (Boneva et al., 2001, pp. 537–538)

Surprisingly, each subsection in the presentation of qualitative interview data begins with more quantitative data in the form of simple descriptive statistics about the interviewees' responses. The interview quotes provided are mainly simple reports of behavior: "Jim: I utilize the computer for entertainment and information. I don't e-mail or any … . I don't e-mail at all" (Boneva et al., 2001, p. 538). This is how the quote appears in the original. It reflects unedited spoken response to an interview question. "There are people I never talk to, like my friend in Alaska. I never talk to him on the phone, we just e-mail each other" (Boneva et al., 2001, p. 541). As far as we can tell from these quotes, the researchers did not exploit the ability of interviews to investigate the meaning of such behaviors to the respondents.

Interestingly, Boneva et al. (2001) provided several quotes and descriptions of the exceptional responses from their interviews. One such example concerns the use of e-mail to chat with geographically close friends:

> Neither women nor men seemed to use e-mail just to chat with local friends. An exception is Jane, who reported preferring e-mail over phone to chat with her closest friend locally:
>
> > I have a friend that lives 10 minutes away and we e-mail back and forth [just to chat] … . I could pick up the phone and talk, but we don't. (p. 541)

Another example concerned the use of e-mail to share emotional communication: "We have preliminary evidence that women may not consider e-mail very suitable for sharing of emotions and personal thoughts … . However at least 2 women judged e-mail more appropriate than the phone for deep-emotionally laden topics with someone far away." The researchers suggested that "although these examples may only be exceptions, they suggest some of the conditions under which e-mail may be preferred over the telephone for sharing deep emotions" (p. 544).

This last quote illustrates the paradoxical and frustrating aspect of this use of interviews. While they are purportedly employed to provide information to further explain the quantitative data, and they presumably ought to illuminate the meaning to participants of the behavior uncovered in the survey findings, the interview data as presented do not in fact address the "Why?" question. The information that emerges from the interviews very much resembles that

conducted quite carefully and thoughtfully. They present interesting and important results and provide useful analyses of the use of the Internet. The HomeNet study, in particular, is a well-known, oft-cited, and highly regarded study. What I hope I have instead illustrated through these examples is the limitations that specifically obtain from the research strategy of combining surveys with qualitative interviews. The "follow-up" interview is a misuse of in-depth qualitative interviewing that obtains none of the usual benefits of that method and may even exacerbate the limitations of the survey method its use purports to strengthen.

Online Interviewing: Using New Media to Study New Media

In studying new literacies, the behaviors and populations we want to study are often online. This can make it difficult to conduct face-to-face interviews given the geographically distributed nature of many online groups. It can also make the idea of instead conducting online interviews seem logical and appealing. While the practice of conducting in-depth qualitative interviews online is still relatively new, several researchers have attempted such research and have written reflections on the advantages and disadvantages. These discussions suggest that while online interviews present some advantages, they should be used with caution and may differ considerably from interviews conducted offline.

The most obvious advantages of online interviewing involve cost. Interviewing people online can decrease travel expenses and travel time, as well as transcription time, since the interview itself produces a written record (Chen & Hinton, 1999). Online interviewing can also enable access to participants who are too busy to consent to an in-person interview or who are uncomfortable discussing the research topic face-to-face (Bampton & Cowton, 2002; Chaney & Dew, 2003). Markham (2005) also suggested that online interviewing may be particularly appropriate when the research focuses on people's online interactions. In such cases, the interview itself becomes a form of participant observation.

Online interviewing actually constitutes a cluster of related methodologies, since a wide range of technologies have been used to conduct online interviews, and these different techniques have a significant effect on both interview process and transcript results. Researchers have conducted one-on-one interviews using e-mail (Bampton & Cowton, 2002; Broad & Joos, 2004), instant messaging (IMing; Chaney & Dew, 2003), and chat rooms (Davis, M., G. Bolding, G. Hart, L. Sherr, and J. Elford, 2004). Researchers have also conducted group online interviews via e-mail listservs (Gaiser, 1997) and through specially downloaded chat software (Madge & O'Connor, 2002). In addition to their difference from face-to-face interviewing, these techniques vary so significantly from each other in the kind and quality of information obtained that referring to them all as online in-depth interviews may be somewhat misleading. One obvious difference is whether interviews are with one person or many. Another key issue is whether interviews are asynchronous (through e-mail and Listservs) or synchronous (through chat and IMing). (In the latter case, it should be noted that although usually referred to as "synchronous," chat and IMing are actually "quasi-synchronous" in that utterances are sequential and cannot overlap.)

Despite these differences, all online interviewing shares some limitations. First, assuming that the interview is taking place through text, it requires literate respondents with access to the Internet. Familiarity with the data-gathering method (e-mail, IMing, etc.) is also usually a requirement, although Madge and O'Connor (2002) successfully introduced net-savvy respondents to new chat software for the purpose of group interviews. (Interviews could also be conducted via voice over the Internet, in which case they would presumably be similar to other sorts of telephone interviews. Video-conferencing software is also available online. I was unable to locate research utilizing these methods, either of which would introduce a host of additional technical issues not considered here.) In order to avoid significant sampling bias, online interviewing thus only makes sense when the population of interest has facility with language and is already online.

Additionally, text-based computer-mediated communication (CMC) does not allow the transmission of such forms of nonverbal communication as tone of voice, mannerisms, gestures, and so forth. One of my interviewees reflected on this at the end of our interview, when he invited me to contact him online if I thought of any further questions:

> Feel free to ask me online. It wouldn't be any different talking online from my perspective from face to face. Of course this [face-to-face] is the most interactive you can get. You get the full range of information, not only the words that I speak, but the inflection and the gestures and the whole nine yards that we have to artificially recreate online by shrieking or howling or smilies or bilies or whatever.

The contradictions in this quote illustrate some of the issues involved in online versus face-to-face interviewing. This participant stated that the online follow-up "wouldn't be any different talking online ... from face to face." The participant also acknowledged, however, that the face-to-face situation allows for "the whole nine yards" and "the full range of information," which must be compensated for online through typing in words such as "shriek" (a practice common in the online forum in which this interviewee was a participant) or by using "smilies."

The lack of nonverbal communication in online textual interviews thus affects how participants communicate and what the researcher can observe. CMC users must find ways to compensate for the lack of richness in communication and must find alternative ways to supply some of the information usually communicated through nonverbal means. Some accomplish this through the addition of specialized language codes (such as "LOL" for "laugh out loud") or emoticons (smiley faces such as ":)"), although conventions for the use of these can vary significantly among different populations and on different online forums. Other users learn to interpret each other's online communication through association over time and shared culture and history (Kendall, 2000). Researchers therefore need to determine interviewees' strategies for online communication. This means that for online interviewing, even more than for offline interviewing, researchers must familiarize themselves with research participants and their online environments.

Researchers have found that e-mail communication constitutes something of a hybrid between written and oral communication. Similarly, e-mail interviews are as much like some forms of open-ended surveys as they are like interviews. As Bampton and Cowton (2002) discussed, interviews through e-mail allow participants to respond at their leisure. This provides an advantage when dealing with busy respondents, but it also makes the interview experience less spontaneous. It is unclear whether the increased time for reflection on answers, as compared with the face-to-face situation, constitutes an advantage or a disadvantage. Further, the e-mail interview does not allow the interviewer to approach the interview situation as a participant observer and take note of more than just the words responding to questions. Denzin (1989) noted that this constitutes an important part of the interview process, as the interviewer is "participating in the life experiences of a given respondent and is observing that person's report of herself during the interview conversation" (p. 118).

Broad and Joos (2004) also noted that the use of e-mail hampers a researcher's ability to conduct an "active interview" in which "the interview guide is a 'conversational agenda' more than a 'procedural directive'" (p. 933), since in Joos' case all of the questions were sent up front to the respondents. Other researchers have conducted interviews through multiple e-mail messages; however, both Bampton and Cowton (2002) and Mann and Stewart (2003) pointed out that continuing such an exchange for too long can lead to interviewee fatigue, potentially causing participants to fail to complete the interview.

Chat and IMing allow for more interaction between interviewer and interviewee, but they raise additional problems of their own. Chat messages are generally short. Because only one message is transmitted at a time, it can feel uncomfortable to type out long messages. The feeling of copresence relies on a constant exchange. As Davis et al. (2004) pointed out, however, turn taking becomes ambiguous online, leading to multiple "threads" within a single conversation and introducing ambiguity into the interpretation of individual utterances. This is difficult to correct because "[c]larification disrupts the flow of an already ambiguous dialogue and takes time in an already protracted engagement. Online interaction is not easily 'repaired' if ambiguity or other distractions arise" (Davis et al., 2004, p. 950).

As the quote from Davis et al. (2004) suggests, chat (or IMing) also takes a considerable amount of time. Most researchers who have employed this method estimate that it takes approximately twice as long as face-to-face interviews (Markham, 2003; Davis et al., 2004). Markham, A. (2003). Even then, the results may not be comparable. Davis et al. found that "a 120-minute online interview produced about seven pages of text" while "a 90-minute face to face interview produced 30 to 40 pages of text" (p. 947). That is a significant loss in quantity, if not quality, of data. Davis et al.'s solution to the issues of both time and ambiguity was to use short, closed questions, which again cause the online interview to more closely resemble a survey than a face-to-face qualitative interview.

Neither chat nor e-mail allows nonverbal feedback, which can be an important form of encouragement to respondents. Attempting to translate nonverbal feedback into text can be problematic. "Each time I felt compelled to react 'nonverbally' to statements the participants made, I had to decide whether or not to risk disrupting their thoughts to let them know I was listening and was engaged in the conversation by verbally signifying a nonverbal behavior" (Markham, 2003, p. 16). Similarly, Madge and O'Connor (2002) noted that "the empathy we held with the woman had to be explicit rather than through utterances and gestures" (p. 99). Sounds such as "mm-hmm" are more ambiguous in meaning when typed and may not feel as encouraging to interviewees. Tone and emotional intent can be difficult to communicate, especially with relative strangers.

Even the information usually communicated verbally changes when typed. Online textual conversations appear to put pressure on participants to produce unique and interesting text. People in various online forums often resist "me too" posts and simple declarations of support, fearing that these sound unoriginal and insincere (Kendall, 2005). The use of small words of encouragement, common in verbal conversation, also changes when typed, and questions that sound innocuous face-to-face may seem blunt in text. Madge and O'Connor (2002) stated, "We felt like our written comments sounded banal or our questions too direct and leading" (p. 99).

These limitations regarding online interviews suggest that they may not be directly comparable to offline qualitative interviews. It also seems likely that pairing online and offline interviews in the same study, as some researchers have done (Henderson & Gilding, 2004; Davis et al., 2004), may be as problematic as combining surveys and in-depth interviews. At the very least, when including quotes from such varied sources, the context of the quote—whether obtained online or offline—should be indicated, something Henderson and Gilding (2004) did not do. These issues suggest that new conventions need to be developed to determine the best practices for the use of online interviews.

CHAPTER 6

The Case of Rebellion: Researching Multimodal Texts

ANDREW BURN

UNIVERSITY OF LONDON, ENGLAND

Rebellion is a computer game created by a 14-year-old boy. Because it affords insights into how multimodal texts are designed (and games are perhaps the most multimodal of texts), I will use it as an instance of how to approach the analysis of such texts.

For me, the most important theoretical and methodological opportunities and problems of social semiotics and multimodality theory are rooted in a claim made by Kress and Van Leeuwen (1992) in a paper critiquing the work of the later Barthes (1978). In it, they made the claim that social semiotics is "the theoretical, analytical and descriptive branch of cultural studies" (p. 28). What might this claim mean?

My reading is that it indicates a desire to operate with the theories of culture emanating originally from the work of pioneers such as Williams (1961), and subsequently from the tradition of cultural studies. It relates this tradition to a theory of textual analysis rooted in the cultural and social function of the text, derived from sociolinguistics, and Halliday (1985), in particular. As a necessary corollary of this, it connects textual meaning with the social interests of its related sign makers—those who make it, and those who use, read, view, or play it. In the context of education, it offers a theory of signification ready for synthesis with the work of scholars of children's media cultures, in particular Buckingham (1996, 2003; Buckingham & Sefton-Green, 1994), who provided influential research in how children engage with media texts (e.g., 1996), as well as proposals for how the pedagogies of media education might be influenced by cultural studies (Buckingham & Sefton-Green, 1994; Buckingham, 2003).

This seems like a marriage made in heaven. The field of cultural studies has been an immensely invigorating development in media research, radically shifting the emphasis from textual structures to lived cultures, from ideal spectators to real audiences, and from abstract textual politics to situated cultural politics. In developing its methodological apparatus from forms of ethnographic investigation, discourse analysis, and social theory, however, it gradually became apparent that it never really developed a new way to think about signification and text. When cultural studies scholars reached for techniques of textual analysis, they reached back in time, as Fiske (1989) and Hebdige (1979) did, for French semiotics in their respective analyses of Madonna and punk.

So the merger Kress and Van Leeuwen (1992) proposed with a new semiotics—which offered to recover some of the clarity of structuralist semiotics, modified by a rigorous attention to social meanings realized as text and discourse characteristic of functional linguistics—seemed timely, to say the least; however, there are some problems.

To the best of my knowledge, no research project has yet truly fulfilled the promise of this merger. No full project has connected a semiotic analysis of media texts with research into the cultures of those who produced them and those who received them. The best I can do here, then, is to use a current funded research project as an example of how I hope such a synthesis might go in the future. The project does not aim for such an accomplishment; however, it has been useful in sharpening my sense of what is needed, and this sense has informed some of my analysis of the data that has emerged so far. I will use a small selection of this data, then, as an example of what questions such an approach might offer, attempt to model them as I go.

Making Games

This is a three-year, funded research project, in its last year at the time of writing. Its aim is to develop—with a software company—authoring software for computer games. The funders are the United Kingdom's Economic and Social Research Council (ESRC) and Engineering and Physical Sciences Research Council (EPSRC), as well as the Department for Trade and Industry. The software has been developed by the industry partners in the project, Immersive Education, Ltd. The researchers are Caroline Pelletier (also project manager), David Buckingham, and myself. In addition to developing the software, a main research aim of the project is to develop a model of game literacy, which would, in principle, be a subset of moves in recent years to expand the notion of literacy beyond print toward multiliteracies (Cope & Kalantzis,

2000; Lankshear & Knobel, 2003), media literacy (Buckingham, 2003), and multimodal literacies (Jewitt & Kress, 2003).

This was not conceived primarily as a research project in multimodal textuality; however, its rationale does refer to the multimodal nature of computer games in particular, drawing on work in earlier projects. In addition, my own contribution to the project has partly been to think how students' gaming experiences (an obvious element of game literacy) can be analyzed in multimodal terms (Burn, 2004); and how the texts they themselves produce (the other obvious component of game literacy) can be analyzed in the same way (Burn, in press).

Furthermore, this project has, for me, helped to focus a range of theoretical and methodological questions in relation to (a) multimodal theory, (b) social semiotic theory, more broadly, and (c) media and cultural studies theory and research at an even more general level. Some of these questions and problems find at least partial answers in this project; others remain for future exploration.

This chapter will, then, select the work of one boy who participated in the project, and consider not only how social semiotic and multimodal theories can help to analyze the games he made, but also how the games realize meanings derived from his own cultural experience, especially in the domain of computer games. The student in question is a Mongolian boy, Ogedei, (pseudonym) who has been involved in each of the three years of this research project. In the first year (when he was 12 to 13 years old), we interviewed him about his gaming experience. In the second year (ages 13 to 14), he created a game in an after-school club, using the second iteration of the software developed in the project, and was also interviewed about his experience regarding the game, book, and film *Harry Potter and the Chamber of Secrets* (Electronic Arts [EA] Games, 2002). In the third (14 to 15 years old), he took the software home and produced a second game, using the third iteration of the software. I have selected data for this chapter from these broad contexts.

When we are confronted with this data, social semiotic and multimodal theories afford us a number of choices:

1. We can approach the data from the point of view of the four strata proposed by Kress and Van Leeuwen (2000) in relation to multimodal texts: (a) discourse (knowledge of some aspect of reality); (b) design (choice of semiotic mode; e.g., language, visual design, music); (c) production (choice of medium; e.g., paper, marble, computer programming); and (d) distribution (getting the text to an audience, sometimes through another layer of technology; e.g., broadcasting or Web display). In addition, I would add *interpretation*—Kress and Van Leeuwen (2000) have a chapter on this, but do not conceive of it as another stratum. For me, however, it is the logical consequence of distribution. Since interpretation, as Kress and Van Leeuwen (2000) argued,

More specifically, Ogedei's references to games he has played invokes a *discourse of horror,* which, as Buckingham (1996) argued, can serve as a testing ground (for teenage boys, in particular). In an interview during Year 8 (the second year of secondary school—high school—in the UK, student ages typically 12 to 13 years), Ogedei was anxious to point out where games have a horror dimension. He emphasized that *Silent Hill* (Konami Computer Entertainment, 1996) is a horror game, and later described the experience of playing *Resident Evil:*

> When we run and he appears, so I start running around. Well it's like the druids are like, they keep turning you around, and they keep running in circles, every time it comes up … You don't know where it comes from. Like black landscape … . It is like they just randomly spring up … Whatever you like, if you have ten seconds or one minute they just spring up. It's weird. And it's like creepy stuff … . I get freaked out by *Resident Evil* (from the author's research interviews with Ogedei).

This account foregrounds the affective thrill of "horror," the only genre named after the emotion it inspires, as noted by film philosopher Noel Carroll (1990). It also, however, relates the affective impact of the game to the modes in which it is designed: the graphic design of the landscape, the dramatic actions available to the player character, and the apparently random design of the appearance of the evil druids (an effect he recreates two years later in his own game, *Rebellion*).

The discourse of horror games appears again a year later, when Ogedei was designing his first game using the second iteration of the authoring software produced by the project. On this occasion, he was designing the game in an after-school club set up by the project, and was talking through his design. He said that his intention was to make his game "more like an actual game." He then immediately referred—as he did a year earlier—to Silent Hill (Konami Computer Entertainment, 1996) as a model: "I've played a game that's really scary—*Silent Hill*" (from the author's research interviews with Ogedei). As we shall see, his game designs reflect intentional adaptations of aspects of these games.

A third discursive theme is what we might call a *proto-critical discourse.* Part of this is an awareness of aspects of the political economy and regulatory domains within which games are produced. In the Year 8 interview (with second year high school students), for example, he claimed that the horror games to which he has referred are certificated as 15, which is indeed the certification for the *Silent Hill* and *Resident Evil* series in the United Kingdom. A year later, he referred to the certification of *Manhunt,* another game he cited as an influence on his design: "I've only played it once, I got it from another country, it wasn't 18 there, it didn't have a rating, then it turned out to be really violent" (from the author's research interviews with Ogedei). This rather elaborate plea of ignorance may well indicate an awareness of the controversial history of this game, certified 18 by the British Board of Film Classification (BBFC) and the subject of a widely publicized murder case in 2004, in which the victim's mother claimed that the murderer had been obsessed by the game.

Within this proto-critical discourse, we can also locate critical judgments Ogedei frequently made about games. In the Year 8 interview, he made critical comments about quality that echo player-review discourses in gaming magazines and online forums: "I play Red Alert on PC which is good. It's better than PlayStation because it's got better graphics" (from the author's research interviews with Ogedei). In a rather different kind of judgment, he disparaged games developed from movies as "rubbish," suggesting that they are developed in a hurry, and relating the quality of games to the length of time it takes to develop them.

In an interview with children who have played the game *Harry Potter and the Chamber of Secrets* (EA Games, 2002; for an analysis of this, see Burn, 2004), Ogedei made specific critical judgments about the game. Unlike other children in the group who compared it with what they see as the originating text, J. K. Rowling's novel, Ogedei judged it inauthentic as compared to other games in the action-adventure genre. It is also clear, however, that his unease with the character (that he is a "teachers' pet") indicates a desire for more subversive images of boyhood and its relation to authority. In particular, he proposed that Harry should have more powerful spells. When asked by a girl in the group whether this could be *Avadakedavra*, the killing spell (a reference to the Harry Potter books), Ogedei replied, "No—a flamethrower." In one sense, this remark displays his critical judgement of the game: It is low in what Van Leeuwen (1999) termed "presentational modality," or truth to its genre; the flamethrower metonymically indicates what a "real" adventure game would be like.

His remark, however, also relates to his wider interests in horror and representations of violence. These interests are the kinds of textual preferences that routinely awaken popular anxieties about media effects. In this respect, it is important to remember the history of such debates. In particular, we can invoke Buckingham's (1996) study of young people's engagement with horror films, as well as his finding that such preoccupations are not the obsessive preserve of a minority of young male delinquents, but a common strategy for young people coming to terms with a range of social anxieties about the world they inhabit and the turmoil of growing up. Ogedei's unfavourable view of Harry Potter indicates similar preoccupations on his part.

Buckingham (1996) also argued that we need to remind ourselves of the fictional nature of such media representations. Play and game theorists make the same point about the nature of games: Their fictional status, and the lack of consequences for the real world, is a shared understanding by those who enter the game world. Sutton-Smith (1997) elaborated the difference, both for animals and humans, between play fighting and real fighting. Salen and Zimmerman (2003) developed the idea of a magic circle, the game world that is governed by clearly defined rules understood by the players. This kind of rational view of games is clearly important to Ogedei; he talks about the logic of games, the strategies needed to defeat end-of-level bosses, and how characters can impart instructions and information to players. In this respect, he engaged with practices and discourses of games in the sense of Roger Caillois' (1958/2001) *ludus:* play as a rule-governed system. His engagement with the discourses of horror games (and films) and the unpredictable, liminal adult pleasures they afford, however, seems much closer to the category Caillois (1958/2001) opposed to ludus, which he termed *paidea:* a looser, more chaotic form of play. Similarly, in the rhetorics of play he identified, Sutton-Smith (1997) isolated a progressive rhetoric that views play as educative, orderly, and rule-governed, one that he called "the rhetoric of Fate," in which more-adult forms of play (from Dionysian rites to gambling) are seen as dangerous and chaotic. It seems plausible that it is the combination of rule-governed, rational mastery and the (safe) experience of forbidden adult pleasures that provides precisely the exhilarating experience sought by teenagers, an experience that grows out of the reassuring structure of playground games and aspires toward the heady risks of adulthood.

Finally, we can identify a *proto-designer* discourse. This is, of course, specifically invited by the nature of the project, since we wanted to find out as much as possible about how the children thought games could be designed. Many of the children were quite uncertain about this in the Year 8 interview. Ogedei, however, made some specific suggestions that were entirely feasible in the light of actual game production practices. For instance, he suggested the following:

> I think one of the first things you need to know is what kind of drama. You have to choose like drama, like the name of a character, like idea about it and develop on that … . Drama, the characters and the storylines. You know, storylines and endings, then you need the stuff for the levels …, and the bad guy on the levels (from the author's research interviews with Ogedei).

Ogedei also suggested that character designs would begin with sketches, which was again entirely consistent with industry practices, especially in the production of, for instance, Japanese role-playing games in which elaborate concept drawings come early in the production process.

Later this same year, after using the first iteration of the project's authoring software, Ogedei had a number of interesting suggestions to make, which showed particular insights into the design process. He made one proposal that, although he presented it as a novel idea, seemed to derive from the so-called "bladder motive" in *The Sims 2* (Maxis, 2004). "None of the other games have this, but after while, they should have a need to go to the toilet." (from the author's research interviews with Ogedei)

Although this game was not released in the United Kingdom until later in the year in which this interview took place, it is possible that Ogedei had read of this feature in the gaming press or on the Internet. It is noteworthy here—perhaps, because it expands the discursive field on which he was drawing—to consider game design beyond the stereotypically male areas of first-person shooters.

He also asked if the future software development will allow characters to talk; again, an area of design that was generally of more interest to the girls in the group:

> If they could talk, if they could give you objectives, or get you involved in objectives, or get new parts of the story of the game and all that, more clearer, clearer what's happening, and then more logical, cos if it just says do this with no reason it'd be weird (from the author's research interviews with Ogedei).

His interest in talk, then, is as one choice of mode the designer can use to convey to the player information about both the representational and ludic aspects of the game.

In general, then, the discursive patterns identified here suggest that Ogedei is deeply immersed in the culture of games. He has played many different titles and genres. He possesses a multimedia PC and a PlayStation 2. He is familiar with recently released titles, in some cases even before they have been released, presumably from previews in magazines, on the Internet, or on television. He has a good sense of the social anxieties that surround games and the regulatory mechanisms that exist to circumscribe them. His interest is not always in games, per se, but in cross-media experiences of narrative and genre, such as the experience of horror in games such as *Resident Evil* and films such as *Jason X;* or quest narratives in the games and films of *The Lord of the Rings.* Finally, he has some sense of how games are designed, belonging to the minority of players who seek out proto-design opportunities such as level editing.

As part of his life, the culture of games intersects with Ogedei's sense of self. On the one hand, he clearly obtains a certain status from his expertise; however, games and other media also serve as semiotic material through which he can articulate subversive meanings that challenge the conventional order of school and the adult world, offering fantasy alternatives to forms of childish obedience that he may wish to leave behind. In one sense, gaming expertise and experience can be seen as a form of cultural capital, though how such capital can be recognized and augmented by school is one question of this project. For conventional schooling, games are largely invisible, in Bourdieu's (1984) sense that to see (*voir*), one has to know (*savoir*): "A work of art has meaning only for someone who possesses the cultural competence, that is,

unpleasant is about to happen. In fact, there is no such ludic consequence (such as the appearance of an enemy or the triggering of a booby trap. The effect, arguably, is a transformation of the word he used two years earlier to describe *Resident Evil:* "creepy." This emotion is his interest and his intention, and he realizes it here through his combination of visual and audio design, in a relation of complementarity across the modes.

The second effect is also representational: it carries forward the narrative, in effect introducing us, albeit enigmatically, to a key character we have not yet met. In this respect, the verbal mode (which *names* the Overlord) augments and anticipates the visual mode, which will *show* us the Overlord soon.

Its final function is ludic. In effect, it gives us an implicit instruction: Our mission is to attack the Overlord. It also warns us that he will be defended. Again, this verbal instruction amplifies the other clues that the game will give us when we meet the Overlord; it anticipates them.

Clearly, then, it becomes hard to disentangle the representational meanings relating to narrative from those relating to game. The landscapes, objects, and sounds help to make up Ogedei's narrative of alien Overlords and rebel commandos. At the same time, they signify familiar game genres, just as elves, orcs, and mages would signify role-playing games and the Tolkienesque cultural history that lies behind them.

The characters Ogedei has chosen also recall earlier games and genres. There are three categories: (a) friendly rebels, (b) enemy stormtroopers, and (c) their leaders, the alien Overlords. Rebel commandos and stormtroopers are familiar figures from commercial FPS games. The idea of rebellion also has earlier gaming connections with science fiction, especially in *Star Wars: Rebellion.* As with the landscapes and objects, the debate raised here is broadly about the virtues and vices of generic reproduction. There is a debate in the industry at the time of writing, for instance, about the extent to which commercial game design might be locked into the conservative reproduction of formulae assumed to appeal to the perceived core demographic (young male gamers). Aleks Krotoski (2006), a UK-based games journalist and researcher, wrote in the *Guardian* newspaper, "At the moment, in-store displays groan under computer games with hackneyed paradigms and established genres" as well as of the need for new ideas from the next generation of game designers.

For Ogedei, the excitement and danger of the FPS and action adventure genres, and the dangerous worlds they present, seem to be connected on the one hand to the discourse of horror in games (and films), which, as we have seen, appeals to him as a transgressive body of texts, offering glimpses of new and independent identities and tastes, distanced from school, authority, and aspects of boyhood he is eager to transcend.

At the same time, it is possible to subject the representational matter here to forms of critical reading which, while they might uncomfortably collide with these social meanings, might also productively challenge them, or at least problematize them. While the male-dominated world of the FPS offers a kind of playground for a certain kind of rite of passage in some ways analogous to paintball, it also raises questions about the limitations of such play. Most particularly, it raises questions about the representation of women. While many girl gamers might enjoy playing male characters in FPS games, and might even find this an experience liberating from stereotypical female social roles (cf. Cassell & Jenkins, 1998, p. 36), it seems entirely reasonable to ask a young games designer the question "Will there be any female characters in your game?" This is the kind of critical question a media-education classroom would routinely raise in relation to representation. This simple but profound issue seems a valuable example of critical thinking for tomorrow's game designers. In a previous research project on role-playing games, we were a little dismayed to work with one company in the United Kingdom that had produced a game which, though inventive and interesting in many respects, had no female characters and was designed entirely by young men, with no real discussion, as far as we could tell, of the rationale for such a representational bias.

What can social semiotics say here? Three things, in my view. First, it can at least demonstrate what has been designed, that is, what processes of signification are in play and what social meanings they convey, or at least wish to make claim to.

Second, it can look at the notion of creativity itself as a rhetorical process, not so much an essential truth, but as a cluster of evaluative discourses and social efforts to negotiate what is valuable and valued, especially in the aesthetic life of the society. In this respect, as we have seen, horror and FPS games may indicate Ogedei's subscription to forms of popular taste that emphatically prefer spectacular, transgressive imagery. In Bourdieu's (1984) inversion of the Kantian aesthetic, this kind of preference is entirely positive; he refers to it as "the expressive content which explodes in the expressiveness of popular language" (p. 34) and "the violence to which the popular spectator consents" (p. 48).

Third, perhaps most usefully here, it can propose a theory of transformation. Signs always adapt signifier material; they never create it out of nowhere. In this sense, Ogedei is like any other creator; however, there are greater and lesser degrees of transformative effort. For Ogedei, the point here is absolutely *not* to transform the FPS genre beyond recognition, but rather to harness it, to produce it as authentically as possible, as we shall see in the next section. The creative work lies, not in the transformation of representational structures, but in the composition of the game, the complexity of this composition, and the well-crafted ludic experience it offers the player, some of the detail of which will be analyzed later in this chapter.

When all is said and done, however, there remains something we might reasonably regard as an aspect of game literacy: the politics of representation. While this may be a distraction from Ogedei's central motivation, and the strong connection of his game with his gaming culture, it can be seen as part of an apparatus of media education that helps the learner to move toward more abstract conceptualizations of text and meaning of the kind Vygotsky called (1986) "scientific."

Interaction. Characters are typically part of the representational system of a text, so that the previous question—"Who is doing what to whom?"—is usually a purely narrative question. Even in games, it can be considered at least partly under the heading of representation; however, to take the protagonist as the main example, while the protagonist fulfils all of the usual narrative functions (e.g., setting out, encountering other characters, overcoming obstacles, doing battle, achieving some kind of resolution), there is a critical—even a *criterial*—difference in games, where the player character is also the "puppet" referred to by the game theorist Gonzalo Frasca (2003) as a kind of "digital dummy" (Burn & Schott, 2004). It is the dramatic point of entrance to the game, and in semiotic terms, it allows the operation of a grammatical sleight of hand, in which one term of the transitive sequence, the *Actor* (in the terminology of functional grammar), becomes the spectator/player. A number of actions performed by the protagonist are passed over to the player. Importantly, they are not all the actions represented in the game, but only those controlled by the interface—typically, *walk, run, jump, shoot,* and *get*. In this sense, we are working not with the infinite number of actions available in a conventional narrative, but with a restricted language, which works like the restricted languages of other games, such as the suits in a deck of cards, as Halliday (1974) described. Neither designer nor player experience this set of actions as restricted, however, as they are juxtaposed with a variety of environments, characters, sounds, and narrative events, and they also undergo forms of semiotic amplification, expanding into wider sets of actions (e.g., *escape, dodge, hide, meet, hover, teeter, blast, kill, make friends, steal, buy,* and so on).

In designing his game, Ogedei is working with a player character that is simply a first-person point of view, with no visible substance other than a hand, a gun or a wand to hover in front of them as a metonymic indicator of agency. Furthermore, most of the player character's actions are predefined by the authoring software (e.g., *jump, walk, crouch, look, get*). In this sense, the ludic design work here is a little like being given a pack of cards and asked to invent a new card game. You can attribute new meanings to the suits and numbers (you must get five black cards to win; or the initial letters of your cards' names must spell a four-letter word); but you cannot change the components with which you are playing. Similarly, you could be given a chess set and invited to make up a new game with new rules; however, the provenance of the components—two differently colored sets representing state, church, and military—are likely to suggest a conflict-based game distantly symbolic of actual historical conflict (though it might be possible to convert chess into a peace game, perhaps by adapting and boosting the powers of the bishops and queens; or a game of proletarian revolution, by boosting the power of the pawns).

In the same way then, Ogedei has been given defined actions with which to work. He makes certain important decisions. He chooses to provide guns and ammunition, consistent with the generic style of his game, and adding the action *shoot* to his player's repertoire. Beyond this, however, his transformative work is in creating the semiotic arrays with which the player character's actions will connect. These include the landscape, which transforms the limited set of actions into a much richer set, through syntagmatic links made provisionally by the designer as possibilities, then by the player as actual combinations in a particular game session. We will next see how this works. Here, we will focus on another semiotic mode, which transforms the actions of the player character through a central interactive function of the game: speech.

At the beginning of *Rebellion*, the player emerges from a transporter pod and meets a friendly ally, one of the rebel commandos. Using the branching dialogue tool of the authoring software, Ogedei has designed the following conversation between player and commando:

Rebel commando: You made it! Quick, we must hurry. Even as we speek [sic] the hunters are teleporting in.

Player: OK, but without weapons I wouldn't be able to do anything.

Rebel commando: Doesn't matter. I have a ray gun and 50 rounds of ammo stashed in the box next to me, I'll follow you after you get them (from the author's research interviews with Ogedei).

This short interchange, in interactive terms, accomplishes a good deal. First, it strikes a balance of mood at the beginning of the game: in terms of the functions of demand and offer, which Kress and Van Leeuwen (1996) have adapted from Halliday (1985), it offers goods (the gun and ammo) and services ("I'll follow you"). It also demands action, both explicitly ("Quick, we must hurry") and implicitly, in what is effectively an instruction to get the gun and ammunition.

Second, however, in addition to the ludic actions already conferred on the player character (*walk, jump, crouch, get*), and the extra one added by Ogedei (*shoot*), it adds another: *speak*. To activate it, the player clicks on the dialogue line as it appears on screen. Again, as with the pack of cards, the player cannot choose what to say, but she or he can choose whether to say it or not; in some cases, a player can choose from a number of different responses, with different consequences for the game. Of course, the dialogue also serves representational purposes, economically sketching in the situation, implying the genre and initial narrative state, and providing character motive.

states, and other ludic features, using the rule editor, a process similar to writing if-clauses, mathematical equations, or high-level computer programming. He has composed dialogue, a process similar to writing a play script, but also like improvised drama.

There are too many aspects of spatial and temporal design, ludic and narrative design, here, to do justice to. We will focus on two: (a) the routes of play designed for the player; and (b) what makes this a coherent text.

The notion of the route through the text invokes Kress and Van Leeuwen's (1996) notion of reading path in visual design: that, while the visual text may indicate a preferred route through by forms of salience attributed to elements of the composition (size, center-margin, foreground-background, etc.), the viewer can choose his or her own route, to some extent. Lemke (2002) extended this idea in relation to hypertext, naming the text's suggested route the *trajectory,* and the player's preferred route the *traversal*, in recognition of the greater possibility of disparity between the two in hypertext, where the designer cannot predict all the possible routes.

The relation between trajectory and traversal is partially realized in popular discourses of gaming as a debate about "linearity," as in this review of the popular Japanese role-playing game, *Final Fantasy VII* (SquareSoft, 1997): "As is typical of the Japanese RPG form, the game is extremely linear. You may not see the train tracks, but the feeling that you've been railroaded is unmistakable" (Burn & Schott, 2004, p. 227).

Ogedei's game offers the player a very clear trajectory. As in many adventure games, there is only one way out of each section of the game, ensuring that the player progresses smoothly from section to section. Within these sections, however, there are choices. In the first level, having encountered the first enemy stormtrooper, the player is offered the choice of surrendering their gun or opening fire. The first option leads to game death, as the stormtrooper pursues you and shoots you until your health level is completely depleted. The second option allows you to kill the stormtrooper and gain a healthpack. You then proceed to the end of a corridor and can turn right or left. If you turn right, you enter a burst of electricity, which kills you. If you turn left, you come to the door to the chamber that contains the Overlord and the route to the next level. You then enter combat with the two stormtroopers in this chamber, after which you meet the Overlord, and are offered the two options just described. If you allow the Overlord to lead you to the door, you follow him, but are then killed as you go through the door. If you kill the Overlord, you are rewarded with his eyeball, which you place in your inventory, and which opens the door for you.

The trajectory is clear, then: there is only one route in each case that leads to the win state and one to the lose state. These options introduce an element of chance: with each double option, you have, in principle, a 50-50 chance of success; however, this simple ludic structure is amplified semiotically by the representational systems of the text. Ogedei has chosen visual designs that will ring alarm bells for the player; and he has, in recording the voice files for their dialogue, used accents and intonations that suggest evil intent: sneering, threatening, and mocking. Here, visual and auditory modes amplify the ludic options to produce warnings and suggestions of characters' intentions. In some cases, these amplifications work as disambiguation: they clarify the options (e.g., the image of an electric storm warns you of a route that will lead to game death). In other cases, they do the reverse (e.g., the "Intruder! Alert!" warning is intended to panic the player and make the ludic route ambiguous and uncertain).

What, then, does the player's traversal consist of? Specific options are available. First, there are the choices outlined earlier, simple twofold choices, in each case. Second, there are choices about routes within the chambers. The chamber containing the Overlord is a large, three-level chamber. We can explore the lower levels (where we will find the barred door leading to the next level, which will inform our understanding of what needs to be achieved next); or we can go straight up the stairs and confront the Overlord. Third, we have choices about time. We can race around frantically, or we can take our time; however, time is constrained in certain places. As we approach the Overlord's chamber, we can see, just inside the entrance, two stormtroopers. Ogedei has placed, just outside the entrance, a trigger volume that, when the player enters it, will make the stormtroopers "seek and destroy" the player. The placing of the trigger volume is critical. It is on the far side of a small bridge so that the player has time and space to approach, see the stormtroopers, and equip a gun before (unknowingly) triggering the seek and destroy action. This allows the player the sense of slowly creeping up, peering into the room, getting prepared, followed by an intense bout of action in which speed and accurate firing makes the difference between winning and losing. The alternation of suspense and energetic release here is, of course, characteristic of horror films. As Carr (2003) argued in the case of *Silent Hill* (Konami Computer Entertainment, 1996), it is also a characteristic of the player's experience of horror games, positioned on the receiving end of the monstrous threat. Here, then, Ogedei's composition carefully balances spatial and temporal dynamics to work toward the ludic experience of the games he seeks to emulate.

What are the organizational features of this game that design the trajectory and make the traversal possible? One aspect of the design can be seen as textual cohesion, defined in the seminal text on this feature of linguistic semantics as "relations of meaning that exist within the text and define it as a text" (Halliday & Hasan, 1976, p. 4); however, the principle of cohesive ties needs to be rethought in the context of complex multimodal texts of this kind. Halliday & Hasan's (1976, p. 4) original five categories—(a) reference, (b) substitution, (c) ellipsis, (d) conjunction, and (e) lexical cohesion—need to be adapted, as Lemke (2002) has suggested.

a coherent narrative sequence, and references to generic patterns in games of this type familiar in the discourses of designer and player.

Redundancy also exists in the repetition of instructions in different modes. As we have seen, we may be cued to attack the Overlord by the visual design of the character, by the intonation of the voice characterization, or by the words used. While the modes complement each other, they also repeat the same message, giving us time to decide. If we see the player in the role of oral performer, who, like Ong's (2002) oral storyteller, must improvise on given formulae, depending on the rhetorical figure of *copia*, stalling devices for performer and reader. The player is, of course, both, like Janet Murray's (1998) notion of the game player as both audience and actor. As the player of *Rebellion* is poised outside the Overlord's chamber, then, the repetition of the figure of the stormtroopers just visible inside the chamber and the ludic sign of the gun in the player's inventory, already used once in the game, serve as repeated formulae that tie the game together. As in the semiotic triad of the referential ties, the meanings made by these clusters of redundant images are potential, dependent on player action to realize their meanings, and hence subject to the performative, improvisatory work of the player, just as the kennings and epithets of oral, formulaic, narrative verse are waiting for assembly by the bard.

Distribution

Like the other strata proposed by Kress and Van Leeuwen (2000), the question of distribution is partly about modes and media, but also about power relations. What has been a process of modal combinations (e.g., animation, sound, speech, game rules) now becomes a relatively fixed final text, but to be sent out into the world, it needs a medium of distribution, frequently more than one medium. In the games industry, this often involves the final contractual stage in the relationship between a developer (often, a small production company) and a publisher (typically, a very large international company); this relationship is marked by (a) forms of content and editorial control, (b) the targeting of markets across age, gender, and cultural and national groupings, and (c) the flow of capital investment and revenue income.

For education, the issue of distribution of media texts made by young people is also about technologies and power. The history of such work is effectively one of simulation, imitations of production practices throughout the world, which most often stop short of distribution. The work is seen by the class, maybe the school, perhaps parents, and sometimes examiners, but it cannot command exhibition opportunities in the prized sites of the media: cinemas, peak-time television, and large-scale production for the retail market. At times, Internet technology seems to provide a solution for this prison of simulation: at last, young people's work can be published to the world. Significant questions remain about who exactly the audience might be, however, both in global and local terms. The exhibition sites that were once considered to be the most prized remain so, in many respects.

The Internet will be the distribution technology for games made by these students, eventually augmented by a free, downloadable player produced by Immersive Education. At present, Ogedei's games are on a password-protected site accessible to other schools, teachers, developers, and researchers in the project.

To return to the world of the simulation, however, the whole question of distribution and interpretation is also, for media education, about how young designers of media texts imagine their audiences. In this regard, the classes and clubs who used the authoring software were encouraged to write walk-throughs for their games, a tentative exploration of the interpretive practices of game fan cultures, which typically produce fan art, writing, text-based games, walkthroughs, and even poems and songs. This aspect of the project is yet to be developed, but Ogedei's walkthrough for his first game (a) displays an anxiety to capture the authentic experience of play, (b) evokes the discourse of hints and cheats that players delight in, and (c) adopts the mantle of the expert shared by the professional designer and the hard-core expert gamer.

Conclusion: Analyzing Games

We can make some conclusions about the game Ogedei has designed. It develops a coherent narrative, consistent with the genres he enjoys and wishes to emulate. It constructs a satisfying experience of play, which can be said to have a high degree of ludic cohesion, also consistent with these game genres. It is closely related to his gaming culture, developing forms of ludic pleasure he has experienced in commercial games, as well as representational and narrative devices typical of his favorite genres. Also related are social meanings with implications for gender, on the one hand, and for popular aesthetic taste, on the other.

The analysis of both the interview data and the game has told us something useful about what kinds of literacy, design process, and learning are going on here. It also answers urgent and pertinent questions about how the interests of literacy in schools might be served by including forms such as computer games alongside film, television, and print media texts in literacy (and literature) curricula. It is clear that one purpose of a multimodal analysis of a text of this kind is to demonstrate what kinds of literacy might be involved in its production. Games represent another example of how we might expand conventional print literacies to fit other representational modes, as Catherine Beavis (2001) argued in her study of the use of games in an Australian classroom. Ogedei's game, produced outside the usual classroom pedagogies of media education, demonstrates that many of the competences usually associated with literacy are in evidence, including certain forms of critical distinction. In answer to the obvious question that arises from this—"What is the value of media edu-

Carroll, N. (1990). *The philosophy of horror: Or, paradoxes of the heart*. New York: Routledge.

Cassell, J., & Jenkins, H. (1998). *From Barbie to Mortal Kombat*. Cambridge, MA: MIT Press.

Cope, B., & Kalantzis, M. (Eds.). (2000). *Multiliteracies: Literacy learning and the design of social futures*. Melbourne, Australia: Macmillan.

Electronic Arts Games. (2002). Harry Potter and the Chamber of Secrets [Video game software]. Redwood City, CA: Author.

Fiske, J. (1989). *Reading the popular*. London: Unwin Hyman.

Frasca, G. (2003). Simulation versus narrative: Introduction to ludology. In M. Wolf & B. Perron (Eds.), *Video/game/theory* (pp. 221–235). London: Routledge.

Free Radical Design. (2002). Timesplitters 2 [Video game software].Redwood City, CA: Eidos.

Halliday, M. A. K. (1974). *Explorations in the functions of language*. London: Edward Arnold.

Halliday, M. A. K. (1985). *An introduction to functional grammar*. London: Edward Arnold.

Halliday, M. A. K., & Hasan, R. (1976). *Cohesion in English*. London: Longman.

Hebdige, D. (1979). *Subculture: The meaning of style*. London: Methuen.

Jewitt, C., & Kress, G. (Eds.). (2003). *Multimodal literacy*. New York: Peter Lang.

Konami Computer Entertainment. (1996). Silent Hill [Video game software]. London, England: Author.

Kress, G., & Van Leeuwen, T. (1992). Trampling all over our unspoiled spot: Barthes' 'Punctum' and the politics of the extra-semiotic, *Southern Review, 25*(1), 27–8.

Kress, G., & Van Leeuwen, T. (1996). *Reading images: The grammar of visual design*. London: Routledge.

Kress, G., & Van Leeuwen, T. (2000). *Multimodal discourse: The modes and media of contemporary communication*. London: Arnold.

Krotoski, A. (2006). 'What they Can't Teach You at Game Design School', The Guardian, Thursday February 23rd, 2006 (accessed online: no page numbers).

Lankshear, C., & Knobel, M. (2003). *New literacies, changing knowledge and classroom learning*. Buckingham, U.K.: Open University Press.

Lemke, J. (2002). Travels in hypermodality. *Visual Communication, 1*(3), 299–325.

Maxis, (2004). The Sims 2 [Video game software]. Redwood City, CA: Electronic Arts Games.

Murray, J. (1998). *Hamlet on the holodeck*. Cambridge, MA: MIT Press.

Ong, W. (2002). *Orality and literacy: The technologizing of the word*. London: Routledge.

Pelletier, C. (2005). The uses of literacy in studying computer games: Comparing students' oral and visual representations of games. *English Teaching: Practice and Critique, 4, 1,* pp. 40–59.

Salen, K., & Zimmerman, E. (2003, November). This is not a game: Play in cultural environments. In M. Copier & J. Raessens (Eds.), *Level up: Digital games research conference, proceedings* (4–6). Utrecht: University of Utrecht.

SquareSoft. (1997). Final Fantasy VII [Video game software]. Tokyo, Japan: Author.

Sutton-Smith, B. (1997). *The ambiguity of play*. London: Harvard University Press.

Van Leeuwen, T. (1999). *Speech, music, sound*. London: Macmillan.

Volosinov, V. N. (1973). *Marxism and the philosophy of language* (L. Matejka, & I. R. Titunik, Trans.). New York: Seminar Press.

Vygotsky, L. S. (1986). *Thought and language* (Alex Kozulin, Ed. & Trans.). Cambridge, MA: MIT Press.

Williams, R. (1961). *The long revolution*. London: Chatto and Windus.

CHAPTER 7

Experimental and Quasi-Experimental Approaches to the Study of New Literacies

JONNA M. KULIKOWICH

THE PENNSYLVANIA STATE UNIVERSITY, USA

Never before has research in literacy been so exciting yet so challenging. Well beyond the advent of the information age, educators are immersed in a knowledge society (Goldman, Wiley, & Graesser, 2005) where information can be accessed and generated at exponential paces by virtual means. While investigators still explore the processes and evaluate the learning outcomes of students as they read offline texts (e.g., magazines, newspapers, and textbooks), researchers of the so-called "new literacies" (Leu, Kinzer, Coiro, & Cammack, 2004) are beginning to embark on lines of inquiry dedicated to the study of performance with (e.g., locating and searching for information) and process of (e.g., comprehension and evaluation) texts of the modern era. These electronic or online texts can be verbal representations read in linear fashion; however, they are as likely to be texts housed with multiple representations including animations, diagrams, graphics, photographs, and mathematical or scientific visualizations that permit nonlinear movement among sources (e.g., Ainsworth, 1999; Jacobson & Archodidou, 2000; Slotta & Linn, 2000). The vast amount of textual information coupled with the varied representations of information makes acts of literacy extremely difficult for students who choose to interact with the systems in linear, nonlinear (Alexander, Kulikowich, & Jetton, 1994), and constructive (i.e., composing texts) ways.

groups on characteristics such as students' ability levels or teachers' experiences prior to comparing them for treatment effectiveness.

For example, suppose a researcher wants to determine if students who use the Internet (i.e., treatment) are able to find relevant references for a term paper to a better degree than students who use the traditional means of going to the library (i.e., comparison/control). Assume one classroom in a school has wireless access to the Internet while another classroom does not. For sheer convenience, the classroom with wireless access would be assigned to treatment while the classroom without would be assigned to control. In this hypothetical case scenario, it is in the best interests of the researchers to match classroom and student characteristics on as many dimensions as possible in an effort to attribute any significant differences in students' performance to the experimental condition.

The definitions or experiment and quasi-experiment are worth revisiting as a reminder of how difficult it is for literacy researchers to conduct these studies. First, to select students randomly from a population of interest (e.g., all elementary or middle-level students enrolled in public or private schools in the United States) is rarely feasible. This would mean every student has the same likelihood of selection. Therefore, it would be as probable for a student in California to participate as it is for a student in Maine. Resources, such as time and personnel, are extremely limited. Therefore, attempting to reach students at different locations across the United States is very unlikely. Of course, with new literacies research, the investigator might consider using a broad network tool like the Internet to select participants, and certainly, given the Internet, a student could participate in any experiment virtually. The experimenter again loses control, however, as the unit of analysis no longer merely becomes the student. The student must work with a computer somewhere and thus the student-computer system must be housed in some larger context such as a classroom, home, or library. With inclusion of the computer alone, experimental control is in question. Further, in the reality of school settings, students are more likely to share computer resources and work together (e.g., Slotta & Linn, 2000).

From a statistical perspective, these realities threaten an important assumption in experimental research, the assumption of independence (Glass & Hopkins, 1996). Simply put, new literacies research not only invites interaction of students with complex learning environments (Young, 1993; Young, Kulikowich, & Barab, 1997) but also emphasizes the importance of cooperation, collaboration, and communication among participants (e.g., Barab, Hay, Barnett, & Squire, 2001; Barron, 2000; Leu et al., 2005; Roschelle, 1992). Essentially, it promotes interdependence, not necessarily independence, among participants as they meet the demands of completing complex tasks.

With the respect to the second characteristic of the experiment, specifying intervention levels with a comparison or control group, new literacy researchers face two dilemmas. First, in the ideal experimental situation, a pure control condition where students receive no form of instruction is the only way many researchers assert that causal claims can be supported in the social sciences (Cronbach, 1982). Establishing causality means that investigators can conclude that a specific intervention (e.g., using prompts to scaffold learning) or element of an intervention (e.g., animation or sound) had an effect on an outcome (e.g., locating or evaluating information) independent of other factors (e.g., parental, peer, or teacher influences) that may influence learning. A control group requires, however, that students who are assigned to the condition do not receive any type of instruction. Students are enrolled in schools to learn. Usually, the best that researchers can do is to compare several manipulated design conditions or instructional interventions against standard regular classroom instruction with no multimedia, hypermedia, or Internet elements (e.g., Leu et al., 2005). As a result, researchers are encouraged to abstain from cause-effect conclusions and, instead, suggest that results are likely or probabilistic based on the introduction of the intervention.

The second dilemma is potentially more problematic. Multimedia and hypermedia platforms as well as instructional paradigms (e.g., jigsaw groups and reciprocal teaching) for new literacy learning are extremely complex. With respect to the former, it is difficult for researchers to know how to manipulate the environments not only because there are so many components of the system (e.g., audio, diagram, graphs, text, videos, and visualizations) but also because systems vary by the amount of information they contain as well as the link and node programming structures that permit movement among information or the construction of new information (e.g., listserv postings or textbox inserts).

Systems that require new literacies can vary greatly based on several characteristics. As mentioned in the introduction, and as I shall review in the next section of this chapter, some systems can be referred to as closed systems. In closed systems (e.g., Ainsworth, 1999; Ainsworth, Bibby, & Wood, 2002; Moreno & Mayer, 1999), there is a manageable, finite amount of information which one is expected to comprehend or understand, and students are expected to interact with all information (e.g., animations, representations, texts) housed in the environment. Comparatively, open-ended systems, such as the Internet and Web site environments (Slotta & Linn, 2000) can contain an ever-emerging stream of information that is held potentially to its limits by only the learner. As such, it is very difficult to impose control parameters on information as can be done in traditional texts where headings or overviews may be included or omitted (e.g., Lorch & Pugzles Lorch, 1996) or seductive details embedded or not embedded in locations where the reader should dismiss unimportant but interesting facts and focus on main ideas (e.g., Garner, Alexander, Gillingham, Kulikowich, & Brown, 1991).

With respect to instructional interventions, researchers must attend not only to design elements of the materials they use, but also to several other major considerations. How long should the intervention last? Should there be multiple sessions? To what degree should scripts be used? To what extent should the teacher or researcher participate in the intervention? Can students work in groups? Can students progress at their own paces? These, of course, are a small set of questions. Each question, however, may lead to important design considerations related to assessment practices, psychometric evaluation of scores, and statistical analysis (Kulikowich, 2005).

The third feature of experimental design is random assignment of participants to conditions. When experimental manipulations can be made within the computer environment, it may be easy to assign students randomly to conditions. Here, researchers must determine whether each student can work autonomously in a setting that does not disrupt completion of tasks. Further, investigators should assess the extent to which participants might converse with one another about their experiences. Reduction in autonomy and discussion of learning experiences may lead directly to violation of the assumption of independence (Beretvas, 2004; Kulikowich, 2005).

Perhaps the most successful program of experimental and quasi-experimental research conducted at the student level in multimedia environments is that of Mayer and colleagues (2001, 2003; Mayer, Mautone, & Prothero, 2002; Moreno & Mayer, 1999, 2002). In these carefully planned studies that largely address the degree to which working memory capacity is taxed during multimedia learning, procedures were very detailed and manipulations of the environment were controlled with utmost precision to isolate effects specific to features (e.g., animation and sound) that could be incrementally added to or deleted from the environment. Students participated in sessions where they worked in individual cubicles to combat violation of independence assumptions. Another stellar feature of this research was the role that replication played to address some of the shortcomings of experimental research presented here, such as lack of a pure control group or numerous gradations in treatment conditions that may make an effect significant in one instance and nonsignificant in the next. Later in this chapter, I will review a study by Mayer and his colleagues; however, characteristics of their research are presented here to contrast it to experimental research that is tied more to classroom instruction interventions.

In classroom-based research, random assignment of students to experimental conditions is impossible, for the intervention is delivered at the classroom level. Random assignment, therefore, should occur at the level of the classroom as students are nested in this higher unit. Fortunately for researchers, statistical procedures such as multilevel modeling (Singer, 1998) or hierarchical linear modeling (HLM; Raudenbush & Bryk, 2002) are available to determine the degree that classrooms vary given the dependent variable of interest.

These multilevel statistical models can be extended readily to address effects due to district (e.g., rural, suburban, or urban) and school characteristics (e.g., amount and quality of computer resources) along with the effects of treatment tested at the classroom level (Beretvas, 2004; Kulikowich, 2005; Lomax, 2004). With every additional level (e.g., schools or districts) of the nested structure of the units of analysis (i.e., students in classrooms), however, the modeling and estimating of parameters becomes more complex (Moerbeek, 2004; Raudenbush & Bryk, 2002).

Control Factors in Experimental Research

Of the many research considerations fundamental to the design of quality experiments, five are particularly important in the study of new literacies. These control factors include (a) sampling of participants to ensure sufficient power; (b) development of study materials to permit replication and generalizability; (c) design of interventions that allow attribution of results to treatment manipulations; (d) defining and operationally defining dependent variables via sound psychometric procedures; and (e) selection of best statistical methods to evaluate intervention effectiveness given the amount and type of data collected.

In the following sections of this chapter, these control factors will be addressed given six studies of new literacies. Further, I select one study for each program of research and review it paying particular attention to why experimental methods were chosen given the topics of interest to the investigators. As indicated in the introduction, researchers' goals vary regarding the use of experimentation. For example, sometimes investigators want to test the degree to which one or more tenets of a theory (e.g., Knowledge Integration Environment [KIE]; Linn, Davis, & Bell, 2004) can be supported. At other times, researchers are interested in whether one or more instructional interventions can promote learning with multimedia and Internet systems (e.g., Azevedo & Cromley, 2004). As I will demonstrate in the review of selected studies, the investigators' purpose leads directly to the type of environment they study as well as the degree of control they impose in manipulating the environment to test experimental hypotheses.

Examples of Experimental Research in the Study of New Literacies

Review of experimental studies which tested the efficacy of one or more interventions on learning outcomes revealed two basic trends about the manners in which experimenters manipulated the literacy environments. One trend that emerged was related to the literacy environment as a closed or open system. Another trend pertained to whether the researchers manipulated one or more elements of the computerized environment to study their effects on learning or whether they introduced an instructional intervention outside of the environment to foster new literacies skills. Often, these two emergent trends coincided. Therefore, in closed systems, it is common for the researchers to program one or more features within the media environment (e.g., animation, feedback menus, and overviews) to examine their effects on students' attention, interest levels, or working memory capacity (Alexander et al., 1995). For open systems, such as the Internet, it is common for researchers to provide direct instruction to students outside of the computer environment in an effort to increase self-regulation and monitoring of a set of strategies (e.g., locating, evaluating, and communicating) that facilitate learning (e.g., Slotta, 2004).

Closed versus Open Systems

A multimedia platform manipulated to study sound and animation and its impact on working memory capacity such as that used in work by Mayer and colleagues (2002) would constitute a closed system. There is a low frequency of links to connect media elements, movement through the system is sequential or linear, and learners are expected to comprehend all information. An open-ended system, by comparison, would be an environment such as the Internet where it is highly probable that no two learners would move and process information in the same way. The amount of information studied is in the control of the reader, and nonlinear, rather than linear, movement among information is the norm (Alexander et al., 1995; Spiro, Feltovich, Jacobson, & Coulson, 1992; Spiro & Jehng, 1990). Also characteristic of open systems is that individuals can contribute their own compositions in the medium. As a result, the text space is constantly changing given the participation of individuals who interact with the system.

Open systems such as the Web and Internet are the media of choice because they preserve the ecological validity of studying a global information highway that permits immediate access to a wealth of information and support systems that can aid in solving real-world problems. For example, in a program called Earth Systems Engineering Management (ESEM; Allenby, 2001, 2004), new literacies are used to connect scholars worldwide in their efforts to tackle important environmental problems (e.g., controlling flooding, maintaining food supplies, and protecting endangered species) in the Everglades (Gorman, 2005).

Interventions within or Interventions outside of the Computerized Environment

The second dimension corresponds directly to the treatment or intervention variable. Some interventions are introduced within the environment to examine the role that design elements have on learning. For example, designers can program inclusion of scaffolding tools to help students acquire domain knowledge that is principled in nature. Investigations by Jacobson (1994; Jacobson, Maouri, Mishra, & Kolar, 1996) typified this kind of research as do studies planned by Linn and colleagues (1992; Slotta & Linn, 2000) that addressed questions pertaining to critical reading of Internet sources.

Other interventions can be characterized as curricular or instructional treatments. In these instances, scripts are often followed and teachers representing the treatment group are trained to provide a specific type of instruction to students (e.g., search and navigation strategies). These classrooms of students are then compared to regular classrooms where instruction on the use of a specific skill set using new literacies is not provided. As such, experimental manipulations are imposed outside of the computerized environment. For example, Winne and colleagues (e.g., Winne & Stockey, 1998) and Azevedo, Cromley, and colleagues (e.g., Azevedo & Cromley, 2004; Azevedo, Cromley, & Seibert, 2004) studied the degree that instruction on self-regulation strategies increases knowledge acquisition during interaction with hypermedia environments. More recently, Leu et al. (2005) adapted the reciprocal teaching program of Palincsar and Brown (1984) to determine its effects on traditional as well as Internet-based reading in the biological sciences. In these studies, students use new literacy resources, however, the treatment variable is an instructional or teaching factor independent of the literacy environment.

In the next section, six studies are reviewed that best represent varying degrees of closed versus open system designs as well as manipulation within or outside of the computerized environment. As one study of a closed system where the intervention is manipulated within the environment, I selected "Maximizing Constructivist Learning from Multimedia Communications by Maximizing Cognitive Load" (Mayer, Moreno, Boire, & Vagge, 1999). As three studies of more open systems where the intervention is still manipulated within the environment, I chose (a) "Reading Strategies and Hypertext Comprehension" (Salmerón et al., 2005); (b) "The Design of Hypermedia Tools for Learning: Fostering Conceptual Change and Transfer of Complex Scientific Knowledge" (Jacobson & Archodidou, 2000); and (c) "The Knowledge Integration Environment: Helping Students Use the Internet Effectively" (Slotta & Linn's, 2000).

While these three studies were similar in terms of the type of environment examined as well as the nature of the experimental manipulation, they differed in terms of the researchers' purposes as well as the primary outcomes of study. Salmerón et al. (2005) were interested in studying hypertext comprehension from a construction integration modeling perspective (Kintsch & van Dijk, 1978). As such, their experimental research traced its historical roots to classical studies of reading comprehension. In contrast, the studies by Jacobson and Archodidou (2000) and Slotta and Linn (2000) typified investigations in cognitive psychology on conceptual change and expert-novice differences. In these investigations, therefore, problem solving is closely linked with new literacies such as critiquing information and using evidence to support a claim (e.g., Slotta & Chi, 2006).

Two examples of experimental studies that focused on instruction outside of a new literacy environment were "Does Training on Self-Regulated

Learning Facilitate Students' Learning with Hypermedia?" (Azevedo & Cromley, 2004) and Leu et al.'s (2005) recent presentation to representatives of the North Central Regional Educational Laboratory (NCREL) in Chicago entitled "Evaluating the Development of Scientific Knowledge and New Forms of Reading Comprehension During Online Learning." The former study has more a closed text environment (e.g., encyclopedia entries) than the latter, where students interacted with information from the Internet. Both studies, however, examined traditional instructional interventions (i.e., self-regulated learning [SLR] and reciprocal teaching).

Mayer and Colleagues (1999)

Mayer et al. (1997) ran two experimental studies following his cognitive theory of multimedia learning. Borrowing from the work of Paivio (1986), Mayer and his colleagues described three key theoretical components that account for student learning. The first of these three components emphasizes that memory processes invoke dual coding where visual and verbal materials operate on different processing systems. The fact that information is processed by different mental mechanisms challenges learners when they encounter multimedia environments leading to cognitive overload.

The second component of the theory relates to why cognitive overload occurs. Essentially, Mayer and colleagues (1999) recognized that working memory is of limited capacity. On this principle, Mayer and colleagues intervened and manipulated the multimedia programming to evaluate potential overload and gauge the degree that information can be presented to optimize learning by operating within the limits of working memory capacity.

The final component emphasizes the value of generative learning (Wittrock, 1990) as a means to combat working memory limitations. Students do not learn best when they are passive participants who receive information and attempt to store it in long-term memory. Generative learning highlights the importance of constructivist learning, and in the multimedia environments created by Mayer and colleagues (1999), students are invited to interact actively with the system trying to make rich connections between the verbal and visual information they encounter.

From this framework, the primary hypothesis espoused by Mayer et al. (1999) was that working memory is limited; however, if the environment can be manipulated to maximize the likelihood that visual and verbal information are processed in working memory at the same time, then learning increases.

The first study evaluated the performance of 60 undergraduate students. Researchers randomly assigned 12 students to one of five experimental conditions. In the first condition, the multimedia environment was programmed to present verbal (sound) and visual information concurrently for manageable amounts of information called "small bites." The verbal information was a narration of how lightning occurs while the visual information was an animation of these processes. In the second condition, animation was followed by narration. In this condition, information was not broken down into segments. Thus, it was referred to as a "successive large bite condition." The third condition reversed the order of modality presentation; narration was followed by animation for successively large bites. The last two conditions broke down the information into a manageable set of 16 segments presented sequentially (i.e., "successive small bites"). The fourth condition presented animation first followed by narration, while the fifth condition was programmed to reverse this order—narration followed by animation. In total, five multimedia programs were developed to allow test of the carefully graded intervention. While the system is arguably closed, the elegance of the design rests in the precision of how the treatment variable was operationally defined to test the researchers' theoretical tenets about how working memory operates during multimedia learning. Small bites should reduce cognitive load. If cognitive load is reduced sufficiently, then learners who can process verbal and visual information concurrently should make richer connections among information than students who are asked to process large chunks of information. Mayer et al. (1999) hypothesized, therefore, that the concurrent and successive small bites groups would do better than the successive large bites groups on a variety of learning outcomes.

Assessment materials used in both studies included a biographic questionnaire and retention, transfer, and matching tests. The retention test measured everything students could recall about lightning. The transfer test included four questions designed to assess how well students could make connections and infer relationships based on the information presented. The matching test evaluated how well students could circle images that represented various meteorological events. Each test was measured on an 8-point scale.

Mayer et al. (1999) treated each outcome variable independently by testing treatment conditions using one-way analysis of variance (ANOVA). The two large bite conditions were collapsed, as there were no differences due to order of modality. Similarly, the small bite conditions were combined after detecting no difference between conditions. After collapsing the groups, the results showed that both the concurrent and small bite groups performed better on the retention, transfer, and matching tasks than the large bite conditions.

One hallmark feature of the program of research developed by Mayer and colleagues (1999) was their use of replication. A pure control condition is not justifiable in their work as they are testing a theory about multimedia learning. Thus, all students must interact with such an environment. To evaluate the credibility of their tenets, therefore, Mayer and colleagues conducted multiple studies to see the degree to which results generalize for similar samples.

The second study was a replication of the first study. This time the cause and effect information focused on a different topic, car mechanics. The same set of treatment levels were defined to examine whether cognitive overload semester. The investigators chose questions that reflected relevant architectural and energy issues.

Students in each condition worked in pairs for five class periods in their physical science program. Slotta and Linn (2000) were interested in three results: to what degree do students in the various groups pose questions that are specific (i.e., focus on evidence) and relevant (i.e., add to their knowledge base and eliminate conceptual gaps) questions that lead to productivity in architectural design.

Student scores were compared via univariate ANOVAs. As expected, the overview group rated information as more credible than the other two groups. The advance guidance groups were more critical in questioning the accuracy and usefulness of information. Further, the advanced guidance and model questions group asked more relevant questions pertaining to design issues and demonstrated better productivity in implementing design principles. Slotta and Linn (2000) concluded, "Having one's attention focused on the relevant science in a piece of evidence leads to heightened estimation of its inherent usefulness" (p. 219).

Azevedo and Cromley (2004)

Azevedo and Cromley (2004) examined instructional interventions rather than environmental design-based ones. Their goal was to teach students how to regulate their learning strategically while interacting with hypermedia environments. They hypothesized that an increase in self-regulation will correlate positively with deep conceptual understanding in science.

Based on previous research (e.g., Azevedo, Guthrie, & Siebert, 2004), five indicators of successful learning were identified. These indicators contributed to the development of their instructional intervention. They included (a) use of effective strategies; (b) planning through articulation of subgoals; (c) activation of prior knowledge; (d) monitoring emerging understanding; and (e) planning of time spent and effort expended to acquire information.

Using these indicators, Azevedo and Cromley (2004) developed their SLR condition. They planned a 30-minute training session on the circulatory system. A four-page script was created along with a table that detailed phases of self-regulation and a diagram of how SLR works. Students also received a table of important SLR variables and their descriptions. Finally, participants were taught how to use the script as they worked within the hypermedia environment.

In their single study, 131 undergraduates participated. They assigned 63 students to the training condition, while 68 undergraduates represented the control group. Both groups of students were given a general learning goal to acquire as much information about the circulatory system they could. The control condition, of course, received none of the SLR guides.

A set of pretest and posttest measures were constructed to address group differences relative to mental models of the circulatory system (e.g., conceptual learning) and eight SLR variables (e.g., planning, monitoring, and strategy use). These tests included a matching task of definitions, labeling a diagram of the heart, and diagramming the flow of blood through the body, and a basic recalling measure (e.g., an essay). The essay and the path diagram of blood flow were scored to represent 1 of 12 mental model profiles (e.g., no understanding to advanced understanding of the heart and blood flow). As two separate scores, students received a point for every correct matching item (e.g., the matching score) and labeling item (e.g., labeling score). The SLR scores were derived from think-aloud protocols examining evidence of the eight key SLR variables.

Participants in both conditions were tested individually. On average, they spent about 45 minutes learning about the circulatory system on a MicroSoft Encarta References Suite 2000 hypermedia system including three articles on the circulatory system that housed multiple representations (e.g., text, diagram, photographs, and animation). In total, the system held 16,900 words, 18 sections, 107 hyperlinks, and 35 illustrations. While it is a very expansive system allowing for varied paths of navigation, it can be considered closed in that information was restricted to one set of articles presented to all participants.

Azevedo and Cromley (2004) ran three—two (training: SLR vs. control) by two (time: pretest vs. posttest)—procedures on the mental model, matching, and labeling scores. The mental models had a significant interaction. SLR students significantly outperformed the control group at posttest while there were no initial differences. Both groups increased their matching scores significantly; however, the SLR group improved significantly on the labeling task compared to their control counterparts.

Chi-square tests were run to determine the degree to which SLR self-regulation protocols contained more key SLR variables than control protocols. There were several differences in favor of the treatment group: increases in planning, monitoring, strategy use, evaluation of task difficulty and demands, and interest. Based on their results, Azevedo and Cromley (2004) concluded that their SLR instructional training was very effective.

Leu and Colleagues (2005)

Leu et al. (2005) designed an experiment to examine the effects of internet reciprocal teaching (IRT) on a variety of traditional and online reading tasks. Of the six studies reviewed in this chapter, Leu et al.'s (2005) investigation not only focused most on the open-ended Internet highway but also looked at the role of classroom instruction on helping students acquire new literacy skills. As such, the treatment variable defined operationally in their investigation does not emerge because of design manipulations in a hypermedia or multimedia environment.

In their investigation, 89 seventh-grade students participated, representing four sections of science at their participating school. Each classroom secof research questions, researchers can plan future studies more effectively by conducting power analyses to determine sample size.

Development of Study Materials

The construction of materials in the study of new literacies is a time-consuming and labor-intensive undertaking. In the studies reviewed in this chapter, however, that all quality design platforms or instructional interventions stem from theoretical frameworks specified by authors based on exhaustive reviews of literature is evident. Mayer's work (e.g., Mayer, et al., 1999) for instance, was rooted in multiple cognitive theories on memory as well as constructivist accounts of learning. Similarly, Leu and colleagues' interventions (Leu, et al, 2005) were based on years of strategy research associated with traditional reading outcomes. Examination of new literacies, therefore, cannot divorce itself from traditional literacy research. That said, experimental researchers are well advised to make efforts to detect where traditional and new literacy processes and products diverge. Leu et al. (2005), for example, determined that general reading achievement scores did not correlate significantly with scores that represented searching, evaluating, and communicating scientific information on the Internet. Materials (e.g., hypermedia systems and instructional scripts) that can isolate where the processes become orthogonal, yet how they can complement one another and promote learning will become especially valuable as the demands placed on students in a knowledge society will increase.

Design of Interventions

With the exception of Salmerón et al.'s (2005) and Azevedo and Cromley's (2004) investigations, all of the experimental studies reviewed in this chapter illustrated the importance of defining interventions that are graded. As such, conditions varied by incrementally adding a design element, principle, or length of the instructional intervention. Specifying levels of an intervention may be easier to do in design-based research with closed systems than in research that evaluates modes of classroom instruction and their impact on learning in Internet or Web-based environments. One recommendation that researchers might consider is the degree to which they can incorporate longitudinal elements in their design. Growth-curve models are becoming more prevalent in reading research (e.g., Francis, Shaywitz, Stuebing, Shaywitz, & Fletcher, 1996). By studying trends that compare treatment and control conditions, researchers may be able to detect where an incremental adjustment in the amount of the intervention starts to show improvement compared to control. Growth-curve models can be tested readily using HLM or multilevel modeling programs. Researchers are encouraged to follow examples outlined by Singer (1998). She also provided SAS programming code to assist investigators in test of their longitudinal effects.

Defining and Operationally Defining the Dependent Variable

Perhaps the largest obstacle confronting experimental design researchers of the new literacies is definition, conceptually and operationally, of one or more dependent variables. With the exception of the Leu et al. (2005) investigation, none of the research teams addressed the reliability and validity of outcome scores. Further, some of the outcomes such as the mental models studied in the works of Jacobson and Archodidou (2000) and Azevedo and Cromley (2004) are likely not only latent but also multidimensional. As such, use of a single score reduces measurement precision and decreases statistical power to estimate treatment effects.

There are exciting new developments in test and task construction that utilize item response theory (IRT) models to scale unidimensional or multidimensional latent variables (Embretson & Reise, 2000). IRT models help researchers detect poor items that do not contribute to measuring an outcome precisely, and they are the only means by which researchers can evaluate whether their outcome truly holds interval-level properties. Without interval scales, results from parametric procedures such as the many ANOVA tests run by researchers of the new literacies are in question.

Use of Statistical Methods to Evaluate Intervention

Finally, the studies reviewed here demonstrated an overreliance on use of univariate procedures to test treatment effects. It is likely the case that many of the multiple measures were correlated. In future research studies where samples of the size described by Slotta and Linn (2000) can be secured, researchers might consider multivariate techniques such as structural equation models (SEM) to examine the relationships among sets of independent and dependent variables. A nice feature of SEM models is that they can compare multiple samples (e.g., treatment and control conditions) to determine whether covariance structures are invariant (Lomax, 2004). This means that the nature of construct relationships may differ between treatment and control groups because of the intervention. For example, the mental models of learners acquiring deep principles because of a design intervention may show stronger relationships between conceptual and procedural knowledge than for students who represented the control group. Multisample SEMs can test for these differences.

Chapter Summary

This chapter focused on experimental and quasi-experimental designs in the study of new literacies. Studies reviewed could be characterized according to two basic characteristics. One characteristic represented the type of literacy environment in which students interacted (closed vs. open systems). The other characteristic reflected the kind of intervention tested (environmental vs. instructional). Features of experiments were introduced and recommendations

Introduction to Part II

The Internet is the largest single repository of information to have been compiled in the history of our civilization. Moreover, as each person contributes to it, the amount of online information grows at a ferocious rate. This poses an interesting paradox: the more information that appears online, the more challenging it is to turn this information into knowledge.

The greater the amount of information, for example, the more difficult it becomes to locate the specific information required to understand a problem. In addition, since anyone may publish anything, we are likely to find multiple answers to any question we might have. Much more is required of us to carefully analyze any information that we locate to determine its reliability. Which sources provide the best information for the questions we have? It is not always easy to tell. It is clear that having access to large amounts of information does not easily translate into knowledge and understanding. For those who study the informational aspects of new literacies, issues of knowledge and inquiry become especially important.

Knowledge and inquiry are topics that have typically been explored within reasonably tight disciplinary boundaries. New literacies research is helping us to understand how incredibly complex these issues are and how we benefit from traversing across traditional disciplinary and theoretical boundaries. The authors in this section show us how including this complexity in research produces much richer and more powerful insights into new literacies.

In each chapter, the authors push evolving conceptions of new literacies into new territory, exploring, in their analyses, several important interstices of research such as reader, text, and task variables during reading; critical pedagogy, reading research, and information studies; culture, learning, instructional design, and human-computer interaction; the discourses of learning, change, and power; and text-image relationships from both learning theory and semiotic perspectives. As much as any section, the next series of chapters will challenge you to think in new ways about your own work. The authors invoke connections between disparate disciplines whose importance we are just now beginning to appreciate.

While the authors bring widely different disciplines together, there is some commonality to the work in this section. Many authors appear to connect their work, either tightly or loosely, to reading comprehension and learning.

There are chapters where the authors draw upon work coming from more quantitative traditions. Mayer (this volume), for example, reviews a tightly designed series of experimental studies to explore how best to design multimedia material to maximize learning. He systematically analyzes one issue and then the next, always building on the previous work.

Lawless and Schrader (this volume), Kuiper and Volman (this volume), Dalton and Proctor (this volume), Young (this volume), and Warshauer and Ware (this volume) also draw upon quantitative methodologies but include qualitative approaches to knowledge generation. At one end of this group, authors such as Lawless and Schrader draw upon more quantitative research traditions. At the other end of this group, Warshauer and Ware appear to favor more qualitative, contextually situated, research though they also note how each framework used to explore the literacy and technology relationship (learning, change, and power) uses somewhat different methodologies to generate knowledge.

Unsworth (this volume) brings the power of sociolinguistic analysis and approaches favored by semioticians. His analysis helps us to understand even wider definitions of text and context as we consider issues of new literacies.

Questions Raised

One reading of these chapters reveals an important transition that has been taking place in new literacies research. Over the past 15 years, work on literacy and technology issues has gradually moved from studying issues of literacy in bounded hypertext environments to issues of literacy in the unbounded context that defines the Internet. We see this pattern in several ways. We see it first, in the historical progression of the studies that are reviewed. Frequently, authors draw upon earlier studies in more restricted hypertext contexts to establish essential issues in their area and then point to more recent work on the issue in the more open context of the Internet. This raises questions about the complexities involved with applying the findings from one literacy and technology context to another. It is an important issue and one that challenges all of us.

The transition, from the more restricted and less social contexts of hypertexts to the more open and social contexts of the Internet, has also prompted the development of the multiple theoretical and multidisciplinary approaches that we discussed previously. As we make this transition, we encounter new disciplinary activity as cognitive psychologists, sociologists, linguists, and educational researchers begin to inhabit the same research space, forging new research connections to work in other fields. By looking carefully at the work being cited in these chapters, you will see the very beginning stages of this development. Much more will take place in upcoming years.

Encounters with new disciplinary, theoretical, and methodological ideas will raise important questions for the training of the next generation of literacy researchers. How can we systematically prepare new scholars for the multiple disciplinary research that will define their future within universities built on a long and established tradition of departmental and disciplinary boundaries?

Common Themes

The issue of change is an important one in these chapters. It is one of several major themes that you will find in this section. We have discussed the change in the contexts of literacy and technology that are being studied in these areas as we move from hypertext to the Internet. There is also another, more important, aspect to this theme of change. Several authors note that change is happening so quickly now that it is increasingly difficult for research to keep up. It may be the case that this rapid pace of change is beginning to drive our research instead of our research driving the changes that take place in the world, an interesting and important reversal for all of us to consider.

A second major theme in these chapters has already been mentioned: the consistent recognition that we require far more serious attempts at interdisciplinary research using more complex and multiple theoretical perspectives. The authors in this section recognize the complexity of the problems they now face. They realize that the only way we can fully understand their complexity is to connect with work taking place in other disciplines and to bring richer, more complex theoretical perspectives to bear on issues of knowledge and inquiry.

There is also a final theme that you will also find in these chapters. In new literacies research, the study of knowledge often focuses largely on what is acquired within informational ICT spaces, not within broader social contexts. This will evolve as our work increasingly takes place on the Internet. Several of the authors have pointed us to what is likely to be an important area of study in the years ahead—the nature of more socially constructed inquiry approaches used to turn the powerful information on the Internet into knowledge. We see work in this area explored most by Kuiper and Volman (this volume) and Dalton and Proctor (this volume), though others also recognize the importance of inquiry approaches to learning in these chapters.

Future Research

Knowledge and inquiry will continue to be central aspects of new literacies research, especially since educational systems will be increasingly looking to our research community to provide them with answers about how best to use the Internet to develop more knowledgeable and more thoughtful citizens. It is likely this will prompt researchers into more direct contact with classrooms, expanding the contexts in which they carry out their research. Future research on knowledge and inquiry will likely possess more of an applied research flavor. This work will benefit from the more complex theoretical frameworks beginning to be called for in these chapters as well as more complex methodological and analytic approaches to research. Classrooms, of course, are amazingly complex contexts in which knowledge and inquiry take place.

We also see in these chapters how research in new literacies will shift to online, Internet contexts. The shift from hypertext and hypermedia to the Internet will raise many new and important questions about knowledge and inquiry.

Finally, as Young (this volume) points out in her chapter, future research on knowledge and inquiry is likely to take greater advantage of cultural aspects that are central to the new literacies of the Internet but have received relatively little attention. As we become increasingly connected to one another, around the world, it will be impossible to deny the powerful impact of culture on both knowledge and inquiry. This will require additional theoretical and methodological complexity in the ways in which we approach these topics. This will, however, help us to more fully appreciate the new intercultural aspects of new literacies that are only now beginning to be recognized. Those insights will be central to preparing a new generation of truly global citizens.

CHAPTER 8

Learning, Change, and Power:

Competing Frames of Technology and Literacy

MARK WARSCHAUER

UNIVERSITY OF CALIFORNIA, IRVINE, USA

PAIGE WARE

SOUTHERN METHODIST UNIVERSITY, USA

As George Lakoff (2004) explained, language always comes with framing. Every word is defined relative to a conceptual framework, and those frameworks shape the word's social significance. The words *technology* and *literacy* are highly contentious ones that can be framed in numerous ways. Historically, literacy has been viewed as the ability to decode print-based texts, and this definition still pervades in many education circles today. Such a view was limited even before the development of new digital technologies, in that typographic literacy extends far beyond decoding and encompasses meaning making, functional use of texts, and critical analysis (see A. Luke & Freebody, 1999). In a rapidly growing digital world, however, such a narrow perspective is even more limiting. We view literacies as plural, consisting of multiple competencies and practices, each shaped by different contexts, purposes, and uses (A. Luke & Freebody, 1999; New London Group, 1996). This perspective recognizes the emergence of new digital literacies that focus not only on foundational skills and practices of reading and writing, but also on the skills, knowledge, and attitudes that enable complex ways of getting and making meaning from multiple textual and symbolic sources (see, e.g., Ba, Tally, & Tsikalas, 2002; International ICT Literacy Panel, 2002; Shetzer & Warschauer, 2000; Warschauer, 2003b).

In this chapter, we consider how the relationship between technology and literacy is commonly framed, and what that means for teaching and learning with digital media. We will examine three of the most common discourses surrounding technology and literacy that we have labeled "learning," "change," and "power." In the learning frame, the emphasis is typically on raising test scores on standardized measures of reading and writing. The change framework turns the lens to an examination of how literacy itself is transforming in radical ways because of revolutions in information communications technology (ICT). Finally, the power framework focuses on the relationship of access and use of technology for social and economic equality. Within our discussion of each framework, we end with a section that highlights examples that illustrate how each of these discourses shape thinking about educational policies and programs. We conclude by discussing our perspective on the implications of these frameworks for teaching and learning and by making recommendations for future research in literacy and technology.

Clearly, the complexity of the issues we address does not easily fit such categorical distinctions, because in the real world people tend to draw from more than one framework. This is certainly true in our own research. Nonetheless, we believe the research on literacy and technology has grown so vast that it is useful to make distinctions among the salient characteristics of current research in order to clarify core ideas and concepts. By synthesizing the vast number of wide-ranging goals, theoretical frameworks, and methods of inquiry within these three frameworks, we ultimately hope to promote interdisciplinary discussion among educators and researchers in identifying possible areas of overlap and conflict among the learning, change, and power frameworks, both within their own work and across disciplines.

Learning Framework: Raising Test Scores

Those who adopt a learning framework are concerned not with how technology is changing literacy, but rather with how student use of technology can enhance learning in general, with outcomes in the area of literacy measured primarily through higher scores on standardized reading and writing tests (see Table 8.1). From this perspective, computers and the Internet are simply new forms of educational media (following radio, film, and television), educational technology (following blackboards and overhead projectors), or learning systems (following programmed instructional kits and audiotape language laboratories used for foreign-language instruction).

With a primary focus on achieving practical and measurable outcomes, the learning framework is driven primarily by quantitative studies. This body of research is grounded in such a broad range of educational theories that it is difficult to point to seminal works in this area. Several of the best known studies on educational technology, such as those of Cuban (e.g., 2001) and

Table 8.1 Learning Framework

Conceptual framework	Learning		
Central Metaphors	**Media in education** Radio Film Television Computer	**Educational technology** Blackboard Overhead Projector Software Programs Digital Whiteboard Computer Internet	**Learning system** Programmed Instructional Kits Language Lab Computer Lab
Representative Journals	*Journal of Technology, Learning, and Assessment*		
Key Works	Becker (2000); Cuban (2001); Fuchs and Woessmann (2004)		
Fields of Inquiry	Educational technology, Educational administration, Educational policy		
Target of Critique	Technology as a match for schools and learners		
Goal	Raise test scores and improve student learning		
Research Interest	Technology's impact on learning and literacy outcomes		

Becker (e.g., 2000), focused on whether or not schools are able to make use of new technologies, and, if so, under what conditions. There is also, though, a growing body of research on what kinds of learning and literacy outcomes students achieve with new technology use at home or school as measured by standardized test scores. A major center of this work is at the Lynch School of Education at Boston College, which hosts the Technology Assessment Study Collaborative and the *Journal of Technology, Learning, and Assessment*, both led by Michael Russell, who has coauthored many of the important studies in this area (Russell & Abrams, 2004; Russell, Bebell, & Higgins, 2004; Russell & Plati, 2002). Most of this research is quantitative in nature, relying on experiments, quasi-experiments, or correlational analysis.

One of the broader studies in this vein, covering students in many nations, was carried out by Fuchs and Woessmann (2004), who analyzed the dataset from the Programme for International Student Assessment (PISA), an international student achievement test conducted in 2000 of 15-year-olds in developed and emerging nations. The PISA assessment had a special focus on reading and literacy, with a dataset covering 174,227 students in 31 countries. The study found a statistically significant and sizable negative correlation with reading scores for students who had a computer at home, once student and family background and schools' resources and institutional features were controlled for. In contrast, Internet access at home caused a positive correlation—and the more frequently students used the Internet to read e-mails or Web pages, the higher their test scores were. No statistically significant effect was noted for school access to computers, whereas school use of computers and the Internet had an inverted U-shape relationship with achievement; some use of computers and the Internet at school had a positive correlation with reading achievement, whereas a good deal of use had a negative correlation.

production, information retrieval and critique, etc.) that go beyond traditional reading and writing (see Warschauer, 2006). The assessments currently available to school districts, however, too narrowly focus on traditional reading and writing measures and thereby limit understanding of digital media's potential. Further, through a washback effect, such tests can even hinder that potential, as witnessed through the previously mentioned example of teachers restricting their use of computers for writing in order to prepare for pencil-and-paper tests. The danger of an overly narrow view of learning and literacy is seen in the following example.

Example: What Counts as Learning and Literacy at an Elementary School?

A university professor organized an after-school computer journalism club at a low-income, and low-performing, elementary school (Seiter, 2004, 2005). The 25 children who joined the club worked together to identify stories of interest, research them, and publish them in a newspaper that was circulated online and also printed and distributed for free to 15,000 community residents. Newspaper stories varied between those of local community interest (about topics such as firefighters, a boys' basketball team, and a nearby pet shop) and those related to popular culture (media stars, wrestling). The children in the project quickly developed a variety of computer skills, including digital photography, keyboarding, and word processing, and honed their reporting, writing, and editing talents.

Unfortunately, though, the school principal had problems with the project, explaining, "This school is about literacy" (E. Seiter, personal communication, December 9, 2004). The journalism project, which allowed students to bring in issues of popular culture, to write articles that might challenge authority, or to carry out community interviews in their own language, apparently treaded on dangerous territory. In the principal's eyes, "literacy" was restricted to activities that stayed close to the school curriculum and helped raise test scores in his low-performing school.

Change Framework: A New Gutenberg Revolution

A critical response to the learning framework can be found in a *change* framework (see Table 8.2). From this perspective, new technologies are seen as bringing revolutionary transformations in reading, writing, communication, and production of knowledge, similar to those last wrought by the development and diffusion of the printing press in 15th-century Europe.

Two central metaphors characterize the discourse of change. On the one hand, information and communication technologies (ICT) are compared to previous human means of communication. In this sense, it represents a "fourth revolution in the means of production of knowledge," following the development of language, writing, and print (Harnad, 1991, p. 39). On the other

Table 8.2 Change Framework

Conceptual framework	Change	
Central metaphors	**Means of communication**	**Carrier of written word**
	Language	Papyrus
	Writing	Codex
	Print	Book
	ICT	Screen
Representative Journals	*Computers and Composition; Kairos: A Journal of Rhetoric, Technology, and Pedagogy;* and *E-Learning*	
Key Works	Bolter (1991); Gee (2003; 2004); Kress (2003); Landow (1992); Murray (1998); New London Group (1996); Tuman (1992)	
Fields of Inquiry	New literacy studies, Cultural and media studies, Game studies, Computers and writing	
Target of Critique	Schools as conservative institutions	
Goal	Make schooling relevant by valuing new literacies	
Research Interest	Relationship between home and school literacy practices	

hand, some scholars make the comparison to prior media of written communication. In this light, the developmental path runs from papyrus to codex to book to screen (see, e.g., discussion in Bolter, 1991).

The revolutionary characteristics of ICT are seen in six of its features (Warschauer, 1997, 1999): (a) it allows interactive written communication, thus bridging the historical divide between text and speech, as evidenced in instant messaging, chat, and e-mail; (b) it allows a global form of many-to-many communication, as witnessed by listservs and bulletin boards; (c) it allows the creation of hypertexts that challenge traditional forms of narrative; (d) it democratizes multimedia creation, taking advantage of a myriad of digital tools for recording, producing, and/or editing audio, music, photographs, video, and animation; (e) it allows those texts and multimedia to be easily self-published for a global audience through means such as home pages, blogs, podcasts, and videoblogs; and (f) it links all this published information in a worldwide interconnected database, bringing an almost limitless amount of navigable information available to any individual.

The change framework finds its natural home in the fields of cultural and media studies (Tyner, 1998), new literacy studies (e.g., New London Group, 1996), game studies (e.g., Gee, 2003; Steinkuhler, this volume), and computers and writing (e.g., Bolter, 1991; Landow, 1992). It finds expression in a number of scholarly journals, such as *Computers and Composition; Kairos: A Journal of Rhetoric, Technology, and Pedagogy;* and *E-Learning.* Key research centers include the University of Southern California's Annenberg Center for Communication, with its focus on digital and multimedia literacies, and the University of Wisconsin School of Education, with its focus on video games and literacies.

(e.g., chat, instant messaging, text messaging), with blogs occupying an intermediary position. Research in electronic communication focuses on issues such as the nature of the genres in each form, the ways that people construct their identities online, and the language choices made by speakers/writers of multiple language or dialects.

For example, Lam (2000, 2003, 2005a, 2005b) has carried out extensive ethnographic studies of Asian immigrants' use of the World Wide Web, e-mail, instant messaging, and chat rooms at home and school in the United States. Her work demonstrated the kind of individual and collective textual identities that immigrants develop and express through the playful switching and mixing of codes, symbols, and roles across and within modes, concluding that these practices stand in sharp contrast to the more restricted set of literacy practices that are valued in school.

Similarly focusing on new literacy and communication practices outside educational settings, Ito and Okabe (2005a, 2005b) have carried out extensive ethnographic investigation of Japanese youths' use of mobile phones, and especially on the expressive functions and styles of text messaging in the particular social and cultural milieu of Japanese teenagers' lives. Their research has demonstrated, for example, the flexible social expectations and rhythms established in text messageing (allowing both intensive conversation and occasional keeping in touch, depending on the particular place and purpose of the communication), the ways that text messaging creates an ambient virtual copresence (by allowing constant intimate exchanges while people are apart), and the nature of augmented flesh meet (in which text messaging helps micro-coordinate physical meetings).

Video-Gaming

Gee's (2003) seminal book, based on extensive game playing and observations of video-gamers, puts forth 36 learning and literacy principles that are embedded in video-games, but are often absent from schools. These include the semiotic principle (understanding interrelations within and across multiple sign systems), the bottom-up basic skills principle (learning basic skills not in isolation or out of context but through a process of discovery while engaging a broader domain), and the affinity group principal (learning through groups that are bonded through shared endeavors, goals, and practices rather than through race, gender, or ethnicity). In a follow-up book, Gee (2004) critiqued more explicitly the contradiction between the types of complex learning that diverse learners achieved through video-games and other new media and the way that schools are structured to fail diverse learners. Gee's work in this area was extended by Steinkuehler's (2005; this volume) ethnographic study of participants in Massively Multiplayer Online Games (also known as MMORGS: Massive Multiplayer Online Role-Playing Games). Steinkuehler examined the array of reading and writing practices that take place both within games (via chats, narratives, and letters) and around games (via discussion boards, blogs, and fan fiction sites), concluding that video-games are actually promoting rather than hindering the types of authentic, creative, and wide-ranging literacies that schools purport to value.

Several outstanding theoretical questions confront literacy theorists from a change framework. The first is: What counts as literacy? In the world of video-gaming, for example, there are now game-based *graphic novels* (Pearce, 2002), in which users take screen shots from their favorite games and annotate them with text to tell a story; *machinima* (Lowood, 2005), in which users render and capture video from games and add audio to produce movies; and *mods* (Sotamaa, 2003), in which users redesign video-games to include new items, weapons, characters, enemies, models, modes, textures, levels, locations, and storylines. The first clearly matches traditional definitions of literacy, albeit in an alternative format; the second and third cause us to rethink whether literacy can be extended to nontextual realms (Kress, 2003) or even to software design.

A second question is: What counts as authorship? Notions of author, audience, and plagiarism were already called into question by the development of hypertexts and the World Wide Web (Landow, 1992; Murray, 1998); now new forms of narrative and storytelling in game playing and design further complicate the matter (Pearce, 2002).

A third question is: What counts as genre? If we consider genre to be a form of conventionalized social action, how do we consider and evaluate genre in a time when conventions are being rapidly undone, and multiple media are being cast together? The instability of genre in 21st-century life has led a group of theorists to promote design as a principle of new media literacy (Kress, 2003; New London Group, 1996), which emphasizes not mastery of conventional forms but rather understanding and application of broad generative concepts.

Finally, there is the question of how to value out-of-school literacies that may not have much social or economic currency. An obvious starting point for answering this question would be for educators to learn more about these out-of-school literacies and find ways to bridge students' engagement with academic literacy through them (see recent examples in Morrell & Duncan-Andrade, 2004; Ware & Warschauer, 2005). Another tack is to create alternative learning spaces where students have caring communities that legitimize their engagement with out-of-school literacies (Hull, 2003; Hull & Schultz, 2002). Such solutions themselves, however, invite further questions pertaining to legitimacy, access, autonomy, community, and academic achievement. The complexities of these various dimensions are seen in the following examples.

Example: What Kind of Change Occurs in Community Technology Projects?

One of the most touted international initiatives to promote informal learning with technology took place in India, where, in 2000, an information technology corporation established a project known as the "Hole-in-the-Wall" to provide computer access to the city's street children (see extended analysis in Warschauer, 2003b). An outdoor five-station computer kiosk was set up in one of the poorest slums of New Delhi. Though the computers themselves were inside a booth, the monitors protruded through holes in the walls, as did specially designed joysticks and buttons that substituted for the computer mouse. Keyboards were not provided. The computers were connected to the Internet through dial-up access. A volunteer inside the booth helped keep the computers and Internet connections running. No teachers or instructors were provided, in line with the concept called *minimally invasive pedagogy*.

The children who flocked to the site taught themselves out how to click and drag objects; select different menus; cut, copy, and paste; launch and use programs such as Microsoft Word and Paint; get on the Internet; and change the background "wallpaper." The program was hailed by researchers and government officials alike as a groundbreaking project that offered a model for how to bring India's and the world's urban poor into the computer age. Visits to the computer kiosk, however, indicated a somewhat different reality. The Internet access was of little use since it seldom functioned. No special educational programs had been made available, and no special content was provided in Hindi, the only language the children knew. Children did learn to manipulate the joystick and buttons, but almost all their time was spent drawing with paint programs or playing uncomplicated games. There was no organized involvement of any community organizations in helping to run the project and the very architecture of the kiosk—based on a wall rather than a room—made supervision, instruction, and collaboration difficult. Parents in the neighborhood expressed concern that their children's schoolwork was suffering because they spent afternoons playing at the kiosks rather than doing their homework.

A second example that echoes these complexities comes from a technology and writing project conducted at a low-income, predominantly African American community site in Chicago. The "Garden Homes" project, as McNamee and Sivright (2002) reported, was developed using a framework called the Fifth Dimension (Cole, 1996; Griffin & Cole, 1987) in which children in community centers play in an elaborate series of educational technology games orchestrated by a fictitious "Wizard." The network has expanded internationally since its inception to include a worldwide network of participants who exchange letters through digital communication. Staff at the Garden Homes project report many benefits for the participating children, including the creation of a community of adults and peers (both physical and online) who help them learn academically relevant skills such as computer operations and analytical problem solving, and who also provide them with opportunities to develop social skills and deal with difficult personal situations.

Despite these benefits, McNamee and Sivright (2002) highlighted many of the limitations of the project, including the limited amount of positive images of African Americans and different dialects in the software programs; the disturbingly self-deprecating images of themselves that the children conveyed to their online peers; and the limited involvement of parents, many of whom faced financial or emotional pressure. Finally, because of their negative experiences in schools, the children generally refused to participate in any activities that resembled schoolwork and often preferred to play outside.

The Hole in the Wall and Garden Homes experiments demonstrated the limitations of the change framework, in and of itself, for guiding educational interventions. Just because literacies are new does not mean that they will benefit—or even engage—those who are exposed to them. Both examples highlight the need for organized involvement among educators, families, community members, and volunteers in order to coordinate efforts at enhancing youth involvement. Because effecting change in the lives of young people often involves academic achievement, educators must look for ways in which youth involvement in new literacies can also directly impact their success in school. To this end, future research must include multiple levels of social and economic analysis to examine critically the extent to which new literacies empower young people to be successful in a range of contexts extending beyond their immediate worlds.

Power Framework: Interacted vs. Interacting

The power framework is perhaps the most complex of the three (see Table 8.3). This perspective shares with the change framework the notion that literacies are in a state of rapid flux, and thus values inquiry into new literacy practices. In contrast to the change perspective, however, it tends to focus on those technology-related literacy practices that it sees as being more closely related to achieving on social, economic, and educational power (such as finding, critiquing, and deploying information in the quest for knowledge, or developing

Table 8.3 Power Framework

Conceptual framework	Power		
Central Metaphors	**Industrial revolution** Steam power Electricity ICT	**Access node** Phone line Internet	**Literacy mode** Print literacy Electronic literacies
Representative Journals	*Information Technology, Education, & Society*		
Key Works	Castells (1996/2000); Cummins and Sayers (1995); Warschauer (1999; 2003b)		
Fields of Inquiry	Sociology, Economics, Development studies, Critical pedagogy		
Target of Critique	Unequal power structures		
Goal	Empower youth through knowledge, access, and skill with socially relevant tools		
Research Interest	Relationship of access and use to educational and social equity		

sophisticated multimedia) rather than those existing on the margins (such as text messaging).

The power framework shares with the learning framework the notion that educational achievement at school is highly important. It views test scores as a highly politicized and contested terrain, however, and focuses on how social, economic, cultural, and linguistic contexts shape students' access to education, literacy, and academic achievement, and to appropriate uses of technology to achieve desired ends.

The sociological analysis of Manuel Castells provides a critical underpinning of the power framework. In his trilogy on the information age (1996/2000, 1997, 1998/2000), Castells outlined the crucial role that new technologies are playing in society, culture, and economics, and how unequal access to these technologies can have devastating consequences for individuals and communities. He posits a future in which the more privileged become the *interacting,* with the skills, knowledge, and resources to select or create their multimedia circuits of communication, while the less privileged become the *interacted,* limited to passive access to prepackaged choices—while the even more technologically isolated fall into "black holes of informational capitalism" (1998/2000, p. 162). Castells' work provided one of the main metaphors of the power framework, that of informational technology as enabling and representing a third stage of capitalism, following steam power of the 18th century and electrification of the 19th century. Some who pursue the notion of technological inequality and access compare campaigns for universal Internet access to earlier campaigns for universal phone access—in other words, a lifeline for full participation in modern society.

A more relevant metaphor from an educational perspective is that of ICT access and literacy being the new print literacy of the 21st century. In other words, those who cannot access and effectively use new technologies are hampered in ways similar to those of people who could not read in an earlier era. This framework has motivated a wide series of attempts to define, assess, and promote digital literacy (see, e.g., Ba et al., 2002; International ICT Literacy Panel, 2002; Shetzer & Warschauer, 2000; Warschauer, 2003b), with literacy in this sense referring not so much to practices (as in the change framework mentioned earlier) but rather to the skills, knowledge, and attitudes that enable meaning making. Another group of researchers examining digital literacy in school settings advocated a New Literacies Perspective (Leu, Kinzer, Coiro, & Cammack, 2004), which outlines a view of in-school literacy to resituate foundational literacies of reading and writing within a much larger set of digital skills and strategies that students need to be successful in the changing knowledge economy. While this research does not draw directly on cultural or social theory to examine issues of power, work on new literacies in schools provides insight into how 21st-century skills are transforming classroom instruction (Coiro, 2003; Labbo & Reinking, 1999; Leu & Kinzer, 2000) and how teachers must rethink pedagogy in light of new literacies and new technologies (Karchmer, 2001; Smolin & Lawless, 2003).

Another major scholar in the power framework is Cummins, whose work on language, literacy, and power (e.g., 1989) predated his major work on new media. In two coauthored books (Brown, Cummins, & Sayers, 2007; Cummins & Sayers, 1995), Cummins and colleagues set out the relationship of new technology use to broader issues of unequal power relations and literacy development in schools. They suggest that only a *transformative* pedagogical approach can unleash the potential of technology for literacy development—both for "traditional" and new literacies. Through such a transformative or critical approach, students make use of technology to analyze their own lives and social problems, develop and publish material that addresses social issues or positively promotes their identities, and collaborate with distant partners to further exploration of social or identity issues.

Several methodological approaches will be useful for conducting research from a power perspective, and many researchers have argued for perspectives that are interdisciplinary and creative (see e.g., Hagood, 2003; C. Luke, 2003; Mackey, 2003; Nixon, 2003; Leander, this volume; Livingstone, Van Couvering, & Thumin, this volume). The approach we have chosen to highlight in this chapter is that of the comparative case study because it includes research methods ranging from highly ethnographic work to mixed-methods approaches that take into account multiple layers of data sources that can illuminate underlying power issues. In *Electronic Literacies* (1999), for example, Warschauer presented four case studies of culturally and linguistically diverse learners using new technologies in language and writing courses that demonstrated how broader issues of social, economic, and political power shaped access to and use of new technologies, and that highlighted examples of empowering practices with culturally and linguistically diverse learners. The book also highlighted how students on the margin—whether immigrants in the United States or international students from developing countries—view the development of technology-based literacies as critical to their economic and social futures.

In two later studies, using a more explicit comparative approach, Warschauer contrasted the use of new technologies in low- and high-socioeconomic-status (SES) K–12 schools (2000; Warschauer et al., 2004). The studies showed how seemingly progressive pedagogy—such as use of computers for collaborative writing and project work—featured very different purposes and content, with low-SES students engaging in more perfunctory tasks and those in high-SES school doing more in-depth critical analysis. In addition, other features of the school context in low-SES schools—such as higher teacher turnover, weaker technical support networks, a greater fear of high-stakes assessments, and less student access to home computers—all complicated effective use of technology for literacy and learning. Some scholars have characterized these differences about the two industries and the condition of workers. At the end of the year, the students held a public presentation, inviting parents and community members to view the multimedia products they had created.

Though no independent evaluation was conducted of Project Fresa, its design reveals the potential benefits of the underlying power framework. Such projects seek to help students actively master technology, rather than use it in a passive manner. They engage students in their own research, data collection, analysis, and interpretation, and in creating quality products such as letters to elected officials and data-based presentations. Such projects also help students learn to speak out and take action on issues of importance to their community. Through gathering and evaluating information from a variety of sources, including workers, nongovernmental organizations, businesses, politicians, and children in other parts of the world, students can gain a better understanding of the broader socioeconomic forces that shape their lives.

Our second example of a power perspective in the classroom is taken from a split-level third- and fourth-grade class at a laptop school in southern California where the teacher presented the class with the challenge of helping prepare their younger second-grade peers for the yearly high-stakes statewide math exam (see extended analysis in Ware & Warschauer, 2005). Equipped with laptops, wireless high-speed Internet access, multiple software programs, and an innovative teacher, the elementary school students, many of whom were non-native speakers of English, designed age-appropriate games targeted to review the types of math tested at the second-grade level.

The pedagogy underlying the production of these educational video games looked very different from a traditional classroom. The students conducted independent research on the Internet and located the appropriate state level standards for second-grade math. They collaborated in groups of four to discuss which types of activities would engage their target second-grade audience and negotiated a collaborative, multiday project plan to guide their decisions and regulate their time. Such autonomy in project-based learning is rarer in conventional classrooms, in which teachers often require that students follow a predetermined sequence of steps. Students used both linguistic means (a direction booklet) as well as multimodal means (digital explanatory videos) to create age-appropriate instructional materials, a step that is rarely taken in elementary school peer-teaching scenarios, in which older students are often given prefabricated scripts to follow as they work with younger peers. Finally, throughout the process, these young children dealt with cognitively complex tasks of breaking down knowledge and repackaging it, of transforming information from one mode to another, and of redesigning the pedagogy of math drills that typically inform test preparation in schools (Kress, 2003; New London Group, 1996). Such multimodal pedagogies position students not as recipients of knowledge, but rather, as Luke (2003) suggested, as students actively involved in drawing on blends of new and old learning styles and practices.

Internationally, many classrooms are beginning to make pedagogical changes that reflect the spirit of a power perspective. D. J. Leu, Karchmer, and D. D. Leu (1999) reported on a number of these transformations in which students and teachers explore new ways of using technology to expand literacy learning (to conduct international e-mail exchanges and develop multimedia portfolios of literacy projects) and to share their work with a range of audiences (local businesses, district and state schools, and international sister schools). As with Project Fresa, no independent evaluation has been conducted on these projects, but we find the projects noteworthy as they mark early attempts to transform classrooms in ways that move well beyond the mandated curricula that characterize much of school-based literacy instruction.

Despite the benefits of such project-based learning, such innovations to the school-based curriculum are not easy to organize. In Project Fresa, for example, though the teachers involved took care to match the project with the state learning standards (in areas such as graphing and letter writing), creating such matches in project-based work is more challenging than simply teaching from the mandated textbooks. Such projects also take a considerable amount of time to set up and manage, and U.S. teachers are provided relatively little time for such collaborative planning, compared to teachers in other developed countries such as Japan (Stigler & Hiebert, 1999). Finally, classroom teachers at low SES schools are under great pressure to raise test scores, and most thus shy away from creative project-based instruction in order to concentrate on more narrowly focused interventions related to state examination material (Warschauer et al., 2004). Project Fresa itself was repeated only one more year until both teachers left the school, one to retire and one to become a vice principal at another elementary school. The latter reported (M. Singer, personal communication, June 9, 2005) that she has been unsuccessful in getting teachers at her school to try similar projects due to their fears about lessening their focus on test scores. It is thus unlikely that such projects will be implemented widely in U.S. schools without a broader repurposing and restructuring of education, moving away from the prescribed and scripted literacy curricula and punitive assessment policies currently in vogue.

To summarize, the frameworks of learning, change, and power dominate the way that academics and educators think about literacy and technology. These three frames can be thought of as corners of a triangle, as of course any individual's perspective is far more likely to fall on a continuum within the triangle rather than at one of its vertices. Indeed, some of the most interesting work on technology-mediated learning in the broad sense of the term has been done by scholars discussed earlier under the change perspective (see Gee, 2003, 2004; Kress, 2003; New London Group, 1996).

Though we consider each of these three frameworks to be legitimate perspectives for researching technology and literacy, in the end we favor a power framework as being best able to integrate the strengths, while minimizing

Ba, H., Tally, W., & Tsikalas, K. (2002). Investigating children's emerging digital literacies. *Journal of Technology, Learning, and Assessment, 1*(4).

Baron, D. (1999). From pencils to pixels: The stages of literacy technologies. In G. E. Hawisher, & C. Selfe (Eds.), *Passions, pedagogies, and 21st century technologies* (pp. 15–33). Logan: Utah State University Press.

Becker, H. J. (2000). Findings from the teaching, learning, and computing survey: Is Larry Cuban right? *Educational Policy Analysis Archives, 8*(51).

Belson, K. (2005, June 21). Dial-up Internet going way of mobile phones. *New York Times*.

Bleha, T. (2005). *Down to the wire*. Retrieved September 5, 2006, from http://www.foreignaffairs.org/20050501 faessay84311–p0/thomas-bleha/down-to-the-wire.html

Bolter, J. D. (1991). *Writing space: The computer, hypertext, and the history of writing*. Hillsdale, NJ: Lawrence Erlbaum Associates.

Brown, K. R., Cummins, J., & Sayers, D. (2007). *Literacy, technology, and diversity: Teaching for success in changing times*. Boston: Allyn & Bacon.

Castells, M. (1996/2000). *The rise of the network society* (2nd ed.). Malden, MA: Blackwell.

Castells, M. (1997). *The power of identity*. Malden, MA: Blackwell.

Castells, M. (1998/2000). *End of millennium* (2nd ed.). Malden, MA: Blackwell.

Coiro, J. (2003). Reading comprehension on the Internet: Expanding our understanding of reading comprehension to encompass new literacies. *The Reading Teacher, 56*, 458–464.

Cole, M. (1996). *Cultural psychology: A once and future discipline*. Cambridge, MA: Belknap Press of Harvard University Press.

Cook, T. D., Appleton, H., Conner, R., Shaffer, A., Tamkin, G., & Weber, S. J. (1975). *"Sesame Street" revisited*. New York: Russel Sage Foundation.

Cuban, L. (1986). *Teachers and machines: The classroom use of technology since 1920*. New York: Teachers College Press.

Cuban, L. (2001). *Oversold and underused: Computers in classrooms, 1980–2000*. Cambridge, MA: Harvard University Press.

Cummins, J. (1989). *Empowering minority students*. Sacramento: California Association for Bilingual Education.

Cummins, J., & Sayers, D. (1995). *Brave new schools: Challenging cultural illiteracy through global learning networks*. New York: St. Martin's Press.

Dewey, J. (1938). *Experience and education*. New York: Macmillan.

Fang, X., & Warschauer, M. (2004). Technology and curricular reform in China: A case study. *TESOL Quarterly, 38*(2), 301–323.

Fuchs, T., & Woessmann, L. (2004). *Computers and student learning: Bivariate and multivariate evidence on the availability and use of computers at home and at school* (CESIFO Working Paper No. 1321). Munich, Germany: Center for Economic Studies at the University of Munich.

Gee, J. (2003). *What video games have to teach up about learning and literacy*. New York: Palgrave Macmillan.

Gee, J. (2004). *Situated language and learning: A critique of traditional schooling*. New York: Routledge.

Giroux, H. (1983). *Theory & resistance in education*. New York: Bergin & Garvey.

Goldberg, A., Russell, M., & Cook, A. (2004). The effect of computers on student writing: A meta-analysis of studies from 1992 to 2002. *Journal of Technology, Learning, and Assessment, 2*(1), 3–51.

Griffin, P., & Cole, M. (1987). New technologies, basic skills, and the underside of education: What's to be done? In J. Langer (Ed.), *Language, literacy, and culture: Issues of society and schooling* (pp. 199–231). Norwood, NJ: Ablex.

Gulek, J. C., & Demirtas, H. (2005). Learning with technology: The impact of laptop use on student achievement. *Journal of Technology, Learning, and Assessment, 3*(2).

Hagood, M. (2003). New media and online literacies: No age left behind. *Reading Research Quarterly, 38*(3), 387–392.

Hargittai, E. (2002). Second-level digital divide: Differences in people's online skills. *First Monday, 7*(4).

Harnad, S. (1991). Post-Gutenberg galaxy: The fourth revolution in the means of production and knowledge. *Public-Access Computer Systems Review, 2*(1), 39–53.

Holloway, D., & Green, L. (2003). *Sesame Street effect: Work, study, play and the family internet.* Paper presented at the Australian and New Zealand Communications Association Conference, Brisbane, Australia.

Hull, G. (2003). AT LAST: Youth culture and digital media: New literacies for new times. *Research in the Teaching of English, 38*(2), 229–233.

Hull, G., & Nelson, M. E. (2005). Locating the semiotic power of multmodality. *Written Communication, 22*(2), 224–261.

Hull, G., & Schultz, K. (Eds.). (2002). *School's out!: Bridging out-of-school literacies with classroom practice.* New York: Teachers College Press.

International ICT Literacy Panel. (2002). *Digital transformation: A framework for ICT literacy.* Retrieved February 28, 2005, from http://www.ets.org/research/ictliteracy/ictreport.pdf

Ito, M., & Okabe, D. (2005a). Intimate connections: Contextualizing Japanese youth and mobile messaging. In R. Harper, L. Palen, & A. Taylor (Eds.), *The inside text: Social, cultural, and design perspectives on SMS* (pp.127–143). Dordrecht, Netherlands: Kluwer Academic Publishers.

Ito, M., & Okabe, D. (2005b). Technosocial situations: Emergent structuring of mobile email use. In M. Ito, D. Okabe, & M. Matsuda (Eds.), *Personal, portable, pedestrian: Mobile phones in Japanese life* (pp. 257–276). Cambridge, MA: MIT Press.

Jeroski, S. (2004). *Implementation of the wireless writing program: Phase 3.* Retrieved June 21, 2005, from http://www.prn.bc.ca/WWP_Report04.pdf

Karchmer, R. (2001). The journey ahead: Thirteen teachers report how the Internet influences literacy and literacy instruction in their K–12 classrooms. *Reading Research Quarterly, 36,* 442–466.

Kelly, T., Gray, V., & Minges, M. (2003). *Broadband Korea: Internet case study.* Geneva, Switzerland: International Telecommunications Union.

Kress, G. (1998). Visual and verbal modes of representation in electronically mediated communication: The potentials of new forms of text. In I. Snyder (Ed.), *Page to screen: Taking literacy into the electronic era* (pp. 53–79). Routledge: London.

Kress, G. (1999). "English" at the crossroads: Rethinking curricula of communication in the context of the turn to the visual. In G. E. Hawisher, & C. Selfe (Eds.), *Passions, pedagogies, and 21st century technologies* (pp. 66–88). Logan: Utah State University Press.

Kress, G. (2003). *Literacy in the new media age.* London: Routledge.

Kress, G., & van Leeuwen, T. (1996). *Reading images: The grammar of visual design.* London: Routledge.

Kress, G., & van Leeuwen, T. (2001). *Multimodal discourse: The modes and media of contemporary communication.* London: Arnold.

Labbo, L. D., & Reinking, D. (1999). Negotiating the multiple realities of technology in literacy research and instruction. *Reading Research Quarterly, 34,* 478–492.

Lakoff, G. (2004). *Don't think of an elephant: Know your values and frame the debate.* White River Junction, VT: Chelsea Green.

Lam, W. S. E. (2000). Second language literacy and the design of the self: A case study of a teenager writing on the Internet. *TESOL Quarterly* (34), 457–482.

Lam, W. S. E. (2003). *Second language literacy and identify formation on the Internet.* Unpublished doctoral dissertation, University of California, Berkeley.

Lam, W. S. E. (2005a). *Re-envisioning language literacy and the immigrant subject in new mediascapes.* Manuscript submitted for publication.

Lam, W. S. E. (2005b). Second language socialization in a bilingual chat room. *Language Learning and Technology, 8*(3), 44–65.

Landow, G. P. (1992). *Hypertext: The convergence of contemporary critical theory and technology.* Baltimore: John Hopkins University Press.

Lankshear, C., & Knobel, M. (2003). *New literacies: Changing knowledge in the classroom.* Buckingham, U.K.: Open University Press.

Leander, K. (2008). Toward a connective ethnography of online/offline literacy networks. In J. Coiro, M. Knobel, C. Lankshear, & D. Leu (Eds.), *Handbook of research on new literacies* (pp. 33–65). Mahwah, NJ: Erlbaum.

Lemke, J. L. (1998). Metamedia literacy: Transforming meanings and media. In D. Reinking, M. McKenna, L. Labbo, & R. D. Kieffer (Eds.), *Handbook of literacy and technology: Transformations in a post-typographic world* (pp. 283–301). Hillsdale, NJ: Erlbaum.

Leu, D. J. , Karchmer, R., & Leu, D. D. (1999). Exploring literacy on the Internet. *The Reading Teacher, 52*(6), 636–642.

Leu, D., & Kinzer, C. (2000). The convergence of literacy instruction with networked technologies for information and communication. *Reading Research Quarterly, 35,* 108–127.

Leu, D. J., Jr., Kinzer, C. K., Coiro, J., & Cammack, D. (2004). Toward a theory of new literacies emerging from the Internet and other information and communication technologies. In R. B. Ruddell & N. Unrau (Eds.), *Theoretical models and processes of reading* (5th ed., pp. 1568–1611). Newark, DE: International Reading Association.

Livingstone, S., Van Couvering, E., & Thumim, N. (2008). Converging traditions of research on media and information literacies: Disciplinary, critical, and methodological issues. In J. Coiro, M. Knobel, C. Lankshear, & D. Leu (Eds.), *Handbook of research on new literacies* (pp. 103–132). Mahwah, NJ: Erlbaum.

Lowood, H. (2005). Real-time performance: Machina and game studies. *The International Digital Media & Arts Association Journal, 2*(1), 10–17.

Luke, A., & Freebody, P. (1999). A map of possible practices: Further notes on the four resources model. *Practically Primary, 4*(2), 5–8.

Luke, C. (2003). Pedagogy, connectivity, multimodality, and interdisciplinarity. *Reading Research Quarterly, 38*(3), 297–314.

Mackey, M. (2003). Researching new forms of literacy. *Reading Research Quarterly, 38*(3), 403–407.

McNamee, G. D., & Sivright, S. (2002). Community supports for writing development among urban African American children. In G. Hull, & K. Schultz (Eds.), *School's out: Bridging out-of-school literacies with classroom practice* (pp. 169–197). New York: Teachers College Press.

Morrell, E., & Duncan-Andrade, J. (2004). What youth do learn in school: Using hip-hop as a bridge to canonical poetry. In J. Mahiri (Ed.), *What they don't learn in school: Literacy in the lives of urban youth* (pp. 248–268). New York: Peter Lang.

Murray, J. H. (1998). *Hamlet on the holodeck: The future of narrative in Cyberspace.* Cambridge, MA: MIT Press.

Nelson, M. E. (2006). Mode, meaning, and synesthesia in multimedia L2 writing. *Language Learning and Technology, 10*(2), 56–76.

New London Group. (1996). A pedagogy of multiliteracies: Designing social futures. *Harvard Educational Review, 66*(1), 60–92.

Nielsen/Net Ratings. (2004). *Three out of four Americans have access to the Internet, according to Nielsen Net Ratings.* Retrieved June 21, 2005, from http://direct.www.nielsen-netratings.com/pr/pr_040318.pdf

Nixon, H. (2003). New research literacies for contemporary research into literacy and new media? *Reading Research Quarterly, 38*(3), 407–414.

O'Dwyer, L. M., Russell, M., Bebell, D., & Tucker-Seeley, K. R. (2005). Examining the relationship between home and school computer use and students' English/language arts test scores. *Journal of Technology, Learning, and Assessment, 3*(3). Retrieved August 11, 2006, from http://www.jtla.org

Paterson, W. A., Henry, J. J., O'Quin, K., Ceprano, M. A., & Blue, E. (2003). Investigating the effectiveness of an integrated learning system on early emergent readers. *Reading Research Quarterly, 38*(2), 172–207.

Pearce, C. (2002). Emergent authorship: The next ineractive revolution. *Computers & Graphics, 26,* 21–29.

Reardon, M. (2005). *China to trump U.S. in broadband subscribers.* Retrieved June 21, 2005, from http://news.zdnet.com/2100-6005_22-5695591.html

Renaissance Learning. (2004). *Accelerated reader.* Wisconsin Rapids, WI: Renaissance Learning.

Russell, M., & Abrams, L. (2004). Instructional effects of computers for writing: The effect of state testing programs. *Teachers College Record, 106*(6), 1332–1357.

Russell, M., Bebell, D., & Higgins, J. (2004). Laptop learning: A comparison of teaching and learning in upper elementary classrooms equipped with shared carts of laptops and permanent 1:1 laptops. *Journal of Educational Computing Research, 30*(4), 313–330.

Russell, M., Higgins, J., & Hoffman, T. (2004). *Examining the effect of text editor and robust word processor on student writing performance (inTASC Publications).* Boston: Lynch School of Education.

Russell, M., & Plati, T. (2002). Does it matter with what I write?: Comparing performance on paper, computer and portable writing devices. *Current Issues in Education, 5*(4), 2–27.

Sandholtz, J. H., Ringstaff, C., & Dwyer, D. C. (1997). *Teaching with technology: Creating student-centered classrooms.* New York: Teachers College Press.

Seiter, E. (2004). Children reporting online: The cultural politics of the computer lab. *Television & New Media, 5*(2), 87–107.

Seiter, E. (2005). *The Internet playground: Children's access, entertainment, and miseducation.* New York: Peter Lang.

Shetzer, H., & Warschauer, M. (2000). An electronic literacy approach to network-based language teaching. In M. Warschauer, & R. Kern (Eds.), *Network-based language teaching: Concepts and practice* (pp. 171–185). New York: Cambridge University Press.

Shiu, E., & Lenhart, A. (2004). *How Americans use instant messaging.* Washington, DC: Pew Internet & American Life Project.

Slayton, J., & Llosa, L. (2002). *Evaluation of the Waterford Early Reading Program 2001–2002: Implementation and student achievement* (Planning, Assessment and Research Division Publication No. 144). Los Angeles: Los Angeles Unified School District Program Evaluation and Research Branch.

Smolin, L. I., & Lawless, K. A. (2003). Becoming literate in the technological age: New responsibilities and tools for teachers. *The Reading Teacher, 56,* 570–577.

Sotamaa, O. (2003, December). *Computer game modding, intermediality and participatory culture.* Paper presented at the New Media? New Theories? New Methods? Conference, Sandbjerg, Denmark.

Steinkuehler, C. (2005). The literacy practices of massively multiplayer online games versus online standards. Paper presented at the Annual Meeting of the American Educational Research Association, Montreal, Canada.

Steinkeuhler, C. (2008). Cognition and literacy in massively multiplayer online games. In D. Leu, C. Lankshear, M. Knobel, & J. Coiro (Eds.), *Handbook of research on new literacies* (pp. 611–634). Mahwah, NJ: Erlbaum.

Stigler, J. W., & Hiebert, J. (1999). *The teaching gap: Best ideas from the world's teachers for improving education in the classroom.* New York: Free Press.

Street, B. (1995). *Social literacies.* Boston: Addison-Wesley.

Taylor, R. (1980). *The computer in the school: Tutor, tool, tutee.* New York: Teachers College Press.

Tuman, M. (1992). *Word perfect: Literacy in the computer age.* Pittsburgh, PA: University of Pittsburgh Press.

Tyner, K. (1998). *Literacy in a digital world.* Mahwah, NJ: Lawrence Erlbaum Associates.

Ware, P., & Warschauer, M. (2005). Hybrid literacy texts and practices in technology-intensive environments. *International Journal of Educational Research.*

Warschauer, M. (1997). Computer-mediated collaborative learning: Theory and practice. *Modern Language Journal, 81*(4), 470–481.

Warschauer, M. (1998). Researching technology in TESOL: Determinist, instrumental, and critical approaches. *TESOL Quarterly, 32*(4), 757–761.

Warschauer, M. (1999). *Electronic literacies: Language, culture, and power in online education.* Mahwah, NJ: Lawrence Erlbaum Associates.

Warschauer, M. (2000). Technology and school reform: A view from both sides of the track. *Education Policy Analysis Archives, 8*(4).

Warschauer, M. (2003a). The allures and illusions of modernity: Technology and educational reform in Egypt. *Educational Policy Analysis Archives, 11*(38).

Warschauer, M. (2003b). *Technology and social inclusion: Rethinking the digital divide.* Cambridge, MA: MIT Press.

Warschauer, M. (2006). *Laptops and literacy: Learning in the wireless classroom.* New York: Teachers College Press.

Warschauer, M., Knobel, M., & Stone, L. (2004). Technology and equity in schooling: Deconstructing the digital divide. *Educational Policy, 18*(4), 562–588.

Warschauer, M., & Ware, P. (2006). Automated writing evaluation: Defining the classroom research agenda. *Language Teaching Research, 10*(2), 1–24.

Wright, C. (2003). Parking Lott: The role of Web logs in the fall of Sen. Trent Lott. *Culture, Communication, and Technology Program, 3*, 1–30.

CHAPTER **9**

The Web as a Source of Information
for Students in K–12 Education

ELS KUIPER
and MONIQUE VOLMAN
VRIJE UNIVERSITEIT AMSTERDAM, THE NETHERLANDS

Introduction

The Web is increasingly omnipresent in the out-of-school lives of many children and adolescents and they seem to be skilful users. They know how to find Web sites that interest them, such as sites about gaming, pop idols, and popular television programs. They know how to make their own Web sites, instant messaging is their favorite way of communicating, and finding images on the Web to illustrate schoolwork is an easy task. Moreover, they often look at the Web as a very user-friendly resource: vast amounts of information is only a mouse click away, and text and pictures can easily be lifted from Web sites and relocated to their own work.

The Web is also increasingly used as an information resource within school settings. More schools are connected to the Internet and in many countries governments have instituted policies to support the use of the Internet in education. American statistics show that in 2003 nearly 100% of the public schools had access to the Internet (NCES, 2005). A multitude of "best practices" can be found on the Web: initiatives by schools and educational-supported institutes aimed at the optimal use of the Web as an information resource in education (see, e.g., Eisenberg & Berkowitz, 1992). Thus, the Web as a new medium has found its place in the lives of young people both at home and at school.

The Web offers children access to large amounts of information and is attractive to children. While it has considerable potential to supplement the educational tools traditionally used in the classroom, it was not designed for children nor was it designed to be used in educational settings. Problems with the validity, thoroughness, and meaning of knowledge acquired through the Web have been pointed out from the outset (e.g., the "butterfly defect," Salomon, 1998). The Web as an information resource is a tool that can only play an adequate role in students' learning processes under certain conditions. These conditions are the focus of this chapter.

The conditions for the effective use of the Web as an educational resource for information have been the subject of research in various, mostly unconnected, bodies of literature under different theoretical perspectives. Scholars in critical pedagogy and reading theorists have analyzed the Web as a new social tool or type of text, requiring new skills and attitudes from its users. Researchers in library and information science (LIS) have studied the Web as a source of information, in addition to books, CD-ROM, etc., while educational researchers have explored its use as a new type of learning tool. In this chapter, we discuss and bring together literature from these different perspectives to find answers to our central research question: How can schools use the Web as a tool that supports students in developing valid and meaningful knowledge?

The chapter is structured as follows. In the next section, we briefly discuss the theoretical perspectives of the three bodies of literature mentioned here, as well as our own theoretical position. In the subsequent three sections we discuss, in succession, research from these three perspectives and their respective utility for addressing our central question. In the last section, we suggest an interdisciplinary approach in which insights from the literature will be integrated.

We focus on the use of the Web as an information resource in K–12 education, with the emphasis on the upper-elementary and middle-school grades. This kind of Web use does not include the use of the Web as virtual-learning space, as is the case in e-learning, nor does it include Web-based learning, or distance learning. All of these support learning processes more directly through some type of instruction delivered via the Web; therefore, we do not discuss them here.

Theoretical Frameworks

Several bodies of literature investigate questions regarding the use of the Web as an information resource in education. In this section, we briefly discuss the theoretical perspectives they employ and the types of research questions they highlight. We argue that the question of how schools can use the Web as a tool to support students in developing valid and meaningful knowledge cannot be fully addressed by any single theoretical perspective and related research, but, rather, requires an integrated approach. We also introduce the socioconstructivist theoretical perspective, which we use in our attempt to bring about this integration.

The first body of literature focuses on questions such as, (a) What demands do the characteristics of the Web make on the knowledge, skills, and attitudes of its users, and (b) how can we deal with this in educational contexts? This theme is mostly addressed by authors with backgrounds in the philosophy of education (e.g., Burbules & Callister, 2000), or reading research (Snyder, 1998; Leu, 2000; Coiro, 2003). This is often combined with a critical pedagogical approach, pointing at power and the way it structures social relations and legitimates knowledge. The authors approach the Web as a new social tool or a new type of text(s), requiring new skills and attitudes from its users. Guidelines for teaching-learning situations in which the Web is used as an information resource are deduced from analyses of Web characteristics such as accessibility, hypertext structure, scope and topicality of information, and the predominantly visual character of the information. More fundamental questions, concerning the conceptualization of information literacy and new literacies are also presented.

A second body of literature asks the question: How do children use the Web in searching for information? This type of question is mainly contemplated by researchers working in the field of the LIS, with its tradition of research into the ways in which people handle information from print resources. From the moment the Web made its appearance in children's lives, scholarly interest focused on how young people handle this medium, whether at school or in leisure activities. Research questions in empirical research predominantly concern the characteristics of children's Web-search behavior, including how they search for information on the Web, the problems that they encounter, and the results of their searching. From the LIS-perspective, the use of the Web is approached as another source of information, in addition to books, CD-ROMs, etc. The strength of this perspective is that it can build on a tradition of research into how people, adults, and children navigate the complexities of locating information.

We also distinguish a third body of research, which studies the answer to the question, How can schools best use the Web as a tool to support students in developing valid and meaningful knowledge? Teachers and educational-support organizations consider the Web a useful, though sometimes problematic, tool for students in an early stage. Educational researchers have responded to this development by setting up studies to evaluate different ways of using the Web in education (e.g., Wallace, Kupperman, Krajcik, & Soloway, 2000; Jones, 2002). The main characteristics distinguishing this type of research from LIS-studies lie in the fact that children's information seeking is embedded in a broader curriculum context; the aim of the studies is to yield recommendations for using the Web to acquire deep and meaningful knowledge instead of merely describing students' Web use behavior. The question of how the Web can be used as a tool contributing to better learning is usually approached by learning theories from a (socio-) constructivist perspective (Duffy & Cunningham, 1996; Simons, van der Linden, & Duffy, 2000).

Although our emphasis is somewhat different, the central question in this chapter is the same as that addressed by the educational researchers mentioned earlier. We share their socioconstructivist perspective on teaching and learning. Constructivist theories stress that knowledge acquisition cannot be conceptualized as the storing of information. Such theories are critical of cognitive-learning theories, in which learning relates to the acquisition of knowledge and cognitive skills as transferable commodities. According to constructivists, people actively construct knowledge by interpreting new information, based on the knowledge they already have, as well as their prior experiences and their personal—but socially rooted—attitudes and values. Consequently, transmission of knowledge is not really possible; people only acquire valid and meaningful knowledge if they are able to transform the information offered to them into something personal. Principles for teaching and learning have been derived from this perspective, suggesting that students should be activated to construct their own knowledge, which builds on what they already know and can do. Moreover, constructing knowledge is seen as a social activity; collaboration with fellow students can enhance knowledge building, since it challenges students to assume an active role and explain their solutions to other students or compare their ideas with those of others (e.g., Van der Linden, Erkens, Schmidt, & Renshaw, 2000). The role of the teacher in constructivist teaching no longer lies in transmitting knowledge, but in providing students with support in the learning processes. Information and communication technology (ICT) is seen as a tool that can support, and contribute to, the transformation of learning and teaching in this direction (Jonassen, 1996; Bransford, Brown, & Cocking, 1999). The use of the Web as a resource is one of the applications now within the reach of many schools, which fits in well with this theoretical perspective. On the Web, students can easily and independently investigate questions that are meaningful to them, which enhances their motivation and stimulates their learning activities.

Socioconstructivist educational theories step even further away from the perspective of cognitive-learning theory. They interpret learning as increasingly competent participation in the discourse, norms, and practices associated with particular communities of practice. They shift the focus from the construction of knowledge to the process of becoming a member of a certain community of practice (Wenger, 1998). Learning not only is a constructive process, but also a socially and culturally situated process. The participation metaphor is often used to characterize this conception of learning as distinct from the acquisition metaphor (Sfard, 1998). The participation metaphor draws attention to the fact that learning is inextricably bound up with identity formation. Becoming a member of a community of practice requires people to see themselves *as* members, taking responsibility for their own actions (including the use of knowledge and skills) in that position. Learning activities are often shaped from this perspective as inquiries in classrooms functioning as communities of learners or communities of inquiry (Wells, 1999). By being involved in such collaborative inquiry-like activities, in which their own questions are the starting point, students are assumed to become stimulated into constructing meaningful knowledge and into developing an inquisitive attitude, enabling them to participate in social practices in a critical way.

Our main thesis in this chapter is that the Web can be seen and used as a new type of tool for teaching and learning that, in fact, fits in well with a socioconstructivist approach. We do, however, plea for incorporating insights from the different bodies of literature just mentioned into such a socioconstructivist approach. In the upcoming sections, we discuss the questions addressed in the literature from these different perspectives and the results research has yielded in a more detailed way. Finally, we propose an interdisciplinary approach, in which insights from these different perspectives are integrated for the design of educational practices that will enable students to use the Web to develop valid and meaningful knowledge.

Relevant Characteristics of the Web and Their Pedagogical Consequences

In this section, we discuss the mostly philosophical and theoretical literature focusing on the distinct characteristics of the Web and its consequences for the teaching-learning situation. We discuss this particular body of literature in four sections: (a) scope and topicality of the Web, (b) Web accessibility, (c) the use of hypertext, and (d) the visual character of the Web.

Scope and Topicality

The Web has assumed enormous dimensions and is growing rapidly. It is also an extremely up-to-date medium compared to written sources of information. It contains specialized and general information, both of which can be accessed exceptionally quickly compared to traditional information sources. Finding the right information on the Web, however, is no simple task. Most people have experienced despair after entering a simple keyboard and discovering numerous sites produced by the search, some of which may be completely irrelevant. As Harada (2001) rightly pointed out, "The sophistication, complexity and specificity of information obtained through electronic resources frequently exceed the comprehension levels of the students as well as their needs" (p.3). Many children, however, find the sheer size of the Web an advantage, based on the idea that they can find "everything and anything" and that "everything and anything" is always available to them and never on loan, as in the library. The seduction of the Web (not only for children) lies in the expectation that one can find an answer to every question and that these answers are only a few mouse clicks away (Todd, 1998). With such an abundance of information, however, it is not only difficult to find what you are looking for, but it is also of paramount importance that you know precisely what you are looking for.

Students must not only have the skills to search for information, but also the skills to process and use the information they find. D. M. Watson (2001) expressed the general concern: "There is a real danger that a fundamental purpose of schooling, to learn to know, is being swept aside by the need to acquire information. Where do the pupils learn the wisdom of how to use information and how to challenge its assumption and sources—indeed the very hegemony of 'Information'" (p. 256)? This view implies that the challenge for education lies in providing a context for that search for information. In this connection, Loveless, DeVoogd and Bohlin (2001) mentioned the problem that Web use involves a demand on students to which they are not accustomed to in traditional forms of education. To be able to use the abundance of information properly, students must be capable of continually making decisions on their own needs for information. Frechette (2002) also made a connection between educational innovation and the use of ICT in the classroom. She stressed the importance of curriculum development for Internet use. In her view, inquiry activities must form the basis of such curricula because they enable students' search processes to acquire a context and make searching for information on the Web not as an end in itself but as an instrument for answering broader questions and solving problems. This approach fits in well with a socioconstructivist perspective as described in the previous section.

Accessibility

The Web is a "democratic" medium from the point of view of both authors (building a Web site is no longer confined to a select group of specialists) and users (in principle, everyone with a computer and an Internet connection has equal access). Nevertheless, there are "haves" and "have nots" in Internet use as well. The well-known digital divide is still there, even if we restrict ourselves to prosperous parts of the world such as the United States and Western Europe. In the United States, inequality is reflected in differences in the way in which computers are used at schools. Songer, Lee and Kam (2002) quoted research data showing that schools with many disadvantaged students, particularly in poor urban areas where children's access to the Internet at home is lower, use their computers mainly for drill and practice, whereas schools in more prosperous areas use computers to solve problems. The latter schools also use the Web more often, as confirmed by recent research (Volman, Van Eck, Heemskerk, & Kuiper, 2005).

The Web is an information resource, which, owing to the way it is accessed, is available at every location with a computer. Looking up information no longer only happens in the library, it happens at home, at school, and at work. Students now have access to information in far more places than was the case with traditional sources of information. Moreover, children's Web use often takes place in the personal domain, without supervision from adults. The fact that the Web is accessible to everyone who wants to post information on it— that is, information not previously assessed by others—has both positive and negative aspects in relation to children. The positive side is that children can easily become authors of information that is accessible to others. They are able to make reports of their inquiry activities available on the Web and no longer write reports just for themselves, their teachers, or their classmates, but for far larger audiences as well. Thus, they obtain the opportunity to participate in cultural practices that were in the past reserved for adults. The negative side of this accessibility is that children may access incorrect or harmful information. This forces schools to make important pedagogical choices. Is it the main task of teachers to protect children by installing filters or other restrictions? Or is it preferable to teach children to approach information critically? Blocking access to certain parts of the Web should not be dismissed as a solution (e.g., Farwick Owens, Hester, & Teale, 2002).

Burbules and Callister (2000) grouped the negative side of Web accessibility under the headings of "misinformation" (wrong or incomplete information), "malinformation" (information that can be harmful, varying from child pornography to instructions for making bombs), "messed-up information" (information that is so badly presented that it is unusable) and "mostly useless information" (information that is of interest to very few people). They emphasized the paradox inherent in the democratic quality of the Web: the Web offers an enormous diversity of perspectives, but such diversity has the potential to scare away users, hence to exclude them. The authors particularly expressed concern about young, inexperienced users who are scared off by certain subject matter, as they lack the ability to interpret it and place it in context. They did not, however, regard censorship or filters as the solution: "How can students learn to make good choices, social and intellectual, if choices are made for them by filtering out things they can and cannot see?" (p. 109). Moreover, filters are the result of choices that in their eyes often have nothing to do with protecting students. Burbules and Callister argued strongly for a much greater emphasis in schools on critical use of the Web. Filters only have a useful function for very young children. With older children, teachers should hold a continuing dialogue about their curiosity, interests, and feelings. This could include why certain texts or illustrations are good or bad. "This, then, is the educational challenge: helping students learn to operate in an environment that is inherently 'dangerous,' to deal with what may be unexpected or unpleasant, to make critical judgments about what they find." (p.118) Frechette (2002) argued in this connection for a critical pedagogy centered on the empowerment of students. By teaching them to deal critically with the form and content of the Web, students will have a greater say in their own knowledge construction.

Web accessibility may be viewed from another perspective. Students now have access to information in far more places than in the past when they only had access to traditional sources of information. As Burnett and Wilkinson (2005) aptly described it, when using the Web in an out-of-school context, children appreciate certain autonomy by accessing information for their own purposes, by interacting with that information, and by solving problems as they do so. Burnett and Wilkinson argued that children's autonomy and innovation in using the Web ought to be acknowledged in education, thus emphasizing the importance of making use of children's own Web experiences and activities at school. Simplifying the Web or controlling Web access by using preselected Web sites or by letting children exclusively use "child-friendly" search facilities may result in Web use at school being less meaningful or even meaningless to the child or in a failure to link certain skills learned at school to Web use in daily life.

Use of Hypertext

Reading researchers, in particular, pay much attention to the hypertext structure of the Web. Web content is not structured in a linear and hierarchical way, but in such a way that texts, opinions, and ideas are interlinked. "Hypertext is essentially a network of links between words, ideas and sources, one that has neither a centre nor an end" (Snyder, 1998, p. 127). This has consequences for reading Web information. Users can choose their own way, to a far greater degree than in printed media, by following particular links. They are partly guided by the links created by Web-site authors, but they are also able to create their own totality of information, completely separate from any author's intentions. The use of hypertext offers the user many possibilities for obtaining information, but also makes it very easy to get lost in a welter of details. It invites users to surf in rather intuitive ways on the Web. An intuitive way of working, however, does not always have the desired result from an educational point of view. In the words of Laurillard (1998), "The paradox of interactive media is that being a user-control medium the learner expects to have control, and yet the learner does not know enough to be given full control" (p. 231).

For education, it is important to know how students can learn to deal with Web texts. Does hypertext require a different way of reading than printed text? If so, what are the consequences for teaching reading comprehension, for example? Burbules and Callister (2000) emphasized the importance of a focal point for students. When students go on the Web with a clear question, preferably their own, their searches for information and their reading are more meaningful. In addition, teachers must realize that using the Web is not first and foremost about the passive acquisition of knowledge but about the active construction of knowledge. Ultimately, this is a question of critical reading—reading while simultaneously evaluating the relevance and reliability of what is being read. Burke (2002) considered students' questions to be central in learning to read Web texts. Students must learn to ask themselves continually what it is they want to know, what is the purpose of knowing it, and what sort of information can contribute to that purpose. Such questions give direction to reading Web sites. Reading comprehension strategies play an important role, for example, in differentiating between facts and beliefs, checking difficult words in a text, etc. Farwick Owens et al. (2002) also emphasized the importance of continual questioning, for example, by learning repeatedly to question whether what you are reading is connected to what you want to know. In this way, students can avoid getting lost on the Web.

Sutherland-Smith (2002) took differences in reading strategies for printed text and Web text as her starting point. Reading a Web text makes greater demands on critical reading skills than reading printed texts, owing to the large proportion of nontextual elements, the possibilities for interactivity, and the demands the nonlinear character of the Web make on the associative ability of the student. Several useful strategies exist to teach students how to deal with Web texts, e.g., the "snatch-and-grab" technique whereby the student quickly checks whether a text includes a certain keyword or sentence and then saves the text. This prevents students from reading every text they find very thoroughly (which is not sensible, owing to the frequently large amounts of information) or, on the other hand, from quickly scanning the text without questioning whether it is useful or not (Sutherland-Smith, 2002).

Coiro (2003) explained how teaching reading comprehension changes when Web texts are used as an information resource. She emphasized the importance of making students aware of what they are doing when they click on a link and quoted Tapscott (1998), who expressed this very appropriately: "It's not just point and click. It's point, read, think and click" (p. 63). In this sense, links are constant decision points. The critical questioning of the motives and factual accuracy of Web texts is even more important than with printed texts. Coiro saw this as part of general critical literacy skills, whereby traditional research skills play an important role. The sheer amount of information and the lack of a clear linear structure can cause problems for weaker readers in particular. Todd (1998) mentioned in this connection that traditional indicators (such as mentioning the author's background and the references quoted) are often not given on the Web. Moreover, information is often presented without a context that can give meaning to the information. Users have to deduce these aspects themselves. To all these new reading skills, the term *new literacies* may be applied.

Visual Character

In printed information, writing is the dominant mode of representing information, while visual elements are used for illustration or decoration. On the Web, this relation between the verbal and visual is different (Ahtikari & Eronen, 2004). Visual elements on the Web have a much more extensive function than

evaluated negatively when the information cannot be found quickly. Large and Beheshti (2000) also found that students very much appreciated the ease of searching on the Web; it is much faster and you do not need to put as much effort into it in comparison to searching in books. Although many students in this study were disappointed with the results of their searches, their overall attitude remained positive. J. S. Watson (1998) questioned nine 8th-grade students in detail about their perceptions of using the Web. These students were positive and full of self-confidence. They liked using the Web, felt extremely sure about their skills, and considered the Web to be a valuable information resource. Students of different ages in the study by Shenton and Dixon (2003) praised the speed of the Web, the abundance of information it offers, and the accessibility of the information. Interestingly, older students had more mixed feelings about the Web: they also considered their difficulties in finding the required information and the variable quality of Web sites.

Children's attitudes toward the Web may influence their Web-searching strategies and their involvement. Kuhlthau (e.g., 1997, 2003) referred to the importance of including the affective characteristics of students during the process of searching for information. Students experience all kinds of emotions that are associated with an information search process and have an important function within that process, such as optimism at the beginning, a feeling of frustration when they cannot find any information, and satisfaction when they succeed.

Children's Web-Search Behavior

Search strategies: browsing or keyword searching. Several studies have looked at the search strategy children use or prefer. Most authors reported a preference for browsing, but greater difficulty in keyword searching. This is, for example, the conclusion Schacter, Chung and Dorr's (1998) came to based on an experimental study with 32 students (fifth and sixth grade). Moreover, the students appeared to be far more successful on an ill-defined task than on a well-defined one. The authors concluded that searching for precise, concrete information makes high demands on the search strategies of the Web user. In contrast, vague, abstract tasks are far more suitable for browsing, which children not only enjoy doing, but also do with ease. Large and Beheshti (2000) conducted research with a group of 50 sixth-grade students involving both student observations and interviews about their experiences using the Web as an information resource for study assignments. The students had a great deal of trouble selecting the right keywords and preferred to browse rather than search with keywords. Bilal (2000, 2001, 2002) studied the use of the American children's search engine Yahooligans! by 17 students aged 12 and 13 (seventh grade) and also found that students spent more time browsing than searching with specific terms.

In contrast, some studies reported that students focused on keyword searching or other search methods. For example, Fidel et al. (1999) observed eight 11th- and 12th-grade students searching for information on the Web for a homework assignment in which they had to answer a number of questions during a biology lesson about a plant of their choice. They often began searching by entering a Web address or a keyword they had used before. When this proved unsuccessful, they tried to formulate different search terms—but finding these terms proved to be a challenge to most students. Hirsh (1999) monitored 10 fifth-grade students seeking information for an assignment in which they had to write a paper on an athlete of their choice. Given the nature of the assignment, these students did not find searching with keywords difficult. Also, in one of Bilal's studies (2000) in which children were given a fact-finding task, most of them initially adopted a keyword-searching approach.

These findings indicate that browsing may be easier for children. Keyword searching is more difficult, particularly when the assignment is more vague and abstract. This may also have to do with the fact that children often have difficulties choosing appropriate and effective keywords. Many simply put in a single keyword that is directly related to the words and phrases used in the assignment. When the assignment is factual and concrete, formulating keywords is easier and the keywords used also have a reasonable chance of being successful. When the assignment is more research-based or ill defined, formulating successful keywords is much more difficult, especially for younger children. Schacter et al. (1998) suggested that browsing may be the preferred strategy for children because using search strategies requires analytic capabilities children do not yet possess. One has to bear in mind that a preference for a certain search strategy does not say anything about the results of that strategy. For example, children can make typing errors and spelling mistakes when using keyword searches. Such searches are bound to prove unsuccessful, and may be one of the reasons why children often prefer browsing. The preference for browsing or searching can also vary during the search for information: although most children in Bilal's (2000) study started with a keyword search, they moved to browsing either when they were unsuccessful or when they found relevant Web sites, which they explored further. The preference for browsing or keyword searching may also differ through time. In recent years, search engines such as Google have gained much popularity even among children.

Search process. Like all Web users, children adopt strategies to cope with the information they encounter. In most studies described in this section, children have to answer a factual or research question or fulfill an assignment. What do they do when confronted with Web information?

Many authors mentioned that children of all ages search for information very quickly and unsystematically, which is aptly illustrated by the following remark by Fidel et al. (1999): "The interactive nature of the Web supported the students' belief that there was no need to plan ahead because the pro-gression of a search would be largely determined by what they saw on the screen" (p.27). The students in this study hardly explored at all and continu-ally "circled around" a few familiar sites. Most students decided very quickly whether certain information was relevant and did not look at the whole text but often just at the beginning. Bilal (2000, 2001, 2002) reported quick and frequent jumps between sites, lots of clicking on links, a lack of orientation, great difficulty with more abstract information and large quantities of textual information as typical of students' search processes. Hirsh (1999) mentioned that students mainly looked for very specific information, quickly judging whether a text would be useful by reading only the first few lines. Shenton and Dixon's (2003) comparative study of youngsters' uses of CD-ROMs and the Web showed a comparable lack of preliminary thoughts: students used one initial keyword, while their subsequent actions were determined by the way the Web responded.

Another frequently mentioned characteristic of children's search process is their focus on finding the correct answer. In Fidel et al.'s (1999) study students were so focused on completing the assignment (answering a number of ques-tions in a biology lesson about a plant of their choice) that they repeatedly changed their question or topic if they could not find exactly the right infor-mation. Students also searched in a highly focused way, looking for actual sentences on the screen that contained the answer to their task. Shenton and Dixon (2003) concluded that students aimed for one article that satisfied their needs, and they were easily disappointed when they were not able to find such an article. In Hirsh's study (1999), students closely adhered to the assignment conditions laid down by the teacher—which also partly explained why they did not explore the Web to a great extent. One of Bilal's studies (2001) showed that when children had to find relevant information for a research assignment, they mainly tried to find a concrete answer instead of collecting information from which they could deduce an answer themselves.

Search results and task characteristics. Surprisingly, only a few studies looked at the results of children's Web searching. Perhaps this is also because the LIS-approach of the studies: in these studies, the focus is not primarily on knowledge construction. Shenton and Dixon (2004) called the two main areas of research in this field the (a) "where" or "what" studies (in which the preferences in terms of exploited sources are investigated), and the (b) "how" studies (in which the focus is on process and users' actual interac-tions with sources). The few studies that did take search results into account concluded that most children have difficulties finding answers in factual as well as research assignments.

A connection may also exist, however, between search results and char-acteristics of the tasks children have to fulfil. In Bilal's studies (2000, 2001,

2002) the same group of students were given a (a) fact-based search task (searching for an answer to a factual question), a (b) research task (searching for information to answer an inquiry) and a (c) fully self-generated task (searching for information on an inquiry they had thought of themselves). The students were most successful and had the least difficulty with the fully self-generated task (Bilal, 2002). Bilal concluded that this was partly because students' own research tasks tended to be simpler than the other tasks and concerned topics which the students already knew something about. In other words, prior knowledge makes searching for information easier. Students also preferred searching for information on their own question, which had a positive effect on their search behavior. Students experienced the most difficulty with the assigned research task. Bilal (2001) blamed this on the complexity of the task and on students' inadequate research skills. The fact that they did not find the research question interesting also seemed to negatively affect on their results.

As mentioned earlier, Schacter et al. (1998) assumed that children would have more trouble with (well-defined) "finding tasks" than (ill-defined) "searching tasks," since the structure of the Web makes it difficult for children to find specific information, and relatively easy to collect information for "ill-defined tasks." The study confirmed their hypothesis—to the effect that children would perform very poorly on the well-defined task, but quite well on the ill-defined task—but contradicts Bilal's findings (2000, 2001). It should be noted, however, that the assignment in Schacter et al.'s study (1998) was more difficult than that of Bilal's (2000) and related to a very different field. This suggests that the literature does not pay enough attention to the degree of difficulty as a task characteristic.

Another element that may be underestimated in the literature is the influence of the meaningfulness of the task on the task results. The assignments in the studies of both Bilal (2000, 2001, 2002) and Schacter et al. (1998) had no links with anything else the students did in the classroom and were not designed or assessed by teachers. Hirsh (1999) commented in this connection: "Students, searching for information needed for a real assignment, may have a different set of goals and a higher motivation level than students performing an artificial search for an external researcher" (p. 1278). We would like to point out here that in a research or ill-defined task, the question of what exactly is expected of students is also relevant. In Bilal's study (2001), the children had to collect information, print out that information, and then indicate on the printout what they thought was relevant to their question. In this way, searching the Web is an objective in itself and does not lead to a product, as is the case in an ordinary teaching-learning situation. This can, of course, influence students' search strategies and search process, as well as their search results.

Gender Differences in Web-Search Behavior

Research by Large, Beheshti, and Rahman (2002b) showed that boys and girls use different search strategies and with different results. Boys used a single keyword more often when searching for information; girls used combinations of keywords more often. Boys' search strategies resulted in many more pages per search than those of girls. Boys also seemed to be more active in their use of the Web, clicking more often on links than girls and also jumping backward and forward between pages and engaging more often in navigation. Boys' groups also spent significantly less time looking at Web pages than girls. One explanation might be that girls' groups might pay more attention to negotiation and cooperation, both of which take time and make Web navigation slower. The fact that boys spend less time on reading the texts may be associated with greater difficulty, and thus less interest in reading. The authors assumed that " … the academic and behavioral differences between boys and girls offline also appear online in the Web environment" (p. 442).

Schacter et al.'s study (1998) also revealed gender differences in search strategies: boys appeared to browse significantly more often than girls did. The researchers presumed that boys may have gone through most of the information quickly or just failed to read it at all. Hirsh (1999) found that boys immediately start searching whereas girls take their time.

Assessing and Evaluating Web Content

Being able to assess the relevance and reliability is, of course, an important point regarding all information, but the use of the Web makes higher demands. As described in the previous section on Web characteristics, children have very easy access to large quantities of information, the reliability and authority of which cannot be assumed. Many studies on children's Web use reported on their inability to assess and evaluate Web content. These studies either did not question the reliability, accuracy, or authority of the information, possibly because researchers did not know how to assess these factors, or used insufficient or wrong criteria for their judgment. The fifth- and sixth-grade students in Schacter et al.'s (1998) study did not seem to realize that false and inaccurate information may be posted on the Web and that the information they found needed to be challenged and questioned. Hirsh (1999) conducted research with a group of fifth graders into the criteria they used when evaluating Web information for a school assignment. The most important criterion proved to be the relevance of the content of the information to the subject. Student interest in the subject was also shown to be important. Students hardly assessed the reliability and authority of the information. This tendency did not appear to improve with age. On the basis of a study involving a group of 15-year-old girls, Agosto (2002b) constructed a theoretical model of the criteria young people use to evaluate Web sites. Students did evaluate sites on their content—the expected relevancy and reliability—but often used inappropriate criteria in the process (e.g., equating quantity with quality). Lorenzen (2001) asked nineteen 10th- and 12th-grade students about their assessment of information on the Web. He concluded that most students either do not look at the reliability and correctness of the information or use incorrect criteria in their assessment. Students assume, for example, that all results of a search engine are qualitatively good and that a Web site with a great deal of text must be good. In Fidel et al.'s (1999) study students used the graphics on a page as a clue to relevance and quality. They also used the amount of information present as a measurement of quality. J. S. Watson (1998) mentioned, on the basis of interviews with 8th-grade students regarding their perceptions during Web use, a level of student confidence only in the use of the Web as a tool. None of the students referred to their evaluation of Web content and few mentioned the accuracy and adequacy of the information obtained. In a more recent study by Shenton and Dixon (2003), no student reported attempting to verify the accuracy of Web information in any way. The authors concluded that for much of the time children do not even realize the need for such verification.

One may assume that assessing and evaluating Web sites proves difficult for anyone confronted with the abundance of information the Web offers. For several reasons, this applies to children in an even greater degree. Children often lack sufficient prior knowledge to which information found on the Web can be related. Prior knowledge of a specific subject makes it easier both to formulate suitable keywords and to evaluate the relevance and reliability of the information (e.g., Fidel et al. 1999). Younger children, in particular, tend to take the information found on the Web literally and are not yet able to question the authority of such information (Hirsh, 1999). Children also often lack sufficient research strategies that can help in the process of distinguishing between relevant and irrelevant information. For example, the tendency, mentioned earlier, of looking for the correct answer prevents a more critical look at the information found. Agosto (2002a) pointed out the importance of constraints in evaluating Web information. Students were not only found to stop searching when they thought they had found enough information of the right quality but also to stop searching due to time constraints, fatigue, or boredom. Children also tended to be easily misled by the appearance of Web sites. Information presented in a way that is attractive to children is more likely to attract their attention and may be assessed more positively. The interviews J.S. Watson (1998) held with eighth-grade students indicated that time also plays an important role with children; the appreciation of a Web site is related to download time. Studies by Agosto (2002a, 2002b) showed that children quickly "click off" Web sites with lots of text and few illustrations. Agosto (2002b) also differentiated between searching for information in the school context and in an out-of-school context: "To the girls in this study, two major categories, or schemata, framed their lives: the school schema and the non-school schema. Web queries, and nearly everything in their lives, fell into

learning in-depth about a topic, and tried to complete the task with as little effort as possible.

Therefore, Wallace et al. (2000), working in the same line of research, looked closer at how students worked within the science unit. They concluded that although the intention of the assignment was to have students learn about something of personal interest by doing research on the Web, students seemed to work on finding a perfect Web page or finding a ready-made answer to their question. Again, students' lack of research skills affected their Web searching. For example, posing and refining research questions was problematic for them. They also overemphasized the Web-search aspect, treating searching and collecting information itself as the centerpiece of their work and not considering how they could use the information to answer their question. Although the resemblance with the research results described in the previous section is striking again, these authors stressed the influence and importance of the wider educational context on students' Web-search behavior. For example, in this study, teachers' support was primarily geared toward completing the task quickly. Wallace et al. (2000) concluded that inquiries on the Web must be incorporated into a broader educational approach: "In many classrooms and schools, students are accustomed to seeking correct answers and producing work that meets clear specifications, laid out in advance. Getting on the Web to "do inquiry" is unlikely to cause a change in that orientation even in the short term" (p. 100).

These results prompted Hoffman et al. (2003) to choose another approach to using the Web for student inquiries. Students used a specially designed interface, which structured and guided both their inquiries and their Web use. Students did not search freely on the Web, but their searches were mediated by the interface, which allowed access to a digital library that contained preselected, preapproved, and age-appropriate online resources. Teachers also received more training in supervision. This led to better learning results in terms of accuracy and depth of content understanding (Hoffman et al., 2003).

Research done by Jones (2002), however, indicated that offering online support and preselected Web sites alone does not diminish students' tendency to look only for the right answer. In this study, ninth- and tenth-grade students searched the Web under two different conditions. In the less-structured condition, students were free to choose between searching freely on the Web or using the Project Web Page that was designed for the project, and on which students could find online support and a selection of Web sites. In the structured condition, students only had access to this Project Web Page. All students were given the same research task within a class project on ecology. Contrary to expectations, the students who were allowed to search freely made little use of this opportunity. They simply expected that the sites selected by the teacher would provide the right answer and were afraid that they would use incorrect information in their paper if they searched for it themselves (Jones, 2002).

This does not necessarily mean that students feel insecure when using the Web for school assignments. Ng and Gunstone (2002) concluded on the basis of interviews with twenty-two 10th-grade students that these students felt the Web gave them control over their learning process, making them less dependent on the teacher and their classmates. Ng and Gunstone (2002) warned of the dangers of the sometimes too technological approach of students to searching for information on the Web.

Summary

The research results mentioned in this section indicate that some aspects of students' Web behavior (for example, their tendency to look for the "right answer") are persistent and reflect a wider educational context in which students are rather passive consumers of information and take the authority of the teacher for granted. This means that this educational context has to be taken into account when thinking about how the Web can be meaningfully used in education. This line of research chooses to simplify the use of the Web for students, by using preselected Web sites or an interface that offers solutions for students' lack of search skills.

Discussion

Much of the research results discussed in this chapter is captured in a paradox. The Web invites students to demonstrate behavior that is the opposite of the behavior necessary for the development of valid and meaningful knowledge. The Web invites students to think that every answer can be found ready-made, given the abundance of information it offers. It also invites students to be more or less passive searchers, because of the speed with which information appears on the computer screen. In contrast, the development of valid and meaningful knowledge assumes that students are actively involved in the learning process, that they construct knowledge by connecting new information to already acquired knowledge, and that they reflect on this process and its results.

Several explanations for this paradox may be given. It is obvious, for example, that the Web is not designed for use aimed at knowledge construction in educational settings. It may also be argued that Web use fits the consumerist attitudes of many students. Finally, it may be the educational culture in many classrooms itself that contributes to students focusing on finding the right answer in as short a time as possible. Although educational innovations have aimed at changes in this culture, it has proven to be a persistent characteristic of education. The question remains as to how the paradox can be resolved.

The educational research mentioned in the previous section tries to solve this problem by simplifying the use of the Web for students, such as by supporting them with an interface offering some solutions for their lack of search skills. This is reflected in the many "best practices" found on the Web offering teachers selections of Web sites on a certain domain or subject. Students do not have to spend time on Web searching, but instead can focus their attention on preselected Web sites with useful information. This solution reflects the focus on the Web as a learning tool that is characteristic for this line of research. Since students show a lack of skills in using the Web, the tool is modified to make its use easier. The solution is understandable if one's primary goal of Web use in education is offering information that can contribute to the construction of knowledge in a certain subject domain.

Such a solution, however, is not conducive to teaching students to use the Web independently and critically—the educational challenge referred to by Burbules and Callister (2000). We make a plea for approaching the Web not only as a tool that can be used in education, but also as a tool that students must learn to master in education. On the basis of theoretical notions as well as empirical research, the literature reviewed in the first two sections argued for making the ability to handle the Web critically an explicit educational goal. We cannot expect students to rely on new literacies when they have never been taught the relevant knowledge, skills, or attitudes, such as knowledge of the structure of the Web and the meaning of hypertext, as well as searching skills (the ability to formulate proper keywords), reading skills (the ability to scan Web texts effectively and to use hypertext elements), and evaluation skills (the ability to critically judge the authority and relevance of information found on the Web).

How then should these new literacies be taught? A socioconstructivist perspective suggests an approach that stimulates students into active construction of knowledge and skills, building on what they already know and can do. One challenge, therefore, is to connect children's in-school and out-of-school Web practices: the ways in which children use the Web at school should take into account their own ways of using the Web at home.

A socioconstructivist approach also suggests that learning is enhanced by students' participation in practices that exist in the real world and are challenging. Using the Web can be seen as a sociocultural practice that is connected with most children's daily lives. From this perspective, Web literacy can be achieved through the actual use of the Web and by confrontation with the problems it involves, such as the abundance of information and the temptation of endless browsing through hypertexts; however, this confrontation alone is not sufficient for learning to take place; reflection on the problems involved in Web use and support in dealing with these is also necessary. In fact, reflection is what education is able to add to mere participation in real-life social practices. In socioconstructivist learning environments, this combination of participation and reflection is often organized in communities of learners or communities of inquiry. In such communities, learning activities are shaped as collaborative inquiries based on students' own research questions. We believe this to be a promising approach to making the development of critical attitudes toward Web information into a meaningful curricular goal.

In this approach, the development of critical Web skills and the construction of subject knowledge go together. Students use the Web to obtain information regarding their research questions. While doing so, they experience the need to transform such information in order to make it meaningful. This encourages them to critically read and evaluate Web content and negotiate its meaning with a view to their own information needs. They may be confronted with all the difficult aspects of the Web we discussed in this chapter—the formulation of adequate keywords to prevent getting endless lists of Web pages from a search engine or being confronted with many pages not primarily designed for children. This requires children to form their own opinions on the usefulness of those pages for their research questions and to translate difficult information into their own words.

In this chapter, we have argued for the integration of several perspectives: (a) theoretical notions on the pedagogical consequences of Web use in education, (b) knowledge about the use of information resources such as the Web, and (c) knowledge about teaching and learning aimed at knowledge construction through inquiry. Such an integrated approach may contribute to gaining insight into how students can be supported in critical Web use for the construction of valid and meaningful knowledge.

We conclude this chapter with some suggestions for future research. First, and above all, research into Web use by children in education should take place from an interdisciplinary perspective.

Research ought to focus on the acquisition of new literacies by children and young learners and the role education can play. How can the development of such complex skills be fostered? Insights from the literature must be translated into characteristics for the guidance of students that can subsequently be tested in research. For the purposes of research, it is advisable to operationalize "umbrella terms" such as Web literacy into a number of subskills. This facilitates the design and study of learning environments aimed at the process of acquiring these skills. It should, however, never be forgotten that, like all literacies, Web literacy is the sum of its parts, irreducible to subskills. Research in this field must, therefore, follow and describe student learning processes and learning results in an integral manner. In this way, insight may also be gained into the conditions under which students acquire such complex skills.

We would, furthermore, like to plea for research focusing on the design of learning environments in which the use of the Web as an information resource is incorporated into different kinds of curriculum contexts. Such research should also explicitly look at the classroom culture and generate recommendations for teachers. An interesting research question is How can students be taught Web literacy, for example, in specific new literacies curricula or embedded in the teaching of subject domains? In this connection, domains other than science should receive research attention. In such research the connection between Web use at school and out of school must be made explicit and the skills children have already mastered must be taken into account.

Research into differences between students in Web use has so far been rare. Future research should focus on these differences, especially with a view to their influence on Web use. For example, how can weak readers and students with short attention spans be supported in their Web use? These groups of students are often more vulnerable to factors such as getting lost on the Web.

Finally, research in the direction indicated should always take into account the constant and rapid changes in the Web, as well as the educational contexts in which the Web is used. "The ... paradox is that technology often changes faster than we can effectively evaluate its utility for literacy and learning." (Leu, 2000, p. 23). This is perhaps a somewhat disconcerting, but challenging, perspective for future research.

References

Agosto, D. E. (2002a). Bounded rationality and satisficing in young people's Web-based decision making. *Journal of the American Society for Information Science and Technology, 53*(1), 16–27.

Agosto, D. E. (2002b). A model of young people's decision-making in using the Web. *Library & Information Science Research, 24*, 311–341.

Ahtikari, J., & Eronen, S. (2004). *On a journey towards Web literacy–the electronic learning space Netro.* Pro Gradu Thesis. University of Jyväskylä, Finland.

Bransford, J. D., Brown, A. L., & Cocking, R. (Eds.) (1999). *How people learn. Brain, mind, experience and school.* Washington, DC: National Academy Press.

Bilal, D. (2000). Children's use of the Yahooligans! search engine: I. Cognitive, physical and affective behaviors on fact-based search tasks. *Journal of the American Society for Information Science, 51*(7), 646–665.

Bilal, D. (2001). Children's use of the Yahooligans! search engine: II. Cognitive and physical behaviors on research tasks. *Journal of the American Society for Information Science and Technology, 52*(2), 118–136.

Bilal, D. (2002). Children's use of the Yahooligans! Web search engine: III. Cognitive and physical behaviors on fully self-generated tasks. *Journal of the American Society for Information Science and Technology, 53* (13), 1170–1183.

Burbules, N. C., & Callister, T. A. (2000). *Watch IT. The risks and promises of information technologies for education.* Boulder, CO: Westview Press.

Burke, J. (2002). The Internet Reader. *Educational Leadership, 60*(3), 38–42.

Burnett, C., & Wilkinson, J. (2005). Holy lemons! Learning form children's uses of the Internet in out-of-school contexts. *Literacy, 39*(3), 158–165.

Coiro, J. (2003). Reading comprehension on the Internet: Expanding our understanding of reading comprehension to encompass new literacies. *The Reading Teacher, 56*(6). Retrieved May 13, 2003, from http://www.readingonline.org/electronic/elec_index.asp?HREF=/electronic/RT/2–03_column/index.html.

Duffy, T. M., & Cunningham, D. J. (1996). Constructivism: Implications for the design and delivery of instruction. In D. Jonassen (Ed.), *Handbook of research for educational communications and technology* (pp. 170–198). New York: Simon & Schuster Macmillan.

Eisenberg, M. B., & Berkowitz, R. E. (1992). Information problem-solving: The big six skills approach. *School Library Media Activities Monthly 8*(5), 27–29, 37, 42.

Farwick Owens, R., Hester, J. L., & Teale, W. H. (2002). Where do you want to go today? Inquiry-based learning and technology integration. *Reading Teacher, 55*(7), 616–625.

Fidel, R., Davies, R. K., Douglass, M. H., Holder, J. K., Hopkins, C. J., Kushner, E. J. et al. (1999). A visit to the information mall: Web searching behavior of high school students. *Journal of the American Society for Information Science, 50*(1), 24–37.

Frechette, J. D. (2002). *Developing media literacy in cyberspace. Pedagogy and critical learning for the twenty-first-century classroom.* Westport, CT: Praeger.

Harada, V. H. (2001). *From instruction to construction: Learning in the information age.* Paper presented at the Ninth Treasure Mountain Research Retreat for School Library Media Programs, Brown County, Indiana.

Hirsh, S. G. (1999). Children's relevance criteria and information seeking on electronic resources. *Journal of the American Society for Information Science, 50*(14), 1265–1283.

Hoffman, J. L., Wu, H.-K., Krajcik, J. S., & Soloway, E. (2003). The nature of middle school learners' science content understandings with the use of on-line resources. *Journal of Research in Science Teaching, 40*(3), 323–346.

Jonassen, D. H. (1996). *Handbook of research for educational communications and technology.* New York: Simon & Schuster Macmillan.

Jones, B. D. (2002). Recommendations for implementing Internet inquiry projects. *Journal of Educational Technology Systems, 30* (3), 271–291.

Kristmundsson, G. (2000). Betekenisvol leren en nieuwe media. [Meaningful learning and new media]. In P. Bemelen, & J. Letschert (Eds.), *Op de schouders van de voorgangers* (pp. 97–106). Enschede, The Netherlands: SLO.

Kuhlthau, C. C. (1997). Learning in digital libraries: An information process approach. *Library Trends, 45*(4), 708–724.

Kuhlthau, C. C. (2003). *Seeking meaning. A process approach to library and information services* (2nd ed.). Westport, CT: Greenwood.

Large, A., & Beheshti, J. (2000). The Web as a classroom resource: Reactions form the users. *Journal of the American Society for Information Science, 51*(12), 1069–1080.

Large, A., Beheshti, J., & Rahman, T. (2002). Gender differences in collaborative Web searching behavior: An elementary school study. *Information Processing and Management, 38,* 427–443.

Laurillard, D. (1998). Multimedia and the learner's experience of narrative. *Computers & Education, 31,* 229–242.

Leu, D. J. (2000). Literacy and technology: Deictic consequences for literacy education in an information age. In M. L. Kamil, P. Mosenthal, P. D. Pearson, & R. Barr (Eds.), *Handbook of reading research* (Vol. III, pp. 743–770). Mahwah, NJ: Erlbaum. Retrieved March 3, 2003, from http://web.syr.edu/djleu/Handbook.html

Lorenzen, M. (2001). The land of confusion? High school students and their use of the World Wide Web for research. *Research Strategies, 18,* 151–163.

Loveless, A., DeVoogd, G. L., & Bohlin, R. M. (2001). Something old, something new ... Is pedagogy affected by ICT? In A. Loveless & V. Ellis (Eds.), *ICT, pedagogy and the curriculum: Subject to change* (pp. 63–83). London: Routledge/Falmer.

Lyons, D., Hoffman, J., Krajcik, J., & Soloway, E. (1997, March). *An investigation of the use of the World Wide Web for on-line inquiry in a science classroom.* Paper presented at the meeting of the National Association for Research in Science Teaching, Chicago, IL.

National Center for Education Statistics (NCES) (2005). *Internet access in public schools and classrooms: 1994–2003.* Retrieved November 2, 2005, from http://nces.ed.gov/pubsearch/pubsinfo.asp?pubid=2004011.

Ng, W., & Gunstone, R. (2002). Students' perceptions of the effectiveness of the World Wide Web as a research and teaching tool in science learning. *Research in Science Education, 32,* 489–510.

Pappas, M. L., & Tepe, A. E. (1998). Media, visual, technology and information: A comparison of literacies. In D. Callison, J. McGregor & R. Small (Ed.), *Instructional interventions for information use: Papers of treasure mountain VI* (pp. 328–347). San Jose, CA: Hi Willow.

Salomon, G. (1998). Novel constructivist learning environments and novel technologies: Some issues to be concerned with. *Research Dialogue in Learning and Instruction, 1*(1), 3–12.

Schacter, J., Chung, G. K. W. K., & Dorr, A. (1998). Children's Internet searching on complex problems: Performance and process analysis. *Journal of the American Society for Information Science, 49*(9), 840–849.

Sfard, A. (1998). On two metaphors for learning and the dangers of choosing just one. *Educational Researcher, 27,* 4–13.

Shenton, A. K., & Dixon, P. (2003). A comparison of youngsters' use of CD-ROM and the Internet as information resources. *Journal of the American Society for Information Science and Technology, 54*(11), 1029–1049.

Shenton, A. K., & Dixon, P. (2004). Issues arising from youngsters' information-seeking behavior. *Library & Information Science Research, 26,* 177–200.

Simons, R. J., van der Linden, J., & Duffy, T. (Eds.). (2000). *New learning.* Dordrecht, Netherlands: Kluwer Academic.

Snyder, I. (1998). Beyond the hype: Reassessing hypertext. In I. Snyder (Ed.), *Page to screen. Taking literacy in the electronic era* (pp. 125–143). London/New York: Routledge.

Soloway, E., & Wallace, R. (1997). Does the Internet support student inquiry? Don't ask. *Communications of the ACM, 40*(5), 11–16.

Songer, N. B., Lee, H.-S., & Kam, R. (2002). Technology-rich inquiry science in urban classrooms: What are the barriers to inquiry pedagogy? *Journal of Research in Science Teaching, 39*(2), 128–150.

Sorapure, M., Inglesby. P., & Yatchisin, G. (1998). Web literacy: Challenges and opportunities for research in a new medium. *Computers and Composition, 15,* 409–424.

Sutherland-Smith, W. (2002). Weaving the literacy Web: Changes in reading from page to screen. *The Reading Teacher, 55*(7), 662–669.

Tapscott, R. (1998). *Growing up digital: The rise of the Net generation.* New York: McGraw-Hill.

Todd, R. (1998). WWW, critical literacies and learning outcomes. *Teacher Librarian, 28*(2), 16–21.

Van der Linden, J., Erkens, G., Schmidt, H., & Renshaw, P. (2000). Collaborative learning. In R. J. Simons, J. van der Linden, & T. Duffy (Eds.), *New learning* (pp. 37–54). Dordrecht, Netherlands: Kluwer Academic Publishers.

Volman, M., Eck, E., van Heemskerk, I., & Kuiper, E. (2005). New technologies, new differences. Gender and ethnic differences in students' use of ICT in primary and secondary education. *Computers & Education, 45,* 35–55.

Wallace, R. M. (2002). The Internet as a site for changing practices: The case of Ms. Owens. *Research in Science Education, 32,* 465–487.

Wallace, R. M. (2004). A framework for understanding teaching with the Internet. *American Educational Research Journal, 42*(2), 447–488.

Wallace, R. M., Kupperman, J., Krajcik, J., & Soloway, E. (2000). Science on the Web: Students on-line in a sixth-grade classroom. *The Journal of the Learning Sciences, 9*(1), 75–104.

Watson, D. M. (2001). Pedagogy before technology: Re-thinking the relationship between ICT and teaching. *Education and Information Technologies, 6*(4), 251–266.

Watson, J. S. (1998). "If you don't have it, you can't find it." A close look at students' perceptions of using technology. *Journal of the American Society for Information Science, 49*(11), 1024–1036.

Wells, G. (1999). *Dialogic inquiry. Towards a sociocultural practice and theory of education.* Cambridge: Cambridge University Press.

Wenger, E. (1998). *Communities of practice. Learning, meaning, and identity.* Cambridge, U.K.: Cambridge University Press.

CHAPTER **10**

Where Do We Go Now?

*Understanding Research on Navigation
in Complex Digital Environments*

KIMBERLY A. LAWLESS

UNIVERSITY OF ILLINOIS AT CHICAGO, USA

P. G. SCHRADER

UNIVERSITY OF NEVADA, LAS VEGAS, USA

Introduction

While hypertext and the ideas surrounding it have clearly been around for decades (see Bush, 1945; Nelson, 1965), the recent and unprecedented growth of contemporary technologies has afforded and necessitated their exploration, development, and deployment (McKnight, Dillon, & Richardson, 1991). Current estimates of the World Wide Web, the most prominent manifestation of hypertext today, indicate that it is comprised of over 60 million servers housing more than 11.5 billion indexed pages (Gulli & Signorini, 2005). This estimate does not account for content that is not indexable by search engines (e.g., Google), sometimes called the "invisible Web," which likely exceeds the amount of indexed content by 400 to 550 times (Lyman & Varian, 2000). These statistics reflect a startling 60,000% increase in quantity in less than 10 years.

In conjunction with the exponential expansion of hypermedia content afforded by the Web, there is also an increasing trend in Internet usage. Well over one billion people worldwide actively participate in online activities (Internet World Stats, 2006). The fastest growing segment of the population to embrace the Web is children ages 9 to 17. Internet usage by children and adolescents of elementary and high school age has intensified, rising from about one third of 9- to 17-year-olds in 1997 to about two thirds in 2001 (U.S. Department of Commerce, 2002) to nearly 74% in 2005 (Pew Internet and American Life Project, 2005). Further, survey research shows that 94% of students ages

12 to 17 with home access to the Internet used the Internet for homework. Nearly 71% used the Internet as the primary source for information on their most recent school report or project, while only 24% reported using standard library materials for the same task (Pew Internet and American Life Project, 2001). These statistics indicate not only that the Internet is a prominent learning tool within the classroom but also that digital resources are rapidly overtaking their more traditional counterparts as the primary information sources in K–12 settings.

Combined, the massive explosion of information available as digital resources and the increasing ubiquity of these resources within the classroom have created a shift in what it means to be literate in today's knowledge society. The computer is more than a medium for the digital transformation of printed resources (J. R. Hill & Hannafin, 2001). Rather, it is a new and ever-evolving context for learning that accommodates a greater variety of learning goals and resources for constructing meaning (D. J. Leu, D. D. Leu, & Coiro, 2005). Citizens in the 21st century must not only know how to decode and comprehend information as they have in the past, but they are also now responsible for efficiently and effectively finding and evaluating information as well as quickly adapting goals in response to the complexities of the environment (Alexander & Fox, 2004; Grabinger, Dunlap, & Duffield, 1997). As such, it becomes clear that online learning both calls on and develops cognitive skills and strategies in addition to those learning apparatuses that are more traditionally required (Kozma, 1991; Mayer, 1997; Shapiro & Niederhauser, 2004).

Many have posited that the key to understanding how we learn from hypermedia environments rests within unpacking the mechanisms through which a user selects one link over another to build a path through the terrain of a hypermedia system—in other words, navigation (Alexander, Kulikowich, & Jetton, 1994; J. R. Hill & Hannafin, 2001; Kozma, 1991; Lawless & Brown, 1997). Although navigational skills are critical for 21st-century learning, there is relatively little research compared to other areas in learning. As stated by McKnight et al. (1991), "For an activity that is routinely performed by all of us, navigation is not a well-studied psychological phenomenon in the same way that reading is." The existing research spans a number of disciplines and methodological approaches, which have shared little cross-pollination. Moreover, each study utilizes environments that vary in terms of domain, structure, and affordances that make transfer of findings difficult.

This chapter attempts to cull these disparate research domains and genres, extracting common findings concerning navigation and its impact on learning. While previous reviews have looked at specific aspects of navigation (C. Chen & Rada, 1996; Dillon & Gabbard, 1998; Lawless & Brown, 1997), the intent of the present analysis was much more broadly defined. Our goal is to provide the reader with a multidimensional review of the continuum of research conducted on navigation across a sundry of digital environments. Using schema theory as a framework, we view navigation as an active, constructive process. It is affected not only by learners' internal knowledge structures but also by the external constraints of the learning environment as well (Kozma, 1991). The following sections of this chapter examine how different internal learner characteristics (e.g., prior knowledge, self-efficacy, and interest) and different external constraints (e.g., learner control, instructional design, and level of control) influence the navigational process. In an effort to extend this research area, we have included a discussion of burgeoning research trends in navigation and their implications for the design and implementation of nonlinear, digital learning environments. Finally, we conclude by providing some recommendations for future research that will help us better understand the skills and strategies involved in navigation and their impact on learning and instruction.

What Is Navigation?

As Whitaker (1998) stated,

> Navigation is a term that describes activities ranging from the first tentative exploration by an infant to the sophisticated calculations and planning which successfully placed a man on the moon. Navigation in its narrow sense means to move through space; in its broader sense, navigation also includes virtual movement through cognitive space made up of data and the knowledge emerging from those data. (p. 63)

Drawn as a parallel between human movement about the physical world and user engagement with electronic environments (H. Kim & Hirtle, 1995), navigation has become the principal metaphor adopted to connote how we interact with hypermedia, the Web, screens of video games, and other immersive and nonimmersive virtual environments (Gamberini & Bussolon, 2001). This basic spatial metaphor has an important influence on how we envision digital environments, what we do when we are using them, and how we design them for others.

The theoretical foundations of the spatial navigation metaphor have their roots in a number of fields. In architecture, the term *wayfinding* has been used synonymously with navigation to account for an individual's understanding of how to move about the physical space of buildings to select a route, monitor progress along this route, and recognize when the target has been reached (Benyon, in press; Downs & Stea, 1973). Similarly, effective navigation through virtual environments also requires users to know where they are, where they need to go, how to get there, and when they have arrived. Navigation, conceived of in this manner, describes not only the behavioral actions of movement (e.g., locomotion from one destination to another), but also elements of cognitive ability (e.g., determining and monitoring path trajectory and goal orientation; Bowman, 1999; Darken, Allard, et al. & Achille, 1999; Passini, 1984).

users engaged with the environment on a very superficial level. They spent very little time navigating and visited a limited number of screens. Their navigational paths tended to be very linear, and indicated that they took the quickest and shortest route through the environment. In subsequent replications of this investigation, which varied in terms of education level of students (Lawless & Kulikowich, 1998), domains of study (Lawless, Mills, & Brown, 2002), and complexity of the computerized environment (Barab, Bowdish, & Lawless, 1997), similar navigational profiles emerged.

MacGregor (1999) triangulated data sources including navigation selections, verbal report and video transcriptions of 10 students (4 seventh graders and 6 eleventh graders) interacting with a science-based, instructional hypermedia system. Using a constant comparative approach, MacGregor (1999) isolated three navigational profiles that were labeled sequential studier, video viewer, and concept connector. However, although each student had a dominant profile that lead to their classification, most of the students used one of the other navigational styles at least once during their session. The sequential studier methodically selected all of the nodes on a particular screen, usually from left to right or top to bottom, before moving onto the next screen. In addition, the sequential studier spent more time on average with each object within the environment than other types of navigators. By contrast, video viewers were primarily interested in the video nodes (still or full motion). These individuals spent about 83% of their time in the environment viewing such resources with little cross-linkage of other modalities. The concept connector was the most flexible navigational profile. These students read carefully at times, skimming at other times, and moved back and forth between text and graphic objects. MacGregor (1999) concluded that only some learners were able to take advantage of the nonlinearity and resources offered by the hypermedia format and that the patterns revealed different motivators attracting students as they navigated through the medium.

More recently, resurgence in the study of user navigation has emerged from the fields of information and computer science. Juvina and van Oostendorp (2004) examined the behavior traces of users' navigation through a personal finance Web site. Using an automated technique for extracting navigation data (e.g., path length, time deviations, etc.), a principal component analysis yielded a four-component solution explaining approximately 86% of the variance in navigational scores. The first of these navigational styles was dubbed flimsy navigation. Users with high scores on this component visited very few pages and did not venture far from the homepage. It was described as a very parsimonious navigational profile, revealing little exploration or nonlinearity. Those individuals that aligned with the content focus approach were deemed the readers, selecting pages with a large amount of text-based content. Furthermore, these individuals not only sought out those types of pages but also allocated time to process them in depth. Laborious navigators intensively used the navigational options availed to them. They were characterized by the high number of back buttons and page revisits selected. Finally, Juvina and van Ostendorp (2004) identified a fourth profile, divergent navigation. These navigators were the explorers, visiting the highest number of unique pages with little or no revisitation to previous sections. In a follow-up study, Herder and Juvina (2004) isolated similar navigation profiles and indicated that understanding these profiles and accounting for them in the design of an environment is a promising means of alleviating a users sense of perceived disorientation in cyberspace.

While each of the studies previously summarized varied in terms of participants, digital environment explored, and methodological approach taken, the findings combine to reveal a common trend highlighting the existence of multiple dominant navigational profiles among users. Across all studies, researchers found one group of navigators that focused on comprehending information, one group that played with the special features, and one group that forced a linear structure onto the nonlinear environment. What is curious about this common finding is that only one study, conducted by Lawless and Kulikowich (1996), included a reference to another in the set (Horney & Anderson-Inman, 1994). This fact may be interpreted by some as an indicator of convergent validity, multiple studies conducted in isolation from one another revealing the same findings. However, one may interpret the lack of cross-referencing among these studies as an indicator of poor communication across academic disciplines conducting research in navigation. This not only narrows our understanding of navigation, but it also clearly contributes to a large amount of redundancy in research efforts.

Influences on User Navigation

While research pertaining to navigation confirms the existence of common navigational patterns, it fails to provide an empirical explanation as to why these different profiles emerge. Knowing that a particular navigational pattern exists does not mean that we understand its impact on task completion or learning from a hypermedia system. The volume of constructs that explain variability in navigational performance and its mediating impact on learning is overwhelming (Juvina & van Oostendorp, 2004). To a certain extent, however, they converge around three primary components: (a) attributes of the user, (b) characteristics of the environment, and (c) features of the learning activity or context. Each of these dimensions is delineated in greater detail in the sections that follow.

User Attributes

Individuals vary in their aptitudes for learning, their willingness to learn, and the styles or preferences for how they learn if they choose to do so. These cognitive and affective differences impact both the learning process and outcome

(Smith, 2001; Webster & Martocchio, 1993). With respect to navigation, macrolevel findings indicate that higher levels of computer self-efficacy are linked to navigational persistence (Murphy, 1988), ease of navigation (Agarwal, Sambamurthy, & Stair, 2000; Ventatesh, 2000), and the selection of more efficient and appropriate navigational strategies (M.-J. Tsai & C.-C. Tsai, 2003). Taking a more microlevel lens, self-efficacy has also been shown to predict the types of individual nodes a user selects, with low-self efficacious navigators displaying an overreliance on the help and support features in a digital information space to aid their navigation (Barab et al., 1997).

Text Characteristics

It has been long argued users' individual experience depends on the configuration of the digital environment (Alexander et al., 1994). In addition to variability among users, each unique arrangement of content, organizational scheme, and enabling scaffolds also impacts the nature of navigational artifacts. In fact, design considerations have often been found to counteract or neutralize many of the individual differences among learners with respect to quality and ease of navigation.

   Domain structure.   Several researchers have highlighted that the manner in which individuals acquire and process information in well-structured domains is different from the way individuals accomplish these tasks in more ill-structured domains (Lawless & Kulikowich, 1996, 1998; Spiro & Jehng, 1990; Spiro, Vispoel, Schmitz, Samarapungavan, & Boerger, 1987). Well-structured domains, such as mathematics or statistics, for example, tend to be more algorithmic or rule based in nature (Alexander, 1997; Kulikowich & DeFranco, 2003). By comparison, domains like psychology and history have been termed *ill structured*. They tend to employ heuristics as procedures and exist as multidimensional composites of other domains. Spiro and Jehng (1990) purported that the more ill structured a domain the more nonlinear the cognitive processing will be (Spiro et al., 1987). This hypothesis is based on the notion that these individuals must acquire associations between different pieces of information in a flexible environment so that connections between disparate schemata can be formed. As such, learners need to be able to explore a domain strategically, from multiple perspectives, in order to study potential relationships (Wittgenstein, 1953). It follows that students would navigate a digital environment representing an ill-structured domain more strategically, seeking out information-based nodes, and comparing and contrasting related screens, in an attempt to discover information linkages and build mental representations.

Some research has supported this view (Lawless & Kulikowich, 1998; Niederhauser, Reynolds, Salmen, & Skolmoski, 2000). However, Spiro et al. (1987) offered cautionary notes on implementing design manifestations of this principle. While an ill-structured domain may lend itself more to easily to nonlinear digital exploration, too many navigational demands on the subject can lead to increased disorientation and too few can lead to misconceptions that arise out of oversimplification. Developers must attend to not only the structure of the domain but also to the overall organizational structure and complexity of the digital representation of the content as well.

Site maps and overviews. Researchers have evaluated several methods to enhance available tools used to interact with and organize information in the digital context (Boiling et al., 1998; Calisir & Gurel, 2003; Chou & Lin, 1997, 1998; Cress & Knabel, 2003; Danielson, 2002; Jonassen & Wang, 1993). Much of this research has been conducted under the premise that a reduction in cognitive load effectively decreases metacognitive demand on the user, thereby improving such factors as navigational performance (speed, accuracy, number of pages accessed, and recall) and comprehension. Typically, in the literature, navigation behavior, navigational errors, and disorientation have been used as proxy measurements of cognitive load (Astleitner & Leutner, 1996; Brünken, Plass, & Leutner, 2003).

Cockburn and Jones (1996) argued that the majority of navigational issues derive from contextual inadequacies. To counteract this, many designers have introduced navigational scaffolding techniques (e.g., site maps; Chou & Lin, 1997, 1998; Danielson, 2002; Puntambekar, Stylianou, & Hubscher, 2003; Schroeder, 1994). Cockburn and Jones (1996) suggested that site maps or other visual aids are invaluable in minimizing memory load, enriching the development of a global mental model of the information space depicting the relationships between pages and their content. As a result, researchers have investigated the link between various forms of site maps (e.g., visual, hierarchical, spherical, and dynamic) and their theorized value to user orientation, wayfinding, and learning.

Schroeder (1994) found that users had difficulty internalizing the structure of the site map and exhibited lower levels of performance when using embedded text links. Schroeder asserted that this might explained by the novelty of the Web combined with the need for some level of navigational expertise or at least proficiency. Considering the findings of later studies, this seems to be the case. For example, Chou and Lin (1998) found that within the context of a complex hypermedia system, site maps had a significant positive influence on performance (e.g., search steps, efficiency, and task completion).

Puntambekar et al. (2003) incorporated external graphical and text-based navigation prompts into a hypertext system pertaining to scientific concepts. The cues (concept maps) updated dynamically as the user navigated through the system and were intended to increase a user's metacognitive awareness. Puntambekar et al. found that the support structure facilitated students' detailed investigation of content. Although there was no significant difference in overall knowledge, students examined adjacent and adjoining information with greater frequency and depth. Similarly, de Jong and van der Hulst (2002) found no significant difference in declarative knowledge across three treatment conditions—(a) visual, (b) hints, and (c) control—but reported significant gains in procedural knowledge and overall knowledge of the system and structure. They argued that graphical map participants did not necessarily show better recall of the content, but exhibited enhanced knowledge of the overall structure and quality of navigational decisions beyond the gains normally attributed to the intervention.

Providing users with a bird's-eye view of the information space has also been found to facilitate information seeking tasks, prompted deeper investigation, diminished the use of the backward navigation (back button), improved local branching, and offered a better conceptual indication of their location (Danielson, 2002). Further Danielson's findings suggested that the integration of a site map allowed users to understand content in their immediate virtual vicinity and allowed them to circumvent redundant visits to content.

Hypertext structure. The organization and intratextual linkage of information is one salient feature of hypermedia that has prompted researchers to explore the nature of navigation performance within the scope of specific hypermedia and encompassing contexts. The structure of information and context evidently are of seminal importance, and as a result, much of the research has been dedicated to understanding the influence of hypermedia structure on navigation and learning (Shapiro & Niederhauser, 2004).

A recurring theme in the literature seems to be that nearly all of available hypermedia structures are appropriate, at least some of the time. For example, McDonald and Stevenson (1996) found that users that had experienced the linear hypermedia structure outperformed users of a nonlinear hypermedia environment. In contrast, Barab, Young, and Wang (1999) suggested that among other things, a nonlinear or generative hypermedia (one that requires user input) is more conducive to the users' goal formation, which in turn, positively influences problem solving and self-determination. In their review of the literature, Shapiro and Niederhauser (2004) expanded on this topic considerably. It follows that like so many other issues associated with hypermedia, there is no consistent, universal design strategy that meets the navigational needs of a true heterogeneous population. Even so, many commonly applied educational contexts demonstrate benefits of one structure over another.

One such context is a hierarchical site structure and similarly designed navigational tool evaluated by Zhang and Salvendy (2001). Zhang and Salvendy examined the site and tool as it interacted with visualization ability pertaining to navigation and information access. They found that both high- and low-visualization participants showed a significant increase in navigational efficiency (identified items and fewer steps) when using the hierarchical site structure. The nature of the task in Zhang and Salvendy's experiment pertained to performance and memory organization when participants performed information search tasks. In this context (e.g., the retrieval of information), evidence supports the use of hierarchical structures for this and similar tasks.

Shapiro (1998) conducted an investigation of 72 undergraduate students as they used one of three hypermedia digital book formats (control or traditional text, loosely structured, and highly structured). She found that the internal representations were significantly influenced because of the hypermedia system. The results indicated that navigators of a loosely structured hypermedia system showed a significantly better recall on an essay posttest than those in a highly structured context. However, Shapiro indicated that there were no significant increases in knowledge gains among the groups.

The issue and relevance of hypermedia structure increases in complexity when individual user differences are taken into account. For example, Calcaterra et al. (2005) found a link between cognitive style, hypermedia structure, and navigation. Specifically, verbalizers visited more pages in a hierarchical condition whereas imagers visited more pages in a relational condition. In an independent study, Lin (2003a) found that older users of the Web experienced more disorientation and navigation difficulty when using referential and mixed hypermedia structures. Lin (2003b) argued that this was due to the overwhelming degree of control over more complex hypertext systems and that for older users a hierarchical structure was superior in facilitating navigational decisions. In addition to age and cognitive style, Schoon and Cafolla (2002) showed significant differences between the ways males and females navigate loosely structured Web sites. Specifically, females on average exhibited greater difficulty in locating closed-task information within Web sites constructed using an ambiguous or arbitrary structure. However, Schoon and Cafolla acknowledged that although experience was not shown to be a significant factor in navigation, the females in the study reported less experience with the Web than their male counterparts did.

Although the empirical research seems at odds with itself, these findings demonstrate important consistencies with the literature on support strategies (site maps and overviews). The results associated with support strategies indicate that the nature of the support system has little bearing on declarative knowledge but has a significant influence on knowledge structures and deep contextual meaning. Similarly, research on system structure indicates that while there is little evidence to support an influence on factual knowledge (declarative), there is a significant influence on the learners' ability to arrive at a deeper contextual meaning. Taken collectively, the literature suggests that for differential goals, a complementary set of structures and support strategies is appropriate.

Design issues. Although disheartening with respect to a single design principle, the previously mentioned findings indicate that hypertext devel-

Curry, as part of the Hypertext Research Group (1999) found that a task goal also affects a user's mental representation of the global information space. Participants received either a general browsing goal or a problem-solving goal that required the identification and synthesis of several distinct bits of information. After interacting with a hypermedia environment based on Lyme disease, participants provided a concept map of their mental representation of the information space. Participants' concept maps generally fell into two distinct structures: hierarchical and relational. Hierarchical maps contained main idea nodes with subordinate ideas listed in the following section (replicating the actual environment), whereas relational maps contained unique links between nodes that did not exist in the original text (representing mental associations between information units). The problem-solving group constructed significantly more relational links than the learners with the general browsing goal. Thus, participants with a specific learning task seem to be better able to make their own unique connections within the material. With respect to navigation, those in the problem-solving task tended to be more nonlinear than the browsing group. These results would seem to indicate that, in the absence of a learning goal, readers' conceptualization of an information space and resulting navigational selections are less integrated than users operating under a specific goal.

Personal intentions.   Unlike user attributes and text characteristics, which are primarily static, learners' intentions are continually created and revised during the process of knowledge acquisition and problem solving and arise from the interaction of the individual and the environment (Young, Kulikowich, & Barab, 1997). A change in users' intention corresponds with shifts in navigational strategies, influencing the direction of linking behavior (Bates, 1989). The navigational path can be thought of as an in situ manifestation of a user's moment-to-moment intentions. Users act on hyperlinks, images, or other navigational objects that are perceived as being most similar to the representation of their current intention (Kitajima, Blackmon, & Polson, 2000). For example, when navigating through a hypertext, an individual can discover a particular node that peaks their interest and maintains their attention. Known as the serendipity effect (Kuhlen, 1991), this increased motivational state makes the user likely to change their navigation strategy and to loose sight of their prior intention (Cress & Knable, 2003). While the serendipity effect may increase incidental learning, it tends to weaken the efficiency of navigational processes and can lead to disorientation. Further, with higher levels of task difficulty, less distractibility can be observed, whereas for low levels of task difficulty the presence of a competing intention leads to an increase in error rates and the amount of time spent on irrelevant information (Gerjets & Scheiter, 2003).

The Future of Navigation in Cyberspace

While the learner has a certain degree of control in a hypertext environment (e.g., over their path), the author is given ultimate control over the design and implementation of the navigational framework by predetermining the intra-textual and intertextual links between nodes (Beasley & Waugh, 1995; S. Chen, 2002; Lawless & Kulikowich, 2006). Implementing a unilateral, intractable navigation structure across heterogeneous populations of users can be viewed as nothing short of problematic. As reviewed in the earlier sections, variables like prior knowledge, field dependence, spatial ability, and experience have been shown to influence the construction of meaning in hypertext environments (Calcaterra et al., 2005; S. Chen, 2002; Lawless & Brown, 1997; Shapiro & Niederhauser, 2004). As a solution to these and other issues, researchers have begun to investigate adaptive navigation schemes that track (actively or passively) the differential abilities and needs of users while customizing a page's navigational support tools (Brusilovsky & Maybury, 2002; S. Chen, 2002). The overall goal of adaptive navigation is to improve usability of hypertext by building "a model of goals, preferences and knowledge of the individual user and use this throughout the interaction for adaptation of the hypertext to the needs of that user" (de Bra, Brusilovsky, & Houben, 1999, p. 2). In essence, its intent is to help relieve cognitive load placed on learners by dynamically supporting navigational decisions.

Work on adaptive navigation within the human-computer interaction (HCI) community has also experimented with social navigation algorithms (Brusilovsky, 2004). Social navigation is an approach to categorizing, collecting, and filtering information on the Web. It is based on propagating word-of-mouth opinions and recommendations from trusted sources about the qualities of particular items (Malone, Grant, Turbak, Brobst, & Cohen, 1987; Maltz & Ehrlich, 1995; Shardanand & Maes, 1995). For example, if deciding on a new restaurant, one would probably ask friends or look at a restaurant guide. This same premise applies to social information filtering and holds promise for constraining and facilitating navigational choices (Maltz & Ehrlich, 1995; Shardanand & Maes, 1995).

In general, social filtering systems approach the problem by estimating the desirability of items under consideration. Desirability can be inferred explicitly by directly soliciting data from users about the quality of items through rating scale items (Herlocker, Konstan, Borchers, & Riedl, 1999), but it may also involve detailed annotations about the resource (W. Hill, Stead, Rosenstein, & Furnas, 1995) and general user demographic information. Desirability estimates can also be inferred implicitly by leveraging information collected for other purposes, usually as a by-product of user navigational actions (Herlocker et al., 1999). For example, the system might infer that desirable items are used more frequently or more recently (Recker this, the unit of assessment has typically been limited to the identification of a particular piece of information as a product of a search task with navigation measured in terms of speed and accuracy (e.g., Bilal & Kirby, 2002; Chou & Lin, 1998; Hölsher & Strube, 2000). Others have used information recall as an indicator of learning (e.g., de Jong & van der Hulst, 2002; Lawless & Kulikowich, 1998; Schwartz et al., 2004). While search success and information recall are important outcomes, they are very simple proxies, not necessarily indicative of the robust levels of knowledge acquisition and learning that hypermedia environments can foster. Because navigation is such a complex enterprise, such basic assessment techniques will not likely help capture the true nature of the relationship between process and product. In the future, we need to be more creative and adventurous in developing outcome measures that encapsulate a much broader definition of learning.

References

Agarwal, R., Sambamurthy, V., & Stair, R. (2000). The evolving relationship between general and specific computer literacy: An empirical assessment. *Information Systems Research, 11*(4), 418–430.

Alexander, P. A. (1992). Domain knowledge: Evolving issues and emerging concerns. *Educational Psychologist, 27,* 33–51.

Alexander, P. A. (1997). Mapping the multidimensional nature of domain learning: The interplay of cognitive, motivational, and strategic forces. In M. L. Maehr, & P. R. Pintrich (Eds.), *Advances in motivation and achievement* (Vol. 10, pp. 213–250). Greenwich, CT: JAI Press.

Alexander, P. A., & Fox, E. (2004). Historical perspective on reading research and practice. In R. B. Ruddell & N. Unrau (Eds.), *Theoretical models and processes of reading* (5th ed., pp. 33–68). Newark, DE: International Reading Association.

Alexander, P. A., & Judy, J. E. (1988). The interaction of domain-specific and strategic knowledge in academic performance. *Review of Educational Research, 58,* 375–404.

Alexander, P. A., Kulikowich, J. M., & Jetton, T. L. (1994). The role of subject-matter knowledge and interest in the processing of linear and nonlinear texts. *Review of Educational Research, 64,* 201–252.

Anderson, R. C., & Pearson, P. D. (1984). A schema-theoretic view of basic processes in reading comprehension. In P. D. Pearson (Ed.), *Handbook of reading research* (pp. 255–291). New York: Longman.

Astleitner, H., & Leutner, D. (1996). Applying standard network analysis to hypermedia systems: Implications for learning. *Journal of Educational Computing Research, 14,* 285–303.

Bandura, A. (1997). *Self-efficacy: The exercise of control.* New York: W. H. Freeman.

Barab, S. A., Bowdish, B. E., & Lawless, K. A. (1997). Hypermedia navigation: Profiles of hypermedia users. *Educational Technology Research and Development, 45*(3), 23–42.

Barab, S. A., Young, M. F., & Wang, J. (1999). The effects of navigational and generative activities in hypertext learning on problem solving and comprehension. *International Journal of Instructional Media, 26*(3), 283–309.

Bates, M. (1989). The design of browsing and berrypicking techniques for the online search interface. *Online Review, 13*(5), 407–424.

Baylor, A. (1999). *Psychological factors influencing World-Wide Web navigation.* Paper presented at the national convention of the Association for Educational Communications and Technology, Houston, TX.

Beasley, R. E., & Waugh, M. L. (1995). Cognitive mapping architectures and hypermedia disorientation: An empirical study. *Journal of Educational Multimedia and Hypermedia, 4*(2/3), 239–255.

Benyon, D. R. (in press). The New HCI? Navigation of information space. *Knowledge-Based Systems.*

Benyon, D. R., & Murray, D. M. (1993). Applying user modeling to human-computer interaction design. *AI Review, 6*, 43–69.

Binder, C. (1989). Hypertext design issues. *Performance Improvement Quarterly, 2*(3), 16–33.

Bilal, D., & Kirby, J. (2002). Differences and similarities in information seeking: Children and adults as web users [Electronic version]. *Information Processing and Management, 38*, 649–670.

Boechler, P. M. (2001). How spatial is hyperspace/interacting with hypertext documents: Cognitive processes and concepts. *Cyberpsychology and Behaviour, 4*(1), 23–46.

Boiling, E., Beriswill, J. E., Xaver, R., Hebb, C., Kaufman, D., & Frick, T. (1998). Text labels for hypertext navigation buttons. *International Journal of Instructional Media, 25*(4), 407–421.

Boiling, E., King, K., Avers, D., Hsu, Y., Lee, J., & Frick, T. (1996). Navigating backward: Concrete vs. abstract representations in hypertext buttons. *Canadian Journal of Educational Communication, 25*(2), 161–176.

Bowman, D. (1999). Interaction techniques for common tasks in immersive virtual environments: Design, evaluation and application. Unpublished doctoral dissertation, Georgia Institute of Technology, Atlanta.

Borges, J., & Levene, M. (1999, August). Data mining of user navigation patterns. Paper presented at the Workshop on Web Usage Analysis and User Profiling, San Diego, CA.

Borgman, C. L. (1986). The user's mental model of an information retrieval system: An experiment on a prototype online catalog. *International Journal of Man-Machine Studies, 24*, p. 47–64.

Breese, J., Heckerman, D., & Kadie, C. (1998). Empirical analysis of predictive algorithms for collaborative filtering. In Editor (Ed.), *Proceedings of the fourteenth conference on uncertainty in artificial intelligence.* New York: Morgan Kaufmann.

Brewer, W. (1987). Schemas versus mental models in human memory. In I. P. Morris (Ed.), *Modeling cognition* (pp. 187–197). Chichester, U.K.: John Wiley and Sons.

Brünken, R., Plass, J. L., & Leutner, D. (2003). Direct measurement of cognitive load in multimedia learning. *Educational Psychologist, 38*, 53–61.

Brusilovsky, P. (2004). Adaptive navigation support: From adaptive hypermedia to adaptive web and beyond. *PsychNology Journal, 2* (1), 7–23.

Brusilovsky, P., & Maybury, M. T. (2002). From adaptive hypermedia to the adaptive Web. *Communications of the ACM, 45*(5), 30–33.

Burbules, N. C., & Callister, T. A. (2000). *Watch IT: The risks and promises of information technologies for education.* Boulder, CO: Westview Press.

Bush, V. (1945). As we may think. *Atlantic Monthly, 76*, 101–108.

Calcaterra, A., Antonietti, A., & Underwood, J. (2005). Cognitive style, hypermedia navigation and learning. *Computers & Education, 44*, 441–457.

Calisir, F., & Gurel, Z. (2003). Influence of text structure and prior knowledge of the learner on reading comprehension, browsing, and perceived control. *Computers in Human Behavior, 19*, 135–145.

Campagnoni, F., & Ehrlich, K. (1989). Information retrieval using a hypertext-based help system. *ACM transactions on information systems, 7*, 271–291.

Carmel, E., Crawford, S., & Chen, H. (1992). Browsing in hypertext: A cognitive study. *IEEE Transactions on Systems, Man, and Cybernetics, 22*, 865–884.

Catledge, L. D. & J. E. Pitkow (1995). Characterizing browsing strategies in the world-wide web. *Proceedings of the 3rd International World Wide Web Conference,* volume 28 of Computer Networks and ISDN Systems, Darmstadt, Germany.

Hill, J. R., & Hannafin, M. J. (2001). The resurgence of resource-based learning. *Educational Technology, Research and Development, 49*(3), 37–52.

Hill, W., Stead, L., Rosenstein, M., & Furnas, G. (1995). Recommending and evaluating choices in a virtual community of use. *Proceedings on Human Factors in Computing Systems* (pp. 194–201). New York: ACM.

Hölsher, C., & Strube, G. (2000). Web search behavior of Internet experts and newbies. *Computer Networks, 33*, 337–346.

Hoeoek , K., & Svensson, M. (1999). Evaluating adaptive navigation support. In M. Maybury (Ed.), *Proceedings of the 1999 International Conference on Intelligent User Interfaces* (p. 187). Redondo Beach, CA: ACM Press.

Horney, M. A., & Anderson-Inman, L. (1994). The ElectroText Project: Hypertext reading patterns of middle school students. *Journal of Educational Multimedia and Hypermedia, 3*(1), 71–91.

Hurtienne, J., & Wandke, H. (1997). How effectively and efficiently do users navigate in the WWW? An empirical study. In D. Janetzko, B. Batanic, D. Schoder, M. Mattingley-Scott, & G. Strube (Eds.), *CAW-97: Workshop cognition & Web.* (pp. 93–104). Freiburg, Germany: IIG Berichte.

Internet World Stats (2006). Retrieved April 20, 2006, from http://www.internetworldstats.com/stats.htm.

Jonassen, D. H., & Wang, S. (1993). Acquiring structural knowledge from semantically structured hypertext. *Journal of Computer-Based Instruction, 20*(1), 1–8.

Jul, S., & Furnas G. W. (1997). Navigation in electronic worlds. *SGCHI bulletin, 29*(4), 44–49.

Juvina, I., & Oostendorp, H. van (2004). Extracting semantic and pragmatic information from web navigation data for user modeling. In Editor (Ed.), *Comprehension of text and graphics: Basic and applied issues* (pp. 102–107). Amsterdam: ACM Digital Library.

Keller, J. M. (1997). Motivational design and multimedia: Beyond the novelty effect. *Strategic Human Resource Development Review, 1*(1), 188–203.

Keller, J. M., & Suzuki, K. (1988). Use of the ARCS motivation model in courseware design. In D. H. Jonassen (Ed.), *Instructional designs for microcomputer courseware* (pp. 401–434). Hillsdale, NJ: Lawrence Erlbaum Associates.

Kim, K. (2001a). Information seeking on the Web: Effects of user and task variables. *Library & Information Science Research, 23*, 233–255.

Kim, K. (2001b). Implications of user characteristics in information seeking on the World Wide Web. *International Journal of Human-Computer Interaction, 13*(3), 323–340.

Kim, H., & Hirtle, S. (1995). Spatial metaphors and disorientation in hypertext browsing. *Behaviour & Information Technology, 14*(4), 239–250.

Kitajima, M., Blackmon, M.H., & Polson, P.G. (2000). A comprehension-based model of Web navigation and its application to Web usability analysis. In S. McDonald, Y. Waern, & G. Cockton (Eds.), *People and Computers XIV-Usability or Else! Proceedings of HCI 2000*, (pp. 357–373). Eindhoven, The Netherlands: Springer-Verlag.

Kozma, R. B. (1991). Learning with media. *Review of Educational Research, 6*, 179–211.

Krapp, A., Hidi, S., & Renninger, K. A. (1992). Interest, learning and development. In K. A. Renninger, S. Hidi, & A. Krapp (Eds.), *The role of interest in learning and development* (pp. 3–26). Hillsdale, NJ: Erlbaum.

Kuhlen, R. (1991). *Hypertext.* Berlin, Germany: Springer-Verlag.

Kulikowich, J. M., & DeFranco, T. C. (2003). Philosophy's role in characterizing the nature of educational psychology and mathematics. *Educational Psychologist, 38*(3), 147–156.

Last, D. A., O'Donnell, A. M., & Kelly, A. E. (2001). The effects of prior knowledge and goal strength on the use of hypertext. *Journal of Educational Multimedia and Hypermedia, 10*, 3–25.

Lawless, K. A., & Brown, S. W. (1997). Multimedia learning environments: Issues of learner control and navigation. *Instructional Science, 25*(2) 117–131.

Lawless, K. A., Brown, S. W., Mills, R. J., & Mayall. H. J. (2003). Knowledge, interest, recall and navigation: A look at hypertext processing. *Journal of Literacy, 35*(3), 911–934.

Lawless, K. A., & Kulikowich, J. M. (1993, October). *Assessment of students' navigation and comprehension of a hypertext document.* Paper presented at the annual meeting of the Northeastern Educational Research Association, Ellenville, NY.

Lawless, K. A., & Kulikowich, J. M. (1996). Understanding hypertext navigation through cluster analysis. *Journal of Educational Computing Research, 14*(4), 385–399.

Lawless, K. A., & Kulikowich, J. M. (1998). Domain knowledge, interest, and hypertext navigation: A study of individual differences. *Journal of Educational Multimedia and Hypermedia, 7*(1), 51–70.

Lawless K. A., & Kulikowich, J. M. (2006). Domain knowledge and individual interest: The effects of academic level and specialization in statistics and psychology. *Contemporary Educational Psychology, 31,* 30–43.

Lawless, K. A., Mills, R., & Brown, S. W. (2002). Children's hypermedia navigational strategies. *Journal of Research on Computing in Education, 34*(3), 274–284.

Lawless, K. A., Schrader, P. G., & Mayall, H. J. (in press). Acquisition of information online: Knowledge, navigational strategy and learning outcomes. *Journal of Literacy Research.*

Leu, D. J., Jr. (2004). Literacy and technology: Deictic consequences for literacy education in an information age. In M. L. Kamil, P. Mosenthal, P. D. Pearson, & R. Barr (Eds.), *Handbook of reading research* (Vol. III, pp. 743–770). Mahwah, NJ: Erlbaum.

Leu, D. J., Jr., Kinzer, C. K., Coiro, J., & Cammack, D. (2004). Toward a theory of new literacies emerging from the Internet and other information and communication technologies. In R. B. Ruddell & N. Unrau (Eds.), *Theoretical models and processes of reading* (5th ed., pp. 1568–1611). Newark, NJ: International Reading Association.

Leu, D. J., Jr., Leu, D. D., & Coiro, J. (2005). *Teaching with the Internet: New literacies for new times* (4th ed.). Norwood, MA: Christopher-Gordon.

Lin, D. M. (2003a). Hypertext for the aged: Effects of text topologies. *Computers in Human Behavior, 19,* 201–209.

Lin, D. M. (2003b). Age differences in the performance of hypertext perusal as a function of text topology. *Behavior & Information Technology, 22* (4), 219–226.

Lyman, P., & Varian, H. R. (2000). How much information? (Technical Report). Berkeley, CA: University of California at Berkeley. Retrieved May 20, 2005, http://www.sims.berkeley.edu/research/projects/how-much-info/how-much-info.pdf.

MacGregor, S. K. (1999). Hypermedia navigation profiles: Cognitive characteristics and information processing strategies. *Journal of Educational Computing Research, 20*(2), 189–206.

Malone, T., Grant, K., Turbak, F., Brobst, S., & Cohen, M. (1987). Intelligent information sharing systems. *Communications of the ACM, 30*(5), 390–402.

Maltz, D., & Ehrlich, K. (1995). Pointing the way: Active collaborative filtering. *Proceeding of the ACM Conference on Human Factors in Computing Systems* (pp. 202–209). New York: ACM Digital Library.

Marchionini, G. (1988). Hypermedia and learning: Freedom and chaos. *Educational Technology, 28*(11), 8–12.

Marchionini, G. (1995). *Information seeking in electronic environments.* Cambridge, U.K.: Cambridge University Press.

Marchionini, G., & Shneiderman, B. (1988). Finding facts vs. browsing knowledge in hypertext systems. *IEEE Computer 21*(1), 70–80.

Mayer, R. E. (1997). Multimedia learning: Are we asking the right questions. *Educational Psychologist, 32,* 1–19.

Tsai, M.-J., & Tsai, C.-C. (2003). Information searching strategies in web-based science learning: The role of Internet self-efficacy. *Innovations in Education and Teaching International, 40,* 1, 43–50.

U.S. Department of Commerce (2002). *A nation online: How Americans are expanding their use of the Internet.* Washington, DC: National Telecommunications and Information Administration. Retrieved February 12, 2006, from: http://www.ntia.doc.gov/reports/anol/index.html.

Venkatesh, V. (2000). Determinants of perceived ease of use: Integrating control, intrinsic motivation, and emotion into the technology acceptance model. *Information Systems Research, 11*(4), 342–365.

Webster, J., & Martocchio, J. J. (1993). Turning work into play: Implications for microcomputer software training. *Journal of Management. 19,* 127–146.

Whitaker, L. A. (1998). Human navigation. In C. Forsythe, E. Grose, & J. Ratner (Eds.), *Human factors and Web development.* Mahwah, NJ: Lawrence Erlbaum Associates.

Wittgenstien, L. (1953). Philosophical investigations. New York: Macmillan.

Wood, F., Ford, N., Miller, D., Sobczyk, G., & Duffin, R. (1996). Information skills, searching behaviour and cognitive styles for student centered learning: A computer-assisted learning approach. *Journal of Information Science, 22*(2), 79–92.

Young, M. F., Kulikowich, J. M., & Barab, S. A. (1997). The unit of analysis for situated assessment. *Instructional Science, 25*(2), 133–150.

Zhang, H., & Salvendy, G. (2001). The implications of visualization ability and structure preview design for Web information search tasks. *International Journal of Human Computer Interaction, 13*(1), 75–95.

CHAPTER 11

The Changing Landscape of Text and Comprehension in the Age of New Literacies

BRIDGET DALTON

VANDERBILT UNIVERSITY, USA

C. PATRICK PROCTOR

BOSTON COLLEGE, USA

Our understanding of what it means to "understand" text is in the process of expanding to reflect a host of new literacies stimulated by accelerating advances in information communication technologies (ICTs) and accompanying changes in social practices and communities (Lankshear & Knobel, 2003; Luke & Freebody, 2000; Leu, Kinzer, Coiro, & Cammack, 2004). We are in a state of disequilibrium as we attempt to integrate our knowledge of reading comprehension based on print technology and the world of books with our emerging knowledge of comprehension in new literacies spaces such as hypertexts and Web sites. This time of change is both exhilarating and daunting, calling for different models of research and development, expanded interdisciplinary and international perspectives, and a more rapid research to practice timeline (Palincsar & Dalton, 2005).

We are faced with an urgent need to expand our understanding of print text, which is linear, static, temporally and physically bounded, often with clear purpose, authorship and authority, to reflect the characteristics of digital text, which is nonlinear, multimodal with a heavy visual orientation, interactive, unbounded in time and space, with murky conveyance of authorship and authority. There is the opportunity for digital text to "read the reader," collecting information through the user's interaction with the text and offering choices of content, help, and interaction accordingly (MacEneaney, 2006). Reciprocally, the user "reads the text environment" and makes active choices about the types of support, content, media, and participation options to access. The characteristics of digital text are made more dramatic on the Internet, where texts live in unbounded time and space and there is no limit to the linkages and paths that can be taken in search of information, entertainment, communication, and community. The use of integrated media is quite sophisticated, with unparalleled access to talent, expertise, experience, and beliefs, in ever-widening circles, from local to global community. Authorship and authority are more elusive, as the democratic space of the Web encourages unvetted publication, bypassing the review and editing processes of established publishing venues, and texts and sites are formed and reformed across multiple authors/designers and over time. Purpose is also less obvious, as websites often have multiple goals, layered and overlapping, overt and covert, in ways not typical of print.

In this new literacies landscape of digital text and the Web, how do we "understand understanding"? How do we teach students to read and understand these texts, becoming both critical consumers and producers? How do we create, or at least inform, the creation of texts designed for educational purposes so that they take advantage of the affordances of flexible digital technologies in service of increased opportunities and rigorous academic learning for diverse students? How do we support teachers so that they are prepared to teach with, about, and through these new texts? The purpose of this chapter is threefold: (a) to offer a scaffolded digital reading framework that reflects a universal design for learning perspective with research on digital- and print-based reading comprehension; (b) to highlight key research on digital text comprehension, much of which has focused on enhancing hypertexts with embedded supports and tools, and connect this work to reading in the context of Internet inquiry; and (c) to suggest practical next steps for applying scaffolded digital reading in the classroom while moving forward an aggressive research and development agenda. We begin the chapter with a brief overview of assumptions, terms, and theoretical perspectives, followed by the presentation of a strategic digital reading framework and review of selected research in key areas. For each area, we offer recommendations for research and practice. We conclude with a discussion of key issues facing the field and suggest priorities for future research and development.

Theoretical Perspectives and Assumptions

Core Assumptions about Diversity and Opportunity in a New Literacies Landscape

Two basic assumptions guide our thinking about designing and teaching for understanding in digital text environments. First, we assume that advances in this arena will require greater attention to issues of diversity and individual difference than has previously been the case, and that this shift in focus to a universal design perspective will produce benefits for the individual and for society (Rose & Meyer, 2002; Dalton & Proctor, 2007). Second, we hold the optimistic view that despite the increased complexities of new literacies spaces, these dynamic and flexible environments offer new opportunities to scaffold and level the playing field so that all individuals are contributing to and benefiting from expanded models of literacy. This should be possible as comprehension processes and outcomes evolve in concert with developing technologies and related social practices, reducing the importance of some reader factors, such as word recognition, that have traditionally operated as gatekeepers to literacy, and increasing the importance of other factors, such as self-regulation (Paris, Cross, & Lipson, 1984) and multimodal abilities (Kress, 2003). In the following section, we expand on these assumptions.

The central role of diversity and individual difference.   It is of paramount importance that digital texts and Web sites be designed to meet the needs of the widest spectrum of learners. This includes children with special needs, struggling readers, and children who speak English as a second language (whom we characterize as "bilingual"). We find this focus on diverse learners to be particularly fruitful. Innovation often takes place in the margins, be they cognitive, social, or linguistic, and is driven by individuals who experience the world in more divergent ways and who are in greatest need of changes to the status quo (Meyer & Rose, 2005).

The role of ICTs in leveling the playing field and promoting high levels of literacy.   While there is promising evidence that technology and digital texts improve students' reading achievement, they also present new challenges (for reviews, see Dalton & Strangman, 2006; National Reading Panel, 2000; MacArthur, Ferretti, Okolo, & Cavalier, 2001; Strangman & Dalton, 2005). For example, students who already struggle in the more constrained world of print may lack the reading speed and critical reading habits that are essential to effective reading on the Internet (Leu & Kinzer, 2000; Eagleton, Guinee, & Langlais, 2003). In addition, many immigrant children who enter school without having had the benefit of extended formal access to schooling, much less school-based Internet access, face a potentially steep ICT learning curve. Thus, it is important that we balance a sometimes romanticized view of new literacies opportunities with interactive learning designed to maximize affordances and minimize hindrances, learning all the while from individuals in the margins. At the very least, we must avoid creating new categories of disability. This notion is not too far-fetched when many at-risk students spend their computer time completing drill-and-practice programs rather than engaging in Internet-inquiry projects (Merrow, 2001).

However, notwithstanding our caution about romanticizing technology, we do, in fact, hold an optimistic view that ICTs are an important, and even essential, vehicle for improving reading and academic achievement for students who are not faring well in print-based schools. We think this is true for students with learning difficulties and language needs, as well as for students who are gifted and languishing within (or struggling against) unchallenging learning environments.

We acknowledge that the ways in which technologies are enacted in schools are purposeful and may maintain current inequities and sustain differential power relations. However, it is our hope that new literacies spaces will, by their very nature, require that issues of social justice and equity be addressed in literacy curricula and ways of "doing school" (Anstey & Bull, 2006). School is a controlled space, and school texts developed by educational publishing companies after intensive state and district screening to eliminate anything remotely controversial are controlled. Further, to some extent, schools are trying to control students' access to the Web, using filtering programs to block content that may be inappropriate and services that provide prevetted educational Web site content. However, the Web outside of school is not a controlled space; the texts are not controlled. This lack of control ups the literacy ante, requiring that students learn to be critical consumers—to deconstruct messages, to identify bias, to ask whose voice is represented, whose is not, and to what end? Critical consumers are also producers of their own messages, skillfully manipulating tools, text, and media with a heightened awareness of agency, audience, and purpose (Hobbs, 2006).

Defining Digital Text

For the purposes of this chapter, we are focusing on comprehension of digital text and approaches to improving comprehension with and through digital text. We do not examine the literature on software programs designed to teach reading comprehension through lessons and skill-building exercises. We will use the term digital text throughout the chapter; while useful, it can be confusing given the variety of things it represents. A digital text may be a linear text in digital format (e.g., a public-domain novel, *Call of the Wild*, by Jack London, retrieved from the online repository Project Guttenberg) , a nonlinear text with hyperlinks (e.g., a Web site about Jack London, with multiple links to other sites about the author, the Yukon, and the Gold Rush), a text with integrated media (e.g., one of the Jack London sites filled with photos, maps, drawings, and film clips from the movie *Call of the Wild*); and a text with response options (e.g., an invitation to join a discussion forum on adventure and how it manifests in the 21st century or to write an e-mail to the designer of a Web site devoted to London). In some cases, text represents a single text, but more often text includes multiple texts, and can be a Web site, a collection of Web sites, etc. The digital text may be client-side and closed (e.g., a CD-ROM Living Books story), or networked and either constrained or open (e.g., accessed via a server, which may or may not provide access to the Internet). Text is not restricted to written prose; text can be primarily visual, such as an animated graphic, video clip, photo slide show, or image with little accompanying verbal information, and verbal information may be presented in auditory rather than written format (e.g., click on a current events slide show and listen to the reporter's narration while viewing the photos). We will be using multiple meanings of this term, digital text, throughout our chapter.

Theoretical Perspectives

This chapter draws on multiple perspectives, an approach we find useful given the comprehensive nature of digital literacies (Labbo & Reinking, 1999). The Rand Reading Study Group's (Snow, 2002) model of reading comprehension serves as a base for conceptualizing a scaffolded digital-reading framework. We situate digital reading comprehension within a new literacies perspective (Lankshear & Knobel, 2003; Leu et al., 2004) and draw on perspectives from the fields of media education, information and library science, and cognitive science. For example, media education efforts have focused on teaching critical viewing and informed production of media messages (Hobbs, 2006), along with studies examining the varying effects of media formats on students' learning (Mayer, 2001). This work offers insight to how digital texts and media might be designed, and how to support students in developing a critical perspective when consuming or producing text/media. Information and library science specialists have taken the lead in thinking about the demands of locating and evaluating information on the Web, creating guidelines for evaluating Web content and developing various online and offline instructional activities to teach children how to search on the Web effectively (American Library Association, 2000). This work highlights characteristics of Web content and structures, suggesting strategies for supporting students in relation to these factors. And finally, cognitive and information scientists and literacy researchers are investigating how students interact with, and learn from digital-literacy environments, with particular attention to the relationships between learner characteristics, domains of study, and various features of the digital environment (McNamara, O'Reilly, Best, & Ozuru, 2006). This work has implications for how we design and teach students to use flexible learning environments that customize the text, activity, and sociocultural context in relation to goals and individual learners' needs and preferences. In addition to integrating knowledge across these disciplines and communities, we find it useful to apply a universal design for learning framework to the design and use of digital texts (Rose & Dalton, 2002; Dalton & Proctor, 2007). We expand on universal design in the next section.

researcher-designed texts with embedded learning supports for diverse learners. We propose a Scaffolded Digital Reading (SDR) framework for thinking about comprehension in new literacies spaces, since digital environments potentially offer a multitude of scaffolds for customizing individual comprehension processes and outcomes. Table 11.1 presents an overview of SDR, focusing on how reader factors morph in relation to text, activity, and context factors. In digital environments, reader, activity, and sociocultural factors can become properties of the digital text experience, changing the relationship of these factors to the advantage of the reader, facilitating access and productive participation in reading and learning. From a universal design perspective, digital features may be characterized in relation to the type of primary support provided: (a) representational (knowing what), (b) strategic (knowing how), and (c) affective (knowing and caring about the why).

Enhancing access and fluency. To read with understanding, the reader must be able to decode the words with a sufficient number of words automatized to allow for the fluency essential to comprehension. With print, students' word-recognition and fluency levels function as a gatekeeper, restricting access to those texts students can read independently, or when the purpose is instructional, read with some assistance from a teacher or more able peers. For struggling readers who are reading two or three grade levels below their grade placement, this essentially blocks access to the texts their peers read, with a resulting adverse impact on their learning and intellectual development (Stanovich, 1986), and engagement as readers and learners. However, digital text turns the concept of readability upside down because access to text is no longer dependent on students' word recognition and fluency levels (Edyburn, 2002; McKenna, Reinking, Labbo, & Kieffer, 1999). Students may use text-to-speech (TTS) or recorded human voice to have the text read aloud at the word, sentence, or passage level. For digital text, listening comprehension may well be a better indicator of the "readability" of the text (although listening and viewing written text is different from, and perhaps more productive than listening to text alone, and the two should not be considered interchangeable constructs). For students with limited fluency and age-appropriate language abilities, TTS and synthetic voice opens up a world of literature and information.

Recognizing the potential of TTS/voice to support struggling readers' comprehension, a number of researchers have investigated this digital tool. Some have been interested in using TTS to bypass decoding difficulties and provide access to content, employing TTS as a compensatory tool to assist in comprehension of a particular text. Others have investigated whether TTS might also serve as a learning tool, going beyond providing access to a particular text, to general improvement of reading comprehension of digital and print texts. In both cases, there is an assumption that offloading the word-recognition task

Table 11.1 Scaffolded Digital Reading (SDR)

Reader factor	Print text (fixed; within text)	Digital text (variable; within and across texts)	New strategies, knowledge and dispositions required for SDR
Word recognition and fluency	Reader's word recognition and fluency key factors in determining reading level and text choices	Read aloud functionality via Text-to-Speech/synthetic voice reduces impact of Reader's word recognition and fluency. Listening comprehension a better indicator of reading level and text choices	Print: Reader varies reading rate according to purpose and genre and applies strategies to decoding unfamiliar words SDR: Reader uses TTS/synthetic voice to access content, varying use in relation to purpose and need. Choices include level (listen to word, sentence, or passage), voice, and speed. Familiarity with tools provides greater options for support via synchronized highlighting and audio text marking.
Vocabulary	Reader's vocabulary knowledge strongest predictor of comprehension; Support via glossary, bolded words, call out boxes with definitions	Influence of Reader's vocabulary knowledge may be mediated by more extensive just-in-time vocabulary supports: Glossary hyperlinks, multimedia representations, access to online tools (e.g., dictionary, thesaurus, encyclopedia, and language translation); and access to social network of experts and peers	Print: Reader applies strategies for figuring out meaning in context, understands structural/graphic cues, and consults glossary as needed. SDR: Reader figures out words in context, integrates multimedia and verbal representations, and flexibly uses glossary and content hyperlinks, online vocabulary tools, and access to experts/peers. Constant updating of knowledge and skill required to keep pace with evolving tools, accompanied by adept social communication skills. Greater need for self-regulation and learning to learn orientation.
General and domain specific prior knowledge	Reader's prior knowledge of content and text structure predicts comprehension. Supplementary aids include graphics, graphic organizers, informational callouts, literary analysis notes, etc.	Influence of Reader's prior knowledge mediated by broader array of just-in-time support: layers of information via hyperlinks within and across hypertexts, multimedia representations, language translation, online encyclopedias, and content websites, tools for RSS feeds and indexing, and access to social network of experts and peers.	Print: Reader has minimal or no support for building prior knowledge with popular print. With educational print, Reader uses supplementary content aids to support weak background knowledge and draws on fixed set of text structures. SDR: Reader flexibly negotiates complex support environment of linked content resources, tools, multimedia, and access to social networks to build background knowledge. Structures are nonlinear and fluid, with more options available. Greater need for self-regulation and 'learning to learn' orientation.

(Continued)

Table 11.1 Scaffolded Digital Reading (SDR) (Continued)

Reader factor	Print text (fixed; within text)	Digital text (variable; within and across texts)	New strategies, knowledge and dispositions required for SDR
Conceptual understanding, inquiry and problem solving	All of PK supports may apply. Lists of resources to extend knowledge, discussion guide questions.	All of PK supports apply, in this case serving the goal of extending knowledge, conducting inquiry and solving problems. Increasing use of search engines to locate content. Inquiry projects and problem solving integrated into digital environment.	Print: Reader flexibly accesses informational resources within text in relation to purpose, and must generate own questions, find related texts externally, etc. SDR: Reader flexibly uses resources and tools described previously, but in an integrated environment where all phases can be conducted interactively and in non-linear fashion. Emphasis on locating information, evaluating information, synthesizing across multiple sources, and collaborative learning.
Cognitive and metacognitive strategies and self-efficacy	Limited strategic support offered. Some knowledge supports previously described serve as cognitive strategies (e.g., graphic organizers). Text may offer questions, main idea statements, summaries, as models of thinking processes and outcomes.	In addition to supports described above that serve as cognitive strategies, there are multiple tools, content, and social supports for strategic learning and self-efficacy. Interactive strategic reading help can be embedded at the text or browser level to prompt strategies and provide models, think alouds, and feedback. Multimedia illustrates dynamic processes, special interest groups share strategies and ways of being in the community.	Print: Reader primarily applies strategies independently in relation to purpose and text. When available, Reader uses strategy supports to aid learning. SDR: Reader flexibly uses tools and social resources to learn about strategies, apply strategies with guidance, and transfer use to independent reading. Requires knowledge of resources, as well as strong orientation to take charge of own learning in face of changing environments.
Affect (interest and motivation; note overlap with self-efficacy)	Reader's interest a function of topic, genre, author, quality of illustrations and aesthetics, writing quality, perceived relevance, text choice, purpose for reading, etc.	Reader's interest is mediated by factors described for print, plus options for multimedia, interactivity, social interaction, hyperlinked content, and choice of supports. Response and production can be seamlessly integrated to promote active involvement.	For both print and SDR, Reader must be able to self-motivate and find ways to develop interest in texts, topics, and tasks. SDR: Reader flexibly uses multiple means for engagement. Requires knowledge of resources and ability to adapt to fluid digital environments.

will free up students' cognitive capacity and allow them to engage more productively in constructing meaning. Whether TTS contributes to reading skill and transfers to print text is likely to be a function of several factors. First, and perhaps key, is how much text is read with TTS. For students whose access to grade-level text has been restricted, the opportunity to engage in sustained reading of multiple texts may contribute to their comprehension abilities generally. For transfer to print to occur, there would need to be some improvement in word recognition and fluency. If students are reading with TTS that has synchronized highlighting, so that they are both viewing and listening to the words simultaneously, it seems reasonable to predict that there would be some improvement in word recognition if sufficiently large quantities of text are processed. Second, the gap between the readability of the text read with TTS and students' instructional reading level of print text may be a factor. A fourth-grade student whose instructional reading level is grade three and who uses TTS to access fourth-grade level text might experience TTS more as a learning tool. In contrast, an eighth-grade student reading on a third-grade level might experience TTS primarily as a compensatory tool. Third, other learner characteristics are likely to affect the outcome, such as language and cognitive abilities, metacognition, and self-efficacy. For example, a recent 16-year-old immigrant who has low levels of literacy in his first language and is reading English on a third-grade level might find that TTS is of limited help in accessing and understanding 10th-grade texts replete with unfamiliar vocabulary and concepts. Finally, a student unused to making choices about accessing help might over or under access TTS, reducing the learning potential.

Unfortunately, the research in this area has not addressed these issues systematically, and the results are variable, with some studies finding positive effects on comprehension and others finding no effect (for a review, see Strangman & Dalton, 2005). There is tremendous variation in the TTS or voice conditions, types of texts, conditions for accessing read aloud help, and formats for providing help. Further, some studies focused on young, beginning readers, while others targeted adolescent readers, and some assessed comprehension only within the read-aloud text condition, and others measured comprehension of both digital and print conditions. Of particular interest is Elkind, Cohen, and Murray (1993) study of adolescent readers with dyslexia. These students read digital literature with TTS over the course of a semester. The authors reported that students were able to engage productively with the literature, and that 70% of the students improved comprehension on a TTS-supported version of the Gray Oral Reading Test by approximately one grade level. For some, the gain was more dramatic, with 40% gaining two to five grade levels on the test. The issue of learner's age was investigated by Lundberg and Oloffson (1993), who found that TTS positively impacted the older students in the study, grade 4 to 6 students with reading disabilities, while having no effect on younger students in grades 2 to 3. The teachers in this study thought that TTS might have been more helpful to the older students, because they were experiencing more of a gap between the readability of the text and their reading-skill level than the younger students. McKenna (1998) and McKenna & Watkins' research (1994) suggested another possible explanation—young students may be less able to determine when they need TTS support, either over or underaccessing support.

In our own research, we have developed several hypertexts with embedded supports, including TTS with synchronized highlighting, strategy instruction, and vocabulary. Results from a study with struggling adolescent readers (Dalton, Pisha, Eagleton, Coyne, & Deysher, 2002) indicated improvement in comprehension, with transfer to an unsupported standardized reading achievement test. It is not possible to know the role of TTS in this improvement, given the multiple supports; however, the hypertexts were far above students' reading levels and were used over several months. Observations and interviews with these adolescent readers strongly suggested that reading engaging, age-appropriate novels was quite motivating, as was the opportunity to focus on the meaning of the text without worrying about lack of fluency. In fact, when asked to rate the usefulness of several features, TTS received the highest positive rating among consistently positive ratings of features (Dalton et al., 2002).

Given the conflicting research findings on TTS and read-aloud support, additional research is needed. However, it seems reasonable to predict that older readers will benefit more than younger readers, and that short-term interventions will be less helpful than longer term interventions.

Read aloud functionality and Internet inquiry. Researchers who focus on students' searching and reading on the Internet typically have not considered the role of TTS or the human voice in providing struggling readers access to information that is grade/age appropriate, but above their reading level. (Note that some of the hypertext research just described is delivered via the Internet, but we consider that to be a different context of use and type of digital text.) In fact, TTS is not mentioned as a factor in Kuiper, Volman, and Terwel's (2005) comprehensive review of the literature on strategies to support students' learning on the Web. From a UDL perspective, we would advocate that TTS be ubiquitous, as common a tool as a pencil. Conducting inquiry on the Web is reading intensive, including generating search terms and browsing, critically reading search results and selecting sites, skimming sites for relevance and credibility, selectively reading information chunks within and across sites, reading embedded hyperlinks, reading navigation menus and text structure cues, reading help information, and so forth. If inquiry and knowledge building are the learning goals, why not offload word-recognition tasks via TTS so that students may focus on reading for meaning, whether it be reading search results, hyperlinks, or more lengthy prose segments? It may be that the current reliance on an independent reading model is simply a holdover from print-based models of successful readers and that it will soon be accepted practice for readers to avail themselves of access tools like TTS. The research on K–12 students' Internet searching and use of information consistently documents that students rarely go beyond a superficial level of searching and engage in minimal reading of actual content (Kuiper et al., 2005). We do not yet know how these processes would be mediated by a TTS tool that changes reading to a hybridized reading-listening process. For struggling readers, TTS changes the readability of the text, giving them increased access to grade-level content (something that is mandated in the United States by the IDEA, 1997, 2006, for students who are considered print disabled). For average readers, a TTS tool might increase their processing speed, a factor considered to be of greater importance on the Web (Leu et al., 2004).

Summary. Clearly, there is a need for further research on read-aloud functionality so that we better understand the relationship between word recognition, fluency, and comprehension in digital environments. At the same time, we recommend that schools and parents move forward now on including TTS as a default tool to support students' access to content in digital format and on the Internet. Just as oral language in the classroom supports literacy learning, the use of TTS and human voice can support literacy learning in digital environments. However, students will need to be taught strategies for using TTS flexibly in relation to needs and task demands.

Enhancing Vocabulary

Reading comprehension is also a function of readers' depth and breadth of vocabulary knowledge; good readers know many more words than struggling readers, and are better able to use contextual cues and morphological knowledge to determine word meaning (Nagy & Scott, 2004). Vocabulary support via hyperlinks to a glossary or annotation is commonplace in hypertext environments, with the assumption that readers will benefit from just-in-time support. It is difficult to assess the unique contribution of vocabulary support to hypertext comprehension, since these supports are often combined with other reading supports.

The most systematic and focused exploration has been in the field of foreign-language learning, where the vocabulary-learning load is quite heavy, especially when reading authentic literature. It is also an opportune context in which to study the effects of multimedia, since it is fairly easy to manipulate representational forms, for example, comparing the effects of verbal, visual, and both verbal-visual information on student learning. Although this research has generally been conducted with college-level students who have high levels of first-language literacy to draw upon, as well as more developed metacognitive skills, the results suggested implications for instructional design with younger learners.

Plass and colleagues have conducted a series of studies to extend Mayer's (1997) generative theory of multimedia learning to address the role of individual differences in abilities and preferences when learning in a second-language multimedia environment (Plass, Chun, Mayer, & Leutner, 1998, 2003). They constructed a hypertext version of an authentic German short story with key word annotations that were either verbal (see a translation of the word in English) or visual (view a picture or video clip representing the word) or both. Consistent with other research on the benefits of multimodal representation, they found that students remembered word translations best when they selected both visual and verbal annotations (Plass et al., 1998). For the more complex task of recalling the story, individual preferences for verbal or visual information came into play, with students understanding better when they received their preferred form of representation, and especially if they were visualizers. In a follow-up study, Plass et al. (2003) manipulated students' access to the media representations to investigate the relationship between student characteristics (e.g., verbal and spatial abilities) and media format of the annotation (e.g., verbal, visual, both verbal and visual, or none). The multimedia effect held true, with students generally demonstrating better vocabulary learning and comprehension when presented both visual and verbal annotations. Results also varied as a function of learner characteristics and format. Low-verbal and low-spatial-ability students learned fewer word translations than their high-verbal and high-spatial-abilities peers when the annotation was visual only; however, they performed comparably when they received verbal annotations, suggesting that this was an easier learning format. For the more difficult story recall task, both high- and low-ability learners did least well when presented with visual-only annotations. From a cognitive-load perspective, this suggests that even when students have strong spatial abilities and may do well with, and enjoy, visual information, that visual information without any accompanying verbal information may draw on cognitive resources at the expense of higher order thinking, such as constructing a coherent model of a story.

We know little about students learning from vocabulary hyperlinks in texts designed for K–12 learners, although such resources are commonplace (Higgins & Boone, 1996; Horney & Anderson-Inman, 1994; MacArthur & Haynes, 1995; Reinking & Schriener, 1985). If we consider studies that include vocabulary support in combination with other reading supports, the results are generally positive, although it is not possible to determine which supports are contributing to the improved vocabulary learning.

Focusing on primary-grade children, Mostow and colleagues (2003) at Project Listen have been developing an intelligent Reading Tutor that supports children as they read text via speech recognition and feedback, verbal and graphical vocabulary information, and embedded questions. Again, supports are confounded, but the overall experience has produced stronger vocabulary gains for grade 2 to 3 children in comparison to peers receiving human tutoring (Mostow et al., 2003). In a study focused on vocabulary learning, Aist (2002) adapted the Reading Tutor to enrich texts with automatically generated vocabulary factoids that provided information about the word and asked a question encouraging students to relate the information to the use of the word in the story context. In comparison to classroom instruction and individual oral reading with an adult, third-grade children reading with the Reading Tutor made significantly greater vocabulary gains than their peers; however, no differences were found for second graders.

Consistent with other research on students' accessing of supplemental information (MacArthur & Haynes, 1995), we found that students tended to underaccess vocabulary links provided in digital novels, although they considered them to be useful, particularly when the definition was accompanied by a graphic (Dalton et al., 2002). Further, some teachers were somewhat reticent to encourage students to access glossary hyperlinks, believing that doing so interrupted the flow of the comprehension process. These kinds of concerns point to the need to better understand the relationship between vocabulary learning and comprehension processes within complex digital environments—when are interruptions helpful, under what circumstances, and for which learners? When are they legitimate cause for concern?

Another factor that may contribute to students' underutilization of vocabulary links is a perception that vocabulary learning is not directly relevant to the task at hand, that is, reading the text. In a recent pilot study of fourth-grade Spanish-English bilingual and English monolingual students reading folktale and informational hypertexts with embedded strategy instruction and vocabulary support, we changed what had essentially been a passive vocabulary experience in our previous hypertexts, providing glossary hyperlinks, to a more active experience (Proctor, Dalton, & Grisham, 2007). This was accomplished via a prereading activity that presented multiple representations of the word and asked students to draw on their own experience to create an association with the word, which they typed and added to their electronic "My Glossary." In addition, during reading, students selected a minimum of three words per text to add to their personal glossary, typing an explanation for their choice. Pedagogical agents were available to provide models and think alouds. Finally, after reading each text, students completed vocabulary assessments designed to tap different levels of vocabulary understanding. This approach did lead to more use of vocabulary supports than we had found previously, as captured by an event usage-tracking log, and higher use was positively associated with vocabulary gain on a standardized reading vocabulary test. Further, those students with lower initial reading achievement tended to use more supports, a finding in contradiction to other research indicating that those in most need of support are less likely to access it appropriately (Horney & Anderson Inman, 1999). While it is not possible to discern the relative contributions of the two types of support (i.e., multimedia representation, personal associations, and active construction of personal glossaries), case studies of bilingual children who made dramatic gains on a standardized reading vocabulary test point to a high level of engagement and personal investment in learning new words.

Vocabulary and Internet inquiry. Students encounter a wide range of vocabulary when carrying out an inquiry task on the Internet. In addition to reading search-result listings, they read URLs containing embedded words, acronyms, and abbreviations signaling the topic and type of site. Once they arrive at a site, students read vocabulary related to structural and interaction elements, as well as content words within the text and related media. They must also understand hyperlinked words within the text on two levels: (a) the immediate meaning within the text, and (b) the meaning in relation to its linked destination. The latter is important since it guides the user in selecting productive links. While the vocabulary level within a site may be somewhat controlled for the intended audience, the inclusion of technical terms related to Internet use and the open access to other sites that are not controlled for vocabulary, substantially increases the complexity of vocabulary demands. Research on students' understanding and use of vocabulary in an Internet inquiry context is a relatively unexplored area. Kamil and Lane's (1998) study of students' understanding of hyperlinks indicated students have difficulty predicting the usefulness of hyperlinks. However, it is not clear whether this difficulty is due to unfamiliarity with the basic meaning of the word, or the meaning of the word as a signal to additional content on the Web.

Vocabulary supports are also available to users on the Internet. First, students may access an online dictionary, thesaurus, or encyclopedia. Some resources are designed for younger students, while others are more appropriate for teenagers. Second, there are free tools such as VoyCabulary that will turn any word on a Web site into a link so that you may access a definition without leaving the text. Third, language-translation tools such as Babel Fish allow bilingual students to view a word or text segment in their first language. Fourth, unfamiliar words may be hyperlinked to explanatory information. Fifth, if students perceive the word meaning as essential to accomplishing an important task, they may take advantage of various "Ask the Expert" forums, or may simply email or instant message a query to a classmate. Finally, the same type of multimedia vocabulary supports just described for digital texts would apply to vocabulary on the Internet.

Note that the first five options require strategic knowledge about how things work on the Internet, and specifically, knowledge of tools and social resources (which are in a state of flux and change). This type of knowledge is typically not taught in the classroom, and in fact, teachers may have limited experience using these tools themselves.

Summary. Studies of vocabulary learning in digital contexts demonstrate the value of multimedia representations and access to word meanings at the point of use in text. However, there has been little empirical research on students' understanding of vocabulary in the more complex context of Internet inquiry, where words are used for multiple purposes—to convey information about content, links to related information, and information on navigation, digital tools, resources, and communities. Further, we know little about the vocabulary-learning strategies that students are bringing to bear in these new literacies spaces. We believe that this is a critical area for inquiry, given the prominent role that vocabulary plays in comprehension and successful learning. At the same time, we advocate that teachers move forward now to teach students Internet vocabulary and strategies for figuring out words in relation to their meaning and function within digital environments, as well as introducing them to online dictionary and thesaurus tools.

Enhancing Comprehension and Strategic Reading

Researchers interested in the potential of digital environments generally have focused on representational and strategic supports. For example, linking to background knowledge, providing a graphic, video, or animation, including an audio-narration track, are all representations, expanding the number and type of pathways into content. If the learner doesn't understand a written verbal description of the water cycle, he or she may listen to the passage read aloud, view a graphic illustrating the water cycle, or observe a video clip showing the impact of droughts in sub-Saharan Africa. For some learners, the written text will suffice; for others, the media will be more supportive of comprehension. For many, it is likely that a multimedia experience will be most helpful (Mayer, 2001).

In addition to offering multiple representations, some researchers have focused on embedding supports for strategic learning within digital environments (Boone & Higgins, 1993; Dalton & Proctor, 2007; Reinking & Schreiner, 1985; Salomon, Globerson, & Guterman, 1989). Successful readers are strategic, flexibly deploying a range of strategies to help them accomplish a variety of reading and learning tasks. They monitor comprehension and goal attainment and take corrective action as needed. The general goal of digital-strategic support is to help learners apply a more strategic approach to understanding a particular text, while simultaneously supporting them in developing and internalizing strategies and dispositions that can be applied to other nonsupported texts. In the remainder of this section, we first highlight work on multimedia representations, and then consider research on strategic learning.

Multimedia learning. When considering the role of multimedia and the potential to enhance students' conceptual understanding and knowledge building,

Mayer's work with animation is particularly instructive (for a summary, see Mayer, 1997, 2001). Mayer's generative theory of multimedia learning posits that the learner actively constructs meaning by selecting and processing visual and verbal information. Following Paivio's (1986) dual-coding theory, visual and verbal information are processed via separate channels. According to Mayer, visual information is selected and organized into a coherent visual mental representation, while verbal information is correspondingly selected and organized into a coherent verbal mental representation. Meaningful multimedia learning occurs when connections are made between the visual and verbal representations to form an integrated knowledge model. Based on extensive research demonstrating positive learning effects of animations and other multimedia, Mayer developed seven design principles: (a) Multimedia principle: students derive greater benefit from visual and verbal presentations than from either presented alone; (b) Spatial contiguity principle—students benefit when visual and verbal information is located in close, rather than far, proximity to one another to aid processing; (c) Temporal contiguity principle—students benefit when visuals and corresponding verbal information is presented simultaneously, rather than in sequence; (d) Coherence principle—Students benefit when presentation is restricted to relevant information, eliminating extraneous content; (e) Modality principle—Students benefit from animations with accompanying oral narration, rather than written narration; (f) Redundancy principle—Students benefit from animations with accompanying oral narration; however, providing both oral and written narration is not helpful; (g) Individual differences principle—Learner characteristics, such as domain knowledge and spatial ability, mediate design effects. This work has obvious relevance to the design of digital text and readers' comprehension. Palincsar and Dalton (2005) pointed out that two caveats are in order when applying Mayer's work to K–12 learning: first, Mayer's research has been conducted primarily with university students and may not hold true for younger learners; second, the work is laboratory-based, testing effects of short-term manipulations in decontextualized contexts (e.g., students view a 30-second animation and are then tested for comprehension). Some of the effects consistently found by Mayer and colleagues (Mayer, 2001; Plas, Chun, Mayer, & Leutner, 2003) may not apply when students use a multimedia environment over time to engage in sustained inquiry or in-depth learning.

In addition to viewing animations, it is also possible for learners to manipulate objects and events depicted in graphics so as to better understand the underlying phenomena. In collaboration with Palincsar, we are studying the role of interactive diagrams and pedagogical agents in supporting fifth-grade readers' comprehension and knowledge building from informational text (Palincsar & Dalton, 2005). Comparison of students' learning from three different versions of a multimedia text on "Light and Vision" indicates that students reading with interactive diagrams and pedagogical agents demonstrated significantly greater vocabulary and concept learning than did their peers reading the same texts with text-to-speech read-aloud functionality and hyperlinked glossary items. Further, the stronger readers appeared to use the pedagogical agents more effectively to support their learning

Strategic reading. Salomon et al. (1989) set the stage for this line of inquiry, developing the Reading Partner, a metacognitive tool to guide 7th-grade students as they read various types of texts. He viewed the computer as a zone of proximal development that could scaffold readers in process so that they internalized metacognitive reading skills that would result in improved comprehension. The control group read the digital text without support; the content question group read the texts with multiple-choice literal and inferential questions that were content related, but not metacognitive; and the Reading Partner group read texts offering metacognitive guidance in the form of general self-guiding questions concerning ways to be a good reader; introduction of four specific strategies (generating an inference from the title; identifying key sentences; engaging in mental imagery; and creating intermediate summaries), along with examples, and repeated presentations of self-monitoring questions. Students were encouraged to read the questions and write a detailed response. The Reading Partner group outperformed the other two groups on a written essay, a standardized reading comprehension test, and a written test of metacognitive reconstruction. Salomon et al. attributed these positive outcomes to the greater mental effort expended by members of the Reading Partner group and their internalization of the metacognitive strategies, as evidenced by increased time spent reading and positive correlation of reading comprehension and the metacognitive reconstruction test outcomes.

Others have continued to investigate the role of strategic support, in concert with representational supports. The majority of these studies have demonstrated a positive impact on students' comprehension for a wide range of learners in elementary, middle-school and high-school grades reading narratives and informational texts (for a review, see Dalton & Strangman, 2005). Strategic supports included such things as main-idea statements (Reinking & Schreiner, 1985), model summaries (MacArthur & Haynes, 1995 Dalton et al., 2002; Proctor et al., in press), visual highlighting of key information, or relations between information (MacArthur & Haynes, 1995; Higgins, Boone, & Lovitt, 1996), and embedded questions or strategy prompts (Anderson-Inman, Horney, Chen, & Lewin, 1994; Dalton et al., 2002; MacArthur & Haynes, 1995; Proctor et al., in press). Two studies, one employing a rereading feature (Swanson & Trahan, 1992) and the other reading-awareness prompts (Leong, 1995) did not yield positive results.

There is some debate as to whether strategic learning aids should be considered scaffolds if the provision of a prompt, explanation or model response allows students to perform at a more advanced level than they would have otherwise. Some contend the answer depends on whether the aid lessens as competence increases, to the point that it is removed altogether and the student performs independently. The presence of the scaffold is contingent upon performance feedback, which is either provided by the system or the learner, or both. Not much attention has been paid to this aspect of developing strategic reading. In a series of studies of hypertext with embedded strategy instruction, we (Dalton et al., 2002; Proctor et al., in press) have taken a middle position, offering several levels of strategy support and collecting students' qualitative-response data so that students and teachers can make decisions about whether to move up or down a level. As students read (or listen via TTS or human voice) to the text, they are periodically prompted to apply a strategy—make a prediction, ask a question, seek clarification, summarize, visualize, make a personal response, or self-evaluate progress. The leveling of the scaffolds is manipulated in three ways: (a) varying the response format (open, constructed and closed), (b) transforming the text (highlighting salient information in the text, listing key information), and (c) varying the level of help offered by computer agent coaches (text specific vs. generic models and think alouds). Results indicate the overall support system generally leads to improved comprehension and engagement of struggling readers. To what extent these particular scaffolds are necessary, we don't know. It may be that fewer levels, or different levels, would produce the same results. Perhaps what is key is that there are levels—that students and teachers know that support is variable, related to need and performance, and that it is possible to customize a personal support system in service of the larger goals of comprehension, engagement, and increasing self-efficacy.

The potential of computer agents to take on the role of instructional coach is an area ripe for further exploration as it becomes increasingly feasible to design an interaction system including the learner, coach, text, and activity whereby the coach mediates the relationships among the components to enhance learning and engagement. Intelligent tutoring, as demonstrated in the I-Start reading comprehension program (McNamara et al, 2006), represents a successful model of strategic instruction using pedagogical agents.

Understanding, strategic reading, and inquiry on the Internet. Alvermann (2002), O'Brien (2001), and Leander (2004) offered compelling portraits of adolescents enacting new literacies in and out of school who were motivated by high interest in a topic of personal relevance and the creative experience of constructing and communicating in new media, often on the Internet. However, we know little about students' comprehension on the Internet. The majority of this research has focused on students' search processes, highlighting the difficulty they encounter generating a research question, creating key search terms, and critically evaluating search results (for a review, see Kuiper et al., 2005). There are limited studies focusing on the next step—what happens when students have found (or are directed to) an appropriate Web site rich with information, media, and interactivity, or a set of such Web sites? Research with adults suggested that reading a Web page is a skimming activity, with occasional plunges into close readings of deep pools of information, depending on the purpose for reading. In a review of research on learning on the Internet, Kuiper et al. (2005) found that students also skim Web sites, often engaging in answer-grabbing techniques, even when the task calls for a more thoughtful and sustained approach. Synthesizing across sites and communicating what you have learned to an audience also poses tremendous challenges. Further, it is not clear to what extent these studies connected students to the variety of tools, resources, and supports designed to promote knowledge building and strategic learning that are outlined in Table 11.1. Eagleton and Castek are tackling this complex problem in different ways. Castek (2005) applied "reciprocal teaching" (Palincsar & Brown, 1984) and "questioning the author" (McKeown, Beck, & Worthy, 1993) strategies to students' inquiry on the Internet. The Internet content serves as the text, and instructional conversations focus on applying these strategies in relation to inquiry processes and knowledge building. This work is in its initial stages; however, preliminary results suggest that students benefit from this kind of instruction and guided practice. Eagleton et al. (2003) also found that middle- and high-school students benefited from a technology-based approach that combined use of a researcher-developed online search tool that guided students in framing a question, generating key terms, and evaluating Web site information, with offline instruction about effective searching and inquiry techniques. A third approach is represented by our work developing and studying a Strategy Tutor browser tool bar that encourages students to apply strategies for comprehension, Web evaluation, critical literacy, and self-reflection as they read on the Internet (Dalton, Hupert, Proctor, Robinson, & Ge, 2005). Students may conduct open-ended searches, or complete a Web-based activity with teacher-authored customized supports for strategies, background knowledge, and vocabulary. We hope to learn whether a tool like this helps bridge the gap between specialized hypertexts designed by researchers and publishers and the open territory of the Internet, where both the content and the activity are unbounded.

Summary. The research on multimedia and supported hypertexts with representational and strategic supports has generally shown positive effects on students' learning. The research on comprehension on the Internet suggests that while students enjoy using the Internet, they encounter difficulties with all aspects of Internet inquiry and new literacies processes. There is a small body of research focusing on improving instruction and developing online tools to support students in this area. Given students' limited opportunities for learning and developing new literacies, it seems premature to characterize reading and inquiry on the Internet as intensely difficult. And, in fact, there are numerous anecdotal accounts of highly successful Internet projects that engage students in reading, viewing, and producing sophisticated digital products. There is a need to conduct research that connects these strands of research on hypertexts and Internet inquiry, and to consider the role of supported Internet-inquiry tools. In the meantime, we recommend that teachers move forward in integrating both kinds of digital comprehension and new literacies into their curriculum, with special attention to developing diverse learners' strategic reading.

Supporting Engagement

The role of affect comes into play on multiple fronts as we consume, interact with, and create meaning in new literacies spaces, using expanded tools for manipulating the emotional impact of our messages. Issues of style, mood, and tone are interwoven along visual, verbal, and interactive dimensions. A scaffolded digital-reading perspective suggests these dimensions are all important and varying configurations can be equally effective in achieving a particular goal, although measurement of goal attainment might be more challenging when there are so many possible combinations of media and interactivity. Perhaps the most dramatic examples can be found in advertising, where the same message can be conveyed with different attention to visual, verbal, and interactive features, depending on the publication vehicle and its targeted audience—a teen magazine, a Discovery channel TV ad, a bill board in the center of the electronics district of Tokyo, and a popular culture Web site. With regard to media consumption and design, media educators have led the way, focusing attention on the methods and purposes, often from a critical literacies stance that questions the intent and methods in relation to how they reflect power relationships and status in the larger society (Hobbs, 2006). Kress (2003) developed a grammar of visual design, and there are numerous how-to books on effective Web design. It seems that practice and art may take a more prominent role in this new literacies space. Just as there is a cognitive advantage to being bilingual, it seems reasonable to expect there is also an advantage to being multimodal—and that learning through, with, and about these various languages, in varying weighted combinations of representation, will be core to new literacies achievement.

In the previous sections, we described digital text approaches and features that support engagement, such as use of multimedia, focus on strategic learning and self-regulation, multiple opportunities for choice, leveled support, diverse means of expression, etc. There are two major affective issues related to representation and communication. The first one relates to individual preferences and prior experiences with various formats: Do I aspire to be a film director and think in terms of moving images? Have I had success as a reader? Do I come from a culture that values oratory and listening skills? In each case, students' experience, values, and skills will influence the choices they make in a multimedia environment, their willingness to persist and invest sustained attention, and finally, the learning outcomes. The second affective issue is whether various media and forms of representation have a differential impact on interest, and in some cases, caring and personal connection. It is one thing to be interested in how the water cycle operates; it is another to have one's curiosity awakened such that it stimulates caring and further action on the part of the learner, leading to seeking out information on global warming and its effect on the water cycle, applying water conservation measures at home, or inventing a new irrigation tool that reduces water run off in high-density developments.

Engagement and Internet inquiry. Clearly, Internet inquiry offers many of the features associated with motivation and engagement, as described previously. Goal setting and choice is a key affective issue, one that is particularly thorny for two different reasons. First, in the unbounded space of the Internet, choices must be made continually about what to learn, how to learn it, and how to communicate that learning. Further, the choice options will continue to evolve, requiring a continual retooling of the learner's choice-making schema and related skills and a disposition toward learning how to learn in ambiguous situations. Thus, teaching for choice and monitoring of goal accomplishment seems critically important for scaffolded digital reading and new literacies. Second, ICTs increasingly have the power to make choices for the learner, reading the student, the text demands, and the activity, and serving up a customized learning space. It points to a future where learners might have less choice, and perhaps fewer opportunities for development and untapping of potential. From an educational perspective, it seems reasonable to predict that constrained choice will be a productive route to follow when students are novice learners, since that is characteristic of successful learning in a variety of domains and apprenticeship. Of course, the challenge is to determine what the constraints should be, under what conditions, for which learners, and for how long. To promote strategic learning and heighten self-efficacy, it would be helpful to make the choice structure visible and explicit so that students are learning about choice and decision making in the context of Internet inquiry.

Summary. Students tend to find reading and learning in digital environments engaging, and as digital natives, they are comfortable interacting with these environments. However, research on academic learning tasks suggests that engagement is often at a superficial level. Research is needed to systematically investigate the ways in which text, activity, and context variables can be manipulated to provide differential affective supports to diverse learners. At the same time, we recommend that teachers move forward in using digital text and the Internet in ways that are more likely to take advantage of features most likely to enhance engagement, such as choice, interactivity, multimedia, and social networking.

Conclusion

The new literacies are not so much a space as an open landscape replete with potential for charting new paths toward learning and achievement. We have drawn on the work of the Rand Study Group (Snow, 2002) to highlight that comprehension occurs at the intersection of the reader, the text, and the activity, all within a distinct sociocultural setting. However, in a scaffolded digital environment, the nature of text is expanded. That is, the digital system that houses a text may contain any number of embedded features, tools, and social networks, which can be accessed by readers in order to scaffold their reading experience. By providing these types of supports, the role of text is increased in relation to the reader and the activity, thus increasing the intersection between reader, text, and activity, and promoting improved comprehension outcomes for students who can make appropriate use of the system. On the Internet, these scaffolds might be external to the text, such as a tagging tool or dictionary, as well as internal to the text in the form of embedded coaches and multimedia representations.

Yet, in order for the role of the text to be expanded as we suggest, learners must avail themselves of the affordances offered. This is not a simple matter, given the evolving nature of digital tools and texts, and the complexities of new literacies. First, learners must be aware of what is available. Second, they must select, use, and monitor scaffolds strategically to accomplish different purposes within and across diverse multimedia texts. While educators agree that "learning how to learn" is core to success in a digital-literacies landscape, little is known about how to develop the relevant knowledge, skills, and dispositions. Issues of choice and self-regulation are central here, and should be a priority for research. Research and development is also needed to develop a more robust model of comprehension that reflects the dynamic nature of text in digital environments and addresses the nature of scaffolding and learning how to learn with customizable texts and tools. We propose a scaffolded digital reading model, situated in a universal design for learning perspective (Rose & Meyer, 2002), as a useful framework for conceptualizing supports to reduce barriers and expand students' capacities for understanding, expression and engagement. It also supports an important social justice goal of inclusion for all learners.

Within the sociocultural realm, recent research indicates that some schools are becoming centers for the development of digital literacies. Children from poor families have significantly less access to computers and the Internet at home in comparison to their more affluent counterparts. However, the access differential is eliminated at school, at least in relation to computer and Internet access (National Center for Education Statistics, 2003). Thus, the challenge is to continue to advance our understanding of what constitutes meaningful engagement with and exploration of the new literacies landscape. We have the infrastructure in place to make access to high-quality scaffolded digital-reading environments a reality for all students, which presents a real opportunity to make a significant impact on the sociocultural environments in which students find themselves on a daily basis. This is the landscape and our newest, and most exciting, frontier.

References

Aist, G. (2002). Helping children learn vocabulary during computer-assisted oral reading [Electronic version]. *Educational Technology and Society, 5*(2).

Alvermann, D. E. (Ed.). (2002). *Adolescents and literacies in a digital world.* New York: Peter Lang Publishing.

American Library Association. (2000). Information literacy competency standards for education. Retrieved September 30, 2006, from http://www.ala.org/ala/acrlstandards/informationliteracycompetency.htm

Anderson-Inman, L., & Horney, M. A. (1998). Transforming text for at-risk readers. In D. Reinking & M. C. McKenna (Eds.), *Handbook of literacy and technology: Transformations in a post-typographic world.* (pp. 15–43). Mahwah, NJ: Lawrence Erlbaum Associates.

Anderson-Inman, L., & Horney, M. A., Chen, D., & Lewin, L. (1994). Hypertext literacy: Observations from the electrotext project. *Language Arts, 71*(4), 37–45.

Anstey, M., & Bull, G. (2006). *Teaching and learning multiliteracies: Changing times, changing literacies.* Newark, DE: International Reading Association and Australian Literacy Educators' Association.

Castek, J. (2005). *Internet reciprocal teaching: Connecting print and new literacies in a science inquiry project.* Paper presented at the 55th National Reading Conference, Miami, FL.

Coiro, J. (2003). Reading comprehension on the Internet: Expanding our understanding of reading comprehension to encompass new literacies. *The Reading Teacher, 56,* 458–464.

Dalton, B., Hupert, N., Proctor, C. P., Robinson, K., & Vue, G. (2005). *Scaffolding strategic reading and viewing of multimedia Websites.* Paper presented at the 55th National Reading Conference, Miami, FL.

Dalton, B., Pisha, B., Eagleton, M., Coyne, P., & Deysher, S. (2002). *Engaging the text: Reciprocal teaching and questioning strategies in a scaffolded learning environment. Final report to the U.S. Department of Education, Office of Special Education Programs.* Peabody, MA: CAST.

Dalton, B., & Proctor, P. (2007). Reading as thinking: Integrating strategy instruction in a universally designed digital literacy environment. In D. S. McNamara (Ed.), *Reading comprehension strategies: Theories, interventions, and technologies.* (pp. 423–442). Mahwah, NJ: Lawrence Erlbaum Associates.

Dalton, B., & Strangman, N. (2006). Improving struggling readers' comprehension through scaffolded hypertexts and other computer-based literacy programs. In D. Reinking, M. C. McKenna, L. D. Labbo, & R. D. Keiffer (Eds.), *Handbook of literacy and technology* (2nd ed.). Mahwah, NJ: Lawrence Erlbaum Associates.

Eagleton, M. B., Guinee, K., & Langlais, K. (2003). Teaching Internet literacy strategies: The hero inquiry project. *Voices from the Middle, 10*(3), 28–35.

Edyburn, D. L. (2002, April/May). Cognitive rescaling strategies: Interventions that alter the cognitive accessibility of text. *Closing the Gap, 1,* 10–11, 21.

Edyburn, D. L. (2005). A primer on universal design in education. Retrieved September 30, 2006, from http://www.uwm.edu/~edyburn/ud.html

Elkind, J., Cohen, K., & Murray, C. (1993). Using computer-based readers to improve reading comprehension of students with dyslexia. *Annals of Dyslexia, 43,* 238–259.

Higgins, K., Boone, R., & Lovitt, T. (1996). Hypertext support for remedial students and students with learning disabilities. *Journal of Learning Disabilities, 29*(4), 402–412.

Hobbs, R. (2006). Multiple visions of multimedia literacy: Emerging areas of synthesis. In M. C. McKenna, L. D. Labbo, R. D. Keiffer, & D. Reinking (Eds.), *International handbook of literacy and technology* (Vol. 2, pp. 15–28). Mahwah, NJ: Lawrence Erlbaum Associates.

Horney, M. A., & Anderson-Inman, L. (1994). The electrotext project: Hypertext reading patterns of middle school students. *Journal of Educational Multimedia and Hypermedia, 3*(1), 71–91.

Horney, M. A., & Anderson-Inman, L. (1999). Supported text in electronic reading environments. *Reading & Writing Quarterly, 15*(2), 127–168.

Individuals with Disabilities Education Act (IDEA) Amendments of 1997, Public Law No. 105–17, 20 U.S.C. § 1400 (1997).

Kamil, M. L., & Lane, D. (1998). Researching the relationship between technology and literacy: An agenda for the 21st century. In D. Reinking, M. C. McKenna, L. D. Labbo, & R. D. Kieffer (Eds.), *Handbook of literacy and technology: Transformations in a post-typographic world* (pp. 323–341). Mahwah, NJ: Lawrence Erlbaum Associates.

Kress, G. (2003). *Literacy in the new media age.* London: Routledge.

Kuiper, E., Volman, M., & Terwel, J. (2005). The Web as an information resource in K–12 education: Strategies for supporting students in searching and processing information. *Review of Educational Research, 75,* 285–328.

Labbo, L. D., & Reinking, D. (1999). Multiple realities of technology in literacy research and instruction. *Reading Research Quarterly, 34,* 478–492.

Lankshear, C., & Knobel, M. (2003). New Literacies: Changing knowledge and classroom learning. Philadelphia: Open University Press.

Leander, K. M. (2004). A spatial history of a classroom literacy event. In K. Leander & M. Sheehy (Eds.), *Spatializing literacy research and practice* (pp. 115–142). New York: Peter Lang.

Leong, C. K. (1995). Effects of on-line reading and simultaneous DECtalk auding in helping below-average and poor readers comprehend and summarize text. *Learning Disability Quarterly, 18,* 101–116.

Leu, D. J., & Kinzer, C. K. (2000). The convergence of literacy instruction with networked technologies for information and communication. *Reading Research Quarterly, 35*(1), 108.

Leu, D. J., Jr., Kinzer, C. K., Coiro, J., & Cammack, D. (2004). Towards a theory of new literacies emerging from the Internet and other ICT. In R. B. Ruddell & N. Unrau (Eds.), *Theoretical models and processes of reading* (5th ed., pp.1570–1613). Newark, DE: International Reading Association.

Luke, A., & Freebody, P. (2000). *Literate futures: Report of the review for Queensland state schools.* Brisbane, Queensland, Australia: Education Queensland.

Lundberg, I., & Oloffson, A. (1993). Can computer speech support reading comprehension? *Computers in Human Behavior, 9,* 283–293.

MacArthur, C. A., Ferretti, R. P., Okolo, C. M., & Cavalier, A. R. (2001). Technology applications for students with literacy problems: A critical review. *The Elementary School Journal, 101*(3), 273–301.

MacArthur, C. A., & Haynes, J. B. (1995). Student assistant for learning from text (salt): A hypermedia reading aid. *Journal of Learning Disabilities, 28*(3), 50–59.

MacEneaney, J. (2006). Agent-based literacy theory. *Reading Research Quarterly, 41,* 352–371.

Mace, R. L. (1998). Universal design in housing. *Assistive Technology, 10*(1), 21–28.

Mayer, R. E. (1997). Multimedia learning: Are we asking the right questions? Educational Psychologist, 32(1), 1–19.

Mayer, R. E. (2001). *Multimedia learning.* Cambridge, U.K.: Cambridge University Press.

McKenna, M. C. (1998). Electronic texts and the transformation of beginning reading. In D. Reinking, M. C. McKenna, L. D. Labbo, & R. D. Kieffer (Eds.), *Handbook of literacy and technology: Transformations in a post-typographic world* (pp. 45–59). Mahwah, NJ: Lawrence Erlbaum Associates.

McKenna, M. C., Reinking, D., Labbo, L. D., & Kieffer, R. D. (1999). The electronic transformation of literacy and its implications for struggling readers. *Reading and Writing Quarterly, 15*, 111–126.

McKenna, M., & Watkins, J. (1994). Computer-mediated books for beginning readers. Paper presented at the annual meeting of the National Reading Conference, San Diego, CA.

McKeown, M. G., Beck, I. L., & Worthy, M. J. (1993). Grappling with text ideas: Questioning the author. *The Reading Teacher, 46*, 560–566.

McNamara, D. S., O'Reilly, T., Best, R., & Ozuru, Y. (2006). Improving adolescent students' reading comprehension with iSTART. *Journal of Educational Computing Research, 34*, 147–171.

Merrow, J. (2001, Spring). Double click: Threat or promise? Technology in Education. *Ed., The Magazine of the Harvard Graduate School of Education*. Retrieved September 30, 2006 from http://www.pbs.org/merrow/news/ed_book_excerpt.html

Meyer, A., & Rose, D. H. (2005). The future is in the margins: The role of technology and disability in educational reform. In D. H. Rose, A. Meyer, & C. Hitchcock (Eds.), *The universally designed classroom: Accessible curriculum and digital technologies* (pp. 13–35). Cambridge, MA: Harvard Education Press.

Mostow, J., Aist, G., Burkhead, P., Corbett, A., Cuneo, A., Eitelman, S., et al. (2003). Evaluation of an automated reading tutor that listens: Comparison to human tutoring and classroom instruction. *Journal of Educational Computing Research, 29*(1), 61–117.

Nagy, W. E., & Scott, J. A. (2004). Vocabulary processes. In R. B. Ruddell & N. Unrau (Eds.), *Theoretical models and processes of reading* (5th ed. pp. 574–593). Newark, DE: International Reading Association.

National Center for Education Statistics; (2003). The nation's report card: Reading. Retrieved January 22, 2004 from: nces.ed.gov/nationsreportcard/reading/results2003/.

National Instructional Materials Standard. (2006). *NIMAS Development Center and Technical Assistance Center*. Retrieved September 30, 2006 from http://nimas.cast.org/

National Reading Panel. (2000). *Teaching children to read: An evidence-based assessment of the scientific research literature on reading and its implications for reading instruction* (NIH Publication No. 00-4769). Jessup, MD: National Institute for Literacy.

O'Brien, D. (2001). "At-risk" adolescents: Redefining competence through the multiliteracies of intermediality, visual arts, and representation. *Reading Online, 4*(11). Retrieved September 19, 2005, from http://www.readingonline.org/newliteracies/lit_index.asp?HREF=/newliteracies/obrien/index.html

Paivio, A. (1986) *Mental representations: A dual coding approach*. Oxford, U.K.: Oxford University Press.

Palinscar, A. S., & Brown, A. L. (1984). Reciprocal teaching of comprehension-fostering and comprehension-monitoring activities. *Cognition & Instruction, 1*(2), 117.

Palincsar, A., & Dalton, B. (2005). Speaking literacy and learning to technology; Speaking technology to literacy and learning. In B. Maloch, J. Hoffman, D. Schallert, C. Fairbanks, & J. Worthy (Eds.), *Invited annual research address, 54th yearbook of the National Reading Conference* (pp. 83–102). Oak Creek, WI: National Reading Conference.

Paris, S. G., Cross, D. R., & Lipson, M. Y. (1984). Informed strategies for learning: A program to improve children's reading awareness and comprehension. *Journal of Educational Psychology, 76*(6), 1239–1252.

Pea, R. D. (1994). Seeing what we build together: Distributed multimedia learning environments for transformative communications. *The Journal of the Learning Sciences, 3*, 285–299.

Plass, J., Chun, D., Mayer, R., & Leutner, D. (1998). Supporting visualizer and verbalizer learning preferences in a second language multimedia learning. *Journal of Educational Psychology, 90*(1), 25–36.

Plass, J. L., Chun, D. M., Mayer, R. E., & Leutner, D. (2003). Cognitive load in reading a foreign language text with multimedia aids and the influence of verbal and spatial abilities. Computers in Human Behavior, 19, 221–243.

Proctor, C. P., Dalton, B., & Grisham, D. (2007). Scaffolding English language learners and struggling readers in a universal literacy environment with embedded strategy instruction and vocabulary support. *Journal of Literacy Research, 39* (1), 71–93.

Reinking, D., & Schreiner, R. (1985). The effects of computer-mediated text on measures of reading comprehension and reading behavior. *Reading Research Quarterly, 20*(5), 536–552.

Rose, D. H., & Dalton, B. (2002). Using technology to individualize reading instruction. In C. C. Block, L. B. Gambrell, & M. Pressley (Eds.), *Improving comprehension instruction: Rethinking research, theory, and classroom practice* (pp. 257–274). San Francisco: Jossey Bass Publishers.

Rose, D. H., & Meyer, A. (2002). *Teaching every student in the digital age: Universal design for learning.* Alexandria, VA: Association for Supervision and Curriculum Development (ASCD).

Salomon, G., Globerson, T., & Guterman, E. (1989). The computer as a zone of proximal development: Internalizing reading-related metacognitions from a reading partner. *Journal of Educational Psychology, 81*(4), 620–627.

Snow, C. (2002). Reading for understanding: Toward a research and development program in reading comprehension. Pittsburgh, PA: Office of Educational Research and Improvement.

Stanovich, K. E. (1986). Matthew effects in reading: Some consequences of individual differences in the acquisition of literacy. *Reading Research Quarterly, 21,* 360–406.

Strangman, N., & Dalton, B. (2005). Technology for struggling readers: A review of the research. In D. Edyburn, K. Higgins, & R. Boone (Eds.), *The handbook of special education technology research and practice* (pp. 545–569). Whitefish Bay, WI: Knowledge by Design.

Swanson, H.L., & Trahan, M. F. (1992). Learning disabled readers' comprehension of computer mediated text: The influence of working memory, metacognition and attribution. *Learning Disabilities Research & Practice, 7*(2), 74–86.

Vygotsky, L. S. (1978). *Mind in society: The development of higher psychological processes.* Cambridge, MA: Harvard University Press.

Wood, D., Bruner, J. S., & Ross, G. (1976). The role of tutoring in problem solving. *Journal of Child Psychology & Psychiatry & Allied Disciplines, 17*(2), 89–100.

CHAPTER 12

Exploring Culture in the Design of New Technologies of Literacy

PATRICIA A. YOUNG

UNIVERSITY OF MARYLAND, BALTIMORE COUNTY, USA

The rapid appearance of new information and communication technologies (ICTs) has complicated the literacy needs of all students, but especially poor and ethnically diverse learners. This has dramatically increased the importance of teacher training, raised academic standards for students across grade levels, changed the delivery of instruction, introduced multimedia curricula, and increased the importance of learning in school settings as well as out of school settings. In essence, the demands imposed by many new technologies of literacy have acutely altered the nature of literacy and what it means to be a literate person in the 21st century (Leu, 2000). Most importantly, equitable access to both technologies, in a general sense, and to learning technologies, in a specific and culturally sensitive sense, continues to be a challenge.

Given this context, the literacy achievement of ethnically diverse learners has become an increasingly important issue. The last 23 years of educational research that intersects issues of race, ethnicity, culture, technology, and literacy has often focused on access and equity as matters that have challenged the academic achievement of ethnically diverse learners in grades K–12 (Becker, 1983a; Hueftle, Rakow, & Welch, 1983; Martinez & Mead, 1988; Office of Technology Assessment [OTA], 1987; U.S. Department of Education and National Center for Education Statistics [NCES], 2005a). In technology, this phenomenon has been labeled the "digital divide" and has been identified as one aspect of technological and literacy inequities between the "haves and have nots" (Monroe, 2004; Warschauer, 2003).

Increased awareness and understanding of the inequities that divide us has generated policy initiatives, such as the *No Child Left Behind Act* of 2001. However, achievement scores on national assessments and high school dropout rates indicate a breakdown in educating a large population of ethnically diverse learners to the levels required by an information age (U.S. Department of Education and NCES, 2005b, 2006). Black and Hispanic students ages 9, 13, and 17 have not fully adapted to taking standardized exams or to the content in these exams as evidenced by student performance indicators (U.S. Department of Education and NCES, 2005b). High school dropout rates remain higher for Black students and youth from lower incomes (U.S. Department of Education and NCES, 2006). These data suggest that some of the outcomes of new pedagogies, professional development, improved curriculum, school restructuring, social programs, interventions, and other reforms do not yet meet the needs of all learners. A basic education to function in society is not yet fully accessible for many ethnically diverse learners. This raises an essential question: How can students who require our assistance the most be fully prepared for the literacy and learning challenges of a technological age?

Researchers have examined culture as a factor to help ethnically diverse learners bridge their understanding and adapt to the academic needs of schools and schooling (Banks & Banks, 2003; Gutiérrez & Rogoff, 2003; Ladson-Billings, 1994; C. D. Lee, 2003; Nieto, 1996). This adaptation has been both educational and technological as the integration of culture would situate learners in their "cultural frame of reference" when learning (Branch, 1997; Gay, 2000; Lave & Wenger, 1991; Mazyck, 2002; Powell, 1997; Thomas, Mitchell, & Joseph, 2002; Young, 2001). In some cases, as explored by this chapter, researchers and practitioners have created programs, products, or online environments to meet the academic needs of ethnically diverse learners (Eglash, 2006; Gates, 1999; Pinkard, 1999a). They have found ways to integrate culture in their designs, and they have done so through the use of technology. This chapter examines how race-, ethnicity-, and culture-related issues have evolved with the new technologies of literacy.

Leu, Kinzer, Coiro, and Cammack (2004) defined new technologies of literacy as the range of ICTs including word processors, World Wide Web browsers, weblogs (blogs), e-mail, instant messaging (IMing), presentation software, listservs, plug-ins, bulletin boards, and so forth. This review further evaluates the meanings behind integrating culture into the design of new literacy technologies and evaluates how the intersection of race, ethnicity, culture, and ICTs changes these meanings.

Finally, what does the future hold for the integration of culture in the design of ICTs? Raising this question is not to advocate that the integration of culture alone would solve the achievement problems of the day; however, researchers keep returning to this important factor for answers (Au, 1980; Gay, 2000; Ogbu, 1995a, 1995b). Au (1980) researched speech events in Hawaiian culture. Gay (2000) posed culture as a factor to improve pedagogy, curriculum, and student achievement. Ogbu (1995a; 1995b) examined culture and its relation to ethnically diverse learners' academic achievements and adjustments in school. In looking forward to what the new technologies of literacy should be and should speak to, it seems necessary that the vision for technology be inclusive of diverse perspectives, ideologies, and epistemologies.

The body of this review of literature examines the last decade or so of new technologies of literacy through exemplary programs, products, and online environments. This review covers both United States and international examples; however, there are more U.S. examples because they meet all of the following requirements. The focus is on how culture is represented in each example and, further, on how it can be replicated in the design of national and international ICTs. The criteria for selection of the programs, products, and online environments in this review were that they needed (a) to be designed for ethnically diverse learners or have ethnically diverse learners as participants; (b) to be situated in school or out of school for grades K–12 or ages 5 to 19; (c) to engage learners in literacy activities using ICTs; and (d) to focus on culture in a generic design or a specialized design.

Borrowing from the field of human-computer interaction (HCI), this review uses two important constructs: generic designs and specialized designs. Generic designs are culture neutral; they seek to eliminate and neutralize culture, generating a more universal design. Specialized designs are culture specific; they tailor products to the needs of a target audience (Horton, 2005). The generic and specialized qualities of the programs, products, and online environments are both included in this review.

The chapter begins with a theoretical frame based in culture, design, and learning. Next, a historical section looks at a series of national studies that laid the ground work for discourse on the digital divide and evaluations of poor and ethnically diverse learners' computer use and access. Then, an examination of exemplary programs, products, and online environments has focused on the academic needs of ethnically diverse learners in relation to ICTs. The review concludes by looking at issues from a more online and globalized point of view.

Theories of Culture, Design, and Learning

Research in the new technologies of literacy benefits from what Labbo and Reinking (1999) referred to as "multiple realities perspective" (p. 481), which offers intersecting or layered hypotheses to inform both research and practice. These hypotheses can be theoretically and methodologically based and seek to enhance and enable discussions across disciplines. This chapter, therefore, operates in this vein by applying multiple theoretical perspectives to the study of race, ethnicity, and culture in the new technologies of literacy. By doing so, this enriches our understanding of the questions asked and explanations offered (Labbo & Reinking, 1999).

This review also draws from theoretical perspectives on culture (e.g., race and ethnicity), learning, instructional design, and HCI. This multiple theoretical lens serves to demonstrate how disciplines have approached similar questions and challenges. This layered complexity may help us to understand how ideologies overlap and how one theory can aid in explaining another's practice. This multiple realities approach serves to advance research in new literacies.

Cultural Perspectives

Culture means many things. Geertz (1973) interpreted culture as a "historically transmitted pattern of meanings embodied in symbols, a system of inherited conceptions expressed in symbolic forms by means of which men [*sic*] communicate, perpetuate, and develop their knowledge about and attitudes toward life" (p. 89). In the area of cultural studies, culture is concerned with how meanings are interpreted and created in a society (Gray & McGuigan, 1997; S. Hall, 1997). R. Williams (1958) believed that "culture is ordinary" (p. 74). It is made in the human mind making effort, examination, and explication possible. That is, culture is what is known (tradition) and what comes to be known through investigation and invention (creativity). These meanings of culture demonstrate its importance as a theoretical construct to explain the composition of humankind but also its malleability as a construct to define or redefine through technological tools.

Theorists have proposed that learning is influenced by culture (Bruner, 1996; Vygotsky, 1978) and that culture is significant to how learners acquire new understanding (DuBois, 1903). These perspectives help us to understand how learners see the world and themselves in it. Learning takes place in a context that is specific to the environment and content information (Bednar, Cunningham, Duffy, & Perry, 1992; Brown, Collins, & Duguid, 1989; Bruner, 1985; Resnick, 1987; Rogoff & Lave, 1984). Thus, learning should be situated from the learner's perspective (Lave & Wenger, 1991; Vygotsky, 1978). In Bruner's (1985) examination of the relationship between learner and learning, he understood that learning is acquired in a variety of ways and that learning happens in a variety of ways. Bruner further argued that learning is "context sensitive" (p. 6). It follows that learning takes place in a context situated from the learner's cultural perspective or a cultural context.

Research supporting a cultural context has been articulated as culturally responsive, relevant, mediated, accommodating, compatible, and congruent (Au & Kawakami, 1994; Gay, 2000; Hollins, 1996; Jordan, 1984; Ladson-Billings, 1994) and multiculturalism (Banks & Banks, 2003; Bennett, 2001; Sleeter & Grant, 1988). These perspectives about culture challenge mainstream notions of teaching and learning, bringing culture to the nexus of discussions and enactments (e.g., what people do and how they do it), and they seek to align teaching and instruction to the cultural contexts of ethnically diverse learners. Gay (2000) argued that "culturally responsive pedagogy" focuses on the needs of ethnically diverse learners by allowing them to use their prior knowledge; situates learning from learners "cultural frames of reference;" incorporates learners' ways of being, seeing, and doing; and integrates learners' histories, language, and learning styles while affirming and validating them (p. xix). Au and Kawakami (1994) hypothesized that cultural congruence is required when ethnically diverse learners perform poorly in school based on the mismatch between school culture and home culture. Ladson-Billings (1994) proposed that culturally relevant teaching assists in sustaining the culture of the learner and transcending norms of the dominant culture; this pedagogy empowers learners using cultural referents that bridge home and school cultures. Hollins (1996) contended that culturally mediated instruction is characterized by the homogeneity of the curriculum, instruction, teacher, and learner—that is, all share the same culture. However, in cultural accommodation the teacher and learner do not share the same culture; academic learning is facilitated through the moderate integration of the student's culture. Cultural compatibility, as defined by Jordan (1984), assumes that there are relationships between the culture of the school and the culture of ethnically diverse learners and that those connections need to be identified, developed within a cultural context, and used to promote academic achievement. Banks' (1995) definition of *multiculturalism* as a theoretical construct provides learners from diverse racial, ethnic, and socioeconomic levels with an equitable educational experience and opportunities for academic achievement and socioeconomic advancement. Collectively, these theories focus on the needs of a target audience, integrate culture, and situate learning from and through the learner as integral to the educational process. They further highlight the usefulness of culture in educating all children.

Design Perspectives

Research in the fields of instructional design (ID) and HCI can best provide the grounding of how to use ICTs to design instruction. ID proposes that learning occurs in a systematic-oriented manner producing measurable outcomes and that there is a process to facilitate this learning (Reigeluth, 1983; Richey, 1986). This process is usually grounded in a generic system of analysis, design, development, implementation, and evaluation, or the ADDIE model. Instructional design translates principles of learning theory and instruction, that is, from the works of John Dewey, Robert Thorndike, B. F. Skinner, Jerome Bruner, and David Ausubel (Saettler, 1990; Seels, 1989; Tennyson, Schott, Seel, & Dijkstra, 1997), into a plan for the design of instructional products, activities, and evaluations (Smith & Ragan, 2005). This process approach is significant for the design of new technologies of literacy because it provides a systematic or structured methodology that all practitioners might follow in the design process. By systematizing or organizing the design of products or online environments, they are more apt to be well-built and researched instruction. This type of "designed instruction" is integral to meeting the needs of learners (Gagne, Briggs, & Wager, 1992, p. 4).

The research in HCI offers a way of classifying and interpreting existing and new technologies of literacy. For almost 20 years, researchers and practitioners in HCI have been examining the cultural differences that inhibit and support the design process (P. A. V. Hall & Hudson, 1997; Taylor, 1992). They have come to realize that meeting the software needs of foreign and domestic markets can be a challenging task and that there needs to be specific frameworks or guidelines to enable product development (Aykin, 2005; P. A. V. Hall & Hudson, 1997; Taylor, 1992). Therefore, there has been a focus on the internationalization and localization of products. Internationalization focuses on globalizing the design process or making it accessible to cross cultural target audiences (Aykin, 2005). The point of internationalization is to eliminate culture (e.g., cultural symbols, religious references, etc.), making the product a more universal design (Horton, 2005). For example, Aykin and Milewski (2005) proposed more than 50 strategies, guidelines, and suggestions that aid in the design of Web pages and product evaluation. They contended that these guidelines are cross-cultural and provide a better understanding of various ways of life. Under the category of guidelines for writing practices that can make the translation of a language easier, Aykin and Milewski suggested the following: "Eliminate culture-specific metaphors; avoid acronyms and abbreviations; avoid jokes, humor and idioms; avoid colloquial language; and avoid gender specific references" (p. 34). Internationalization seeks to create a homogenous technological product that is useable across cultures or that is culture neutral. Localization seeks to specialize products and/or services, making them acceptable to target groups through "culture-specific" design (Aykin, 2005; Degen, Lubin, Pedell, & Zheng, 2005, p. 314).

Culture specific design focuses on meeting the needs of a target audience through authentic or true representations. Establishing an authentic design can be assisted through the use of qualitative research methods where the target audience is studied in their natural settings (Bogdan & Biklen, 1992; Denzin & Lincoln, 2000). Foucault, Russell, and Bell (2004) incorporated ethnographic methods in finding out about their target audience Chinese consumers; in an effort to "develop culturally sensitive or culturally appropriate products, services and technologies" (p. 1481). This ethnographic fieldwork consisted of visiting and interacting with the target audience in their country, gathering nonfiction materials that documented the target audiences history and culture, and creating video documentaries of the history of the region.

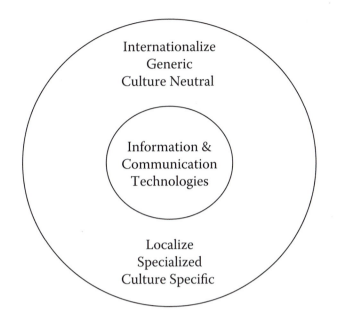

Figure 12.1 Culture-based circumference for use when designing ICTs.

If the goal of the project is to internationalize, then the design specifications are often generic and culture neutral (Figure 12.1). Generic features can be generalized across cultures but they are still culture based. If the goal of the project is to localize, then the design specifications are specialized and culture specific. Specialized features focus on meeting the needs of the target audience, and they are also culture based. For practitioners, this means that culture based design specifications exist within a circumference of the generic to specialized; therefore, there is a much broader palette in which to design (Young, in press-a; Young, in press-b).

A focus on multiple realities can advance the field of new literacies by providing direction for the design of new technologies of literacy. Theories and methods about culture provide a foundation to concepts of culture. Learning theory informs what is known about educating all children and how this education can be improved upon. Research in ID presents an example of a generic model for understanding the design process—that is, moving systematically or methodically from idea to innovation. HCI offers the concepts of generic and specialized designs, thereby classifying and evaluating designs for improvements or reinventions.

Early Studies on Ethnically Diverse Learners and ICTs

National studies of student performance have had an important impact on the fabric of American society (Becker, 1983a, 1983b, 1983c, 2000; Martinez & Mead, 1988; U.S. Department of Education and NCES, 2005a, 2005b;

OTA, 1987). In particular, the outcomes of these studies have influenced the lives of poor and ethnically diverse learners and their acquisition of knowledge and other opportunities. Large-scale educational surveys have altered the direction of public policy, funding for poor and minority communities, school improvements, district and school reforms, pedagogical practice, and instructional content. The history behind these studies chronicles a path of difference and deficit.

In examining these studies, the tests apparently changed, but the outcomes remained the same. Poor and ethnically diverse learners have the least access and use of ICTs but have the greatest need. This represents one version of history, but it does not seal the fate of academic achievement for ethnically diverse learners.

The initial studies focusing on student performance and ICTs began in the early 1980s where preliminary data appeared for what has come to be known as the digital divide (Becker, 1983a, 1983b, 1983c). Becker's reports examined inequities in access and computer use. Becker (1983a) sought to determine the number and main uses of microcomputers in public, private, and parochial elementary and secondary schools. The data indicated that, by January 1983, 51% of elementary and 56% of secondary schools had more than one microcomputer out of a national sample of 2,209 schools. However, public schools in poorer communities were less likely to own a computer. This study suggested that the number of computers used in schools was sparse and that poor communities most likely had little to no access to computers.

Becker (1983b) reported on the frequency of use of microcomputers by teachers and students in elementary and secondary schools. Only one or two teachers even used the microcomputer regularly in a little less than 50% of the 1,082 reporting schools. In a week, student use of microcomputers was very low at 16% in elementary and 13% in secondary; student time on the microcomputer was 12 to 19 minutes for elementary students and 11 to 55 minutes for secondary students. Elementary schools used the microcomputer for mostly drills and remedial work (54%); secondary schools used the microcomputer for mostly writing programs and computer literacy (81%). Becker concluded that computer use served to provide a better understanding of the computer than of subject matter. This is indicated in that students had limited time on the computer and the unknown effectiveness of computer programs. School use of computers apparently focused mostly on drill and practice in elementary and programming on the secondary level, and student time on the computer was very limited.

Becker (1983c) focused on school ownership and use of computers and found that minority students engaged in drill and practice activities 33% of the time while White students spent only 9% of the time on drill and practice. In contrast, minority students spent 10% of the time on programming activities while White students spent 49% of the time on programming. Elementary schools in minority communities used computers to improve the academic achievement of students whereas equally poor White communities used computers for individualized instruction in computer programming that supported the academic achievement of the best and brightest students. Becker's (1983a, 1983b, 1983c) studies chronicled the limited computer access and use in elementary and secondary schools. When computer technology was available, poor and ethnically diverse learners received a remedial education through the use of ICTs. Computers functioned as rote teaching machines for some but sophisticated teaching and learning tools for others.

The evolving data of difference and deficit continued into the late 1980s. However, these studies provided more comprehensive data in support of a digital divide (Martinez & Mead, 1988; OTA, 1987). The National Assessment of Educational Progress [NAEP], as authored by Martinez & Mead (1988), 1985 to 1986 reported on computer competence among students in grades 3, 7, and 11 and across Black, White, and Hispanic ethnic groups. Martinez and Mead's (1988) findings indicate that most of the students in grades 7 and 11 had little or no engagement with computers. Given these findings, how was competence judged without engagement in the activity? For example, Martinez and Mead asked, "How often do you use a computer to: write letters, stories and reports; make graphs and make a database" (p. 23)? Therefore, the results would have yielded lower levels of competence amongst ethnically diverse learners, which it did. To judge computer competence, learners must first have access.

OTA (1987) issued a report on computer use in schools and found an 18 to 20% increase in the number of computers in American schools from 1981 to 1986. In terms of equity and access, in 1985, Black students were more likely than White students were to attend schools that did not have computers. During 1985, students in poorer schools spent more time with drill and practice than students in richer schools. OTA found that teachers who worked at elementary and secondary schools with low socioeconomic status (SES) were less likely to use computers than teachers at other schools. In addition, 69% of the software available focused on drill and practice, 35% tutorial and 20% games; these limitations also attributed to the use of software programs for remediation versus academic advancement. The OTA report illustrated the imbalance in access to computers and technologically under prepared teachers. Further, limitations were apparent in the lack of academically suitable computer software to move ethnically diverse learners out of drill and practice activities and on to educationally appropriate tasks. One could assume that teachers used the software that they had available or that their schools could afford.

The continued search to understand student access to computers in school and at home is evident in Becker's (2000) examination of three national surveys in the late 1990s (e.g., *Teaching, Learning and Computing: 1998-A National Survey of Schools and Teachers*; Center for Research on Information

Technology and Organizations, 2000) and the Supplements from the *U.S. Census Bureau's Current Population Survey Computer Ownership* (U.S. Census Bureau, 1997, 1998). The conditions of low SES schools and the ethnically diverse learners who attend these schools remained similar to those of 1983. Low SES schools had slower or no Internet connections. Computer to student ratio averaged 1 to 12, and modernizing technology was difficult. Teachers from low SES schools reported a high frequency or weekly computer use; however, this use was mainly for remediation and mastering basic skills. Becker found that how teachers judged a class's ability influenced teaching and learning. That is, a class of students considered low achieving received more drill and practice activities, whereas a class of students considered high achieving received spreadsheet and e-mail activities. Overall, Becker argued that school computer use failed to provide a high level of competency.

For better or worse, poor and ethnically diverse learners were seemingly limited to drill and practice, received limited access to computers and limited time in use, suffered from technologically underprepared teachers, obtained a lower quality education and would not ultimately be prepared for technological positions in society (Becker, 1983a, 1983b, 1983c, 2000; Martinez & Mead, 1988; OTA, 1987; Sutton, 1991). These reports describe what the future of computer literacy appeared to be for poor and ethnically diverse learners; they highlighted the existing racial and economic divides between the "haves and have nots" (Sutton, 1991). If the data of the past 23 years are the only indicators of student performance and the potential success of ethnically diverse learners and poor school communities, then the stigma of difference and deficit will continue to inhibit educational innovation in the new millennium. It may be best to see standardized assessments as one history and not a given to the situations plaguing the academic performance of ethnically diverse learners. Examples of the types of reinvention needed to alter educational futures are demonstrated in the following exemplars where ingenuity, culture, learners, learning, and ICTs intersect.

New Envisionments

Leu et al. (2004) proposed that the deictic nature of literacy includes "envisionments of new literacy potentials within new technologies" (p. 1591). These envisionments are constructed when new technologies are used for "literate acts" (p. 1592; see also Leu, Karchmer, & Leu, 1999). Envisionments can be programs, products, or online environments as envisionments require a vision, the construction of that vision, and sharing the creation with others. The last decade has seen the enactment of these envisionments for ethnically diverse learners in a variety of ways and means. This section explores the meanings behind the integration of culture in the design of new technologies of literacy, and how the intersection of race, ethnicity, culture, and ICTs changes these meanings. Although most of the envisionments represented here focus on United States examples, the intersection of culture and ICTs is significant for the design of national and international products and meeting the needs of ethnically diverse learners worldwide.

These envisionments are categorized according to programs, products, and online environments. All of these envisionments focus on technology, culture and ethnically diverse learners and most are supported by empirical data. Highlighted in each review are its cultural contexts and meanings and what the data suggests for educating ethnically diverse learners.

Programs

The programs reviewed here include both in school and out of school where ethnically diverse learners engage in structured activities designed to improve academic achievement (see Table 12.1). The ICTs used in these programs included video, audio, Internet, online games, and CD-ROMs. The programs focused on meeting the needs of ethnically diverse learners in grades K–12 or ages 4 to 19. Three out of four programs were specialized and one was generic.

Hull and Zacher (2004) found that after school programs can offer learners opportunities to use multimedia technology, develop learners identities, provide opportunities for linguistic and cultural expression, and engage in social relationships and practices. This is exemplified in the Digital Underground Storytelling for Youth (DUSTY, 2007) program that is a partnership between the University of California and several community and school organizations. In the DUSTY after-school program, multiethnic middle and high school students create digital poems as part of a multimedia (e.g., computers, video, and music) project (Hull, 2003; Hull & Zacher, 2004). Hull and Nelson (2005) analyzed Randy Young's, a DUSTY participant, digital story. Randy's "Lyfe-N-Rhyme" multimodal project is a compilation of images and video with music and voice narration; it combines the language of social critic using poetry, rap, and autobiography. Hull and Nelson examined the images and language of "Lyfe-N-Rhyme" to understand the "meaning-making affordances of multimodality" (p. 239). Specifically, they looked at the technical (e.g., titles, subtitles, font, and color) and linguistic symbols (e.g., written and spoken) of the digital story. Hull and Nelson found that the meanings produced and the perceptions of viewers via multimodal compositions are unique and different. Through the digital story, Randy expressed his personal identity as a young Black man, his visions of African American history, and his lived culture using symbolic images (e.g., Malcolm X, Tupac Shakur, and Marcus Garvey). These "authentic symbols" resulted in a multisemiotic experience (Hull & Nelson, 2005) between the medium and the message (McLuhan & Fiore, 1967). The cultural context in the lives of learners is readily apparent as learners engage in activities where they are allowed to express themselves.

Table 12.1 Programs

| | | | | PROGRAMS | | | | |
| | | | | | | | Generic | Specialized |
Author/ year	Program name	Location/goal	ICT	Participants race/ethnicity	Grade level			
Hull & Zacher (2004)	DUSTY	After school Use multimedia to promote literacy	Multimedia formats	Multiethnic	7–12		Students bring their cultural frame to the program	n/a
Vasquez (2003)	La Clase Magica	After school Use technology to promote academic achievement and self-esteem	Computer	Latino	K–12		n/a	Uses content and context specific to Latino history and culture
Dickerson et al. (1995)	Saturday Science Academy	Weekend Science enrichment using technology	Computer, games, and simulations	African American	7		n/a	Uses culturally sensitive, social context to learning, holistic education
Gates (1999)	MLK, Jr. After-School Program	After school Use technology to learn the history of Africans throughout the diaspora	Computer Internet	African American	7–12		n/a	Uses content and context specific to African American history and culture

Ethnically diverse learners fall back on their cultural frame or schema and bring forth cultural and creative expressions particular to their identities, languages, and families and their communities' ways of being, acting, and seeing the world. This research suggests that learners bring their own meanings to ICTs and their interactions with technology changes the outcomes and the intended meanings. These changes in outcomes can be good in that they offer learner and educator opportunities for new understandings.

La Clase Magica (2007) is a Fifth Dimension (Fifth Dimension Distributed Literacy Consortium, 2007) based learning model that is a collaboration between the University of San Diego and the Latino community. The Fifth Dimension is a network of national and international sites. La Clase Magica is an afternoon school program that uses computer-mediated activities to help Latino learners in grades 7 through 12 improve their academic skills and self-esteem. An online maze game (El Laberinto Mágico) is an integral part of the program; in this task, students use their reading, writing, and problem-solving skills to answer questions related to Mexican history and culture (Vásquez, 1994, 2003). Vásquez's (2003) findings, from almost a decade of research, indicate that, for such programs to be successful and culturally relevant, attention must be made to the local language, social contexts, and maintenance of financial resources, and they must offer flexibility in educational opportunities. In terms of the Mexican students in this study, Vasquez found that there is a need to consider the cultural and linguistic assets of learners. Learners' lived experiences aid them in creating meaning, and this meaning making, in turn, enables learning to happen. These data suggest that the needs of the target audience must be central to build and sustain a culturally relevant after-school program. Further, ICTs can be developed within cultural contexts. La Clase Magica was able to accomplish this culturally relevant context through their bilingual and bicultural online maze and by providing an environment that nurtured Latino culture. This programs' format is consistent with Ladson-Billings (1994) theory that culturally relevant teaching assists in sustaining the culture of the learner.

Dickerson, Bernhardt, Brownstein, and Copley's (1995) study of African American seventh graders in a Saturday Science Academy at Clark Atlanta University concluded that creative writing enabled the students to articulate their attitudes and ideas about science, mathematics, and computers as they were engaged in the practical applications of these content areas. The findings indicate that through creative writing students found meaning, gained understanding, and articulated the science, mathematics, and computer principles and methods. Inherit in the design of the program was the educational philosophy that "all children can learn" (Dickerson et al., 1995, p. 142). Instruction was guided by a holistic type of education where interdisciplinary pursuits were integrated into the curriculum such as creative expression and computer science. Researchers and historians who write about the history of education for African Americans describe this education as being holistically based (Ihle, 1990; Webber, 1978; Whiteaker, 1990) in that it is defined in terms of community life, social gatherings, family life, and things learned outside these personal settings (Young, 1999). More specifically, creative expression was seen as a conduit to learning, and computers were seen as a tool that could aid in this learning (Dickerson et al., 1995; M. W. Lee, 1986). There was a focus on being culturally sensitive to their students, and literacy skills were situated in a "social context" aligned with the background of the student (Dickerson et al., 1995, p. 152). The entire functioning of the program centered on a cultural context. This research suggests that a comprehensive learning environment can be designed around the cultural needs of a target audience. This is consistent with Jordan's (1984) research on cultural compatibility in that there are relationships between the culture of the school (or learning environment) and the culture of ethnically diverse learners; those connections need to be identified, developed within a cultural context, and used to promote academic achievement.

One program designed to bridge the digital divide and to present ethnically diverse learners with content from a Black perspective is the Martin Luther King, Jr. After-School Program: Content to Bridge the Digital Divide (http://www.mlkafterschool.org). This multisite project is founded by The National Netcasting Foundation and the W. E. B. DuBois Institute for African and African American Research at Harvard University. The cultural context of the program is to provide middle and high school learners with historical and cultural content specific to people of African descent. The program is housed in Black community centers and churches where computers are set up with Internet access. Integral to the program is the CD-ROM encyclopedia *Encarta Africana,* which also provides content about Africa and African people throughout the diaspora (Gates, 1999). (This software is discussed further within the following section about products.) The format of the Martin Luther King, Jr. After-School Program is consistent with Hollins (1996) research on cultural accommodation where academic learning is facilitated through the integration of the student's culture. Goldsmith and Sherman (2002) conducted a formative evaluation of the Martin Luther King, Jr. After-School Program with the goal of providing insight into future directions. This evaluation took place at the Boston, Massachusetts location. The findings indicated that 80% of the 51 students who participated in the program came from families that owned computers. Of the students, 60% reported using the Internet at home, and only 7% reported using the computer in school. According to Goldsmith and Sherman, these students were unlike those found in national studies in that they owned computers and used the Internet; this is indicated in Becker's (2000) national surveys, which found that African American and Hispanic children were "far less likely to have a computer or Internet access at home than other children" (p. 57). Goldsmith and Sherman speculated how representative the students were of the poor and ethnically diverse learners in the larger community and, further, how students with less access might fair in the program. Although students reported having computer access and use, Goldsmith and Sherman found that student skill level varied in terms of navigating the Internet, operating the computer, and accessing and saving computer files. The Martin Luther King, Jr. After-School Program format integrated the learning of computer technology in a structured academic program focused on African American history and culture. The program effectively provided a "context for learning" (p. 43) about and through technology and created authentic examples to motivate student interest in technology. Oddly, Goldsmith and Sherman recommended the use of drill and practice to help students with learning the keyboard and short activities that focused on a single skill (e.g., importing music into a PowerPoint presentation). The Martin Luther King, Jr. After-School Program's state-of-the-art equipment enabled student learning to operate smoothly. High parent interest and participation also supported the program. One important piece of data missing from the Goldsmith and Sherman study was the SES of students; this would have brought clarity to the relationship between computer ownership and student access and use in the home. That is, just because students have computers at home does not mean that they actually use the computers. The study suggests that programs with a focus on meeting the needs of ethnically diverse learners may have to develop creative recruitment and retention plans. Otherwise, the point of bridging a digital divide will not be accomplished.

The structure of the Martin Luther King, Jr. After-School Program is also somewhat controversial in that there is a student dress code, homogenous classes, and a parent requirement to attend monthly meetings over the 12-week course period (Goldsmith & Sherman, 2002). Will this type of structure meet with the needs of poor and ethnically diverse communities? If not, then how will those who are most in need acquire the technological skills needed for the 21st century? According to national studies, like Becker's (2000), computer use and access is isolated among low SES and minority children. Could it be that ethnically diverse learners across socioeconomic levels are not receiving the technological skills they need?

Programs can supplement the curricula provided by in-school settings or provide a totally unique learning experience. They can offer a cultural and technological experience unlike that in schools. Cummins (2005) found that the most innovative ICTs for ethnically diverse learners are found in out-of-school settings because of the standardized and assessment driven focus in schools. Further, research from the *Harvard Family Research Project (HFRP): Out-of-School Time Learning and Development Project* (HFRP, 2007) at Harvard University has found that programs with a technology focus do attract and engage students. However, they have experienced some challenges in getting older students to move into programming, updating and obtaining new software to keep students interested, and locating technology of interest for diverse learners. These programs are also challenged by the financial means to maintain Internet connections, the ability to update and repair equipment, being able to retain and recruit staff with adequate technology skills, and being able to provide programs with both technology and academic enrichment (Wimer, Hull, & Bouffard, 2006).

Products

Products refer to instructional products that incorporate ICTs. These products can be used for in-school or out-of-school settings. The products in this review seek to improve the academic achievement of learners (see Table 12.2). All of the products are computer-supported applications some with or without Internet links. Finally, all of these products focus on meeting the needs of ethnically diverse learners in grades K–12 or ages 5 to 19. Three of the four products were specialized and one was classified as generic.

Pinkard (1999a, 1999b) created two instructional products that were culturally responsive computer-mediated environments—*Say, Say Oh, Playmate* (Pinkard, 1998) and *Rappin' Reader* (Pinkard, 1996). These programs sought to use students' oral language to improve their literacy skills and draw on their cultural experiences to enhance learning. *Rappin' Reader* used the lyrics of rap songs to engage learners in a reading task. In a study of 30 students in grades 1 through 4, Pinkard (1999a) found that the use of *Rappin' Reader* increased students' sight word recognition between pre- and posttests. Moreover, African American students, across grade levels, made equal or greater gains in sight word recognition than European American students. The second program, *Say, Say Oh, Playmate,* used African American clap routine lyrics, performed by an avatar, as a basis for reading acquisition; the clap routines are rooted in African American hand-clapping songs (Gaunt, 2006). In a study of 12 first and second grade students, Pinkard (1999a) field-tested *Say, Say, Oh Playmate* to determine students' sight word-recognition learning. Students gained, on average, 2.4 more words than students who used *Rappin' Reader.*

Pinkard (1999a) argued that ethnically based differences on national assessments such as NAEP could be explained by the reading material selections. That is, most reading selections prevalent in standardized assessments are based on Eurocentric views; therefore, culturally relevant reading selections might aid in helping ethnically diverse learners perform better on standardized assessments. Pinkard found that the culturally responsive elements in these reading programs included the audience, rap music, hand-clapping games, language use, and the motivational intent.

This research is supported by Gay's (2000) theorizing that culturally responsive pedagogy (and learning) focuses on the needs of ethnically diverse learners by allowing them to use their prior knowledge, situates learning from learners cultural frames of reference, incorporates learners' ways of being,

Table 12.2 Products

			PRODUCTS			
Author/ year	Product name	Goal/purpose	ICT	Participants race/ethnicity	Grade level	Generic	Specialized
Pinkard (1999a)	*Say Say Oh Playmate* and *Rappin' Reader*	After school Improve reading skills and motivate learners	Computer	Multiethnic	1–4	n/a	Content of software specific to African American cultural experience
Leonard et al. (2005)	*Underground Railroad*	In school Improve science and mathematics achievement	Computer	African American	4	n/a	Content of software specific to African American historical and cultural experience
Gates (1999)	*Encarta Africana*	After school Improve computer skills and knowledge of Africa and people of African descent	Computer Internet	Multiethnic	K–12	n/a	Content of software specific to African and African American historical and cultural experience
Cummins (2005)	*e-Lective Language Learning Program*	In school/after school Improve academic language learning	Computer	Multiethnic	9–12	Content of software allows learner to input their language samples	n/a

Table 12.3 Online Environments

			ONLINE ENVIRONMENTS				
Author/year	Online name	Goal	ICT	Participants race/ethnicity	Grade level	Generic	Specialized
Barab et al. (2005)	Quest Atlantis	In school/after school Engage in educational tasks	Online virtual environment	Multiethnic	3–6	Help children learn about other cultures. Use of ethnically diverse characters in online environment	n/a
Eglash (2006)	Culturally Situated Design Tools	In school Understand standards based mathematics	Online environment	Multiethnic	7–12	Content of online environment is multiethnic, historical, and cultural	n/a
Massey et al. (2005)	International Children's Digital Library	In school/after school Provide a multicultural digital library	Online environment	Multiethnic	preK–6, ages 3–13	Content of online environment is multiethnic, multilingual, and multicultural	n/a
L. C. Williams (2003)	Kidlink	In school/after school Provide a global online learning environment	Online environment	Multiethnic	K–10, ages up to 15	Students bring their cultural frame to the online environment	n/a
Abbott (2005)	iEARN	In school/after school Provide a global online learning environment	Online environment	Multiethnic	K–12, ages 5–19	Students bring their cultural frame to the online environment	n/a

are used in both in-school and after-school settings. Across these examples, the goal seemed to be engaging learners in an interactive educational task. The Internet provided access to an online 3-D world, virtual games, computer simulations, a digital library, and international online learning environments. These online environments focused on meeting the needs of ethnically diverse learners in grades preK–12 or ages 5 to 19. All of the examples are generic designs because of their cross-cultural focus.

Quest Atlantis (QA) is an online, 3-D, virtual environment where students engage in interactive educational activities (http://atlantis.crlt.indiana.edu/start/index.html). It has been implemented in multiple sites both nationally and internationally. QA is part education, part entertainment, and also a socially responsive game (Barab, Thomas, Dodge, Carteaux, & Tuzun, 2005, p. 86). Students, usually third to sixth grade, engage in literacy practices through experiential and inquiry based learning. Other online literacy supplements include comic books, a QA novel, activity charts, and trading cards. The cultural context is addressed through the variety of virtual universes with their ethnically diverse characters and discourses. QA hopes to help students learn about and from other cultures, thereby fostering a "multicultural appreciation" (Barab et al., 2005, p. 104). Barab et al. believed that QA could help build school and community relations, as students must use real world examples to complete quests. This may foster cultural compatibility of home and school connections (Jordan, 1984). Barab et al.'s findings reveal that QA can be motivational to students and provide meaningful educational experiences. This intervention has been successfully implemented with both in-school and out-of-school settings (e.g., classrooms in Australia, Denmark, Malaysia, and Singapore and two after-school programs in the United States). Some of its design specifications lead to this effectiveness as it provides a "flexibly adaptive" innovation that functions well in multiple learning contexts, connects to educational standards, uses an online game structure, supports 3-D technologies, infuses interdisciplinary curriculum content, and builds connections with the real world (Barab et al., 2005, p. 103). The specific quantitative academic gains in science, math, reading, social studies, and language arts are not specified in these studies (Barab et al., 2005; Barab, Thomas, Dodge, Squire, & Newell, 2004). This research provides an example of the type of virtual online environments needed to appeal to a highly visual and technology-oriented youth population. Addressing the needs of target audiences across cultures requires captivating graphics, sound, characters, content, and maybe an interactive game-like learning environment. Innovation in designing ICTs will cost much more than traditional designs (Bates, 1995). However the investment has greater potential for longevity because online environments can be revised and updated without fully reproducing the original design.

Eglash, Bennett, O'Donnell, Jennings, and Cintorino (2006) examined culturally situated design tools (CSDT) to teach mathematics through culture terpretations across cultures. These international sites provide an important context for globalized learning and thinking.

Online environments are versatile forms of technology that can provide access and use to ethnically diverse learners around the world. This type of globalized learning appears to enhance teaching and instruction and provide opportunities for an in-depth understanding of diverse peoples. The possibilities are many—as students are able to interact with an educational game, virtual world, simulation, or reference Web site.

A Summary

Learners respond and interact with technology based on their cultural frames of reference (Gay, 2000), and thus, these interactions are neither predictable nor fixed. When ethnically diverse learners interact with ICTs, the outcomes change and meanings are changed because their lived reality, in most cases, is different from the design of the programs, products, and online environments.

Building on these cultural frames of reference begins with the creation of generic or specialized designs. The programs, products, and online environments in this review were categorized according to whether they provided a more generic or specialized design. In Tables 12.1, 12.2, and 12.3, the generic designs appear to provide a culture neutral educational experience where ethnically diverse learners bring their cultural frame to the context. The infrastructure of DUSTY is culture neutral because it is designed for a broad audience and student participants bring their cultural frames to the program. Hull and Nelson's (2005) research found that students pulled from their life experiences to interact and engage in educational tasks.

The *e-Lective Language Learning Program* is also culturally neutral. Learners bring their language samples to the e-Lective program for translation. In addition, the online environments described here also represent culturally neutral infrastructures. QA replicates a fictionalized culture in an online 3-D environment with ethnically diverse avatars that provide a cross-cultural experience for learners (Barab et al., 2005). CSDT uses simulations to teach learners mathematical concepts inclusive of both historical and societal traditions of multiple ethnic groups (Eglash et al., 2006). ICDL provides learners with a digital children's library that is multiethnic, multilingual and multicultural (Massey et al., 2005). With Kidlink and iEARN, learners also bring their cultural frames to these online environments, and they engage in mostly teacher lead educational activities and projects (Abbott, 2005; Willliams, 2002).

Specialized designs are culture specific because they focus on the needs of the learner or the target audience; make the ethnicity of the target audience integral to the design; incorporate the target audiences' histories, learning styles, and preferences; and provide a culturally supportive environment in which to learn. In Tables 12.1 and 12.2, specialized designs provide a setting where the cultural needs of the target audience are specified. La Clase

Magica, according to Vásquez (2003), focuses on the needs of the Latino community and its student participants. The Saturday Science Academy, according to Dickerson et al. (1995), created an environment infused with holistic learning experiences that imparted a cultural sensitivity toward African American students. The Martin Luther King, Jr. After-School Program incorporates African and African American history throughout all program components (Gates, 1999). *Say, Say Oh Playmate, Rappin' Reader* (Pinkard, 1999a, 1999b), and the *Underground Railroad* (Leonard et al., 2005) focuses on content specialized to African Americans, their history, and their cultural experiences. *Encarta Africana* contains content specific to Africa and people of African descent (Gates, 1999). The next section elaborates further on culture in the design of ICTs.

Culture, Design, and ICTs

The integration of culture in the design of ICTs has the potential to improve learning for ethnically diverse learners (Cummins, 2005; Lee, C. D., 2003). However, the exclusion of culture in the design of ICTs apparently happens for several reasons. First, there may be a need to clarify understandings of what is means to design with culture in mind. Culture, as defined in Dickerson et al.'s (1995) study, focused on the social and individual aspects of culture. This perspective on culture is consistent with that of physical anthropologists who study humans and human behavior (Haviland, 1987). For the practitioner, an examination of an individual's culture could include understanding, studying, or replicating human characteristics. In Squire, MaKinster, Barnett, Luehmann, and Barab's (2003) study, culture is perceived environmentally as the culture of the classroom. This perspective on culture is consistent with that of cultural anthropologists who examine a society's ways of life (Haviland, 1987). For the practitioner, an examination of environmental cultures could include understanding, studying, or replicating a society's way of life. The design of ICTs includes the reproduction, simulation, or virtualization within the space of design; therefore, a complete picture of designing with ICTs must be inclusive of environmental and physical definitions of culture. That is, people and place must both be considered.

A second issue in the design of ICTs is how to represent culture in the design process, what to look for, and what to include. Traditionally, as evident from this review, the integration of culture has focused on features such as identity (Hull & Zacher, 2004); language and language use (Cummins, 2005); community (Vásquez, 2003); cultural sensitivity (Dickerson et al., 1995); cultural responsiveness (Gay, 2000); culturally relevant teaching and learning (Ladson-Billings, 1994); histories (e.g., educational, ethnic, familial, social, and ancestral) (Eglash et al., 2006; Gates, 1999; Leonard et al., 2005); attitudes (Massey et al., 2005); institutions (e.g., schools, church, family, and work); and religion, traditions, race, ethnicity, socioeconomic status, and gender (Pinkard, 2004). This is a good beginning. However, what these terms mean in the design of ICTs and, further, how they should translate into design specifications is unclear.

Sometimes, the inclusion of cultural contexts may not have been seriously considered as an important factor in the design process. Most designs of programs, products, and online environments focus on a generic—culturally neutral design. Generic designs can reach broader audiences where as specialized designs are much more narrow. However, targeting designs to the needs of specialized audiences appears to be where the design of ICTs is headed (Aykin, 2005). There is much to consider as the integration of culture in ICTs must be an explicit goal throughout the design process.

Globalized Learning

If knowledge were globalized, then the inclusion of culture within the design of ICTs would seem a natural course. As it stands in many western circles, culture seems an abstract concept devoid of design considerations, confused in teaching situations, and tolerated as a learning strategy. In a globalized society, culture would be at the forefront of e-learning. This focus is exemplified in the recent publication of *Globalized E-Learning Cultural Challenges* (Edmundson, 2006). Scholars around the world are trying to figure out how to internationalize and localize design. It is imperative that literacy educators find a space for this work in the new millennium.

Cheng (2002) argued that globalized learning means that learning is provided through many avenues including national and international resources. This type of learning provides access to instructional materials, educators, peers, and experts around the world; this approach appears to advance scholarship, learning, and instruction in the new literacies.

The integration of culture in the design of ICTs is a move to improve learning and instruction. The design of culture based ICTs is more than simply helping students with their identities or helping learners with examples that come from their cultures (Eglash et al., 2006). It is much broader in that the design of culture based ICTs aids learners in bringing their creativity to educational tasks, taking responsibility for their learning, seeing themselves as producers of knowledge, and globalizing their learning experiences. Learners need to reach and interact with the world and begin to understand and appreciate differences and similarities. It is about creating a world community through the engagement of technology where this type of instantaneous connection, information, and education was never possible before in history. Education does not have to be limited to the classroom and textbooks because the Internet provides opportunities for worldwide educational access and activity (Leu et al., 2005; Leu, 2002).

Concluding Thoughts

The last 23 years of surveys in the United States would have one to believe that the academic fate of ethnically diverse learners is a losing battle and that digital, economic, and social divides continue to exist. The numbers do not speak to the grassroots efforts of after school programs in communities that are trying to address the digital divide by providing a culturally enriching environment, academic assistance, and hands-on computer technology exposure (Dickerson et al., 1995; Hull & Nelson, 2005; Vasquez, 2003). Other innovators are developing products that meet the needs of specialized audiences of students in order to incorporate culture in the teaching of academic content (Cummins, 2005; Gates, 1999; Leonard et al., 2005). Online environments have been generated by national and international organizations to begin the process of globalized learning (e.g., Kidlink; iEARN). More of these grassroots, in-school, out-of-school, and online efforts are needed to supplement classroom instruction and improve teaching and learning.

The integration of culture in the design of technologies of literacy is not a new idea. However, it is a concept that has not maintained any longevity or consistent support. Young's (1999, 2001) research identified primary source documents created through print technology, dating back to 1792, as evidence that African Americans created culture based technologies of literacy to educate their own. These early documents were produced in many forms such as newspapers, magazines, religious matter, and later textbooks used in historically Black colleges. These materials exemplify the feasibility of ICTs in creating localized products. More contemporary examples are the Rough Rock English-Navajo Language Arts Program (RRENLP) that focused on improving student achievement through bilingual and bicultural language arts instructional strategies (McCarty, 1993). The program included teacher made authentic Navaho children's literature written in the Navaho language. The findings of this program, from 1990 to 1991, saw gains of 12 percentage points for students in grades K–3. During 1992, the K–3 median California Test of Basic Skills (CTBS) scores doubled in the area of vocabulary, although these scores were still below national averages. Further, teachers became confident in themselves and the work they were doing (Dick, Estell, & McCarty, 1994).

Another important culture based technology of literacy was *Bridge: A Cross-Cultural Reading Program* (Simpkins, Holt, & Simpkins, 1977). *Bridge* was developed as an intervention reading program that sought to improve the reading levels of Black junior and senior high school students in America's public schools. *Bridge* was extensively tested in 1975 in Chicago, Illinois; Phoenix, Arizona; Washington, DC; Memphis, Tennessee; and Macon County, Alabama. Using the Iowa Test of Basic Skills in Reading Comprehension level 12 as the final assessment, students who received instruction in *Bridge* made higher gains than those who received instruction via the basal reader (e.g., grade 7 experimental gain 4.9 and control gain 2.8; grade 8 experimental gain

9.3 and control gain 3.5; grades 9–12 exhibited gains of 5.2 months and control loss of 4.9 months; Simpkins, 1976, 2002; Young, 1999). These studies suggest the opportunities inherent in integrating culture based ICTs that can improve the academic achievement of ethnically diverse learners. Whether it is old or new technology, the integration of culture in the design of technologies of literacy has potential to improve the academic performance of all learners. This chapter has attempted to demonstrate that possibility.

Thinking Ahead

The significance of culture in the design of new technologies of literacy will be important as national and international relationships increase and the need to know and interact with other ethnic groups becomes imperative for human survival. This globalization illustrates the need to internationalize our thinking in terms of meeting and exceeding the educational needs of our students. In the final analysis, issues of race, ethnicity, culture, and technology are not local but global concerns. Taken in these terms, there is much work to do. New envisionments must provide both internationalized and localized products, programs, and online environments. Innovation must be at the forefront of this thinking for all learners to be fully prepared for life in a global, online world.

According to Aykin (2005), the "concept of cross-cultural design" (p. xx) needs to become a priority issue. Important new questions lie ahead of us: How can educators begin to see culture as an integral part of the design of new technologies of literacy? What changes in mindset, instructional practices, curriculum, and/or policy need to take place before we systematically integrate globalized, culturally sensitive thinking into the curriculum? How will the integration of culture be a contributing factor to improve learning experiences in all technologies of literacy?

In a Vygotskyian (1978) interpretation, change is not limited only to technology but also to society. In that sense, change must begin with people. People must change in mindsets and then those changes will be reflected in our uses and interactions with technology. Perhaps that is our greatest challenge. Our duty as educators is to be transformative (Hooks, 1994) and initiators of this forward thinking.

It is clear that equity and access will not cease to be issues in the social fabric of the technological revolution. Nor will these issues be resolved in the next generation. Therefore, finding alternative interventions, preventions, and conventions seems to be a proactive step in making the margins the middle. The content of new technologies of literacy can replicate the past or transform the future. Ultimately, it will take a conscientious effort to change ways of thinking, ways of doing, and ways of believing. If new technologies of literacy are to transform, they must first begin with its creators, builders, and soothsayers. Only then can issues of equity and access be bridged.

References

Abbott, L. (2005). The nature of authentic professional development during curriculum-based telecomputing. *Journal of Research on Technology in Education, 37*(4), 379–398.

Appiah, K. A., & Gates, H. L. (Eds.). (1999). Microsoft Encarta Africana [Computer software]. Redmond, WA: Microsoft Corporation.

Au, K. H. (1980). Participation structures in a reading lesson with Hawaiian children: Analysis of a culturally appropriate instructional event. *Anthropology & Education Quarterly, 11*(2), 91–115.

Au, K. H., & Kawakami, A. J. (1994). Cultural congruence in instruction. In E. R. Hollins, J. E. King, & W. C. Hayman (Eds.), *Teaching diverse populations: Formulating a knowledge base* (pp. 5–23). Albany: State University of New York Press.

Aykin, N. (2005). Overview: Where to start and what to consider. In N. Aykin (Ed.), *Usability and internationalization of information technology* (pp. 3–20). Mahwah, NJ: Lawrence Erlbaum Associates.

Aykin, N., & Milewski, A. E. (2005). Practical issues and guidelines for international information display. In N. Aykin (Ed.), *Usability and internationalization of information technology* (pp. 21–50). Mahwah, NJ: Lawrence Erlbaum Associates.

Banks, J. A. (1995). Multicultural education: Historical development, dimensions and practice. In J. A. Banks & C. A. Banks (Eds.), *Handbook of research on multicultural education* (pp. 3–24). New York: Macmillan.

Banks, J., & Banks, C. (Eds.). (2003). *Handbook of research on multicultural education*. San Francisco: Jossey-Bass Publishers.

Barab, S., Thomas, M., Dodge, T., Carteaux, R., & Tuzun, H. (2005). Making learning fun: Quest Atlantis, a game without guns. *Education Technology Research and Development, 53*(1), 86–107.

Barab, S. A., Thomas, M. K., Dodge, T., Squire, K., & Newell, M. (2004). Critical design ethnography: Designing for change. *Anthropology & Education Quarterly, 35*(2), 254–268.

Bates, A. W. (1995). *Technology, open learning and distance education*. London: Routledge.

Becker, H. J. (1983a). *School uses of microcomputers. Reports from a National Survey. Issue No. 1*. Baltimore: Johns Hopkins University.

Becker, H. J. (1983b). *School uses of microcomputers. Reports from a National Survey. Issue No. 2*. Baltimore: Johns Hopkins University.

Becker, H. J. (1983c). *School uses of microcomputers. Reports from a National Survey. Issue No. 3*. Baltimore: Johns Hopkins University.

Becker, H. J. (2000). Who's wired and who's not: Children's access to and use of computer technology. *Children and Computer Technology, 10*(2), 44–75.

Bednar, A. K., Cunningham, D., Duffy, T., & Perry, J. D. (1992). Theory into practice: How do we link? In T. M. Duffy & D. H. Jonassen (Eds.), *Constructivism and the technology of instruction* (pp. 18–34). Hillsdale, NJ: Lawrence Erlbaum Associates.

Bennett, C. (2001). Genres of research in multicultural education. *Review of Educational Research, 71*(2), 171–217.

Bogdan, R. C., & Biklen, S. K. (1992). *Qualitative Research for Education: An introduction to theory and methods*. Boston: Allyn and Bacon.

Branch, R. M. (1997, March/April). Educational technology frameworks that facilitate culturally pluralistic instruction. *Educational Technology, 37*, 38–41.

Brown, J. S., Collins, A., & Duguid, P. (1989). Situated cognition and the culture of learning. *Educational Researcher, 18*, 32–42.

Bruner, J. (1985). Models of the learner. *Educational Researcher, 14*(6), 5–8.

Bruner, J. (1996). *The culture of education*. Cambridge, MA: Harvard University Press.

Center for Research on Information Technology and Organizations (2000). *Teaching, learning and computing: 1998—A national survey of schools and teachers (TLC-1998)* [Electronic version]. Irvine: University of California Irvine.

Chascas, S., & Cummins, J. (2004). The e-Lective language learning program [Computer software]. Rhodes, Greece: Morphes, Inc.

Cheng, Y. C. (2002). *New paradigm of borderless education: Challenges, strategies, and implications for effective education through localization and internationalization.* Paper presented at the International conference on learning and teaching: Challenge of learning and teaching in a Brave New World: Issues and opportunities in borderless education, Hatyai, Thailand.

Cummins, J. (2002). Learning through target language texts. In K. Nakajima (Ed.), *Learning Japanese in the network society* (pp. 105–122). Calgary, Canada: University of Calgary Press.

Cummins, J. (2005). *Technology, literacy and young second language learners: Designing educational futures.* Retrieved June 15, 2006 from http://www.ucop.edu/elltech/background.html

Cummins, J., Ardeshiri, M., & Cohen, S. (February 3, 2007). Computer-supported scaffolding of literacy development. Retrieved June 22, 2007, from http://www.multiliteracies.ca/index.php/folio/viewProject/109

Degen, H., Lubin, K. L., Pedell, S., & Zheng, J. (2005). Travel planning on the web: A cross-cultural case study. In N. Aykin (Ed.), *Usability and internationalization of Information Technology* (pp. 313–343). Mahwah, NJ: Lawrence Erlbaum Associates Publishers.

Denzin, N. K., & Lincoln, Y. S. (2000). Introduction: The discipline and practice of qualitative research. In N. K. Denzin & Y. S. Lincoln (Eds.), *Handbook of qualitative research* (2nd ed., pp. 1–28). Thousand Oaks, CA: Sage Publications, Inc.

Dick, G. S., Estell, D. W., & McCarty, T. L. (1994, Spring). Saad naakih bee'enootihji na'alkaa: Restructuring the teaching of language and literacy in a Navajo community school. *Journal of American Indian Education, 33*(3), 31–46.

Dickerson, T., Bernhardt, E., Brownstein, E., & Copley, E. (1995). African American children reflecting on science, mathematics and computers through creative writing: Perspectives from a Saturday science academy. *Journal of Negro Education, 64*(2), 141–153.

Digital Underground Storytelling for Youth (DUSTY). (2007). Retrieved January 16, 2007, from http://oaklanddusty.org/

DuBois, W. E. B. (1903). The talented tenth. In *The Negro Problem: A series of articles by representative American Negroes of To-day* (pp. 33–75). New York: James Pott & Co.

Edmundson, A. (Ed.). (2007). *Globalized e-learning cultural challenges.* Hershey, PA: Information Science Publishing.

Eglash, R. (2006). Ethnocomputing with Native American Design. In L. E. Dyson, S. Grant, & M. Hendriks (Eds.), *Information technology and indigenous people* (pp. 210–219). Hershey, PA: Information Science Publishing.

Eglash, R., Bennett, A., O'Donnell, C., Jennings, S., & Cintorino, M. (2006). Culturally situated design tools: Ethnocomputing from field site to classroom. *American Anthropologist, 108*(2), 347–362.

Fifth dimension distributed literacy consortium. (2007). Retrieved January 16, 2007, from http://129.171.53.1/blantonw/5dClhse/clearingh1.html

Foucault, B. E., Russell, R. S., & Bell, G. (2004, April 24–29). *Techniques for research and designing global products in an unstable world: A case study.* Paper presented at the Computer Human Interaction, Vienna, Austria.

Frank, M. J. (2000, January 24). MLK after-school programs would teach children about computers, Black history. *The University Record 55*(17). Retrieved June 23, 2007, from http://www.umich.edu/%7Eurecord/9900/Jan24_00/10.htm.

Gagne, R. M., Briggs, L. J., & Wager, W. W. (1992). *Principles of instructional design.* Fort Worth, TX: Harcourt Brace Jovanovich College Publishers.

Gates, H. L. (1999). An Essay on Encarta Africana. *The Black collegian, 30*(1), 140–143.

Gaunt, K. (2006). *The games Black girls play: Learning the ropes from double dutch to hip-hop.* New York: New York University Press.

Gay, G. (2000). *Culturally responsive teaching.* New York: Teachers College Press.

Geertz, C. (1973). *The interpretation of cultures.* New York: Basic Books.

Goldsmith, L., & Sherman, A. (2002). *Evaluation of the pilot year of the Martin Luther King, Jr. after-school program.* Newton, MA: Education Development Center, Inc.

Gray, A., & McGuigan, J. (1997). Introduction. In A. Gray & J. McGuigan (Eds.), *Studying culture: An introductory reader* (pp. xi–xv). New York: Arnold, A member of the Hodder Headline Group.

Gutierrez, K. D., & Rogoff, B. (2003, June/July). Cultural ways of learning: Individual traits or repertories of practice. *Educational Researcher, 32*(5), 19–25.

Hall, P. A. V., & Hudson, R. (1997). *Software without frontiers: A multi-platform, multi-cultural, multi-nation approach.* New York: John Wiley & Sons.

Hall, S. (1997). Introduction. In S. Hall (Ed.), *Representation: Cultural representations and signifying practices* (pp. 1–11). London: Sage Publications.

Harvard Family Research Project (HFRP). (2007). *Out-of-school time learning and development project.* Retrieved January 16, 2007, from http://www.gse.harvard.edu/hfrp/projects/afterschool/about.html

Haviland, W. A. (1987). *Cultural anthropology* (5th ed.). New York: Holt, Rinehart and Winston.

Hollins, E. R. (1996). *Culture in school learning: Revealing the deep meaning.* Mahwah, NJ: Lawrence Erlbaum Associates.

Hooks, B. (1994). *Teaching to transgress: Education as the practice of freedom.* New York: Routledge.

Horton, W. (2005). Graphics: The not quite universal language. In N. Aykin (Ed.), *Usability and internationalization of information technology* (pp. 157–188). Mahwah, NJ: Lawrence Erlbaum Associates.

Hueftle, S., Rakow, S., & Welch, W. (1983). *Images of science: A summary of results from the 1981–1982 National Assessment in Science.* Minneapolis: University of Minnesota.

Hull, G. A. (2003). Youth culture and digital media: New literacies for new times. *Research in the Teaching of English, 38*(2), 229–233.

Hull, G. A., & Nelson, M. E. (2005). Locating the semiotic power of multimodality. *Written Communication, 22*(2), 224–261.

Hull, G. A., & Zacher, J. (2004). What is after-school worth? Developing literacy and identity out of school. *Voices in Urban Education, 3.* Retrieved January 16, 2007, from http://www.annenberginstitute.org/VUE/spring04/Hull.html

Huppert, J., & Lomask, S. M. (2002). Computer simulations in the high school: Students' cognitive stages, science process skills and academic achievement in microbiology. *International Journal of Science Education 24*(8), 803–821.

Hutchinson, H. B., Rose, A., Bederson, B., Weeks, A. C., & Druin, A. (2005). The international children's digital library: A case study in designing for a multi-lingual, multi-cultural, multi-generational audience. *Information Technology and Libraries, 24*(1), 4–12.

Ihle, E. L. (1990). Education of the free blacks before the civil war. In H. G. Neufeldt & L. McGee (Eds.), *Education of the African American adult: An historical overview* (pp. 11–23). New York: Greenwood Press.

Jordan, C. (1984). Cultural compatibility and the ducation of ethnic minority children. *Educational Research Quarterly, 8*(4), 59–71.

Labbo, L. D., & Reinking, D. (1999). Negotiating the multiple realities of technology in literacy research and instruction. *Theory and Research into Practice, 34*(4), 478–492.

La Clase Magica. (2007). Retrieved January 16, 2007, from http://communication.ucsd.edu/LCM/Coming_Soon.html

Ladson-Billings, G. (1994). *The dreamkeepers: Successful teachers of African American children.* San Francisco: Jossey-Bass Publishers.

Lave, J., & Wenger, E. (1991). *Situated learning: Legitimate peripheral participation.* Cambridge, MA: Cambridge University Press.

Lee, C. D. (2003). Toward a framework for culturally responsive design in multimedia computer environments: Cultural modeling as a case. *Mind, Culture and Activity, 10*(1), 42–61.

Lee, M. W. (1986). The match: Learning styles of Black children and microcomputer programming. *The Journal of Negro Education, 55*(1), 78–90.

Leonard, J., Davis, J. E., & Sidler, J. L. (2005). Cultural relevance and computer-assisted instruction. *Journal of Research on Technology in Education, 37*(3), 263–284.

Leonard, J., & Leonard, D. (2002). Interactive journeys in mathematics and science: Riding the freedom train (field test 2) [Computer software]. Ann Arbor, MI: Renaissance Micro.

Leu, D. J. (2000). Literacy and technology: Deictic consequences for literacy education in an information age. In M. L. Kamil, P. B. Mosenthal, P. D. Pearson, & R. Barr (Eds.), *Handbook of reading research* (Vol. 3, pp. 743–770). Mahwah, NJ: Lawrence Erlbaum Associates.

Leu, D. J. (2002). The new literacies: Research on reading instruction with the Internet and other digital technologies. In A. E. Farstrup & S. J. Samuels (Eds.), *What research has to say about reading instruction* (3rd ed., pp. 310–337). Newark, DE: International Reading Association.

Leu, D. J., Castek, J., Coiro, J., Gort, M., Henry, L. A., & Lima, C. O. (2005). Developing new literacies among multilingual learners in the elementary grades. *Technology in support of young second language learners*. Retrieved June 15, 2006, from http://www.ucop.edu/elltech/background.html

Leu, D. J., Karchmer, R., & Leu, D. D. (1999). The Miss Rumphius effect: Envisionments for literacy and learning that transform the Internet. *The Reading Teacher, 52,* 636–642.

Leu, D. J., Kinzer, C. K., Coiro, J. L., & Cammack, D. (2004). Toward a theory of new literacies and other information and communication technologies. In R. Ruddell & N. J. Unrau (Eds.), *Theoretical models and processes of reading* (pp. 1570–1613). Neward, DE: International Reading Association.

Martinez, M. E., & Mead, N. A. (1988). *Computer competence: The first national assessment* (No. Tech. Rep. No. 17–CC-01). Princeton, NJ: National Assessment of Educational Progress: Educational Testing Service.

Massey, S. A., Weeks, A. C., & Druin, A. (2005). Initial findings from a three-year international case study exploring children's responses to literature in a digital library. *Library Trends, 54*(2), 245–265.

Mazyck, M. (2002, March/April). Integrated learning systems and students of color. *Tech Trends, 46*(2), 33–39.

McCarty, T. L. (1993). Language, literacy, and the image of the child in American Indian classrooms. *Language Arts, 70*(3), 182–192.

McLuhan, M., & Fiore, Q. (1967). *The medium is the massage.* New York: Bantam Books.

Monroe, B. (2004). *Crossing the digital divide: Race, writing and technology in the classroom.* New York, NY: Teachers College Press.

No Child Left Behind Act of 2001. Public Law No. 107–110, 115 Stat. 1425 (2002).

Nieto, S. (1996). *Affirming diversity: The sociopolitical context of multicultural education.* White Plains, NY: Longman Publishers.

Ogbu, J. U. (1995a). Cultural problems in minority education: Their interpretations and consequences—Part one: Theoretical background. *Urban Review, 27*(3), 189–205.

Ogbu, J. U. (1995b). Cultural problems in minority education: Their interpretations and consequences—Part two: Case studies. *Urban Review, 27*(4), 271–297.

Office of Technology Assessment. (1987). *Trends and status of computers in schools: Use in chapter 1 and use with limited English proficient students.* Washington, DC: Author.

Pinkard, N. (1996). Rappin' Reader [Computer software]. Evanston, MI: Northwestern University.

Pinkard, N. (1998). Say say oh playmate [Computer software]. Ann Arbor: University of Michigan.

Pinkard, N. (1999a). Learning to read in culturally responsive computer environments (Ciera Report No. 1-004). Ann Arbor: Center for the Improvement of Early Reading Achievement, University of Michigan.

Pinkard, N. (1999b). Lyric reader: An architecture for creating intrinsically motivating and culturally responsive reading environments. *Interactive Learning Environments, 7*(1), 1–30.

Pinkard, N. (2004). *Exploring the effects of learners' cultural and social histories on the practices of learning scientists.* Paper presented at the proceedings of the sixth international conference of the learning sciences: Embracing diversity in the learning sciences, Santa Monica, CA.

Powell, G. C. (1997, March/April). Understanding the language of diversity. *Educational Technology, 37*(2), 15–18.

Reigeluth, C. M. (1983). Instructional design: What is it and why is it? In C. M. Reigeluth (Ed.), *Instructional-design theories and models: An overview of their current status* (pp. 3–36). Hillsdale, NJ: Lawrence Erlbaum Associates.

Resnick, L. (1987). Learning in school and out. *Educational researcher, 16*(9), 13–20.

Richey, R. (1986). *The theoretical and conceptual bases of instructional design.* London: Kogan Page.

Rogoff, B., & Lave, J. (1984). *Everyday cognition: Its development in social context.* Cambridge, MA: Harvard University Press.

Saettler, P. (1990). *The evolution of American educational technology.* Englewood, CO: Libraries Unlimited, Inc.

Seels, B. (1989). The instructional design movement in educational technology. *Educational Technology, 29*(5), 11–15.

Simpkins, G. A. (1976). *The cross-cultural approach to reading.* Unpublished doctoral dissertation, University of Massachusetts, Amherst.

Simpkins, G. (2002). *The throwaway kids.* Brookline, MA: Brookline Books.

Simpkins, G., Holt, G., & Simpkins, C. (1977). *Bridge: A cross-culture reading program.* New York: Houghton Mifflin.

Sleeter, C. E., & Grant, C. A. (1988). *Making choices for multicultural education.* Columbus, OH: Merrill.

Smith, P. L., & Ragan, T. J. (2005). Instructional design (3rd ed.). Hoboken, NJ: John Wiley & Sons, Inc.

Squire, K. D., MaKinster, J. G., Barnett, M., Luehmann, A. L., & Barab, S. L. (2003). Designed curriculum and local culture: Acknowledging the primacy of classroom culture [Electronic version]. *Science Education, 87,* 468–489.

Sutton, R. E. (1991). Equity and computers in the schools: A decade of research. *Review of Educational Research, 61*(4), 475–503.

Taylor, D. (1992). *Global software: Developing applications for the international market.* New York: Springer.

Tennyson, R. D., Schott, F., Seel, N., & Dijkstra, S. (Eds.). (1997). *Instructional design: International perspectives* (Vol. 1). Mahwah, NJ: Lawrence Erlbaum Associates.

Thomas, M., Mitchell, M., & Joseph, R. (2002). The third dimension of ADDIE: A cultural experience. *Tech Trends, 46*(2), 40–45.

U.S. Census Bureau. (1997). *Current population survey: Computer ownership supplement– 1997 Internet usage-methodology and documentation.* Retrieved January 16, 2007, from http://www.bls.census.gov/cps/computer/1997/smethdoc.htm

U.S. Census Bureau. (1998). *Current population survey: Computer ownership supplement– 1998 Internet and computer use-methodology and documentation.* Retrieved January 16, 2007, from http://www.bls.census.gov/cps/computer/1998/smethdocz.htm

U.S. Department of Education and National Center for Education Statistics. (2005a). *Internet access in U.S. public schools and classrooms: 1994–2003* (NCES 2005-015). Washington, DC: U.S. Government Printing Office.

U.S. Department of Education and National Center for Education Statistics. (2005b). *The Nation's Report Card™. NAEP 2004: Trends in academic progress: Three decades of student performance in reading and mathematics* (NCES 2005-0464). Washington, DC: U.S. Government Printing Office.

2005d). We have conducted dozens of experiments intended to determine the best ways to promote understanding of short scientific explanations. Without knowing it at first, we have been contributing in a modest way to the field of multimedia literacy because we have generated a collection of 10 principles for how to design multimedia messages. These principles have implications for teaching students how to generate multimedia messages that others can comprehend and, therefore, constitute an example of what it means to teach for multimedia literacy. My thesis is that these 10 design principles should be taught to students to improve their communication skills, that is, to improve their multimedia literacy.

What Is the Rationale for Teaching for Multimedia Literacy?

How can we help students develop multimedia literacy? As an example, consider one aspect of multimedia literacy—producing a scientific explanation that others can comprehend. Scientific explanations are at the heart of scientific discourse and represent an essential form of scientific communication. A scientific explanation tells how some cause-and-effect system works, such as a physical system (e.g., how lightning storms develop), a biological system (e.g., how the human lungs work), or a mechanical system (e.g., how an electric motor works). A cause-and-effect system consists of parts that interact with one another in a principled way such that a change in the state of one part causes a change in the state of another part and so on. For example, Table 13.1 contains a verbal explanation of how lightning storms develop (Mayer, 2001).

The desired learning outcome is that the learner builds a mental model of the causal system, which would enable the learner to mentally run the mental model when solving transfer problems. Deep understanding of a scientific explanation is indicated by improvements in the learner's performance on tests of problem solving transfer. For example, if learners understand the lightning explanation in Table 13.1, they should be able to answer transfer questions including troubleshooting questions (e.g., "Suppose you see clouds in the sky but no lightning. Why not?"), redesign questions (e.g., "What could you do to decrease the intensity of lightning?"), prediction questions (e.g., "What does air temperature have to do with lightning?"), and principle questions (e.g.," What causes lightning?").

My focus on multimedia literacy is based on the premise that people understand more deeply when scientific explanations are presented with words and pictures than with words alone. I refer to this idea as the multimedia principle, and in nine out of nine experiments (Mayer, 2001), my colleagues and I have found that students perform better on a problem-solving transfer test when they study a scientific explanation consisting of words and pictures (i.e., illustrations and text, or animation and narration) than words alone (i.e., text or narration alone). The median effect size was 1.50, which is considered a large effect (Cohen, 1988). Similarly, in a recent review, Fletcher and Tobias (2005)

Table 13.1 An Explanation of Lightning Formation

When the surface of the earth is warm, moist air near the earth's surface becomes heated and rises rapidly, producing an updraft. As the air in these updrafts cools, water vapor condenses into water droplets and forms a cloud. The cloud's top extends above the freezing level. At this altitude, the air temperature is well below freezing, so the upper portion of the cloud is composed of tiny ice crystals.

Eventually, the water droplets and ice crystals in the cloud become too large to be suspended by updrafts. As raindrops and ice crystals fall through the cloud, they drag some of the air from the cloud downward, producing downdrafts. The rising and falling air currents within the cloud may cause hailstones to form. When downdrafts strike the ground, they spread out in all directions, producing gusts of cool wind people feel just before the start of the rain.

Within the cloud, the moving air causes electrical charges to build, although scientists do not fully understand how it occurs. Most believe that the charge results from the collision of the cloud's light, rising water droplets and tiny pieces of ice against hail and other heavier, falling particles. The negatively charged particles fall to the bottom of the cloud, and most of the positively charged particles rise to the top.

The first stroke of a cloud-to-ground lightning flash is started by a stepped leader. Many scientists believe that it is triggered by a spark between the areas of positive and negative charges within the cloud. A stepped leader moves downward in steps, each of which is about 50 yards long, and lasts for about 1 millionth of a second. It pauses between steps for about 50 millionths of a second. As the stepped leader nears the ground, positively charged upward-moving leaders travel up from such objects as trees and buildings, to meet the negative charges. Usually, the upward moving leader from the tallest object is the first to meet the stepped leader and complete a path between cloud and earth. The two leaders generally meet about 165 feet above the ground. Negatively charged particles then rush from the cloud to the ground along the path created by the leaders. It is not very bright and usually has many branches.

As the stepped leader nears the ground, it induces an opposite charge, so positively charged particles from the ground rush upward along the same path. This upward motion of the current is the return stroke and it reaches the cloud in about 70 microseconds. The return stroke produces the bright light that people notice in a flash of lightning, but the current moves so quickly that its upward motion cannot be perceived. The lightning flash usually consists of an electrical potential of hundreds of millions of volts. The air along the lightning channel is heated briefly to a very high temperature. Such intense heating causes the air to expand explosively, producing a sound wave we call thunder.

found strong research-based evidence for the multimedia principle. For example, Figure 13.1 shows selected frames from a narrated animation explaining how lightning storms develop.

Although words have been the conventional medium for scientific explanations (e.g., Table 13.1), our research (Mayer, 2001) shows a strong increase in learner understanding when pictures are added (e.g., Figure 13.1). Yet, not all multimedia messages are equally instructive, so students need to learn how to use words and pictures to maximize learner understanding; that is, students need to learn to maximize the effectiveness of their multimedia communications. In order to understand how to generate effective multimedia messages, it is useful to understand how people learn (Mayer, 2001, 2005a).

How Do People Learn from Multimedia Messages?

The principles I present in this chapter are based on research and inspired by the cognitive theory of multimedia learning (Mayer, 2001, 2005a; Mayer & Moreno, 2003) and cognitive load theory (Paas, Renkl, & Sweller, 2003; Sweller, 1999, 2005). These theories are based on three fundamental prin-

"The charge results from the collision of the cloud's rising water droplets against heavier, falling pieces of ice."

"The negatively charged particles fall to the bottom of the cloud, and most of the positively charged particles rise to the top."

"A stepped leader of negative charges moves downward in a series of steps. It nears the ground."

"A positively charged leader travels up from such objects as trees and buildings."

"The two leaders generally meet about 165-feet above the ground."

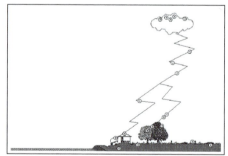

"Negatively charged particles then rush from the cloud to the ground along the path created by the leaders. It is not very bright."

"As the leader stroke nears the ground, it induces an opposite charge, so positively charged particles from the ground rush upward along the same path."

"This upward motion of the current is the return stroke. It produces the bright light that people notice as a flash of lightning."

Figure 13.1 Selected frames from a multimedia lesson on lightning formation.

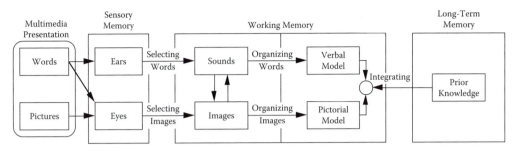

Figure 13.2 A cognitive theory of multimedia learning.

ciples of cognitive science: (a) dual channels, (b) limited capacity, and (c) active processing. First, the dual channels assumption is that humans have two somewhat separate channels for processing information—an auditory/verbal channel and a visual/pictorial channel (Baddeley, 1999; Paivio, 1986). Second, the limited capacity assumption is that people can process only a limited amount of material in a channel at any one time (Baddeley, 1999; Sweller, 1999). Third, the active processing assumption is that meaningful learning involves cognitive processing such as attending to relevant incoming information, mentally organizing the material, and mentally integrating the material with knowledge from long-term memory (Mayer, 2001; Wittrock, 1989).

Figure 13.2 shows a representation of the human cognitive system. Spoken words enter the system through the ears, whereas printed words and pictures enter through the eyes. If learners pay attention (i.e., indicated by the selecting words and selecting images arrows), some of the words and pictures enter working memory for further processing. The selected words and images are organized into coherent representations (i.e., indicated by the organizing words and organizing images arrows). Then, the resulting verbal and pictorial representations are integrated with each other and with relevant prior knowledge from long-term memory (as indicated by the integrating arrow). As you can see, multimedia learning requires that the learner engage in five major cognitive processes: (a) selecting relevant words, (b) selecting relevant images, (c) organizing words, (d) organizing images, and (e) integrating. Multimedia messages that foster these processes are more likely to lead to meaning learning than are those that do not.

The challenge for multimedia authors is to create multimedia messages that foster the five cognitive processes shown in Figure 13.2, but do not overload the capacity of the learner's cognitive system. Sweller (1999, 2005) and Mayer (2005a) distinguished among three types of cognitive load:

Extraneous processing. Extraneous processing, or what Sweller (1999, 2005) calls *extraneous load,* is cognitive processing that does not support the learner's construction of knowledge and that is attributable to confusing instructional design.

Essential processing. Essential processing, or what Sweller (1999, 2005) calls *intrinsic load,* is cognitive processing needed for receiving the basic material (corresponding to the processes of selecting words and selecting images).

Generative processing. Generative processing, or what Sweller (1999, 2005) calls *gemane load,* is deeper cognitive processing needed for making sense of the basic material (corresponding to the processes of organizing words, organizing images, and integrating).

When learners engage mainly in extraneous processing, no learning occurs as indicated by poor performance on tests of retention and transfer. When learners engage in appropriate essential processing (but insufficient amounts of generative processing), rote learning occurs as indicated by good retention and poor transfer performance. When learners engage in essential and generative processing, meaningful learning occurs as indicated by good retention and good transfer performance.

The implications of the cognitive theory of multimedia learning and cognitive load theory are that multimedia authors should reduce extraneous processing, manage essential processing, and promote generative processing. First, given that the total amount of cognitive capacity is limited, learners who must engage in large amounts of extraneous processing because of poor instructional design may not have sufficient capacity remaining for essential and generative processing. Therefore, one important goal of multimedia literacy is to create multimedia messages that minimize the need for the learner to engage in extraneous processing. Second, in cases where the material is inherently complex—requiring large amounts of essential processing—learners may not have sufficient remaining capacity to engage in generative processing. Therefore, an important goal of multimedia literacy is to create messages that manage essential processing in ways that enable concurrent generative processing. Finally, even when cognitive capacity is available, learners may not engage in generative processing. Thus, an important goal of multimedia literacy is to encourage appropriate generative processing.

In each of the following sections, I explore principles for reducing extraneous processing, managing essential processing, and fostering generative processing. For each principle, I give a definition, explain the theoretical basis for the principle, evaluate the supporting evidence, and offer some instructional implications.

Principles for Reducing Extraneous Processing in Multimedia Learning: Coherence, Signaling, Redundancy, Spatial Contiguity, and Temporal Contiguity

General Goal: Minimize the Learner's Extraneous Processing

Extraneous processing occurs when the learner must engage in cognitive processing that does not directly contribute to the learner's building of a mental representation of the target material (e.g., a mental model of how lightning storms develop). When a multimedia message is poorly designed (e.g., containing distracting irrelevant material), the learner must allocate cognitive capacity to cognitive processing that does not support learning (i.e., extraneous processing), which leaves less remaining cognitive capacity for cognitive processing that does support learning (i.e., essential and germane processing). Therefore, authors of multimedia explanations should be sensitive to anything that would cause learners to engage in extraneous processing.

Coherence principle: Weed out extraneous words, sounds, and pictures. In creating a multimedia explanation (e.g., how lightning storms develop), it might be tempting to add entertaining sentences (e.g., short stories about near-death experiences involving lightning), attention grabbing graphics (e.g., video of a lightning storm), or background sounds (e.g., lightning sounds or instrumental loops). Based on years of experimental research, I can offer this advice: Do not do it. (Mayer, 2005c). The number one multimedia literacy skill that students need to learn is to keep the multimedia explanation focused. I refer to this idea as the *coherence principle*.

In 10 out of 11 experimental tests that we conducted, students learned more deeply (i.e., scored higher on a test of problem-solving transfer) from a multimedia explanation (i.e., consisting of illustrations and text or animation and narration presentation) that was concise (i.e., containing mainly core material) rather than embellished (i.e., containing interesting but irrelevant words, sounds, or pictures). The median effect size favoring the concise presentation was 1.32, which is considered large. For example, students performed better on transfer tests when the text in a multimedia presentation on lighting described only the main steps in the process of lightning formation rather than also containing some supporting details (Mayer, Bove, Bryman, Mars, & Tapangco, 1996, Expts. 1, 2, & 3), when entertaining sentences about near-death experiences with lightning and entertaining pictures involving lightning were excluded rather than included (Harp & Mayer, 1997, Expt. 1, 1998, Expts. 1, 2, & 3) and when interesting video segments showing lightning storms and interesting background sounds and music were excluded rather than included (Mayer, Heiser, & Lonn, 2001, Expt. 3; Moreno & Mayer, 2000a, Expts. 1 & 2).

Overall, multimedia authors need to resist the temptation to embellish their messages with extras that distract the learner from processing the main steps in the cause-and-effect explanation. When learners focus on extraneous material, however entertaining, they are not processing the core material.

Signaling principle: Highlight the essential material. Sometimes it might not be possible to eliminate all of the potentially extraneous material from a multimedia explanation. In these cases, I suggest guiding the learner's cognitive processing by highlighting the essential material, such as adding an organizational sentence that lists the main steps in the process, inserting headings that correspond to the main steps in the process, inserting pointer words (e.g., first, second, third, or because of this) to pinpoint each respective step and the relations among them, and using extraordinary font style, size, or color or different intonation for essential words. I refer to this idea as the *signaling principle*. The goal is to draw the learner's attention to the essential material, such as the main steps in the cause-and-effect chain.

In three out of three experimental tests, my colleagues and I found that people performed better on transfer tests when they received multimedia explanations that were signaled rather than nonsignaled (Mayer, 2005c). The mean effect size was .60, which is considered medium to large. For example, learners performed better on a transfer test when the lightning lesson was signaled by adding an organizational sentence listing seven basic steps and pointer words for each step (e.g., "1" for the first step; Harp & Mayer, 1998, Expt. 3a). Similarly, students better understood multimedia explanations of how an airplane flies when the text was signaled using an organizing sentence keyed to headings (Mautone & Mayer, 2001, Expts. 3a & 3b).

Overall, multimedia authors need to provide cues to learners concerning what material is important and how it is organized. When learners are scanning a lesson looking for the essential material, they are wasting cognitive capacity that they could have used for learning. In short, the multimedia author's job includes clearly highlighting how to process the presented material.

Spatial contiguity principle: Place corresponding words and pictures near each other on the page or screen. Multimedia explanations consist of words and pictures. When the words are printed text, they should be placed next to the pictures they describe. For example, when there is a series of static frames depicting the steps in lightning formation, the text descriptions should be placed within the frames next to the elements to which they refer. I call this idea the *spatial contiguity principle*—place printed words next to the pictures to which they refer. The rationale for the spatial contiguity principle is that learners attempt to build mental connections between corresponding words (e.g., "negatively charged particles fall to the bottom of the cloud") and pictures (e.g., an animation depicting circles with minus signs in them moving downward in a cloud). If corresponding words and pictures are separated, learners must scan the multimedia lesson looking for elements of the pictures that correspond with elements of the words. This scanning activity is a form of extraneous processing that wastes cognitive capacity that otherwise could be used to build cognitive representations.

In eight out of eight experimental tests, my colleagues and I, as well other researchers, found evidence for the spatial contiguity principle; that is, students performed better on transfer tests when they learned from multimedia explanations in which corresponding words and pictures were integrated rather than separated (Mayer, 2005c). The median effect size was 1.11, which is considered large. For example, students performed better on a transfer test when they read a booklet about lightning formation in which the words describing each step were printed next to the corresponding pictures depicting each step than when the pictures were on a different page than the words (Mayer, Steinhoff, Bower, & Mars, 1995, Expts. 1, 2, & 3). Similarly, students performed better on a transfer test when an animation depicting the steps in lightning formation had corresponding words printed next to the elements they described than at the bottom of the screen (Moreno & Mayer, 1999, Expt. 1). Similar effects were reported for multimedia lessons involving braking systems (Mayer, 1989, Expt. 2), a mathematical procedure (Sweller, Chandler, Tierney, & Cooper, 1990, Expt. 1), and an engineering procedure (Chandler & Sweller, 1991, Expt. 1; Tindall-Ford, Chandler, & Sweller, 1997, Expt. 1).

Overall, multimedia authors should exercise care in the layout of the page or screen so that words are placed next to the corresponding portion of the picture. An integrated layout reduces the need for learners to engage in extraneous processing and thereby maintains the cognitive capacity available for learning.

Temporal contiguity principle: Present corresponding narration and pictures simultaneously. When the words are in printed form, then spatial contiguity is important. However, when the words are in spoken form, then temporal contiguity is important. The *temporal contiguity principle* is that corresponding narration and pictures should be presented simultaneously rather than successively. For example, in a narrated animation on lightning formation, as the narrator's voice says, "Negatively charged particles move to the bottom of the cloud" the animation should show circles with minus signs in them moving downward in the cloud. The rationale for the temporal contiguity principle is that learners are attempting to mentally connect corresponding words and pictures. When corresponding words and pictures are separated in time the learner must use cognitive capacity to mentally hold words in memory until the corresponding picture is presented or vice versa. Using cognitive capacity to temporarily hold words or pictures in working memory is a form of extraneous processing—processing caused by suboptimal presentation of the material. The capacity used for this representational holding could be put to better use—that is, in building mental representations.

In eight out of eight experimental tests that my colleagues and I conducted, students performed better on transfer tests when a narration and animation were presented simultaneously rather than successively (Mayer, 2005c). The median effect size was 1.31, which is considered large. For example, students who viewed a narrated animation of how lightning storms develop performed better on a transfer test than did students who received the animation followed by the narration or vice versa (Mayer, Moreno, Boire, & Vagge, 1999, Expt. 1). Similar results were obtained for narration and animation explain-

clicked on the button. Students who received the segmented narrated animation performed better on a transfer test than students who received the continuous narrated animation. Similar results were obtained with a narrated animation explaining how an electric motor works (Mayer, Dow, & Mayer, 2003, Expts. 2a & 2b).

Overall, segmenting is a technique intended to manage essential cognitive processing. It is consistent with van Merrienboer's (1997; van Merrienboer & Kester, 2005) four-component instructional design model. When presenting the entire explanation would overload the learner, it is better to break it into meaningful segments that can be presented individually.

Pretraining principle: Begin by explaining the operation of each part. A complex system consists of parts that interact in a principled way. Two aspects of learning about a complex system such as how a car's braking system works are component models and the causal model. Learning about component models involves learning the name and location of each part along with the possible states of the part. For example, the master cylinder consists of a piston in a cylinder; the piston can be forward or backward. The causal model is a cause-and-effect chain in which a change in the state of one part affects a change in the state of another part and so on. For example, when the piston moves forward in the master cylinder, brake fluid is pushed into the brake tube, and so on. The *pretraining principle* is to explain component models before explaining the causal model. In short, learners need to know the name, location, and possible states of each part before they are given a narrated animation explaining how the system works. The rationale is that when a narrated animation about a complex system is presented at a rapid pace, the learner has to mentally build component models and a causal model at the same time—a situation that can easily overload the learner. When the narration says, "The piston moves forward in the master cylinder," the learner must build a component model of how the master cylinder works and at the same time must build a causal model of how the piston's movement affects the brake fluid in the tube and so on. Pretraining in the component models can reduce this load, and make essential processing more manageable.

In seven out of seven experimental tests, students who received pretraining performed better on transfer tests than did students who did not (Mayer, 2005b). The median effect size was 0.92, which is considered a large effect. The same pattern was obtained for multimedia lessons involving brakes (Mayer, Mathias, & Wetzell, 2002, Expts. 1 & 2), tire pumps (Mayer et al., 2002, Expt. 3), an engineering procedure (Pollock, Chandler, & Sweller, 2002, Expts. 1 & 3), and a geology game (Mayer, Mautone, & Prothero, 2002, Expts. 2 & 3).

Overall, students learn how a complex system works more easily if they already know about the components in the system. Multimedia authors should make sure that learners are familiar with the parts of the system before they present a multimedia explanation of how the system works.

Modality principle: Present words in spoken form rather than printed form. The best-established principle for multimedia design is the *modality principle:* Present words in spoken form rather than printed form. This principle is particularly important when an animation or series of still frames is presented at a rapid pace and the material is complex. The rationale for the modality principle is that printed words and pictures both must enter through the eyes and therefore must compete for processing in the learner's visual channel. When the words are presented in spoken form, the words can be processed through the ears in the verbal channel whereas the pictures can be processed through the eyes in the visual channel. Thus, some of the load on the visual channel is offloaded onto the verbal channel.

In 21 separate tests, students performed better on a transfer test when they learned from pictures and spoken text than from pictures and printed text (Mayer, 2005b). The median effect size was 0.97, which is considered large. For example, researchers (Craig et al., 2000, Expt. 2; Mayer & Moreno, 1998, Expt. 1; Moreno & Mayer, 1999, Expts. 1 & 2) presented a narrated animation explaining lightning formation or the same animation with on-screen text. Students generated more acceptable answers on a transfer test if they learned with spoken rather than printed text. Similar results were obtained in an multimedia explanation of how an electric motor works (Mayer, Dow, & Mayer, 2003, Expt. 1), how braking systems work (Mayer & Moreno, 1998, Expts. 1 & 2), how an aircraft fuel system works (O'Neil et al., 2000, Expt. 1), how plants grow (Moreno, Mayer, Spires, & Lester, 2001, Expts. 4a, 4b, 5a, & 5b; Moreno & Mayer, 2002b, Expt. 1a, 1b, 1c, 2a, & 2b), an engineering procedure (Kalyuga et al., 1999, Expt. 1; Kalyuga et al., 2000, Expt. 1), and a mathematical procedure (Jeung, Chandler, & Sweller, 1997, Expts. 1, 2, & 3).

Overall, the format of words matters. One way of managing essential load is to make use of the processing capacity of both the visual and verbal channels. When words are presented in printed form, they can compete with pictures for limited processing capacity within the visual channel. When words are presented in spoken form, they can be processed in the verbal channel, thus freeing capacity in the visual channel for processing of pictures. Multimedia authors should question the common sense idea that words are the same whether spoken or printed, and instead should be sensitive to ways of managing essential processing.

Principles for Fostering Generative Processing: Personalization and Voice Principles

General Goal: Foster the Learner's Generative Processing

Meaningful learning depends on appropriate essential processing—paying attention to the relevant words and pictures—and generative processing—efforts to make sense of the relevant words and pictures by making connections between them and with prior knowledge. Even though multimedia authors are careful to reduce extraneous processing and manage essential processing, we cannot be assured that learners will use the remaining available capacity for generative processing—making sense of the material. How can we encourage learners to engage in deeper processing? One technique is to create a social partnership between the learner and the computer. When the learner accepts the computer as a social partner, the rules of human-to-human conversation come into play in which the learners try harder to understand what their social partner is saying (Reeves & Nass, 1996). In this section, I explore two techniques for fostering social presence and hence fostering generative processing with narrated animation: (a) personalization principle and (b) voice principle.

Personalization principle: Present words in conversational style rather than formal style. One way to create a sense of social presence is to present words in conversational style. I refer to this idea as the *personalization principle*. For example, the formal text about lightning formation presented in Table 13.1 can be made more conversational by using first and second person constructions (i.e., *I* and *you*). For example, in the sentence, "The cloud's top extends above the freezing level, so the upper portion of the cloud is composed of tiny ice crystals," we can replace *the* with *your* in two places. We can also add a preceding sentence: "As you watch, you tilt your head skyward." The point of these changes is to prompt a social response in the learner, which in turn will result in the learner trying harder to understand what the computer is saying.

In 10 out of 10 experimental tests that my colleagues and I conducted, students learned more deeply with conversational text than with formal text. The median effect size on a transfer test was 1.29, which is a large effect. For example, when the lightning passage was changed from formal to conversation text, learners scored higher on the transfer test (Moreno & Mayer, 2000b, Expts. 1 & 2). A narrated animation explaining how the lungs work was changed from formal to conversational form by changing a "the" to "your" in 12 places (Mayer, Fennell, Farmer, & Campbell, 2004, Expts. 1, 2, & 3). This modest change was enough to cause a large increase in correct answers on the transfer test. Finally, the same personalization effect was found in a computer game that contained narrated animations about plant growth (Moreno & Mayer, 2000b, Expts. 3 & 4; Moreno & Mayer, 2004, Expts. 1a & 1b).

Overall, a modest change from formal to conversational style improves problem-solving transfer. Personalization is an attempt to foster generative processing by creating a sense of social presence. The underlying assumption, which warrants further testing, is that people try harder to make sense out a presented multimedia explanation when they see the author as a social partner. Multimedia authors should be sensitive to their social relation with the learner.

Voice principle: Present narration with a standard-accented human voice. Finally, another way to create a sense of social presence concerns the nature of the voice in narrated animations. According to the voice principle, the narration should be in a standard-accented human voice. When a machine voice or a foreign-accented voice is used, learners may be less able to form a social connection with the computer. Thus, they may not try as hard to make sense of the material, that is, they may not engage in as much generative processing.

In four out of four experimental tests, students performed better on transfer tests when they learned from a narrated animation consisting of a standard-accented human voice rather than a machine voice or a foreign-accented human voice. The median effect size was 0.79, which is considered large. For example, when the lightning lesson summarized in Figure 13.1 was presented in a machine voice or a foreign-accented voice, learners performed more poorly on a transfer test than when a standard-accented human voice was used (Mayer, Sobko, & Mautone, 2003, Expts. 1 & 2). Supplemental studies demonstrated that the words were easily discernible in all conditions. Similar results were obtained with a multimedia lesson on mathematics by Atkinson, Mayer, and Merrill (2005, Expts. 1 & 2).

Overall, the speaker's voice is an important social cue that can prime the learner to exert more effort. Multimedia authors should take advantage of the social power of voice in multimedia explanations.

Conclusion

Table 13.2 summarizes the 10 research-based principles for how to produce multimedia explanations that people can understand. These 10 principles should be included in any program intended to improve students' multimedia literacy. The underlying theme is that presenting the necessary information is not sufficient; multimedia authors must present the message in a way that encourages appropriate cognitive processing and is sensitive to demands

Table 13.2 Ten Principles of Multimedia Message Design

Principles for Minimizing the Learner's Extraneous Processing
1. Coherence principle: Weed out extraneous words, sounds, and pictures.
2. Signaling principle: Highlight the essential material.
3. Spatial contiguity principle: Place corresponding words and pictures near each other on the page or screen.
4. Temporal contiguity principle: Present corresponding narration and pictures simultaneously.
5. Redundancy principle: Do not add printed on-screen text to a narrated animation.
Principles for Managing the Learner's Essential Processing
6. Segmenting principle: Break an explanation into bite-size parts.
7. Pretraining principle: Begin by explaining the operation of each part.
8. Modality principle: Present words in spoken form rather than printed form.
Principles for Fostering the Learner's Generative Processing
9. Personalization principle: Present words in conversational style rather than formal style.
10. Voice principle: Present narration with a standard-accented human voice.

on the learner's cognitive capacity. In short, as new forms of media become widespread, educators should expand their conceptions of what it means to be literate. Multimedia literacy is a new form of literacy whose time has come. A major goal of promoters of multimedia literacy is to help students develop skills for how to produce multimedia messages that others can understand. A first step toward this goal is represented in the 10 research-based principles listed in Table 13.2.

A major limitation of the principles presented in this chapter is that they are intended to support only one type of multimedia message—explanations. Explanative messages provide cause-and-effect explanations of how some system works. They can be represented as flow charts and are based a rhetorical structure sometimes referred to as process. Further research is needed to determine how well these principles relate to other genres.

References

Atkinson, R. K., Mayer, R. E., & Merrill, M. M. (2005). Fostering social agency in multimedia learning: Examining the impact of an animated agent's voice. *Contemporary Educational Psychology, 30*, 117–139.

Baddeley, A. D. (1999). *Human memory.* Boston: Allyn & Bacon.

Chandler, P., & Sweller, J. (1991). Cognitive load theory and the format of instruction. *Cognition and Instruction, 8*, 293–332.

Clark, R. C., & Mayer, R. E. (2003). *E-learning and the science of instruction.* San Francisco: Pfeiffer.

Cohen, J. (1988). *Statistical power analysis for the behavioral sciences* (2nd ed.). Hillsdale, NJ: Lawrence Erlbaum Associates.

Craig, S. D., Gholson, B., & Driscoll, D. M. (2002). Animated pedagogical agents in multimedia educational environments: Effects of agent properties, picture features, and redundancy. *Journal of Educational Psychology, 94*, 428–434.

Fletcher, J. D., & Tobias, S. (2005). The multimedia principle. In R. E. Mayer (Ed.), *Cambridge handbook of multimedia learning* (pp. 117–134). New York: Cambridge University Press.

Harp, S. F., & Mayer, R. E. (1997). The role of interest in learning from scientific text and illustrations: On the distinction between emotional interest and cognitive interest. *Journal of Educational Psychology, 89*, 92–102.

Harp, S. F., & Mayer, R. E. (1998). How seductive details do their damage: A theory of cognitive interest in science learning. *Journal of Educational Psychology, 90*, 414–434.

Jeung, H., Chandler, P., & Sweller, J. (1997). The role of visual indicators in dual sensory mode instruction. *Educational Psychology, 17*, 329–343.

Kalyuga, S., Chandler, P., & Sweller, J. (1999). Managing split-attention and redundancy in multimedia instruction. *Applied Cognitive Psychology, 13*, 351–371.

Kalyuga, S., Chandler, P., & Sweller, J. (2000). Incorporating learner experience into the design of multimedia instruction. *Journal of Educational Psychology, 92*, 126–136.

Mautone, P. D., & Mayer, R. E. (2001). Signaling as a cognitive guide in multimedia learning. *Journal of Educational Psychology, 93*, 377–389.

Mayer, R. E. (1989). Systematic thinking fostered by illustrations in scientific text. *Journal of Educational Psychology, 81*, 240–246.

Mayer, R. E. (2000). The challenge of multimedia learning. In A. W. Pailliotet & P. B. Mosenthal (Eds.), *Reconceptualizing literacy in the age of media, multimedia, and hypermedia* (pp. 363–376). Norwood, NJ: JAI/Ablex.

Mayer, R. E. (2001). *Multimedia learning.* New York: Cambridge University Press.

Mayer, R. E. (2003). *Learning and instruction*. Upper Saddle River, NJ: Merrill Prentice Hall.

Mayer, R. E. (2005a). Cognitive theory of multimedia learning. In R. E. Mayer (Ed.), *Cambridge handbook of multimedia learning* (pp. 31–48). New York: Cambridge University Press.

Mayer, R. E. (2005b). Principles for managing essential processing in multimedia learning: Segmenting, pretraining, and modality principles. In R. E. Mayer (Ed.), *Cambridge handbook of multimedia learning* (pp. 169–182). New York: Cambridge University Press.

Mayer, R. E. (2005c). Principles for reducing extraneous processing in multimedia learning: Coherence, signaling, redundancy, spatial contiguity, and temporal contiguity principles. In R. E. Mayer (Ed.), *Cambridge handbook of multimedia learning* (pp. 183–200). New York: Cambridge University Press.

Mayer, R. E. (2005d). Principles of multimedia learning based on social cues: Personalization, voice, and image principles. In R. E. Mayer (Ed.), *Cambridge handbook of multimedia learning* (pp. 201–211). New York: Cambridge University Press.

Mayer, R. E., & Anderson, R. B. (1991). Animations need narrations: An experimental test of a dual-coding hypothesis. *Journal of Educational Psychology, 83*, 484–490.

Mayer, R. E., & Anderson, R. B. (1992). The instructive animation: Helping students build connections between words and pictures in multimedia learning. *Journal of Educational Psychology, 84*, 444–452.

Mayer, R. E., Bove, W., Bryman, A., Mars, R., & Tapangco, L. (1996). When less is more: Meaningful learning from visual and verbal summaries of science textbook lessons. *Journal of Educational Psychology, 88*, 64–73.

Mayer, R. E., & Chandler, P. (2001). When learning is just a click away: Does simple user interaction foster deeper understanding of multimedia messages? *Journal of Educational Psychology, 93*, 390–397.

Mayer, R. E., Dow, G., & Mayer, R. E. (2003). Multimedia learning in an interactive self-explaining environment: What works in the design of agent-based microworlds? *Journal of Educational Psychology, 95*, 806–813.

Mayer, R. E., Fennell, S., Farmer, L., & Campbell, J. (2004). A personalization effect in multimedia learning: Students learn better when words are in conversational style rather than formal style. *Journal of Educational Psychology, 96*, 389–395.

Mayer, R. E., Heiser, H., & Lonn, S. (2001). Cognitive constraints on multimedia learning: When presenting more material results in less understanding. *Journal of Educational Psychology, 93*, 187–198.

Mayer, R. E., Mathias, A., & Wetzell, K. (2002). Fostering understanding of multimedia messages through pre-training: Evidence for a two-stage theory of mental model construction. *Journal of Experimental Psychology: Applied, 8*, 147–154.

Mayer, R. E., Mautone, P., & Prothero, W. (2002). Pictorial aids for learning by doing in a multimedia geology simulation game. *Journal of Educational Psychology, 94*, 171–185.

Mayer, R. E., & Moreno, R. (1998). A split-attention effect in multimedia learning: Evidence for dual processing systems in working memory. *Journal of Educational Psychology, 90*, 312–320.

Mayer, R. E., & Moreno, R. (2003). Nine ways to reduce cognitive load in multimedia learning. *Educational Psychologist, 38*, 43–52.

Mayer, R. E., Moreno, R., Boire, M., & Vagge, S. (1999). Maximizing constructivist learning from multimedia communications by minimizing cognitive load. *Journal of Educational Psychology, 91*, 638–643.

Mayer, R. E., & Sims, V. K. (1994). For whom is a picture worth a thousand words? Extensions of a dual-coding theory of multimedia learning? *Journal of Educational Psychology, 86*, 389–401.

Mayer, R. E., Sobko, K., & Mautone, P. D. (2003). Social cues in multimedia learning: Role of speaker's voice. *Journal of Educational Psychology, 95*, 419–425.

including their understanding of how the resources of language, images, and other modalities are deployed to make meanings. Such understanding goes beyond using the various semiotic resources of language, image, sound, and other symbolic system separately and in combination to make meanings. It involves knowledge of the nature of semiotic systems and their meaning-making potential—metasemiotic knowledge. It includes, but extends beyond, knowledge of the grammatical and discourse systems of language to similar systems dealing with visual, audio, gestural, spatial, and multimodal semiotics. To develop this kind of metasemiotic knowledge as part of a multiliteracies pedagogy what is required is "a metalanguage that describes meaning in various realms. These include the textual, the visual, as well as the multimodal relations between different meaning-making processes that are now so critical in media texts and the texts of electronic multimedia" (New London Group, 2000, p. 24).

Teachers and students need this kind of metalanguage for talking about language, images, sound, and so forth, and for their meaning-making interactions. It is a significant (but not sufficient) resource for developing students' understanding of how the "interestedness" of all texts is frequently naturalized or deemed invisible by the semiotic choices that are made in constructing the text. This kind of metalanguage gives students and teachers a means of comparing texts, of determining what semiotic choices were made in constructing particular meanings, what alternatives might have been chosen, and the effects of particular choices rather than others.

The problem, of course, is that, despite strong advocacy for its development and some research in this direction, there is, as yet, no such comprehensive, intermodal metalanguage. The obvious overarching questions relate to how such a metalanguage might be developed. Further questions relate to how such a project would take account of the "deictic" nature of new literacies (Leu, Kinzer, Coiro, & Cammack, 2004). This refers to the rapidly changing forms and functions of new literacies, as new ICTs seem to be constantly emerging and people devise innovative literacy practices using the affordances of new technologies. In suggesting an approach to these questions, the second section in this chapter will outline a transdisplinary perspective on the theoretical frameworks that seem most powerful in informing the relevant research; the third section will indicate reasons for focusing the discussion here on image/text relations; the fourth section will summarize the support for the role of metalanguage in multimodal literacy education; and the fifth section reviews research on the nature of image/text relations and the nature of an emerging metalanguage as an interpretive resource for negotiating multimodal texts. Educational implications of the development of such a metalanguage are discussed briefly in the last section, and the final section sketches a number of research challenges in progressing a "futures-oriented" multiliteracies pedagogy.

A Transdisciplinary Theoretical Framework Exploring Multiliteracies and Metalanguage

New literacies integrate multiple meaning-making systems, such as language, image, sound, and movement; multiple "text"-generation devices, such as digital cameras, scanners, and computer software such as multimedia authoring systems; and multiple communication formats such as computer screens, iPods, handheld/pocket personal electronic organizing devices, and mobile phones. Developing an understanding of the pedagogic impact and potential of new literacies necessitates a framework that encompasses their multiple dimensions as a unified resource. The implication of this for educational research is to emphasize the importance of adopting a "transdisciplinary" perspective. Transdisciplinary research, according to Halliday (2003), is very different from "inter-" or "multidisciplinary" research. The latter imply that one still pursues research focused within the disciplines while building bridges between them and/or assembling the research efforts into a "collection," whereas the real alternative is to transcend disciplinary boundaries to achieve the kind of integrated focus necessary to research issues in the fields such as new literacies research. This means that educational researchers need to commit to reading and participating in the discourses of research beyond the discipline(s) in which they were trained and in which their prestige is established.

Such an enterprise seems to be emerging as researchers in disciplines such as literacy education, systemic functional linguistics (SFL), social semiotics, and information and ICT in education, begin to find common, compatible, or complementary theoretical frameworks productive in progressing research initiatives. The beginnings of this transdisciplinary orientation is partially reflected in this chapter through the growing integrative theorizing and research endeavors linking multiliteracies, new literacies, deictic perspectives of literacy, SFL, multimodal perspectives, and semiotic theory. The following sections outline some key aspects of this transdisciplinary work in relation to image/text relations.

Core Elements of a Social Semiotic Theory of Image/Text Relations

The fundamental theoretical tenets for a wide range of social semiotic work dealing with aspects of intersemiosis such as image/text relations derive from SFL. SFL posits the complete "interconnectedness" of the linguistic and the social. According to SFL, the structures of language have evolved (and continue to evolve) as a result of the meaning-making functions they serve within the social system or culture in which they are used. Halliday (Halliday & Hasan, 1985) emphasized that language is only one semiotic system among many, however, which might include forms of art such as painting, sculpture, music, and dance, and other modes of cultural behavior not usually classified as art, such as modes of dress, structures of the family, and so forth. All of these modes of meaning-making interrelate and their totality might be thought of as a way of defining a culture (Halliday & Hasan, 1985, p. 4).

This conceptualization of language as one of many different interrelated semiotic systems, and hence the assumption that the forms of all semiotic systems are related to the meaning-making functions they serve within social contexts, indicates the strength of SFL in contributing to frameworks for the development of intersemiotic theory. The SFL-related theorizing proposes that the meaning-making functions of all semiotic systems can be grouped into three main categories, or metafunctions: (a) ideational, (b) interpersonal, and (c) textual. These three kinds of meaning-making, or metafunctions, are related to three corresponding situational variables that operate in all communicative contexts: (a) field, (b) tenor, and (c) mode.

Any communicative context can be described in terms of these three main variables that are important in influencing the semiotic choices that are made. *Field* is concerned with the social activity, its content, or its topic; *tenor* is the nature of the relationships among the people involved in the communication; and *mode* is the medium and channel of communication. In relation to language, mode is concerned with the role of language in the situation—whether spoken or written—accompanying or constitutive of the activity, and the ways in which relative information value is conveyed. These situational variables are related to the three overarching areas of meaning, or metafunctions—"ideational," "interpersonal" and "textual." For example, if I say "My daughter is coming home this weekend," ideationally this involves an event, a participant, and the circumstances of time and place associated with them. Interpersonally it constructs me as a giver of information and the reader/listener as a receiver (as well as perhaps suggesting I have at least some acquaintance with the listener). Textually, it locates "my daughter" as the theme, orientation, or point of departure for the interaction, simultaneously suggesting that "my daughter" is given information that we both know about (given), and the new information is that she is coming home "this weekend" (new). If I say "Is my daughter coming home this weekend?", the ideational meanings remain the same—the event, the participant, and the circumstances have not changed. The interpersonal meanings, however, have certainly changed. Now I am demanding information, not giving it (and there may be some suggestion of estrangement between the listener and me). Similarly, if I say, "This weekend my daughter is coming home," the ideational meanings are still the same, but this time the textual meanings have changed. Now the orientation (theme) is the weekend and this is the given or shared information. What is new or unknown concerns what my daughter is doing. So the different structures reflect different kinds of meaning, which in turn reflect different aspects of the context. The metalanguage of systemic functional grammar derives from this linking of language structure, meaning, and context.

It is this metafunctional aspect of SFL and its link to the situational variables of social contexts that has provided a common theoretical basis for the development of similar "grammatical" descriptions of the meaning-making resources of other semiotic modes. Extrapolating from SFL on this basis, Kress and van Leeuwen (1996) proposed that images, like language, also always simultaneously realize three different kinds of meanings. Images construct not only representations of material reality but also the interpersonal interaction of social reality (such as relations between viewers and what is viewed). In addition images cohere into textual compositions in different ways and so realize semiotic reality. More technically, the "grammar of visual design" formulated by Kress and van Leeuwen (1996) adopted from SFL the metafunctional organization of meaning-making resources:

- *representational/ideational* structures verbally and visually construct the nature of events, the objects and participants involved, and the circumstances in which they occur;
- *interactive/interpersonal* verbal and visual resources construct the nature of relationships among speakers/listeners, writers/readers, and viewers, and what is viewed;
- *compositional/textual* meanings are concerned with the distribution of the information value or relative emphasis among elements of the text and image.

Similar extrapolations from SFL have provided social semiotic descriptions of "displayed art" (O'Toole, 1994), music and sound (van Leeuwen, 1999), and action (Martinec, 1999, 2000a, 2000b).

Many researchers exploring image/text relations explicitly acknowledge the grounding of their work in the SFL metafunctional hypothesis (Baldry, 2000; Lemke, 1998a, 1998b, 2002; Macken-Horarik, 2003a, 2004; Martin, 2002; O'Halloran, 2004; Royce, 1998, 2002). This provides a useful commonality in theorizing meaning in very broad terms across different semiotic systems. This does not mean, however, that existing theories of meaning and communication are sufficient to describe the interrelations among different semiotic modes. This latter descriptive capacity is what is required for a metalanguage of multiliteracies. The development of such a metalanguage presupposes adequate social semiotic descriptions of the contributing modes in multimodal compositions, but needs to draw on and extend beyond them to detail the range of possible ways in which intersemiotic synergies are involved in the design of texts. This chapter reviews research relating to image/language interaction as one dimension of this enterprise. One further significant issue in developing a theoretical framework for a metalanguage of multiliteracies, however, is its capacity to deal with the deictic nature of New Literacies (Leu et al., 2004). A useful contribution by SFL scholars toward theorizing this kind of inherent and ongoing change in the meaning-making potential of evolving intersemiotic systems is outlined later in this chapter.

the production and consumption of images than reading and writing of either hypertextual or linear prose" (p. 7), and that written elements on screen are now considered to be only what cannot be done in images (Boulter, 1999).

The need to redefine literacy and literacy pedagogy in the light of the increasing influence of images has been widely advocated in the international literature (Russell, 2000). The *Handbook of Reading Research* noted as particularly important that research be undertaken in the comprehension of graphics and text and the study of whether (and how) referential connections between visuals and text can be explicitly taught (Kamil, Intrator, & Kim, 2000). While the multimodal nature of electronic texts and Internet communication has drawn attention to the blurring of relations between verbal and visual media of textuality (Richards, 2001), this changed visual/verbal dynamic has also emerged as a key issue in the changing nature of text in books. Writing about *Books for Youth in a Digital Age,* Dresang (1999) noted, "In the graphically oriented, digital, multimedia world, the distinction between pictures and words has become less and less certain" (p. 21), and that "in order to understand the role of print in the digital age, it is essential to have a solid grasp of the growing integrative relationship of print and graphics" (p. 22). In both electronic and paper-media environments, then, "Although the fundamental principles of reading and writing have not changed, the process has shifted from the serial cognitive processing of linear print text to parallel processing of multimodal text-image information" (Luke, 2003, p. 399).

Recently, Andrews (2004) has explicitly noted the importance of the visual/verbal interface in both computer and hardcopy texts: "It is the visual/verbal interface that is at the heart of literacy learning and development for both computer-users and those without access to computers" (Andrews, 2004, p. 63).

Metalanguage and Metasemiotic Work as Criterial to New Literacies Learning

The quest for an appropriate metalanguage facilitating the kind of metasemiotic work required in new literacy pedagogy, although intensified in recent years, has been on the agenda for some time. In the 1980s, Nodelman (1988) pointed out that the narrative art of children's picture books might be better explicated if there were a system underlying visual communication that was something like a grammar similar to that which defines the relationships and contexts that makes verbal communication possible (Nodelman, 1988).

More recently Gee's (2003) work in *What Video Games Have to Teach Us About Learning and Literacy* noted that the combination of images and text communicates things that neither of the modes does separately. But he also noted that for learning to be critical as well as active the learner not only needs to be able to understand and produce meanings but also how to think about meaning-making in particular contexts at a "meta" level as a complex system of interrelated options (Gee, 2003, p. 23).

Gee (2003) went on to indicate the need for a metalanguage to facilitate this kind of meta-activity, which he outlined in terms of internal and external design grammars. Internal design grammars allow individuals to recognize what is acceptable or typical content in a semiotic domain, while external design grammars enable one to recognize what is acceptable or typical social practice and identity in regard to the affinity group associated with the semiotic domain. In exemplifying the principles of these grammars, what Gee strongly emphasized was their pedagogic role. He noted that for active learning, understanding, and use of the internal and external design grammar, at least unconsciously, is essential. "But for critical learning, the learner must be able consciously to attend to, reflect on, critique, and manipulate those design grammars at a metalevel" (p. 40).

Such a role for metalanguage is essential to the effective critical negotiation of "new texts" since the acquisition of metalanguage through which to talk about texts puts learners in a position "to say—and think—even more" (Bearne, 2000, p. 148). The New London Group emphasized the role of metalanguages as a defining aspect of the overt instruction element of their pedagogy of multiliteracies (New London Group, 2000, p. 34).

There seems to be significant support for the view that redefining literacy in the electronic age entails the development of a metalanguage that will facilitate metatextual awareness of image/text relations (Kamil et al., 2000; Kress, 2003b; Macken-Horarik, 2004; Richards, 2001; Russell, 2000). The work on grammars for exploring the coarticulation of image and verbiage, however, is in its infancy (Kress, 2001; Macken-Horarik, 2003a). These early efforts (Kress & van Leeuwen, 1996; New London Group, 2000) have drawn on the social semiotic theories of SFL (Halliday, 1994; Martin, 1992; Matthiessen, 1995). Little classroom research has been done on the pedagogic use of such emerging grammars, although there is some evidence that young children can learn and productively use aspects of Kress and van Leeuwen's visual grammar in work with picture books and with multimedia CD-ROMs in curriculum-area learning (Callow & Zammit, 2002; Howley, 1996). There is also a good deal of evidence of the efficacy of the metalanguage of SFL in literacy development and learning in primary/elementary- and secondary/high-school contexts (Quinn, 2004; Schleppegrell, 2004; Schleppegrell, Achugar, & Oteiza, 2004; Torr & Harman, 1997; Williams, 1999, 2000). What is suggested here is that the theoretical bases of the social semiotic research arising from SFL are providing a generative and inclusive framework for the transdisciplinary development of a metalanguage of multiliteracies.

Toward a Metalanguage of Image/Text Relations: Researching Intermodal Meanings

The formulation of a metalanguage of multiliteracies needs to entail both the description of the specific characteristics of each participatory semiotic cate that the visual and verbal modes provide much more than a duplication of meanings. A similar analysis of an explanation of the water cycle from a high-school science textbook produced findings consistent with the earlier study (Royce, 2002). Royce (1998, 2002) described these results as indicating intersemiotic complementarity, but they are consistent with, and may now be more appropriately considered as indicating, ideational concurrence. "Crossmodal" cohesive links were also described by Lemke (2002) to indicate the role of these image/text relations on science Web sites in enabling the viewer to derive meanings. In fact, interpreting the contribution of the image component depended on these intermodal ties, since the construction of meaning from the image necessitated integrating information from the caption texts.

A further perspective on ideational concurrence can be seen the work of Macken-Horarik (2003a) who analyzed newspaper reports of the "children overboard" affair, which occurred in the context of the apprehension of asylum seekers attempting to reach Australia by sea. [This notorious incident, in which Liberal Party government ministers wrongly claimed that the asylum seekers threw their children overboard in an effort to coerce the navy to offer them sanctuary, was front-page news in Australian newspapers for some time.] One part of Macken-Horarik's investigation of the coarticulation of image and verbiage related to the depiction of people specifically or generically:

> Specification is often realized in language through the definite article (e.g., "the Australian frigate"), by the demonstrative ("this") or by means of a numerative (e.g., "one woman"). "Genericisation" in language is most typically realized through the plural (e.g., "children" or "asylum seekers") or collective nouns (e.g., "the navy" or "the government") (Macken-Horarik, 2003a, p. 8).

Overwhelmingly in the media reports, asylum seekers were genericised while the government ministers and officials were specified. The visual depictions of asylum seekers were predominantly distant views, and where individuals could be seen, their faces were left blurred. In fact, the government Defense Minister, Peter Reith, banned the taking of photographs that could "humanise or personalize asylum seekers."[1] In these texts the ideational concurrence resides in the genericising of asylum seekers through the strategies of "homogenization in language and indetermination in image" (Macken-Horarik, 2003a, p. 9).

The final means by which ideational concurrence is achieved is the phenomenon of "homospatiality" (Lim, 2004), and refers to texts where two different semiotic modes co-occur in one spatially bonded homogenous entity. One example shows the linguistic representation, "snaaap," which visually appears with the "sna" segment forming one arm of an inverted "V" shape and the

---

[1] Macken-Horarik (2003a, p. 9) noted, "As Defence Officials reported to the Senate Inquiry in April, 2002, Mr. Reith and his staff did not want to allow photographs to create sympathy for asylum seekers" (Parliament of Australia, 2002).

Figure 14.2 An illustration of homospatiality.

"aap" segment forming the other arm, so that it appears that the word itself has "snapped," as indicated in Figure 14.2.

Another example shows an image of a campfire with the heat arising from the fire represented by curved lines, which can be read to spell the word *hot*.

Ideational complementarity. In multimodal texts what is represented in images and what is represented in language may be different but complementary. Kress (1997, 2000b, 2003a, 2003b) and Lemke (1998b) have explicated what they call the "functional specialization" of language and image. According to this specialization principle the resources of language are most apposite to the representation of sequential relations and the making of categorical distinctions, while the resources of images are most apposite to the representation of spatial relations and for formulating "degree, quantity, gradation, continuous change, continuous covariation, noninteger ratios, varying proportionality, complex topological relations of relative nearness or connectedness, or nonlinear relationships and dynamical emergence" (Lemke, 1998b, p. 87).

Kress (1997, 2000b, 2003a, 2003b) has provided many illustrations of this principle. For example, he analyzed a textbook page dealing with electronics:

> The language is about events: relatively simple sentences (one or two clauses), which are about actions—what had been done; what is to be done; what might happen if … The diagrams represent the core information of this bit of the curriculum: what a circuit consists of, and in what relation its components stand to each other (Kress, 2000b, p. 197).

Language and images are not restricted to the areas of representation indicated by the functional specialization principle, but as images are becoming more frequent in a wide range of texts, functional specialization is likely to characterize the ideational complementarity of these two modes.

A related perspective on ideational complementarity arises from adapting SFL-based descriptions of the logical relations of enhancement, extension, and elaboration (Halliday & Matthiessen, 2004; Martin, 1992) to consideration of the linking of verbiage and images. In a study comparing school science explanations in books on CD-ROMs and on the World Wide Web (Unsworth,

2004), the relationships between illustrations and the main text were classified as (a) indicating how or why about an event in the main text (enhancement), (b) providing additional information to that in the main text (extension), or (c) restating or specifying what was in the main text (elaboration). The categories of image/text relations did not distinguish among books and electronic media texts. A number of the image/text relations were classified as elaboration and hence indicate ideational concurrence, however those classified as extension and enhancement indicate ideational complementarity. For example, the explanation of the water cycle on the Classroom of the Future Web site (http://www.cotf.edu/ete/modules/wateM/cycle.html) included evaporation from the soil and the movement of clouds in its diagram but did not mention these in the main text. The explanation of the greenhouse effect on the *USA Today* Web site (http://www.usatoday.com/weather/tglwhrmng.htm) relied on the mouse-activated, rollover, dynamic image and accompanying captions to explain how the greenhouse effect is created by "the natural blanket of gases that traps heat in the atmosphere," as indicated in the main text. The effectiveness of dynamic images such as these in electronic texts in dealing with sequence suggests some modification of the functional specialization principle in the case of digital texts.

In the study of newspaper reports of the "children overboard" affair introduced earlier in this chapter (Macken-Horarik, 2003a), ideational complementarity can also be seen to be a crucial aspect of the media depiction of the asylum seekers reflecting the perspective constructed by government control of images and nature of comment. This is evident in the analysis of the roles allocated to social actors and the value attached to these roles' (Macken-Horarik, 2003a, p. 11). In the verbal texts, asylum seekers are agentive in processes seen to be hostile ("heading for Australian territory" and "throwing their children into the sea"). Where the asylum seekers are patients, the processes in which others are agentive are seen to be benevolent ("picking up asylum seekers" and "helps a child and woman"). The images show the asylum seekers floating in the sea while navy personnel swim toward them to rescue them. The propagandistic effect of the text is achieved through ideational concurrence, genericising asylum seekers visually and verbally while specifying government personnel, and through ideational complementarity, foregrounding negative role allocation to asylum seekers and positive role allocation to navy and government representatives.

Intersemiotic complementarity is fundamental to the construction of interpretive possibilities in picture books. From an ideational perspective this can be seen in picture books in which significant segments of the narrative are conveyed by several pages that consist of images alone. In *Where the Wild Things Are* (Sendak, 1962), for example, the conduct of the "wild rumpus" is conveyed by images alone in three consecutive double-page spreads. In addition, where images and text are copresent, frequently significant elements of the action of the story occur within the images only. For example, in Anthony Browne's (1983) *Gorilla,* on page nine, the text foreshadows subsequent events: "In the night something amazing happened." Then the images on this page are exclusively responsible for conveying just what the amazing event was. It is these images only that depict Hannah's toy gorilla growing into a real gorilla (Gill, 2002). Juxtaposed images and text in picture books have also been shown to jointly construct activity sequences. Gill described the nature of this joint image/text construction of meaning as "distribution." According to Gill, there are two types of distribution. *Intraprocess distribution* refers to the portrayal by images and text of different aspects of a shared process. For example, the image(s) might depict the result of a process described in the verbal text. This occurs in *Gorilla* when the text indicates that Hannah and the gorilla crept downstairs and Hannah put on her coat and the gorilla put on her father's hat and coat. The image shows them standing in the doorway so dressed. Interprocess distribution occurs when images fill a gap in the ideational flow of meaning in the verbal text. For example, later in the story of *Gorilla,* the text indicates that it is time to go home and then indicates that they danced on the lawn, which is clearly in front of Hannah's home. The text does not refer to their actually going home, however. This is conveyed by the image of the gorilla walking along the street with Hannah on his shoulders.

Ideational divergence. Ideational divergence is not addressed in research dealing with intersemiotic concurrence and complementarity. Nevertheless, it is important in picture books. For example, in the "Shirley" books by John Burningham (1977, 1978) the text and images of Shirley's parents convey a narrative of a typical beach visit or of a child taking a bath, while the images of Shirley depict her participation in exciting adventures such her encounter with pirates. Similarly, McCloud (1994) has drawn attention to the role of ideational divergence in the narrative art of comic books with his category of image/text relations he refers to as "parallel combinations" in which "words and pictures seem to follow very different courses—without intersecting" (p. 154).

Interpersonal Meaning

Interactive and evaluative meaning. Interpersonal meaning in SFL includes interactive and evaluative meaning. *Interactive meaning* refers to the roles of interactants in giving information (making statements) or goods and services (making offers), or demanding information (asking questions) or goods and services (giving commands). These interactive roles are realized grammatically by the mood system (Halliday, 1994). The grammar of visual design (Kress & van Leeuwen, 1996) indicates that visually only two interactive roles can be portrayed. A "demand" image has the gaze of one or more represented participants directed to the viewer and hence "demands" some kind of response in terms of the viewer entering into some kind of pseudo-interactive relation with the represented participant; an "offer" does not have the gaze of any represented participant directed to the viewer and hence provides a portrayal for the viewer's contemplation.

Evaluative meaning in SFL has traditionally been confined to commentary on the truth of what is represented linguistically. This is realized by polarity (yes or no) and by the system of modality, which realizes possibilities between positive and negative polarity, such as degrees of certainty and probability (perhaps/of course; possibly/probably/certainly), and degrees of usuality and frequency (sometimes/usually/always). In the grammar of visual design, evaluation also focuses on the truth or credibility of images, also referred to as "modality" (Kress & van Leeuwen, 1996). Modality value however is related to "coding orientation." Within a naturalistic coding orientation, high modality is a reflection of the fidelity of the representation with the natural world, such as that achieved in a high-quality color photograph. Within a scientific coding orientation, fidelity may be calibrated more in relation to the representation of conceptual clarity rather than naturalistic reality.

Martin has extended SFL perspectives on evaluation by proposing an "appraisal network" including three main systems: attitude, engagement, and graduation (Martin, 2000; Martin & Rose, 2003). Here I will deal with attitude only. Within attitude there are a number of subcategories: *affect* refers to the expression of feelings, which can be positive or negative, and may be descriptions of emotional states (e.g., happy) or behaviors that indicate an emotional state (e.g., "crying"). Subcategories of affect are "happiness," "security," and "satisfaction." *Appreciation* relates to evaluations of objects, events, or states of affairs and can also relate to the characteristics of people but not to their behavior. Appreciation is further subdivided into "reaction," "composition," and "valuation." Reaction involves the emotional impact of the phenomenon (e.g., thrilling, boring, enchanting, depressing). *Composition* refers to the form of an object (e.g., coherent, balanced, haphazard) and *valuation* refers to the significance of the phenomenon (e.g., groundbreaking, inconsequential). *Judgment* can refer to assessments of someone's capacities (brilliant, slow), their dependability (tireless, courageous, rash), or their relative normality (regular, weird). Judgment can also refer to someone's truthfulness (frank, manipulative) and ethics (just, cruel, corrupt). Recent research on interpersonal meaning in image/text relations has noted the joint construction of interaction, but the main impact of these intermodal relations from an interpersonal perspective seems to be oriented to the construction of evaluative stance in multimodal texts.

Image/Text Relations and the Construction of Interpersonal Interaction.

The *Economist* magazine advertisement analyzed by Royce (1998) showed a medium-to-close-up, eye-level view of a young woman whose gaze is directed at the viewer, and whose frontal plane is parallel with that of the viewer. These visual features realize a pseudo-interpersonal relation of direct involvement at a personal level with a demand for a response. Positioned immediately above this image is the following question in the largest font on the page: "Does your environmental policy meet your granddaughter's expectations?" Royce points out that the second-person address and similar features in the subsequent text, effects a joint image/text initiation of interaction, which he refers to as "Reinforcement of Address." Similar work by Cheong (2004) showed how the medium-to-close-up, eye-level demand image of a smiling young woman whose frontal plane parallels that of the viewer is juxtaposed with the written text positively evaluating the products of the M1 telecommunications company, so that she appears to be the speaker of the quotation: "I get the feeling that M1 wants me to enjoy value—and enjoy life. Everything they offer is brighter, nicer and more fun!" In texts of this kind the image/text relations are jointly constructing evaluative stance as well as interaction.

Evaluation in Image/Text Relations: Interpersonal Resonance and Complementarity

Gill (2002) described a resonance of interpersonal meaning that could occur across image/verbiage juxtapositions. For example, on pages 27–28 of Anthony Browne's (1983) *Gorilla,* the ideational content does not concur. There is a resonance, however, between the image and text in the affect portrayed between Hannah and her father. The father says, "Happy birthday, love," and the image shows Hannah with her father putting his hands on Hannah's shoulders. Gill's analysis showed many examples of resonance of appraisal content, such as affect. For example, on page 11 of *Gorilla,* the text indicates that "Hannah was frightened," corresponding to the image of a frightened Hannah with the bedclothes drawn up over part of her face. On pages 17–18 where Hannah and the gorilla visit the orangutan and the chimpanzee in the zoo, the text indicates, "She thought they were beautiful. But sad."—corresponding visually to the expression of the orangutan and, to a lesser extent, that of the chimpanzee. Similarly, instances of interpersonal resonance with appraisal content were found in the picture book, *the baby who wouldn't go to bed* (Cooper, 1996). For example, the images consistently depict the other participants as looking down on the baby from a high vertical angle, positioning them as having power over her. This resonates with the mood structure of the text, where the other participants make statements that serve as indirect disciplinary comments about the baby's behavior.

The intermodal construction of interaction, which entails the systems of contact (offer/demand) and social distance, discussed earlier in relation to the work of Royce (1998, 2002) and Cheong (2004), and intermodal explorations of Martin's appraisal network (Martin, 2000; Martin & Rose, 2003), broached in relation to Affect in Gill's (2002) work in the immediately prior paragraph, are drawn together in Macken-Horarik's (2004) study of the interpersonal meanings in two matriculation students' artworks presented in a Sydney exhibition called ArtExpress. The study analyzed the complementary contribution of image (artwork) and verbiage (text panel) to the meanings of the multimodal displays. One of the displays was a photographic work called *Gloria* and the other was a painting called *Elaboration*.

> *Gloria* is a monumental photographic image of an older female nude presented in two views: an oblique (side-on) view in the left-hand image and a back view (though front-posed) in the right-hand image. This black and white photograph has a documentary quality. The artist uses high-contrast lighting to model the shapes, curves, lines and folds of "the older body." This figure stands in a contrastive relationship with other nudes more familiar in the artist's contemporary "youth culture" (an issue explored in her text panel). She conceals her subject's identity while revealing something of the solid and imposing grandeur of the older woman.
>
> *Elaboration* is a painting of human hands opening to the viewer and suggesting prayer, joy or supplication. These hands have a particular salience as a result of the diagonal vectors they create through a centric hold-release movement and the warm light which bathes them from above. This image combines a sensory orientation in the treatment of the setting (with its intense red flowers, green foliage and deep blue background) with a naturalistic coding orientation (verging on the hyper-real) in the artist's treatment of the hands (Macken-Horarik, 2004, p. 9).

Macken-Horarik (2004) concluded that in relation to interactive roles, two kinds of contact embodied in the system of "person" were found in each mode: the visual "you" in *Elaboration* and "she" in *Gloria;* and the verbal "I" in the text panels for each work. There are two kinds of vision corresponding to two kinds of social distance in the two modes. Firstly, there is the private vision of the artist in the images. In *Gloria* this is distancing achieved by the long distance view of the whole length of the body, the oblique horizontal angle of the left-hand image, the rear view of the right-hand image, and the positioning of the head to preclude facial identification, presenting both images as offers. In *Elaboration* the private vision of the artist is more intimate and interactive. This is achieved by the close-up view of the hands reaching toward the parallel frontal plane of the viewer as a demand image. The complementary public vision in each case is expressed in the text panels. In *Elaboration* this is distanced through a very public language style. In *Gloria* the emphasis in the text panel on "beauty" contests the objectifying viewpoint on the nude encouraged by the image presentation, and through the language the viewer is invited to "look again" from a more aesthetic perspective. Macken-Horarik suggested that the complementary image/text relations provide complex interpretive possibilities for the multimodal texts—in the case of *Gloria* by opposing the visual "medical-style" portrayal with the verbal aesthetic appreciation, and in the case of *Elaboration* verbally infusing the visual demand with opportunities for contemplation and spiritual edification. Thus her analysis "highlights the power of the multimodal text in the creation of a third semantic space and the importance of fashioning tools of analysis adequate to this" (p. 24).

In respect to interpersonal meaning, verbiage/image relations are more concerned with evaluation than interaction (Martin, 2002). Martin argued that a key function of images is to coarticulate attitude (including affect, judgment, and appreciation). In doing so, images operate in a similar way to imagery, provoking an evaluative reaction in readers, and the images are typically positioned to do this so that they foreshadow the value positions to be constructed in the subsequent verbiage. One example is taken from Nelson Mandela's "The Illustrated Long Walk to Freedom" (Mandela, 1996). In the section dealing with the 1976 Soweto uprising, the well known photo of the body of 13-year-old Hector Pieterson being carried from the fray is positioned as a full-page image on page 147, preceded by its caption in the right-hand margin of the previous page. The main text dealing with the Soweto uprising then appears overleaf on page 148. The photo previews and amplifies the reaction induced by Mandela's verbal imagery. In SFL terms, Martin suggested that the photo functions as an evaluative interpersonal theme, naturalizing the stance from which the remaining verbiage can be read. Additional examples are provided by Martin's (2002) analysis of other sections of this text and further examples from his analysis of the Australian Government Report (Commission, 1997) *Bringing Them Home* on the generations of Aboriginal children taken from their families and placed in alternative care. This report similarly deploys images and imagery to establish evaluative orientations to the ensuing text. On the basis of this work, Martin (2002) suggested that for multimodal texts the Given/New elements of the compositional meaning-making resources of images (Kress & van Leeuwen, 1996), need to be augmented to include a visual version of the SFL concept of Interpersonal Theme. As Martin reasoned, "The left is not simply Given, but has a positive forward looking function, instigating and naturalizing a reading position for the evaluation of verbiage/image texture that ensues" (Martin, 2002, p. 334).

Image/Text Relations and the Construction of Textual/Compositional Meanings

The descriptions of compositional meanings in images by Kress and van Leeuwen (1996) have been extensively applied by them to image/text relations. Further studies of school science books have shown how layout resources of Given/New, Ideal/Real, and Framing are deployed to structure pedagogic texts (Veel, 1998). Typically what is likely to be familiar to students, whether in the form of language or image, is placed in the Given position on the left and that which deals either visually or verbally with unfamiliar, technical information is placed in the New position on the right. While these Given/New structures are consistent with the usual left-to-right progression in reading, the Ideal/

Real structures in school curriculum texts do not necessarily map strategically onto our practice in working from top to bottom of the text. Students might be advised to examine the specific, concrete information of the Real positioned at the bottom of the layout before addressing the more abstract, conceptual, and generalized information of the Ideal positioned at the top. Often the salience of concrete images in the Real will influence students to adopt such a reading path (Unsworth, 2001).

It has been noted, in Martin's (2002) work earlier, that the descriptions of the compositional meanings in multimodal texts need to be extended to take account of the role of images as Interpersonal Theme. Further extensions are suggested in the work by Jewitt (2002) dealing with the compositional resources for constructing character in the "Novel as CD-ROM" version of Steinbeck's *Of Mice and Men* (Steinbeck, 1996/1937), and by issues of "framing" raised in Macken-Horarik's (2003b) study of texts which were central to the "children overboard" affair.

From her *Of Mice and Men* study, Jewitt (2002) has suggested that the spatial relationship between image and verbiage on each of the screens is itself a meaning-making resource. She argued that writing serves as a visual element, a block of "space" that makes textual meaning beyond its content. Jewitt indicated that on the CD screens, the blocks of writing are positioned in different places: the left or right side, along the bottom or top length of the screen, or in the top or bottom corner. The size and position of the block and its location combine to reveal or conceal different parts of the image layered "beneath" it. In this way a block of writing emphasizes different aspects of the image on screen. According to Jewitt, the image at times cuts across the lexis and grammar of the written text to create a visual mood and rhythm, which she illustrated with one image of George and Lenny that runs across four screens of changing text:

> In the first screen, the block of writing sits above George's head as he talks to Lennie about what he could do if he left him. In the second screen Lennie is visually obliterated by George's angry talk of leaving, visually foregrounding George. In the third screen, as George's anger subsides, the block of writing is placed on the screen so that both George and Lennie are visible (Jewitt, 2002, p.184).

Jewitt (2002) suggested that it is through the visual arrangement of image and writing on screen that the narrative construct of character, indicates intensity of emotion to suggest the alignment of the viewer with George's point of view, and to emphasize the agency/passivity of the characters in the novel.

The use of framing was discussed in the study of the "children overboard" texts (Macken-Horarik, 2003b). One aspect of this is demonstrated by comparison of two images of the same event. The first shows four indistinct figures viewed from above and surrounded by the sea. There is a wide expanse of sea around the figures so the image is not closely cropped. There is nothing within the frame to show why these people are in the sea. This is the image released by the navy, which appeared in the newspaper reports. There is no indication of the origin of the photo, but it was captioned in the newspaper, "A female sailor from HMAS Adelaide helps the woman and the child from the people smuggling boat." Immediately above this image is the uppercase screamer headline "THE CRUEL SEA" and to the right of the image the smaller headline "Proof that people threw children overboard." There is nothing in the image to suggest the veracity of the screamer headline since the sea appears to be quite calm, so the implication is one of displacement of the cruelty. At the same time the grammar of the smaller headline presents a claim that is both unattributable and unarguable, with no indication of "who said?" or "who proved?" The original framing in the taking of the photograph and its reframing by the verbiage of the headlines constructs the propagandist perspective on the incident which aligned with comments by government ministers.

The second image of the same incident was released after the Australian Federal Government elections. This shows the same event with a widened visual frame and a very long distance view. The four figures can be seen in the water, but in the foreground there is also a rescue boat and in the background can be seen another boat partially submerged. Including the sinking boat within the frame of the image changes the significance of the women and children in the water. Macken-Horarik (2003b) also analyzed the "voicing" of the interpretive and evaluative comments included in the newspaper report, suggesting an analogous relationship between the voicing and the framing of the images. Both voicing and framing can specify or obfuscate the saying or imaging of representations of events into being. According to Mackin-Horarik the interactivity of image and verbiage is crucial to our analysis of framing in multisemiotic texts:

> Analysis of framing in this sense takes us beyond consideration of visual devices that connect or disconnect one part of an image with another (Kress and van Leeuwen, 1996, 1998). We need a notion of framing that allows us to analyze both images in isolation (visual framing) and images in interaction with other semiotic modes (multisemiotic framing) (Macken-Horarik, 2003b, p. 288).

Educational Implications of an Emerging Metalanguage of Image/Text Relations

A meaning-based metalanguage, which maps the ways image/text relations can be used to construct meanings in a variety of media and across a range of social contexts, is a resource for enabling critical interpretive engagement with the design of multimodal texts and the social and ideological work they do. I shall deal briefly with two kinds of educational implications of the development of such a metalanguage. The first concerns renovating current pedagogic practices that do not adequately accommodate multimodal texts. Here I shall illustrate the potential for immediate reform by reference to studies dealing with issues of multimodal texts in school literacy assessment. The second kind of implication refers to the changing role for teachers in the emerging contexts of new literacies, to which many young students will bring relevant expertise in particular areas well beyond that of their teachers.

Current educational practice demonstrates an awareness of the increasing prominence of images, but a shared metalanguage explicating the meaning-making resources of image/text relations is necessary to facilitate more systematic teaching, enhanced learning, and informed approaches to evaluation. This was evidenced in a study of the mandatory year-five reading test for government schools in one Australian State that examined the relationships among the types of images included in the test passages, the multiple choice questions, and reported reading strategies targeted (Unsworth, Thomas, & Bush, 2004). In Australia, all states conduct statewide group literacy tests for students in government schools at three age levels—usually when students are in the third, fifth, and seventh years of their schooling. This study concerned the New South Wales test for students in year five. In this test the students received a color magazine containing different kinds of illustrated texts relevant to school subject areas like English, Science, and Social Studies, and a multiple-choice question book with test items derived from each of the texts in the magazine. In 1998, about one tenth of the total questions in the test booklet involved images. In 1999 this proportion rose to one fifth, and in 2000 more than one third of the test items involved the reading of images. In both 1999 and 2000 the number of test items explicitly targeting images was very similar, and more than double the number of such items in 1998. These results reflect recognition of the importance of reading images as a part of reading comprehension across the school curriculum. The study also determined questions which entailed the use of images to obtain the correct answer, but which were not so designated by the test constructors. These showed a marked increase in 2000. In addition the study found a marked emphasis on test items that involved conceptual rather than narrative images. More than twice the number of conceptual images than narrative images were involved in test items in each of the tests over the three years. The number of test items involving narrative images was almost nonexistent in 1998 and 1999, and in 2000 the number of test items addressing conceptual images was nearly twice the number addressing narrative images. Why were the narrative images virtually ignored in the test samples of school curriculum area reading materials? The research noted earlier by Martin (2002) and Macken-Horarik (2003b) indicated that narrative images played a crucial role in the construction of the interpretive possibilities of the texts they studied.

Apparent inconsistencies and lack of a systematic approach were also revealed in a study of matriculation-writing assessment tasks in the final-year high-school public examination in English in one Australian state (Callow & Unsworth, 1997). In one examination paper, in response to a cartoon pamphlet promoting blood donation among teenagers, students were asked, "How do the language and layout of the pamphlet persuade young people to become blood donors?" Another examination provided a newspaper story about collecting crocodile eggs for farming and asked students, "Do the article and the picture tell the same story? Discuss both the text (including the headline) and the photograph in your answer." The published marking criteria and accompanying sample student answers evidenced inconsistent grading with two clearly equivalent student responses being graded "average" in one case and "excellent" in the other. The published examiners' comments give no real clue as to any perceived differences between the papers, making it difficult for teachers to explain the discrepant marks to their students. Situations such as these in tests of students' interpretation of multimodal texts suggest the kind of immediate renovation that could be achieved by an accessible, shared metalanguage of image/text relations, but they are indicative only of the extensive reforms that are necessary in the many multimodal dimensions of literacy education. For example, Lemke (1998a) emphasized the urgency with respect to pedagogies of multimedia text production, indicating, "We do not teach students how to integrate even drawings and diagrams into their writing" (p. 288), and, to date, little seems to have changed in this respect.

The second kind of implication that arises from work on a metalanguage of multiliteracies pertains to the role of the teacher in new learning contexts that are emerging in response to the exponential rate of change in available technologies and the associated changes in new literacies. A growing body of research indicates that, increasingly, students are coming to school more literate in some dimensions of the new literacies and ICTs than their teachers (Leu et al., 2004). There is a need for curriculum design and classroom teaching to be responsive to these changes and, in so doing, to acknowledge the relevant experience and expertise of children. Leu et al. (2004) have indicated the importance of social learning strategies with teachers, no longer the sole source of literacy knowledge, orchestrating literacy-learning opportunities between and among students and themselves. They have appropriately argued in such contexts that teachers will become even more important to the development of literacy in a world of new literacies. It is also obviously the case, however, that teachers are in a position to mediate areas of new knowledge and understandings that are not so readily accessible to children. A clear example of this is the theoretically articulated functional grammars of language and image and the emerging metalanguage of image/text relations that facilitate explicit discussion about the interpretive possibilities constructed by multimodal texts and strategies for negotiating their critical comprehension and composition.

The work of Burn and Parker (2003) indicated the urgency of preparing teachers to take on this role of explicitly teaching students how the "grammars"

working with traditional and new literary forms, it may well be that "teachers themselves, exploring in their own classrooms hunches and intuitions about the implications for their teaching" can "provide the strongest lead as to how the future research agenda should be formulated" (p. 148). This could be practically encouraged by the provision of widely accessible supportive and facilitative frameworks for teachers interested in conducting such investigations.

One such framework is a collaborative-action research project described in a recent book dealing with children's literature and computer-based teaching (Unsworth, Thomas, Simpson, & Asha, 2005). The project is based on the story world of J. R. R. Tolkien's "Middle Earth" and Web sites devoted to it, such as the Middle Earth story palace (Sorenson, 2000 to 2004, online). Action research guidelines and possibilities for classroom work to be explored are provided in the book, which invites teachers to try a project they adapt from the suggestions for exploring the potential of digital technologies in the literacy classroom. A Web site maintained by one of the authors provides practical support including a discussion forum and provision to publish the results of the studies. These and other kinds of informal, widely participatory collaborative research strategies would seem to be an important complement to the more traditional, university-based, funded studies, which typically require an extended preparatory period prior to implementation. Not only are social learning strategies central to the development of new literacies pedagogies in contexts of schooling, but such strategies are also central to researching the continuous change in what actually needs to be taught and learned.

References

Andrews, R. (2004). Where next in research on ICT and literacies. *Literacy Learning: The Middle Years, 12*(1), 58–67.

Baldry, A. (Ed.). (2000). *Multimodality and multimediality in the distance learning age.* Campobasso, Italy: Palladino Editore.

Bearne, E. (2000). Past perfect and future conditional: The challenge of new texts. In G. Hodges, M. Drummond, & M. Styles (Eds.), *Tales, tellers and texts* (pp. 145–156). London: Continuum.

Bolter, J. (1998). Hypertext and the question of visual literacy. In D. Reinking, M. McKenna, L. Labbo, & R. Kieffer (Eds.), *Handbook of literacy and technology: Transformations in a post-typographic world* (pp. 3–14). New Jersey: Erlbaum.

Boulter, D. (1999). *Writing space: The computer, hypertext, and the history of writing.* Hillsdale, NJ: Erlbaum.

Browne, A. (1983). *Gorilla.* London: Julia MacRae.

Burn, A., & Parker, D. (2003). Tiger's big plan: Multimodality and the moving image. In C. Jewitt & G. Kress (Eds.), *Multimodal literacy* (pp. 56–72). New York: Peter Lang.

Burningham, J. (1977). *Come away from the water, Shirley.* London: Cape.

Burningham, J. (1978). *Time to get out of the bath, Shirley.* London: Cape.

Callow, J., & Unsworth, L. (1997). Equity in the videosphere. *Southern Review, 30*(3), 268–286.

Callow, J., & Zammit, K. (2002). Visual literacy: From picture books to electronic texts. In M. Monteith (Ed.), *Teaching primary literacy with ICT* (pp. 188–201). Buckingham, U.K.: Open University Press.

Cheong, Y. (2004). The construal of ideational meaning in print advertisements. In K. O'Halloran (Ed.), *Multimodal discourse analysis: Systemic functional perspectives* (pp. 163–195). London: Continuum.

Commission, H. R. a. E. O. (1997). *Bringing them home: National inquiry into the separation of aboriginal and torres strait islander children from their families.* Sydney, Australia: Human Rights and Equal Opportunities Commission.

Cooper, H. (1996). *The baby who wouldn't go to bed.* London: Doubleday/Picture Corgi Books.

Dresang, E. (1999). *Radical change: Books for youth in a digital age.* New York: Wilson.

Gee, J. (2003). *What computer games have to teach us about learning and literacy.* New York: Palgrave Macmillan.

Gill, T. (2002). *Visual and verbal playmates: An exploration of visual and verbal modalities in children's picture books.* Unpublished B.A., Honours, University of Sydney.

Halliday, M. A. K. (1992). Language as system and language as instance: The corpus as a theoretical construct. In J. Svartvik (Ed.), *Directions in corpus linguistics: Proceedings of Nobel symposium 82, Stockholm, 4–8 August 1991* (pp. 61–77). Berlin, Germany: De Gruyter.

Halliday, M. A. K. (1993). Language in a changing world. *Applied Linguistics Association of Australia Occasional Paper, 13,* 62–81.

Halliday, M. A. K. (1994). *An introduction to functional grammar* (2nd ed.). London: Edward Arnold.

Halliday, M. A. K. (2003). New ways of meaning: The challenge to applied linguistics. In J. Webster (Ed.), The collected works of M. A. K. Halliday: Vol. 3. *On language and linguistics.* (pp. 139–174). London/New York: Continuum.

Halliday, M. A. K., & Hasan, R. (1976). *Cohesion in English.* London: Longman.

Halliday, M. A. K., & Hasan, R. (1985). *Language, context and text: Aspects of language in a social-semiotic perspective.* Geelong, Australia: Deakin University Press.

Halliday, M. A. K., & Martin, J. R. (Eds.). (1993). *Writing science: Literacy and discursive power.* London: Falmer Press.

Halliday, M. A. K., & Matthiessen, C. M. I. M. (1999). *Construing experience through meaning: A language-based approach to cognition.* London: Cassell.

Halliday, M. A. K., & Matthiessen, C. (2004). *An introduction to functional grammar* (3rd ed.). London: Arnold.

Howley, P. (1996). *Visual literacy: Semiotic theory, primary school syllabus documents and classroom practice.* Unpublished Bachelor of Education Honours, University of Sydney, Sydney.

Jewitt, C. (2002). The move from page to screen: The multimodal reshaping of school English. *Visual Communication, 1*(2), 171–196.

Kamil, M., Intrator, S., & Kim, H. (2000). The effects of other technologies on literacy and learning. In M. Kamil, P. Mosenthal, P. Pearson, & R. Barr (Eds.), *Handbook of reading research* (Vol. 3, pp. 771–788). Mahwah, NJ: Erlbaum.

Kress, G. (1997). Visual and verbal modes of representation in electronically mediated communication: the potentials of new forms of of text. In I. Snyder (Ed.), *Page to screen: Taking literacy into the electronic era* (pp. 53–79). Sydney: Allen and Unwin.

Kress, G. (2000). Multimodality: Challenges to Thinking About Language. *TESOL Quarterly, 34*(3), 337–340.

Kress, G. (2000a). Design and transformation: New theories of meaning. In B. Cope & M. Kalantzis (Eds.), *Multiliteracies: Learning literacy and the design of social futures* (pp. 153–161). Melbourne: Macmillan.

Kress, G. (2000b). Multimodality. In B. Cope & M. Kalantzis (Eds.), *Multiliteracies: Literacy learning and the design of social futures* (pp. 182–202). Melbourne: Macmillan.

Kress, G. (2001). Sociolinguistics and social semiotics. In P. Cobley (Ed.), *Semiotics and linguistics* (pp. 66–82). London: Routledge.

Kress, G. (2003a). Genres and the multimodal production of 'scientificness'. In C. Jewitt & G. Kress (Eds.), *Multimodal literacy* (pp. 173–186). New York: Peter Lang.

Kress, G. (2003b). *Literacy in the new media age.* London: Routledge.

Kress, G., & van Leeuwen, T. (1996). *Reading images: A grammar of visual design.* London: Routledge.

Lemke, J. (1998a). Metamedia literacy: Transforming meanings and media. In D. Reinking, M. McKenna, L. Labbo, & R. Kieffer (Eds.), *Handbook of literacy and technology: Transformations in a post-typographic world* (pp. 283–302). New Jersey: Erlbaum.

Lemke, J. (1998b). Multiplying meaning: Visual and verbal semiotics in scientific text. In J. R. Martin & R. Veel (Eds.), *Reading science: Critical and functional perspectives on discourses of science* (pp. 87–113). London: Routledge.

Lemke, J. (2002). Travels in hypermodality. *Visual Communication, 1*(3), 299–325.

Leu, D. J., Jr. (2000). Literacy and technology: Deictic consequences for literacy education in an information age. In M. L. Kamil, P. Mosenthal, P. D. Pearson, & R. Barr (Eds.), *Handbook of reading research* (Vol. III, pp. 743–770). Mahwah, NJ: Erlbaum.

Leu, D., Kinzer, C., Coiro, J., & Cammack, D. (2004). Toward a theory of new literacies emerging from the Internet and other information and communication technologies. In R. Ruddell & N. Unrau (Eds.), *Theoretical models and processes of reading* (Vol. 5, pp. 1570–1613). Newark, DE: International Reading Association.

Lim, V. F. (2004). Developing an integrative multi-semiotic model. In K. O'Halloran (Ed.), *Multimodal discourse analysis: Systemic functional perspectives* (pp. 220–246). London and New York: Continuum.

Locke, T., & Andrews, R. (2004). ICT and literature: A Faustian compact? In R. Andrews (Ed.), *The impact of ICT on literacy education* (pp. 124–152). London: Routledge/Falmer.

Luke, C. (2003). Pedagogy, connectivity, multimodality and interdisciplinarity. *Reading Research Quarterly, 38*(10), 356–385.

Macken-Horarik, M. (2003a). A telling symbiosis in the discourse of hatred: Multimodal news texts about the 'children overboard' affair. *Australian Review of Applied Linguistics, 26*(2), 1–16.

Macken-Horarik, M. (2003b). Working the borders in racist discourse: The challenge of the "children overboard affair" in news media texts. *Social Semiotics, 13*(3), 283–303.

Macken-Horarik, M. (2004). Interacting with the multimodal text: Reflections on image and verbiage in *artexpress. Visual Communication, 3*(1), 5–26.

Mandela, N. (1996). *The illustrated long walk to freedom: The autobiography of Nelson Mandela.* London: Little, Brown and Company.

Martin, J. R. (1992). *English text: System and structure.* Amsterdam: Benjamins.

Martin, J. R. (2000). Beyond exchange: Appraisal systems in English. In S. Hunston & G. Thompson (Eds.), *Evaluation in text: Authorial stance and the construction of discourse* (pp. 142–175). Oxford, U.K.: Oxford University Press.

Martin, J. R. (2002). Fair trade: Negotiating meaning in multimodal texts. In P. Coppock (Ed.), *The semiotics of writing: Transdisciplinary perspectives on the technology of writing.* (pp. 311–338). Begijnhof, Belgium: Brepols & Indiana University Press.

Martin, J. R. (2003). Voicing the 'other': Reading and writing indigenous australians. In G. Weiss & R. Wodak (Eds.), *Critical discourse analysis: Theory and interdisciplinarity* (pp. 199–219). London: Palgrave.

Martin, J. R., & Rose, D. (2003). *Working with discourse: Meaning beyond the clause* (1 ed., Vol. 1). London/New York: Continuum.

Martinec, R. (1999). Cohesion in action. *Semiotica, 1/2,* 161–180.

Martinec, R. (2000a). Rhythm in multimodal texts. *Leonardo, 33*(4), 289–297.

Martinec, R. (2000b). Types of process in action. *Semiotica, 130*(3/4), 243–268.

Matthiessen, C. (1995). *Lexicogrammatical cartography: English systems.* Tokyo, Japan: International Language Sciences.

McCloud, S. (1994). *Understanding comics: The invisible art.* New York: Harper Collins.

New London Group. (2000). A pedagogy of multiliteracies: Designing social futures. In B. Cope & M. Kalantzis (Eds.), *Multiliteracies: Literacy learning and the design of social futures.* Melbourne, Australia: Macmillan.

Nodelman, P. (1988). *Words about pictures: The narrative art of children's picture books.* Athens: University of Georgia Press.

O'Halloran, K. (Ed.). (2004). *Multimodal discourse analysis: Systemic functional perspectives.* London: Continuum.

O'Toole, M. (1994). *The language of displayed art.* London: Leicester University Press.

Quinn, M. (2004). Talking with Jess: Looking at how metalanguage assisted explanation writing in the middle years. *Australian Journal of Language and Literacy, 27*(3), 245–261.

Richards, C. (2001). Hypermedia, Internet communication, and the challenge of redefining literacy in the electronic age. *Language Learning and Technology, 4*(2), 59–77.

Royce, T. (1998). Synergy on the page: Exploring intersemiotic complementarity in page-based multimodal text. *Japan Association Systemic Functional Linguistics Occasional Papers, 1*(1), 25–50.

Royce, T. (2002). Multimodality in the TESOL classroom: Exploring visual-verbal synergy. *TESOL Quarterly, 36*(2), 191–205.

Russell, G. (2000). Print-based and visual discourses in schools: Implications for pedagogy. *Discourse: Studies in the cultural politics of education, 21*(2), 205–217.

Schleppegrell, M. (2004). *The language of schooling: A functional linguistic perspective.* Mawah, NJ: Erlbaum.

Schleppegrell, M., Achugar, M., & Oteíza, T. (2004). The grammar of history: Enhancing content-based instruction through a functional focus on language. *TESOL Quarterly, 38*(1), 67–93.

Sendak, M. (1962). *Where the wild things are.* London: The Bodley Head.

Steinbeck, J. (1996). *Of mice and men.* New York: Penguin Electronics. (Original work published 1937.)

Torr, J., & Harman, J. (1997). Literacy and the language of science in year one classrooms: Implications for children's learning. *Australian Journal of Language and Literacy, 20*(3), 222–237.

Unsworth, L. (2001). *Teaching multiliteracies across the curriculum: Changing contexts of text and image in classroom practice.* Buckingham, U.K.: Open University Press.

Unsworth, L. (2004). Comparing school science explanations in books and computer-based formats: The role of images, image/text relations and hyperlinks. *International Journal of Instructional Media, 31*(3), 283–301.

Unsworth, L. (2006). *E-literature for children: Enhancing digital literacy learning.* London: Routledge/Falmer.

Unsworth, L., Thomas, A., & Bush, R. (2004). The role of images and image-text relations in group 'basic skills tests' of literacy for children in the primary school years. *Australian Journal of Language and Literacy, 27*(1), 46–65.

Unsworth, L., Thomas, A., Simpson, A., & Asha, J. (2005). *Children's literature and computer based teaching.* London: McGraw-Hill/Open University Press.

van Leeuwen, T. (1999). *Speech, music, sound.* London: Macmillan.

Veel, R. (1998). The greening of school science: Ecogenesis in secondary classrooms. In J. R. Martin & R. Veel (Eds.), *Reading science: Functional and critical perspectives on the discourses of science.* London: Routledge.

Williams, G. (1999). Children becoming readers: Reading and literacy. In P. Hunt (Ed.), *Understanding children's literature* (pp. 151–162). London: Routledge.

Williams, G. (2000). Children's literature, children and uses of language description. In L. Unsworth (Ed.), *Researching language in schools and communities: A functional linguistic perspective.* London: Cassell.

PART **III**
Communication

Introduction to Part III

Anderson (Chapter 3) observes that the terminology used to refer to the technology of new media had changed from talk of "computers," "information technology," or "IT," which prevailed during the 1980s, to talk of "information and communication technology" by the late 1990s. "The integration of the Internet and multimedia with computer technology made many more comfortable with calling it ICT" (ibid. p. 67). Some researchers have gone further still, withdrawing entirely from reference to "information," preferring to speak of computing and communications technologies, or CCTs (cf. Bigum, 2002). This throws even greater weight on communication as a defining social purpose and constellation of human practices associated with the new technologies. Mortensen (p. 461) maintains, "[O]ur most recent, most sophisticated technology is built for communication." Moreover, the ethos of Web 2.0 reflects the insights of Michael Schrage (1997/2001), among others, who talked about "the relationship revolution" and "relationship technologies" in preference to the language of "information." Schrage suggested that "anyone trying to get a handle on the dazzling technologies of today and the impact they'll have tomorrow, would be well advised to re-orient their worldview around relationships."

The four chapters in the following section instantiate the extent to which communication and relationship are integral to social practices that are increasingly becoming the objects of research attention. They also bespeak an inherent difficulty involved in reviewing dimensions of the new that are genuinely recent. In the case of practices like weblogging and instant messaging, we have phenomena that are simply too recent for sizable corpora of research to have emerged—a circumstance that recurs in the research on popular culture, community, and citizenship and is discussed in the Introduction to that section. At the same time, these phenomena are so widespread and central to everyday literacy engagements that they cannot be ignored. The fact that they cannot be ignored, however, is not to say that they will necessarily be researched, or researched in familiar academic terms, as we find in the case of Torill Mortensen's (Chapter 16) chapter on weblogging, for example.

This section addresses three different types of focus in its four chapters. Two, as mentioned, are popular everyday practices. Torill Mortensen (Chapter 16) addresses weblog literacy from the standpoint of a researcher who has integrated blogging into her mainstream practice as a researcher. Gloria Jacobs (Chapter 17) discusses cross-disciplinary research on instant messaging through the lens of the New Literacies Studies. The remaining chapters address an area of learning and a social equity category respectively. Steven Thorne (Chapter 15) addresses the considerable body of research literature that has been generated around the incorporation of networked computers as mediating technologies in second language learning. Finally, Jonathan Marshall (Chapter 18) reviews research into the production, performance, and effects of gender as it mediates online communication.

Theoretical Perspectives

The authors in this section are all qualitative researchers, writing out of backgrounds spanning applied linguistics, sociology, social anthropology, literature studies, cultural studies, media studies, and sociocultural studies of language and literacy. The research addressed in their reviews falls mainly within these parameters, although the specific theoretical perspectives encompassed in the research reviewed in each chapter are diverse. These perspectives range across psycholinguistics, sociolinguistics, sociocultural studies of literacy, feminist theory, gender theory, performativity theory, activity theory, narrative theory, ethnology, diffusion theory, reader response theory, hypertext theory, ethnology, and cultural studies, to name the most commonly cited. Interestingly enough, however, there is relatively little carry-over at the level of specific theoretical positions cited in the discrete research corpora from one chapter to the next. For example, feminist theory informs the research on gender in online communications but is evident nowhere else. Reader response theory informs Mortensen's (Chapter 16) account of weblogs, but makes no further appearance in other chapters in this section. Psycholinguistic theories inform research in second language learning but are not referred to otherwise. Activity theory travels across research on instant messaging and second language learning, which is to be expected given that instant messaging is an obvious tool for use in second language learning, at least within nonformal and tertiary education settings. In addition, elements of linguistic theory concerned particularly with grammatical constructions, syntax, communicating interpersonal meanings, and the relationship between oral and written language can be discerned in common across research on second language learning and instant messaging, although the emergent state of research on instant messaging renders this commonality more one of in principle than in practice.

Notwithstanding the relative discreteness of the theories informing research in these different areas, the research addressed overwhelmingly sustains conceptions of literacy in terms of social practices and processes. This entails that meanings are always about much more than texts and wordings alone, but are inseparable from contexts, from cultural ways, from Discourse (Gee, 1996). This plays out in interesting ways across the chapters. Marshall (Chapter 18), for example, concludes that it is a common theme across the extensive body of research he has surveyed that "literacy in all of its forms ... is an interactive social process" and "gender provides an important context within which communications are interpreted, actions contested, and people organized" (p. 513–514). Thorne (p. 425) notes that inextricability of language and culture is integral to the conceptualization of second language learning and use as primarily a process of intercultural communication—whether online or offline. From this perspective, written and spoken language alike "are always produced and interpreted in relation to historically formed cultural practices and speech situations" that vary from one "languaculture" (Agar, 1994) to another. Intercultural communication, therefore, demands that participants negotiate situationally adequate systems "of (inter)cultural standards and linguistic and pragmatic rules of interaction" (Sercu, 2004, p. 116). Jacobs (Chapter 17) concludes from the research she has reviewed that instant messaging as a literacy must, in fact, be understood as so many context-specific social practices. From study to study, setting to setting, social network to social network, instant messaging practitioners cocreate their own versions of instant messaging, with variations occurring on almost every variable—from uses of away messages and emoticons to choice of register and, indeed, the very purposes for which instant messaging is appropriated. Mortensen (p. 459) similarly depicts the multiple forms that blogging takes as blogs "keep breeding shamelessly with other media," and as one moves from one blogging community (e.g., edu-bloggers) to others (e.g., video bloggers, academic bloggers, fiction bloggers, etc.).

Research Approaches and Methods

The range of research approaches and methods employed across the fields of inquiry covered in this section of the book is wide. The most common variants of quantitative research used include quasi-experiments and quantitative analysis of linguistic features (second language learning) and surveys (gender in online communication and instant messaging). Diverse forms of linguistic and sociolinguistic methods have been used to research computer-mediated communication in second language learning and gender in online communication and instant messaging. These include corpus linguistics involving conversation analysis, variants of discourse analysis, microgenetic analysis, and contrastive analysis. Logs of telecollaborative exchanges, instant messaging, e-mail exchanges, and discussion forums have been subjected to different kinds of analysis of language features, ranging from a focus on the use of emoticons and abridgements in instant messaging to analysis of linguistic elements used to develop, negotiate, and maintain social relationships within second language learning. Interviews and participant observation have been employed in studies of instant messaging and gender in online communication. From the perspective of this *Handbook*'s raison d'être it is evident that there are rich possibilities for cross-disciplinary conversations across the fields of inquiry represented in this section. Forms of theory and analysis employed in the study of gender online might usefully inform work in second language learning, for example, and vice versa. There are obvious possibilities for mutually informing conversations and collaborations between researchers investigating computer-mediated communication in second language learning and researchers investigating instant messaging as a domain of social practice. Equally, forms of telecollaboration in weblogging and second language learning might well find fruitful points of intersection.

Mortensen's (Chapter 16) account of researching weblogs raises some very interesting and timely questions on a number of levels with respect to received conceptions of academic research and its conventions. At one level, researching weblogs involves a user-oriented immersive methodology that constitutes researching weblogs as a metalogue—"a conversation in which the form of the discussion embodies the subject being discussed" (Lunenfeld, 1999, as cited in Mortensen, this volume, p. 452). Reading and learning about research on weblogs involves reading weblogs and keeping one, since the weblog is the best vehicle for researching weblogs. This has a number of implications for common research conventions. For example, peer review becomes a process where peers can be anyone, and the process of review is formative, immediate, and collaborative. Consequently, researchers do not guard their "intellectual property" jealously, although citation is appreciated. Referencing goes "online" and displaces ritualized print-based styles with the literal insertion of a hyperlink direct to the source.

Common Themes

Despite the somewhat eclectic nature of the areas of research addressed in this section some common themes are evident across the four chapters. One of these is the authors' shared conception of the Internet as so many culturally variant tools and not a monolithic neutral technology, as is so often assumed by formal educators and by researchers who speak of the Internet as a learning technology and treat the internet as an "it." Indeed, as we have seen in the case of instant messaging and as is abundantly evident in the case of weblogs, even the more specific communication tools of the Internet are constituted differently and assume different meanings within different contexts of appropriation. This has far-reaching implications for how we conceive teaching and learning new literacies, and the sense we make of what it would mean to assess this learning.

A second common theme is a deep awareness of the roles and significance of social networks in the constitution of new literacies and our understanding of them and of their implications for teaching and learning. At one level, this is closely related to the previous theme, but goes beyond it to take account of relations of power and authority as inscribed in particular constructions of Internet tools as "cultural artifacts." Thorne (Chapter 15) notes that for large numbers of young people who have grown up "with (and through) the use of Internet information and communication tools" (p. 438), scholastic and social communication alike increasingly involve participation in networks that are mediated by social software (e.g., MySpace, Facebook), online games, blogs, IM, telephone texting, MP3 players, and so forth. The way they use these tools, the meanings these tools have for them, the contexts in which they use them, and the artifacts they produce when using them, may conflict with the ways these tools are constituted as "cultural artifacts" within the cultures-of-use of educators, policymakers, education administrators, test designers, and so on. One way of dealing with such discrepancies is for educators to impose their meanings as official and legitimate them through curriculum, pedagogy, and assessment. Another way is to treat the difference educationally and to see it as a dimension along which learning, innovation, negotiation, and problem solving might occur. This accords with our conception here of new literacies as deictic: since one of the most powerful engines of technological change consists in the insistence that tools be pushed beyond their present "interactional and relational associations [and] preferred uses" (Thorne, p. 438).

Future Research

A number of lines for future research development are suggested by the authors. One is that although research often identifies context as integral to using cultural tools like instant messaging, the nature of context and its relationship to instant messaging as social practice is rarely discussed in any depth and needs to be problematized.

A second recommendation is that researchers pay greater attention to what new technologies mean to users and less attention to specific new technologies per se. This will involve investigating technologies within varying cultures of use, mapping where these cultures fit into the local and global scenes, and the implications of this "fit" for particular cultures of use.

With respect to the study of gender in online communications, there needs to be further research into uses of online gender emerging from non-Anglo cultures, on changes and variations across generations, and on how online activity melds with life offline from the standpoint of gender matters. Furthermore, greater attention should be paid in research to the circumstances in which people are acting online and to the circumstances under which behavior changes, instead of assuming that what is observed is necessarily the case more generally.

More needs to be known about how Internet tools are actually used for schoolwork, and greater consideration needs to be given to understanding how Internet use might inform school learning cultures. The currently amplified generation gap between "top-down processes and pedagogies" operating within formal education settings and "the bottom-up life experiences" of students needs to be addressed by researchers.

Finally, there is a need for research into the relationship between self-publishing via weblogs and similar media and the established media. As technologies create channels for distributing content faster than official news media can adapt gaps emerge. The question is what happens in those gaps, and whether publics are capable of exploiting the channels for their own use. Similarly, the transmission model of communication is rendered increasingly ineffective by weblogs and allied media. A new image of the user arises with the development of Internet communication tools and begs a new model to describe it and new concepts to capture the new configurations.

References

Agar, M. (1994). *Language shock: Understanding the culture of conversation.* New York: William Morrow.

Bigum, C. (2002) Design sensibilities, schools, and the new computing and communications technologies. In I. Snyder (Ed.), *Silicon literacies* (pp. 130–149). London: Falmer-Routledge.

Gee, J. P. (1996). *Social linguistics and literacies: Ideology in discourses* (2nd ed.). London: Falmer.

Schrage, M. (2001). *The relationship revolution.* (Original work published 1997). Retrieved June 7, 2007, from http://www.yi-tan.com/wiki/yi-tan/the_relationship_revolution.

Sercu, L. (2004). Intercultural communicative competence in foreign language education: Integrating theory and practice. In O. St. John, K. van Esch, & E. Schalkwijk (Eds.), *New insights into foreign language learning and teaching* (pp. 115–130). Frankfurt, Germany: Peter Lang.

CHAPTER 15

Mediating Technologies and Second Language Learning

STEVEN L. THORNE

THE PENNSYLVANIA STATE UNIVERSITY, USA

Across the variegated history of human social organization, information and communication technologies have proven to have complex effects on the processes they mediate. Some technologies have scaled up familiar activities in the areas of impact, breadth, or speed, while others have given rise to genuinely unique informational, communicative, and social practices (see Marvin, 1990). In the current era, global networks enable memes (in the sense of Dawkins, 1976) of art, music, image, and of course language to propagate, cross-pollinate, mutate, and refract across media and communicative modalities. Massive sociological analyses have documented that the Internet has qualitatively transformed everyday communication and information practices in commercial, financial, professional, educational, recreational, and interpersonal realms (e.g., Castells, 1996, 1997, 1998, 2004). All of these issues raise questions as to how educators and researchers should orient themselves to the changing contexts and conditions of additional language learning.

While Internet access remains unequally distributed across social classes and geopolitical regions (see Van Dijk, 2005; Warschauer, 2003), user populations continue to expand around the world as life becomes increasingly mediated by established and emerging genres of Internet-mediated communicative activity, many of which vary substantially from predigital epistolary conventions (e.g., Crystal, 2001; Herring, 1996; Thorne & Payne, 2005; Werry, 1996). Of course, at this point in history, more than a decade beyond the widespread

Internet-mediated practices was common to the point of complete transparency for habituated late modern communicators.

Review Of Research

Networked Communication Tools in Language Education

The ability to link students by networked computers has created a variety of opportunities for language-based social interaction in L2 education. The pedagogical impetus behind educational uses of CMC (both Internet-mediated and earlier, within local-area networks) has been, and continues to be, language development through textually mediated, generally peer-focused communication.

Reports of L2 uses of Internet and local-area network communication technologies began emerging in the early 1990s. These accounts suggested a number of pedagogical benefits from CMC use, many of which were not readily available in conventional L2 language (Cononelos & Oliva, 1993) or composition (Colomb & Simutis, 1996) classrooms. Reported findings included a greater opportunity for expression of ideas than in face-to-face discussions and more time for reflection in the production of messages (Kern, 1995), more linguistic production overall (Kelm, 1992; Beauvois, 1992), and increased participation by students who do not participate as frequently in face-to-face classroom discussion (Sullivan & Pratt, 1996). The conventional subject positions of teachers and students were also argued to have shifted dramatically through the intervention of technology. Speaking about this issue, Kelm (1996) stated, "Technology allows language instructors to function in new roles: designer, coach, guide, mentor, facilitator. At the same time the students are able to be more engaged in the learning process as active learners, team builders, collaborators, and discoverers" (p. 27). While such shifts may have occurred in some cases, the early euphoria surrounding technology use as the panacea assuaging the challenges of education and language learning is striking (for a critical treatment of this issue, see Knobel, Lankshear, Honan, & Crawford, 1998).

Synchronous CMC Use in L2 Education

The use of synchronous CMC (SCMC), commonly referred to as *chat*, has been the basis of a large number of second-language acquisition (SLA) studies. Throughout the early 1990s, Kern (1995) used a SCMC tool called Daedalus Interchange, a local-area network application, with sections of university second-semester French foreign-language students. Based on his observations of in-class SCMC use, Kern attempted to quantitatively assess the impression that foreign-language students were producing more language output in SCMC environments than was the case in large group face-to-face classroom settings. Using a quasi-experimental methodology, Kern analyzed a 50-minute

French foreign-language SCMC session and compared it to an oral in-class discussion by the same language students on the same topic. The SCMC treatment produced between two and three times more turns per student and a higher total number of sentences and words compared to the large-group oral discussion (see also Abrams, 2003). Kern also examined the linguistic quality of the discussions and found that students' SCMC language output was more sophisticated in terms of the range of morphosyntactic features and variety of discourse functions expressed (1995, p. 470). These findings are supported by Chun's (1994) study of fourth-semester German students in which SCMC use promoted increased morphological complexity and a greater ratio of complex sentences in non-SCMC written coursework over the course of one semester. More recent research has also suggested that SCMC language use is more accurate than face-to-face interaction (Salaberry, 2001).

While Kern and Chun's research on L2 uses of large-group SCMC have demonstrable strengths, Ortega (1997) noted limitations to comparing computer-mediated classroom and whole-class oral discussions. Ortega (1997) posited that the variables of group size and communicative task were not accounted for in the early SCMC research (e.g., Beauvois, 1992; Chun, 1994; Kelm, 1992; Kern, 1995). She argued,

> It is justified to hypothesize that group size and equality of participation are negatively related in traditional oral interactions and positively related in computer-assisted interactions, and that the benefits of electronic over non-electronic interactions will increase with the size of groups ... . In other words, the positive equalizing effect of the electronic mode will be accentuated when comparing larger groups, as in the comparisons of teacher-fronted, whole-class discussion with whole-class electronic discussion. (p. 86)

This observation in no way obviates early SCMC research efforts, but it constructively suggested attention to key pedagogical and group-size variables and also set the stage for future work that examines the possibility of cross-modality transfer between SCMC use and oral-language production.

Cross-Modality Transfer

A growing number of L2 SCMC investigations explore cross-modality transfer between spontaneous SCMC and oral L2 language production (e.g., Abrams, 2003). Indeed, one of the alluring characteristics of SCMC for L2 teachers and learners has been its perceived resemblance to oral conversational language (e.g., Chun, 1994; for an argument against this claim, see Johanyek, 1997; see also Yates, 1996). Since a major goal of foreign-language instruction is the development of oral conversational ability, the possible connection between spontaneous L2 language production via text and speech has been a long-standing focus of L2 SCMC research (Beauvois, 1997; Payne & Whitney,

2002; Abrams, 2003; Payne & Ross, 2005). Payne and Whitney (2002) applied psycholinguistic models of language production and working memory to cross-modality transfer and found a significant difference in the oral proficiency gains between experimental (+SCMC) and control (–SCMC) groups. In a follow-up study, Payne and Ross (2005) augmented this psycholinguistic approach with discourse and corpus analytic techniques to explore how individual differences in working memory capacity may affect language use in SCMC. A principal finding was that learners testing at lower levels of measured phonological working memory were able to utilize the scrolling on-screen messages from other students as they generated their own contributions. Payne and Ross hypothesized that SCMC creates a "bootstrapping effect" that reduces the cognitive demand of L2 language production and may enable students with measured low-span working memory to produce more complex language than would otherwise be the case. New possibilities in cross-modality research include emerging CMC tools that support bimodal chat (i.e., a combination of both text and voice communication; see Blake, 2005) that may prove promising as environments to support a variety of learning styles and media preferences.

Interactionist SLA Research

A large number of SCMC studies have adopted the interactionist or "negotiation of meaning" framework, an approach to SLA initially designed for analysis of negotiation of meaning in oral interaction (e.g., Varonis & Gass, 1985) and subsequently has been applied to SCMC learner data and task configurations. Briefly described, the interactionist hypothesis suggests that nonnative speakers benefit from negotiation processes, such as modifications to linguistic input, that subsequently increase comprehension and promote interlanguage development (e.g., Long, 1985; Pica, 1987; Varonis & Gass, 1985; for a critique of the interactionist SLA paradigm, see Block, 2003). Pellettieri's (2000) interactionist research on Spanish L2 learners using SCMC finds that dyadic groupings promote an increase in corrective feedback and negotiation at all levels of discourse, a condition that prompts learners to produce form-focused modifications to their turns. Additionally, task type, specifically goal-oriented closed tasks, is positively correlated to the quantity and type of negotiations produced. In a similar study from the same period, Blake (2000) assessed the SCMC interactions of 50 intermediate learners of Spanish. Participants were arranged in dyads and asked to carry out three task types: (a) decision making, (b) information gap, and (c) jigsaw. Like Pellettieri (see also Smith, 2003), Blake found that jigsaw tasks produced the greatest number of negotiations, but nearly all negotiations were lexical in focus with very few addressing problems in syntax or larger units of discourse. In a 2005 study, Sotillo examined the use of Yahoo! Instant Messenger to assess the nature of negative feedback (e.g., error correction) occurring in native speaker (NS)—nonnative speaker

(NNS) and NNS-NNS interaction. This study indicated the availability of negative feedback within SCMC, particularly among the NNS-NNS dyads, with some evidence of learner uptake catalyzed by these direct and indirect (e.g., recasts) corrective feedback moves.

Building on earlier negotiation of meaning research in both CMC and face-to-face settings, Smith (2003) expanded the Varonis and Gass (1985) four-part model of face-to-face negotiated interaction—(a) trigger > (b) indicator > (c) response > (d) optional reaction to response—by explicitly incorporating two additional phases to represent delayed reactions to response turns that are so frequent in SCMC discourse. Smith termed these *confirmation* and *reconfirmation* phases, elements that explicitly conclude a given negotiation routine and which act as discourse markers suggesting the possibility of resuming nonnegotiation interaction. Smith's augmentation of the interactionist model provides a more modality-relevant framework for research on computer-mediated negotiated interaction.

While the interactionist SLA framework constitutes a significant or even majority market share of CMC L2 research and has produced interesting findings, the assumption that negotiation of meaning results in increased comprehensibility, which then is posited to promote language learning, has been strongly contested (Block, 2003; related to CMC, see Reinhardt, in press). Swain (2000), an early proponent of and contributor to the interactionist paradigm, recently contested these correlations, stating, "[V]irtually no research has demonstrated that the greater comprehensibility achieved through negotiation leads to second language learning" (p. 98). Interactionist researchers are aware of this problem and subsequently often make only descriptive claims confirming the presence of negotiation in SCMC discourse. For example, in a recent NNS-NS SCMC study, Lee (2006) concluded that, while her study supported the interactionist hypothesis, it "did not address whether responses to implicit feedback led to L2 development," but rather, it "simply identified feedback features used by both NSs and NNSs to negotiate meaning and form in the immediacy of ongoing [SCMC] dialogue" (p. 171). Another challenge to the interactionist paradigm is its traditionally exclusive focus on linguistic elements and encapsulated discoursal moves with little attention to, or provision for, the goal-directed pragmatic and cultural dimensions of communicative activity as they may relate to language learning (Kern, 2006). Researchers committed to the interactionist hypothesis, however, are addressing these limitations, for example, by focusing on cognitive processes such as noticing and attention to form that more robustly correlate negotiation of meaning to measurable gains in linguistic and communicative competence (e.g., Ellis, Basturkmen, & Loewen, 2001). Within CMC L2 research, an inspiring research article by O'Rourke (2005) frontally addresses the constraints of interactionist CMC research by contrapuntally contrasting it to Vygotsky (1997) inspired sociocultural theory (SCT; the latter is discussed next). O'Rourke utilized interactionist methodologies as an aid in uncovering language phenomena associated with metalinguistic awareness. At the same time, he openly acknowledged interactionism's tendency toward determinisms—both that technology can be seen to determine linguistic functions and that negotiation of meaning can be, somewhat ironically, presented as a set of predefined categories of nonnegotiable discoursal moves. He also problematized SCT as overstating the plasticity of social relations, interpretation of tasks, contexts (and by extension, subjectivities), and cultural significances associated with particular technologies. For research on technology-mediated L2 language use, O'Rourke suggested careful attention to the "features of artifacts and environments [that] can be graded according to the strength of their tendency to promote attention to form" (p. 435). This approach could allow interactionist methodology greater responsivity to the flexibility and local cultural qualities of the activity and artifacts at hand while also accepting the "relatively identifiable contours" of historically stable contexts, language practices, and technologies.

Sociocultural Theory and CMC L2 Research

L2 technology researchers have found SCT to be a useful theoretical framework due in large part to its serious attention to the symbolic and material mediators of human activity (e.g., Belz, 2002; Darhower, 2002; Oskoz, 2005; Thorne, 2004; Warschauer, 1997, 2005). The vast majority of technology-related SCT-oriented L2 studies, however, address the specific context of Internet-mediated *intercultural* L2 education, an area of pedagogical innovation that has become so vibrant as to warrant separate attention and thus will be addressed in the following section. To briefly describe essential elements of theory, SCT—also referred to as cultural-historical activity theory (for discussion of this terminological difference, see Thorne, 2005)—is rooted in the writings of the Russian psychologist Vygotsky (1997) and his colleagues (e.g., Leont'ev, 1981; Luria, 1976; Volosinov, 1973). SCT argues that human mental functioning is fundamentally a mediated process that is organized by cultural artifacts, activities, and concepts (Ratner, 2002). Humans are understood to utilize historically developed repositories of existing—as well as to create new—semiotic and conceptual artifacts that allow them to regulate their biological and behavioral activity. In this sense, individual and communal practices are, on one hand, articulations of historical continuance; on the other hand, however, they possess revolutionary potential for individual and collective change (see Sawchuk, Duarte, & Elhammoumi, 2006). Language use, as well as language organization and conceptual structure, are the primary of these social-semiotic mediational tools (for an SCT-informed linguistic model of communicative activity, see Thorne & Lantolf, 2007). While human neurobiology is an obvious and necessary condition for higher order thinking, human cognitive activity develops and is qualitatively transformed through interaction with, and contributions to, social and material environments (see Lantolf & Thorne, 2006, 2007; Stetsenko & Arievich, 2004; Tomasello, 1999).

SCT has been used to frame a number of areas of L2 CMC inquiry. Darhower (2002) examined the use of SCMC in two fourth-semester, university-level Spanish courses. His analysis illustrates that students were able to appropriate the chat environment to produce a personally meaningful, highly intersubjective discourse community that included the performance of nonstudent identities, theatrical role play, sarcasm and recurrent forms of humor, and strategic uses of the L1 to support more sophisticated dialogue, all of which extended the discourse possibilities substantially beyond those available in the face-to-face classroom setting. In a multisite research project that resulted in the text *Electronic Literacies,* Warschauer (1999) examined technology use in linguistically and ethnically diverse college-level ESL, Hawaiian language, and English writing courses. His emphasis was to assess the impact of technology-mediated learning activities across divergent contexts, with a focus on understanding the limits and possibilities of computer-mediation as a potentially transformative force in the development of computer literacy, L2 communicative competence, and L1 writing. Warschauer's analysis shows that the processes and outcomes of technology use differed greatly across the various contexts, suggesting constitutive ecological relationships (e.g., Bateson, 1972) between institutional mission and culture, teacher beliefs about the processes and expected outcomes associated with learning, and student-participants as subjects with agency and independent life goals. To take two of the cases, the undergraduate ESL course emphasized discrete point surface-level grammatical accuracy and subsequently, computer-mediated activities involved primarily grammar drills and attention to linguistic form. The Hawaiian language course, by contrast, was ideologically committed to writing as a form of collective empowerment, with computer-mediated activities involving linkages to the community and the production of applied research that could support Hawaiian language revitalization and maintenance. In terms of technology integration into formal educational contexts, Warschauer's (1999, 2005) work suggests that socially and/or professionally relevant "strong purpose activities" are more productive, but equally, that the uses of various technologies should include modality specific and rhetorically appropriate opportunities for expression.

Engeström and Miettenin (1999) pointed out the problem that "[a]ctivity-theoretical studies of work and communication have thus far mainly dealt with development and learning within well-bounded activity systems" (p. 32). Yet, demonstrably, life and learning are not composed of isolated or strictly isolatable moments and spaces (e.g., Leander & Lovvorn, 2006; Roth, Elmesky, Carambo, McKnight, & Beers, 2005). Addressing this issue, Thorne (1999, 2000a) focused on the interpenetrations occurring between microinteractional activity and macrosocial and cultural structures through an examination of social and formal educational uses of Internet communication technologies. Based on log file transcripts and ethnographic interviews with participants, Thorne presented evidence that for a number of students, the discursive framing of L2 educational activity is differentially configured when mediated by synchronous Internet communication tools. The question posed was, why is this the case? Although prior research on CMC use in L2 contexts (e.g., Beauvois, 1998; Chun, 1994; Warschauer, 1997) provided important descriptive analyses of uses of CMC for educational purposes, this work was limited by its lack of attention to macrocultural processes also at work (cf., Warschauer, 1999, previously discussed). Addressing this problem, Thorne proposed a two-level theoretical framework for the study of CMC that draws and expands upon theoretical treatments of mediation and interactivity system analysis. This approach to human activity mediated by artifacts distinguishes the "genotype" of an artifact's essential features and functional from its "phenotype," or observable characteristics as it is used within goal-directed activity.[1] While artifacts always possess a discrete functional materiality—their brute observable genotypic existence—in practice, artifacts are meaningfully and differentially defined by their historical patterns of use. Within the context of CMC L2 use, a phenotypic approach frames in-class digital interaction within the larger context of participants' prior and everyday use of Internet communication tools. Through a focus on divergent communities mediated by common mediational artifacts—in this case Internet communication tools—the relevance and importance of interactivity system analysis becomes both obvious and necessary. Extensions of this line of research will be further discussed in the next section of this chapter.

Internet-Mediated Intercultural L2 Education

The use of Internet technologies to encourage dialogue between distributed individuals and partner classes proposes a compelling shift in L2 education, one that moves learners away from simulated classroom-based contexts and toward actual interaction with expert speakers of the language they are studying. The conceptualization of L2 learning and use as foremost a process of intercultural communication, in both online and offline contexts, has received significant attention in recent years (e.g., Belz & Thorne, 2006a; Belz & Reinhardt, 2004; Brammerts, 1996; Byram, 1997; Furstenberg, 2003; Furstenberg, Levet, English, & Maillet, 2001; Kinginger, 1998, 2004; Kramsch, 1998; O'Dowd, 2003; Sercu, 2004; Tella, 1991; Thorne, 2003, 2006). Indeed, with greater Internet access across more of the world, there has been the suggestion that Internet-mediated intercultural communication constitutes a "second

---

[1] Genotype and phenotype are terms from biology that Thorne analogically applies to the discussion of artifact mediation. The definition of genotype is the basic genetic structure of an organism while phenotype describes the observable characteristics of an organism resulting from the interaction of its genotype with the environment.

wave" of computer-mediated L2 pedagogy (Kern, Ware, & Warschauer, 2004, p. 243). To refer to the wide diversity of approaches in this area, the umbrella term *Internet-mediated intercultural L2 education* (ICL2E; note that "Internet-mediated" is assumed, and thus ellipted from the acronym) will be used.

While intercultural approaches to language education constitute a vibrant but minority position in North America, Europe has begun to attune its education systems to acknowledge growing diaspora populations and multilingualism as core characteristics of the modern nation state (Council of Europe, 2001). Displacing the long-standing goal of L2 communicative competence, the "objective of foreign language teaching is now ... 'intercultural competence'" (Sercu, 2004, p. 115). Elaborating on this shift, Sercu argued,

> Seen from the intercultural perspective, it can be said that what a foreign language learner needs to learn in order to attain communicative competence is not how to adapt to any one of the foreign cultures present, and forget about his/her own cultural identity. Rather, the task of the participants in such an intercultural situation will be to negotiate, by means of implicit or explicit cues, a situationally adequate system of (inter)cultural standards and linguistic and pragmatic rules of interaction. (p. 116)

In reference to the larger goals of L2 education, Byram and Zarate (1997) described intercultural competence as the capacity to mediate multiple cultural identities and situations, a perspective that includes, but extends far beyond, the mechanics of surface-level grammatical accuracy.

Many ICL2E researchers and educators have benefited from the work of linguistic anthropologist Michael Agar (1994), who brought together language and culture into a dialectical unity through the construct "languaculture" (Agar, 1994, p. 60). Agar emphasized that utterances are always produced and interpreted in relation to historically formed cultural practices and speech situations; thus, the "langua" in "languaculture" is to be understood as the local inscription of more holistic frames of reference, examples of which include discourse grammar and language use as discursive practice (see also Carter, 1998; Gee, 1992, 1996; McCarthy & Carter, 1994; Scollon & Scollon, 2001). For L2 learners, perhaps especially those at more advanced levels, the growing realization of the subtle and obvious differences between their own and others' languacultures produces what Agar termed "rich points," the opportunities to collaboratively forge a heightened awareness of self and other that is fueled by the contestations and confusions that arise during communication (explicitly "intercultural" and otherwise). Agar conceptually shifted culture from the status of object to that of a process: "Culture happens when a problem in language has to do with who you are" (p. 48). A "problem" in the sense meant by Agar (see also Belz & Müller-Hartmann, 2003) is not something to avoid or ignore; it is a catalyst for development. As has been suggested by practitioners of cultural-historical activity theory (Engeström,

research should address not only the processes through which participants jointly construct online discourse, but also how participants construe the larger context of their participation.

In a study that imparts a complementary perspective on the issue of divergent communication styles, Belz (2003) carried out a linguistic analysis of telecollaborative exchanges between one American and two German participants. Belz utilized a variety of Hallidayian systemic functional analysis called *appraisal theory,* a specialized approach used to analyze the linguistic elements at play in the development, negotiation, and maintenance of social relationships. Appraisal theory provides tools to examine epistemic modality and other linguistic resources that communicators use to display and negotiate feelings, judgments, and valuations (see Martin & White, 2005). This study involved a quantitative analysis of linguistic features in the asynchronous CMC interactions illustrating that while overall rates of appraisal were similar for the three participants, there were marked differences in the distribution of positive and negative appraisals between the Germans and the American. To summarize, Belz demonstrated in fine-grained linguistic detail that Anke and Catharina, the German partners, showed a tendency toward "negative appraisal, categorical assertions, and intensification [that] may be reflective of broader German interactional patterns of directness, explicitness, and an orientation toward the self" (Belz, 2003, p. 91). In contrast, Eric, the American, exhibited "patterns of self-deprecating judgments, positive appreciation, and the upscaling of positive evaluations [that] may index broader [American] communicative patterns of indirectness and implicitness" (Belz, 2003, p. 91). Belz clearly stated that these differences dialectically interrelate with cultural and institutional communicative patterns but that languacultural norms do not determine discourse in any absolute fashion. Rather, historically established languacultural systems represent social semiotic resources that inform interactional preferences. Building on Byrnes (1986), the pedagogical implication to be drawn is not that students need necessarily change their discourse preferences. Rather, intercultural communicators would benefit from greater awareness of their own interactional style(s) and the development of heightened attunement to the communicative preferences of their interlocutors. The instructor would have multiple roles in this process, such as acting as a critical mediating resource and sounding board to facilitate consciousness raising and modeling what Kramsch (1999; Ware & Kramsch, 2005) described as an intercultural stance. Belz provided the following description of the role of the ICL2E educator:

> [T]he teacher in telecollaboration must be educated to discern, identify, explain, and model culturally contingent patterns of interaction in the absence of paralinguistic meaning signals, otherwise it may be the case that civilizations ultimately do clash—in the empirical details of their computer-mediated talk. (pp. 92–93)

Put another way, the role of the L2 teacher in ICL2E setting is "to prepare students to deal with global communicative practices that require far more than local communicative competence" (Kramsch & Thorne, 2002, p. 100).

ICL2E research has also addressed issues of pragmatic and linguistic development that have been argued to be consequences of participation in significant, meaningful, typically age-peer personal relationships. In a case of language learning fostered by interpersonal mediation, Thorne (2003) described a student in a university-level fourth-semester French grammar course participating in an ICL2E exchange with university students in France. In a post-semester interview, the student described a transition that began with frustration over the slow start to her key pal relationship but which culminated with a one-week period of prolific dialogue. The exchange began with an e-mail message but quickly moved to another Internet communication tool, America Online Instant Messenger (IM). The student reported that the first IM interaction went on for nearly 6 hours and included the use of both English and French. Subsequent to this, the interactions continued in 20- to 30-minute sessions, often two or three times per day. Two issues are highly salient—the shift to IM, which is the clear communication tool of choice for peer interaction among university-aged youth in the United States, and the subordination of French language study as an educational activity to the use of French (and English) for the building of a personally meaningful relationship. Not discounting the importance of the flirtatious nature of this relationship, the American student reported that her linguistic and pragmatic performance in French showed significant shifts. Through interaction with and goading from her French key pal, the American student eventually gained command of appropriate tu-vous (T/V) pronoun use, a facility that had eluded her throughout years of French study. More dramatically, the American student had always thought of herself as "horrible" at French grammar and had little confidence in her capacity to carry out meaningful communication in the language. When asked about the specific linguistic gains arising from her interactions with her French interlocutor, she made the following remarks:

Interviewer: What else beside the tu/vous stuff did he help you with?

Kirsten: Usage of "au" versus "en" versus "dans" versus "à" versus, you know, that kinda stuff. A more in-depth vocabulary, for sure. … it's kind of nice to have a human dictionary on the other end too … I was like "how am I supposed to say?" like for example … So the "de" and "à" thing, "de la campagne," "à le cité," whatever, stuff like that. I was like "wow," you know, eeeeee [vocalization of glee; laughs]. Because I couldn't get that from a dictionary.

Interviewer: That's something you have to have a little help with, yeah?

Kirsten: Yeah, yeah, and how am I supposed to learn it? That's not in the grammar books, you know [laughing], expressions like that, and other things. It was fun. (Thorne, 2003, pp. 50–51)

In these excerpts, the American student described the interaction that allowed her access to the French prepositional system that she allegedly "couldn't get … from a dictionary" and that is "not in the grammar books." Many French-language students have successfully developed the ability to use French prepositions of location from grammar texts or instructor-provided grammar explanations. This student, however, seemingly required interpersonal mediation, specifically from a desirable age peer who was willing to provide immediate corrective feedback as part of an ongoing social relationship. During her initial IM conversation with her French partner, she crossed a threshold that marked the first time she was consciously aware of her capacity to communicate meaningfully in French, stating "that was the first time that I was like, 'I made a connection in French.' I was so proud. It was like, 'wow, that's me, in French, and he understood me!'" (Thorne, 2003, p. 53) This brief case study suggests that interpersonal dynamics construct differing capacities to act, which, in turn, are associated with a range of possible developmental trajectories.

The power of social relationships also has a hand to play in one of the strongest examples of pragmalinguistic learning outcomes reported in ICL2E research. In a series of SCT-informed studies on telecollaboration, Belz and Kinginger (2002, 2003) and Kinginger and Belz (2005) described the development of address forms used in French and German (*tu/vous* and *du/Sie*, hereafter T/V). Current sociolinguistic research indicates that T/V usage has become destabilized in the French and German languages (Morford, 1997). Additionally, the specialized contexts of foreign-language textbooks and classroom discourse tend to radically simplify the sociopragmatic ambiguity around T/V usage. Perhaps for this reason, nearly all of the American student participants in these transatlantic interactions exhibited free variation of T/V at the start of the intercultural communication process. Employing the Vygotskian methodology of microgenetic analysis, Belz and Kinginger tracked usage over time in both e-mail and synchronous CMC sessions and found that after critical moments within exchanges with expert speaker-age peers, the American participants began to systemically modify their usage. These critical moments included explicit feedback and rationales for T-form usage from German and French peers. Additionally, the American students had myriad opportunities to observe appropriate pronoun use by native speakers across synchronous and asynchronous CMC modalities. In this way, pragmatic awareness of T/V as an issue (i.e., "noticing", see Schmidt, 1993) led to the approximation of expert speaker norms in most cases. Belz and Kinginger argued that the American students' desire to maintain positive face (in essence, wanting to be liked) with age peers helped to focus their attention on the role of linguistic form in the performance of pragmatically appropriate communication. In further research, the importance of the social relationships built in these transatlantic partnerships have been linked to positive development of other grammatical and morphological features, namely *da*-compounds in German (Belz, 2004, 2006), modal particles in German (Belz & Vyatkina, 2005), and lexical and morphological development in Spanish (Dussias, 2006).

Methodological Affordances: Corpus Analysis and CMC as Persistent Conversation

As we have discussed, ICL2E is premised on the notion of language learning through intercultural communication. A significant problem with the teaching of language as culture, as well as language form, is that the more obvious manifestations, such as grammatical constructions or formulaic pragmatics, are relatively simple to isolate and may require only modest explication. On the other hand, the historically structured resources (i.e., culture) that inform the subtleties of everyday communication can remain difficult to access or even invisible. Internet mediation provides a number of affordances in this area. In addition to the process ontology of unfolding activity, the actual moment-by-moment participation in a chat-dialogue box or even the first reading of an asynchronous post, most CMC tools also produce a digital record that has been described as "persistent conversation" (Erickson, 1999). Erickson provided the following insightful description:

> [D]igital conversation may be synchronous or asynchronous, and its audience intimate or vast. Its persistence means that it may be far more structured, or far more amorphous, than an oral exchange, and that it may have the formality of published text or the informality of chat. The persistence of such conversations also opens the door to a variety of new uses and practices: persistent conversations may be searched, browsed, replayed, annotated, visualized, restructured, and recontextualized, with what are likely to be profound impacts on personal, social, and institutional practices.

The persistence of (relatively) spontaneous language production is useful for L2 learners on at least two levels. The first is the immediate rerepresentation of a message that has been typed and submitted to a synchronous or asynchronous forum. In the case of SCMC, for example, messages are first entered into a discrete composition window and then, when posted, take their place in the publicly shared window as a turn at talk in an ongoing two- or multiparty discussion. This representation of one's message as a unified and emplaced utterance objectifies it in a way that is distinctive from the experience of having produced it. Learners often see gaps, problems, or a need for revision in their own messages when rereading them just moments after they have been posted (Thorne, 2000a). For example, in the following excerpt, a student describes learning from e-mail interactions with a French friend:

Eric: *e-mail is kind of like not a written thing … when you read e-mail, you get conversation but in a written form* so you can go back and look at them … . I've had that experience where conversational constructions appear in an e-mail form from a native speaker of French, which is really neat. Because it doesn't fly by you and kind of "look at that." (Kramsch & Thorne, 2002, p. 97)

A second use of persistence is that transcripts can be intensively searched and analyzed after the fact. If we understand language use as a form of social action (Heritage, 1984), CMC makes these actions visible and durative. This creates significant opportunities for reflection and analysis that would otherwise not be possible. From a conversation analytic perspective, Brouwer and Wagner (2004) described working with "collections of phenomenological similarity," meaning recurrent patterns of communicative activity that share structural and functional features and are used as a "resource for constructing intersubjective meanings in social life" (p. 31). One approach for making visible such "collections of phenomenological similarity" is to utilize computational tools that can search, produce collocations, and variably sort large volumes of real-language data that reflect specific genres or communicative contexts of interest. This approach is called *corpus linguistics* (e.g., Biber, Conrad, & Reppen, 1998; Granger, Hung, & Petch-Tyson, 2002; McCarthy, 1998; Sinclair, 1991, 2004).

Within ICL2E, Belz (2004, 2006) and her collaborators used corpus analytic techniques to query large volumes of Internet-mediated intercultural language conversations to ascertain the precise differences between expert and learner discourse in difficult-to-teach (and learn) areas (e.g., *da* compounds and modal particles for German). Belz used corpus-informed contrastive analysis, sometimes described as data-driven learning (e.g., Johns, 1991), to ascertain subtle differences in uses of discrete linguistic elements and collocations (i.e., common patterns of lexical affiliation) across learner and expert corpora of language use (see also Thorne, Reinhardt, & Golombek, in press). Assessing variance in the frequency and distribution of linguistic elements between expert and learner language use is especially relevant for ICL2E projects as issues of pragmatic appropriacy and cultural misalignments are all recorded in persistent textual form. With ecologically aligned corpora of both learner and expert language use, Belz and Thorne (2006b) suggested that L2 teachers can better:

capitalize on the blended quality of telecollaborative pedagogy in conjunction with the results of contrastive learner corpus analysis to convey an understanding of L2 competence that is rooted in frequency of use as well as grammatical accuracy, to construct quantitative profiles of learners' linguistic development over time, and to design individualized, corpus-based pedagogical interventions for underused or misused features. (p. xv)

This review of ICL2E research has attempted to show that the goals of various projects and interventions are diverse, but often include linguistic and pragmatic development as well as increasing awareness about one's own cultural background, those of one's interlocutors, and the processes involved in carrying out extended, developmentally productive, and ultimately meaningful dialogue with persons who are primary speakers of other languages. While correspondence with expert speakers of the language of study is a pedagogical method with a long history (e.g., Freinet, 1994), the recent surge in pedagogical and research efforts in this area suggests that ICL2E is exerting a significant and broad-based influence on the character, processes, and goals of mainstream L2 language education.

Open Internet Communities and Affiliative Networks

People have interests, passions, hobbies, idols, fetishes, problems, addictions, and aspirations that they want to communicate, share, argue about, and bond over. The Internet has created compelling opportunities to engage in all of these (and more) that include discussion fora associated with newspapers such as *Le Monde* (Hanna & de Nooy, 2003), fan fiction sites (Black, 2005, 2006), and fan Web sites (Lam, 2000, 2004; Lam & Kramsch, 2003). To begin with a project that most closely relates to instructed L2 learning, in a finely crafted study, Hanna and de Nooy (2003) reported on four students of French who participated in public Internet discussion forums associated with the Parisian newspaper *Le Monde*. The authors presented a strong rationale for opting to use public discussion forums rather than more conventional telecollaboration partnerships. While it is a debatable point, Hanna and de Nooy argued that while telecollaboration has many virtues, students are still "safely within the classroom, virtual though it might be" (p. 73) and limited by the fact that they occupy, and predominantly speak from, the institutionally bounded subject position of student or learner. *Le Monde* discussion fora, by contrast, exist to support argumentation and debate about mostly contemporary political and cultural issues. One forum in particular, labeled *Autre sujets* (other topics), included a wide range of participants and topics and was selected as the venue for the study.

The French language learners in Hanna and de Nooy's (2003) study were David and Laura, both American, and Eleanor and Fleurie, who were English. Each student's opening post to the *Autre sujets* forum was analyzed and followed for the number and content of the responses received. Each of the four students opened with a gambit that positioned them as learners of French, but they differed in their tone and affect. Eleanor and Fleurie opted to create new, stand-alone messages on the forum, with the respective subject lines *Les Anglais* ("The English") and *Une fille anglaise* ("An English girl"). In the content of their posts, Eleanor and Fleurie each made explicit requests for conversational partners to help them improve their French. They received a few cordial as well as abrupt replies, each of which suggested that they actually say something or take a position in the ongoing discussion. Neither did and both disappeared from the forum.

David and Laura, in contrast, both opened with a response to another message, *de facto* entering into a turn exchange system as their messages were marked by the subject line header of the message they had responded to (e.g., *Réf: Combattre le modèle américain*—"Fight the American model"). They also each began by apologizing for the limitations of their French-language ability. Hanna and de Nooy (2003) interpreted this as a clever strategy that "reinstates certain cultural borders" and that provided them with "a particular speaking position" (p. 78) that may have yielded advantages in the debate culture of the forum. It is also salient that, immediately following their language-apology gambits, they each contributed position statements on the themes of racism and cultural imperialism. David, in fact, primarily used English in his posts, but with coaching and support from forum participants, he maintained a significant presence on the forum, suggesting, "[N]either politeness nor linguistic accuracy is the measure of intercultural competence here" (Hanna & de Nooy, 2003, p. 78). Rather, in the circumstances of *Le Monde* discussion forums, participation in the genre of debate is the minimum threshold for membership. The critically important message from this study, framed in the vernacular, is that if you want to communicate with real people, you need to self-present as a real person yourself. From an instructional perspective, encouraging (or requiring) students to participate in noneducationally oriented online communities would involve teaching students how to recognize genres, and subsequently, how to engage in discussion that does not ultimately revolve around "the self ... as the exotic little foreigner/the other" (Hanna & de Nooy, 2003, p. 73).

Hanna and de Nooy's (2003) study illustrates that participation in open and thematically oriented Internet communities supports the very processes L2 education ostensibly seeks to provide, such as the use of language as a resource for ongoing identity formation and personally meaningful communication in the service of goals that extend beyond "practice" or "learning" in the restrictive senses associated with institutional settings. In related research investigating diaspora and immigrant youth engaged in nonacademically structured uses of the Internet, Lam (2000, 2004) ethnographically documented a number of developmental trajectories. One individual, an immigrant from Hong Kong, struggled with English, was tracked as a low-achieving student, and expressed significant trepidation about English, the language of his new home in the United States. In high school, however, he began to explore the Internet, developed a Web site devoted to the Japanese pop (J-pop) singer Ryoko and started to converse over e-mail and SCMC with a number of other J-pop fans. This process was mediated largely in English but also included transcultural expressive features such as emoticons, Web-page design, and elements from other languages (e.g., Chinese). Participation in a vibrant online community elevated Almon's confidence and enhanced his capacity to use a genre of English appropriate to online communication. As Almon's semiotic repertoire expanded, he developed the ability to construct a complex online identity and to build and sustain meaningful relationships. Commenting on the differences between Almon's developmental progress in English in school and in the Internet peer group, Lam and Kramsch (2003) argued that while Almon's textual identity on the Internet was a positive and empowering discursive formation, his position in the U.S. high school "is also symbolically constructed, this time as a low-pride 'low-acheiver'" (p. 155). In other words, noted Lam and Kramsch, the sophisticated genre of English language use Almon demonstrated online may not meet the selection criteria necessary to pass the high-school exit composition test. This case presents a number of challenges to the conventional goals and processes of language education, such as the rigidity of the gatekeeping mechanisms of high-stakes testing, the disconnect between and the prescriptivist epistemology of schooling and language use that is appropriate in other contexts (Internet-mediated and otherwise), and what should or could be done to leverage, and perhaps formally acknowledge, a plurality of communicative practices that are currently considered stigmatized linguistic varieties. In an age marked by transcultural and hybrid genres of communication, these issues will increase in intensity and complexity and will necessarily have to inform the L2 educational frameworks of the future.

New(er) Technologies and L2 Education

A number of recent techonologies, namely wikis, blogs, and gaming, are rapidly being appropriated into L2 educational contexts. There is currently very little research on the use of these tools for L2 learning, presenting an obvious opportunity for future work.

Blogs and Wikis

Blogs and wikis are considered second-generation Web applications and represent relatively modest technological advancements over their static Web page predecessor (for a review of these technologies, see Thorne & Payne, 2005). *Wiki* (from the Hawaiian *wiki wiki* meaning "quick") describes a Web-based environment that supports collaborative writing. Wikis are designed to be intensely collaborative and allow multiple users to edit content and contribute to the production of continually evolving texts and informational resources. The radical dimension to wiki use is its challenge of the notion of authorship. In the archetypal wiki, there is no distinction between "author" and "audience" per se since readers of a wiki page can spontaneously opt to become a collaborating author. Individual wiki pages can be password limited to one or a group of users using an access-control list, but wiki technology is premised on the idea of universal write/access. Within the context of group and educational uses, wikis obviate the need to laboriously merge individual contributions in order to avoid deleting one another's work. Most wiki engines track each addition, deletion, and modification so that changes can be assessed against earlier versions of the text. Furthermore, determining the amount of individual participation in a group project for assessment purposes need not rely exclusively on self- and peer-assessments by group members or observational hunches by the teacher. Like an archaeological tell, a wiki's current content is but the top layer of temporally stratified laminations of text that record the history of the writing process (Thorne & Payne, 2005).

Blogs and *blogging* are terms describing use of a Web application that displays serial entries with date and time stamps. Most blogs include a comments feature that allows visitors to post responses. In its short history—the first use of the term *blog* (from "Weblog") is variably reported to have occurred in either 1996 or 1997 and blogging as a populist movement dates only from the turn of the millennium—the rise of blogging as a form of communicative and informational expression has been mercurial. To take one example, LiveJournal (http://www.livejournal.com) reports over 7 million blogs created, approximately 5 million of which have been updated at least once. LiveJournal reports that female-presenting bloggers outnumber users presenting as males by approximately 2 to 1 (67.3% vs. 32.7%, respectively). The ages of LiveJournal users span from 13 (35,856 blogs created by this age group) to 55 (1,229). The 15- to 20-year-old age group produces the majority of the blogs on this site, which suggests that the everyday digital literacy practices of current high school and college students differ significantly from those of earlier generations. Within L2 education contexts, blogging provides an alternative to writing assignments that would normally be presented only to the instructor. The chronological ordering of blog entries creates for each student an archive of his or her personal work that can be revisited and reflected upon. In addition to its intraclass use as a journaling tool, blogging is also being used to link together study abroad students and those still at their home universities. While still in the exploratory phase, such uses of blogs serve a number of functions, such as providing predeparture cultural exposure for students still at their home university, helping students currently abroad to synthesize and put into narrative form their cultural and linguistic experiences, and for creating predeparture-orientation materials that represent student specific experiences and points of view.

While a large number of additional mediated social networks exist, such as facebook (www.facebook.com), MySpace (www.myspace.com), and Friendster (www.friendster.com), to date, their potential as sites for affiliative interaction and L2 learning has gone entirely unexplored.

Gaming and Virtual Environments

A genre of digital environment that will likely emerge as the premier L2 educational technology in the immediate future is virtual environment games (Gee, 2003), which provide the opportunity for temporary immersion in linguistic, cultural, and task-based settings. One variety of gaming involves interaction within preprogrammed (but sometimes customizable) environments, the best-selling example of which is The Sims. A game that simulates the activities and responsibilities of everyday life, The Sims is now produced in a number of languages. In an informal assessment of The Sims as a foreign-language learning tool, Purushotma (2005) found that the vocabulary and tasks comprising the game were highly aligned with the content of conventional foreign-language course content. The difference between instructed foreign-language learning and a game like The Sims, suggested Purushotma (2005), is that exposure to the target language is always linked to carrying out tasks and social actions, which concomitantly embeds vocabulary and constructions in rich associative contexts.

A second variety of virtual immersion is massive multiplayer online videogames (MMOGs, see Steinkeuhler, 2006). These Internet-mediated environments are immensely popular, especially among adolescents and younger adults, and are already educational in the sense that gamers must learn to negotiate complex scenarios, be socialized into culturally specific discursive formations, and be capable of negotiating play in real time with environment-driven elements as well as other copresent gamers. MMOGs log a gamer's activity such that there is an ontogenetic developmental component to one's online character or avatar. In essence, a gamer's character becomes more capable and more powerful based on experience. In addition, gamers can accumulate (virtual) property, commodities with set exchange values within a given MMOG, and in some instances, properties and commodities with exchange value recognized by nongaming global capital (e.g., in-game resources such as weapons, currency, property, and even completely developed advanced characters can be bought and sold on eBay). Many MMOGs are multilingual and involve thousands, and, in some cases, millions, of gamers from around the world (e.g., World of Warcraft). For the growing number of individuals participating in MMOG-based cultures, the international, multilingual, and task-based qualities of these social spaces, where language use is literally social action, may one day make them *de rigueur* sites for language learning (see Thorne, in press). Or perhaps, somewhat ironically, students will study foreign languages to enhance their gaming skills and interactional capacity in these largely language organized action-scapes.

Technology as Cultural Artifact and Challenges to L2 Education

This section addresses two final issues relating to technology use in L2 education. The first is (hopefully) a reminder that the Internet does not exist as a neutral medium. The second issue is the widening gap between real-world communication and the anachronistic epistemological prescriptivism that remains dominant in educational institutions.

The Internet has enabled multiple new opportunities for information gathering, enhanced possibilities for producing and disseminating information to others, and has provoked changes in the granularity of information sharing between spatially dispersed coworkers, friends, and family members. By definition, such communicative practices are made possible through technological mediation. As the research of Jones (2004), Miller and Slater (2000), and Scollon and Scollon (2004) made clear, a dichotomized view of face-to-face and Internet-mediated life, and certainly a rigid dichotomization between "real" and "virtual," completely dissolves under close examination of lived communicative practice. Especially among the digital native generation (Prensky, 2001), a descriptor for individuals who quite literally grew up with (and through) the use of Internet information and communication tools, it is apparent that social as well as academic communication increasingly involves participation in community networks mediated by Facebook, MySpace, blogs, vlogs (video blogs), instant messaging, MMOGs, and voice and text messaging over cell phones (for discussions, see Thorne & Payne, 2005; Thorne, 2006). The rise in mediated communication in the service of community building and maintenance suggests that for many students across the world, performing competent identities in second and additional language(s) may now involve Internet-mediation as or more often than face-to-face and nondigital forms of communication. However, for an obstinate majority of L2 CMC researchers, the variable meanings and significances of the Internet are masked by the *doxa,* or taken-for-grantedness, of its use in routine, everyday cultural practice (e.g., Bourdieu & Eagleton, 1992). Internet communication tools are, like all human creations, cultural tools (e.g., Cole, 1996; Nardi, 1996; Wartofsky, 1979) that carry interactional and relational associations, preferred uses (and correspondingly, dispreferred uses), and expectations of genre-specific communicative activity. Kramsch and Anderson (1999) noted that information and communication "has become more mediated than ever, with a mediation that ever more diffuses and conceals its authority. The role of education, and FL [foreign language] education in particular, is precisely to make this mediation process visible" (p. 39). Cultures-of-use of Internet communication tools build up over time in relationship to use in particular discursive settings and to mediate specific social functions. The suggestion is that technologies, *as culture,* will have variable meanings and uses for different communities. While Internet communication tools carry the historical residua of their use across time, patterns of past use do not determine present and future activity, just as gender, mother tongue, or social class do not determine present and future activity. Rather, the cultures-of-use framework provides another axis along which to perceive and address cultural conflict, variation, and similarity (Thorne, 2000a, 2003, 2006).

A telling example of the malleability of Internet communication and information tools involves wiki technology (previously described). Emigh and Herring (2005) found that despite the potential of wiki environments to transform notions of authorship and processes of writing, wiki use does not necessarily promote the production of heterogeneous, creative, or nonstandard genres of text. Based on a corpus analysis of Wikipedia and Everything2 (another wiki-based encyclopedia), Emigh and Herring found that structures of postproduction and editorial control resulted in homogeneous, formal, and standardized text types despite the expectation that multiple authors would produce a diversity of text genres. As with all technologies described in this chapter, task design and procedural processes, in interface with exogenously developed cultures of use and expectations of appropriate Internet communication tool use, are critical elements that contribute to the ways that mediated language-learning activity plays out.

The second aforementioned challenge precipitated by the Internet is that there now exists an amplification of the conventional generation gap between top-down processes and pedagogies that operate in formal learning environments and the bottom-up life experiences of students in secondary and university environments (e.g., Lankshear & Knobel, 2003). This gap has been confirmed in recent research by the Pew Internet and American Life Project (Levin & Arafeh, 2002) based on focus groups (136 students in gender-balanced and racially diverse clusters) and voluntary participation data (200 students who submitted online essays describing their use of the Internet for school). The 2002 Pew report revealed that while nearly all students used the Internet as a regular part of their educational activities, little is known about how the Internet is actually used for schoolwork nor has there been adequate consideration of Internet use as it might substantively inform school policies, practices, and pedagogies. As Internet users expand numerically and geographically, and as Internet information and communication tools continue to evolve, research and pedagogical innovation in the area of CMC and language education will need to continually adapt in response to new populations, communication tools, and emerging communicative needs.

Final Points

While in the 1990s the use of the Internet was often treated as a proxy or heuristic environment to assist with the development of "real" communicative performance (i.e., face-to-face communication, aural comprehension, and nondigital epistolary conventions such as essay writing), textual Internet-mediated communication now presents its own set of high-stakes contexts and modalities. Commercial activity is conducted via asynchronous and synchronous channels, job interviews take place over instant messaging, university courses are now mediated by course-management systems, and chat, blogs, wikis, and podcasting, among other technologies, are increasingly being incorporated into general education and L2 course activities. Furthermore, with the proliferation of digital multimedia technologies (e.g., digital-video cameras and video-editing software, Web-publishing technologies that support audio and video, and cell phones that record still images and video), mediated communication now includes a large number of small footprint devices that have little to do with what has been conventionally referred to as a *computer*. Education generally, and language education particularly, will need to accommodate emerging communication tools and their attendant communicative genres that are, and have been for some years, everyday dimensions of competent social and professional activity.

While there exists a large volume of research on CMC in foreign and second-language education, this field is something of a shape shifter, a research area that is polymorphous both across time and within and between bounded areas of inquiry. The population of Internet users has expanded geographically and numerically, Internet information and communication technologies continue to evolve at increasing rates, and for many individuals around the world, daily social and professional activity is mediated by ubiquitous computing. This observation is not meant to hype these transformations as universally positive or superior to earlier patterns of communicative and informational activity. On the contrary, the point is that with the increasing opportunity to choose and engineer Internet mediation for educational purposes, the responsibility to make informed decisions—at the levels of classroom use, curricular innovation, institutional policy, and even region or nation state agenda setting—is more critical now than ever before.

References

Abrams, Z. I. (2003). The effects of synchronous and asynchronous CMC on oral performance. *Modern Language Journal, 87*(2), 157–167.

Agar, M. (1994). *Language shock: Understanding the culture of conversation.* New York: William Morrow.

Bateson, G. (1972). *Steps toward an ecology of mind: Collected essays in anthropology, psychiatry, evolution, and epistemology.* Chicago: University Of Chicago Press.

Beauvois, M. H. (1992). Computer assisted classroom discussion in the classroom: Conversation in slow motion. *Foreign Language Annals, 25*(5), 525–534.

Beauvois, M. H. (1997). Computer-mediated communication: Technology for improving speaking and writing. In M. D. Bush & R. M. Terry (Eds.), *Technology-enhanced language learning* (pp. 165–184). Lincolnwood, IL: National Textbook Company.

Beauvois, M. H. (1998). Write to speak: The effects of electronic communication on the oral achievement of fourth semester French students. In J. A. Muyskens (Ed.), *New ways of learning and teaching: Focus on technology and foreign language education.* Boston: Heinle & Heinle.

Belz, J. A. (2002). Social dimensions of telecollaborative language study [Electronic version]. *Language Learning & Technology, 6*(1), 60–81.

Belz, J. A. (2003). Linguistic perspectives on the development of intercultural competence in telecollaboration [Electronic version]. *Language Learning & Technology, 7*(2), 68–117.

Belz, J. A. (2004). Learner corpus analysis and the development of foreign language proficiency. *System, 32*(4), 577–591.

Belz, J. A. (2006). At the intersection of telecollaboration, learner corpus analysis, and L2 pragmatics: Considerations for language program direction. In J. Belz & S. L. Thorne (Eds.), *Internet-mediated intercultural foreign language education* (pp. 207–246). Boston: Thomson Heinle Publishers.

Belz, J. A., & Kinginger, C. (2002). The cross-linguistics development of address form use in telecollaborative language learning: Two case studies. *Canadian Modern Language Review/Revue canadienne des langues vivant, 59*(2), 189–214.

Belz, J. A., & Kinginger, C. (2003). Discourse options and the development of pragmatic competence by classroom learners of German: The case of address forms. *Language Learning, 53*(4), 591–647.

Belz, J. A., & Müller-Hartmann, A. (2003). Teachers as intercultural learners: Negotiating German-American telecollaboration along the institutional faultline. *Modern Language Journal, 87*(1), 71–89.

Belz, J. A., & Reinhardt, J. (2004). Aspects of advanced foreign language proficiency: Internet-mediated German language play. *International Journal of Applied Linguistics, 14*(3), 324–362.

Belz, J. A., & Thorne, S. L. (Eds.). (2006a). *Internet-mediated intercultural foreign language education*. Boston: Heinle & Heinle.

Belz, J. A., & Thorne, S. L. (Eds.). (2006b). Introduction: Internet-mediated intercultural foreign language education and the intercultural speaker. In J. Belz & S. L. Thorne (Eds.), *Internet-mediated intercultural foreign language education* (p. iix–xxv). Boston: Thomson Heinle Publishers.

Belz, J. A., & Vyatkina, N. (2005). *Computer-mediated learner corpus research and the data-driven teaching of L2 pragmatic competence: The case of German modal particles* (CALPER Working Papers, 4, 1–28). Retrieved June 10, 2005, from http://calper.la.psu.edu/downloads/download.php?143

Berners-Lee, T. (1998). *What the semantic web isn't but can represent*. Retrieved June 10, 2005, from http://www.w3.org/DesignIssues/RDFnot.html

Bernstein, B. (1996). *Pedagogy, symbolic control and identity*. London: Taylor & Francis.

Biber, D., Conrad, C., & Reppen, R. (1998). *Corpus linguistics: Investigating language structure and use*. Cambridge, U.K.: Cambridge University Press.

Black, R. W. (2005). Access and affiliation: The literacy and composition practices of English language learners in an online fanfiction community. *Journal of Adolescent & Adult Literacy, 49*(2), 118–128.

Black, R. W. (2006). Language, culture, and identity in online fanfiction. *E-learning, 3*(2), 170–184.

Blake, R. J. (2000). Computer mediated communication: A window on L2 Spanish interlanguage. *Language Learning & Technology, 4*(1): 120–136.

Blake, R. J. (2005). Bimodal CMC: The glue of language learning at a distance. *CALICO Journal, 22*(3), 497–512.

Blake, R. J., & Zystik. E. (2003). Who's helping whom?: Learner/heritage speakers' networked discussions in Spanish. *Applied Linguistics 24*(4), 519–544.

Block, D. (2003). *The social turn in second language acquisition*. Washington, DC: Georgetown University Press.

Bolter, J. D. (1991). *Writing space: The computer, hypertext, and the history of writing*. Hillsdale, NJ: Erlbaum.

Bourdieu, P., & Eagleton, T. (1992). Doxa and common life. *New Left Review, 191*, 111–121.

Brammerts, H. (1996). Language learning in tandem using the Internet. In M. Warschauer (Ed.), *Telecollaboration in foreign language learning* (pp. 121–130). Honolulu: University of Hawaii Second Language Teaching and Curriculum Center.

Kinginger, C. (1998). Videoconferencing as access to spoken French. *Modern Language Journal, 82*(4), 502–513.

Kinginger, C. (2004). Communicative foreign language teaching through telecollaboration. In K. van Esch & O. St. John (Eds.), *New insights into foreign language learning and teaching* (pp. 101–113). Frankfurt am Main, Germany: Peter Lang.

Kinginger, C., & Belz, J. A. (2005). Sociocultural perspectives on pragmatic development in foreign language learning: Microgenetic case studies from telecollaboration and residence abroad. *Intercultural Pragmatics, 2*(4), 369–422.

Knobel, M., Lankshear, C., Honan, E., & Crawford, J. (1998). The wired world of second-language education. In I. Snyder (Ed.), *Page to screen: Taking literacy into the electronic era* (pp. 20–50). New York: Routledge.

Kötter, M. (2002). *Tandem learning on the Internet: Learner interactions in online virtual environments.* Frankfurt, Germany: Lang.

Kramsch, C. (1998). *Language and culture.* Oxford, U.K.: Oxford University Press.

Kramsch, C. (1999). Thirdness: The intercultural stance. In T. Vestergaard (Ed.), *Language, culture, and identity* (pp. 41–58). Aalborg, Denmark: Aalborg University Press.

Kramsch, C., & Andersen, R. (1999). Teaching text and context through multimedia. *Language Learning & Technology, 2*(2): 31–42.

Kramsch, C., & Thorne, S. L. (2002). Foreign language learning as global communicative practice. In D. Block & D. Cameron (Eds.), *Globalization and language teaching* (pp. 83–100). London: Routledge.

Lam, W. S. E. (2000). Second language literacy and the design of the self: A case study of a teenager writing on the Internet. *TESOL Quarterly, 34*(3), 457–483.

Lam, W. S. E. (2004). Second language socialization in a bilingual chat room. *Language Learning & Technology, 8*(3), 44–65.

Lam, W. S. E., & Kramsch, C. (2003). The ecology of an SLA community in computer-mediated environments in leather. In J. Leather & J. van Dam (Eds.), *Ecology of language acquisition.* Dordrecht, Netherlands: Kluwer Publishers.

Landow, G. (1992). *Hypertext: The convergence of contemporary critical theory and technology.* Baltimore: Johns Hopkins.

Lanham, R. (1993). *The electronic word: Democracy, technology, and the arts.* Chicago: University of Chicago Press.

Lankshear, C., & Knobel, M. (2003). *New literacies.* Buckingham, U.K.: Open University Press.

Lankshear, C., Peters, M., & Knobel, M. (1996). Critical pedagogy and cyberspace. In H. Giroux, C. Lankshear, P. McLaren, & M. Peters (Eds.), *Counter narratives: Cultural studies and critical pedagogies in postmodern spaces.* New York: Routledge.

Lantolf, J. P., & Thorne, S. L. (2006a). *Sociocultural theory and the genesis of second language development.* Oxford, U.K.: Oxford University Press.

Lantolf, J. P., & Thorne, S. L. (2006b). Sociocultural theory and second language acquisition. In. B. van Patten & J. Williams (Eds.), *Explaining SLA.* Cambridge, U.K.: Cambridge University Press.

Leander, K., & Lovvorn, J. (2006). Literacy networks: Following the circulation of texts, bodies, and objects in the schooling and online gaming of one youth. *Cognition and Instruction, 24*(3), 291–340.

Lee, L. (2006). A study of native and nonnative speakers' feedback and responses in Spanish-American networked collaborative interaction. In J. Belz & S. L. Thorne (Eds.), *Internet-mediated intercultural foreign language education* (pp. 147–176). Boston: Thomson Heinle Publishers.

Leont'ev, A. N. (1981). The problem of activity in Soviet psychology. In J. V. Wertsch (Ed.), *The concept of activity in Soviet psychology* (pp. 37–71). Armonk, NY: Sharpe.

Levin, D., & Arafeh, S. (2002). *The digital disconnect: The widening gap between Internet-savvy students and their schools.* Washington, DC: Pew Internet & American Life Project.

Long, M. (1985). Input and second language acquisition theory. In S. M. Gass & C. G. Madden (Eds.), *Input in second language acquisition* (pp. 377–393). Rowley, MA: Newbury House.

Luria, A. R. (1976). Cognitive development. Cambridge, MA: Harvard University Press.

Marvin, C. (1990). *When old technologies were new: Thinking about electric communication in the late nineteenth century.* New York: Oxford University Press.

Martin, J. R., & White, P. R. R. (2005). *Language of evaluation: Appraisal in English.* New York: Palgrave Macmillan.

McCarthy, M. J. (1998). *Spoken language and applied linguistics.* Cambridge, U.K.: Cambridge University Press.

McCarthy, M., & Carter, R. (1994). *Language as discourse: Perspectives for language teaching.* London: Longman.

Miller, D., & Slater, D. (2000). *The Internet: An ethnographic approach.* Oxford, U.K.: Berg.

Morford, J. (1997). Social indexicality in French pronominal address. *Journal of Linguistic Anthropology, 7*(1), 3–37.

Nardi, B. (Ed.). (1996). *Context and consciousness: Activity theory and human-computer interaction.* Cambridge, MA: MIT Press.

Noblitt, J. (1995). The electronic language learning environment. In C. Kramsch (Ed.), *Redefining the boundaries of language study.* Boston: Heinle & Heinle.

O'Dowd, R. (2003). Understanding the "other side": Intercultural learning in a Spanish-English e-mail exchange. *Language Learning & Technology, 7*(2), 118–144.

O'Rourke, B. (2005). Form focused interaction in online tandem learning. *CALICO Journal, 22*(3), 433–466.

Ortega, L. (1997). Processes and outcomes in networked classroom interaction: Defining the research agenda for L2 computer-assisted classroom discussion. *Journal of Language Learning & Technology, 1*(1), 82–93.

Oskoz, A. (2005). Students' dynamic assessment via online chat. *CALICO Journal, 22*(3), 513–536.

Payne, J. S., & Ross, B. (2005). Synchronous CMC, working memory, and oral L2 proficiency development. *Language Learning & Technology, 9*, 35–54.

Payne, J. S., & Whitney, P. J. (2002). Developing L2 oral proficiency through synchronous CMC: Output, working memory, and interlanguage development. *CALICO Journal, 20*(1), 7–32.

Pellettieri, J. (2000). Negotiation in cyberspace: The role of chatting in the development of grammatical competence. In M. Warschauer & R. Kern (Eds.), *Network-based language teaching: Concepts and practice* (pp. 59–86). New York: Cambridge University Press.

Pica, T. (1987). Interlanguage adjustments as an outcome of NS-NNS negotiation interaction. *Language Learning, 38*(1), 45–73.

Prensky, M. (2001). Digital natives, digital immigrants. On the horizon. *NCB University Press, 9*(5).

Purushotma, Ravi (2005). Commentary: You're not studying, you're just ... . *Language Learning & Technology,* (9)1: 80-96.

Ratner, C. (2002). *Cultural psychology: Theory and method.* New York: Kluwer/Plenum.

Reinhardt, J. (in press). Negotiating meaningfulness: Face, solidarity, and support in computer-mediated learning environments. In S. Magnan (Ed.), *Mediating discourse online.* Amsterdam: John Benjamins.

Rheingold, H. (1993). *The virtual community.* New York: Addison-Wesley.

Roth, W. M., Elmesky, R., Carambo, C., McKnight, Y. M., & Beers, J. (2005). Re/making identities in the praxis of urban schooling: A cultural historical perspective. *Mind, Culture, and Activity, 11*, 48–69.

Salaberry, M. R. (2001). The use of technology for second language learning and teaching: A retrospective. *Modern Language Journal, 85*, 39–56.

Savignon, S. (1983). *Communicative competence: Theory and classroom practice.* Reading, MA: Addison-Wesley.

Sawchuk, P., Duarte, N., & Elhammoumi, M. (2006). *Critical perspectives on activity: Explorations across education, work, and everyday life.* Cambridge, U.K.: Cambridge University Press.

Schmidt, R. (1993). Awareness and second language acquisition. *Annual Review of Applied Linguistics, 13,* 206–226.

Schneider, J., & von der Emde, S. (2000). Brave new (virtual) world: Transforming language learning into cultural studies through online learning environments (MOOs). *ADFL Bulletin, 32*(1), 18–26.

Schneider, J., & von der Emde, S. (2006). Conflicts in cyberspace: From communication breakdown to intercultural dialogue in online collaborations. In J. Belz & S. L. Thorne (Eds.), *Internet-mediated intercultural foreign language education* (pp. 2–30). Boston: Thomson Heinle Publishers.

Schwienhorst, K. (2003). Learner autonomy and tandem learning: Putting principles into practice in synchronous and asynchronous telecommunications environments. *Computer-Assisted Language Learning, 16*(5), 427–443.

Scollon, R., & Scollon, S. (2001). *Intercultural communication* (2nd ed.). Cambridge, U.K.: Blackwell.

Scollon, R., & Scollon, S. (2004). *Nexus analysis: Discourse and the emerging Internet.* New York: Routledge.

Sercu, L. (2004). Intercultural communicative competence in foreign language education: Integrating theory and practice. In O. St. John, K. van Esch, & E. Schalkwijk (Eds.), *New insights into foreign language learning and teaching* (pp. 115–130). Frankfurt, Germany: Peter Lang Verlag.

Sinclair, J. (1991). *Corpus, concordance, and collocation.* Oxford, U.K.: Oxford University Press.

Sinclair, J. (Ed.). (2004). *How to use corpora in language teaching.* Philadelphia: John Benjamins.

Smith, B. (2003). Computer-mediated negotiated interaction: An expanded model. *The Modern Language Journal, 87*(1), 38–57.

Sotillo, S. (2005). Corrective feedback via instant messenger learning activities in NS-NNS and NNS-NNS dyads. *CALICO Journal, 22*(3), 467–496.

Steinkuehler, C. (2006). Massively multiplayer online videogaming as participation in a discourse. *Mind, Culture, & Activity, 13*(1), 38–52.

Stetsenko, A., & Arievich, I. (2004). The self in cultural-historical activity theory. *Theory & Psychology, 14*(4), 475–503.

Sullivan, N., & Pratt, E. (1996). A comparative study of two ESL writing environments: A computer-assisted classroom and a traditional oral classroom. *System, 29,* 491–501.

Swain, M. (2000). The output hypothesis and beyond: Mediating acquisition through collaborative dialogue. In J. Lantolf (Ed.), *Sociocultural theory and second language learning.* Oxford, U.K.: Oxford University Press.

Tella, S. (1991). *Introducing international communications networks and electronic mail into foreign language classrooms: A case study in Finnish senior secondary schools.* Helsinki, Finland: Yliopistopaino.

Thorne, S. L. (1999). *An activity theoretical analysis of foreign language electronic discourse.* Unpublished doctoral dissertation, University of California, Berkeley.

Thorne, S. L. (2000a). Beyond bounded activity systems: Heterogeneous cultures in instructional uses of persistent conversation. In Editor (Ed.), *Proceedings of the Thirty-Third Annual Hawaii International Conference on System Sciences* (HICSS-33). Los Alamitos, CA: IEEE Press.

Thorne, S. L. (2000b). Second language acquisition and the truth(s) about relativity. In J. Lantolf (Ed.), *Sociocultural theory and second language acquisition* (pp. 219–244). New York: Oxford University Press.

Thorne, S. L. (2003). Artifacts and cultures-of-use in intercultural communication. *Language Learning & Technology, 7*(2), 38–67.

Thorne, S. L. (2004). Cultural historical activity theory and the object of innovation. In O. St. John, K. van Esch, & E. Schalkwijk (Eds.), *New insights into foreign language learning and teaching* (pp. 51–70). Frankfurt, Germany: Peter Lang Verlag.

Thorne, S. L. (2005). Epistemology, politics, and ethics in sociocultural theory. *Modern Language Journal, 89*(3), 393–409.

Thorne, S. L. (2006). Pedagogical and praxiological lessons from Internet-mediated intercultural foreign language education research. In J. Belz & S. L. Thorne (Eds.), *Internet-mediated intercultural foreign language education* (pp. 2–30). Boston: Thomson Heinle Publishers.

Thorne, S. L. (in press). Transcultural communication in open Internet environments and massively multiplayer online games. In S. Magnan (Ed.), *Mediating discourse online*. Amsterdam: John Benjamins.

Thorne, S. L., & Lantolf, J. P. (2007). A linguistics of communicative activity. In S. Makoni & A. Pennycook (eds.), *Disinventing and reconstituting languages* (pp. 170–195). Clevedon: Multilingual Matters.

Thorne, S. L., & Payne, J. S. (2005). Evolutionary trajectories, Internet-mediated expression, and language education. *CALICO Journal, 22*(3), 371–397.

Thorne, S. L., Reinhardt, J., & Golombek, P. (in press). Mediation as objectification in the development of professional discourse: A corpus-informed curricular innovation. In J. Lantolf & M. Poehner (eds.), *Sociocultural theory and the teaching of second languages*. London: Equinox.

Tomasello, M. (1999). *The cultural origins of human cognition*. Cambridge, MA: Harvard University Press.

Van Dijk, J. (2005) *The deepening divide: Inequality in the information society*. London: Sage.

Varonis, E., & Gass, S. (1985). Non-native/non-native conversations: A model for negotiating meaning. *Applied Linguistics, 6*(1), 71–90.

Vološinov, V. N. (1973). *Marxism and the philosophy of language*. New York: Seminar Press.

Vygotsky, L. S. (1997). *The collected works of L. S. Vygotsky, Volume 4: The history of the development of higher mental functions*. New York: Plenum.

Ware, P. (2005). "Missed" communication in online communication: Tensions in a German-American telecollaboration. *Language Learning & Technology, 9*(2), 64–89.

Ware, P., & Kramsch, C. (2005). Toward in intercultural stance: Teaching German and English through telecollaboration. *Modern Language Journal, 89*(2), 190–205.

Warschauer, M. (Ed.). (1996). *Telecollaboration in foreign language learning*. Honolulu: University of Hawaii Second Language Teaching and Curriculum Center.

Warschauer, M. (1997). Computer-mediated collaborative learning: Theory and practice. *Modern Language Journal, 81*, 470–481.

Warschauer, M. (1999). *Electronic literacies: Language, culture, and power in online education*. Mahwah, NJ: Lawrence Erlbaum Associates.

Warschauer, M. (2003). *Technology and social inclusion: Rethinking the digital divide*. Cambridge, MA: MIT Press.

Warschauer, M. (2005). Sociocultural perspectives on CALL. In J. Egbert & G. M. Petrie (Eds.), *CALL Research Perspectives* (pp. 41–51). Mahwah, NJ: Lawrence Erlbaum Associates.

Warschauer, M., & Kern, R. (2000). *Network-based language teaching: Concepts and practice*. Cambridge, U.K.: Cambridge University Press.

Wartofsky, M. (1979). *Models*. Boston, MA: D. Reidel.

Werry, C. (1996). Linguistic and interactional features of Internet relay chat. In S. Herring (Ed.), *Computer-mediated communication: Linguistic, social and cross-cultural perspectives*. Philadelphia: John Benjamins.

Yates, S. (1996). Oral and written aspects of computer conferencing. In S. Herring (Ed.), *Computer-mediated communication: Linguistic, social and cross-cultural perspectives*. Philadelphia: John Benjamins.

Roland Barthes (1975), hypertext theory grounded in the ideas of Vannevar Bush (1945) and developed from there, and a user-oriented immersive methodology highly informed by ethnology. I started to use a blog in 2001 to support my own research on computer games. I found that it was such a valuable tool, both for my own reflection and development as a scholar and for communication and discourse with other academics and laymen with an interest in my topics, that I have continued writing the weblog since. It works as an outlet for the more personal side of life as an academic, a log of my academic activities including travels and lectures, and a place where I can informally test and shape thoughts and theories before I take them further. This creates an eclectic, personal mixture and gives me a presence in the online research community that would be impossible to maintain without this tool.

The main advantages of the weblog to my more traditional academic writing are immediacy, memory, and community.

Immediacy. I learn to write down an idea and leave it open and vulnerable for discussion. While fully formed hypotheses with the whole formal apparatus of discussion are good, they are also quite frightening and off-putting, and they make academic writing appear distant and unapproachable for a more public debate. Opening the process of research or analysis to the public makes it easier for others to understand and participate: the distance between the scholar and the public diminishes when our thoughts are presented without the mystery of formulas.

Memory. While I work on a larger research topic, a lot of my time is spent saying, "No, that's a great idea, but it does not belong here." In most cases, it means that these thoughts or ideas will then be lost forever in the stream of new, similar thoughts that keep being set aside. By writing some of these thoughts or ideas in the blog, I can either recapture and reintroduce them at a later point, or I can have the pleasure of seeing somebody else write the paper I always wanted to read, connected more or less loosely to what I blogged some time in the past.

Community. This leads us to a point that I find is a major advantage but many traditional academics find dangerous and threatening. I like to share ideas and I enjoy seeing others write something I thought about but on which I never acted. The idea of having my thoughts stolen is not a threat; it is a benefit. If a person took thoughts directly from my archives, I would appreciate a nod to my weblog in a reference, just as I try to acknowledge my sources of inspiration. The idea of the Net as a communal working area for questioning, critical minds is so attractive, however, that I would rather see my informal work used than insist on ownership of ideas that I have already deliberately set free.

While weblogs can be very informal, they need not be any less rigidly open and transparent when it comes to citing sources and being clear about where ideas come from and in which context they are being discussed. The nature of the Web allows a weblog writer ("blogger") to link directly to the source cited. Whereas a printed, scholarly article uses a highly ritualized form of citing and quoting such as the *Publication Manual of the American Psychological Association*, a weblog can just as easily, quickly, and openly cite online texts using hyperlinks directly to the quoted, cited, or otherwise referenced text. When referring to a book, it is common to link to a presentation of the book somewhere, frequently at the online bookstore Amazon. While this might not be the correct style of academic writing, it adheres to the original idea: it makes it easy for people to check the writer's sources and thus see for themselves if they agree or disagree with the writer's interpretation.

This chapter is, in some ways, influenced by this informal ease of references. My sources are mostly online because the subject (weblogs), the academic publishing about weblogs, and both the academic and popular discussions about weblogs take place, to an extremely high extent, on the Internet. Many of my sources are not traditionally published, but instead are blogs themselves, as much of the practice of blogging is also a metapractice: a process of self-definition and a way of inscribing the individual on the global Net. Since the weblogs are online and the research on weblogs is published online, the mass of literature grows at a speed unavailable to paperbound books. This may at one side be a weakness: already, genres and fields of weblog research that appear isolated and self-sufficient have developed. Fed by their own prolific production, they experience no need to look outside narrow fields for inspiration or community. At the same time, it is an immense advantage; even the narrow-minded or the hidebound cannot avoid the occasional discovery of new clusters of engaging research and critical debate as search engines increasingly support our research and academic development.

The Beginning of the Blog

The early history of the weblog, from 1998 to 2000, is told online by Rebecca Blood (2000), and it is a story of her near past and her experiences. It is the first history of the weblog, and she first posted it in her blog, *Rebecca's Pocket*. Rich with links to the posts that make up the events that become the blog history, her blogpost is a metahistory; history intertwined with the events it describes, making history out of the events by naming them. It is also a manifesto, however, as it points toward a future where weblogs change the world:

> We are being pummeled by a deluge of data and unless we create time and spaces in which to reflect, we will be left with only our reactions. I strongly believe in the power of weblogs to transform both writers and readers from "audience" to "public" and from "consumer" to "creator." Weblogs are no panacea for the crippling effects of a media-saturated culture, but I believe they are one antidote. (Blood, 2000, para. 30)

This is an optimistic vision of a future in which weblogs change our culture and set the consumers free, a huge task for a Web client, but a claim that has been frequently repeated. In addition, the weblog boom of 2003 and 2004 implies that there is something to the blogs beyond what the geek communities of deep cyberspace feel.

A true-born child of the computer medium, the weblog may have its roots in the research journal, the ship's log, the private diary, and the newspapers, all at the same time; however, like a mongrel hunting the dark alleys of the digital city, the weblog is nothing if not adaptive and unique. It is not a fancy thoroughbred too rigid to be put to other use than its intention, nor is it bred for beauty or for hunting wolves on the Russian tundra; rather, it is a bastard child of all personal writing, breeding wildly as it meets others of its ilk online.

Peter Lunenfeld (1999) foresaw this development in the article "Unfinished Business," in which he pointed out the unfinished nature of digital media: "The business of the computer is always unfinished. In fact, 'unfinish' defines the aesthetic of digital media" (p. 7). Weblogs are, if anything, unfinished business. A weblog may be abandoned and left to languish in the misery of no updates. It may be discontinued with a note from the writer about his or her change of heart, change of interests, or lack of time. It may even be erased in an attempt to rewrite the past and remove all traces of what was; however, it is never finished.

This metastate is, however, typical for a weblog. Almost invariably, a blog will at some point contain metareflection. It often happens right at the beginning: "I want to write this weblog because ...;" however, it also frequently permeates the process of writing. Typically, research on weblogs cannot resist this metalogue: "The great cybernetic anthropologist Gregory Bateson speaks of the metalogue—a conversation in which the form of the discussion embodies the subject being discussed: a metalogue about the nature of passion is impassioned" (Lunenfeld, 1999, p.7). In the spirit of the metalogue, the most common way to read and learn about research on weblogs is by reading weblogs and, preferably, by keeping one yourself. The nature of weblogs invites metalogues, and the research community keeps this metalogue running through a network of links, exchanges, comments, and notes between the weblogs of the participants. The weblog itself is the best tool for researching and learning about weblogs.

Not Always a Simple Practice

Weblogs, or blogs, are both deceptively simple—or even minimalistic—and surprisingly complex. The definition written by Jill Walker for the *Routledge Encyclopedia of Narrative Theory* (2005, p. 45) starts out with the simple part:

A weblog, or *blog, is a frequently updated website consisting of dated entries arranged in reverse chronological order so the most recent post appears first (see temporal ordering). Typically, weblogs are published by individuals and their style is personal and informal. Weblogs first appeared in the mid-1990s, becoming popular as simple and free publishing tools became available towards the turn of the century. Since anybody with a net connection can publish their own weblog, there is great variety in the quality, content, and ambition of weblogs, and a weblog may have anywhere from a handful to tens of thousands of daily readers.

Walker's definition describes weblogs from a user perspective: how they are organized, who writes them, and how simple they are due to the free publishing tools available. For a regular weblog user who wants to know how to create a simple way to publish information online, this is all they need to know. The Perseus Development Corp. estimated that there were 31.6 million hosted blogs as of April 4, 2005, and that the number would increase to 53.6 million by the end of the year (Perseus Development Corp., 2005). *Technorati,* the weblog search engine, watched 20.4 million weblogs (*Technorati,* 2005) (in 2007 Technorati no longer gives a number for the blogs the engine tracks, they simply use "zillions"). The weblogs themselves, however, are not easy to describe and pin down. They span the length of the publishing continuum from organized weblogs belonging to traditional media by way of group efforts of varying size, such as *Metafilter* (1999-2007), *Slashdot: News for nerds* (1997-2007), *Boing boing:* A *directory of wonderful things* (2000-2007), *Terra Nova* (2003-2007) and *Grand Text Auto* (2003-2007), to personal pages maintained by anyone from professional writers (Gaiman, 2001-2007), journalists (Allbritton, 2002-2007), and academics (Walker 2000-2007) by way of more or less competent communicators among special interest groups of every kind to personal pages of a character, which might at times be best kept strictly private. The focus on the practice of blogging, with very simple, formal demands to the forms and content of a blog, permits the Walker definition to cover all these different types of weblogs.

Jill Walker's user-oriented definition, which focuses on how the reader and writer both relate to and experience the blog, contrasts with the other school of understanding weblogs, which we can say is represented by the *Technorati* approach:

> *Technorati* is a real-time search engine that keeps track of what is going on in the blogosphere—the world of weblogs.

A few years ago, Web search was revolutionized by a simple but profound idea—that the relevance of a site can be determined by the number of other sites that link to it, and thus consider it 'important.' In the world of blogs, hyperlinks are even more significant, since bloggers frequently link to and comment on other blogs, which creates the sense of timeliness and connectedness one

it is dominated by individual efforts. Several lanes are being explored, and we have looked at the structure-based research, the practice-based research, the educational use of weblogs, and the combinations: weblogs as community, as text, and as a force for social change. More directions are open than have been covered, and even as researchers address them, weblogs mutate into video blogs or "vogs"/"vlogs," mobile-phone blogs or "moblogs," photoblogs, and audio-blogs, not to mention the versions connected to sites offering social software services including weblogs. There are, however, a few major directions to the academic discussion of weblogs.

I maintain the two main directions: structure and practice. Among the typical structure-oriented research, there are several active agents focusing mainly on structure. "The weblog ecosystem" from *The Truth Laid Bear* (Bear, 2005) is an example of structure-based ranking of weblogs. This very popular site is not created by a researcher who desires professional recognition by attracting readers from all over the world but a programmer who, due to the frequently sharp commentary on his site, prefers to write anonymously as N. Z. Bear (ibid).

What exactly is the TTLB Blogosphere Ecosystem?

The TTLB Blogosphere Ecosystem is an application which scans weblogs once daily and generates a list of weblogs ranked by the number of incoming links they receive from other weblogs on the list.

In 2007 the site has been remodelled, and now contains much more than the original ranking list, although the list can still be found at http://truthlaidbear.com/ecosystem.php (Bear 2007).

A more formal approach to this was expressed in the articles from the WWW2004 workshop on the weblogging ecosystem in New York. In the workshop program committee was Cameron Marlow of MIT, who created a very early system for weblog tracking and indexing: Blogdex.

The Blogdex aggregator has been collecting data on the referential information contained within weblogs for the past 3 years, namely the hypertext links contained within webloggers' writing. Using the links between weblogs as a proxy to social structure, we construct a representation of the social networks of the weblog community and employ social network analysis to describe the aggregate effects of status. Two measures of authority are explored: popularity, as measured by webloggers' public affiliations and influence measured by citation of each others writing. These metrics are evaluated with respect to each other and with the authority conferred by references in the popular press. (Marlow, 2004, p. 1)

Marlow's Blogdex, *Technorati,* the weblog ecosystem, and the game *Blogshares* (Rasavi, 2003) all track links and connections in different manners, and these systems exemplify a growing genre of weblog research that is easily applicable to any online publishing system. In order to stick to the simple dichotomy I sketched at the beginning, however, I will also introduce some researchers who focus on the practice of blogging.

The practice of blogging is the particular focus of the group who call themselves "edu-bloggers." Blogging has become a tool not only for research, but also for teaching. What most edu-bloggers teach is some type of writing, and they use weblogs in order to activate the students and raise their consciousness about the writing process, publishing, and feedback from the reading public. In order to teach writing through blogging, the edu-bloggers need to understand what blogging is, how it is done, what the aesthetics of blogs are, and what impact blog writing has on the readers. This is a rich source of different research approaches for weblog literacy and an active network of bloggers who link to each other and follow and comment on each other's teaching and blogging practice.

In a peer-reviewed online (of course) collection of scholarly articles on weblogs, *Into the blogosphere* (Gurak, Antonijevic, Johnson, Ratliffe, & Reyman 2004), Charles Lowe described how weblogs are useful tools for teaching because they give instant and free access to the public domain (Lowe, 2004). True to form, however, bloggers question these advantages. Jill Walker teaches blogging at the University of Bergen, Norway. Her weblog (Walker 2000 to 2007) reflects the practice of teaching in the same way that it reflects her research and her life in general. Using weblogs to teach writing and digital media awareness is natural to her because it is a medium with which she is deeply involved. One of her posts discussed the ethics of making the students write online:

> In a way my post the other day about a student's blog with lots of great links on fictional blogs ran in to the same problem when my sending unexpected readers to this student resulted in her sloppy citation practice being exposed. Such public exposure of learners' mistakes (and of course learners will make mistakes, that's the whole point of learning) can lead to far direr consequences than the harshest disciplinary measures taken by a university. Which would you rather: fail an exam or have your name indelibly connected to something bad on the internet? Which could potentially affect your future the most? (Walker, 2005b)

Many teachers use weblogs to teach blogging, and quite a few of them reacted to this question. It aims at the center of the blogging practice: As Lowe (2004) pointed out, weblogs are great to teach writing, and particularly writing in the public sphere, because it puts the students right out there in the middle of it quickly, cheaply, and easily. At the same time, that is the problem: It puts the students right out there, quickly, cheaply, and easily—and not always particularly well prepared.

Another blogging teacher, Barbara Ganley, linked to this post and described the dilemma when students have no sense of the possible consequences of their public actions:

> Little did I know that my own students' in their first post-semester creative-writing-blog posting would find themselves playing around with both boundaries, commenting under just-for-the-occasion pseudonyms on a blank posting, comments that crossed into some pretty offensive sexually explicit trash. They knew enough to adopt pseudonyms (except for the post's originator) for their off-color commentary, thereby protecting themselves, but also thereby releasing themselves from a certain level of accountability. Almost all of my students post under their names, taking public pleasure in and responsibility for their work and their responses. (Ganley, 2005)

Ganley (2005) went on to describe how the experience still turned into a learning experience; the students realized that they were destroying not only their own future reputations, but also the work of their companions and the community spirit. These posts are typical of the weblogs of teachers teaching blogging. The discussion between the teaching bloggers using weblogs flow back and forth in the same manner as they try to encourage their students to work. Some examples of webloggers who adopt this strategy of living what they teach are Dennis Jerz with his well established English teaching weblog *Literacy weblog*, Alex Halavais with his *thaumaturgical notes,* and Mike Edwards of *Vitia,* all participants in a public conversation on weblogs and education, which in itself is an exploration and a learning process.

Weblogs as an educational practice is a fairly new concept, but it has grown as quickly as the weblog field in general. When Anne Bartlett-Bragg wrote "Blogging to Learn" in 2003, the article was a simple overview of different types of weblogs and a description of the blogging process, with very few references to writing on weblogs or others who used blogs in teaching. Since 2004, however, several articles bringing examples of how teachers used weblogs in the classroom reached the net through *Into the Blogosphere* (see articles by Brooks, Nichols, & Priebe), Internet research conferences (Ferdig & Trammel, 2004), and in panels at conferences with a teaching focus.

Diversity beyond Dualism

As we start looking at the actual research areas, it is obvious that the lines between structure and practice are not clear. Researchers who look at the structure of weblogs and track the links and references in order to gain an overview of the networks use tools based on Boolean searches in order to understand the meaning behind these links (Nilsson, 2003; Efimova & de Moor, 2004; Efimova & Hendricks, 2005). They use links, language, and words as markers for social connections between the weblogs in their studies.

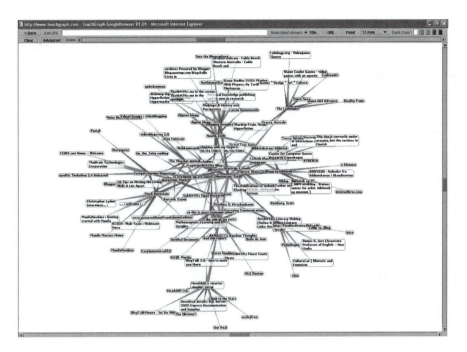

Figure 16.1 Touchgraph 2005: Map of connections to Thinking with my fingers.

Tracking the links and comparing signifiers, which can be found by the use of a search engine, invites interpretation beyond scripted ranking systems. Put into different contexts and made visible, the links between weblogs create a web that not only contains meaning, but also beauty.

One generator of network connections is Google's Touchgraph (See Figure 16.1), which makes the connections visual in a lovely display that moves and lives in the screen and invites the viewer to touch, expand, and manipulate the image (TouchGraph Google Browser V1.01). You can put any URL in the center of the search, but if you put in a weblog, the links and connections become visible and almost tangible.

Another creative use of URLs can be seen in *The World as Blog* (Figure 16.2), a map of the world that continuously tracks two changing states of the world: one visible to the naked eye wherever you are geographically and the other only detectable online by computer users. The latter tracks the change of daylight and when changes to weblogs are being posted. Michael Maron (2005), creator of the map and blog combination, generates several different combinations of maps where the physical world and the space of weblogs overlap.

The dots, red changing to blue as time passes, represent newly updated weblogs, which the users have registered according to a certain procedure that lets geoblogs register any updates.

Weblogs keep breeding shamelessly with other media, and an old version is the vog (or vlog), or the video blog as it was described by Adrian Miles in his vog manifesto, or *Vogme* (2000):

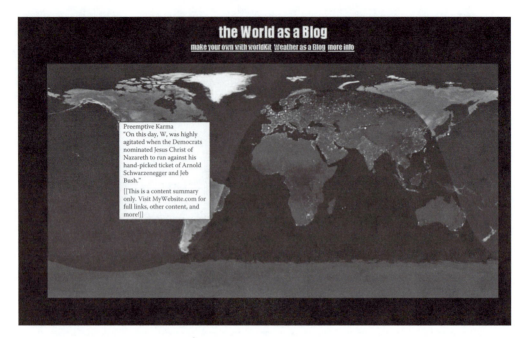

Figure 16.2 Weblogs updated around the world, while we watch the map.

Vogme Manifesto

First published December 2000.

A vog respects bandwidth. A vog is not streaming video (this is not the reinvention of television). A vog uses performative video and/or audio. A vog is personal. A vog uses available technology. A vog experiments with writerly video and audio. A vog lies between writing and the televisual. A vog explores the proximate distance of words and moving media. A vog is dziga vertov with a mac and a modem. A vog is a video blog where video in a blog must be more than video in a blog. (Miles 2000)

The *Vogme* demands something more than simple video put into a blog, and it refers to Barthes' distinction of writerly and readerly (Barthes, 1975, p. 5). This expresses how, under the many different approaches to the weblogs, we can trace a connection backward to the theories of the reader and the increasingly active reader. Rebecca Blood's (2000) vision of the readers and writers as public and as creators gains precision and strength when it passes the filters of theory devoted to the study of the readers, writers, and texts.

The traditions of literature theory are present in the weblog research community as more than the occasional hints. The hypertext tradition that Lunenfeld (1999) represents, is pursued by several webloggers, perhaps the most obvious and visible example being the *Grand Text Auto* (n.d.) group; however, very little is as yet written about it. With Jill Walker, I wrote some on this topic in the article "Blogging Thoughts" (Mortensen & Walker, 2002). "Blogging

Thoughts" is mainly concerned with the practice of blogging and the new opportunities for dialogue that blogging represents. Within the argument, however, there is a pointer toward the study of interactive and distributed narrative, which is the direction of research that Jill Walker has since chosen to pursue (Walker, 2004).

The Versatile User

The human being is an animal that desires meaning. Meaning is so important that if we perceive that it is lost in our lives, the loss can be fatal. Even when we build calculating machines, we find ways to interpret the numbers beyond and outside mathematics and put the numbers to work to generate more ways to communicate meaning.

The modern human being is not just a thinking being—Homo sapien—but also a communicating being. Our most recent, most sophisticated technology is built for communication. From the vision of Vannevar Bush (1945) to the desire of the newbie blogger (Natalie, 2005), the computer-mediated information flowing through the Internet is an opportunity for the individual to find, share, and contribute information. Recent research into the development of weblogs indicates that with the right tools, the net offers exactly that: an opportunity for individuals to express themselves.

One direction of research that is extremely interesting, but so far has mainly been the field of popular media and journalistic coverage, is the connection between self-publishing through media such as weblogs and the established media. In 2004 and 2005, two books on journalism and weblogs were published: *We, the Media* (Gillmor, 2004), which mainly is a presentation of the many online agents making personal publishing available to the public, and *Blog* (Hewitt, 2005), which is a description of the author's blogging practice and the narrative of some of his experiences from the liminal space between personal publishing and institutional publishing. What neither of these interesting descriptions contains is a more thoroughly researched report of the changes the explosion of self-publishing provokes in the news industry and an analysis of the discovery. This is the period of change; healthy newsagents are suffering economically as the public turns to the Net for news. New channels for pushing information are appearing every year through the development of increasingly sophisticated cell phones or hybrid creations such as the *Gizmondo*, which, according to the company's pitch, is a combination of a handheld game, cell phone (SMS and MMS ability), GPS, GPRS, MP3 player, movie player, and PDA with Bluetooth. The technology is creating channels through which content can be distributed faster than the news industry can possibly adapt, and this leaves gaps. What enters into these gaps? What fills the niches? Will the public be able to adapt such channels for their own use in the manner Rheingold describes in *Smart Mobs* (2002) or are the organized media sufficiently powerful and innovative to take over these niches despite their late start?

The second direction—as I see it—of current new media research is along this vein, but more generally addresses the users and not the producing institutions; the field of practice is still open to exploration beyond the classroom and the intermedia dialogue where it dwells now. Weblogs are changing the concept of the sender-message-receiver model, a transmission model of communication conceived by Shannon & Weaver (1949), with such a force that even the modifications added by Stuart Hall (1990), considered radical in the power they give to the reader, are made to look archaic and conservative. The new image of the user emerges from the personal publishing power that the Internet gives to the individual, and it needs a new model to describe it: new theory and new concepts to express the new constellations. Literature and more general media and communications theory need to look toward the task of creating new aesthetics for online texts because the old concepts and categories appear clumsy and unwieldy as they are forced to fit the new literatures of games, chats, weblogs, cell phones, and other media-carrying and media-communicating texts. If observations and criticism are not to appear disconnected from the objects of study, researchers delving into the online texts need a language with which to work and research and theoretical tools made for the purpose.

The magical third direction for future research is the eternally fruitful direction of human behavior. In this case, a culture sociology of the Net should not be disconnected from the understanding of culture and text. In order to communicate online, everything needs to be translated into text (in a wide sense) and mediated through a channel that is separate from the human body. The main distinction between the online community and the offline community is that while the physical world can offer you real sustenance, the computer-mediated world can offer you nothing but symbols structured in some kind of text. While symbols are sufficiently powerful to buy you physical sustenance, they do not satisfy your hunger. The story of Midas is as relevant in this context as in any other: you may be able to create an online illusion as good as gold, but you cannot eat it. Therefore, all study of human behavior online becomes a study of the human exchange of symbols online. This demands a fusion between academic directions that started with the cultural studies tradition and continues today in interdisciplinary departments and research centers. In Europe these academic directions are currently often grouped under the umbrella notion of "media theory." The sociologist needs to understand how to interpret a text and the literature critic needs to understand the context and the social and technological restraint under which a text is produced, because the sender institutions are no longer monolithic and the audience and the senders are all becoming participants.

And They Lived Happily Ever ...

I wanted to tell a story of the weblog research because life, in our heads, is made of little stories. We innocently go through the day experiencing all those mundane things that make up life. Living in rural Norway, I feel blessed as I walk from home to the college and see sheep, mountains, the fjord, the ferry, a few cars, several cats and dogs, some cows, a river, and yes, all that common green stuff and all those nice little houses and gardens that make up a human dwelling in a country not all that far from the polar circle. Though I notice all these things, I hardly ever reflect on them as agents in a story; they are just their own objects, perceived sometimes only at the edge of my vision as I plod along planning an early morning lecture, usually running a little late.

Ask me later how my walk was, however, and suddenly it all snaps into narrative focus and a drama enfolds. It gains structure, purpose, and direction, as well as resistance and perhaps even a certain touch of danger. This is what the weblog does to the everyday thought process. By offering a box to fill, the weblog agent asks you, "So, what was that thought you wanted to share?" Perhaps it is the blinking instant messenger window, the chat room filled with other humans you want to impress, or the picture upload service inviting you to search through the pictures that would otherwise have gone into the forgotten file and upload something to share. Through communication and the sharing of information, we repeatedly recreate the story of our life in interaction with others. Now we do the same online with a potential audience of millions.

The computer lets us store fragments of knowledge and then reconnect them into different arguments. There is nothing particularly new about this realization; it is what the Memex machine was planned to do (Bush, 1945), what Ted Nelson envisioned in Literary Machines (Nelson, 1981), what Tim Berners-Lee (1994) developed the World Wide Web to accommodate, and what hypertext theorists hold up as the main innovation of computerized hypertexts. All the little bits and pieces of information can be repeatedly restructured into new paradigms, sets of understanding, or even worldviews. This is a change in the way we think of research and a far cry from the idea of the scientist as an individual whose genius constructs a whole new paradigm and shatters the understanding of the world. It can, at first glance, look like a very postmodern understanding of the academic process through its emphasis on fragments and reuse; however, what the Net invites us to do is not to kill the understanding of the great modern narrative, but to open the scope of it indefinitely. From a situation where bits and pieces of the collected world knowledge were only available on paper in certain bookstores and libraries, existing as isolated fragments within certain fields of competence and specialization, the Internet permits rapidly increasing access and, with access, a constant reuse that recreates the great story of the world of research for each researcher and user.

Merriam-Webster online dictionary (2004). Retrieved May 14, 2005, from http://www.m-w.com/

Metafilter. (1999-2007) Retrieved May 17, 2005, from http://www.metafilter.com/

Miles, A. (2000). Vogma; vog manifesto. Retrieved July 2nd, 2007, from http://vogmae.net.au/content/blogcategory/26/47

Mortensen, T., & Walker, J. (2002). Blogging thoughts: Personal publication as an online research tool. In A. Morrison (Ed.), *Researching ICTs in context*. Oslo, Norway: Inter-Media Report. Retrieved May 17, 2005, from http://www.intermedia.uio.no/konferanser/skikt-02/docs/Researching_ICTs_in_context-Ch11-Mortensen-Walker.pdf

Natalie (2005). *Bacon and blue cheese*. Retrieved May 17, 2005, from http://baconandbluecheese.blogspot.com/

Nelson, T. H. (1981). *Literary machines*. Sausalito, CA: Mindful Press.

Nilsson, S. (2003). *The function of language to facilitate and maintain social networks in research weblogs*. Umeå, Sweden: University of Umeå. Retrieved May 15, 2005, from http://www.eng.umu.se/stephanie/web/LanguageBlogs.pdf

Ooi, J. (2004). Blogs give Dan Rather '60+1 Minutes'. In *Screenshots*. Retrieved May 14, 2005, from http://www.jeffooi.com/archives/2004/09/september_8_cbs.php

Pax, S. (2003). *The Baghdad blog*. London: Guardian Books.

Perseus Development Corp. (2005). The Blogging geyser. In *Perseus*. Retrieved May 14, 2005, from http://www.perseus.com/blogsurvey/geyser.html

Rasavi, S. (2003). *Blogshares, fantasy stockmarket for blogs*. Retrieved May 16, 2005, from http://www.blogshares.com/index.php

Rheingold, H. (2002). *Smart mobs; The next social revolution*. Cambridge, MA: Basic Books.

Shannon, C. E., & Weaver, W. (1949). *The mathematical theory of communication*. Urbana: University of Illinois Press.

Slashdot: News for nerds. (n.d.). Retrieved May 17, 2005, from http://slashdot.org/

Technorati (2005). Retrieved May 14, 2005, from http://www.technorati.com/

Terra nova. (2003-2007). Retrieved May 17, 2005, from http://terranova.blogs.com/

The guardian. (2005). Retrieved May 16, 2005, http://blogs.guardian.co.uk/online/

TouchGraph Google Browser V1.01. (n.d.). Retrieved May 16, 2005, from http://www.touchgraph.com/TGGoogleBrowser.html

Weblogg. (2005). Dagbladet.no. Retrieved May 16, 2005, http://www.dagbladet.no/weblogg/

Walker, J. (2004). *Distributed narrative*. Retrieved May 17, 2005, from http://jilltxt.net/txt/distributednarrative.html

Walker, J. (2005a). Weblog. In D. Herman, M. Jahn, & M.-L. Ryan (Eds.), *Routledge encyclopedia of narrative theory*. London: Routledge.

Walker, J. (2005b). Should we tell our students to blog pseudonymously? Retrieved May 16, 2005, from http://jilltxt.net/?p=1376

Walker, J. (2000-2007) *Jill/txt*. Http://jilltxt.net/

Walsh, J. (2005). Who killed Dan Rather? In *Salon.com*. Retrieved May 14, 2005, from http://www.salon.com/opinion/feature/2005/03/09/rather/

CHAPTER 17

People, Purposes, and Practices
*Insights from Cross-Disciplinary
Research into Instant Messaging*

GLORIA E. JACOBS

ST. JOHN FISHER COLLEGE, USA

Instant messaging (IMing) is an ontologically new literacy (Lankshear & Knobel, 2003) that has captured the public imagination through its association with youth culture and nonstandard writing conventions. Although the popular press in the United States has published seemingly endless anecdotes that connect adolescent use of IMing and the demise of adolescent academic writing skills (Jacobs, 2004), to date little research empirically supports a connection between IMing use and academic or school-based writing skills. The majority of extant literature into IMing is primarily in the fields of psychology and sociology (Hu, Wood, Smith, & Westbrook, 2004; Lenhart, Rainie, & Lewis, 2001) , linguistics (Baron, 2004; Baron & Ling, 2003; Baron, Squires, Tench, & Thompson, 2003; Hård af Segerstad, 2002a, 2002b; Hult & Richins, 2005), communications (Park, 2003), and human computer interaction (Schiano et al., 2002; Voida, Newstetter, & Mynatt, 2002) and computer-supported collaborative work (Grinter & Palen, 2002; Isaacs, Walendowski, & Ranganthan, 2002; Nardi, 2005; Nardi, Whittaker, & Bradner, 2000). Methods of investigation include examination of text logs, observations, interviews, surveys, and videotaping of IM conversations.

A portion of the research is related to commercial concerns around improving IMing interfaces for use in the workplace (Herbsleb, Atkins, Boyer, Handel, & Finholt, 2002; Nardi, 2005; Nardi et al., 2000; Voida et al.,

2002). A few studies have worked to identity the linguistic features of IMing, and there has been some discussion of IMing as part of the spectrum of digital literacy practices that people engage in (Lankshear & Knobel, 2003; Leander & Johnson, 2002; Leander & Sheehy, 2004; Livingstone, 2002; Livingstone & Bovill, 1999, 2001). Lewis and Fabos (2000, 2005) and Jacobs (2004, 2005) are among the few literacy researchers who have looked specifically at adolescent use of IMing and what engagement in IMing means in terms of literacy learning.

In this chapter, I examine the research into IMing to provide an understanding of what IMing looks like, why it is used, and what some implications are for literacy research. I argue that, although the current research points to context as a central aspect of IMing use, the majority of the literature fails to problematize the nature of context and its relationship to IMing. Because of the paucity of studies into IMing, I necessarily draw from studies across disciplines, methodologies, and theoretical frameworks. I also include unpublished dissertations as well as an undergraduate honors thesis. Because of the newness of IMing and the relative lack of authoritative studies, making confident assertions about the outcomes of IMing use is difficult. This review, therefore, should be read as an early exploration into the field rather than a definitive account of the nature and significance of IMing use.

Contextualizing Instant Messaging Use

While my selection of studies to include in this chapter is eclectic, the review I make of them is by no means atheoretical. I approach this review from a stance that how we use language and literacy is informed by local and global contexts. Specifically, my thinking about the research and IMing is informed by the traditions of the new literacy studies (Hull & Schultz, 2001, 2002; Lankshear & Knobel, 2003; Street, 1995, 2003). That is, literacy involves the ways in which we use text for culturally meaningful purposes within culturally meaningful activities (Gee, 2000a). I define text as both speech and writing (Fairclough, 1995) and as "sets of potential meanings and signifying practices adhering for readers and writers in both local and larger discourse communities" (Neilsen, 1998, p. 4). I appeal to the new literacy studies because of the clear way in which it links the microanalysis of language use to larger contexts.

Context has, in fact, been the project of the new literacy studies. The new literacy studies was part of what Gee (2000a) identified as the social turn in language and literacy research and scholarship. That is, the new literacy studies shifts our concept of literacy from reading and writing as a psychological or individual act toward more of a sociological focus on using text as part of a meaning making system within localized sociocultural, historical, and political contexts (Lankshear & Knobel, 2003; Street, 1995; 2003). It makes explicit the connection between the literacy event and the literacy practice. Whereas the literacy event is an event in which text use is central to the interaction (Heath, 1982, 1983), literacy practices as defined by Street (1995) "refer to both behavior and the social, and cultural conceptualizations that give meaning to the uses of reading and/or writing" (p. 2). Text takes its meaning from what people do with it and what social and cultural meanings they bring to it and take from it. These connections remain unexplored if we limit our thinking to the cognitive or psychological because making sense of IMing becomes a matter of decoding the message, rather than understanding why people would bother learning a new form of communication.

Rather than imposing this view on the research literature, I found that despite the disparate origins of the studies, most researchers pointed to the problem of context in attempting to understand the nature of IMing. As the Swedish linguist Hård af Segerstad (2002b) argued, "There does not seem to be one variable that is the most important in all modes; rather, language use is adapted to several parameters that vary from situation to situation" (concluding chap., section 1.4.2, last para.). This finding is echoed throughout the literature as quantitative and qualitative researchers alike seek to identify characteristics of IMing and variables that affect IMing use. While coming from different theoretical and disciplinary traditions, the findings across the research literature support, at least obliquely when not directly, the new literacy studies argument that literacy (and language) is a locally situated social practice embedded within and informed by global ideologies (Street, 1995, 2003).

Recognition of the contextual nature of IMing allows us to transcend and move beyond attempts to label IMing as speech, writing, or a new genre. We are able, instead, to understand IMing as a social practice in which written text plays a significant role rather than being an autonomous form of writing that retains meaning across multiple contexts. Furthermore, by researching IMing from the perspective of a locally situated social practice (Barton, Hamilton, & Ivanic, 2000), we can turn our interpretive gaze to the practices afforded by the technology. This leads us to consider what participation (or nonparticipation) in those practices means for people in today's information society. As Lewis and Fabos (2005) eloquently argued,

> We think it is important that educators focus on shifting dimensions of practice rather than on new technological tools (Lewis, Alvermann, & Leander, 2004). Most of our suggestions ... relate to broader-based shifts—the kind that one experiences through many forms of popular culture that depend on interactivity, pastiche, intertextuality, and other qualities associated with the Internet (comics, videos, reality TV) ... Focusing pedagogical reform on shifting dimensions of practice that apply to new forms of media and communication beyond those that depend on Internet access is one way to make sure that individuals without access can be full participants in the instruction. (p. 497)

I argue similarly that research into IMing, as well as other digital literacy practices, should be used to inform pedagogy so that educators can integrate digital ways of knowing (Lankshear & Knobel, 2003) into instruction in ways that reimagine existing literacy roles and practices, rather than simply technologizing existing ways of doing school.

Chapter Organization

I have organized this chapter around the issues raised by the current research. I first discuss the literature that identifies some linguistic features of IMing as well as the research into who uses IMing and why. This latter research comes from a variety of disciplines and draws on psychology, anthropology, communications, and computer-supported collaborative work/human-computer interface (HCI). A consistent theme appears throughout both sets of literature; how people use IMing and for what purposes is unpredictable and dependent upon the multiple layers of context that permeate any individual's life or the community to which they belong. An overview of the literature reveals that IMing cannot be essentialized and that despite attempts to identify universal conventions of language use, how people use IMing is dependent upon the context of the communities of which they are members. Identified similarities of use appear to be related to the lack of diversity between the studied populations rather than inherent qualities of the technology. I conclude by discussing the implications of research into IMing for education and argue that researchers should turn their attention to the practices afforded by technologies such as IMing rather than focusing on specifics of an ever changing technology.

The Technological and Linguistic Features of Instant Messaging

IMing is part of a larger use of language generally referred to as "computer-mediated communication." Computer-mediated communication refers to the practice of using networked computers and alphabetic text to transmit messages between people or groups of people across space and time (Baron, 1998a, 2000; Herring, 1996; Jones, 1995; Mann & Stewart, 2000). IMing is a peer-to-peer (P2P) system that allows computers to communicate directly and thus allows for private, synchronous, and dyadic exchanges rather than having to go through public Internet spaces as is the case with chat rooms. IMing now includes affordances for the use of images and sound files as well as visual and audio connection via webcams, but how these are integrated into IMing practices remains unstudied.

There are a number of IMing software programs available; at the beginning of the 21st century, America Online Instant Messenger (AIM) was the most popular program among youth in the United States. ICQ (pronounced I Seek You), the original IMing program, was created in 1996 by an Israeli firm and retains a high level of popularity throughout the wired world (The ICQ Story, 2005). Although AIM and ICQ are not interoperable, both systems are owned by America Online. There are also a number of other programs, but lack of interoperability between systems remains an issue. That is, in order to converse online with someone, both interlocutors must be registered with and signed on to the same system. There have been efforts to address the issues of interoperability, but at the time of this writing, cross-platform applications have not yet been commercially successful. IMing programs are free to users, but like much of the Internet, the interfaces carry advertisements. My description of IMing is based on how it is configured at the time of this writing, and is based primarily on AIM because it is the most popular program among youth in the United States and is the program most commonly associated with IMing in the popular press. Like most software programs, IMing interfaces are continually being upgraded by the parent companies. As such, any description of the software functions will most likely differ from what is in use at the time this chapter is read.

In general, IMing interfaces contain a buddy list or list of the screen names of the user's contacts; symbols that alert the user as to who is online; an interface for posting an online profile, personal statement, or biographic information; a window for posting away messages which alert others that the user is not available for online conversations; and a window for conversation. These multiple windows provide the user with numerous options for configuring his or her experience. These can include avatars or buddy icons, which are graphic representations of the user; choice of font style and size; color selection: time stamping of incoming and outgoing messages; message notification methods; and the aforementioned profiles and away messages.

Profiles

Profiles can be used for a wide range of purposes. Shiu and Lenhardt (2004) found that 34% of IMing users posted a profile that others can see, but at the time of this writing, the only published research that examines the use of online profiles was Lewis and Fabos (2005). The software design allows users to post personal information and sets of interests so that people with similar interests can make contact. Lewis and Fabos began their study in 1999 and found that their participants, who ranged from 13 to 17 years old, used profiles to remain "hyperconnected" (p. 490). They would post cell phone numbers and party announcements as well as biographical information such as gender, general location, and interests. They also did not block their profiles from being viewed by people they did not know and indicated that they were not concerned about the media hype about the dangers of the Internet. In 2002, I began a study of a 15–year-old girl in the northeastern United States and found that she and her friends did not post personal information on profiles, nor did they make their profiles accessible to the general public. Instead the study participants used the profile's text space to construct a representation of self through the posting of song lyrics, quotes from movies, and snippets of conversations copied from IMing sessions with friends.

Although both studies indicated that profiles were used for identity construction, how the affordances of profiles were used differed. The differences between the two studies lie in context; the actual variables, however, are not easily identifiable. It may be that the adolescents of 2002 were more cautious about sharing personal information than the adolescents of 1999 were. It may be the age differences between the two study populations. It could be regional differences, or the differences could be in the different purposes the participants ascribe to profiles. In order to understand these differences and even if these differences matter, we need to conduct additional research into the nature of online profiles. We should be asking what purposes do profiles serve for those who use them and what social semiotic resources are called upon during the construction of profiles?

Away Messages

Away messages can be used for different purposes, one of which is to remain connected to the IMing service while indicating that the participant is busy doing something other than sitting at his or her computer (Baron et al., 2003; Nardi, 2005; Nardi et al., 2000). When a user is away, he or she can still receive messages. These messages appear on the user's desktop and act much like voice mail or a message on an answering machine. Because the person who posted the away message is already logged in to IMing, however, he or she does not have to make any additional steps to view messages, unlike voice mail, which requires a series of commands before the message can be heard. Messages are on the computer screen ready to be read unless a software glitch causes the system to shut down. If that occurs, the messages are lost. The person who sent the message receives the away message automatically in return. If the person who has the away message has a profile, the profile will also appear on the initial sender's desktop.

Baron et al. (2003) studied undergraduate students' uses of away messages at a university on the east coast of the United States and found that away messages are used to keep track of friends, for entertainment purposes, and to keep friends aware of one's activities. The participants in Lewis's and Fabos's (2005) study also used away messages to keep friends up-to-date on one's whereabouts. Awareness and entertainment were intertwined among Baron's participants in that some of the activities posted were fictitious. This was not troublesome to the participants in Baron's study; in fact, they indicated that there were expectations that away messages should be humorous and expectations for receiving real information were low. Lewis and Fabos (2005) also found that their participants enjoyed witty away messages even though their own messages tended toward the succinct. I found that my participants, who were all high school students, similarly used away messages to keep track of friends and to post their activities, but tended not to post humorous or fictitious away messages (Jacobs, 2003; 2005). Instead, away messages were used primarily to post the individual's current activity or occasionally to ask for information about homework. None of the participants in either Baron's (2003) or Lewis's and Fabos's (2005) study used away messages to obtain homework help.

Nardi (2000), who studied the use of IMing in the workplace, found that, like the high-school and college students in the previously mentioned studies, those in the workplace kept track of one another's whereabouts using away messages, but humor was not as evident as it was in Baron's study. Nardi suggested that her adult participants used away messages to establish availability for contact or keep open a zone of communication. Entertainment was of less importance to the participants in Nardi's study.

Although these studies show similarities to the extent that away messages were used to keep track of friends and colleagues, there were differences in expectations regarding quality of information and expectations for humor and veracity. The reasons for these differences remain unexplored, but the findings indicate that like the literacy events studied by numerous scholars in the new literacy studies the particulars of away messages are specific to the community in which they are used even as they also reflect in common more global practices and the constraints and affordances of the technology.

Linguistic Features of Instant Messaging

Although the use of away messages has been identified as being an important aspect of IMing, the conventions associated with IM conversations are most often discussed in the popular press. Jacobs (2005) analyzed 18 articles published over a 2–year period in United States national and regional newspapers. Jacobs found that most of the public conversation surrounding IMing was about the nonstandard writing conventions associated with IMing, and the attitudes parents and educators have adopted toward these conventions.

Analysis of IMing text logs at a university in the United States indicate that, contrary to popular opinion, college students tend not to use the abbreviations and acronyms associated with IMing (Baron, 2004; Baron & Ling, 2003). Moreover, as part of a larger study of the differences between American college students' use of online and face-to-face communication, Baron (2004) found that IM users tended to use more conventional language than not. Baron's study consisted of 22 undergraduates or recent college graduates and 23 separate IMing conversations made up of 9 male-male, 9 female-female, and 5 male-female exchanges. The most consistent deviation noted by Baron was that apostrophes were seldom used within IMs, although they were used more often by the women in the study than by the men. Jacobs (2005) found that 6 participants (4 female and 2 males), who were college bound high school students, also used few of the conventions associated with IMing, tended to use more standard writing conventions in their IMs, and eschewed apostrophes in conversations but included them in profiles.

Deaf and Hard of Hearing Adults Connect to Each Other and the Hearing

Deaf and hard of hearing adults indicated that IMing was preferable to assistive technologies such as TTY and relayed conversations (Bowe, 2002) because IMing most closely simulated the real time dyadic nature of face-to-face conversation. Although some respondents said that they disliked the expectation that they would respond immediately to a posting or found IMing to be distracting, the majority of respondents found IMing to be advantageous. Specifically, Bowe (2002) found that the respondents liked IMing because of its visual nature, interactivity, immediate response, and the ability to request clarification immediately after receiving a message. Interestingly, the respondents also reported using emoticons to convey emotion, something TTY and relayed conversations did not afford. The respondents in Bowe's study also reported adapting IMing software to set up private chat rooms in order to conduct conference calls.

Primarily, IMing was seen as breaking down communicative barriers. One respondent said, "IM levels the playing field far better than any relay service could, for it removes a third party and any sense of [a] 'deaf,' 'hard of hearing,' or 'speech impaired' person on the conversation" (p. 9), and it is "the closest thing to real time communication between friends" because of its informal nature (p. 9). Bowe (2002) argued that because IMing has become a powerful means of communication for the deaf and hard of hearing community, teachers of students who are deaf or hard of hearing need to place a greater emphasis on instruction in reading and writing. As such, IMing holds the potential for transcending the schism between the deaf and hard of hearing community and the hearing community and for addressing issues of marginalization faced by members of the deaf and hard of hearing community. Whether this is in fact the case is open for additional research.

Instant Messaging for Building Personal Connections

The way in which IMing simulates face-to-face interaction is also noted by Boneva et al. (2006). Using a national telephone survey and interviews conducted in the Pittsburgh area the authors investigated how IMing satisfies two major needs for adolescents: (a) maintaining individual friendships and (b) belonging to peer groups. They claimed that one of the reasons IMing is so popular among adolescents is that it simulates the experience of spending time with friends offline without the pressure of the acceptance rules that are part of face-to-face experiences. Drawing on theories that propose that adolescence is a time of identity construction (cf., Erickson, 1968) and that young people accomplish this through association with groups of people, the authors claimed that IMing serves as part of the construction of youth's social identity by allowing them to build and maintain connections with their peers.

IMing as a cultural tool for building connections is a particularly promising concept when coupled with Bowe's (2002) argument that IMing technology may be a way to meet the communicative needs of a historically marginalized group such as the deaf and hard of hearing. We need to remember, however, that Bowe's study, as well as the majority of studies discussed in this chapter, is limited to the extent that the studies typically include only those who have access to the Internet. As previously noted, this limitation is common to the survey and interview studies on IMing and other forms of computer mediated communication. Consequently, it is necessary to look beyond users of IMing or computer-mediated communication to those who choose not to use the technology or do not have access to the technology.

The Role of Critical Mass in Instant Messaging Use

By limiting our research to only those who use a technology like the Internet or, in particular, IMing, we may be also limiting the discourse communities we are studying. This becomes apparent in Park's (2003) study of the determinants of IMing use. Park used diffusion theory to understand who will adopt IMing and what adopter characteristics are. Diffusion theory argues that the "adoption of technological innovations is a function of people's social locators, media use patterns, uses of other technologies, and peoples' communication needs" (p. 7). Park's quantitative study was conducted via a survey of college students that looked at adoption rates, demographics, media use, technology clusters, communication needs, innovative attitude, user satisfaction, and network effects or how the value of a product or service to one user is dependent on how many other users there are. The author found that adopters tend to be younger, have a higher disposable income, and have more education than nonadopters. The survey results indicated that communication needs did not have a significant impact, but the sense that everyone else was using IMing was important. In sum, the characteristics of early adopters are related to socioeconomic status, opportunity, and a critical mass of peers who also use the technology (Park, 2003); therefore, adopters of IMing tend to be of the same socioeconomic group and do so because others in their group have also adopted the technology.

The importance of a critical mass of people who must use a technology like IMing for it to be worthwhile engaging with was also found to hold true within geographically distributed workgroups (Herbsleb et al., 2002). Participants in the study, which involved over 200 semistructured interviews and numerous on-site observations, included technical staff, supervisors, managers, and executives. The authors found that the perceived usefulness of the technology depended upon how much the users value informal communication. Those who did not take up IMing found it superfluous and did not understand why people did not just use the telephone. Other respondents had concerns about privacy issues and the potential use of the software for surveillance. Those who used IMing did so primarily in order to gather quick information concerning a work task or to determine whether a coworker was available to discuss a work related question. Overall, IMing use was dependent upon how it fitted into the value system of the work place.

Using Instant Messaging for "Outeraction"

Based on an ethnographic study of IMing use in a work environment, Nardi and colleagues (2000; Nardi, 2005) proposed that IMing is used less to exchange information (what she called interaction) and is used more to engage in "outeraction" or "a set of communicative processes outside of information exchange, in which people reach out to others in patently social ways to enable information exchange" (Nardi et al., 2000, p. 79). Nardi (2005) proposed that this outeraction consists of three dimensions of connection that keep the participants ready to carry on a conversation: (a) affinity, (b) commitment, and (c) attention. IMing, she argued, supports a field of connection by allowing users to constantly monitor, negotiate, and manage social bonding (affinity), to let their coworkers know that they are committed to being connected and that they are paying attention to the needs of their coworkers. Nardi suggested that social bonding in IMing is often oriented toward renewing rather than creating bonds, and commitment is expressed simply by being available. Ultimately, the maintenance of these dimensions prepares people for further communication which in turn is necessary for the complex collaboration demanded of knowledge workers in today's information society.

Who Gets Messaged and Who Does Not

The negotiation of availability is also a consistent theme among college students (Boorshtein, 2004). For her honors thesis, Boorshtein (2004), an undergraduate in the Schreyer Honors College at Pennsylvania State University, conducted a random survey of 100 undergraduates in order to gain an understanding of their IMing use. She found that students use IMing to stay in touch with friends and family, to feel more connected, to get quick answers while in class or at work, and to talk to people in close proximity. Both Boorshtein & Santoro (2004) and Thorne (2003), a professor also at Pennsylvania State, found that college students were selective about the medium they used for communication. Boorshtein's respondents indicated that IMing was for communication between peers and used e-mail to conduct correspondence with professors. Thorne's students resisted using e-mail to contact peers in France and insisted on using IMing, even at the risk of impacting their course grade. This phenomenon may be unique to the students at Pennsylvania State University, but when taken in conjunction with Nardi's (2005) argument that IMing allows for the maintenance of the three dimensions of communication, we can begin to understand how the specifics of IMing use carry less weight among users than the purposes for which it can be used.

Building Friendships through Instant Messaging

The use of IMing as a tool for social interaction rather than a tool for transmitting information was also found among teens. Grinter and Palen (2002) conducted in-depth interviews of 16 teenagers from technologically rich communities in the United States and the United Kingdom. Their participants indicated that IMing is used to build social relationships, a sense of belonging, and for learning how to be a communicator. These qualitative findings are supported by a quantitative study conducted by Hu et al. (2004). Drawing on data collected from a wide scale survey, Hu et al. examined the relationship between the amount of IMing use and the level of perceived intimacy between friends. After controlling for age and gender, the authors found that IMing use was positively associated with verbal, affective, and social intimacy. Specifically, they argued that IMing promotes rather than hinders intimacy and that frequent IMing use increases desire to meet face to face. Findings by Gross, Juvonen, and Gable (2002), however, indicated that this argument might be simplistic. Using IMing text logs, interviews, and a psychometric tool to measure the sense of well-being among seventh graders in a middle-class public school in California, Gross et al. found that time spent online is not associated with a teen's sense of daily well-being; instead, IMing can foster a sense of connectedness or a sense of loneliness depending upon whether it supports or replaces meaningful contact among peers.

In sum, it becomes clear not only that are the language and literacy practices of IMing context specific but also that the purposes of IMing are specific to the community in which it is used. Even though the literature indicates that IMing is an effective tool for keeping members of a community or work group connected, the underlying framework of the tool's effectiveness develops out of the nature of the preexisting relationships, not the nature of the tool itself. Overall, the technical aspects of IMing appear to be less salient for users than the ability to maintain connections with people with whom they already have a relationship. Hence, our research should focus on the purposes of IMing, and the implications these purposes have for the supporting technologies (including literacy) as well as the roles performed by the people who use IMing.

Instant Messaging and Literacy Learning

Little research in the field of education directly examines the use of IMing to support literacy instruction; the majority of research approaches IMing as an out-of-school literacy. If we think beyond the obvious questions of letter strings and abbreviations and probe the larger practice of IMing, we are led to a multitude of questions for future research and practice. For instance, Lewis and Fabos (2000, 2005) provided a clear demonstration of how studying IMing can be used to inform literacy instruction.

Critiques of the new literacy studies raise the concern that we have collected ethnographies of local uses of literacy but that we have failed to make connections between those local practices and the more distant or imposed forms of literacy as often instantiated in schools and imposed by policy (Brandt &

Clinton, 2002; Collins & Blot, 2003). In what has rapidly become a seminal literature review, Hull and Schultz (2001) pointed to the "false dichotomy" (p. 577) that had been set up in the research literature between in-school and out-of school literacies and work to transcend the dichotomy by calling for researchers to examine the relationship between the two. By carefully examining the historical development of literacy research through the research traditions of ethnography of communication, Vygotskian and activity theory perspectives, and the new literacy studies, Hull and Schultz (2001) showed how research into out-of-school literacies has expanded our concepts of literacy. They asked, "How can research on literacy and out-of-school learning help us to think anew about literacy teaching and learning across a range of contexts, including school?" (p. 577). In the remainder of this chapter, I explore some questions that arise out of rethinking the relationship of IMing and in-school literacy learning.

Second Language Learning

Carmen Lee's (2002) discussion of the ways the e-mail and ICQ (a form of IMing) texts of Cantonese speakers differ provides some insight into the connections between in-school and out-of-school literacy learning. She identified microlevel language and literacy forms used within computer-mediated communication and suggested that a "thorough study of computer mediated communication textual features should go beyond the general features of computer mediated communication to the cultural-specific features" (p. 22). Lee argued for a consideration of the variations in features of different computer-mediated communication systems and the cultural and linguistic backgrounds of the computer-mediated communication users. Such a consideration may help provide ways to think about how students negotiate the demands of a writing technology within the contexts of their cultural and linguistic background. Lam (2000), for example, analyzed the way Alnon, a Chinese immigrant, used computer-mediated communication to develop English skills and to build his identity as a Chinese person now living in the United States. She demonstrated the cultural forces at play in Alnon's construction of self, as well as the ways he appropriated the English language for his own nonschool sanctioned but highly meaningful purposes. Alnon developed an identity outside of school in which he was a successful user of English. Within school, however, he continued to be positioned as a second language learner and deficient. How might the authentic practices in which Alnon was engaged outside of school be used to promote a successful in-school identity?

New Ways of Thinking about Reading and Writing

Research into IMing can also be used to raise questions and provide additional understandings similar to those suggested by Lee (2002) and Lam (2000). For instance, Lewis and Fabos (2005) connected IMing as a literacy event to the literacy practices in which IMing is embedded. With respect to IMing as a literacy event, they found,

> [Participants] were neither absorbed nor reliant on IM lingo; in fact, they often cared about using conventional spelling and punctuation. They were also acutely aware of the various audiences they were addressing, adapting their subject matter and writing style accordingly. Moreover, our participants viewed their entire IM sessions—including simultaneous exchanges that often lasted for hours—not as individual, separate exchanges but as a larger, entwined narrative. Beyond a singular window of exchange with one buddy, IM users were engaged in a larger dialogue reliant upon their knowledge of and participation within an offline network of friends, and upon the various tools and options connected with the IM platform. (p. 493)

Lewis and Fabos (2000, 2005) also found IMing to be a multimodal literacy that includes elements of linguistic, audio, spatial, gestural, and visual design (New London Group, 1996). Using the framework of multiliteracies, Lewis and Fabos showed that the literacy practices apparent in IMing are the "performative and multivoiced nature of the IM experience" (2005, p. 493). That is, the participants used language, literacy, and software affordances to enact a version of self, to enhance their social standing, and to expand their social network. Their observations and interviews with the participants revealed that they were using sophisticated literary techniques such as tone, nuances of vocabulary choice, and voice to attain social ends. Their work demonstrated that young people know and are able to use the literary devices that are often laboriously taught in the secondary classroom.

Lewis and Fabos (2005) carefully delinated a number of ways in which the understandings garnered from research into IMing can inform the schooling of literacy. They argued that schools need to prepare students for changing epistemologies, identities, and practices without appropriating the technologies young people have embraced. They suggested that one way to do so is to engage students in discussing the ways they use literacies in and out of school as a means for unearthing what it is about the various activities that is engaging, demanding, and rewarding. Furthermore, Lewis and Fabos (2005) pointed out that the ways of reading IMs is different than the linear and deep or reflective reading valued in schools and academia. They argued that being able to read multiple simultaneous IMs is not a deficient or surface form of reading; it is simply a different form of reading. They claimed that students develop a repertoire of reading behaviors. As a way to address this "lateral" (p. 497) reading style in the classroom, Lewis and Fabos suggested that teachers explore the use of online materials that require lateral reading across genres and modes as well as collaborative activity-based projects that require students to draw on a variety of texts and modalities.

Lewis, C., & Fabos, B. (2005). Instant messaging, literacies, and social identities. *Reading Research Quarterly, 40*(4), 470–501.

Livingstone, S. (2002). *Children's use of the internet: A literature review.* London: National Children's Bureau.

Livingstone, S., & Bovill, M. (1999). *Families and the internet: An observational study of children and young people's internet use.* Retrieved March 9, 2002, from http://www.lse.ac.uk/collections/media@lse/whosWho/soniaLivingstonePublications2.htm

Livingstone, S., & Bovill, M. (2001). *Young people, new media.* Retrieved March 9, 2002, from http://www.lse.ac.uk/collections/media@lse/pdf/young_people_report.pdf

Mann, C., & Stewart, F. (2000). *Internet communication and qualitative research: A handbook for researching online.* Thousand Oaks, CA: Sage.

Nardi, B. (2005). Beyond bandwidth: Dimensions of connection in interpersonal communication. *Computer Supported Collaborative Work, 14*(2).

Nardi, B., Whittaker, S., & Bradner, E. (2000). *Interaction and outeraction: Instant Messaging in action.* Retrieved August 18, 2003, from http://portal.acm.org/citation.cfm?id=358975

Neilsen, L. (1998). Playing for real: Performative texts and adolescent identities. In D. Alvermann, K. Hinchman, D. Moore, S. Phelps, & D. Waff (Eds.), *Reconceptualizing the literacies in adolescents' lives* (pp. 3–26). Mahwah, NJ: Erlbaum.

New London Group. (1996). A pedagogy of multiliteracies: Designing social futures. *Harvard Educational Review, 66*(1), 60–92.

Park, N. (2003). *Determinants of Instant Messaging use.* Kansas City, MI: Proceedings of the Annual Meeting of the Association for Education in Journalism and Mass Communication (ERIC Document Reproduction Service No. ED481267).

Rogoff, B. (2003). *The cultural nature of human development.* New York: Oxford University Press.

Schiano, D., Chen, C. P., Ginsberg, J., Gretarsdottir, U., Huddleston, M., & Isaacs, E. (2002). *Teen use of messaging media.* Retrieved August 18, 2003, from http://portal.acm.org/citation.cfm?doid=506443.506500

Shaughnessy, M. P. (1977). *Errors and expectations: A guide for the teacher of basic writing.* New York: Oxford University Press.

Shiu, E., & Lenhart, A. (2004). *How Americans use instant messaging.* Retrieved September 7, 2005, from http://www.pewinternet.org/pdfs/PIP_Instantmessage_Report.pdf

Street, B. V. (1995). *Social literacies.* London: Longman.

Street, B. V. (2003). What's 'new' in new literacy studies? Critical approaches to literacy in theory and practice. *Current Issues in Comparative Education, 5*(2).

Thorne, S. L. (2003). Artifacts and cultures-of-use in intercultural communication. *Language Learning & Technology, 7*(2), 38–67.

Voida, A., Newstetter, W. C., & Mynatt, E. D. (2002). *When conventions collide: the tensions of instant messaging attributed.* Retrieved August 18, 2003, from http://portal.acm.org/citation.cfm?id=503376.503410

CHAPTER **18**

Gender in Online Communication

JONATHAN PAUL MARSHALL

UNIVERSITY OF TECHNOLOGY, SYDNEY, AUSTRALIA

Introduction

Whatever media is employed, communication is not simply about the transfer or exchange of information; all communication involves context, interpretation, and error. Context often involves situating ourselves with respect to others in a social field (e.g., status, role, proficiency, recognized dangers, etc.) with the aim of getting these others to behave in ways which are either intended or predictable, so that we too can act. Communication, therefore, is intertwined with relations of power or cooperation, and efforts to increase certainty, and it is always social.

These contexts, relations, and outcomes can seem much vaguer and more problematic online than they seem offline. Presence and activity is not witnessed or reinforced without the emission of communication, so that people are not exactly present or absent, but what I have called "asent." They may feel they are continually on the verge of slipping away. Reception of messages may not be confirmed. Feedback is often desultory and unclear. The actions of others may be hidden. Even when others think that what we have written is wonderful, we may not get the feedback common in offline communication. Resolving these kinds of ambiguities, and the anxieties they produce, becomes an important part of online life and of efforts to situate oneself socially (J. Marshall, 2000, chap. 6; 2004a). One method of reducing these ambiguities is through emphasizing common offline contexts and channels for expectation, such as gender.

Gender, as context, is connected not only with issues of identity and its truth or of power, privilege and proficiency, but also with issues around finding intimacy and support online and the complex shifting divisions of public versus private events. Gender gives us experiences of ways of conversing, and these seem to be transferred to life online. It also affects the way people interact with computers, what they use the Internet for, and how they interpret the behavior of others.

Paul ten Have (2000, n.p.) argued that social categories are used by people

to orient themselves and others in their dealings with one another. That is, a substantial part of the social knowledge that members of society use, is organized in terms of categories of persons ... . Members count on each other in terms of those categories and the properties associated with them.

When a person gains category information about another, they gain knowledge about how they should behave, what they can expect, how wary they should be, how much they might have in common, what kind of projects might be pursued together, and so on. The salience of a category will vary with situation and context.

Gender is a major category with which people organize knowledge about each other and themselves, regulate the ways that they interact, and claim access to cultural privilege, knowledge, and status. Thus, it will be of continuing importance online, especially when other ways of gaining knowledge about others remain relatively undeveloped. Gender also seems to condense much of the anxiety and strangeness of online communication and requires careful research, tracing the complex ways in which it is deployed and the factors that affect salience, without expecting that these deployments will necessarily be uniform, or open to immediate inspection. Gender may even take new importance, as it becomes potentially vaguer online. The precise focus of these issues may change as new generations work out their own conventions, but there is little to suggest that the effects of gender will disappear.

Gender Theory and Internet Research

There is a large body of theoretical work about the nature and functions of gender and the way it intersects with divisions of labor, power, social roles, sexuality, language use, philosophy, and technology. To caricature, some claim that gender is constructed (whether based on a given biological difference or not), that gender inclines us to certain types of behavior and experience, that there are multiple types of gender (not just male and female), that gender is a social institution like class, and there are various combinations of these positions. Good summaries of some of the arguments and positions can be found in Alsop, Fitzsimons, and Lennon (2002), Connell (2002), B. L. Marshall (2000),

Mascia-Lees and Black (2000), and Pilcher and Whelehan (2004). Many other works could be suggested. Whatever the state of theory, it seems that Westerners tend to regard gender as an essential part of a person's being, which informs us of the way they should, and will, act. It seems sensible to bear all of these factors in mind when studying the influences of gender in online life and not to foreclose our investigation by assuming that we already know what gendered behavior is.

Rather than spend this chapter arguing with this huge body of theory, I will assert that the study of gender is not the study of women or men in isolation. Gender is produced within an interactive process between people of the same and other genders. It is a dynamic category and set of conventions emerging from continuing interactions and comparisons and is thus not separable from the history of gender relations. This gender system is expressed in many aspects of social life including art, religion, violence, education, and knowledge (tacit or otherwise). Gender creates not only needs but also ways that are supposed to give satisfaction. People may increase or mark gender differences as part of the way to these satisfactions.

Gender is a process of both categorizing and organizing people and it exists prior to and independent of any individual. How people identify a person as gendered is as important as how the person identifies him- or herself, and needs to be investigated. Not all members of a gender will identify with each other all of the time. Gender identity will be cross cut by class, income, education, ethnicity, nationality, sexuality, context, work, kinship, problems of survival, and so forth. Gender may not be abstractable from these factors or be able to be treated as a completely independent variable. There may not be a single uniform gender code. Unfortunately, as researchers, we are all embedded within our cultural preconceptions about gender; we are not outside, and thus we have to be careful in research and reflect upon our own reactions, rebellions, privileges, interpretations, and effects on research.

Online gender is not isolated from offline gender or offline social life, experience, power relations, and conventions and, thus, will likely vary depending on the societies and subgroups involved. Several specific questions relating to gender in online forums are how does a person's offline gender and gendered interaction influence how they are likely to behave online, how they are likely to find life online, and how they will present themselves online? How are people likely to use gender online? How are they likely to decode the gender of others? Under what circumstances does gender become increasingly or decreasingly relevant? How do the results of online gender interaction affect offline interaction and vice versa?

Any gendered differences in behavior we find will probably be, like most human differences, distributed statistically. One example of a gender-linked difference is height. The average man is taller than the average woman, but there is considerable overlap and no categorical difference. There is only a

"spivak." MOOs also allow people to build characters, while on the mailing lists that I have been on, identification of others, communication with others, and perhaps attributable status was part of the purpose of posting. In many MOOs, MUDs, and so forth, it is possible to get a list of characters by their assigned gender. This can mean that anyone who is listed as female may be subject to harassment, which will lower the number of females identifying as female. However, when people move out of a relatively brief contact into a longer term, more private contact, offline gender seems to become much more important. Mowbray (2001) stated that people who were indeterminately or specially gendered on MOOs "generally told me that their online friends knew their offline gender—or correctly guessed it from their online behaviour—and reacted to their characters as though the characters were of that gender" (p. 6).

Wright (2000) studied gender impersonation in online games through surveys and responses to an initial article via posts to Slashdot. A small number of responses (33) were posted to the original survey. However, most people responding (60%) claimed that they played female characters for game advantage either because of social conventions of males helping, protecting, or being careless when fighting females or because of technical features built into the game or imagined to be built in the game—for example, some people expected female characters to be smaller targets in some games, but they were not. Only 19% said they did it for reasons of gender exploration. Those responding often claimed not to role-play the characters at all, although some claimed to read books detailing expected male and female differences in order to pass. Offline gender of the player again became more relevant as people bonded through their characters and began to move into friendship and intimacy.

Kibby (2001, n.p.) likewise asserted that "gender policing" becomes common "in sex entertainment forums," something which would not be expected if the sex was simply play, but would be if it really was about establishing intimacy, relationship, or using one's true gender identity and its conventions. Vagueness tends to become more problematic the more people become close, and finding the truth about others becomes a problem to be solved, not an uncertainty to be celebrated (Slater, 1998, p. 92). Vagueness seems particularly rare when people already know each other from offline meetings.

This suggests that gender is an important regulator of intimacy online and offline. This association of the private with femininity and intimacy seems contrasted with publicity, masculinity, and exposure, even though the terms shift rather than oppose one another. Discovering that someone with whom you have been intimate is not female when you thought he or she was female changes the relationship from the realm of intimate and private into public display. Our private role and its vulnerabilities have broken into the public male domain and betrayal, as well as possibly dislocating self-identity around sexuality. In primarily non-heterosexual domains gender will probably play differently.

In general, the offline body seems to be associated with the real person. The closer we approach the offline, then the more real things seem to be: from on group, to off group, to phone calls, and to face-to-face. The more important the relationship, the more people want to check its reality by comparison with the offline and the offline body. This suggests that people look for an authentic self, beyond that presented in online interactions. The relatively common explanation that people who engage in gender impersonation are closet homosexuals (e.g., "A vocal portion of the gaming population seems to believe that if a male plays as a female character, he is a homosexual," Wright, 2000; cf., Curtis, 1997, p. 128) assumes not only that homosexuality is a gender disorder, foreign to those with real gender identity, but also that impersonation itself indicates a hidden authentic truth, rather than identity play or potential, as would be expected if people are abiding by a postmodern theory of selves. O'Brien (1999a) even worries that conventional sexual ghettos will be replicated online and that conventions about the embodied offline will be taken as really real. Ultimately, identity and truth seem to be associated with the body. As Kendall (1998) wrote, people "privilege offline identity information over information received online ... This allows them to continue to understand identity in the essentialized terms of a persistent and consistent self, grounded in a particular physical body" (p. 130). When people already know each other offline before meeting online, as in a classroom, the existent gender dynamics are likely to translate directly to the online.

Although we may not be able to experience life as the other gender, people can learn about the other gender's experience. Suler (1999) gives the example of a woman who wanted to find out how other females acted with men and who came to feel that other women were somewhat silly and boring and that men had more pressure on them to be entertaining. Another woman who had played as a man remarked, "I hadn't truly appreciated how much a guy has to constantly maintain the facade of strength. One slip of weakness and the women crush you like a walnut." But in these cases, it was probable there was mutual role-playing; a person who played like a clichéd man might induce other people to play like a clichéd woman. Similarly, Campbell (1994) described his experiences when he used a woman's account to get free access to a bulletin board service. Immediately after logging on, he received 31 requests from one male with whom he had no prior contact and whose message descriptions repeatedly included sex. Another man sent him his phone number without it being requested. People who were initially helpful ended up requesting cybersex as recompense, and so on. Campbell had apparently not attempted to pass as a woman; it was just assumed to be so by others, and they evoked their power automatically.

Cross-cultural aspects of gender vagueness have largely not been explored. Taking advantage of this vagueness may be less compelling in some cultures than in others, as may the levels of disruption experienced. Gender categorization may have importance in different aspects of life and may carry different knowledge. Different languages can also make gender vagueness harder, as they may require the person to gender him- or herself and to gender others in order to speak, thus requiring much more deliberation. As a result, gender vagueness may not be a universal issue, and certainly not an issue in the same circumstances.

Indeed, despite its importance as a myth of cyberspace, some evidence shows that not much gender play occurs. Herring (2000, n.p.) wrote, "Claims of widespread gender anonymity have not been supported by research on online interaction." Roberts and Parks (2001), in a survey of MOO users, claimed that even on MOOs, despite the varieties of automatic gender on offer, deliberate gender changing involves a minority of users and is relatively infrequent and conventional—78% of those who used gender variety simply switched gender (p. 275). They suggested that this offers "little ammunition for those who argue that online interaction is being used to 'break the binaries' in our approaches to gender" (p. 280; cf., Deuel, 1996, p. 133). Cooper, Scherer, Boies, and Gordon (1999) reported that, in a survey they conducted of 9,177 people on MSN, "only 5% of the sample indicated pretending to be a different gender, and most of them (4%) said that they do so only occasionally" (p. 158). In contrast, Mowbray (2001) claimed that, by looking at active characters on two MOOs, she was able to determine that "at least 18% had online genders other than 'male' and 'female'" (p. 5), although it was possible that these people could have been influenced by gender studies and were trying to live their theories. They may well have been perceived by others and interacted with as really male or female, whatever their MOO gender. In any case, new freedoms found online may not translate to the offline.

Gender in Online Groups: Interaction Styles and Power

There is a large body of online folklore and research into the ways that males and females behave online. That such differences exist should be expected. It is probably inevitable that people with high status offline might carry their modes of converse online, and either deliberately or unconsciously keep subordinate people in their places. The supposedly disinhibiting effects of partial anonymity and removal from physical retaliation might even free some members of that dominant group from the normal restraints on attitudinal violence towards those 'beneath' them.

This lack of restraint can be seen in frequent reports of sexual or other harassment. Ferris (1996) referred to a survey of 1,150 women online that found that 26% reported being sexually harassed in the past year. Cyberstalking is a new crime category largely affecting women (Ogilvie, 2000). Women may be subject not only to this kind of harassment but also to "challenges to 'prove' they are female, unwanted offers of help, and 'babying' by male-presenting characters" (LaPin & Bharadwaj, 1998). Definition of harassment may depend not only on the gender observing but also on the place of occurrence. Thus, Biber, Doverspike, Baznik, Cober, and Ritter (2002) claimed that people can have more stringent standards online than they do offline, implying again that online life is not necessarily less inhibited or less affecting than offline.

Early research often reported that groups with a female focus, especially newsgroups, would be dominated by men. Thus, Gladys We (1994) wrote that, of 303 posts to alt.feminism, 11% were from women, 83% from men, and 6% were undeterminable. Most of these posts seemed to be abusive. Balka (1993) also described men overwhelming women's issue newsgroups, and the founding of the mailing list Femina to deal with those problems. Frederick (1999) showed that these problems mean that feminist newsgroups have difficulties being inclusive, and moderation is useful in increasing inclusion. Herring, Job-Sluder, Scheckler, and Barab (2002) gave an account of a man attempting to attack (troll) a women's mailing list by getting people involved in futile arguments and abuse while pretending sincerity and victim status. It also seems that men may perceive requests for a polite, less aggressive discourse as a form of censorship, and this is boosted by a common presence on the Net of U.S. libertarian philosophy, which basically asserts that if you are not inclined to fight, or not strong enough to succeed, you deserve what you get.

The locus classicus of research into online gendered differences in communicative behavior is the work of Susan Herring (1993). In her initial research on the mailing lists LINGUIST and Mega Byte University, she found that women participated at rates far lower than their percentage of membership, especially when the discussion was generally theoretical. If messages by women approached 50% of the postings, then at least some men would object strongly to the discussion happening at all. Furthermore, women's messages were shorter than men's were, and both men and women responded more to men's posts. Herring added that men tended to discuss issues, while women contributed most to personal discussions, for example, discussing linguists rather than linguistics. She also argued that women produced mail with more features of "women's language" than men and that men produced mail with more features of "men's language" than women. Good outlines of the kinds of linguistic features found in male and female languages offline are in Herring (1993), Ferris (1996), Hatt (1998), Witmer (1996), and Sussman and Tyson (2000).

Herring (1994) argued that women and men have different communicative ethics, men valuing aggression more. Lists devoted to feminized subjects or careers are more likely to have women posting in line with their proportion on list, and these lists had "little or no flaming, and cooperative, polite exchanges." She added, "The simple fact of the matter is that it is virtually only men who flame."

Herring (2000, n.p.) summarized her position as follows:

> In asynchronous CMC ... males are more likely to post longer messages, begin and close discussions in mixed-sex groups, assert opinions strongly as "facts," use crude language (including insults and profanity), and in general, manifest an adversarial orientation towards their interlocutors ... In contrast, females tend to post relatively short messages, and are more likely to qualify and justify their assertions, apologize, express support of others, and in general, manifest an "aligned" orientation towards their interlocutors

> In mixed-sex public discussion groups, females post fewer messages, and are less likely to persist in posting when their messages receive no response...Even when they persist, they receive fewer responses from others (both females and males), and do not control the topic or the terms of the discussion except in groups where women make up a clear majority of participants.

Clerc (1996, pp. 81–82) also pointed out that not being responded to on early posts can be discouraging for people, and they may not get involved with the group as a result. If women tend to be responded to less often, then new female members may be discouraged and female populations decline.

However, not all researchers have observed the same results as Herring (2000). Thus, Jenkins (1998) reported that on her (presumably private) friends list,

> It is actually the men on the list who are more likely to initiate gossipy conversations, for instance, discussing the activities of friends not on the list, while many of the more serious, academic conversations are begun by the women.

Vaughn Trias (1997, n.p.) studied 487 minutes of transcripts from the IRC channel Atheism, excluding all of those of unknown gender and concluded, "Males produce more messages and spend more time online, but females produce more messages while online."

In my own study of 6,126 posts over 4 months made on the mailing list Cybermind, it seemed that the percentage of the population which could be identified as female was the same as the percentage of the population of female posters. Women were represented among the most prolific posters in accordance with their proportion of the population. There was little difference in the response rates of men and women to each other or in men and women starting a thread. Posters responded to 85% of male posts and to 87% of female posts. Males wrote an average of 13.43 lines of text per post, and the females wrote an average of 13.48 lines of text per post (J. Marshall, 2000, Appendix I).

Witmer (1996, n.p.) collected 3,000 messages from newsgroups and commercial chat rooms to test the following hypothesis:

(i) Women use more graphic accents (i.e., graphic expressions of emotions, emoticons, etc.) than men do in their CMC, (ii) men use more challenging language in CMC than do women, and (iii) men write more inflammatory messages than do women. Results indicate that only the first hypothesis is partially supported and that women tend to challenge and flame more than do men in this sample group.

Savicki, Lingenfelter, and Kelley (1996) also reported that, although groups with large numbers of women tended to engage in more tension reduction, there was no gender difference in flames or challenging behavior. They concluded their six year study by arguing (Savicki & Kelley 2000) that context was important. In particular the gender composition of the group was highly significant in producing styles of communication, but these styles were quite variable in individuals. Sussman and Tyson (2000) looked at newsgroups the subjects of which they defined as masculine, feminine, or neutral. Postings by nongenderable people were ignored. They found that males did tend to make longer posts and were more opinionated, but that females tended to post more often—especially in feminine newsgroups. Topic seems to provide a further context for gender usage.

Patterns of communication can change over time. Thus, Colyer (1997) reported that, after an absence of 3 years on the Cinema-L list, on her return, she found that women were much more active. The average number of messages from women per day had doubled, the most active poster was female, and women posted more messages than men did. That the historical trajectory of this change could not be documented to show the circumstances in which the change occurred is a pity.

Some anecdotal evidence shows that women are more likely to communicate off the group in private than are men or that men are not as likely to maintain lengthy interactions with other men off the group (Colyer 1997, chap. 7; J. Marshall, 2000). As Colyer remarked, this may mean that surveys that are answered in private are much more likely to have an overrepresentation of women. The question as to whether men can expand their gender conventions by becoming more open to expressing their emotional or confused sides has not really been explored beyond assertions that gender switching might allow this. However, Bennett (1998), in an investigation of the possibilities of private communication with the extremely small sample of six men, suggested that the conventions of gender, privacy, and intimacy might allow more openness. Some of the men remarked that they had told her things that they had never previously said to anyone, including their wives. Bennett remarked, "The fact that I was a female researcher was of significant value with regards to the degree and type of data which was generated by participants" (1998, n.p.).

Whatever the accuracy of these results (some of the research was extremely short term with little appreciation of normal group politics), it shows that a fair level of different gender behavior can be observed. This suggests that there are many factors to consider, and perhaps, gender does not operate in simple uniform kinds of ways everywhere, but it does seem to have effect.

In doing this kind of research, given that people will evaluate the same text differently depending upon whether it is attributed to a male or a female, then it is vitally important to code messages for features of language without the coder being aware of the gender of the writers. Whether most of the research previously described has done this is not clear. It is also difficult to code a text for things like aggressiveness, interactivity, support, or opinionatedness, as these are largely matters of opinion. People often regard the comments of others as flames, when their own, which may be even more aggressive, are not. Likewise, what is opinion to some is simply fact to another. Despite trying, I found it impossible to classify mails in such ways when trying to investigate gendered behavior on Cybermind.

Single Gender Lists

Because of these social difficulties, women have attempted to find online groups confined to women. Research in this field is limited partly because the groups are, in some sense defined as private and closed. Some of the groups reportedly admit only people who they know from offline contact to be female; others engage in gender policing so that people who behave in ways that are not considered to be feminine are expelled (Hall, 1996). Thus, offline definitions of being female are maintained and enforced. To engage in such expelling, list moderation must be strict, so it is difficult to tell whether the lower levels of flame and high levels of politeness reported for such groups emerge from gender or result from enforcement. In her account of the list Systers, Borg (1993) remarked, "[The] forum will need a strong leader/moderator, committed to the encouragement of productive discussion and willing to stop unproductive argument," which implies that unproductive argument does occur naturally among women, as reports of schoolgirls using the Internet or mobile phones to attack and bully their classmates also suggest.

Gender and Bodies Online

Theorizing bodies is notoriously complicated, and there are many different approaches. Here a naïve perspective is taken. Even if bodies are separate from minds, they are not inert or uncommunicative. People have a dialogue or multilogue with their bodies, which do not necessarily speak in the same language or format as they do. Bodies communicate largely in feelings, sensations, and images. As a result, everything we might know about our bodies arises from nonisomorphic translations, motivated by our personal experience through cultural decoding procedures, conventions, and actions. Bodies are not simply inscribed, but they inscribe in return—we are already dynamic (but ultimately entropic) networks of flows, transmutations, pulsions, symbols, and signs. This becomes more ambiguous and oscillatory online, although the presence of physical pain offline can disrupt the sense of online engagement or immersion.

In the West, bodies are popularly seen as underlying, as subject to control, and as rebelling against control. Emotional states seem to be considered real in the way that statements might not be. The stronger the emotional state the more real it is. Minds are also considered real, and there is a long and complex history of the way that people have divided minds from bodies. The mind is often portrayed as being like an immaterial ghost. In some respects, the separation of minds and bodies seems to have increased in the presence of computer models of the mind where the program is seen as equivalent to the mind and hardware to the body. People have proposed gaining immortality by downloading the mind into a computer, and this is a common theme in science fiction. Another common model for the body is the cyborg (the cybernetic organism), which in practice is often blurred with androids and robots. As the idea of downloading minds implies, cyborgs and ghosts can also meld, and the cyborg is not inherently liberating or postgendered as can be claimed but is also implicated in the history in which the mind and technology has been identified with the masculine and the body with the feminine (J. Marshall, 2004b).

Ghost or parallel universe versions of being online, which deny the importance of space and place, are inaccurate in that people are situated in the offline world; they do need keyboards, a wired or wireless infrastructure, a history of laying this structure, and a history of approach to technology. Ignoring this ignores the offline politics both of getting online and of the ways that space is used to further sectional aims and dominance. Communication between humans is necessarily embodied and emotional, with bodily reactions and possible physical consequences. However, there can be different experiences of space online, largely determined by structures of communication and by the rhetorical function of that space (J. Marshall, 2001). By thinking of online as space—as in cyberspace, as in surfing the Web, or as in going to different places online—people think in terms of bodies moving and being contained and of themselves as speaking rather than typing. They can think of themselves as extended or without boundaries, or with different boundaries. Online space is never without some structure that dictates ease of movement or interaction, and the type of space may ground the experience of embodiment. Space might also be gendered by its association with gendered activities.

Bodies most obviously appear symbolically online in the use of emoticons, or graphic images of emotion, and in netsex, all of which anchor communication in reference to offline bodies.

In the West, three emoticons are mainly used: ":)," ";)," and ":(." The first indicates good humor or a request to read carefully as the writer is not trying to be offensive; the second indicates a knowingness which is sometimes taken

people can not only interact and get to know each other, but can also attempt to maintain the presence of the other before them via interactive narration and via reference to a commonly available and sustainable bodily reaction. Netsex could be used to restore contact and the sense of presence between people when the dialogue slides out of areas of mutual interest. As such, it can be like sharing a drink or watching a film offline (J. Marshall, 2002).

Netsex is not abstracted from offline social life. As Albright and Conran (n.d.) wrote, "Online communities accelerate the expansion of opportunities for relationships begun by personals, video dating, and telephone chat line" (n.p.). Here, netsex can be seen as part of wider social processes, and it suggests that pairing and sexuality are extremely important in the construction of gender and self-identity (particularly as sexual activity is usually gendered) or in ensuring survival in the contemporary world. In this case, online groups, more generally, are also ways that people can find some level of contact and support in a world in which the institutions which help survival are becoming run down, temporary, and perhaps more hostile.

Gender and Growing Up Online

People who have grown up with the Internet may use it in significantly different ways to those who came to it as adults. New conventions may develop and different constructions of gender may be in use depending upon the person's generation. These usages may change as they move through the life cycle. Change does not have to mean that there is less sexism but simply that sexisms may change as well.

One change that has been intensely discussed in Australia recently is the growing success of girls at school and the growing failure of boys. When this was the other way round, in expectations with hierarchy, we would frequently hear explanations suggesting that girls were not as intelligent, were interested in people and babies rather than ideas, and so forth. These changes, while powerfully activating attempts to restore order, do not seem to have moved into success in the out-of-school world yet. Perhaps the power structures are too ingrained for them to do so, but it does mean that some of the strangeness that using computers seems to have had for women may be changing in schools, even though familiarity with tool use is not the same as gaining technical proficiency.

Familiarity, may also mean that, rather than being used to extend the circle of acquaintance, the Internet is only one of many media, such as mobile phones, used to maintain contact between already existing acquaintanceship, so there is no longer easy distinction between online and offline life. Questions that I have asked to classes of University students have suggested that they tend to see the Internet as primarily the World Wide Web and e-mail. Mailing lists (other than one-way commercial lists and educational lists at the University), newsgroups, and even MOOs seem to be largely unheard of. If this is the case, then issues of role-playing might be largely abandoned, as people are already communicating with those who already know them. Communication could become primarily a one-way broadcast, as seems to be the case with personal Web sites and blogs, which might of course attract people with which to converse. However, it may mean that online communication is becoming less distinguishable from everyday life, and thus, even less subversive of it, even if separate languages and competencies develop to indicate in-group membership in this world of instant communication at a distance. This new language may also depend on gendered contexts.

Angela Thomas (2000) set up an online graphical chat environment in the Palace in order to ethnographically investigate over 4 years how children, particularly girls, between ages 8 and 16 dealt with issues around growing up and writing their bodies and themselves. She used transcripts of their interactions, interviews, screenshots, and recordings of actions (p. 666). Thomas (2004) saw these modes of discourse as empowering, even though they are primarily determined by acceptance of or reaction to Western discourses of femininity, sexuality, and beauty (pp. 358–359, 379). Thomas suggested that girls use imaged avatars as an ideal mirror in which to display/construct what they desire and dream of becoming (p. 376). These fantasies seem very conventionally gendered indeed. She remarked, "Children were more inclined to exaggerate their real gender, and perform, as Butler termed, 'hyperbolic exhibitions' of their gender, with girls giggling incessantly, and boys talking about decidedly masculine topics" (p. 369). Similar results were found in Clark's (1998) study of teenagers using the Internet for dating. Children also learn from each other or work out together how to socialize and how to use the Palace and its props (Thomas, 2000, p. 668), and we might expect gender will guide the kinds of interactions they have in this learning. Learning seems a matter of discovering how to fit in, what behavior, and what revelations are acceptable. As such, the children seem to place a great value on literacy or attractive use of words, word arrangement, and word style together with the ability to craft a cool avatar image and use the other parts of Palace software. Online appearance, as expressed in a form of literacy, does count, as may offline appearance and the oscillations and vagaries between them.

Gender and the Web

In some ways, Web sites are also presentations of self and, thus, are probably gendered. As Kibby (1997) pointed out, women were often targeted by other Web sites, such as "Babes on the Web," which evaluated them by the attractiveness of the photos included on their Web sites. As a result, Kibby wondered why, despite the Internet giving women the "opportunity to present themselves in ways which are not bound by such categories as 'sex object' …

on so many women's home pages was the sexualised body chosen as a primary image of self?" She concluded that many women "present a sexualised self on their home pages because for them sexuality and identity are not easily separated, and nor is such a separation desired." Separation of body and self may be something that comes easier to males in our society. The lack of faces that she mentions and the common observation of faces without bodies, however, implied that people might be more ambivalent than this position suggests.

Arnold and Miller's (1999) study of the pages of academics also shows this ambivalence. They reported, in their earlier work, that men's pages tended to be relatively short, and there was "more variety in length and self-reference in women's pages" and more awareness of the reader. They also found that, even when Web pages were dictated by house style, gender differences were present "in the cyberspace equivalent of 'fluffy' feminine (such as the use of a substitute picture, e.g., 'flowers') compared to technical 'images' (e.g., a computer) used by men." Women also tended to be more prone to list all of their qualifications and memberships on the front page than men were. This perhaps indicated some uncertainty about academic identity, or a need to reinforce it. Arnold and Miller (2000, n.p.) reported that women academics seemed ambiguous about the use of photographs "most wanted to avoid it, but found it friendly and validating on other women's pages." As opposed to the pages that Kibby was looking at, here the threat of being appropriated by appearance or having status affected by appearance is more worrying. Borders between the public self and the private self seemed more fraught for female academics. Monitoring the potential reader is also a form of self-monitoring and self-regulation. Men are apparently less concerned about this or less vulnerable and, thus, have more options for self-presentation (Arnold & Miller, 2001, n.p.). Interestingly,

> Most respondents volunteered that they were not 'neutral' in their approach to gender in their use of the Web and many had noticed at a practical level that patterns of use, time spent and range of uses, were possibly different for them compared to their male colleagues. (Arnold & Miller, 2000)

This needs further investigation.

Further Research

Further research needs to be done on the uses of online gender which emerge from non-Anglo cultures (to check our own preconceptions), on generational changes, and on the ways that online activity is melded with offline life or interacts with divisions like class or ethnicity and with modes of language and symbolization use. Otherwise, literacy remains abstract, rather than something with which people engage in their daily lives. To uncover relations between gender and communication, researchers need to get people in the wild, and recognize the complexities and contradictions of people's lives. More care needs to be given to the circumstances within which people are acting and to note the circumstances in which behavior changes, rather than simply assuming that what we have observed is always the case. Simple questions include when do people engage in flame, when are references to the body made and what are their consequences, what happens as the group's population changes, when does gender become important to self-presentation, or to interaction with others, and do these events involve interaction between offline and online life? In investigating power relations, we need at least to ask who is involved, when does it occur, how does it occur and what patterns are activated. Such research can be done only through extended long-term investigation, not in a matter of days or weeks. We also need to be sensitive to our own enculturation and biases, as we are interpreters of what others mean, and gender is an important part of this. It is conceivable that, through no fault of their own, the researchers' results will be affected by their genders, as the reactions of people to them will be influenced by these genders. People will even respond differently to a machine if it has gendered attributes (Reeves & Nash, 1996, chaps. 14 and 15). Although conventions of gender are constantly contested in the contemporary world, gender is not something that has been transcended or avoided, and although it may not feature in exactly the same ways or in the same communicative contexts of previous years, that does not mean that it can be ignored or assumed.

Online Gender and Literacies

All the work previously mentioned suggests that gender provides an important context within which communications are interpreted, actions contested, and people organized; that the prime drivers of online gender are still offline conventions, offline privileges, offline survival strategies, and the need to fit in, cooperate, or be understood. Communication is social and the offline social world cannot be dismissed from consideration, even after its limiting affects on access, experience, proficiency, status, leisure, and its relation to the politics of offline space have been taken into account. Gender still provides a dynamic matrix that guides interaction and meaning.

Gender conventions and roles appear to become more salient when issues of intimacy, privacy, emotionality, minds, bodies, power, occupation of space, and argumentation arise and are possibly more likely to activate the more that people know each other in an offline environment. These contexts are not passive but active, in that they shape responses and are brought forward by people in order to define what is going on, irrespective of the intention of others. Multiplicity is not a savior as it can still be reduced to what is acceptable and what is not, to a special occasion, or to what everyone already knows is the case. Forms of violence are still present even in a primarily textual environment, especially when that environment translates into offline life. Harassment, stalking, and threat cannot be ignored, anymore than can friendship and love, and they shape the kind of communications produced.

Much has been claimed for technology as mode of liberation. This has a long history in the West, but this history is gendered and we cannot solve issues of gender by ignoring them, hoping the technology deletes them, or by claiming that technology itself is the solution. We also cannot assume that all forms of digital media are equivalent in the uses they enable and restrict. The ways that communication is organized, and the kinds of forms of literacy encouraged will have different effects, as will the proportion of the genders involved within that particular media forum. Literacy in all its forms is still an interactive social process, with aims and applications—it is not a thing in itself, and it also relates to the technology deployed and its gendered history of proficiency. Hypertext, for example, does not inevitably lead to radical or subversive communication or learning practices—to be effective it has to use conventions—neither does it solve problems around gendered interaction and gendered learning. The possibility of combining images with texts or turning texts into images is not something completely new which radicalizes literacy (after all children in the West have been doing this for at least the last century), especially when the literacy still has to function within the same offline social conventions. Expertise in certain forms of the new literacy may already be encoded within such gender conventions as women being more competent with decoration or design and men in providing information or art. Such conventions may be quite robust and survive a new literacy for quite some while.

Online communication, in itself, does not free a person from the expectations of a socially conditioned audience and their conventions, especially when that audience interacts with them offline. People are still likely to imagine an audience or to fall into the conventions they associate with having an audience, especially when projects are being marked or otherwise evaluated. Part of learning to use an online environment is learning to fit in and to use common reference points. Even if students are encouraged to express their own beliefs, they do not gain complete power over their words and perspectives because they know the words are to be read or perceived. Those being educated are not free of their relation to a teacher and that teacher's gendering or to their immediate social background. Even if that background may look quite different to an older generation, it will still probably be gendered. Even communicative styles or communicative ethics may differ by gender and result in certain genders being predominant in different circumstances and other genders being silenced. Because the silencing may be expected, it may even be invisible, and the labor of, or expertise in, apologizing, supporting, arguing, or responding may also be invisibly distributed by gender. If the learning work becomes collaborative or open to discussion, this collaboration may also silence work which is not conventional, from the right people (however defined), or again fall easily into the existent gender conventions. The collaboration may divide the collaborator's tasks by gender expectations as there are competences required for the collaboration to function, and these may not be equally socially distributed or expected. In any case, a successful violation of gender codes does not mean that the codes are overthrown or no longer relevant; they could be reinforced by that violation being carefully situated in a particular place or time or given a dubious moral value by the participants.

Given the speed with which events surrounding new literacies proceed, it is more important to be aware of the questions, the problems, and the complications around gender than it is to think that there are fixed answers to any of these issues.

References

Abbate, J. (2003). Women and gender in the history of computing. *IEEE Annals of the History of Computing, 25*(4), 4–8.

Albright, J., & Conran, T. (n.d.). *Online love: Sex, gender, and relationships in cyberspace.* Retrieved April 15, 2006, from http://www.eff.org/pub/Net_culture/Virtual_community/online_love.article

Alsop, R., Fitzsimons, A., & Lennon, K. (2002). *Theorizing gender.* Cambridge, U.K.: Polity Press.

American Association of University Women. (2000). *Tech-savvy: Educating girls in the new computer age.* Retrieved April 15, 2006, from http://www.aauw.org/member_center/publications/TechSavvy/TechSavvy.pdf

Arnold, J., & Miller, H. (1999). *Gender and Web home pages.* Retrieved April 15, 2006, from http://ess.ntu.ac.uk/miller/cyberpsych/cal99.htm

Arnold, J., & Miller, H. (2000). *Same old gender plot? Women academics' identities on the Web.* Paper presented at Cultural Diversities in/and Cyberspace Conference, University of Maryland, Campus Park, Washington, DC. Retrieved April 15, 2006, from http://www.aber.ac.uk/~jmcwww/Identact/Papers/paper80.doc

Arnold, J., & Miller, H. (2001). Academic masters, mistresses and apprentices: gender and power in the real world of the Web. *Mots pluriels, 19.* Retrieved April 15, 2006, from http://www.arts.uwa.edu.au/MotsPluriels/MP1901jahm.html

Austin, J. L. (1962). *How to do things with words.* Oxford, U.K.: Oxford University Press.

Balka, E. (1993). Women's access to on-line discussions about feminism. *Electronic Journal of Communication, 3*(1). Retrieved April 15, 2006, from http://www.cios.org/getfile/Balka_v3n193

Benedikt, C. L. (1995). Tinysex is safe sex. *Infobahn Magazine, 1*(1), 13–14.

Bennett, C. M. (1998). *Men online: Discussing lived experiences on the internet.* Honors thesis, Department of Social Sciences, James Cook University, North Queensland, Australia. Retrieved April 15, 2006, from http://www.hotkey.net.au/%7Ecarolineb/

Biber, J. K., Doverspike, D., Baznik, D., Cober, A., & Ritter, B. A. (2002). Sexual harassment in online communications: Effects of gender and discourse medium. *CyberPsychology & Behavior, 5*(1), 33–42.

Borg, A. (1993). Why systers?. *Computing Research News.* Retrieved April 15, 2006, from http://cec.wustl.edu/~cs142/articles/GENDER_ISSUES/why_systers--borg

Bruckman, A. (1993). Gender swapping on the Internet. *Proceedings of INET'93.* Retrieved April 15, 2006, from http://www.cc.gatech.edu/elc/papers/bruckman/gender-swapping-bruckman.pdf

Butler, J. (1990). *Gender trouble: Feminism and the subversion of identity.* New York: Routledge.

Butler, J. (1993) *Bodies that matter: On the discursive limits of 'sex'.* New York: Routledge.

Campbell, K. K. (1994). Attack of the cyber-weenies.*Wasatch Area Voices Express*. Retrieved April 15, 2006, from http://kumo.swcp.com/synth/text/cyberweenies.html

Canada, K., & Brusca, F. (1992). The technological gender gap: Evidence and recommendations for educators and computer-based instruction designers. *Educational Technology Research & Development, 39*(2). Retrieved April 15, 2006, from http://www.arielpcs.com/resources/articles/etrd.shtml

Castranova, E. (2003). *The price of 'man' and 'woman': A hedonic pricing model of avatar attributes in a synthetic world* (CESifo Working Paper Series No. 957). Retrieved April 15, 2006, from http://ssrn.com/abstract=415043

Clark, L. (1998). Dating on the Net: Teens and the rise of 'pure' relationships. In S. Jones (Ed.), *Cybersociety: Revisiting computer-mediated communication and community* (pp. 159–183). Thousand Oaks, CA: Sage.

Clerc, S. (1996). Estrogen brigades and 'big tits' threads: Media fandom online and off. In L. Cherney & E. R. Weise (Eds.), *Wired women* (pp. 73–97). Seattle, WA: Seal Press.

Connell, R. W. (2002). *Gender.* Cambridge, U.K.: Polity Press.

Colyer, A. (1997). Gender issues in cyberspace. *A Trip Through Cyber-Cinema Fandom.* Retrieved April 15, 2006, from http://www.outreach.psu.edu/users/afc1/thesis/eth.contents.html

Cooper, A., Scherer, C. R., Boies, S. C., & Gordon, B. L. (1999). Sexuality on the internet: From sexual exploration to pathological expression. *Professional Psychology Research and Practice, 30*(2), 154–164.

Cooper, J., & Weaver, K. D. (2003). *Gender and computers: Understanding the digital divide.* Mahwah, NJ: Laurence Erlbaum.

Corneliussen, H. (2002). The multi-dimensional stories of the gendered users of ICT. In A. Morrison (Ed.), *Researching ICTs in context, InterMedia report 3* (pp.). Retrieved April 15, 2006, from http://www.intermedia.uio.no/ konferanser/skikt-02/docs/Researching_ICTs_in_context-Ch8-Corneliussen.pdf, pp. 161–184.

Curtis, P. (1997). MUDding: Social phenomena in text-based virtual realities. In S. Kiesler (Ed.), *Culture of the Internet* (pp. 121–142) . Mahwah, NJ: Erlbaum.

Deuel, N. (1996). Our passionate response to virtual reality.In S. Herring (Ed.), *Computer mediated communication: Linguistic, social and cross-cultural perspectives* (pp. 129–146). Amsterdam: John Benjamin.

Dibbell, J. (2001). Samantha, among others. *Mots pluriels,* 19. Retrieved April 15, 2006, from http://www.arts.uwa.edu.au/MotsPluriels/MP1901jd.html

Ernst, S. (2003).*Gender, power, and leadership: Perspectives from figurational sociology.* Paper presented at the 5th European Feminist research conference, Gender and Power in the New Europe, Lund University, Sweden.

Eubanks, V. (2000). Paradigms and perversions: A women's place in cyberspace. *CPSR Newsletter, 18*(1). Retrieved April 15, 2006, from http://www.cpsr.org/publications/newsletters/issues/2000/Winter2000/eubanks.html

Fallows, D. (2005). How Men and Women use the Internet. Pew Internet and American Life Project. Retrieved, 5th August 2006 from http://www.pewinternet.org/pdfs/PIP_Women_and_Men_online.pdf

Ferris, S. P. (1996). Women online: Cultural and relational aspects of women's communication in online discussion groups. *Interpersonal Computing and Technology: An Electronic Journal for the 21st Century,* 4, 29–40. Retrieved April 15, 2006, from http://www.helsinki.fi/science/optek/1996/n3/ferris.txt

Fredrick, C. A. N. (1999). Feminist rhetoric in cyberspace: The ethos of feminist usenet newsgroups. *Information Society, 15*(3), 187–198.

Ghosh, R. A., Glott, R., Krieger, G., & Robles, B. (2002). *Free/libre and open source software, survey, and study, part IV.* Maastricht, The Netherlands: International Institute of Infonomics, University of Maastricht.

Gurak, L. (1997). *Persuasion and privacy in cyberspace: The online protests over lotus market place and the clipper chip.* New Haven, CT: Yale University Press.

Hall, K. (1996). Cyberfeminism. In S. Herring (Ed.), *Computer mediated communication: Linguistic, social and cross-cultural perspectives* (pp. 147–170). Amsterdam: John Benjamins.

Hatt, D. F. (1998). *Male/female language use in computer dyadic interactions.* Unpublished master's thesis, Lauretian University, Ontario, Canada. Retrieved April 15, 2006, from http://www.fortunecity.com/boozers/princessdi/302/Lang.html

Herring, S. (1993). Gender and democracy in computer mediated communication. *EJC/REC, 3*(2). Retrieved April 15, 2006, from http://dc.smu.edu/dc/classroom/Gender.txt

Herring, S. (1994, June 27). *Gender differences in computer-mediated communication: Bringing familiar Baggageto the new frontier.* Keynote address at the American Library Association annual convention, Miami, FL. Retrieved April 15, 2006, from http://cpsr.org/cpsr/gender/herring.txt

Herring, S. (2000). Gender differences in CMC: Findings and implications. *CPSR Newsletter, 18*(1). Retrieved April 15, 2006, from http://www.cpsr.org/publications/newsletters/issues/2000/Winter2000/herring.html

Herring, S., Job-Sluder, K., Scheckler, R., & Barab, S. (2002). Searching for safety online: Managing "trolling" in a feminist forum. *The Information Society, 18,* 371–384.

Jenkins, S. (1998). *Gender differences in the use of the internet as a means of personal communication.* Unpublished master's thesis, University of London. Retrieved April 15, 2006, from http://www.agari.org/summer/

Kendall, L. (1996). 'MUDder? I hardly know er'! Adventures of a feminist MUDder. In L. Cherny & E. R. Weise (Eds.), *Wired women* (pp. 207–223) . Seattle, WA: Seal Press.

Kendall, L. (1998). Meaning and identity in cyberspace: The performance of gender, class, and race online. *Symbolic Interaction, 21*(2), 129–153.

Kendall, L. (2000). 'Oh no! I'm a nerd!' Hegemonic masculinity on an online forum. *Gender and Society, 14*(2), 256–274.

Kibby, M. (1997). Babes on the Web: Sex, identity, and the home page. *Media International Australia, 84,* 39–45. Retrieved April 15, 2006, from http://www.newcastle.edu.au/department/so/babes.htm

Kibby, M. (1999). Sex entertainment for women on the Web. *Sexuality & Culture, 3,* 89–103.

Kibby, M. (2001). Women and sex entertainment on the Internet: Discourses of gender and power. *Mots pluriels, 19.* Retrieved April 15, 2006, from http://www.arts.uwa.edu.au/MotsPluriels/MP1901mk.html

Kibby, M., & Costello, B. (1999). Displaying the phallus: Masculinity and the performance of sexuality on the Internet. *Men & Masculinities, 1*(4), 352–364.

Kibby, M., & Costello, B. (2001). Between the image and the act: Interactive sex entertainment on the Internet. *Sexualities: Studies in Culture and Society, 4*(3), 353–369.

King, L. J. (2000). Gender issues in online communities. *Computer Professionals for Social Responsibility Newsletter, 18*(1). Retrieved April 15, 2006, from http://www.cpsr.org/publications/newsletters/issues/2000/Winter2000/king.html

Kramarae, C. (1988). *Technology and women's voices: Keeping in touch.* New York: Routledge.

LaPin, G. (1999). *Shapeshifters: Why women must adapt in the computer world to succeed.* Retrieved April 15, 2006, from http://www.fusion-studio.com/soc/shapeshifters.html

LaPin, G., & Bharadwaj, L. (1998). *Pick a gender and get back to us. How cyberspace affects who we are.* Retrieved April 15, 2006, from http://www.fusion-studio.com/soc/pick_a_gender.html

Margolis, J., & Fischer, A. (2003). *Unlocking the clubhouse: Women and computing.* Cambridge, MA: MIT Press.

Marshall, B. L. (2000). *Configuring gender: Explorations in theory and politics.* Ontario, Canada: Broadview Press.

Introduction to Part IV

Popular culture, community, and citizenship are important lines of investigation that bear directly on our understanding of new literacies as key elements in everyday practices. There are seven chapters in this section. The section itself can be divided roughly into three subsections. The first two chapters focus on particular demographic groups: Margaret C. Hagood (Chapter 19) focuses on adolescents, literacy, and popular culture, and Dana J. Wilber (Chapter 20) reviews research on college students, literacy, and technology. The next three chapters focus on literacies and popular practices associated with particular digital technologies and digital "affinity" spaces or groups. Rebecca Ward Black (Chapter 21) analyzes research on anime, manga, and fanfiction writing, Constance A. Steinkuehler (Chapter 22) reviews research in cognition, literacy, and massively multiplayer online games, and Kurt D. Squire (Chapter 23) discusses methodological, theoretical, and pedagogical issues within video games and literacy research. The final two chapters in this section focus on ways in which people can be engaged as active members of local and distributed communities whose interests and projects are mediated in some way by new digital technologies. Angela Thomas (Chapter 24) discusses research and theory with respect to young people building and sustaining cyber-communities. Bertram C. Bruce and Ann P. Bishop (Chapter 25) discuss what research has to say about the role digital technologies can play in grassroots-level, community-based projects.

Collectively, this set of chapters is characterized by sociocultural analyses of people's engagement with popular culture and new forms of social participation mediated by a range of resources and digital technologies. All of the chapters are distinguished by the attention their authors pay to "insider" perspectives on new literacies within a range of social contexts. These insider—or emic—perspectives span adolescents and their engagement with popular culture and digital technologies in their everyday lives, college-age students' literacy and new technology practices, fanfiction writers, video game and massively networked game players, cybercitizens, and participants in community-based initiatives that aim at addressing a range of social and well-being needs. Literacy is defined in terms of social practices or processes by all seven authors; that is, in order to be able to theorize and investigate literacy effectively, these authors argue that literacy cannot be reduced to the study of texts and reading and writing processes alone. New literacies thus are conceptualized in terms of either engagement with new social practices (e.g., *producing* popular culture in multimediated ways, establishing and maintaining social networks and affinity spaces using a range of technologies), or in terms of social process (e.g., collectively solving problems; establishing, resourcing, and participating in spaces framed by affinities).

Hybridizing Theoretical and Methodological Orientations

It is not surprising in one sense that all of these chapters share noticeable similarities in terms of theoretical orientations, researcher stance, and key assumptions about new literacies. The selective processes involved in compiling an edited collection generally mean certain networks of colleagues are tapped into instead of others. What is remarkable, nevertheless, is the broad sweep of fields and disciplines represented collectively by this section. To we four editors, this speaks directly to an emerging trend within new literacies research at the intersection of popular culture, community, and citizenship toward increasingly hybrid theoretical and methodological research orientations. For example, Hagood (Chapter 19) draws on cultural studies, communication and media studies, and sociology. Wilber (Chapter 20) employs concepts and positions from sociology, psycholinguistics, and anthropology in framing her analysis of research. Black (Chapter 21) orients her chapter by means of theoretical terrain provided by the New Literacies Studies and critical discourse theories. Steinkuehler (Chapter 22) locates her own position as a researcher within cognitive science, discourse theory, and sociology. Squire (Chapter 23) melds theory, research, and methods from game studies, educational technology studies, learning sciences, and literacy studies. Thomas (Chapter 24) frames her review of cyber-community research using critical sociology, ethnography, sociolinguistics, cyberfeminist studies, and cultural and media studies. Bruce and Bishop (Chapter 25) draw on ideas and theories from the philosophy of education, social cognition, and critical sociology to frame their review. Clearly, these hybrid theoretical positions are not random pastiches of just any old theories and concepts. Each author provides excellent justification for why existing off-the-shelf theories do not suffice with respect to explaining the phenomena under study. For example, Black explains and demonstrates the limits of literary theory in explaining fanfiction writing practices and affinity spaces. Squire bridges traditional divides between ludolgy and narratology to create a hybrid position on design, narrative, and pleasure that neither field of study on its own can deliver.

In keeping with the authors' own declared hybrid theoretical positions, the research they identify as relevant to their focus in their respective chapters surveys popular culture, community, citizenship, and literacy research conducted from a broad swathe of theoretical positions. Collectively, these include theories from critical cultural studies, cyber feminist theories, theories used in literary, communication and media studies (e.g., film analysis, literary criticism, audience response theory, and narratology), game studies theories (e.g., ludology), social cognition and collective intelligence theories, theories from cultural studies (e.g., gender theories), theories from sociology (e.g., critical theory, space theory, social capital theory, and social network theories), psychology (e.g., psychoanalysis theories), philosophy (e.g., education philosophy and analytic philosophy) semiotic and design theories, sociolinguistic and discourse theories (e.g., Hallideayan systemic functional linguistics, Gee's D/discourse theory, critical discourse analysis), and community inquiry theories, among others. This multiplicity of theoretical orientations adds depth and breadth to the study of literacy, popular culture, community.

This same multiplicity and hybridity can also be found in the research methodologies surveyed in this section. For example, the corpus of studies discussed in this section includes field-based observation designs, large-scale quantitative surveys, case studies, online ethnographies, design principle analysis methods, discourse analysis studies, narrative analysis methods, ludology analysis methods, semiotic analysis, genre and text analysis methods, and literary criticism, to name a few. While some studies surveyed by the authors do include quantitative data collection tools and analysis, the majority of studies referenced in these chapters can be categorized as largely qualitative in nature. That being said, this set of chapters does not argue for a single, unified "best" theory or research methodology for investigating new literacies. Instead, it can be said that the authors of these chapters are in many ways calling for new literacies researchers to be well-versed in a range of theoretical positions and to be familiar with an array of research design types and approaches, so that they can explore what hybrid approaches have to offer with respect to useful interpretations, insights, and suggestions for future research trajectories. A particular strength of this section, then, is the possibilities the chapters sketch for new literacies researchers to "try on" new approaches and theoretical frameworks in their own work.

Common Concepts

A number of concepts recur across the seven chapters in this section. Examining these concepts helps to identify the scope and "shape" of the terrain covered by the authors. For example, the concept of "popular" takes on two distinct—albeit related—meanings in this set of chapters. One conception of "popular" is drawn from a historically long-standing distinction between "high culture" and "mass culture." Mass culture is often set as the polar opposite of high culture and generally refers to mass-produced items of consumption or mass-produced experiences that can be afforded or accessed by the general populace. Historically, mass culture has been disparaged as "low brow" (rather than highbrow) and soporific (rather than analytic and "educated"). The chapters in this section pay attention to this high-culture/

mass-culture distinction only in the sense of championing mass culture as an important resource on which more and more young people are drawing in their lives outside school. Indeed, Hagood's (Chapter 19) analysis of what adolescents do with popular culture, Wilber's (Chapter 20) reminder that college-age students are often early adopters of mass-marketed digital devices which they often turn to purposes unintended by the producers of these items, Black's (Chapter 21) focus on media mixing and writing process, Steinkeuhler's (Chapter 22) analysis of the complexities involved in playing massively multiplayer online games, Squire's (Chapter 23) analysis of the multiple dimensions associated with game design and play, Thomas' (Chapter 24) focus on culture and cultural artifacts in the lived experience of cybercitizens, and Bruce and Bishop's (Chapter 25) keen interest in grassroots community inquiry projects stand as strong arguments that schools are *not* keeping up with the complex, informal learning and literacy practices taking place in community settings and affinity spaces distributed across online and offline contexts.

The second sense of "popular" found in this set of chapters can be described as a focus on what Henry Jenkins (2006a) calls "folk culture" (see also Hagood, Chapter 19) or "participatory culture" (Jenkins, 2006b). For Jenkins (2006a), folk culture practices refer to those "creative skills and artistic traditions [that are] passed down mother to daughter, father to son" (p. 135). These folk practices were largely displaced or pushed underground by mass media and commercial entertainment industries in the 20th century. Collectively, however, the chapters in this section suggest that folk culture is on the rise again, with digital technologies making it possible for *consumers* to be *producers* of culture, too. The authors' emphases on participation, collaboration, and active citizenship mean that passive audience and reception theories, for example, have reached their use-by date when it comes to understanding popular culture. This emphasis also means—as Black (Chapter 21) usefully phrased it in her chapter—that the current attention paid to propositional knowledge in schools may well need to move toward valuing *procedural* knowledge much more (e.g., ways of knowing, doing, writing, and producing artifacts or resources valued by others within everyday contexts).

Space precludes extended discussion of other concepts that appear across all or most of the chapters in this section. That being said, three additional concepts do stand out because they are used by the authors to construct what they variously refer to as "expanded" notions of literacy and what it means to be literate in a digitized and thoroughly social world. These concepts include "identity," "participation," and "collaboration." Collectively, identity is conceptualized by the authors as dynamic and shifting constructions and presentations of self. Steinkuehler (Chapter 22), for example, construes identity as something that is achieved through shared social, virtual, material, and discursive practices. As such, one's identity can change across social contexts, spaces of engagement, and purposes. Thomas (Chapter 24) examines how research shows young people "tinkering" with and exploring identities online through their written fanfictions, their multimedia representations of ideas, their uses of different digital communications media, and their role-plays. In a very real sense, the authors in this section are staking a claim for the importance of taking identity into account in any documentation and analysis of new literacies and culture or community.

As mentioned, another concept in common to all seven chapters in this section is *participation*. That is, the authors underscore the communicative and interactive affordances of digital technologies across people's interests and needs. Squire (Chapter 23), for example, argues that the research on video games suggests strongly that the interactive dimensions of game playing itself, and the participatory practices that often take place online with respect to gamers sharing affinity spaces they have resourced with game playing tips, walkthroughs, game-play strategy analyses, "cheats," back story, help forums, and the like, are reshaping traditional text practices. Bruce and Bishop (Chapter 25) see participation as a central element of community inquiry research and, as such, refer not so much to "new literacies" in their chapter, but to "new community-based literacies." They argue that literacy needs once again to be seen as inherent in the practice of engaged citizenship. For Bruce and Bishop, focusing on people's participation in solving real, situated, and local problems helps redress a text-centric imbalance in literacy research and thinking. Participation is highlighted in the works of the five other authors, such as in contrasting schools' focus on information rather than communication when it comes to using digital technologies.

Another in-common concept within this section is *collaboration*. Collaboration is conceptualized by the authors as a key dimension of learning and community building. That is, the affordances of social digital networks enable people to work together on projects in ways not necessarily possible in the past due to distance, time, age, or language constraints. Wilber (Chapter 20), for example, uses an implied concept of collaboration (and personal agency) to critique dominant research designs in college-level studies of digital technology use that focus on "required participation" in university-sanctioned course content interfaces, in online group work for a grade, and in discussion forums. Steinkuehler (Chapter 22) uses the concept of collaboration in her analysis of research on massively multiplayer online games to explain how players actively co-construct "worlds of meaning" within and beyond the games they play. This collaborative universe is a rich site for learning and for developing a collective intelligence pertaining to a game and playing it well.

To sum up, the conceptions of popular culture, identity, participation, and collaboration employed by the authors in this section collectively disrupt a text-centric view of literacy and advocate for a social, dynamic and complex approach to studying new literacies.

Future Research

In closing, many of the authors pointed to the difficulty they encountered in following the brief we editors gave them with respect to locating research work published primarily in English-language journals. Most of the areas discussed in this section are still relatively embryonic with respect to attracting sustained academic attention, and many scholars in these rapidly developing areas find publishing in journals too delayed and static a process to be of sufficient use to them. These scholars turn to the Internet instead as a place to post their work and to comment on the work of others. This "finding" in itself is an interesting one and may point toward changing conceptions of what it means to "publish" academically in terms of the dissemination and take-up of ideas.

The relative newness of this field also means that the authors of the chapters in this section are able to identify multiple directions in which future research studies fruitfully could move.

These include asking or inferring, for example, the following questions:

- What is the correlation between traditional measures of literacy competency and the competencies required to consume and produce popular culture?
- How can we best build fruitfully on young adults' literacies in preparing them for a world of work and adult life?
- In what ways are young people becoming active global citizens through their online discursive and social practices, which also blend into their offline worlds?
- What is so engaging about these media (e.g., manga) and networked, informal learning sites that youth willingly devote hours to participation in and around them—even in fanfiction writing spaces where participation involves many school-based literacy practices such as composition, editing, and peer review?
- In what ways might the patterns of participation in informal, online learning spaces be linked to larger shifts in our increasingly globalized, networked, and linguistically and culturally diverse societies?
- What are the actual practices (especially, the forms of literacy) that constitute massively multiplayer online games and how do they align (or fail to align) with valued practices elsewhere, including those we purport to foster in schools?
- How do people author new identities within online spaces, what role do these identities play in the transformation of self, and how do they compare to those we make currently available in formal and informal educational environments?
- What are the implications of an interactive medium for literacy and learning?
- How does access to globally distributed communities change traditional notions of meaning making?

- How will a gaming generation react to traditional schooling with its grammar of teacher/text as authority and student as product, when outside school this generation relives historical eras, leads civilizations, conducts forensic investigations, or earns a real wage by buying and selling virtual currencies?
- In what ways do literate activities arise out of experiences in communities (and which include dimensions of morality and social justice)?
- How do people create and live new roles as they appropriate technologies into their lived experiences?
- How might we or even should we bring such understandings (of new literacies) to bear on literacy pedagogy in classrooms?

References

Jenkins, H. (2006a). *Convergence culture: Where old and new media collide.* New York: New York University Press.

Jenkins, H. (2006b). *Fans, bloggers and gamers: Exploring participatory culture.* New York: New York University Press.

moving screen, still images, video games, and cultural artifacts (Cowan, 2004; Gee, 2004; Kress, 2003; Messaris, 2001).

Second, increased daily access to and the preponderance of media in developed countries makes texts of popular culture seemingly unavoidable to people of all ages, as these texts are experienced through ever increasingly available technologies—television, radio, Web sites (including weblogs), magazines, cell phones, and so forth (Kamil, Mosenthal, Pearson, & Barr, 2000; Roberts, Foehr, & Rideout, 2005). Readers' access to a plethora of popular culture texts has increased researchers' interests in ascertaining how users engage popular culture as production and consumption resources (Hagood, 2003).

Third, the acknowledgement that literacy develops not only by cognitive but also by social and cultural factors has provided opportunities to study how literacy is socially situated, culturally constructed, and dependent upon uses of texts within communities (Barton, Hamilton, & Ivanic, 2000; Street, 1999). The sociocultural and sociocognitive influences of literacy in community contexts have helped researchers delve into uses of popular culture as part of community life and, thus, as part of identity construction tied to community. A significant number of literacy researchers are examining readers' in-school and out-of-school popular culture literacies and the relationship between the two within and across contexts as readers' identities shift and change with their text use (Hagood, 2002; Mahari, 2004; Morrell, 2004).

Because identity is context specific, it is not a stable category across time and space (Weedon, 1997). People share and articulate different characteristics of themselves with different groups, and identities shift depending upon context. Therefore, the discursive formations of identities as sociocultural processes must be studied using the cultural forms and social relations within a collective space (Holland, Lachicotte, Skinner, & Cain, 2001). Hall (1996) asserted that identity studies—as multiply situated and context specific—should focus on the process of how and why people identify with other people, ideals, or concepts. Thus, research on identity construction and uses of popular culture includes more than just the process of being; it should document the process of becoming, and in so doing, should connect people's actions to the larger social context.

Research at the intersection of readers' literacy practices, popular culture, and identity construction has revolved around the three aforementioned areas, and studies have been conceptualized around several key questions: (a) What texts do readers access in their day-to-day lives? (b) What media do readers employ in their uses of popular culture? and (c) How do readers read and use popular culture to form and to inform identities? To date, some studies have revealed the quantitative nature of readers' access to popular culture and stratified those texts by media genres, which has provided some grist for responding to the first two questions (e.g., Livingstone & Bovill, 2001; Roberts et al., 2005). Researchers have begun to explore answers to the third question within studies that examine the relations between the production and consumption of readers' uses of texts, especially in relation to identity. The remainder of this chapter examines this research.

In this chapter, I review the postpositivist research on the intersections of literacy, popular culture, and identities. I begin from the stance that embraces multiliteracies (Cope & Kalantzis, 2000) and metalanguages (New London Group, 1996), both of which draw on cognitive, psychological, sociocultural, and linguistic theories and give depth to understanding how texts are read and used within and across contexts. Using a historical approach, I align how researchers have used three overarching theories of popular culture developed over the past 50 years to represent different perspectives of the relation between popular culture and identity construction on readers' acceptance, resistance, and negotiation of texts. These views of popular culture reflect different theories and the range of foci toward which research on identity, youth, and literacy practices of popular culture has tended to apply itself. Within each section, I relate the overall perspectives of popular culture described to the components of the Four Resources Model (Freebody & Luke, 1990; Luke, 1997) to illustrate how literacy research has tended to focus on some but not all of the necessary literacies to be successful readers in the 21st century. Then, I conclude the chapter with several directions for future research.

Tracing Perspectives of Popular Culture and Mapping Identity Construction

The diverse range of images, discourses, narratives, and codes related to race, gender, class, age, and experience found in popular culture influences the creation of socially constructed identities. These past and present experiences influence the positioning individuals take up with texts (McRobbie, 1994). It is through the process of reading and identifying with particular texts that readers form identities. Readers use the array of popular culture texts to stake claims to particular kinds of knowledge, to define identities, to form allegiances, to set boundaries for inclusion and exclusion, and to create alternative ways of being. Popular culture texts, therefore, are tools for understanding individual and group identities and dynamics and are formed through production and consumption of texts.

For decades, cultural theorists have argued that people's constructions and understandings of their worlds may be studied through popular culture (Fiske, 1989; Turner, 1996; Willis, 1978). But views and theories of popular culture, much like *text, reading,* and *literacy,* are multiplicitous. These perspectives conflict in terms of three areas: (a) views of media and audiences' control of knowledge, power, and pleasures in popular culture, (b) views of text circulation through modes of production and consumption, and (c) readers' formations of identity through their uses of popular culture. A closer examination of popular culture characterized as mass culture, folk culture, and everyday of reading outside of higher education (Lankshear & Knobel, 2003; Sefton-Green, 2000). Schools, for example, teach literacy in the same ways it has been taught for the past century, focusing primarily on the instruction of print-based reading mastery derived from a print-based curriculum (Arthur, 2005; Comber, 2000; Marsh & Millard, 2006; Sefton-Green, 1998).

Furthermore, literacy researchers' analyses of the role that popular culture plays in the formation of readers' identities are often unrealized by larger educational communities. Some research has shown that students' literacy resources related to popular culture are invisible to or avoided by teachers and disconnected from the curriculum (Hagood, 2002). When this happens, students' literate identities associated with those resources are not perceived as valuable or appropriate for school-based learning (Comber, Badger, Nixon, & Pitt, 2002). Or teachers often see the use of popular culture in opposition to their responsibilities to teach students traditional, print-based literacy (Lambirth, 2003). Even when educators recognize popular culture texts as valid and relevant to students' personal identities (Mahar, 2003), teachers frequently shy away from using popular culture texts in literacy instruction (Finders, 2000; Marsh, 2006; Marsh & Millard, 2001; Xu, 2004), thus continuing the split between in-school and out-of-school literacies (Gallego & Hollingsworth, 2000). Researchers' documentation of teachers' views of popular culture from a mass culture perspective have shown that teachers often perceive that students passively accept stereotypical gender identities such as helpless princesses and violent male superheroes because educators see these story lines shape children's identities during sociodramatic play (Arthur, 2005). The framework of viewing identities as part of mass culture is so strong that teachers habitually do not see outside it to form other interpretations (Tobin, 2000).

Parents' and children's ideas about popular culture regularly mirror teachers' perspectives. Expanded definitions of reading that include popular culture texts are likely to be considered outside of both adult and youth perceptions of what counts as real literacy (Alvermann et al., 2007). Furthermore, parents continue to be concerned about the negative identity effects of what their children might learn from using popular culture. Concerns about violent behavior (Marsh & Thompson, 2001) and an overemphasis on consumerism (Arthur, 2005) continue to influence parents' perspectives on youngsters' uses of popular culture and their identity formation.

Findings from these studies on teachers', parents', and students' views of popular culture relate to three components of mass culture: (a) that the produced meaning of popular culture is more powerful and influential than the readers' uses of text, (b) that popular culture is too mundane to be included in the high culture of school literacies, and (c) that popular culture does not address the most salient components of school literacies, which are print based in nature. In summary, research that views popular culture as mass culture has shown that critics of popular culture value teaching readers how to read text as forms of print, desiring code breaking over any other literate resource. Readers must become strong code breakers, able to read text for its intended meaning produced for consumption. This view forms the basis of many media literacy programs that focus predominantly on the ability to read media based upon texts' implied messages related to identities.

Popular Culture as Folk Culture

Unlike the top-down model of mass culture that produces popular meaning for the people and delineates culture along class lines, a *folk culture* perspective on popular culture celebrates a bottom-up, authentic popular culture of the people (Storey, 1998). Begun in the 1960s by British Cultural Studies in response to mass cultural views of popular culture, research from a folk cultural view examines how different social groups construct alternate uses of popular culture that differ from, and perhaps resist, the dominant, mainstream views in and uses of texts. A folk culture view of popular culture emphasizes audiences' appropriations of media-produced texts and users' text creations to satisfy their own purposes. Audiences' everyday production practices—their "production-in-use"—demonstrate how readers work outside the mass culture perspective of holistic consumption (Fiske, 1989; Storey, 1996).

Contrary to the view of mass culture that forces particular readings onto audiences and produces negative effects, a theory of popular culture as folk culture views the audience as those who hold power and who are knowledgeable about text uses. Audiences use their power to actively construct meanings, to produce new uses of texts, and to form new identities through their text uses.

This form of literacy research highlights readers' uses of texts that extend beyond passive consumption of media. Identity construction from a folk culture standpoint is active and group defined. Audiences create meanings and uses from the text and form identities that are potentially different from and unlike those presented in the text. This view of the impact of audience on popular culture for identity construction has influenced the investigations of researchers interested in subcultural groups' text uses. Researchers working from this perspective acknowledge pleasure in texts and focus their study on how readers construct group identities through the transformation of texts and practices set forth by the culture industry (Buckingham, 1991). Research in this area seeks to document and analyze how users give meaning to texts within a particular culture.

Trying to locate themselves apart from others, youth orient themselves toward popular culture to express themselves and to find commonalities with peers. Often, readers manipulate shared interests to create new meanings of texts reflected in identities ascribed to the text by a group. Appropriating popular culture for their own uses, readers form affinity groups (Gee, 2002), youth cultures, and allegiances that situate them within and apart from other peers and age groups (Valentine, Skelton, & Chambers, 1998). Individuals form identities for themselves from nuanced meanings and pleasures in texts that are in agreement with or in resistance to the text, or they may form wholly new identities that reflect neither agreement nor resistance. Speaking to this point, Buckingham and Sefton-Green (1994) claimed, "In sharing what [youth] read, readers also define themselves … . It is through these processes that young people develop their cultural competencies as readers, while simultaneously constructing identities for themselves" (p. 31).

Several studies have investigated the ways readers use popular culture as a framework to form their own cultures and to negotiate the intricacies of inclusions and exclusions based upon their readings and interpretations of texts. According to Massey (1998), a "hybrid culture" is not "a closed system of social relations but a particular articulation of contacts and influences drawn form a variety of places scattered, according to power relations, fashion and habit" (p. 124). Research from this perspective documents how readers use popular culture to locate meaning, to construct individual and group identity, and to define that identity within a larger landscape of peer relations.

Vasquez (2003), for example, through observation and interviews over 5 years, documented Curtis's uses of Pokémon. He collected Pokémon cards, played the Pokémon game, and formed a Pokémon club with several of his friends. After some time spent studying and playing the commercially created game, Curtis and his friends used the cards' template and created their own cards, which held greater power than the manufactured cards. These cards became part of the game within their club and were traded along with the manufactured cards. Although Curtis and his buddies consumed Pokémon cards as part of mass culture, their folk culture uses of the cards gave them the power to change the game according to their rules and standards formed in the Pokémon club. Vasquez noted that she "was not arguing that everything learned from playing Pokémon is good" (p. 125). Rather, she focused on the pleasurable and powerful literacies Curtis formed from Pokémon so as to understand both the Pokémon community and the connections between identity and literacy.

Similarly, Mahar (2003) used a folk cultural perspective to ascertain how middle school students used Japanese anime as literacy resources in school to find pleasure in their multiliteracy practices. As a *kopai,* Mahar welcomed the students' expertise to teach her the intricacies of anime, which included video game and card playing; graphic novel, comic, and fanfic writing; anime drawing; and much print-based reading of favorite Internet Web sites and magazines. As part of her observational and informal interview study of students' out-of-school literacies used for in-school practices (e.g., writing papers), Mahar documented their rich and complex literacies and associated identities as being *senpais:* They found pleasure in being more knowledgeable authorities of anime texts during in-school lunch anime group that a group of students formed in her classroom. As she learned about anime from the students, she learned about the genre (both artistic and writing) and came to appreciate how her students, as anime users, created identities as readers and writers—producing stories, artwork, or games. From her newfound appreciation of students' identities as anime experts, she welcomed their uses of anime in her English class as she came to see the complementary skills developed across in-school and out-of-school literacies.

Studying the relation between popular culture and identity formed from lowriding (the practices associated with a particular form of customizing cars), Cowan (2004) explored Latino identities and relations to gangs and cholos. Using interviews as a primary form of data gathering, Cowan met with custom builders of lowriders to learn about the art and culture of lowrider car building. Then, using artwork produced by students he taught in a summer school program, Cowan interviewed Latino youth and recorded their reflections on the social world of lowriders, which was depicted in the drawings. He demonstrated that uses and meanings of texts are bound to discourse communities. Meanings of lowriding texts, which are often associated with gang membership and violence in mainstream communities unassociated with Latino life, are over-generalized and perpetuate negative stereotypes of Latino youth. Cowan's research assisted in his own growing knowledge of a discourse community about which he knew little, and what little he knew had been based on stereotypes—in short, on his own perceptions of lowriding from a mass cultural perspective. Research from a folk cultural perspective respects the discourse communities' uses and meanings of texts. This perspective-taking allowed the author to understand the Latino identities associated with text uses of lowriding, not from a mass cultural perspective but from one that valued the folk cultural uses of lowriding in the Latino community. Aesthetic appreciation for the visual literacies of this community forced the author to question his own assumptions and to reflect upon the stereotypes related to lowriding culture. His analysis documented how someone outside the subculture could well misunderstand the popular culture practices of and identities formed from association with lowriding.

Other researchers have investigated how readers use popular culture to negotiate fantasy and real life experiences as outlets for discovering alternative identity constructions. Imagining oneself as someone else by identification with characters in popular culture texts highlights the desires that readers have to form multiple identities and recognizes the pleasures that folk cultural perspectives bring to readers' engagement with text. Through creations of multiple selves, readers escape the boundaries of lived realities and explore new territories in textual spaces beyond what is available to them in their daily lives.

Crafting multiple selves, defined as "a convergence of past experiences and future visions that influence current activity" (Fisherkeller, 1997, p. 484), shows how youth envision identities that exceed the borders of the identities offered to them in their own cultural surroundings and that affect their current and future perceptions of themselves. For example, Fisherkeller (1997) found that youth analyze television characters to imagine desired identities different from the identities exhibited in their home, peer, and school lives.

Fisherkeller (1997) argued that youth implemented "imaginative strategies" learned and developed in identity creations to cope with dilemmas in daily lives and to envision different realities. For example, strong and independent female television characters became girls' role models, showing them how to dress and act and providing them with examples of alternative female lifestyles they considered viable for the future. In this way, readers crafted possible identities that positioned them outside of the narrow construction of identity felt within the local culture.

Fisherkeller (1997) also found that creations of multiple selves assisted youth in managing current life experiences. Like children in other studies who fashioned selves from their affinity for superheroes (Dyson, 1996, 2003) or from their readings of romance novels (Cherland, 1994; Christian-Smith, 1993), Fisherkeller found that youth used traits they identified and valued in popular culture that they knew were fictitious to create identities to cope with real difficulties in their lives, such as a relocation to a new neighborhood. Reading and interpreting characters bolstered youth's desires to enact aspects of the characters lives.

Pahl (2005) also found that young children used popular culture to insert themselves into and to create spaces for identity work in their play of video gaming. In this observational research on youngsters uses of video games, Pahl showed how, as gamers, the children drew on familiar characters and story lines in their play and inserted their personal identities into the game. Their abilities to insert themselves into the texts gave them agency in a figured world. The games allowed the children to play with identity and to refashion identity through avatars (imaginary characters created within the playing of video games). Pahl noted that gaming "allows children a space to shift and to improvise on identity" (p. 129).

Reading popular culture texts as a form of folk culture provides opportunities to challenge the status quo and to assert voices that resist particular identities. In this way, popular culture is not a passive acceptance of what is read; rather, it is an active engagement of personal meaning making. A folk cultural view of research on popular culture moves beyond Freebody and Luke's (1990) "code breaking" resource of reading as consumption of text based on media production of text and into readers' productions of text meaning. Research on uses of text from a folk cultural perspective illustrates readers' abilities to be both "text participants" and "text users" according to the Four Resources Model. As text participants, readers participate in the meaning making of text. They understand how to use texts according to a particular system or culture and how texts change according to different community standards and uses, as illustrated in Vasquez (2003) and Cowan's (2004) work. Readers as "text users" know when and how to use texts functionally with appropriate identities for various cultural and social functions as with the students in Mahar's (2003) class who demonstrated for her how identities shifted in their production of anime and in Fisherkeller's (1997) work. Research on popular culture from a folk cultural perspective illustrates how readers form identities as text participants and text users that reflect the cultural values and models that resonate with their created identities.

Popular Culture as Everyday Culture

Popular culture is also defined as everyday culture. This perspective, developed out of the work of the Contemporary Centre for Culture, locates popular culture in the study of everyday life. Williams (1976) explained that its study involves interrogating relations of the constant give and take between media and audiences' production and consumption of popular culture. Literacy researchers who examine popular culture as everyday culture attend to both media and audience text uses in order to understand readers' multiplicitous and contextualized identities formed within the production and consumption of popular culture. Such research examines the delicate balance of the circulation of knowledge, power, and pleasure related to identities within the circuit of production and consumption of texts.

The polysemic nature of popular culture as everyday culture ensures that readers may interpret and use texts differently and derive various pleasures from texts dependent upon the context. Walkerdine (1997) explained that audiences' meaning making of texts is neither wholly resistant nor fully duped, but rather individual and group uses of texts combine both consumption and production. Thus, audiences may at times look like cultural dupes who passively accept the ideologies of the popular culture texts, while at other times audiences may produce novel readings from popular culture texts (Buckingham, 1998).

By highlighting audiences' negotiations of consumption and production of popular culture within different contexts, researchers can examine both media's power to control cultural markets' access to products and audiences' power to choose whether or not to give value to or to form uses for popular culture. Furthermore, research on identity formation using the perception of popular culture as everyday culture situates the social and political discourses of how readers' "literacy practices shape their identities, the way in which already formed identities limit to some extent the kinds of literacy practices which they take up and the intense dialectic between self and others" (Marsh, 2005, p. 33).

Because engagement in and with popular culture texts is an ongoing social practice, research on readers' uses of texts as everyday life explores temporary, hybrid identities that shift and change by context. Readers sometimes use popular culture texts to work out contradictions between identities they see portrayed in texts and ones they have constructed in other aspects of their lives. This kind of research studies readers' understanding that texts are not neutral, that particular points of view privilege some while silencing other voices, and that readers can both critique and redesign texts in contextually significant ways.

Interrelations of popular culture as everyday culture and identity formation are found in several studies that highlight categorical identities such as ethnicity, race, and gender. Mahiri (2004) examined how five urban adolescents' used street scripts to make sense of their urban identities. Using rap and hip-hop popular culture, these African American youths created texts (e.g., documentaries, screenplays, rap lyrics, poetry, and videos) that demonstrated their awareness of urban life. Explorations of racial stereotyping as well as drug use, gang violence, and family hardship were prevalent themes and showed how these adolescents consumed and produced texts as both expressions of and responses to their urban lives. For example, Reggie demonstrated critical literacy through his creation and production of *Hiphopumentary,* a hip-hop documentary. Voice over, images, and symbolism included in the text show both his visual literacy capabilities and his understanding of political, economic, and aesthetic qualities of hip-hop music. Similarly, Keisha's screenplay, *Jus' Living,* highlights themes of the social world of urban life to explore issues of race, class, and gender. Keisha displays through her writing an exploration and critique of identities associated with day-to-day gang life.

Hagood's (2005) research on the everyday uses of popular culture for identity construction illustrates how adolescent boys also used popular culture and cultural norms in society as a way to play with expected gendered identities. Following these two boys in various in-school and out-of-school contexts, she documented how they used their popular culture interests to ascertain and ultimately to question acceptable gendered, male identities tied to their ethnicities. A, an immigrant to Australia from China, excelled in all sports in school and worked diligently to maintain that status of an athletic boy, which was a highly prized identity in Australia. Tommy, an Australian native, who was often excluded from playing sports on the oval during morning tea due to his small stature and diminutive and effeminate features, was further ostracized by his peers because of his interest in Japanese anime. Ultimately, the two boys used their popular culture literacies of athleticism and anime to question the stereotypical male identities and to open up spaces for constructing new identities that cut across race, ethnicity, and gender.

In a different study on transnational culture, Lam (2004) found that a Chinese adolescent boy's uses of reading of comic books illustrated the situated nature of literacy, which enabled the boy to construct alternative subject positions and identities. Willis, a 15-year-old who migrated to the Western United States from Hong Kong, created a "third space" through his reading of Japanese comic books translated into Chinese. By reading these texts, he functioned outside other menial and subordinate identities he felt as an immigrant student in school and immigrant minority in his community. Lam found that the comics that Willis used positioned him differently and offered different identities to him. From an identity of betweenness, Willis reflected on other identities in his life including his critique of identities in Hong Kong and in the United States. From this perspective, Lam illustrated how "people actively mobilize their diverse sources of identification to resist subordination, and where new subject positions emerge out of cross-cultural exchange and the negotiation of difference" in their uses of popular culture of everyday life (p. 95).

Some research on identity and popular culture has illustrated how readers use parody, play, and performativity with text to analyze, question, and potentially transform identities. Lewis (1998) documented how young boys tried on various male constructs of socially constituted gendered identity in a discussion of horror texts. Lewis explained that, within a masculinist horror genre, only two kinds of male characters are present: violent and vengeful males or strong and protective ones. The rigidity of character identities available led Lewis to speculate that boys are left little room for exploring aspects of their own fears elicited from horror texts and of male identities that exhibit emotions that exceeded feelings of violence or courage. To make room for examination of stereotypical male identities hailed in this popular culture genre, Lewis argued that the boys used parody to playfully combine dangerous and harmless characters and violent characters with themselves to explore their own feelings of fear. In Lewis's observations, the all-male audience questioned the constructed meaning of a text to include a place for exploration of a fearful male identity, albeit through play and parody. Others have also found that audiences' interaction using social performances of text assists in inquiring into established identities and societal norms (Grace & Tobin, 1997; Urquhart, 1996).

Marsh's research has also studied performativity in uses of popular culture in early childhood. In one such study, Marsh (2000) illustrated how 6- and 7-year-old girls explored agency and autonomy when they actively positioned themselves as heroic females in the sociodramatic play center focused on superheroes. In their play, they actively resisted taken-for-granted, stereotypical female identities: the helpless beauty and the evil woman. Instead, they were assertive female superheroes, choosing not to emulate male superheroes. In a different study of young children's home uses of popular culture, Marsh (2005) found that children used popular culture texts and narratives to perform various identities. Children used popular culture to perform gendered identities. These performances both replicated and resisted traditional gendered identities. Marsh also documented how parents' inclusion of popular culture and media texts in the home allowed children to perform identities of competent media users.

Readers use popular culture as everyday culture to negotiate identity, combining interests in a particular popular culture genre with desires to be part of a particular peer group. Chandler-Olcott and Mahar (2003) and Lewis and Fabos (2000) documented the social practices of online communication between adolescent girls and the peer group of which they desired to be a part. Chandler-Olcott and Mahar found that girls not only used the Internet to become part of an affinity group to learn how to draw particular anime or to create Web pages, but once they were members, they used their identities to shape the online community, moving beyond mass culture and into uses of popular culture as everyday culture. Similarly, Lewis and Fabos studied adolescent girls and their friends' uses of instant messaging (IMing). The girls used IMing to learn about appropriate IM identities and to establish a peer network. By tracking and analyzing the flow and form of conversations, the girls could shift their identities to engage in different IM groups simultaneously.

For instance, the girls monitored and analyzed the verbiage and slang used in IM conversation before joining them. They learned from this activity that before speaking online, they had to understand the appropriate discourse to use, and the discourse changed by groups of IM users. Learning how to alter their identities by conversation allowed them to juggle and manipulate multiple conversations simultaneously. Engagement in many conversations afforded them membership in the group of IM users. The more IM conversation they managed, the more popular they felt themselves to be among the group.

Researchers' examination of popular culture as everyday culture reveals readers' uses of text as they are text analysts. According to Freebody and Luke (1990), text analysts scrutinize and transform texts as they see fit, understanding that texts represent a particular point of view. In their uses of popular culture, readers, as text analysts, consume and produce texts to work within their identities. They realize, albeit sometimes tacitly without an associated metalanguage for their efforts, that their uses of texts convey particular ideas about identities and influence others in certain ways. Therefore, although research on popular culture as everyday culture may attend to "text analysis," that analysis might often more likely fall into readers "text use" and/or "text participation."

Future Directions for Research on Popular Culture and Identities

I return here to the questions posed at the beginning of this chapter, and discuss what we know about the answers from a historical framework of popular culture, and then address the gaps needed to be addressed in future research through both questions to be posed and methodologies to be used.

What Texts Do Readers Access in Their Day-to-Day Lives?

Though we understand from survey data the kinds of media readers employ in their uses of popular culture, implicit within these questions is the assumption of a broadened notion of text, one that includes print, semiotic, and oral. Immersed now in the 21st century, what continues to be unclear is the answer to a more fundamental question: How do *readers* define *text* and *reading* in the 21st century? And relatedly, how do readers define popular culture? Specifically, how do teachers, parents, and students define these terms both for themselves and for others? Perhaps the field of literacy has expanded its definitions of text, reading, and literacy to include both print and nonprint texts inclusive of popular culture based upon theories of multiliteracies and studies in new literacies, but the explicit examinations and uses of text, reading, and popular culture as they are defined and used by teachers, parents, and students across in-school and out-of-school settings has not been undertaken. Do readers who have been schooled in traditional forms and definitions of print-based literacy embrace a broadened definition and use of text in their day-to-day lives? And do readers (teachers, parents, children alike) perceive their readings of nonprint texts as a form of reading at all? And, finally, how do students' definitions of reading and of texts align with their definitions of popular culture, and how do these definitions align with their perceptions of themselves as readers in the 21st century? Without answers to these questions, the field of literacy research does not know the impact of the practices of multiliteracies in the 21st century. Working from different definitions and uses of these terms between the researcher and the participants affects the overall study.

Relatedly, not only does the field need a large-scale study to determine teachers, parents, and students' definitions of text and reading and their related literacy practices, but researchers must also formulate studies to understand the kinds of popular culture that teachers and parents use to construct their own identities. Studies that examine how adults use popular culture in their own lives will assist in opening up the ways that popular culture is explored with students. These studies need to be tied to teachers' approaches to students' popular culture in their classroom instruction, and they will begin to answer some questions about the intergenerational understandings and uses of popular culture.

What Media Do Readers Employ in Their Uses of Popular Culture?

Much remains to be explored in terms of understanding the relations between new literacies and traditional forms of reading (Coiro, 2005). Specifically, what is the relation between reading practices of new literacies and those of popular culture? What are the relations between traditional reading strategies and practices and those of popular culture? Which literacy strategies are most conducive for working with popular culture and why? And what is the correlation between traditional measures of literacy competency and the competencies required to consume and produce popular culture? These questions lend themselves to study through new literacies methodologies such as design work (Cope & Kalantzis, 2000), the pedagogy of multiliteracies

Deleuze, G., & Guattari, F. (1987). *A thousand plateaus: Capitalism and schizophrenia* (B. Massumi, Trans.). Minneapolis: University of Minnesota Press. (Original work published 1980.)

Dimitriadis, G. (2001). "In the clique": Popular culture, constructions of place, and the everyday lives of urban youth. *Anthropology & Education Quarterly, 32*(1), 29–51.

Dyson, A. H. (1996). Cultural constellations and childhood identities: On Greek gods, cartoon heroes, and the social lives of schoolchildren. *Harvard Educational Review, 66*(3), 471–495.

Dyson, A. H. (1997). *Writing superheroes: Contemporary childhood, popular culture, and classroom literacy.* New York: Teachers College Press.

Dyson, A. H. (2003). Popular literacies and "all" children: Rethinking literacy development for contemporary childhoods. *Language Arts, 81,* 100–109.

Finders, M. (1996). Queens and teen 'zines: Early adolescent females reading their way toward adulthood. *Anthropology and Education Quarterly, 27*(1), 71–89.

Finders, M. (2000). "Gotta be worse": Negotiating the pleasurable and the popular. *Journal of Adolescent and Adult Literacy, 44*(2), 146–149.

Fisherkeller, J. (1997). Everyday learning about identities among young adolescents in television culture. *Anthropology and Education Quarterly, 28*(4), 467–492.

Fiske, J. (1989). *Understanding popular culture.* Boston: Unwin Hyman.

Flood, J., & Lapp, D. (1995). Broadening the lens: Toward an expanded conceptualization of literacy. In K. A. Hinchman, D. J. Leu, & C. K. Kinzer (Eds.), *Perspectives on literacy research and practices* (pp. 1–16). Chicago: National Reading Conference.

Freebody, P., & Luke, A. (1990). Literacies programs: Debates and demands in cultural context. *Prospect: Australian Journal of TESOL, 5*(7), 7–16.

Gallego, M., & Hollingsworth, S. (2000). *What counts as literacy: Challenging the school standard.* New York: Teachers College Press.

Gee, J. P. (1996). *Social linguistics and literacies: Ideology in discourse* (2nd ed.). London: Taylor & Francis.

Gee, J. P. (2002). Reading as situated language: A sociocognitive perspective. *Journal of Adolescent and Adult Literacy, 44,* 714–725.

Gee, J. P. (2004). *What video games have to teach us about learning and literacy.* New York: Palgrave Macmillan.

Gordon, D., Underwood, A., Wiengarten, T., & Figueroa, A. (1999, May 10). The secret life of teens. *Newsweek,* 45–50.

Grace, D. J., & Tobin, J. (1997). Carnival in the classroom: Elementary students making videos. In J. Tobin (Ed.), *Making a place for pleasure in early childhood education* (pp. 159–187). New Haven, CT: Yale University Press.

Hagood, M. C. (2001). Media literacies: Varied but distinguishable. In J. Hoffman, D. Schallert, C. Fairbanks, J. Worthy, & B. Maloch (Eds.), *National Reading Conference yearbook* (pp. 248–261). Chicago: National Reading Conference.

Hagood, M. C. (2002). Critical literacy for whom? *Reading Research and Instruction, 41*(3), 247–266.

Hagood, M. C. (2003). New media and online literacies: No age left behind. *Reading Research Quarterly, 38*(3), 386–413.

Hagood, M. C. (2005). Bodily pleasures and/as the text. *English Teaching: Practice and Critique.* Retrieved May 14, 2006, from http://education.waikato.ac.nz/journal/english_journal/view.php?article=true&id=78

Hall, S. (1996). Introduction: Who needs identity? In S. Hall & P. du Gay (Eds.), *Questions of cultural identity* (pp. 1–17). London: Sage.

Heath, S. B. (1991). The sense of being literate: Historical and cross cultural features. In R. Barr, M. L. Kamil, P. B. Mosenthal, & P. D. Pearson (Eds.), *Handbook of reading research* (Vol 2., pp. 3–25). New York: Longman.

Hirsch, E. D. (1988). *Cultural literacy: What every American needs to know.* New York: Vintage Books.

Holland, D., Lachicotte, D., Skinner, D., & Cain, C. (2001). *Identity and agency in cultural worlds*. Cambridge, MA: Harvard University Press.

Horkheimer, M., & Adorno, T. (1999). *Dialectic of enlightenment* (J. Cumming, Trans.). New York: Continuum. (Original work published 1972.)

Kamil, M., Mosenthal, P., Pearson, P. D., & Barr, R. (2000). Preface. In M. Kamil, P. Mosenthal, P. D. Pearson, & R. Barr (Eds.), *Handbook of reading research* (Vol. 3, pp. ix–xiv). Mahwah, NJ: Lawrence Erlbaum Associates.

Knobel, M. (2006). Technokids, koala trouble and Pokémon: Literacy, new technologies, and popular culture in children's everyday lives. In J. Marsh & E. Millard (Eds.), *Popular literacies, childhood, and schooling* (pp. 11–28). New York: Routledge.

Kress, G. (2003). *Literacy in the new media age*. New York: Routledge.

Lam, W. S. E. (2004). Border discourses and identities in transnational youth culture. In J. Mahiri (Ed.), *What they don't learn in school* (pp. 79–98). New York: Peter Lang.

Lambirth, A. (2003). "They get enough of that at home": Understanding aversion to popular culture. *Reading, 37*(1), 9–13.

Lankshear, C., & Knobel, M. (2003). *New literacies: Changing knowledge and classroom learning*. London: Open University Press.

Lefebevre, H. (1991). *The production of space*. Cambridge, MA: Blackwell.

Lewis, C. (1998). Rock 'n' roll and horror stories: Students, teachers, and popular culture. *Journal of Adolescent and Adult Literacy, 42*(2), 116–120.

Lewis, C., & Fabos, B. (2000). But will it work in the heartland? A response and illustration. *Journal of Adolescent and Adult Literacy, 43*, 462–469.

Livingstone, S., & Bovill, M. (Eds.). (2001). *Children and their changing media environment: A European comparative study*. Hillsdale, NJ: Lawrence Erlbaum Associates.

Lonsdale, M., & McCurry, D. (2004). *Literacy in the new millennium*. Adelaide, South Australia: Department of Education, Science, and Training.

Luke, C. (1991). Media and popular culture in education and society. *Teaching Education, 5*(2), 41–56.

Luke, A. (1997). When basic skills and information processing just aren't enough: Rethinking reading in new times. *Teachers College Record, 97*, 95–115.

Mahar, D. (2003). Bringing the outside in: One teacher's ride on the anime highway. *Language Arts, 81*, 110–117.

Mahiri, J. (Ed.). (2004). *What they don't learn in school: Literacy in the lives of urban youth*. New York: Peter Lang.

Marsh, J. (2000). "But I want to fly too!": Girls and superhero play in the infant classroom. *Gender and Education, 12*(2), 209–220.

Marsh, J. (2005). Ritual, performance, and identity construction. In J. Marsh (Ed.), *Popular culture, new media, and digital literacy in early childhood* (pp. 28–50). New York: Routledge Falmer.

Marsh, J. (2006). Tightropes, tactics, and taboos: Pre-service teachers' beliefs and practices in relation to popular culture and literacy. In J. Marsh & E. Millard (Eds.), *Popular literacies, childhood and schooling* (pp. 179–199). New York: Routledge.

Marsh, J., & Millard, E. (2001). *Literacy and popular culture: Using children's culture in the classroom*. London: Paul Chapman Educational Publishing.

Marsh, J., & Millard, E. (2006). *Popular literacies, childhood, and schooling*. New York: Routledge.

Marsh, J., & Thompson, P. (2001). Parental involvement in literacy development: Using media texts. *Journal of Research in Reading, 24*(3), 266–278.

Massey, D. (1998). The spatial construction of youth cultures. In T. Skelton & G. Valentine (Eds.), *Cool places: Geographies of youth cultures* (pp. 121–129). London: Routledge.

McRobbie, A. (1994). *Postmodernism and popular culture*. New York: Routledge.

Messaris, P. (2001, February). New literacies in action: Visual education. *Reading Online, 4*(7). Retrieved July 25, 2005, from http://www.readingonline.org/newliteracies/lit_index.asp?HREF=/newliteracies/action/messaris/index.html

CHAPTER 20

College Students and New Literacy Practices

DANA J. WILBER

MONTCLAIR STATE UNIVERSITY, USA

Introduction

Surprisingly, the new literacy practices of college-age students comprise a much underresearched area, despite a growing interest in new literacy research and the early and heavy uptake of new digital technologies within higher education settings from the 1960s onward. This absence in the research literature is perhaps even all the more surprising given that college-age students, defined here as those young people aged 17 to 25 years, are regarded widely as likely to be the "first adopters" and users of many new digital technologies. High-profile digital technology researchers like Steve Jones, for example, call for a much more sustained research focus on college-age students, because this demographic has long played an important role in shaping how new technologies are taken up, changed, modified, and reworked to suit a range of social and literacy practices (Madden & Jones, 2002; see also, Howe & Strauss, 2000; Rheingold, 2002). As such, this demographic is clearly worth paying attention to and can offer researchers and educators valuable insights into future trends and patterns of new technology development and use.

The published research currently found at the intersection of college-age students and new technologies seems to fall into two main bodies of work: (a) evaluative studies concerning the effective integration of digital technology across a university and/or as a component of campus life (e.g., Jones, 2003; Dutt-Doner & Powers, 2000; Gustafson & Kors, 2004; Landow, 2002; Shuchat Shaw & Giacquinta, 2000; Yellowlees Douglas, 2002); and (b) studies that document and evaluate the integration of a particular digital technology or digital interface function into a course at the college level (e.g., Abrams, 2003; Hara, Bonk, & Angeli, 2000; Miall & Dobson, 2001; Reed, 1990; Smith, Coldwell, Smith, & Murphy, 2005; Wells, 2000). The bulk of both of these research strands or trajectories has focused mainly on student attitudes toward digital technologies encountered in their coursework, rates of participation in online contexts associated with coursework (e.g., as measured by quantity of posts to a discussion boards), or the "effectiveness" of new technology inclusion in terms of student perceptions of enhanced course quality or increased performance outcomes.

Little of this research, however, focuses on the systematic study of college students' *everyday literacy practices* involving digital technologies. This contrasts markedly with the now sizable and growing amount of research that has a sociocultural orientation and focuses on the new literacy and technology practices of adolescents and children in a range of contexts (see, for example, chapters by Black, Hagood, and Merchant in this volume). Therefore, this chapter maps out a possible research agenda for investigating college-aged students' literacy and digital technology practices within a range of contexts, including a variety of types of colleges and universities. It begins with a discussion of the ways in which sociocultural theories of literacy and technology use provide a fruitful theoretical orientation that is for all intents and purposes missing from the current research literature within this focus area. This discussion is followed by a general overview and analysis of the current state of this research terrain. This overview comprises three sections: (a) college-age students and their "everyday" digital technology practices, (b) college-age students and their digital technology practices within "formal learning" contexts associated with their college studies, and (c) college-age students and their literacy practices in general with a view to outlining possible future research trajectories that explicitly involve a focus on college-age students and their new literacy practices involving digital technologies.

Of course, drawing a distinction between college students' "personal" or "everyday" lives and their "formal-learning" courses is overly simplistic in spatial terms. There is no clear distinction when documenting what occurs where and when (e.g., is a college student blogging on his or her personal blog an idea generated out of an in-class discussion practicing a personal literacy or a formal-learning literacy?). Nevertheless, the distinction does offer a useful heuristic for examining existing literature. For example, this distinction can help us see that much of the existing research is too often limited in scope and focused too closely on professors, pedagogy, and measurable learning outcomes, rather than on the emic perspective of students as expert, adaptive users. Therefore, this chapter will call for a new research agenda for grounded, mixed-method research to capture new literacies from the perspectives of users whose practices have an immediate and powerful impact upon their literate lives.

Defining the Demographic

For the purposes of drawing boundaries, albeit loosely, around the scope of this review, "college-age students" is taken to mean those young people aged between 17 and 25 years. Using age to define a particular cohort of young people is always problematic (Alvermann, 2002), and is especially so in this case since not all young people aged 17 to 25 years enroll in formal postsecondary education, and not all students enrolled in these institutions are 17 to 25 years old. Even the term *college* is difficult to pin down with any certainty, because it can include a wide range of education institutions such as technical colleges, community colleges, universities, and institutes. While I use the term *college-age students* throughout this chapter, I do not mean college to denote a single type of educational institution, but rather a range of types of schools, students, and technological practices.

Boundaries are nevertheless needed in any report on the current state of a certain body of literature, and in this chapter, age helped in locating as wide a range of studies as possible by including those studies not necessarily conducted on a college campus but that nevertheless investigated a particular demographic known for its early adoption of new digital technologies in their everyday lives. Therefore, this chapter draws on studies concerning both young people ages 17 to 25 *and* college students. The first group focuses on an age demographic and includes investigations of people between the ages of 17 and 25 years where the studies themselves do not specify which participants were college students. The second group includes students attending some kind of postsecondary school where the study does not specify an age range. This relative looseness helps to maximize the number of the studies that can be counted as falling within the scope of this chapter.

The specific target demographic for this chapter was born between 1983 and 1987. As a point of reference, the Internet first began to be used in compulsory schooling in developed countries from roughly 1995 onward (cf., Tapscott, 1998; Suoranta & Lehtimaki, 2004), when these young people were 7 to 13 years old. Outside of school, digital technology often has been a part of their lives since the very beginning, especially in the case of young people from White, middle-class homes. Many of these young people have no memories of life without digital technologies. Of course, the young people within this demographic are not a homogenous group; they include a wide variety of cultural backgrounds, races, ages, and classes as well as experiences with digital technologies. Not all current college students have had the same access to technologies, and college well may be their first opportunity to develop the new literacies demonstrated by their peers. In addition, as already mentioned, these new literacies practices may be complex and cutting-edge indeed. Jones (2002), for example, pointed out that many of the new, and extremely popular, technological tools and services mentioned in broadcast media headlines, such as music downloading services like Napster.com and social-networking Web sites like Facebook.com, were developed by college students. The diversity of this demographic is unquestionably important, although a review of relevant research literature to date suggests that little of this diversity has been taken into account.

New Literacies in Theory and Practice

In order to obtain a deeper, empirical sense of the kinds of new literacies and new technologies college-age young people are using, surveying the U.S. scene alone provides plenty of material. For example, Madden and Jones' (2002) large-scale survey of Internet use by U.S. college students found that even in 2002, 75% of participants used the Internet for four or more hours per week. This is a significantly higher rate of use than that for the general U.S. population, which tallied a total of 59% of the population who use the computer more than four hours a week in 2002 (Madden & Jones, 2002). Eighty-five percent of participants in Jones' college survey also reported owning their own computer (Jones, 2003).

In terms of perceptions of technology, according to a study of 25 students at The Pennsylvania State University, most participants considered Web browsing, instant messaging (IMing), and the Internet to be "neutral" rather than specific technologies in their own right (Roberts, 2005). That is, students did not view these as distinct technologies in the same way that they viewed televisions and telephones, but simply as elements of the online mix these students use in conducting their everyday lives. While this study involved an admittedly tiny sample of students, it remains nonetheless indicative of more widespread dispositions. Collectively, research on college-age students within the United States suggests that most students own or have access to a cellular telephone, a digital music player, digital cable television perhaps with a broadband Internet connection, a video-game player, and a range of other technologies such as a computer, an external, portable data-storage device, a digital camera, and so on, which students use for a wide variety of purposes (Jones, 2003).

In terms of these uses, students often layer tools and practices. When studying, a college-age student may be listening to digital music, surfing the Internet either for research or personal interest (or both), updating a weblog, chatting with friends using a chat or instant-messaging program, participating in an interest-driven discussion forum, using a word-processing program to write an assigned paper, and reading/responding to e-mail messages (cf., Jones' 2003 findings on multitasking; see also Cammack, 2005a; Lohnes, 2005).

In another example, students use digital technologies to reach out to one another. Many U.S. university students now have a profile on Facebook.com. Facebook is a popular online directory of college students particular to each school that is used by a reputed 85% of college students within the United

States (Hass, 2006). On Facebook, students can list a wide variety of information about themselves. This can include everything from their class schedules to their favorite songs, photographs, and links to friends' Facebook pages. Within Facebook, users can leave comments on each other's pages, follow up the Facebook pages of friends of friends, make new friends, or search for long-lost friends.

Even this small set of examples suggests the extraordinary range of new technologies and literacy practices with which many college and college-age students are engaging. Focusing on their new technology uses from a "new literacies" orientation is important, especially within the current climate of growing accusations that college students' literacy levels are declining rapidly (cf., claims in Romano, 2005). Defining *new* is always tricky, although the field of new literacies studies is beginning to offer up a number of substantive definitions of "new" that are useful constructs for research. Lankshear and Knobel (2003), for example, identified three ways in which new literacies may be new: (a) chronologically, (b) ontologically, and (c) paradigmatically. Thus, some literacies are new because they have been newly developed (i.e., *chronologically* new); this includes, for example, knowing how to read and navigate a Web page. Others are considered new because they are *new in kind* in that they simply were not possible prior to the development of certain digital technologies and services; this includes, for example, literacy practices such as blogging (see Mortenson, this volume). This second "take" on new is concerned with *ontologically new* literacies. Yet, other literacies can be considered "new" due to the development of a sociocultural stance within literacy studies that now recognizes a range of social practices as being "literacies" of one kind or another. That is, these literacies are *paradigmatically* new and involve, for example, scenario planning, zineing, and fan-fiction writing, among others (see also Knobel & Lankshear, 2005).

In my work with Leu, Kinzer, and others, we have used Leu's concept of "deictic literacies" to help explain the rise of the term *new* itself and its employment as a concept that marks off one set of literacy practices and understandings from another. *Deixis* is a linguistic term used to categorize those words such as *today, tomorrow, here,* and *there* that take their meaning directly from the context in which they are used. Thus, what it means to say "today" at any given time is specific to that particular point in time. Literacy practices, we argue, are deictic in that they change in relation to the tools and contexts in which they are practiced (Leu, Kinzer, Coiro, & Cammack, 2004). Therefore, the addition of new tools in the forms of digital technologies necessarily means a change in existing literacy practices when seen from a particular point in time. New literacies—as both a concept and a practice—are thoroughly deictic in that they depend for their meaning on new developments that inform and shape them. Arguably, current "new" literacies will no longer be so when a new set of tools and use contexts come along.

The intersection of a deictic stance on new literacies and Lankshear and Knobel's (2003) concept of ontologically new literacies, in particular, provides a useful theoretical framework for examining studies of college-age young people's new literacy and digital technology practices as well as studies bounded by college contexts and purposes. This focus on ontologically new and always changing, yet context-dependent literacies enables researchers to better understand how new literacies are being defined and taken up in college contexts. This framework also offers useful leverage for critically comparing studies of new technologies and literacies in college contexts with studies of how college-age young people define and use literacies and digital technologies (cf., Cammack, 2005a, 2005b; Lohnes, 2005, 2006). This theoretical orientation toward new literacies affords insight into ways of bridging the in- and out-of-school literacy practices of college students in particular, thereby shedding important light on the student as user and obtaining an emic perspective on literacy and technology developments that could prove to be important resources for effective higher education. This emic perspective is glaringly absent from the bulk of research concerning college-age students, which, as stated before, tends on the whole to focus on new technologies as curriculum resources or as somehow tied to enhanced student performance outcomes, rather than as everyday practices.

The following three sections review the research literature from three different angles: (a) college-age young people and their new technology uses in general, (b) college students and college-driven new technology uses, and (c) college-age students and their literacy practices in general. The absence of a fourth review section that focuses on college-age students and their new literacies practices speaks volumes about the lack of research in this particular area. It is possible, however, to draw important implications for new literacies research by surveying studies of college-age students' general literacy practices, as well as their personal and college-driven technology practices.

"Just ping, IM, txt, or call me": College-Age Students and Their New Technology Use in General

Jones' (2002) study, "The Internet goes to college: How students are living in the future with today's technology," is the largest survey study of the technology uses of college students conducted thus far. It included over 2,000 participants from across the United States and reported not only on Internet use in general, but also on college students' uses of instant messaging and other digital technologies. Part of the rationale for Jones' study was the fact that the Internet proper was developed by users from a range of networked U.S. university campuses during the 1970s and onward, and that the Internet became more or less ubiquitous on U.S. college campuses in the 1990s. Jones argued that the widespread adoption of the Internet and other subsequent digital technologies and services has had a significant impact on college life, both academically and socially.

Jones found that 20% of respondents began using computers between the ages of 5 and 8 years and all of the respondents had used a computer by the time they were between 16 and 18 years old. Interestingly, almost half of the respondents only began using the Internet in college (49%), while roughly the other half (47%) had used the Internet at home prior to college. Seventy-nine percent of these student respondents believed that Internet use has had a positive impact on their college experience and 73% reported using the Internet more than the library to conduct research for their assignments. Thus, it seems that a relatively low precollege use of the Internet within this sample of respondents has not stopped many of them from embracing the Internet as an important resource within their college lives. What would have been an interesting added dimension to Jones' study is a sense of what effects easy access to the Internet had on participants' lives in a range of areas (i.e., not just in terms of academic research purposes). Small-scale qualitative case study evidence certainly suggests that these effects are widespread and sizable (Cammack, 2005a).

Indeed, reports issued by groups such as Educause and their Center for Applied Research (ECAR), and others, show that students' uses of technology for personal purposes are much more widespread than for academic or college-driven purposes (see, for example, Carroll, Howard, Vetere, Peck, & Murphy, 2002; Jones, 2003). Even with the advent of online registration and course-management systems such as Blackboard or WebCT at most colleges within the United States, students' uses of technology for nonacademic reasons far outweigh their uses for academic purposes. Research also shows us that what many professors and researchers would regard as chronologically "new" literacies are not necessarily or even intrinsically regarded as better or preferable practices by college-age students, due to their personal practices beyond or outside college-required uses of new technologies. Steve Thorne's research is a case in point. Thorne (2003, as cited in Knobel & Lankshear, 2004) documented the use of e-mail in a French-language class. The U.S. students enrolled in this class were required to exchange a number of e-mails written in French with "key pals" in France. Two of the students interviewed by Thorne admitted that even the threat of a reduced grade for not sending a certain amount of e-mails was not enough to induce them to e-mail their key pal, even though they liked him very much. For these students, e-mail was too slow as a mode of communication, and one that they associated most closely with e-mailing professors or their mothers, than with striking up and maintaining a social relationship with a peer. Even though the French teachers in this college class felt they were including cutting-edge new technologies in their teaching, the use of e-mail to communicate with native-language speakers missed the mark for at least these two otherwise hard-working and committed students.

A small, but growing body of studies is beginning to document college-age students' personal purposes for using a range of entertainment, communication, and information technologies. As with Thorne's (2003) study just described, all of these studies have important implications for the adoption of new technologies within college instructional settings. Prensky (2001), for example, reported that most college graduates in the United States have spent more than 10,000 hours of their college lives playing video games. A second, large-scale survey study conducted by Jones focused on college students and their digital gaming practices (Jones, 2003). Jones found that 65% of respondents defined themselves as regular or occasional gamers—with slightly more women than men reporting they play computer-based games (60% to 40%), while about the same number of women and men reported playing video or console games (p. 6). Interestingly, and contrary to popular perceptions of game players and their use of time, these same students reported studying, on average, the same amount as other nongame playing college students (p. 2). Findings such as these suggest that digital gaming comprises a significant part of college-age youths' lives, and warrants closer examination with respect to what gaming might offer for enhancing or impacting college-level teaching and learning. This point is discussed again toward the end of this chapter.

An ongoing student-research project at Stanford University has students investigating their own and their peers' new uses of technology. The Mercury Project for Instant Messaging (IM) Studies was created in 2003 and acts as a kind of clearinghouse for undergraduate student-research projects that comprise part of their Program Writing and Rhetoric class (see www. stanford.edu/class/pwr3-25/group2/main.html). Although the validity and reliability of these studies is unlikely to match that of research reported in peer-reviewed journals, the studies themselves offer an important window onto students' personal uses of new technologies. For example, in his piece titled, "A note to Mom: Why I use IM," Chu (2005) reported the results of a survey of 120 of his fellow Stanford University students about using IM. He found that most respondents limited their IM time to 5 hours or less per week, and that they often weighed the rapidity and relative nonintrusiveness of using IM against the directness and intimacy of face-to-face or phone conversations in making decisions about which mode to use. Ninety-one percent of respondents reported that their principal purpose for IMing was to participate in and maintain a range of social networks that spanned on- and off- campus contexts. Similarly, and also included in the Mercury Project, Nachbaur's study of IM focused on the use of away messages and flirting (Nachbaur, 2003). He found that IM served to strengthen social bonds and foster a sense of a campus community. Both of these studies, and others reported via the Mercury Project, begin from the assumption that IMing is a key component of their peers' everyday lives.

Concerning another medium, usage statistics suggest college-age students represent a significant demographic within the world of weblogs. Forty-eight percent of active bloggers are under the age of 30, while overall, 7% of all U.S. Internet users have created blogs, and 27% of U.S. Internet users read blogs (Rainie, 2005). According to the Live Journal homepage, 9.6 million journals or blogs have been created on their site since 1999 (information retrieved 2/24/06). Trevino's (2005) study of 14 college-student bloggers found that participants often began their blogs because other friends and family had one, and that they used their blogs to maintain contacts with one another. Trevino found that study participants used blogs to "document their lives" even as they wrestled with posting private thoughts in a very public forum (p. 10). My own study of a college-age blogger (see, for example, Cammack, 2005b) suggests that one important purpose for keeping a blog concerns relationships, rather than sharing "information" or paying close attention to "truth," despite what pundits in the past have claimed *should* be important with respect to all people's Internet use (cf., Burbules, 1997; Gilster, 1998).

Mobile technologies comprise yet another growing area of research attention with respect to college-age young people's digital technology use. At present, readily accessed mobile technologies include mobile phones or cell phones (that increasingly are Internet enabled), portable music players (e.g., iPods, MP3 players), personal digital assistants (PDAs, which include devices like the BlackBerry and the Treo), portable global-positioning system devices, and the like. An Australian study of 34 young people ages 16 to 22 focused specifically on participants' mobile technology use (Carroll et al., 2002). Data collection methods included demographic questionnaires, scrapbooks, disposable cameras with which to record their personal "takes" on the role of mobile technologies in their own lives, online diaries that documented mobile technology use, and participant observation. The researchers found that mobile phones, in particular, were "seamlessly woven into [participants'] lives, [and were] almost invisible and mundane in their ordinariness" (p. 5). With respect to identifying mobile technology "attractors," the researchers found that freedom from time and location constraints afforded by mobile technologies made them most attractive to participants. Interestingly, participants also nominated style and design as an important part of their mobile technology choices, especially where mobile phones were concerned. Participating in mobile (and even not-so-mobile) technology-mediated networks was also regarded as extremely important by participants: "One participant described young people's technologies such as mobile phones, SMS [text messaging], chat and email as *'our stuff'* and contrasted it with conventional technologies such as televisions, video recorders and the content of Information Technology subjects taught at school" (Carroll et al., 2002, p. 4).

to improve course delivery or access to college programs (e.g., Daugherty & Funke, 1998; Warschauer, 2000; Yellowlees-Douglas, 2002).

A sizable number of studies focus on evaluating general effects of increasingly technologized curricula and campuses within postsecondary education. In 1998, the National Survey of Information Technology in Higher Education reported that 30% of classes used Internet resources and 46% of all higher education institutions in the United States had mandatory student computing fees. These percentages continue to increase each year, as reported in the 2004 National Survey of Information Technology in U.S. Higher Education (Campus Computing Survey, 2004). Large-scale reviews of the extant research literature, however, suggest that little research systematically documents the effects of technology integration across an academy or even across a given faculty (cf., criticisms in Flowers, Pascarella, & Pierson, 2000; Nespor, 2006). In 2000, Flowers et al. published a metareview of existing research that focused on the "promise of information technologies" with respect to enhancing cognitive or learning outcomes for students in their first year of college. They claimed causal connections between enhanced academic performance and computer use was a common rationale for investing in digital technologies for higher education at the turn of the last century. Flowers et al. (2000) found, however, that the bulk of the published studies were conducted within individual college courses, and often by the instructing professor. As such, the researchers found little support in the published research for new technologies as a positive influence on learning at the time of their review. Not only did they find little information on the impact of campus uses of computing on overall student achievement, but in attempting to replicate previous work to determine if computer and e-mail use influenced standardized measures of cognitive or intellectual growth, Flowers et al. also found no significant cognitive impact on students.

When the findings of Flowers and colleagues' (2000) study were broken down according to type of institution, however, students at 2-year colleges specifically received a positive significant effect from computer use as measured in cognitive development and reading comprehension. Since no concurrent work was done to compare or contrast the literacy practices of students at the 2-year and 4-year institutions involved in this study or to research attention paid to students' nonacademic uses of technology, the potential impact of these two factors was not taken into account. It seems possible that students at 4-year institutions may have engaged in more sophisticated uses of digital technologies and had more experience in using them but that did not register in the survey data as having a significant effect on reading comprehension; yet, neither the ways in which 4- versus 2-year college students *used* technologies or had different experiences with them was measured in this study. Instead, Flowers and colleagues simply attributed the difference in findings to the additional writing support students at 2-year institutions were receiving and that used word processing as the writing medium, rather than trying to untangle the relationship between the technology uses, cognitive development, and literacy practices of the students involved.

In short, it seems that the bulk of the studies conducted to date on college students and new technologies focus almost exclusively on evaluating the degree to which the *addition* of new technologies to a course has improved student learning in some way. This research is dominated by psychological and cognitive theoretical orientations that seem to assume causal links between digital technologies and effective learning, or rather, between digital technologies and enhanced content delivery (see criticisms of these assumptions in Noble, 1998; Nespor, 2006). By not conducting research on the ways technologies are *used* by students either for nonacademic purposes, or for academic purposes not stipulated by the professor, we risk missing the multiple ways college-age students have learned to adapt new technologies to their lives.

Looking More Closely at Studies of Digital Technologies, Reading and Writing, and College Students

A distinct subset of the "college students and college-directed uses of new technologies" research focuses on conventional conceptions of academic reading and writing. This includes studies that explore using technology to support college students in basic skills or developmental-reading classes (e.g., Lansford, 1999; Wepner, 1990; Maloney, 2003); studies of college reading in general (e.g., Valeri-Gold & Commander, 2000-2001; Stahl & King, 2000), and reading comprehension in particular (e.g., Yaworski, 2000); and studies reporting the impact on student learning of particular reading-related, academic technology resources, such as e-textbooks (e.g., Simon, 2001).

Despite the sizable number of studies focusing on new technologies, some aspect of reading and writing, and college students, this research nonetheless tends to operate within the narrow confines of a single college course, or from a conception of literacy as a skill that students either already have and are using, or, as in the case of developmental academic reading studies, as a skill to be mastered. Moreover, this research also seems to assume that digital technology is a socially "neutral" tool (that is, it does what it does, regardless of context, users, and user purposes). Little or no attention is paid to exploring the ways in which digital technologies themselves mediate and shape—or are mediated and shaped by—users' literacy practices. This latter point is important because digital technology is not a neutral tool, and it is not being integrated equally into all postsecondary settings or being used by all students in the same way for the same end. Digital divide issues between who knows how to use digital technologies, who has access to them, and how they are being used are shaping the college landscape even as we do little to research them from the perspectives of the users themselves.

Many of the studies that do focus on some aspect of reading and writing seem to be simply reinscribing predigital academic literacy practices, with little or no attention given to the ways in which academic reading and writing practices themselves may have changed with the advent of the Internet, word-processing software, e-mail, and other digital technologies. One study that seems to treat the complex network of the Internet as merely a repository of texts is Burton and Chadwick's (2000) investigation of the ways in which a sample of college-student researchers used the Internet for writing class-assigned research papers. Their study of 543 college students found that some students used information found online irresponsibly; that is, without properly citing the source or evaluating the validity of the information (p. 324). They found that students in the main quickly skimmed online references, located main ideas, and copied information without first fully evaluating the resource's credibility and currency (p. 310). The assumption within this study, however, is that literacy is a singular skill, marked by, in this case, the ability to locate and evaluate information online compared to locating and evaluating information in more traditional book form. Little or no attention is paid to the multimedia and hyperlinked affordances of information online or to how those affordances might be better used by students and faculty. Studies of young adults' news reading online and the more complex connections they make between ideas, events, and key figures (see, for example, Eveland et al., 2004) do not seem to have made their way into Burton and Chadwick's study as an important feature worth studying. The focus of their research concerned *how* written information is or, perhaps more accurately, *should be* used by students, as though the Internet and a written book were the same media (see also Cammack, 2005a).

This is not to say that researching and writing college-valued, successful academic texts is no longer important or necessary for college success—far from it. What is interesting, however, is these researchers' assumption that the Internet has not wrought significant changes in students' reading practices (see discussions in Leu, Kinzer, Coiro, & Cammack, 2004). For these researchers, the ability to locate and evaluate information both online and offline in the same ways is the key factor in a good-quality college-student essay rather than looking at the quality of the essay task itself, or establishing students' existing abilities to synthesize information.

Duffelmeyer (2000) offered a useful alternate research perspective to that mapped out by the work of Burton and Chadwick by focusing explicitly on identifying and analyzing the ways in which different technologies shape how people think and act, just as the ways in which how people think and act shape how technologies are taken up and used (which may or may not coincide with the developers' original purposes for these devices). This study, which focused on the computer practices of students in six sections of a first-year composition course or unit, asked students to compose "technology narratives" about their experiences with technology up to that point. The 140 students in the course who completed the prompt represented a range of experiences with computers spanning oppositional to ambiguous and mutable positions.

Duffelmeyer (2000) focused on the concept of "critical computer literacy" to emphasize the interplay between digital technologies and the information they deliver. That is, as mentioned before, technologies are not value-neutral objects but devices and interfaces that carry meanings and values associated with them. Duffelmeyer used her research to argue that to use technologies without thinking about them more deeply is simply to engage in a surface interaction with their potential. According to Duffelmeyer, fully competent users of computers and digital networks must also be able to identify how the technologies themselves affect their lives, as well as how these technologies shape the information users obtain from them. In focusing on the computer as both a tool and locus of study, Duffelmeyer identified the need to develop a sense of critique as a part of what she considered critical computer literacy (p. 304).

Even though Duffelmeyer's study went well beyond the kinds of "direct transfer of literacy skills" studies that pay little attention to technologies themselves as social practices, her work still focused on college-classroom contexts and not on students' everyday literacy and digital technology practices. Academic analysis of these everyday practices, I argue, can offer important insights into the political or "interested" nature of language, text, and technology uses that can work to some people's benefit while simultaneously excluding others from formal recognition of success in postsecondary education settings. For example, discursive analysis of the social and language practices of IMing can show how choice of language, symbols, and interface shapes a particular literacy practice (cf., Jacobs, 2004; Lewis & Fabos, 2005). At the same time, discursive analysis can help students to understand how context-bound this practice is and that IM language conventions rarely translate successfully into academic text practices.

New technologies and college composition comprise another sizable group of studies within this field. Quarshie-Smith (2004), for example, conducted a teacher-research study of the writing practices of nontraditional college students (i.e., those students returning to college after time spent working or raising a family) in what she called a "networked setting:" the Internet-connected computer labs on campus. As part of her study, conducted within the context of a degree-program course, her students wrote memoirs recounting the role of technology in their lives, with technology defined in these memoirs in whatever way each student wanted to define it. Her results suggested that her students struggled less with issues of access than they did with how to appropriate the technologies in ways that allowed them "to develop creative uses, to produce knowledge, to intervene on one's own behalf or on behalf of others, and to orient one's self in a world that is in flux" (Quarshie-Smith,

2004, p. 93). Students then worked over the course of the semester to bridge any distance they felt existed between themselves and the technologies.

Quarshie-Smith's (2004) findings are important in terms of highlighting the discomfort older, nontraditional students often feel in using technology and, especially, how digital-divide issues affect these students in more complicated ways than just accessing digital technologies. Her research is also important in that it worked from the position of the students as users. The main problem, from a new literacies perspective, is that the study is located in academic skills and contexts as a point of departure and reference. While the study mentioned that students used digital technologies for recreational as well as vocational purposes, Quarshie-Smith sidelined those purposes in favor of educational uses, particularly those associated with her students' academic literacy skills. Due to this preference, academic literacy remained a static, singular skill measured by an association with the academy and a skill that many of her students felt dissociated from or unable to fully attain. In short, while participating students perceived a difference between academic and recreational uses of technology, their proficiency with recreational uses was not built upon in any way that facilitated their engagement with more academically rewarded uses of these new technologies.

In sum, it seems that the bulk of the research on new digital technologies within college settings is really about documenting "business as usual," where the business of teaching or delivering content is simply more technologized (Lankshear & Knobel, 2003). Anecdotal and commentary evidence suggests that this may be changing, however; that is, developments within new digital-technology practices and devices in the world beyond postsecondary institutions may be having an important impact on higher education pedagogy and learning. This particular area concerns the burgeoning use of digital game technologies to create expert learning environments for college students. The implications for effective literacy pedagogy at the college level are sizable, and this point is taken up in the final section of this chapter. First, however, it is important to understand what we currently know about literacy research more generally, as it concerns college-age students.

College-Age Young Adults and Literacy Research

Two recent studies, one conducted by the American Institutes for Research (Baer, et al., 2006) and the other by the National Endowment for the Arts (Bradshaw & Nichols, 2004), are the first full-scale attempts to quantify U.S. college-age students' literacy abilities in any way, and both define literacy much too narrowly. Both studies state that college graduates are more literate than the general population, but less literate than might be expected. However, literacy "levels" within both studies were identified by means of specific, decontextualized, and narrow measures. For example, according to the American

Institutes for Research study, while students at 2- and 4-year institutions had significantly higher levels of literacy than adults without comparable levels of education, average scores for nonquantitative literacy (i.e., generally taken to mean the ability to read literary works, procedural texts, expository prose texts, etc.), still registered as less than proficient. For the purposes of the AIR study, *proficient* was defined as those "skills necessary to perform more complex and challenging literacy activities" (p. 13). The examples of proficient reading given in the report included being able to read, synthesize, and analyze information found in "dense, complex documents." It also meant being able to analyze "abstract prose texts" in terms of "comparing viewpoints in two editorials," and "interpreting a table about blood pressure, age, and physical activity" (p. 13). In contrast, the NEA survey asked respondents, whether "during the past 12 months, they had read any novels or short stories, plays, or poetry" (p. 1). Any affirmative response to this survey item was counted as reading literature, regardless of "quality."

In the AIR study, literacy was measured as a skill or set of skills rather than a series of practices. The focus of the study was fixed firmly on respondents' strategies for gathering and using information from specific texts for specific purposes. In the NEA study, literacy was simply a behavior involving a particular type of text. In neither instance were contexts or practices taken into account. Nevertheless, the NEA study went on to posit a positive correlation between literary reading and civic participation without knowing anything more than the amount of books read by respondents in the previous year. In the AIR study, *prose literacy* was defined as the ability to read and use information from "continuous texts." *Document literacy* was defined in this study as the ability to gather and use information from "non-continuous texts" (p. 3). The use of texts for other than informational purposes was lost in this study, which signals strongly that reading for other than informational purposes is unimportant in the eyes of the researchers who designed this study.

The AIR study, a part of the National Survey of America's College Students, collected data from more than 1,800 students at 2- and 4-year institutions across the United States using an assessment instrument developed for the 2003 National Assessment of Adult Literacy. This instrument was designed to "focus on a broad range of tasks that adults perform in order to function at work, at home, and in the community" (p. 9), thereby limiting literacy to a discrete set of skills relating to functionality. The NEA study, in contrast, specifically studied the literature reading practices of college graduates. It found that 35.2% of college graduates did not choose to read literature, a percentage that has dropped 16.5% from 1982 to 2002. To invert the findings, this means that 63.1% of college graduates do engage in literary reading, and that 39% of books for adults are bought by those with at least a college degree. These findings were gathered through a survey of more than 17,000 respondents that was designed to elicit information about "public participation in the arts"

(Bradshaw & Nichols, 2004, p. 1). Compared to the AIR study, the NEA survey eliminated any literacy practices involving technology or information gathering and focused solely on the reading of novels, short stories, plays, and poetry. The survey also asked respondents if "they had read any books and how many"—a finding that was reported separately from respondents' literary reading practices. While 56.6% of adults reported reading "any book," this information was not broken down according to level of education, so it is impossible to know if this rate is higher (or lower) for college graduates.

At any rate, both studies reported confusing and even contesting information. What exactly are the practices that the NEA and AIR studies capture? What definitions of literacy are embedded in those studies, and how do they interrelate with the literacy practices of students' lives? More importantly, what do we know about the literacy practices of college-age students, and the role of technology in those practices through surveys like these?

The unnecessarily narrow definitions of literacy embedded in the AIR and NEA studies missed much of the rich, contextualized literacy practices in college-aged students' lives. These studies also missed documenting the role digital technologies play in important new and emerging literacy practices. Although studies of young adults' everyday literacy and technology practices are only now beginning to appear in peer-reviewed journals, this small-but-growing body of research may well have much to say about the extent to which young adults' literacy and technology proficiencies have been significantly and, perhaps wastefully, underestimated in the research literature to date, as well as in curriculum applications of new technologies within higher education settings. While large-scale studies of how few novels college-age students are reading make good news copy, they illustrate only a small slice of the literate lives of students today.

Implications of This Review

To underscore my argument for the centrality of new literacy practices in any consideration of college students and digital technology uses, it is useful to first distinguish between insider and outsider mindsets with respect to people's everyday conceptions and uses of new digital technologies. Lankshear and Knobel (2003) used the concept of mindsets to characterize particular, reasonably well-defined stances on something. Mindsets shape what people see and how they see it, how they act subsequently in terms of decision making, and so forth. Two mindsets on digital technologies that they explored are the outsider mindset and the insider mindset. *Insider mindsets* generally belong to those who have grown up with digital technologies simply as part of their everyday world. *Outsider mindsets* tend to belong to those people who are relative newcomers to digital technologies, who are often acutely aware of digital technologies, and who often have to consciously and carefully learn how to use new digital technologies (and even then, often never master a range of functions built into devices). Many of today's college students are very much the insiders in relation to new literacies, while many of their professors constitute a cadre of outsiders who are learning how to teach in a digital world. This difference is key as many faculty struggle with implementing new technologies in their teaching, yet never feel as though they have caught up with their students. In other cases, some students unfamiliar with new technologies may feel at an academic and social disadvantage in comparison with more insider peers. In many ways, the existing literacy practices of the university stand in direct contrast to the new literacies of some students. It is an open question as to whose literacy practices will come to shape what it means to know and be able to do things in the world at large, and at this point, it seems that the academy in general—save for those few centers devoted to new technology development—is already out-of-touch with the new literacies of many of its students.

Many of our college students' lives are mediated by literacy practices and technologies that are qualitatively different from what they were 10 years before. Gathering data on the demonstration of students' skills in prose literacy or the percentage of college graduates who prefer reading novels to other activities is a minute part of the picture. By the same token, studying the college-directed technology uses of university students tends to focus too closely on the tools themselves and loses essential information about the ways in which these tools shift the literacy practices of students (i.e., how students learn to create multimedia papers with embedded hyperlinks, photos, and even video for a presentation requirement in a class). Historically, research on the uses of technology in relation to students' specific literacy practices (e.g., essay writing, evaluating information sources) has been limited in scope and has tended toward the specific with respect to documenting technology use in individual university courses. While this research has nonetheless forged inroads into understanding the impact of technologies on the literacy practices of college students, these literacy practices have been limited for the main part to conventional academic practices associated with coursework. The nonacademic technology and literacy practices of college students outside of classes or class-driven purposes have been lost as researchers have focused on evaluating the integration of technology in academic settings and its effects on student learning or proficiency in a specified area.

Positive inroads nonetheless are being made toward richer conceptions and understandings of what it means to be a young adult insider with respect to new technology use. For example, new developments in gaming and cognition research have been informing a small-but-steadily growing area of curriculum development and learning research at the college level; this area holds much potential as a model of how personal expertise with new technologies and a range of new literacies can be harnessed to effective professional learning within postcompulsory education contexts. (cf., Gee 2003; D. Oblinger, 2004;

Squire, this volume; Steinkeuhler, this volume). The Massachusetts Institute of Technology (MIT) is taking college students' game-playing practices seriously and some faculty members have been testing course-content delivery using games as a medium and aimed at honing students' professional expertise (see, for example, educationarcade.org). MIT uses purpose-built multiplayer online games to orient new students to the sprawling campus and to teach about a particular historical time (the American Revolution, for example). MIT is currently also using a range of 3D environment, simulation, and arcade-style games—many built by students themselves—to teach concepts and principles from physics, environmental engineering, biology, epidemiology, chemistry, and so on. While much of this work is still being tested and tweaked, innovations like these nonetheless mark a significant signpost for future directions for technology integration within higher education contexts (see Jones, 2004, for an example of this kind of work).

Thinking about Literacy and Technology in More Complex Ways

A complex picture of literacy and technology practices as codetermined and thoroughly social has been drawn by Hawisher and Selfe (2004) in their work on the literacy life histories of men and women who have grown up in the information age. Patterned after Brandt's (2001) *Literacy in American Lives*, Hawisher and Selfe have collected the narrative histories of participants not only about their literacy practices but also their technological experiences and development. Hawisher and Selfe (2004) theorized technology as "an essential component of literate activity" (p. 642) in their move from their early work in composition studies to their belief in a need to study electronic literacies as shaped by multiple contexts. They referred to this matrix as the "cultural ecology" of literacy practices (p. 644). While this work is not specific to college-age students, it is an argument for the study of literacy practices as technological. The narratives of participants highlight the agency available to them in shaping new literacies through their technology practices. These narratives also suggest participants did not always find schools or colleges to be "gateways" to new literacies. While, in the 1970s, college served as the point of introduction to computers for a select few, studies conducted in the past few years show quite clearly that children from a wide range of family types and socioeconomic backgrounds have sent e-mails, loaded software or Web sites to a computer to play games, or have had onscreen text read to them, drawn pictures onscreen, or digitally manipulated images in some way, independently loaded and watched DVDs on television and computer screens, and so on even before beginning school (Kaiser Family Foundation, 2003; Marsh, 2006).

With each subsequent generation in their study, Hawisher and Selfe (2004) found an increased connection between literacy and technology practices as well as the development of new practices within respondents' everyday lives. This closer connection was not necessarily matched in respondents' experiences at school, however. One participant, Brittney, described how she used a friend's computer for homework and school projects because she didn't have one at home, nor did she have ready access to one at school: "I didn't have a computer of my own until I was a sixth grader, so the only time I used the computer was when I was at her house" (p. 658). Examples such as this remind educators and researchers of the need to understand thoroughly what Hawisher and Selfe referred to as a "double life in terms of literacy practices and values" (p. 661). That is, there seems to be an ongoing discrepancy between the literacy and technology practices required of college students for academic purposes in formal-education contexts, and the technology practices these same students pursue as part of their own interests and in their own time (see also, Cammack, 2005c; Lewis, et al., 2005; Snyder, 2004). Hawisher and Selfe's ecological orientation gave rise to the idea that, "literacies have *lifespans*. Specific literacies emerge; they overlap and compete with preexisting forms; they accumulate, especially, perhaps, in periods of transition; they also eventually fade away" (2004, p. 665).

The idea of literacies emerging over time dovetails nicely with a deictic notion of new literacies, where literacy practices are in a state of constant flux and change. My own research has explored the deictic nature of new literacies with respect to college contexts specifically. For example, my study of the technology and literacy practices of college students in a history course in a private, Eastern U.S. university focused on documenting tensions between old and new literacies that became apparent over time in a particular history course (Cammack, 2005a, 2005c). The original rationale for this study concerned a multimedia environment developed by a consortium of experts and designed specifically to enhance college students' engagement with the classic U.S. text, *The Autobiography of Malcolm X*. A key component of this study, however, was also the collection of general data concerning participating students' literacy and technology practices both within and outside the classroom.

This small-scale, ethnographic study included close observations of three focal students over the course of one semester. Observations were conducted during classes and three times outside this context for each student. Open-ended interviews were held along with out-of-class observations; the interviews focused on understanding the students' literacy and technology practices from their perspective and the ways in which the multimedia environment used in the history course could be integrated with those practices. Findings suggest that these three students' literacy practices, across all of the contexts in which they were observed, were a mix of both traditional and new literacies. They engaged not only in the traditional academic literacies of a college course, but also in new literacies associated with this multimedia environment in active and proficient ways. These literacies included reading online texts that were a mix of linguistic and multimodal information; navigating online spaces to find information; reading by skimming and activating hyperlinks; copying, cutting, and pasting information from online texts into word-processed writing; using online multimedia resources as a part of in-class oral presentations; posting comments to the course bulletin board and reading others' thoughts; e-mailing other students and the teaching assistants; and understanding the relationship of the components of the multimedia tool to one another (i.e., how the footnotes related to the main text and then to the interviews with historians and sociologists as well as cultural critics). All three students' new literacies were marked by speed, flexibility, intertextuality, multiplicity, and nonlinearity—especially when compared with the professor's more traditional literacy practices. These new literacies mirrored the practices that students engaged in outside of the classroom. Their uses of the multimedia environment were much more like their uses of the Internet more generally, and less like their ways of reading paper-based course texts. The new literacy practices associated with the multimedia environment related to their other literacy and technology practices by bridging their out-of-school literacies, developed through the uses of media like e-mail and Instant Messaging as well as hypertext, with their traditional literacies used in conducting research for a course.

Of course, such a small-scale study can only suggest possible avenues of further study. More work like this needs to be conducted in order to create any sort of systematic understanding of the new literacies of college students and college-age young adults, whether from a life history approach like Hawisher and Selfe, through survey research as with Jones' (2002) study, or through direct-observation qualitative methodologies. Once we, as a research community, have a strong sense of what the literacy practices of college students are, and the extent to which these practices constitute new literacies and in what ways, we can begin to better understand how to build fruitfully on young adults' literacies in preparing them for a world of work and adult life that will no doubt be quite different than that of today.

Conclusion

New technologies shift literacy practices and create the opportunity for new literacies to develop. College students, as early adopters and innovators of new digital technologies in particular, are a key population for research aimed at understanding new literacies. While little research has been done through this lens to date, the continuing development of innovations such as Facebook.com and simulation and role-play gaming keep this a rich field of inquiry. By adding the theoretical lens of new literacies to the grounded study of technology practices through the eyes of the students themselves, we can, as a research community, gain a deeper understanding of the ways in which students use literacy in daily, immersive, and personally productive ways. We can also begin to understand potential disconnects between the practices of students and faculty, and how those disconnects in literacy practices can contribute to issues of power, access, and knowledge in university settings. Given the pace of technological development, it's never too late to begin asking questions of students and watching what they do—the innovation of today may very well be the quotidian practice of tomorrow, nearly invisible but nonetheless essential.

References

Abrams, Z. (2003). The effect of synchronous and asynchronous CMC on oral performance in German. *Modern Language Journal, 87*(2), 157–167.

Alvermann, D. (Ed.). (2002). *Adolescents and literacies in a digital world. New literacies and digital epistemologies.* New York: Peter Lang.

Anson, C. (1999). Distant voices: Teaching and writing in a culture of technology. *College English, 61*(3), 261–280.

Aviles, K., Phillips, J., Rosenblatt, T., & Vargas, J. (2005). If higher education listened to me. Speech presented at ELI Meetings, (01/24./2005) Retrieved at: http://connect.educause.edu/library/abstract/IfHigherEducationLis/42623 on June 1, 2006.

Baer, J., Cook, A., & Baldi, S. (2006). *The literacy of America's college students.* Denver, CO: American Institutes for Research.

Barone, C. (2005). The new academy. In D. Oblinger & J. Oblinger (Eds.), *Educating the net generation* (pp. 14.1–14.16). Boulder, CO: Educause.

Bradshaw, T., & Nichols, B. (2004). *Reading at risk: A survey of literary reading in America.* Washington, DC: National Endowment for the Arts.

Brandt, D. (2001). *Literacy in American's lives.* Cambridge, MA: Cambridge University Press.

Brown, M. (2005). Learning spaces. In D. Oblinger & J. Oblinger (Eds.), *Educating the net generation* (pp. 12.1–12.22). Boulder, CO: Educause.

Burbules, N. (1997). Misinformation, malinformation, messed-up information, and mostly useless information: How to avoid getting tangled up in the 'Net. In Lankshear, C. and Bigum, C. (Eds.), *Digital rhetorics: Literacies and technologies in education: Current practices and new directions* (pp. 109–120). Canberra, Australia: Department of Employment, Education, Training, and Youth Affairs/Brisbane, Queensland University of Technology.

Burton, V., & Chadwick, S. (2000). Investigating the practices of student researchers: Patterns of use and criteria for use of internet and library source. *Computers and Composition, 17*(3), 309–328.

Cammack, D. (2005a). By any means necessary: Understanding the literacy and technology practices of using multimedia in a college history course (Doctoral dissertation, Teachers College, Columbia University, 2005). *Dissertation Abstracts International, 66,* 229.

Cammack, D. (2005b). Multiple modes, one life: A semiotic analysis of a blogger and her blog. Paper presented to the National Reading Conference, Miami, FL.

Cammack, D. (2005c). No straight line: Wrinkling binaries in literacy and technology research. *eLearning, 2*(3), 153–168.

Carroll, J., Howard, S., Vetere, F., Peck, J., & Murphy, J. (2002). Just what do the youth of today want? Technology appropriation by young people. *Proceedings of the 35th International Conference on System Sciences,* Hawaii. Retrieved (05/2006) , from ieeexplore.ieee.org/iel5/7798/21442/00994089.pdf

Chu, E. (2005). A note to Mom: Why I use IM. The Mercury Project for Instant Messaging Studies. Retrieved on 06/2006.

Colbeck, C., Campbell, S., & Bjorklund, S. (2000). Grouping in the dark: What college students learn from group projects. *The Journal of Higher Education, 71*(1), 60–83.

Daugherty, M., & Funke, B. (1998). University faculty and student perceptions of web-based instruction. *Journal of Distance Education/Revue de l'enseignement à distance, 13*(1). Retrieved July 25, 2006 from http://cade.athabascau.ca/vol13.1/daugherty.html

Davies, J. (2006). Escaping to the borderlands: An exploration of the Internet as a cultural space for teenaged Wiccan girls. In K. Pahl & J. Rowsell (Eds.), *Travel notes from the new literacy studies: Instances of practice* (pp. 57–71). Clevedon, U.K.: Multilingual Matters.

Duffelmeyer, B. B. (2000). Critical computer literacy: Computers in first-year composition as topic and entertainment. *Computers and Composition, 17*, 289–307.

Dutt-Doner, K., & Powers, S. (2000). The use of electronic communication to develop alternative avenues for classroom discussion. *Journal of Technology and Teacher Education, 8*(2), 153–172.

Electronic Publishing Initiative at Columbia (EPIC). (2003). *Executive summary of student survey.* Retrieved May 26, 2006, from http://epic.columbia.edu/eval/eval04frame.html

Eveland, W., Marton, K., & Seo, M. (2004). Moving beyond "just the facts:" The influence of online news on the content and structure of public affairs knowledge. *Communication Research, 31*(1), 82–108.

Flowers, L., Pascarella, E. T., and Pierson, C. (2000). Information technology use and cognitive outcomes in the first year of college. *The Journal of Higher Education, 71*(6), 637–667.

Gee, J. P. (2003). *What video games have to teach us about learning and literacy.* New York: Palgrave Macmillan.

Gilster, P. (1998). *Digital literacy.* New York: Wiley.

Glenn, L., Jones, C., & Hoyt, J. (2003). The effect of interaction levels on student performance: A comparative analysis of web-mediated versus traditional delivery. *Journal of Interactive Learning Research, 14*(3), 285–301.

Gustafson, K. (2003-4). The impact of technologies on learning. *Planning for Higher Education, Society for College, and University Planning, 32*(2), 37–43.

Gustafson, K., & Kors, K. (2004). Strategic implications of an educational technology assessment. *EDUCAUSE Quarterly, 27*(2). Retrieved May 5, 2006, from http://www.educause.edu/pub/eq/eqm04/eqm04210.asp?bhcp=1

Hara, N., Bonk, C., & Angeli, C. (2000). Content analysis of online discussion in an applied educational psychology course. *Instructional Science, 28*(2), 115–152.

Hartman, J., Moskal, P., & Dziuban, C. (2005). Preparing the academy of today for the learner of tomorrow. In D. Oblinger & J. Oblinger (Eds.), *Educating the net generation* (pp. 6.1–6.15). Boulder, CO: Educause.

Hawisher, G. E., & Selfe, C. L. (2004). Becoming literate in the information age: Cultural ecologies and the literacies of technology. *College Composition and Communication, 55*(4), 642–692.

Howe, N., & Strauss, W. (2000). *Millennials rising: The next great generation.* New York: Vintage.

Jacobs, G. E. (2004). Complicating contexts: Issues of methodology in researching the language and literacies of instant messaging. *Reading Research Quarterly, 39*(4), 394–406.

Jones, S. (2003). *Let the games begin: Gaming technology and entertainment among college students.* Retrieved July 8, 2003, from http://www.pewinternet.org/reports/toc.asp?Report=93

Jones, G. (2004). 3D On-line distributed learning environments: An old concept with a new twist. In C. Crawford et al. (Eds.), *Proceedings of society for information technology and teacher education international conference, 2004* (pp. 507–512). Chesapeake, VA: AACE.

Kaiser Family Foundation. (2003). *Zero to six: Electronic media in the lives of infants, toddlers, and preschoolers.* Retrieved March 17, 2004, from www.kff.org/entmedia/loader.cfm?url=/commonspot /security/getfile.cfm&PageID=22754

Kapitzke, C. (2000). [Review of the book *Network science a decade later: The Internet and classroom learning*]. *Teaching Education, 11*(2), 233–235.

Knobel, M., & Lankshear, C. (2004). Planning pedagogy for i-mode: From flogging to blogging via wi-fi. *English in Australia, 139*, 78–102.

Knobel, M., & Lankshear, C. (2005). "New literacies": Research and social practice. In B. Maloch, J. Hoffman, D. Schallert, C. Fairbanks, & J. Worthy (Eds.), *54th yearbook of the National Reading Conference* (pp. 22–50). Oak Creek, WI: National Reading Conference.

Landow, G. (2002). Educational innovation and hypertext: One university's successes and failures in supporting new technology. In I. Snyder (Ed.), *Silicon literacies: communication, innovation, and education in the electronic age* (pp. 101–115). London: Routledge.

Lankshear, C., & Knobel, M. (2003). *New literacies: Changing knowledge and classroom learning.* Philadelphia: Open University Press.

Lansford, C. E. (1999). Using pre-test/post-test data to evaluate the effectiveness of computer-aided instruction (A study of CAI and its use with developmental reading students). Paper presented at the SITE 99: Society for Information Technology & Teacher Education International Conference, San Antonio, TX.

Larson, B. E., & Keiper, T. A. (2002). Classroom discussion and threaded electronic discussion: Learning in two areas. *Contemporary Issues in Technology and Teacher Education, 45–62.*

Leu, D., Kinzer, C., Coiro, J., & Cammack, D. (2004). Toward a theory of new literacies emerging from the internet and other information and communication technologies. In R. B. Ruddell, & N. J. Unrau (Eds.), *Theoretical models and processes of reading* (pp. 1570–1613). Newark, DE: International Reading Association.

Lewis, C., & Fabos, B. (2005). Instant messaging, literacies, and social identities. *Reading Research Quarterly, 40*(4), 470–501.

Ling, R. (2001). *Adolescent girls and young adult men: Two sub-cultures of the mobile telephone* (R&D report r 34/2001). Kjeller, Norway: Telenor Research and Development. Retrieved July 25, 2006, from http://telenor.no/fou/program/nomadiske/articles/rich/(2001)Adolescent.pdf

Lohnes, S. (2005). Blogging within the system: Exploring undergraduate literacy practices in school-sanctioned blogs. Paper presented to the National Reading Conference, Miami, FL.

Lohnes, S. (2006). To IM or not: Exploring the contexts of undergraduates' literate engagement with technology on campus. Paper presented at the annual meeting of the National Reading Conference, Los Angeles, CA.

Lupia, A., & Philpot, T. (2005). Views from inside the Net: How websites affect young adults' political interest. *Journal of Politics, 67*(4), 1122–1142.

Madden, M., & Jones, S. (2002). *The internet goes to college: How students are living in the future with today's technology.* Washington, DC: Pew Internet and American Life Project. Retrieved July 25, 2006, from http://eric.ed.gov/ERICDocs/data/ericdocs2/content_storage_01/0000000b/80/28/22/3c.pdf

Maloney, W. H. (2003). Connecting the texts of their lives to academic literacy: Creating success for at-risk first-year college students. *Journal of Adolescent & Adult Literacy, 46*(8), 664–672.

Marsh, J. (2005). *Popular culture, new media and digital literacy in early childhood.* London; New York: Routledge Farmer.

McNeely, B. (2005). Using technology as a learning tool, not just the cool new thing. In D. Oblinger & J. Oblinger (Eds.), *Educating the net generation* (pp. 4.1–4.10). Boulder, CO: Educause.

Metzger, M., Flanagin, A., & Zwarun, L. (2003). College student Web use, perceptions of information credibility, and verification behavior. *Computers & Education, 41,* 271–290.

Miall, D., & Dobson, T. (2001). Reading hypertext and the experience of literature. *Journal of Digital Information, 2*(1), Electronic resource. Retrieved (06/2007), from http://journals.tdl.org/jodi/article/view/jodi-36/37

Nachbaur, A. (2003). College students and instant messaging: An analysis of chatting, flirting, & using away messages. *Mercury Project for Instant Messaging Studies at Stanford.* Retrieved (06/2006), from http://www.stanford.edu/class/pwr3-25/group2/projects/nachbaur.html#

Nespor, J. (2006). *Technology and the politics of instruction.* Mahwah, NJ: Lawrence Erlbaum.

Noble, D. (1998). Digital diploma mills, part 1: The automation of higher education. *October, 86,* 107–117.

Oblinger, D. (2004). The next generation of educational engagement. *Journal of Interactive Media in Education, 8,* pp. 1–18.

Oblinger, D., & Oblinger, J. (Eds.). (2005). *Educating the net generation.* Boulder, CO: Educause.

Prensky, M. (2001). Digital natives, digital immigrants. *On the Horizon, 9.*

Quarshie Smith, B. (2004). Genre, medium, and learning to write: Negotiating identities, enacting school-based literacies in adulthood. *Journal of College Reading and Learning, 34*(2), 75–96.

Rainie, L. (2005). *The state of blogging.* Washington, DC: Pew Internet and American Life Project.

Reed, W. M. (1990). The effect of computer-and-writing instruction on prospective English teachers' attitudes toward and perceived uses of computers in writing instruction. *Journal of Research on Computing in Education, 23*(1), 3–27.

Rheingold, H. (2002). *Smart mobs: The next social revolution.* New York: Basic Books.

Roberts, G. (2005). Technology and learning expectations of the net generation. In D. Oblinger & J. Oblinger (Eds.), *Educating the net generation* (pp. 3.1–3.7). Boulder, CO: Educause.

Romano, L. (2005, December 25). Literacy of college graduates is on decline: survey's finding of a drop in reading proficiency is inexplicable, experts say. *Washington Post,* A12. Retrieved May 25, 2006, from http://washingtonpost.com/wp-dyn/content/article/2005/12/24/ AR2005122400701.html

Satchell, C., & Singh, S. (2005). The mobile phone as the globalizing icon of the early 21st century. *Smart Internet Technology Cooperative Research Centre.* Retrieved (04/2007), from ucd.smartinternet.com.au/Documents/MobilePhone_Globalizing.pdf

Shuchat Shaw, F., & Giacquinta, J. (2000). A survey of graduate students as end users of computer technology: New roles for faculty. *Information Technology, Learning, and Performance Journal, 18*(1). Retrieved May 5, 2006, from http://osra.org/itlpj/shuchatshawgiacquinta.PDF

Simon, E. J. (2001, Winter). Electronic textbooks: A pilot study of student e-reading habits. *Future of Print Media Journal,* pp. 1–5.

Smith, P., Coldwell, J., Smith, S., & Murphy, K. (2005). Learning through computer-mediated communication: A comparison of Australian and Chinese heritage. *Innovations in Education and Teaching International, 42*(2), 123–134.

Snyder, I. (2004). *Pattern recognition: Learning from the technoliteracy research.* Paper presented to the National Reading Conference 54th annual Meeting, San Antonio, TX.

Stahl, N. A., & King, J. R. (2000). A history of college reading. In R. F. Flippo & D. C. Caverly (Eds.), *Handbook of college reading and study research* (pp. 1–24). Mahwah, NJ: Lawrence Erlbaum Publishers.

Suoranta, J., & Lehtimaki, H. (2004). *Children in the information society: The case of Finland.* New York: Peter Lang.

Tao, L., & Moon, J. (1996). Electronic messages: Can we expect them to be coherent? Paper presented to the Annual Meeting of the College Reading Association, Charleston, SC.

Tapscott, D. (1998). *Growing up digital: The rise of the net generation.* New York: McGraw-Hill Companies, New York.

Tenopir, C. (2003). *Use and users of electronic library resources: An overview and analysis of recent research studies. Executive summary.* Washington, DC: Council on Library and Information Resources. Retrieved May 26, 2006, from http://clir.org/pubs/execsum/sum120.html

Thorne, S. (2003, April). The internet as artifact: Immediacy, evolution, and educational contingencies, or "The wrong tool for the right job?" Paper presented at the American Educational Research Association annual meeting, Chicago, IL.

Thorne, S., & Payne, J. S. (2005). Evolutionary Trajectories, Internet-mediated Expression, and Language Education (Special issue). *CALICO Journal,* 371–397.

Trevino, E. M. (2005). Blogger motivations: Power, pull, and positive feedback. Internet Research 6.0, Annual Meeting of Association of Internet Researchers, Chicago, IL.

Valeri-Gold, M., & Commander, N. E. (2000-2001). An examination of at-risk college students' sexist attitudes toward reading. *The Journal of College Literacy and Learning, 30,* 1–9.

Warschauer, M. (2000). *Electronic literacies: Language, culture, and power in online learning.* Mahwah, NJ: Erlbaum.

Weiler, A. (2001). "Two-year-college-freshmen and the internet: Do they really know all that stuff?" *Libraries and the Academy.* Volume 1, Number 2, April 2001, pp. 161-167. Baltimore, MD, Johns Hopkins University Press.

Wells, J. (2000). Effects of an on-line computer-mediated communication course, prior computer experience and internet knowledge, and learning styles on students' internet attitudes computer-mediated technologies and new educational challenges. *Journal of Industrial Teacher Education, 37*(3). Retrieved May 8, 2006, from http://scholar.lib.vt.edu/ejournals/JITE/v37n3/wells.html

Wepner, S. B. (1990). Do computers have a place in college reading courses? *Journal of Reading, 33*(5), 348–354.

Windham, C. (2005a). "Father Google and mother IM: Confessions of a net gen learner." *EDUCAUSE Review,* 42–58.

Windham, C. (2005b). The student's perspective. In D. Oblinger & J. Oblinger (Eds.), *Educating the net generation* (pp. 5.1–5.12). Boulder, CO: Educause.

Yaworski, J. (2000). Using computer-based technology to support the college reading classroom. *Technology and College Reading, 31*(1), 19–41.

Yellowlees-Douglas, J. (2002). Here even when you're not: Teaching in an internet degree program. In I. Snyder (Ed.), *Silicon literacies: communication, innovation and education in the electronic age* (pp. 116–129). London: Routledge.

CHAPTER 21

Just Don't Call Them Cartoons
The New Literacy Spaces of Anime, Manga, and Fanfiction

REBECCA WARD BLACK

UNIVERSITY OF CALIFORNIA, IRVINE, USA

Introduction

Recent scholarship across a range of academic disciplines has started to explore the contours of a media and cultural landscape that is in constant flux because of new information and communication technologies (ICT) that allow for traversal across temporal and spatial boundaries (Leander & McKim, 2003; Leander & Sheehy, 2004), traditional linguistic and cultural borders (Lam, 2000), as well as long-established divisions between producers and consumers of intellectual property (Jenkins, 2006). Such scholarship underscores the importance of attending, not only to the nature of new technologies and tools, but also to the uses within and across networked life spaces to which these new media and tools are being put. A robust understanding of these digital technologies situated in authentic everyday practice is necessary if we, as educators and researchers, aim to successfully engage new generations of students who are entering, currently attending, or indeed are dropping out of schools with "mindsets" (Lankshear & Knobel, 2003) that in many ways are in direct opposition to the mindsets underpinning traditional systems of education.

New Literacy Studies scholars (New London Group, 1996) have pointed out that many schools still operate from a mindset rooted in the Industrial Revolution that is "forged in physical space" and organized around the production of material goods (Lankshear & Knobel, 2003). Whereas, contemporary students are entering classrooms with a mindset that is "forged in cyberspace" and organized around the production and distribution of information and various texts, including traditional print documents, graphic arts, spoken and embodied language, and other forms of online and post-typographic communication (Castells, 1996; Lankshear & Knobel, 2003). Most students today are accustomed to active participation in such information-based economies, where graphic art and online publishing software enable new forms of semiotic engagement and symbolic manipulation of media. Many of them are also well versed in new ICTs such as synchronous chatting, webcams, avatars, blogs, and personal Web sites that make possible the sort of public performance of self that provides social and intellectual cachet in today's multicultural, multilingual, and multitextual networked spaces.

This chapter explores three topical phenomena: (a) *anime* (Japanese animation), (b) *manga* (Japanese graphic novels), and (c) *fanfiction* (texts created by fans that are derived from popular media), in terms of historical background, content, existing research, and related fan practices. These three phenomena provide salient examples of how new ICTs have led to the development of literacy and social practices that traverse accustomed national, cultural, linguistic, and producer-consumer boundaries. Moreover, they illustrate how new ICTs have facilitated the global dispersion of a range of fan-produced cultural and intellectual products via circulation in online communities. The chapter begins with a general introduction to the development and history of anime and manga and an overview of the artistic and generic characteristics of these media. This introduction is followed by a review of anime and manga-related research—research that primarily is guided by historical time lines, focused on generic content and audience reception, and directed at adults. The focus then moves to research devoted to fan activities surrounding these media, ultimately narrowing in scope to emphasize the small amount of work that explicitly addresses how school-age fans are integrating these media into their daily social and literate interactions.

Interestingly enough, as the latter portion of the chapter will detail, one of the most salient ways that anime and manga have been integrated into school-age fans' lives is through the production of online, anime and manga-based fanfiction. Moreover, research on fanfiction has followed a similar trajectory to that of anime and manga studies—with primary foci being genre, audience reception (and production), and adult fans. Following a review of adult-oriented fanfiction studies, the chapter then turns to work that explores *school-age* fans' literacy and social practices surrounding online fanfiction. The chapter concludes with discussion of how anime, manga, and fanfiction have coalesced in various fan communities as a sort of "third space" (Bhabha, 1994) where adolescents engage in meaningful learning and participation that is not dependent on common cultural, historical, or linguistic background, but instead relies on a shared discourse and semiotic repertoire linked to popular media and fan culture. In conclusion, the chapter addresses the need for hybrid, interdisciplinary perspectives on literacy, popular culture, and learning that acknowledge and can adequately address the multidirectional flows of information, the hybrid, multilingual, and multimodal forms of communication, and the temporal, spatial, and cultural fluidity of these new media and literacy landscapes.

Theoretical Framework

As researchers, our understandings of new ICTs and digital literacies have been and will continue to be shaped extensively by our epistemic frameworks for literacy and the sort of questions that we ask about emerging forms of online, post-typographic communication. My own research, which centers on the literacy and communication practices of adolescent English language learners (ELL) writing online fanfiction, is firmly grounded within a sociocultural or "new" approach to literacy studies. I find a New Literacy Studies (New Literacy Studies) theoretical orientation particularly apt for looking at the everyday use of emerging ICTs in online spaces, and for relating such work to teaching and learning both in and outside of formal-education settings, for many reasons. To begin, sociocultural perspectives have effectively expanded our notions of literacy beyond discrete, rule-governed decoding and encoding skills to include consideration of many shifting forms of semiotic and textual meaning-making practices, such as those that develop in tandem with new technologies, contexts, and the intentions of individual and collective-literacy users (New London Group, 1996).

This notion of literacy as a social practice (Street, 1984) has helped us to move away from "autonomous" models of language and learning. Such models tended to attribute failure to learn standard and academic forms of literacy to individual, cognitive deficits, and/or the deficiencies of entire cultural groups. A social practice paradigm, on the other hand, facilitates exploration of how an individual or group's willingness and ability to take on forms of literacy are closely tied to the relevance of various literacies or discourses (Gee, 1999) to the literacy users' personal, social, cultural, historical, and economic lives (Heath, 1983; Scribner & Cole, 1981). In so doing, this paradigm also turns our research view toward the ways in which literacy as a nonneutral entity might carry and transmit a wealth of historical and ideological perspectives that play a part in reproducing certain social and material contexts, and how individuals, as active, agentive literacy users, take up dominant forms of literacy and refashion them to suit the particular needs and perspectives of local contexts. Such a paradigm is crucial to understanding key issues emerging in research related to anime, manga, and fanfiction, including (a) the fact that media such as Japanese anime and manga carry with them certain generic, ideological, cultural, and literate conventions; (b) how, as these media become part of global flows of information and spectacle, they are taken up by fans and are revised and recontextualized through local literate and social interactions; and (c) how these reworked texts, in turn, are shared and redisseminated into global networks via new ICTs.

In terms of literacy and learning, there has been a recent push within the New Literacy Studies (Alvermann, 2002; Hull & Schultz, 2002; Lankshear & Knobel, 2003) to develop vistas extending beyond traditionally accepted contexts for literacy research—primarily those that are temporally and geographically bounded—in order to gain a clearer view of students' out-of-school literacy practices and engagement with forms of online and post-typographic communication. A sociocultural framework for literacy is broad enough to allow literacy pedagogy to be informed and enhanced by models of learning developed within other component "movements" of the "social turn" toward conceptualizing and theorizing literacy (Lankshear, 1999). As such, it allows for a fair measure of theoretical and methodological flexibility in approaching informal, grassroots learning spaces, such as anime and manga-based fanfiction writing sites, in order to best answer key questions that are emerging as a result of the aforementioned push, as well as in response to the growing salience of media, popular culture, and technology in youths' lives, including such queries as (a) What is so motivating about these media and networked, informal learning sites that youth willingly devote hours to participation around them—even in fanfiction writing spaces where participation involves many school-based literacy practices such as composition, editing, and peer review? (b) How might the patterns of participation in these informal, online learning spaces be linked to larger shifts in our increasingly globalized, networked, and linguistically and culturally diverse society? (c) What are the effective and motivating forms of learning and teaching that are taking place around media and popular culture in these sites? (d) What sorts of identities do these spaces recruit, recognize, and reward? (e) And, given what we have learned so far in answer to these questions, how might we or even should we bring such understandings to bear on literacy pedagogy in classrooms?

More than Just Cartoons: Japanese Anime and Manga

Neither *anime*, which began emerging in Japan in the early 20th century (Clements & McCarthy, 2001; Napier, 2001; Patten, 2004), nor its graphic counterpart *manga*, which has been traced as far back as the "sequential storytelling" picture scrolls from medieval Japan (K. Ito, 2005; Pandey, 2000) can be held up as novel in terms of the chronological development of "new literacies." The term manga was coined at the start of the 19th century with Hokusai's multicolored woodblock prints (K. Ito, 2005), and over time the medium has become ubiquitous in Japanese culture. Contemporary manga genres (these categories apply to anime as well) address markedly diverse target audiences and can be broadly categorized in the following ways: (a) *josei/*

redikomi manga which are, as a rule, created by female artists and feature the daily aspects of Japanese women's lives, (b) *seinen,* created by and for men with texts ranging from horror to war stories to mild pornography. Other types include the whimsical and fantasy laden (c) *kodomo,* which is intended mostly for children, (d) *shōjo* geared toward young females with its romantic themes and strong magical girl characters, and the high-action (e) *shōnen* for young and teenage boys (K. Ito, 2005; Wikipedia, 2005). In Japan, manga also encompass an array of informative texts ranging from government-produced pamphlets on the economy to instructional texts on how to do home or auto repairs (K. Ito, 2005). Clearly, the relatively low manufacturing costs and flexibility of the medium allow for creative experimentation across myriad landscapes, character styles, and artistic techniques and facilitate the expression of all types of information in a widely accessible format (Napier, 2001).

While short animated films were produced throughout the early 20th century in prewar and postwar Japan, the manga-influenced productions that most of us associate with contemporary anime began decades later with the release of Osamu Tezuka's *Tetsuwan Atomu (Astro Boy)* in Japanese theatres in 1963 (Leonard, 2004). Whereas the cartoon industry in many countries confined the medium mostly to the realm of childfare, comedy, and action-hero adventures, as anime scholar Gilles Poitras (1999) has pointed out, "[T]he Japanese have been using anime to cover every literary and cinematic genre imaginable" (p. viii) for years. Prevalent genres of anime vary across the sexually explicit *hentai,* to the highly popular *science-fiction* productions and its subgenres of *mecha* or giant robots, *cyberpunk* with its dystopian representations of the ills of corporate greed and technology, and the quasi-historical *steampunk* (K. Ito, 2005; Wikipedia, 2005). Anime genres also include biting humor, heart-wrenching drama, historical samurai-era productions, and sports-inspired shows to name just a few. Characterized by its vibrant colors, fine lines, and the exaggerated expressions of its characters, Japanese animation has attracted the worldwide attention of fans and researchers alike as an alternative to the sort of commodified and child-oriented narratives that dominate the animation market in other countries (Napier, 2001).

Manga and anime have become some of Japan's most important cultural exports (Napier, 2001). Achieving international reach, these media have been translated into many languages in countries across the globe, including China, France, Germany, Italy, the United Kingdom, Spain, and the United States (K. Ito, 2005). Outside of Japan, the United States has one of the largest markets for anime (Napier, 2001; Patten, 2004), as it offers many fans an alternative to American animation monoliths such as Disney. In recent years, Japanese animation and manga have made a conspicuous return to mainstream media space in several countries with popular children's television *shōnen* genres such as *Pokémon, Yugioh!, Ramna* 1/2, and *Dragonball Z,* and *shōjo* genres such as *Sailor Moon, Card Captor Sakura,* and *Inuyasha.* Major motion pictures such as the blockbuster hit *Spirited Away* and other popular films such as *Princess Mononoke, Castle in the Sky, My Neighbor Totoro,* and *Kiki's Delivery Service* have brought the stunning graphics, complex themes, and often whimsical nature of kawaii or "cute" culture (Allison, 2004) and the fantasy genre into the 21st-century spotlight.

Manga and Anime Research

While manga and anime are often derided for being violent and pornographic or dismissed as being child-fare, manga and anime scholars, aficionados, and fans concur that these media are far more than just cartoons. Anyone who has watched a significant amount of anime or read enough manga must at minimum cede to these media a wealth of complex, believable characters, intricate narrative structures, and many themes that address the light and dark aspects of the human condition. To date, scholarship has examined anime and manga primarily in terms of existing genres and past trends, artistic characteristics, and in relation to the social and historical contexts of production of these media. Identifiable categories of academic writing include introductory works that offer historical, cultural, and thematic overviews of both manga (Mizuno, 1991; Schodt, 1983, 1996; Shimizu, 1991) and anime (Drazen, 2002; Levi, 1996; Poitras, 2001) in relation to specific series and/or to the work of individual creators/artists (Ledoux, 1997). In addition, the "explosion" of anime in recent years has inspired some scholars to expand readers' knowledge about anime via exposition on the cultural and historical significance of objects such as "historical personages, organizations, corporations, [and] gestures" that are found in and across different genres of anime (Poitras, 1999), or through broad surveys of and guides to the numerous anime and manga series produced in the last several decades (Pelletier, 2000; Clements & McCarthy, 2001; Ledoux & Ranney, 1997; McCarthy, 1996). Much of this research, interestingly enough, has occurred outside education fields.

Susan Napier (2001), a well-known name in anime research and Japanese studies, used a cultural and literary lens to explore how anime might move audiences to consider contemporary issues in Japanese society in ways that older art forms might not be able to. She explored the unique narrative and aesthetic qualities of contemporary anime in terms of characteristic modes such as the *apocalyptic* (end of the world), *elegiac* (melancholy or nostalgia), and *festival* (play or ritual) that reflect the complex and sometimes conflicting cultural backdrops of historical and modern Japan (Napier, 2001). Other scholars have also examined the apocalyptic in these media in terms of representations of disaster (Napier, 1993), war, and the bombings of Hiroshima and Nagasaki (Crawford, 1996; Freiberg, 1996). Many studies also focus on issues such as ideology (Kinsella, 1998, 2000; Morris-Suzuki & Rimmer, 2002; Napier, 2001, 2002; Newitz, 1995), gender representation

(Erino, 1993; Fujimoto, 1991; Grigsby, 1998; K. Ito, 1994, 2003; Ledden & Fejes, 1987; Napier, 1998; Ogi, 2001; Orbaugh, 2003; Shiokawa, 1999), sex (Buckley, 1991; Napier, 2001; Perper & Cornog, 2002), and the representation of sexuality (Matsui, 1993; McLelland, 2000a, 2000b; Sabucco, 2003) in anime and manga. Recent work also is beginning to address these media in terms of their global spread as pop culture (Grigsby, 1998; Lai & Dixon, 2001), the broader topic of Japan's place within global flows of information in the 21st century, and the complex and multimodal literacy practices used by college students reading manga (Allen & Ingulsrud, 2003).

All of these studies, while focused primarily on adult anime and manga, highlight the sophistication and complexity of these "cartoons" and work toward establishing their legitimacy as media productions that are worthy of increased academic attention as their popularity and mainstream visibility grows. Additionally, such broad surveys and in-depth explorations of these increasingly popular media genres have relevance for literacy education in that they provide insight into the sort of generic conventions and narrative structures with which students are becoming familiar. Moreover, such work details the various representations of sexuality, gender, culture, and history—representations that often present a stark contrast to those of mainstream U.S. animation—that are becoming part of many youth's pop-cultural repertoires and may influence the possibilities for social and narrative action that they envision for themselves.

Otaku Fandom

Otaku is a much contested term that appears frequently in conversations around Japanese media and is used in Japan as a derisive label to describe a fan who is "so involved with a particular type of fan subculture that he or she becomes obsessed, even insane" (Newitz, 1994, p. 1). The meaning of *otaku* has shifted, over time and space, to a more positive connotation for anime and manga fans outside of Japan (Eng, 2001a, 2001b, 2002; Volker, 1990). The genesis of organized anime and manga fandom in the United States has been located in the late 1970s and early 1980s with the grassroots establishment of science-fiction/fantasy fan clubs and conventions (Patten, 2004). While these fan clubs were created with the purpose of promoting preexisting anime media in the United States, they also centered on the production and distribution of a wide range of fan-created texts. Such fan texts engage an array of sophisticated literacy practices such as *fansubbing,* which is when fans synchronize the video signals from the television, a VCR, and computer to write and inscribe their own subtitles onto anime videos with a Japanese soundtrack, or *digisubbing,* which essentially describes the modern version of fansubs that are created entirely on the computer (Leonard, 2004). Fan practices also include creating fanzines and producing *dōjinshi,* or amateur works such as manga, fan-art collections, and fan guides, and writing fanfiction that, in spite of their present-day prominence and widespread dissemination on the Web, remain largely unexplored in academic research. The following section will include a brief introduction to the ways that anime and manga have been taken up within fan communities and then will discuss how academic research has approached such fannish activities.

Many self-identified *otaku* or aficionados have entered the global flows of information surrounding anime and manga by forming Web sites and mailing lists devoted to metadiscussion of the artistic, thematic, and social elements of these media. These sites include articles and commentary by the Web site or list administrators and links to scholarship, which is published and disseminated via fan networks, on the Web, and in online journals. These sites also serve as clearinghouses or guides for finding the aforementioned sorts of fan texts such as *digisubs* and *dōjinshi*. Some of the more prominent sites include AnimeResearch.com, the Anime Manga Research Circle, (groups. yahoo.com/group/amrc-l), the Anime Manga Web Essay Archive (corneredangel.com/amwess), Matt Thorne's encyclopedic Web site (matt-thorn.com), and AnimeFandom.org. Such spaces should not be overlooked by researchers, as the fans running and participating in these sites provide a unique brand of metacommentary and nuanced perspectives that are informed by years of devoted consideration and appreciation of anime and manga. Moreover, if we are truly to understand how students use new literacies and operate from a mindset rooted in digital space, then we must begin to think about the online proliferation of networked, participatory "centers of learning" (Purves, 1998) and to understand the roles they might play in global flows of information surrounding media and popular culture. In addition, in terms of education, perhaps it is time to address how such prolific, networked, and interactive sources of information may influence students' attitudes toward and facility with more traditional, structured, and enclosed "centers of learning" such as books, encyclopedias, classrooms, and even libraries.

Sean Leonard (2004) took a unique perspective on fan-produced texts in terms of globalization. Leonard analyzed the aforementioned practice of fan-subbing as a driving force in the licensed distribution of subtitled anime in the U.S. market, essentially positing that fan practices "pulled" licensed copies of these media to the West. While Leonard provided a thorough discussion and overview of fansubs, from their debut in American fandom in 1989 through subsequent eras of anime production and distribution both in Japan and the United States, his primary focus was on the historical, legal, and global, rather than literacy-related aspects of fansubbing. Albeit outside the scope of Leonard's article, fansubbing and its contemporary online counterparts, such as digisubs and Web sites that provide translations and/or "cliffnotes" (i.e., succinct summaries of storylines) for various anime and manga, are complex new literacy practices involving sophisticated processes of "translation, reconstitution, and reproduction" of the original texts (Leonard, 2004) and are worthy of exploration in their own right. Moreover, such practices have much to offer in understanding the role of such literacy practices in Western youths' understandings and perceptions of Japanese history, culture, and society.

Once a fandom dominated primarily by over-30-something males, the contemporary otaku demographic has shifted to include a substantial base of young school-age males and females alike, and a limited amount of research is beginning to follow suit. For example, popular anime series such as *Pokémon, Digimon,* and *Yu-Gi-Oh!* have received a fair amount of academic attention for their unique status as media mixes (M. Ito, 2001), media franchises (Lemke, 2005), or as sets of cultural practices (Buckingham & Sefton-Green, 2004) that, combined with technological advances and new ICTs, make it possible for children to integrate fandom into multiple aspects of their daily lives. Over the course of a day, or in some cases simultaneously, children can eat Pokémon candy, play Digimon games on handhelds as they ride in the family car, sleep with a Pikachu stuffed animal, watch *Yu-Gi-Oh!* on a laptop, and/or IM with their friends about what might happen on the next Pokémon episode. As Lemke pointed out, such media franchises facilitate and, in the interest of profit, encourage fans' engagement with the worlds of popular culture across "multiple timescales" and a range of networked social spaces. Such networks and confluence of media also enable fans to engage in a range of productive activities through which the division between producer and consumer is blurred. For instance, fans can actively participate in a pop-cultural imaginary while they trade paper playing cards with their friends on the playground (just as the *Yu-Gi-Oh!* characters do in the series), gather online in fan Web rings to discuss discrete characteristics of different Pokémon, create and post fan art, design personal Web pages, and publish their own anime-based fanfictions online for other fans to read and respond to.

In response to the widespread visibility of the Pokémon craze, the University of Hawaii sponsored a conference in 2002 devoted entirely to the consideration of this anime phenomenon and emphasized school-age children's interactions with the series. J. Tobin (2000, 2004), an authority on children's engagement with media and popular culture, edited a volume of proceedings from the conference that features discussion from teachers and researchers across fields including anthropology, sociology, cultural, and media studies. Individual essays addressed such diverse topics as the implications for cultural identity as anime and manga are increasingly consumed by nonJapanese audiences (Iwabuchi, 2004; Katsuno & Maret, 2004; Yano, 2004), how children productively engage with Pokémon in local cultural contexts (Brougere, 2004; Lemish & Bloch, 2004) and use their interactions around these media to construct and enact multiple identities through narrative play (Bromley, 2004; S. Tobin, 2004) and through writing (Willett, 2004) in schools. As a whole, this work addressed issues that have clear implications for education, such as how

cultural, and intellectual practice, as evidenced by the research and metacommentary on fanfic that has started appearing online on personal fan sites as well as in academic texts and journals. These shifts, brought about by new advances in media and communication technologies, have placed fanfiction squarely within the flows of information and social exchange that are being passed between new generations of adolescents across national, cultural, and linguistic spaces.

Academic attention to fanfiction has varied widely in terms of disciplinary approach and focus, with studies stemming primarily from cultural, communication, media, and literature studies. Also, because fanfiction is derivative work based on copyrighted intellectual property, the genre has also been looked at from legal (McCardle, 2003; Tushnet, 1997) and ethical standpoints (Pugh, 2004), with such studies serving as references for fans who wish to defend their right to continue producing fictions. Early academic writers on fanfiction such as Joanna Russ, (1985), Patricia Frazier Lamb and Diana L. Veith (1986), and Camille Bacon-Smith (1992) centered their feminist-inflected work primarily on fanzines and the genre of slash fiction—that is, fiction depicting noncanonical homosexual relationships, such as pairing the Star Trek characters Kirk/Spock—with the *slash* between the names denoting romantic pairing. When these studies were conducted, the majority of fanfiction, including slash, was produced by middle-aged females. Thus, their works conceive of slash primarily as female erotica or "pornography by women, for women" (Jenkins, 1992; Russ, 1985) and a means by which these fans are able to project their own feminine romantic and sexual fantasies/desires onto the masculine bodies of the series characters (Jenkins, 1992). Constance Penley (1991) added an interesting dimension to research on Star Trek slash with her piece on "Brownian Motion" in which she focused on the genre as a site of debate about male domination in the arenas of technology as well as sex.

Without a doubt, Henry Jenkins' ethnographic work *Textual Poachers* (1992) continues to be the authoritative text on fan culture. In this text, Jenkins, writing as a self-identified fan, drew on Michel de Certeau's notion of "poaching" to liken fans' interpretive and productive practices to a form of "cultural bricolage through which readers fragment texts and reassemble the broken shards according to their own blueprints, salvaging bits and pieces of the found material in making sense of their own social experience" (de Certeau, as cited in Jenkins, 1992, p. 26). Through case studies, interviews, and the voiced impressions of numerous fans, Jenkins provided an empathetic and nuanced perspective of fan culture that challenges short-sighted stereotypes of fans as "cultural dupes" who passively ingest the messages of mainstream media or as obsessive followers who need to "get a life." In so doing, Jenkins consciously sought to redefine public conceptions of fandom and raised seminal questions about the nature of fan culture and audience reception that have spurred years of subsequent fan-related research.

Contemporary work has turned to the multiplicity of online fanfiction archives and discussion boards as data for exploring assorted fandoms, new canons, and different genres of fanfiction. Many such studies are canon-specific investigations of the genre of *shipper* or relationship-based fictions that explore issues such as how women use these fictions to take a counter-hegemonic stance against "producers' commercial imperatives, a separate spheres dichotomy, devaluation of the feminine/private sphere, and masculine generic conventions" on series such as the X-files (Scodari & Felder, 2000, p. 238). Other studies explore why some women write *het,* or fictions with heterosexual pairings of certain couples, within canons such as *Star Trek Voyager* that generally inspire slash fiction (Somogyi, 2002). Or, in a similar vein, Rosemary Coombe (1998) looked at shipper fanzines as forms of social critique and satire that enable women to explore their position in patriarchal society.

Over the years, expanding canons of slash fiction, ranging from *Xena the Warrior Princess* and *Buffy the Vampire Slayer* (Cicioni, 1998) to more obscure manga series (McClelland, 2000a, 2000b) have continued to draw the attention of researchers and fans alike. Anne Kustritz (2003) looked at slash from a literary perspective and posited that as a genre, slash "offers its own particular challenge to normative constructions of gender and romance, as it allows women to construct narratives that subvert patriarchy by reappropriating those prototypical hero characters who usually reproduce women's position of social disempowerment" (p. 371). Additionally, new forms of hybrid academic texts created by fanfiction authors who are also academic researchers are emerging with explorations of female/female or *femmeslash* as a means of contesting and dialoging with hegemonic mass culture and a way of challenging the primacy of representations of heterosexuality in the media (Busse, 2005; Russo, 2002).

For the most part, what these studies all share is continuous movement toward some understanding of the many ways in which fans are taking up elements of pop culture and then redistributing them in new forms that are imbued with meanings that are grounded in the lived realities and social worlds of fans. However, considering how the demographics of fanfiction have shifted with the advent of online publishing—from a base primarily made up of adult science fiction and daytime soap-opera fans to a transnational and multilingual population that is dominated by adolescents from across the globe—it is somewhat surprising that more academic attention to fanfiction has not followed suit. As evidenced by the aforementioned studies, the vast majority of the research corpus to date has focused on adult-authored fictions within certain genres and centers on a largely English-speaking population. In contrast, prominent archival fanfiction sites as well as the vast numbers of personal fan sites on the Web feature fictions based on a range of culturally diverse canons, composed of multiple languages, and posted mostly by fans between the ages of 13 and 18. The following section will introduce the small amount of research that has looked at literacy-related aspects of youths' engagement with fanfiction. It also identifies some key elements of on- and offline fan writing and fan culture that have great potential to shed light on how adolescents are using technology to simultaneously learn from and contribute to global flows of information and to meaningfully participate in discourses that are steeped in culturally, linguistically, and semiotically diverse forms of literacy.

Fanfiction, Literacy, and Research

Interestingly enough, the relatively few studies examining adolescents' literacy and social practices surrounding fanfiction mostly center on canons related to anime and manga (Black, 2005a; 2005b, and 2006); Chandler-Olcott & Mahar, 2003a, 2003b). For example, Kelly Chandler-Olcott and Donna Mahar (2003a, 2003b), a university researcher and educator team, recently conducted a classroom-based enthnographic inquiry into adolescent girls' use of digital technologies in which they found pop-cultural texts, particularly anime and manga, to be central to participants' literacy practices. The authors drew from work in the New Literacy Studies tradition (Cope & Kalantzis, 2000; New London Group, 1996) as analytic lenses for viewing focal participants' creative-design practices of crafting amateur manga, developing anime-based Web sites, and writing fanfiction. Design is a particularly apt construct for looking at adolescents' engagement with media texts, as it emphasizes the relationships between source texts, the often hybrid and intertextual forms that redesigned texts take, as well as the creative and potentially transformative process of reworking and reshaping existing modes of meaning (Chandler-Olcott & Mahar, 2003a, 2003b; New London Group, 1996; Cope & Kalantzis, 2000).

Chandler-Olcott and Mahar (2003a, 2003b) used the notion of design to explore multimodal aspects of one participant's development of anime-inspired Web pages and fanfiction, and another's creation of manga and participation in an online amateur manga mailing list, focusing on the visual, spatial, and embodied aspects of their engagement with these technology-mediated activities. The authors made a valuable contribution to fanfiction research in that they are among the first to apply a literacy-related and educational lens to examining anime, manga, and fanfiction. Additionally, their analyses provided insight into the ways in which some adolescent girls may draw from "conflicting discourses about gender and relationships" in both media and print texts to explore and possibly expand female spaces in a patriarchal society, such as through the construction of fanfictions that feature strong female characters in roles generally reserved for men. Their analyses also provided insight into how these youth used popular culture as a resource in their ongoing social interactions and conversations about "issues such as friendship, loyalty, power, and sexuality" (Chandler-Olcott & Mahar, 2003a).

In terms of academic value, Chandler-Olcott and Mahar (2003a) depicted fanfiction as a possible entry point for discussions about differences between fanfiction genres and traditional academic text. They also discussed fanfiction's potential value as a diagnostic measure that might help teachers understand students' composition capabilities in nonacademic genres. While the authors saw the value of fanfiction in terms of motivation for and engagement with writing, they constructed the genre as both separate and dissimilar from school-based literacy practices. This may be a result of the authors' limited exploration of or exposure to the larger fanfiction writing community that exists online, as their data consisted of one focal participant's fictions that were created primarily for her friends and family or were posted on a personal Web site and intended for a limited audience. Thus, while this piece is consonant with many of the emerging perspectives on the role that digital and fanfiction often plays in helping young adolescent girls to construct and enact powerful, online identities (Thomas, 2004, 2006; see also Thomas, this volume), it takes a different stance on fanfiction's relevance to school-based literacies (Black, 2005a; 2005b; Jenkins, 2006).

For instance, Jenkins (2006) provided an overview of one home-schooled student's experiences creating and editing *The Daily Phoenix*, an online "school newspaper" for the fictional Hogwarts Academy from Harry Potter. In this work, he explained why the focal student, Heather, and many other fanfiction authors can write—pointing to their participation as *Daily Phoenix* staff and in various online affinity spaces, such as the archival site *Fanfiction Alley*, as a formative part of their writing and literacy development. In these affinity spaces, members have the opportunity to take on identities as writers, editors, reporters, proofreaders, and columnists. Additionally, Jenkins pointed out that "through online discussions of fan writing, the teen writers develop a vocabulary for talking about writing and learn strategies for rewriting and improving their own work" (pp. 183). Moreover, when they talk about the original Harry Potter text, "[T]hey make comparisons with other literary works or draw connections with philosophical and theological traditions; they debate gender stereotyping of the female characters; they cite interviews with the writer or read critical analysis of the works" (pp. 183) and essentially engage in literate and analytical activities that they normally would not encounter until college.

Jenkin's (2006) work with these fan sites helps to illustrate how popular culture and media technologies are often the crux of interaction in such affinity spaces where new generations of adolescents are spending more and more time. Jenkins drew on Gee's (2004b) work to point out that online affinity spaces represent the cutting edge of effective learning environments in several respects. First, they are organized around a common endeavor or interest rather than temporal or spatial proximity, and therefore are able to span differences in gender, race, class, age, and education level. Also, because knowledge is both *intensive,* with some members bringing specialized information about discrete aspects of a site, and *extensive,* with other members understanding the site at a broader level, leadership turns out to be "porous" in such spaces, as different activities and functions provide multiple opportunities for *all* members to both teach and learn (Gee, 2004b, p. 87). Thus, multiple forms of participation, knowledge, and experience are valued, and knowledge is both *distributed* across various "people, tools, and technologies, not held in any one person or thing" (Gee, as cited in Jenkins, 2006, p. 177) within the space, and *dispersed,* meaning that ICTs provide access to other "centers of knowledge" (Purves, 1998) that can be linked to outside of the space.

Other affinity spaces, such as fanfiction help and *beta-reading* sites have also started to attract some academic attention (Black, 2005a, 2005b; Jenkins, 2006). In the fanfiction community, a person who edits or proofs a fiction is known as a *beta-reader.* To submit a fiction to many beta-reading sites, authors must fill out a form specifying the genre (e.g., poetry, adventure, romance) and canon (e.g., Harry Potter, Pokémon) for the fiction and indicate which elements of the fiction they would like feedback on (e.g., plot development, characterization, adherence to genre, or grammar and spelling). Thus, a situation is set up in which a beta-reader is qualified to read fictions from the genre, and can provide the sort of focused feedback that the author wants. Moreover, many fanfiction help sites, such as the now defunct Writer's University feature metadiscussion on elements of fanfiction, writing, and reviewing that mirror school-based composition practices, such as peer review, giving constructive feedback, editing, proofreading, effective plot development, robust characterization, and constructing effective rhetorical structures, to name just a few (Black, 2005a, 2005b; Jenkins, 2004, 2006).

My own work extends fanfiction and anime research into a different but related arena with a focus on ELLs' literate and social practices on *Fanfiction.net,* the largest multifandom archive on the Web. Fanfiction.net is a prime example of the prevalence and popularity of online fanfiction, as it currently houses well over a million pieces of fanfiction spanning 2,000 different media. Canons such as Harry Potter seem to grow exponentially overnight, with over 175,000 fictions at last count. The site also hosts an impressive collection of over 350,000 anime-inspired fanfictions stemming from 300 different series. Due to the widespread popularity of these media, the anime canons attract a great many adolescents. And, while English is the primary language of the site, the interface supports the posting of fictions in seven different languages, thus offering many nonnative English speakers the opportunity to post fictions and interact in their first languages. Moreover, primary foci of the site are writer/reader interaction, peer-review, and improving writing skills, thus providing a context for in-depth inquiry into many fan activities that are aligned with school-based literacy practices (Black, 2005a; 2006). Drawing primarily from case studies and ethnographic data collected over 2 years of participant observation, I have been exploring online fanfiction both as a genre and as a social practice, situated in relation to the context of Fanfiction.net, networked technology, and the broader fan community. Such explorations have enabled me to characterize aspects of this online community that promote the development of collaborative, meaningful forms of language and learning over time, as well as to understand how such spaces both enable and motivate adolescent ELLs to enact identities as successful and critical writers, readers, and users of English (Black, 2006).

As can be seen through this review, currently there is very little research on school-age students who are engaging with online fanfiction. This may be due in part to a general tendency in educational settings to dismiss or even outlaw popular culture, deriding it and the media as frivolous pursuits that distract students and take time away from more worthy pursuits such as reading literature, studying, and learning about "high culture" (Jenkins, McPherson, & Shattuc, 2003). While fanfictions are derivative in the sense that their design is mediated through fans' interpretations of media and popular culture, as can be seen from this small amount of scholarly work, the genre lends itself to a great deal of literate innovation that is intimately tied to issues of literacy, learning, and identity that certainly call for further exploration.

New Research Vistas

The notion of a "third space" (Bhabha, 1994) entails a meeting place or a convergence of sorts where diverse mindsets, perspectives, and materialities can come together and be articulated into new interconnected and hybrid frames of mind. New forms of communication and media increasingly offer opportunities for the articulation of hybrid perspectives, the synergy of multiple modes of representation, and the development of pluralistic forms of literacy and identity. Affinity spaces such as online fanfiction communities provide a wealth of such articulations for study. However, inquiry into such sites calls not only for hybrid approaches to research, but also for researchers who will approach these spaces with mindsets that enable them to selectively cull from established methodologies and traditions that are best suited for exploring multiple and shifting terrains. Moreover, culling with such a mindset necessarily requires that researchers themselves are able to effectively navigate ICTs and these third spaces that they are investigating (Steinkuehler, Black, & Clinton, 2005; Lankshear & Knobel, 2004).

As research described within this chapter has shown, modern social shifts and technological advances have led to the development of many third spaces where school-age youth are doing a great deal of learning and "identity work" that is mediated through their online, literate interactions, various forms of semiotic meaning making, and their activities surrounding popular culture. The New Literacy Studies is based on a tradition of interdisciplinary inquiry, traversing such fields as social cognition, anthropology, and sociolinguistics. As such, a New Literacy Studies lens provides the sort of theoretical and methodological flexibility needed for gaining more nuanced perspectives of such activities in relation to broader social, political, historical, and educational climates, and also for judiciously drawing from diverse traditions in order to best answer the critical "next" questions in the areas of anime, manga, and fanfiction research.

Anime-based fanfiction sites are a clear example of such third spaces in which cultural, historical, ideological, and semiotic elements of available media often simultaneously converge, are redesigned, and then redistributed via various ICTs. Thus, traditional offline, single-site approaches to ethnography may prove inadequate for capturing the geographical, temporal, and semiotic fluidity of these networked, online spaces. However, recent work within literacy (Leander & McKim, 2003), communication (Hine, 2000), and anthropological studies have put forth a more connective approach to inquiry that moves beyond "the single sites and local situations of conventional ethnographic research designs to examine the circulation of cultural meanings, objects, and identities in diffuse time-space" (Marcus, 1995, p. 96). As George Marcus (1995) pointed out, this sort of research necessarily "arises in response to empirical changes in the world and therefore to transformed locations of cultural production" (p. 97) where the computer is not only an object of, but also a context for study (Hine, 2000). Such an approach enables the researcher to follow "cultural products" such as Japanese anime and manga texts from inception to uptake to redistribution in order to better understand issues raised in previous research related to media producers' structure and promotion of dominant messages versus consumers' or fans' agency, uptake, and/or lack thereof. With the ever-reaching spread of mass media, such issues have been a cause of concern for parents, educators, and policymakers and such research has crucial implications for the development of curriculum and pedagogy in critical media literacy.

A New Literacy Studies theoretical framework is also particularly helpful as I return to the questions from the start of the chapter in order to parse out some compelling new research vistas in these areas. First, it seems crucial to begin with questions such as, *What is so engaging about these media and networked, informal learning sites that youth willingly devote hours to participation around them—even in fanfiction writing spaces where participation involves school-based literacy practices such as composition, editing, and peer review?* In my own research, I have found it helpful to understand motivation in these spaces by looking at the sorts of powerful identities that adolescents, particularly ELLs, are able to take on and successfully enact through their literacy and social practices surrounding fanfiction and popular culture. James Gee's (1999) big-D Discourse—defined as "ways of behaving, interacting, thinking, believing, speaking, and often reading and writing that are accepted as instantiations of particular roles (or 'types of people' by specific *groups of people*)" (p. *viii*)—is highly applicable to such research in that it foregrounded literacy and identity as crucially interrelated components of social practice and interaction. A big-D discourse approach provides an analytic lens through which to examine how adolescents use language and other modes of meaning making to "pull off" certain socially situated identities in anime-based fanfiction sites.

The New London Group's (1996) notion of hybridity—defined as "rearticulating conventionally accepted modes of meaning such as discourses, genres in order to create new meanings"—would also be useful for such analysis in looking at how diversity and multiple forms of expertise are valued rather than marginalized in anime-based fan communities, thus helping fans to pull off desirable identities that are not necessarily open to them in classrooms. For instance, as Black (2005a) pointed out, because anime is a Japanese cultural production, Japanese language and cultural elements are highly valued in these fictions; thus, ELLs with Asian backgrounds often have insider or expert status in this regard and will integrate such knowledge into their fictions to create linguistically and culturally hybrid texts. Moreover, it is not uncommon for authors to ask other fans with a great deal of knowledge about anime or Japanese language or culture to beta-read their fictions or help them integrate culturally congruent elements into their texts (Black, 2005a). This creates a situation where ELLs who are often at a disadvantage in English-based writing and reading activities in classrooms have the opportunity to take on powerful, identities as experts on anime, manga, and Asian language or culture within this social space.

In addition, it is worthwhile to look at how such spaces offer options for ELLs and struggling writers to display talents in areas other than print-based literacy. Because the nature of online publishing allows for hybrid and multimodal forms of meaning making, performance does not wholly depend on facility with written language, as tech-savvy fans can often supplement their writing with images, sound, and/or other digital elements in order to create fictions that are valued within the community or create personal Web sites to display their artistic talents or Web-publishing skills (Chandler-Olcott & Mahar, 2003a, 2003b; Black, 2005a, 2005b). So, while interaction in online fanfiction sites centers on writing and improving composition skills, successful participation is not determined solely by traditional, print-based literacy skills, and there are multiple opportunities for members to take on powerful identities as technical experts, artists, designers, and webmasters, and to help other fans in ways that are recognized and valued within the community.

Another crucial question emerging in this area is *How might the patterns of participation in these informal, online learning spaces be linked to larger shifts in our increasingly globalized, networked, and linguistically and culturally diverse society?* A great deal of work within the New Literacy Studies has foregrounded the relationship between literacy and context in terms of how economic and social changes are linked to new global capitalism and a "knowledge economy" (Lankshear & Knobel, 2003). However, work within critical cultural studies can also be particularly helpful for locating such practices within larger patterns in an increasingly globalized, networked, and information-oriented context. As an example, Eva Lam's (2005) innovative work on diasporic populations of adolescent, Chinese-American ELLs draws from work in the New Literacy Studies as well as from cultural studies to examine how "trans-border social networking" and cultural flows of information via new ICTs enable immigrant youth to create online "imagined worlds" or *mediascapes* that serve as "new contexts for language learning, literacy development, and socialization" (p. 1).

What work within cultural studies enables us to more clearly see is how youths' online literacy practices are related to emerging economic and social patterns of globalized participation and communication that carry across national borders. And, as Lam (2005) argues, within literacy and second-language studies, such connections make us aware of larger patterns of movement away from strict nationalism and compel us to consider how approaching language instruction in terms of *acculturation* or assimilation to the culture of one's adopted country perhaps should be replaced with one of *transculturation* or socialization into multiple languages, modes of meaning making, and of belonging. Moreover, work within cultural studies that theorizes the new formations of our globalized, networked society (Appadurai, 2001; Castells, 1996) can also help us to more clearly apprehend the parallels and discrepancies between the sort of learning and participation taking place in informal learning sites and the sort of learning and participation valued in contemporary global workplaces as well as social spaces. Ideally, this knowledge could then be applied to the development of curriculum and pedagogy in formal learning sites such as schools that would also mirror and offer students options for successful participation in transnational society.

Another worthwhile direction for future inquiry that is clearly indicated by earlier research involves exploring the question, *What are the effective and motivating forms of learning and teaching that are taking place around media and popular culture in these sites?* Of late, there has been a push for Critical Discourse Analysis (CDA) to account for "matters of learning" (Rogers, 2004, p. 14) in educational research. In response, Gee (2004a) expanded the CDA framework and drew from a range of social theories of cognition to posit that learning is "changing patterns of participation in specific social practices" (p. 38). Coupled with such a social perspective on learning, CDA applied to texts from the fanfiction community, such as fanfictions, peer reviews of fictions, interactions between writers and beta-readers, and columns featuring metacommentary about composition, can serve as information-rich artifacts of analysis, providing insight into how and why adolescents voluntarily engage in such patterns of participation in online affinity spaces, as well as how such social and self-directed patterns of participation aid in learning.

In terms of application to education, Gee (2004a) pointed out that notions from learning sciences and social cognition "like 'distributed cognition', 'collaborative practice', 'networked intelligence' and 'communities of practice'" (p. 165) have yet to be taken up in any serious way in schools, in spite of the fact that such forms of learning are related to the needs of modern workplaces and the value system of fast capitalism and a knowledge economy. Interestingly enough, as evidenced by the earlier review of research, such forms of learning are readily apparent in many informal fan spaces and activities. For example, while fanfiction authors and anime fans engage in a range of school-related literacy practices (e.g., reading, reviewing, providing feedback, editing, writing, and proofreading), they are all part of authentic social and communicative activities that are meaningful and contribute positively to powerful identities in these shared learning spaces. Fanfiction writers also draw from knowledge that is distributed across the Web and other offline sites. Moreover, they solicit help in thinking through their ideas and collaborate with other authors and actively participate in a space that is organized around common affinity for anime where many different forms of expertise are recognized and valued within the community. This can be juxtaposed with many classrooms, where literacy is often viewed as a mere tool for content-area learning; research is often confined to textbooks and materials in the library; learning is viewed as an individual process; there are established standards for what counts as expertise and successful participation; such standards are determined by administrators and policy makers outside of classroom community; and failure to achieve such standards often has negative effects on students' identities.

Finally, the baseline question that likely hinges on answers to all the preceding queries is, *How might, could, or even should we integrate such forms of learning into formal school curriculum and pedagogy?* I believe our answers to this question, like our approaches to new literacies research, will depend largely on our epistemic frameworks for what counts as literacy and learning. Lankshear and Knobel (2003) pointed out that with the advent of new ICTs and the widespread movement toward globalization, there perhaps have been profound changes, not only in the world of literacies *to be known* but also in *how to know* the literacies of world. Moreover, they pointed out that as literacy educators and researchers, at minimum, we ought to take note of these changes, and optimally, learn from these changes and integrate them into our understandings of literacy instruction in schools. Based on the implications emerging from much of the research in the chapter, this would most likely involve movement away from the current emphasis in classrooms on *propositional* knowledge, which primarily involves the learning of content-area facts and figures, toward a greater emphasis on *procedural* knowledge,

Cicioni, M. (1998). Male pair-bonds and female desire in fan slash writing. In C. Harris & A. Alexander (Eds.), *Theorizing fandom: Fans, subculture, and identity* (pp. 153–177). Cresskill, NJ: Hampton Press.

Clements, J., & McCarthy, H. (2001). *The anime encyclopedia: A guide to Japanese animation since 1917.* Berkeley, CA: Stone Bridge Press.

Coombe, R. J. (1998). *The cultural life of intellectual properties: Authorship, appropriation, and the law (Post-contemporary interventions).* Durham, NC: Duke University Press.

Cope, B., & Kalantzis, M. (2000). *Multiliteracies: Literacy learning and the design of social futures.* London: Routledge.

Crawford, B. (1996). Emperor Tomato-Ketchup: Cartoon properties from Japan. In M. Broderick (Ed.), *Hibakusha cinema: Hiroshima, Nagasaki and the nuclear image in Japanese film* (pp. 75–90). New York: Kegan Paul International.

Drazen, P. (2002). *Anime explosion!: The what? why? and wow of Japanese animation.* Berkeley, CA: Stone Bridge Press.

Dyson, A. H. (1997). *Writing superheroes: Contemporary childhood, popular culture, and classroom literacy.* New York: Teachers College Press.

Eng, L. (2001a). *The politics of otaku.* Retrieved April 24, 2005, from http://www.cjas.org/~leng/otaku-p.htm

Eng, L. (2001b). *The current status of "otaku" and Japan's latest youth crisis.* Retrieved May 1, 2005, from http://www.cjas.org/~leng/hikiko.htm

Eng, L. (2002). *Otak-who? Technoculture, youth, consumption, and resistance: American representations of a Japanese youth subculture.* Retrieved May 1, 2005, from http://www.rpi.edu/~engl/otaku.pdf

Erino, M. (1993). *Rediisu komikku no joseigaku* [Gender studies of ladies' comics]. Tokyo: Kosaido Shuppan.

Freiberg, F. (1996). Akira and the postnuclear sublime. In M. Broderick (Ed.), *Hibakusha cinema: Hiroshima, Nagasaki and the nuclear image in Japanese film* (pp. 91–102). New York: Kegan Paul International.

Fujimoto, Y. (1991). A life-size mirror: Women's self-representation in girls' comics. *Review of Japanese Culture and Society, 4.*

Gee, J. P. (1999). *An introduction to discourse analysis.* London: Routledge.

Gee, J. P. (2004a). Discourse analysis: What makes it critical? In R. Rogers (Ed.), *An introduction to critical discourse analysis in education* (pp. 19–50). Mahwah, NJ: Lawrence Erlbaum Associates.

Gee, J. P. (2004b). *Situated language and learning: A critique of traditional schooling.* New York: Routledge.

Grigsby, M. (1998). Sailormoon manga (comics) and anime (cartoon) superheroine meets Barbie: Global entertainment commodity comes to the United States. *Journal of Popular Culture, 32*(1), 59–80.

Heath, S. B. (1983). *Ways with words: Language, life, and work in community and classrooms.* Cambridge, MA: Cambridge University Press.

Hine, C. (2000). *Virtual ethnography.* Thousand Oaks, CA: Sage.

Hull, G., & Schultz, K. (2002). *School's out: Bridging out-of-school literacies with classroom practice.* New York: Teachers College Press.

Ito, K. (1994). Images of women in weekly male comic magazines in Japan. *Journal of Popular Culture, 27*(4), 81–95.

Ito, K. (2003). Japanese ladies' comics as agents of socialization: The lessons they teach. *International Journal of Comic Art, 5,* 425–436.

Ito, K. (2005). A history of manga in the context of Japanese culture and society. *Journal of Popular Culture, 38,* 456–475.

Ito, M. (2001). *Technologies of the childhood imagination: Media mixes, hypersociality, and recombinant cultural form.* Paper presented at the Society for the Social Studies of Science meeting, Boston, MA. Retrieved April 25, 2005, from http://www.ssrc.org/programs/publications_editors/publications/items/online4-4/ito-childhood.pdf

Iwabuchi, K. (2004). How Japanese is Pokémon? In J. Tobin (Ed.), *Pikachu's global adventure: The rise and fall of Pokémon* (pp. 53–79). Durham, NC: Duke University Press.

Jenkins, H., McPherson, T., & Shattuc, J. (Eds.). (2003). *Hop on pop: The politics and pleasures of popular culture*. Durham, NC: Duke University Press.

Jenkins, H. (1992). *Textual poachers: Television, fans, and participatory culture*. New York: Routledge.

Jenkins, H. (2004). Why Heather can write. *Technology Review*. Retrieved September 28, 2005, from http://www.technologyreview.com/articles/04/02/wo_jenkins020604.asp?p=1

Jenkins, H. (2006). *Convergence culture: Where old and new media collide*. New York: New York University Press.

Katsuno, H., & Maret, J. (2004). Localizing the Pokémon TV series for the American market. In J. Tobin (Ed.), *Pikachu's global adventure: The rise and fall of Pokémon* (pp. 80–107). Durham, NC: Duke University Press.

Kinsella, S. (1998, Summer). Amateur manga subculture and the otaku panic. *Journal of Japanese Studies*.

Kinsella, S. (2000). Adult *manga: Culture and power in contemporary Japanese society*. Honolulu: University of Hawaii Press.

Kustritz, A. (2003). Slashing the romance narrative. *Journal of American Culture, 26*, 371–384.

Lai, C. S. L., & Dixon, H. W. W. (2001). Japanese comics coming to Hong Kong. In B. Harumi & S. Guichard-Anguis (Eds.), *Globalizing Japan: Ethnography of the Japanese presence in Asia, Europe, and America* (pp. 111–120). London: Routledge.

Lam, W. S. E. (2000). Literacy and the design of the self: A case study of a teenager writing on the Internet. *TESOL Quarterly, 34*, 457–482.

Lam, W. S. E. (2004). Second language socialization in a bilingual chat room: Global and local considerations [Electronic version]. *Language Learning and Technology, 8*(3), 44–65.

Lam, W. S. E. (2005). *Re-envisioning language, literacy, and the immigrant subject in new mediascapes*. Paper presented at 2005 meeting of American Educational Research Association, Montreal, Canada.

Lamb, P. F., & Veith, D. L. (1986). Romantic myth, transcendence, and Star Trek zines. In D. Palumbo (Ed.), *Erotic universe: Sexuality and fantastic literature* (pp. 235–255). New York: Greenwood.

Lankshear, C. (1999). Literacy Studies in Education. In M. Peters, Ed. *After the Disciplines*. Greenwood Press. http://www.geocities.com/c.lankshear/literacystudies.html

Lankshear, C., & Knobel, M. (2003). *New literacies: Changing knowledge and classroom learning*. Philadelphia: Open University Press.

Lankshear, C., & Knobel, M. (2004). *New literacies: Research and social practice*. Paper presented at the Annual Meeting of the National Reading Conference, San Antonio, Texas. Retrieved May 3, 2005, from http://www.geocities.com/c.lankshear/nrc.html

Leander, K. M., & McKim, K. K. (2003). Tracing the everyday "sitings" of adolescents on the Internet: A strategic adaptation of ethnography across online and offline spaces. *Education, Communication, & Information, 3*, 211–240.

Leander, K. M., & Sheehy, M. (Eds.). (2004). *Spatializing literacy research and practice*. New York: Peter Lang.

Ledden, S., & Fejes, F. (1987). Female gender role patterns in Japanese comic magazines. *Journal of Popular Culture, 21*, 155–176.

Ledoux, T. (Ed.). (1997). *Anime interviews: The first five years of Animerica anime & manga monthly (1992–1997)*. San Francisco: Viz Communications.

Ledoux, T., & Ranney, D. (1997). *The complete anime guide*. Issaquah, WA: Tiger Mountain Press.

Lemish, D., & Bloch, L. R. (2004). Pokémon in Israel. In J. Tobin (Ed.), *Pikachu's global adventure: The rise and fall of Pokémon* (pp. 165–186). Durham, NC: Duke University Press.

Lemke, J. (2005). Critical analysis across media: Games, franchises, and the new cultural order [CD-ROM edition]. In M. Labarto Postigo (Ed.), *Approaches to critical discourse analysis*. Valencia, Spain: University of Valencia.

Leonard, S. (2004). *Progress against the law: Fan distribution, copyright, and the explosive growth of Japanese animation*. Cambridge: Massachusetts Institute of Technology.

Levi, A. (1996). *Samurai from outer space: Understanding Japanese animation*. Chicago: Open Court.

Marcus, G. E. (1995). Ethnography in/of the world system: The emergence of multi-sited ethnography. *Annual Review of Anthropology, 24*, 95–117.

Matsui, M. (1993). Little girls were little boys: Displaced femininity in the representation of homosexuality in Japanese girls' comics. In S. Gunew & A. Yeatman (Eds.), *Feminism and the politics of difference* (pp. 177–196). St. Leonards, Australia: Allen & Unwin.

McCardle, M. (2003). Fanfiction, fandom, and fanfare: What's all the fuss? *B.U. J. Sci. Tech. L., 9*(2). Retrieved May 1, 2005, from http://www.bu.edu/law/scitech/volume9issue2/McCardleWebPDF.pdf

McCarthy, H. (1996). *The anime! movie guide*. Woodstock, NY: Overlook Press.

McLelland, M. (2000a). Male homosexuality and popular culture in modern Japan. *Intersections, 3*. Retrieved March 23, 2005, from http://wwwsshe.murdoch.edu.au/intersections/issue3/mclelland2.html

McLelland, M. (2000b.) No climax, no point, no meaning? Japanese women's boy love sites on the Internet. *Journal of Communication Inquiry, 24*, 274–291.

Mizuno, R. (1991). *Manga bunka no uchimaku* [The inside of manga culture]. Tokyo: Kawade Shobo Shinsha.

Morris-Suzuki, T., & Rimmer, P. (2002). Virtual memories: Japanese history debates in manga and cyberspace. *Asian Studies Review, 26*, 147–164.

New London Group. (1996). A pedagogy of multiliteracies: Designing social futures. *Harvard Educational Review, 66*, 60–92.

Napier, S. J. (1993). Panic sites: The Japanese imagination of disaster from Godzilla to Akira. *Journal of Japanese Studies, 19*, 327–351.

Napier, S. J. (1998). Vampires, psychic girls, flying women, and sailor scouts: Four faces of the young female in Japanese popular culture. In D. Martinez (Ed.), *The worlds of Japanese popular culture: Gender, shifting boundaries and global cultures* (pp. 91–109). Cambridge, MA: Cambridge University Press.

Napier, S. J. (2001). *Anime: From Akira to Princess Mononoke: Experiencing contemporary Japanese animation*. New York: Palgrave.

Newitz, A. (1994). Anime otaku: Japanese animation fans outside of Japan. *Bad Subjects*, 13. Retrieved May 1, 2005, from http://bad.eserver.org/issues/1994/13/newitz.html

Newitz, A. (1995). Magical girls and atomic bomb sperm: Japanese animation in America. *Film Quarterly, 49*(1), 2–15.

Ogi, F. (2001). Gender insubordination in Japanese comics (*manga*) for girls. In J. Lent (Ed.), *Illustrating Asia: Comics, humor magazines, and picture books* (pp. 171–186). Honolulu: University of Hawaii Press.

Orbaugh, S. (2003). Busty battlin' babes: The evolution of the shojo in 1990s visual culture. In J. Mostow, N. Bryson, & M. Graybill (Eds.), *Gender and power in the Japanese visual field* (pp. 201–228). Honolulu: University of Hawaii Press.

Pandey, R. (2000). The medieval in manga. *Postcolonial Studies, 3*(1), 19–32.

Patten, F. (2004). *Watching anime, reading manga*. Berkeley, CA: Stone Bridge Press.

Pelletier, C. J. (Ed.). (2000). *Anime: A guide to Japanese animation (1958–1988)*. Montreal, Canada: Protoculture.

Penley, C. (1991). Brownian motion: Women, tactics, and technology. In C. Penley & A. Ross (Eds.), *Technoculture* (pp. 135–161). Minneapolis: University of Minnesota Press.

Perper, T., & Cornog, M. (2002). Eroticism for the masses: Japanese manga comics and their assimilation into the U.S. *Sexuality & Culture, 6*(1), pp. 3–126 (Special Issue).

Poitras, G. (1999). *The anime companion: What's Japanese in Japanese animation?* Berkeley, CA: Stone Bridge Press.

Poitras, G. (2001) *Anime essentials: Everything a fan needs to know.* Berkeley, CA: Stone Bridge Press.

Pugh, S. (2004). The democratic genre: Fanfiction in a literary context. *Refractory,5.* Retrieved October 26, 2005, from http://www.refractory.unimelb.edu.au/journalissues/vol5/pugh.htm

Purves, A. (1998). Flies in the web of hypertext. In D. Reinking, M. McKenna, L. Labbo, & R. Kieffer (Eds.), *Handbook of literacy and technology: Transformations in a post-typographic world* (pp. 235–251). Mahwah, NJ: Lawrence Erlbaum.

Rogers, R. (Ed.). (2004). *An introduction to critical discourse analysis in education.* Mahwah, NJ: Lawrence Erlbaum Associates.

Russ, J. (1985). *Magic mommas, trembling sisters, Puritans and perverts: Feminist essays.* Trumansburg, NY: Crossing. Retrieved May 1, 2005, from http://www.totse.com/en/erotica/erotic_fiction_o_to_p/pornogra.html

Russo, J. L. (2002, August). NEW VOY 'cyborg sex' J/7 [NC-17] 1/1: New methodologies, new fantasies. *The Slash Reader.* Retrieved May 1, 2005, from http://www.julielevinrusso.org/asmic/fanfic/

Sabucco, V. (2003). Guided fanfiction: Western "readings" of Japanese homosexual-themed texts. In C. Berry, F. Martin, & A. Yue (Eds.), *Mobile cultures: New media in queer Asia* (pp. 70–86). Durham, NC: Duke University Press.

Scodari, C., & Felder, J. L. (2000, Fall). Creating a pocket universe: "Shippers," fanfiction, and the X-Files online. *Communication Studies*, 51. Retrieved October 26, 2007, from http://findarticles.com/p/articles/mi_qa3669/is_200010/ai_n8926461

Schodt, F. L. (1983). *Manga! manga! The world of Japanese comics.* New York: Kodansha International.

Schodt, F. L. (1996). *Dreamland Japan: Writings on modern manga.* Berkeley, CA: Stone Bridge Press.

Scribner, S., & M. Cole (1981). *The psychology of literacy.* Cambridge, MA: Harvard University Press.

Shimizu, I. (1991). *Mangano rekishi* [The history of manga]. Tokyo: Iwanami Shoten.

Shiokawa, K. (1999). Cute but deadly: Women and violence in Japanese comics. In J. Lent (Ed.), *Themes and issues in Asian cartooning: Cute, cheap, mad, and sexy* (pp. 93–125). Bowling Green, OH: Bowling Green State University Popular Press.

Steinkuehler, C. A., Black, R. W., & Clinton, K. A. (2005). Researching literacy as tool, place, and way of being. *Reading Research Quarterly*, 40(1), 7–12.

Street, B. (1984). *Literacy in theory and practice.* Cambridge, MA: Cambridge University Press.

Super Cat. (1999). A (very) brief history of fanfic. *The Fanfic Symposium.* Retrieved May 1, 2005, from http://www.trickster.org/symposium/colyear.html#2003

Thomas, A. (2004). Digital literacies of the cybergirl. *E-Learning*, 1, 358–382. Retrieved May 1, 2005, from http://www.wwwords.co.uk/pdf/viewpdf.asp?j=elea&vol=1&issue=3&year=2004&article=3_Thomas_ELEA_1_3_web&id=65.30.211.33

Thomas, A. (2005). Positioning the Reader: The affordances of digital fiction. For: *Reading the Past, Writing the Future.* Brisbane, Queensland Council for Adult Literacy Inc,. pp. 24–33.

Thomas, A. (2006). "MSN was the next big thing after Beanie Babies": Children's virtual experiences as an interface to their identities and their everyday lives. *E-Learning*, 3(2), 126–142.

Tobin, J. (2000). *Good guys don't wear hats: Children's talk about the media.* New York: Teachers College Press.

Tobin, J. (Ed.). (2004). *Pikachu's global adventure: The rise and fall of Pokémon.* Durham, NC: Duke University Press.

Tobin, S. (2004). Masculinity, maturity, and the end of Pokémon. In J. Tobin (Ed.), *Pikachu's global adventure: The rise and fall of Pokémon* (pp. 241–256). Durham, NC: Duke University Press.

Tushnet, R. (1997). Legal fictions: Copyright, fanfiction, and a new common law. *Loyola of Los Angeles Entertainment Law Journal, 17.* Retrieved May 25, 2005, from http://www.tushnet.com/legalfictions.pdf

Vasquez, V. (2003). What Pokémon can teach us about learning and literacy. *Language Arts, 81,* 118–125.

Volker, G. (1990). *"I'm alone, but not lonely": Japanese Otaku-kids colonize the realm of information and media.* Retrieved May 1, 2005, from http://www.cjas.org/~leng/otaku-e.htm

Wikipedia. (2005). *Anime.* Retrieved May 1, 2005, from http://en.wikipedia.org/wiki/Anime#Genres

Willett, R. (2004). The multiple identities of Pokémon fans. In J. Tobin (Ed.), *Pikachu's global adventure: The rise and fall of Pokémon* (pp. 226–240). Durham, NC: Duke University Press.

Yano, C. R. (2004). Panic attacks: Anti-Pokémon voices in global markets. In J. Tobin (Ed.), *Pikachu's global adventure: The rise and fall of Pokémon* (pp. 108–140). Durham, NC: Duke University Press.

CHAPTER 22

Cognition and Literacy in Massively Multiplayer Online Games

CONSTANCE A. STEINKUEHLER

UNIVERSITY OF WISCONSIN-MADISON, USA

For the current youth generation, the Internet has *always* existed. Online technologies have profoundly contributed to a dramatic technocultural shift in contemporary society, transforming how we learn, work, play, and socialize. Information from multiple sources on everything from Athabascan birch bark baskets to the calculation of z-scores is there for the Googling. Global social networks—made visible, designable, and searchable via services such as Friendster (http://www.friendster.com/), Facebook (http://www.facebook.com), and MySpace (http://www.myspace.com/)—are increasingly becoming the must-have/must-do activity for business people, college students, and fan communities alike. And whether it is collaboration on a formal project or informal socializing among peers, our modus operandi has shifted from face-to-face get-togethers, a couple of e-mails, and the occasional phone call to the overlapping "multimodal, multi-attentional spaces" (Lemke, n.d.) on today's computer screen—e-mail in-boxes, Web pages, collaborative authoring software (e.g., wikis and blogs), multiple instant messaging (IMing) windows of conversation, video streaming, file sharing, voice over IP (VoIP), and even shared online 3-D environments where players can fashion digital versions of their corporeal selves and get together in a server-stored tavern for a virtual beer. For those who have grown up with such technologies, this heterogeneous, networked, online, global, "flat" (Friedman, 2005) world is the unremarkable mainstream. While the older, "world on paper" natives gasp, wonder, and worry about the furious pace and penetration of online technologies into everyday life, the younger generations just adopt them, adapt them, and move on to the next (Lankshear & Bigum, 1999; Lankshear & Knobel, 2003).

The American education system has done its best to keep pace, providing Internet connections to virtually all schools (99% in 2001), 87% of which are accessible to students via classrooms, libraries, computer labs, and other regulated spaces (Kleiner & Farris, 2002). Still, the *culture* of schooling carries on with business as usual—as it was 10 or 20 years ago, that is. As a Pew Internet and American Life Report (Levin & Arafeh, 2002) on the digital disconnect between children and their schools details with excruciating clarity, what students do with online technologies *outside* the classroom is not only markedly different from what they do with them in schools (e.g., IMing, blogging, sharing files, consuming and producing media, engaging in affinity spaces, gaming, building social networks, downloading answers to homework, and researching for school projects and assignments); it is *also* more goal driven, complex, sophisticated, and engaged. If we care to understand the current and potential capacities of technology for cognition, learning, literacy, and education, then we must look to contexts *outside* our current formal education system rather than those within.

Video games are an excellent starting point for such investigation. We know that video games are a *push technology,* providing people entrée into other important technologies, such as computers. For example, games precede computers at every step of adoption in the home (see Figure 22.1), and these days have become nearly ubiquitous to the everyday life of the American child:

> More than eight in ten (83%) young people have a video game console at home, and a majority (56%) have two or more. About half (49%) have one in their bedroom, and just over half (55%) have a handheld video game player. (Rideout, Roberts, & Foehr, 2005, p. 36)

More importantly, the online affinity groups that emerge around games function as a kind of *push community*, engaging members in identities, values, and practices markedly similar to the intellectual and social practices that characterize high-level, conceptual communities of innovation in fields such as science, technology, and engineering—Discourses (Gee, 1999) that American schools currently fail to provide young learners access to (in the wake of the Bush administration and their return to "skill and drill"), that the global market demands, and that some other countries (e.g., India and China) now offer to between 2 and 6 times as many individuals as the United States currently does (Gates, 2005). Beneath the veneer of fantasy and seeming childishness (e.g., "l337 speek"), video games are sites for socially and materially distributed cognition, complex problem solving, identity work, individual and collaborative learning across multiple multimedia and multimodal "attentional spaces" (Lemke, n.d.), and rich meaning making. For the (now K–12) millennial gen-

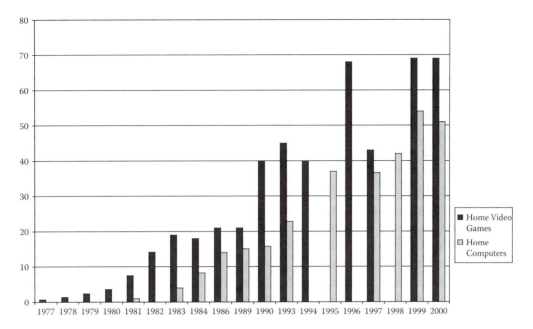

Figure 22.1 Video games as a push technology for computers in the home (reprinted with permission from Williams, 2004).

eration, video games are a—if not *the*—leading form of entertainment, despite their complexity and the considerable cognitive investment they exact from those who play (Gee, 2003).

Massively Multiplayer Online Games

Massively multiplayer online games (MMOGs) are the quintessential example of such communities. They share the same features as other game worlds with one important exception—they are *played online,* allowing individuals, through their self-created digital characters or "avatars" within the game space, to interact not only with the *gaming software* (the designed environment of the game and the computer-controlled characters within it) but with *other players' avatars* as well. Thus, they are a thoroughly collaborative space, not only *beyond* the game (in fan sites, discussion boards, game information databases, etc.) but also *within* the game itself. Moreover, given that they are persistent virtual spaces played in real time yet instantiated in digital graphics and architectural code, they function as a highly visible and, therefore, thoroughly traceable medium (Moore, Ducheneaut, & Nickell, 2005) for the study of cognition, learning, and literacy in online digital contexts.

Conceptually, MMOGs are part of the rich tradition of alternative worlds that science fiction and fantasy literature provide us (e.g., Tolkien's, 1938, *The Hobbit*). Technically, they are the evolutionary next step in a long line of social games that runs from paper-and-pencil fantasy games (e.g., Gygax & Arneson's, 1973, *Dungeons & Dragons*) to main-frame text-based multiuser dungeons (e.g., Trubshaw & Bartle's, 1978, famous first *MUD1*) through sors—who have grown up with such technologies and tend to readily post their work online (primarily, blogs, and Web sites) long before publishing in traditional print journals (if they publish there at all). Although this may seem troubling for some, the reality is that "game studies" is a nascent field growing at an incredible rate. In some respects, then, the print journal publication process is simply too slow for scholars to get their work out to the public rapidly enough for substantive conversation and feedback on their ideas while they are still relevant and of practical and intellectual use. Given the pace with which technologies and practices change, holding out for print publication often means having your work seen only after your object of study is grossly out of date.

This rise of formal study of the economics of virtual worlds, largely published online, has been accompanied by an equal number of companies and entrepreneurs who now make their living from online out-of-game trade of virtual in-game virtual goods (e.g., Book, 2004; Dibbell, 2003b, in press; companies like IGE, http://www.ige.com). The in-game effects, in some cases, have been profound. For example, entire "sweat shops" of "adena farmers" in China now earn lucrative salaries by earning virtual currency within *Lineage* and selling it online, with whole territories of the game world now inaccessible to the leisure gamer and core game mechanics for which the game was once famous (between-clan sieges for castles in the virtual world) effectively transformed into Americans versus Chinese raids on said farmers by a community desperately trying to rid themselves of what they see as a "cancer" to the virtual world (Steinkuehler, 2004a). If our world is indeed increasingly "flat" (Friedman, 2005), then the MMOG is, in some respects, our proverbial canary in the coalmine.

The legal implications of virtual worlds, not just in terms of out-of-game trade of in-game items but also, and as crucially, in terms of intellectual property rights, in-game governance, and the legal jurisdiction of play, are still being worked out (Balkin, 2004; Balkin & Noveck, in press; Castronova, 2004; Crawford, 2003; Dibbell, 2003a; Hunter, 2003; Johnson, n.d.; Lastowka & Hunter, 2004, 2005; Noveck, 2004; Shirky, 2003). Issues such as *who has intellectual property rights to what* in the context of MMOGs are far more complicated than they at first appear to be. In some contexts, the MMOG is owned by a company in one nation, with legislation based on one set of definitions of notions like ownership and value, yet inhabited by citizens in other nations with very different legislation based on very different understandings of such concepts. Moreover, important aspects of the "content" of games are, in fact, the work of *gamers*, not game companies (Herz, 2002; Hunter & Lastowka, 2005; Taylor, 2002, in press). In actual practice, the game player communities that inhabit the worlds to which game companies declare sole ownership create much of the substance that makes such virtual worlds what they are. As Humphreys (2004) pointed out,

Player activities are being commodified by the publishers and structured into their business models. This shift in "consumer"/publisher relations requires a reconsideration of how the relationship is theorized. Most discussion of games and the law characterize commodification as the process of giving "real world" value to in-game items such as the virtual swords and armour accumulated by a player. The initial bedrock process of harnessing player productivity (Herz, 2002) in all its forms, including the social and emotional, is the commodification that is ignored. (p. 3)

In theories of cognition and literacy, this blur between production and consumption is a familiar one, as it lies at the heart of all constructivist theories of human sense making (e.g., Cobb & Bowers, 1999; Piaget, 1978; Von Glasersfeld, 1995; Vygotsky, 1930/1978). People actively construct the world around them, engaging in what Certeau (1984) called the "hidden production" of consumption. Yet in the context of MMOGs, this blurred relationship between production and consumption is caught up with the broader economic, legal, social, and ethical dilemmas of a world that is increasingly networked and accessible, yet corporate owned (Boyle, 1996; Coombe, 1998; Lessig, 1999). In MMOG communities, as with other participatory cultures (Jenkins, 1992, 2004), *consumption is production*, manifested in gamer-authored practices, products, and social networks that are then commodified by corporations and sold back to the very groups that authored them in the first place. Through their in- and out-of-game activities, game communities effectively assert their right "to form interpretations, to offer evaluations, and to construct cultural canons. … fans raid mass culture, claiming its materials for their own use, reworking them as the basis for their own cultural creations and social interactions" (Jenkins, 1992, p. 18). Yet, to date, game companies (with the exception of Second Life, http://secondlife.com/) claim full ownership of all content within the virtual worlds they publish, and often ban the account of any enterprising player who is caught selling in-game materials for out-of-game profit, even when the object of trade is, for example, the gamer's own digital body, their online avatar. The grand irony, of course, is that the games companies themselves freely borrow not just from their players but also from other literary and creative sources (e.g., the orc characters that appear in many of MMOGs, which are the explicit property of Tolkien estate, Taylor, 2002), including other games (e.g., yellow exclamation marks used to denote quest-giving characters—a design feature first used in *World of Warcraft*, then magically appearing in *Lineage* just a few months later with their next software update).

From this perspective, the difference between game players and game companies appears more a matter of access to power (in shaping legislation) than rightful claim to authorship/ownership per se: Both game players and game designers actively appropriate and rework the cultural resources at hand, with

Stivale, 1997; Yee, 2005b) and, of course, sex (Dibbell, 1998; Kaufman, 1996; Van Gelder, 1996). Yet, as Walls (2005) remarked, "It is through MMOGs that players have the greatest ability/responsibility to explore, construct, and resist those concerns of dominant culture's representations" (¶ 1). And it is through such semiotic, virtual, and sociocultural resources that participants in virtual worlds reify themselves on screen in a process of "becoming and being, which centers around images and text projected and manipulated on a screen" (Nash, 2004, ¶ 3; see also Filiciak, 2003).

Psychology

To date, MMOG research from the domain of psychology has largely focused on issues of addiction (not discussed here as such research tends to rely on a deficit model in which gamers, through their online participation, make up for something their real life purportedly lacks) and, more recently, motivational factors and patterns of use (Yee, 2005a, 2005b). By far the most influential work on the psychology of MMOGs is Turkle's (1995) early work, *Life on the screen: Identity in the age of the Internet*, based on psychoanalytic perspective. In it, Turkle outlined how MUDs (and therefore MMOGs, their technological descendants) function as laboratories for individual identity play (see also Kitchin, 1998; Suler, 1996) by providing a "psychosocial moratorium" (Erikson, 1963) where one can have meaningful experiences without the consequences accompanying them in everyday real life. Such spaces function as a "window" (Turkle, 1995, p. 184) where individuals can project themselves into roles that may not be available to them in the everyday offline world—not just fantasy roles, like those of an elf or princess, but also sociocultural roles, like the powerful leader of a successful campaign. According to Turkle, this ability to create alternate personas in alternative "windows" or frames allows individuals to cycle through multiple versions of who they are—an experience of self not readily available in life offline where "lifelong involvement with families and communities kept such cycling through under fairly stringent control" (p. 179). In her words,

> [Virtual worlds] imply difference, multiplicity, heterogeneity, and fragmentation. Such an experience of identity contradicts the Latin root of the word, *idem,* meaning "the same." But this contradiction increasingly defines the conditions of our lives beyond the virtual world. [Virtual worlds] thus become objects-to-think-with for thinking about postmodern selves. Indeed, the unfolding of all [virtual world] action takes place in a resolutely postmodern context … . Since [virtual worlds] are authored by their players, thousands of people in all, often hundreds at a time, are all logged on from different places; the solitary author is displaced and distributed. Traditional ideas about identity have been tied to the notion of authenticity that such virtual experiences actively subvert. When each player can create many characters and participate in many games, the

self is not only decentered but multiplied without limit. (Turkle, 1995, p. 185)

Based on such reasoning, MMOGs become the instantiated means with which individuals can think *about* and *with* a thoroughly postmodern conception of the self, one marked by "multiplicity, heterogeneity, flexibility, and fragmentation" (Turkle, 1995, p. 178).

It has been a decade, however, since Turkle's (1995) foundational publication and important aspects of MMOGs, in particular, and the role of technology in everyday life, in general, have evolved. In the last 10 years, we have witnessed increasing economic, sociocultural, and technological *convergence* (Jenkins, 2001). MMOGs are no exception: "Real-world" companies now advertise in virtual worlds (Book, 2004) and entrepreneurs and corporations can now trade their in-game "loot" for out-of-game profit (as previously discussed). References to MMOGs such as *World of Warcraft,* for example, increasingly show up in the mainstream media, as in the stand-up routines of popular comedians (Thorsen, 2005) and televised game shows (Lees, 2005), and large percentages of MMOGers play online with "real-life" romantic partners, family members, coworkers, and friends (Seay, Jerome, Lee, & Kraut, 2005; Yee, 2005a). Even the technological "magic circle" that once bounded the virtual world from life beyond has become increasingly porous thanks to recent innovations like VoIP software (that allow real-time verbal communication during game play) and integrated IM (e.g., the in-game chat system of *Lineage II* is now consolidated with MSN's instant messaging service, allowing individuals to slay dragons while attending online meetings with coworkers at the same time). In truth, the discursive space of MMOGs is one with fuzzy boundaries that expand with continued play: What is at first confined to the game alone soon spills over into the virtual world beyond it (e.g., Web sites, chat rooms, e-mail) and even life offscreen (e.g., telephone calls, face-to-face meetings), and the communities such practices serve likewise expand from collections of in-character playmates to real-world affinity groups. Thus, not only does offline life bleed into virtual worlds, but virtual worlds bleed back into offline life as well. Caught up in such economic, sociocultural, and technological convergence, MMOGs function less and less as "laborator[ies] for experimenting with the constructions and reconstructions of self" (Turkle, 1995, p. 180) and more and more as just another of the many "figured worlds" (Holland et al., 1998) we inhabit. From this perspective, then, it is not the self that is "decentered [and] multiplied without limit" (Turkle, 1995, p. 185) but our interpretive frames.

Turkle's (1995) argument that virtual worlds instantiate concepts in postmodern theory (e.g., the fragmentation and fluidity of the self) and render them accessible to the public has served the last decade of research well. Still, given the changing face of today's world both within virtual environments and beyond, it would seem worthwhile to reconsider what theory MMOGs actually instantiate in the lived-in worlds of those who inhabit them. I argue that they instantiate the broad notion of *social construction* rather than postmodernity per se. MMOGs are highly visible mediums for understanding the way in which specific cultures shape individual sense making (i.e., cognition) and vice versa (Steinkuehler, 2006; cf., Nasir, 2005). Through participation in and reflection on such worlds we are better able to understand how it is that the sense we make of events, contexts, and other people are not fixed and inevitable "truths" out in the world but, rather, interpretations that are created, maintained, and transformed by specific groups of people at specific historical times for specific reasons. MMOGs allow us to discern, both as researchers and as "just plain folk" (Lave, 1988), how it is that socially constructed worlds of meaning are collaboratively achieved.

A Proposal for Research on Cognition and Literacy in MMOGs

MMOGs function as highly visible and therefore traceable mediums by providing "near-total data on all player activities" (Moore et al., 2005, ¶ 1) both within the game and within the game's surrounding online fandom. As such, they provide both participants and researchers powerful contexts for observing and theorizing individual participation in the creation and interpretation of culture, which is to say, in the social construction of "figured worlds" (Holland et al., 1998). As contexts for the study of cognition, learning, and literacy, however, the "virtual omniscience" (Moore et al., 2005, ¶ 1) afforded by MMOGs alone cannot suffice—we need both theory and method that can provide analytical insight into the coconstitution of individual meaning making and macrolevel cultural norms and values. Gee's (1992, 1996, 1999) "big-D" Discourse theory and method is one such analytical framework. Coming out of new literacy studies (e.g., Barton, 1994; Cazden 1988; Cook-Gumperz, 1986; Gumperz, 1982; Heath, 1983; Knobel, 1999; Kress, 1985; Lankshear, 1997; Street, 1984, 1993), Gee's Discourse theory maintains a focus on individuals' (inter)action in the social and (virtual) material world, but, by foregrounding the role of d/Discourse (language-in-use/"kinds of people") in such interactions, it provides a fulcrum about which theory and method can be coherently leveraged to gain insight into the situated meanings individuals construct, the definitive role of communities in that meaning, and the inherently ideological nature of both.

"Big-D" Discourse Theory

To begin, we need a more robust account of meaning-making process itself. The meaning of a symbol, event, or activity is not a stable, abstract, entity transparently encoded from the environment; rather, it is *situated* (Gee, 1992, 1999): It is multiple, varying across different situations, integrally tied to specific contexts of use, and based on how the current context and prior experiences are construed (Agar, 1994; Barsalou, 1991, 1992; Clark 1993, 1996; Kress, 1985;

Levinson, 1983). What guides an individual's sense making is (often tacit) assumptions about how the world works, assumptions that hang together to form cultural models (Holland & Quinn, 1987), explanatory theories or story lines of prototypical people and events. Such "emblematic visions of an idealized, 'normal,' 'typical' reality" (Gee, 1996, p. 78) allow us to get on with the business of interpreting in the world by setting up what counts as normal and typical (and, therefore, what counts as marginal and nontypical as well). Such cultural models are exceedingly community specific (i.e., what counts as normal varies wildly depending on what community of people one is, here and now, calling from), change over time, compete with one another (especially when the distribution of goods are at stake), overlap or connect up with one another in complex ways, and are distributed across individuals heads, other people, practices, and material resources (Gee, 1992, 1996, 1999). The sense we make of our world at any given time, then, is contingent on the cultural models we bring to bear on it. Yet these cultural models are created, maintained, and transformed by specific social groups whose ways of being in the world underwrite them (Gee, 1999). These "ways of being in the world" or "forms of life" (Wittgenstein, 1958) are what Gee (1992, 1996, 1999) called "big D Discourses." They are similar to what various other theorists have called ("small d") discourses (Foucault, 1966, 1980), communities of practice (Lave & Wenger, 1991), discourse communities (Miller, 1984), distributed knowledge systems (Hutchins, 1995), thought collectives (Fleck, 1979), practices (Bourdieu, 1977, 1990; Heidegger, 1927/1996), cultures (Geertz, 1973, 1983), and actor networks (Latour, 1987).

> [Big-D Discourses are] different ways in which we humans integrate language with non-language "stuff," such as different ways of thinking, acting, interacting, valuing, feeling, believing, and using symbols, tools, and objects in the right places and at the right times so as to … give the material world certain meanings … make certain sorts of meaningful connections in our experience, and privilege certain symbols systems and ways of knowing over others. (Gee, 1999, p. 13)

A "big D" Discourse is the social and material practice of a given group of people associated around a set of shared interests, goals, and/or activities (e.g., gamers within a particular MMOG community). These practices include shared discursive resources such as word choice and grammar (e.g., "l337 speek") and other communicative devices involved in language-in-use (e.g., text conventions for prosody, gestures, or emotes); shared textual practices for both production and interpretation (e.g., in-game letters, unofficial player written manuals, and discussion board flame wars); customary practices for social interaction (e.g., social conventions for in-game group hunts); characteristic ways to coordinate and be coordinated by material resources such as tools, technologies, and systems of representation (e.g., conventions for the use

Such thick description, however, must be augmented by microanalysis of how group members' utterances construe the world in particular ways and not others in order to infer the Discourses as play. Therefore, data collected from the cognitive ethnography are analyzed using discourse analysis procedures (Fairclough, 1989, 1995; Gee, 1999; Gumperz, 1982; Halliday & Hasan, 1989)—"the analysis of language as it is used to enact activities, perspectives, and identities" (Gee, 1999, pp. 4–5) in order to unpack how the meaning of events, practices, and people is constructed, maintained, and transformed. Such analyses focus on the configurations of linguistic cues used in spoken or written utterances in order to invite certain interpretive practices (Gee, 1992)—for example, word choice, foregrounding/backgrounding syntactic and prosodic markers, cohesion devices, discourse organization, contextualization signals, and thematic organization. Configurations of such devices signal how the language of the particular utterance is being used to construe reality in terms of (a) *semiotics*—what symbol systems are privileged, how they construe the relevant context (the world), and on what epistemological basis; (b) *the material world*—what objects, places, times, and people are relevant and in what way; (c) *sociocultural reality*—who is who and what their relationships are with one another, including the implied identity of the speaker/writer and who the audience is construed to be, all in terms of affect, status, solidarity, and (shared or disparate) values and knowledge; (d) *activities*—what specific social activities the speaker and his or her interlocutors are taken to be engaged in; (e) *politics*—what social goods are at stake and how they are and ought to be distributed; and (f) *coherence*—what past and future interactions are relevant to the current communication (Gee, 1999). Particular configurations of linguistic cues prompt specific situated meanings of these six aspects of reality, meanings that are indelibly linked to particular Discourses, allowing speakers and hearers to display and recognize the kind of people each purports to be. Through such discourse-analysis based ethnographic work, we can better capture the sense human beings make of virtual worlds and their (inter)action with/in them. And, in so doing, we may very well discover something new about cognition and literacy in this increasingly heterogeneous, networked, online global, "flat" (Friedman, 2005) world of ours.

Questions for Research

Toward the development of an understanding of MMOGs as Discourses that are created, maintained, and transformed by individuals who participate in them, I propose the following five areas of research: (a) investigation into the complex ways in which the small, routine activities of participants constitute, and are constituted by, macrolevel Discourses within the game (Steinkuehler, 2004a, 2005a, 2005c), (b) exploration into the cultural resources game community participants leverage in the authoring of identities (both their own and others) within such virtual worlds (Steinkuehler, in press), (c) research that examines how individuals are enculturated into such Discourses (Steinkuehler, 2004b), (d) analysis of the literacy practices within and beyond such virtual spaces and how they operate to create and maintain a coherent world of both practice and perspective (Steinkuehler, 2003, 2004c, 2004d, 2005b, 2005d, 2005e), and (e) exploration of how the Discourse of MMOGs is caught up in conversation with other Discourses and how participation in them is situated within gamers' everyday lives (Steinkuehler, 2004a; Steinkuehler & Williams, 2005). This list of areas for further research is surely not complete, yet my hope is that they might start us down paths toward research that, on the one hand, will explicate the function and meaning of MMOGs in the lives of those who inhabit them while, on the other hand, will better inform our theories of cognition and literacy within the globally networked, technologically mediated, "figured worlds" (Holland et al., 1998) we increasingly call home.

Key research questions specifically related to education emerge across all five research areas: What are the actual practices (especially, the forms of literacy) that constitute MMOGs, and how do they align (or fail to align) with valued practices beyond it, including those we purport to foster in schools? What are the ways of believing and valuing that characterize MMOG Discourses, and how are they in conversation with Discourses beyond them (e.g., science in classrooms; Steinkuehler & Chmiel, 2005)? How do individuals come to understand the notion of social construction and the epistemological and ideological issues it raises? How do people author new identities within such worlds, what role do these identities play in the transformation of self, and how do they compare to those we make currently available in formal and informal educational environments? And, finally, what are the mechanisms for learning built into MMOGs, both as designed object and emergent culture, and how might they inform our theories of learning and schooling? Answering such questions is crucial for addressing the current digital disconnect between the uses of online technologies in and out of classrooms. By demonstrating the potential of such online worlds/cultures rather than reifying the current impoverished use of such technologies in schools, we might one day change the very culture of schooling into something more relevant, promising, and transformative for all. Besides, if my hunch is correct and MMOGs are, indeed, push communities that function as our proverbial canaries in the coalmine when it comes to their life in the globalized online world, then research on them *now* can only better prepare us for the radical changes to come—regardless of whether schools respond or render themselves further obsolete.

References

Agar, M. (1994). *Language shock: Understanding the culture of conversation.* New York: William Marrow.

A model economy: Economics and gaming (2005, January 22). *The Economist, 374*(8410), 85.

Balkin, J. M. (2004). Virtual liberty: Freedom to design and freedom to play in virtual worlds. *Virginia Law Review, 90*(8), 2043–2098.

Balkin, J. M. & Noveck, B. (Eds.). (in press). *The state of play: Law and virtual worlds*. New York: New York University Press.

Barsalou, L. W. (1991). Deriving categories to achieve goals. In G. H. Bower (Ed.), *The psychology of learning and motivation: Advances in research and theory* (Vol. 27, pp. 1–64). New York: Academic Press.

Barsalou, L. W. (1992). *Cognitive psychology: An overview for cognitive scientists*. Hillsdale, NJ: Erlbaum.

Bartle, R. (1996). Hearts, clubs, diamonds, spades: Players who suit MUDs. *Journal of MUD Research, 1*(1).

Bartle, R. (2004). *Designing virtual worlds*. Indianapolis, IN: New Riders Publishing.

Barton, D. (1994). *Literacy: An introduction to the ecology of written language*. Oxford, U.K.: Blackwell.

Book, B. (2004). *These bodies are FREE, so get one NOW!: Advertising and branding in social virtual worlds*. Social Science Research Network (SSRN No. 536422). Retrieved June 28, 2005, from http://ssrn.com/abstract=536422

Bourdieu, P. (1977). *Outline of a theory of practice* (R. Nice, Trans.). Cambridge, U.K.: Cambridge University Press.

Bourdieu, P. (1990). *The logic of practice* (R. Nice, Trans.). Stanford, CA: Stanford University Press.

Boyle, J. (1996). *Shamans, software, & spleens: Law and the construction of the information society*. Cambridge, MA: Harvard University Press.

Bruckman, A. S. (1993, August). *Gender swapping on the Internet*. Paper presented at The Internet Society, San Francisco, CA.

Carlstrom, E. L. (1992). *Better living through language: The communicative implications of a text-only virtual environment*. Unpublished manuscript. Retrieved July 1, 2005, from ftp://ftp.game.org/pub/mud/text/research/communicative.txt

Castronova, E. (2001). *Virtual worlds: A first-hand account of market and society on the cyberian frontier* (CESifo Working Paper Series No. 618). Retrieved September 15, 2005 from http://ssrn.com/abstract=294828

Castronova, E. (2002). *On virtual economies* (CESifo Working Paper Series No. 752). Retrieved September 15, 2005 http://papers.ssrn.com/sol3/papers.cfm?abstract_id=338500

Castronova, E. (2004). The right to play. *New York Law School Law Review, 49*(1), 185–210.

Cato, G. (2004, December 15). *MMOs: It's the economy, stupid*. Retrieved July 1, 2005, from http://overanalyzed.com/portal.php?topic_id=19

Cazden, C. (1988). *Classroom discourse: The language of teaching and learning*. Portsmouth, NH: Heinnemann.

Certeau, M. de. (1984). *The practice of everyday life* (S. Rendall, Trans.). London: The University of California Press.

Cherney, L. (1999). *Conversation and community: Discourse in a social MUD*. Stanford, CA: CSLI Publications.

Clark, A. (1993). *Associative engines: Connectionism, concepts, and parallel distributed processing*. Cambridge, MA: MIT Press.

Clark, A. (1996). *Using language*. Cambridge, U.K.: Cambridge University Press.

Clodius, J. (1994). *Concepts of space and place in a virtual community*. Unpublished manuscript. Retrieved July 1, 2005, from http://dragonmud.org/people/jen/space.html

Clodius, J. (1995). Ritual and religion on DragonMud. Unpublished manuscript. Retrieved July 1, 2005, from http://dragonmud.org/people/jen/ritual.html

Clodius, J. (1996a). Orality in a text-based community. Unpublished manuscript. Retrieved July 1, 2005, from http://dragonmud.org/people/jen/oral.html

Clodius, J. (1996b). Shar's return: Performance as gifting. Unpublished manuscript. Retrieved July 1, 2005, from http://dragonmud.org/people/jen/shar.html

Clodius, J. (1997, January 15). Creating a community of interest: "Self" and "other" on DragonMud. Paper presented at the Combined Conference on MUDs, Jackson Hole, WY.

Cobb, P., & Bowers, J. (1999). Cognitive and situated perspectives in theory and practice. *Educational Reasearcher, 28*(2), 4–15.

Cook-Gumperz, J. (Ed.). (1986). *The social construction of literacy.* Cambridge, U.K.: Cambridge University Press.

Coombe, R. J. (1998). *The cultural life of intellectual properties: Authorship, appropriation, and the law.* Durham, NC: Duke University Press.

Crawford, S. (2003, November 13–15). Who's in charge of who I am: Identity and law online. Paper presented at First Annual State of Play Conference, New York Law School, New York.

Curtis, P. (1992). Mudding: Social phenomena in text-based virtual realities. In P. Ludlow (Ed.), *High noon on the electronic frontier: Conceptual issues in cyberspace* (pp. 347–374). Cambridge, MA: The MIT Press.

Danet, B. (1998). Text as mask: Gender, play, and performance on the Internet. In S. G. Jones (Ed.), *Cybersociety 2.0: Computer-mediated communication and community revisited* (pp. 129–158). Thousand Oaks, CA: Sage Publications.

Dibbell, J. (1998). *My tiny life: Crime and passion in a virtual world.* New York: Henry Holt.

Dibbell, J. (2003a, November 13–15). Owned!: Intellectual property in the age of dupers, gold farmers, eBayers, and other enemies of the virtual state. Paper presented at first annual State of Play Conference, New York Law School, New York.

Dibbell, J. (2003b, January). The unreal estate boom. *Wired, 11*(1), Retrieved September 1, 2006 from http://www.wired.com/wired/archive/11.01/gaming.html

Dibbell, J. (in press). *Play money. Or how I quit my day job and set out to strike it rich selling imaginary castles and make-believe gold.* Cambridge, MA: Basic Books.

Ducheneaut, N., Moore, R. J., & Nickell, E. (2004). Designing for sociability in massively multiplayer games: An examination of the "third places" of *SWG.* In J. H. Smith & M. Sicart (Eds.), *Proceedings of the other players conference* (pp.). Copenhagen, Denmark: IT University of Copenhagen. Retrieved January 1, 2007 from http://itu.dk/op/proceedings.htm

Erikson, E. (1963). *Childhood and society* (2nd ed.). New York: Norton.

Fairclough, N. (1989). *Language and power.* London: Longman.

Fairclough, N. (1995). *Critical discourse analysis.* London: Longman.

Filiciak, M. (2003). Hyperidentities: Postmodern identity patterns in massively multiplayer online role-playing games. In M. J. P. Wolf & B. Perron (Eds.), *The video game theory reader* (pp. 87–102). New York: Routledge.

Fleck, L. (1979). *The genesis and development of a scientific fact.* Chicago: University of Chicago Press.

Foucault, M. (1966). *The order of things: An archaeology of human sciences.* New York: Random House.

Foucault, M. (1980). *Power/knowledge: Selected interviews and other writings 1972–1977* (C. Gordon, L. Marshall, J. Meplam, & K. Spoer, Eds.). Brighton, U.K.: The Harvester Press.

Fransella, F., & Bannister, D. (1977). *A manual for repertory grid technique.* London: Academic Press.

Friedman, T. L. (2005). *The world is flat: A brief history of the twenty-first century.* New York: Farrar, Straus, and Giroux.

Galarneau, L. (2005, June 16–20). *Spontaneous communities of learning: A social analysis of learning ecosystems in massively multiplayer online gaming (MMOG) environments.* Paper presented at the Digital Games Research Association Conference (DIGRA), Vancouver, British Columbia, Canada.

Gates, B. (2005, February 26). *Speech to the National Education Summit on High Schools.* Retrieved October 1, 2005, from http://www.gatesfoundation.org/MediaCenter/Speeches/BillgSpeeches/BGSpeechNGA-050226.htm

Gee, J. P. (1992). *The social mind: Language, ideology, and social practice.* New York: Bergin & Garvey.

Masterson, J. T., III. (1996). Nonverbal communication in text based virtual realities. Unpublished master's thesis, University of Montana. Retrieved July 1, 2005 from http://www.johnmasterson.com/thesis/toc.html

Miller, C. R. (1984). Genre as social action. *Quarterly Journal of Speech, 70*(2), 151–167.

Moore, R., Ducheneaut, N., & Nickell, E. (2005, June 23–24). *Leveraging virtual omniscience: Mixed methodologies for studying social life in persistent online worlds.* Workshop presented at the Games, Learning, and Society Conference, Madison, WI.

Morningstar, C., & Farmer, F. R. (1991). The lessons of Lucasfilm's Habitat. In M. Benedikt (Ed.), *Cyberspace: First steps* (273–302). Cambridge, MA: MIT Press.

Mulligan, J., & Patrovsky, B. (2003). *Developing online games: An insider's guide.* Indianapolis, IN: New Riders Games.

Nakamura, L. (1995). Race in/for cyberspace: Identity tourism and racial passing on the Internet. *Works and Days, 25/26,* 13(1–2), 181–193.

Nash, S. S. (2004, December 8). *Stop! You're scaring me! Hyperidentities in e-learning.* Retrieved July 1, 2005, from http://www.xplanazine.com/archives/2004/12/stop_youre_scar.php

Nash, J., & Schneyer, E. (2004). *Virtual economies: An in-depth look at the virtual world of Final Fantasy XI: Online.* Unpublished manuscript. Retrieved July 1, 2004, from http://lgst.wharton.upenn.edu/hunterd/VirtualEconomies.pdf

Nasir, N. S. (2005). Individual cognitive structuring and the sociocultural context: Strategy shifts in the game of dominoes. *The Journal of the Learning Sciences, 14*(1), 5–34.

Noveck, B. (2004). Unchat: Democratic solution for a wired world. In P. Shane (Ed.), *Democracy online: The prospects for democratic renewal through the Internet* (pp. 21–34). New York: Routledge.

Piaget, J. (1978). *Success and understanding.* Cambridge, MA: Harvard University Press.

Rathedan, P. (2001, May 14). *A real player economy.* Retrieved June 28, 2005, from http://swg.stratics.com/content/feature/editorials/editorials.php?Cat=1&uid=13

Raybourn, E. M. (1998, February). *The quest for power, popularity, and privilege in cyberspace: Identity construction in a text-based multi-user virtual reality.* Proceedings of the Western Speech Communication Association Conference, Denver, CO.

Reid, E. M. (1994). *Cultural formations in text-based virtual realities.* Unpublished master's thesis, University of Melbourne, Australia.

Rheingold, H. (1993). *The virtual community: Homesteading on the electronic frontier.* Reading, MA: Addison.

Rideout, V., Roberts, D. F., & Foehr, U. G. (2005). *Generation M: Media in the lives of 8–18 year-olds* (Publication No. 7250). Washington, DC: The Henry J. Kaiser Family Foundation.

Rollings, A., & Adams, E. (2003). *On game design.* Indianapolis, IN: New Riders Publishing.

Rosenberg, M. (1992). *Virtual reality: Reflections of life, dreams, and technology. An ethnography of a computer society.* Unpublished manuscript. Retrieved June 28, 2005, from http://www.eff.org/Net_culture/MOO_MUD_IRC/rosenberg_vr_reflections.paper

Schaap, F. (2002). *The words that took us there: Ethnography in a virtual reality.* Piscataway, NJ: Transaction Publishers.

Seay, A. F., Jerome, W. J., Lee, K. S., & Kraut, R. E. (2005). *Project massive.* Retrieved July 1, 2005, from http://www.projectmassive.com/

Shirky, C. (2003, November 13–15). *Constitutional experimentation in online social spaces.* Paper presented at First Annual State of Play Conference, New York Law School, New York.

Squire, K. D., & Steinkuehler, C. A. (2005). Meet the gamers. *Library Journal, 130*(7), 38–41.

Squire, K. D., & Steinkuehler, C. A. (in press). Generating cyberculture/s: The case of star wars galaxies. In D. Gibbs & K. L. Krause (Eds.), *Cyberlines: Languages and cultures of the Internet* (2nd ed., 177–198). Albert Park, Australia: James Nicholas Publishers.

Steinkuehler, C. A. (2003). *Massively multiplayer online videogames as a constellation of literacy practices*. Paper presented at the International Conference on Literacy, Ghent, Belgium.

Steinkuehler, C. A. (2004a, October 28–31). *The culture of play*. Paper presented at the State of Play Conference, New York University Law School, New York.

Steinkuehler, C. A. (2004b). Learning in massively multiplayer online games. In Y. B. Kafai, W. A. Sandoval, N. Enyedy, A. S. Nixon, & F. Herrera (Eds.), *Proceedings of the sixth international conference of the learning sciences* (pp. 521–528). Mahwah, NJ: Erlbaum.

Steinkuehler, C. A. (2004c). *The literacy practices of massively multiplayer online gaming*. Paper presented at the annual meeting of the American Educational Research Association, San Diego, CA.

Steinkuehler, C. A. (2004d). *Providing resources for MMOG guild leaders*. Paper presented at the MUD Developers Conference, San Jose, CA.

Steinkuehler, C. A. (2005a, January 21). *Cognition & learning in massively multiplayer online games: A critical approach*. Paper presented at the Learning Sciences Colloquium, University of Wisconsin–Madison.

Steinkuehler, C. A. (2005b, April 11–15). *The literacy of massively multiplayer online gaming versus national standards*. Paper presented at the annual meeting of the American Educational Research Association, Montreal, Canada.

Steinkuehler, C. A. (2005c, June 16–20). *Styles of play: Gamer-identified trajectories of participation in MMOGs*. Paper presented at the annual Conference of the Digital Games Research Association (DIGRA), Vancouver, British Columbia, Canada.

Steinkuehler, C. A. (2005d, April 4–6). *(Tech)tual play: Literacy learning in massively multiplayer online games*. Paper presented at CAL05 Virtual Learning? Conference, University of Bristol, U.K.

Steinkuehler, C. A. (2005e, May 11). *Why should libraries care about videogames?* Paper presented at the Online Computer Library Center (OCLC) annual meeting, Washington, DC.

Steinkuehler, C. A. (2006). Why game (culture) studies now? *Games and Culture, 1*(1), 1–6.

Steinkuehler, C. A. (in press). Massively multiplayer online videogaming as participation in a discourse. *Mind, Culture, & Activity*.

Steinkuehler, C. A., & Chmiel, M. (2005). *Fostering scientific habits of mind in the context of online play*. Manuscript submitted for publication.

Steinkuehler, C. A., & Williams, D. (2005). *Where everybody knows your (screen) name: Online games as 'third places.'* Manuscript submitted for publication.

Stivale, C. J. (1997). Spam: Heteroglossia and harassment in cyberspace. In D. Porter (Ed.), *Internet culture* (pp. 133–144). New York: Routledge.

Street, B. (1984). *Literacy in theory and practice*. Cambridge, U.K.: Cambridge University Press.

Street, B. (Ed.). (1993). *Cross-cultural approaches to literacy*. Cambridge, U.K.: Cambridge University Press.

Suler, J. (1996). *The psychology of cyberspace*. Retrieved July 1, 2005, from http://www.rider.edu/~suler/psycyber/psycyber.html

Taylor, T. L. (2002). Whose game is this anyway?: Negotiating corporate ownership in a virtual world. In F. Mäyrä (Ed.), *Computer games and digital cultures conference proceedings* (pp. 227–242). Tampere, Finland: Tampere University Press.

Taylor, T. L. (in press). Pushing the borders: Player participation and game culture. In J. Karaganis & N. Jeremijenko (Eds.), *Network_netplay: Structures of participation in digital culture*. Durham, NC: Duke University Press.

Terdiman, D. (2003, August 8). Commerce drives virtual world. *Wired, 11*(8), Retrieved January 1, 2006 from http://www.wired.com/gaming/gamingreviews/news/2003/08/59941

Terdiman, D. (2004, January 23). Virtual cash breeds real cash. *Wired, 12*(1), Retrieved January 1, 2006 from http://www.wired.com/gaming/gamingreviews/news/2004/01/61999

Thompson, Z. B. (2000, March). *The in-game economics of Ultima Online*. Paper presented at Computer Game Developer's Conference, San Jose, CA.

Thorsen, T. (2005, June 29). *Dave Chappelle loves World of Warcraft: Famed and elusive comic praises Blizzard's popular MMORPG at San Francisco nightclub appearance*. Retrieved July 1, 2005, from http://www.gamespot.com/news/2005/06/29/news_6128319.html

Tolkien, J. R. R. (1938). *The Hobbit*. Boston: Houghton Mifflin.

Trubshaw, R., & Bartle, R. (1978). *MUD1*. Essex, U.K.: University of Essex. Retrieved Oct. 1, 2004, from http://www.british-legends.com/

Turkle, S. (1994). Constructions and reconstructions of self in virtual reality: Playing in the MUDS. *Mind, Culture, & Activity, 1*(3), 158–167.

Turkle, S. (1995). *Life on the screen: Identity in the age of the Internet*. New York: Touchstone.

Van Gelder, L. (1996). The strange case of the electronic lover. In R. Kling (Ed.), *Computerization and controversy: Value conflicts and social choices* (pp. 533–549). San Diego, CA: Academic Press.

Von Glasersfeld, E. (1995). *Radical constructivism: A way of knowing and learning* (Studies in Mathematics Education Series, No 6). London: The Falmer Press.

Vygotsky, L. S. (1978). *Mind in society: The development of the higher psychological processes*. Cambridge, MA: The Harvard University Press. (Original work published 1930).

Walls, D. (2005, June 16–20). *Just who wears the tights in this household?: Technological dramas, gender trouble, and Cryptic Studio's City of Heroes*. Paper presented at the Digital Games Research Association Conference (DIGRA), Vancouver, British Columbia, Canada.

Williams, D. (2004). *Trouble in river city: The social life of video games*. Unpublished doctoral dissertation, University of Michigan.

Wittgenstein, L. (1958). *Philosophical investigations*. Oxford, U.K.: Basil Blackwell.

Wong, G. (2000). A working mud economy. *Imaginary Realities, 3*(5), Retrieved January 1, 2006 from http://www.mud.co.uk/dvw/workingmudeconomy.html

Yee, N. (2005a). Playing together. *The Daedalus project, 3*(3). Retrieved July 1, 2005, from http://www.nickyee.com/daedalus/archives/001338.php

Yee, N. (2005b, June 16–20). *Motivations of play in MMORPGs*. Paper presented at the Digital Games Research Association Conference (DIGRA), Vancouver, British Columbia, Canada.

Zackariasson, P., & Wilson, T. L. (2004). Massively multiplayer online games: A 21st century service? In J. H. Smith, & M. Sicart (Eds.), *Proceedings of the other players conference*. Copenhagen, Denmark: IT University of Copenhagen. Retrieved January 1, 2007 from http://itu.dk/op/proceedings.htm

CHAPTER 23

Video-Game Literacy
A Literacy of Expertise

KURT D. SQUIRE

UNIVERSITY OF WISCONSIN-MADISON, USA

Why Video Games Literacy?

"Reading" competence is at risk, or so reports (in the United States at least) from the National Endowment from the Humanities (NEA, 2004), popular press, and news reports would have one believe (Sanders, 1995). Authors of the NEA report *Reading at Risk* write, "If one believes that active and engaged readers lead richer intellectual lives than non-readers and that a well-read citizenry is essential to a vibrant democracy, the decline of literary reading calls for serious action" (p. 9). The assumptions behind this message are clear. The world can be divided into two types of people: the readers and the nonreaders, with literary readers holding the highest status. Nonreaders, who lead "lesser lives" than readers, are threatening the state of democracy. In an influential *New York Times* article, Solomon (2004) described this "crisis in reading" as a "crisis in national health." Note that critics like Solomon and the NEA are concerned not that millions *cannot* read; it is that people are *choosing* not to read. Ironically perhaps, proponents of this (possibly hegemonic) position are especially concerned that citizenry read the *right* kinds of "literary" texts (presumably not the lyrics of rapper, 50 Cent, or the manga series, *Sailor Moon*), lest the health of democracy suffer. The message underlying these critiques is clear: The rise of popular media in the digital age is at the heart of this decline (cf., Sanders, 1995).

As critics lament the "decline of the book" (with Harry Potter presumably not counting as literature), those few scholars who have touched video-game controllers are noting that games are surprisingly long, difficult, and complex, requiring and developing new digital literacies (Gee, 2003; Squire, 2003). The term *video games* is used throughout this chapter as an umbrella term that covers a wide range of digital-gaming media, including computer-based games that are downloaded from the Internet or contained on a storage media (e.g., CDs or DVD), free and subscription-based online games, handheld electronic games and console-based video games played on televisions. Psychologists have long noted that video games require fine-motor skills and sophisticated navigation skills, but recent studies have focused on the games' complex problem-solving requirements, much as an earlier generation of scholars studied checkers or chess (Greenfield, 1984; Rosser et al., 2004; Squire, 2003; Steinkuehler, in press-a). Video games incorporate both closed-ended and open-ended problem-solving tasks, require navigation across complex systems, productivity with digital media, and collaboration with others (Squire, 2002; Steinkuehler, in press-b). As one example among many, some video games, like the award-winning role-playing game, *Star Wars: Knights of the Old Republic*, actually include classic cognitive-psychology problems such as Tower of Hanoi that require a pyramid of three disks to be moved from one peg to another using two additional pegs between the starting and finishing points. Indeed, research comparing video-game playing practice to traditional academic literacy and technology standards suggests that gaming *is* thoroughly a literacy practice, requiring players to produce meaning with texts and become expressive with technology in multiple forms (Steinkuehler, 2005). As a generation of kids raised on games and the Internet enters the academy—not as students, but as tenure-track faculty—our understandings of literacy are changing as well.

Those unfamiliar with games (frequently "baby boomers," those born in developed countries during the 1950s, as well as older people) are usually surprised to learn of the developments in game technology and design over the past 35 years (cf., Williams, 2005). When most people think of video games, they think of *Pac-Man* or *Pong* (the latter, coincidentally, was released in 1972, the year I was born). Today's games have evolved far beyond early stand-alone, purpose-wired arcade games, which were (necessarily) designed to be played by anyone with a coin in his or her hand and in a relatively short time (the time factor was deliberately kept short in order to increase the number of games that could be played in a day, which in turn increased profits). For an amusing illustration of this, see "Kids Review Classic Games," published by the *Electronic Gaming Monthly*, which features transcripts of today's kids reviewing the games their parents played. The following exchange typifies these young reviewers' (who are purported to be real children) responses to *Pong*:

John: I'd sooner jump up and down on one foot. By the way, is this supposed to be tennis or Ping-Pong? *Becky:* Ping-Pong. *Gordon:* It doesn't even go over the net. It goes through it. I don't even think that thing in the middle is a net.

With the appearance of the Atari home entertainment system and personal computer in the mid-1970s, games began diversifying. Games soon included genres spanning action, adventure, sports, role playing, movie tie-ins (most notably, *E.T.* in the early 1980s), and puzzles, with games like *Pac-Man* and *Donkey Kong* introducing Japanese-made games into the global gaming marketplace. On the PC around this time, games took a more cerebral tack than did their console-based counterparts, with games like *Zork* aspiring to a form of interactive fiction (with similar games later done with graphics), and a host of role-playing games inspired by offline, dice-based Dungeons and Dragons role-playing games.

While we can see traces of today's video games in these early titles, they were incredibly simple by today's standards. They were usually designed and programmed by one person and took up less than a few kilobytes of storage space (roughly the size of one image file on a contemporary Web page today). These early games also lacked key features characteristic of current games—such as the ability to "save" partly played games. Indeed, in 1984, poor-quality games and consumer disillusionment caused a collapse of the games industry, and it did not fully recover until the Nintendo Entertainment System (NES) began gaining in popularity in the late 1980s (Herman, 1997; Sheff, 1994). The fast rise of the NES, a console product made by Nintendo, a Japanese games and toy manufacturer, and its many commercial tie-ins surprised and concerned many parents. As Hertz (1997) described, Nintendo pioneered many business practices common today, including its aggressive marketing of ancillary products (e.g., lunchboxes, snack items) along with company-owned "companion" media, such as the Nintendo-owned *Nintendo Power* magazine and its 1-900 call-in phone lines. The result of all of this was that Nintendo largely captured the hearts of a generation (born more or less in the early to mid-1970s and also referred to as the "Nintendo generation"). By 1992, for example, Mario (Nintendo's flagship character) was more recognizable and popular with American children than Mickey Mouse (Sheff, 1994).

It is fair to say that a major driver in the growth of the games industry has been the Nintendo generation itself. As this generation grows older and begins to enter middle age, members of this generation are bringing their video games with them. The average age of video-game players is now over 30 years old (10 years ago, the average age of video-game players was 16 to 18 years). It is this generation that played the much maligned *Mortal Kombat* as preteens, and bought PlayStations as they entered high school and college in the 1990s.

This same generation also made the GameBoy the best-selling gaming platform to date, ringing up sales of over 100 million of these handheld devices worldwide. The late 1980s and early 1990s witnessed a range of developments and innovations in the PC industry, including the rise of PC-simulation games (like *Flight Simulator, Sim City,* or *Civilization*), the birth of Internet-mediated multiplayer gaming via the PC (like *Modem Wars,* released in 1988), the continuing maturation of narrative-driven games, and the birth of 3-D gaming with *DOOM* and *Ultima Underworld.*

As the Nintendo generation grows up, markets for games appear to be only expanding in order to meet demands brought about by the rising average age of game players and the corresponding rise in the number of game players overall, the increasing number of women playing games, and the increasing globalization of the games marketplace. Gaming developments over the last decade, which are largely the focus of this chapter, might well be described as a phase of maturation and consolidation with some diversification thrown in for good measure. For certain, the core features of games as we know them today (e.g., 3-D graphics, simulated worlds, Internet connectivity, distributed game play) were established during this time, but it is during this same time period that the SONY Corporation released the PlayStation, a new and eminently affordable console-based video-game player. The PlayStation was remarkable for bringing real-time 3-D-interface rendering to the masses and for solidifying the market for games targeted at the 18- to 30-year-old market. In 2002, Microsoft entered the fray with its Xbox machine, turning the video-game console wars into the war over the entertainment system (and software) that runs the living room. At the time of writing this chapter, the Nintendo Revolution, Sony PlayStation 3, and Microsoft Xbox 360 are all jockeying for first position as the entertainment console that will become the centerpiece of living rooms around the world.

Over the past decade, the popular press, media scholars, and now educators have been paying closer attention to computer and video games (hereafter referred to as video games; Hertz, 1997; Cassell & Jenkins, 1998). Creatively, video games push the boundaries of interactivity, immersive environments, community design, and digital storytelling. Technologically, games push the boundaries of consumer-grade real-time simulation and artificial intelligence. Culturally, they are changing the way we play, learn, and interact and quintessential sites of broader shifts in knowledge consumption and production (de Castell & Jenson, 2007; King, 2001; Scholder & Zimmerman, 2003; Squire, 2003). Games are in a transitional phase of cultural status, and it is no longer unusual to see game exhibits at art museums or university courses on gaming. The last 18 months have brought us dozens of academic, government, and industry conferences focused on the academic study of games, a substantial portion of which are dedicated to games and learning. It is beyond the scope of this chapter to identify all the major conferences related to games currently running each year, but noteworthy U.S. industry conferences include the biannual Serious Games summits held in Washington, DC and in conjunction with the Game Developer's Conference, and the Education Arcade, held in conjunction with the Electronic Entertainment Exposition. Although the latter was founded in the United States, there are or have been similar conferences in Europe, Japan, and Australia. Academically, there are at least a dozen relevant conferences every year including the regular meeting of the Digital Games Research Association (DiGRA), and the University of Wisconsin-Madison's annual Games, Learning, and Society Conference. The Games and Learning research centers at the Massachusetts Institute of Technology, the University of Southern California, the University of Texas-Austin, and the University of Wisconsin-Madison are becoming more established, and are formalizing into degree programs at the undergraduate, master's, and doctoral level (for more on such developments within academia, see Carlson, 2003; Schiesel, 2005).

Games are one—although perhaps *the* quintessential—site for studying digital literacies as a medium of *interactivity,* both with respect to the human-computer interface and among constellations of users. Video games are the medium of the computer, and in understanding them, we can understand what it means to think, act, and learn in simulated worlds (cf., Starr, 1994). However, researchers are only beginning to theorize how games operate and understand what the medium will mean for learning, schooling, and society. Key questions that currently shape this growing field of studies include (a) What are the implications of an interactive medium for literacy? (b) How does access to globally distributed communities change traditional notions of meaning making? (c) How will a gaming generation react to traditional schooling with its grammar of teacher text as authority and student as product, when outside school this generation relives historical eras, leads civilizations, conducts forensic investigations, or can earn a real wage by buying and selling virtual currencies (Castronova, 2001; Shaffer, Squire, Halverson, & Gee, 2005; Squire, 2003; Steinkuehler, 2004a, this volume)?

This review of gaming research begins by examining the study of *games as artifacts,* and discusses the assumptions academics have made about and approaches they have used to study games. This section is followed by an examination of studies of *game playing as a social practice.* This focus encompasses research that investigates gaming in communities and social contexts. The final section of this review explores the implications of games for literacy, learning, schooling, and education writ large, and focuses in particular on studies of games in educational contexts. Across all three sections, I argue that games are an experiential, interactive medium where we participate (and cocreate) new worlds. Although these worlds are synthetic, simulated worlds, they are worlds constructed to provide particular kinds of experiences, which might be called *designed experiences.* Games literacy can be defined as developing *expertise* in designing rewarding experiences for oneself within a gameworld (particularly within the game's semiotic and rule systems). Notably, there is no one rubric by which expertise can be judged, and through studies of gaming communities we see how different meanings are created, negotiated, and given legitimacy. Like video games themselves, gaming communities are interactive in nature, frequently functioning as spaces for participating in social practices with a life beyond the boundaries of the game itself. To date, efforts to create such programs in schools have shown some successes, but have fallen short of creating the kind of participatory culture that characterizes the contemporary popular culture landscape.

Games as Artifacts: Synthetic Spaces for Action

Video games' interactivity presents major challenges for literacy researchers. This includes asking how we can best treat authorship in a medium in which players have *agency* in creating the unfolding of events and in changing the very symbols and representations that comprise the game on screen (Jenkins, in press; LeBlanc, 1999/2006; Robison, in press). In other words, without the player, there literally is no game. This leads to a core challenge for literacy researchers: How do we study a phenomenon that cannot exist without its players? For example, in the case of *Grand Theft Auto: San Andreas,* a first-person shooter game, the much publicized example of a player stealing a car, hiring a prostitute, and running her over is an emergent property of interacting rules; however, most players may never explore this aspect of the game and certainly would not use it as a regular strategy. Choosing a single set of interactions in a game for scrutiny is unproductive and disingenuous although it is a common tactic of mainstream media reporting of games. Yet, clearly, there is a difference between *Grand Theft Auto* and *Sim City.* Just how to categorize, conceptualize, and understand the characteristics of games has been a core concern in games and literacy research.

Perhaps not surprisingly, then, much of the early (and current) theoretical work in video-game studies has aimed at defining what a game is and how games ought to be studied. The core organizing debates have centered on whether games should be studied from the perspectives of media studies (this orientation has been characterized as "narratology") or as a form of play (this orientation is often called "ludology"; cf., Frasca, 1999). These theoretical issues take on practical significance as researchers deal with questions concerning violence and media in games like, *Grand Theft Auto: San Andreas.* While media theorists tend to emphasize the importance of characters in a game and the narrative (and rule-based) consequences of game actions, ludologists tend to emphasize the psychosocial dimensions of play (cf., Wardrip-Fruin & Harrigan, 2004; Frasca, 1999).

The so-called narratology/ludology debates have been unfortunate, since the interaction between "narratology" (taken here to mean characters, backstory, and symbols) and "play" (fantasy, removal of everyday rules and constraints, goal-driven activity) is just what makes games so intriguing (Juul, 2001; Squire, 2005c; Squire & DeVane, 2006). To continue with the case of *Grand Theft Auto: San Andreas,* part of its playful and theoretical allure is that it is a stylized representation of a ghetto; a representation that codifies symbols such as gang colors and allegiance into game concepts such as loyalty, respect, and giving players a set of symbols and icons to play with. Reports of research focusing on players suggest that gamers do wildly different things with the worlds available to them with this game and, in fact, appear to conceptualize the worlds and themselves within them according to their own lived histories (Squire & DeVane, 2006; Vargas, 2005). One player interviewed by Squire and DeVane used the game as little more than a "pimp your ride" car-customization kit (he wanted to pursue a career in car customization), one used the game as a chase-scene simulator as a relief from school, and another as fantastical escape from the suburbs. Thus, both technologically and conceptually, it is the (usually) seamless blending of agency, interactivity, narrative, semiotic domains, and expansive worlds that makes video games so interesting (Gee, 2003; Mateas, 2004; Murray, 2004; Perlin, 2004).

Games as Spaces

Jenkins (1993, 2002) argued that one useful way to understand games-as-interactive objects is to study them as spaces. Writing about Super Nintendo's *Mario* games, Jenkins and Fuller (1995) argued that the narrative structure of video games is like those of travel narratives. A game such as *SuperMario* is organized around exploration; the core game pleasures involve visiting exotic lands, meeting unusual characters, and unlocking secret passages. Jenkins and Fuller (1995, p. 61) argued that structurally, this kind of exploration game shares much in common with John Smith's travel writing:

> Nintendo®'s central feature is its constant presentation of spectacular spaces (or "worlds," to use the game parlance). Its landscapes dwarf characters who serve, in turn, primarily as vehicles for players to move through these remarkable places. Once immersed in playing, we don't really care whether we rescue Princess Toadstool or not; all that matters is staying alive long enough to move between levels, to see what spectacle awaits us on the next screen. Most of the criteria by which we might judge a classically constructed narrative fall by the wayside when we look at these games as storytelling systems. In Nintendo®'s narratives, characters play a minimal role, displaying traits that are largely capacities for action: fighting skills, modes of transportation, pre-established goals.

Thus, while many cultural critics may look at Nintendo's games and see impoverished potential for interaction, Jenkins and Fuller reminded us that not all "classic" literature is as taught in freshman English; different narrative forms have served different purposes and taken on different forms/interpretations across different times. For example, in the early 1700s, most fiction novels of the time were regarded as having dubious quality, or, as in the case of Daniel Defoe's *Robinson Crusoe* (1719)—which was described as a "true history" and not a novel—as having little value as a resource to be used in schooling children.

According to Jenkins and Fuller (1995), the task for games scholars is not to argue *how* games necessarily fit within traditional forms, but to better understand how games are *transforming* previous forms. Taking (and fueling) the narratology/ludology debate, Jenkins (2002) argued that many games do, in fact, aspire to tell stories, but they do so by means of "space." Jenkins saw a basic contradiction between the linearity of traditional narrative structures and interactivity, which leads designers to telling stories through the arrangement of space so as to produce compelling narrative moments—or *experiences*. Jenkins found four ways that games use space to create narrative: (a) evocative stories (stories that reshape based on previous characters and media), (b) enacted stories (stories where players enact specific plot points), (c) embedded narratives (games where narrative events are embedded in artifacts in the world), and (d) emergent narratives (narrative experiences that emerge as the result of simulation). Jenkins situates his argument for understanding stories and games within a *pragmatic* framework that tries to account for how games are designed and played, drawing on interviews with game designers as well as a close reading of video games.

In "The Art of Contested Spaces," Jenkins and Squire (2002) expanded on this notion of understanding games through spatial terms, describing different aesthetic approaches for creating *conflict* within space. Responding to critics who want to see a theory of digital games rooted in play and games (e.g., Eskelinen, 2004), Jenkins and Squire described how *contestation* is at the core of game design. Many video games, such as *Civilization,* remediate board games, while others, such as sports games, are about contestations of space on a metaphoric or strategic level (e.g., a basketball team that uses floor spacing well or defends the lane well). Enemies, puzzles, and a character's inability to move or affect the world obstruct access to space. Much of game play can be seen as "opening" new spaces—both physical ones (levels) and abstract ones (possibilities, or new experiences within the same physical space). Jenkins and Squire also emphasized the social space surrounding the machine, arguing that interfaces and game mechanics from the guild-user interfaces in the medieval-like *Asheron's Call* to the hand-held maracas in the music game, *Samba de Amigo,* are designed to promote social interaction. A critical feature of these spaces for Jenkins and Squire was that they evolve in response to users' actions. In role-playing video games like *Morrowind,* players' actions open new lands, social networks, and possibilities for action (cf., Hayes, 2005; Kadakia, 2005). In snowboarding games, the camera, snow, and crowds all respond with exaggerated feedback on players' actions (e.g., crowds will cheer or moan according to the quality of the gamer's turn, slide, jump, etc.; the camera follows the player as she makes decisions about which downhill run to take and how to complete it). Or, perhaps most dramatically, in *Black & White,* the physical features of the world literally evolve in response to players' actions, potentially becoming everything from a tropical paradise to a barren desert, making the world a physical manifestation of players' actions.

Game Time: Games as Dynamic Systems

Games are dynamic systems, operating similarly to simulations, which begin with a particular set of initial conditions and then evolve through time in response to players' actions. Of particular interest to game theorists has been how game players reported transformations of their experience of time while engrossed in game play. Csikszentmihalyi (1990) described this phenomenon in terms of flow; the condition under which a player's skill level is optimally matched with the level of challenge faced, creating conditions in which the participant reports a feeling of being in the zone. Researchers such as Bowman (1982) have shown how video games are especially good at inducing and maintaining these flow states by adjusting complexity in response to users' actions. Myers (1991, 1992) sought to extend this hypothesis concerning play and time, and posited that game play unfolds through *semiotic transformations;* transformations where players' goals and oppositional structures iteratively evolve, resulting in an emergent, semiotically more complex self over time.

More recently, some researchers have begun to use *time* itself as an analytic axis when examining games and game playing. Jesper Juul's (2004) project, for example, has been to build a descriptive theory of digital games that uses time as one lens for examining game aesthetics. Juul is especially interested in how players interact with the *game state* over time. Juul uses the term, "game state," to describe how the "game" may be static code on a computer, but as game play unfolds dynamically, the game and player together generate unique game situations. Sim City, for example, consists of no actual city, but rather a virtual parcel of land, a set of nouns (e.g., land, road), a set of actions (e.g., zoning), a rule set describing relations among these things, and the ability to watch these relations grow and evolve over time. Juul categorized games in terms of how game *play time* (time experienced by the player) relates to *game time* (whatever chronological system is employed in the game). Juul's work suggests that there is no one "static" game to be studied, only game *states* that emerge through the interaction of preset rules and player choices. Indeed, replaying a video game never unfolds exactly the same way as it did originally; therefore, issues concerning author, audience, and meaning making are only amplified in game studies (Church, 2000; LeBlanc, 1999/2006; Robison, in press).

Interactive "texts." This lack of a stable "text" poses one of the greatest challenges for educators. Designers of educational games, such as

Aldrich (2004), have observed that the single biggest obstacle to creating educational games is moving from linear to dynamic content. Aldrich's model for designing educational games is built around *cycles of action* (cf., Games-to-Teach Team, 2003; Salen & Zimmerman, 2003; Squire, 2005c). These cycles of action consist of feedback loops whereby the player iteratively develops goals, takes an action, experiences feedback on that action, and shifts goals and actions accordingly. Similarly, Betrus's (1995, 2005) chainsaw model is another time-based approach to understanding games that emphasizes the cyclical, recurring nature of game play (see Figure 23.1). Betrus' model—which is particularly appropriate for action games—focuses on the relationship between relatively short events (e.g., moves), sets of moves (e.g., sequences), and entire levels. Betrus used this model to examine the ways in which these elements were linked together by means of a theory of how they unfold over time. For Betrus, games were marked by small, repeating challenges punctuated by more difficult challenges that require a consolidation of previous skills (see Figure 23.1). This chainsaw model suggested how games are designed for learning; the player begins with small, relatively easy challenges, which are paced to produce automaticity. These regular events are punctuated with more challenging sequences, which serve to both disrupt and then strengthen or add to players' knowledge (cf., Gee, 2005).

Good games build on themselves by taking these smaller units and combining them to create increasingly complex situations that coalesce to become a holistic experience for the player-as-game-character. Gee (2004), examined *Ninja Gaiden* as one such game that is designed to produce mastery. Gee showed how the first hour of *Ninja Gaiden* is constructed as a *de facto* tutorial, teaching the player how to read the game environment, perform isolated skills, perform sequenced skills, and finally, produce mastery by the first boss battle. Gee argued that *Ninja Gaiden,* when taken as a piece of instruction, is artfully constructed to produce learning, learning that is not just of any sort, but in this case, teaches the player to play like a ninja (as opposed to like Rambo).

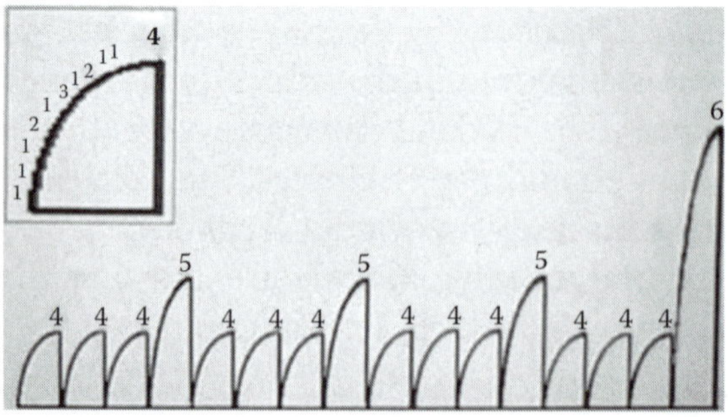

Figure 23.1 A screenshot of Betrus' Chainsaw model. (Image used with permission from the author.)

Cycles of choices and consequences. Games are driven by these overlapping, interacting cycles of action; as legendary game designer Sid Meier (n.d.) has widely been quoted as saying, "Games are a series of interesting choices." Most any game—from turn-based strategy games such as *Civilization* to massively multiplayer games such as *World of Warcraft* (worldofwarcraft.com)—can be analyzed in terms of overlapping cycles of choices and consequences (Salen & Zimmerman, 2003). Games such as *World of Warcraft* excel at just this type of play phenomenon; players are constantly developing overlapping goals, so that a player begins a quest with the idea of earning experience points, but midway decides to gather materials needed to create a new weapon, as well. Once the quest is completed, the player might have nearly enough raw materials (e.g., a certain amount of copper) to craft a new weapon, so she keeps playing in order to gather what is needed in order to meet her "new weapon" goal. Just before she gathers enough copper, however, she discovers a new land that she wants to explore. These overlapping cycles of choices and consequences are in part what make games so "addictive." In *Civilization*, as another example, players report a "just-one-more-turn" phenomenon, whereby a player develops a web of interlocking goals that overlap in such a fashion that she stays playing for hours on end, hoping to experience the results of one set of decisions (e.g., completing a quest to obtain new equipment), but in the mean time, becomes engrossed in experiencing another (e.g., collecting flowers to raise herbalism skills). In this fashion, many good games are specifically designed so that players always feel as if they are on the verge of "doing something interesting." Roughly translated, this means being put in a novel situation with the opportunity to think creatively while solving a problem (McKenzie, 2005; Shaefer, 2004). This need to keep the player in a constant state of "nearly doing something interesting" is what drives game designers to constantly iterate and reiterate game designs through play testing, so as to achieve a fluid game experience for the player.

Games remediating music. Emerging from this work on games and time is a sense that games are a deeply *rhythmic* medium that may share as much with music and dance as they do with visual storytelling. This is not to suggest that there is no rhythm in storytelling (e.g., oral storytelling is especially rhythmic), film editing, visual composition or theater. It does however, persuade us to go beyond games' graphics and consider them as experiences that are fundamentally multimodal (cf., Lemke, 1998).

Squire (2002, 2005c) and Smith and Squire (2002) connected games with a tradition largely overlooked in game studies: virtual soundscapes. Building on Jenkins' notion of narrative architecture, Squire and Smith described games as a sort of *sonic architecture,* operating much like music, which, in the words of Ong (2002), places the listener at the center of the world. Like music, the aesthetics of many games is less about the unfolding of a plot than it is about the *feeling of being* somewhere. Games from *Samba de Amigo* to *Quake* operate through aesthetics of *rhythm* and a feeling of empathy with the game system (cf., Gee, 2005). For example, in *Arcadia,* a Web-based game developed by Gamelab, players play simplified versions of four "classic" games simultaneously, each of which has its own distinct rhythm, producing a polyrhythmic sensation in the player. Friedman (1999) argued that a primary pleasure of playing *Civilization* is entering the system, developing an almost cyborg relationship with the computer whereby the game world is one that we inhabit via the game controls, which, in turn, become an extension of the self. Even though *Civilization* is a turn-based game, its turns and overlapping cycles of interaction have their own cycles and rhythms, producing a particular kind of feeling (which notably, the designers have sped up in the current version, *Civilization IV).* Gee (2005), as well as Jenkins, Squire, and Tan (2004), have argued that designing video games where we can enter physical, biological, or social systems is a promising future for the design of educational games, as in the case of *Supercharged!,* a game developed at MIT where players can literally enter the world of electromagnetism, thereby gaining a sense for how scientists think.

Not coincidentally, the Holy Grail for many game designers has been to create "interactive jazz," whereby players can spontaneously act and react in meaningful ways with the computer (or one another via the computer). By giving the player access to the controller, games place the player as both a listener and a participant in the orchestra. Indeed, at first glance players may seem to be largely constrained by game interfaces, but examinations of rhythm/action/dance players show how players use the space outside of the game to be creative, constructing elaborate dance moves with their hands, arms, and heads, treating the game as a *performative* space. On at least some level, to be literate with games means being competent, if not good with them, as games are ultimately something one does. When we study games, on some level we are also studying the game performance.

Game as performance. Fundamental to any notion of a game-based literacy is that the player is actively engaged in producing not just meanings, but tangible actions on screen and in real spaces. To be literate in the gaming medium means to be able to do things with games; one cannot imagine claiming to be "literate" with games, yet never have finished a game (or substantial portion thereof). Squire (2005b) noted that this emphasis on performance permeates much of gamer discourse, drawing on analyses of the forum-listed Frequently Asked Questions (FAQ) for *Viewtiful Joe* to argue that underlying many games' community discourses is a *functional epistemology,* whereby *doing* in the game world organizes all accompanying literacy activities (game cheats, FAQs, and discussion). Gee (2003, 2004, 2005) contrasted this notion of literacy with the ones found in school; imagine a science classroom where students first do scientific investigations and then read books, research cheats, and discuss with peers to aid their "doing" science. Games push our theoretical notions of learning and literacy, firmly unseparating knowing from doing.

As evidence of this performative, functionalist nature of games, Clinton (2004, analyzing *Prince of Persia*) noted that the first thing gamers do when picking up a new game is to press different buttons on the game controller (e.g., console control or computer joystick), seeing what each character (or other player role) *can* do in the world, because it is through what we *do* in game worlds that we come to know them. Also analyzing *Prince of Persia,* Davidson (2005) described this opening portion of game play as *involvement,* where the player is generally involved in the unfolding of action but is yet to be immersed, invested, or really controlling the action in a meaningful way. Through the careful, ever increasing orchestration of obstacles, narrative events, rewards, and new capacities, games usher the player into a state of immersion and eventual completion. Davidson observed that the final stage (perhaps most interesting for educators) is one of *investment,* where the player has been immersed in the game world, has committed to being the character for a sustained period of time.

Transformations over time.   Gee (2005) argued that it is these transformations into "player as game player" (e.g., "James Paul Gee as Lara Croft") that are of most interest to educators. As discussed earlier, the timescales of video games are interesting themselves and are tied to a player's investment in the game. A board game (like a book or film) might be played in a few hours; however, a common commercial single-player video game such as *Viewtiful Joe* is usually played over a number weeks. Strategy games such as *Civilization* or action games such as *CounterStrike* are more akin to hobbies or sports and are played over months and even years (cf., Wright, 2001). Similarly, the average massively multiplayer gamer plays any one title for 6 months to a year, on an average for 20 hours a week (see Steinkuehler, this volume). Timescales may be a production notion for educators who seek to understand the transformations that occur through game play, as they suggest how different game experiences might create different learning trajectories (Lemke, 2004; Squire, 2005d).

Indeed, Lemke (2004) argued that games are especially interesting laboratories because they allow us to examine learning over timescales, zooming from the microaction to macroparticipation in communities of practices. As we shift the timescales of game activities, we see different trajectories of participation. On the microsecond level, we can analyze a specific move within a game environment (e.g., a kick or punch in a fighting game). Building on Lemke's (2000) framework of learning over timescales, we can see how any particular game practice (e.g., executing a kick or punch) forms through the affordances of actions occurring at smaller intervals timescales (visual percep-

CounterStrike is a fan-produced modification for the game that has attracted a dedicated following of millions of players, and for years was the dominant competitive multiplayer squad-based shooter game. As Wright (2001) noted, at first glance, *CounterStrike* is an incredibly violent game with juvenile-discourse patterns. Wright and his colleagues' studies revealed not anarchy but, rather, a complex social world with rules and social conventions organized around an ethos of "having fun." This core feature of *CounterStrike* communities is constituted through creative-player actions, which include players' verbal banter and one-up-manship, creative reappropriation of game actions (such as committing suicide in a humorous manner to amuse one's peers), and production of original art that can be viewed in-game. Wright (2001) argued that the meaning of *CounterStrike* is generated by its players who have created a set of mores that are socially reproduced and handed down from one generation to the next. Player *production* is at the core of this community, and the ability to entertain and amuse is held in highest regard.

Player production was also the focus of Zhan Li's (2003) master's thesis research: *The Potential of* America's Army *as Civilian Public Sphere*. *America's Army* is the controversial $8 million video-game/recruiting tool built and distributed by the U.S. Army. The goals of the project were to "support Army recruiting efforts, particularly of teenagers with high-tech aptitude and skills; raise the positive profile of the Army as an interesting, high-skilled organization; and to promote the revival of military-civilian grassroots contact" (Li, 2003, p. 8). Li's ethnography examined how the activities of three exceptional gamer groups—(a) real-life soldiers and veterans, (b) Evangelical Christians, and (c) hackers—intersected with the stated and unstated purposes of the game.

Li (2003) found that *America's Army* functions as neither propaganda for the state, nor as a site where hacker culture wholly subverts the culture of the game, but rather as a (contested) *liminal* space that where everyday relations can be (and are) reconfigured for the purposes of play. Li's notion of liminality differs somewhat from that of Wright and colleagues (2002), in that whereas Wright's notion of liminality was largely about activity within the game space, Li situated player's activities within other social spheres (i.e., military service, religious). Even though the formal game-play elements of *CounterStrike* and *America's Army* are essentially the same, the forms of play that unfolded in each were quite different. Li argued that *America's Army* functioned as a space where the "rationalities" of the state, military, commodity, and people's lived experiences are in collision. For example, Li observed that many players stayed away from *America's Army* during the initial phases of Gulf War 2, wanting to preserve the "gameness" of the space; that is, they did not want the seriousness of the actual war to be compromised by "playing at war." Similarly, Li described soldiers and veterans gamers in the *America's Army* community as soldiers acting at playing soldiers. That is, these soldiers and war veterans were using *America's Army* as a context for inhabiting stylized identities as soldiers. Li used the lens of army, Christian, and hacker groups to show how the space of *America's Army* is a peculiar mix of both the intentions of its designers (a military-owned space for civilian/military relations) and the ideologies of its inhabitants.

These studies suggest that games' most potent social value may be their *liminality*, their capacity to function as contexts within which participants can play with new identities and ideologies. As role-playing game designer Warren Spector (1999) has argued (building on the work of Frederick Turner), every culture has provided spaces where the dominant social order is temporarily reshaped, and people have (at least temporarily) the ability to pursue experiences with reduced (or removed) social consequence (cf., Jenkins, 2006). Li's (2003) study suggested how games are coconstructions of the designer and participant, in that emergent activity reflects the goals of the participant constrained within the parameters of the game spaces, which are the residue of designers' goals. In *America's Army,* for example, it matters greatly that the representations, symbols, game rules, social rules, and capacities for action are based on those of the military. However, as researchers, we know little about their meanings until we examine how they are taken up by players.

Games as Affinity Spaces for Learning

Gee (2003; 2004) argued that video games are powerful models for learning. We can examine the technical design of games, how games are *designed as experiences* to produce certain feelings, skills, and knowledge; games can also be studied as social *spaces;* spaces where people congregate to learn. Examining forums for *Age of Mythology,* Gee (2004) proposed that games are affinity spaces, spaces where learners congregate based on personal interests rather than on race, class, economic status, or background. Gee described several key features of such forums: (a) participation is open to any user; (b) newbies and veterans share a common space; (c) participants have the power to shape and transform the environment; (d) knowledge and expertise is distributed across players; (e) multiple routes for participation, success, and status are presented; and (f) participation in the affinity space reshapes the "attractor" (i.e., game) itself. Gee contrasted these affinity spaces with communities of practice, arguing that affinity spaces are much more common to today's digitally mediated society where technologies make social boundaries permeable, participation open, and knowledge production decentralized.

As such, affinity spaces are more than just intriguing places to spend our off hours; they are exemplars of the social organization in the modern digital world, which are changing contemporary notions of literacy. Gee (2004) connected the rise of affinity spaces to broader patterns in the new capitalist world (cf., Squire, 2005a); others (e.g., Jenkins, in press) have described similar trends cutting across entertainment, political, and educational media. Today's digital consumers do not have a stereo or piano; they have a suite of digital tools where they can "rip, burn, mix," and then publish their creations via the Web, using digital services to even turn a profit if their work is good. Core to such affinity spaces are opportunities and expectations for *participation*. The rise of digital production and communication tools make participants producers, not just consumers of media, and games are a leading technology for such changes (Squire & Steinkuehler, 2005).

Self-organizing communities for learning. These studies of affinity spaces beg the question of how to design learning systems for a digital age. Although substantial learning occurs in such affinity spaces, these spaces are not designed explicitly for learning. What might a game-based learning system built on these principles look like? To better understand this, Squire and Giovanetto (in press) have been examining Apolyton University, an online community of game players that has evolved to teach other players to become expert gamers. Squire and Giovanetto argued that unlike most other institutions of higher education, the system is driven by *learning,* with class practices, courses, and administrative structures all taking a backseat to the demands of learning. The core practices driving the community are playing *Civilization III* and (a) redesigning a common game modification to improve its playability; (b) conducting During Action Reports that capture participants' cognitive activity and serve as the basis for discussions, and (c) proposing and developing new "courses" for the community. As players create and change courses, they create custom game modifications to illustrate their arguments about the game, and collaboratively build a "master" curriculum/game file.

Squire and Giovanetto (in press) argue that participating in Apolyton University is a process of transitioning from a game player to a game producer. Players enroll as advanced players, having spent dozens, if not hundreds of hours with the game and having mastered its basic rules. As players begin to identify and exploit loopholes, they propose and implement changes to the games' rules, identify superior strategies, and invent new game-rule systems, including custom modifications and scenarios. In one course, lead artificial intelligence designer for the game, Soren Johnson, joined the discussion to correct a misconception about how the game's artificial intelligence works. As a result of the ensuing discussion, several players from the community were recruited to participate in the game play testing and balancing, completing the cycle from game consumers to producers.

Self-organizing learning environments are unlike traditional online learning environments in that they are open systems with permeable boundaries (Squire & Giovanetto, in press; Wiley & Edwards, 2002); participation is open to anyone and the "classroom" activities are both transparent to outsiders and expected to have an impact on broader social practice. In the case of self-organizing game communities such as Apolyton University (but there are other ones, including Civfanatics, Madden Football forums, or specific sites within the Warcry network) sites of learning spontaneously organize around authentic, meaningful questions and typically result in changing the design practice, effectively reshaping the context of their learning (which Gee would call the "reshaping the attractor"). As such, self-organizing learning communities share much more in common with cutting-edge research communities than with formal classrooms. Their existence suggests an implicit critique of schools: Why should I study computer science or writing classes in order to get a job in the entertainment industry, when I can participate in learning communities that offer trajectories of participation where I might enter the industry? Game-based self-organizing learning systems are intriguing to educators for how they are at the cusp of participatory media culture; in today's digitally mediated media environment, meaningful participation involves opportunities for participating in the *production* of media. These examples also suggest design patterns for the design of game-based learning environments, which will be discussed in the final section.

The consequences of participation in gaming practice for literacies. Studies of digital-gaming communities as liminal spaces (e.g., Li, 2003) affinity spaces (e.g., Gee 2004), and self-organizing learning systems (e.g., Squire & Giovanetto, in press) suggest how games are more than a technology; they are a maturing medium with attendant social practices. The preceding studies suggest profound shifts in participants' relation to knowledge, media, information, and social institutions (cf., Squire & Steinkuehler, 2005). These practices include (a) *producing* as well as consuming information, (b) the strategic use and critique of digital spaces that promote their particular values, (c) the ability to produce meanings across multiple representational forms (i.e., texts, visuals graphs, charts, game modifications), (d) texts that circulate within and across communities, (e) trajectories for participation in social systems, including game journalism, design, and criticism, and (f) the repositioning of written texts from objects of authority to resources that are used in support of (digitally mediated) practice. The lasting social consequences of these shifting practices are only beginning to be understood.

Preliminary survey work on the games' generation suggests that these discourses are powerful, shaping our notions of learning, literacy, and expertise. Surveys of gamers show that they have an increased appetite for risk, a greater comfort with failure, a stronger desire for social affiliations, a preference for challenges, a capacity for independent problem solving, and a desire to be involved in meaningful work when compared with nongamers (Beck & Wade, 2004). Underlying Beck and Wade's argument is a notion of changing literacies; gamers have grown up with a medium built on assumptions unlike those in print cultures (e.g., a game engine can be tinkered with, a text is not necessarily print based or defined by book covers); game players are coauthors along with game designers, coconstructing the game-as-text through their own action (cf., Robison, in press). Gamers have grown up in simulated worlds, worlds where anything is possible, and where learning through trial and error is expected, information is a resource for action, and expertise is enacted through both independent and collaborative problem solving in self-directed tasks (Simpson, 2005).

How students will react to traditional schooling in this digital era is a question of increasing importance that digital-literacy scholars are beginning to ask. Kevin Leander and colleagues investigated the in and out of school literacy practices of one gaming youth, finding that texts and literacies operate quite differently in and across these contexts, and which actually serve to bring down traditional home/school conceptual divides in education research (Leander, 2005). Using Actor Network Theory, Leander and Lovvorn (2006) found that multimodal texts in gaming environments function as resources for action. These texts come from official and nonofficial sources and different media (strategy books, Web sites, in game text and nontext resources; cf., Squire & Steinkuehler, 2005; Steinkuehler, 2005). Within a game environment, the meaning of texts (and their legitimacy) arises in response to their efficacy for action. Leander and Lovvorn contrasted this type of meaning in texts with those in classrooms, where texts are given authority by their *distance* from the student; the teacher's notes (wherever they came from) and published works are given the most authority, and students' work is to effectively reproduce those notes for legitimized authority. In contrast, texts in game cultures are "lively," flowing across boundaries and borders as they serve social functions, texts in classrooms are remarkably *static*, designed for a student or teacher's consumption, but having little impact outside of the classroom. Leander and Lovvorn showed how in the case of one typical student (Steve), text (and all of its associated artifacts, e.g., notes) is prepared and produced exclusively for a teacher's consumption, and its life ends abruptly when the teacher grades it, having no discernable impact on the field, the teacher's thinking, other students' thinking, or Steve's life.

The preceding studies of gaming cultures suggest how emerging game literacies are a product of both games-as-designed-artifacts as well as the game cultures in which they are created and enacted. Indeed, the values that are expressed in the design of games do not emerge from thin air; they are the product of particular technological cultures that spawned them, which, as Stephen Levy (2001) argued, can be traced principally to hacker cultures in terms of origin. Games are then enacted in cultural contexts, where such values are promulgated. Through sites such as Apolyton University or Game FAQs, we can see examples of gamers creating social structures that initiate newcomers into these cultures. The affinity spaces that Gee (2004) described are the result of a co-evolving structure of emerging technologies (games and modification or "modding" software, the Internet, wiki software, online-community software) and the communities that spawn them. If the games themselves serve as attractors, then educators may benefit by studying learners' trajectories through these spaces, focusing on how values and identity emerge in practice. To date, there are still comparatively few such studies, but future literacy scholars might benefit by examining how participants learn through participation in these structures.

Games in Schools

Thus far, the discussion of games and learning has focused largely on learning and literacy outside of classrooms. As Warschauer (this volume) observes, emerging literacy scholars have generally sought to understand (a) how literacies are changing in response to emerging technologies, frequently with a focus on how traditional schools are failing to respond to these changes (b) the power structures and dynamics behind literacy regimes, and (c) how literacy can be improved (or the impact of media on learning). The incongruency between emerging game and school-based literacies has meant that necessarily, the bulk of the research on games literacies has taken place outside of classroom contexts. There are, however, examples of research programs where game literacies are examined in classroom contexts, usually occurring with a design-based research framework. Design-based research studies seek to posit and test hypotheses by creating learning contexts and then examining the processes by which they function (Barab & Squire, 2004; Cobb, Confrey, diSessa, Lehrer, & Schauble, 2003; Design-Based Research Collective, 2003). Studies of games in classroom settings suggest that game play can be the basis of meaningful academic learning experiences, but the epistemological assumptions of learning through game play are at odds with those of schooling. This suggests a need for radical transformations of schooling to meet the needs of a digital age (Squire, 2005e).

Games, simulations, and play have a long history in education and the study of human learning more generally. Legendary game designer Chris Crawford (2003) remarked that games are "the original" educational technology, reminding us that most mammals learn through play—creating and playing within spaces set apart from the every day. This rhetorical framing of game—such as, play as development—is but one of many rhetoric of play. In his magnum opus, *The Ambiguity of Play*, Sutton-Smith (1997) argued for the centrality of play in human experience, contending that play has been conceived primarily along seven or so rhetorical lines: the ancient four, (a) fate, (b) power, (c) communal identity, and (d) frivolity, and the modern discourses of (e) progress, (f) imaginary, and (g) the self. Sutton-Smith used this notion of rhetoric to describe the different theoretical frames that we bring to a phenomenon that then determine what we count as play (particularly how much of a context we count as play; i.e., is it an individual or an individual in context, or

research. Groups are interdisciplinary and structured to include participants with media, business, and design expertise. Core to this project is the students' real-life approximation of an actual "pitch" session, so that the criteria for an effective project are aligned closely with those institutions outside of school (for-profit game companies, nonprofits, and foundations).

These three sets of examples are but three examples of games literacy projects that attempt to blend close, critical reading of games with transitioning students from thinking as media consumers to media producers. Combined, they pose interesting questions for media literacy: How far do we go in insisting that students understand "the production" of media? How many English teachers would be considered *literate* in writing, if understanding the economics, politics, and social ramifications of book or newspaper publishing were considered a prerequisite to teaching English? Further, such projects, by attempting to tie to the commercial games industry, may risk focusing on issues (profitability, market share) while overlooking others (underrepresented voices). Regardless, these studies also emphasize that the biggest challenge in developing a critical vocabulary around games may not be with students, but with teachers, parents, and administrators who treat games as trivial, rather than influential cultural artifacts and practices.

Games as Designed Contexts for Studying Learning

Although there is a long tradition of games in education (particularly instructional design), historically there has been very little useful research into the effectiveness of games and simulations in instruction, with common critiques being that games research has lacked a coherent theoretical focus (Gredler, 1996, 2004; Rieber, 1996). One of the few fruitful paths of research has been psychological studies by Mark Lepper and colleagues, who used games as sites for studying highly motivated learning. Malone (1981) and Malone and Lepper (1987) examined games to build a theory of intrinsic motivation, finding that "good" games create highly motivated learning through challenge, curiosity, control, fantasy, competition, and collaboration. Cordova and Lepper (1996) built prototypes of educational games in mathematics that leverage these properties in order to increase motivation, finding that more highly motivated students performed better than their peers on similar mathematics tasks. These well-designed studies suggest how design-based approaches can lead to fundamental insights into cognition that improve the quality of instructional materials.

Building game-based learning environments. The most overt attempt at designing learning environments based on the technologies, learning principles, and social values of games to date has been MIT's Microsoft-funded Games to Teach Project. The Games-to-Teach Team (2003) was grounded in the premise that for too long, educational technologists have treated computers as technology rather than as media, thereby missing opportunities for designing powerful learning environments in the process. Holland, Jenkins, and Squire (2003) described their 15 conceptual prototypes as ideal sites for generating and testing game theory, using prototypes as sites for identifying and exploring new avenues for game theory. These prototypes range from historical role playing to physics-simulation games to massively multiplayer engineering games, each of which seeks to both explain how games work and to argue for new models of games.

One such game, *Supercharged!*, situates the student in the role of piloting a spaceship that has the power to adopt the properties of a charged particle; this design is in keeping with research that found expert physicists reason by imagining themselves literally "inside" physics problems. Students work through a series of maze-based levels based on popular platform game conventions that are designed to build their conceptual understandings of electrostatics, starting with Coulumb's law and moving through most of an advanced high-school physics electrostatics curriculum (Barnett, Squire, Higgenbotham, & Grant, 2004). Squire and colleagues found that students not only developed better conceptual understandings of physics, but a better understanding of *why* representations in their textbooks look the way that they do. Further, Squire et al. found that lower achieving students emerged as leaders in their classes and showed the highest gains on pre- and posttests. Teachers interviewed believed lower achieving students outperformed high-achieving students because the activities and assessments in the unit did not primarily involve reading, interpreting and producing text, unlike most school activities.

Similarly, Dede and colleagues (2002) developed *Riverworld*, an interactive 3-D environment where students investigate a host of environmental problems in an early 20th-century village. The purpose of *Riverworld* is to help low-achieving students perform better in science through complex inquiry-based tasks where they must identify problems, collect data, synthesize information, and generate conclusions based on their understandings. Dede and colleagues found that not only did students learning in *Riverworld* perform better than students in a control group, but attendance rates were higher, there were less disruptions in class, and teachers and students alike reported higher levels of motivation. Importantly, students showed improved understanding of scientific inquiry as a result of participating in the program.

In another effort to apply gaming principles to formal learning environments, Barab and colleagues (Barab & Squire, 2004; Barab et al., 2005) designed *Quest Atlantis*, a 3-D environment aimed at helping elementary- and middle-school students learn science more effectively. Just as games are designed according to the values of a particular media property, *Quest Atlantis* is designed according to social commitments including an affirmation of diversity, personal agency, social responsibility, environmental awareness, healthy communities, and compassionate wisdom. The tasks and challenges of *Quest*

Atlantis are designed to foster these virtues, creating a liminal space where students can inhabit a world that acknowledges and fosters these values. Barab and colleagues (2005) argued that students participate in *Quest Atlantis* out of a desire to help others, which suggests that contemporary models of motivation have omitted altruism as a powerful source of learning and virtue for designing learning environments.

These studies point to the rich pedagogical potential of games, but also to some of the limitations of creating pedagogical programs based on game-based principles in formal learning environments. All of these projects, while well funded, are very primitive compared to even the most basic commercial video games. Whereas role-playing games are designed to be played over 40 or more hours, most of the "units" developed with classrooms in mind were forced to work within a traditional school environment where students have a dozen hours at most for learning about a particular topic or concept. When compared to a contemporary massively multiplayer game, where participants *average* 20 hours per week online, students have significantly less time to become involved and to develop identities and investments within these virtual environments. Last, while engaging, such environments frequently pale in design sophistication compared to commercial games. As a result, a number of games researchers have begun experimenting with using commercial games in classrooms, hoping to use such games as "attractors" for academic intellectual work.

Teaching and learning with commercially available entertainment games. Despite the broad popularity of management simulation, historical strategy, and games such as *Sim City,* there have been very few studies to date of such games being used in classrooms. In perhaps the first study of such a game being used in a classroom environment, Squire (2004) created custom historical scenarios for the game *Civilization III.* Squire's scenario was designed to build on the game's underlying geographical/materialist simulation model in order to help low-achieving high-school students understand key processes in world history (cf., McNeil, 1968). Squire found that the game created a liminal space for students to explore world history, leading to basic background conceptual understandings in history, as well as deeper historical understandings of broad causes in history, which Dunn (2000) has called the "patterns of change" model of world history. Students previously marginalized from the study of history found spaces for their identities and lived histories to enter historical narratives. In particular, they found exceptionally rewarding that the "Rise of the West" might be seen as a particular product of its geographic location and access to trade networks (and ensuing colonization).

Attempting to use complex games in school-based learning environments also poses substantial challenges, however. Squire (2005e) reported many of these challenges: A single game of *Civilization* can take up to 20 hours to complete. The interface is opaque to new users, as it employs conventions built up over generations of strategy-game iterations. Many girls do not immediately read the game as a girl-friendly play space, as games have been historically gendered male, as has game playing culture. Further, research on games suggest the existence of the game-privileged literacies (e.g., generating original interpretations of history) that schools devalue. As Squire described, the game "changes the rules of the game" on students, and it can be difficult to establish entirely new learning cultures for a traditional classroom environment.

In 2005, Egenfeldt-Nielsen conducted a similar study in Denmark, using *Europa Universalis* as a tool for studying European history. Egenfeldt-Nielsen reported implementation obstacles similar to Squire and noted some conceptual problems in experiential game-based learning approaches. These conceptual problems include a mismatch between learning outcomes through games and state curricular goals, time constraints in setting up games, differential learning outcomes across students, and the complexity of game interfaces for novices. Egenfeldt-Neilsen described learning through game-based environments as a hermeneutic process whereby students observe phenomena, interact with game rules, and draw interpretations based on previous understandings of history, just-in-time information provided by teachers and outside resources, and experiences in the game environment. As such, game-based learning in intentional learning environments is a hermeneutic process that resembles learning in a research lab. Learning is driven by a combination of students' questions, emerging experiences and findings, and historical interpretations.

Based on these findings, Squire and colleagues have been examining the potential of *Civilization III* and *Civilization IV* in after-school environments (Squire, Giovanetto, DeVane, & Durga, 2005). Whereas previous game development and curricular enactment programs have struggled to accommodate the demands of schools, formal after-school environments offer intriguing possibilities for rethinking educational practice for a digital age. Squire and his colleagues' program engages students iteratively in building and playing historical "mods" or scenarios for *Civilization III* and *Civilization IV*. They reported the processes by which students learn to build these historical mods as a process of (a) developing interest in the game, (b) developing advanced knowledge of the game systems, (c) seeing iterative models of the game tailored in response to students' play, (d) adapting scenarios to enhance their play, in particular, to create games for other students to enjoy, and (e) building models to highlight particular game dynamics, such as the domination of the Vikings in medieval Europe. Squire and colleagues are finding that in controlled environments, students can and do develop literacies as game producers, which is marked by a systemic level understanding of game systems and design. Squire and colleagues posited that such literacies could be developed in classrooms, but would require systemic changes that give teachers and students more freedom in choosing what they study and more flexibility within the curriculum.

Conclusions

A recent *New York Times* piece describing the rise of academic programs in higher education quotes former Senator and current president of the New School Bob Kerry. Kerry argued that, "The skills and methods of video-games are becoming a part of our life and culture in so many ways that it is impossible to ignore," (as cited in Schiesel, 2005) suggesting an alternative narrative to the predominant broadcast media story that "games are bad for you." Each year that the Nintendo generation ages, the average age of gamers rises, and some reports suggest that aging Generation Xers and baby boomers are turning to games as a way to stay social when there are children in the house (you may not be able to go out every night, but you can log into *World of Warcraft*), or ward off the effects of aging (Sheff, 1994; Oblinger & Oblinger, 2005; Steinkuehler, 2005). As games become increasingly mainstream, literacy scholars are looking to video games as sites for studying emerging digital literacies.

Perhaps the alarm bells sounding the decline of "reading" do not signal a "loss" of literacy, but the emergence of a new constellation of literacy practices that could someday transform our social institutions. If the history of media holds true, video games, like film or television, are not going to replace books but live along side them (cf., Thorburn & Jenkins, 2004). Games are becoming ingrained within a range of political, military, commercial, and—at least for now on the margins of—education systems, bringing with them attendant changes in cultural practices. Cases such as *America's Army* show how a game made for military recruitment purposes operates differently from a 30-second recruiting advertisement run during a televised football game, which, in turn, changes what it means to brand and recruit new military personnel. Similar examples can be found in politics: (e.g., *The Mass Balance* game where citizen-players are challenged to try and balance the budget), advertising (e.g., YaYa Media's *Jeep* driving game, where salespeople and consumers can test drive new vehicles), or military training/entertainment (e.g., *Full Spectrum Warrior,* a game that challenges you to lead squadrons through urban militarized zones; Gee, 2005; Squire, in press). These examples suggest how emerging literacies are about more than physical (or digital) materials; they are about emerging cultural practices that reciprocally transform people and social institutions.

Perhaps not surprisingly, schools have been slower than the military and industry in taking advantage of the opportunities in games. The literacies that schools are based around include "mastery" over predetermined, increasingly federally mandated content, reading and writing traditional school-based genres of text (i.e., the five- paragraph essay, the term paper), ritualized performance on decomposed tasks, participation in activity cleaved from other social processes and institutions. Game-based literacies include a constellation of literacy practices that are quite different: texts are spaces to inhabit, learning as a productive, performative act, knowledge is legitimized through its ability to function in the world, participation requires producing as well as consuming media, expertise means leveraging digital spaces to further one's goals, and social systems have permeable boundaries with overlapping trajectories of participation.

As games become more culturally entrenched, the idea of using games in education may be passing from an *opportunity* to an *imperative,* if we are to create an education system that adequately prepares students for life in an information/knowledge rich economy. Games are only rising in cultural prominence and acceptance as SONY, Microsoft, and Nintendo, and Electronic Arts all vie to expand their markets beyond traditional gamers and seemed poised to become even more mainstream. At the same time, schools are being regarded by students as less relevant than ever; for the first time in the United States' history, for example, a majority of students—even successful ones—see school as little more than credentialing spaces (Baines & Stanley, 2003). In schools, we label those students who exhibit the qualities of gamers—increased independence, preference for multitasking, decreased respect for authority—as ADHD; outside schools, these same students are championed as leaders of the new economy (Gee, Hull, & Lankshear, 1996). The history of education also suggests that if these emerging literacies do prove to be foundational to success in the new economy, upper-middle-class parents will make sure that their children develop these skills, and in particular, have access to not just games but the affinity spaces and self-organizing learning systems that are crucial to becoming producers of and with digital media. The real question will become how will underfunded and overlooked urban schools respond.

References

Aldrich, C. (2004). *Learning by doing: A comprehensive guide to simulations, computer games, and pedagogy in e-Learning and other educational experiences.* New York: Wiley.

Anderson, C. A., & Bushman, B. J. (2001). Effects of violent games on aggressive behavior, aggressive cognition, aggressive affect, physiological arousal, and prosocial behavior: A meta-analytic review of the scientific literature. *Psychological Science, 12,* 353–358.

Anderson, C. A., & Dill, K. E. (2000). Video games and aggressive thoughts, feelings, and behavior in the laboratory and life. *Journal of Personality and Social Psychology, 78,* 772–790.

Baines, L. A., & Stanley, G. K. (2003). Disengagement and loathing in high schools. *Educational Horizons, 81,* 165–168.

Barab, S. A., & Squire, K. D. (2004). Design-based research: Putting a stake in the ground. *The Journal of the Learning Sciences, 13*(1), 1–14.

Barab, S. A., Thomas, M., Dodge, T., Carteaux, R., & Tuzon, H. (2005). Making learning fun: Quest Atlantis, a game without guns. *Educational Technology Research and Development, 53*(1), 86–107.

Barnett, M., Squire, K., Higgenbotham, T., & Grant, J. (2004). Electromagnetism supercharged! In *Proceedings of the International Conference of the Learning Sciences.* Los Angeles: UCLA Press.

Jenkins, H., Squire, K., & Tan, P. (2004). You can't bring that game to school: Designing supercharged! In B. Laurel (Ed.), *Design research* (pp. 244–252). Cambridge, MA: MIT Press.

Juul, J. (2001). Games telling stories: A brief note on games & narratives. *Games Studies*, 1(1). Retrieved January 26, 2006, from http://www.gamestudies.org/0101/juul-gts

Juul, J. (2004). Introduction to game time. In P. Harrington & N. Frup-Waldrop (Eds.), *First person* (pp. 131–142). Cambridge, MA: MIT Press.

Juul, J. (in press). *Half real*. Boston: MIT Press.

Kadakia, M. (2005). Increasing student engagement by using *Morrowind* to analyze choices and consequences. *Technology Trends, 49*(5), 29–33.

Leander, K. (2005, February 19). Imagining and practicing internet space-times with/in school. Keynote address to the National Council of Teachers of English Assembly for Research Annual Mid-Winter Conference, Columbus, OH.

Leander, K., & Lovvorn, J. (2006). Literacy networks: Following the circulation of texts and identities in the school-related and computer gaming-related literacies of one youth. *Cognition & Instruction, 24*(3), 291–340.

LeBlanc, M. (2006). *Formal design tools* [Electronic version]. Paper presented at the annual Game Developers' Conference, San Jose, CA. (Original work presented 1999).

Lemke, J. L. (1998). Metamedia literacy: Transforming meanings and media. In D. Reinking, L. Labbo, M. McKenna, & R. Kiefer (Eds.), *Handbook of literacy and technology: Transformations in a post-typographic world* (pp. 283–301). Hillsdale, NJ: Erlbaum.

Lemke, J. (2000). The long and the short of it: Comments on multiple timescale studies of human activity. *Journal of the Learning Sciences, 10*(1–2), 193–202.

Lemke, J. (2004). *Why study digital gameworlds? Notes toward a basic research agenda for learning technologies*. Retrieved December 11, 2004, from http://www-personal.umich.edu/~jaylemke/games.htm

Levy, S. (2001). *Hackers: Heroes of the computer revolution*. New York: Penguin.

Li, Z. (2003). *The potential of America's army as civilian public sphere*. Unpublished master's thesis, MIT, Cambridge, MA. Retrieved from http://www.gamecareerguide.com/features/230/masters_thesis_the_potential_of.php

Malone, T. W. (1981). Toward a theory of intrinsically motivating instruction. *Cognitive Science, 4*, 333–369.

Malone, T. W., & Lepper, M. R. (1987). Making learning fun: A taxonomy of intrinsic motivations for learning. In R. E. Snow & M. J. Farr (Eds.), *Aptitude, learning, and instruction, III: Conative and affective process analysis* (pp. 223–253). Hillsdale, NJ: Lawrence Erlbaum Associates.

Mateas, M. (2004). A preliminary poetics for interactive drama and games. In P. Harrington & N. Frup-Waldrop (Eds.), *First person* (pp. 19–22). Cambridge, MA: MIT Press.

McKenzie, N. (2005). *Searching for the intangible: Commercial game designers wrestle with educational games*. Paper presented at the 2005 Games, Learning, and Society Conference, Madison, WI.

McNeil, W. H. (1968). *The rise of the west*. Chicago: University of Chicago Press.

Meier, S. (n.d.). Quoted in Wikipedia. Retrieved January 26, 2006, from http://en.wikiquote.org/wiki/Sid_Meier

Murray, J. (2004). From game-story to cyberdrama. In P. Harrington & N. Frup-Waldrop (Eds.), *First person* (pp. 2–10). Cambridge, MA: MIT Press.

Myers, D. (1991). Computer game semiotics. *Play and culture, 4*, 334–346.

Myers, D. (1992). Time, symbol, transformations, and computer games. *Play and Culture, 5*, 441–457.

National Endowment for the Arts (NEA). (2004). *Reading at risk: A survey of literary reading in America*. Retrieved November 22, 2005, from http://www.nea.gov/pub/ReadingAtRisk.pdf

New London Group. (2000). A pedagogy of multiliteracies: Designing social futures. In B. Cope & M. Kalantzis (Eds.), *Multiliteracies: Literacy learning and the design of social futures* (pp. 9–37). New York: Routledge.

Oblinger, D., & Oblinger, J. (2005). *Boomers, gen-xers, and millenials: The new generation.* Retrieved November 27, 2005, from http://www.educause.edu/ir/library/pdf/erm0342.pdf

Ong, W. (2002). *Orality and literacy: The technologizing of the word* (2nd ed.). New York: Routledge.

Perlin, K. (2004). Can there be a form between game and a story? In P. Harrington & N. Frup-Waldrop (Eds.), *First person* (pp. 12–18). Cambridge, MA: MIT Press.

Prensky, M. (2001). *Digital game-based learning.* New York: McGraw Hill.

Provenzo, E. F. (1992, December). What do video games teach? *Education Digest, 58*(4), 56–58.

Rieber, L. P. (1996). Seriously considering play: Designing interactive learning environments based on the blending of microworlds, simulations, and games. *Educational Technology Research & Development, 44*(2), 43–58.

Robison, A. (in press). What videogame designers can teach literacy instructors. In R. Matzen & J. Cheng-Levine (Eds.), *Reformation: The teaching and learning of English in electronic environments.* Taipei, Taiwan: Tamkang University Press.

Rosas, R., Nussbaum, M., Cumsille, P., Marianov, V., Correa, M., Flores, P., et al. (2003). Beyond Nintendo: Design and assessment of educational videogames for first and second grade students. *Computers and Education, 40*(1) 71–94.

Rosser, J. C., Jr., Lynch, P. J., Haskamp, L. A., Yalif, A., Gentile, D. A., & Giammaria, L. (2004, September). *Are video game players better at laparoscopic surgery?* Paper presented at the Serious Games for Health Conference, Madison, WI.

Salen, K., & Zimmerman, E. (2003). *Rules of play: Game design fundamentals.* Cambridge, MA: MIT Press.

Sanders, B. (1995). *A is for ox: The collapse of literacy and the rise of violence in an electronic age.* New York: Vintage.

Schiesel, S. (2005, November 22). *Video games are their major, so don't call them slackers.* Retrieved November 22, 2005, from http:/www.nytimes.com/2005/11/22/arts/design/22vide.html?ex=1290315600&en=f26dbe96bc527f0e&ei=5088

Scholder, A., & Zimmerman, E. (2003). *RePlay.* New York: Peter Lang.

Sefton-Green, J. (2003). Informal learning: Substance or style? *Teaching Education, 13*(1), 37–51.

Sefton-Green, J. (2004). Initiation rites; A small boy in a poke-world. In J. Tobin (Ed.), *Pikachu's global adventure: The rise and fall of Pokemon* (pp. 141–164). Durham, NC: Duke University Press.

Shaefer, E. (2004). Blizzard Entertainment's *Diablo II.* In A. Grossman (Ed.), *Postmortems from game developers: Insights from the developers of Unreal Tournament, Black & White, Age of Empires, and other top-selling games* (pp. 79–90). San Francisco: CMP Books.

Shaffer, D. W., Squire, K. D., Halverson, R., & Gee, J. P. (2005). Video games and the future of learning. *Phi Delta Kappan, 87*(2), 104–111.

Sheff, D. (1994). *Game over: How Nintendo conquered the world.* London: Vintage.

Simpson, E. (2005). Here come the gamers. *Technology Trends, 49*(5), 17–22.

Smith, J., & Squire, K. (2002, May 10–12). "Sound screen:" Points of convergence in recorded sound and digital gaming. Paper presented at Media in Transition 2: globalization and convergence. MIT, Cambridge, MA.

Solomon, A. (2004, July 10). *The closing of the American book.* Retrieved November 22, 2005, from the New York Times Web site: http://www.nytimes.com/2004/07/10/opinion/10SOLO.html?ex=1090460203&ei=1&en=819cb83606a96f4f

Spector, W. (1999). Remodelling RPGs for the New Millenium, Game Developer (Feb.). Retrieved January 28, 2006, from http://www.gamasutra.com/features/game_design/19990115/remodeling_01.htm

Squire, K. D. (2002). Cultural framing of computer/video games. *Game Studies, 2*(1). Retrieved July 25, 2006, from http://gamestudies.org/0102/Squire/

Squire, K. D. (2003). Video games in education. *International Journal of Intelligent Simulations and Gaming, 2*(1), 49–62.

Squire, K. D. (2004). Sid Meier's civilization III. *Simulations and Gaming, 35*(1), 135–140.

Squire, K. D. (2005a). *The future is Sweden.* Retrieved July 25, 2006, from http://www.joystick101.org/story/2005/2/6/22938/72327

Squire, K. D. (2005b). Educating the fighter. *On the Horizon, 13*(2), 75–88.

Squire, K. D. (2005c). Toward a theory of games literacy. *Telemedium, 52*(1-2), 9–15.

Squire, K. D. (2005d). Recessitating educational technology research: Design based research as a new research paradigm. *Educational Technology, 45*(1), 8–14.

Squire, K. D. (2005e). Changing the game: What happens when video games enter the classroom? *Innovate, 1*(6). Retrieved January 26, 2006, from http://www.innovateonline.info/index.php?view=article&id=82

Squire, K. D. (in press). Game-based learning: Present and future state of the field. *Performance Improvement Quarterly.*

Squire K. D., & DeVane, B. (2006, April 8–12). *Pimping my ride and representing my hood: GTA as a sandbox for constructing identity and representing race.* Keynote presentation to the Media, Culture, and Communications Special Interest Group at the annual meeting of the American Educational Research Association.

Squire, K. D., & Giovanetto, L. (in press). *The higher education of gaming.* eLearning.

Squire, K. D., & Steinkuhler, C. A. (2005). *Meet the gamers: Games as sites for new information literacies.* Retrieved July 25, 2006 from the Library Journal Web site: http://www.libraryjournal.com/article/CA516033.html

Squire, K. D., Giovanetto, L., DeVane, B., & Durga, S. (2005). From users to designers: Building a self-organizing game-based learning environment. *Technology Trends, 49*(5), 34–42.

Starr, P. (1994). Seductions of sim. *The American Prospect, 5*(17), n.p.

Steinkuehler, C. A. (2004a, October 28–31). *Emergent play.* Paper presented at the State of Play Conference, New York University Law School, New York. Retrieved June 29, 2005, from mywebspace.wisc.edu/steinkuehler/web/papers/SteinkuehlerSoP2004.pdf

Steinkuehler, C. A. (2004b, April). *The literacy practices of massively multiplayer online gaming.* Paper delivered at the annual meeting of the American Educational Research Association, San Diego, CA.

Steinkuehler, C.A. (2005, October). *Guild leadership.* Presentation made to the Austin Game Developers' Conference, Austin, TX.

Steinkuehler, C. A. (in press-a). The new third place: Massively multiplayer online gaming in American youth culture. *Tidskrift Journal of Research in Education.*

Steinkuehler, C. A. (in press-b). Learning in massively multiplayer online games. *Mind, Culture, and Activity.*

Sudnow, D. (1983). *Pilgrim in the microworld: Eye, mind and the essence of video skill.* London: HeinemannWeise.

Sutton-Smith, B. (1997). *The ambiguity of play.* Boston, MA: Harvard University Press.

Thorburn, D., & Jenkins, H. (Eds.). (2004). *Rethinking media change: The aesthetics of transition.* Cambridge, MA: MIT Press.

Vargas, J. A. (2005, September 27). *Gamers' intersection. Grand Theft Auto: San Andreas' plays to a generation from the streets to suburbia.* Retrieved September 27, 2005, from the Washington Post Web site: http://www.washingtonpost.com/wp-dyn/content/article/2005/09/26/AR2005092601697_pf.html

Weise, M. (2004). *Understanding meaningfulness in videogames.* Unpublished master's thesis, MIT Comparative Media Studies, Cambridge, MA.

Wiley, D. A., & Edwards, E. K. (2002). Online self-organizing social systems: The decentralized future of online learning. *Quarterly Review of Distance Education, 3*(1), 33–46.

Willett, R. (2003). New models for new media: Young people learning digital culture. *Medienpädagogik, 4.*

Williams, D. (2003). The video game lightning rod: Constructions of a new media technology, 1970–2000. *Information, Communication, and Society, 6*(4), 523–550.

Williams, D. (2005). A brief social history of video games. In P. Vorderer & J. Bryant (Eds.), *Playing computer games: Motives, responses, and consequences* (pp. 197–212). Mahwah, NJ: Lawrence Erlbaum.

Williamson, B., & Facer, K. (2004). More than 'just a game': The implications for schools of children's computer games communities. *Education, Communication, & Information, 4*(2/3), 255–270.

Wright, W. (2001). Design plunder. Keynote address at the 2001 Gaming Developer's Conference, San Jose, CA.

Wright, T., Bouria, E., & Breidenbach, P. (2002). Creative player actions in FPS online video-games: Playing Counter-Strike. *Game Studies, 2*(2). Retrieved January 26, 2006, from http://www.gamestudies.org/0202/wright/

CHAPTER 24

Community, Culture, and Citizenship in Cyberspace

ANGELA THOMAS

UNIVERSITY OF SYDNEY, AUSTRALIA

Introduction

Hine's (2000) notion of cyberspace as both culture and cultural artifact (Hine, 2000; Bell, 2001) is a useful starting point for thinking about cultures and communities in cyberspace. On one hand, understanding cyberspace involves understanding *culture*—that is, the politics and meanings (Bakhtin, 1981) inherent in cybercommunities, and the subject positioning of the members within them (drawing on Foucault, 1980; Heidegger, 1977). On the other hand, it involves understanding *cultural artifacts*—the multimodal texts (Kress & van Leeuwen, 1996) and everyday practices (de Certeau, 1984) that shape the communities. According to Bell, considering cyberspace as an artifact requires exploring and understanding the lived experiences and stories of cybercitizens. The stories, experiences, and issues reported in this chapter are partly my stories, reflecting multiple roles as feminist, linguist, literacy educator, role player, ethnographic Internet researcher, educator, blogger, and long-term cybercitizen. They include accounts of meeting and researching ordinary young people who build and sustain communities, explore, play, resist, and tinker with their identities and engage in sophisticated and multiple forms of literacy practices.

Accordingly, the chapter draws on theoretical understandings that seem to best accommodate these multiple roles. I draw on studies of cybersociety and

> You can be whoever you want to be. You can completely redefine your-self if you want. You can be the opposite sex. You can be more talkative. You can be less talkative … you can just be whoever you want really. (pp. 184–185)

The issue of tinkering with sexuality was and is of interest to many scholars (e.g., Bruckman, 1992; Danet, 1998; Spender, 1998). Danet asserted that, from early childhood, individuals learn to signal their gender identity in accord with gender stereotypes. They learn to *perform* "masculinity" or "femininity." The medium of online chat can be very liberating for many users, both male and female, since the anonymity allows one to explore all aspects of one's identity and sexuality. Identity tinkering online opens the possibility and potential for cybercitizens to take risks and to explore all aspects of their personalities. Courage to take risks is fostered by a sense of anonymity by users. Work by Herring (1996a; 1996b) about gender online, however, raised concerns about the reification of the gender divide in cybercommunities, from the ways women use language to communicate, to the ways girls and women are silenced or devalued in communities such as the blogging community (cf. Herring et al., 2004).

To think of cyberspace as only a playground for the mind is to forget that intimate connection between body and mind, as emphasized by Stone (1991):

> Cyberspace developers foresee a time when they will be able to forget about the body. But it is important to remember that virtual community originates in, and must return to the physical … Even in the age of the technosocial subject, life is lived through bodies. (p. 113)

Over the past decade, researchers have further explored the notion of the body and how it experiences the worlds of cyberspace. The new found freedom and seeming lack of consequences also resulted in some cases where users were reported to be more aggressive and to be more overtly critical or even cruel to other users. This type of behavior, labeled "flaming" (Reid, 1994), was found to occur typically in groups that have little or no overt moderation, rules, or regulations to control such behavior. A majority of online groups, however, has established acceptable social norms of behavior for that particular group, and offenders are reprimanded or simply removed from the group by the community. Each community will decide which social norms it will enforce according to its purpose. This may change over time, as in the case of Jakobsson's (1999) report about how a boy in his palace was upset about the hierarchical structure of wizards and the fact that he could not become one. The boy hacked into the palace and killed one of the programmed bots, destroying months of Jakobsson's work. Jakobsson investigated the hacking, and when he discovered the reasons behind it, he decided to eliminate the hierarchical power structure completely (see Dibbell, 1998; Everard, 2000, for other relevant examples).

The term embodiment is defined as "an incorporation of the interrelationships which constitute experience into the constantly evolving body" (Cranny-Francis, Waring, Stavropoulos, & Kirkby, 2003, p. 83), whereby experiences are "inscribed" onto the body within social practices and power relations (McNay, 1994). Balsamo (2000) argued that the body should not be seen as a product, but more a process. Hence, embodiment could be considered an effect of such a process (cf. Foucault, 1977, p. 148).

T. L. Taylor, a leading researcher linking cyberspace and embodiment, examines the nature of identity in graphical communities and massively multiplayer online role-playing game (MMORPG) communities. She notes that in visual cybercommunities the use of visual representations of self, avatars, heightened the degree of embodiment (Taylor, 1999, 2002). Taylor's work, following Bruckman and Turkle, has significantly influenced understandings about that nature of the body, the screen and cyberspace. Explaining virtual embodiment, Taylor commented,

> Users create digital presences, either via textual descriptions or graphical representations and all of these actions are done not by just an amorphous self in the space, but by a body imbued with certain characteristics and properties. The bodies users create and use in virtual spaces become inextricably linked to their performance of self and engagement in the community. ... Avatars and textual bodies facilitate interaction, shape and solidify identity, as well as more generally mediate users' engagement with the world. (Taylor, 1999, p. 438)

Taylor's (1999) ideas open up more possibilities for considering the notion of online identities as embodied selves in three ways: first, from the connectedness between the corporeal body and the perceptions and experiences lived out on the screen and its associated cyberworlds; second, from the visual embodied image of the self as represented through the avatar on the screen; and third, from the dimension of identity performance.

More recently, Shinkle (2003) has argued that we need to think beyond the notion of the screen as a mediating device between the body and cyberspace; rather, she defined the technology user as an "interfaced being." Further, she insisted that "the embodied and affective character of interfaced being is articulated through the concept of the *anamorphic* subject" (Abstract section, para. 1). Her concern with both historical and some current accounts of cyberspace is that, "the trope of the distanced, disembodied eye/I lingers, implicitly or explicitly, in twenty-first century notions of virtuality, and the subject of virtual space, by some accounts, differs little from its Renaissance predecessors" (Shinkle, 2003, Introduction section, para. 1).

Tracing a historical overview of the perception of Cartesian space, Shinkle (2003) contended that virtual reality provides a simulation of reality, which requires reflexive and embodied engagement with the space. Using the video game, *Rez,* as an example of virtual reality, she stated,

Being, in *Rez* means being (as) an instrument, being *in time*—engaged, entranced, and embodied in/by one's environment. *Rez* requires an ana-morphic subject, one whose rational sensibility is understood to cohabit with its affective presence in the lifeworld ... . Technology does not "come between" body and subject, the three maintain a relation of mutual mate-rial and ontological proximity, a reflexive and multistable condition of *technological embodiment*. (Phenomenology, virtuality, and the anamor-phic subject section, para. 5)

This notion of an "interfaced being" seems much more apt given our increas-ingly mobile society, with wearable technology and new fashion trends for the young in which clothing is manufactured to hold mobile phones, iPods and mini game consoles (see wearable computing at http://www.wearablecomput-ing.com/). Fashion designers working in technology at the MIT lab are also inventing playful fashion that integrates touch-responsive technology such as the "Closer Pullover" designed by Alison Lewis (MIT, 2005, Closer section, para. 1), who designed a number of items such as the pullovers, which she defined as "snuggly, huggably soft garments that respond to positive touch interactions" (MIT, 2005, Closer section, para. 1). The MIT lab holds regular fashion shows with the aim of creating "a fashion event featuring innovative and experimental works in computational apparel design, interactive clothing, and technology-based fashion" (MIT, 2005, Motivation section, para. 1).

In fact, it seems to me that technology has become the new fashion acces-sory, so much so that, to adapt a common phrase, "digital is the new black." Parent and Leech (2004) contended,

Over the past few years, technological prostheses have gradually encroached upon the world of clothing by combining with the surfaces that protect and personalize our bodies. Communications and enter-tainment devices, such as cellular phones and mp3 players, have become new forms of adornment, connecting our inner world with our sur-roundings and profoundly altering our relationship with the world. These increasingly multifunctional and powerful accessories have con-tributed to a process of layering our personal boundaries with multiple strata of information and sensation while offering others the image of a hardware-equipped body. (Smart clothes, fashionable technologies sec-tion, para. 1)

Mobile technology, wearable technology, and digital fashion have the power to profoundly impact the ways in which we both construct our own identi-ties and communicate with others (e.g., Harrill, 2002). Smart fabrics and "e-Textiles" (Parent & Leech, 2004) are being developed to break down the physical hardness qualities associated with the hardware packaging currently housing technology. With miniaturization and wireless technologies, it is now possible to embed the hardware into soft textiles and to use the skin as a conducting device (Moriwaki, 2004). With the potential for bodies to be inscripted with the technologies of mass communication, it is possible to imagine a future where the bodies are always and already online; a new type of interfaced body.

"Interfaced beings" resonates with Donna Haraway's (1991) notion of the cyborg and posthumanism. Haraway coined the term *cyborg* to represent her vision of the intersection of the body and technology. Her work moved away from the genres of cyberpunk and closer to a possible vision for the present and future of our bodies, arguing that "the boundary between science fiction and social reality is an optical illusion" (p. 149). She claimed that distinctions between the organism and the machine are fruitless since we are all now existing as cyborgs—"fabricated hybrids of machine and technology" (p. 150). "Cyborg Manifesto" initiated a new wave of feminist thinking about identity, embodiment, and the portrayal of females in technological spaces. Haraway saw any form of feminine "identity" as being fractured, declaring that there is no such thing as a common feminine identity, only a coalition of affinity. Furthermore, identities now seem "contradictory, partial and strategic" (p. 155). The concept of the cyborg offers women alternative ways to make sense of the multiple identities they must adopt. According to Haraway, the cyborg offers the notion of an assemblage of identities that combines fantasy, desire, and myths about identity, with science, technology and a multitude of other ways of considering identity (cf. p. 163).

Biocca (1997) talked also about the cyborg conceptualizations of the coupling between the physical body and the computer interface. He discussed the notion of mediated bodies with respect to cyberspace and virtual reality bodies, and stated the following:

> To the degree that cognition and identity are embodied in the simulations run by our sensors and effectors, then the mind in advanced virtual environments becomes also adapted to a mediated body, an avatar, a simulation of the cyborg body. Observing the day-to-day movements of our consciousness between the experience of our unmediated body and our mediated virtual bodies, we may come to ask: Where am "I" present? (The Cyborg's Dilemma section, para.7)

Rosi Braidotti (2005) recently revisited the writings of both Donna Haraway (1991) and N. Katherine Hayles (1999) on posthumanism, technology, materiality, and the link between body and machine to explore the political consequences of the cyborg. One the one hand, she claimed,

> Post-humanism is a fast-growing new intersectional feminist alliance … Feminist cultural studies of science attempt to disengage biology from the structural functionalism of DNA-driven linearity and to veer it instead towards more creative patterns of evolutionary development (p. 178).

for offering, as Gurak (1999, p. 259) termed it, "expressions from the *vox populi*." Mele (1999), however, argued that few disenfranchised social groups have been able to utilize the resources of the Internet to challenge or subvert societal inequalities. He states that to be successful and actuate real change requires, "vast commitments of time, resources, and unflagging dedication, a clear sense of purpose, and a flexible course of action in the face of over-whelming obstacles" (p. 304).

While Mele (1999) claimed that the Internet and its related virtual communities and networking of social groups were creating a new kind of civil society based on a technologically disposed form of democratic interaction, he cited a number of obstacles to social change posed by the new types of inequality and divisions being created by these very networks. Such obstacles included equality of access and equality of technical knowledge, and as Gurak (1999) pointed out, the issues of accuracy of available information and the assumptions that making fast-quick responses (so easy to do in a few keystrokes), may, in fact, lead to hasty decision-making rather than careful and deliberated decisions made through due time and process.

Acknowledging that there are obstacles to democratic interaction, there are nonetheless instances in which online communities have successfully activated change and/or pursued issues of social justice. One example of grassroots change comes from the efforts of Thomas, an 11-year-old boy, who started a "save our looney toons" Web site in response to Warner Brothers announcing a proposed change to cartoon characters like Bugs Bunny and the Tasmanian Devil. Thomas's site attracted so much support and attention that Warner Brothers revised its prototype sketches to give the characters a softer image. The online community, drawn together through its common goal, had the power to influence a major commercial corporation (Associated Press, 2005).

At another level, Guzzetti and Gamboa (2004) described an online community of young adolescent girls who created their own punk rock zine to write against stereotypical notions of gender, race, and class. The researchers noted the significance of punk rock to the girls' identities. Although the girls were all friends offline, the online space of the zine allowed a new space of projection for their ideologies, and opened up the potential for readers from all over the world to respond and connect with the girls and their ideas.

In some of my own research (e.g., Thomas, 2004a, 2004b, 2005a, 2005b) I have found that groups of young people tend to flow over into multiple communities, reflecting their multiple and changing identities. Violetta, one of the focus girls in my study, explained her involvement in various communities:

> Well, Sarah and I go home, and she calls me on the phone when she's ready to log on later. We keep the phone conversations going while we log on and decide where to go. We're always on my talker, but sometimes we go idle there to visit other places. I keep telling dad I need a bigger monitor, because I end up with so many windows open that I can't always

follow what's going on in each one. Then we do about six different things at the same time.

We'll have my talker open, our icq on, we have the role-playing MOO we've just joined open, we have our homework open (which I am pleased to report, we both get done at the end of the night, and its sooooo much more fun doing it this way!), we have the palace open, we have our own private conversation windows open for different friends, and we have our phone conversation going on at the same time. And that is not to mention having conversations with mom or dad, popping out for drinks and nibbles, and having my music on in the background. Then, depending what's going on, we have hysterics over the phone together as we manage the activities going on in each window (Thomas, 2004a, pp. 154–155).

Many young people I have studied belonged to different groups for different purposes and would traverse between them according to mood, inclination, and who else was present at any particular time. Some communities also spread across multiple sites. The Middle Earth community in one of my studies (Thomas, 2005a), for example, had a graphical synchronous world—a palace—for people to meet and interact in real time, several forum based role-playing sites for asynchronous interactions, and an e-mail list for sending out notices to members. Some members of the palace never went to the forum, some members of one forum tended to be the younger members of the palace, and some members of the other forum never subscribed to the e-mail lists. Each site had a loose kind of membership of its own, but the core of the community was made up of people who were engaged in each site.

What Is Cyberculture?

Like the concepts of both cyberspace and cybercommunity, that of cyberculture is highly complex. Cyberculture researchers were initially quick to use metaphors like "global village" to describe the ways users would act, behave, and interact—each person taking on a community role and contributing to the life and well-being of that "village." With the popularization of the Internet, however, cyberspace has become increasingly fragmented and a multiplicity of diverse cultural, ethnic, gender, and economic spaces have emerged and flourished. With youth cultures moving toward mobile media, technologies and communications devices there is no simple way to describe cyberculture. In a way, cyberculture and cybercommunity are really the same thing—communities shape and are shaped by their cultures. For every type of community online, a different culture could be described, researched, and theorized. In this section, I will emphasize the historical stages of research that have marked the field of cyberculture studies. It will become very obvious that throughout these stages educational research of cyberculture has been very thin or even absent.

Table 24.1 Examples of Cyberculture Studies Research (adapted from Silver, 2000)

Field of study	Examples of cyberculture studies research
Sociologists	- examining the Internet as social networks (Wellman, 1997; Wellman et al., 1996) - employing the sociological traditions of interactionism and collective action dilemma theory (Kollock & Smith, 1996; Kollock, 1999)
Anthropologists	- cyborg anthropology, devoted to exploring the intersections between individuals, society, and networked computers (Downey & Dumit, 1998; Escobar, 1996)
Ethnographers	- studying what users do within diverse online environments, ranging from online lesbian bars and Usenet newsgroups to Web-based "tele-gardens" and online cities (Baym, 1995, 1998; Correll, 1995; McLaughlin, Osbourne, & Ellison, 1997; Collins-Jarvis, 1993; Silver, 2000)
Linguists	- analyzing writing styles, Netiquettes, and (inter)textual codes used within online environments (Danet, Ruedenberg-Wright, & Rosenbaum-Tamari, 1997; Herring, 1996a, 1996b, 1996c)
Feminists	- used textual analysis and feminist theory to locate, construct, and deconstruct gender within cyberspace (Cherny & Weise, 1996; Consalvo, 1997; Dietrich, 1997; Ebben & Kramarae, 1993; Hall, 1996)
Community Activists	- exploring the intersection of real and virtual communities in the form of community networks, including the Public Electronic Network (PEN) in Santa Monica, California, the Blacksburg Electronic Village (BEV) in Blacksburg, Virginia, and the Seattle Community Network (SCN) in Seattle, Washington (Cohill & Kavanaugh, 1997; Schmitz, 1997; Schuler, 1994, 1996; Silver, 1996, 1999, 2000)

David Silver (2000) identified three stages or generations of research, which he called (a) "popular cyberculture," (b) "cyberculture studies," and (c) "critical cyberculture studies." He described popular cyberculture as characterized by research about the new spaces that was marked by description and was somewhat limited in scope. In cyberculture studies, new scholars built on earlier work by people like Rheingold (1993, 1994) who first wrote about cybercommunities to explore cyberculture from a multiplicity of perspectives and methodologies.

A typical example of research in cyberculture studies concerns the ways women have challenged the dominance of masculine discourse in online cultures and have made the Internet a space that serves them, rather than their male counterparts. Silver (2000) explained that the solution for many women was to create spaces of their own, including academic spaces, political spaces, and more indie do-it-yourself fan and hobby sites. Covering a long list of other examples of the diversity of research into cyberculture studies, Silver pointed out the differing methodological and theoretical perspectives adopted for the study of all aspects of the Internet. Table 24.1 adapts Silver's list to illuminate the varying fields of research into cyberculture.

Finally, Silver (2000) claimed that the third generation of cyberculture studies has been approached from more critical perspectives. Particular foci include the multiplicity of social contexts in which online interactions occur; discourses surrounding such interactions; issues of access and equity to such interactions, including issues related to social, cultural, political, and economic factors; and the ways in which varying technological interfaces affect interactions. Furthermore, in this latest generation of research into cyberculture, the issue of power is being explored across all disciplines.

A recent study falling within this third-generation research of critical cyberculture studies focuses on power in the blogosphere. Its results are astounding and reveal explicitly how marginalization and silencing occurs in and around cyberspace. Herring et al. (2004), working in the library and information sciences lab at Indiana University, reported their research in a paper titled *Women and Children Last: The discursive construction of weblogs*. They conducted a content analysis of 357 blogs and discovered that women and young people (particularly adolescent girls) comprised over 50% of the demographics of bloggers, and tended to write blogs that were categorized into the genre of journal writing or personal blog type. When examining media reportage during 2003 of the blogging phenomena, the researchers found that,

- more males (88%) are mentioned in the media articles than females (12%)
- males are mentioned multiple times in the same article more often than females
- males are mentioned earlier in the articles than females
- males are more likely to be mentioned by name than females
- all 94 males mentioned are adults, except for one adolescent male blogger (Herring et al., 2004, Mass Media Reports section, para. 2).

Such reporting in effect defines blogging "in terms of the behaviour of a minority elite (educated, adult males), while … marginalizing the contributions of women and young people" (Herring et al., 2004, Mass Media Reports section, para. 3). A further examination into the nature of scholarly research about blogging revealed that blogs produced by educated adult males and, in particular, blogs that could be categorized as "knowledge" and "filter" blogs (that might be providing an alternative news service for example) were dominant as subjects for research and analysis. Personal and journal-type blogs are given little attention in the scholarship to date, and the treatment given to them is one of trivialization or disregard. Herring et al. (2004) argued that this combination of public, media, and scholarly disdain serves to minimize and discriminate against women's and teen's contributions and experiences in the blogosphere. As a significant demographic in this space, women and young people have had a significant impact and have actually shaped what we know of as the blogosphere, so to privilege a very small subset of adult male bloggers, which is, in fact, a representation of the exception, rather than the norm, is a form of discursive silencing. Herring et al. called for a broader conception and discussion about weblogs to counteract the inequitable discursive constructions of woman and young people.

Such studies provide valuable critical analysis of the construction of a particular group or groups in the broader spectrum of a global society. In one of my own studies about blogging (Thomas, 2005b), I record detailed stories of two adolescent girls. I analyze their social and discursive practices using a multiple-perspectives approach, including closely looking at the narratives the girls tell about their experiences online and using systemic functional grammar to conduct linguistic analyses of the language they have used to construct their fan fiction, their relationships with each other, and the multiple aspects of their identities. Such accounts contribute to countering the dominance of the "White American over-30s male" story. Educators don't need to know how members of privileged groups can build and participate in an online community. They may well benefit, however, from knowing more about how young people, girls, and marginalized groups can successfully use the Internet and technology to enhance, improve, and enrich their lives, both in the here and now, and into the future.

This work also endorses the arguments of Bell (2001) and numerous other Internet researchers (e.g., Jones, 2004) that Internet research should concentrate on close examinations of the experiences and stories of individuals in order to understand the social, economic, and political complexities and implications of all aspects of the Internet and its role within the broad context of a global society. By scrutinizing these experiential stories, it becomes possible to contextualize the significance of the Internet within all aspects of global citizenship.

Livingstone, Bober, and Helsper (2005) report research related to a national survey in the United Kingdom about teenagers' civic and political action online. In their survey of approximately 1,000 teenagers in Britain, they found that only 31% of girls and 23% of boys visit Web sites related to civic issues (government, environment, and so on), and that even fewer participate in any way on such sites where participation is an option. Quantitative studies are useful in exploring trends, yet the extent to which they can capture what is really happening online is questionable. In every online community I have studied over the past decade, whether the focus was on fan fiction, role playing, or simply chat, the young people participating were interested, enthused, and active in sharing their ideas about civic issues. All these forums have had multiple sections, for various types of role playing, for sharing personal information, and so on. At least one or more has been devoted to civic issues, and a high percentage of members participate in these sections, as much as they do in the role playing or general chat sections.

At one site, young people were involved in heavy debate about the environment. They would post up (for example) a link to a scientific report about the ozone layer, which each member would read and then comment on. Sometimes the conversation would go on for 300+ postings as they deconstructed the meanings of the report and discussed the implications it had for them and the future. The point is, young people care very much about civic issues, but they may not go to an established "civic Web site" to engage in discussion or to express their opinions. They prefer to do it within their own community, with friends they have made through common interests and with whom they have built trust over many months or even years. Frequently, these discussions are password protected because the community administrators (other teens) want all their members to feel safe and free to express whatever opinions, no matter how controversial. As a researcher it has been a joy to have access granted to me to these private conversations.

Similarly, Sally Humphrey (2006), who researches youth activism, reported that new media such as weblogs, MSN, zines, and online discussion boards have, in fact, contributed to new forms of social activism among young people. These often occur in what are known as "submerged networks" (Melucci, 1989), which are often not obvious to or valued by adults (Humphrey, 2006).

With respect to the blog of a young activist in Australia concerned with raising awareness of the issues of mandatory detention of asylum seekers, Humphrey wrote,

> Zahra's weblog, which she began in October 2004, functions primarily as a forum for an overtly political agenda. Through her entries she seeks to share her concerns with other like-minded young people: by giving her opinions of social issues such as teenage drinking; excessive money spent on pets; stereotypical representations of global events by the media; by celebrating values, such as the rights of women and forgiveness or by making a direct plea for change (eg. Somebody there can STOP da HUNGER from it's ROOTS!). In these overtly political and persuasive texts, Zahra played the role of advocate, appealing to the reader either to agree with her point of view about how the world is or to take action to change things. (Humphrey, 2006, p. 145)

Humphrey (2006) suggested that looking at the blog through a teacher's eyes might result in focusing on the nonstandard spelling, unfamiliar prosodic expressions, the popular text-speak, and unusual typographical choices. Yet, a close examination of the blog reveals a passionate and articulate young girl who is able to express a remarkable and touching depth of feelings about her own experiences as a refugee, while at the same time calling for a halt to the mandatory detention of women and children asylum seekers. This study affirms the increasingly common finding that adolescents' out-of-school literacy practices (both online and offline, and across modes) are more compelling than official school-sanctioned literacy practices, and provide young people with opportunities for citizenship and activism at a level beyond anything that could be achieved in the classroom.

Indeed, many social practices associated with new digital literacies are not school-sanctioned practices (Sefton-Green, 2001; Kenway & Bullen, 2001).

Sefton-Green pointed out the widespread banning practices adopted by many schools with respect to digital toys such as Tamagotchis, and cards such as Pokémon cards. More recently, there has been a widespread ban on iPods, chatrooms, blogging, role-playing forums, and photography communities online such as Flickr by schools at an International level. Kenway and Bullen argue that when children bring such practices to schools, they create their own communities; communities of literate practice in which digital texts and technologies are explored and exploited for as much fun and pleasure as they can afford. Many children spend hours helping each other learn these practices, willingly volunteering their time and efforts to help their friends become insiders of the communities. Besides becoming active creators of multimedia texts, young people are developing values, citizenship, and ethics through their participation in the communities in which such texts are produced.

The Phenomenon of Web 2.0: New Ways of Thinking about Culture, Community, and Citizenship in Cyberspace

A recent wave of research argues for a conceptualization of the current trends of the internet as Web 2.0 (Cuene, 2005). Web 2.0 means slightly different things to different people. It is used here to signal the new wave of social practices and new types of communities that are mushrooming across cyberspace. Richard McManus claimed,

> Web 2.0 is everyday, non-technical people using the Web to enhance their lives and businesses. The fact that so many more people are now creating and building on the Web is what the "2.0" signifies. (McManus, 2005, para. 1)

Similarly, Ian Davis stated, "Web 2.0 is an attitude, not a technology. It's about enabling and encouraging participation through open applications and services" (Davis, 2005, para. 3). The shift is from conceptualizing the Web as a source for downloading information to seeing it as a place for uploading, building, and creating. Kevin Kelly (2005, online) argued that we are now seeing a "bottom-up takeover" of the Web. The key principles of Web 2.0 identified by Davis (2005, paras. 1–5) are participation, openness, and communication. While these principles have been active over the past 10 years or so of the Web, they were not significantly widespread or adopted by everyday people. In education particularly, there seems to have been an emphasis on encouraging children to access information (the "I" of ICT) but, by contrast, a reluctance to use the Web for participation or communication. Now that the everyday (young) person has embraced the spirit of Web 2.0, it is an opportune time to call for a shift in mindset, to admit the "C" of ICT: namely, Communication.

Web 1.0 (the first Internet "moment") might be characterized as individuals using the Internet to find information, make Web pages, read other Web pages, and so on. More Net-savvy people were involved in communities such as role playing (e.g., MUDs and MOOs), but, in general, the content that shaped the online space was coded by computer programmers, and for some time the Net was considered the domain of the "geek." But with Web 2.0, this new "moment" of the Internet is motivated more by social action and movement, and symbolized through the discourses of giving, contributing, and sharing. Rather than just reading Web pages, people are highly involved in creating their own communities and spaces. McManus (2005) termed it the "read/write web." The content that shapes the Web as we are coming to know it now is written by the everyday person and is no longer the domain of the geek. People are no longer solely consumers, but are at the same time producers. This is in part due to emerging applications that require little or no technical knowledge, and in part due to the wave of the "gift-giving economy" I previously mentioned (Smith & Kollock, 1999). People provide their services for free, willingly giving of their time and resources.

Cybercitizens are involved in volunteer participation, support, and networking to build and share significant resources. These include a free online suite of encyclopedias that anybody can edit and add to; networked blogging communities; social bookmarking and tagging of documents and sites with keywords for the enabling of comprehensive search results; goal-setting sites where people support and cheer each other on to succeed at their goals, and a host of other software, sites, and community practices that devolve responsibility, power, and spaces to end users.

A range of very different forms of communities can be used to illustrate the spectrum of practices symbolizing Web 2.0. Some of these are Wikipedia (the editable encyclopedia). del.icio.us (a bookmarking and cataloging system), and Flickr (a photograph community in which users have extended the basic idea of an online photo album to create an entirely revolutionary and innovative community with a social consciousness). At another level, blogs have reinvented notions of academic networking, debate, and discussion to reflect the educational power and potential of the Web 2.0 phenomenon.

Wikipedia

The communities of Web 2.0 reflect the ideas I mentioned previously because they push the boundaries of our assumptions about communities. Some of these communities don't have any concept of interactivity in the traditional sense of people communicating with known others. Wikipedia, a freesource online encyclopedia, is an example of tens of thousands of individuals contributing freely for the sole purpose of producing an online library. Yet, the sense of community and active citizenship in Wikipedia is highly significant to its success.

Wikipedia has a community of users who are proportionally few, but highly active. Emigh and Herring (2005, p. 9) argue that "a few active users, when acting in concert with established norms within an open editing system, can achieve ultimate control over the content produced within the system, literally erasing diversity, controversy, and inconsistency, and homogenizing contributors' voices." In a page on researching with Wikipedia, its authors argue that Wikipedia is valuable for being a social community. That is, authors can be asked to defend or clarify their work, and disputes are readily seen. Wikipedia editions also often contain reference desks in which the community answers questions.

The software (known as "wiki") that enables Wikipedia is free, and in the past few years, wikis have been constructed for a multiplicity of purposes other than the encyclopedia. Wikis are being used by students to collaboratively construct and share content of their respective fields of study. Authors are using them to collaboratively write books. Fan communities are using them to build and share resources. As members work together to edit and refine the collective knowledge and consciousness of their communities, the quality of their wikis becomes increasingly more sophisticated, making them highly valuable resources. What is, perhaps, remarkable, is less the wikis themselves than the dedication and commitment of members to share and work together to improve the quality of their community. This social citizenship is the essence of Web 2.0.

Del.icio.us

Some examples of other social communities based on sharing and building up resources for the good of the community at large include del.icio.us, a system of social bookmarking, whereby articles and sites are categorized and tagged by multiple users for the benefit of all; Yahoo's (originally Ludicorp's) flickr.com, a site for posting, sharing, and discussing digital photographs; and All Consuming's 43things.com, a site where people list, share, and discuss their personal goals. A description from the del.icio.us site, explaining why it is classed as a social community, claims,

> What makes del.icio.us a social system is its ability to let you see the links that others have collected, as well as showing you who else has bookmarked a specific site. You can also view the links collected by others, and subscribe to the links of people whose lists you find interesting. (del.icio.us, 2005, About del.icio.us section, para. 1)

One of the significant new developments in these new forms of social online communities is this practice of "tagging," sometimes called "folksonomy." This is a process where user networks (normal "folks") ascribe tags and categories to create "taxonomy" to their photographs, Web sites, online articles, bookmarks, blog posts, goals, and so on. Through this process, people with similar interests (whether it be research interests or photography interests, for example) come to know each other, develop communities within communities, comment on each other's works, ideas, photographs or lists, and encourage each other to achieve their personal goals.

Flickr

Flickr was only established in 2004 and already has had an enormous impact and take up by over a million members worldwide. What started as a site for interactive gaming (Hicks, 2004) has turned into a buzzing community with a strong social conscience and with members sharing images that contribute to global understandings of the issues that affect their everyday lives. Flickr has a number of characteristic features that contribute to the experience of being part of the community. These include tagging—so that users can search for other people's images of any particular topic (the tag "Hurricane Katrina" yields thousands of images of the catastrophe from ordinary photographers, for example); commenting—the facility to praise, laugh, be touched by, and to discuss other people's images, and also to get angry with and engage in debate over images that reveal injustices; notes—the ability to code in pop-up text to hotspot elements of a photo, which can also include hyperlinks (e.g., one of my photos is of four colleagues, and running the mouse over each of their faces yields four individual pop-up windows with their names and hyperlinks to their Web sites); and groups—to enable people with a common interest to upload photographs to share and discuss, as well as to make political commentary over issues (such as the group "Hoody Moral Panic," where users parody U.K. media concerns over the "gangs" of young people wearing hoodies by uploading images of themselves wearing hoodies).

Davies (2006) identified a number of types of groups that are being formed on Flickr. These range from absurdist groups—groups where members, or "Flickrites," take a second look at a common object and find a comic way of shooting it; socio-political jokes (such as the Hoody Moral Panic group); political journalism—activist groups such as the one against whaling, and so on. Davies argues,

> "Flickrites" bring to the Flickr space contributions such as digital images; comments about photographs (comments on photo content, composition, format, source, meanings); technological solutions and suggestions; as well as all kinds of information. These contributions are brought to the Flickr space thus constituting the fabric of the Flickr space. This space is therefore in a state of both constant affirmation and renewal; for contributions can be seen to both sustain the existing values as well as to develop them. These contributions include glimpses of everyday lives; representations of artifacts; observations and commentaries, and are sourced from the everyday experiences of Flickr members, representing what Moll (2000) refers to as "Funds of Knowledge" or what Gee refers to as "Discourses." (Davies, 2006, p. 219).

The degree of debate over images that reflect injustices in the world and in media reporting of events of the world is striking. This was most evident in the recent Hurricane Katrina tragedy, when a Flickrite posted two similar images that had been captioned differently by the media: (a) one of a White person "finding food," (b) the other of a Black person "looting for food." The anger over the captions and their apparent racial discrimination caused a major controversy.

The images and links to the controversy being debated on the Flickr site were circulated around the world and within hours of being posted were featured on several lists to which I subscribe. People from each of the mailing lists debated about the images, the language in the captions, and the Flickr debate itself, and the story was even picked up by the ABC's "Media Watch" television program in Australia. The controversy ended with the photographer making an extensive public apology and explanation of how he had seen the events occur in real time. The power of one ordinary person's Flickr site and the ensuing Flickrite debate to incite global and widespread community action where an injustice was observed was astounding.

Blogging

Weblogs, or blogs, have become a new Web phenomenon over the past few years. Kelly (2005) wrote that the incredible rise of participant media such as blogs has shocked media experts, and envisioned that in the near future, "everyone alive will (on average) write a song, author a book, make a video, craft a weblog, and code a program" (Kelly, 2005, online). The impact of blogging in particular has been profound across the world, with its power to showcase the everyday experiences of people from all circumstances and contexts. One of the most surprising consequence of writing my own blog, *i-Anya* (Thomas, 2004c) has been the new international network of colleagues I have made, and the stimulating level of intellectual debate, scholarship, discussion, and friendships that have developed. Many academics are now blogging and are experiencing the same exciting stimulation. According to Farrell, a writer for the U.S. *Chronicle of Education,*

> The majority [of academics who blog], see blogging as an extension of their academic personas. Their blogs allow them not only to express personal views but also to debate ideas, swap views about their disciplines, and connect to a wider public. For these academics, blogging isn't a hobby; it's an integral part of their scholarly identity. They may very well be the wave of the future ... academic blogs also provide a carnival of ideas, a lively and exciting interchange of argument and debate that makes many scholarly conversations seem drab and desiccated in comparison. Over the next 10 years, blogs and bloglike forms of exchange are likely to transform how we think of ourselves as scholars. While blogging won't replace academic publishing, it builds a space for serious conversation around and between the more considered articles and monographs that we write. (Farrell, 2005, para. 3)

The willingness of others to share their intellectual ideas, to engage in constructive debate, and to link academic works in progress provides many academics with access to a type of scholarship they might not otherwise experience regularly in the frantic daily grind of academic life. Academic blogging and engagement in blogging affinity spaces affords opportunities to build, refine, and sharpen intellectual ideas and to find like-minded colleagues to enter into dialogue with on a regular basis about academic work. From this standpoint, Web 2.0 is about far more than creating content together with others, it's also about creating new spaces for all forms of social, emotional, and intellectual engagement with others. If academic blogging is "the wave of the future," as Farrell (2005) suggested, then research should be conducted to explore the conditions under which this works most effectively.

Conclusion

In a commerce talk for e-businesses, Cuene (2005, online) posed the question, "Is it a whole new internet?" The notion that we are living with a new and different form of the Internet, a different "moment" of the Internet, is exactly what I have been arguing for in this chapter. It is one that traverses traditional boundaries of space, divisions, communities, cultures, bodies, and subjectivities. The rise of media consumerism, wireless technology, mobile culture, wearable technologies, and new and innovative ways of using spaces for multiple social purposes signals new times ahead that will continue to change the ways in which people interact, communicate, build relationships, and construct new global identities. The role of Internet researchers is to continue to be alert to the ways in which these changes serve to build and construct power, or not, for disenfranchised societal groups.

I want to point out what I see as the three main concerns for educators in general and literacy educators in particular to consider. These are (a) critically examining the new literacies associated with Web 2.0; (b) critically examining the affordances of technology, cyberspace, cybercommunities, and cyberculture within the broader social, discursive, and embodied contexts of global citizenship; and (c) raising the profile of literacy and technology research. With media-savvy, mobile-networked, "interfaced beings" in today's classrooms, teachers would be well served to understand the ways in which new youth cultures impact upon their everyday lives and identities.

One of the shifts I have observed informally in teachers I work with is how previously teachers looked at how their students could learn *from* the Internet. Now, however, teachers are exploring what their students can learn *with* the Internet, through utilizing all of its affordances, manipulating media, and producing their own online/offline communities, multimedia digital texts, and sites for identity exploration and experimentation. Reports highlighting this dynamic shift in thinking are included in this volume and reflect the diverse and exciting depth and breadth of current research. Unfortunately, there seems to be an underrepresentation of these studies in circulation within both the education profession and the professional groups of critical cybercultures researchers (such as the Association of Internet Researchers [AoIR]). Literacy educators admittedly have an incredibly daunting task, given the breadth and scope of the social and discursive practices inherent in Web 2.0 coupled with their concerns about an ever-increasing digital divide. The challenge as I see it is to raise the significance of individual groups and their experiential narratives with technology and all things cyber-related, and to emphasize the effects on the "nodes"—the people—who are at each end of the screens, wires, and online networks. We need to tell more stories about how young people are becoming active global citizens through their online discursive and social practices, which also blend into their offline worlds. Through raising local social consciousness and awareness, I believe we stand a better chance of providing a relevant, equitable, and critical education for all.

As Kelly (2005) has argued, the first 10 years of the Internet are just a warm-up act for what's about to happen in this new Web moment, Web 2.0. Education as an institution generally hasn't even begun to tap into the potentials of Web 1.0, let alone Web 2.0. Getting the principles and potentials of Web 2.0 across to policymakers, curriculum designers, and teachers is crucial at this moment in time if we are to engage young people in their education, utilize the skills many are developing in out-of-school contexts, and teach them to be critical consumers of media. We need to find out how young people are interfacing with technology and manipulating its affordances for their own purposes. We need to find ways of engaging them into the collective conscious building principles of Web 2.0. We need to give them the tools for producing: blogs, music, videos, wikis, wearable technologies, and digital cameras. In a world where media production is overtaking the rate of consumption, teachers need to think not only of how to teach children to be critical consumers, but also to provide meaningful purposes for production so that children become critical producers as well. The tools of critique are vital in this process. The fan-fiction community is a good proxy for this notion. One of my research participants said that within a week of posting a piece of fan fiction, she received over 100 responses of critical feedback about all aspects of her writing, from plot development to spelling. Yet, in a classroom, she might get a piece of work she handed in to the teacher returned to her with a mere "good work" comment on it. Web 2.0 is truly a dialectical process between the individual and the collective.

Children need to be taught about the semiotics of media design so they understand both how to produce and how to critique. They need to be given a metalanguage for speaking about media. The implication for this for researchers includes (a) the need to examine, define, and report on the semiotics of all forms of digital media; and (b) the need to find examples of collective critiquing cultures such as the fan-fiction community, learn how they work, and find ways of implementing such practices within an educational setting.

Finally, Internet research should be focused on contemporary issues of social justice. Ways of supporting local communities from education to business with an emphasis on social inclusion should be explored. A revisioning of education where students are fully empowered citizens should be imagined, implemented, and researched from multiple perspectives. Initiatives to build global collaborations between schools, teachers, and students should be established. The use of both digital media and other media technologies to enable global collective dialogue and action is now possible. The conditions under which it is effective for everyday citizenship practices should be scrutinized, researched, and documented.

References

Associated Press. (2005). Cartoon controversy. Retrieved May 31, 2005, from http://www.cnn.com/2005/SHOWBIZ/TV/04/27/cartoon.controversy.ap/

Bakhtin, M. M. (1981). *The dialogic imagination: Four essays* (C. Emerson & M. Holquist, Trans.). Austin: University of Texas Press.

Balsamo, A. (2000). The virtual body in cyberspace. In D. Bell & B. M. Kennedy (Eds.), *The cybercultures reader* (pp. 489–503). London: Routledge.

Baym, N. K. (1995). From practice to culture on usenet. In S. L. Star (Ed.), *The cultures of computing* (pp. 29–52). Oxford, U.K.: Blackwell Publishers.

Baym, N. K. (1998). The emergence of on-line community. In S. G. Jones (Ed.), *Cybersociety 2.0: Revisiting computer-mediated communication and community* (pp. 138–163). London: Sage Publications.

Bell, D. (2001). *An introduction to cybercultures.* London: Routledge.

Biocca, F. (1997). The cyborg's dilemma. Progressive embodiment in virtual environments. *The Journal of Computer-Mediated Communications, 3*(2), 12–26 .

Braidotti, R. (2003). Cyberfeminism with a difference. In A. Jones (Ed.), *The feminism and visual culture reader* (pp. 531–533). London: Routledge.

Braidotti, R. (2005). A critical cartography of feminist post-postmodernism. *Australian Feminist Studies, 20*(47), 169–180.

Bruckman, A. (1992*). Identity workshop: Emergent social and psychological phenomena in text-based virtual reality.* Unpublished article. Retrieved May 31, 2005, from MIT, Media Laboratory Web site: ftp://ftp.cc.gatech.edu/pub/people/asb/papers/identity-workshop.rtf

Cherny, L., & Weise, E. R. (Eds.). (1996). *Wired women: Gender and new realities in cyberspace.* Seattle, WA: Seal Press.

Cohill, A. M., & Kavanaugh, A. L. (Eds.). (1997). *Community networks: Lessons from Blacksburg, Virginia.* Norwood, MA: Artech House, Inc.

Collins-Jarvis, L. A. (1993). Gender representation in an electronic city hall: Female adoption of Santa Monica's PEN system. *Journal of Broadcasting & Electronic Media, 37*(1), 49–66.

Consalvo, M. (1997). Cash cows hit the web: Gender and communications technology. *Journal of Communication Inquiry, 21*(1), 98–115.

Correll, S. (1995). The ethnography of an electronic bar: The lesbian cafe. *Journal of Contemporary Ethnography, 24*(3), 270–298.

Cranny-Francis, A. (2005). *Multimedia.* London: Sage Publications.

Cranny-Francis, A.,Waring, W., Stavropoulos, P., & Kirkby, J. (2003). *Gender studies: Terms and debates.* New York: Palgrave MacMillan.

Cuene. (2005, June 5). *Web 2.0: Is it a whole new internet?* Retrieved September 20, 2005, from http://cuene.typepad.com/blog/2005/05/web_20_at_mima.html

Danet, B. (1998). Text as mask: Gender, play, and performance on the internet. In S. G. Jones (Ed.), *Cybersociety 2.0: Revisiting computer-mediated communication and community* (pp. 129–158). London: Sage Publications.

Danet, B., Ruedenberg-Wright, L., & Rosenbaum-Tamari, Y. (1997). Hmmm ... Where's that smoke coming from?: Writing, play and performance on internet relay chat. *Journal of Computer-Mediated Communication, 2*, 4.

Davies, J. (2006). Affinities and beyond! Developing ways of seeing in online spaces. *E-Learning, 3*(2), 217–234.

Davis, I. (2005, July 4). Talis, Web 2.0, and All That. *Internet Alchemy Weblog.* Retrieved September 20, 2005, from http://internetalchemy.org/2005/07/talis-web-20-and-all-that de Certeau, M. (1984). *The practices of everyday life* (S. Rendall, Trans.). Berkeley: University of California Press.

Del.icio.us Social Bookmarks Manager. (2005). Retrieved May 31, 2005, from http://del.icio.us/

Dibbell, J. (1993). *A rape in cyberspace or how an evil clown, a Haitian trickster spirit, two wizards, and a cast of dozens turned a catabase into a society.* Retrieved May 31, 2005, from http://ftp.game.org/pub/mud/text/research/VillageVoice.txt

Dibbell, J. (1998). *My tiny life. Crime and passion in a virtual world.* New York: Henry Holt Company.

Dietrich, D. (1997). (Re)-Fashioning the techno-erotic woman: Gender and textuality in the cybercultural matrix. In S. G. Jones (Ed.), *Virtual culture: Identity and communication in cybersociety* (pp. 169–184). London: Sage Publications.

Donath, J. S. (1999). Identity and deception in the virtual community. In M. A. Smith & P. Kollock (Eds.), *Communities in cyberspace* (pp. 25–59). London: Routledge.

Downey, G. L., & Dumit, J. (Eds.). (1998). *Cyborgs and citadels: Anthropological interventions in emerging sciences and technologies.* Santa Fe, NM: The School of American Research Press.

Ebben, M., & Kramarae, C. (1993). Women and information technologies: Creating a cyberspace of our own. In H. J. Taylor, C. Kramarae, & M. Ebben (Eds.), *Women, information technology, and scholarship* (pp. 5–27). Urbana, IL: Women, Information Technology, and Scholarship Colloquium.

Emig, W., & Herring, S. (2005). Collaborative Authoring on the Web: A Genre Analysis of Online Encyclopedias. *Proceedings of the Thirty-Eighth Hawaii International Conference on System Sciences* (HICSS-38) (pp.1-10). Los Alamitos: IEEE Press.

Escobar, A. (1996). Welcome to cyberia: Notes on the anthropology of cyberculture. In Z. Sardar & J. R. Ravetz (Eds.), *Cyberfutures: Culture and politics on the information superhighway* (pp. 111–137). New York: New York University Press.

Everard, J. (2000). *Virtual states: The internet and the boundaries of the nation-state.* London: Routledge.

Farrell, H. (2005, October 7). The blogosphere as a carnival of ideas. *The Chronicle of Higher Education.* Retrieved October 22, 2005, from http://chronicle.com/free/v52/i07/07b01401.htm

Foucault, M. (1977). *Discipline and punish: The birth of the prison.* London: Penguin Books.

Foucault, M. (1980). *Power/knowledge.* New York: Pantheon.

Gibson, W. (1986). *Neuromancer.* New York: Ace Books.

Gurak, L. (1999). The promise and the peril of social action in cyberspace. In M. A. Smith & P. Kollock (Eds.), *Communities in cyberspace* (pp. 243–263). London: Routledge.

Guzzetti, B. J., & Gamboa, M. (2004). Zines for social justice: Adolescent girls writing on their own. *Reading Research Quarterly, 39*(4), 408–436.

Haraway, D. (2003). A cyborg manifesto: Science, technology, and socialist-feminism in the late twentieth century. In A. Jones (Ed.), *The feminism and visual culture reader* (pp. 475–496). London: Routledge.

Haraway, D. J. (1991). *Simians, cyborgs, and women: The reinvention of nature*. New York: Routledge.

Harrill, R. (2002). Latest fall fashion includes wearable technology. *University Week, 20*(1). Retrieved May 31, 2005, from the University of Washington Web site: http://admin.urel.washington.edu/uweek/archives/issue/uweek_story_small.asp?id=611

Hayles, K. N. (1999). *How we became posthuman: Virtual bodies in cybernetics, literature, and informatics*. Chicago: University of Chicago Press.

Heidegger, M. (1977). *The question concerning technology and other essays* (W. Lovitt, Trans.). New York: Harper and Row.

Herring, S. (1996a). Gender and democracy in computer-mediated communication. In R. Kling (Ed.), *Computerization and controversy: Value conflicts and social choices* (pp. 476–489). San Diego: Academic Press.

Herring, S. (1996b). Posting in a different voice: Gender and ethics in CMC. In C. Ess (Ed.), *Philosophical perspectives on computer-mediated communication* (pp. 115–146). Albany: State University of New York Press.

Herring, S. (1996c). Two variants of an electronic message schema. In S. C. Herring (Ed.), *Computer-mediated communication: Linguistic, social, and cross-cultural perspectives* (pp. 81–106). Amsterdam: John Benjamins.

Herring, S. (Ed.). (1996d). *Computer-mediated communication: Linguistic, social, and cross-cultural perspectives*. Amsterdam: John Benjamins.

Herring, S., Kouper, I., Scheidt, L. A., & Wright, E. (2004). Women and children last: The discursive construction of weblogs. In L. Gurak, S. Antonijevic, L. Johnson, C. Ratcliff, & J. Reyman (Eds.), *Into the blogosphere: Rhetoric, community, and culture of weblogs*. Retrieved May 31, 2005, from http://blog.lib.umn.edu/blogosphere

Hicks, M. (2004). *Online collaboration borne from multiplayer game*. Retrieved October 5, 2005, from http://www.eweek.com/article2/0,1759,1526440,00.asp

Hine, C. (2000). *Virtual ethnography*. London: Sage Publications.

Holeton, R. (1998). *Composing cyberspace: Identity, community, and knowledge in the electronic age*. Boston: McGraw-Hill.

Humphrey, S. (2006). Getting the reader on side – Exploring adolescent online political discourse. *E-Learning, 3*(1), pp. 143-157.

Jakobsson, M. (1999). Why Bill was killed – understanding social interaction in virtual worlds. In A. Nijholt, O. Donk, & B. van Dijk (Eds.), *Interactions in virtual worlds. Proceedings of the fifteenth Twente workshop on language technology*. Enschede, The Netherlands: Twente University. Retrieved July 2, 2007, from http://www.informatik.umu.se/~mjson/files/bill.pdf

Jakobsson, M. (2001). Rest in peace, Bill the bot. Death and life in virtual worlds. In R. Schroeder (Ed.), *The social life of avatars. Presence and interaction in shared virtual environments* (pp. 63–76) London: Springer.

Jenkins, H. (1992). *Textual poachers: Television fans and participatory culture*. New York: Routledge.

Jenkins, H. (2004, February). Why Heather can write. *MIT Technology Review*. Retrieved July 2, 2007, from http://www.technologyreview.com/Biztech/13473/

Jones, S. G. (Ed.). (1998). *Cybersociety 2.0. Revisiting computer-mediated communication and community*. Thousand Oaks, CA: Sage Publications.

Jones, S. G. (2004). Conclusion: Contexting the network. In P. N. Howard & S. G. Jones (Eds.), *Society online: The internet in context* (pp. 325–334). Thousand Oaks, CA: Sage Publications.

Kelly, K. (2005). We are the web. *Wired, 13*(8), Retrieved October 22, 2005, from http://www.wired.com/wired/archive/13.08/tech.html

Kenway, J., & Bullen, E. (2001). *Consuming children*. London: Open University Press.

Kollock, P. (1999). The economies of online cooperations: Gifts and public goods in cyberspace. In M. A. Smith & P. Kollock (Eds.), *Communities in cyberspace* (pp. 220–239). London: Routledge.

Kollock, P., & Smith, M. (1996). Managing the virtual commons: Cooperation and conflict in computer communities. In S. C. Herring (Ed.), *Computer-mediated communication: Linguistic, social, and cross-cultural perspectives* (pp. 109–128). Amsterdam: John Benjamins.

Kress, G., & van Leeuwen, T. (1996). *Reading images: The grammar of visual design.* London: Routledge.

Livingstone, S., Bober, M., & Helsper, A. J. (2005). Active participation or just more information? *Information, communication, & society, 8*(3), 287–314.

Ludicorp Research & Development Ltd. (2004/2005). *Flickr.* Retrieved May 31, 2005, from http://www.flickr.com

Marshall, J. (2004). Governance, structure, and existence: Authenticity, rhetoric, race, and gender on an internet mailing list. *Proceedings of the Australian Electronic Governance Conference*, Centre for Public Policy, University of Melbourne. Retrieved October 5, 2005, from http://www.publicpolicy.unimelb.edu.au/egovernance/papers/21_Marshall.pdf

Mazzarella, S. R. (2005). *Girl wide web: Girls, the internet, and the negotiation of identity.* New York: Peter Lang.

McLaughlin, M. L., Osborne, K. K., & Ellison, N. B. (1997). Virtual community in a telepresence environment. In S. G. Jones (Ed.), *Virtual culture: Identity and communication in cybersociety* (pp. 146–168). London: Sage Publications.

McManus, R. (2005, August 6). Web 2.0 is not about version numbers or betas. *Read/Write Web.* Retrieved October 22, 2005, from http://www.readwriteweb.com/archives/002791.php

McNay, L. (1994). *Foucault: Critical introduction.* Cambridge, U.K.: Polity Press.

Mele, C. (1999). Cyberspace and disadvantaged communities: The internet as a tool for collective action. In M. A. Smith & P. Kollock (Ed.), *Communities in cyberspace* (pp. 290–310). London: Routledge.

Melucci, A. (1989). *Nomads of the present: Social movements and individual needs in contemporary society.* London: Hutchinson.

MIT. (2005). Seamless. Retrieved July 2, 2007, from http://seamless.sigtronica.org/2005/projects.html

Moll, L. (2000). Inspired by Vygotsky: Ethnographic experiments in education. In C. Lee & P. Smagorinsky (Eds.), *Vygotskian perspective on literacy research: Constructing meaning through collaborative inquiry* (pp. 256–268). Cambridge, MA: Cambridge University Press.

Moriwaki, K. (2004, July/August). Between the skin and the garden: New modes of interaction in the wearable data environment. *HorizonZero, 16.* Retrieved May 31, 2005, from http://www.horizonzero.ca/textsite/wear.php?is=16&file=7&tlang=0

Parent, S., & Leech, A. (2004, July/August). Wear: Smart clothes, fashionable technologies. *HorizonZero, 16.* Retrieved May 31, 2005, from http://www.horizonzero.ca/textsite/wear.php?is=16&art=0&file=0&tlang=0

Reid, E. (1994). Cultural formations in text-based virtual realities. In P. Ludlow (Ed.), *High noon on the electronic frontier: Conceptual issues in cyberspace* (pp. 326–345). Retrieved May 31, 2005, from http://semlab2.sbs.sunysb.edu/Users/pdludlow/highnoon.html

Rheingold, H. (1993). *The virtual community: Homesteading on the electronic frontier.* Reading, MA: Addison-Wesley. Retrieved May 31, 2005, from http://www.rheingold.com/vc/book/

Rheingold, H. (1994). *The virtual community: Finding connection in a computerized world.* London: Secker & Warburg.

Schmitz, J. (1997). Structural relations, electronic media, and social change: The public electronic network and the homeless. In S. G. Jones (Ed.), *Virtual culture: Identity and communication in cybersociety* (pp. 80–101). London: Sage Publications.

Schuler, D. (1994). Community networks: Building a new participatory medium. *Communications of the ACM, 37*(1), 39–51.

Schuler, D. (1996). *New community networks: Wired for change*. Reading, MA: Addison-Wesley Publishing Co.

Sefton-Green, J. (2001). The 'end of school' or just 'out of school'? ICT, the home, and digital cultures. In C. Beavis & C. Durant (Eds.), *P(ICT)ures of English* (pp. 162–174) . Kent Town, SA: Wakefield Press/AATE.

Shinkle, E. (2003, September). Gardens, games, and the anamorphic subject: Tracing the body in the virtual landscape. *Fineart Forum* , *17*(9). Retrieved May 31, 2005, from http://www.fineartforum.org/Backissues/Vol_17/faf_v17_n09/reviews/shinkle.html

Silver, D. (1999). Localizing the global village: Lessons from the blacksburg electronic village. In R. B. Browne & M. W. Fishwick (Eds.), *The global village: Dead or alive?* (pp. 79–92). Bowling Green, OH: Popular Press.

Silver, D. (2000). Margins in the wires: Looking for race, gender, and sexuality in the blacksburg electronic village. In B. E. Kolko, L. Nakamura, & G. B. Rodman (Eds.), *Race in cyberspace: Politics, identity, and cyberspace* (pp. 133–150). New York: Routledge.

Smith, M. A., & Kollock, P. (Eds.). (1999). *Communities in cyberspace*. London: Routledge.

Spender, D. (1998). Gender-bending. In R. Holeton (Ed.), *Composing cyberspace - Identity, community and knowledge in the electronic age* (pp. 69–75). New York: McGraw-Hill.

Stone, A. R. (1991). Will the real body stand up?: Boundaries stories about virtual cultures. In M. Benedikt (Ed.), *Cyberspace. First steps* (pp. 81–118) . Cambridge, MA: MIT Press.

Taylor, T. L. (1999). Life in virtual worlds: Plural existence, multimodalities, and other online research challenges. *American Behavioral Scientist, 3*(43), 436–449.

Taylor, T. L. (2002). Living digitally: Embodiment in virtual worlds. In R. Schroeder (Ed.), *The social life of avatars: Human interaction in virtual worlds* (pp. 40–62). London: Springer-Verlag.

Thiel, S. (2005). "IM me": Identity construction and gender negotiation in the world of adolescent girls and instant messaging. In S. R. Mazzarella (Ed.), *Girl wide web: Girls, the internet, and the negotiation of identity* (pp. 179–202) . New York: Peter Lang.

Thomas, A. (2004a). *e-selves@palace.kids: Literacy and identity in a virtual community*. Unpublished manuscript, Charles Darwin University, Australia.

Thomas, A. (2004b). Digital literacies of the cybergirl. *E-Learning, 1*(3), 358–382.

Thomas, A. (2004c). *i-Anya*. Personal weblog. http://angelaathomas.com

Thomas, A. (2005a). Children online: Learning in a virtual community of practice. *E-Learning, 2*(1), 27–38.

Thomas, A. (2005b, May). Fictional blogging and the narrative identity of adolescent girls. Paper prepared for *Blogtalk Downunder Conference*, Sydney, Australia.

Turkle, S. (1995). *Life on the screen*. New York: Simon and Schuster.

Wellman, B. (1997). An electronic group is virtually a social network. In S. Kiesler (Ed.), *Culture of the internet* (pp. 179–205). Mahwah, NJ: Lawrence Erlbaum Associates Publishers.

Wellman, B., Salaff, J., Dimitrova, D., Garton, L., Gulia, M., & Haythornwaite, C. (1996). Computer networks as social networks: Collaborative work, telework, and virtual community. *Annual Review of Sociology, 22*, 213–238.

Wenger, E. (2002). *Communities of practice: Learning, meaning, and identity*. London: Cambridge University Press.

Wikipedia. (2001–2005). *Wikipedia: The free encyclopedia*. Retrieved May 31, 2005, from http://en.wikipedia.org/wiki/Wikipedia

CHAPTER 25

New Literacies and Community Inquiry

BERTRAM C. BRUCE
and ANN PETERSON BISHOP
UNIVERSITY OF ILLINOIS AT URBANA-CHAMPAIGN, USA

Be the change you want to see in the world. (Gandhi)

Introduction

Community inquiry research focuses on people participating with others, on the lived experiences of feeling, thinking, acting, and communicating. It sees literacy as part of living in the world, not simply as a skill to be acquired in the classroom. Inquiry is central, because as people live, they encounter challenges. Through inquiry, people recognize a problem, mobilize resources, engage actively to resolve it, collaborate, and reflect on the experience. Making sense of experience in this way, and doing so in concert with others in embodied, historical circumstances, is fundamental to learning.

This chapter reviews literature addressing the following question: What is the relationship of new literacies to community inquiry? We are concerned with how new technologies highlight enduring issues of community and, conversely, how communities change new technologies. These concerns are embedded within larger issues of participation, citizenship, cooperation, community membership, change, and collective memory. The chapter speaks from the perspective of progressive education's emphasis on understanding the deep connections among literacy, learning, technology, and community but does not limit its view to work explicitly in that tradition.

Approach to the Review

Around a century ago, a set of ideas and practices shaped a radical vision for education as a keystone for all social life. It was called "progressive education" in the United States, with parallels in other countries; this new way of thinking was built upon the assumption of an integral connection between democracy and education (Cremin, 1964; Dewey, 1939/1991; Graham, 1967). The conception of democracy at that time diverged considerably from that commonly taught in schools today. The latter most often views democracy as a purely political process or views democracy as something to be fought for, especially when one nation tries to impose its will on another or one group seeks power over another. Instead, progressive education in the early to mid-1900s envisaged democracy from the ground up, as a process involving every aspect of living. It meant active participation by all citizens in social, political, and economic decisions (Addams, 1893/2002). Both Jane Addams and John Dewey realized that practices promoted under the name of progressive education varied widely, often being reduced to a romanticized notion of undirected learning. We argue that the version of progressive education presented in the following section is closer to Dewey's original meaning and, perhaps even more importantly, is a useful encapsulation of a philosophy of education for today. Benson, Harkavy, and Puckett (2007) make a similar argument with respect to the relation between universities and communities.

Connecting New Literacies and Community

The progressive education movement appeared in response to an era of massive immigration, disorienting technological change, and questions about the nature of civic governance; these are not unlike the conditions and corresponding concerns voiced today (Boyte, 2003; Bruce, 2002). There was a core belief that education could not succeed by avoiding these complexities. Instead, the opposite was needed. Students must be given the opportunity to engage with life as it is, not as it was imagined or might be someday. Progressive education offered ideas about how to develop the ability to cope with complexity, but more importantly, there was an assumption throughout that connecting community, work, social values, nature, and all the other aspects of lived experience was a fundamental necessity for meaningful learning.

A central thesis of this movement was that education is about the development of engaged citizens. Today the individualist conception of literacy is dominant in educational discourse and policy. In contrast, the progressives saw individual growth as important, but inseparable from issues of democratic participation and social change. Key elements of this kind of education include the following:

- respect for diversity, meaning that each individual should be recognized for his or her own abilities, interests, ideas, needs, and cultural identity, and

- the development of critical, socially engaged intelligence, which enables individuals to understand and participate effectively in the affairs of their community in a collaborative effort to achieve a common good (John Dewey Project on Progressive Education, 2002).

As we consider the role of new media and technologies in literacy it may at first seem strange to look back over a century to a time before iPods, the Internet, computers, television, and movies for insights into how we teach, learn, and live today. Yet, beyond the usual rule that it is useful to examine the present in light of the past, the experiences of the progressive education period may be especially salient today. In many ways, we have lost the deep connections between school literacy and community, which the progressive education movement sought to foster. We have lost the ability to see literacy as inherent in the practice of engaged citizenship, rather than a simple objective to be attained. New literacies have the potential to reestablish those connections; both their benefits and their drawbacks can be better understood by considering the larger communities in which formal learning is embedded (Bruce, 2003).

Research within the community inquiry framework overlaps with other research on new literacies and shares many core assumptions. This body of research highlights aspects of literacy and technology that may be less visible when one looks at only formal learning settings. This is because much of formal learning today provides limited opportunities for students or teachers to participate fully in creating, selecting, appropriating, or modifying the tools of learning. It separates the learning of skills and concepts from daily life. And it studiously avoids the aesthetic, moral, ethical, political, and economic dimensions of knowing. Attention to community brings those dimensions forward. In so doing, it expands our conception of new literacies and what they mean for schools, communities, and life in general.

Challenges for the Review

Any review poses challenges: how to balance breadth and depth, how to discuss incommensurable studies in one venue, how to do justice to work based on unshared assumptions, how to integrate theory with empirical work, and how much to cover early work versus the most recent. But this one raises additional issues, primarily because it refers to an emerging discipline concerned with new community-based literacies, which calls for not only new research but also new ways of thinking.

Our topic might suggest a focus on separate categories of literacy, technology, and community; however, this organizational scheme turns out to be simplistic upon further consideration. The first problem is that there are divergent conceptions of literacy, technology, and community, which make it difficult to compare and contrast research across these areas. While we concentrate on lived experience in geographic communities in this review, the purpose, temporal and spatial scope, and very definition of community are all in question (Wellman, 2001), as we discuss later in this chapter. There are similar divergences in the definitions of literacy and technology. As Lankshear and Knobel (2004) argued, it soon becomes clear that we need to avoid narrow statements, such as equating new literacy with literacy using information and communication technologies.

Whatever definitions we adopt, another problem for any review is that research in any one of these categories often remains unconnected to that in the other two categories. Although there are classic, peer-reviewed, data-driven, published journal articles in each of these category areas, they typically fail to speak to the integration of these areas. For example, few studies examine how community projects might become more aware of literacy issues or how school-based new literacies might connect with community problems. Moreover, there is relevant work that does not fit neatly into any of the categories. For instance, Moje (2000) talked about life beyond the school in her discussion of graffiti and rap, but does not frame the work as community-oriented per se. Similarly, graffiti and rap are new technologies but do not fit the more common definitions that focus on electronic devices.

Thus, in the present review, we strive to provide a substantial grounding in community inquiry as a means to bring together work in the community, technology, and literacy. And we highlight work such as Moje's (2000) work, which demonstrates creative and meaningful integration across the categories and suggests, in our minds, the power of community inquiry as an analytic lens. In addition to reports of research published in scholarly journals, much of the best work is found in books (e.g., Druin, 1998; Eglash, Croisant, & di Chiro, 2004), Web sites (e.g., the *TECFA Community Portal* at http://tecfaseed.unige.ch/door, the Public Sphere Project's *Liberating voices! A pattern language for communication revolution* at http://trout.cpsr.org/program/sphere/patterns, and *infed* at http://www.infed.org/), technical reports, newsletters, conference proceedings, and other nonjournal venues.

Organization of the Review

The challenges encountered in participating in community inquiry might be summarized as those inherent in paradigm-shifting science, as distinct from normal science. We are talking about community inquiry in this *Handbook* because we feel there is an important body of work that ought to be integral to new literacies but has not yet been explicitly recognized in much of the literature. The community inquiry perspective is noteworthy because it brings certain things to the foreground: learning as lived experience, literacy as community participation, and technology as construction of the means of inquiry. We present that work here and try to make the connections clear, highlighting their importance for research on new literacies. We address the shift in science that community inquiry commands in part by including a substantial discussion of contributions to theory in this review. While we try to let the research speak on its own terms, our selection and presentation necessarily reflects our own specific values and theoretical orientations, as well as our own community inquiry practice.

In an effort to make our orientations explicit, we present the research in terms of three key themes central to community inquiry: (a) learning and lived experience, (b) community, and (c) technology. It is important to note that, for community inquiry, these are not three separate realms; they function in a coordinated way. The best way to show that is to present examples in the form of vignettes, small but rich slices of research in which the three themes come together. Thus, following an account of the themes, we examine a set of research vignettes that are organized according to aspects of an inquiry cycle and that embody possible ways of bringing together effectively considerations of learning, community, and technology. These research vignettes are drawn from community inquiry in which we have participated, so that we are able to speak from our own lived experiences. We use the vignettes both to help explain what community inquiry is but also to provide a base for linking community inquiry to a broader spectrum of new literacies research.

Learning and Lived Experience

Studies of communities solving problems or developing better communication practices have shown two clear findings regarding literacy. First, literacy is vital to community well-being, especially if one sees literacy as a set of cultural practices involved with making and communicating meaning through a variety of socially defined symbol systems. The ways in which people communicate within the community and with those outside are central to both community functioning and to our understanding of those communities. Second, and somewhat paradoxically, a focus on literacy may be counterproductive. For the community, especially underserved ones, a literacy focus often leads to a deficit view, in which one catalogs the various ways that members of a particular community lack literacy skills needed within the larger society. From an analytical perspective, the focus can lead us to ignore the surround in which literacy is practiced. For these reasons, and because literacy is addressed more directly in other chapters, we want to start here with a consideration of learning and lived experience. As the case studies near the end show, literate activities are central to community life, but we need to understand them within a context of lived experience, community building, and political struggles.

Situation

In his autobiography, Myles Horton (1990) described the work of the Highlander Folk School in New Market, Tennessee, which helped guide Martin Luther King, Jr., Rosa Parks, Eleanor Roosevelt, Pete Seeger, and many others involved with labor and civil rights movements in the 20th century. Writing about social goals and personal goals as they developed within the labor, civil rights, and antiwar work of the school, Horton argued, "Goals are unattainable in the sense that they always grow," and this is a good thing because "you die when you stop growing" (p. 228).

The Highlander School is a prime example of a holistic approach to education that encompasses social well-being and change. Horton, for example, deliberately placed education goals within a broader perspective on larger social change:

> Instead of thinking that you put pieces together that will add up to a whole, I think you have to start with the premise that they're already together and you try to keep from destroying life by segmenting it, over-organizing it and dehumanizing it. You try to keep things together. The educative process must be organic, and not an assortment of unrelated methods and ideas. (1990, p. 130)

Horton learned from Jane Addams and Hull House, which embodied a similar approach to democratic education, that people actively shape their own learning as they work on real problems within their own communities. In doing so, people sought to realize democracy in its social, as well as its political, expression. This resulted in an educational philosophy in which learning starts with lived experience:

> If you listen to people and work from what they tell you, within a few days their ideas get bigger and bigger. They go back in time, ahead in their imagination. You just continue to build on people's own experience: it is the basis for their learning. (Horton, 1990, p. 137)

For Horton, goals arise because "in any situation there will always be something that's worse, and there will always be something that's better, so you continually strive to make it better" (1990, p. 228). Both this positioning of goals within problematic situations and the equation of goals with living hark back to John Dewey and his theory of inquiry.

For Dewey (1938/1991), *situation* is not something we enter into, nor does it exist independent of inquiry. We are a part of, not spectators of, this dialectical situation. We change a problematic situation, and we, in turn, are changed through our actions. In his classic reflex arc paper, Dewey (1896/1972) showed how, under this view, conventional distinctions between organism and environment, stimulus and response, body and mind, or cause and effect need to be reconsidered. Bentley (1941) further showed that even the distinction between "knower" and the "known" relies on an incomplete understanding of situation, positing the knower as separate from the environment. This theory is articulated further in Dewey's major works (e.g., Dewey & Bentley, 1949). Indeed, Dewey's (1938/1991) definition of *inquiry* uses his concept of situation to provide a descriptive account of how we survive in the world: "Inquiry is the controlled or directed transformation of an indeterminate situation into one that is so determinate in its constituent distinctions and relations as to convert the elements of the original situation into a unified whole" (p. 108).

Indeterminate situations are those in which a person finds conflict between current needs and realities. The indeterminacy can range from feeling cold to being puzzled about an historical event. That feeling of indeterminacy is then the driving force of inquiry, causing the individual to put on a coat in the former case or to make a trip to a library, in the latter. In each case, the inquirer seeks to establish a unified whole, one that replaces the indeterminacy with a unity. It is important to note that, for Dewey (1938/1991), inquiry is not a purely mental act, separate from action. Putting on a coat can be as much an instance of "directed transformation" as is reading a book. In fact, the integration of mind and body in action constitutes the transformative aspect of inquiry.

It is also important to note that this account is descriptive, not prescriptive. That is, Dewey did not argue that we *should* transform indeterminate situations or that a good way to help people learn or participate with others is to have them do so. Instead, the "controlled or directed transformation" of indeterminate situations is simply what we do as purposive organisms. Learning is our capacity to reflect upon that transformation and to realize that we can achieve a "unified whole" when faced with similar situations in the future. In that sense, *inquiry-based learning* is not a method or an option to consider for teaching and learning; instead, it is what happens when people *do* learn.

The emphasis in Dewey's (1938/1991) definition of inquiry and his use of "situation" is on transformation, on remaking the world along with ourselves. Because situations often include interactions with others, inquiry typically involves collaborative practices within geographically defined communities. The usual categories (i.e., teacher/student, technology/concept, and knowledge/skill) are replaced with a need to understand the process of transformation: What means are employed to transform an indeterminate situation? What are the varied roles played by tools, ideas, and people in inquiry? How does an inquirer evaluate the unity of a situation? How do multiple inquirers coordinate their activities? How do individual experiences and needs coordinate with those of the community?

For Dewey, Bentley, Addams, Horton, and others involved with this educational praxis, the problems of education were not located in what we teach or how we teach, but rather in the breakdown of connections between individual and community, between formal learning and lived experience, and between the means and ends of problem solving. From this perspective, the situation set up within formal education is often so far removed from the situation of life outside that learning has no meaning and remains in what Dewey (1938/1991) called a "water-tight compartment" (p. 48). It leads to the notion that the school (or library, after-school program, museum, etc.) should be a social center for addressing the real and present problems within the community (Dewey, 1902).

The Inquiry Cycle

We can think of inquiry as a cycle in which each question leads to an exploration, which in turn leads to more questions to investigate (Bruce & Davidson, 1996). Thus, there is a process of asking, investigating, creating, discussing, and reflecting, and then asking again (Bruce & Bishop, 2002), as shown in Figure 25.1.

We need to interpret the cycle as suggestive only. Inquiry rarely proceeds in a simple, linear fashion. The five dimensions in the process—ask, investigate, create, discuss, and reflect—overlap, and not every category or step is present in any given inquiry. Each step can be embedded in any of the others, and so on. In fact, the very nature of inquiry is that these steps are mutually reinforcing and interrelated. Thus, reflection on solving a problem may lead to reformulating the problem or posing a new question. Similarly, action in the world is closely tied to dialogue with others. Despite this fuzziness, the steps and cycle outlined in Figure 25.1 can be helpful in highlighting aspects of an otherwise opaque process.

- *Ask* reminds us that inquiry begins with a question or problem arising out of experience. The "indeterminate situation" Dewey (1938/1991) refers to is part of that experience, including an individual's participation in a community. It is not something that can be delivered from "outside" this participation. This is why there is "an enormous pedagogical difference between answering someone else's question and formulating your own" (Olds, Schwartz, & Willie, 1980, p. 40).
- *Investigate* relates to the varieties of experience possible and the many ways in which we become part of an "indeterminate situation." It suggests that opportunities for learning require diverse, authentic, and challenging materials and problems. Because experience includes

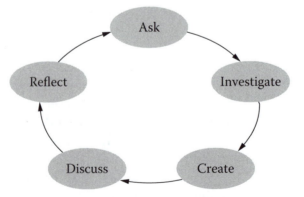

Figure 25.1 The inquiry cycle.

interactions with others, there is also a moral dimension to inquiry. Similarly, physical, emotional, aesthetic, and practical dimensions are inherent in inquiry, and are not merely enhancements or add-ons.

- *Create* picks up the "controlled or directed transformation" part of Dewey's (1938/1991) definition. This term insists that inquiry means active, engaged hands-on learning. Inquiry thus implies active creation of meaning, which includes new forms of collaborating and new roles for collaborators.

- *Discuss* highlights an implicit part of Dewey's (1938/1991) definition, which is developed in great detail in his writing, especially in his later work. Although inquiry has a personal aspect, it is also part of our participation in social arrangements and community. The "discuss" aspect in the inquiry approach involves listening to others and articulating our own understandings. Through discussion (or dialogue), construction of knowledge becomes a social enterprise.

- *Reflect* tells us that it is the inquirer who recognizes the "indeterminate situation" and can say whether it has been transformed into "a unified whole." Reflection (later articulated in the work of Schön, 1983, and others) means expressing experience and thereby being able to move from new concepts into action. Reflection may also mean recognizing further indeterminacies, leading to continuing inquiry.

As previously discussed, these steps are only one way to describe effective community inquiry. Together, they comprise a cycle that can be used to inform and guide educational experiences for learners.

Inquiry-Based Learning

Participation in the cycle of inquiry is crucial to inquiry-based learning, but the integral connection to lived experience outside school walls must not be obscured. As Addams learned at Hull House, the best education constantly reconstructs experience, relating it to both the past and to contemporary life. This view is captured in an oft-quoted passage written by Dewey (1938/1991):

> We always live at the time we live and not at some other time, and only by extracting at each present time the full meaning of each present experience are we prepared for doing the same in the future. This is the only preparation which in the long run amounts to anything. (p. 51)

Thus, inquiry requires active learning in authentic contexts. Authentic contexts require that teachers, students, and community members become partners in inquiry, including inquiry into the world and inquiry into pedagogy. This principle carries through from the individual classroom to the whole school. As Owen, Cox, and Watkins (1994) said, "For communities to rethink and redesign their schools so that all students develop successfully, the entire community must have the opportunity to be involved in inquiry about teaching, learning, and assessing" (p. 15).

Antecedents of this idea can be seen in the work of Lucy Sprague Mitchell, a leader of progressive education, who extended the work of both Addams and Dewey (Smith, 2000). In New York, in 1931, she started what was later known as the Cooperative School for Teachers, which exemplified a commitment to collaboration and inquiry. She saw the need for both children and teachers to develop a scientific attitude toward work and life:

> Our aim is to turn out teachers whose attitude toward their work and toward life is scientific. To us, this means an attitude of eager, alert observation; a constant questioning of old procedure in light of new observations; a use of the world, as well as of books, as source material; an experimental openmindedness, an effort to keep as reliable records as the situation permits, in order to base the future upon accurate knowledge of what has been done. Our aim is to equally turn out students whose attitude toward their work and toward life is that of the artist. To us this means an attitude of relish, of emotional drive, a genuine participation in some creative phase of work, and a sense that joy and beauty are legitimate possessions of all human beings, young and old. If we can produce teachers with an experimental, critical, and ardent approach to their work, we are ready to leave the future of education to them. (Mitchell, 1931, p. 251)

Inquiry-based learning is sometimes described as a philosophical and pedagogical response to the changing needs of the information age, but its roots are much deeper. It assumes that all learning begins with the learner. That is, what people know and what they want to learn are not just constraints on what can be taught; they are the very foundation for learning. Dewey (1900/1915) described the impulses (or instincts) of the learner, which are available resources for the school, and underlie the cycle of inquiry:

- Social instinct—conversation, personal intercourse, and communication;
- Instinct of making—the constructive impulse;
- Instinct of investigation—doing things and watching to see what happens; and
- Expressive impulse—the desire to extract meaning from experience (pp. 42–44).

Dewey (1900/1915) saw these four interests as the natural resources, or the uninvested capital of education, out of which active learning grows. If people are to understand and participate fully in the complex world in which they live, they need to have opportunities to engage with challenging problems, to learn through hands-on investigations, to have supportive experiences, to articulate their ideas to others, and to explore a variety of resources in multiple media (Boyer Commission on Educating Undergraduates in the Research University, 1998; Minstrell & van Zee, 2000; Shavelson & Towne, 2002). These ideas have established at least a toehold in formal education but have become an imperative in community-based learning.

Concept of Community

The term *community* has been used to refer to a classroom or a global movement, to groups of people defined by location or interests, or in terms of communion (Smith, 2001; Wellman, 2001). There are learning, disciplinary, and professional communities, as well as historically defined, place-based communities. Hutchins (1952) used the term for a scholarly conversation across centuries, cultures, nations, and languages. There are also imagined (Anderson, 1991) and online or virtual communities (Rheingold, 1993). To some, community is a warm concept, akin to family and neighborhood. For such people, more community is thus a good thing. A corollary of this is that in much of the literature within education, "community" is something to be created, developed, and nurtured (Cuthbert, Clark, & Linn, 2002; Joseph & Edelson, 2002; Joseph & Nacu, 2003; Renninger & Shumar, 2002). In the management literature, some ask how to create a community of practice (Wenger, McDermott, & Snyder, 2002). Conversely, others see community as divisive, or as a site of struggle (Hoggett, 1997). Nancy (1991) described community as the site of political resistance against immanent power. At the same time, he also saw the potential of communities to become oppressive, and asks how we can conceive community in a nontotalitarian manner.

Cohen (1985) argued that communities are best approached as *communities of meaning*. A community, from this perspective, plays a crucial symbolic role in our sense of belonging. That is, "People construct community symbolically, making it a resource and repository of meaning, and a referent of their identity" (p. 118). For Cohen, members of a community have something in common with each other, and that thing in common distinguishes them from the members of other groups (p. 12). The boundaries of community may be established formally, but often exist symbolically "in the minds of the beholders" as well (p. 12). As such, boundaries may be seen in very different ways by members of the same community as well as by those outside the community.

Thus, community implies both similarity and difference, a property Knorr-Cetina (1999) found in her work with scientific groups as well; that is, a group engages actively in defining both how it is the same and how it is different from other groups. Her account of a group is similar to what Zacklad (2003) called "a community of action" (p. 193). He proposed this term for

> dealing with small groups which actively and thus to some extent rationally pursue explicit goals while relying on a tightly woven fabric of relationships to promote mutual sympathy and the mimetic learning

that is assumed to characterize primary groups and communities of practice. (p. 193)

Thus, his concept contrasts with *community of practice* (Lave & Wenger, 1991), which is nonintentional in its original conception, even though recent formulations have moved them closer.

A definition of similarity and difference is necessary for a group to be a community but it is not sufficient. Communities also have an intrinsic relation to *place*. This is at the heart of the debate over whether online groups are truly communities: Do they need a physical place, or can place exist in online geographies? Moreover, communities have *histories,* typically with complex tapestries of relations to communities before them. The ease with which online groups can be formed calls into question our prior notions of place and history in relation to our understandings of community.

For Dewey (1927), communities develop through reciprocal processes of individual and community inquiry. Thus, a community can change and develop, but not through top-down engineering; a democratic community must be created through democratic processes. His concept of community is then central to learning. Making it possible for everyone to share in a common life—creating the Great Community, as he called it—is the central aim of education. Viewing conditions in the world in 1934, he identified two principal reasons for this. One was to counter the effects of "the economic regime of modern capitalistic industry" (Dewey, 1934, p. 214):

> In a world that has so largely engaged in a mad, often brutal, race for material gain by means of ruthless competition the school must make ceaseless and intelligently organized effort to develop above all else the will for cooperation and the spirit which sees in every other individual an equal right to share in the cultural and material fruits of collective human invention, industry, skill and knowledge. (p. 214)

The second was to exorcize racism:

> Unless the schools of the world can unite in effort to rebuild the spirit of common understanding, of mutual sympathy and goodwill among all peoples and races, to exorcise the demon of prejudice, isolation and hatred, they themselves are likely to be submerged by the general return to barbarism. (p. 214)

These reasons remain valid today. Surrounded by the larger contexts of capitalism and racism, communities today also face internal challenges in areas of health, education, economic development, sustainable environments, and social order. Nevertheless, and regardless of the difficulty of these challenges, a necessary task for communities is to find ways for members to work together in addressing problems and issues. Too often, according to Dewey (1927), both within their communities and in relation to the larger society, people work at cross-purposes resulting in "the eclipse of the public" (p. 110). Over 90 years later, the "eclipse of the public" is even more salient as we consider relations between Muslims and Christians, racism throughout the world, and struggles for economic equality.

Communities of Inquiry

Community inquiry provides a theoretical and action framework for thinking about and working on these issues. It emphasizes the need for people to come together to develop shared capacity and work on common problems in an experimental and critical manner. It thus has much in common with action research (Greenwood & Levin, 2006; McNiff & Whitehead, 2006; Stringer, 1999), especially participatory action research (McTaggart, 1991; Reardon, 1998; Whyte, 1991). It emphasizes, however, seeing the community as an organic whole. Action research by some members of a community focusing on a particular problem would be a key component of community inquiry. But communities of inquiry tend to connect specific problem solving activities. For example, a community wellness program leads to the creation of a farmers' market, which is itself an opportunity to address divisions within the community through concerted action; the farmers' market leads to market baskets for low-income people and those who are shut in; all of these activities are tied to community economic development, cultural heritage, and community pride; the various activities become the curriculum for the schools; and so on. This is a capsule description of some of the community inquiry activities in Paseo Boricua, the setting for one of our research vignettes. It is also evident in new directions for the (U. S.) National Writing Project (Berdan, et al., 2006).

To recap briefly, the word *community* signals support for collaborative activity and for creating knowledge that is connected to people's values, history, and lived experiences. *Inquiry* points to support for open-ended, democratic, participatory engagement. Communities of inquiry thus involve several key elements. They

- respond to human needs by democratic and equitable processes;
- view community problems as an *opportunity* for the community to come together, to build capacity for problem solving, and to learn about the community and its situation;
- recognize that every member of the community has knowledge which may be critical to solving a problem, but can be discovered only if that individual has a voice; and
- help communities become learning organizations.

A successful *community of inquiry* (Garrison, Cleveland-Innes, & Fung, 2004) therefore is not one in which everyone is the same, but instead is one that accommodates plurality. As Clark (1994) argued, a learning community needs to maintain equitable relations among participants and render "the progress of expertise in a community secondary to a relational and epistemological practice of confronting differences so that its participants can come to understand how the beliefs and purposes of others can call their own into question" (p. 74). This is often easier said than done, and a key challenge that every community of inquiry will face concerns how to maintain a focus on addressing a given problem without sidelining the contribution of individual experiences, perceptions, and values.

We do not need to assume that "normal" learning is that which occurs in a classroom, with hyphenated versions of learning occurring outside (service-learning, community-based learning, lifelong-learning, project-based learning, etc.). *Communities of inquiry* situate learning in a broader frame than that assumed in much of educational research. This can be seen in recent studies emphasizing outside of school literacies, particularly with the use of new media (Garner, Zhao, & Gillingham, 2002; Hull & Schultz, 2002). Learning is then seen as a condition of all lived experience, with the classroom as a special case.

Community and Social Change

If we accept Dewey's definition of *technology* as encompassing tools for problem solving—everything from a computer to a process to a definition of a term (Hickman, 1990)—it is clear that Horton's Highlander School employed and developed many technologies. For example, Highlander workshops developed a set of assumptions that were used to guide decision making and learning. These assumptions included the following: (a) There should be a goal arising out of a perceived social problem; (b) people have the capacity to solve their own problems; (c) dialogue in a larger context is important; (d) teachers need to interact in the field with students; (e) facts and analyses need to be tailored to the students' needs; and (f) follow-up to an implemented change is essential. The enactment of these assumptions constituted a technology for learning as much as any courseware or simulation tool might today.

However, tools were always regarded by Dewey and his colleagues as provisional and subject to change by participants, particularly when participants discovered that the tools failed to address identified social goals. This position differs markedly from the current dominant discourse about educational methods and technologies, which are typically conceived as independent of social change and not open to revision by students or teachers.

In many schools, the environment beyond the school walls might as well not exist. The culture of the community is irrelevant to the fixed curriculum; there is no recognition of the *funds of knowledge* (Moll, Amanti, Neff, & Gonzalez, 1992) a community might provide for a school. Local history is deemed secondary to the authorized history of the textbook or not acknowledged at all. Students' lived experiences, their personal and family goals, and their questions often are ignored. In some cases, however, the larger environment is recognized. It may be used prior to a lesson to "generate student interest" or to "activate prior knowledge." It may be used after a lesson as a way to "apply what is learned" or to "extend learning." The language here reveals that the environment beyond the classroom is at most a supplement to the "real" learning that occurs in a lesson.

Highlander inverts this hierarchy. Although one might say that everything this school does concerns learning, it is a learning that grows out of issues central to the lives of participants (e.g., "forums on war, the importance of defending and extending democracy against fascism, race problems, the social teachings of the Bible, old and modern Russia, social developments in Scandinavian countries, the labor movement in the South;" Horton, 1990, p. 75). Today, the National Issues Forums (nifi.org) similarly looks to community-based deliberation as a cornerstone of both learning and democracy. Community knowledge, existing practices, and felt needs become the core, with formal methods as one means to foster community and individual growth. This inversion is also evident in other community-based learning programs, including the Freirean literacy campaigns (McLaren & Lankshear, 1994; Robert, 1998), Bolívarian circles in Venezuela (Bello, 2006), science shops in Europe (Fischer, Leydesdorff, & Schophaus, 2004), Scandinavian study circles (Oliver, 1987), ActionAid's Reflect approach to adult learning and social change (actionaid.org.uk/323/reflect.html), the appreciative inquiry approach as used in community development (Elliott, 1999), the Alternative Schools Network in Chicago (asnchicago.org), and in the University of Chicago Laboratory School (Tanner, 1997).

Technology

Online Learning

There is a large body of research on online learning appearing in journal articles, books, government reports, and other publications. This research highlights the details of specific software, pedagogical approaches, curricula, or learning situations (Haythornthwaite & Kazmer, 2004; Linn, 1996; Mishra, Koehler, & Zhao, in press).

Some of these studies speak to community inquiry and digital technologies. Henri (1992), for example, studied the relationship between teaching and learning in networked collaborative learning environments by focusing on the social activity and the interactivity of individuals in the participating group. Gunawardena, Lowe, and Anderson (1997) used a modification of Henri's framework to explore social negotiation in online learning environments. Garrison, Anderson, and Archer (2000) developed a model of critical thinking and practical inquiry that illustrates the multifaceted components of teaching and learning in text-based environments. M. J. Hannafin, K. M. Hannafin, Land, and Oliver (1997) argued that the best online learning projects follow principles of grounded design, which has shown promise in meeting community needs.

On the whole, the research portrays a field with many intriguing demonstrations, but with many unanswered questions as well, especially in the context of community inquiry. The research is fragmented and noncumulative in part because the frameworks for analysis and comparison are underdeveloped. Hartley (1998), Anglin and Morrison (2002), and others noted a lack of studies based on theoretical frameworks of learning. These authors called for more studies based on significant research questions, and less reliance on participant reaction surveys alone.

However, online environments are often driven more by the nature of the technology or by commercial imperatives than by a commitment to learning and to equity. These problems are exacerbated when one takes seriously the use of online technologies outside of formal learning contexts, or for contexts that connect formal learning and community action. Indeed, most online learning research deals with cost or effectiveness of learning environments, narrowly defined.

Community Technologies

People have developed a diverse array of technologies in the service of community inquiry—from cave paintings to Post-it notes on refrigerators, from stone cairns to newsletters, from books to Web sites. Language itself might be defined as the primary means for community inquiry, inasmuch as it embodies through its essential social aspect both the means and ends for community members to engage one another in addressing their problems. Moreover, the ongoing reinvention of language and its various manifestations represents the story of community inquiry as well.

It is beyond the scope of this chapter to review all the many new forms of hardware for communication available and the research being done on these. Let it suffice to mention not only computers and the Internet, but also mobile phones, personal digital assistants (PDAs), iPods, wireless technologies, and digital cameras, as but a few of the devices that are reshaping community interactions, marking new fault lines within communities, and creating new ways of connecting one community with another. Often, these new tools are combined with older ones in novel ways. For example, *Netti-Nysse* is an Internet bus in Tampere, Finland (Harju, 2005). It offers a mobile technology for community members in general when it visits a public square or for specific communities when it makes a requested visit. The bus contains a small auditorium and 10 computer stations with Ethernet connections. The bus itself connects to the Internet via a wireless link to 1 of 10 WLAN antennas in Tampere. *Netti-Nysse* provides computer/Internet instruction for 1,000 people and access for 5,000 to 12,000 others each year. Its activities are coordinated with the city libraries, NetSquares (fixed community technology centers; see http://tampere.

fi/kirjasto/sampola), and Mansetori, a community Web site (http://mansetori. uta.fi). Together, these resources provide basic computer education, the means for communication among community groups, access to information, and e-government services. It will be interesting to see how projects such as this might provide support for community inquiry, with active involvement of community members in design, appropriation, and evaluation of the technologies.

A related effort on a global scale is UNESCO's International Initiative for Community Multimedia Centres (Creech, Berthe, Assubuji, Mansingh, & Anjelkovic, 2006). Each Community Multimedia Centre addresses local development needs in education, training, health, and income generation. It does this by combining community radio broadcasts which are produced by local people in their own languages and community technology centers that host Internet-capable computers and provide phone, fax, and photocopying services as well. The low-cost radio broadcasts inform, educate, and entertain, but also empower the community by encouraging public participation and greater accountability in public affairs. It is linked with the Internet through programming that discusses useful Web sites. A recent evaluation found,

> [L]onger term benefits are already being realized within individual communities, such as the gradual removal of barriers to social inclusion, the stimulation of poverty alleviation through access to knowledge of better health, resource management and agriculture practices, through the establishment of listeners clubs as self help groups (a direct connection between CMC [Community Multimedia Centre] work and the generation of income from small savings and credit operations), and the creation of new livelihoods opportunities. The CMC role in fostering cultural resilience—the capacity of a community to retain critical knowledge and at the same time adapt to external influences and pressures–is particularly remarkable. (Creech, et. al., 2006, p. 6)

Since 2001, UNESCO has established nearly 100 CMCs in developing countries in Africa, Asia, and Latin America/Caribbean. There are efforts to establish countrywide networks of 50 or more CMCs each in Mali, Senegal, and Mozambique.

The Internet is of course a prime venue for new literacies in service of communities. Web resources can promote learning for many community members. On one hand, users can learn about history and culture related to their investigations through images and stories. Through interactive software, they can engage in simulated investigations that would be too expensive, dangerous, or lengthy to pursue in other ways. Web sites can help people see their current ideas in a new light and encourage the creation and expression of new ones. On the other hand, people can be frustrated by the gap between their ordinary experiences and codified technical knowledge. The latter can seem static and different in kind from the knowledge gained through daily living. One way of addressing this issue, we propose, is to think of technology use as representing the ongoing processes of community inquiry (Tardieu, 1999). This way, the conflict between personal, situated knowledge and historically constituted, communal knowledge becomes a problem of melding and connecting, not of choosing one over the other.

Appropriating Technology

Technology appropriation is a familiar phenomenon. People appropriate all kinds of technologies in their lives: cell phones as ways to avoid phone solicitations or digital video cameras to produce "pandacam" shots of the San Diego zoo, to name a few. The deaf community has appropriated instant messaging (IMing) technology in a particularly clever way; deaf teenagers can "talk on the phone" with their friends after school. These conversations can be with both hearing and nonhearing friends, unlike the situation with the earlier teletypewriters. Their parents appreciate the writing and typing practice that this use affords. The designers of these technologies may not have envisioned these uses, nor may have the users when they first purchased the item.

Eglash, Croisant, di Chiro, and Fouché (2004) emphasized the importance of using two-way bridges across the digital divide. This contrasts with the one-way bridge, which assumes that experts need to deliver the technology and the knowledge to users. The one-way-bridge model stereotypes individuals and communities and overlooks the valuable resources they possess, an attitude that runs counter to asset- and capacity-based approaches that have become the norm in community development (Kretzmann & McKnight, 1993). The definition of a two-way bridge relies on a model that recognizes two intersecting axes: (a) high to low social power and (b) production to consumption. In this model, two-way bridges comprise a shift for those with low social power

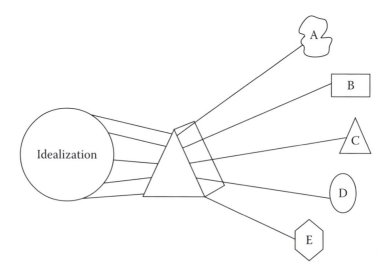

Figure 25.2 The idealization to realization process.

from being just consumers to being producers of science or technology through reconceptualizing professional products that are provided by producers with high social power. If the appropriation process is supported and examined, the result can be new opportunities for local communities to make use of powerful new resources. This is similar to the *alternate realizations* process (Bruce, Peyton, & Batson, 1993; Bruce & Rubin, 1993) as shown in Figure 25.2.

Here, the innovation (which can be read as computer technology, curriculum, teaching practice, or other method) appears as a discrete and well-defined *idealization*. But as community members incorporate it (or not) into their own lived experience, they transform it to fit their own beliefs and practices. This process may occur consciously, but usually occurs through unreflective acts of interpretation and adaptive use. The result is that each situation results in a different reading of the innovation and a different *realization* of it in practice.

Community Informatics

Community informatics is an emerging field of research, action, and policy that aims to understand how information and communication technologies are employed to help communities achieve their goals in a wide range of domains, such as health care, civic engagement, preserving cultural heritage, agriculture, economic development, environmental planning and protection, and education (Bieber, Civille, Gurstein, & White, 2002; Bishop & Bruce, 2005; Gurstein, 2004; Keeble & Loader, 2001). Community informatics is concerned with geospatial communities and helps conceive of the entire community as a unit of analysis when considering literacy and technology issues, practices, and outcomes. It provides a natural framework for looking at how technologies are linked to social change in communities (Grabill, 2003, in press). Moreover, community informatics prompts us to consider critically the role that technology plays in communities (Granqvist, 2005; Stoecker, 2005).

Community informatics research is conducted internationally in settings that range from inner-city neighborhoods to rural villages, and explores how individuals and institutions (e.g., schools, libraries, grassroots groups, health agencies, etc.) come together to work on common problems. It addresses questions of community development, learning, empowerment, and sustainability in the context of efforts to promote a positive role for computers and the Internet in society (see http://community.telecentre.org). Community informatics highlights issues of social justice, prompting literacy researchers to consider the cultural reproduction of digital inequality (Kvasny, 2006) and the development of a radical praxis for "rewiring" the social order" (Venkatesh & Owens, 2006) and creating more livable communities (Schuler, 1996).

Technology as Lived Experience

We can summarize much of the research on literacy technologies in communities by saying that it concerns how people live in the world, how they engage with others, and how they articulate and make sense of their experiences. *Technology* is a central player in these processes (McCarthy & Wright, 2004). Research on technology design, development, distribution, use, and evaluation within communities has highlighted this role for technology and in the process identified several revisions to the ordinary view of technology:

1. Technologies are often construed as tools to solve problems, but problem solving also creates technologies (regardless of whether the solution is a new term, an artifact, a process, a machine, etc.). Technologies are thus constructions and reconstructions through use.

2. Problem solving is a technology when we envision future needs to address similar problems (e.g., workshop activities become an agenda, then a model, then tangible materials, e.g., a Web site, poster, handout, then online technology). Thus, *being* a technology is a relative property expressing the assessment of the fixity of a process and its reusability in future contexts.

3. A device, such as a personal computer, is not a particular technology until it comes into use, after which it can realize any of an indefinite set of possibilities. In that sense, the user is not the recipient of the developer's work but the ultimate creator of the technology; that is, if I use my PC as a doorstop, I have constructed a kind of doorstop technology out of available resources.

4. The cycle of problem solving to technology to next problem solving to next technology, and so forth means that at any given point one can view a technology as a description of the process of past problem solving or as a means for future problem solving.

5. Artifacts manifest the problem-solving activities that give rise to them; compare Madeline Akrich (1992) on the thickness of the metal in a car body, while simultaneously providing the structure for future activity. This view counters both a naïve constructivism that views all activity as totally fluid and agentive. It also counters naïve determinism, which argues that all action is fixed, independent of experience and human action.

Technology is thus the reconstruction of lived experience, which is essentially the definition of learning found within progressive education. Technology has impact, and we become conscious of its meaning. It prepares us for future experiences. It helps us perform tasks, but more fundamentally, it is in a sense a definition of learning. A corollary of this is that users participate in technology design and use, even if they are not engineers. They do so because the continual design of technology is lived experience. Design is what happens when people incorporate technology into their lives.

Progressive education centers the discourse on living life in a democratic society. From that center, we look out to terms like informatics, learning, and literacy as aspects of democratic participation. The question shifts from "does this tool help people develop literacy skills?" to "how does this research inform our understanding of relations between literacy, community, and technology for people desiring to participate in a democratic society?"

Research Vignettes: New Literacies and Community Inquiry

In this section we examine five cases in which the themes of literacy and lived experience, community, and technology recur. We use the five elements of the inquiry cycle presented previously to avoid recapitulating the division into academic disciplines that has stood in the way of deeper understanding in this field. The case studies exemplify a diverse array of community inquiry projects in terms of five focal questions:

- *Ask:* How do literate activities arise out of experiences in communities, including dimensions of morality and social justice?
- *Investigate:* How do communities both use and construct the tools for literacy?
- *Create:* How do people create and live new roles as they appropriate technologies into their lived experience?
- *Discuss:* How do communities address conflicts or bring multiple perspectives together? What are the reciprocal relations between the individual and the community in these processes?
- *Reflect:* How do individuals in communities make sense of their experiences for themselves and for others?

While each vignette represents the ways that multiple technologies are created and used to transform situations, all draw on the *Inquiry Page* (http://inquiry.uiuc.edu), a collective endeavor in research and practice that began over a decade ago to support community inquiry (Benson & Bruce, 2001; Bruce & Easley, 2000). Participants in the site include community activists, teachers, museum educators, librarians, university students and faculty, scientists, and others engaged in a variety of lifelong and informal learning activities.

An extension of the *Inquiry Page* is the *Community Inquiry Laboratory or iLab,* which is free, open source, collaboratively designed software that allows people to craft their own interactive Web sites (http://ilabs.inquiry.uiuc.edu). Their Web sites provide a place where members of a community can come together online to develop shared capacity and collaborate in identifying and addressing problems. Thus, users are developers through their creation of the site content, their contributions to the interface, and their evaluations, and often simply by discussion within the inquiry community of its usefulness, as well as their reports of what works and what does not work in the context of their own settings of use (Bruce, 2001; Bruce & Bishop, 2002; Bruce et al., 2003; Comstock, Bruce, & Harnisch, 2003).

Ask: Literate Activities Arising out of Experience

Our first case study is of the Paseo Boricua neighborhood in Chicago, where we have been learning from, and collaborating with, teachers, students, and youth activists for several years, largely through work with the Dr. Pedro Albizu Campos High School and the Café Teatro Batey Urbano. We chose this example because it arises from a vital, multigenerational urban collective whose community inquiry has produced stunning benefits for local residents, university learners, and scholarship alike (Alicea, 2001; Antrop-González, 2003; Arocho, 2001; de Genova & Ramos-Zayas, 2003; Flores-Gonzalez, 2001, 2002; Flores-Gonzalez, Rodriguez, & Rodriguez-Muniz, 2006; Johnson, 2004, 2005; Perez, 2001; Rinaldo, 2002). With its guiding principles of "the community *is* the curriculum" and "live and help others to live," it also represents significant and interesting relations between a minority community and new literacies. Some of these relations recapitulate what many others have found about young people and the use of new technologies, and all of their positive and negative aspects. But some of these relations reveal quite different uses of new technologies and different stances toward them. We devote some space to considering the diverse set of practices found in this high school and the surrounding community because it is important to begin any investigation of communities such as this on the terms of the community itself, rather than employing *a priori* assumptions about what new literacies are, how they are typically enacted, and what their value is.

For example, the Café Teatro Batey Urbano is a youth-led venue for cultural expression and social action in the community. One evening, Juan David Martinez, aka Ghost—a student at Dr. Pedro Albizu Campos High School—performed the following poem (Copyright 2006, Juan David Martinez, used with permission).

Cyberwashed

I can't stand this anymore

Young people selling their souls

To the devil in the streets

To the one-eyed monster cable,

Satellite, video, DVD.

If you want you can even pause live T.V.

Looking @ the real world through a

One-sided glass box,

MTV

BET

ABC

123

LMNOP

QRXYZ

Just let me be,

Maybe I'll tune into a station when it's

Called free,

Free of stereotypes and scripted reality shows

That don't represent my surreal life,

Having to deal with BIG Brother

Looking over my shoulder,

Or whether I will be a survivor

In this RAT RACE.

Welcome to the Cyber Revolution

You got mail

You got mail

You got mail

I don't need your freakin' mail

AOL

MSN

And Net Zero,

Leaving the money in your pocket

At a total of zero,

Yahoo,

Black Planet,

& MiGente*.

Not really being MiGente,

Because you see,

If you really want to see MiGente,

You can go to the streets,

also consider research on how people use technology as they investigate problems in the context of their community. This research shows that people use a diverse variety of information and communication tools and materials as they learn, collaborate, and communicate. These tools are the most valuable when they speak in a language and with a purpose that matches the lived experience of participants. We need more research on what materials are authentic, challenging, and productive, for different situations. This research on tools and materials must be done in partnership with the people affected (Alkalimat & Williams, 2001).

For our second vignette, we turn to SisterNet, a grassroots organization of Black women in Champaign, Illinois, founded by Imani Bazzell. SisterNet has developed many programs for women that nurture both healthy lifestyles and community activism. These are akin to community-based research at Hull House, which involved women in empirical investigations of local conditions in their neighborhoods, such as child labor and tenement deaths resulting from the city's lack of garbage services (Addams, 1912).

The Afya project united SisterNet women with university affiliates in a process of community inquiry. Its primary aim was to engage Black women in investigating and improving health information and services, while simultaneously nurturing their interest, proficiency, and participation related to computers and the Internet. Afya was concerned with developing new social technologies as well as new digital tools and resources for community-based learning (Bishop, Mehra, Bazzell, & Smith, 2003). Afya experimented with action circles and community-based workshops as social arrangements to make productive use of difference in pursuing both health and technology literacy; *Inquiry Page* technologies were recreated in the process.

Scenarios collected in focus groups helped to understand the social context of Afya members' investigations into health care and technology. We were able to identify the most pressing problems (i.e., provider relationships, common diseases, lack of relevant health information, and lack of culturally relevant and appealing health information on the Internet). These scenarios reveal something of the lifestyle, knowledge, and capacity of SisterNet women.

Scenario examples

It's hard to know if it is really racism or if the healthcare providers are being pushed. The fact that if a Black woman presents with abdominal pains the first thing they want to do is run a series of venereal disease tests on her, whether that is the issue or not.

[Doctors] walk in there, and they start spurting off these words in their lingo, and they're saying this and that. Talk to me in layman's terms because I don't know what's going on. They really do rely on us not to ask too many questions. Luckily for me, like I said, I have an aunt who has been through everything possible, and she asks more questions. That's what's really good about having people like that in your lives.

The scenarios also helped us develop a community action plan, based on SisterNet's action circle model. This plan was designed to address the identified needs of this group and to respond to their desire for building capacity. Community action plan items included the following:

> Establish an action circle to develop a website featuring jargon-free, culturally appropriate health information for our physical, emotional, spiritual, and intellectual well-being; chat and bulletin board space; news; tips; and public policy information. Establish an action circle to organize an African American women's health fair designed to increase knowledge about health concerns and resources and provide opportunities for interaction between health information and service providers and community women.

The action plan highlights SisterNet women as participating in both the construction and the use of tools for literacy. SisterNet women's investigations into health and technology were intertwined. The project picked up momentum when community inquiry was explicitly recognized as our theoretical framework. SisterNet workshops conducted at the annual health fairs and symposia moved from a model of training in Internet searching to developing and using tools to support learning. SisterNet action circle members, who included SisterNet women along with faculty and students, used the *Inquiry Page* to develop an online Inquiry Unit that was to create a personal health action plan, a practice that was established as an ongoing feature of annual SisterNet symposia.

The "Investigate" section of the online Inquiry Unit contained a list of resources, both online and offline, that would help SisterNet women learn how to achieve better health. The resources were assembled and annotated by all action circle members. In symposia workshops led by SisterNet women, participants learned how to access the personal action plan Inquiry Unit and browse items in the "Investigate" portion of the unit. Then, they discussed the rationale behind creating a simple action plan to help them pursue small improvements in their daily lives, before "spinning off" their own Inquiry Unit and entering their personal action plans in its "Create" section:

Instructions for creating an action plan

Are you ready to create your own personal financial health plan?

Here we go ...

Let's start by writing down three things you will do or would like to accomplish in the next three months to improve your financial health.

Personal action plan created by one SisterNet woman

- Find out my pension options and rollover pension into Roth IRA
- Acquire a copy of my credit report
- Contact VA to find out what my housing options are
- Begin a peace of mind fund

The "Discuss" section of the Inquiry Unit was used to prompt discussion in the workshop about barriers to successful action and how they could be overcome. The "Reflect" section invited women to think about what they had learned in the workshop.

To prepare for a SisterNet health fair, another action circle was charged with developing an activity that would help women investigate water quality while gaining additional exposure to digital resources. Here, an Inquiry Unit was created that outlined a process for collecting and testing local water samples and then entering the data online. Another Inquiry Unit was devoted to learning more about the importance of drinking water and critically assessing the benefits of store-bought bottled water. Women and girls attending the health fair conducted water quality tests and entered their data.

The collaboration with SisterNet fed into significant design investigations and enhancements for the *Inquiry Page*. One was the development of several different Inquiry Unit templates, including one with less academic jargon. SisterNet women also wanted their Inquiry Units to be more seamlessly integrated into their SisterNet Web site. Working through this problem led to an increased focus on how to promote what we came to call "distributed inquiry" and, in fact, to prototyping the first version of *iLabs*.

Taking a larger view, our work with SisterNet helps us interrogate the public role of professionals and the manner of their professional preparation (Cuban & Hayes, 2001; Curry, 2005; Hawisher & Selfe, 1999; Hyland & Noffke, 2005; Regenspan, 2002; Smith, 1994). Framed within community inquiry, educators and new media designers have a responsibility to society that goes beyond conveying so-called technical expertise (Boyte, 2000; Sullivan, 2004). Professionals also need to capitalize on the knowledge and commitment that novice community members contribute. Addams (1912) employed women's club members around the country to collect data on child labor because they were the ones who both cared enough to conduct the investigation and were knowledgeable enough to accurately gauge the age of the children they observed in factories. Similarly, SisterNet women contributed to the design and implementation of iLab software because they cared about creating software to support community inquiry and they knew what functionality and usability features would be appropriate for its intended users.

Create: Appropriating Technology

In this section, we consider research linked with action, following Dewey's (1938/1991) argument that inquiry is both thinking and action in the world.

How do people appropriate technologies, engage in collaborative learning, create, and live new roles? Our example is the *Inquiry Kit* (http://gslis.org/index.php?title=Inquiry_kit), which was developed as a class project in a graduate-level course on inquiry-based learning. Graduate students had engaged in a lively discussion following their viewing of the video documentary, *A Private Universe*. This video shows that even Harvard graduates had not learned basic astronomy concepts taught in elementary school, such as the reason we have seasons. Watching others work through the concepts provoked curiosity about those ideas but, more importantly, about how anyone learns and whether familiar models based on transmission and individual learning really work. This led to their choosing the Moon as the focal point for a class inquiry and project.

To begin with, the abstract conceptualization of the Moon was questioned. Students asked the following questions: "How can one teach the Moon's phases?" "What are the various translations and meanings for the word 'Moon'? Are the words 'Moon' and 'month' correlated in all languages?" "What are the representations of the Moon in our lives?" "How complex is learning about the Moon's motions?" "Are there cultural icons of the Moon?" "Are there specific cultural events to celebrate the Moon?" "How old are the explanations about the Moon, and what are their histories?" The diversity of these questions reflected the cultural and subject-oriented variety in the students' community of inquiry. As they asked about the Moon as a social, cultural, and educational phenomenon, they considered various issues:

- the discrepancies between the scientific view of the Moon as universal and the cultural approaches and various interpretations of the Moon;
- the tension between learning about the Moon as a scientific phenomenon and personal understandings/meanings given to the Moon;
- alternative educational ways in understanding Moon's motion, color, existence, measurement, and so on;
- the Moon as a particular phenomenon in different disciplines; and
- the Moon as stereotype in social contexts.

The inquiry conducted to address these issues soon became an action project—to build a kit representing their own learning and providing resources for others. The kit was both physical, a box with various objects and books, and an electronic text in the form of a wiki. Its design drew from diverse published sources, such as Eleanor Duckworth's (1987) "Teaching as Research" essay, Web instructional references, learning and information technologies, and course readings, but also from a variety of community resources, such as the community college planetarium, the art museum, and the host of the astronomy program on a local public radio station. In addition, its motive force was the desire to create something useful for communities beyond the classroom. These included local teachers, planetarium visitors, after-school programs, individuals with interests either in the moon or in inquiry in general, and anyone with Web access who might find something of value in the kit.

Students drew upon a wide variety of digital technologies, such as e-mail, a bulletin board, collaborative document sharing, wikis, Web searching, as well as others specific to the project, such as astronomy image files and simulations. They also used many nondigital tools, for example, to make various solar system models. As they used these technologies, they also transformed them, or appropriated them to their purposes. In some cases, this meant creating hybrid technologies, such as a digital photo library showing pages from a paper-based journal. This was done in order to communicate the inquiry process as well as to provide a model for others who might do similar projects. Figure 25.3 shows one page from one of those journals.

Here is a sample entry:

3/13/06 This past Friday in Indiana, I glimpsed an almost full moon. It was very bright, and wispy clouds floated across. What was most interesting was the wide halo around it. The inner circle was whitish-yellow, then turning into orange, and then a reddish-pink. Why those colors? Does it have to do with refraction through clouds?

The moon study showed that when people have the opportunity to create and to be actively involved, they can build a community of inquiry, design practices and artifacts that extend beyond what they could have envisioned originally, contribute to larger community needs, and learn more in the process. Yet, questions remain for the moon project and for similar classroom-centered activities: Can that kind of collaborative activity extend to the community beyond the protective wall of the school? Can we transform research on this kind of learning by involving participants more? Can we begin to see the community as the curriculum?

Discuss: Multiple Perspectives Meeting in Community Dialogue

In this section, we look at research emphasizing collaboration and dialogue in inquiry where learning, community, and technology intersect. This research shows the importance of dialogue and community participation; it also reveals some of the challenges in developing more effective dialogue and how to support it (Day, Farenden, & Goss, 2006; Lissonnet & Nevile, 2007; McQuillan, 2006; Merkel, Clitherow, Farooq, & Xiao, 2005). Further, it shows that people learn through listening and talking (articulating their own understandings). We need more research on how dialogue operates, how different communication tools support dialogue in different ways. And it needs to be participatory—research with a strong basis in dialogue across differences among research participants.

The next case is an after-school, homework-help program established for the children of new Spanish-speaking immigrant families at the B. T. Wash-

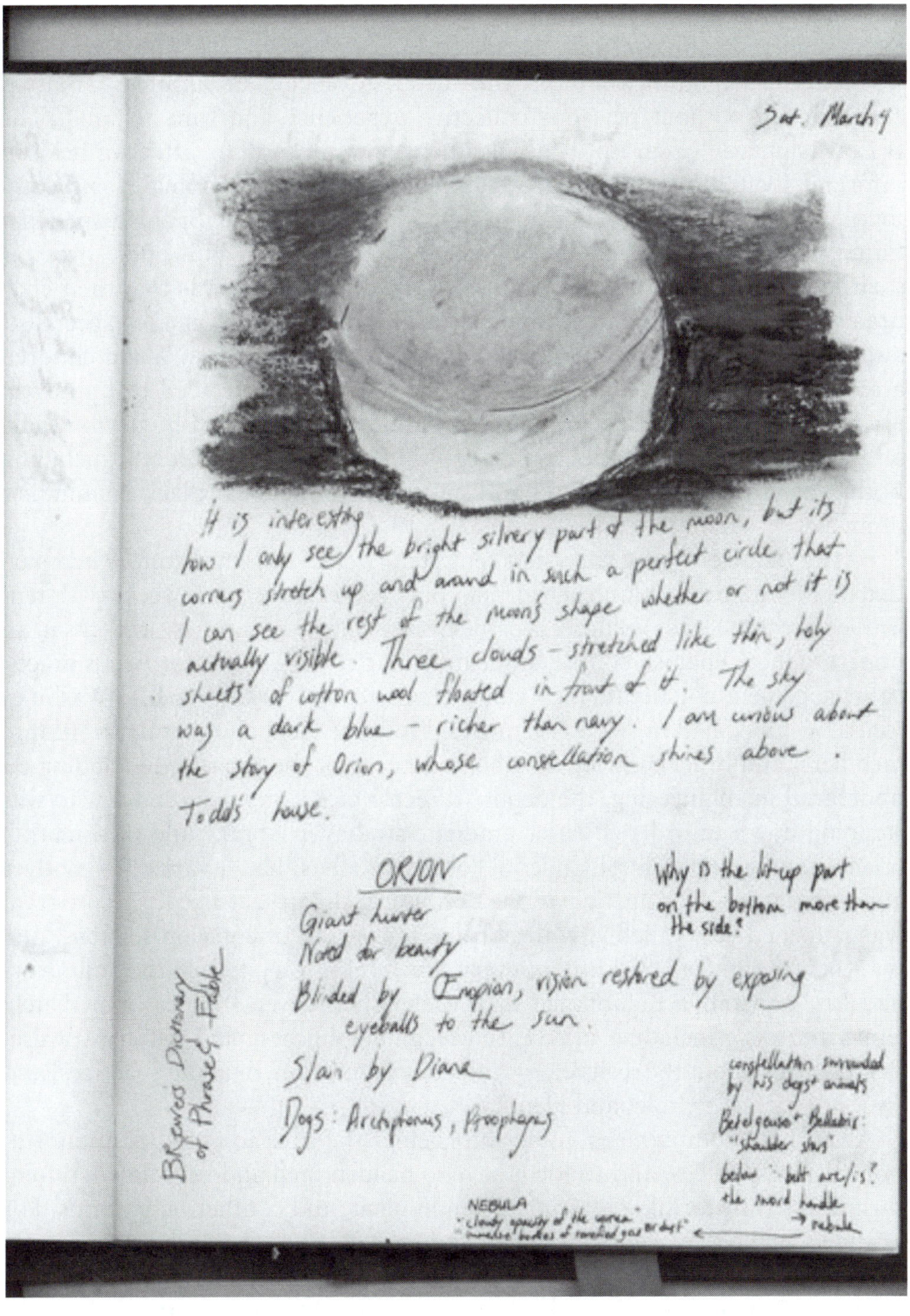

Figure 25.3 Excerpt from a moon journal.

ington Elementary School in Champaign, Illinois. It illustrates the potential and challenge of meaningful communication across difference with technologies (Monroe, 2004; Nardi & O'Day, 1999). In contrast to Paseo Boricua, the community of inquiry formed very quickly, in response to mutual concern, but without previous collective experience and time to bind. The B.T. Washington program came into being several months after we held an informal focus group with parents at Shadow Wood, a mobile home community in which about 60% of the residents are recent Spanish-speaking immigrants who are struggling to make ends meet and build new lives for their families. The primary concern expressed by parents was that their children were falling behind in school. The principal, librarian, literacy specialist, and teachers at B.T. Washington, which many of the Shadow Wood children attended, were eager to help and very supportive. We decided to house the all-volunteer run program in the school's library and offered homework help and other learning activities 3 days a week for about 14 children, including both those from Shadow Wood and several from the local Black community immediately surrounding the school.

By the end of the program's first semester, over 25 volunteer tutors had participated, with each volunteer working only several hours per week, with tenures of 2 to 12 weeks. Volunteers came from a variety of sources: students in an undergraduate Spanish course, students in our community informatics practical engagement course, literacy volunteers already working at B.T. Washington, long-time Shadow Wood volunteers from the local community, fraternity members, and other individuals who had heard of the program, including an undergrad in engineering, the deputy director of a campus museum who was stepping down in order to enter graduate studies in library and information science, and a high school student. Volunteers, thus, had a variety of motives and expectations for participation. Because of the urgent need, the program was launched very quickly, with no time for overall orientation sessions, and with new volunteers trickling in every few weeks. Very few of the volunteers had any previous acquaintance with each other. Several issues immediately came into play, including differential technology access and patterns of use, assumptions about the technology and communication, existing practices, and issues of hierarchy, role, and identity.

When new communities come into being, the myriad roles, communication patterns, values, and so forth have to be identified and negotiated. Often, this means transforming existing, often implicit, and conflicting patterns. For example, while they were very active and engaged in their one-on-one interactions with the children, some of our undergraduate student tutors saw their roles as minimal engagement in designing program activities, requiring commitment overall. For example, a crisis arose when only one tutor out of six showed up on the day before spring break. It became apparent that e-mail and the Web would be crucial to sharing information and building common base of knowledge among the diverse and loosely bound volunteer participants. We created an iLab for the B.T. Washington program, which housed schedules, participant rosters, rules and guidelines, a volunteer pledge, program forms, worksheets for specific activities, and so forth. While our iLab and e-mail use did not solve all of our volunteer coordination, communication, and community-building problems, at least it allowed for core knowledge to be accessed and disseminated, and it provided a common home base for volunteers, where no physical base existed.

Another situation desperately calling for discussion across difference was perceived cultural, ethnic, and literacy gaps inherent in the group of children and in their relationships with the volunteers. Girls sat together, apart from the boys. Mexican children sat together, apart from the Black children. Slights were noted, as in the complaint from one of the Black children that "You let the Mexican kids on the computer more than us." All of the children were much more proficient with verbal communication than reading and writing, and few had any experience with computers and the Internet.

To address this situation, we took an asset-based approach, modeled on Moll's community funds of knowledge work, which illustrates how members of the community have deep funds of knowledge which are often disjoint from those of mainstream disciplinary communities and mainstream schools (Moll et al., 1992). We wanted to emphasize what the kids knew and were good at, like chess, origami, and magic tricks, and to use that to build positive self-image, respect for each other, and literacy. The kids expressed interest in learning how to make their own Web pages, so we introduced them to the B.T. Washington iLab and showed them how to make Inquiry Units. They showed incredible patience with stubborn technology, spending a lot of time laboriously striving to enter their passwords correctly. They liked making Inquiry Units and were more amenable to writing with the computer than with pencil and paper. And the world came into their writing as they expressed their feelings about being different:

Example 1: Calling Names

Kyla Morris thats my name poeple at school call me names I go home and tell my mom but when I go to school they throw me in the pond

Kyla Morris thats my name count to three its still the same turn the rope and watch me spin quick desiree jump on in.

Example 2: Michael

I am a good preson I like to play kickball and soccer. When I go home I am going to go outside and play wath cyria malky lacyria and shacyria and khiri

Example 3: Exploring Rosa

How much they pay to the soccer team. What T-shirt you need to use. We need to buy are shoes to play soccer.

http://www.womensoccer.com/gsw

I Like to play soccer. I want to be a star of soccer.

Example 4: Exploring Juan

Hi, my name is Juan Munoz. I like to play soccer and like to watch wrestling. My favorite wrestler is Ray Mysterio

[with links to images from a wrestling Web site]

Interactions around literacy expanded when an undergraduate art student joined the volunteer group to do an independent study—making with the children a film that documented what they were good at doing. Children gained technical and social skills in the process of making the movie. They also expanded their literacy skills by writing memos to their parents requesting permission to participate in the filmmaking. Further, the video spurred the creation of an iLab video archive for a variety of similar community-based projects. This video archive has now come to serve the needs of other community projects.

Reflect: Making Sense of Experiences

Jane Addams and others working in the Hull House community saw that education is a reconstruction of daily experience, which relates it to both the past and contemporary life. Diversity of experiences among community members was not an obstacle, but instead, a resource for learning, especially when there were opportunities for dialogue and critical engagement with others. In an essay on the education of immigrant children, Addams (1908/2002) noted, "We send young people to Europe to see Italy, but we do not utilize Italy when it lies about the schoolhouse" (p. 238). She realized that there were enormous funds of knowledge within the community (cf. Moll et al., 1992). Building upon that knowledge was the only approach to education and social change that had any chance of success.

One cannot look at the experiences of Hull House or contemporary community action projects, such as the Youth Action Research Institute (Berg & Schensul, 2004; Schensul, 2005; http://www.incommunityresearch.org/research/yari.htm) without being struck by the separation between much of life in communities and life in formal education, including universities; this, despite the fact that the rhetoric of education at all levels refers consistently to meeting the needs of individuals and communities. "Learning communities" in the school setting are remarkably immune from the communities lying about the schoolhouse.

If we ask the question "what does the university know?" we might say that it claims to know everything. Certainly, it embodies through its libraries, research facilities, courses, and people the knowledge of diverse disciplines. But it is curious that the typical university does poorly at reconstructing its own daily experience. It knows little about itself (its learning community). It knows even less about its relation to the communities in which it participates. Moreover, these limitations in its knowledge are perpetuated by the fact that it knows little about how to inquire within and beyond its walls on these topics.

One example of a project to address this separation of university and community is *Ethnography of the University Initiative (EUI)* (http://www.eotu.uiuc.edu). It began with two primary motivations. One was to engage undergraduates in research. The second was to build a repository of knowledge about the university from the experiences of those living within it. This repository would supplement the usual contents of a university archive, such as addresses by the Chancellor, budgets, organizational charts, course syllabi, and so forth. To date, there have been 50 courses in various disciplines participating in the project. It is now expanding to other campuses. Students gather data through photographs, video, interviews, document analysis, surveys, and discussions. They create Inquiry Units for ethnographies to represent what they have learned. Their studies have led to changes in the courses involved and for themselves. They are helping to change the definition of what a university archive can be, and their findings can change the university or the surrounding communities. Thus, they are exemplifying inquiry as transformation of an indeterminate situation.

The project also illustrates what happens when users are not merely recipients of a design for inquiry, but take an active role in creating that design. The project became a major driver of the *Inquiry Page* and the *Community Inquiry Labs* as students and faculty discovered new ways of defining an inquiry cycle and using online Inquiry Units. They wanted different terms for aspects of inquiry and greater flexibility in defining steps in the process. They also sought tools to support more collaboration, such as comments on Inquiry Units. A major need was a more elaborate scheme for access, one that would permit sharing of findings across groups where that was appropriate, but also privacy for participants where that was needed. In this process, participants in Ethnography of the University recreate the very technologies they are using, their own tools for further inquiry. This is the essence of the pragmatic technology idea. Table 25.1 shows a set of student ethnographies of the university, which were presented at a student conference in Spring 2006.

In EOTU, students learn about themselves and responsible action in the community. Many learn about how to make positive social change. In the end, most faculty report that they learn more about the disciplines as well.

Table 25.1 Student Ethnographies of the University

Author, Title
Michael Cozza, The Introduction of a Neophyte into Gaming Culture
Kaitlin Sulkowski, A Look into the Social Phenomenon of Facebook
Aly Marchetti, The Daniels Street ATM on Wednesday Nights
Jonathan Wassell, The Life of the Off-Campus Student
Christina Miceli and Kari Schmehil, Two Tattoo Parlors
Jennifer Mull, Unethical Treatment of Volunteers
Amy Franco, Technology in the Illini Union Vending Room
Ben Krop, Justin Meyer, and Nipa Patel, University Grading Issues and Policies
Kurt Rottunda, Chinese Students on the U of I Campus
Louis Morton, Coffee Talk: Language in Cafes Across Campus
Suzanne Perkins, Ethnography of the Language of Creative Writers
Nate Harmann, Acting and Acting Myths
Nicholas Murphy, The MTD 22 Illini
Christine Travers, Ethnography of the Urbana Fire Department
Andrew Meyer, Three Hours that Changed the World: T. K. Cureton
Tiffany White, Student Workouts at WIMPE
John Noble, The Canopy Club and Its Culture
Bryan Calip and Laura Haning, Scott Hall and Video Gaming
Cole Cullen, Residents' Use of the Gregory Drive Computer Lab
David Lai, College Gamers: Their Technology, Their Academics
Allie Wyler, Technology Used in Special Education
Angela Marconi, WPGU: Technology and Tension of Corporate Media
Daniel Edgerton, The UIUC Account Billing Office
Joe Bottalla, The Behavior of Aviation Students
Maria Frias, Coming Out Stories at the U of I
Lissette Uriostegui, The Technology and Creativity of the Metal-Smithing Community
Andrea Henderson, Greenhouse Workers in the Plant Biology Conservatory and Their Technology
Chris Manna, Those Who Work out in the ISR Weight Room

Conclusion

The research discussed in this chapter echoes Ladson-Billings' (2006) call to frame immediate issues of achievement in education within the larger issue of education debt, within which she included the historical, income, wealth, socio-political, and moral debts accumulated by (United States) society with respect to African American, Latino/a, Native American, and other groups. Starting with community as a key term reminds us that learning and literacy are always embedded within social and economic structures and processes (see also Oakes & Rogers, 2006).

Writing about the conditions necessary for the Great Society to become a Great Community, Dewey (1927) wrote,

The highest and most difficult kind of inquiry and a subtle, delicate, vivid and responsive art of communication must take possession of the physical machinery of transmission and circulation and breathe life into it. When the machine age has thus perfected its machinery it will be a means of life and not its despotic master. Democracy will come into its own, for democracy is a name for a life of free and enriching communion. It had its seer in Walt Whitman. It will have its consummation when free social inquiry is indissolubly wedded to the art of full and moving communication. (p. 184)

Two generalizations emerge from this review: First, beyond the acquisition of specific skills and knowledge, education entails that individuals develop in a reciprocal relationship with the development of community and society. Second, the development of responsible citizens requires a process of community inquiry, one that occurs across people from all occupations, social classes, and in all situations. Given this, it is puzzling that so little research focuses explicitly on the processes of community inquiry. One explanation is that the lack of an inquiry perspective makes it all too easy to fragment or separate aspects of activity.

To take a concrete example, service-learning, which might be considered as the epitome of engaged citizenship, is often reduced, in both research and practice, to a narrowly defined activity with discrete and limited curriculum goals. Thus, researchers might ask questions about whether students learned specific skills and developed self-esteem. But they shy away from bigger questions of whether the activity truly transforms society or the students. The same argument could be made for research in community informatics, literacy acquisition, technology design, and related areas. Our academic disciplines, with systems of rewards and punishments, are political forces that marginalize any challenges to the established order. And our strongly ingrained habits to look at minute but easily achievable goals, all conspire to make us keep a little distance from larger questions such as: What kind of society should we have? How can we truly achieve full participation? What are the real conditions for full development of individuals and society?

When we speak about literacy we need to do so with the view of the world we hope to inhabit. We hope that this chapter indicates the value of looking beyond established modes of thinking about these questions and itself fosters community inquiry in a deep and collaborative way.

References

Addams, J. (1912). *Twenty years at Hull-House with autobiographical notes.* New York: MacMillan.

Addams, J. (2002). The subjective necessity for social settlements. In J. B. Elshtain (Ed.), *The Jane Addams reader* (pp. 14–28). New York: Basic. (Original work published 1893.)

Addams, J. (2002). The public school and the immigrant child. In J. B. Elshtain (Ed.), *The Jane Addams reader* (pp. 235–239). New York: Basic. (Original work published 1908.)

Akrich, M. (1992). The description of technical objects. In W. E. Bijker & J. Law (Eds.), *Shaping technology/building society—studies in sociotechnical change* (pp. 205–224). Cambridge, MA: The MIT Press.

Alicea, M. (2001, Fall). Cuando nosotros viviamos ... : Stories of displacement and settlement in Puerto Rican Chicago. *Centro Journal, 13*(2), 167–195.

Alkalimat, A., & Williams, K. (2001). Social capital and cyberpower in the African American community: A case study of a community technology center in the dual city. In L. Keeble & B. Loader (Eds.), *Community informatics: Shaping computer mediated social relations* (pp. 177–204) . London: Routledge. Retrieved November 30, 2006, from http://www.communitytechnology.org/cyberpower/

Anderson, B. (1991). *Imagined communities: Reflections on the origin and spread of nationalism* (2nd ed.). London: Verso.

Anglin, G. J., & Morrison, G. R. (2002). Evaluation and research in distance education. In C. Vrasidas & G. Glass (Eds.), *Distance education and distributed learning* (pp. 157–180). Greenwich, CT: Information Age.

Antler, J. (1987). *Lucy Sprague Mitchell: The making of a modern woman.* New Haven, CT: Yale University Press.

Antrop-González, R. (2003). This school is my sanctuary—the Dr. Pedro Albizu Campos Alternative High School. *Centro Journal, 15*(2), 233–255.

Arocho, E. (2001). They wear Zapatos de Arco-Iris (rainbow shoes) to the Epiphany/Rumba Time Bomb. *Centro Journal, 13*(2), 96–97.

Bello, W. (2006, March 3). Military radicalism in Venezuela: How relevant for other developing countries? *Focus on the Global South.* Retrieved December 14, 2006, from http://www.focusweb.org/content/view/833/26/

Benson, A. P., & Bruce, B. C. (2001). Using the Web to promote inquiry and collaboration: A snapshot of the Inquiry Page's development. *Teaching Education, 12*(2), 153–163.

Benson, L., Harkavy, I., & Puckett, J. (2007). *Dewey's dream: Universities and democracies in an age of education reform.* Philadelphia, PA: Temple University Press.

Bentley, A. F. (1941). The human skin: Philosophy's last line of defense. *Philosophy of Science, 8*(1), 1–19.

Berdan, K., Boulton, I., Eidman-Aadahl, E., Fleming, J., Gardner, L., Rogers, I., & Solomon, A. (2006). *Writing for a change: Boosting literacy and learning through social action.* New York: Jossey-Bass

Berg, M. J., & Schensul, J. J. (Eds.). (2004). Approaches to conducting action research with youth [Special issue]. *Practicing Anthropology, 26*(2).

Bieber, M., Civille, R., Gurstein, M., & White, N. (2002). *A white paper exploring research trends and issues in the emerging field of community informatics.* Retrieved November 30, 2006, from http://www.is.njit.edu/vci/vci-white-paper.doc

Bishop, A. P., & Bruce, B. C. (2005). Community informatics: Integrating action, research and learning. *Bulletin of the American Society for Information Science and Technology, 31*(6). Retrieved November 30, 2006, from http://www.asis.org/Bulletin/Aug-05/bishopbruce.html

Bishop, A. P., Mehra, B., Bazzell, I., & Smith, C. (2003). Participatory action research and digital libraries: Reframing evaluation. In A. P. Bishop, B. Buttenfield, & N. Van House (Eds.), *Digital library use: Social practice in design and evaluation* (pp. 161–189). Cambridge: MIT Press.

Boyer Commission on Educating Undergraduates in the Research University. (1998). *Reinventing undergraduate education: A blueprint for America's research universities.* Retrieved November 30, 2006, from http://naples.cc.sunysb.edu/Pres/boyer.nsf/

Boyte, H. C. (2000). *Public engagement in a civic mission: A case study.* Washington, D.C.: The Council on Public Policy Education.

Boyte, H. C. (2003). A different kind of politics: John Dewey and the meaning of citizenship in the 21st century. *The Good Society, 12*(2), 1–15.

Bruce, B. C. (2001). The Inquiry Page: A collaboratory for curricular innovation. *Learning Technology, 3*(1).

Bruce, B. C. (2002). New technologies and social change: Learning in the global cyberage. In L. Bresler & A. Ardichvili (Eds.), *Research in international education: Experience, theory, and practice* (pp. 171–190). New York: Peter Lang.

Bruce, B. C. (Ed.). (2003). *Literacy in the information age: Inquiries into meaning making with new technologies.* Newark, DE: International Reading Association.

Bruce, B. C., & Bishop, A. P. (2002). Using the Web to support inquiry-based literacy development. *Journal of Adolescent and Adult Literacy, 45*(8), 706–714.

Bruce, B. C., Bishop, A. P., Heidorn, P. B., Lunsford, K. J., Poulakos, S., & Won, M. (2003). The inquiry page: Bridging digital libraries to learners. *Knowledge Quest, 31*(3), 15–17.

Bruce, B. C., & Davidson, J. (1996). An inquiry model for literacy across the curriculum. *Journal of Curriculum Studies, 28*(3), 281–300.

Bruce, B. C., & Easley, J. A., Jr. (2000). Emerging communities of practice: Collaboration and communication in action research. *Educational Action Research, 8*(2), 243–259.

Bruce, B. C., & Hogan, M. P. (1998). The disappearance of technology: Toward an ecological model of literacy. In D. Reinking, M. McKenna, L. Labbo, & R. Kieffer (Eds.), *Handbook of literacy and technology: Transformations in a post-typographic world* (pp. 269–281). Hillsdale, NJ: Erlbaum.

Bruce, B. C., Peyton, J. K., & Batson, T. W. (Eds.). (1993). *Network-based classrooms: Promises and realities.* New York: Cambridge University Press.

Bruce, B. C., & Rubin, A. D. (1993). *Electronic quills: A situated evaluation of using computers for writing in classrooms.* Hillsdale, NJ: Lawrence Erlbaum.

Clark, G. (1994). Rescuing the discourse of community. *College Composition and Communication, 45*(1), 61–74.

Cohen, A. P. (1985). *The symbolic construction of community.* London: Tavistock.

Comstock, S. L., Bruce, B. C., & Harnisch, D. (2003). Scientists becoming teachers: Lessons learned from teacher partnerships. In *Proceedings of the Society for Information Technology and Teacher Education, International Conference.* Norfolk, VA: Association for the Advancement of Computing in Education.

Creech, H., Berthe, O., Assubuji, A. P., Mansingh, I., & Anjelkovic, M. (2006). *Evaluation of UNESCO's community multimedia centres: Final report* (Report No. IOS/EVS/PI/54). Paris: United Nations Educational, Scientific, and Cultural Organization.

Cremin, L. (1964). *The transformation of the school: Progressivism in American education, 1876–1957.* New York: Vintage Books Editions.

Cuban, S., & Hayes, E. (2001). Perspectives of five library and information studies students involved in service-learning at a community-based literacy program. *Journal of Education for Library and Information Science, 42*(2), 86–95.

Curry, A. (2005). Action research in action: Involving students and professionals. *Proceedings of World Library and Information Congress: 71st IFLA General Conference and Council.* Oslo, Norway: International Federation of Library Associations and Institutions. Retrieved November 30, 2006, from http://www.ifla.org/IV/ifla71/Programme.htm

Cushman, E. (2006). Toward a praxis of new media: Sustainability and capacity building in an Cherokee nation collaborative. *Reflections: A Journal of Writing, Community Literacy, and Service Learning, 4*(3), 254-70.

Cuthbert, A., Clark, D., & Linn, M. (2002). WISE learning communities: Design considerations. In K. A. Renninger & W. Shumar (Eds.), *Building virtual communities: Learning and change in cyberspace* (pp. 215–248). New York: Cambridge University Press.

Day, P., Farenden, C., & Goss, H. (2006, October 9–11). Maps, networks and stories: A community profiling methodology. Paper presented at the 3rd Prato International Community Informatics Conference, Prato, Italy. Retrieved November 30, 2006, from http://www.ccnr.net/files/day.pdf

Joseph, D. M., & Nacu, D. (2003). Designing interesting learning environments: When the medium isn't enough. *Convergence, 9*(2), 84–115.

Keeble, L., & Loader, B. (Eds.). (2001). *Community informatics: Shaping computer mediated social relations.* London: Routledge.

Knorr-Cetina, K. (1999). *Epistemic cultures: How the sciences make knowledge.* Cambridge, MA: Harvard University Press.

Kretzmann, J. P., & McKnight, J. L. (1993). *Building communities from the inside out: A path toward finding and mobilizing a community's assets.* Evanston, Ill.: Center for Urban Affairs and Policy Research, Northwestern University; Chicago: ACTA.

Kvasny, L. (2006). The cultural (re)production of digital inequality. *Information, Communication and Society, 9*(2), 160–181.

Ladson-Billings, G. (2006). From the achievement gap to the education debt: Understanding achievement in U.S. schools. American Educational Research Association presidential address, San Francisco. Retrieved December 14, 2006, from http://www.cmcgc.com/Media/WMP/260407/49_010_files/Default.htm

Lankshear, C., & Knobel, M. (2004, December). "New" literacies: Research and social practice. Plenary address at the Annual Meeting of the National Reading Conference, San Antonio, TX.

Lave, J., & Wenger, E. (1991). *Situated learning: Legitimate peripheral participation.* Cambridge, U.K.: Cambridge University Press.

Linn, M. C. (1996). Cognition and distance learning. *Journal of the American Society for Information Science, 47*(11), 826–842.

Lissonnet, S., & Nevile, L. (2007). A forum for indigenous culture building and preservation. In J. Trant and D. Bearman (eds), *Museums and the Web 2007: Proceedings.* Toronto: Archives & Museum Informatics, published March 31, 2007 at http://www.archimuse.com/mw2007/papers/lissonnet/ lissonnet.html

McCarthy, J., & Wright, P. (2004). *Technology as experience.* Cambridge, MA: MIT Press.

McLaren, P., & Lankshear, C. (Eds.). (1994). *Politics of liberation: Paths from Freire.* London: Routledge.

McNiff, J., & Whitehead, J. (2006). *All you need to know about action research.* London; Sage.

McQuillan, H. (2006, October). As others see us—As we see ourselves: Culture, identity, and representation in a community technology project. Paper presented at the 3rd Prato International Community Informatics Conference, Prato, Italy. Retrieved November 30, 2006, from http://www.ccnr.net/files/McQuillanfinal.zip

McTaggart, R. (1991). *Action research: A short modern history.* Geelong: Deakin University Press.

Merkel, C. B., Clitherow, M., Farooq, U., & Xiao, L. (2005). Sustaining computer use and learning in community computing contexts: Making technology part of who they are and what they do. *The Journal of Community Informatics, 1*(2).

Minstrell, J., & van Zee, E. (Eds.). (2000). *Inquiry into inquiry learning and teaching in science.* Washington, DC: American Association for the Advancement of Science.

Mishra, P., Koehler, M., & Zhao, Y. (Eds.). (in press). *Faculty development by design: Integrating technology in higher education.* Greenwich, CT: Information Age.

Mitchell, L. S. (1931). Cooperative schools for student teachers. *Progressive Education, 8,* 251–255.

Moggridge, A. (2000) Research and practice in community information systems: Learning through human inquiry. In *Fourth international conference of the International Society for Third Sector Research.* Dublin, Ireland: International Society for Third Sector Research. Retrieved November 30, 2006, from http://www.istr.org/conferences/dublin/workingpapers/moggridge.pdf

Moje, E. B. (2000). 'To be part of the story': The literacy practices of 'gangsta' adolescents. *Teachers College Record, 102,* 652–690.

Moll, L. C., Amanti, C., Neff, D., & Gonzalez, N. (1992). Funds of knowledge for teaching: Using a qualitative approach to connect homes and classrooms. *Theory into Practice, 31*(2), 132–141.

Monroe, B. (2004). *Crossing the digital divide: Race, writing, and technology in the classroom.* New York: Teachers College Press.

Nancy, J.-L. (1991). *The inoperative community.* Minneapolis: University of Minnesota Press.

Nardi, B., & O'Day, V. (1999). *Information ecologies: Using technology with heart.* Cambridge, MA: MIT Press.

Oakes, J., & Rogers, J. (with Lipton, M.). (2006). *Learning power: Organizing for social justice.* New York: Teachers College Press.

Olds, H. F., Schwartz, J. L., & Willie, N. A. (1980). *People and computers: Who teaches whom?* Newton, MA: Education Development Center.

Oliver, L. P. (1987). *Study circles: Coming together for personal growth and social change.* Bethesda, MD: Seven Locks Press.

Owen, J. M., Cox, P. L., & Watkins, J. M. (1994). *Genuine reward: Community inquiry into connecting learning, teaching, and assessing.* Andover, MA: Regional Laboratory for Educational Improvement of the Northeast and Islands.

Perez, G. M. (2001). An upbeat West Side Story: Puerto Ricans and postwar racial politics in Chicago. *Centro Journal, 13*(2), 47–71.

Reardon, K. (1998). Participatory action research as service learning. *New Directions for Teaching and Learning, 7,* 57–64.

Regenspan, B. (2002). *Parallel practices: Social justice-focused teacher education and the elementary school classroom.* New York: Peter Lang.

Renninger, K. A., & Shumar, W. (Eds.). (2002). *Building virtual communities: Learning and change in cyberspace.* New York: Cambridge University Press.

Rheingold , H. (1993). *The virtual community: Homesteading on the electronic frontier.* New York: Harper Collins.

Rinaldo, R. (2002). Space of resistance: The Puerto Rican Cultural Center and Humboldt Park. *Cultural Critique, 50,* 135–174.

Robert, P. (1998). Extending literate horizons: Paulo Freire and the multidimensional word. *Educational Review, 50*(2), 105–114.

Schensul, J. (2005). Strengthening communities through research partnerships for social change: Perspectives from the Institute for Community Research. In S. Hyland (Ed.), *Community building in the twenty-first century* (pp. 191–218). Santa Fe, NM: School of American Research.

Schön, D. A. (1983). *The reflective practitioner: How professionals think in action.* New York: Basic Books.

Schuler, D. (1996). *New community networks: Wired for change.* Reading, MA: Addison-Wesley.

Shavelson, R. J., & Towne, L. (Eds.). (2002b). *Scientific research in education.* Washington, DC: National Research Council, National Academy Press.

Smith, M. K. (1994). *Local education: Community, conversation, action.* Buckingham, U.K.: Open University Press.

Smith, M. K. (2000, Fall). Who was Lucy Sprague Mitchell ... and why should you know? *Childhood Education.* Retrieved November 30, 2006, from http://www.findarticles.com/p/articles/mi_qa3614/is_200010/ai_n8907594/

Smith, M. K. (2001). Community. *The encyclopedia of informal education.* Retrieved December 14, 2006, from http://www.infed.org/community/community.htm

Srinivasan, R. (in press). Indigenous and ethnic articulations of new media. *International Journal of Cultural Studies.*

Stoecker, R. (2005). Is community informatics good for communities? Questions confronting an emerging field. *Journal of Community Informatics, 1*(3). Retrieved November 30, 2006, from http://www.ci-journal.net/index.php/ciej/article/view/183/129

Stringer, E. T. (1999). *Action research* (2nd ed.). Thousand Oaks, CA: Sage.

Introduction to Part V

For many, a central issue within the field of new literacies is how best to prepare students for the new literacies of online learning. The chapters in this section reflect the complexities associated with designing and implementing instruction as new technologies enter the classroom and the home. The authors in this section seek to challenge existing classroom practices in relation to ICT use and the digital literacies illuminated in their work; they introduce new ideas about how readers construct meaning from text, they question the role of the classroom teacher, and they challenge traditional understandings of what constitutes and is valued as text. In addition, many of the authors repeatedly highlight the notion that literacy education is undergoing a major paradigm shift. They allude to this shift by describing the gap between current classroom practices and a growing understanding that something different has emerged in the experiences of children and the ways in which they learn with information and communication technologies (ICT).

The authors in this section take full advantage of the complexities of classroom contexts. They provide examples that span a range of age groups (e.g., young children, adolescents, secondary school students, and higher education) and focus on diverse areas of content (e.g., digital writing, popular culture texts, science and math, information research, English, and distance learning). They also urge educators, researchers, and policymakers to go beyond thinking about technology only in terms of tools and implements to integrate the cognitive, social, and cultural dimensions of how digital technologies are used. Collectively, their work illustrates the rich and complex interpretations made possible by observing learners through multiple lenses. From their own perspectives, each contributor acknowledges that we still know far too little about the nature of literacy in relation to ICT and remind us of the urgency to learn more. Further, the authors conceive of learners as agentive, critical, and resourceful and, consequently, encourage educators to think innovatively when designing effective pedagogies that support and extend children's interactions with ICT in both home and school contexts.

The eight chapters in this section introduce a wide range of conceptions of how best to support and extend classroom literacy practices in relation to ICT.

egies required to manage information, solve problems, analyze resources, communicate, and collaborate with new technologies.

Common Themes

In looking across the chapters in this section, at least four common themes are evident. First, the authors bring to the forefront a series of competing discourses about how we define and conceive of literacy and of ICT in schools. There are multiple frameworks, for instance, for thinking about writing instruction, distance learning, technology uses in the classroom, or assessment tasks that capture complex learning with computers in particular domains. Some authors have conceived of these frameworks as either acceptable or unacceptable, while other authors see them as situated along a continuum with levels of appropriateness dependent upon particular curriculum goals or learning purposes. Likewise, the authors clarify the multiple meanings assigned to concepts such as critical literacy, popular culture texts, or learning with technology that may otherwise prompt confusion about how these ideas are integrated into classroom practices. Importantly, the authors in this section note that most current conceptions do not adequately capture the range of new skills or new potentials available. Many illustrate how contemporary texts and audiences are rapidly changing in ways that complicate design efforts, prompt new vocabulary, or otherwise have significant implications for literacy classrooms.

Ironically, a second pattern is that the authors in this section acknowledge that the literacy community has much to learn in understanding the particular skills, practices, processes, and strategies that effectively characterize the rapid and transformative nature of new literacies. The authors stress the urgency required to document the changing needs and skills required of young people growing up in a context where reading and writing onscreen is pervasive. Fabos (Chapter 29), for example, urges people to become aware of the underlying battles for media control and its impact on student access to and use of information. Others recommend more attention be focused on defining the role that motivation and interest play in learning with ICT. Many authors highlight the need to better understand the ways learners collaboratively construct new information rather than just interpreting the texts presented to them.

A third commonality among the authors in this section is summed up by Merchant's (Chapter 26) observation that it is no longer an issue of *if*, but rather *how* educators should provide classroom opportunities that may support, extend, and document literacy work with ICT. These opportunities should reflect the complexity of authentic online experiences and be flexible enough to adapt to the continuous changes prompted by new technologies, new global learning communities, and new ways of thinking. Several authors touch on the importance of fostering critical literacy skills that prepare learners to position themselves in relation to the texts they read. Many also emphasize the multimodal competencies required to move within and across multiple sign systems and forms of communication. Further, the authors urge educators and researchers to recognize the rich diversity of resources and knowledge that learners, even very young ones, bring to school contexts from their daily lives.

Finally, the authors in this section describe the struggle to balance new skills and curriculum goals against current understandings about how students learn literacy and what is appropriate at different stages. Many describe the tensions between meeting calls for innovative teaching that responds to young people's lives and meeting demands for high stakes assessment and educational policy. Several authors acknowledge the limitations set forth by federal mandates and ask us to consider new ways of documenting the complexities of online learning while also thinking about if and how to prompt the transfer of new literacies back to those currently measured in classrooms. Still others describe the challenge of finding a balance between the structure of teaching particular objectives and the need to integrate student dialogue as a purposeful, constructive, and valued aspect of learning.

Questions and Recommendations

The authors in this section also pose a number of questions and recommend next steps for literacy educators, researchers, and policymakers. Several authors wondered, as Pippa Stein (Chapter 30) wrote, if we are "documenting a dying set of practices" (p. 888) by looking only at traditional reading and writing processes rather than teaching young people to comfortably contribute and participate with the multiple text formats and forms of communication they find in global networked environments. More dialogue needs to consider precisely what sort of experiences we want students to have in terms of curriculum goals and instructional models, and further, what pedagogies and resources are needed to support these different sets of curriculum goals.

Another recommendation is to seek pedagogical models that encourage critical engagement with culture and language while finding innovative ways to ensure students have the capacity to assume a critical and informed approach toward information and technology. Many of the authors prompt us to think carefully about how we should most effectively transport new texts and literacy practices from nonschool to school contexts in ways that inform curricular decisions and welcome disenfranchised learners back into the classroom literacy community. Learners of all ages should be provided access to a rich and diverse body of information for them to critically evaluate and synthesize and assessments should be designed to document their ability to do so.

A third recommendation is to continually examine our abilities to prepare students for living and working in a world saturated with ICT. In order to do this, we first need to reach consensus on the knowledge, skills, and practices that constitute new literacies. This will be particularly challenging because new technologies will continue to emerge. Then, we require much more research on ways to flexibly assess new literacies in both formative and summative ways that capture how students apply their abilities in a range of contexts and domains. It is vital that we continue to develop new performance based rubrics that validly and reliably capture the complexities of problem solving in online environments. Further, to address the needs of policymakers, we must think creatively about how best to scale up assessment procedures in order to document effective practices and new applications of knowledge across large groups of students and multiple classroom contexts.

Finally, all eight authors in this section express a deep sense of urgency with respect to the need to take up new definitions and ways of thinking about literacy education in classrooms. Change is upon us, and we must respond. Several authors point out that a failure to embed the range of new literacies of ICT into classroom practices and curriculum goals may simply perpetuate disadvantage and alienation among learners. Yet, at the same time, each chapter provides examples of the potentials inherent in integrating ICT into our literacy programs if we pay attention, work together, think innovatively, and accept the new ways that contemporary children engage with their literacy worlds.

CHAPTER 26

Digital Writing in the Early Years

GUY MERCHANT

SHEFFIELD HALLAM UNIVERSITY, ENGLAND

We live in times of considerable uncertainty—uncertainty about what is important in education, and uncertainty about what matters in the upbringing of young children. Rapid social change makes it difficult for us to envisage the future worlds that the next generation may inhabit, so it is hard for us to know which dispositions, values, and practices will remain important and which new ones may be required. This uncertainty is reflected in the education systems of postindustrial economies, locked, as they are, in a struggle between the valorization of traditional routines and the lure of radically different futures. Technological innovation is a significant force in this struggle and is sometimes seen as a threat to highly valued skills. At other times, it is seen as a way of changing educational practices. Perhaps it is not surprising, then, to find that these positions are played out in the field of literacy education.

Since it is generally accepted that the acquisition of literacy is a prime function of compulsory schooling, the impact of screen-based communication, which has revolutionized the social practices of literacy, demands the serious attention of educationists (Kress, 2003). As new technoliteracy practices become more deeply embedded in society, they impact on ever-younger age groups (Marsh, 2003). What we have come to call "new technology" is ubiquitous in the everyday lives of children, from birth to maturity. A considerable part of the technological environment they inhabit directly involves literacy, both in the broadest sense of the term, and in the more specific domain of alphabetic writing. This chapter focuses on young children's onscreen encounters with lettered representation, the productive aspect of writing with new technology, and the implications that this has for writing pedagogy. Whilst different tools and technologies for screen-based communication continue to be developed, here I use the terms *digital* or *onscreen writing* to refer to alphabetic meaning-making practices that are digitally mediated, whether those practices involve the use of laptop or desktop computers, online or offline practices, or word processing or messaging software.

The following is based on a view of what currently constitutes writing, although it may be worth acknowledging at this point, that theorists are beginning to envision radically different futures for writing, from the design of multimodal texts (Kress, 2003) to the potential for alternative systems of computer-mediated symbolic communication (Harris, 2000). Nevertheless, the very nature of recent changes in written communication has led to the development of new theoretical perspectives about the role of literacy in everyday life and in childhood, and this is an important starting point for this review. Here, I overview some of the more influential of these.

Theorizing Changes in Written Communication

It is not just the case that patterns of communication are changing; our social lives are changing, too. However, these changes are not simply a *result* of technological innovation (Robins and Webster, 1999). In fact, it is more accurate to say that new tools for communication have emerged out of a changing social world (Kress, 2003). This is a world that places people in different relationships with one another and even engenders an altered sense of who we are (Giddens, 1991). Therefore, communication needs have changed along with the capacity to communicate in new ways. Digital media in general, and digital writing in particular, have begun to reinforce this sense of a new social order and, as a result, are of central importance to those concerned with the welfare and education of children and young people. As Gee (2000) pointed out, networking within distributed systems is a key characteristic of new capitalism and one that is exerting an influence on business and labor markets and causing us to rethink what we mean by knowledge and knowledge building. From this point of view, the wide-reaching impact of new media on everyday life highlights the importance of social theory in understanding and interpreting the changes that are taking place.

While new information and communication technologies (ICTs) fundamentally change the ways we write and communicate, it becomes clear that they also change how we interact and who we interact with. As Nixon (2003) suggested, a theoretical perspective that focuses on literacy as a social practice is likely to be helpful here. The work of Barton (1994) and Barton and Hamilton (1998) is particularly influential in this respect. Their explorations of literacy as a social practice show how specific activities (such as sending an e-mail or contributing to a discussion board) are linked to the wider social structures in which these events are embedded and help to shape (Barton, 1994). Specific "situated" literacy acts or events can then be analyzed—for instance, by looking at the participants and settings, and the particular artifacts, activities, and technologies that are used (Hamilton, 2000). These are aspects of literacy practices that are linked to broader sets of values, attitudes, feelings, and relationships (Street, 1993).

Another useful perspective comes from paying closer attention to text, design, and communication. As we have seen, new technology involves new ways of meaning making, and these challenge the authority of the book and the page as dominant sites for representation (Kress, 2003). The sociosemiotic approach developed by Kress (1997; 2000; and 2003) has led us to carefully consider the characteristics of screen-based communication. His work has highlighted the affordances of the screen and the facilities of different media, and this, in turn, has helped us to understand the visual nature of the screen and how its characteristics differ from that of the page. An emphasis on the materiality of new textual forms has shifted our attention to the multimodal design features of screen-based texts such as Word documents and Web pages.

My own work (Merchant, 2006), and my collaborative work with colleagues and teacher-researchers (described in Larson and Marsh, 2005) is shaped by Kress's ideas about the changing nature of literacy, the different affordances of page and screen, and the increasing importance of multimodality (Kress, 2003). This perspective enables us to sharpen the focus on the nature of the texts that can be produced by children working onscreen. It also uncovers the rich diversity of resources and knowledge about text that young learners bring to the school context. In adopting this approach, questions about the materiality of digital writing are brought to the fore (Merchant, 2005a). We are also faced with the challenge of developing new analytical frameworks to apply to digital texts produced by children (Bearne, 2003).

The dramatic shifts in the forms, uses, and technologies of writing that have taken place over the last 20 years raise fundamental issues about the nature of literacy and the role of education in promoting literacy. A significant amount of the existing body of writing and research on the topic acknowledges the possibility that ICT might *help* in instruction, or in the acquisition, of literacy; but this rests on the assumption that literacy is somehow separate from technology—that it exists, or is applied to practices of meaning making associated with conventional print-based text. An alternative perspective, and one captured in part by the term "new literacy" (Lankshear & Knobel, 2003a) implies that there is an intimate relationship between technology and new communicative practices and suggests that, because literacy is radically changed by new practices, we need to redraw the literacy maps of schooling. At the same time, of course, we need to turn our attention to the relationship between literacy and ICT in the school curriculum.

Central Questions

The relationship between literacy and ICT is called into question by any serious consideration of digital writing in the school curriculum. The ways in which we conceive of ICT are particularly relevant here. In the United Kingdom, there are a number of competing discourses that see ICT either as a set of skills (the National Curriculum for ICT, QCA, 2000), as a tool or vehicle for learning (DfES, 2004), or as transformative influence affecting all aspects of schooling (DfES, 2005). The New Zealand directive, Interactive Education (Ministry of Education, New Zealand 1998) contains similar contradictions, conceiving of ICT as a "range of tools," a way of enriching the existing curriculum framework and on occasions as transformational— particularly with respect to a more flexible vision about the time and place of learning and the nature of communication within schools and between schools and communities. By contrast, the U.S. Partnership for 21st Century Skills Assessment Report (Partnership for 21st Century Skills, 2004) gave a systematic analysis of how new technologies can be used to transform the *content* of four curriculum subjects (geography, science, mathematics, and English), showed how tools can be applied, and provided examples of learning outcomes in 4th, 8th, and 12th grade.

These discourses influence thinking about the relationship between new technology and literacy. Seeing ICT as a set of skills suggests that there are specific items of procedural knowledge that can then be applied in other contexts (such as cutting and pasting in word-processing). ICT as a tool for learning suggests an emphasis on software and transferable strategies (such as practicing specific writing skills), whereas transformative views, often broader in outlook, envision new kinds of learning, communication, and interaction, and emphasize embedded and pervasive uses of ICT. Each of these views will, of course, determine the questions asked and the kinds of research needed.

The first serious writing about the use of ICT to promote literacy in the classroom emerged in the 1980s (e.g., Johanson, 1988). This was followed by considerable speculation, much of it focusing on the influence of new technology on traditional literacy skills (Cochran-Smith, Paris, & Kahn, 1991). As computers became more commonplace, the concerns of many educators and policymakers shifted to a consideration of the social implications of screen-based interaction. Work on ICT and collaborative writing, and pupils' interactions when working onscreen attracted the interest of researchers (Vass, 2002; Wegerif & Scrimshaw, 1997), who were driven by an interest in collaborative learning as much as by a reaction to the idea of the isolated technosubject (Luke & Luke, 2001). At the same time, there was considerable experimentation with educational software, such as reading and writing packages that were child friendly, reflecting the growing recognition by software designers of an emerging market created by educational policy and investment in computing. An emphasis on digital writing as a way of motivating learners—a way of helping those with general or specific difficulties—from the reluctant to the gifted and talented; from the marginalized to the isolated or the digitally disadvantaged has continued to grow (Kamil, Intrator, & Kim, 2000). This all follows a trend toward a more integrated (or domesticated) view of new technology in education; however, there are still relatively few examples of how ICT might transform literacy in educational contexts, and radically change how we learn to write. Yet, as we have seen, when we look at screen-based communication in the world outside the school, its impact on literacy practices is hard to ignore (Kress, 2003; Lankshear & Knobel, 2003a).

I want to move now to a consideration of the key issues at stake in promoting digital literacy in the early years and through the initial stages of children's compulsory schooling. To begin, I focus on what we know about the experiences of digital writing that children bring with them to the learning environment. I then move on to the question of what sort of experiences we want children to have in terms of curricular goals and instructional models. This leads into a discussion of the pedagogies and resources needed to support different sets of curriculum goals.

Children's Experience with Digital Writing

Although digital writing now plays a central role in many everyday informal and occupational settings, a number of commentators (following Tapscott, 1998) have expressed concern over the unevenness of pupils' out-of-school experience. They suggest that a lack of experience, or even experience of the "wrong kind," may create or compound disadvantage in the education system. The notion of a "digital divide" (Tapscott, 1998) has provoked considerable debate, but in reality, the situation may be far more complex than a simple binary divide separating the "haves" from the "have-nots." As a recent study of children and computing in the home pointed out, some children are excluded from the world of ICT and some exclude themselves (Facer, Furlong, Furlong, & Sutherland, 2003). However, the researchers went on to demonstrate that "a significant minority of children are excluded from home-based access to ICT because of cost; cost is a major feature in the initial purchase of a computer and in on-going maintenance and upgrading" (2003, p. 227). They also showed, however, that family settings vary in the extent to which they recognize and promote educational uses of new technology. Therefore, while it is important to map the new textual worlds of childhood (Carrington, 2005; Marsh, 2003), competence within these textual worlds is likely to be unevenly distributed (Snyder, Angus, & Sutherland-Smith, 2002). The challenge for the education system, then, is to recognize and respond to the rapidly changing world of digital communication and to build on children's varied experience and interest (Merchant, 2006). This can only be achieved through a re-examination of curriculum goals and pedagogical approaches, accompanied, of course, by appropriate resource and professional development.

Curriculum Goals and Models of Instruction

The curriculum goals of English-language education systems frame literacy in terms of book-reading and paper-based print media. Primacy is given to the pen and pencil as tools for writing and, where new technology is mentioned, it is referred to in terms of a supplement or extension to traditional literacy practices. Similarly, where reference is made to developing children's experience of different text types, or genres, these are predominantly print-based forms. For example, curriculum guidance for 3- to 5-year-olds in England and Wales, encourages practitioners to "provide a variety of writing tools and paper" (ICT is not mentioned) and "give children extensive experience" so that they are able to "use a pencil and hold it effectively to form recognizable letters" (DfEE, 2000, pp. 66–67). Elsewhere, in a section dedicated to ICT, teachers are told to help children "find out about and identify everyday technology"—examples given include the use of a "talking word processor" and a "paint program to develop early mark making" (DfEE, 2000, pp. 92–93).

Much the same is found in the curriculum for 5 to 11-year-olds in England and Wales, and indeed, in other English-language education systems. For example, the language curriculum in the Canadian state of Ontario emphasizes the importance of being able to print legibly and "leave spaces between words" (Ministry of Education, Ontario, 1997). Interestingly, though, this skill is categorized under visual representation. In New Zealand, "visual language" is given prominence in the English curriculum, although, again, clarity and fluency of handwriting is emphasized (Ministry of Education, New Zealand, 2002). These are systems that reify print and book-based literacies, and take cognizance of digital writing either as a way of enriching conventional print-based practices or as part of the more specialist domain of technology studies.

This response to new technology does, of course, provide one possible model for the development of digital writing. The model uses pencil-and-paper technology as a starting point, privileging pencil control over keyboard skills, and print over screen-based text. In essence, this is a sequential model whereby digital writing is gradually introduced as children progress through the system, and this progression is supported by work in the ICT curriculum. The model assumes that a certain degree of control over traditional writing processes is desirable or even necessary *before* the introduction of new technology. There are a number of problems with this model. First, and most significantly, it fails to take into account the pervasive influence of digital writing in the practices that constitute the literacy environment of young children (what was once referred to as the "print environment", Whitehead, 1997). By doing this, it simply ignores the literacy capital (Bearne, 2003) of significant numbers of pupils. Moreover, it enshrines a belief in the primacy of traditional literacy practices, creating an unhelpful dichotomy between school-based and out-of-school practices (Hull & Shultz, 2001).

A second possible model would seek to balance out the emphasis on old and new technologies for writing. In this parallel approach, specific aspects of digital writing would be used alongside print-based skills, forming an identifiable and progressive strand in the literacy curriculum. For example letter recognition and letter formation would be learned at the same time as basic keyboard skills. This approach would involve revisiting curriculum guidance in literacy and ICT and seeking to identify parallel paths of progression in learning. An obvious difficulty here stems from the fact that we already have good reason to question standard unilinear models of literacy development (Dyson, 2001). Similar problems exist with ICT in the curriculum. Tying together two highly contested developmental sequences would be inadvisable. Of course, in common with the sequential model, the parallel model implies that there is a separation between literacy and the technologies of literacy. As we have seen, this separation is in itself problematic.

A third and alternative model would be one in which new technology infuses the curriculum, providing young children with planned opportunities to engage with ICT as a writing tool from the very earliest stages of schooling. This would include the use of digital tools for early mark making and necessitate a reconceptualization of emergent writing (Merchant, 2005a; Turbill, 2001) and subsequent paths of literacy development. The infusion model would include traditional print-based practices and would need to address issues of choice and appropriacy in the use of different writing tools. Making such choices would presumably need careful and critical thinking about communicative purpose, the affordances of specific media, and resultant design choices (Bearne, 2003). This could be a way of avoiding the temptation to base our view of digital literacy on old print-based models. The need to think of future patterns and developmental paths for literacy is captured by Labbo (2000), who pointed out, "It is likely that multi-age and cross-age collaborative projects will place increasing pressure on curriculum developers to reconceptualise how children acquire and develop digital literacy in ways that challenge traditional notions of development" (p. 10). This suggests a more radical view of digital literacy, and one in which new relationships and ways of learning come into play. It seems, then, that there is a need for exploratory research that looks at how digital literacy can infuse and transform both pedagogy and the curriculum.

Implications for Pedagogy and Resources

The relationship between curriculum goals, pedagogy, and resource provision is complex at the best of times. When we consider the rapidly changing world of digital writing, this relationship becomes even more complex. Nonetheless, we can begin to trace the implications of the three models just presented in terms of the pedagogy and resources that would be needed to develop them. Table 26.1 summarizes this.

Table 26.1 The Pedagogical and Resource Implications of Curriculum Responses to Digital Writing

Curriculum model	Pedagogy	Resources
Sequential introduction of digital writing	Existing approaches with updating in the light of new knowledge and resources	Routine upgrading of hardware and software with regular pupil access
Parallel introduction of digital writing	Specific approaches related to the development of screen-based writing practices	Increased investment in new hardware and software with increased pupil access
Infusion of curriculum with digital writing	New approaches based on a changed view of literacy and the possibilities of new technology	Heavy investment in hardware and software with pupil access at all times

Of course, any significant change of policy or emphasis is dependent upon substantial professional development and accompanying reforms in the preparation of new teachers and teaching assistants. Initiatives like Ireland's Schools IT 2000 (Ireland Department of Education and Science, 1998) pledge support to new policy directives with an investment in professional development. Based on a view that there is no single formula for integrating ICT into the school curriculum and recognizing the importance of "appropriate professional development," the Irish initiative has developed a school-focused approach that provides an ICT infrastructure with resource and support mechanisms for policies developed at school level. In a similar vein, current work by eMINTS (2000) in the United States illustrates the significant impact of inquiry-based peer coaching and ICT use on pupil-learning outcomes.

Nonetheless, educational innovation in the use of ICT has tended to be resource driven. Over the last 20 years, national governments and local administrators, often in partnership with entrepreneurs, have invested large sums of money in purchasing hardware and software for schools and classrooms. According to Torgerson and Zhu (2004), over £1billion has been spent by the U.K. government in the last 5 years alone; whereas it is estimated that the Australian government has invested half a billion dollars a year since 2003, and this pattern is repeated elsewhere. Unfortunately, as critics have pointed out, this investment in new equipment has not always been matched by a similar investment in professional development (Torgerson & Zhu, 2004). Teachers' confidence in their personal use of ICT is generally quite low. Research commissioned by the Scottish Office (Williams, Wilson, Richardson, Tuson, & Coles, 1998) suggested that teachers "are still in the early stages of ICT development." A similar pattern emerged from the NCES report on teacher quality in the United States (NCES, 1999), and a more recent review on barriers to the uptake of ICT by teachers suggests that confidence, along with time and access, are crucial determining factors (Becta, 2004). Partly as a result of this, the development of innovative classroom practice has largely been the province of enthusiasts. Nevertheless, any meaningful exploration of digital writing in the school system is, of necessity, dependent upon technology, so the resource issue certainly warrants close attention.

In considering the resource dimension of digital literacy, it is useful to separate some distinct, yet interrelated elements (see Holloway & Valentine, 2002, for a useful exploration of these issues). For example, there are issues of *provision*—what hardware and software is provided and how it is updated; *location*—where this equipment is situated in schools or classrooms; *access*—how and when teachers and pupils can get to the hardware and software; and *use*—the actual practices that are promoted in, and outside of, the formal curriculum. There is growing recognition that these factors work together to constitute classroom practices, and that changes in ICT policy need to take account of their interplay (Becta, 2004; Holloway & Valentine, 2002). Future research that focuses on school-, district-, or system-level innovation in ICT will need a design and research tools that are sufficiently robust to cope with this complexity.

Reviewing the Research

The following review of research on children and digital writing is divided into four parts. I begin by giving an overview of recently published research reviews concerned with children's use of ICT in general, before moving onto a closer consideration of three specific aspects of digital writing. The first of these is concerned with studies that concentrate on children's experience of digital writing in different contexts. This includes work on access and activity around new technology in the home alongside studies that have attempted to give voice to children's attitudes and thinking about digital communication. The following section looks at the use and application of various forms of ICT in classroom settings and draws on a variety of studies that focus on children's engagement with new tools and technologies for writing. In the final section, I review the work that has examined the development, use, and evaluation of hardware and software specifically designed for classroom environments and educational purposes

Reviews of General ICT Use among Young Children

As Leu (2000a) observed, a relatively small amount of work on digital literacy has been published in journals that addresses the development of reading and writing in educational contexts. In fact, Kamil and Lane (1998) identified only 9 out of 437 research papers in four leading research journals that dealt with technology and writing in a 5-year period (1990 to 1995). More recently, along with a growing academic interest in the field, a number of research reviews have been published, and although none of them focuses directly on digital writing in the early years, they provide a background for the more specific review that follows. Reviews of literacy and ICT include the work of Lankshear and Knobel (2003b) who analyzed existing studies of ICT in early-childhood education (0 to 8 years); Labbo and Reinking's (2003) review of the use of computers in early literacy education; and the EPPI review of the impact of ICT on literacy learning in English in the 5 to 16 age range (Andrews, 2004). Finally, following Cochran-Smith (1991) and Bangert-Drowns (1993), Goldberg, Russell, and Cook (2003) reported on a metaanalysis of research on the impact of the word processor across a similar age range.

Lankshear and Knobel (2003b) identified the limitations found in the relatively small corpus of empirical studies and specifically observed that "the corpus of studies is swamped by an emphasis on developing a generic capacity to encode and decode print rather than to promote competence as 'insiders' of practices and discourse communities that extend beyond conventional classroom reading and writing" (p. 77). More often than not, this so-called generic capacity is measured in terms of conventional paper-based skills—a flawed approach, which has been subject to critique in the work of Reinking (1994), Leu (1996), and Leu, Kinzer, Coiro, and Cammack (2004). The Lankshear and Knobel (2003b) study also showed how, even in the context of the relatively low levels of published work in mainstream literacy research journals (as identified by Kamil and Lane, 1998; Kamil et al., 2000), only a fraction were concerned with new technology in early childhood.

The prevalence of this conventional view was also supported by Labbo and Reinking's (2003) review of computers and early literacy education, which addressed a range of topics including early writing, the development of phonological abilities, independent reading, collaboration, and new literacy skills. Labbo and Reinking suggested that there is not only a growing body of research in the area of computers and young children, but also a pressing need to acknowledge the complexity of computer learning environments. They argued that "context counts when it comes to effective use of computers in early childhood classrooms" (p. 348), and in this sense their work contrasts sharply with earlier overviews such as that given by Bangert-Drowns (1993) which, by nature of its design, excluded classroom and individual case studies. Assumptions about what counts as relevant research in this field are called into question by Labbo and Reinking in a way that suggests that attention may be beginning to turn from considering *whether* to use new technology to *how* to use new technology in classrooms.

The EPPI review, set up in 2001, attempted to address the question, "What is the impact of ICT on literacy learning in English, 5–16?" (Andrews, Robinson, & Torgeson, 2004). In the EPPI study (Andrews, 2004), a subreview looked at the effectiveness of ICT in improving young people's literacy. The subreview focused on 5 to 16-year-olds and on the basis of its systematic review and analysis of randomized control trials concluded that there was no evidence to support the claim that ICT-based literacy instruction and resources were any more effective than non-ICT approaches (English Review Group, 2004). Although this suggests some caution, particularly with respect to resource investment, it is interesting that the research question itself constructs ICT as distinct from literacy: that is, as a way to become literate rather than a site for literacy in its own right.

In this sense, this is similar to the results found in Goldberg et al.'s (2003) meta-analysis of studies that compared writing with computers to pencil-and-paper writing in grades K–12. Goldberg et al. limited their review to quantitative studies conducted in the 10 years up to 2002 and concluded that word processing had a positive impact on learning to write. Although there was no evidence to support the claim that learners were more engaged and motivated when using word processors (as compared to pencil-and-paper writing), the studies did show that writing with a word processor resulted in texts of greater length and higher quality. Furthermore, similar to the earlier findings of Cochran-Smith (1991) and Bangert-Drowns (1993), they observed how writing on computers tended to be more of a social process with more collaboration and sharing of text than in pencil-and-paper work. They also found a tendency for students to make more revisions during text production when using a word processor.

Children's Experiences with Digital Writing in Their Everyday Lives

A number of studies and large-scale surveys have documented the changes in children's engagement with new technology and the impact of new media on their everyday lives. These include the work of Livingstone and Bovill (1999); Roberts, Foehr, Rideout, and Brodie (1999); Roberts, Foehr, and Rideout (2005); Facer et al. (2003); and Livingstone, Bober, and Helsper (2005). Such studies are typified by their tendency to address a wide range of technologies and usually only provide a fleeting glimpse of children's engagement with digital writing; however, they are helpful in capturing the changing nature of the communication environment that children are growing up in, and developing an appreciation of the literacy capital that children may, as a result, draw on in school settings. Furthermore, these studies are useful in helping us to place what we are beginning to learn about digital literacy in the context of the wider arena of new media.

The ScreenPlay project (Facer et al., 2003) was based on a survey of 855 secondary and primary pupils and used follow-up interviews and case studies to illuminate the impact of home computer ownership on the everyday lives of children and young people. This study explored some of the variations in children's engagement with new technology (see previous disussion), but also provided good evidence about the impact of new media on childhood. The researchers showed how children and their families inhabit an increasingly digitalized world typified by interactivity and rapid information flow. This contrasted with children's experience of ICTs in school where "computers are primarily seen as a *resource* for learning rather than a *context* for learning" (Facer et al., 2003, p. 232). In turning their attention to digital writing, the

ScreenPlay team noted that all the case-study children used onscreen writing at one time or another. Despite a diverse pattern of practices and software use, children in the study tended to be driven by interest rather than skill acquisition, and the screen was primarily perceived as a visual space, in which design and text features (such as font color and size) were highly prized. These researchers suggested that children's use of e-mail and chat was constrained both by Internet availability and, in some cases, by an absence of online social networks. However, they also predicted a rise in home e-mail usage in the United Kingdom, and, as we shall see, this is supported by more recent work.

Livingstone et al. (2005) concentrated on the online experiences of the 9 to 19 age group in the United Kingdom. Their data illustrate the increased use of interactive and peer-to-peer communication, but clearly shows that online opportunities are unevenly distributed, varying according to socio-economic status and age and in some instances, such as instant messaging and texting, according to gender. They also suggest that Internet literacy is influenced by access, in that "one opportunity leads to another in a virtuous circle of online experiences, so the benefit of enhancing online opportunities is magnified" (p. 3). Data of a similar nature is produced by the Kaiser Family Foundation (Roberts et al., 2005) who focused on 8- to 18-year-olds' engagement with new media in the United States. They reported rapid increases in the uses of video gaming and the Internet; in addition to this, 66% of their sample used instant messaging on a regular basis. The study described how a majority of young people from each of the major ethnic and socioeconomic groups have Internet access, but outlined how there are marked differences between groups. Roberts and colleagues distinguished between the consumption of screen media (TV, DVD, video and movies) and what is read (i.e magazines, newspapers and books). The research does not undertake a focused examination of digital writing but does provide good evidence of the widespread use of instant messaging, e-mail and chat.

An important, yet significantly underresearched area relates to younger children's experience of digital literacy. For example, Labbo and Reinking (2003) commented on the ubiquitous nature of digital communication in young children's lives, but suggested that research into computers in early literacy is "broad" and "shallow"—broad in the sense that ICT has some application in most aspects of early literacy, but lacking the depth of an established tradition that draws on a repertoire of methodologies. It is not surprising then to find that studies based on a view of literacy as a social practice are few in number. Snyder et al. (2002) provided an interesting model with their series of case studies that look at computer-mediated literacy events in home and school, but this, like the work of Facer et al. (2003) related to older children.

In contrast, Marsh (2003) took an in-depth view of the emergent technoliteracy practices of 44 young children between the ages of 2.6 and 4.0 years of age and found widespread engagement in a variety of literacy practices associated with new media in the home context. Marsh's work documented literacy practices related to television and film, computer games, mobile phones, and music. Similarly, my own study of young children in an early-years' setting shows the richness of children's experience of digital communication through observations of their spontaneous integration of portable technology in routine play scenarios (Merchant, 2005a).

However, the gap between what children know and engage with in their out-of-school lives is in stark contrast with the conventional view of literacy and literacy development. As Marsh (2003) concluded, "when children attend nursery, only very selective areas of their home literacy experiences are normally focused on" (p. 61). The disjuncture between home and school literacies, which has become a recurrent theme in the literature is, then, no less true with younger children as it is with older children.

Research that explores children's own views of digital communication at home and school provides another interesting dimension to this topic. An example of this is the work of Selwyn and Bullon (2000), who focused on two groups of children, eliciting their views about engaging with ICT at home and in school. As with other research, they found different levels of access to computer culture. The children in this study reported that their engagement in school was dominated by the use of word processing and drawing programs, but also expressed considerable frustration with respect to their school experience of using ICT, which they felt was sporadic and overregulated. The children reported that they had little sustained engagement with writing on screen.

Using ICT in the Writing Classroom

As Labbo and Reinking (2003) suggested, there is some evidence to suggest that technology can support young children's writing development in the classroom. The problem with the research is that it is unable to answer some of the basic questions that classroom practitioners ask. These include, for example, how to organize early learning environments in order to maximize opportunity and learning, whether to use child-friendly word processors, and how and when to introduce keyboard skills. In addition, there are many unresolved questions about the use of ICT as an instructional tool. There is conflicting evidence concerning the effectiveness of pedagogical applications and programs designed to practice literacy skills, such as letter identification, sound-symbol correspondence, and word recognition. Despite this, there is some evidence on the value of word processors in the development of early writing (Breese, Jackson, & Prince, 1996; Dalton & Hannafin, 1987; Dauite, 1986), and in a critical review of the literature, Cochran-Smith (1991) highlighted some of these (particularly with respect to drafting, reviewing, and editing), suggesting that the quality of children's digital writing is dependent on teachers' strategies and the social organization of the classroom.

Word processors allow developing writers important flexibility and freedom to experiment with what they have written, whether this consists of revising texts without the chore of copying out, including illustrative material, or simply deciding on appropriate presentational features. Examples of this sort of work are given in classroom case studies of ICT and writing (Moseley et al., 1999). Here there are descriptions of 6-year-olds using a talking word processor (Clicker), and creating visual stories onscreen (using KidPix). However, despite extensive documentation of this sort of practice in English-language settings internationally, practice still remains patchy. An observational study of practice in nine classrooms in England by Mumtaz and Hammond (2002) concluded that word processors, while being the most commonly used software in literacy teaching, were not well used in many classrooms. They found that on the occasions in which word processing was used, it was mainly for presentational purposes, for individualized "writing-up" activities, and for onscreen punctuation and spelling practice.

Relatively little work addresses the use of new technology in the very early stages of writing. Researchers have grappled with how to provide experiences that are appropriate to young children's physical and cognitive development (Labbo, 1996), as well as how to introduce digital literacy into the distinctive kinds of learning environments and curricula that are provided for young children. Turbill (2001) carefully described some of the challenges and frustrations of integrating ICT into existing early years' routines. She identified some of the possibilities, but also concluded that there is a need for more hardware, more technical support, and more professional development time for early years' teachers. Work that has focused on ways of integrating ICT into existing routines seems particularly worthwhile. For example, Labbo, Sprague, Montero, and Font (2000) conducted an action-research study into the effective use of a computer center for supporting literacy in a kindergarten. Labbo and her colleagues identified three specific teaching strategies. These include (a) "targeted moments" (10 to 15 minutes) with a specific skill focus tailored to children's needs; (b) "spur-of-the-minute ideas," in which teachers use digital writing in response to spontaneous, incidental or child-initiated topics; and (c) "thematic connections," which are planned in relation to overarching curricular goals. These are seen as ways of reversing the trend toward unproductive time spent on computers in early years' classrooms (Labbo et al., 2000; Turbill, 2001).

In a case study of preschoolers' uses of digital writing (Merchant 2005a), I show how laptop computers can easily be integrated into imaginative play. The texts produced by young writers in these sorts of contexts call into question established developmental models of emergent literacy (Clay, 1975; Teale and Sulzby, 1986). As Turbill (2001) suggested, there are many parallels between being a "beginning computer user" and "beginning to use print." However, there is a need to revisit Clay's (1979) "concepts of print," which are derived from observations of young children's interactions with conventional texts.

The equivalent concepts of screen-based text would need to consider keyboard use, the mouse-cursor relationship, screen navigation, and so on (for further exploration, see Merchant, 2005a). It becomes clear that there is a need for more detailed work on the role of ICT in the early stages of writing development. This is, of course, not just the case for English-language education systems. In an overview of ICT in Finland, Kankaanranta and Kangassalo (2003) reported that ICT is "invisible" in early years' curricula. In an attempt to redress this, their work is based on case studies of innovative uses of ICT in early-childhood settings that involve the use of games and paint programs to develop children's visual, numerical, and linguistic skills. Kankaanranta and Kangassalo reported on two projects, one that aims to infuse early years' settings with new technology and another which involves sharing digital portfolios between schools. This work illustrates the potential for using technological tools in early education settings, but suggests that computer access and levels of teacher competence and confidence are barriers to progress. They concluded that ICT in early childhood education "has yet to achieve the same status that it enjoys in the education of older children" (Kankaanranta & Kangassalo, 2003, p. 292).

Examining the characteristics of children's onscreen writing has attracted the attention of a number of researchers. Matthewman and Triggs (2004) reported on children's use of visual features in onscreen writing. Their study suggested that visual elements (such as font size and color, layout and use of image) may be significant at all stages of composition. Merchant (2005b) reported similar findings in his analysis of children's onscreen work that focused on the production of multimodal texts. He found that children's ongoing attention to the visual appearance of texts, at all stages in their development, contrasted with traditional models of writing that associate presentational features with the production of a final draft.

Classroom explorations of the interactive, communicative potential of screen-based technology have been comparatively well documented. It is widely acknowledged that e-communication opens up new opportunities for children and involves them in the production of new kinds of written text (Merchant, 2006). Several studies focus on pupil involvement in international communication through e-mail (Garner & Gillingham, 1998; Tao & Reinking, 2000; Tao, Montgomery, & Pickle, 1997), whereas others have put children in contact with adults (Harris & Kington, 2002; McKeon, 1999; Merchant, 2003; Merchant, 2005b). McKeon's study of 23 children's e-mail interactions with preservice teachers looked at the balance between purely social exchanges and topic-focused exchanges (in this case book-talk). Roughly half of the exchanges of these 9- and 10-year-olds fell into each category. Harris and Kington reported on a case study of 10-year-olds in e-mail contact with employees at a mobile phone factory some 30 miles away from the school. "Epals" learned about children's interests and in turn offered insights into the world of work. Teachers involved in the project commented on how they found out more about their pupils when reading the messages they exchanged. A more formal evaluation also showed gains in pupil motivation and social skills.

These studies all draw attention to the social nature of e-mail exchange. This is not surprising, since e-communication is a transparent example of literacy as a social practice. Educators' concerns have tended to focus on whether such social interaction has an educative function, or whether frivolous message exchange is the equivalent of unproductive classroom talk (Merchant, 2003). Further concerns have centered on the use of informal language, abbreviation, and the kinds of linguistic innovation shared in chatrooms, on SMS, and in instant messaging (Merchant, 2005b). My work, based on work with 9- and 10-year-olds in a classroom setting, shows how informal digital communication can be used to develop new and more conventional literacy practices (Merchant, 2005b). This research shows how pupils draw on their knowledge of popular digital communication in e-mail message exchanges and how their awareness of the affordances of new media and their perceptions of audience influence the ways in which they write. In a close analysis of the frequency and content of e-mail exchanges between 301 eleven-year-olds, Van der Meij and Boersma (2002) also drew attention to the social nature of this communication. The researchers draw attention to the need for more work in this area, observing in passing that "email is not yet the integrated communication tool that it is in business settings" (p. 199). In short, the ubiquity of interactive written discourse in work and leisure—and even in some educational settings—finds few parallels in most primary classrooms.

A final, but important strand in classroom-based research places the emphasis on face-to-face pupil interaction in computer-based activities. As we have already seen from the work of Cochran-Smith (1991) and Bangert-Drowns (1993), screens are often more public spaces for written text, and as a result seem to prompt more shared behavior. Placing the emphasis on talk as a tool for thinking, Mercer, Fernandez , Dawes, Wegerif, and Sams (2004) looked at children's literacy work in settings where computer software is used as a resource for organizing collaborative activity. They provided vignettes that show how new technology can be embedded in collaborative classroom routines. A similar theme is pursued by Vass (2002) who looked at the talk and collaborative activity of 8-year-olds engaged in joint poetry writing. Here data on collaborative talk were gathered from observations of classroom and IT suite activity, which enabled the author to draw up a framework for the relationship between aspects of the writing process and discourse forms in children's talk. However, the extent to which the different technologies mediated the process of collaborative writing was not explored. Clearly, this is a rich and important area for future research.

Using and Developing Purpose-Built Classroom Applications

Much has been written about the development, use, and evaluation of hardware and software specifically designed for classroom environments and educational purposes. However, little of this places an explicit focus on children's writing development. As a result, there are some unanswered questions about which kinds of writing interfaces, hardware, and software are most appropriate for young writers. Some of the studies previously discussed in this chapter have employed specific educational software. For example, Labbo and colleagues (2000) used KidPix Studio Deluxe; Moseley et al. (1999) described the use of Clicker (a talking word processor), and KidPix; and I described the use of the First Class e-mail system and Powerpoint (Merchant, 2005b). Other studies either use "standard" software packages, such as Microsoft Word and PowerPoint, or did not specify the software used. Professional opinion is divided when it comes to the use of software specifically designed for educational purposes, and consequently on when and how to introduce the more widely used packages associated with adult use. In the arena of early childhood education these issues come into focus in the debate around developmentally appropriate software (Bredekamp & Rosegrant, 1994) with some practitioners and researchers arguing for the use of simplified keyboards and age-appropriate word processors, and others suggesting that children should be given a staged introduction to the tools they will be using later on in their school careers and in later adult life.

But of course, both hardware and software *can* be modified, adapted, or specifically designed for young learners. In their review of research on ICT and preschool children, Plowman and Stephen (2003) highlighted the learning needs of the under-5s, making the point that, "Design for young children is not simply a matter of scaling down the hardware, however, as preschool users are not scaled-down adults but have specific requirements of equipment, such as robustness and mobility" (p. 56). They go on to describe a number of electronic and communicative toys, interfaces, and developmentally appropriate software specifically designed to meet the needs of young children. This may cause us to reconsider the emphasis that has been placed on desktop computers in work on early digital writing. Newer technological developments in the form of portable and handheld equipment may, in fact, turn out to be more adaptable and more appropriate for younger learners. Moving in a rather different direction, Lingau, Hoppe, and Mannhaupt (2003) described roomware environments for beginning writers that make use of new embedded interfaces such as large touchscreens and modified interactive classroom furniture as tools for the collaborative production of written text. Clearly there is much potential for development as technology continues to evolve, but enthusiasm needs to be tempered by a clear sense of what we are trying to achieve with young writers.

The Internet has had a profound effect on the literacy lives of much of the adult population and, as we have seen, is becoming influential in children's lives in out-of-school contexts. There is now a sense of a developing research base that addresses the educational implications of reading online (Leu, 2000b; Leu et al., 2004), although less attention has been given to writing online. As connectivity becomes faster and more widespread in schools and classrooms, more possibilities exist for writing and publishing online. We have already seen that there are a number of accounts that show how e-mail has been creatively woven into the fabric of classroom life (Merchant, 2003; Merchant, 2005b). Explorations of other forms of online writing are not so well documented. Johnson (2002) catalogued 15 net-based resources that can be used to connect pupils in dispersed locations and provide opportunities for publishing on the Web and argued that children can use online environments to communicate in significant ways, but acknowledged that more work is needed in this area if we are to understand the processes, benefits, and possible pitfalls of this kind of work. In a similar vein, Watts and Lloyd (2004) described work with an online multimedia service that functioned as a resource for the development of the journalistic writing of 11-year-olds. The results of this work show how rapidly children became autonomous and active learners, developing important literacy skills in a new context. The researchers observe that the project raises important issues in the organization and management of classroom teaching as control is devolved to the learner. There is clearly a pressing need for more work that looks at ways of writing and publishing onscreen using Net-based resources. Furthermore, the implications that this has for how we organize and instruct pupils and even how we conceive of teacher-pupil and pupil-pupil relationships are only just beginning to receive attention.

Future Directions

This chapter has outlined the growing body of research in the field of digital writing, but as the review shows, there are still many unanswered questions. We urgently need exploratory research that looks at how digital writing can infuse and transform the early years' curriculum. Such research should focus on young children's experimentation and text production and aim to identify pedagogies that support and extend children's onscreen work. In particular, we need to know how to best organize early-learning environments to maximize the benefits of new technology for writing. This will help us develop ways of structuring children's earliest encounters with digital writing in the school that are sensitive to children's existing knowledge and skills.

Underpinning much of the work described here is a distinction between seeing ICT as a medium for literacy—a new literacy in its own right (Lankshear & Knobel, 2003a) and as a means for achieving literacy (Torgerson & Zhu, 2004). In advocating a view of digital literacy as a social practice, I have favored the former view, following Bigum (2002) who presented a curriculum model which embeds new technology in authentic meaning-making practices. It, therefore, seems that the time is now right for literacy researchers to engage more systematically with digital literacies, particularly with respect to the integration of new technologies into classroom life. We need to know more about the diversity of young children's experience of digital writing in out-of-school contexts in order to better understand their literacy capital, but we also need to understand how to build on that so that new technology can be used to motivate and develop children's meaning making in early education.

At the levels of policy, curriculum change, and professional development, there is much work to be done. The academic community is already taking the lead in describing and debating the ways in which English and literacy are being defined (and redefined) in everyday life. We are beginning to develop an understanding of the needs of young people growing up in a context in which reading and writing onscreen are pervasive. As Labbo (2000) outlined,

> To be digitally literate will mean to learn skills necessary to navigate, locate, communicate on-line, and participate in digital, virtual and physical communities. Therefore, literacy will be seen as *informatic*, involving a range of meaning-making strategic abilities required to navigate through and assemble knowledge from various informational sources in cyberspace." (p. 6)

In reflecting the general shift of emphasis from *whether* to use ICT to *how* to use ICT in literacy, there is a need for careful consideration of digital writing. In particular, there is scope for more work that shows how digital writing can be embedded in classroom practice in ways that provide authentic contexts for learning, meaning making, and communication. Because digital writing involves new kinds of skills and new kinds of social practices, however, it cannot simply be grafted on to existing instructional practices and curricular objectives. We need to re-evaluate the ways in which writing is taught and develop our understanding of what actually constitutes writing development in digital environments. This will involve more exploration of what experiences, resources, and guidance are most helpful in the early stages of emergent literacy and working toward an understanding of the appropriate balance between investigation and skill instruction (such as keyboarding skills and menu navigation). However, curriculum development must also be balanced against current understandings about early learning and what is appropriate at different stages of physical and cognitive development.

Further questions concerning how and when children are best introduced to different genres of digital texts, e-communication, and online environments will need to be addressed and these questions will require a view of literacy that transcends traditional views of reading and writing. As Leu (2000b) suggested,

Research time might be better spent on exploring issues of how to support teachers' efforts to unlock the potentials of new technologies, and not demonstrating the learning gains from technologies we already know will be important to our children's success. (p. 3)

In the meantime, most children and young people are apprenticed to digital writing through informal learning in out-of-school contexts. Given the centrality of new literacies in everyday life and the unevenness of provision, access and use, a failure to embed digital writing in classroom practices may simply perpetuate disadvantage. Alternatively, we can rise to the challenge by accepting the wide-reaching changes in written communication that are taking place and looking for new ways to extend the experience of young writers in school settings.

References

Andrews, R. (Ed.). (2004). *The impact of ICT on literacy*. London: Routledge Falmer.

Andrews, R., Robinson, A., & Torgerson, C. (2004). Introduction. In R. Andrews (Ed.), *The impact of ICT on literacy* (pp. 1–33). London: Routledge Falmer.

Bangert-Drowns, R. L. (1993). The word processor as an instructional tool: A meta-analysis of word processing in writing instruction. *Review of Educational Research, 63*(1), 69–93.

Barton, D. (1994). *Literacy: An introduction to the ecology of written language*. Oxford, U.K.: Blackwell.

Barton, D., & Hamilton, M. (1998). *Local literacies: Reading and writing in one community*. London: Routledge.

Bearne, E. (2003). Rethinking literacy: Communication, representation, and text. *Reading Literacy and Language, 37*(3), 98–103.

Becta (2004). *A review of the research literature on barriers to the uptake of ICT by teachers*. Retrieved October 16, 2005, from http://becta.org.uk/research

Bigum, C. (2002). *Managing new relationships: Design sensibilities, the new information, and communication technologies and schools*. Retrieved February 23, 2005, from http://www.apapdc.edu.au?2002/archive/ASPA/2000/paapers/art429.html

Bredekamp, S., & Rosegrant, T. (1994). Learning and teaching with technology. In J. L. Wright, & D. D. Shade (Eds.), *Young children: Active learners in a technological age* (pp. 53–61). Washington, DC: NAEYC.

Breeze, C., Jackson, A., & Prince, T. (1996) Promise in impermanence, children writing with unlimited access to word processors. *Early Childhood Development and Care* 118, 67-91.

Carrington, V. (2005). New textual landscapes, information, and early literacy. In J. Marsh (Ed.), *Popular culture, new media, and digital literacy in early childhood* (pp. 13–27). London: Routledge Falmer.

Clay, M. (1975). *What did I write?* London: Heinemann Educational.

Clay, M. (1979). *The early detection of reading difficulties* (2nd edition). Auckland, New Zealand: Heinemann Educational.

Cochran-Smith, M. (1991). Word-processing and writing in elementary classrooms: A critical review of related literature. *Review of Educational Research, 61*, 107–55.

Cochran-Smith, M., Paris, C. L., & Kahn, J. L. (1991). *Learning to write differently*. Norwood, NJ: Ablex.

Dalton, D., & Hannafin, M. (1987). The effects of word processing on written composition. *Journal of Educational Research, 80*(6), 338–342.

Dauite, C. (1986). Physical and cognitive factors in revising: Insights from studies with computers. *Research in the Teaching of English, 20*, 141–159.

DfEE. (2000). *Curriculum guidance for the foundation stage*. London: QCA.

DfES. (2004). *Learning and teaching using ICT: Example materials from foundation stage to year 6*. London: DfES.

DfES. (2005). *Harnessing technology: Transforming learning and children's services*. London: DfES.

Dyson, A. H. (2001). Where are the childhoods in childhood literacy? An exploration of outer (school) space. *Journal of Early Childhood Literacy, 1*(1), 9–39.

eMINTS. (2000). *Teacher comments about working in an eMINTS classroom 12.08.00*. Retrieved October 17, 2005, from http://www.emints.org/evaluation/reports/index.shtml

English Review Group. (2004). *A systematic review and meta-analysis of the effectiveness of ICT on literacy learning in English, 5-16' EPPI-Centre*. Retrieved March 16, 2005, from http://eppi.ioe.ac.uk/EPPIWeb/home.aspx?page=/reel/review_three.html

Facer, K., Furlong, J., Furlong, R., & Sutherland, R. (2003). *ScreenPlay: Children and computing in the home*. London: Routledge Falmer.

Garner, R., & Gillingham, M. G. (1998). The Internet in the classroom: Is it the end of transmission-orientated pedagogy? In D. Reinking, L. D. Labbo, M. C. McKenna, & R. D. Kieffer (Eds.), *Handbook of literacy and technology: Transformations in a post-typographic world* (pp. 221–241). Mahwah, NJ: Erlbaum.

Gee, J. P. (2000). New people in new worlds: Networks, the new capitalism, and schools. In B. Cope & M. Kalantzis (Eds.), *Multiliteracies: Literacy learning and the design of social futures* (pp. 43–68). London: Macmillan.

Giddens, A. (1991). *Modernity and self-identity: Self and society in the late modern age*. Cambridge, U.K.: Polity Press.

Goldberg, A., Russell, M., & Cook, A. (2003). The effect of computers on student writing: A meta-analysis of studies from 1992 to 2002. *Journal of Technology, Learning, and Assessment, 2*(1), 1–24.

Hamilton, M. (2000). Expanding the new literacy studies: Using photographs to explore literacy as a social practice. In D. Barton, M. Hamilton, & R. Ivanic. (Eds.), *Situated literacies: Reading and writing in context* (pp. 16–34). London: Routledge.

Harris, R. (2000). *Rethinking writing*. London: Continuum.

Harris, S., & Kington, S. (2002). Innovative classroom practices using ICT in England. Retrieved February 27, 2005, from http://nfer.ac.uk/research/down_pub.asp

Holloway, S., & Valentine, G. (2002). *Cyberkids: Youth identities and communities in an on-line world*. London: Routledge Falmer.

Hull, G., & Shultz, K. (2001). Literacy and learning out of school: A review of theory and research. *Review of Educational Research, 71*(4), 575–611.

Ireland Department of Education & Science. (1998). *Schools IT 2000*. Retrieved October 16, 2005, from http://195.7.52.179/overview/it2k.htm

Johanson, R. P. (1988). Computers, cognition, and curriculum: Retrospect and prospect. *Journal of Computing Research, 4*, 1–30.

Johnson, D. (2002). Web watch: Writing resources. *Reading Online, 5*(7). Retrieved March 8, 2005, from http://www.readingonline.org/electronic/webwatch/writing/index.html

Kamil, M. L., Intrator, S., & Kim, H. (2000). The effects of other technologies on literacy and literacy learning. In M. L. Kamil, P. Mosenthal, D. Reason, & R. Barr (Eds.), *Handbook of reading research* (Vol. 3, 771–788). Mahwah, NJ: Erlbaum.

Kamil, M. L., & Lane, D. M. (1998). Researching the relationships between technology and literacy: An agenda for the 21st century. In D. Reinking, M. McKenna, L. Labbo, & R. Kieffer (Eds.), *Handbook of literacy and technology: Transformations in a post-typographic world* (pp. 323–343). Mahwah, NJ: Erlbaum.

Kankaanranta, M., & Kangassalo, M. (2003). Information and communication technologies in Finnish early childhood environments. *Childhood Education, 79*(5), 287–292.

Kress, G. (1997). Visual and verbal modes of representation in electronically mediated communication: The potentials of new forms of texts. In I. Snyder (Ed.), *Page to screen: Taking literacy into the electronic age* (pp. 53–79). London: Routledge.

Kress, G. (2000). Multimodality. In B. Cope & M. Kalantzis (Eds.), *Multiliteracies: Literacy learning and the design of social futures* (pp. 182–202). London: Macmillan.

Kress, G. (2003). *Literacy in the new media age.* London: Routledge.

Labbo, L. D. (1996). A semiotic analysis of young children's symbol making in a classroom computer centre. *Reading Research Quarterly, 31*, 356–385.

Labbo, L. D. (2000). *'Towards a vision for the future role of technology in literacy education.'* Report commissioned by the US Department of Education. Retrieved March 16, 2005, from http://www.air.org/forum/abLabbo.htm

Labbo, L. D., & Reinking, D. (2003). Computers and early literacy education. In N. Hall, J. Larson, & J. Marsh (Eds.), *Handbook of early literacy education,* (pp. 338–354). London: Sage.

Labbo, L. D., Sprague, L., Montero, M. K., & Font, G. (2000). Connecting a computer centre to theme's literature and kindergarteners' literacy needs. *Reading Online, 4*(1). Retrieved March 8, 2005, from http://www.readingonline.org/electronic/labbo/index. html

Lankshear, C., & Knobel, M. (2003a). *New literacies: Changing knowledge and classroom learning.* Buckingham, U.K.: Open University Press.

Lankshear, C., & Knobel, M. (2003b). New technologies in early childhood research: A review of research. *Journal of Early Childhood Literacy, 3*(1), 59–82.

Larson, J., & Marsh, J. (2005). *Making literacy real: Theories and practices for learning and teaching.* London: Sage.

Leu, D. J. (1996). Sarah's secret: Social aspects of literacy and learning in a digital information age. *The Reading Teacher, 50*, 162–165.

Leu, D. J. (2000a). Our children's future: Changing the focus of literacy and literacy instruction. *Reading Online.* Retrieved March 11, 2005, from http://www.readingonline. org/electronic/RT/focus/

Leu, D. J. (2000b). Literacy and technology: Deictic consequences for literacy education in an information age. In M. Kamil, P. Rosenthal, P. Pearson, & R. Barr (Eds.), *Handbook of reading research* (Vol. 3, pp. 743–770). Mahwah, NJ: Erlbaum.

Leu, D. J., Kinzer, C. K., Coiro, J. L., & Cammack, D. W. (2004). Towards a theory of new literacies emerging from the Internet and other information and communication technologies. *Reading Online.* Retrieved October 16, 2005, from http://www.readingon-line.org/newliteracies/lit_index.asp?HREF=/newliteracies/leu

Lingau, A., Hoppe, H. U., & Mannhaupt, G. (2003). Computer supported collaborative writing in an early learning classroom. *Journal of Computer Assisted Learning, 19*, 186–194.

Livingstone, S., Bober, M., & Helsper, E. (2005). *Internet literacy among children and young people: Findings from the U.K. children go online project.* London: London School of Economics.

Livingstone, S., & Bovill, M. (1999). *Young people, new media.* London: London School of Economics.

Luke, A., & Luke, C. (2001). Adolescence lost/childhood regained: On early intervention and the emergence of the techno-subject *Journal of Early Childhood Literacy, 1*(1), 91–120.

Marsh, J. (2003). The techno-literacy practices of young children. *Journal of Early Childhood Research, 2*(1), 51–66.

Matthewman, S., & Triggs (2004). Obsessive compulsory font disorder: The challenge of supporting writing with computers. *Computers and Education, 43*(1-2), 125–135.

McKeon, C. A. (1999). The nature of children's e-mail in one classroom. *The Reading Teacher, 52*(7), 698–706.

Mercer, N., Fernandez, M., Dawes, L., Wegerif, R., & Sams, C. (2004). Talk about texts at the computer: Using ICT to develop children's oral and literate abilities. *Reading, Literacy, and Language, 37*(2), 81–89.

Merchant, G. (2003). E-mail me your thoughts: Digital communication and narrative writing. *Reading, Literacy, and Language, 37*(3), 104–110.

Merchant, G. (2005a). Barbie meets Bob the Builder at the workstation: Learning to write on screen. In J. Marsh (Ed.), *Popular culture, new media, and digital literacy in early childhood* (pp. 183–200). London: Routledge Falmer.

Merchant, G. (2005b). Digikids: Cool dudes and the new writing. *E-Learning, 2*(1), 50–60.

Merchant, G. (2006). A sign of the times: Looking critically at popular digital writing. In J. Marsh & E. Millard (Eds.), *Popular literacies, childhood, and schooling* (pp. 93–109). London: Routledge Falmer.

Ministry of Education, New Zealand. (1998). *Interactive education: An information and communication technologies strategy for schools.* Wellington, New Zealand: Ministry of Education.

Ministry of Education, New Zealand. (2002). *English in the New Zealand curriculum.* Wellington, New Zealand: Ministry of Education. Retrieved October 17, 2005, from http://www.tki.org.nz/r/language/curriculum

Ministry of Education, Ontario. (1997). *Ontario curriculum: Grades 1-8.* Ontario, Canada: Ministry of Education. Retrieved October 17, 2005, from http://www.ed.gov.on.ca

Moseley, D., Higgins, S., Bramald, R., Hardman, F., Miller, J., Mroz, M., et al. (1999). *Ways forward with ICT: Effective pedagogy using information and communication technology for literacy and numeracy in primary schools.* Newcastle-upon-Tyne, U.K.: University of Newcastle.

Mumtaz, S., & Hammond, M. (2002). The word processor re-visited: Observations on the use of the word processor to develop literacy at key stage 2. *British Journal of Educational Technology, 33*(3), 345–347.

NCES. (1999). *Teacher quality: A report on the preparation and qualifications of public school teachers.* Retrieved October 16, 2005, from http://nces.ed.gov/pubsearch/pubsinfo.asp?pubid=1999080

Nixon, H. (2003). New research literacies for contemporary research into literacy and new media? *Reading Research Quarterly, 38*(3), 407–413.

Partnership for 21st Century Skills. (2004). *ICT literacy maps.* Washington, DC: Partnership for 21st Century Skills. Retrieved October 16, 2005, from http://www.21stcenturyskills.org

Plowman, L., & Stephen, C. (2003). A 'benign addition'? Research on ICT and pre-school children. *Journal of Computer Assisted Learning, 19,* 149–164.

QCA. (2000). *Information and communication technology, the national curriculum for England.* London: Qualifications and Curriculum Authority.

Reinking, D. (1994). *Electronic literacy. Perspectives in Reading Research No.4.* Athens, GA: University of Georgia, National Reading Research Centre.

Roberts, R. F., Foehr, U. G., Rideout, V., & Brodie, M. (1999). *Kids and media @ the new millenium.* Menlo Park, CA: Kaiser Family Foundation.

Roberts, R. F., Foehr, U. G., & Rideout, V. (2005). *Generation M.: Media in the lives of 8-18 year-olds.* Menlo Park, CA: Kaiser Family Foundation.

Robins, K., & Webster, F. (1999). *Times of the Technoculture: From the information society to the virtual life.* London: Routledge.

Selwyn, N., & Bullon, K. (2000). Pimary school children's use of ICT. *British Journal of Educational Technology, 31,* 321–332.

Snyder, I., Angus, L., & Sutherland-Smith, W. (2002). Building equitable literate futures: Home and school computer-mediated literacy practices and disadvantage. *Cambridge Journal of Education, 32*(3), 367–383.

Street, B. (Ed.). (1993). *Cross-cultural approaches to literacy.* Cambridge, U.K.: Cambridge University Press.

Tao, L., Montgomery, T., & Pickle, M. (1997). Content analysis in e-mail research: A methodological review. In C. K. Kinzer, K. A. Hinchman, & D. J. Leu (Eds.), *Inquiries into literacy theory and practice* (pp. 474–482). Chicago: National Reading Conference.

Tao, L., & Reinking, D. (2000). E-mail and literacy education. *Reading and Writing Quarterly, 16,* 169–174.

Tapscott, D. (1998). *Growing up digital: The rise of the net generation.* New York: McGraw-Hill.

Teale, W. H., & Sulzby, E. (Eds.). (1986). *Emergent literacy: Writing and reading.* Norwood, NJ: Ablex.

Torgerson, C., & Zhu, D. (2004). Evidence for the effectiveness of ICT on literacy learning. In R. Andrews (Ed.), *The impact of ICT on literacy* (pp. 34–68). London: Routledge Falmer.

Turbill, J. (2001). A researcher goes to school: Using technology in the kindergarten literacy curriculum. *Journal of Early Childhood Literacy, 1*(3), pp. 255–279.

Van der Meij, H., & Boersma, K. (2002). E-mail use in elementary school: An analysis of exchange patterns and content. *British Journal of Educational Technology, 33*(2),189–200.

Vass, E. (2002). Friendship and collaborative creative writing in the primary classroom. *Journal of Computer Assisted Learning, 18,* 102–110.

Watts, M., & Lloyd, C. (2004). The use of innovative ICT in the active pursuit of literacy. *Journal of Computer Assisted Learning, 20,* 50–58.

Wegerif, R., & Scrimshaw, P. (1997). *Computers and talk in the primary classroom.* Clevedon, U.K.: Multilingual Matters.

Williams, D., Wilson, K., Richardson, A., Tuson, J., & Coles, L. (1998). *Teachers' ICT skills and knowledge.* Aberdeen, U.K.: Robert Gordon University. Retrieved October 16, 2005, from http://www.scotland.gov.uk/library/ict/append-title.htm

Whitehead, M. (1997). *Language and literacy in the early years.* London: Paul Chapman.

CHAPTER 27

Teaching Popular-Culture Texts in the Classroom

RICHARD BEACH
and DAVID O'BRIEN

UNIVERSITY OF MINNESOTA, USA

In this chapter, we explore the kinds of new literacy practices involved in understanding, producing, and critiquing popular-culture texts. Although the focus is on the role of schooling and teachers' support of students' engagement with these texts, we make the case that because popular-culture texts are ubiquitous, intertexual, and intermedial, they are themselves creating pedagogical spaces within and outside of school, spaces in which students acquire a range of literacy practices about which we know very little.

These are the central questions we address in this chapter: (a) What popular-culture texts are youth and adolescents investing in the most and why? (b) What kinds of literacies do K–12 students acquire and enact through their experiences with these popular-culture texts in school and outside-of-school spaces? (c) What strategies serve as the basis for a curriculum framework that fosters a critical analysis and production of popular-culture texts?

Theoretical Frameworks

Based on research on space and learning (Ellsworth, 2004; Leander & Sheehy, 2004), we believe that popular-culture texts and the media cultural space in which they reside are a powerful form of pedagogy that goes beyond what students acquire from the official school curriculum. In the last 20 years or so, one could say that popular culture is what is left after "high culture" is subtracted "from the overall totality of cultural practices" (Giroux & Simon, 1988, p. 10). The new popular culture, however, is not so easily subtracted, because it is now so constantly added in, constructed and reconstructed, and so seamlessly manifested through digital media that the distinction between popular culture and high culture seems to give way more to the notion of an ubiquitous mediasphere (Rushkoff, 1999) constituted by a larger global intertext.

While much of mass-media popular culture consists of homogenized, standardized texts or artificial "pseudo-places" such as Disney World™ (Cresswell, 2004, p. 8), what is "popular" in popular culture, is partly defined by audiences' desires and needs—things we want to own, pleasures we want to experience, people we want to be like or be with, images we want to project, and notions as to what constitutes normality in cultures. The reasons we seek popularity—the reasons we seek attention (Lankshear & Knobel, 2003) and membership in affinity groups (Gee, 2003)—however, are implicit, interlinked pedagogical moments. The pedagogical power of popular media texts is evident in how effectively audiences readily acquire images, scenarios, and discourses involved in participating in brand communities (Schor, 2004; Twitchell, 2004) or multiple affinity groups, such as popular-culture music scenes (Bennett & Peterson, 2004; for different theories of popular-culture texts, see Strinati, 2004; Weaver, 2005).

Moje and van Helden (2004) described three ways in which meanings are assigned to popular-culture texts. A values-based critique perceives popular culture as low, trashy, deviant, or immoral relative to what is assumed to be "high" culture that represents more ennobling values. The second economic critique perceives popular culture as a seductive tool of a consumer, capitalist society (Grossberg, 1997). A third "romantic" or "agentic" critique argues that popular culture fosters innovative thinking that challenges traditional, hegemonic norms and practices (Dolby, 2003). Moje and van Helden (2004) argued that each of these critiques represent reductive categorization of popular culture that fails to recognize that popular culture "cannot be reduced to categories of good *or* bad, self-expression *or* other-exploitation, deviance *or* innovation, resistance *or* domination" (p. 219). These overdetermined categories do not capture the ways in which popular culture involves both individuals' imaginative expressions and institutional or economic forces seeking to manipulate individuals. Based on their ethnographic studies of adolescents' complex, conflicted uses of popular culture, Moje and van Helden posit "that youth both use and are used by popular culture, and that working this tension, rather than simply avoiding it by avoiding popular culture, is the job of educators" (p. 220). The young people they study simultaneously enjoy and disdain popular-culture texts, leading them to ask the question as to whether enjoyment and critique are mutually exclusive.

The dominant official discourse of schooling has at best disregarded popular culture and at worst positioned it as detrimental. However, the pervasiveness of the new popular culture in the mediasphere—constructed, interconnected, and distributed through ICTs and digital multimodalities—has become as equally powerful as the official discourse of schooling, shaping how students learn, what they choose to learn, and how they view themselves as learners. In a Kaiser Family Foundation study (Foehr, 2006), using diary accounts collected in 2003 to 2004 from a subsample of 694 young people, ages 8 to 18, and survey data from the larger sample of 2032 7th to 12 graders, 80% of the respondents were more likely to engage in some form of multitasking (using multiple forms of media simultaneously), particularly when reading. During reading they reported surfing the Net, IMing, and playing computer games. About 30% reported that they multitask "most of the time" while doing homework. They were less likely to multitask while watching TV or while playing video games. Females were more likely to multitask than males.

Another study of college students ages 18 to 24, the Alloy Collect Explorer Study (Alloy Marketing, 2006) conducted in 2006 by Harris Interactive, found that college students are spending an average of 11 hours a day involved in some sort of media or digital communications, including an average of 20 minutes a day devoted to IMing, and 6 ½ hours a week on social networking sties such as MySpace. Of the 41% of students who own an MP3 player, 85% listen to the MP3 daily.

About 40% of media users are engaged in other tasks while they are viewing, including 28% who often go online to access material related to their viewing. About one fourth of young people are multitasking in their media use, and about 30% multitask with media as they work on homework. This raises questions about how they work and how new perspectives on attention explain how they split attention while doing homework. Increased media use means that bedrooms have become increasingly popular media spaces or scenes for using texts (Bennett & Kahn-Harris, 2004) with an increase in use of TV and all digital devices including computers and game consoles in that space. Media-use perspectives that envision users splitting time across media types rather than multimediating can now reach erroneous conclusions: For example, calls for reducing TV viewing so that youth and adolescents free up time for other activities fail to consider how adolescents now experience TV: they may watch programs and also engage in online chat via chat rooms organized around TV programs even while viewing a program (Mackey, 2003).

What are the pedagogies inherent in these multimediating bedroom spaces? Youth not only prefer to be constantly connected, but also express cravings and feelings of discomfort and isolation when they are not connected, via the Web, cell phones, text messaging, and IMing. This strong desire for constant connection to the digital-media collective, a bit reminiscent of the Borg on *Star Trek*, is both a social and physiological phenomenon. Brain plasticity theorists, including neurologists (Restak, 2003) and cognitive scientists (Clark, 2003) offer a cyborg explanation for youth's desire to be constantly connected and stimulated with multimedia. They suggest that the neural networks in kids' brains are changing to allow more efficiency in multimediating. This increasingly efficient multimediating requires an engagement in the new literacies practices (Lankshear & Knobel, 2003). In short, youth engage in multimediating not simply because they have become highly competent in doing so. Further, their demonstration of multimediating related to continuous connections to peers, through, for example, simultaneously IMing with multiple audiences (Lewis & Fabos, 2005) is now refined as a social imperative constituting newer notions of popular culture.

Hence, we contend that the concept of media "multitasking" discussed in the response to the Kaiser Family study is somewhat anachronistic and based on productivity efficiency models that don't work here; what the young people are doing is actually multimediating (Lankshear & Knobel, 2003; O'Brien, 2006)—that is, simultaneously engaging in multimediating as part of the natural order of the life in the mediasphere. They listen to MP3 files while typing on a word processor in between checking for text messages on a cell phone. The mediasphere is the new pedagogy because its digital information and channels provide the multiple, interconnected teaching and learning moments youth experience and share with one another. It is how they learn about the world and themselves in the world. Although much of this multimediating occurs outside of school, we will make the case that particular approaches and strategies in school can facilitate it or connect it to explicit school curricula in useful ways.

These multimediating practices afford students multiple mediations for constructing ways of knowing and valuing the world. Multiple mediations do more than simply represent the world. They afford different, often fragmented, limited constructions, of, for example, the horrific nature of the Holocaust as mediated through *Schindler's List*; *Life is Beautiful*; or *The Complete Maus: A Survivor's Tale* (Hirsch & Kacandes, 2005; Spiegelman, 1996). This suggests the need to understand how students' construction of knowledge and cultural models are mediated through their uses of popular-culture texts. Through their experiences with *Lord of the Rings* or *Harry Potter*, early adolescent students are transported into imagined fantasy worlds that alter their perceptions of lived worlds (Blackford, 2004). Children employ popular-culture texts, particularly television characters, to construct fantasy/make-believe experiences. Analysis of 9 to 10 year-old children's construction of make-believe worlds through drawings and talk indicated traces of the popular-culture texts in two thirds of the material (Götz, Lemish, Aidman, & Moon, 2003).

A further pedagogical affordance inherent in multimediating practices is that students are accustomed to communicating through the combination of print with visual, sound, and tactile texts. This requires an increased focus on the materiality of texts, the interplay between the way physical text is laid out and accessed and the way readers assemble and reassemble it to construct mental representations of it. The new materiality, wherein the text physically resides in both actual and virtual spaces is evident not only in contemporary conceptual art, but also in the multimodal texts produced in students in writing classes (Hull & Nelson, 2005). As Anne Wysocki (2004) noted,

> We should call "new-media texts" those that have been made by composers who are aware of the range of materialities of texts and who then highlight the materiality: such composers design texts that help readers/ consumers/viewers stay alert to how any text—like its composers and readers—doesn't function independently of how it is made and in what contexts. (p. 15)

Students know that to engage contemporary audiences accustomed to multimediating, they need to emphasize the materiality inherent in hypermedia presentations, Web sites, or blog entries. It also involves learning multimodal transduction (Kress, 2003, p. 36) across different texts in which texts from one mode are transformed by putting them into another mode. For example, when young children used animated characters in print mode in digital animated mode, they became aware of how their animated version differed from their original print version of their stories (Marsh, 2005).

Despite the extensive and increasing use of popular-culture texts outside of school among youth, current school practices continue to revolve almost exclusively around print-based traditional, formalist conceptions of literacy and autonomous notions of literacy achievement (Street, 2005). This mismatch between students' out-of-school practices with popular-culture texts and their in-school, print-centric practices constituted by the "deep grammar of schooling" (Lankshear & Knobel, 2003, p. 30; O'Brien & Bauer, 2005), contributes to their increasing disengagement with print-only curricula. In short, school-sanctioned traditional pedagogies will be increasingly ineffective with students who are adapting more and more to engaging with popular-culture pedagogies. Rather than assume an artificial binary between in-school and out-of-school worlds (Hull & Schultz, 2002), we posit the need to reformulate school curricula to teach students the "ability to understand the power of images and sounds, to recognize and use that power, to manipulate and transform digital media, to distribute them pervasively, and to easily adapt them to new forms" (New Media Consortium, 2005, p. 4).

At the same time, we are not recommending abandoning traditional, formalist print literacies. Unfortunately, there is little research on the transfer of teaching popular-culture texts to traditional print literacies. In one study, Hobbs and Frost (2003) found that students in a media-literacy treatment group had higher reading comprehension scores, wrote longer paragraphs, and were better able to identify construction techniques, point of view, and omitted information; they were also better able to infer message purpose and target audiences than nontreatment peers. In another study, Hobbs (2004;

2007) found that 11th graders who were taught to critically analyze advertising were better able to identify an ad's target's audience, the verbal and visual techniques employed in ads, and the implied messages compared to students who did not receive this instruction.

In spite of the sparse evidence that engaging with popular-culture texts can improve competence with print, we must challenge views that engaging with popular-culture texts undermines students' academic achievement. There is little empirical support for the position that television viewing has negative effects on academic achievement except for very heavy viewers (more than 4 hours per day; Center for Children and Technology, 2004). For example, viewing television programs such as *Sesame Street* requires children to draw on multiple modes of learning and language development through interacting with television characters (Fisch, 2004). In addition, critiques of the mindlessness of viewing popular-culture texts such as prime-time television have been challenged by the argument that, in contrast to television programs of the 1960s and 1980s, more recent programs such as *The Sopranos* require audiences to attend to multiple narrative tracks and interpret shifting social relationships between characters (Johnson, 2005).

Teachers are often reluctant, however, to teach popular-culture texts assumed to have negative effects on students (Sternheimer, 2003). An analysis of a classroom in which English-language learners made references to Pokémon was perceived as not valid "content" for inclusion in second-language instruction in a second-grade classroom (Rymes, 2004). In addition, the presumed decline in reading of print literature is erroneously blamed on the increased use of mass-media popular-culture texts (National Endowment for the Arts, 2004), even though the same report found that while heavy TV viewers are less likely to be readers, frequent readers do not watch less TV than less frequent readers.

In the first section, we have attempted to establish that popular culture and its texts have morphed considerably based on digital media and multimediating. The increasingly intermedial and intertextual fabric of popular culture, played out in the mediasphere, is a powerful form of pedagogy in and of itself. In rejecting negative views that pit popular culture against youth and adolescents' engagement in more "legitimate" schooled texts, we offer some strategies that support the use of and creation of popular-culture texts in school.

Strategies for Interpreting and Producing Popular-Culture Texts

In the remainder of the chapter, we focus on teaching six intersecting strategies involved in interpreting and producing popular-culture texts: (a) searching for and organizing text material based on critical inquiry; (b) interpreting and using genre features; (c) linking, connecting, and revising texts; (d) sharing responses to and constructing popular-culture texts; (e) constructing identities through uses of popular-culture texts; and (f) critiquing popular-culture texts (for specific methods for teaching of popular-culture texts, see Beach, 2006; Evans, 2005; Schwarz & Brown, 2005; Xu, 2005).

We illustrate the use of these strategies based on examples from others' work and some examples from our recent or current research projects. For example, a range of these strategies were explored in studies of the Literacy Lab, a media-based, inquiry-oriented program for learners "at-risk" of failing in reading (O'Brien, Springs, & Stith, 2001). In a current project, (O'Brien, Beach, & Scharber, 2007) we are in the second year of studying seventh- and eighth-grade students' literacy practices in a media-rich, language-arts class in a suburban middle school. The students engage in a range of traditional and new literacies practices including whole-class reading and individual reading, journaling, media authoring (radio plays, PowerPoint™ presentations), Web browsing, use of an online course-management system, wikis, and playing video games in an after-school game club.

Searching for and Organizing Texts Based on Critical Inquiry

While in the past, popular-culture texts were accessible through limited venues, these texts are now ubiquitous due to their availability on the Web. Web sites themselves are forms of popular culture. Students, therefore, need to know how to search for information, images, video clips, print texts, or ideas for use in producing texts, for example, noncopyrighted images available on Google™ or images or social-networking tools such as Flickr™ for storing, searching, organizing, and sharing photographs. They also need to know how to search out and scan or copy texts from one media form that can be used to convey a different meaning in a different media form. For example, high-school students in the Literacy Lab program worked on an inquiry project that we termed the *Violence Project*. The inquiry was a response to this question: "How does violence in the media impact adolescents?" In responding to the question, students drew extensively on popular-culture texts to construct hypermedia productions. The students were required to select among popular-culture genres (e.g., film, television, video games) and to use popular-culture texts from the selected genre to show how those media defined, portrayed, and amplified violence that had an impact on adolescents.

As part of the project, one group of students read the newspaper piece for critical information about the broad media project. One pair of students focused on the *The Program*, a controversial film blamed for the death of a teenager in Philadelphia who unsuccessfully mimicked a scene from the film in which a teen laid down in the middle of a highway and traffic rolled harmlessly over him. Another pair selected a newspaper article charging that an episode of *Beavis and Butt-Head* motivated for a 5-year-old to light his house on fire, resulting in death of his little sister. A third pair constructed a rubric that classified different types of violence displayed in the *Beavis and Butt-Head* series overall.

The group that chose to work on *The Program* decided that it wanted to depend more on visual text than print after researching and gathering a range of print and visual media on the topic. They storyboarded an idea in which they scanned juxtaposed images of Michael Shingledecker, the high-school student from Pennsylvania who was killed when he lay down in the middle of a highway, mimicking the film. The Literacy Lab students juxtaposed a news photo of the highway death scene next to Michael's yearbook photo. The contrasted images were of a death on a lonely stretch of highway against a smiling image of a student with his future before him. The two scenes together depicted a hopeful life senselessly taken away. To the right of these images, they placed a picture of his friends grieving at the cemetery. The intertextual fabric of the whole visual text was somebody who would be greatly missed, who was gone forever possibly because of the power of media to influence his decisions and actions.

One of the pairs that chose violence types in *Beavis and Butt-Head* brought in multiple videos from their home VHS libraries. They set up a screening station, repeatedly viewing segments of the videotapes. As they viewed the tapes, they discussed what they were seeing and jotted down descriptions of the segments. They tabulated and charted different types of violence in a table and digitized the video segments that represented those categories. They wrote descriptions to accompany the video clips and put all of the media in Hyper-Studio™ to display the project to peers and parents during open-house night. The other group found more information about the fire that was allegedly connected to kids watching an episode of the series and referenced a story in *USA Today* (della Cava, 1993) and included the video clips from the episode that was referenced in the newspaper article.

In this work, students were learning to search for and select thematically related multimodal popular-culture texts to convey their beliefs about violence. This project required them to frame selections in terms of relevancy to their topic.

Interpreting and Using Genre Features

A second strategy involves the ability to interpret and use genre features that constitute genres of popular-culture texts such as mystery, science fiction, horror, romance, comedy, soap opera, music video, rap, musical, news, and reality television. Interpreting these texts entails applying knowledge of prototypical roles, settings, imagery, plot, and themes to texts, as well as noting instances of inventive deviation from status-quo conventions operating in these genres. They also explore audience appeal of genres, for example, how *The Harry Potter* series, which features Harry as the marginalized orphan or *The Spiderman* comic and film series, in which Spiderman is an "outsider" high-school student, may appeal to outsider, loner students (Scott, 2002). Or they explore how the appeal of manga—Japanese comics—may be related to the need for escape from the pressures of school, the pleasures of vicarious experience, acquiring knowledge of language employed in school contexts, and ease of reading (Allen & Ingulsrud, 2003).

Analyzing aspects of form also includes semiotic analysis of the visual codes of composition (framing pictures), movement (pan shots, zooms, close ups), and sequence (editing/juxtaposing of images; Bordwell & Thompson, 2004). This includes learning to analyze the use of film techniques used in video production, which, in turn, enhances students' ability to analyze the use of the techniques. For example, in analyzing a horror film, a teacher may demonstrate how the use of close-up shots of characters' anguished faces functions to portray characters' fears as a means of building suspense. Then, from learning to analyze purposes for use of certain techniques, students may know why they are using those techniques in creating their own video productions.

Learning to determine a purpose for use of film techniques is related to the larger pedagogical notion of purposeful viewing of video in the classroom in which students intentionally focus on certain content or techniques, as opposed to adopting a passive stance toward what is assumed to be effortless viewing (Kozma, 1991). Teachers can enhance student learning by defining specific purposes for viewing through the use of previewing, scaffolding, and postviewing discussions (Fisch, 2004).

Students may also explore the characteristics and development of specific music genres (blues, jazz, rock, country, Cajun, soul, rap, etc.) using clips from iTunes™, which is organized according to genres and historical periods to note genre patterns characteristic of certain genres or historical periods (Alvermann, Hagood, & Williams, 2001). They could also listen to podcasts available through iTunes™ or create podcasts (audio files published on the Internet and downloadable to iPods) about certain kinds of music or other popular-culture texts for sharing with peers by using online tutorials for creating the podcasts using Apple's Garageband™ (http://www.apple.com/ilife/tutorials/garageband/). Students' analysis of genre features in popular-culture texts can transfer to analysis and construction of written narratives. Adolescents apply genre knowledge for playing, for example, the *Starship Titanic* games (Mackey, 2005), writing of genre texts (Dyson, 2003; Rowe, Fitch, & Bass, 2003), or constructing talk-show presentation texts (Kamberelis & Dimitriadis, 1999). For example, based on a case-study analysis of his brother's strong interest in professional wrestling, one high-school English teacher, Andrew Huddleston, constructed story-writing activities based on students' knowledge of professional wrestling as a form of narrative melodrama (Alvermann, Huddleston, & Hagood, 2004). The teacher's brother graphed the plot lines associated with particular matches related to rising action, climax, and moment of last suspense, as well as comparison of these plots to literary texts.

In the Literacy Lab, Katie, a sophomore, became interested in the 60s music culture by talking with her parents and perusing their considerable music collection. After the death of Jerry Garcia, the leader of the Grateful Dead, she read all about Garcia and the band created replicas of the band's symbols and put them on her school gear, and critiqued the 60's music scene. For several weeks, Katie read everything she could find about the band in *Rolling Stone* and other music publications. Via her reading, she became fascinated with images of the band, both the pictures and the various symbols the band used. She scanned in pictures of Garcia working with the band and relaxing at home. She mimicked the genre of their music/lifestyle by creating a text with pictures of the band placed around a narrative she wrote by using San Francisco font as well as images and symbols from the band's albums.

In our research on early adolescents assigned to a class for struggling readers (O'Brien et al., 2005), we found that many of the students drew on their knowledge of prototypical narrative patterns and characters derived from video games in constructing and responding to stories. For one comic-book writing assignment using Comic Life™, software for creating comics, students who were active gamers drew not only these patterns and character types, but also the game-playing strategies to develop their comics using the software program. For example, one 8th-grade student, David, created a comic book entitled, "Die," derived from his experience playing the Mortal Combat™ and Dragon Ball Z™ games. A key strategy in playing these games involves one player teaming up with another player to acquire additional power to beat an opponent. In his comic book, David drew on this strategy to have his two "good guy" heroes join forces to oppose the monster, "Gore." He also drew on another game strategy—creating a clone to deceive one's opponents, but having his "good guy" heroes believe that they had killed the monster, Gore, when they actually had just killed Gore's clone. And, when the heroes are fighting the actual monster, the monster uses "Real Form" to transform himself into an even more powerful monster by draining everyone else's power. David noted that this can be a precarious move in that the monster can overpower himself and die or be killed. David ended his comic-book story by having the good guys escape through a portal into their own realm.

David's use of these strategies in constructing his story suggests that students acquire more than simply knowledge of prototypical narrative patterns and character types from video games. He is also acquiring conditional, problem-solving strategies, that, when given a certain type of challenge, his story hero needs to employ a certain action that typically addresses this challenge. This allows him to create a narrative sequence and dialogue exchange that dramatize the problems facing the hero and hero's skill in overcoming these problems. As these examples show, using genre features means not only manipulating features of texts via intertextual connections to popular media text genres, but also drawing on multiple genres features to create hybrid texts.

Linking, Connecting, and Revising Texts

Another basic strategy in understanding and producing popular-culture texts involves learning to define links or connections between texts, as well as revising texts associated with, for example, hypermedia production. In doing so, students acquire an intuitive understanding of three basic principles of digital media, what Lev Manovich (2001) defined as modularity, automation, and variability. *Modularity* refers to the fact that samples or data bits—e.g., stills, QuickTime™ video clips, and sounds, etc., can function as separate objects or modules that can be combined together in different ways without losing their independence so that material can then be readily added, deleted, or revised without having to completely redo the overall Web site or digital text. *Automation* refers to the ways in which the combination of these modular parts is often completed through the use of highly automated systems so that digital images can be automatically edited to improve their quality. *Variability* refers to variations in how the same texts can also be automatically created in different versions to suit individual users' needs or interests, as evident in hypertext literature in which users can select different paths for reading a hypertext novel.

Knowledge-construction links.   At one level, links to films, television, music, and video games provides knowledge to help students define concepts or understand certain ideas. A physics teacher uses examples from superhero comic books to give students problems to solve related to, for example, the speed with which superheroes fall to save someone (Kakalios, 2005). In her analysis of children's appropriation of popular-culture texts in "literacy jams" in primary grade classrooms, Anne Dyson (2003) found that children continually appropriate popular-culture texts into the "permeable curriculum." For example, in creating a radio play, students drew on knowledge of music genres/rap, deejay announcing/humor, interviewing, and celebrity performances. Or, in their writing, students drew on texts such as the *Goosebumps* television show to create character voices for a radio-show dialogue in ways that appropriated "scary story" genre conventions and social language from the television show. Dyson argued that while low-income students of color are particularly eager to import popular-culture texts, dominant notions of official literacy shaped by White, middle-class notions of literacy learning often preclude importation of the very texts that engage these students, which further alienates them from school cultures.

In her work on "cultural modeling," Carol Lee and her colleagues (Lee, Spencer, & Harpalani, 2003) examined how urban high-school students drew on their knowledge of metaphoric and symbolic language use in rap and hip-hop popular-cultural texts to interpret literary texts. By transferring their experiences with the uses of which metaphors and symbolism in everyday speech and rap music to the interpretation of symbolic language in Shakespeare's plays, students learned how to perceive the relevancy of literary texts to their own lives. An 8-year study of a curriculum designed for urban adolescents that incorporated hip-hop music, culture, and films into a high-school poetry unit found that students examined subordinate groups' challenges to

Studying scenes for use of popular-culture texts.   Researchers studying social uses of popular music have focused on what they define as *scenes.* Bennett and Peterson (2004) distinguished between three types of scenes: (a) the "local scene," which is organized around a particular geographic/physical space constituted by uses of popular-culture texts reflecting the unique feature of that space; (b) the "translocal scene," which is constituted by scattered local scenes that share a common interest in a particular type of popular text medium or genre; and (c) the "virtual scene," in which participants of the local scene share experiences about popular-culture texts through online fan clubs, zines, and chat rooms. In the classroom, students study particular music scenes in terms of how the music of a particular scene reflects certain genre conventions, local cultural practices, and promotional efforts (Bennett & Kahn-Harris, 2004; Bennett & Peterson, 2004).

Online contexts for use of popular-culture texts.   Students also learn literacies involved in responding to and constructing texts in online sites: chat rooms, blogs, MOO's (Multi-Object Orientation), MUD's, MUVES (Multiuser virtual environment), IMing, wikis, online fan clubs, or podcasts. For example, the Quest Atlantis project draws on students' shared background mythological knowledge of "quests" in characters through participation in MUVES (Barab, Thomas, Dodge, Squire, & Newell, 2004). The PalacePlanet MUVE site (see http://www.palaceplanet.net) represents a situated learning arena mediated by popular-culture texts in which participants adopt roles, language, and practices based on their popular-culture experience (Thomas, 2004). Adolescent Harry Potter fans manage an online "school newspaper," *The Daily Prophet* (www.dprophet.com; Jenkins, 2004), which can be used by students to construct their own online classroom fan site. Adolescent manga fans construct their own Manga (Black, 2005; Chandler-Olcott & Mahar, 2003), particularly in terms of female producers who challenge what is a largely male genre with male representations of females. And, zine production provides adolescents with a means of appropriating and parodying popular-culture representations. For example, a group of San Francisco adolescents produce the zine, Bamboozled (see http://www.bamboozled.org) to comment about contemporary issues in their lives and to express their counter-culture perspectives (Guzzetti & Gamboa, 2004; Knobel & Lankshear, 2002).

Students also produce online zines (e.g., http://zinebook.com ; http://etext. org/zines ; http://directory.google.com/Top/Arts/online_writing/E-zines/) as a means of actively expressing their counter-culture perspectives (Guzzetti & Gamboa, 2004; Knobel & Lankshear, 2002). Through e-zining, they are using online zines to challenge what they perceive to be status-quo sexist and racist norms in the culture, often through parody, satire, and spoofs. One study of three adolescent girls who published their own zine, *Burnt Beauty*, found that they employed intertextual links to other magazines, newspapers, and the Web both in terms of clips and critical reviews (Guzzetti & Gamboa, 2004). The zine focused on issues of feminism and featured reviews of TV programs, films, and music, as well as popular-culture portrayals of females, such as a critique of Barbie dolls. However, Knobel and Lankshear argued that given the subversive nature of zines, assigning zines in the classroom can be counterproductive.

As part of their participation in online sites, students are also engaged in constructing fan fiction—written narratives that often import and appropriate popular-culture texts as a bricolage of intertextual references, particularly from games, films, and television (Jenkins, 1992; Merchant, 2005). The fanfiction.net site fosters sharing fan fictions as well as sharing of users' favorite authors, stories, bands, video games, anime series, and home-page links. Users also post reviews that can be linked back to reviewers' biographical information (Black, 2005). Fan fictions have also become increasingly multimodal. For example, in constructing fantasy narratives about heroes and villains, 8- and 9-year-olds brought in video clips of films such as *The Wizard of Oz* and *Star Wars,* which portray villains, and then used this material to create their villain characters (Millard, 2005). One study of ELL students' construction of fan fictions based on the anime series *Card Captor Sakura* found that many of their stories contain issues such as pregnancy, violence, or suicide not found in the original anime stories (Black, 2005).

Students also create fan fiction in the classroom (Chandler Olcott & Mahar, 2003; Trainor, 2003). An ESL 13-year-old student who migrated from Taiwan to Australia created an elaborate adventure narrative with characters from the Nintendo games Mortal Kombat, The Ultimate Evil, Dungeon Keeper II, DOOM, and the Fighting Fantasy Gamebook role-play game series (Thomas, 2004). More recently, adolescents have turned to the use of hypermedia fan fiction through IMing, blogs (see http://anyaka.blogspot.com/), or trailers about new fan-fiction episodes (Thomas, 2004; this volume).

Students also participate in MOO's as simulations of literary text in which they assume that characters' roles operating in different settings draw from a text. In a MOO developed for studying *Brave New World*, students created their own fictional roles and shared discussions of the novel in fictional rooms (Rozema, 2003). Students can also go to the Literary Worlds site (http://brn227.brown.wmich.edu/literaryworlds/index.html) to participate in virtual settings based on frequently taught literary works in which they assume the roles of character-avatars.

In another Literacy Lab project, Eddie and Ron, both freshmen who read considerably below grade level, developed a Web site about Jim Harbaugh, who at this time was the star quarterback of the Indianapolis Colts. Eddie found images of Harbaugh in the *Indianapolis Monthly* magazine, which was running a feature story on Harbaugh. Ron located video clips of some of Harbaugh's best plays from television sports highlights that he had taped, saved these highlights into files, and wrote captions for them. Eddie rounded up some biographical information and news stories about Harbaugh from the *Indianapolis Monthly*, *Sports Illustrated* and other sources and synthesized it.

As Eddie and Ron worked together, they continued to sort out the text and images and modify their plan for Web pages. They collaborated using Super-Card™, an authoring package they were both learning that allowed them to mock-up the Web pages with displays of text, pictures, and video clips. Eddie looked up information in the SuperCard™ documentation to help Ron as Ron used menus to explore button options, select background colors, and put hyperlinks on pages. Eddie served as the format editor, double checking Ron's layouts of the objects on each page. The final product was a Super-Card™ stack that logically and aesthetically displayed text and pictures about Harbaugh's personal life, the evolution of his career, and key plays, which played as video clips in windows on separate pages with captions and descriptions. As the boys progressed on the project, they periodically called over one of the teachers to see what they had done, a reflection of the importance of social display of competence mediated by creation of this text.

These various social uses of popular-culture texts suggest the need for researchers to examine the practices and norms operating in these tool-mediated social worlds or communities, particularly in terms of how participants transfer practices across different worlds or communities. Researchers may examine how constructing imaginative language in adopting characters in fan-fiction transfers to the use of language in everyday social interactions.

Constructing Identities through Uses of Popular-Culture Texts

Another instructional strategy involves the use of popular-culture texts to help students explore aspects of their identities related to race, class, and gender differences (Knobel, 1999). By adopting voices, practices, genres, or discourses associated with uses of popular-culture texts, students construct different identities of, for example, a "blues fan" or an online "Buffy fan." By adopting musical tastes or listening practices based on certain music genres or performers, students construct a "sound identity" associated with their identities as fans of particular music genres or performers (McCarthy, Hudak, Miklavcic, & Saukko, 1999). For example, two adolescent African American males used hip-hop texts to construct allegiances to family members and attachment to a small Midwestern city (Dimitriadis, 2001). Analysis of their use of "Southern rap" indicated that they associated certain rap genres and rappers with certain geographic regions, rejecting what they perceived to be the violent aspects of the East Coast and West Coast rap conflicts between rappers Biggie Smalls and Tupac Shakur. They noted that rappers from the South are less likely to "diss" other rappers given what they perceived to be a sense of respect associated with identification with one's local neighborhood or community.

In producing videos, students expropriate popular-culture images to assign their own meanings to these images consistent with their identity construction (Goldfarb, 2002; Goodman, 2002). For example, a case-study analysis of Mani, an adolescent Tamil male living in Switzerland focused on his construction of collages and videos based on his responses as an avid fan of Jackie Chan films (Schneider, 2005). Mani admired Chan's ability to make films in a range of different cultural settings as an Asian male living in a largely White culture. Mani also admired the fact that Chan included outtakes on the DVDs of accidents and mistakes in his martial-arts stunts, a reflection of Chan's willingness to publicly reveal his limitations or vulnerabilities, an alternative perspective to that of the authoritative, omniscient male. Mani was therefore using his fan-based appropriation of Jackie Chan materials to construct his identities in terms of race and gender through his video productions.

Students also explore how the narratives, discourses, and language of popular-culture texts mediates identity construction. For example, they explore how a discourse of Whiteness in Hollywood films is often the invisible norm against which identities as "others" are constituted (Macarthy, Rodriquez, Meecham, David, Wilson-Brown, Godina, et al, 2004; Roediger, 2002). For example, films such as *Menace II Society, Higher Learning,* and *Falling Down* foster negative, racist representations of urban people of color in ways that serve to fuel suburban White resentment toward the inner city. In a study in which White and Native American participants rewrote prime-time television drama scripts about race relations, the White groups' scripts continued to perpetuate dominant White discourses, while the Native American groups altered the scripts to challenge White discourses (Bird, 2003).

Popular-culture texts also mediate hybridity in identity construction. Immigrant students moving between different racial or ethnic cultures experience shifts whereby the original meaning of popular-culture texts in their home culture no longer holds the same meaning in their new culture. Yemini female adolescents in a Detroit suburb used popular music as an unofficial expression of their negotiating alternative identities outside of their traditional Yemini culture (Sarroub, 2005). Canadian-African adolescents living in Alberta, Canada, employed American and Canadian popular culture to mediate their identity construction as Canadians (Kelly, 2004). Elsewhere, MTV World is adding three new channels, MTV Desi for Asian-Americans; MTV Chi, for Chinese-Americans; and MTV K, for Korean-Americans, that provide music and video appealing to these hybrid audiences (Sontag, 2005).

In addition to race, students' class backgrounds also shape their responses to, and construction of, popular-culture texts. Working-class White fourth graders' responses to horror fiction reflected ways in which they were grappling with the complexities of their everyday, often difficult lives (Hicks, 2005). In responding to the difficulties experienced by female characters in confessional magazines, working-class female readers adopted a stance of "flexible moral realism"—an "elastic code of ethics" used to accept the realistic portrayals of problematic aspects of relationships and to avoid imposing rigid moral standards to judge characters' practices (Greer, 2004).

Students' gender also influences their responses—gender defined as a free floating, fluid set of practices or performances that position people to adopt different versions of the self across different cultural contexts (Butler, 1999; Schweichert & Flynn, 2004). In studying portrayals of gender in teen magazines, students go beyond simply identifying sexist portrayals to consider how gender portrayals mediate their gender performances through uses of language and genres. In some cases, magazine ads address readers as "you" in an attempt to create a "synthetic sisterhood" in imaginary communities of consumption (Currie, 1999, p. 65). Or, they employ "quizzes" to position readers to adopt certain stances and beliefs about femininity in these magazines (Currie, 2001). One 8th-grade female responded positively to the magazine quizzes as a means of establishing a link to a larger community of female adolescents based on certain assumed norms for what it means to be popular (DeBlase, 2003). At the same time, researchers cite instances of adolescent females moving beyond being positioned as passive dupes of consumerism to their active construction of identity through parody of consumerism in zines and or Web sites (Guzzetti & Gamboa, 2004; Knobel & Lankshear, 2002).

There has also been a strong interest in males' construction of popular-culture texts in terms of the social need to perform culturally constructed masculine identities (Newkirk, 2002; Smith & Wilhelm, 2002). While teachers often object to the violence portrayed in popular-culture texts for boys, Newkirk (2002) argued that students should be allowed to read or write texts with violent content as a means of examining their attitudes toward such content.

In the Literacy Lab, Dario and Juan, both recent immigrants from Mexico, worked together writing a story about "terrorist drug runners." The story, inspired by numerous films and media stories about drug production and drug cartels in Columbia, enabled Juan and Dario to project themselves into the story as savvy, dangerous drug lords in a large cartel. Their collaborator, Scott, who was writing the story with them (Scott sat behind Juan and Dario who were at the keyboard, watching what they wrote about him) was positioned by them in the story as a bumbling coward whom they roughed up and captured. When Scott protested the way that they had characterized him in the story, they enacted the story in real time in the Lab, threatening Scott until he left the group and went back to his seat as Dario and Juan laughed and made jokes about him in Spanish. As we wrote in previous analysis of this incident (Moje, Dillon, & O'Brien, 2000), Dariio and Juan used the story as a shared text to construct and affirm their cultural identity amplified by the machismo in violent drug films. The strategy of providing time for students in the Lab to write about themselves in ways that helped them explore and enact various identities amplified through popular media worked to engage them in reading and writing. The incident with Scott shows how the discourse of the film played out in their story was connected both temporally and spatially to their real lives when they played out the scene in the story.

Critiquing Popular-Culture Texts

While students may be knowledgeable about popular culture, they may not know how to critique the ideological and institutional forces shaping popular culture (Ogdon, 2001). They could examine how popular-culture texts reflect and perpetuate values of consumerism and conservative political agendas in which private, individual needs take precedent over the larger public good related to a sense of shared community. And, younger children can reflect on how they are socialized into consumer "youth-market" culture through uses of commodified, branded popular-culture texts (Schor, 2004) or the use of "pester power" on adults to purchase products (Kenway & Bullen, 2001, p. 47).

Students also critically examine how corporate ownership often limits content to highly predictable, homogenized, "safe," genre material. Students keep media logs of their viewing television programs, listening to radio stations or CDs, or reading books, magazines, or newspapers (Beach, 2007). They then note which of these texts are produced by corporate conglomerates such as TimeWarner™ (CNN/AOL), Disney™ (ABC) the News Corporation™ (Fox), GE/Vivendi™ (NBC, RCA/Arista), Viacom™ (CBS, MTV), Clear Channel™ (1,200 radio stations), Bertlesmann™ (Columbia/Epic Records).

Students can also analyze ideological assumptions and discourses inherent in these corporate systems. Philip Green (2005) argued that the commercial-network-drama programs produced in this system promote the values of "national unity, individual competition, the ultimate goodness of the social order, and the sovereignty of commercial television itself" (p. 79); an ideology contradicted by racial, class, and gender conflicts, the negative effects of competition, the breakdown of the social order, and the failure of the system to challenge political misrepresentations. Green also noted that, given the need to fill up a 24-hour broadcast schedule, commercial television continually recycles material from a limited reservoir of genres or storylines. To avoid boring their audiences, programs must portray increasingly more sensationalized or graphic material to maintain audiences' attention, while at the same time avoiding "being caught saying anything that is not conventionally acceptable" (p. 84).

Students could also examine how popular-culture texts are related and serve to construct the binaries of the "local" versus the "global" in a global economy. Popular-culture texts are often created by international conglomerates to sell to a global market with little attention to variations in local cultures. Maira and Soep (2005) cited the state of California as a site of increasing cultural immigration from Asia and Latin America in which young people experience hybrid mixtures of both local and global youth cultures. An analysis of the Diva Starz interactive dolls (designed for 6 to 11-year-old girls) showed

further research that examines instructional methods for fostering these ironic or subversive links and the degree to which they foster adopting a "culture-jamming" (Lankshear & Knobel, 2003) critical stance.

We also need to understand how the multimediating itself serves to represent students' understanding of the world, particularly, how students combine their experience of different texts that mediate experiences from different perspectives leading to different understandings of events or experiences. We need to understand how students then sort through competing perspectives on such an event and determine differences in the validity of these competing perspectives. We need to know more about the levels of focused concentration and attention versus interruption in formulating ideas through linking texts. And, we need to know more about the social incentives for making intertextual connections, as reflected in the complex rhetorical readings involved in, for example, simultaneously responding to multiple windows of IMing audiences to maintain social ties with these different audiences (Lewis & Fabos, 2005).

Popular-Culture Texts versus Print Texts

Teachers' use of popular-culture texts is often limited by the pressure on schools to prepare students for NCLB-mandated standardized reading or writing tests. Teachers often assume that because they must focus on reading or writing of print texts to prepare students for these tests, instruction involving reading or writing of popular-culture texts will not adequately prepare students for these tests. Unfortunately, other than the Hobbs and Frost (2003) research, there is little research examining the ways in which instruction using popular-culture texts can actually benefit students' test performance. There is, therefore, a need for more research that examines the transfer of acquired literacy practices from interpretation and production of popular-culture texts to performance on more traditional measures of reading and writing such as what is assessed on standardized reading and writing tests.

This research may challenge the false bifurcation of popular-culture texts and print texts given the blurring of the two. At the same time, the traditional curriculum framework that presupposes distinctions between reading, writing, speaking, listening, and viewing, needs to be replaced with a curriculum framework based on the strategies involved in understanding and producing texts such as those cited in this chapter. In this framework, literacies acquired in analysis of texts transfer to literacies involved in text production and vice versa. Students would then be evaluated based on their ability to transfer what they learned in critiquing texts to producing texts as well as what they learned in producing texts to critiquing texts.

Transporting Popular-Culture Texts from Nonschool to School Contexts

Transporting popular-culture texts from nonschool to school contexts can be challenging, and, as may be the case with zines, not necessarily productive. As soon as popular-culture texts are imported into the classroom, they no longer retain their original meanings constituted by how they serve to resist school and authority. Squire (2005) cited the example of requiring students to play *Civilization III* when the appeal of games often lies in the fact that they allow for many choices; restricting choices via the school curriculum robs them of their appeal to students. Importing popular-culture texts into school also creates a challenge for teachers attempting to assume the role of "expert" on popular-culture texts, when, in fact, their students often know far more about these texts than teachers do, as reflected in their discussions of playing *Civilization III* on the Apolyton site (http://apolyton.net) (Downes, 2005).

An alternative approach repositions students as the "expert" teachers of popular-culture texts (Hull & Schulz, 2002). In an observation study of five high-school teachers who integrated popular-culture texts into their teaching, students most valued activities that provided them with critical concepts and approaches for analyzing the texts, as well as instances in which *they* were perceived as authorities (Callahan & Low, 2004). In one of the classes dealing with hip-hop culture, the teacher readily admitted his lack of knowledge as a "cultural outsider," which led students to formulate their theory of language use in hip-hop texts. As a result, students were positioned as authorities and language use was recontextualized and reinvented for alternative uses.

At the same time, teachers can share their own knowledge of how their identities were mediated by experience with popular-culture texts as members of different races, classes, gender, or generational groups or as someone socialized through popular-culture texts in a different cultural context. For example, Walter Jacobs (2005) used a "teacher as text" (p. 9) approach to describe how, as an African-American, he brought certain experiences with racism to constructing the meaning of popular-culture texts. Then, when his predominately White students noted that he may be biased about his perceptions and was therefore racist, he argued that there are multiple forms of racism representing different forms of institutional power and authority shaping the construction of texts.

Having Students' Study Their Own Uses of Texts

We have argued that the meaning of popular-culture texts is constituted by how those texts are used in certain social contexts or "scenes" (Bennett & Peterson, 2004). This suggests the value of having students study their own uses of texts in school, family, peer group, community, or virtual worlds, and how these texts represent these worlds. Thus, rather than analyzing texts per se, students could conduct small-scale media ethnography studies of peers' or their own uses of texts as tools for constructing their identities and attitudes, as well as participation in cultural events, scenes, or virtual online worlds (Beach, 2005; Bird, 2003). For example, students could study how the meaning of certain popular-culture songs by a particular group are influenced by their social participation in that group's online fan-club site, participation in which they assume social status given their knowledge about the group. And, consistent with current multimodal presentation of ethnographic results, they may present their findings using hypermedia productions. Research is needed to examine how having students conduct studies of their uses of popular-culture texts enhances their understanding of how their identities and beliefs are constituted through their uses of texts.

Understanding the Values Acquired from Popular-Culture Texts

In interpreting and constructing popular-culture texts, students are ultimately defining attitudes and values. The students in the Violence Project were examining their beliefs about violence in society. Much of the research on the values acquired from popular-culture texts has been narrowly focused on studying what are assumed to be negative behaviors or attitudes related to violence and sex (Sternheimer, 2003). We know little about the nature of other larger attitudes or values related to identities, world views and political beliefs (Moje & van Helden, 2004).

We also need to know more about how experiences with texts representing values of past historical periods or generations are perceived by students in terms of being consistent with or different from their values in contemporary society. Gee (2002) compared the values of the baby boomer generation as reflected in *Sesame Street* versus the millennial generation as reflect in *Blues Clues* and *Babar*.

We also need to know more about how students in different cultural contexts acquire different values that may or may not transfer across different contexts, given value hierarchies in society. Can students step outside the pervasive commercial popular-culture mediasphere to formulate alternative cultural perspectives? For example, students in urban cultures may acquire certain values associated with hip-hop culture that, in some cases, has not been coopted by the commercial mediasphere. Can these students use hip-hop texts to formulate new, alternative cultural perspectives? Do those perspectives transfer into other cultures? If so, why or why not?

Finally, critiquing and producing popular-culture texts leads students to challenge status-quo cultural values. Critical pedagogy theorists posited the need to move beyond critique to action through production of counter-hegemonic texts and activities (McCarthy et al., 2004). Given the conservative climate of many schools, teachers need to develop strategies to effectively construct these texts that result in social change (Pardue, 2004). They also need to help students examine successes and failures of uses of popular-culture texts in the past to challenge the status quo, for example, rock music in the 1960s.

In discussing popular-culture texts and strategies for teaching these texts in schools, we have argued that popular-culture texts are so ubiquitous, interconnected, and recursive that it is almost an anachronism to try to distinguish popular-culture texts from other texts. However, if we take the stance that new literacies practices are part of uses of popular-culture texts in the mediasphere, then we need to support students use, production, and critique of those texts. We must also acknowledge that the official discourse of schooling, the schooled literacies, and deep grammar of schooling (Lankshear & Knobel, 2003) if not permeated by popular-culture texts and new literacies practices they engender, will increasingly alienate the students of the mediasphere. In proposing strategies to facilitate engagement with, and construction and critique of popular-culture texts, we hope that some possibilities for linking the new literacies of popular-culture texts and traditional print literacies can be realized. Inherent in those approaches, of course, are new areas of inquiry that we are only just beginning to realize.

References

Allen, K., & Ingulsrud, J. E. (2003). "Manga" literacy: Popular culture and the reading habits of Japanese college students. *Journal of Adolescent & Adult Literacy, 46*(8), 674–683.

Alloy Marketing. (2006). *College students surf back to campus on a wave of digital connections.* Retrieved September 10, 2006, from http://www.alloymarketing.com/investor_relations/news_releases/index.html

Alvermann, D. E., Hagood, M. C., & Williams, K. B. (2001). Image, language, and sound: Making meaning with popular culture texts. *Reading Online, 4*(11). Retrieved June 12, 2007 from http://www.readingonline.org/newliteracies/lit_index.asp?HREF=/newliteracies/action/alvermann/index.html

Alvermann, D. E., Huddleston, A., & Hagood, M. C. (2004). What could professional wrestling and school literacy practices possibly have in common? *Journal of Adolescent & Adult Literacy, 47*(7), 532–540.

Alvermann, D., Moon, J., & Hagood, M. (1999). *Popular culture in the classroom: Teaching and researching critical media literacy.* Newark, DE: International Reading Association.

Barab, S. A., Thomas, M. K., Dodge, T., Squire, K., & Newell, M. (2004). Critical design ethnography: Designing for change. *Anthropology & Education Quarterly, 35*(2) 254–268.

Beach, R. (2005). Researching response to literature and the media. In A. Goodwyn & A. Stables (Eds.), *Learning to read critically in language and literacy* (pp. 123–148). Thousand Oaks, CA: Sage.

Beach, R. (2007). *Teachingmedialiteracy.com: A web-linked guide to resources and activities.* New York: Teachers College Press.

Beach, R., & Myers, J. (2001). *Inquiry-based English instruction: Engaging students in life and literature.* New York: Teachers College Press.

Beach, R., & O'Brien, D. (2005). Playing texts against each other in the multi-modal English classroom. *English in Education, 39*(2), 50–65.

Bennett, A., & Kahn-Harris, K. (Eds.). (2004). *After subculture: Critical studies in contemporary youth culture.* New York: Palgrave Macmillan.

Bennett, A., & Peterson, R. A. (Eds.). (2004). *Music scenes: Local, translocal, and virtual.* Nashville, TN: Vanderbilt University Press.

Bhabha, H. (1994). *The location of culture.* New York: Routledge.

Bird, E. (2003). *The audience in everyday life: Living in a media world.* New York: Routledge.

Black, R. W. (2005). Access and affiliation: The literacy and composition practices of English language learners in an online fan-fiction community. *Journal of Adult and Adolescent Literacy, 49*(2), 118–128.

Blackford, H. (2004). *Out of this world: Why literature matters to girls*. New York: Teachers College Press.

Bordwell, D., & Thompson, K. (2004). *Film art: An introduction* (7th ed.). New York: McGraw Hill.

Brooker, W., & Jermyn, D. (Eds.). (2003) *The audience studies reader*. New York: Routledge.

Butler, J. (1999). *Gender trouble: Feminism and the subversion of identity* (2nd ed.). New York: Routledge.

Callahan, M., & Low, B. E. (2004). At the crossroads of expertise: The risky business of teaching popular culture. *English Journal, 93*(3), 52–57.

Carrington, V. (2003). "I'm in a bad mood. Let's go shopping": Interactive dolls, consumer culture and a "glocalized" model of literacy. *Journal of Early Childhood Literacy, 3*(2), 83–98.

Center for Children and Technology. (2004). *Television goes to school: The impact of video on student learning in formal education*. Retrieved October 2, 2005, from http://www.cpb.org/stations/reports/tvgoestoschool/

Chandler-Olcott, K., & Mahar, D. (2003). Tech-savviness' meets multiliteracies: Exploring adolescent girls' technology-mediated literacy. *Reading Research Quarterly, 38*(3), 356–385.

Clark, A. (2003). *Natural-born cyborgs: Minds, technologies, and the future of human intelligence*. New York: Oxford University Press.

Cresswell, T. (2004). *Place: A short introduction*. Malden, MA: Blackwell.

Currie, D. (1999). *Girl talk: Adolescent magazines and their readers*. Toronto: University of Toronto Press.

Currie, D. (2001). Dear Abby: Advice pages as a site for the operation of power. *Feminist Theory, 2*, 259–281.

DeBlase, G. (2003). Acknowledging agency while accommodating romance: Girls negotiating meaning in literacy transactions. *Journal of Adolescent & Adult Literacy, 40*(8), 624–635.

della Cava, M. R. (1993, October 21). Taking aim at TV violence: Lawmakers tell industry: Clean up act. *USA Today*, 1A.

Dimitriadis, G. (2001). *Performing identity/performing culture: Hip hop as text, pedagogy, and lived practice*. New York: Peter Lang.

Dolby, N. (2003). Popular culture and democratic practice. *Harvard Educational Review, 73*(3), 258–284.

Downes, S. 2005. Places to Go: Apolyton. Innovate 1(6). Retrieved June 12, 2007, from http://www.innovateonline.info/index.php?view=article&id=198

Dyson, A. H. (2003). *The brothers and sisters learn to write: Popular literacies in childhood and school cultures*. New York: Teachers College.

Ellsworth, E. (2004). *Places of learning: Media, architecture, pedagogy*. New York: Routledge.

Evans, J. (2005). Introduction: The changing nature of literacy in the twenty-first century. In J. Evans (Ed.), *Literacy moves on: Popular culture, new technologies, and critical literacy in the elementary classroom* (pp. 1–12). Portsmouth, NH: Heinemann.

Fairclough, N. (2003). *Analysing discourse: Textual analysis for social research*. New York: Routledge.

Fisch, S. M. (2004). *Children's learning from educational television: Sesame Street and beyond*. Mahwah, NJ: Lawrence Erlbaum.

Foehr, U. G. (2006). *Media multitasking among American youth: Prevalence, predictors and pairings*. Kasiser Family Foundation. Retrieved June 12, 2007 from http://www.kff.org/entmedia/upload/7592.pdf

Gee, J. P. (2002). Millennials and bobos, Blues Clues, and Sesame Street: A story for our times. In D. E. Alvermann (Ed.), *Adolescents multiliteracies in a digital world* (pp. 51–67). New York: Peter Lang.

Gee, J. P. (2003). *What video games have to teach use about learning and literacy.* New York: Palgrave MacMillan.

Giroux, H. A., & Simon, R. I. (1988). Schooling, popular culture, and a pedagogy of possibility. *Journal of Education, 170*(1), 9–26.

Goldfarb, B. (2002). *Visual pedagogy: Media cultures in and beyond the classroom.* Durham, NC: Duke University Press.

Goodman, S. (2002). *Teaching youth media: A critical guide to literacy, video production, and social change.* New York: Teachers College Press.

Götz, M., Lemish, D., Aidman, A., & Moon, H. (2003). The role of media in children's' make-believe worlds: A cultural comparison of Germany, Israel, the USA, and South Korea. *Munich: International Central Institute for Youth and Educational Television.* Retrieved May 3, 2005, from http://www.bronline.de/jugend/izi/english/televizion/16_2003_1/e_goetz_ua.htm

Green, P. (2005). *Primetime politics: The truth about conservative lies, corporate control, and television culture.* Lanham, MD: Rowan & Littlefield.

Greer, J. (2004). "Some of their stories are like my life, I guess": Working-class women readers and confessional magazines. In P. Schweickart & E. Flynn (Eds.), *Reading sites: Social difference and reader response* (pp. 135–165). New York: Modern Language Association.

Grossberg, L. (1997). *Dancing in spite of myself: Essays on popular culture.* Durham, NC: Duke University Press.

Guzzetti, B., & Gamboa, M. (2004). Zines for social justice: Adolescent girls writing on their own. *Reading Research Quarterly, 39*(4), 408–436.

Hall, S. (Ed.). (1997). *Representation: Cultural representations and signifying practices.* Thousand Oaks, CA: Sage.

Hicks, D. (2005). Cultural hauntings: Girlhood fictions from working-poor America. *Qualitative Inquiry, 11*(2), 170–190.

Hills, M. (2002). *Fan cultures.* New York: Routledge.

Hirsch, M., & Kacandes, I. (Eds.). (2005). *Teaching the representation of the Holocaust.* New York: Modern Language Association.

Hobbs, R. (2004). Analyzing advertising in the English language arts classroom: A quasi-experimental study. *Studies in Media & Information Literacy Education, 4*(2). Retrieved May 3, 2005 from http://www.utpress.utoronto.ca/journal/ejournals/simile

Hobbs, R. (2007). Reading the media in high school. New York: Teachers College Press.

Hobbs, R., & Frost, R. (2003). Measuring the acquisition of media-literacy skills. *Reading Research Quarterly, 38*, 330–356.

Hull, G. A. (2003). Youth culture and digital media: New literacies for new times. *Research in the Teaching of English, 38*(2), 229–233.

Hull, G. A., & Nelson, M. E. (2005). Locating the semiotic power of multimodality. *Written Communication, 22*(2), 224–261.

Hull, G., & Schultz, K. (Eds.). (2002). *School's out: Bridging out-of-school literacies with classroom practices.* New York: Teachers College Press.

Jacobs, W. (2005). *Speaking the lower frequencies: Students and media literacy.* Albany, NY: SUNY Press.

Jenkins, H. (1992). *Textual poachers: Television fans and participatory culture.* New York: Routledge.

Jenkins, H. (2004). Why Heather *can* write. *Technology Review, 2.* Retrieved October 4, 2005, from http://www.technologyreview.com/articles/04/02/wo_jenkins020604.asp

Johnson, S. (2005). *Everything bad is good for you: How today's popular culture is actually making us smarter.* New York: Riverhead Books.

Kaiser Family Foundation. (2005). *Generation M: Media in the lives of 8-18 year-olds.* Washington, DC: Kaiser Family Foundation. Retrieved June 21, 2005, from http://www.kff.org/entmedia/entmedia030905pkg.cfm

Kakalios, J. (2005). *The physics of superheroes.* New York: Penguin.

Schrøder, K., Drotner, K., Kline, S., & Murray, C. (2003). *Researching audiences.* London: Arnold.

Schwarz, G., & Brown, P. (Eds.). (2005). *Media literacy: Transforming curriculum and teaching. 104th Yearbook of the National Society for the Study of Education.* Malden, MA: Blackwell.

Schweickart, P. P., & Flynn, E. A. (Eds.). (2004). *Reading sites: Social difference and reader response.* New York: Modern Language Association.

Scott, A. O. (2002, June 16). A hunger for fantasy, a movie empire to feed it. *The New York Times, 1,* 26.

Smith, M. W., & Wilhelm, J. D. (2002). *"Reading don't fix no Chevy's": Literacy in the lives of young men.* Portsmouth, NH: Heinemann.

Sontag, D. (2005, June 19). I want my hyphenated-identity MTV. *The New York Times, 2,* 1.

Spiegelman, A. (1996). *The complete Maus: A survivor's tale.* New York: Pantheon.

Squire, K. (2005). Changing the game: What happens when video games enter the classroom? *Journal of Online Education, 1*(6). Retrieved November 9, 2005, from http://innovateonline.info/index.php?view=article&id=82

Sternheimer, K. (2003). *It's not the media: The truth about pop culture's influence on children.* Boulder, CO: Westview Press.

Street, B. (2005). *Literacy: An advanced resource book for students.* New York: Routledge.

Strinati, D. (2004). *An introduction to theories of popular culture* (2nd ed.). New York: Routledge.

Thomas, A. (2004). Digital literacies of the cybergirl. *E-Learning, 1*(3), 358–382.

Trainor, J. (2003). Critical cyberliteracy: Reading and writing *The X-Files*. In J. Mahiri (Ed.), *What they don't learn in school: Literacy in the lives of urban youth* (pp. 145–156). New York: Peter Lang.

Twitchell, J. B. (2004). *Branded nation: The marketing of megachurch, college Inc., and museumworld.* New York: Simon and Schuster.

Vasquez, V. (2005). Creating opportunities for critical literacy with young children: Using every issues and everyday text. In J. Evans (Ed.), *Literacy moves on: Popular culture, new technologies, and critical literacy in the elementary classroom* (pp. 83–105). Portsmouth, NH: Heinemann.

Weaver, J. A. (2005). *Popular culture.* New York: Peter Lang.

Wysocki, A. (2004). Opening new media to writing: Openings and justifications. In A. Wysocki, J. Johnson-Eilola, C. L. Selfe, & G. Sirc (Eds.), *Writing new media: Theory and applications for expanding the teaching of composition* (pp. 1–42). Logan, UT: Utah State University Press.

Xu, S. H. (2005). *Trading cards to comic strips: Popular culture texts and literacy learning in grades K–8.* Newark, DE: International Reading Association.

CHAPTER **28**

Using New Media in the Secondary English Classroom

ILANA SNYDER
and SCOTT BULFIN
MONASH UNIVERSITY, AUSTRALIA

Introduction

Since desktop computers were introduced into schools in the late 1970s, increasingly grandiose claims have been made about their implications for education. Writers predicted that computer technologies would transform education, altering things for the better. Perelman (1993), for example, declared that "hyperlearning" will enable "virtually anyone … to learn anything … anywhere, anytime" (p. 23), making schools as material institutions a thing of the past. Such claims that characterized the early days of uncritical boosterism, however, have been critiqued as ignoring the deeply complex and contextualized ways in which information and communication technologies (ICT) are embedded in local and global structures of commerce, industry, and education (e.g., Snyder, 2002; Snyder & Beavis, 2004). The dismantling of schools still does not seem imminent—even less so in the developing world than in the developed world. At the same time, however, the rapidly expanding use of knowledge-based information technologies to enhance and accelerate the production of knowledge and information means that most domains of life are affected. Moreover, as the Internet becomes a universal tool of interactive with new cultural forms might mean for schools and for critical education. Of contemporary importance is researchers' interest in how teachers might handle the tension between calls for more innovative teaching and responsiveness to young people's lives and meeting demands for more high-stakes assessment and greater centralized control of educational policy and curriculum.

Useful Theoretical Approaches

In this section, some theoretical frameworks useful for investigating new media in secondary classrooms are identified. Frameworks that help explain the new multimodal textual formations that dominate the communication landscape receive particular attention as understanding them, together with the literacy practices associated with their production and use, have implications for curriculum and pedagogical practices. Although the New Literacy Studies (NLS) offers a generative framework for thinking about the complex issues involved, no one theory is adequate to engage the richness, complexity, variety, and novelty inherent in the literacy practices associated with the use of new media (Snyder, 2002). The reality is that understanding the use of ICT in secondary-English classrooms is often an interdisciplinary endeavor. In their variety, the different theoretical approaches identified here suggest multiple ways to analyze, evaluate, and critique the new spaces, the emerging cultural forms, and the experiences young people have when interacting with them. They also suggest new pedagogies that take account of the forms of knowledge and information associated with the use of ICT.

The New Literacy Studies

Social accounts of literacy as represented in the NLS offer a potent framework for investigating the use of ICT in the secondary-English classroom. Researchers who have taken the "social turn" recognize that reading and writing are always situated within specific social contexts, and that it is these contexts that give meaning to the practices of reading and writing. The NLS, conceived as a body of independent yet linked work produced over the past 20 years across a number of disciplines, including anthropology, history, psychology, and sociolinguistics exemplifies the social approach to literacy research (Barton & Hamilton, 1998; Barton, Hamilton, & Ivanic, 2000; Gee, 1996; Heath, 1983; Scribner & Cole, 1981; Street, 1984).

Increasingly, the NLS has directed attention toward the understanding that there is a need to move beyond limited psychological accounts of literacy to ones that capture the complexity of literacy practices in contemporary society. Rather than defining literacy as a set of static skills taught in schools and associated with books and writing, NLS research examines literacy practices and events looking at the role of literacy in people's everyday lives, in their homes, at work, and at school (Barton & Hamilton, 1998; Pahl & Rowsell, 2005; Prinsloo & Breier, 1996; Snyder, Angus, & Sutherland-Smith, 2002; Street,

1995, 2001). The NLS rejects the dominant view of literacy as a "neutral" technical skill, conceptualizing it instead as "an ideological practice, implicated in power relations and embedded in specific cultural meanings and practices" (Street, 1995, p. 1).

The NLS presents a framework for rethinking what teachers might do with new-media cultures and with globalized flows of information and text, as well as how to engage students' diverse backgrounds and understandings of the world (Luke, 2005). Once the framework is understood, teachers can find the resources, grounds, and normative purposes for teaching literacy, not from textbooks and skills taxonomies, but by attending closely to what children and communities actually do with texts, old and new, print and multimodal, traditional and radical.

Multimodality

As well as the ideas that shape the NLS, the work of social semioticians such as Kress (1995, 2003) is also significant. Not only has there been a social turn in literacy studies; there has also been what Kress called a "visual turn," which is changing the ways communication and meaning making are understood. In short, researchers working in this area argued that communication and learning are becoming more and more multimodal (Jewitt & Kress, 2003; Kress & van Leeuwen, 1996, 2001).

In an electronically mediated world, literacy practices include multiple forms of representation: to be literate means recognizing how different modalities are combined in complex ways to create meaning. These other modes incorporate diagrams, pictures, video, gesture, speech, and sound. In an increasingly multimodal communication landscape, understandings of language are no longer limited to grammar, lexicon, and semantics: communication often comprises a wider range of semiotic systems that cut across reading, writing, viewing, and speaking (Snyder, 2001b; Street, 2001). In the context of new media, what looks like the same text or multimedia genre on paper or on screen is not functionally the same. The multimedia text follows different meaning conventions and requires an interdisciplinary range of methods of analysis: linguistic, semiotic, social, cultural, historical, and critical.

The collaboration between Kress and van Leeuwen (1996, 2001) has produced systematic accounts of the ways in which multimodal texts communicate meaning. Drawing on a broad range of examples, including children's drawings, textbook illustrations, photojournalism, advertising images and fine art, as well as three-dimensional forms such as sculpture and toys, the authors have examined the differences and similarities between the grammar of language and that of visual communication. They have also outlined an approach to social discourse in which color plays an equal role to language and how two different but related thought processes interact in the design and production of communicative messages: "design thinking" and "production thinking," the kinds of thinking that occur in direct interaction with the materials and media

Nixon, 2003). In their move away from cognitive models to concentrate on cultural and social aspects of language use, many of the studies represented in this chapter share common ground with the theoretical approaches and ethnographically oriented methodologies of the NLS.

While the review begins with a brief overview of the first 2 decades of research (the 1980s and 1990s), with particular attention given to a major Australian project and to a body of work that represents critical approaches to technology, the focus is on the 21st century, an analysis and synthesis of more recent research provoked and guided by the questions outlined earlier.

Research 1980 to 2000

The first decade of research was dominated by a plethora of studies that set out to determine whether the use of computers improved writing and in the main drew upon accounts of literacy conceived predominantly in psychological terms. By the mid-1980s understandings of literacy as social practice became more widely accepted. With this increased sensitivity to the social setting in which the computers were used, some researchers shifted the focus from the isolated writer to the writer in context (e.g., Eldred, 1991; Susser, 1993); some began to explore the possibilities of the computer as a site for the social construction of knowledge (Dickinson, 1986; Herrmann, 1987). A number of studies began to adopt multiple perspectives (e.g., Hawisher & Selfe, 1989, 1991), while others examined computer-mediated literacies through a particular ideological lens (Goodson & Mangan, 1996). More generally, there was a growing recognition that computers in classrooms appeared "unlikely to negate the powerful influence of the differential socialization of students by social class and its effects on their success or failure in school" (Herrmann, 1987, p. 86).

The social approach to computers and their use made gender issues central to discussions of technology (Haraway, 1991; Kramarae, 1988; Reinen & Plomp, 1997). Early research on computers and gender focused on women's exclusion from the computer revolution (Gerrard, 1999). Women and girls were found to be anxious about computers (Collis, 1985; Gerrard, 1999), unchallenged by the unstimulating assignments and lack of hands-on experience they received in school (Levin & Gordon, 1989), discouraged from pursuing a career in technology, and stereotyped as phobics in advertising (Hawkins, 1985). A Scandinavian study showed that adolescent girls were rejecting computers in disproportionate numbers, presumably because of their lack of sympathy for the control ideology that drives the construction and invention of computers, and because of the obstacle to quality interaction between people that they may erect (Staberg, 1994). Research also examined ways to inform the computer-based classroom with a feminist approach to pedagogy (Selfe, 1990; Sofia, 1998), considered the computer conference as a medium that promotes or shuts out women's voices (Flores, 1990; Romano, 1993), and investigated girls' use of the Internet (Kaplan & Farrell, 1994). A number of studies have pursued gender issues in relation to video and computer games (Cassell & Jenkins, 1998; Cunningham, 1995; Gray, 1992).

Also informed by a social approach, researchers examined computer-mediated communication (CMC). They observed that the electronic spaces in which writers and readers create, exchange, and comment on texts have the potential for supporting student-centred learning and discursive practices that can be different in form, and, some claim, more engaging and democratic than those in more traditional classrooms (Batson, 1988; Sandholz, Ringstaff, & Dwyer, 1997).

The *Digital Rhetorics* study (Lankshear, Bigum, Green, Honan, Durrant, Morgan, et al., 1997; Lankshear & Snyder, 2000) exemplifies research informed by the understanding of literacy as social practice. The 2-year study investigated the relationship between literacy and technology in teaching and learning and argued that education must enable young people to become proficient in operational, cultural, and critical dimensions of literacy (Green, 1988). The investigation of 11 research sites, representing a range of circumstances, policy, and resourcing arrangements and professional knowledge bases, identified five broad patterns of practice: (a) complexity, (b) fragility, (c) discontinuity, (d) conservation, and (e) limited authenticity. The analysis suggested five principles for practice when ICT are used: (a) teachers first, (b) complementarity, (c) workability, (d) equity, and (e) focus on trajectories. The project found little critical emphasis in the sessions observed that suggested the extent to which classroom practices involving ICT were being exhausted on "operational" matters. This was understandable given the relatively limited prior experience many teachers had had with ICT, but the telling finding reinforced the importance of attending to all the patterns and principles identified in the study in future policy directions, teacher-education programs, and professional-development initiatives.

Increasingly, the Internet has become a site for research (e.g., Jones, 1999; Warschauer, 1999). Informed by the understanding of literacy as a set of social practices, investigations have focused on (a) new literacy practices (Gilster, 1997; Lankshear, 1997; Mosenthal & Watts-Pailliotet, 1999; Snyder, 1997); (b) issues of identity (Sudweeks, McLaughlin, & Rafaeli, 1998; Turkle, 1995); (c) class and access (Castner, 1997; Grabill, 1998; Selwyn, Gorard, & Williams, 2001); and (d) the maleness of the Web (Takayoshi, Huot, & Huot, 1999). The findings of research emphasize the need to teach students how to critically assess the reliability or value of the information they find on the Web by understanding not only its textual but also its nontextual features such as images, links, and interactivity (Bruce & Hogan, 1998; Burbules, 1997; Burbules & Callister, 2000; LeCourt, 1998).

Although it might appear that research and related policies have moved from the somewhat narrow approaches of the late 1970s to the more recent one way and instrumental: it is always two-way and relational. These under-standings, of course, are not universal.

Before the five themes are presented, it is salutary to point out that, as in most research areas, indeed, as this handbook epitomizes, there are available overviews of the research literature (e.g., Leu, Kinzer, Coiro, & Cammack, 2004; Snyder, 2000). Rather than undertake a "review of the reviews," just one is given some attention as it focuses directly on the use of ICT in English. As suggested earlier, although not all the research discussed in this section relates exclusively to the secondary English classroom, it seems reasonable to extrapolate from studies concerned more broadly with young people's engage-ment with new media and the implications for education.

Andrews' (2004) comprehensive and thorough review, based on reports written by different researchers as part of the Evidence-Informed Policy and Practice Initiative in the United Kingdom (REEL, 2003), is useful for prospec-tive researchers as it has collected much of the work in the area. The analysis of the learning effects of applying ICT in literacy teaching concludes with a mixed set of findings. For some learners, ICT bring no improvement in edu-cational outcomes, while in some instances it seems that educational practices and learning are made worse.

Included in Andrews' (2004) edited collection is a review of the relation-ship between ICT and moving images. Burn and Leach (2004) reported on 12 small qualitative case studies that suggest the beneficial effects of engagement with digital moving media in the English classroom. Several of the studies found a connection between media literacy and the cultural experiences of young people, suggesting that curriculum content that recognizes this factor is "more likely to motivate high quality work, to locate learners as determiners of their own meanings, and to be aware of ways in which the developing social identities of young people are implicated with their media cultures" (Burn & Leach, 2004, p. 164). Second, several studies found that the incorporation of moving-image media in the curriculum led to gains in literacy broadly defined, in some cases specific gains in print literacy. Third, four of the studies reported findings related to the collaborative nature of media production. A major con-clusion is that moving-image production should be part of professional learn-ing for teachers.

In addition, Locke and Andrews (2004) found that ICT can positively affect social interaction among learners in the context of literature-related literacies, but probably because the use of ICT is mediated by teachers. A similar conclu-sion is reached in connection with learners of English as a second language (ESL) (Low & Beverton, 2004). For these learners, English literacy acquisi-tion was enhanced when the ICT had a specific and identifiable pedagogical function, rather than a random application. As far as specific technologies are concerned, Low and Beverton reported that speech synthesis and word-processing functions of ICT have had the most positive consequences for literacy teaching, that Computer Assisted Language Learning (CALL) typically supports more code-centered and lower levels of literacy development best, and that non-ICT-mediated educational practices are in no way inferior to ICT based or ICT influenced literacy teaching.

As a caution against unthinking technological optimism, Andrews (2004) proposed that randomized trials should precede further investments in ICT for literacy education; however, Andrews' confidence that rigorously designed randomized trials evaluating the impact of ICT on literacy learning across all age groups will attach scientific evidence to direct future policy settings is perhaps too hopeful. Early attempts to evaluate *the effects* of the use of computers *on* writing quality used experimental designs but the results were equivocal. Experimental designs do not capture the interactive, iterative, and dialogical character of literacy learning and teaching (Hawisher & Selfe, 1998). Although such designs persist, researchers who subscribe to a social view of literacy implement different kinds of studies (e.g., Lankshear & Snyder, 2000; Schultz, 2002) and are informed by the understanding that literacy is socially constructed and not technologically determined. They prefer qualitative approaches to provide nuanced pictures of what happens when ICT are used in English classrooms.

Overall, Andrews' (2004) collection of research reports suggested that the policy environment surrounding the use of ICT in literacy education is becoming increasingly oriented toward research favoring a more psychological or cognitive perspective on language and learning. In this kind of environment, it may become more difficult to attract funding for literacy research that attempts to go beyond these approaches and toward more sociocultural ways of knowing. But Andrews' work also pointed to the possibility of a future research landscape where teachers and researchers may consider approaches to the study of literacy and technology that bring together both social and cognitive perspectives.

Changing Texts and Changing Practices

As in the world beyond the classroom, working with texts in English classrooms requires a complex set of literacies: not only the verbal literacy of the recent past, but also visual and audiovisual literacies. New text types, new language practices, and new social formations have emerged as young people use mobile phones, text messaging, the Internet, instant messaging, online games, blogs, search engines, Web sites, e-mail, peer-to-peer technologies, digital video, music and imaging, and more. Working with the texts produced by these new ways of communicating requires among other things an understanding of layout and design, not often recognized as necessary with logocentric texts. Finding the language to talk about these practices and discerning how meanings are made with them is a preoccupation of the research included in this section (cf. Jewitt, 2002; Snyder, 2003).

Abbot (2002), for example, examined the ways in which young people, including those with special needs, make eloquent use of the visual in their online texts, forming representations of themselves, their practices, and their aspirations. Also interested in issues of Web design, O'Hear and Sefton-Green (2004) examined online culture and Web authoring by young people. In addition to a consideration of the technical, institutional, aesthetic, and generic determinants influencing the precise nature of new Web-based productions, they pay attention to the fusion of visual, textual and structural elements, especially those relating to any nonlinear navigation features. Similarly, Hammett (2004) described students' complex hypermedia projects, based on prescribed texts, that were characterized by close attention to design aesthetics and to the multimodal possibilities of using image, sound, written text, and layout. Chandler-Olcott and Mahar (2003) argued that opportunities to create multimodal texts had positive benefits for students who came to see themselves as capable text producers, especially when such texts were constructed for an audience of peers as well as for teachers.

Implicit in much of this research are notions of critical literacy, broadly defined, but often mobilized in different ways in online spaces. Such research has a long heritage, but continues to argue that ICT require new and different ways of reading the Web and the world. Cranny-Francis (2004) maintained that young people need to know not only how to approach sites as readers looking for information and/or entertainment, but also how, as text producers, they may understand the kinds of meanings different sites generate. She explored how various semiotic modes (verbal, visual, and aural) contribute to the meaning making potential of Web sites, and the associated new meaning-making practices.

By contrast, Walton (2004) was interested in what goes on *behind* the screen, claiming that it is just as important for users as what is visible *on* the screen. With a focus on the database and on design and interactivity, she suggested some adjustments to Kress and van Leeuwen's (1996, 2001) grammar of visual design, drawing on evolving conventions in the field of Web design, to account theoretically for the peculiar characteristics of new media. Walton also considered search-engine logic and the ways in which it shapes online knowledge and experience (cf. Gerhart, 2004). Much of this amounts to a version of critical literacy that presents a designer's view of the Web, where the seamlessness of new-media environments (cf. Manovich, 2001) are understood as the composited and constructed worlds that they are (cf. Lemke, 2002).

Walton argued that without a designer's view, which, for example, might include understanding how a search engine ranks and displays results and how to read such rankings critically, any analysis of the Web or new forms of multimodality is incomplete. New literacies require teachers and their students to look carefully at what lies behind the screen into the domain of programmers and designers who develop the coding schemes and languages and evolve the systems of categorization that are needed to organize and to communicate on the Web. Without careful scrutiny, users are left to the mercy of the people who create the conventions, standards, and languages that shape what can be said on the Web and how. Technical details can be introduced into the English classroom at a level suited to the goals and skills of the learners concerned but need to be framed in a nontechnical way if students are to form independent, critical, and creative views of the Web.

In a similar way, Burbules (1997, 2002) looked at hyperlinks and the ways that they can become invisible and neutral. He considered their dual character as semantic connectives and as actual navigation elements, suggesting new metaphors for thinking about learning with, through, and about ICT; metaphors that posit learning as a kind of mobility that has special import for reconceptualizing education in an information age. Lemke (2002) postulated a "politics of hypermodality" (p. 321), asking questions about "the degree of importance assigned to different media and their combinations," suggesting that the privileging of "linguistic meaning to the point of excluding or denigrating pictorial modes … must have a politics" (p. 321). While acknowledging that images can be misused, Lemke (2002) argued that ambiguity in visual images, rather than representing a problem, "affords a greater display of complexity" (p. 322) in allowing differences of degree; by contrast, language is premised upon categorization and degrees of kind (cf. Snyder, 2005). As English teachers and students consider how some semiotic modes are privileged and others excluded and how these modes can also be combined in various ways for various purposes, possibilities for thoughtful and critical engagement with a range of new text types become available.

Digital Literacy Practices in and out of School

The pervasive take up and presence of ICT, at least in the developed world, mean that young people's experience of literacy is shaped by multiple engagements with ICT and global digital cultures. As a result, their use of ICT in out-of-school and community contexts has implications for equity and identity formation as well as for a range of other important issues. Research examining the complex connections between school literacies and out-of-school literacies can provide important insights for English teachers and teacher educators about the experiences and expectations of online and print-based literacy practices students bring to formal studies in school and beyond (e.g., Beavis, Nixon, & Atkinson, 2005; Freebody, 2001; Hull & Schultz, 2002; Lankshear & Knobel, 2003; Moss, 2001; Snyder et al., 2002; Sorensen, 2005).

In a number of large-scale studies that have examined young people's use of old and new media, Livingstone and her colleagues (Livingstone, 2002; Livingstone & Bovill, 2001) provided insight into the complex relationships between the media and childhood, the family, and the home. The U.K. project, *Children, young people, and the changing media environment* (Livingstone, 2002), represents a contextualized analysis of the meanings and contexts of new media use within young people's daily lives. Using a multimethod design, the study investigated how far gaining access to media goods determines or frames subsequent use, tracing the slippage between access and use. As Burbules and Callister (2000) have also emphasized, access to new media cannot be seen merely as having a way to use a computer with an Internet connection. Access also includes issues of who can afford a computer with an online connection, who knows how to operate the technologies, and who knows how to judge what is good and what is not. Users who cannot operate effectively across the full range of opportunities that new media represent cannot be said to have "true" access, even if they have a computer with an Internet connection. Researchers and teachers need to ask questions that take account of this more nuanced notion of access.

Livingstone's study saw the contexts of leisure, home, and family increasingly aligned but also in tension, particularly in terms of the individualization of leisure, the loss of public leisure, together with the privatization of everyday life, even within the home, and the democratization of cross-generational relationships within the family. A comparative European study (Livingstone & Bovill, 2001) asked similar questions, but included researchers from 12 countries. The study was based on interviews and a detailed comparative survey of 6- to 16-year-olds across Europe and in Israel. The findings, too elaborate and complex to report here, are similarly illuminating and generative.

Livingstone's more recent work (Livingstone & Bober, 2005; Livingstone, Bober, & Helsper, 2005) examined the online risks, opportunities, inequalities, and digital divides associated with 9- to 19-year-olds' Internet use. In the United Kingdom, at least, although considerable regional differences exist, home access is growing and school access is near universal; many young people are daily or weekly users. While parents generally underestimate children's negative experiences with Internet technology, more than half of the young people in the study had seen pornography online. Livingstone and her colleagues concluded that opportunities and risks go hand in hand and that Internet literacy is crucial. Further, the authors suggested that rather than a divide, a more useful idea is a continuum from hesitant, narrow, or unskilled use to diverse, confident, and skilled use.

Similar findings have emerged from other large-scale survey studies. The *Pew Internet and American Life Project* has found that more than half of American teenagers have created content for the Internet and that most think that getting free music files is easy to do. The young people also think that it is unrealistic to expect people to self-regulate and to avoid free downloading and file sharing (Lenhart & Madden, 2005). They have created a blog or Web page, posted original artwork, photography, stories or videos online, or remixed online content into their own new creations. Moreover, teenage bloggers are more fervent Internet users than nonbloggers and have more experience with almost every online activity in the survey.

A study of Generation M by the Kaiser Family Foundation (Rideout, Roberts, & Foehr, 2005) asked questions that ranged from broad societal issues to health concerns to issues of cognitive development. They found that young people live media-saturated lives and have access to an unprecedented amount of media in their homes. Those with easy access tend to spend more time using those media, but age, gender, and race influence the amount of time they spend. For most young people, parents don't impose rules about their use of media, and they continue to use old media such as television. Those with the poorest grades spend the most time with video games. And television and listening to music remain more important in their media lives than the Internet. Although they continue to read, they now spend less time with books.

The implications of the findings of such surveys for secondary English teachers are clear. To make responsive and meaningful changes to curriculum and pedagogy, teachers need to understand the young people who populate their classrooms. They need to know what they do in their out of school lives; they need to know what engages their interest and what does not. They also need to know what sophisticated skills young people bring to classrooms and how these might be better used for language and literacy learning.

As a useful counterpoint to large survey studies, in-depth case studies of young people both at school and at home provide deeper understanding of the ways in which computers are taken up and used in the real world of inequitable distribution. While the rhetoric of access and opportunity means that households from widely different socioeconomic situations are feeling the necessity of computer ownership, the translation of such ownership into real-world equity is far from clear (cf. Compaine, 2001; Saloman, 2002). Gaps between home, community, and school usage are exacerbated by the invisibility of much of students' out-of-school expertise in the school context, and by the diversity of expectations and assumptions that are made about which practices are educationally advantageous or desirable and those that are not. Despite the obvious difficulties that these challenges pose, especially to culturally marginalized groups, Auld (2002) has documented the work of a minority Australian Aboriginal group working to maintain cultural stories with the aid of computerized "talking books." The study demonstrates how the technological transformation of Indigenous texts supported the linguistic rights of speakers of minority Indigenous Australian languages. The participants were able to make new choices about texts that mediated their threatened languages.

The ScreenPlay project (Facer, Furlong, Furlong, & Sutherland, 2003) examined what young people do with computers at home, how parents and children negotiate access to and use of the computer, and the role the computer plays in the day-to-day lives of families. The case studies question commonplace assumptions about the use of technology by children at home and highlight issues of equality and access in a wider social context (cf., Murdock, 2002; Norris, 2001; Warschauer, 2003). On a smaller scale, Snyder and colleagues

often ignored in English curriculum design. Such texts are often denigrated as vehicles of entertainment, belonging in the domain of leisure. Intrinsic to this view is the belief that the texts represent "low" culture and do not belong in a curriculum that should be dedicated to the literary canon. These texts are also ignored in literacy assessment. Due to "institutional arrangements for assessment" (Bearne, 2003), teachers are often prevented from giving multimodal, multidimensional texts their full value in the classroom. Assessment regimes have narrowed the pedagogical focus and required increased accountability. They not only devalue what young learners know and can do, but also close down future possibilities (see DfES, 2005).

Gee's (2003, 2005) approach to video gaming is particularly interesting as it embodies some of the significant work in cognitive science and literacy studies about learning. Rather than investigating the impact of games, he asked how the industry sells so many games, which are both time consuming and difficult. After examining the theory of learning underpinning "good" video games, Gee concluded that it most closely resembles the best kinds of science instruction in schools. Gee did not argue that what people learn when playing video games is always good; rather, what they are doing when they are playing good video games often involves good learning (cf. Consalvo, 2003; Prensky, 2001). Gee's research suggested that there are a number of lessons teachers might learn from games designers about situated learning, reducing the consequences of failure, the power of affinity groups, and the benefits of information given on-demand or just in time rather than just in case (Gee, 2003).

ICT-Mediated Innovation and Change in English Classrooms and Schools

When researchers write about the possibilities for creative changes to pedagogical and institutional practices when ICT are used, they often ask several questions: What are the optimum conditions under which innovation can thrive? Is conflict between institutional goals and pedagogical objectives inevitable? They raise these questions within the context of the culture of institutionalized education that champions innovation at the same time as it honors the value of preserving the traditional. This is further complicated by those who have a vested interest in commodifying education and who often promote technological innovation as an appealing selling point (Snyder, 1999). However, the research suggests that efforts at innovative practices can have positive results even though the best outcomes are often unexpected.

A prerequisite for effective innovation and change is a strong knowledge and understanding of the history of the new literacies. Bruce (2002) took a historical perspective on the notion of new literacies, asking how literacies, technologies, and social circumstances co-evolve and what changes in literacy practices mean for young people today. He argued that literacy becomes inextricable from community, from the ways that communities and society change and from the material means by which knowledge is negotiated, synthesized, and used. Also valuing the lessons to be learned from history, while arguing a case for "changing knowledge and classroom learning," Lankshear and Knobel (2003) outlined how the field moved from reading to the NLS, pointing out that just 30 years' ago, the term literacy hardly featured in formal educational discourse.

Interested in the nexus between schools and the communities within which they are located, Bigum (2002, 2004) critiqued the widely held assumption that the more schools spend on technology, the better the outcomes. A similar view was once held in business and industry; however, analyses have demonstrated that there is little or no association between spending on ICT and increased productivity and profitability. Bigum suggested that schools have embraced a design sensibility (Schrage, 2000) based on information and its delivery—a mindset consistent with the powerful capacities of schools to "domesticate" new technologies. Rather than rethink schooling, schools have adapted the technologies to make them school-like. Bigum's research on "knowledge producing schools" (cf. Lankshear & Knobel, 2004) argued for the development of a relationship-based design sensibility for schools that shifts the focus from how to integrate ICT into the curriculum toward a consideration of schools as social organizations that have relationships with local communities, government, and other schools.

Bigum (2002, 2004) provided a salutary example of a school's engagement with this agenda. The school invested in digital-still and video-recording technologies. When a broad base of expertise had developed among the teachers and students, groups of students produced products directed at audiences beyond the school: a video for the principal to use at a state conference and a CD to offer advice to students about bullying. As Bigum suggested, schools and classroom teachers can actively seek to build productive relationships by embedding the goals in school policy and fostering the building of knowledge producing networks in the local communities for specific projects.

With an even broader focus, Luke (2002) discussed new literacies as an object of state educational policy. He described a state policy in Australia that included some of the available discourses on both print and new literacies among particular generational cohorts of teachers and the implications of current patterns of neoliberal educational policy for the appropriation and remediation of new literacies. Despite the New London Group's (1996) vision of how ICT and multiliteracies might be situated within a rigorous theorization of school education, Luke despaired that,

> educational systems will awaken from their generational slumber and begin the serious task of domesticating the new literacies, of developing standardized measures on multiliteracies to ensure and verify their inequitable production through the deployment of the first generation of IT-based multinational curriculum packages. (p. 203)

He argued that the appropriation of the new texts, practices, and identities described in this chapter by the forms of governance that have led schools and education systems to their present "retro state" (Luke, 2002, p. 203) must be avoided at all costs. Of course, Luke's call for resistance comes at a time when teachers are under enormous pressure and not just to technologize learning. Teachers' work has been intensified, there is continual erosion of their conditions, and interested groups conspire to undermine confidence in public schools by manufacturing successive "crises" in school performance and imposing narrow assessment and testing regimes. Resistance is difficult under such conditions. However, teachers need to be aware of these broad-based assaults on education so that they are able to do all that they can to ensure that their profession does not become a servant to a neoliberal ethos dedicated to policy directions abhorrent to those committed to contributing to building the best and most humane of all possible worlds (Lankshear & Snyder, 2000).

Following Williams (1976), Snyder (2003) identified the keywords involved in understanding what an innovative literacy pedagogy designed to take account of the new media might look like. Such an approach would provide students with opportunities to learn how to communicate effectively when using the new media. It would also encourage students to respond critically to the changing material and cultural conditions in which literacy education—both formal and informal—is situated. Through the study of texts, both print and electronic, a subtle, tough, and humane pedagogy would aim to provide learners with a sense of their place in the world and give them the capacity to develop strategies for making it a better place.

Examples of what such classrooms might look like are already available. In a 7-year search for classrooms in which teachers might, on a daily basis, be attempting to weave new literacies into the regular framework of everything they do, Kist (2005) travelled through the United States and Canada:

> I was not looking for teachers who do a video production unit once a year or who ask their students to do occasional PowerPoint presentations, but rather for teachers who talk with their students every day about all kinds of texts and who together with them become "readers" and "writers" of those various texts. (p. 4)

Seeking answers to questions like, "How were these teachers doing it?" and "How were they assessing kids in a system that demands that grades be given in some kind of report card?" Kist (2005) wrote case studies of those teachers and the classes he found. These case studies, while not heroic tales, are full of insights about how this kind of work might be done. But, of course, there is no magic bullet.

In a secondary English classroom project focused on writing, Beavis and Charles (2005) investigated the popular "god game," *The Sims*. They argued that young people can learn a great deal from playing and critiquing the game.

In some schools in Australia and the United Kingdom, the game is used to teach aspects of the ways in which society works, including issues of family, work, and socialization. For example, a student who creates a Sim who lives to shop will soon discover the downside of mindless consumerism. Beavis and Charles describe *The Sims* as an online continuation of much older forms of play that children have engaged in for generations: building imaginary worlds in the hedge, the backyard, vacant lots, down by the river, building cubby houses, playing dress-ups, or playing with dolls.

Integrating Multimodal and Sociocultural Approaches to New Literacies in the Classroom

Two recent books that deal directly with contemporary English classrooms and take account of the theoretical positions outlined in this chapter highlight how theory and practice can work together effectively. Both books see learning as a shared enterprise between teachers and students rather than as an individual cognitive activity concerned with the acquisition of a set of skills that can be transferred with ease from context to context. *Literacy and education: Understanding the New Literacy Studies in the classroom* has already been mentioned (Pahl & Rowsell, 2005). The book offers a practical guide to applying the NLS within primary, secondary, and family-literacy contexts. It suggests ways to rethink, redefine, and redesign language and literacy in the classroom to meet the contemporary needs of students. Its feature most relevant here is that it succeeds in integrating the digital with print effectively.

Pahl and Rowsell (2005) outlined multiple ways for teachers to find the resources, grounds, and purposes for teaching literacy, not from textbooks and skill taxonomies, but by attending closely to what children and communities actually do with texts, old and new, print and multimodal, and traditional and radical. They argued that the systematic engagement with everyday texts, discourses, and practices is at the heart of teaching and learning. They also argued that by acknowledging students' identities in their literacy practices, teachers can support and sustain their engagement with schooling. In the book, Pahl and Rowsell suggested that teachers bring contemporary literacy practices such as the text message, the email, and the instant message into the classroom, and engage with them in relation to the teaching of literacy. When literacy is seen as embedded within a wider communicational landscape of meaning and when the flows between different meanings are acknowledged, they argued that changes to secondary English teaching can be initiated.

English in urban classrooms (Kress et al., 2005) examines many of the language issues that confront contemporary English teachers: spoken and written, but also other modes of representation and communication including image, gesture, gaze, movement, and spatial organization. The research was shaped by four questions: (a) How is English made? (b) What is it like? (c) How is it experienced in specific classrooms? and (d) What is the best way of looking at English? To explore the questions, the team considered the ways in which English is influenced by policy, institutions, and the social relations of classrooms. The study provides a detailed account of the characteristics of urban multicultural schools, teacher formation and tradition, the ethos of school English departments, the institutional changes that have affected school English in urban classrooms, and students' experiences of learning. The book examines matters of history and of social and political context within the theoretical framework of multimodal semiotics. It is a fitting study with which to conclude the review of the research literature as it provides a textured examination of the here and now in ICT-mediated English education.

Conclusions for Teaching and Learning

This review of the research in the field of literacy and technology studies reveals that the communication landscape is changing, as it has always done, but more rapidly and more fundamentally. Contemporary texts are being shaped by the new uses they have been put to. They cross communication domains and are remediated to make new texts. These changes mean that the literacies required for the future will no doubt be different and thus have significant implications for the English classroom.

Teachers and researchers are thinking about the possibilities of ICT for literacy learning. There is growing recognition that ICT cannot be simply dismissed as new tools, employed to do what earlier technologies did, only faster and more efficiently. Researchers and teachers acknowledge the cultural significance of ICT, warning against overlooking their material bases and the expanding global economic dependence on them. However, opportunities to use ICT in the secondary English classroom that exploit their affordances are happening unevenly, within and between nation states, in both the developed and the developing world.

The studies reported in this chapter explore the complexity of technology-mediated secondary English classrooms in local settings. The findings demonstrate that the changes to literacy practices can be understood only when they are examined within their social, political, economic, cultural, and historical contexts. When ICT are available in schools, secondary English teachers have an important role to play. Finding ways to use them well, informed by the theoretical understandings and practical strategies documented here, represents the best goal. And, in situations where resources are scarce, the imperative for teachers is to find creative ways to do more with less. As young people are engaging with these technologies in contexts beyond the boundaries of formal education and in the various realities and trajectories of their lives, teachers need to ensure that their students have the capacity to assume a critical and informed approach while they are still accessible to the secondary English classroom.

This chapter does not presume to prescribe the components of a quality English education in the age of the Internet, but aims to encourage English teachers and researchers to "think outside the box" and "remove themselves from where they have been placed by curriculum regimes" (Pahl & Roswell, 2005, p. 138). It is through a dialogue between teachers, researchers, and policymakers that change has the best possibility of success. At the end of their guide to applying the NLS in the classroom, Pahl and Roswell reminded researchers and teachers alike that, above all else, "literacy is about meaning" (p. 139). Young people in secondary English classrooms use literacy, mediated by technologies, to make meaning and to explore the constraints and possibilities of their worlds.

Questions to Guide Future Research

The research agenda is rich with possibilities. The challenge is to devise research initiatives that will inform effective practice in the secondary English classrooms mediated by the use of ICT, as well as informing policy changes that might enable the kinds of innovation and change reviewed in this chapter.

It would be salutary to concentrate on students who have grown up with the technologies. A longitudinal approach to the study of young people immersed in computer culture, at school, at home, and in the community would produce new understandings of computer-mediated literacy practices. Attention also needs to be directed toward the intersection between multiple languages and the multiple modalities of the new technologies. There are many schools in which the presence of multiple languages is present both inside and outside classrooms. Research could investigate the place of multilingualism and multiculturalism in the ICT-mediated secondary English classroom.

Further research aimed at investigating the complex relationships between the verbal and the visual in communication and representation would also provide opportunities to closely examine new literacy practices in real contexts: to observe teachers and students, to discuss the emerging computer-mediated communication practices with them, and to apply to those understandings which draw on the work of theorists such as Kress and van Leeuwen, Bolter and Grusin and Gee. Such research would contribute to rethinking English teaching and learning—reframing it as something broader than "English-as-literature" and "English-as-language" to include "English-as-communication," "English-as-semiosis" and "English-as-rhetoric."

Issues of access and equity have been explored from a number of perspectives. The need for further research investigating the complex relationships between literacy, ICT, and disadvantage is manifest. Prompted by similar concerns about equity, Livingstone and Bober (2005) recommended that research needs to keep up with technological and market developments in relation to access: to track shifting and diversifying contexts of use, including the institutional and social influences on young people's Internet use and to critically examine causes and consequences of exclusion.

Above all else, making literacy education better is the main game. If this is true, then the challenge for researchers and teachers is how to restructure

Compaine, B. M. (Ed.). (2001). *The digital divide: Facing a crisis or creating a myth?* Cambridge, MA: MIT Press.

Consalvo, M. (2003). Zelda 64 and video game fans: A walkthrough of games, intertextuality, and narrative. *Television and New Media, 4*(3), 321–34.

Cranny-Francis, A. (2004). Spinning the Web: An analysis of a website. In I. Snyder & C. Beavis (Eds.), *Doing literacy online: Teaching, learning and playing in an electronic world* (pp. 145–62). Creskill, NJ: Hampton Press.

Cuban, L. (1986). *Teachers and machines: The classroom use of technology since 1920.* New York: Teachers College Press.

Cunningham, H. (1995). Moral Kombat and computer game girls. In D. Buckingham & C. Bazalgette (Eds.), *In front of the children: Screen entertainment and young audiences* (pp. 188–200). London: British Film Institute.

DfES (Department for Education & Skills). (2005). *The standards site.* Retrieved December 22, 2005, from http://www.standards.dfes.gov.uk/

Dickinson, D. K. (1986). Cooperation, collaboration, and computers: Integrating a computer into a second grade writing program. *Research in the Teaching of English, 20*(4), 357–78.

Eldred, J. M. (1991). Pedagogy in the computer-networked classroom. *Computers and Composition: An International Journal for Teachers of Writing, 8*(2), 47–61.

Facer, K., Furlong, J., Furlong, R., & Sutherland, R. (2003). *Screenplay: Children and computing in the home.* London: RoutledgeFalmer.

Faulkner, J. (2004). 'It gives you an image of yourself that you can reflect on': Literacy, identity, and new media. In I. Snyder & C. Beavis (Eds.), *Doing literacy online: Teaching, learning and playing in an electronic world* (pp. 207–24). Creskill, NJ: Hampton Press.

Flores, M. J. (1990). Computer conferencing: Composing a feminist community of writers. In C. Handa (Ed.), *Computers and community: Teaching composition in the twenty-first century* (pp. 106–17). Portsmouth, NH: Boynton Cook.

Freebody, P. (2001). Theorising new literacies in and out of school. *Language and Education: An International Journal, 15*(2-3), 105–16.

Freebody, P. (2005). Critical literacy. In R. Beach et al. (Eds.), *Multidisciplinary perspectives on literacy research* (2nd ed., pp. 433–454) Cresskill, NJ: Hampton Press.

Gee, J. P. (1996). *Social linguistics and literacies: Ideology in discourses* (2nd ed.). London: Taylor and Francis.

Gee, J. P. (2003). *What video games have to teach us about learning and literacy.* New York: Palgrave Macmillian.

Gee, J. P. (2005). Learning by design: Good video games as learning machines. *E-Learning, 2*(1), 5–15.

Gerhart, S. (2004). Do Web search engines suppress controversy? *First Monday, 9*(1), Retrieved January 5, 2005, from http://www.firstmonday.org/issues/issue9_1/gerhart/index.html

Gerrard, L. (1999). Letter from the guest editor. *Computers and Composition: An International Journal for Teachers of Writing, 16*(1), 1–5.

Gilster, P. (1997). *Digital literacy.* New York: John Wiley & Sons.

Godwin-Jones, B. (2005). Messaging, gaming, peer-to-peer sharing: Language learning strategies and tools for the millennial generation. *Language, Learning and Technology, 9*(1), 17–22.

Goodson, I. F., & Mangan, J. M. (1996). Computer literacy as ideology. *British Journal of Sociology of Education, 17*, 65–79.

Grabill, J. T. (1998). Utopic visions, the technopoor, and public access: Writing technologies in the community literacy program. *Computers and Composition: An International Journal for Teachers of Writing, 15*(3), 297–315.

Gray, A. (1992). *Video playtime: The gendering of a leisure technology.* London: Comedia, Routledge.

Green, B. (1988). Subject-specific literacy and school learning: A focus on writing. *Australian Journal of Education, 32*(2), 156–79.

Gurak, L., Antonijevic, S., Johnson, L., Ratliff, C., & Reyman, J. (Eds.). (2004). *Into the blogosphere: Rhetoric, community, and culture of weblogs.* Retrieved April 4, 2005, from the University of Minnesota Web site: http://blog.lib.umn.edu/blogosphere/

Hammett, R. F. (2004). Words and windows: Using technology for critical literacy. In B. R. C. Barrell, R. F. Hammett, J. S. Mayher, & G. M. Pradl (Eds.), *Teaching English today: Advocating change in the secondary curriculum* (pp. 117–31). New York: Teachers College Press.

Haraway, D. (1991). *Simians, cyborgs, and woman: The reinvention of nature.* New York: Routledge.

Hawisher, G. E., & Selfe, C. L. (Eds.). (1989). *Critical perspectives on computers and composition instruction.* New York: Teachers College Press.

Hawisher, G. E., & Selfe, C. L. (Eds.). (1991). *Evolving perspectives on computers and composition studies: Questions for the 1990s.* Urbana, IL: National Council of Teachers of English.

Hawisher, G. E., & Selfe, C. L. (1998). Reflections on computers and composition studies at the century's end. In I. Snyder (Ed.), *Page to screen: Taking literacy into the electronic era* (pp. 3–19). London: Routledge.

Hawkins, J. (1985). Computers and girls: Rethinking the issues. *Sex Roles, 13,* 165–80.

Heath, S. B. (1983). *Ways with words: Language, life and work in communities and classrooms.* Cambridge, U.K.: Cambridge University Press.

Herrmann, A. (1987). An ethnographic study of a high school writing class using computers: Marginal, technically proficient, and productive learners. In L. Gerrard (Ed.), *Writing at century's end: Essays on computer-assisted composition* (pp. 79–91). New York: Random House.

Hull, G. A., & Schultz, K. (Eds.). (2002). *School's out! Bridging out-of-school literacies with classroom practice.* New York: Teachers College Press.

Jewitt, C. (2002). The move from page to screen: The multimodal reshaping of school English. *Visual Communication, 1*(2), 171–96.

Jewitt, C., & Kress, G. (Eds.). (2003). *Multimodal literacy.* London: Peter Lang.

Jones, S. (Ed.). (1999). *Doing Internet research: Critical issues and methods for examining the net.* Thousand Oaks, CA: Sage.

Kaplan, N., & Farrell, E. (1994). Weavers of webs: A portrait of young women on the net. *The Arachnet Electronic Journal on Visual Culture, 2*(3), Retrieved June 5, 2005, from http://www.infomotions.com/serials/aejvc/aejvc-v2n03-kaplan-weavers.txt

Kellner, D. (1995). *Media culture.* New York: Routledge.

Kellner, D. (2002). Technological revolution, multiple literacies, and the restructuring of education. In I. Snyder (Ed.), *Silicon literacies: Communication, innovation and education in the electronic age* (pp. 154–69). London: Routledge.

Kellner, D. (2004). Technological transformation, multiple literacies, and the re-visioning of education. *E-Learning, 1*(1), 9–37.

Kist, W. (2005). *New literacies in action: Teaching and learning in multiple media.* New York: Teachers College Press.

Kramarae, C. (1988). *Technology and women's voices: Keeping in touch.* New York: Routledge & Kegan Paul.

Kress, G. (1995). *Writing the future: English and the making of a culture of innovation.* Sheffield, U.K.: National Association for the Teaching of English.

Kress, G. (2003). *Literacy in the new media age.* London: Routledge.

Kress, G., Jewitt, C., Bourne, J., Franks, A., Hardcastle, J., & Jones, K. (2005). *English in urban classrooms: A multimodal perspective in teaching and learning.* London: RoutledgeFalmer.

Kress, G., & van Leeuwen, T. (1996). *Reading images: The grammar of visual design.* London: Routledge.

Kress, G., & van Leeuwen, T. (2001). *Multimodal discourse: The modes and media of contemporary communication.* London: Arnold Publishers.

Lankshear, C. (1997). *Changing literacies.* Buckingham, U.K.: Open University Press.

Lankshear, C., Bigum, C., Green, B., Honan, E., Durrant, C., Morgan, W., Murray, Snyder, I., & Wild, B. (1997). *Digital rhetorics: Literacies and technologies in education – current practices and future directions.* Canberra, Australia: Department of Employment, Education, Training, and Youth Affairs.

Lankshear, C., & Knobel, M. (2003). *New literacies: Changing knowledge and classroom learning.* Buckingham, U.K./Philadelphia: Open University Press.

Lankshear, C., & Knobel, M. (2004). Planning pedagogy for i-mode: From flogging to blogging via wi-fi. *English in Australia, 139,* 78–102.

Lankshear, C., & Snyder, I. (with Green, B.). (2000). *Teachers and techno-literacy: Managing literacy, technology and learning in schools.* Sydney: Allen & Unwin.

Lather, P. (2004). This *is* your father's paradigm: Government intrusion and the case of qualitative research in education. *Qualitative Inquiry, 10*(1), 15–34.

Leander, K., & Sheehy, M. (Eds.). (2004). *Spatializing literacy research and practice.* London: Peter Lang.

LeCourt, D. (1998). Critical pedagogy in the computer classroom: Politicizing the writing space. *Computers and Composition: An International Journal for Teachers of Writing, 15*(3), 275–95.

Lemke, J. (2002). Travels in hypermodality. *Visual Communication, 1*(3), 299–325.

Lenhart, A., & Madden, M. (2005). *Teen content, creators, and consumers. PEW Internet & American Life Project: Family, friends, and community.* Retrieved December 22, 2005, from http://www.pewinternet.org

Leu, D. J., Kinzer, C. K., Coiro, J., & Cammack, D. A. (2004). Toward a theory of new literacies emerging from the Internet and other information and communication technologies. In R. B. Ruddell & N. Unrau (Eds.), *Theoretical models and processes of reading* (5th ed., pp. 1568–611). Newark, DE: International Reading Association.

Levin, T., & Gordon, C. (1989). Effect of gender and computer experience on attitudes towards computers. *Journal of Educational Computing Research, 5,* 69–88.

Livingstone, S. (2002). *Young people and new media: Childhood and the changing media environment.* London: Sage.

Livingstone, S., & Bober, M. (2005). *UK children go online: Final report of key project findings.* London: London School of Economics and Political Science. Retrieved June 2, 2005, from http://www.children-go-online.net

Livingstone, S., Bober, M., & Helsper, E. (2005). *Inequalities and the digital divide in children and young people's Internet use: Findings from the UK children go online project.* London: London School of Economics and Political Science. Retrieved June 2, 2005, from http://www.children-go-online.net

Livingstone, S., & Bovill, M. (Eds.). (2001). *Children and their changing media environment: A European comparative study.* Mahwah, NJ: Lawrence Erlbaum.

Locke, T., & Andrews, R. (2004). ICT and literature: A Faustian compact? In R. Andrews (Ed.), *The impact of ICT on literacy education* (pp. 124–52). London: Routledge Falmer.

Low, G., & Beverton, S. (2004). ICT, literacy learning, and ESL learners. In R. Andrews (Ed.), *The impact of ICT on literacy education* (pp. 91–123). London: RoutledgeFalmer.

Luke, A. (2002). What happens to literacies old and new when they're turned into policy. In D. E. Alvermann (Ed.), *Adolescents and literacies in a digital world* (pp. 186–203). New York: Peter Lang.

Luke, A. (2005). Forward. In K. Pahl & J. Rowsell (Eds.), *Literacy and education: Understanding the new literacy studies in the classroom* (pp. x–xiv). London: Paul Chapman.

Manovich, L. (2001). *The language of new media.* Cambridge, MA: MIT Press.

Marsh, J. (Ed.). (2005). *Popular culture, new media, and digital literacy in early childhood.* London: Routledge Falmer.

Merchant, G. (2001). Teenagers in cyberspace: Language use and language change in Internet chatrooms. *Journal of Research in Reading, 24*(3), 293–306.

Monroe, B. (2004). *Crossing the digital divide: Race, writing, and technology in the classroom.* New York: Teachers College Press.

Mosenthal, P., & Watts-Pailliotet, A. (Eds.). (1999). *Reconceptualising literacy in a new age of media, multimedia, and hypermedia*. Greenwich, CT: JAI Press.

Moss, G. (2001). On literacy and the social organisation of knowledge inside and outside school. *Language and Education: An International Journal, 15*(2–3), 146–61.

Murdock, G. (2002). Review article: Debating digital divides. *European Journal of Communication, 17*(3), 385–90.

New London Group. (1996). A pedagogy of multiliteracies: Designing social futures. *Harvard Educational Review, 66*(1), 60–92.

Nixon, H. (2003). New research literacies for contemporary research into literacy and new media? *Reading Research Quarterly, 28*(3), 407–14.

Norris, P. (2001). *Digital divide: Civic engagement, information poverty, and the Internet worldwide*. Cambridge, U.K.: Cambridge University Press.

O'Hear, S., & Sefton-Green, J. (2004). Style, genre, and technology: The strange case of youth culture online. In I. Snyder, & C. Beavis (Eds.), *Doing literacy online: Teaching, learning and playing in an electronic world* (pp. 121–43). Creskill, NJ: Hampton Press.

Pahl, K., & Rowsell, J. (2005). *Literacy and education: Understanding the new literacy studies in the classroom*. London: Paul Chapman.

Perelman, L. (1993). *School's out*. New York: Avon Books.

Postman, N. (1993). *Technopoly: The surrender of culture to technology*. New York: Vintage.

Postman, N. (1995). Virtual students: Digital classroom. *The Nation, 26*, 377–82.

Prensky, M. (2001). *Digital game-based learning*. New York: McGraw-Hill.

Prinsloo, M., & Breier, M. (Eds.). (1996). *The social uses of literacy: Theory and practice in contemporary South Africa*. Amsterdam: John Benjamins.

REEL. (2003). *Research evidence in education library*. Retrieved August 19, 2006, from http://eppi.ioe.ac.uk

Reinen, I. J., & Plomp, T. (1997). Information technology and gender equality: A contradiction in terminis? *Computers in Education, 28*, 65–78.

Rideout, V., Roberts, D. F., & Foehr, U. G. (2005). *Generation M: Media in the lives of 8-18 year-olds*. Retrieved December 22, 2005, from http://www.kff.org/entmedia/entmedia030905pkg.cfm

Robertson, H. -J. (1998). *No more teachers, no more books: The commercialisation of Canada's schools*. Toronto: McClelland & Stewart.

Rochlin, G. I. (1997). *Trapped in the net: The unanticipated consequences of computerization*. Princeton, NJ: Princeton University Press.

Romano, S. (1993). The egalitarianism narrative: Whose story? Whose yardstick? *Computers and Composition: An International Journal for Teachers of Writing, 10*(3), 5–28.

Roszak, T. (1994). *The cult of information: A neo-luddite treatise on high tech, artificial intelligence, and the true art of thinking*. Berkeley: University of California Press.

Saloman, G. (2002). Digital equity: It's not just about access anymore. *Technology and Learning, 22*(9), 18–26.

Sandholz, J. H., Ringstaff, C., & Dwyer, D. C. (1997). *Teaching with technology: Creating student-centred classrooms*. New York: Teachers College Press.

Schrage, M. (2000). *The relationship revolution*. Retrieved June 4, 2005, from http://web.archive.org/web/20030602025739/http://www.ml.com/woml/forum/relation.htm

Schultz, K. (2002). Looking across space and time: Reconceptualising literacy learning in and out of school. *Research in the Teaching of English, 36*(3), 356–90.

Scribner, S., & Cole, M. (1981). *The psychology of literacy*. Cambridge, MA: Harvard University Press.

Selfe, C. (1990). Technology in the English classroom: Computers through the lens of feminist theory. In C. Handa (Ed.), *Computers and community: Teaching composition in the twenty-first century* (pp. 118–39). Portsmouth, NH: Boynton Cook.

Selwyn, N., Gorard, S., & Williams, S. (2001). Digital divide or digital opportunity? The role of technology in overcoming social exclusion in U.S. Education. *Educational Policy, 15*(2), 258–77.

on content, they ceased school programming completely and instead began producing more profitable daytime soap operas. Perhaps the final blow was the manner in which NBC radio executive David Sarnoff and others cynically positioned all commercial radio as "educational" by introducing the term *life-long learning*. This interpretation of radio programming thus excused NBC (the largest radio network at the time), and its competitor CBS (and later ABC) of any educational or democratic obligation to the public whatsoever (Fabos, 2004; McChesney, 1994). What began as a promising public movement to serve democracy was turned into a vehicle for commercial enterprise.

Television Mimics Radio

TV continued on the same path commercial radio had established. The television industry advanced a profitable commercial environment and left little room for education. PBS programming was an exception. The establishment of the Corporation for Public Broadcasting in 1967, which later fostered PBS and National Public Radio, marked at least partial support for public interest broadcasting, more than 30 years after Congress initially rejected it.

There have been other attempts to bring education back into the commercial broadcasting environment. After years of public interest group lobbying to get more educational programming on commercial television, the Federal Communications Commission in 1990 finally required the networks to program 3 hours of children's educational programming a week. "This sounds like a dramatic gain," McChesney (1999) wrote, "until one realizes that these three hours of kids' TV are advertising supported and determined by the same business minds that created the current monstrosity that is commercial children's television" (p. 71). Similar to connecting lifelong learning with soap operas in the age of radio, television executives slyly labeled large portions of their existing programming educational, used youth targeted shows as a branding opportunity, and soundly got away with it.

Channel One is another cynical attempt to use the rhetoric of education as a front for the objective of directly marketing to youths. The 12-minute news programs, played in 40% of schools across the United States each school day, are filled with forgettable magazine-style packages that often promote new technology and 2 minutes of punchy (and memorable) teen-targeted advertising. Channel One schools have no control over the programming content and are contractually required to make their students watch the show each day. When Channel One was first launched in 1989, it caused perhaps the most explosive anticorporate response among teachers since the radio era (Molnar, 1996). And yet, the programming has made amazing inroads into public schools. Many teachers tacitly accept Channel One, as it gives them a built-in, 12-minute break in their hectic schedules.

The biggest lure of Channel One was its promise to give each school a free satellite dish to download the daily Channel One feed, and place free television monitors in every classroom to show the program. Of course, television is just a technology. How technology is deployed (particularly its content) makes all of the difference. The case of Channel One illustrates much about the relationship of mass media technology in U.S. schools. Many educators want good pedagogical technology. Corporations see the technology as something akin to a trojan horse (bearing the friendly mantle of "public-private partnership" to gain the exclusive attention of young people). Finally, educators have mixed opinions about the appropriateness of commercial media content in schools, and the ability of their students (and themselves) to adequately deal with those messages.

The Internet: Another Education "Bait and Switch"

The Internet is indeed a much different technology than radio, but it did follow a similar developmental path. Like radio, the Internet was closely allied with education in its early years and blossomed in educational circles before it became harnessed for commercial purposes. As with radio, educators could easily produce, disseminate, and control content, making it especially appealing to teachers. And, as with radio, the intensive efforts of a powerful industry, and a lack of government regulation and further investment in educational content have diminished its value as a medium for education.

The Internet's origins can be traced back to developmental support by the U.S. Defense Department's Advanced Research Projects Agency (ARPA) in the 1960s. Although the Internet had been used by some members of higher education in the 1970s and 1980s, it did not begin to break through as a mass medium until the arrival of the World Wide Web software and graphical Web browsers in the early 1990s. This is the point when both educators and the corporate sector began to imagine vastly different uses for the Internet.

The process of government sanctioned corporate control of the Internet began in the early 1990s with the Clinton Administration. A handful of public officials, including Vice President Al Gore, had championed the Internet as a government project to aid democratic public life and education. However, by 1993, the heavy lobbying of commercial interests had already converted the Internet into a private sector initiative with government encouragement, well before the Internet became a well-known, Web-driven mass medium (Aufterheide, 1999).

As a media studies scholar, I was first interested in looking at the way the Internet was marketed in the mass media as an educational panacea during this formative period, the mid-1990s. As if someone had turned on a switch, many beautifully edited advertisements, ambitiously marketed by MCI, Microsoft, Oracle, and AT&T, began appearing on prime-time television (Martin & Fabos, 1998). They were placed in high-profile programs such as the Super Bowl and the 1996 Olympics and showed students at school engaged in the breathtaking world of Internet learning, a world of golden sunlight and ooohing kids. The ads featured children e-mailing astronauts and float-ing around classrooms, as if in outer space themselves. They showed students peering at images of human hearts (invoking medicine), planets (invoking sci-ence), and Martin Luther King, Jr. (invoking democracy).

Even though I was studying advertising messages, this research informed my understanding of the way the Internet was being framed as a cultural tool. I was interested in looking at the telecommunication and computer companies, who was doing the framing, (and why the Internet was being framed as an educational, not a business or e-commerce tool. These industries, I found, stra-tegically framed the Internet as an education tool and played up the rhetoric of democracy in order to get the schools and the homes of school-aged children wired. The strategy tapped into middle class parents' fears that their children would be left behind in the educational abyss if they did not follow suit—what Barbara Ehrenreich (1989) termed "the fear of falling." The strategy worked. The Internet was connected to the majority of U.S. schools by 2000, and Inter-net penetration into more than half of the nation's households happened in those same 5 years—more quickly than any media technology to date.

Meanwhile, the major Internet players (including the government) were quietly paving the way toward Internet privatization and commercialization (Fabos, 2004). In other words, the Internet was being set up to serve business while the rest of society was seeing the Internet in the lofty light of education. The ironic part was that no substantial public investment was made toward online educational *content* during this time. However, there was plenty of public (and private) investment toward school and library wiring. By achieving critical mass, the "real" commercial Internet could *stop* being an educational tool and *start* being an advertising medium for products and services. Think commercial radio here; think commercial television. History simply repeats.

While educators were celebrating the new medium in their classrooms, learning HTML, publishing their students' work online, joining support groups, and, especially in the case of librarians, building subject gateways, the consolidating Internet industry was solving their next problem. They needed to get Internet users—suddenly renamed "consumers"—to shop online. Gone was the Internet-for-education discourse. Dot-com became the new buzzword. Print and television ads began showing online shoppers at home, in pajamas and bunny slippers, buying flowers for their mothers from new online flower services. News reports, many in the form of successfully planted press and video news releases, celebrated the ease and convenience of online shopping. These reports were especially noticeable around the Christmas holidays with news anchors offering online shopping tips, taking viewers on virtual shop-ping excursions, and interviewing spokespeople from Yahoo!

The process of repositioning Internet citizens as consumers (who only buy things) rather than users (who consume but also make Internet content) started in the early 1990s, as the private sector pushed to control the Internet's backbone of main fiber optics lines—a government-led project until 1995. By the late 1990s, the term Internet "users" in popular discourse was almost categorically replaced with the word "consumers," a premonition of how the Internet would be shaped in the coming decade (Gray & Brunette, 1999).

A Commercial Highway in Every Classroom

This research on Internet framing led me to question the changing nature of Internet content. Was it becoming excessively commercialized? Since studies showed that students were overwhelmingly using search engines to conduct their research, what were the economic and political forces driving the search engine industry? In turning my attention to the political economy of the commercial search engine industry, I hoped to find out some implications of commercialization and conglomeration on information access and education.

Search Engines: From Syndicators to Ad Brokers

Search engines were initially information navigation services that made their money through syndication (i.e., providing search services for other Web sites). Google had cornered the market in search engine relevance since the company released its first algorithm in 1998. Google's constantly updated (and somewhat mysterious) PageRank algorithm broadly treats relevance like popularity: the more pages linking to your page, the more relevant (or popular) the page will be in Google's search result listings. Google also factors in the relative popularity or significance of the pages doing the linking. A link on *USA Today* pointing to your page, for example, carries more weight than a link from a student Web site. The year Google was born, search engines began trying to generate more revenue beyond syndication. Commercial search engines, such as GoTo (renamed Overture), began experimenting with paid placement within search results in 1998. In this enhanced search engine model, advertisers bid to be associated with particular key words, which are then accounted for in any given search. Their Web sites then appear next to (or within, depending on the search engine or search portal) the "organic" search result list, which is presumed to be ranked according to Web site relevance to the key terms typed into the search engine "search" box. By 2003, both Google and Overture had perfected keyword advertising as an essential marketing tool for any business—be it local, regional, national, or global (Fabos, 2006a).

With such a successful advertising strategy, Google, then Yahoo!, which acquired Overture in 2003, and later Microsoft began investing heavily in the advertising part of their business, acquiring thousands of advertising clients and cross-listing these clients with applicable search terms. Thus, the syndication/content-provider model was replaced by an advertising-broker model (Battelle, 2005). Instead of bringing information to *users* (which was how they continued to market their services), commercial search engines were bringing narrowly targeted *consumers* to their advertiser clients. Every search became

glomerates. By 2006, Google, Yahoo! and MSN formed what had become a search engine market oligopoly, with the three corporations respectively controlling 42.7%, 28%, and 13.2% of all Web searches (Graham, 2006). Given, their assets, it is hard for any company to keep up with them. Every month Google, Yahoo!, or Microsoft unveils another impressive-looking content service with which to better understand, profile, and then market to those of us seeking online information. Meanwhile, most of us are generally oblivious to the online advertising environment, and generally trust that Google, Yahoo!, or MSN are the best means for locating relevant information. The Pew Internet and American Life Project (Fallows, 2005) surveyed 2,200 adult users of search engines in 2005. The findings must have buoyed the spirits of search engine executives: 62% of respondents were unaware of the distinction between paid and unpaid results; 70% were nonetheless agreeable with the concept of paid or sponsored results; 68% said that search engines are a fair and unbiased source of information; and 92% were confident about their searching abilities. Thus, the general public's trust in commercial search engines is evident.

In fact, the Big Three are putting their commercial interests front and center, before their commitment to deliver objective and relevant search results, before any firm commitment to a user's privacy, and before ethical considerations to make all information freely available. What incentive does a publicly owned company, committed to bringing profits to its shareholders and in intense competition with like companies, have for offering a democratic selection of information? True, one must deliver some decent content to make search engines *seem* relevant. However, every time a consumer clicks on a sponsored link, the search engine, along with any hosting portal, earns money. Even if there is a supposed firewall between Google's sponsored and organic search results (where there is none with Yahoo! and MSN), commercial (or paying) pages still find a way to artificially influence page rank.

Google, which contends that it has the best, most relevant search results, is the constant target of search engine optimization services (SEOs), which work 24 hours a day to crack the Google algorithm and boost page ranks for their paying clients (Gaither, 2006). In fact, Google would just prefer these clients went through Google's advertising program, and the company spends considerable energy cracking down on these SEO practices. However, another way commercial pages find their way into "organic" search lists is through Google's own contextual linking service, called AdSense, which brokers the sponsored links that appear at the bottom of nearly every online article in a commercial publication and that match the context of the main Web site. Small as they are, contextual links are effective far beyond the advertising spot on a given page. For example, a contextual link for a cat-food company on a *USA Today* page serves as an endorsement of the product. By linking the lesser known cat food to the popular news site, it increases the sponsor's PageRank standing in Google organic search results. As a result of contextual linking, Google (Yahoo! and MSN have similar services) undermines the relevance of its own search results by allowing a commercial transaction (benefiting Google and its client) to define the "popularity" of a client Web site (see Fabos, 2006b).

Now, consider what these commercial search engine practices mean for the political economy of information. Imagine a public library where, instead of nonjudgmentally serving patrons with a wide array of texts, the library's primary motive was to make money. To do this, the library accepted payments (without the patron's knowledge) from a handful of authors who paid every time their books were checked out of the library. The public library would understandably steer its patrons toward these books, and not others. Search engines operate in much the same way. They have much to gain by bringing consumers to their advertiser client pages rather than to the "poorer" pages that cannot afford the price for access. It is no surprise, then, that a search result list is stacked with commercial pages.

Today, hugely successful Internet powerhouses such as Google, Yahoo!, Microsoft, the entire telecommunication industry, and the countless businesses that now depend on the Internet for their promotion, marketing, and data collection, would like to continue along the same path of government sanctioned privatization in a way that solidly benefits corporate enterprise. At the core of this issue is the question of democratic public space. Should the Internet indeed be for everyone? Or should it serve business? How can we ensure that we have access to the kind of information we need to make informed decisions about our world if this communication medium will supplant public libraries as the foremost information resource? If literacy is a primary goal of education, do we ask students to be literate consumers or literate citizens? And, what does it mean to be literate in this age of information?

Educators Respond to the Commercialized Internet

In the late 1990s, commercial search engines were becoming the first place K–12 and college students would go to find information for their research projects (Fabos, 2004; Griffiths & Brophy, 2005). A number of educators and librarians began to voice concerns. First, they wondered about their students' growing reliance on these services for most, if not all, of their research (e.g., Gibson & Tranter, 2000; Holt, 1995; Kirkwood, 1998). What were the ramifications of students rejecting other forms of information, such as books, online databases, and reference materials found in libraries? Was online searching via search engines detrimentally easy? Second, educators were concerned that students were not finding the "right" kind of information via search engines, which they defined as objective material based on truthful reporting and academic inquiry rather than mere opinion. Numerous reports emerged in education and library journals stating that students were prone to getting ineffective search results (e.g., Arnold & Jayne, 1998; Blandy & Libutti, 1995; Claus-Smith, 1999). They were becoming overwhelmed by the amount of information they found online and constantly wandered off "into the glitter-paved, hypertext-linked pathways of the Web" (Arnold & Jayne, 1998, p. 43). Perhaps most significantly, observers noted that students were not adequately questioning the validity or context of the material they found online (e.g., Berger, 1998; Carter, 1999; Minkel, 2000; Noakes, 1999; O'Sullivan & Scott, 2000).

Applying Information Literacy to the Web

The solution to students' uncritical search engine wandering, according to most of these educators and librarians, was information literacy. This view recommended that existing information literacy practices be expanded to the Web and students be taught information literacy as part of their overall research orientation. Three main strategies emerged with this kind of information literacy.

First, teach students about the value of other library holdings, such as books and online databases purchased by the library for their use (Cox & Vander-Pol, 2004; Haycock, 2006; Walker & Engel, 2003). One path toward this end is to advocate far more intense collaboration between students and teacher-librarians to help young people develop disciplined and long-lasting inquiry and research strategies. Cox and VanderPol (2004), for example, asked their students to critically reflect upon their research practices and generate discussions about library holdings. Another method is to generate research exercises for students to emphasize the relative usefulness of various library resources. Walker and Engel (2003) developed a series of short research exercises for their freshman library orientation students at Grinnell College. First, they asked their students to each tackle the same difficult research question on their own, such as "Is filtering software (e.g., Net Nanny, CyberPatrol, SurfWatch) effective in restricting access to objectionable Web sites to children?" (p. 140). Then they modeled informed and disciplined research practices for their students based on these questions and exposed their students to library databases (digital-journal archives), scholarly books, and reference materials that took students beyond the world of commercial search engines. In the end, Walker and Engel reported that their students unanimously agreed that scholarly books contained the highest quality of information for their research purposes, with scholarly journals coming in second. Moreover, working through the series of exercises with the support of these two instructors, students' reassessed their faith in search engines. They no longer believed commercial search engines gave them the wide breadth of ideas and information they needed for solid research inquiry and preferred to first investigate books and scholarly journals instead.

A second method was to help students learn advanced (Boolean) search syntax, using terms such as "and," "or," and "not," to narrow down an unwieldy search. A more succinct search meant more relevant results and less chance of students wandering off into the Web's "glitterpaved pathways" (e.g., Brandt, 1996; Bailey & Lumley, 1999; Kennedy, 1998; Kohut, 2000). Brandt (1996) wrote, "Obviously, the more one knows about Boolean operators and strategies for narrowing a search, the more successful the result" (p. 35–36). Kohut, for example, referred to the benefits of teaching "advanced search syntax" and pointed to two metasearch engines, MetaCrawler and SavvySearch (now defunct), which responded to such Boolean syntax as quotation marks, and +/– signs.

Third, information literacy lessons teach students Web-page evaluation skills, so they can better assess the quality of each Web site they encounter. The purpose of Web-page evaluation, according to educational and information science discourse, is to isolate "quality" (objective) information. In other words, in a cluttered search environment containing many biased resources, Web-page evaluations skills allow students to identify what is true. Borrowing from the already established librarian evaluation code for print resources, librarians and educators began to discuss, beginning in the mid-1990s, the necessity of evaluating Web pages according to Authorship, Accuracy, Objectivity, Currency, and Coverage (e.g., Alexander & Tate, 1999; Bailey & Lumley, 1999; Bos, 2000; Salpeter, 2003). Students were instructed, for example, to consider ".edu" pages as generally but not always more trustworthy than ".com" pages; to be suspicious of typos, grammatical, and spelling errors and shoddy page design; to note the date of the page's last update; and to evaluate the depth or bias of information available on the site. Again, the overarching goal was to help students find *reliable, objective* (i.e., "true") online information for fact-based educational projects.

Interestingly, the bulk of concern about search engine use in this discourse has had to do with students' ability to properly evaluate personal home pages. Educators characterized these home pages as unfiltered and, therefore, undesirable. They have no affiliation to any legitimate business or organization, so consequently they are seen as imposters in the online environment (e.g., Safford, 1996; Solock & Wells, 1999). The Web pages that were most suspicious overall were "vanity" pages that were marked by the potentially deceptive tilde symbol (~). Often affiliated with a legitimate university or educational site, these educators warned that tilde pages may also indicate that a single person with little authority is behind the information (e.g., Reynolds & Plucker, 1999; Safford, 1996). Henderson's (2000) warning was typical: "If you see a tilde (~) as part of the URL, be aware that the website is a personal page likely created by someone who was given space on the Web server in an unofficial, unauthorized capacity" (p. 2). Therefore, suspicious individual pages trumped the abundance of commercial pages as an area of educational concern.

Limitations of Information Literacy

I found the solutions offered by educators and librarians just outlined to be a good first step in understanding—and becoming literate in—our evolving information environment. However, these solutions are hardly enough, and certainly don't penetrate the most urgent question presented by Internet commercialism and confronting our information environment: what is to become of our democratic information environment? Next, I offer some concrete criticisms of information literacy practices, and then offer some alternative critical literacy solutions.

Web-page evaluation strategies are no match for today's Web. Over the past decade, a Web information and design aesthetic has evolved for most professionally crafted Web sites that incorporates all of the check points (Authorship, Accuracy, Objectivity, Currency, and Coverage) to project the aura of believability. This "credibility aesthetic" is, no doubt, a result of the Web-page evaluation discourse, which basically promotes validity guidelines. Any institutional Web site routinely lists its page author, page-update information, and links to other objective-seeming Web sites; they also exhibit decent writing, balanced-*sounding* arguments (to the unaware), and even Web site awards (no matter if they are minor, or perhaps, completely bogus) that may increase the chances of the Web page *appearing* legitimate and objective. The typical Web-evaluation criteria, for example, has done little to prevent a student from thinking a public relations page with a well-crafted design and the aesthetics of objectivity is valid and factual information.

Webpage evaluation practices privilege fact-based assignments and the search for objective truth. Not knowing one's subject is the typical student's research scenario for most class-based research assignments. Students have no or barely any prior knowledge of their subject and are meant to glean "facts" amidst opinions and slick public relations pages (which, I should add, tend to cluster at the top of search engine result lists). They must determine objective information from biased information, and, as Watson (2001) observed, are nervous about evaluating Web pages when they are unfamiliar with the topic they are investigating. As such, I will make a case that Web-page evaluation and the fact-based assignments they support offer students a limited understanding of a student's topic area, as well as our broad world of ideas. First, one can easily argue that all information is biased. However, since "biased" in Web-page evaluation discourse is always interpreted as "bad," students too easily reject important arguments without understanding the guts of the issue they are attempting to study. Because Web-evaluation discourse privileges fact-based assignments and the replication of an "objective" truth, students are never given a chance to understand the more complex perspectives of their world.

Information literacy dismisses Internet commercialization. Information literacy has scorned tildes and has characterized personal Web pages as *the* major threat to credible online information. And yet, this literature does not attempt to account for the larger, and arguably far more significant, commercial patterns that had begun to dominate online information as early as 1999. According to a piece published in *Nature*, 83% of Web content was dominated by commercial enterprise (Lawrence & Giles, 1999). Worse, these pages are the bulk of what students are finding and using in their research. Communication studies researcher Samuel Ebersole (2000) documented the huge proportion of commercial Web pages that high-school students were clicking on as they conducted their in-school research via search engines. First, Ebersole found that students tended to select commercial Web pages far above any other domain. Second, he found these sites to have no or little relationship to students' academic objectives, and rated these sites the lowest in terms of their educational value.

Despite these problems, which are easily observable in the classroom (Fabos, 2004), educators have focused on Web-page evaluation, not Web evaluation. They have expressed concern about that which is most tangible: how to find individual pages in the current information environment, and then, once found, how to evaluate them, page by page. By focusing on the evaluation of individual pages (Are they biased? Are they credible?), information literacy inherently ignores the larger issues that concern online information access: the overwhelmingly commercial (and problematic) environment of Internet search. It ignores recent Internet conglomeration, the huge success and increasing competition between Google, Yahoo!, and Microsoft, keyword advertising, contextual linking, the drive of SEOs to influence search engine results, the business discourse among advertisers, indeed, the entire political economy of the Internet.

There are reasons for this lack of critique. One is that many librarians and educators continue to see the Internet overall in neutral terms—as a new technology owned by all and free for anyone with Internet access to use (or abuse). In this discourse, technology is always good. It advances society. It simply exists (Carey, 1997). The Internet, they believe, will get better for education in the coming years as the technology improves. Recall also that corporate interests had successfully visualized the Internet in the public imagination as a necessary tool for *education*. Many educators have accepted this notion as well. Apart from concerns about the digital divide (i.e., disparities in Internet access along age, class, race, and geographic lines), the Internet still resonates as a democratic tool for everyone, and a little commercial input "to pay the bills" is fine—we are immune to commercial messages anyway, they seem to conclude. Furthermore, today there are so many good noncommercial sites accessible via search engines that one could effectively argue the Internet's possibilities for education have already trumped commercial incursions (the Benkler, 2006, argument). The information explosion is real, this position concludes, and we should embrace the huge amounts of information we can now access online (Burbules & Callister, 2000). The fact that search engines are rolling out an array of philanthropic-sounding services such as Google

Meanwhile, plenty of competing voices reflect a position of "personal responsibility" and take on a private conception of democracy. Perhaps big business has the most to gain by portraying obesity as an individual and not a social problem. By successfully blaming individuals for making their own "bad" lifestyle choices, Big Food and Big Pharma can more easily avoid culpability for obesity rates and can comfortably continue their highly profitable business as usual. The commercial media system, it turns out, also revealingly skews its "objective" news reports about obesity in favor of personal responsibility. Because the news media are so dependent on advertising revenue, they are far more comfortable spinning stories that champion new drugs, new treatments, and individual responses to obesity rather than conducting investigative reports into the types of larger social issues that would upset the status quo.

With a better understanding of the political nature of the obesity topic, students can begin to question the political bias of all their information sources, including those coming from commercial search engines. Anyone who types in the word "obesity" in Google, for example, will be flooded with sites. Not surprisingly (given the previous analysis on the political economy of the Internet), there are numerous Web sites within the first three pages of a search result list selling health-treatment plans, supersize clothing, and "individual" solutions to the obesity epidemic. However, what about the other legitimate-looking pages that would meet the approval of Web page evaluation guidelines? At number one, two, and three on a recent Google search using the term "obesity" are the "American Obesity Association" (www.obesity.org/) "CDC Overweight and Obesity" (www.cdc.gov/node.do/id/0900f3ec80007302) and "The Obesity Society" (http://www.obesityresearch.org/). They seem to provide factual, evenhanded, objective information, offering causes and solutions to the "obesity epidemic." However, only a student well-versed in the political discourse outlined in Step 1 would recognize that these sites represent only one perspective in the obesity debate (envisioning obesity as a medical issue, which can be addressed only by individual action), and determine the need to search further. The number 6 listing, a link to the nonprofit Wikipedia's entry on obesity, was the only Web site in the first three pages of the search result list that discussed obesity as a public interest/social issue as well as a medical/personal responsibility issue. The next Web site in the results list to discuss obesity as a public interest/social issue was the Center for Media and Democracy, which came in at number 99; at the ninth page, this would not be seen by most searchers.

Step 3: Understanding the Political Economy of Information

This step asks students to consider the whole political economy of information. Why is there so little breadth of information in the obesity search? Could it be that the commercial Internet works in the same way as our other commercial media outlets? Money drives content in the world of commercial search. A more complicated way of looking at this is that beyond the many commercial advertisements inundating our search results list, Google gives us the most popular views on the obesity topic. And, in the world outside of Google, the most popular views typically are not the dissenting views. Indeed, Google gives us a world much like the mainstream news media, where commercially controlled and industry sanctioned positions dominate, and dissent is marginalized. That does not mean that dissenting opinions are not valid—they could be the best take on an issue. However, if they are marginalized in the rest of the mass media, they will also be marginalized on Google.

A search result list like the one for "obesity" can be a launching point for a critique of commercial search engines as an information resource. Educators can help students understand the reality of search engine conglomerates as advertising brokers, not information brokers. They can discuss the state of Internet conglomeration and competition, which will surely turn many free services to paid services; the effects of SEOs; and debates over the future of information (e.g., Benkler, 2006; Bollier, 2002; Lessig, 2002).

In our overall discussion of "obesity," it is no surprise that the fullest range of information comes from university library books, political magazines, and public interest Web sites—all of which are typically off a student's radar—that advocate alternative views to the usual fare of the mainstream commercial media. Wikipedia is an excellent example of how a *nonprofit* information resource handles information. The open source encyclopedia offers diverse coverage with plentiful updates and a platform that is committed to disseminating many, often competing, views. In a nonprofit information universe, ideas can coexist more easily without economic ramifications.

As McClaren and Lankshear (1993) advised, "[Critical literacy] teachers must themselves be widely enough read to know where to locate content that can help learners investigate curriculum issues from a more critical standpoint than those represented in prescribed texts" (p. 47). Teachers need to point their students to a range of well-argued opinions. That means books (print or online). That also means databases either within the public library or on the Internet. The growing movement of nonprofit digital libraries—a movement that at its core supports critical literacy—should be of paramount interest to all educators and librarians (Fabos, 2004). In the political economy of information, where commercial interests are encroaching more and more into the role of librarians, these collaborative, citizen and librarian-driven databases play a critical role in the future of information.

Toward a Critical Literacy Movement

David Bollier (2002), the cofounder of Public Knowledge, an advocacy group for Internet and intellectual property issues, spoke to the need of a public information commons. He advocated an online collaboration-rich sphere teeming with a full range of human expression, as opposed to a centralized, corporate-controlled alternative. The central issue, Bollier argued, is the way information flows in society and who will pay for it.

Because the Internet is clearly the central medium of the new information environment, educators must also confront this issue. We cannot just hope that Google, Yahoo!, and Microsoft will do the right thing—our present experience and history tells otherwise. Critical literacy helps to show us what is wrong with the current information environment. However, it also points the way toward a more ideal information environment, and advocates a growing movement of democratic alternatives to the commercial Internet.

One of the leading alternatives is the digital archiving movement, which is about shaping tomorrow's Internet—at least a portion of it—for public good and education. Thousands of citizens, digital librarians, and subject experts across the world are quietly building nonprofit subject gateways so that potentially marginalized information can be made accessible. Wikipedia, the world's largest open source reference Web site, is one example of this movement, as are INFOMINE (infomine.ucr.edu/), ibiblio (www.ibiblio.org/), the Oaister project (oaister.umdl.umich.edu/o/oaister/), and the Internet Archive (www.archive.org)—all nonprofit initiatives based in the United States but with global implications. In the United Kingdom, across continental Europe and in Australia, in particular, concerted government investment has gone into building digital archives for the purpose of education, such as the United Kingdom's Resource Discovery Network (www.rdn.ac.uk/) and Renardus (www.renardus.org/), a European-Union-funded subject gateway project. Another key to this movement is cross-searching technology, which allows digital archives to combine and become searchable, much like a search engine interface.

It is critical that educators know about these significant initiatives, steer their students toward these databases, and build a broader discourse around the digital archiving movement so that these public interest initiatives become highly valued. Keeping these efforts visible and understanding why they need to be there is a worthy fight. And, it seems that the idea of an "information commons" is gaining ground.

The commercial sphere would like to control information. But there is a price for this, sometimes with actual monetary fees, but always with barriers to the widest possible range of ideas. Critical literacy reveals the truth about our information environment and leads us to the idea of a networked public sphere. The important condition is that there will always be a struggle if the public wants a stake in controlling it.

References

Alexander, J. E., & Tate, M. A. (1999). *Web wisdom: How to evaluate and create information quality on the Web*. Mahwah, NJ: Lawrence Erlbaum Associates.

Alterman, E. (2003). *What liberal media?* New York: Basic Books.

Arnold, J. M., & Jayne, E. A. (1998, January). Dangling by a slender thread: The lessons and implications of teaching the World Wide Web to freshmen. *The Journal of Academic Librarianship, 24*(1), 43–52.

Aufderheide, P. (1999). *Communications policy and the public interest: The telecommunications act of 1996.* New York: The Guilford Press.

Bagdikian, B. (2004). *The new media monopoly.* Boston: Beacon Press.

Bailey, G. D., & Lumley, D. (1999, January). Fishing the net. *Electronic School,* A20–A23.

Battelle, J. (2005). *The search: How Google and its rivals rewrote the rules of business and transformed our culture.* New York: The Penguin Group.

Benkler, Y. (2006). *The wealth of networks: How social production transforms markets and freedom.* New Haven, CT: Yale University Press.

Berger, P. (1998). *Internet for active learners: Curriculum-based strategies for K–12.* Chicago: American Library Association.

Berlin, J. A. (1993). Literacy, pedagogy, and English studies: Postmodern connections. In C. Lankshear & P. McClaren (Eds.), Critical literacy, politics, praxis, and the postmodern (pp. 247–270). Albany: State University of New York Press.

Blandy, S. G., & Libutti, P. O. (1995, Fall). As the cursor blinks: Electronic scholarship and undergraduates in the library. *Library Trends, 44*(2), 279–305.

Bollier, D. (2002, June 15). *Saving the information commons: Remarks by David Bollier.* Paper presented at the ALA Convention, "Pirates on the Commons" Panel, Atlanta, GA. Retrieved July 30, 2006, from http://www.ala.org/ala/acrlbucket/copyrightcommitt/copyrightcommitteepiratesbollier.htm

Boostrom, R. (2005). *The foundation of critical and creative learning in the classroom.* New York: Teachers College Press.

Bos, N. (2000). High school students' critical evaluation of scientific resources on the World Wide Web. *Journal of Science Education and Technology, 9*(2), 161–173.

Brandt, D. S. (1996, September). Relevancy and searching the Internet. Computers in Libraries, 16(8), 35-7.

Brandt, D. S. (1996, May). Evaluating information on the Internet. *Computers in Libraries, 16*(4), 44–46.

Breivik, P. S., & Senn, J. A. (1998). *Information literacy: Educating children for the 21st century* (2nd ed.). Washington, DC: National Education Association.

Burbules, N. C., & Callister, T. A., Jr. (2000). *Watch it: The risks and promises of information technologies for education.* Boulder, CO: Westview Press.

Carey, J. (1997). *James Carey: A critical reader.* Minneapolis: University of Minnesota Press.

Carter, D. S. (1999). Internet public library (IPL). In A. Wells, S. Calcari, & T. Koplow (Eds.), *The amazing Internet challenge: How leading projects use library skills to organize the Web* (pp. 121–143). Chicago: American Library Association.

Claus-Smith, D. (1999, November/December). Starting small, dreaming big: The OSLIS Project brings resources statewide. *Multimedia Schools, 6*(5), 29–31.

Cox, J. L., & VanderPol, D. (2004). Promoting information literacy: A strategic approach. *Research Strategies, 20*(1–2), 69–76.

Curran, J., & Gurevitch, M. (2004). *Mass media and society* (4th ed.). Oxford, U.K.: Oxford University Press.

Douglas, S. (1987). *Inventing American broadcasting, 1899–1922.* Baltimore: Johns Hopkins University Press.

Ebersole, S. (2000, September). Uses and gratifications of the Web among students. *Journal of Computer-Mediated Communication, 6*(1). Retrieved May 18, 2003, from http://www.ascusc.org/jcmc/vol6/issue1/ebersole.html

Ebersole, S. E. (2005). On their own: Students' academic use of the commercialized Web. *Library Trends, 53*(4), 530–538.

Ehrenreich, B. (1989). *Fear of falling: The inner life of the middle class.* New York: Harper Perennial.

Fabos, B. (2004). *Wrong turn on the information superhighway: Education and the commercialization of the Internet*. New York: Columbia University Teachers College Press.

Fabos, B. (2006a). Search engine anatomy: The industry and its commercial structure. In C. Kapitske & B.C. Bruce (Eds.), *Libr@ries: Changing information space and practices* (pp. 229–252) . Mahwah, NJ: Lawrence Erlbaum Associates.

Fabos, B. (2006b). For the love of facts: Misguided searching on the information superhighway. In J. Lockard & M. Pegrum (Eds.), *Brave new classrooms: Educational democracy and the Internet* (pp. 169–188). New York: Peter Lang.

Fallows, D. (2005). Search engine users. *Pew/Internet & American life project*. Retrieved July 1, 2006, from http://www.pewinternet.org

Fones-Wolf, E. A. (1994). *Selling free enterprise: The business assault on labor and liberalism, 1945–60*. Urbana: University of Illinois Press.

Fones-Wolf, E. A. (2006). *Waves of opposition: The struggle for democratic radio, 1933–58*. Champaign-Urbana: University of Illinois Press.

Gaither, C. (2006, May 22). The one bit of info Google withholds: How it works. *Los Angeles Times*, p. 1.

Gerhart, S. L. (2004, January). Do Web search engines suppress controversy? *First Monday*, 9(1). Retrieved January 23, 2004, from http://firstmonday.org/issues/issue9_1gerhart/index.html

Gibson, S., & Tranter, J. (2000, Summer). Internet information: the whole truth? *Canadian Social Studies*, 34(4), 77–80.

Giroux, H. A. (1987, February). Critical literacy and student experience: Donald Graves' approach to literacy. *Language Arts, 64*, 175–81.

Giroux, H. A. (1998). Education in unsettling times: Public intellectuals and the promise of cultural studies. In D. Carlson & M. W. Apple (Eds.), *Power/knowledge/pedagogy: The meaning of democratic education in unsettling times* (pp. 41–60). Boulder, CO: Westview Press.

Graham, J. (2006, April 21). Google's quarterly revenue nearly doubles from last year. *USA Today*, p. 28.

Grassian, E. S., & Kaplowitz, J. R. (2001). *Information literacy instruction: Theory and practice*. New York: Neal-Schuman Publishers, Inc.

Gray, P., & Brunette, K. (1999, March). *Re: U.S. perspectives on consumer protection in the global electronic marketplace, comment P994312*. Retrieved June 10, 2006, from the Internet Consumers Organization (ICO) Web site: http://www.ftc.gov/bcp/icpw/comments/ico1.htm

Griffiths, J. T., & Brophy, P. (2005). Student searching behaviour and the Web: Use of academic resources and Google. *Library Trends*, 53(4), 539–554.

Hall, S. (1977). Culture, the media and the ideological effect. In J. Curran, M. Gurevitch, & J. Woolacott (Eds.), *Mass communications and society* (pp. 315–348). London: Edward Arnold.

Hansell, S. (2006, June 23). Google is testing ads for video service. *New York Times*, p. 7.

Haycock, K. (2006, February) Information literacy programs can foster disciplined inquiry. *Teacher Librarian*, 33(3), 38.

Henderson, J. R. (2000, June 13). *ICYouSee: T is for thinking*. Retrieved November 7, 2000 from the Ithaca College Library Web site: http://www.ithaca.edu/library/Training/hott.html

Hindman, M., Tsioutsiouliklis, K., & Johnson, J. (2003). *"Googlearchy": How a few heavily-linked sites dominate politics on the Web*. Retrieved April 10, 2004, from www.princeton.edu/~mhindman/googlearchy--hindman.pdf

Holt, G. (1995, September 15). Catalog outsourcing: No clear cut choice. *Library Journal*, 120(15), 32–34.

Introna, L., & Nissenbaum, H. (2000). Shaping the Web: Why the politics of search engines matters. *Information Society, 16*(3), 189–186.

Jhally, S. (1990). *The codes of advertising*. Oxford, U.K.: Routledge.

Kapitzke, C. (2001, February). Information literacy: The changing library. *Journal of Adolescent & Adult Literacy, 44*(5), 450–456.

Kennedy, S. D. (1998). *Best bet Internet: Reference and research when you don't have time to mess around.* Chicago: American Library Association.

Kim, W. (2006, March-April). Trends in the uses of the Internet—2006. *Journal of Object Technology, 5*(2), 55–60.

Kinchloe, J. (2006). Forward. In D. Macedo (Ed.), *Literacies of power: What Americans are not allowed to know* (pp. xi–xvi) . Boulder, CO: Westview Press.

Kirkwood, H. P. (1998, July/August). Beyond evaluation: A model for cooperative evaluation of Internet resources. *Online, 22*(4), 66–84.

Kohut, R. (2000, March). MetaSearching the net. *Learning and Leading with Technology, 27*(6), 18–21.

Lankshear, C., & McClaren, P. (1993). *Critical literacy: Politics, praxis, and the postmodern.* Albany: State University of New York Press.

Lawrence, S., & Giles, C. L. (1999, July 8). Accessibility of information on the Web. *Nature, 400*(6740), 107–109.

Lessig, L. (2002). *The future of ideas: The fate of the commons in a connected world.* New York: Vintage.

Lewis, C. (2001). *Literacy practices as social acts.* Mahwah, NJ: Lawrence Erlbaum Associates.

Livingstone, D. W. (1987). *Critical pedagogy and cultural power* (D. Livingstone, Ed.). New York: Bergin & Garvey Publishers.

Martin, C. R., & Fabos, B. G. (1998). Wiring the kids: The TV ad blitz to get the Internet into home and school. *Images: A Journal of Film and Popular Culture, 6* (September), [Online]. Available: http://www.imagesjournal.com/issue07/features/wiringthekids.htm

McChesney, R. W. (1994). *Telecommunications, mass media, & democracy: The battle for the control of U.S. broadcasting, 1928–1935.* London: Oxford University Press.

McChesney, R. W. (1997). *Corporate media and the threat to democracy.* New York: Seven Stories Press.

McChesney, R. (1999). *Rich media, poor democracy: Communication politics in dubious times.* Urbana: University of Illinois Press.

McColl, J. (2006, February 8). Google challenges for academic libraries [Electronic version]. *Ariadne, 46,* 1–6.

Minkel, W. (2000, October). Burden of spoof. *School Library Journal, 46*(10), 49.

Modahl, M. (1999). *Now or never: How companies must change today to win the battle for Internet consumers.* Cork City, Ireland: Collins.

Molnar, A. (1996). *Giving kids the business: The commercialization of America's schools.* Boulder, CO: Westview Press.

Mosco, V. (1996). *The political economy of communication.* London: Sage.

Noakes, A. (1999). Argus Clearinghouse (Argus). In A. Wells, S. Calcari, & T. Koplow (Eds.), *The amazing Internet challenge: How leading projects use library skills to organize the Web* (pp. 17–35). Chicago: American Library Association.

O'Sullivan, M., & Scott, T. (2000, March/April). Teaching Internet information literacy: A critical evaluation (part I). *Multimedia Schools, 7*(2), 40–44.

Pungente, J. J., Duncan, B., & Andersen, N. (2005). The Canadian experience: Leading the way. In G. Schwarz & P. I. Brown (Eds.), *Media literacy: Transforming curriculum and teaching* (pp. 140–160). Malden, MA: Blackwell Publishing.

Quinn, S. (2006). *Conversations on convergence: Insiders' views on news production in the 21st century.* New York: Peter Lang.

Reynolds, E., & Plucker, J. (1999, May). Panning for gold (creatively) on the new frontier: Locating and evaluating educational resources on the Internet. *NASSP Bulletin, 83*(607), 8–15.

Safford, B. (1996, November). The problem with the Internet is NOT the information highway. *School Library Media Activities Monthly, 13*(3), 42–43.

Salpeter, J. (2003). Web literacy and critical thinking: A teacher's tool kit. *Technology & Learning, 23*(8), 22–34.

Samoriski, J. (2000, Winter). Private spaces and public interests: Internet navigation, commercialism and the fleecing of democracy. *Communication Law and Policy, 5*(1), 93–114.

Schuler, D., & Day, P. (Eds.). (2004). *Shaping the network society: The new role of civil society in cyberspace.* Boston: The MIT Press.

Sehr, D. T. (1997). *Education for public democracy.* Albany: State University of New York Press.

Shannon, P. (1992). *Becoming political: Readings and writings in the politics of literacy education.* Portsmouth, NH: Heinemann.

Sholle, D., & Denski, S. (1993). Reading and writing the media: Critical media literacy and postmodernism. In C. Lankshear & P. McClaren (Eds.), *Critical literacy: Politics, praxis, and the postmodern* (pp. 297–322). New York: State University of New York Press.

Solock, J., & Wells, A. T. (1999). Scout report signpost (signpost). In A. Wells, S. Calcari, & T. Koplow (Eds.), *The amazing Internet challenge: How leading projects use library skills to organize the Web* (pp. 203–222). Chicago/London: American Library Association.

Spring, J. (1997). *The American school, 1642-1996.* New York: McGraw-Hill Companies.

Sullivan, E. V. (1987). Critical pedagogy and television. In D. Livingstone (Ed.), *Critical pedagogy and cultural power* (pp. 57–75). New York: Bergin & Garvey Publishers.

Tedeschi, B. (2006, June 26). As online ads grow, eyeballs are valuable again on the web. *New York Times*, p. 6.

The Age. (2003, November 4). Melbourne, Australia, p. 16.

Walker, H. M., & Engel, K. R. (2003). Research exercises: A sequenced approach to just-in-time information literacy instruction. *Research Strategies, 19*(2), 135–147.

Walker, J. (2005, Spring). Links and power: The political economy of linking on the Web. *Library Trends, 53*(4), 524–529.

Watson, J. S. (2001, October). Students and the World Wide Web. *Teacher-Librarian, 29*(1), 15–19.

Won, K. (2006, March-April). Trends in the uses of the Internet—2006. *Journal of Object Technology, 5*(2), 55–69.

Young, J. (2005, October 7). *Microsoft, joining growing digital-library effort, will pay for scanning of 150,000 books.* Retrieved June 6, 2006, from The Chronicle of Higher Education Web site: http://chronicle.com/free/2005/10/2005102701t.htm

CHAPTER 30

Multimodal Instructional Practices

PIPPA STEIN

UNIVERSITY OF WITWATERSRAND, SOUTH AFRICA

Introduction

Multimodality as a field of study is concerned with how human beings use different modes of communication, like speech, writing, image, gesture, and sound, to represent or make meaning in the world. The study of multimodality within the social sciences and linguistics has been developed in different ways: in discourse analysis (Norris, 2004; Scollon & Wong Scollon, 2003), sociocultural paradigms (Lemke, 2000) and Systemic Functional Linguistics (O'Halloran, 2004). This chapter looks at the relationship between multimodality, learning, and teaching in relation to a particular theoretical perspective— multimodal social semiotics (Kress and van Leeuwen, 1996, 2001; Kress, 1997, 2003; van Leeuwen, 2005). It explores how certain key ideas from multimodal social semiotics have been taken up in educational research and applied to aspects of teaching and learning, across curriculum subjects and academic disciplines, and in formal and informal educational environments. The majority of these studies investigate multimodality in relation to literacy and literacy education.

Multimodal social semiotics reframes instructional practice as multimodal: teaching and learning happens through the modes of speech, writing, sound, movement, gesture, image, and space. These modes work in different ways with different effects, to create multilayered, communicational ensembles. These different effects affect what it means to learn and to teach in contemporary classrooms. It is important to stress that while the theoretical domain of mul-

through the windows and the view of the Thames below. On my way out, I pick up a free blue booklet with photographs, text, and images from the show. I will read it on my way home.

As I leave this exhibition, I am struck by how much I have learned about Frida Kahlo from the experience of the interactive multimedia tour. If I had done what I usually do—simply walked around the exhibition, reading the information blocks on the walls, and viewing the paintings—the experience would have been more private, "purer," less shaped and positioned by the different voices and intertexts, which were there for me to pull up at the touch of a button. The only images I would have viewed would have been the paintings on the museum walls, the only sounds I would have heard would have been the sounds in the museum—people chatting and whispering as they strolled through the large rooms. The experience of the entity Frida Kahlo is not one thing: as Frida Kahlo is represented through different media and modes, who she is and what she does, shifts and changes. This impacts on my experience as a viewer and consumer of her work.

In both the classroom and the museum, some important learning is taking place, incorporating many of the best learning principles outlined by Gee (2003). The designers of these pedagogical environments (curators and teachers) understand that there is a relationship between learning and the semiotic forms through which learning occurs. All learning is multimodal. While in most classrooms, the range of options open for meaning making is limited to language, through speech and writing, there is a recognition here that purposeful learning can occur through a whole range of modes: image, speech, sound, writing, performance, action, movement, space, and a range of materials and media: books, screens, oil paintings, artifacts, video, Web pages, booklets, photographs, film, and three-dimensional models. The curators and teachers recognize that curriculum concepts or "content" occurs in the complex interrelations produced within and across multiple sign systems (images, words, symbols, artifacts, gestures, and body movements), and learners' own knowledge and resources. In both of these learning environments, knowledge is situated and embodied, and there is an awareness of the learner as agentive, critical, and resourceful. There is also recognition that different modes offer different potentials for representation: some modes are better for certain tasks than others are. In shifts across modes, the meanings of entities change and are transformed. In both environments, the body, emotions, and synesthesia are integral: human beings have a highly sophisticated capacity to move across the senses, "to dance the pathway of sound."

A Multimodal Social Semiotic Approach to Learning: Some Key Ideas

This chapter explores how key ideas in multimodal social semiotic theory have been applied to questions of teaching and learning. Social semiotic theory is concerned with how human beings make meaning in the world through using and making different signs, always in interaction with someone. A written text is a sign. An advertisement on a billboard is a sign. A child's drawing is a sign. Signs are multimodal: they can draw on language, image, gesture, sound, and action, in different configurations and for different effects. Modes are "culturally shaped resources for making meaning" and the prefix "multi-" refers to the fact that modes never occur by themselves but always with others in ensembles (Kress et al., 2005). Signs are always conjunctions of meaning and form. They are never neutral but socially and culturally produced and motivated—meaning is always made and read *in* culture. We produce signs according to our interests:

> Signs arise out of our interest at a given moment, when we represent those features of the object which we regard as defining of that object at that moment ... This interest is always complex and has physiological, psychological, emotional, cultural, and social origins. It gets its focus from factors in the environment in which the sign is being made. (Kress, 1997, p. 11)

This perspective on communication as sign production, reception, and transformation has been elaborated to take account of systems of meaning making other than speech and writing, including the resources of music/sound (van Leeuwen, 1999), action (Kress et al, 2001; Martinec, 2000), visual communication (Kress & van Leeuwen, 1996; 2006), and their arrangement as multimodal ensembles (Kress & van Leeuwen, 2001; van Leeuwen, 2005).

The application of this theory of signs to learning has been called a *multimodal social semiotic approach* to learning. It assumes that pedagogical environments, in and out of school, are semiotic environments: teachers and learners are constantly engaged in reading and creating signs across a range of genres, modes, and discourses. All texts are multimodal. Pedagogic processes can be understood as the selection and configuration of the semiotic resources available in the learning environment (Jewitt, 2006; Kress et al, 2005). Another basic assumption is that language is not the only mode sufficient and possible for representing meaning. Increasingly, image is as important as language. This has important implications for teachers' attention to and understanding of the visual in the curriculum (Unsworth, 2001).

The notion of design is fundamental. Teachers and students are *designers* of meaning (Cope & Kalantzis, 2000; New London Group, 1996): this means that teachers are involved in making particular choices about how and what to teach. Students make decisions about how to represent what they understand and wish to communicate. In all instances, the idea of design means that people choose how to represent meaning from a range of possible options. These options are continuously shaped within the history of a culture and its available technologies for representation, as well as by an individual's relationship to identity and history. How people represent their meanings may be limited by the semiotic resources available, what Kress (1997) called "what is to hand" and by students' competence in design. These choices communicate important information to teachers about students' learning and have implications for instructional and assessment practices.

A multimodal social semiotic approach to learning is based on the following assumptions:

- All acts of communication are multimodal: there is no monomodal communication.
- Modes are the effect of the work of culture in shaping materials into resources for meaning making.
- Human beings, as agents of meaning making, shape and transform available materials for representation.
- Different modes have affordances and potentials that make them better for certain tasks than others.
- In shifts across modes (transduction), the meanings of "entities" change and transform.
- Each mode is partial in relation to the whole of the meaning.
- Any mode may become foregrounded in a particular representation (Jewitt & Kress, 2003, pp. 1–4).

A social semiotic approach to learning is interested in the following questions about modes:

- How do modes shape what is represented?
- How do differences in modal representation reshape what is represented?
- How are learners and learning affected, changed, and shaped by the differences in mode, the material differences entailed, and the different senses called upon or engaged in the use of a mode?
- How do differences in mode interact with difference in media to affect ways and possibilities of learning (*media* is defined as technologies for making and distributing messages such as book, screen, radio, and billboard)?

This chapter presents an overview of research that has developed these key ideas, and applied them to multimodal instructional practices. The first section is an overview of foundational work that opened up the field. The second section reports on research in which a multimodal analysis or "lens" is used to examine multimodal texts produced in learning environments. The third section reports on research into pedagogy and curriculum design where teachers have consciously incorporated multimodal pedagogies/instructional practices into their classrooms. The fourth section reports on developments in multimodal assessment practices, and the final section looks at the implications of this research for teacher education.

Foundational Work in Multimodal Social Semiotics and Education

Foundational work in the area of multimodal social semiotics and education was undertaken by Gunther Kress and Theo van Leeuwen and focused on language and image. In *Reading Images* (1996, 2006), they put forward a grammar of visual design based on M.A.K. Halliday's (1978) social semiotic theory of communication. About the same time, the New London Group (1996) launched its influential "Pedagogy of Multiliteracies" in the *Harvard Educational Review,* in which the concept of multimodality and the designing of meaning was central (Cope & Kalantzis, 2000; Kress, 2000). While a "Pedagogy of Multiliteracies" is built on the concept of multimodality and multiple literacies of the new information age, it draws on other important ideas including citizenship, fast capitalism, globalization, and diversity. It puts forward a framework for rethinking pedagogy, which includes "Situated Practice," "Overt Instruction," "Critical Framing," and "Transformed Practice." It is important to note that a multimodal social semiotic approach to learning is *not* a framework for pedagogy but a reconceptualization of learning, which can lead to rethinking pedagogy.

In 1997, Kress published *Before writing: Rethinking the paths to literacy,* a groundbreaking book that explores the multimodality of young children's meaning making in their everyday play. This book explores the relationship between literacy, learning, and multimodality and challenges the idea that learning occurs through language alone. Kress demonstrated how, in learning to read and write, children come as thoroughly experienced sign makers who have already engaged in complex ways with a multitude of semiotic resources—toys, pens and paper, scissors, paste, mud, grass, clay, stones, bottles, pots, and pans—to express their meanings in play. Kress focused on the multimodality of writing in its concern with directionality, spatiality, font, and layout of the page. On the basis of this, Kress made suggestions on how to use children's capacity for creativity and resourcefulness to reimagine a literacy curriculum for the 21st century that prepares children for productive futures within the context of global diversity.

In a special edition of *Linguistics and Education* edited by Lemke (2000), researchers examined multimodality in subjects across the curriculum, particularly mathematics and science. O'Halloran (2000; 2004) used a systemic-functional perspective to dissect the multiple sign systems operating in the mathematics classroom, which make the pedagogical discourse very dense. She demonstrated how teaching and learning math involves drawing on the semiotic resources of mathematical symbolism, visual display, and language. There is a constant movement between these resources, as well as shifts across oral and written modes. Each of these resources has its own unique lexico-grammar system for making meaning and its own discourse, making the mathematics classroom a highly complex semiotic environment. This analysis of the multimodality of mathematics is very useful in making visible the inherent difficulties in the teaching and learning of mathematics. Recent work by Baker and Street (2006) investigated multimodal numeracies as a social practice and has identified different modes of representation in mathematics education, including actional, diagrammatic, and symbolic modes. They suggested, like O'Halloran, that problems of switching between such modes may be a source of children's difficulties in the subject.

Lemke (2000) and Wells (2000) focused on the science classroom. Investigating students in their final year of secondary school, Lemke found that students were expected to meet stringent demands for mastery of multiple, hybrid multimedia genres and their associated genre-specific literacies at an advanced level. How fluently and quickly students master scientific concepts in verbal, mathematical, and visual-graphical literacies is fundamental to academic success. The key point Lemke made is that it is not enough to gain mastery of one modality: scientific concepts, as in mathematics, are articulated *across* these modes and media:

> It is only in the integration of these various aspects that the whole concept exists ... So we do not have so much an exact translatability among verbal statements, mathematical formulas, and visual-graphical or material-operational representations as a complex set of co-ordinating practices for functionally integrating our uses of them. And these co-ordinating practices must be learned in each case as a difficult and specialized form of multi-literacy. (Lemke, 2000, p. 246)

In 2001, Kress et al. produced an important study on multimodal teaching and learning in the science classroom that provided a set of conceptual tools for analyzing multimodality in pedagogical settings. Interaction in the science classroom is put under the spotlight in order to analyze "the complexity of what goes on." A key finding is the extent to which teachers shape students' conceptions of the world through acting rhetorically: *rhetoric* refers to how teachers present a plausible, integral, and coherent account of the world through the orchestration of a range of modes and means in an attempt to persuade students to view an aspect of the world in a particular way (p. 20). They also found a prevalence of metaphors and modes where teachers ask learners to "imagine the everyday as strange" so that learners can see the need for explanation. This study presents a detailed account of how teachers use action, gesture, modeling, speech, writing, image, and role play to communicate scientific knowledge, and the importance of materiality as a resource for representing meaning. In one example, they use a multimodal lens to look at texture, color, and shape in how students represented "the cell" and are able to extrapolate aspects of students' learning from the analysis of these multimodal texts. Kress et al. made clear the integral connection between formal issues of representation, such as genres and modes, and the shaping of knowledge: certain modes are used to convey particular content in ways that other modes cannot. For example, the genre of "a conceptual map" to represent the circulation of the blood represents the entity "blood circulation" in a way that is different from the genre of "a story of the journey of the blood." This study opens up important questions about which mode to use to best represent particular content: is the structure of an electronic circuit best represented in writing or in image? It also explores what it means to "talk" or "write" like a scientist, in other words, how learners take on the discourses or social languages (Gee, 1996) of science in ways that make sense.

The English classroom in *English in Urban Classrooms* (Kress et al., 2005) is a focused study, from a multimodal perspective, of contemporary-school English in three-state co-educational, ethnically diverse secondary schools in inner London. This study asks, How is English made? What is it like? How is it experienced when it appears in actual classrooms shaped by new curriculum policy, the school's response to that policy, the variety of department traditions in the school, the social and geographical environment in which the school operates, the kinds of students who come to the school, and the different histories and professional trainings of the teachers?

> The English classroom is about meaning ... the social participants in the construction of the entities in the English classroom have an effect on the shape of the entity, a situation that cannot readily be imagined in subjects such as mathematics, science, geography and others ... In the counterposing of science and English, we posit a re-emergence of a split between a world of "fact" and a world of "value." (Kress et al., 2005, p. 5)

While previous studies of the English classroom have focused on the role of "talk" and on language in its written and spoken form as the main mode of communication, this study paid attention to all the culturally shaped resources through which the subject is realized, including image, gesture, layout, writing, and speech. The varied visual displays and spatial arrangements of classrooms can be understood as multimodal signs that inflect a particular relationship to history and culture around what constitutes the subject English. Texts are a critical resource in the teaching of English and which texts are selected is a politically charged arena. In a chapter on the "textual cycle" of the English classroom, the authors examined the selection of texts, their presentation and reproduction to and for students, and the teacher's production of new texts. A significant finding in this study is the disappearance of the text through its fragmentation into extracts, annotated notes, and summaries: the text as a literary or textual entity is replaced by a focus on text as the site of "mechanically performed operations" (p. 164). It appears that the book's role has waned, if not collapsed, in English. The importance of this study is not only in its findings, but also in its methodological framework: It presents a multimodal perspective as a new methodology or "way of looking" at subject English, "so that we might actually get a full understanding of its reality, in all ways, in the experience of students and teachers alike, in any one classroom" (p. 1).

Analyzing Semiotic Resources in Meaning Making: Applying a Multimodal Lens to Learning

Since 2000, the field of multimodal semiotics in education has developed substantially. Numerous studies now draw on and develop the conceptual tools developed in the foundational work to explore the relationship between learning and the multisemiotic forms through which meaning is made. Applying a multimodal analysis or "lens" to the range of texts produced in learning environments gives us valuable insights into how learners use different semiotic resources to interpret learning activities and to formulate their relation to objects, phenomena, and experiences (van Leeuwen, 2000). We learn more about different semiotic potentials: this is important for developing instructional practices that actively work with multimodality to enhance learning. Many of these studies combine micro levels of textual analysis with interviewing and observation as well.

The majority of studies to date have focused on visual communication and investigate how different genres and discourses of the visual shape meaning making. As pointed out by van Leeuwen (2000), the analysis of words and images is not new. Until the advent of a visual grammar (Kress & van Leeuwen, 1996), however, such analyses were organized into discrete compartments in discrete disciplines: linguistics for language and art history for pictures. This made it difficult to compare, for example, a photograph and its caption, within the same underlying construction of reality. A social semiotic analysis attempts to look for common principles, semiotic functions, and organizing functions across different modes, drawing on Halliday's (1978) systemic functional grammar.

While children's drawings have long been a focus of interest among art educators and art therapists, literacy researchers are using multimodal social semiotics to analyze children's use of image and text (Bearne, 2003; Unsworth, 2001). Researchers are interested in the choices children make in relation to modes, in the differences in affordances between image and language, and the potentials these modes offer for communication. Much of this work explores the relationship between choice of mode, materials, and the shaping of identity.

van Leeuwen (2000) analyzed 56 texts produced by 8 to 10 year-old children, from three different schools, after the children had visited London's Science Museum's Launch Pad section of interactive exhibits for children. The Science Museum set a series of writing and drawing tasks mainly focused on the children's subjective, emotional responses to the exhibition, such as "What do you remember best?" In the final task, children were asked to draw the exhibit. Thus, the structure of the task was multimodal in its combination of writing and drawing. van Leeuwen was interested in how the children integrated writing and drawing, what markers of subjectivity and affectivity they used in their drawings, and how the drawings "described" the exhibits. In their writing, he was interested in the range and kind of generic variation in the writing, how the children incorporated themselves into their texts, and how they approached the tasks of describing the exhibits. He found the different approaches of individual children and the differences between the three groups striking, and made the point that children's acts of sign making are not isolated instances of meaning making: their writing and drawings should be seen as part of an intertextual chain, as stages in a dialogic process, in which the children are responding to the social and cultural context in which they are making meaning. He showed the links between modes and learning: The verbal and visual choices they made are motivated by the same interests, and these preoccupations are a complex negotiation between the demands of the task and the habitus they themselves bring to the task.

Mavers (2003) reported on what happened when 9- and 10-year-olds were given 30 minutes in which to draw image-based mind maps on the topic, "Computers in My World." Children were given a specific audience and purpose: "Draw all the things you want to tell people about." They were also told that drawing is a useful way of communicating ideas. In follow-up interviews, Mavers asked children to reflect on their mind maps in terms of their intentions and the meanings these maps had for them. She clearly demonstrated how perceptual, experiential, and conceptual matters are interwoven in the semiosis of drawing, through the children's use of spatial arrangement in relation to the resources of size and positioning of image on the page, their use of image, composition, and links. Children made full use of the spaciality of the image as against the linearity of writing, and acting with an astute awareness of audience, strove to make themselves "maximally understood." Mavers concluded that the nature of such drawing is "intensely meaningful" (p. 31).

In a study exploring children's relationship to literacy and identity through modes other than language, Kendrick, McKay, and Moffatt (2005) asked 162 children from grades 1 to 6 from diverse backgrounds, to draw images of literacy "as a window on their constructions of self" (p. 185). Children were asked to "draw a picture of reading and writing" and to talk about their drawings afterwards. These explanations were used to verify and deepen interpretations of the content and meanings of the drawings. Drawing on Rose (2001), the analysis of the drawings involved using an interactive process that meant moving back and forth between the content of the drawings and the meaning evident in the children's descriptions of what they drew. The children depicted themselves as readers of popular culture, as writers of multiple genres, including map stories, fairy tales, sports scores, e-mail, computer diaries, stories and games; and they imagined themselves as teachers, hockey players, news anchors, children's writers, and office-tower builders. Importantly, children

critical question for learning: what does it mean to get better at multimodal representation? This research has important suggestions for pedagogy and teacher education in the area of multimodality.

While there is a marked interest in looking at multimodality in terms of images and words, studies of other modes are emerging. Lancaster (2003) investigated the role played by the coordinated use of physical and bodily resources in the structuring of semiotic events, showing how a 2-year-old uses language, gaze, and action in the process of making a greeting card. The child's use of gaze is particularly significant in mediating the "reflective recall of images, enabling past experiences to inform present thinking and decisions about future actions" (p. 121). Prinsloo (2004) explored the multimodal, multilingual resources of children's skipping games in unsupervised, child-choreographed play in Kwezi Park in Cape Town, demonstrating how children draw freely on local, regional, and global popular-culture sources. Multimodal dramatic performance is the focus of a study by Franks (2003), who used a multimodal semiotic perspective to observe a progressive sequence of action that involves the dramatization of a Shakespeare text in a classroom. This begins with the teacher establishing the purposes of the lesson, the students familiarizing themselves with an extract of the Shakespearian text through the utterance of lines, and moves into drama-animated dramatic action. Franks' focus on the role and function of the body as socially organized, situated in particular places and settings is a locus of multimodal meaning-making activity.

An important aspect of multimodality is what Kress et al. (2001) called *transduction*: the processes involved in how knowledge transforms when it moves from one mode to another. In this transduction across modes, Kress et al. have shown how the "entity" changes its shape and, therefore, its meaning. In her investigation into children's text making at home, Pahl (1999; Pahl & Rowsell 2005) demonstrated that shifts across modes produce not only variations in content and meaning, but also shifts in the child's subjectivity and identity. She described how a 6-year-old child effortlessly manipulated different materials and media, creating new signs in the process of playing Pokèmon, and constructing his own Pokèmon factory. Through exploring Sam's imaginative worlds beyond language, Pahl revealed his complex pattern of links across communicative practices. Pahl argued that Sam's movements across modes can be linked to the shifts in identity, which he achieved through each leap. She advocated that school environments should be supporting this kind of multimodal creative work.

Stein (2003; 2004; 2007) described a similar project in a school environment where marginalized children from poor communities in Johannesburg produced a series of narratives about characters in their neighborhoods in a sequence of planned movements across a semiotic chain. This involved drawing a character, creating the same character as a 3D doll figure, using the 3D doll figure in an improvisational play, and writing a story involving the same character. In making these artifacts, children drew on local and family knowledge of making traditional fertility dolls. Referring to the multimodal textual products as "points of fixing in the semiotic chain," Stein showed how the meanings attached to the "character" are fluid and unstable across the semiotic change. In other words, as the drawing of the character transforms into a 3D object, then into a character in a play and in a written narrative, the character is not the same entity—the differences in modal representation reshape what is being represented. She argued for a closer relationship between homes, communities, and schools where children's local cultural knowledge can be more highly valued for its potential to speak back to the school. Through such synergies, new forms of learning can take place.

Multimodal Instructional Practices: Instances of Practice

The concept of multimodality opens up meaning-making to a multiplicity of modes of communication. This is a very generative idea when applied to curriculum and pedagogy. The majority of studies focusing on multimodal instructional practices are critical of the narrowness of what counts as learning and communication in contemporary classrooms.

Numerous researchers and educators (Bearne, 2003; Cope & Kalantzis, 2000; Cummins, 2001; Heath, 1983; Hull & Schultz, 2002; Lankshear & Knobel, 2003; Millard, 2006; Pahl & Rowsell, 2005; Street, 2005) have made strong cases for crossing the boundaries between formal learning in schools and learning in everyday settings. In technologically rich societies, the gap between young people's use of technologies in and out of school is widening. Teachers are being urged to go beyond thinking of technology only in terms of tools and implements and to attend to the social and cultural dimensions of how this technology is being used. Lankshear and Knobel (2003), in *New Literacies: Changing Knowledge and Classroom Learning*, challenged existing classroom practices in relation to digital literacies in state schools in North America, Britain, and Australasia. Their research showed the increasing gap between teachers' cultural identities and those of their students, who have grown up immersed in digital technologies. Such learners are experiencing forms of disadvantage as their digital knowledge and e-proficiency are unacknowledged in mainstream classroom arrangements. They advocated new epistemologies in classrooms where teachers work more actively with the kinds of knowledge and capabilities young people are doing and using outside the confines of school in order to make effective pedagogical connections to them in class. They were highly critical of the use of new ICTS within school settings, "new wine in old bottles" syndrome, in which long-standing school-literacy routines have a new technology attached to them "without in any way changing the substance of the practice"—for example, using computers to produce neat final copies. New literacies and the social practices associated with them "are being invented on the streets" (p. 31) as "screenagers" engage on the Internet in weblogging, e-zining, and culture jamming.

Studies working within a critical pedagogical tradition use multimodality to take forward a social justice and equity agenda. They are interested in making classrooms more democratic, inclusive spaces in which the histories, identities, cultures, languages, discourses, and epistemologies of students whose lives and lifeworlds are excluded or marginalized from classrooms' spaces, can be made visible. Multimodality opens up the possibilities for multiple, diverse forms of meaning making and the process of hybridizing students' resources for representation and dominant classroom practices can produce "transformative" or "fusion" pedagogies (Stein, 2007; Millard, 2006).

Rogers and Schofield (2005) worked with students in a Learning Center that houses a Youth Literacy Program for at-risk youth alienated from traditional schooling, who are completing a diploma. Arguing for the redesigning of curricula" that are rich and inclusive for all students" (p. 219), they maintained that most traditional secondary schools "do not provide programming that engages struggling students in curricular projects that allow them to creatively draw on the material contexts of their lives and their multiple literacies to narrate their stories." In this project, the authors worked with students to produce emergent narratives through language, art, print, and multimedia. These included multimedia digital videos and CD compositions. Students developed storyboards, composed, acted, danced, filmed, and edited their own work. The authors' definition of youth-literacy pedagogy moves away from a focus on print alone toward "a braiding of multimodal texts into narratives—stories constructed on the playing fields of curriculum—that draw on adolescent biographies, imaginations, and their multiple and hybrid identities" (McCarthey & Moje, 2002, see p. 220). Multimedia and multiple literacies allow for the creative and constant interplay across spatial boundaries. The students' narrative artifacts are conceived of as "socially produced spaces that represent the interstices of students' in and out of school lives." In this way, multimodal narratives become spatial tours (de Certeau, 1984) of students' biographies and identities, their imaginations and multiple literacies, which they draw upon to reimagine, resist, and critique their experiences.

Similarly, Brenner and Andrew (2007) described their use of multimodal instructional practices in their visual literacy course aimed at preparing university students from previously disadvantaged backgrounds for entry into mainstream degree programs in the performing and visual arts. This course aimed to develop students' critical engagement in visual discourses and their academic writing in English. In developing essay-writing competence, they combined the process of writing with other modes, like "walking" and "performing the space." In one such project where students had to write an essay on an animated film by a local artist, students went on walks across the city locating, photographing, and discussing monuments and aspects of the city that were central to the film. They watched a video interview with the artist and made individual short, animated films using a technique similar to the artist's technique. They read historical documents and extracted from local literature on the theme of the city to help shape their writing. The authors, both practicing artists, found that, far from being anything near a methodical process,

> It is this ambulatory, controlled and convoluted approach that enables students to achieve in ways they need to ... working with students in a close-knit and ongoing way—a bit like having a group of apprentices—is what enables multiple capacities to congeal, gaps to heal and students to grow (2007, p. 212).

In another example of the potential of using multimodality as an instructional practice to explore identities with at-risk students, Smagorinsky, Zoss, and O'Donnell-Allen (2005) described the mask composing process of a male student, Peta, whose primary identity was Native American, and who maintained traditional Native American beliefs and practices. Peta made a gauze-and-plaster mask using traditional, low-technology methods practiced in Native American communities. The mask-making project was part of a year-long exploration of self in the senior curriculum. When presenting the mask activity, the teacher told students "masks serve as identities because when you put on a mask you become what the mask represents—we become our mask" (p. 67). Preparatory activities included completing writers' notebooks, reading logs on literary texts they were reading, writing portfolios, life maps, childhood memories, and mirrors to construct how they saw themselves and how others saw them.

Peta's approach to his mask design was emergent in relation to the available materials for production as a form of "materials-based decision making" (p. 68). He also engaged in nonlinear thinking, where he made new decisions as his design emerged. From an identity perspective, Peta's mask showed how his experiences had caused him to develop "a rage from deep inside." He used the mask as an emotional mediator as well as a spiritual mediator to express his broader connection to the earth. Using writing as part of the composing process, he produced a poem in conjunction with a mask, which put into words some of the ideas he was trying to express through his mask. The authors link multimodal meaning making to the long tradition of creativity in English classrooms, arguing for the incorporation of the arts into the curriculum "in the face of current high-stakes standardized-testing movement that has overtaken U.S. schools" (p. 62).

In a similar attempt to engage at-risk students in a South-African township school, an English teacher, Robert Maungedzo, consciously worked with multimodal pedagogies to stimulate his disaffected grade 11 students into creative production, hoping that this might stimulate them to returning to poetry, which they had abandoned in the school because it was "too difficult"

beck novel *Of Mice and Men* to a CD-ROM, Jewitt analyzed how reading or watching the novel as CD-ROM introduced new resources and practices for navigating, constructing, and understanding the entity "character." In the screen representation, the literary notion of character as realizing a particular moral, aesthetic, ethical, and dramaturgical function within the novel is transformed and represented as "person," authorial intent, and sociocultural entity (p. 98). Jewitt argued that to assess the newly configured entity on the CD-ROM within the same modal and generic framework of linguistic assessment is to ignore the transformation of the meaning of the entity. If a teacher only focuses on written language to assess how students engage in a multi-layered way with the entity character through a variety of semiotic resources (the novel in print, CD-ROM, class discussion, gesture, or images), traces of students learning that are apparent through modes other than written essay or multiple choice tests will be invisible.

The detailed multimodal analysis of school science and English classrooms by Kress et al. (2001; 2005) has provided evidence of how a great deal of the curriculum is represented in modes other than speech or writing. *More than Words: Multimodal Texts in the Classroom* (UKLA/QCA, 2004) worked with actual examples from classroom practice to develop assessment criteria for assessing multimodal texts and learning. Building on existing assessment strands to see how they can be applied to multimodal texts, the research team focused on the extent to which teachers can draw on their existing knowledge of texts and assessment ways to describe children's texts that use more than one mode, in this case, language and images. They worked with the Qualifications and Curriculum Authority writing assessment focuses that underpin the mark schemes for assessing writing rather than using text mark schemes to evaluate texts, as they "wanted to see how far the different aspects of writing identified in the focuses would help in describing texts that use pictures as well as words to communicate ideas" (p. 3). The focuses are combined into the following strands at all key stages:

- composition and effect
- text structure and organization
- sentence structure and punctuation (plus spelling)

UKLA/QCA (2004) provides an example of how teachers might use these strands to describe a child's multimodal text. In this task, a year 6 class was asked to produce posters advertising a new mobile phone. In preparation for the task, students explored examples of mobile-phone advertisements, paying attention to the linguistic and visual features of this genre. In pairs, children discussed ideas for new designs for mobile phones. Individually, they had to produce rough sketches of a new phone, list its design features, and make a plan of their poster, before using A3 paper to present their final posters (UKLA/QCA, p. 16). The research group found that the writing assessment strands could fruitfully be applied to describing the pictorial and verbal parts of a multimodal text, except for sentence structure, which they suggest is more likely to help in describing the verbal parts of a text (p. 18). The authors concluded that teachers have a great deal of knowledge to draw on as a basis for describing children's production of texts that use more than one mode. An important next step is to work out how to apply these strands in terms of assessing these multimodal texts.

In relation to assessing students' multimodal online texts, Wyatt-Smith and Kimber (2005) drew on research from a 5-year Australian national study (2003 to 2007) (see http://www.griffith.edu.au/centre/callcs/ecl) of first- and third-year high-school students, examining how well students research existing knowledge and use it to create and represent new knowledge in the form of online multimodal texts. Arguing that traditional theoretical and policy frameworks for literacy and assessment are orientated toward reading and print and do not readily transfer to technology-mediated literacies as actually practiced (2005, p. 230), Wyatt-Smith and Kimber posed the question: what are relevant and useful assessment criteria to inform teachers' and students' efforts at *talking about* and *determining quality* in students' multimodal online texts? The authors worked closely with the idea of giving students agency and developing their critical literacy to develop a set of criteria that included e-proficiency, cohesion, content, and design. These criteria can be used to identify and talk about the elements of multimodal texts, focusing on the component parts of the text, with each criterion given separate consideration. In addition to this, they developed a category, "transmodality," in order to examine the text more holistically. Transmodality captures the essence of working within and across modes, as well as the "synergistic dynamics" of text production online. They claimed that a focus on transmodal operation, in conjunction with explicitly defined assessment criteria, allows a more concentrated focus on human agency in designing.

Concepts of agency and resourcefulness were also at the center of Newfield et al.'s (2003) approach to multimodal assessment, based on their experience of working with disaffected Soweto high-school students who, as a group, produced a "multimodal identity text," the handmade TEBUWA cloth. The cloth as an artwork containing visual, verbal, and three-dimensional artifacts, was composed of individually written poems, as well as collaboratively produced elements such a multiple layers of stitching and embroidery. The authors argued that new criteria need to be developed that address the fact of multimodality: what multimodality is and what it does to achieve its effects. One of the categories they engage with is multimodal cohesion: this echoes van Leeuwen's (2005) discussion on dialogic cohesion in a multimodal text, where he asked whether we can we look at images and sounds in terms of simultaneous dialogue. Can word and image be in "social unison" or in "polyphonic relationship"? In many examples of multimodal texts, like the TEBUWA cloth, the individual voices have less value in themselves, but are meaningful in terms of their function with respect to the whole. In discussing the assessment of the TEBUWA cloth, Newfield and colleagues stated they were interested in,

> The assessment of the cloth as product and process that speaks to the complex orchestration of its voices and modes, to evidence of its learning and creativity, in a sensitive and flexible way, that is able to celebrate the profundity of its achievement (p. 73).

Drawing on assessment practices in art education, which emphasize the relationship between process and reflection, Newfeld et al. (2003) included a more participatory, ethnographic-style dimension to the assessment process where discussions with students took place on their interpretations of how they could make different modes work for them, in order to realize their projected interests through the overall design. The authors suggested that assessment should explore the idea of "resourcefulness" as an overarching category. Resourcefulness would signal the learner's engagement in relation to his or her "representational resources" and would include the extent to which students are able to recruit apt resources for making their meaning and their ability to use them generatively and productively with evidence of linkages and cohesion across modes and genres.

In an analysis of the shifts since the 1990s in what constitutes "text" in the Advanced Level English Language examination papers in the United Kingdom, Shortis and Jewitt (2005) explored the changes in the construction of subject English and its assessment. Before 2000, the texts used for analysis were reset in a word-processed format that stripped them of their original materiality and design including their use of image, font, layout, and color. Since 2001, the texts have been consistently reproduced in facsimile form in a state of "ecological materiality" in which the linguistic is set alongside and within other signifiers: these include the original graphology, use of image and layout. While the questions set on the text still require students to pay attention mainly to the linguistic features, there is some focus on the multimodal features of the text, even if this is somewhat "peripheral." By according value to everyday texts such as postcards, e-mails and handwritten notes, for example, and by loosening the boundaries between the visual and the linguistic in textual practice, the "picket-fence demarcations" around the sub-Englishes of English Language, communication, and media studies are challenged. The authors argued that these changes to how texts are represented in examination contexts point to small shifts in thinking about what constitutes text, textual practices, and textual responses in the English classroom: that "text is made in artifacts and not made exclusively by language," and "by always showing layout, the linguistic becomes embedded within a multimodal semiotic" (p. 86–88). They conceptualized an "ecology of texts and literacy practices" on "a continuum of multimodality" demonstrating how any classroom study of contemporary texts inevitably challenges traditional notions of textual boundaries and, therefore, the kinds of assessment procedures that accompany classroom practice.

Ferreira (2007) complemented this work by showing how spaces for multiliteracies and multimodality can be "prised open" in standardized examinations, citing examples of political cartoons, advertisements, and postcards from the national school-leaving English Language examination in South Africa. As chief examiner, she provided a rare insight into examination practices from behind the scenes, showing how it is not enough to simply select multimodal texts: much hinges on the types of questions that are posed about these texts. In one example, an advertisement for Boystown, a well-known boarding home for boys with behavioral problems, the text in its entirety consists of a written narrative and a parallel visual narrative in the use of font and style. The overlap between the verbal and visual semiotic is central to the meaning being conveyed. In the examination, students were asked to comment on the multimodal design of the advertisement and to discuss how the visual impact of the writing reflects the "journey of the writer." Ferreira argued that standardized tests can be enhanced by a multiliteracies pedagogy, and, in so doing, can encourage innovation and change.

Multimodal Instructional Practices: Implications for Teacher Education

The importance of the concept of multimodality in rethinking instructional practices in contemporary learning environments cannot be underestimated. The emergence of new relationships between modes of representation and communication means that the idea of literacy education is undergoing a paradigm shift in terms of how texts work to make meaning (Bearne, 2003). Multimodality is a key component of this paradigm shift and research in this vast area is rapidly growing. Much of the research reviewed in this chapter has demonstrated the importance of developing students' flexibility across knowledge domains in relation to modes, genres, and discourses. It is also crucial to develop young people's critical perspectives in forms of critical literacy and enquiry. To do this effectively, teachers need to extend their subject knowledge in relation to multimodality and multimodal texts, and their pedagogical knowledge in terms of how to use multimodality to improve students' learning. An important starting point is to include visual communication as an essential component of any teacher-education curriculum. Teachers can also deepen their understanding of popular culture in order to appreciate how students draw on the multimodal semiotic resources present in their everyday worlds to make meaning. Teacher education can extend teachers' knowledge of how to build on these resources to extend students' existing boundaries in relation to dominant school literacies. It is clear that multimodal assessment is an urgent, key area for research. While written and oral assessment has been the subject of intense scrutiny and research over decades, developing assessment tools that take into account the complex interrelationship of modes in a text is only just beginning. Without reliable assessment tools, multimodal instructional practices carry little weight and authority where it really matters.

References

Archer, A. (2006). Opening up spaces through symbolic objects: Harnessing students' multimodal resources in developing English academic literacy in an Engineering course. *English Studies in Africa*, 49(1), pp. 189–206.

Baker, D., & Street, B. (2006). 'So, What about Multimodal Literacies?' in K. Pahl, & K. J. Rowsell, (Eds.). Travel Notes from the New Literacy Studies. Clevedon: Multilingual Matters, pp. 219–233.

Barthes, R. (1974). *S/Z*. New York: Hill and Wang.

Barton, D., Hamilton, M., & Ivanic, R. (2000). *Situated literacies: Reading and writing in context*. London: Routledge.

Beach, R., & O'Brian, D. (2005). Playing texts against each other in the multimodal English classroom. *English in Education*, 39(2), 44–59.

Bearne, E. (2003). Rethinking literacy: Communication, representation, and text. *Reading: Literacy and Language*, 37(3), 98–103. Retrieved September 10, 2006 from http://www.ukla.org/site/publications/pdf/literacypapers

Bearne, E. (2005). Multimodal texts: What they are and how children use them. In J. Evans (Eds.), *Literacy moves on: Using popular culture, new technologies, and critical literacy in the primary classroom* (pp. 13–29). London: David Fulton.

Brenner, J., & Andrew, D. (2006). 'Be an artist in words, that you may be strong, for the tongue is a sword': Developing academic writing in a visual literacy course. *English Studies in Africa*, 49, 207–215.

Comber, B., Nixon, H., Ashmore, L., Loo, S., & Cook, J. (2005). Urban renewal from the inside out: Spatial and critical literacies in a low socioeconomic school community. *Mind, Culture and Activity: Semiotic, Dialogic and Material Spaces* (special issue), 13(3), 226-243.

Cope, B., & Kalantzis, M. (Eds.). (2000). *Multiliteracies: Literacy learning and the design of social futures*. London: Routledge.

Cope, B., Kalantzis, M., & Harvey, A. (2003, March). Assessing multiliteracies and the new basics. *Assessment in Education*, 10(1), 15–26.

Cummins, J. (2001). *Negotiating identities: Education for empowerment in a diverse society* (2nd ed.). Los Angeles: California Association for Bilingual Education.

de Certeau, M. (1984). *The practice of everyday life* (S. Rendell, Trans.). Berkeley: University of California Press.

Doneman, M. (1997). Multimediating. In C. Lankshear, C. Bigum, C. Durrant, B. Green, E. Honan, W. Morgan, et al. (Eds.), *Digital rhetorics: Literacies and technologies in education – current practices and future directions* (pp.). Canberra: Department of Employment, Education, Training, and Youth Affairs. [Vol 3, *Children's Literacy National Projects*, pp. 131–148,]? Brisbane: QUT/DEETYA.

Ferreira, A. (2006). Multiliteracies and standardized examinations: A personal reflection on the South African matric English language examination. *English Studies in Africa*, 49, 163–188.

Franks. A. (2003). Palmer's kiss: Shakespeare, school drama, and semiotics. In C. Jewitt & G. Kress. (Eds.). *Multimodal Literacy*, (pp. 155–172). New York: Peter Lang.

Gee, J. P. (1996). *Social linguistics and literacies: Ideology in discourses* (2nd ed.). London: Taylor and Francis.

Gee, J. P. (2003). *What video games have to teach us about learning and literacy*. New York: Palgrave Macmillan.

Halliday, M. A. K. (1978). *Language as social semiotic*. London: Arnold.

Heath, S. B. (1983). *Ways with words: Language, life, and work in communities and class-rooms.* Cambridge, UK: Cambridge University Press.

Hull, G., & Schultz, K. (Eds.). (2002). *School's out! Bridging out of school literacies with classroom practices.* New York/London: Teachers College Press.

Jewitt, C. (2003). Rethinking assessment: Multimodality, literacy and computer-mediated learning. *Assessment in Education: Principles, Policy, Practice, 10*(1), 83–102.

Jewitt, C. (2006). *Technology, literacy, learning.* London: Routledge Falmer.

Jewitt, C., & Kress, G. (Eds.). (2003). *Multimodal literacy.* New York: Peter Lang.

Johnson, D., & Kress, G. (2003, March). Globalization, literacy and society: Redesigning pedagogy and assessment. *Assessment in Education, 10*(1), 5–14.

Kendrick, M., Mckay, R., & Moffatt, L. (2005). The portrayal of self in children's drawings of home, school, and community literacies. In J. Anderson, M. Kendrick, T. Rogers, & S. Smythe (Eds.), *Portraits of literacy across families, communities, and schools: Intersections and tensions* pp. 185–204. New Jersey and London: Lawrence Erlbaum Associates.

Kenner, C. (2003). Embodied knowledges: Young children's engagement with the act of writing. In C. Jewitt & G. Kress (Eds.), *Multimodal literacy* (pp.). New York: Peter Lang.

Kenner, C. (2004). *Becoming biliterate: Young children learning different writing systems.* Cambridge, UK: Stoke on Trent.

Kress, G. (1997). *Before writing: Rethinking the paths to literacy.* London: Routledge.

Kress, G. (2000). Multimodality. In B. Cope & M. Kalantzis (Eds.), *Multiliteracies: Literacy, learning, and the design of Social Futures* (pp. 182–202). London: Routledge.

Kress, G. (2003). *Literacy in the new media age.* London: Routledge.

Kress, G., & van Leeuwen, T. (1996). *Reading images: The grammar of visual design.* London: Routledge.

Kress G., & van Leeuwen, T. (2001). *Multimodal disourse.* London: Arnold.

Kress, G., & van Leeuwen, T. (2006). *Reading images: The grammar of visual design* (2nd ed.). London: Routledge.

Kress, G., Jewitt, C., Bourne, J., Franks, A., Hardcastle, J., Jones, K., et al. (2005). *English in urban classrooms.* London: Routledge Falmer.

Kress, G., Jewitt, C., Ogborn, J., & Tsatsarelis, C. (2001). *Multimodal teaching and learning: Rhetorics of the science classroom.* London: Continuum.

Lancaster, L. (2003). Beginning at the beginning: How a child constructs time multimodally. In C. Jewitt & G. Kress (Eds.), *Multimodal literacy* (pp. 107–122). New York: Peter Lang.

Lankshear, C., & Knobel, M. (2003). *New literacies: Changing knowledge and classroom learning.* Buckingham, UK: Open University Press.

Lemke, J. (2000). Multimedia literacy demands of the scientific curriculum. *Linguistics and Education, 10*(3), 247–271.

Martinec, R. (2000). Construction of identity in Michael Jackson's 'Jam.' *Social Semiotics, 10*(3), 313–29.

Mavers, D. (2003). Communicating meanings though image composition, spatial arrangement, and links in primary school student mind maps. In C. Jewitt, & G. Kress (Eds.), *Multimodal literacy* (pp. 19–33). New York: Peter Lang.

McCarthey, S. J., & Moje, E. (2002). Conversations: Identity matters. *Reading Research Quarterly, 27*(2), 228–238.

Millard, E. (2006). Transformative pedagogy: Teachers creating a literacy of fusion. In K. Pahl, & J. Rowsell (Eds.), *Travelnotes from the new literacy studies: Instances of practice* (pp. 228–238). Clevedon, U.K.: Multilingual Matters.

New London Group. (1996). A pedagogy of multiliteracies: Designing social futures. *Harvard Educational Review, 66*(1), 60–92.

Newfield, D., Andrew, A., Stein, P., & Maungedzo, R. (2003, March). No number can describe how good it was: Assessment issues in the multimodal classroom. *Assessment in Education: Principles, Policy, and Practice, 10*(1), 61–81.

Norris, S. (2004). *Analyzing multimodal interaction*. London: Routledge.

O'Halloran, K. (2000). Classroom discourse in mathematics: A multisemiotic analysis. *Linguistics and Education, 10*(3), 359–388.

O'Halloran, K. (Ed.). (2004). *Multimodal discourse analysis*. London: Continuum.

Ormerod, F., & Ivanic, R. (2002). Materiality in children's meaning making practices. *Visual Communication, 1*(1), 65–91.

Pahl, K. (1999). *Transformations: Children's meaning making in nursery education*. Cambridge, UK: Stoke on Trent.

Pahl, K., & Rowsell, J. (2005). *Literacy and education*. London/Thousand Oaks, CA/New Delhi: Paul Chapman Publishing.

Pahl, K., & Rowsell, J. (Eds.). (2006). *Travelnotes from the new literacy studies: Instances of practice*. Clevedon, UK: Multilingual Matters.

Prinsloo, M. (2004). Literacy is child's play: Making sense in Khwezi Park. *Language and Education, 18*(4), 291–303.

Rogers, T., & Schofield, A. (2005). Things thicker than words: Portraits of youth multiple literacies in an alternative secondary program. In J. Anderson, M. Kendrick, T. Rogers, & S. Smythe (Eds.), *Portraits of literacy across families, communities, and schools: Intersections and tensions* (pp. 205–223). New Jersey/London: Lawrence Erlbaum Associates.

Rose, G. (2001). *Visual methodologies*. London: Sage.

Scollon, R., & Wong-Scollon, S. (2003). *Discourses in place*. London: Routledge.

Shortis, T., & Jewitt, C. (2005). A 'multimodal ecology of text' in advanced level English language examinations? *English in Education, 39*(2), 76–96.

Smagorinsky, P., Zoss, M., & O'Donnell-Allen, C. (2005). Mask-making as identity project in a high school English class: A case study. *English in Education, 39*(2), 60–75.

Stein, P. (2003). The Olifantsvlei fresh stories project: Multimodality, creativity, and fixing in the semiotic chain. In C. Jewitt & G. Kress (Eds.), *Multimodal iteracy* (pp. 123–138). New York: Peter Lang.

Stein, P. (2004). Representation, rights, and resources: Multimodal pedagogies in the language and literacy classroom. In B. Norton & K. Tooney (Eds.), *Critical pedagogies and language learning* (pp. 95–115). Cambridge, UK: Cambridge University Press.

Stein, P. (2007). Multimodal Pedagogies in Diverse Classrooms: Rights, Representation and Resources. London: Routledge (in press).

Street, B. (Ed.). (2005). *Literacies across educational contexts*. Philadelphia: Caslon Inc.

Street, B., & Baker, D. (2006). So, what about multimodal numeracies? In K. Pahl & J. Rowsell (Eds.), *Travelnotes from the new literacy studies: Instances of practice* (pp. 118–146). Clevedon, UK: Multilingual Matters.

Thesen, L. (2001). Modes, literacies, and power: A university case study. *Language and Education, 15*(2/3), 132–145.

Unsworth, L. (2001). *Teaching multiliteracies across the curriculum: Changing contexts of text and image in classroom practice*. Buckingham, UK: Open University Press.

United Kingdom Literacy Association [UKLA]. (2004). *More than Words: Multimodal Texts in the Classroom*, London: Qualifications and Curriculum Authority. Retrieved June 12, 2007 from http://www.qca.org.uk/9054.html

van Leeuwen, T. (1999). *Speech, music, sound*. London: Macmillan.

van Leeuwen, T. (2000). It was just like magic: A multimodal analysis of children's writing. *Linguistics and Education, 10*(3), 273–305.

van Leeuwen, T. (2005). *Introducing social semiotics*. London/New York: Routledge.

Wells, G. (2000). Modes of meaning in a science activity. *Linguistics and Education, 10*(3), 307–34.

Wemmer, K., & Drew, M. (2004). *Designing think trails: Using multiliteracies pedagogy to reshape academic knowledge into clinical reasoning*. Unpublished paper, Department of Audiology, University of the Witwatersrand, Johannesburg.

Wyatt-Smith, C., & Kimber, K. (2005). Valuing and evaluating student-generated online multimodal texts: Rethinking what counts. *English in Education, 39*(2), 22–44.

CHAPTER 31

Multimodal Reading and Comprehension in Online Environments

CLAIRE WYATT-SMITH
and JOHN ELKINS
GRIFFITH UNIVERSITY, AUSTRALIA

Few would challenge the idea that we are in a critical period in human history characterized by an unprecedented and increasingly rapid change in technologies and communication processes. It is fair to say that we are in a communication revolution every bit as radical and significant as the advent of the printing press. To adopt Selfe and Hawisher's (2004) title, our *Literate Lives in the Information Age* have been fundamentally altered from those of preceding generations. We have quick access to what can be an overwhelming amount of information online, information delivered at the touch of keyboard and with a speed and currency not previously imaginable. Further, our lives have become entangled with computers and related technologies so that our work, leisure, and home activities not only involve these devices, but also in many respects depend on "going online," being technologically literate.

Against this backdrop, the chapter starts with the international imperative to reconceptualize the nature of knowledge, its generation and production in what has come to be known as the information economy (Castells, 1996, 1997, 1998). While the growing importance of technological literacy is widely recognized, to the point of being foundational to social and economic access and participation, also acknowledged is the paucity of research on how and why young people acquire and develop, or fail to acquire and develop, such literate capabilities, both in school and beyond (Selfe & Hawisher, 2004). The goal of this chapter is to draw on available research to probe what we might count as multimodal reading and comprehension in online environments.

When we consider reading comprehension in its traditional sense, we are easily tempted to think of it as a unitary concept, whereas it changes, qualitatively as well as in magnitude, as readers progress from primary to high-school levels and beyond. We may easily lose sight of the fact that reading, and comprehension of what is read, takes place in physical and sociopolitical contexts. It is therefore a situated social and cultural practice at the same time that it is a psychological skill that contains cognitive and affective elements. This mix of context and skill elements would seem to apply to multimodal online reading and the process of comprehending that is our focus.

While there have been concerted calls in the last decade for new theorizations of literacy online, considerable terminological confusion has grown around literacy and its interface with technology. This is evident in the proliferation of such terms as *new literacies* (Leu, Kinzer, Coiro, & Cammack, 2004), *digital literacy* (Tyner, 1998), *multiliteracies* (Kress, 2003; Luke, 2000, 2003; New London Group, 2000; Cope & Kalantzis, 2000), *information literacy* (Kuiper, Volman, & Terwel, 2005), and *the literacies of technology* (Selfe & Hawisher, 2004), with each of these terms attending to literacy practices in online environments, broadly speaking.

In this chapter, multimodal reading and comprehension are situated in direct relationship to what has come to be known under the umbrella term, new literacies, discussed in the following section, and in particular to the literacies of technology[1], both offering "an all-encompassing phrase to connect social practices, people, technology, values, and literate activity, which, in turn, are embedded in a larger cultural ecology" (Selfe & Hawisher, 2004, p. 2). This emphasis on connectedness is taken to be central to ways of reading online where interactivity occurs—between reader/user and screens, and also among readers/users, within local community spaces as well as across virtual and global spaces. It is therefore in this mix of dimensions that visual, audio, and spatial semiotic systems come together in what is in effect a new grammar (Cope & Kalantzis, 2000; Kress & van Leeuwen, 2001; Unsworth, Martin, Painter, & Gill, in press).

Existing research shows an increasing interest in identifying and mapping different aspects of literate practice, reflecting at least in part the prominence given literacy as a marker of quality education provision and international standing (Chandler-Olcott & Mahar, 2003; Green, 1988, 1999; Hasan, 1996; Luke, Freebody, & Land, 2000; Smolin & Lawless, 2003; Unsworth, 2002). While there are points of difference in these writings, of more immediate

---

[1] In this chapter, technological literacies are taken in their widest sense to be both receptive and generative, involving visual, audio, and text-based communications and representations (digital gaming; the Internet; chat rooms; e-mail; text-messaging; creating multimedia including web pages, video clips etc.).

interest is the shared recognition of how learners need to develop a range of literate capabilities that allow them to engage effectively within educational, workplace, leisure, and community settings.

Further, several writers including Lankshear and Knobel (2003a) and Leu (2000) have pointed to the limited research about new literacies of the Internet (see also Coiro, 2003; Coiro & Dobler, 2007), and other information communication technologies (ICTs). Leu et al. (2004) made the strong statement that "what we know about new literacies from the traditional research literature must recognize that we actually know very little" (p. 1571). As a corollary, other writers, including Lankshear and Knobel (2003a), Tiene (2002), and Williamson and Facer (2004), argued that literacy theorists and educators have, to date, failed to give due consideration to the implications of new literacies that are emerging from technological, economic, and other changes including globalization.

Over the last 5 years, however, there has been an upsurge of policy, research, and teacher interest and teacher engagement with how reading is changing in a networked age. Researchers including those with The New Literacies Research Team at the University of Connecticut have focused teacher attention across K–12 on ways to integrate what is referred to as *the new literacies of online reading comprehension* into classroom practice. Members of this research team share considerable work on using the internet for innovative approaches to literacy education. For example, you can find videos of new literacy instructional models at http://ctell.uconn.edu/canter/canber_video.cfm?; you can view examples of new literacy instruction applied to grades 3 to 5 at http://www.learner.org/channel/workshops/teachreading35/session5/index. html; and Karchmer, Mallette, Kara-Soteriou, & Leu (2005) provide several chapters of award-winning teachers who have successfully integrated new literacies instruction into their classroom.

Additionally, various frameworks have been developed to conceptualize and analyze teaching and learning through multimedia and technology-related literacies, including sociocultural, semiotic, psychological, structural, and organizational materialistic perspectives. This is discussed in more detail later in this chapter. Of note here is that these approaches have as yet not been integrated or applied to large data sets, with most studies being descriptive or small scale. Despite this, education systems throughout the world continue to invest heavily in physical infrastructure so that schools are able to enhance learning with ICTs. This move parallels the increasing availability of digital technologies in the home. More than one billion readers are now online every day at home, in the workplace, and at school (AFP, 2007).

In effect, the home has become a key site for ICT entertainment and learning, with parents directly co-opted as buyers of a diverse and expanding range of associated commodities. In addition, digital technologies including mobile phones, e-mail, text messaging, and LAN (Local Area Network) gaming, have changed the modes and patterns of interaction for leisure, work, and learning purposes. Essentially, young people are afforded opportunities to develop multiliterate capabilities, including online reading comprehension skills not only in school, but also through participation in other communities. Current research suggests that while print literacy skills are incorporated into online environments and are central to how informal teaching and learning occur there, they are only part of the repertoire of skills and strategies needed to handle the multimodal representations of meaning that are found in online environments (See Carrington, 2005, for a discussion of texting; and Beavis, Nixon, & Atkinson, 2005, for LAN cafes).

Given this, it seems that we are never simply reading—we are always reading something, in some context or situation, and reading for some purpose. Four questions therefore emerge as relevant from the start of this chapter: (a) *Reading what and where?* (b) *Reading how?* (c) *Reading why?* and (d) *Reading with what possible consequence?* Throughout the chapter, these serve to anchor our thoughts and are key, given the research finding of "a wide and widening gulf ... between the forms of literacy students engage in within school settings, and the manner in which they engage in them, and those they encounter in the worlds beyond school" (Lankshear & Knobel, 2003b, p. 1). Studies of home and school (Chandler-Olcott & Mahar, 2003; Hinchman, Alvermann, Boyd, Brozo, & Vacca, 2004) have emphasized that the digital divide exists not only in terms of access but also in the gap between ICT practices at home and school. This disjunction has significant implications for the development of online reading comprehension and consequent success in school (Sunderland-Smith, Snyder, & Angus, 2003, p. 5) and beyond. In addition, recent studies of multiliteracies involving teenagers in a range of countries including the United States (Thorne, 2003), Japan (Ito, 2003), and Canada (Parks, Huot, Hamers, & H.-Lemonnierr, 2003) have pointed to tensions between the pedagogy associated with school learning, including learning to read multimodal texts online, and the cultural practices and values integral to young people's identities.

Currently, however, it remains unclear how, and how well, schools are preparing students for living and working in an ICT-saturated world in which young people, in outside-of-school contexts, are already enthusiastic users of a wide range of technologies demonstrating an extensive repertoire of multiliterate capabilities. Also unclear is the nature and extent of the disconnections between literacies practiced at home, at school, and in other communities, especially in the middle years. Some Australian research suggests that any lack of such connectivity has significant implications for student learning (Lankshear & Bigum, 1999; Luke, 1998, 2003; Unsworth, 2002). In discussing this issue as it relates to education in the United Kingdom, Millard (2003) claimed:

> The disjunction between the multimodal world of communication which is available to school children in the wider community and the consti-

pated, book bound modes of the standard curriculum has resulted in the increasing alienation of pupils from the schooling on offer (p. 4).

In related work, Bousted and Ozturk (2004) explored the intersection of visual and textual literacies with preservice teachers in the United Kingdom. They reported that the study enabled them "to reaffirm ... their commitment to maintaining a creative approach to literacy that builds on the multiple experiences of the different literacies, which are an essential element of the cultural capital that children bring with them to the classroom" (p. 56). Further, they asserted that "the failure to make these connections could ... result in dangerous disjunctions between school literacy, children's implicit and existing literacy abilities and the literacies which are essential in order to make sense of the 'real world' outside the classroom" (p. 56). Such disjunctions have clear implications for young people's life trajectories in social, employment, and leisure spheres, and, in turn, national well-being and prosperity in the broadest sense. Moreover, they also have implications for how curriculum and pedagogy attempt to maintain relevance and continuity to practices and knowledges valued outside schooling. It also raises the issue of the relative "comfort" of those involved in the teaching of literacy in new times. Lankshear and Bigum (1998, cited in Lankshear & Knobel, 2003a) described some of these issues by reference to a distinction made by Barlow (in Tunbridge, 1995) between "immigrant" and "native" mindsets for new technologies. Here the distinction is between those who have "been born and grown up" in the IT world (i.e., approximately under 30 years of age) and those who were migrated into this world (i.e., approximately over 30 years of age). One (immigrant) affirmed the world as the same as before, only more technologized: the other (native) affirmed the world as radically different, precisely because of the operation of new technologies (Lankshear & Bigum, 1998, p. 11). Lankshear and Knobel (2003a , p. 6) went on to explain that "schools already face sizable cohorts of natives largely indifferent to and bemused by the quaint practices of schooling ... [where] the deep grammar of school—embedded in its administrative systems, policy development, curriculum and syllabus development, systemic planning etc., as well as in its daily enactment within classroom routines and relations— institutionalizes the privileging of the immigrant mind-set over the native mind-set." Against this background, we move to outline the theoretical perspectives that we use in considering the nature of reading and reading comprehension online.

Theoretical Perspectives

In writing this chapter, we considered various ways of framing the review. One approach would start with present understandings of print reading comprehension and the knowledge, capabilities, and attributes traditionally associated with being a fluent reader. These include understanding the resources of alphabetic writing, speech, and the visual, and having a sense of the potentials of all these resources in use—traditionally regarded as essential in mastering acts of decoding and encoding print that are typically the goals of reading. While we regard this approach as useful, we decided to frame our discussion of what online reading comprehension and successful engagement with multimodal text might require by pulling together various strands of theoretical argument. Motivating our thinking is the need for multiperspectival, multitheoretical approaches to reading research that take account of sociolinguistic concerns as well as the cognitive, critical, or evaluative, and aesthetic design aspects of new literacies. To begin, we outline four key propositions as follows:

1. Reading and literacy are embedded in social processes and cultural contexts.
2. Cultural and linguistic pluralism, as well as the ease of global communication, demand new forms of literacy and ways of reading that enable people to negotiate diversity and difference for productive effect.
3. Schools are located at the confluence between traditional, conventional approaches to meaning making and reading, and new understandings about the multiple modes operating in online reading. The latter includes how linguistic representation (e.g., text, oral presentation), visual representation (e.g., shapes, icons, colors, foregrounding, backgrounding; font size), audio representation (sound effects), spatial representation (perspective) and gesture (New London Group, 1996) combine.
4. Reading online is not readily separable from writing, the latter ranging from the most basic acts of moving cursors and entering search terms through to using located and accessed information for problem-based inquiry and communication purposes. If this is accepted, then research on reading is best understood as being concerned with both using and creating knowledge, individually and collaboratively.

As suggested earlier, influential in our thinking is the writing of United States, British, and Australian critical linguists working with a sociocultural theory of language, such as Fairclough (1989, 1992), Johnson and Kress (2003); Kress (1985, 2003), Gee (1991), and Street (1984, 1993), who take up the social, political, multiple, dialogic, and dynamic nature of literacies. The already strong and growing series of writing in both research and practice, known as the New Literacy Studies (NLS), treats literacies as social practices rather than as universal technical skills to be learned in schooling. The term *social literacies* (first used by Street, 1995) refers to "the nature of literacy as social practice and to the plurality of literacies that this enables us to observe" (Street, 2001, p. 147). Since the early 1980s, there has been considerable elaboration of the key concepts of this influential series of writings, in both research and in practice, including the plurality of literacies and the intrinsic relationship between *literacy practices* and *social processes* (Heath, 1983; Heath & Mangiola, 1991; Street, 1993, 2000; Barton & Hamilton, 1998).[2] Given this relationship, literacy practices inevitably vary with social contexts and with cultural norms. Street and others (e.g., Kress, 1997) argued strongly against literacy being understood as a single, fixed and essential thing—a predetermined body of knowledge and skills. Similarly, they were careful to highlight "a danger when talking of a plurality of literacies of appearing to associate *a literacy* with *a culture*" (Street, 2001, p. 148). In focusing on schooling, Street wrote,

> That literacy is a social practice is an insight both banal and profound: banal, in the sense that once we think about it, it is obvious that literacy is always practiced in social contexts and that even the school, however "artificial" it be accused of being in its ways of teaching reading and writing, is also a social construction. The school, like other contexts, has its own social beliefs and behaviours into which its particular literacy practices are inserted. The notion is, in this sense, also profound in that it leads to quite new ways of understanding and defining what counts as literacy and has profound implications for how we teach reading and writing. If literacy is a social practice, then it varies with social context and is not the same, uniform thing in each case (p. 147).

From this perspective, literacy practices vary with social context, cultural norms, and discourses regarding gender, belief, age, and social class, for instance. Moreover, the uses of literacy are always inevitably bound up with relations of power. We believe that such an ideological perspective on literacy has profound implications for how reading is taught and assessed/valued in formal and informal learning, and even more fundamentally, how reading comprehension comes to be researched. From a NLS approach, there is a need for taking a situated approach to studying acts of reading, individually and in groups, as they occur both in and outside schooling. In relation to online reading comprehension then, legitimate sites for research extend to LAN cafés for communal gaming, as well as multiplayer synchronous online gaming sites with players potentially across the globe.

In writing this, we are mindful that there are numerous challenges associated with undertaking empirical studies of online reading in school contexts and we discuss this later in the chapter. Even more so, we acknowledge the even greater challenges associated with gaining access to and collecting empirical data on actual online reading practices outside school. Given this,

---

[2] Readers interested in writing on variation in literacies from the NLS are advised to see Heath's (1983) account of three literacies associated with communities in the piedmont Carolinas: Roadville, Trackton and maintown literacies; Street's (1984) writing on literacies in an Iranian village (schooled literacy, 'Qoranic literacy and commercial literacy'), and writing on local and community literacies (Barton, 1991; Barton & Hamilton, 1998).

Street's words about the ideological nature of literacy are particularly salient, especially as they extend to considerations about what comes to be valued for assessment and grading in formal education. On this point, Street (2001) made a useful distinction between *literacy practice*, which may refer to classroom behaviors, and the term *literacy practices* that "allows us to adopt a broader and more culturally relative perspective, and thereby to see and value varieties of literacy practices that we might otherwise miss, and that would certainly remain marginalized through such lack of attention" (p. 149).

The conception of new literacies outlined above reflects the current expectation in the field of reading research that new theoretical perspectives will emerge from actual practices studied in-situ, especially how students read and engage with the visual, linguistic, spatial, and audio resources available in online environments. The expectation also holds for the field of multiliteracies assessment where there is growing recognition that, just as being literate with print involves more than knowledge and skill, say, in phonics, being literate with ICTs involves more than technical competence. This is a view put forward from various perspectives including the assessment of "iSkills Literacy" being developed by the Educational Testing Service (2004). Drawing on the paper, Katz (2005) made the strong claim that "the risks for college students who leave higher education without ICT literacy skills are substantial. More than in the past, skills in researching and communicating information via technology are part of what is needed to function in society" (p. 2). While this point has been made previously in this chapter, of special interest in the chapter here the elaborated point about critical or evaluative capabilities as central in ICT literacy, as follows:

> Just because someone can navigate to a Web site, or even knows how to construct Web sites, it does not mean that the person can identify reliable, authoritative resources from the Web or know how to best interpret and communicate a Web site's content via a well-supported argument. In other words, technological competence alone does not equal ICT literacy. (p. 2)

Beginning work in the assessment field (Johnston, 2003; Jewitt, 2003; Wyatt-Smith & Kimber, 2005; Kimber & Wyatt-Smith, 2006) has already emphasized the potentially interrelated aspects of visual, audio, gestural, and spatial modes of meaning that challenge the privileging of any single mode, and in particular, the long-held dominance of the written linguistic mode as the determinant of literate accomplishment. This work points to how multiliteracies assessment calls for a deliberate connecting of reading and writing online for inquiry purposes, where what is valued extends to how students use the information they have accessed and located online. Then, reading and writing assessment together, can attend to multimodal design where assessment focuses on students' demonstrated capabilities to work within and combine different meaning systems and channels of communication for critical inquiry and engagement.

Central to our theoretical framing, therefore, is a belief that there is an urgent need to reconceptualize reading online broadly, taking account of what is involved in making meaning of a myriad of representational resources online and the contexts in which meaning is both shaped and shared. Consistent with this, we draw on the work of Johnson and Kress (2003) in placing "text-as-social process and entity as the central category from which other categories derive their sense, use and function in the text" (p. 12). From this vantage point, a strong sense of interrelation can be established across knowledge domains, the social and representational, and the cognitive and evaluative, in what we count as reading comprehension online.

The discussion that follows is presented in three parts. Part One focuses on conceptual frameworks for new literacies, reading, and comprehension. Part Two considers research on the relationship between reading practices associated with print materials (sometimes themselves multimodal), and ways of reading hybrid, multimodal texts online. Part Three then reviews research on online reading and writing, both in and outside of school contexts.

Review of Literature

Part One: Conceptual Frameworks

We begin with the observation that there is a paucity of empirical research to support the development of conceptual frameworks on multimodal reading and comprehension online. This situation reflects how, currently, "we lack a precise definition of what new literacies are" (Leu et al., 2004, p. 1571), and even more fundamentally, we lack a precise definition of reading online.

Drawing on Kramarski and Feldman (2000) and Kymes (2005), it seems that the use of technology or online resources may not of itself improve student comprehension. Kramarski and Feldman found that "although the Internet environment contributes significantly to the motivation of the students, ... no real contribution was found ... in English reading comprehension" (p. 149). Andrews (2004) noted from a systematic review of the research, that "gains in reading comprehension are negligible: most of the advances are at basic skills levels—in general, ICT is good for basic skills but not for higher order literacy capabilities" (p. 59). A word of caution is appropriate here. Despite their claims to be about comprehension and ICT use, several writers including Andrews, Kramarski and Feldman (see Figure 31.1), and Kymes (see Table 31.1) appeared to be located on traditional ground, offering a print dependent construct of reading tied predominantly to school tasks. This is reflected, for example, in how the writers' vocabulary for addressing the demands of reading and comprehension online does not extend beyond traditional concerns to engage with features such as the verbal/visual interface and multimodal operations instrinsic to the Internet or other digital technologies more generally.

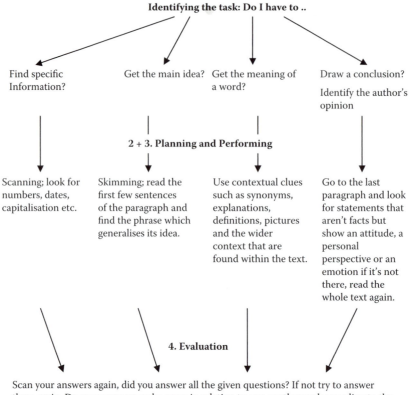

Identifying the task: Do I have to ..

Find specific Information?

Get the main idea?

Get the meaning of a word?

Draw a conclusion?
Identify the author's opinion

2 + 3. Planning and Performing

Scanning; look for numbers, dates, capitalisation etc.

Skimming; read the first few sentences of the paragraph and find the phrase which generalises its idea.

Use contextual clues such as synonyms, explanations, definitions, pictures and the wider context that are found within the text.

Go to the last paragraph and look for statements that aren't facts but show an attitude, a personal perspective or an emotion if it's not there, read the whole text again.

4. Evaluation

Scan your answers again, did you answer all the given questions? If not try to answer them again. Do your answers make sense in relation to one another and according to the text? If not, try to answer the problematic questions following the model.

Figure 31.1 A metacognitive strategy for reading comprehension.

In contrast, a recently completed study by Coiro and Dobler (2007) adopted a multitheoretical approach, combining theoretical perspectives on literacy, technology, and learning, to study online reading comprehension strategies used by sixth- grade skilled readers to search for and locate information on the Internet. These writers also wanted to develop an understanding of the rationale behind the choices the young people made during their Internet reading experience. In undertaking this work, Coiro and Dobler posited that older notions of knowledge domains used to interpret and predict the meaning of printed texts no longer sufficiently explain the knowledge domains required of readers in Web-based contexts. An important feature of this work is its clear recognition that the priority is less with reading as a generic activity, than with what is being read—the knowledge domain and modes that combine to constitute the text and that necessarily shape how acts of reading occur. If this premise is accepted, then by extension, we necessarily open up the issue of how acts of reading come to be shaped by the available technologies, and, therefore, narrative technologies such as instant messaging or e-mails, for example, may

Table 31.1 Comparison of Reading Strategies

Awareness of purpose

Print texts:	Online texts:
"I need to find a quote or a fact that will support my ideas about what should be done about acid rain."	"I need to log on to the Web and do a Google search to find information about acid rain. Maybe there will be a chart or graph or something else that will help, too. If I can't find that with Google, I might need to use a different search engine that will let me search specifically for multimedia besides just text. I need to be careful not to get distracted by anything that is flashing, or by chasing links, or even checking my e-mail, because I don't have too much time today."

Discovering new meanings of words

Print texts:	Online texts:
"I don't know what that word means. It seems like it is important because it is used several times in the next few sentences. Let me reread that to see if it makes more sense. Was it explained earlier and I missed it or is the definition coming up? If I can't figure this out, I am going to need to get a dictionary, check the back of this book, or ask someone else for help."	"I am not really sure what that word means. Let me click on it—it's blue so I think there is a link to something else. Hopefully, it will tell me what it means or send me somewhere else where the word is explained better than it is here. I just don't want to go away from this page too far and forget where I am!"

Interpreting the text and conversing with the author

Print texts:	Online texts:
"I wonder if there is something in this author's background or experiences that has made him write the text this way? I guess I will have to ask the teacher or try to find a biography or another book or article that talks about the author and why he writes this way."	"I wonder why the author said that. Maybe there will be an e-mail address somewhere on this page where I can write and ask him. Or maybe there is a bulletin board where I can look to see if anyone else has ever had this same question before."

well call for different reading practices from those relevant to reading informational texts on the Internet.

Coiro and Dobler's (2007) research provided some much needed empirical evidence of how Internet reading is more complex than print and requires skills that are similar to but more complex than print. They make evident how online readers were engaged in an overwhelmingly complex and integrated reading comprehension process as they searched for information. Specifically, they showed four key elements as being central to information hypertext comprehension: (a) prior knowledge of website structures and search engines; (b) inferential reasoning (reading between the lines) similar to print based media; (c) self-regulation; and (d) affective variables related to efficacy and motivation. A key finding of this work is that compared to reading printed texts, Internet reading seemed to demand many more attempts to infer, predict, and evaluate reading choices (e.g., hyperlinks followed) while anticipating the relevance of information. A related finding is that comprehending Internet text required readers to orient themselves in a new and dynamic three-dimensional space to figure out how to get back to where they were. This work suggests that "directionality" or how to self-monitor reading pathways and site selection choices may be an important attribute of a skilled online reader.

More broadly, the Coiro and Dobler (2007) study highlighted how existing theoretical frameworks for literacy, originally conceptualized in relation to reading print, do not automatically have relevance to or easily transfer to new and emerging literacies of the Internet and other ICTs. Further support for this stance can be found in the reported "Hole in the Wall" experience (Mitra, 2004) in which *untutored* Indian children learned to do a diverse range of tasks, for example "browse and search the Internet, ... set up e-mail accounts, send and receive e-mail, chat on the Internet, download and play streaming media and download games"(p. 22). This observation provided an opening for considering how the acquisition and development of such capabilities do not necessarily depend on their being taught in the classroom as part of the formal curriculum. The corollary of this, however, is that if a curriculum and pedagogy are to claim that they enable students to be effective readers online, including on the Internet, then strategies for teaching and learning Internet reading, for example, need to be focal. Sutherland-Smith (2002) and Kuiper et al. (2005) took up these matters and consistently suggested that we should rethink our classroom reading practices.

Generally, literacy frameworks, including those influential in many countries' curriculum documents and standardized testing programs, have tended to extrapolate from a conventional print base. Some examples are useful here. Consider, for example, Freebody and Luke's (1990; 1999) conceptual framework that identified how the desired repertoire of literate capabilities can be thought of in four interrelated "roles": (a) *Code Breaker*: the practices required to "crack" the codes and systems of written and spoken language and visual images; (b) *Meaning Maker*: the practices required to build and construct cultural meanings from texts; (c) *Text User*: the practices required to use texts effectively in everyday situations; and (d) *Text Analyst*: the practices required to analyze, critique, and evaluate texts, through to the point of values promoted by the text. In its initial formulation, the four resources model was designed to apply to reading of print, with the expanded application to literate capabilities being a more recent development.

Similarly, Green's *3 Dimension* model (1988; 1999) shared with the four resources model the notion of literacy as an ensemble of social practices, the former including three dimensions: (a) operational, (b) cultural, and (c) critical, taken to overlap, intersect, and be interdependent. This framework was influenced in its development by Green's (1988) research into the relationships between literacy and subject or content area learning and was subsequently developed in response to the increasing "technologization" of literacy (see Bigum & Green, 1993).

Both models have relevance to research efforts that examine the resources readers bring to acts of reading, offering frameworks for considering the textual-linguistic and visual features of hybrid multimodal texts online. To date, however, while literacy writers have sought to link available literacy frameworks such as the four resources model to pedagogy (see for example, Healy & Honan, 2004), there are no reported large-scale, longitudinal studies showing how they have been applied for analyzing reading and comprehension processes, either inside or outside of schooling. It is possible however, to reinflect the elements as they relate to online multimodal environments. Questions to be asked include, What is involved in being a Code breaker when searching the Internet? For example, code breaking would additionally involve understanding functions of icons and ways of moving around a screen, between screens and being able to track journeys around sites. Similarly, meaning making would extend to how linguistic, visual, and auditory language could combine to convey particular representations of people, places, points in time, and so on.

While recognizing the scope and utility of these frameworks, a current Australian study of digital curricular literacies (Castleton & Wyatt-Smith, 2005) drew on multiliteracy concepts of the New London Group (NLG) (1996) to analyze a large corpus of video-screen records (over 500 hours) showing students searching the Internet and reading and writing online in classroom activity. The Australian researchers drew on the concepts of (a) *design* and its related concern with multimodality, (b) *hybridity,* and (c) *intertextuality.* The first of these, *design*, gives emphasis to how any semiotic activity uses "Available Designs." These are taken to include linguistic, visual, audio, gestural, spatial, and multimodal resources for meaning making, and are used to create "The Redesigned," which is a new set of meanings. The NLG members suggested that this Designing process,

> transforms knowledge by producing new constructions and representations of reality. Through their coengagement in Designing, people transform their relations with each other, and so transform themselves ... Transformation is always a new use of old materials, a rearticulation and recombination of the given resources of Available Designs. (NLG, 1996, p. 76)

From this perspective, research on reading and comprehending multimodal texts (as well as text construction or composition online) necessarily involves consideration of what readers do as they interact with what they read and write online, this being a "blend" of an individual creative process and a social cognitive process.

The two other concepts *hybridity* and *intertextuality* refer to related processes. *Hybridity* is defined as the articulation in new ways of "established practices and conventions," and intertextuality is "the potentially complex ways in which meanings ... are constructed through relationships to other texts, discourses, genres, and modes of meaning" (NLG, 1996, p. 82). With regard to the Internet, Zembylas and Vrasidas (2005) argued that its hyper-text/hypermedia nature "allows users to move with unprecedented ease from document to document, accessing images, text, and sound, and to form new paths as they explore connections and co-construct knowledge" (p. 70). The Australian study (Castleton & Wyatt-Smith, 2005) is of interest here, as a part of the procedures engaged students in (1) using the Web for problem-solving inquiry activities and (2) constructing a multimodal text as a learning outcome. While the work is ongoing and scheduled for completion in 2007, analyses to date lend support to the literature review findings presented by Kuiper et al (2005), namely that (a) the use of the Web makes specific demands on readers, especially in relation to navigational and access skills; information processing strategies, and selecting information of relevance for purpose, including both written and visual data; (b) in general terms, students need support in acquiring Web-search skills and more specifically, skills necessary to identify and examine perspectives on offer in online materials; and (c) when students do find the right information, it is also difficult for them to use it to solve a problem (p. 309). The Australian study further showed that even if students can propose a solution to a problem, the skills and strategies involved in composing an online multimodal text to convey the solution are different again from those necessary to draw on Web-based evidence to develop the solution.

This final observation links with current theory on new literacies and reading by Leu and colleagues (2004) who also connected reading to communicating answers, though the written mode was not directly named:

> The new literacies of the Internet and other ICTs include the skills, strategies, and dispositions necessary to successfully use and adapt to the rapidly changing information and communication technologies and contexts that continuously emerge in our world and influence all areas of our personal and professional lives. These new literacies allow us to use the Internet and other ICTs to identify important questions, locate information, critically evaluate the usefulness of that information, synthesize information to answer those questions, and then communicate the answers to others (p. 1571).

In keeping with this observation, Martin (2004) argued that the Internet and other forms of ICT have changed conceptions of knowledge as well as the ways in which we acquire knowledge, exemplifying his point by noting how the use of search engines mediates the process of finding knowledge.

While large- and small-scale studies using both qualitative and quantitative methodologies are underway in several countries including the United States and Australia, at the time of this writing, empirically based understanding of what new literacies and related reading look like, is limited. This observation lends support to the call put forward by Leu and colleagues (2004) for developing new theorizations of these literacies that make ICTs focal, rather than importing perspectives evolved in other contexts to the ICT environment. Such theorizations, drawn from empirical data, are needed to provide an evidence-based foundation for developing new frameworks for reading comprehension online.

Part Two: Reading Print and Online Texts

Rouet (1993) sought to review studies of how nonlinear reading online might facilitate understanding. Apart from the use of hypertext to explore a topic in greater depth (or breadth), he noted that online definitions also provide nonlinearity and that comprehension is aided when the readers are mature (and don't need to use definitions often), when the words are important, and the process of obtaining the meanings is unobtrusive to the overall reading process. However, the use of layered text, with the importance fading by successive layers, was not always helpful, depending on purpose, familiarity of the topic, and the use of hypertext. He noted a study by Alessi, Anderson, and Goetz (1979), however, that reported how "look backs" facilitated by the computer were helpful if the process was easier than would be true of book reading. Overall, the authors concluded that the usefulness of hypertext in aiding comprehension depended on individual learner characteristics, how it is used, and what sort of text is read.

Based on the inconclusive results of previous research, Macedo-Rouet, Rouet, Epstein, and Fayard (2003) compared the effects of print and online presentation of popular science content on several variables including comprehension. They argued that hypertext diminished comprehension and increased cognitive load, and that using graphics often makes reading more effortful without necessarily improving understanding. Using real-world texts, they noted poorer comprehension for online reading, particularly related to questions about information in documents not immediately visible on the main screen. The authors surmised that improved design of hypertext might increase cognitive efficiency. However, another study investigated the effects of highlighting hyperlinks to dictionary definitions on, among other things, comprehension (de Ridder, 2002). While highlighting increased the use of additional information, it did not affect comprehension or incidental vocabulary.

At times, reading from a computer may consist of activities little different from reading printed texts, with an extreme example being opening a file containing only print and reading it with familiar purpose and strategies. Accomplishing a task such as browsing the Web to find information and weighing its relevance and trustworthiness, then incorporating it in some other context, perhaps an entry in a crossword puzzle, or a sentence in an essay, however, seems quite different. Sutherland-Smith (2002) noted,

> Students perceive Web text reading as different from print text reading. Jake (age 11) said, "On the Internet, you have to be really quick and can go lots of places to find out heaps of stuff, but with books, you need to go slower." Similar comments indicated that students felt there was a neces-

sity for speed in an Internet reading task. There was almost a snatch-and-grab philosophy adopted by students in the Web text classroom that was not apparent in print text environments. (p. 664)

If we go back to traditional reading of print, the construct of reading comprehension has served well both in theory and practice. While not all researchers would agree with the simple model of reading—i.e., comprehension = decoding + language understanding—it is often reflected in testing programs that consist of one or more measures that assess word identification (e.g., phonic knowledge and syllabification), along with a test of comprehension involving finding specific information, locating main ideas, drawing conclusions, and inferencing.

Once we are beyond the early school years, reading comprehension is the chief goal of literacy instruction and the focus of testing programs. Reading comprehension tests are mostly attempts to produce evidence that a covert mental activity has taken place. Thus, questions are asked at various levels (e.g., explicit, implicit) to enable inferences about understanding of text to be made. Other techniques have been tried, including retellings, cloze procedure, and sentence verification (Royer, Greene, & Sinatra, 1987), but generally the results are similar across techniques (i.e., test intercorrelations are moderately high). Another approach has been to stimulate readers to produce verbalizations of their thinking during the act of reading. These verbal protocols are analyzed to provide evidence of the associations, predictions, and confusions that can occur (Pressley & Afflerbach, 1995).

The Cambridge Handbook of Multimedia Learning (Mayer, 2005) is a rich source of information on teaching and learning material, and its focus on learning is anchored firmly in instructional psychology. Of direct relevance to the present chapter is Reinking's chapter in the *Handbook* on multimedia learning of reading. This chapter identifies some ways in which online reading has been shown to influence comprehension. These include enhanced strategic engagement, diminished comprehension through distractive aspects of multimedia, and increased awareness of aspects that might require a critical stance. For example, Reinking (2005) cited Miller and Gildea's (1987) early study of learning vocabulary meanings that showed viewing a video clip increased learning of target words and work. He also cited Reinking and Rickman (1990), that found text comprehension as well as vocabulary meanings were aided by allowing online access to the meanings of technical terms while reading. In addition, Reinking (2005) also cited the Young Sherlock project and a history learning study by Stahl, Hynd, Britton, McNish, and Bosquet (1996) as showing promising improvements in comprehension through multimedia access to additional information while reading from a screen, but noted that teacher follow-up may be needed to secure the use of new strategies.

Other research reviewed by Reinking (2005) offered further insights into learning to read, but even more, it opened up issues such as the role of interest and motivation in multimedia reading, and conditions under which multimodal elements such as sound effects and animation may help or hinder understanding and retention. Little if any of the cited research, however, involved activities that appear to be as potentially influential as online explorations of topics that are commonplace for millions of students.

Overall, we consider that Reinking's (2005) chapter needs to be read in parallel with our account of online reading and comprehension, with his being dominated by multimedia situations that are contrived by the researcher or teacher, while we focus more on the agency of the user of online resources both in formal school and out-of-school contexts. One avenue for researching such agency that may be productive is the multiliterate analogue of reading procedural text. Keystrokes, mouse clicks, or cursor moves may signal attainment of meaningful steps toward a goal. Also, newer screen capture software (e.g., Camtasia) has potential for the development of tasks that may help illuminate the complex nature of Web activities. By replaying screen sequences that accurately record real-time activities including talk, as is being done in the Australian study of digital curricular literacies (Castleton & Wyatt-Smith, 2005), mentioned earlier, such software has potential to facilitate the development of metacognitive reflection and illuminate how effective use of the Internet occurs. There is perhaps a role for the well-tried expert-novice paradigm to be used. To date, the study has shown that reading practices are varied both within cohorts and across year levels (years 8 to 12, being the first and last years of high school), and include, though are not restricted to, skimming and scanning, cutting and pasting, noting paratextual elements such as fonts, bolding, italicizing, and underlining. More challenging for students are interpreting pictures, graphs and diagrams, separately and in combination. Then, there are text structure analyses at levels from word to sentence to complete text, linked to response to genre. Often there are interpretive, affective, and intertextual activities. As shown in Freebody and Luke's (1990, 1999) Four Resources model discussed earlier, readers working on the Web in inquiry approaches to activities do need to move among the four roles, variously combining them.

There are some other differences between traditional and computer-mediated reading. The printed book still requires extended time periods of reading, and the ability to link memories of previous sessions with the current information. While it is easy to flick through pages in a book, it may be hard to locate and relocate information in a computer search. Computer-mediated reading is usually episodic, and the physical characteristics of PCs, and even most laptops, is less conducive to extended reading than the book, which is suited to be read in page sequence, with eye movement directions typically occurring in predictable ways consistent with cultural norms for textual layout. ICTs, however, provide better supports for gathering information from a range of diverse hypertextual sources. Further, hypertext is a format better suited to ICT, with distinct comprehension strategies, such as using search engines, databases, and selecting the likely best (or more appealing) "lead" to follow.

Rather than trying to create a single construct of reading comprehension, there may be potential in considering screens as inherently interactive with reading practices being shaped by the nature of the medium as well as reading purpose. By way of example, instant messaging, e-mail, 3D avatar-based environments and online role playing simulations invite users to take up particular reading positions and practices in response to the affordances of the medium.

Given this complexity, how can we develop a "theory" of ICT comprehension? Stockl (2004, p. 12) has schematized printed media as visual language and image modes, both static, with submodes such as type size and fonts, these having features such as form and style. He extended this to film and TV by adding dynamic modes and an auditory channel (see Figures 31.2 and 31.3).

This analysis is largely complete for ICT applications such as using the Web, but a motor channel is needed to allow for the participatory aspects of mouse clicking, screen drawing, and managing software choices. As speech recognition advances, the motor channel will encompass speaking.

We next consider the human elements of ICT activities for reading print and online texts. Listening/speaking involves the simultaneous processing of verbal language and the nonverbal such as gesture and facial expression. Writing/reading of print is inflected by typeface and layout, with alternating processing of images of many kinds. Some non-ICT situations have similar complexity, such as enjoying opera with subtitles. Interrelationships among modes need more investigation. Indeed, we still do not know enough about how printed material with illustrations is processed, and how the brain stores verbal and visual information. We also do not know enough about the relative efficiency of these modes for different types of information, nor about how to best portray these modes on the page/screen. Examination of print and screen structure suggests that there is a wide range of organization. For example, academic text is likely to have explicit cross-referencing so the reader is directed between text and illustration. An extreme example is the Anatomy Coloring Book (Kapit & Elson, 2001) in which the reader is told to mark anatomical features on line drawings in particular colors. At the other extreme are magazines like *Smithsonian* in which illustrations and their often extensive captions have no explicit links to the print. This has the advantage of permitting browsing of the illustrations before, after, or during the act of reading, but the disadvantage is that readers are not cued to examine the illustrations. The challenge of extending analysis of these issues to complex, multimodal ICT environments is daunting.

Stockl (2004) suggested that the following elements need to be incorporated into an account of multimodal communication:

- Hallidayan metafunctions (ideational, interpersonal, textual)
- Segmentation into elements that are linked syntactically

Channels, Modes and Sub-modes in Printed Media

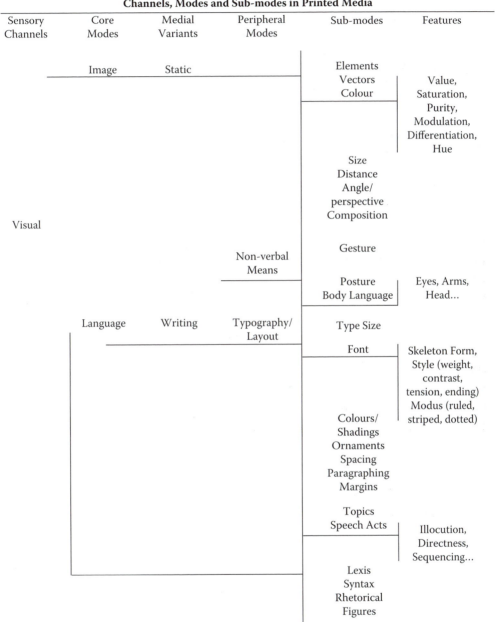

Sensory Channels	Core Modes	Medial Variants	Peripheral Modes	Sub-modes	Features
Visual	Image	Static		Elements Vectors Colour	Value, Saturation, Purity, Modulation, Differentiation, Hue
				Size Distance Angle/ perspective Composition	
			Non-verbal Means	Gesture	
				Posture Body Language	Eyes, Arms, Head...
	Language	Writing	Typography/ Layout	Type Size	
				Font	Skeleton Form, Style (weight, contrast, tension, ending) Modus (ruled, striped, dotted)
				Colours/ Shadings Ornaments Spacing Paragraphing Margins	
				Topics Speech Acts	Illocution, Directness, Sequencing...
				Lexis Syntax Rhetorical Figures	

Figure 31.2 Channels, modes, and submodes in printed media.

Channels, Modes and Sub-modes in TV- and Film Media

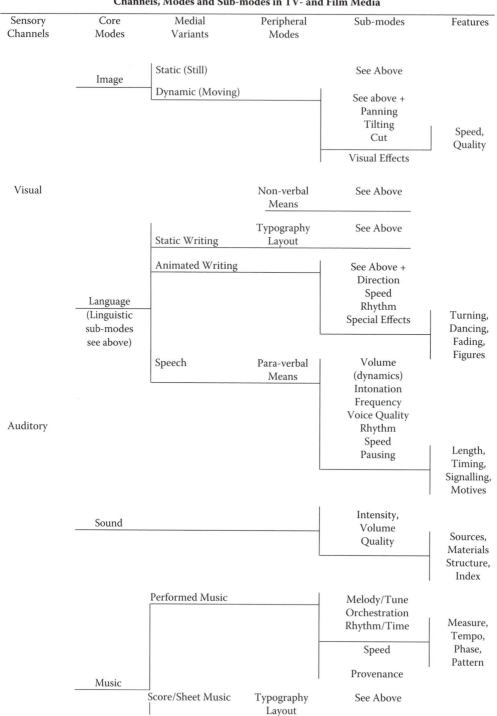

Sensory Channels	Core Modes	Medial Variants	Peripheral Modes	Sub-modes	Features
	Image	Static (Still)		See Above	
		Dynamic (Moving)		See above + Panning Tilting Cut	Speed, Quality
				Visual Effects	
Visual			Non-verbal Means	See Above	
		Static Writing	Typography Layout	See Above	
		Animated Writing		See Above + Direction Speed Rhythm Special Effects	Turning, Dancing, Fading, Figures
	Language (Linguistic sub-modes see above)	Speech	Para-verbal Means	Volume (dynamics) Intonation Frequency Voice Quality Rhythm Speed Pausing	
Auditory					Length, Timing, Signalling, Motives
	Sound			Intensity, Volume Quality	Sources, Materials Structure, Index
		Performed Music		Melody/Tune Orchestration Rhythm/Time	Measure, Tempo, Phase, Pattern
				Speed	
				Provenance	
	Music	Score/Sheet Music	Typography Layout	See Above	

Figure 31.3 Channels, modes, and submodes in TV and film media.

- Differential involvement of modes in denotation, connotation, and association
- Semantic relations within and across modes
- Meaning expressed iconically, indexically, and symbolically
- Gestalt similarities and analogies

Stockl's elements suggest that a mix of structural and other grammatical features, modalities, semiotics, and cognitive aspects are at play in working multimodally. Collectively this mix highlights how using ICTs may require a new style of reading that is inherently more fragmented than reading print. Reader supports to facilitate understanding could include word/sentence/passage pronunciation, dictionary definitions, and etymology while maintaining attention to the screen. Additionally, support could focus on scaffolding how users may digress to Web sites giving information about the work, the author, or reviews by other users.

Part Three: Online Reading and Writing in Formal and Informal Learning

In terms of a definition, the Rand Reading Study Group (2002) defined reading comprehension as "the process of simultaneously extracting and constructing meaning through interactions and involvement with written language" (p. xiii) and developed a four-part way of exploring reading comprehension: through the reader, through the text, and through the activity and context in which comprehension is embedded. Broadly speaking, we take this definition as a useful starting point and, in relation to the Internet, lend support to Coiro's (2003) argument "that the Internet forces us to expand our understanding of each of the elements by considering new aspects of comprehension that are clearly related to traditional comprehension areas ... but also require fundamentally new thought processes" (p. 2). The point is that in acts of reading that involve technologies, the technological dimension of reading cannot be overlooked. From this vantage point, what counts as reading and reading comprehension can no longer be regarded as a fixed set of skills.

This observation is strongly to the fore in the *Handbook of Research on Literacy in Technology at the K–12 Level* (Tan Wee Hin & Subramaniam, 2005). The 35 chapters in the handbook represent research writing from 9 countries and have been helpfully grouped under three broad sections including (a) Perspectives on Technological Literacy, (b) Teaching and Learning with Technology, and (c) Issues Related to Teacher Education and School-Based Matters. While each chapter takes a particular focus, all explore how literacy, education, and technology are converging (or could converge), and the implications of this for curriculum, pedagogy, and formal and informal learning. Collectively, the chapters show how traditional metrics of literacy and language (reading, writing, listening, and speaking) are now inadequate and how, to use the words of the editors, "the new age metrics for literacy leverages on a range of computer-related skills." Further, the chapters show the enabling nature of technologies for learning and call for a new definition of learning and teaching at the K–12 level.

Broadly speaking, *the Handbook of Research on Literacy in Technology at the K–12 Level* presents a clear case for how crucial skills required for the knowledge age include a mix of verbal, visual, and digital literacy capabilities, the latter including but not restricted to knowing the technicist or operational management aspects of working with technologies. Also necessary are information retrieval skills including location, interpretation, synthesis, and transformation of information, gained from often complex sources, into meaningful knowledge (Johnson & Kress, 2003). At play here is the mix of capabilities and knowledge necessary not only to locate and retrieve knowledge, but also to interrogate it, extending to creating new knowledge. To this end, valued skills extend to Web-site construction skills and creative ways of combining audio, video, data, multimedia, and text; online collaboration skills; familiarity in using digital media such as computers, digital cameras, mobile phones, and knowing how to work in the convergence of such media.

Current research has shown that in the most effective types of digital learning environments, sociocognitive, constructivist approaches are adopted for students' active meaning making, with communicative interactions and problem-solving purposes central to the learner-centered classrooms. For example, Gibson (2005) promoted this idea in relation to how WebQuests can facilitate constructivist learning if they are carefully designed to encourage student-directed learning, higher order thinking, perspective taking, and collaborative learning on authentic real-world tasks. Similarly, Huffaker (2004) argued that blogs can promote verbal, visual, and digital literacy skills, with the technology enabling robust instructional approaches. Jonassen, Peck, and Wilson (1999) also argued strongly for learning and critical inquiry *with* technology. In their model where technologies are used as tools for learning, particularly in representational mediums, students are more engaged in the active searching for, reading, and processing of information, as well as in constructing personal and socially shared understandings of the phenomena they are exploring. For these writers, meaningful reading and learning result when technologies engage learners in "knowledge construction, not reproduction; conversation, not reception; articulation, not repetition; collaboration, not competition; [and] reflection, not prescription" (p. 16).

An investigation of learning science on the Internet that highlights new forms of reading comprehension has been reported by Leu et al. (2005). The authors examined changes in reading comprehension, both online and traditionally measured, as well as the extent of science learning in seventh-grade students. Four classes in one middle school were assigned at random to one of four conditions: three levels of Internet use with Internet Reciprocal Teaching in the two higher levels, and a control condition. Online reading comprehension was measured in two ways: instant messaging and weblogs. Of particular interest in this chapter is that the treatments had predicted effects on online reading comprehension measured using both instant messaging and weblogs. Correlations between conventional and online reading comprehension were low, and the treatments did not facilitate performance on traditional reading comprehension. This study offers important insights into ways of measuring online reading comprehension, and points to ways that standardized assessments of online activities should be developed. Further, the study shows that given sufficient intensity, online learning facilitates understanding of important content knowledge. There is a clear link between this study and Leu's (2000) earlier writing that highlighted Mayer's (1997) caution,

> about generalising findings from traditional texts to different forms of hypermedia because each technology contains different contexts and resources for constructing meanings and requires somewhat different strategies for doing so … What is clear is that the two contexts will be substantially different, requiring new strategies to effectively exploit new resources, permitting different opportunities for communication. (p. 749)

Savery and Duffy (1995) also stressed the complex interplay of content, context, learner activity, and learner goals in the learner acquisition of knowledge, advocating a problem-based learning model as their foundation to learning with hypertext. It is through an emergent process of knowledge acquisition aided by both personal reflection and communication with others that the learner is able to move from low-level factual details to higher order concepts (Bruce, 1997).

Additionally, as mentioned in our fourth key proposition (see p. 7), the notion of problem-based inquiry as underpinning the learning processes in digital environments has been quite widely endorsed (Gee, 2003; Johnson & Liu, 2000; Jonassen et al., 1999; Leu & Kinzer, 2000; Leu et al., 2004). Gee (2003), in particular, drew on insights derived from observation of and participation in video gaming to propose new learning principles. In these principles, active playfulness and risk-taking are key in working multimodally. Also strongly evident is the agency of the student/gamer in shaping how learning occurs. Other researchers have similarly stressed the interdependence of communicative interaction and new technologies, as well as the design elements of computer-based tasks and focused activity for learners to become critical thinkers and creators of knowledge (Bliss & Säljö, 1999; Johnson & Liu, 2000; Lankshear & Knobel, 2003b; Meredyth, Russell, Blackwood, Thomas, & Wise, 1999; Wells, 2002). If as research suggests, students' problem-solving abilities, analytical and creative thinking, understanding, assimilation, and creation of new knowledge can be promoted in digital-learning environments (Gee, 2003; Meredyth et al., 1999), this small percentage indicates a major challenge for teachers to redress. Designing activities that effectively apply collaborative inquiry to electronic learning tasks for deepening student knowledge remains crucial, whatever the content area, student age, or software choices (Jonassen et al., 1999; Mercer & Wegerif, 1997; Scrimshaw, 1997). To date at least, the activities are, in the main, not prepackaged. Instead, the teacher is best understood as the curriculum designer for such activities, placing teacher agency as critical to their imaginative development and implementation (Kimber & Wyatt-Smith, 2006).

Indications suggest that teacher-generated, computer-based tasks and commercially available technological tools can assist students in their construction of meaning and knowledge, especially in developing the higher order cognitive processing associated with value-adding. Research has shown that ideas-processing software used individually and collaboratively has been advantageous in assisting students to become active, effective creators of meaning, moving to higher levels of thinking and understanding (Anderson-Inman & Ditson, 1999; Johnson & Liu, 2000; Kimber, Pillay, & Richards, 2001). When metacognitive aids like concept maps, decision-making matrixes, or retrieval charts are incorporated into computer-based tasks, students can be encouraged to pause and reflect on the information or issue with which they are engaged, thereby assisting their internal negotiation of meaning and/or personal representation of meaning. By using any number of different "attention structures," devices designed to trigger students to pause and pay attention (Lanham, 1994, 1997), students can become more effective knowledge creators while working online (Kimber & Wyatt-Smith, 2006). Overall, there is a growing body of writing that points to how acts of pausing, reflecting, and going on to compose and design multimodal representations of knowledge are at the heart of learning in a digital environment, though Kuiper et al. (2005) were clear in stating that much more research is needed to connect reading to writing (referred to here as including design).

In summary, the research shows that networked computers that incorporate Web-authoring and ideas-processing software and that are used in a collaborative, problem-solving manner can help generate learning processes that encourage students to think more deeply about the task at hand. In this way, students can more actively engage in the learning process. More specifically, they can be better equipped to access and transform information into thoughtful solutions to problems worth communicating to others (Lepani 1998, Leu & Kinzer 2000, Leu et al., 2004). In effect, students are not just learning operational skills with using these types of software; they are developing a strategic knowledge base that includes a repertoire of technological options for accessing, evaluating, and transforming information into new knowledge designs and representations.

Next, we open the space for considering reading and the information exchange and social interaction that occur in digital spaces where informal learning is in the hands of young people. This part of the chapter presents some main research findings relating to these spaces, taken to include online fan-fiction Web sites, messaging, massively multiplayer online games (MMOGs), and single-player video games.

Informal Learning

Several recent studies including Sefton-Green's (2004) review of informal learning with technology have focused attention on what Beavis et al. (2005) referred to as "the overall ecology of learning," arguing that it is constituted by "flows between formal and informal sites and practices" (p. 41). In considering such "flows," one issue is the arbitrariness of divisions between learning in formal institutions and beyond, a point mentioned earlier. Young people access technology outside of school for varying reasons. A study by Yelland (2001) showed that out of every 30 minutes spent on a computer, children are spending an average of 21 minutes having fun with out-of-school activities and games. Currently, little is known about the mix of cognitive, metacognitive, aesthetic, and critical capabilities that young people develop as they participate online outside of school, though a desire for social connectivity seems a primary reason for the reading and writing that young people report doing online. For example, in a study focusing on adolescent girls' participation in cyberspace, Merchant (2001) discussed the reasons the participants accessed chat rooms, e-mail, and instant-messaging sites. The reported reasons varied from belonging to a specific community of game players, to accessing technical gaming information; to keeping in contact with friends overseas, to generally having someone to chat with. Essentially, these literacy events where reading and writing coalesce were about communication, with friends, virtual friends, and strangers, often not for a specific purpose other than to establish and maintain social contact.

New technologies connect individuals and communities in ways not available to previous generations. At the same time, sudden emphasis on being connected through technologies excludes and alienates those who do not actively participate in the information age. Rheingold (2003) foresaw a new kind of digital divide in 10 years whereby those who know how to use new technology will be banded together, separate from those who do not. Currently, users belong to two types of communities: (a) *real-world communities*, such as family, clubs, classes; and (b) *electronic communities*, such as chat rooms, e-mail buddies, and news groups (Andrews, 2003; Merchant, 2001). Similarly, Merchant made the distinction between actual friends and virtual friends; the former often communicated with through e-mail and phones and the latter more associated with chat rooms and instant messaging. "Meeting up" with virtual friends is usually a virtual experience involving meeting online at a particular time. Not only does this change the way we think about community, but also, as Merchant discovered, it allows for users to develop a large group of friends (typical teenagers have about 50 friends on their personal list that they regularly meet), some they may never meet face to face, that they communicate with in a variety of ways.

Also evident is change around the once recognized and valued line between written and spoken language, the line now blurring with new "technolanguages" emerging to suit communication purposes and contexts. Merchant (2001) made the point, for example, that teenagers "write more or less as they speak … and talk more or less as they write in chat rooms, often with little thought for the accuracy of keystrokes, spelling conventions, traditional punctuation or grammatical completeness" (p. 296). This new communication is not confined to alphanumeric text. Chat room conversations and messaging often incorporate symbols, pictures, sounds, moving images, and Web surfing. Consider, for example,

hoopy_da_hula: 19/m/uk [age/sex/location]

hoopy_da_hula: bus driver has the best mullet!

hoopy_da_hula: bald on top, 12inches long at the back. tasteful

cherry_dot: oh that's good check out www.mullet.co.uk

hoopy_da_hula: you?

cherry_dot: 16/f/England

hoopy_da_hula: where in England?

cherry_dot: Sheffield

hoopy_da_hula: Bristol

cherry_dot: cool

cherry_dot: how are you then?

hoopy_da_hula: nice pics, btw! [btw = by the way]

(Merchant, 2001, p. 303)

This conversation, although far from correct in its traditional language forms, requires the participants to have a repertoire of literate capabilities and comprehension strategies. They must, for example, navigate through text, and compose image and hyperlinks, and manage a print conversation at the same time. This opens a space for considering the potential of computer-based communication for developing a range of composing and comprehending skills and strategies that typically remain unacknowledged in educational settings.

From this vantage point, it seems that the composing and comprehending that is taking place in real/digital worlds is quite "other" than those traditionally valued in schooling, the corollary of this being that we are entering an age of "linguistic conservatism" (Merchant, 2001) whereby "legitimate language" comes to be protected by the education system (Bourdieu, 1991).

Working from a related position, it is widely recognized that from a very young age children are exposed to literacies in forms other than print that equip them with a range of narratives, mythologies, assumptions, and expectations. Often, upon entering school, the literacies children are accustomed to, and the texts they routinely read as part of their home and community interactions, may be very different from those they experience and are expected to work with in schools. Beavis (2002) made this point, stating that "the world of texts inhabited by young people, the literacies the texts teach and the nature of the texts, are significantly different from those with which English and Literacy teaching practices and curriculum have been traditionally associated" (p. 47). This raises the issue of the mismatch between school expectations and the reading events young people are participating in outside the classroom, a point mentioned earlier.

In exploring what is involved in accessing and engaging with online multimodal texts, new metaphors for literacy are emerging in attempts to capture "the semiotic work and play" that occurs in various digital spaces. By way of example, Steinkuehler, Black, and Clinton (2005) drew on Markhan's (2003) metaphoric framework to discuss *literacy* as *tool*, as *place*, and as *way of being*. In discussing literacy as tool, for instance, the writers draw attention to how "doing" online fan fiction involves fans in adopting and adapting "tools such as genres, forms of media, and digitally mediated modes of representation to create texts that are culturally, linguistically, and multimodally hybrid" (Steinkuehler et al., p. 98). The metaphor of literacy as place focuses attention on research on game playing as it works to "constitute a complex of nuanced set of social, material, and discursive practices, tied to particular communities and consequential for membership and identity" (p. 98). Finally, the writers' use of the metaphor of literacy as way of being serves as an entry into research on "new forms of reading and writing emerging as people experience such semiotic resources as three-dimensional spaces, stereo sound, virtual objects, interface icons, representational bars, symbols, and (perhaps most crucially) avatars" (p. 99).

Although viewed with suspicion, and sometimes even moral panic by some, the skills students are honing through their out-of-school "readings" with technology have considerable potential and application in the new labor market (Kalantzis, Cope, & Harvey, 2003). Perhaps it is not, at the core, a mismatch between in- and out-of-school technoliteracies and their related reading and writing practices, but rather a mismatch between the demands of school and the demands of the labor market in the "new capitalism" (Cope & Kalantzis,

2000; Gee, 2000, 2003,). According to polls in the United States, students of the new capitalism like school less and less (Gee, 2004). Though they see it as important for their future to achieve the credentials schools provide, Gee (2004) made the point that "they are well aware that many of the core credentials, skills, experiences, and identities necessary for success in that world are not gained in school, but rather outside school at home, in activities, camps, travel, and on the Net" (p. 104).

Though there is reported unease about the influx of new technologies on the lives of students both in and outside school, fears regarding heightened access to information and how to use it are not new. In fact, Socrates made claims that the new technology of writing would allow students to "receive a quantity of information without instruction" (translated by Hamilton, 1973, p. 96). Again, with the invention of the printing press, concerns about the sudden availability of information and the obvious dramatic change that it brought led to worries and concerns about how the way we know and understand the world would change. It was schools, in this case, that normalized books through their introduction of the textbook. This time, it seems, schools are just trying to keep up. We now move toward a proposal for reframing reading comprehension online.

Toward a Reframing of Reading Comprehension Online

Much has been written about the credibility challenges posed by the Web. Haas and Wearden (2003) reviewed the literature on credibility from a range of fields and identified how a network of factors contributes to what they referred to as "e-credibility difficulties" (p. 169). Readers interested in this topic are advised to see the full article. Of interest here is Haas and Wearden's point that e-credibility entails deliberately and critically discerning "the qualities of trustworthiness, accuracy, completeness and timeliness that entail a sense of 'believability'" (p. 170).

According to Burbules (2001), "one of the most-discussed topics about the World Wide Web is how users can be expected to assess the credibility of information they find there" (p. 441). Several writers have identified that such challenges stem from the commercialism of the Web, its speed and size, as well as its fluidity, with links able to change, expand, and to "decay speedily" (Bruce, 2000, p. 99). The latter image gives the Web an organic attribute that is no doubt in keeping with its dynamic, networked nature where commercial and noncommercial sites coexist, and search engines, commercial, and governmental interests interact, with potential for high impact on users and local and global markets. Bruce went on to argue that there is no easy solution to the issue of determining quality or credibility of Web resources, the reason being that,

> there is no resort to any kind of recognised textual authority, no board
> of editors as for a respected encyclopaedia, who invite authors and vet

articles for publication. And authority is a highly disputable term on the Web. When students, or anyone for that matter, actually do find relevant information on the Web, it is all too easy to copy that material without attribution. (p. 100)

In response to the absence of "any kind of recognised textual authority," researchers, educators, and those in education policy have taken up the challenge of formulating criteria to assist readers to determine the credibility and utility of Web materials, and even to put in place certain protocols for blocking access. While recognizing the value of surveillance protocols on school and system networks, we want to refocus the topic of credibility within the larger issue: How should one read the Web and comprehend online resources more generally? To engage with this question, we draw on three elements: first, Kress's (1985) notions of reading positions and practices; second, Bruce's (2000) application of Walter Kaufmann's (1977) modes of reading, as presented in his essay, "The Art of Reading"; and third, insights from what has come to be known as "critical literacy" (Gee, 1990; Lankshear & McLaren, 1993; Morgan & Wyatt-Smith, 2000). Our approach in what follows is to lay out different ways of knowing multimodal reading and comprehension and ask questions about how these ways interact and with what effects. In taking this approach, we have been influenced by the image of "boundary conversations" as used by McCarthy and Fishman (1991) in their dual-focused study of conflicting ways of knowing in philosophy and interdisciplinary research. McCarthy and Fishman (1991) described "boundary conversations" as follows:

In boundary conversations we envision ourselves ... encountering unfamiliar languages or opposing approaches to the world. These engage our attention and, at first, invite our scrutiny from across the border. We may, however, at some point, decide to step gradually into the unfamiliar neighborhood, at first listening closely, then perhaps deciding to try some phrases of the new language, first mimicking them, then examining them critically ... But it is not in abandoning our old ways of knowing and points of view that learning occurs. Rather it is in preserving and contrasting our various discourses, moving back and forth among them, clarifying and repositioning them, that we create conflict and force reconstruction of ourselves. (p. 422)

Our approach to engaging in "boundary conversation" is not to resolve difference, but to put into dialogue perspectives drawn from literary studies and critical-cultural theory, to explore answers to the question: What are different ways of reading and engaging with multimodal texts online? In keeping with this purpose, the discussion that follows introduces the concept of reading positions (Kress, 1985), and is then organized around Bruce's (2000) reading framework, originally drawn from Kaufmann (1977).

From the outset of the discussion, readers may be interested in knowing that Kaufmann's taxonomy of reading was originally developed in a larger work on the future of humanities and sought to engage with the question of whether it is possible to read "the great works" (Bruce, 2000, p. 103) in different ways. According to Bruce, Kaufmann's (1977) concern was with "characterising and promoting humanistic education, which he defines as including the preservation and appreciation of the great works of civilisation, the realisation of personal autonomy through reflection and the acquisition of a personal vision" (p. 103). In drawing on Kaufmann's framework, Bruce sought to engage with the question: what are different modes of reading the Web?

The Concept of Reading Position

According to Kress (1985), texts address and position readers by constructing a dominant reading position that constructs the social subject: "about who, what, and how to be in a given social situation, occasion, interaction" (p. 39). A reading position is the dominant position from which a text appears meaningful, coherent, logical, and even beyond question. By occupying the reading position on offer in a text, the reader or subject identifies with and accepts the discourses or values and representations on offer in the text. However, if the reader rejects the discourses on offer in the text, he or she is said to be a resistant reader. From this position, the act of multimodal reading and comprehending takes account not only of the demands of vocabulary, generic structure, and linguistic/graphic features, but also extends to the transaction that occurs between the text and the reader. Meaning making then, or comprehending, can be said to occur centrally in the transaction; the primary understanding being that meaning is not singular and that the text, of itself, does not guarantee how meaning will be made. From here, we move to consider Bruce's (2000) four distinct ways of reading, considering each one in terms of the related reading position and practices that each makes available, and critically, where it locates "meaning" and agency in meaning making.

The Exegetical Reader: Web-Site as a Sperior Representation

According to Bruce (2000), the exegetical reader "assigns superior merit to the Web. Compared to print sources, the Web is seen to represent meaning through multimedia that gives richness and authenticity" (p. 103). Further, this reader

- regards the text as definitive
- considers that the role of the reader is to study the text thoroughly to divine its true value
- highly values the rapid updating of Web sites in the understanding that it brings to the sites freshness and accuracy not afforded by print
- is authorized to impose his or her own values on the text.

In elaborating on the last characteristic, Bruce (2000) identified that exegetical readers shut down, or at least do not draw on, critical inquiry when reading Web texts. Instead, they choose the elements that reflect their own preferences and then employ the text to legitimize those preferences. They typically select and appropriate specific Web resources to illustrate the excellence of the Web for a given purpose, conveniently ignoring the lesser sites that others bemoan. Essentially, this is a reading practice that serves to promote the identity of the reader as being "in the know," having ready access to current knowledge, simply because he or she draws on online materials. Further, within this reading practice, the reader is selective in using located material, valuing primarily the "excellence of the Web" as tool and resource, in and of itself.

The Dogmatic Reader: Web-Site as Inferior to Print

Unlike exegetical readers, dogmatic readers are described as being suspicious of the Web, assuming the superiority of print media. Bruce (2000) went on to state that "where the exegetical reader sees bounty in the multiple sites on a given topic, the dogmatic reader sees chaos and the inability to judge good from bad. The more the Web grows, the more the dogmatic reader sees its flaws" (p. 104). Both the dogmatic and exegetical readers, however, "selectively analyse the web to suit their prior beliefs. Neither engages fully with questions such as how Web as media really differs from print, or with what confidence one can make encompassing assumptions about the quality of Web resources" (p. 104).

Both categories of reading practice (exegetical and dogmatic) highlight how reading is value laden. More specifically, they highlight the agency of the reader and how he or she brings to the Web text preexisting values and attitudes that shape the transaction that occurs between reader and text. Working from this position, it is the reader and the assumptions that the reader brings to the Web that shape in part how reading and meaning making occur.

The Agnostic Reader: Web-Site as Subject to Selection, Analysis, Measurement, and Categorization

The agnostic reader brings what Bruce (2000) referred to as a "technical stance toward Web quality" (p. 104). In elaborating, he wrote that "they acknowledge that there are both good and bad resources, and so develop schemes for finding good sites and separating one from the other. The agnostic mode entails attention to developing and finding better tools for accessing the Web, to conducting effective Web searches, and to evaluating the quality of Web-sites" (p. 104). Of prime interest to them are ways of improving technologies for Web searches and ways to improve search practice. What is valued, therefore, is evaluative information about the relative performance of different search tools; the choice of search engine; the effectiveness of respective search directories in relation to a given task; and evaluative information about chosen Web sites. Bruce identified that "Once a Web-site has been found the agnostic user applies a scheme for evaluating it, typically expressed as a series of questions, sometimes with point values to assign for each" (p. 105). For these readers, he stated that consideration deserves to be given to a suite of issues: ease of navigation, accessibility, readability of layout, relevance of images, indications of the source of information, acknowledgement of biases, the reputation of the author, the site's primary purpose, and the time of its writing. Essentially, the agnostic reader sees "a technocratic solution" as appropriate to and necessary for solving "the problem of Web variety" (p. 105), with the solution including applying a formula or specified criteria for selecting tools, locating sites, and determining their relative merit.

In critiquing the practice of agnostic readers, Bruce (2000) highlighted that while it may have appeal, searching online is a far more complicated process than simply looking up information. Referring to his own searching, he wrote that "it appears to be part of a general process of inquiry, which is tentative and fallible. There is no absolute starting point, nor is there any sure way to reach the end, assuming such a point exists" (p. 106). Further, the preoccupation with applying a technocratic solution is that it tends to occlude the potential of the Web to "open up our questions" (Bruce, 2000, p. 106), making spaces for different ways of thinking and understanding. Such spaces are valued within the dialectical reading practice.

The Dialectical Reader: Web site as Facilitation of New Understandings

According to Bruce (2000), this category of reader "enters into a relationship with the text in which there is an openness to new values and ways of making meaning. The result is a process of accepting discomfort, examining alternatives, and searching for new understandings. Thus meaning is not static, but constructed out of evolving activities of thinking and doing" (p. 107). To realize this skilled practice, the reader draws on coding, semantic, and pragmatic competence. The reader is knowledgeable of the properties of Web sites including the genres operating on the Web and the textual conventions that apply. Beyond this, the reader reads critically, attending to the values and representations on offer in the text, recognizing that Web texts promote particular interests and understandings about the world, groups, and individuals. Additionally, the dialectical reader is aware of the dominant reading position on offer in Web texts, knowingly accepting or rejecting that position. In this way, the reader can critically discern how the texts work to promote particular interests (and not others), making available certain accounts and perspectives, while remaining silent about others. Of interest to the reader are not only what is in the text, therefore, but also what is omitted from the text, and how texts may offer different, even contradictory, information about a phenomenon or event.

Carrying forward the work of Kuiper et al. (2005), this is the terrain where perspective becomes important, and the formulation of perspective by the reader and in the working of the text can be taken into account. Several other writers from diverse theoretical orientations have pointed in this direction, highlighting the need for explicit instruction in critical-thinking skills and strategies online. For example, Coiro (2003) suggested the need for online reading instruction that helps readers move beyond their current level of shallow, random, and minimally strategic online reading practices. Similarly, Goldsborough (1998) claimed that students "need to learn how to apply critical thinking in evaluating the information they come across—critical thinking that will help them throughout their school years, career and personal life" (p. 32). Overall, there is growing recognition that the ability to make informed judgments about what is found online is part of the art of critical thinking.

The move to reframe reading comprehension is offered as a first step to understanding how text and reader can mutually influence how words are read and meaning ascribed. Further, we suggest that the theoretically eclectic approach of this chapter illustrates how perspectives previously kept apart can align in new ways to enable insights not otherwise available. Finally, we turn to consider needed directions in research.

Essential Next Questions

Learning to read and learning through reading are expected to happen at school. Further, education authorities throughout the world spend many millions of dollars and commit extensive human resources documenting the nature of expected, valued learning, and normalizing it through curricular and assessment materials. Further, standardized large-scale tests and related scores remain influential, promoting the view that they measure and account for learning in schools. In this context, several reading researchers have identified how the early years of the new century have been marked by what Paris (2005) has described as "a greater than ever reliance on scientific evidence to guide educational policies for assessment and instruction" (p. 184). He further claimed that while,

> the attention and new credibility given to reading research have been hard won by the academic community and have great promise, ... there are also pitfalls to avoid in the rush to use basic research for legislated policies and educational prescriptions. (p. 184)

While Paris's caution about basic research applies to many policy contexts across countries, also critical is the challenge facing the literacy research community to present rigorous "scientifically based" research about digital spaces. This situation is reflected in Steinkuehler et al. (2005) comment:

> Poised as we are at the edge of an expanding wave of digital technologies, researchers are faced with the task of finding firm footing within a rapidly changing landscape of computer-mediated communication and

given the common research focus on Internet literacy, student class-room learning, and task design.

References

AFP. (2006). One billion people have Internet access. Retrieved June 14, 2006 from http://www.Breitbart.com/news/na/060518163500.mk2075cs.html

Alessi, S. M., Anderson, T. H., & Goetz, E. T. (1979). An investigation of lookbacks during studying. *Discourse Processes, 2,* 97–212.

Anderson-Inman, L., & Ditson, L. (1999). Computer-based concept mapping, a tool for negotiating meaning. *Learning and Leading with Technology, 26*(8), 6–13.

Andrews, R. (2003). Where next in research on ICT and literacies? Joint IFTE issue. *English in Australia, 139* & *Literacy Learning: The Middle Years, 12*(1), 58–67.

Andrews, R. (Ed.). (2004). *The impact of ICT on literacy education.* London: Routledge Falmer.

Barton, D., & Hamilton, M. (1998). *Local literacies: Reading and writing in one community.* London: Routledge.

Beavis, C. (2002). Critical engagement: Literacy, curriculum, and ICTs. *Idiom, 38*(2), 42–50, VATE Melbourne.

Beavis, C., Nixon, H., & Atkinson, S. (2005). LAN cafes: Cafes, places of gathering, or sites of informal teaching and learning? *Education, Communication, & Information, 5*(1), 41–60.

Bigum, C., & Green, B. (1993). Technologizing literacy or interrupting the dream of reason. In A. Luke & P. Gilbert (Eds.), *Literacy in contexts: Australian perspectives and issues* (pp. 4–28). St. Leonards, NSW: Allen & Unwin.

Bliss, J., & Säljö, R. (1999). The human-technological dialectic. In J. Bliss, R. Säljö, & P. Light (Eds.), *Learning sites: Social and technological resources for learning* (pp. 1–13). Kidlington, Oxford: Elsevier Science Ltd.

Bourdieu, P. (1991). *Language and symbolic power.* Cambridge, MA: Harvard University Press.

Bousted, M., & Ozturk, A. (2004). 'It came alive outside my head.' Developing literacies through comparison: The reading of classic text and moving image. *Literacy, 38(1),* 52–57.

Bruce, B. (2003) *Literacy in the Information Age: Inquiring into meaning-making with new technologies.* Newark, DE: International Reading Association.

Bruce, B. C. (2000) Credibility of the web: Why we need dialectical reading. *Journal of Philosophy of Education, 34*(1), 97–109.

Burbules, N. (2001). Paradoxes of the Web: The ethical dimensions of credibility. *Library Trends, 49,* 441–453.

Carrington, V. (2005). Txting: The end of civilization (again)? *Cambridge Journal of Education, 35*(2), 161–175.

Castells, M. (1996). *The information age: Economy, society, and culture, Vol 1.* The rise of the network society. Malden, MA: Blackwell.

Castells, M. (1997). *The information age: Economy, society, and culture, Vol 2.* The power of identity. Malden, MA: Blackwell.

Castells, M. (1998). *The information age: Economy, society, and culture, Vol 3.* The end of the millennium. Malden, MA: Blackwell.

Castleton, G., & Wyatt-Smith, C. (2005). Investigating digital curricular literacies: Resolving dilemmas of researching multimodal technologically mediated literacy practices. *Yearbook of the National Reading Conference, 54,* 144–156.

Chandler-Olcott, K., & Mahar, D. (2003). "Tech-savviness" meets multiliteracies: Exploring adolescent girls' technology-mediated literacy practices. *Reading Research Quarterly, 38*(3), 356–385.

Coiro, J., & Dobler, E. (2007). Exploring the online reading comprehension strategies used by sixth-grade readers to search for and locate information on the Internet. *Reading Research Quarterly*,42(2), 214–257.

Coiro, J. (2003). Reading comprehension on the Internet: Expanding our understanding of reading comprehension to encompass new literacies. *The Reading Teacher, 56(5)*, 458–464.

Cope, B., & Kalantzis, M. (2000). *Multiliteracies: Literacy learning and the design of social futures*. London: Routledge.

de Ridder, I. (2002). Visible or invisible links: Does the highlighting of hyperlinks affect incidental vocabulary learning, text comprehension and the reading process? *Language Learning and Technology, 6(1)*, 123–146.

Educational Testing Service [ETS]. (2004). Iskills assessment (The former ICT Literacy Assessment). Retrieved June 16, 2007, from http://www.ets.org/portal/site/ets/menuitem. 1488512ecfd5b8849a77b13bc3921509/?vgnextoid=fde9af5e44df4010VgnVCM100 00022f95190RCRD&vgnextchannel=cd7314ee98459010VgnVCM10000022f95190R CRD

Fairclough, N. (1989). *Language and power*. London: Longman.

Fairclough, N. (1992). *Discourse and social change*. Cambridge, UK: Polity Press.

Freebody, P., & Luke, A. (1990). "Literacies" programs: Debates and demands in cultural context. *Prospect, 5(3)*, 7–16.

Freebody, P., & Luke, A. (1999). A map of possible practices: Further notes on the four resources model. *Practically Primary, 4(2)*, 5–8.

Gee, J. P. (1990). *Social linguistics and literacies: Ideology in discourses*. London: Falmer Press.

Gee, J. P. (1991). What is literacy? In C. Mitchell & K. Weiler (Eds.), *Rewriting literacy: Culture and the discourse of the other* (pp. 77–102). New York: Bergin & Garvey.

Gee, J. P. (2000). Teenagers in new times: A new literacy studies perspective. *Journal of Adolescent and Adult Literacy, 43(5)*, 412–423.

Gee, J. P. (2003). *Power up! What video games have to teach us about learning and literacy*. New York: Palgrave.

Gee, J. P. (2004). *Situated language and learning: A critique of traditional schooling*. London: Routledge/Taylor and Francis.

Gibson, N. (2005). *Production, Inc!* Queensland, Australia: Smart Classrooms ICT Teacher Awards. Retrieved June 29, 2006, from http://education.qld.gov.au/smartclassrooms/ teacherawards/2005awards.html

Green, B. (1988). Subject-specific literacy and school learning: A focus on writing. *Australian Journal of Education, 32(2)*, 156–179.

Green, B. (1999). The new literacy challenge? *Literacy Learning: Secondary Thoughts, 7(1)*, 36–46.

Goldsborough, R. (1998, January). Teaching healthy scepticism about information on the Internet. Technology and Learning, 32.

Haas, C., & Wearden, S. (2003). E-Credibility: Building common ground in web environments. *L1 - Educational Studies in Language and Literature, 3*, 169–184.

Hamilton, W. (Trans.). (1973). Plato. (1973). *Phaedrus and Letters VII and VIII*. Translated by W. Hamilton. Harmondsworth, UK: Penguin.

Hasan, R., & Williams, G. (1966). Literacy, everyday talk, and society. In R. Hasan and G. Williams (Eds.), *Literacy in society*. London: Longman.

Healy, A., & Honan, E. (2004). *Text next: New resources for literacy learning*. Sydney, Australia: Primary English Teaching Association.

Heath, S. B. (1983). *Ways with words*. Cambridge, NY: Cambridge University Press.

Heath, S. B., & Mangiola, L. (1991). *Children of promise: Literate activity in linguistically and culturally diverse classrooms*. Washington, DC: National Education Association.

Hinchman, K., Alvermann, D., Boyd, F., Brozo, W., & Vacca, R. (2004). Supporting older student's in-and out-of-school literacies. *Journal of Adolescent and Adult Literacy, 47(4)*, 304.

Huffaker, D. (2004). *Gender similarities and differences in online identity and language use among teenage bloggers.* Unpublished master's thesis, Georgetown University Graduate School of Arts and Sciences, Washington, DC.

Ito, M. (2003, March). *A new set of social rules for a newly wireless society.* Retrieved June 22, 2007, from www.ojr.org/japan/wireless/1043770650.php

Jewitt, C. (2003) Re-thinking assessment: Multimodality, literacy, and computer-mediated learning. *Assessment in Education: Principles, Policy, & Practice, 10*(1), 83–102.

Johnson, D., & Kress, G. (2003). Globalization, literacy, and society: Redesigning pedagogy and assessment. *Assessment in Education: Principles, Policy, & Practice, 10*(1), 5–14.

Johnson, D. L., & Liu, L. (2000). First steps toward a statistically generated technology integrated model. In D. L. Johnson, C. Maddux, & L. Liu (Eds.), *Integration of technology into the classroom: Case studies* (pp. 3–12). New York, NY: The Haworth Press, Inc.

Johnston, P. (2003). Assessment conversations. The Reading Teacher, 57(1), 90-92.

Jonassen, D. H., Peck, K. L., & Wilson, B. G. (1999). *Learning with technology. A constructivist perspective.* Upper Saddle River, NJ: Merrill Prentice Hall.

Kalantzis, M., Cope, B., & Harvey, A. (2003). Assessing multiliteracies and the new basics. *Assessment in Education: Principles, Policy, & Practice, 10*(1), 15–26.

Kapit, W., & Elson, L. M. (2001). *The anatomy colouring book.* Menlo Park, CA: Benjamin-Cummings Publishing Company.

Karchmer, R. A., Mallette, M. H., Kara-Soteriou, J., & Leu, D. J., Jr. (Eds.). (2005). *Innovative approaches to literacy education: Using the Internet to support new literacies.* Newark, DE: International Reading Association.

Katz, I. R. (2005). *Beyond technical competence: Literacy in information and communication technology.* An issue paper from ETS. Retrieved July 5, 2007 from http://search.live.com/previewx.aspx?q=%22higher+education+without+ICT+literacy+skills%22&FORM=CBPW&first=1&noredir=1

Kaufmann, W. (1977). The art of reading. In W. Kaufmann (Ed.), *The future of the humanities* (pp. 47–83). New York: Thomas Y. Crowell.

Kimber, K., & Wyatt-Smith, C. (2006). Using and creating knowledge with new technologies: A case for students-as-designers. *Learning, Media and Technology, 31*(1), 19–34.

Kimber, K., Pillay, H., & Richards, C. (2001). Learning through ICT: An analysis of the quality of knowledge developed through computer-mediated learning tools. In P. Singh & E. McWilliam (Eds.), *Designing educational research: Theories, methods and practice:, Faculty of education postgraduate student conference proceedings* (pp. 95–114) Flaxton, Australia: PostPressed.

Kramarski, B., & Feldman, Y. (2000). Internet in the classroom: Effects on reading comprehension, motivation, and metacognitive awareness. *Educational Media International, 37*, 149–155.

Kress, G. (1985). *Linguistic processes in sociocultural practice.* Geelong, Australia: Deakin University Press.

Kress, G. (1997). Visual and verbal modes of representation in electronically mediated communication: The potentials of new forms of text. In I. Snyder (Ed.), *Page to screen: Taking literacy into the electronic era* (pp. 53–79). St. Leonards, Australia: Allen and Unwin.

Kress, G. (2003). *Literacy in the new media age.* London/New York: Routledge.

Kress, G., & van Leeuwen, T. (2001). *Multimodal discourses.* London: Arnold.

Kuiper, E., Volman, M., & Terwel, J. (2005). The Web as an information resource in K–12 education: Strategies for supporting students in searching and processing information. *Review of Educational Research, 75*(3), 285–328.

Kymes, A. (2005). Teaching online comprehension strategies using think-alouds. *Journal of Adolescent & Adult Literacy, 48*(6), 492–500.

Lanham, R. (1994). *The economics of attention.* Proceedings of 124th Annual Meeting, Association of Research Libraries. Retrieved June 2, 2000 from http://sunsite.berkeley.edu/ARL/Proceedings/124/ ps2econ.html

Lanham, R. (1997, Spring). *The economics of attention.* Retrieved August 18, 2004, from http://www.rhetoricainc.com/

Lankshear, C., & Bigum, C. (1998, July). *Literacies and technologies in school settings: Findings from the field.* Paper presented at the Australian Literacy Educators National Conference, Canberra, Australia.

Lankshear, C., & Bigum, C. (1999). Literacies and new technologies in school settings. *Curriculum Studies, 7*(3), 445–465.

Lankshear, C., & Knobel, M. (2001a). *New technologies, social practices, and the challenge of mindsets.* Paper presented at the AERA Conference, Seattle, WA. Retrieved June 22, 2007 from http://www.geocities.com/c.lankshear/mindsets.html

Lankshear, C., & Knobel, M. (2003a). *New literacies: Changing knowledge in the classroom.* Buckingham, U.K.: Open University Press.

Lankshear, C., & Knobel, M. (2003b). *Planning pedagogy for i-mode: from flogging to blogging via wi-fi.* Paper presented at the IFTE Conference, Melbourne.

Lankshear, C., & McLaren, P. (Eds.). (1993). *Critical literacy: Politics, praxis, and the postmodern.* Albany: State University of New York Press.

Lepani, B. (1998, December). *The challenge of the digital age.* Paper presented at the Third National Information Literacy Conference, Canberra, Australia.

Leu, D. J., Jr. (2000). Literacy and technology: Deictic consequences for literacy education in an information age. In M. L. Kamil, P. B. Mosenthal, P. D. Pearson, & R. Barr (Eds.), *Handbook of reading research* (Vol. 111, pp. 743–770). Mahwah, NJ: Erlbaum.

Leu, D. J., Castek, J., Hartman, D. K., Coiro, J., Henry, L. A., Kulikowich, J. M., et al., (2005, June). *Evaluating the development of scientific knowledge and new forms of reading comprehension during online learning.* Final report to the North Central Regional Educational Laboratory/Learning Point Associates, Albany, NY.

Leu, D. J., Jr., & Kinzer, C. K. (2000). The convergence of literacy instruction with networked technologies for information and communication. *Reading Research Quarterly, 35,* 109–127.

Leu, D. J., Jr., Kinzer, C. K., Coiro, J., & Cammack, D. W. (2004). Towards a theory of new literacies emerging from the Internet and other information and communication technologies. In R. B. Ruddell & N. Unrau (Eds.), *Theoretical models and processes of reading* (pp. 1570–1613). Newark, DE: International Reading Association.

Luke, A. (1998). Literacy teaching as work in new times. *Language Arts, 75*(4), 305–314.

Luke, A., Freebody, P., & Land, R. (2000). *Literate futures: Review of literacy education.* Brisbane, Australia: The State of Queensland.

Luke, C. (2000). Cyber-schooling and technological change: Multiliteracies for new times. In B. Cope, & M. Kalantzis (Eds.), *Multiliteracies - Literacy learning and the design of social futures* (pp. 69–92). London/New York: Routledge.

Luke, C. (2003). Pedagogy, connectivity, multimodality, and interdisciplinarity. *Reading Research Quarterly, 38*(3), 397–403.

Macedo-Rouet, M., Rouet, J. -F., Epstein, I., & Fayard, P. (2003). Reading and understanding a science report through paper and hypertext. *Science Communication, 25,* 99–128.

Markhan, (2003). *Images of Internet: Tool, place, way of being.* Paper presented at the fourth annual conference of the Association of Internet Researchers (AoIR), Toronto, Canada.

Martin, A. (2004). Review of the book 'New literacies: Changing knowledge and classroom learning.' *Journal of eLiteracy, 1,* 61–65.

Mayer, R. E. (1997). Multimedia learning: Are we asking the right questions? *Educational Psychologist, 32,* 1–19.

Mayer, R. E. (Ed.). (2005). *The Cambridge handbook of multimedia learning.* New York: Cambridge University Press.

McCarthy, L. P., & Fishman, S. M. (1991) Boundary conversations: Conflicting ways of knowing in philosophy and interdisciplinary research. *Research in the Teaching of English, 25,* 419–469.

Mercer, N., & Wegerif, R. (1997). Is 'exploratory talk' productive talk? In R. Wegerif & P. Scrimshaw (Eds.), *Computers and talk in the primary school* (pp. 79–101). Clevedon: Multilingual Matters Ltd.

Meredyth, D., Russell, N., Blackwood, L., Thomas, J., & Wise, P. (1999). *Real time computers, change, & schooling.* Retrieved May 14, 2003, from http://detya.gov.au/archive/schools/Publicatgions/1999/realtime.pdf

Merchant, G. (2001). Teenagers in cyberspace: An investigation of language use and language change in internet classrooms. *Journal of Research in Reading, 24,* 293–306.

Millard, E. (2003). Towards a literacy of fusion: New times, new teaching and learning? *Reading, Literacy, and Language, 37(1),* 3–8.

Miller, G. A., & Gildea, P. M. (1987). How children learn words. *Scientific American, 257(3),* 94–99.

Mitra, S. (2004, September). The hole in the wall. *Dataquest,* Retrieved June 22, 2007 from http://www.dqindia.com/content/industrymarket/2004/104092301.asp#i

Morgan, W., & Wyatt-Smith, C. M. (2000). Improper accountability: Towards a theory of critical literacy and assessment. *Assessment in Education: Principles, Policy & Practice, 7(1),* 124–142.

New London Group. (1996). A pedagogy of multiliteracies: Designing social futures. *Harvard Educational Review, 66,* 60–92.

New London Group. (2000). A pedagogy of multiliteracies: Designing social futures. In B. Cope & M. Kalantzis (Eds.), *Multiliteracies: Literacy learning and the design of social futures* (pp. 9–37). London: Routledge.

Parks, S., Huot, D., Hamers, J., & H.-Lemonnierr, F. (2003). Crossing boundaries: Multimedia technology and pedagogical innovation in a high school class. *Language Learning and Technology, 7(1),* 28–45.

Paris, S. G. (2005). Reinterpreting the development of reading skills. *Reading Research Quarterly, 40,* 184–202.

Pressley, M., & Afflerbach, P. (1995). *Verbal protocols of reading: The nature of constructively responsive reading.* Hillsdale, NJ: Erlbaum.

RAND Reading Study Group [RRSG]. (2002). *Reading for understanding: Towards an R&D program in reading comprehension.* Santa Monica, CA: RAND.

Reinking, D. (2005). Multimedia learning of reading. In R.E. Mayer (Ed.), *The Cambridge handbook of multimedia learning* (pp. 355–374). New York: Cambridge University Press.

Reinking, D., & Rickman, S. S. (1990). The effects of computer-mediated texts on the vocabulary learning and comprehension of intermediate-grade readers. *Journal of Reading Behavior, 22,* 395–411.

Rheingold, H. (2003). *Smart mobs: The next social revolution.* New York: Basic Books.

Rouet, J-F. (1993). *Cognitive processing of hyperdocuments: When does nonlinearity help?* Paper presented at ACM conference on Hypertext, Milan, Italy. Retrieved July 5, 2007 from http://portal.acm.org/citation.cfm?id=168466.168508

Royer, J. M., Greene, B. A., & Sinatra, G. M. (1987). The sentence verification technique: A practical procedure teachers can use to develop their own reading and listening comprehension tests. *Journal of Reading, 30,* 414–423.

Savery, J. R., & Duffy, T. M. (1995, September/October). Problem-based learning: An instructional model and its constructivist framework. *Educational Technology,* 31–38.

Scrimshaw, P. (1997). Computers and the teacher's role. In B. Somekh & N. Davis (Eds.), *Using information technology effectively in teaching and learning. Studies in pre-service and in-service teacher education* (pp. 100–113). London/New York: Routledge.

Sefton-Green, J. (2004). *Literature review in informal learning with technology outside school.* Retrieved June 23, 2007 from www.futurelab.org.uk/resources/documents/lit_reviews/Informal_Learning_Review.pdf

Selfe, C. L., & Hawisher, G. E. (2004) *Literate lives in the information age.* Mahwah, NJ:. Lawrence Erlbaum.

Smolin, L., & Lawless, K. (2003). Becoming literate in the technological age: New responsibilities and tools for teachers. *The Reading Teacher, 56*(6), 570–577.

Stahl, S. A., Hynd, C. R., Britton, B. K., McNish, M. M., & Bosquet, D. (1996). What happens when students read multiple source documents in history? *Reading Research Quarterly, 31,* 430–436.

Steinkuehler, C. A., Black, R. W., & Clinton, K. A. (2005). *Researching literacy as tool, place, and way of being. Reading Research Quarterly, 40*(1), 7–12.

Stockl, H. (2004). In between modes: Language and image in printed media. In E. Ventola, C. Charles, & M. Kaltenberger (Eds.), *Perspectives on mutlimodality* (pp. 9–30). Amsterdam: John Benjamins.

Street, B. (1984). *Literacy in theory and practice.* Cambridge, New York, NY: Cambridge University Press.

Street, B. (Ed.). (1993). *Cross-cultural approaches to literacy.* Cambridge, New York, NY: Cambridge University Press.

Street, B. (1995). *Social literacies: Critical approaches to literacy in education, development, and ethnography.* London: Longman.

Street, B. (2000). Contexts for literacy work: The 'new orders' and the 'new literacy studies'. In J. Crowther, M. Hamilton, & L. Tett (Eds.), *Powerful literacies* (pp. 13–22). London: NIACE.

Street, B. (2001). Literacy demands of the Curriculum in the Post-Compulsory Years. In J. Cumming & C. M. Wyatt-Smith (Eds.). *Literacy and the Curriculum: Success in senior secondary schooling* (pp. 146-156). Melbourne Australia: Australian Council for Educational Research.

Sunderland-Smith, W., Snyder, I., & Angus, L. (2003). The digital divide: Differences in computer use between home and school on low socio-economic households. *L1 - Educational Studies in Language and Literature, 3,* 5–19.

Sutherland-Smith, W. (2002). Weaving the literacy web: Changes in reading from page to screen. *The Reading Teacher, 55*(7), 662–669.

Tan Wee Hin, L., & Subramaniam, R. (2005). *Handbook of research on literacy in technology at the K-12 level.* Singapore: Idea Group Reference.

Thorne, S. (2003, April). *The Internet as artifact: Immediacy, evolution, and educational contingencies or "The wrong tool for the right job?"* Paper presented at the American Educational Research Association, Chicago, IL.

Tiene, D. (2002). Addressing the global digital divide and its impact on educational opportunity. *Education Media International, 39*(3/4), 211–222.

Tunbridge, N. (1995, September). The cyberspace cowboy. *Australian Personal Computer* (pp. 64–68).

Tyner, K. (1998). *Literacy in a digital world: Teaching and learning in the age of information.* Mahwah, NJ: Lawrence Erlbaum Associates.

Unsworth, L. (2001). *Teaching multiliteracies across the curriculum: Changing dimensions of text and image in classroom practice.* Buckingham, U.K.: Open University Press.

Unsworth, L., Martin, J. R., Painter, C., & Gill, T. (in press). *Image/text relations in book and computer-based versions of literary narratives for children: Towards a functional intermodal semiotic description.*

Wells, G. (2002). Inquiry as an orientation for learning, teaching, and teacher education. In G. Wells, & Claxtohn (Eds.), *Learning for life in the 21st century* (pp. 197–210). Oxford, U.K.: Blackwell Publishing.

Williamson, B., & Facer, K. (2004). *More than 'just a game': The implications for schools of children's computer games and communities.* Unpublished draft paper, Bristol. Retrieved April 1, 2004, from the NESTA FutureLab Web site: http://www.nestafuturelab.org/research/draft_articles.htm

Windschitl, M. (2000). Using the WWW for teaching and learning in K–12 classrooms: What are the interesting research questions? *Cyber Psychology & Behavior, 3*(1), 89–96.

Winne, P. H. (2006). How software technologies can improve research on learning and bolster school reform. *Educational Psychologist, 41,* 5–17.

Wyatt-Smith, C. M., & Kimber, K. (2005) Valuing and evaluating digitally-mediated texts: Rethinking what counts. *English in Education, 39*(2), 22–43.

Yelland, N. (2001). *Teaching and learning with information and communication technologies (ICT) for numeracy in the early childhood and primary years of schooling.* Report prepared for the Research and Evaluation Branch Department of Education, Training and Youth Affairs, Canberra, Australia.

Zembylas, M., & Vrasidas, C. (2005). Globalization, information, communication technologies, and the prospect of a global village: Promises of inclusion or electronic colonization. *Journal of Curriculum Studies, 37*(1), 68–83.

CHAPTER 32

Assessing New Literacies in Science and Mathematics

EDYS S. QUELLMALZ

WESTED, USA

GENEVA D. HAERTEL

SRI INTERNATIONAL, USA

The breathtaking proliferation of information and communication technologies being used in school, work, personal, and civic activities speaks to the centrality of these powerful, transformative tools in today's world. International studies document the increased use of technologies in schools, despite competing demands on school budgets and entrenched, traditional views of learning and instruction (Pelgrum & Anderson, 1999). Policymakers throughout the world recognize the transformative consequences of technologies for economic, civic, and global progress, as well as the concomitant need for coherent educational policies to promote and implement skills characterized as new literacies, 21st-century skills, or information and communication technology (ICT) skills (Partnership for 21st Century Skills, 2005; Kozma, McGhee, Quellmalz, & Zalles, 2004). As technologies and contexts of use expand, views of ICT are moving beyond operation of computer productivity tools to examine individuals' use of the Internet, specialized software, and facility with handheld and wireless devices. "New literacies," from our perspective, refer to expertise in the use of a range of digital media and information and communication technologies exercised in academic and applied settings.

Technologies are increasingly recognized as transforming schooling because of their capacity to extend students' opportunities to access rich repositories of knowledge and to engage in deep, extended problem solving (U.S. Department of Education, 1996). Large-scale national and international studies are providing evidence that technologies are truly changing and improving schools by enriching curricula, tailoring learning environments, offering opportunities for embedding assessment within instruction, and providing collaborative tools to connect students, teachers, and experts locally and globally (Bracewell, Breuleux, Laferriere, Benoit, & Abdous, 1998; Bransford, Brown, & Cocking, 2000; Coley, Cradler, & Engel, 1999; Kozma, 2003; Means & Olson, 1995; Wenglinski, 1998). Despite this groundswell of enthusiasm for technology, neither traditional large-scale assessment methods nor curriculum-embedded, formative methods are designed to measure the impacts of ICT on learning (Burns & Ungerleider, 2002; McFarlane et al., 2000; Quellmalz & Kozma, 2003).

Debate is rampant about definitions of ICT knowledge and skills; their relationships to knowledge and processes in academic, vocational, and functional domains; the contexts in which ICT should be taught and tested; and the extent to which the knowledge and skills about technologies to be used within a domain-based problem or context can be distinguished from the domain-specific knowledge and skills required (Bennett, Jenkings, Persky, & Weiss, 2003; Quellmalz & Kozma, 2003). Assessments *of* technology, such as the International Computer Driving License and technology proficiency tests in some states, test the facts and procedures needed to operate common tools, while the content or the academic or applied problem and context are considered irrelevant (Crawford & Toyama, 2002; Venezky & Davis, 2002).

Assessments of learning *with* technology, in contrast, can present problems and items that *integrate* measurement of technology operations, strategic use of ICT, and subject-matter knowledge and processes through carefully designed sets of tasks and items related to complex problems. Assessments of learning with technology can vary along a continuum from static to animated and dynamic displays of information, data, and phenomena and from static to interactive ways for students to solve problems and enter responses (Koomen, 2006). At the beginning of the continuum would fall technology-based assessments intended to replicate paper counterparts. Assessments that would fall at a midpoint on the continuum may permit students to construct tables and graphs or they may present animations of science experiments or phenomena, such as chemical reactions, for students to observe. Assessments presenting dynamic simulations that allow students to interact by manipulating multiple variables would be placed at the most transformative end of the continuum.

An important distinction must be made between assessments *by* technology and assessments *with* technology. Assessments *by* technology are increasing rapidly in large-scale state, national, and international testing, where technology is being embraced as a means to reduce the costs and logistics of assessment functions such as test delivery, scoring, and reporting. Online, large-scale testing programs focus on measuring academic knowledge and skills such as statistics or composition. They typically assume that skills needed to use supporting technology tools, such as calculators, spreadsheets, or word processors, are confounding or construct-irrelevant processes. These types of testing programs seek comparability of paper and online tests. As such, designs of these tests tend to present static stimuli and use traditional constructed-response and selected-response item formats. For the most part, conventional, online tests remain limited to measuring knowledge and skills that can be easily assessed on paper. Consequently, they do not take advantage of technologies that can measure more complex knowledge structures and extended inquiry and problem solving. This chapter is concerned with assessments *with* technology, not assessments *by* technology.

The quest to provide powerful evidence of the impacts of technologies on learning and to assess new learning enabled by technology is further complicated by three issues: (a) multiple definitions of new literacies as indicated in this book; (b) overlapping frameworks that address assessment of technology within multiple academic and practical areas, also in this book and throughout the rest of our chapter; and (c) the dearth of alternative assessment designs and prototype assessments of ICT use. Clearly, there is a need for innovative assessments that capture new forms of learning associated with ICT use in ways that distinguish them from students' ability to simply manipulate features of the tools.

Differences in the ways that ICT skills are defined and tested and the role of ICT in the constructs to be measured will be recurring issues in this chapter. We begin with a brief summary of cognitive science research and basic principles of assessment design that guided our beliefs about how best to assess new literacies. Then, we identify findings from three areas of research conducted by the Center for Technology in Learning at SRI International that informed the development of our assessment framework, called the Coordinated ICT Assessment Framework. These areas of research include: (a) analyses of studies focused on the role of technology; (b) analyses of educational frameworks and standards; and (c) analyses of classroom technology practices. After proposing our ICT Assessment Framework as a means to guide and support future studies of new literacies, we discuss extant examples of assessments *of* technology and of assessments *with* technology and describe newer designs and prototypes we have explored as part of a 3-year project, (Coordinated, Innovative Designs for International Information Communication Technology (ICT) Assessment in Science and Mathematics Education) funded by the National Science Foundation. The goals of the project were threefold: first, to forge an interdisciplinary ICT assessment framework; second, to design ICT performance assessments for a planned international study *of* technology use in education; and third, to develop prototypes of assessments of science and mathematics learning *with* technology. Toward the end of the chapter, we describe principled assessment designs and prototype assessments developed in SRI projects for these two different testing purposes. We conclude with recommendations for further research, design, and development.

Background

Assessments are designed to serve a multitude of purposes. Assessments of ICT may look different from paper-based tests used to measure achievement in a narrowly defined subject area. However, all assessments share certain common principles. The publication of *Knowing What Students Know: The Science and Design of Educational Assessment* (Pellegrino, Chudowsky, & Glaser, 2001) signaled a new way of thinking about the design of high-quality assessments. It presented advances in measurement science that integrate findings from the cognitive-learning sciences about how people learn into systematic test design frameworks that specify an evidence-based assessment argument. The framework and assessment design principles presented in this chapter for assessing new literacies in science and mathematics are grounded in learning science theory and in measurement science methods of evidence-centered design. Our assessment designs and exemplars presuppose explicit identification of what knowledge and skills are to be tested. They also assume that features of problems and items will elicit observable evidence of the desired knowledge and skills, and they indicate the method by which responses will be evaluated and reported. The assessments may serve formative or summative purposes, but they must be based on principled design, as will be defined next.

Cognitive Science Research

The report *How People Learn* summarizes decades of learning research and identifies fundamental cognitive processes such as access, storage, and retrieval (Bransford et al., 2000). The report suggests skilled individuals are those who go beyond accumulation of factual information and routine procedures to exhibit adaptive expertise by integrating knowledge, skills, and procedures in ways that are useful for solving problems in new situations. Therefore, skill and expertise require not only possessing declarative knowledge and procedural skills, such as facts and concepts, but also using strategies to determine when and how to apply them. Assessments of interconnected knowledge structures and reasoning processes are generally acknowledged to require more complex tasks that can reveal how learners use knowledge, skills, and processes to accomplish significant, recurring tasks in key settings, such as school, work, and community (Pellegrino et al., 2001). The implications of cognitive research for the assessment of new literacies in academic domains such as science and mathematics are that the specifications of the knowledge, procedures, and strategies to be tested should go beyond basic facts and skills to include testing of strategic uses of the technologies in the types of problems and contexts important in a domain and setting.

Evidence-Centered Assessment-Design Principles

Knowing What Students Know (Pellegrino et al., 2001) characterizes the assessment of the knowledge and skills that individuals possess as a process of reasoning from evidence. The reasoning required to make inferences about an individual's knowledge and skills is best developed through the specification of an assessment argument. This assessment argument connects three components including: (a) the specific knowledge and skill constructs in the particular domain to be measured; (b) the features of assessment activities that will require examinees to use that knowledge and those skills; and (c) the data derived from student responses that will count as evidence of the level of knowledge and skills demonstrated (Baxter & Mislevy, 2005; Messick, 1994; Mislevy et al., 2003).

Evidence-centered assessment-design structures an assessment argument by relating the learning to be assessed, specified as a *student model*, to a *task model* that specifies features of tasks and questions that would elicit observable evidence of learning, and to an *evidence model* that specifies the quality of student responses and scores that would indicate levels of proficiency (Messick, 1994; Mislevy et al., 2003; Pellegrino et al., 2001). Specifying student, task, and evidence models as part of assessment development represents a best practice in the field of assessment (Pellegrino et al., 2001). This advancement has shifted assessment development from being a "craft" toward being a systematically applied science of design.

Assessments of new literacies, then, should specify an assessment framework with these three components: (a) student model, (b) task model, and (c) evidence model. The student model would identify the ICT domain knowledge and processes that define the constructs to be measured. These would include students' declarative knowledge about technology tools, such as their purposes and features, and students' procedural knowledge, or proficiency for operating particular technology tools. The ICT domain would also define strategies such as information processing, knowledge management, problem solving, and communication; each of these are strategies that individuals must draw on to make use of technologies to address significant, recurring problems in general, applied contexts, and in academic disciplines. For new literacy assessments aiming to measure technology use and also to measure academic knowledge and skills, the student model would need to specify both ICT and domain knowledge and skills.

The second component of evidence-centered design for the assessment of new literacies, the task model, would then specify the features of tasks and items that would elicit observations of achievement of the ICT and domain knowledge and skills of interest. The types of assessment tasks and items would represent the fundamental contexts, problems, and activities in which examinees use technology in school and applied settings.

The third component of evidence-centered design, the evidence model, would specify: (a) the evidence of student learning that needs to be extracted from student responses to the assessment tasks and items; (b) how the responses will be scored; and (c) the details of the statistical models needed to calibrate items and create proficiency estimates and reports of students' knowledge and skills.

In addition, each assessment produced would require empirical studies that provide evidence of its validity and reliability (American Educational Research Association, American Psychological Association, & National Council on Measurement in Education, 1999). A rigorous evidence-centered assessment framework would be supplemented by studies confirming that assessment items and tasks align with the knowledge and skills in the framework and/or content standards. Documentation of the technical quality of the assessment would provide evidence that items and tasks: (a) elicit the cognitive processes that the developers believe they should; (b) are instructionally sensitive; and (c) have established technical qualities related to their reliability and validity (Haertel, Lash, Javitz, & Quellmalz, 2006; Quellmalz & Haydel, 2002, Quellmalz & Kreikemeier, 2004).

Informed by these three components of evidence-centered design (student, task, and evidence models), we sought to create assessment designs situated within the types of problems and epistemologies of science and mathematics learning in which technology plays an integral role. Consequently, our efforts to develop an innovative and coordinated framework for assessing new literacies in math and science (i.e., The Coordinated ICT Assessment Framework) focused on three areas of research, each of which are summarized in the next section. First, we drew on research in learning sciences to study the role of technology in learning. Second, we drew on analyses of frameworks and standards that specified student learning outcomes for 21st-century skills and student models for skills in science and math. Third, we reviewed studies of technology use in schools and in science and math curricula to identify cross-cutting knowledge and strategies. These reviews helped identify particular features of curriculum and assessment activities that could serve as design templates for a new breed of assessment tasks.

Studies of the Role of Technology in Learning

How People Learn (Bransford et al., 2000) summarizes research on the benefits of new technologies for enhancing student learning, stressing that technologies do not guarantee effective learning, but that technologies can make it easier to create research-based environments that students can manipulate as they acquire and consolidate new understandings. Technologies can help learners to access, structure, connect, store, retrieve, and process information en route to becoming experts in a given content area.

In many fields, new technologies allow representation of domains, systems, and data in new ways. Technologies such as three-dimensional models of ecosystems or molecular structures help people to visualize difficult-to-understand concepts. This move from static to dynamic models has profoundly changed the nature of inquiry in mathematics and science, for researchers as well as for students. For example, spatial, causal, and dynamic relationships can now be made visible (Gobert & Clement, 1999). Representational technologies have expanded the phenomena that can be considered and the nature of argumentation and acceptable evidence (Bachelard, 1984; Holland, 1995). Communication technologies enable socially constructed dialogues of learning among distributed collaborators, learners, and experts set within extended projects (Pea, 1993). As a result, designs of formative assessments embedded in science and math curricula could make use of these advanced technologies and open environments to gather evidence of student learning. Unfortunately, formal, large-scale assessments are currently limited to testing more traditional uses of technologies commonly available in all schools.

Analyses of Frameworks and Standards

The purpose of the Coordinated ICT Assessment Framework was to integrate measurement of technology use and subject matter. Consequently, a second area that informed the design of our assessment framework involved the analyses of frameworks and standards documents for direct assessments *of* technology skills and frameworks for assessments of science and mathematics. As mentioned earlier, development of the Coordinated ICT Assessment Framework was one component of a 3-year study conducted by the Center for Technology in Learning at SRI International and funded by the National Science Foundation (NSF) (Quellmalz & Kozma, 2003). The project was to design and pilot test ICT performance assessments that could be administered as a national option in an international study that was planned for the third stage of the Second International Technology in Education Study (SITES). (SITES is supported by the International Association for the Evaluation of Educational Achievement, or IEA.) Goals of the NSF project were to forge a framework that would guide the development of a performance assessment of ICT that could be used across a range of school subjects documented in IEA SITES Modules 1 and 2 (Pelgrum & Anderson, 1999).

To these ends, a working group of international experts in ICT representing Chile, Finland, Norway, Singapore, and the United States was formed. The group aligned standards documents that specified important technology proficiencies with those that focused on mathematics and science and the role of technology within the domains. These standards documents were meant to shape the "intended curriculum." They also often integrated the use of technology. Rather than focusing on technology features and basic operations (e.g., how to save a document or write a Web-search query), however, these frameworks focused on the strategic deployment of technology in school curricula and learning environments (e.g., conducting analyses using graphing tools) to support the learning of complex skills such as information management, problem solving, analysis, communication, and collaboration. These are the skills required in 21st-century economy and society (European Commission, 2000; Organization for Economic Co-operation and Development [OECD], 2000a; Partnership for 21st Century Skills, 2005). In addition, the working group examined assessment frameworks that shaped major national and international achievement studies in science and mathematics. In aligning these various frameworks and standards documents, the group classified the knowledge and skills identified in the frameworks according to the cognitive demands it required of students (declarative, procedural, schematic, and strategic knowledge), aspects of technology, and the subject matter (Pellegrino et al., 2001).

To create the Coordinated ICT Assessment Framework, the descriptions and classifications of problem solving and inquiry from the math and science frameworks were incorporated into the more general categories of information processing, knowledge management, and communication categories in the technology proficiency frameworks. From these frameworks, the project team culled common categories of ICT use that could shape the coherent collection of evidence across studies of students' abilities to use ICT in academic domains.

Technology Proficiency Frameworks

The ICT strategies that were chosen for inclusion in the Coordinated ICT Assessment Framework appeared throughout technology proficiency frameworks and were differentiated from the facts and skills that were needed to operate the technology tools. The International Society for Technology in Education (ISTE), for example, proposed that as a result of ICT integration in the curriculum, students should be: (a) capable information technology users; (b) information seekers, analyzers, and evaluators; (c) problem solvers and decision makers; (d) creative and effective users of productivity tools; and (e) communicators, collaborators, publishers, and producers (ISTE, 2000). The National Educational Technology Standards (NETS) recommended that students effectively use productivity tools, research tools, and communication tools for purposes such as enhancing learning, collaborating, publishing, and communicating (ISTE, 2000). The NETS framework also calls for demonstrations of basic technology operations and concepts. Recently, the Programme for International Student Assessment (PISA) proposed a definition of ICT literacy as the interest, attitude, and ability of individuals to appropriately use digital technology and communication tools to access, manage, integrate, and evaluate information, construct new knowledge, and communicate with others to participate effectively in society (Lennon, Kirsch, Von Davier, Wagner, & Yamamoto, 2003).

The development of our cross-cutting Coordinated ICT Framework was built around these various definitions of 21st-century knowledge and skill constructs, as specified by national and international organizations. In addition, the analyses documented the range of technology programs to which the ICT framework could be applied.

Math and Science Standards and Assessment Frameworks

Because the performance assessments for the international technology study were to be developed within math and science contexts, the SRI project team focused on national and international math and science frameworks. These analyses classified the types of problem-solving and inquiry skills that appeared in the math and science frameworks into the general information processing and reasoning strategies appearing in the technology proficiency frameworks.

The National Science Education Standards (NSES) describe a science and technology partnership that establishes connections between the natural and designed worlds and provides students with opportunities to develop decision-making abilities (National Research Council, 1996). The science-inquiry abilities, such as posing problems, analyzing and interpreting data, and communicating findings, fit clearly within more generic technology proficiency frameworks. In the National Council of Teachers of Mathematics' (NCTM) document *Principles and Standards for School Mathematics* (NCTM, 2000), technology is one of the six principles. The standards document makes the point that technologies allow students to focus on decision making, reflection, reasoning, and problem solving. The assessment frameworks for the IEA Trends in International Mathematics and Science Study (TIMSS) and PISA science and mathematics present similar types of knowledge and reasoning categories that could be classified within more generic information processing and problem-solving categories (OECD, 2000b). SRI incorporated research from learning science and our analyses of technology and science and mathematics frameworks into the Coordinated ICT Assessment Framework.

Analyses of Technology Practices in Schools

In this section, we describe our examination of international and national studies and curriculum projects that document the ways in which ICT strategies are being implemented in schools. Attention focused primarily on the nature and role of standards and assessments as they relate to students and teachers, as well as the impacts of technologies on emerging pedagogical practices and student outcomes. We analyzed these studies to determine how well the planned Coordinated ICT Assessment Framework would represent current and emerging technology use in schools—that is, how well the framework specified proficiencies of a student model that can be broadly applicable. Our analyses also enabled us to identify recurring types of classroom assignments to represent in assessment-task designs. Analyses of the types of problems students address by using technology informed the design features of the task models intended to elicit student outcomes specified in the ICT assessment framework.

Technology Surveys

Recent national and international technology surveys provided a general picture of technology use in schools. The SITES Module 1 surveys of technology coordinators were used to identify promising innovative pedagogical practices using technology (Pelgrum & Anderson, 1999). The surveys were used in part to identify innovative classrooms that might be included in case studies in SITES Module 2. The surveys found that students in most countries were expected to be able to use word processors and spreadsheets by the time they finished secondary school, if not earlier.

In the United States, a national study found that teachers used a wide variety of software with their students (Becker, 1999). Teachers were apt to see information acquisition and written expression as primary objects of computer use. Data-analysis goals were addressed through the use of spreadsheets, databases, and simulations. In the Integrated Studies of Educational Technology (ISET) survey of 1,300 U.S. teachers (Adelman et al., 2002), 66% of the secondary mathematics teachers reported having students use computers to solve problems and analyze data. The study found that less-traditional teachers were more likely to use technology in the classroom. Teachers reported an increase in achievement in students' research skills (76%), breadth and depth of understanding of subjects taught (64%), problem-solving skills (57%), and quality of writing (59%). These findings corroborated the ICT strategies and tools included in our coordinated framework.

Technology Case Studies

The OECD Centre for Educational Research and Innovation (CERI) conducted a survey of teachers' technology practices and their students' use of technologies. Study questions probed how technology served as a catalyst for organizational change throughout a school. Ninety-four case studies were conducted, approximately 3 to 6 per country. Twenty-one countries that were OECD members participated in the case studies, plus Israel and Singapore, which had participated in other OECD studies. Findings included that the most successful implementations relied on teacher competence with the technologies and that ICT became a lever for new classroom methods based on ICT. The study found that ICT was used to change or enhance curriculum, to improve access to learning, to implement new teaching methods, to reform the school organization, and to improve staff support (Venezky & Davis, 2002).

The SITES Module 2 study provided a more detailed picture of how ICT was being used to support innovative teaching practices around the globe. SITES Module 2 was an IEA project that collected and analyzed 174 case reports of innovative classroom practices from 28 countries in Europe, North America, Asia Pacific, Africa, and South America. The analysis of these case reports found interesting patterns in how technology was used to support instructional change around the world (Kozma, 2003).

The 174 cases indicated that, across countries, ICT had become integrated throughout the curriculum. A large majority of the innovations used productivity tools (78%), Web resources (71%), and e-mail (68%). Many (52%) used multimedia software. Some used Web-design tools (34%). Very few used specialized educational software, such as simulations and microcomputer-based laboratories (13%). In almost all cases (94%), computers were used in regular school settings, such as the classroom, library, or computer laboratory. In relatively few cases (28%), technology was used outside of school. Software packages were widely used to create products or presentations (80%), Web browsers or CD-ROMs were used to search for information (77%), and e-mail was used to support communication (55%). Less commonly, teachers used ICT to plan or organize instruction (26%) or to monitor or assess student work (22%). In a small number of cases, ICT was used to support student collaboration (17%), or simulations or modeling software packages were used for research or experimentation (13%). Although the student-learning outcomes in this study were not directly measured by the research teams, the kinds of impact reported by students, teachers, and administrators indicated the need for novel assessment approaches that can show how technology-supported practices are influencing student learning of these advanced skills.

These broad findings from surveys and case studies about technology use in schools contributed to our formulation and confirmation of the significance and relevance of the ICT knowledge, skills, and strategies specified in the Coordinated ICT Assessment Framework that would form the student model component of assessment designs for ICT.

Technology-Based Curricula

Detailed analyses of innovative curricula that integrated tools of science, mathematics, and information technology into instructional activities were analyzed to yield further information about potential designs for assessments of learning *with* technology. The innovative curricula tended to represent deeper, more significant uses of technologies in the domains. Often, these curriculum programs attempted to engage students in uses of technologies typically employed by professionals in the workplace. Innovative curricula also tended to foreshadow the types of classroom technology integration that will become commonplace within a few years. The uses of technologies in these curricula served as referents for student and task models of more advanced uses of learning tools, uses of more complex tools, and the completion of more meaningful, complex tasks.

Technology-based science curricula. In a different project funded by NSF titled 21st Century Assessment (Quellmalz & Haertel, 2004), SRI International examined cutting-edge science curricula to find ways to take advantage of embedded technologies that (a) structure formal assessment tasks and (b) elicit evidence for the kinds of conceptual understanding and extended science inquiry that were promoted in the programs. We expected that many of the technologies embedded in science curricula could be used or adapted to elicit, collect, document, analyze, appraise, and display kinds of student performances that are not readily accessible through traditional paper-based testing methods. Furthermore, we explored ways that the technologies might support ongoing, formative assessment of investigations in progress, in addition to the design of summative accountability measures. We concluded that a number of the technology applications that supported science learning could be extracted, tuned, generalized, and repurposed or redesigned for assessment purposes.

Figure 32.1 presents a conceptual model that relates technologies embedded in innovative science curricula (as found in our analyses) to seven key components of project-based science inquiry curricula: (a) rich environments and authentic problems; (b) collaboration; (c) planning; (d) investigating; (e) analysis and interpretation; (f) communication and presentation; and (g) monitoring, reflection, and evaluation. Technology applications have also been developed for assembling electronic notebooks or digital portfolios and digital libraries. These can be used to document an individual student's problem-solving efforts; archive data for a research team, classroom, or school; or collect examples of instructional resources, instructional activities, or assessments. These technologies could be incorporated into formative or summative assessments of students' abilities to engage in more complex conceptual problems involving more science inquiry processes. Such designs for assessments of learning *with* technology would fall at the far end of the continuum of technology-enhanced assessment where technologies play integral, transformative roles.

Technology-based mathematics curricula. Our project also analyzed innovative mathematics curricula that incorporated technologies to identify student and task models that could be repurposed for either formative or summative assessments. For example, SimCalc *MathWorlds* is a suite of curriculum units integrated with software designed to help middle- and high-school students make the intellectual connections necessary to understand conceptually complex aspects of the mathematics of change (Roschelle, Kaput, & Stroup, 2000). The software dynamically links the simulations of moving objects, the associated position and velocity graphs, and tables and formulas. Students were presented with challenging problems and made connections among the various

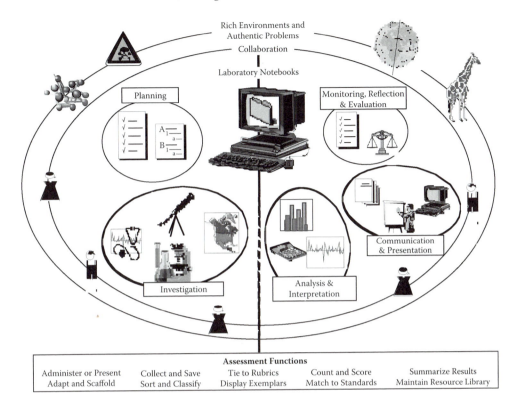

Figure 32.1 Conceptual model for technology-based science assessment.

representations, a process that supported their developmental understanding of rate of change. The domain of interest for assessment purposes was rate and proportionality at the middle-school level. The Scaling Up SimCalc project distinguished conceptually simple aspects of proportionality from complex aspects (Shechtman, Roschelle, Haertel, Tatar, & Knudsen, 2005). Students were required to use the computer-based simulations, but their proficiency in using the technology was not directly tested. Neither the end-of-unit nor the embedded assessments that accompanied this intervention were technology supported, although some of the simulations presented in the curriculum were available during the exploratory, embedded assessments for the student to use in solving the problems. From our perspective, technology-based assessment tasks could be designed for either formative or summative purposes to test the more complex aspects of proportionality and allow direct assessments of students' proficiency with the technology.

In another innovative math curriculum funded by NSF, Foundational Tools for Data Literacy (Zalles & Vahey, 2005), fourth- and sixth-grade students carried out data-rich tasks in two integrated math/life science units: pulse rate and plant growth. In a unit on pulse rate, fourth-grade students collected, organized, and analyzed data about pulse rate from samples of people drawn from different populations. In a unit on plant growth, sixth-grade students

Table 32.1 Coordinated ICT Assessment Framework

General cognitive demands	ICT knowledge and strategies	Sample component strategies
Declarative knowledge	Identify/list required domain information Identify features and functions of technology tools Identify uses of tools	Identify features Identify functions For each tool group and specific tool, identify appropriate uses
Procedural knowledge	Perform steps Operate tools	Follow directions Use algorithm Produce component and complete operations
Schematic and strategic knowledge	Plan strategies and procedures Access and organize information and data Represent and transform information and data Analyze and interpret information and data Critically evaluate Communicate ideas, findings, arguments Design product Collaborate to solve complex problems and manage information	Analyze problem Identify needed and given information Pose questions Specify design for data/information collection Specify analysis plan Choose appropriate tools Specify product form and content Specify search purpose/topic Navigate directories Generate Web searches Search multiple representational formats Generate representations from data or phenomena Transform data from one form to another Take and record measurements Identify information/data Apply quantitative and qualitative procedures Understand and compare data and information Infer trends/patterns Produce solutions/findings Use modeling and visualization tools to investigate, compare, test Evaluate relevance, credibility of information, data, representations Evaluate quality of plan, conduct, analysis, argument, conclusions Express questions, ideas clearly and appropriately Present ideas, findings in alternative formats appropriate for audience Present supported argument/findings Compose product to fit constraints, appropriate for audience, purpose Plan project work and roles Contribute relevant information Fulfill task assignment Incorporate and integrate others' information and views

The ICT strategies of interest in the Coordinated ICT Assessment Framework fall in the schematic and strategic knowledge category, which identifies organized knowledge structures (schematic) and systematic methods (strategic) to assess where students are taking advantage of the capabilities of technologies to solve key, complex problems. Planning strategies for a problem on how to save endangered species, for example, could involve analyzing the problem presented according to information given in various representational forms, (e.g., visualizations, maps, and tables of endangered species populations), and developing plans for collecting information and data from a range of databases and Web sites. Components of the ICT strategy for critical evaluation might include evaluating the credibility of reports by game preserves and sporting clubs on the need for stabilizing animal populations. Students might search the Web for more information about the membership and views of the organizations and also exchange critiques of others' reports with remote collaborators.

We propose that the Coordinated ICT Assessment Framework can support coherent, cross-cutting studies of student outcomes in new literacies across subject domains. The framework also defines and organizes constructs that comprise the model of student outcomes to test. Although our project applied the framework to design new literacy assessments in science and math, the framework clearly addresses outcomes commonly called out in frameworks for other academic domains, such as reading. For example, the PISA reading literacy framework includes aspects of reading such as forming a broad understanding of text, retrieving information, developing an interpretation, and reflecting on the content, structure, and form of a text. The ICT framework strategies for identifying needed and given information, posing questions, accessing and organizing information, understanding and comparing information, inferring trends and patterns, and evaluating relevance and credibility of information all relate to these aspects of reading in the PISA reading literacy framework. Similarly, the ICT framework's strategies for communicating findings, ideas, and arguments are relevant to writing frameworks for generating persuasive and informational text and in broader communication contexts involving collaboration among distributed partners.

Designs and Prototypes of Technology-Enhanced Assessments

In this next section, we describe ways in which the designs of assessments of new literacies can build on extant designs of assessments *of* technology skills, in which knowledge and use of technologies are the focus, as well as the few examples of assessments of learning *with* technology, in which academic domain knowledge and skills (e.g., math and science) are the focus and technologies such a calculators, graphing tools, and modeling tools are used to help solve problems. Analyses of assessment examples revealed the student constructs that are tested directly and potential constructs, types, and features of assessment tasks that could be incorporated into designs of student and task models for richer, multidimensional assessments.

Designs of Assessments of Technology

Assessments *of* technology target students' abilities to operate and deploy technologies in basic and advanced problems. Typically, the assessment designs limit the content required to familiar background knowledge or to well-taught, well-learned domain knowledge. Generally, the assessments address relatively basic ICT skills. The assessment formats may be paper-based or brief performance tasks.

A number of international, national, and state assessments test basic procedures required to use common Internet and productivity tools in simple, applied problems. The tests are typically designed to certify basic technology skills in school or in the workplace. Within the Coordinated ICT Assessment Framework, these assessments tend to emphasize declarative knowledge about the features and functions of tools and procedural knowledge for performing steps to operate the tools. For example, the International Computer Driving License, in use in more than 140 countries, tests competence in common computer applications and basic information technology concepts (see http://www.acs.org.au/icdl). These basic skills tests can be implemented across vendor platforms to test baseline technical competencies such as managing files, spreadsheets, databases, word processing, and presentations. A similar international technology test, the Internet and Computing Core Certification (IC3), has been developed for Microsoft Windows platforms.

Recently, PISA conducted a feasibility study of ICT literacy assessments (Lennon et al., 2003). Six tasks were developed to test students' abilities to access, manage, integrate, evaluate, construct, and communicate in tasks labeled *e-mail*, *database*, *Web abstract*, *Web search*, and *simulation*. The task designs varied the problem contexts, the ICT processes, and the technology environments. ICT knowledge and skills generally related to declarative and procedural knowledge.

A few assessments of students' abilities to use technology tools test more than basic technical skills. As part of an evaluation of the World Links for Development (WorLD) program funded by the World Bank, SRI developed sets of performance assessments requiring use of technology in brief, project-based learning activities (Quellmalz, 1987; Quellmalz & Zalles, 1998). The student performance assessments were to serve as outcome measures in an evaluation of the WorLD program in developing countries and also as models for the design of new assessments tailored to specific technology-enhanced curricular programs within the participating countries. The assessments provided evidence of secondary students' proficiencies in technology use, reasoning with information, and communication—student outcomes specified by the WorLD program. These proficiencies served as the student models for the WorLD assessments. The performance-assessment task designs employed an integrated problem-based structure (Quellmalz & Hoskyn, 1997). The approach reflected research and best practice on promoting higher order reasoning and communication strategies within a project-based learning paradigm (Quellmalz, 1987; Collins, Brown, & Newman, 1989). A modular-design task model was developed to allow the subject matter, technologies, tasks, and questions to be tailored to varying levels of technology implementation and integration in school curricula in the participating countries. The assessments were also fashioned to be widely applicable across the range of World Links for Development implementations.

A field test of one set of the tasks with 200 WorLD and non-WorLD students in Uganda revealed advantages in reasoning and communication for WorLD students who had opportunities to experience ICT in their schools (Quellmalz & Zalles, 2001). The field test also provided data supporting the discriminative validity of the performance assessments and acceptable levels of raters' agreement on use of the scoring rubrics.

In a project for the U.S. Department of Education, prototype online performance-assessment tasks were designed to assess Internet-research skills, reasoning, and communication (Means, Penuel, & Quellmalz, 2000). The performance assessments of technology use were developed and pilot tested with middle-school students in the United States (Quellmalz & Zalles, 2002; Zalles & Yarnall, 2000; see http://ipat.sri.com). The tasks were intended to serve as models that could be used or adapted by evaluators or teachers in Department of Education programs such as Technology Challenge Grants and Preparing Tomorrow's Teachers to Use Technology.

ISTE and Microsoft have developed a set of twelve 30-minute performance tasks for grade-eight students to test the NETS standards for analysis, production, and communication. The assessment battery is available on the ISTE Web site and tests abilities to perform applied tasks using Microsoft Office productivity applications (http://www.iste.org/resources/asmt/msiste).

We referred to the features of the assessments developed by others and the ICT skills they aimed to measure as we created the student, task, and evidence models for the innovative, prototype ICT assessments we developed for the NSF ICT project.

Designs of Assessments of Learning with Technology

The designs of assessments of new literacies, as just described, are few and differ markedly from each other. We propose that the development of innovative assessments of new literacies should be grounded in systematic methods and the learning and measurement sciences; such an approach is likely to increase the validity and technical qualities of any assessment. Evidence-centered design principles can shape assessments of new literacies according to a coherent and systematic process.

The evidence-centered design approach is being applied by SRI and the University of Maryland in a 5-year project, Principled Assessment Designs for Inquiry (PADI; see http://padi.sri.com), funded by the Interagency Education Research Initiative. The project is devoted to the development of a conceptual framework and a collection of development resources, including an online design system, to support the design of assessments of science inquiry (Riconscente, Mislevy, Hamel, & PADI Research Group, 2005). Drawing on the expertise of a multidisciplinary team, the project advances an evidence-centered approach to assessment design to demonstrate the relevance of its principles to all types of assessment. PADI provides assessment-design structures that are aimed specifically at the development of assessments of science inquiry (Baxter & Mislevy, 2005).

The PADI project uses an object-modeling approach to software design, innovative technologies, and powerful measurement methods in its components, including (a) an online system for developing reusable assessment-task templates, organized around schemas of inquiry from research in cognitive psychology and science education; (b) generally stated rubrics for recognizing and evaluating evidence of inquiry skills; (c) an organized set of assessment development resources; (d) an initial collection of design patterns, and exemplar task templates produced in the context of the BioKIDS, FOSS, and GLOBE projects; and (e) a statistical model that will support rigorous analyses of student learning. Researchers involved with the three curriculum projects have been using the PADI system to design assessments that incorporate technologies in some of their instructional and assessment tasks. The PADI system and software are being readied to support the design of a wide range of assessments in various domains. In the following section, we apply evidence-centered design principles to the design of ICT assessments.

Principled assessment designs for new literacies would identify and relate important components of the assessment argument: (a) the student model—what knowledge and skills to test, (b) the task model—the types of tasks that will elicit the knowledge and skills, and (c) the evidence model—the evidence to be used to support the argument that the proficiencies have been achieved.

ICT Assessment Student Models

Our reviews of research on learning with technology, alignments of technology, and subject matter standards and frameworks, and the studies of technology implementation in schools (as summarized earlier in the chapter) were the bases for the student knowledge and skills (student model) specified in the Coordinated ICT Assessment Framework.

ICT Assessment Task Models

The analyses of technology use in schools and technology-based curricula yielded features to build into assessment task models to elicit evidence of student proficiencies in ICT. We applied the innovative performance-assessment design approach we had developed in previous SRI national and international projects that aimed to measure students' 21st-century skills. From these projects emerged the Integrative Performance Assessments in Technology (IPAT) design approach, which extended the problem-based, modular design (Quellmalz & Hinojosa, 2000). The aim of IPAT (see http://ipat.sri.com) was to further develop an assessment-design framework of modular components that could provide "templates" or task models for new or modified assessments addressing similar outcome areas. The IPAT design approach provides a framework for structuring key components or modules of the assessment. The IPAT task template incorporates modules specifying the problem posed for an academic or applied area, the technology tools (e.g., Web tools and productivity tools), the types of reasoning and problem-solving strategies (e.g., analysis, comparison, inference, evaluation), and the communication form (e.g., report, letter, presentation). The IPAT design includes a research-based, problem-based activity flow: posing an authentic problem, gathering relevant information and data, analyzing and interpreting information and data, and communicating findings and conclusions (Quellmalz, 1987). IPAT assessment prototypes were designed according to templates or authoring shells that could be used or adapted by evaluators and teachers to customize the materials, presentation, and work products that are aligned with the content and skills that have been taught.

The modular structure of the assessment task components allows assessments to be tailored to the examinee population. Features of the task models can be varied by adding or deleting a module (if students are inexperienced with technologies required in a module, for example) or by varying the task complexity within a module, while maintaining the logical flow of the problem-solving activities. One IPAT assessment model presents modules in which students conduct research on the Internet; gather relevant information; use reasoning strategies to analyze and interpret the information; use productivity tools such as graphics programs, word processors, and presentation tools; and communicate findings.

For our NSF assessment project, we applied the IPAT generic design to develop more extensive prototype ICT assessments. Our assessment development efforts addressed two quite different assessment purposes. One purpose was to develop ICT performance assessments *of* technology skills that could be administered as one component of the design proposed for SITES Module 3. That design called for school, teacher, and student surveys of technology use, as well as administration of an ICT performance assessment to a small sample of students in classes who had passed a paper-and-pencil technology test intended to screen students for familiarity with basic operations of technology tools. These problem-driven ICT performance assessments were developed according to the Coordinated ICT Assessment Framework and designed

For this prototype, the science and mathematics required were well-taught, well-learned material.

Questions and tasks within modules in this prototype were designed to capture student responses dynamically as they employ ICT strategies to accomplish a subtask by using various technologies. First, the problem is presented and hypothetical student team members from another school who will be virtual collaborative partners are introduced.

- Module 1 assesses ICT planning strategies through questions and tasks for analyzing the problem by examining data on hare and lynx populations, while selecting from a set of technology tools. Module 1 assesses collaborative planning through tasks and questions in which the student uses e-mail to examine hare and lynx population data sent by virtual team members. Evidence of skills in operating the technology tools is a by-product of students' use of the tools in the problem-solving tasks.

- Assessment of strategies for using technology to access and organize information is tested in Module 2 in a series of tasks in which the student formulates a search query, gathers information and data from Web pages, and organizes them in a table. Critical evaluation, tested throughout the modules, is assessed by questions on the credibility of information from a Web report produced by a fur trading company and by questions on the effectiveness of Web-search results.

- Module 3 assesses the ICT strategies for using technologies to represent and transform information and data. Questions and tasks ask students to convert data sent in an e-mail text message by virtual collaborators to data on a spreadsheet and then transform the data into a graph.

- Module 4 tests the ICT strategies for using technologies for analysis and interpretation of information and data. Questions and tasks ask students to read specified data presented in tables and graphs and to interpret trends.

- Module 5 tests analysis and interpretation by using a modeling tool that displays the pattern of hare and lynx populations. Students answer questions about output of the model at specified years, predict trends, and manipulate population values in the model to test predictions.

- In Module 6, uses of ICT strategies and technologies for planning a presentation and communicating findings and results are tested. Questions and tasks ask students to develop a plan that specifies a recommendation for reintroducing lynx into the park. The recommendation is to be supported by data and evidence students gather from Web searches. Students are asked to prepare a presentation by using a word processor or presentation tool and appropriate graphics and charts. The presentation is evaluated according to the quality of the argument and its organization. Module 6 also assesses critical evaluation by asking students to critique a presentation prepared by another group. Students are asked to prepare their critique and send it electronically to the other group.

This predator-prey scenario describes one prototype that has been developed using the IPAT modular design. The task model variables for the modules can be changed to adjust the complexity of the problem and the cognitive demands of the tasks and technologies. Each module was designed to allow students to select appropriate tools. Modules can be combined in various ways to accommodate time and logistical constraints. Since the prototypes are delivered over the Web or by CD, the configuration of modules for an administration can be tailored for different needs.

Students' responses to questions and tasks can be captured electronically. Because the responses are recorded as students are in the midst of problem solving, the ICT performance assessments can provide a rich set of data on students' problem-solving and technology proficiency. As in previous IPAT projects (Quellmalz & Zalles, 2002), scores (evidence model) can be reported for ICT strategies and for tool use. Rubrics have been developed to rate the quality and appropriateness of student responses. Rater training and standardized online scoring procedures were developed to establish and maintain interrater reliability. In pilot testing of the prototypes, "think-alouds" and subsequent cognitive analyses were used to examine the thinking and reasoning students employed related to the ICT strategies, domain content and processes, and operation of technology tools. Analyses of these data provide preliminary evidence of each assessment's content and construct validity.

Examples of Designs and Prototypes of Assessments in Math and Science with Technology

Another task in our NSF ICT assessment project was to draw on the Coordinated ICT Assessment Framework and the modular-design approach to fashion prototype performance assessments that would tap transformative uses of learning *with* technology in advanced science and mathematics (e.g., visualizations, modeling). These prototypes could be used as models for teachers and evaluators to assess student learning in innovative technology-supported curricula.

One prototype was designed to test the ability of two classes of high-school physics students to apply the laws of motion to solve an authentic problem (designing a freeway car crash barrier) with a widely used commercial modeling tool, *Interactive Physics*. The student model variables included: (a) physics concepts related to force, mass, acceleration, and velocity; (b) ICT inquiry strategies for planning/design, conduct of investigations (running the simulation), analysis and interpretation (of acceleration and velocity graphs), evaluation of possible design solutions, and communication of a recommendation; and (c) technology proficiencies related to using the modeling tool, graphing tool, and presentation tools. The task model consisted of a series of modules in which students planned their design, iteratively predicted and tried out designs using the simulation, interpreted results, evaluated a proposed design, and developed a presentation for their recommended design. The evidence model produced scores for student work related to physics knowledge, the component inquiry skills, and technology use. Cognitive analyses of teacher and student responses during the tasks provided initial content and construct validity evidence.

Another prototype designed according to the IPAT modular-design approach tested a student model for secondary students to solve an applied problem by using a widely available commercial visualization tool, *ArcView*. The student model included: (a) science and math knowledge; (b) inquiry skills for planning and conducting investigations, analyzing and interpreting data, and communicating recommendations; and (c) technology use. The task model involved presentation of the problem (Which states meet requirements to apply for solar power funds?); accessing, analyzing, and combining visualizations of different types of data (for solar energy); interpreting data; and presenting a recommendation. The evidence model consisted of scores for the three outcome areas and their components.

In two other ongoing NSF projects, SRI is applying and extending these systematic-design approaches for the assessment of new literacies in math and science. In these projects, we are designing performance assessments of students' learning *with* technology. In *Calipers: Using Simulations to Assess Complex Science Learning*, we are using the principles of evidence-centered design to create assessments that can measure two significant science standards (student model) not well addressed in paper-based tests: understanding of interrelated concepts (schematic-knowledge structures) and the ability to use inquiry strategies in extended, problem-based tasks (Quellmalz et al., in press). The Calipers assessments focus on the capacity of the technology to present a complex environment and to allow the students to interact with multiple aspects and phenomena in order to probe structural, dynamic, and causal aspects of the system. The task model describes the dimensions of the simulated-domain environment, sets of task activities and questions, and the format of anticipated student responses. For example, the template on the survival requirements of species in an ecosystem identifies which components of the simulation environment need to be specified, such as type of ecosystem, number and type of moving species, type of food for consumption, and abiotic factors and time changes that affect rate of growth of food and health of the species. In addition, the template identifies formats for questions and tasks designed to assess the dynamic interactions in an environment that could not be captured by traditional paper-based test formats.

The evidence models for Calipers templates specify the scoring criteria that will be used to evaluate student responses to the explicit questions and prompts identified in the task model and how scores are combined. The project classifies these questions according to the concepts, the interrelationships, and the inquiry strategies they test. We will extract and combine student responses into these knowledge and strategy types. Rubrics will be used for rater training and evaluation of student work by teachers to generate scores on the assessment items and tasks. The project aims to contribute principled design methods and benchmark performance-assessment exemplars using appropriate simulation environments under student control to measure complex science understanding and reasoning.

In another NSF funded project, Using Geoscience Data Sets for Inquiry, SRI is collaborating with Concord Consortium to design curriculum models and performance assessments in which secondary-level students address important geoscience problems requiring use of real data sets and visualizations (Zalles, Quellmalz, & Gobert, 2006). Standards addressed (student model) include geoscience concepts, inquiry abilities in NSES (NRC, 1996) and in *Benchmarks for Science Literacy* (AAAS, 1993), NCTM standards (NCTM, 2000), 21st-century skills, and technology proficiencies (ISTE, 2000). We are developing design principles, task templates, and prototypes for technology-based performance assessments in Earth science.

The prototype performance assessments described above exemplify the use of the general evidence-centered design approach. The Coordinated ICT Assessment Framework shaped the student models; the IPAT modular design shaped the task models. In addition, evidence models were developed to provide scores for new literacies required to access, manage, investigate, analyze, interpret, and communicate. The problems and component tasks take advantage of the affordances of technology tools to support the problem-solving processes. Some of the assessment tasks could not have been accomplished without the technologies. Many of the assessment tasks required strategic use of the technologies—that is, knowing when and how to deploy them to solve problem components. We suggest that the use of a principled assessment-design approach can offer a powerful strategy for designing assessments *of* technology and of learning *with* technology. Such an approach involves (a) a framework that allows coordination of new literacy knowledge and skills across programs and disciplinary areas; (b) assessment task models that take advantage of modular components to integrate technologies into assessment activities; and (c) evidence models that extract data for multiple proficiencies.

Next Steps

The development of assessments of new literacies is in its early stages. Multiple frameworks, contexts, and points of view both invigorate and complicate design efforts. Educators differ as to whether or not technology should be assessed as a distinct domain (Quellmalz & Kozma, 2003). Expert panels need to reach consensus on the knowledge and skills that constitute new literacy skills and how those skills align with the knowledge and skills in subject-matter frameworks and standards (*student model*). Research is needed on how to design tasks that integrate the use of technologies into subject matter tests (*task model*) and how to directly test, extract, and report the skill with which technologies are operated and strategically used (*evidence model*). Experts need to identify the features and functions of technologies that are relevant to academic and 21st-century constructs of interest as well as those features that need to be controlled because they interfere with performance on targeted knowledge and skills. Studies are needed to examine student performance on items and tasks in which technology is assumed to enhance or hinder performance.

Educators also differ as to whether or not there are general ICT processes that pertain across applications of technologies in domains (Quellmalz & Kozma, 2003). Studies could ask expert panels to align what are thought to be cross-cutting items with ICT and subject-matter frameworks to judge, for example, whether an item that tests evaluation of the credibility of a source (an ICT skill) is also classified as a reading skill. Empirical studies could compare student performance on items aligned with ICT strategies and items aligned with problem solving in subject-matter frameworks. Cognitive analyses of student reasoning in problems involving use of technologies could reveal the extent to which students' thinking involves selecting, operating, and manipulating the technology and the role technology plays in solving the problem presented.

Work with technology-based assessments that scaffold learning and performance in complex tasks while adapting to student responses is in its early stages. Research on ways that these adaptive modules can serve as formative and summative assessments is greatly needed. Changes in scaffolding would be features that are varied in the task model of an assessment. Research would examine how changes in the scaffolding levels of assessment task designs relate to student performance. Such efforts would provide the field with interdisciplinary ICT assessment frameworks, principled assessment designs, exemplary assessments, and evidence of their validity.

We advocate that the design of assessments of new literacies follow a systematic, evidence-centered design approach. The framework that defines the student model should clearly specify desired knowledge and skills and document their relationship to research and best practice. The types of assessment tasks designed according to features of a task model should be clearly representative of significant types of classroom, applied, or workplace activities in which students have learned to use technologies. Tasks designed for summative purposes are likely to develop task models of technology use in defined environments. For example, summative assessments of skills related to Internet search and evaluation of credible sources are likely to deliberately limit and define the Web sites and the Web-site features to search, so that scoring rubrics to evaluate the quality of searches can anticipate the range of possible search options. Formative assessments of the same skills could allow students more leeway to search a variety of sites, with scoring guidelines applied by teachers to the broader array of possible appropriate responses. Studies relating opportunity to learn about and with technologies should be conducted along with assessments of students' abilities to use the technologies in similar ways and contexts. Soon, The design system developed in the PADI project is available to offer online support or the development of assessments of technology and of learning *with* technology.

New assessments of the new literacies related to ICT use should routinely collect evidence of their validity and reliability. Prototype assessments can document qualitative reviews of their content validity. Prototype assessments that are pilot-tested with small student samples can include cognitive laboratories in which students think aloud as they respond to assessment items and tasks. Cognitive analyses of students' thinking can provide some documentation of the content and construct validity of the assessments. It will be important to study how students orchestrate their knowledge and manipulations of technology as they engage in extended problem-based tasks. These small-scale tryouts can also allow refinement of scoring rubrics and rater training procedures, and documentation of interrater agreement. Assessments ready for larger-scale administrations should collect data needed to document their validity and reliability. In these large-scale studies, research will be needed to compare the types of student understanding and problem solving elicited in technology-based tasks that can also be paper based. Also needed are studies of the types of student learning that can be assessed only in technology-based tasks (e.g., model-based reasoning).

Currently, there are few examples and studies of students using a variety of technologies in extended, problem-based tasks. Studies of how students choose and use technologies strategically would inform questions about the kinds of higher order thinking and transfer employed. Studies of how the technologies represent complex, hard-to-understand phenomena and support interactive inquiry will be important. Expert panels could be asked to judge the alignment of the content and cognitive demand of technology-enhanced items and tasks with the more challenging standards in academic standards and frameworks. Cognitive interviews could investigate whether items elicit deeper, more connected knowledge and hard-to-measure inquiry and communication skills. Findings from expert panel reviews that show critical-thinking skills are being addressed, along with evidence of achievement of challenging academic standards and 21st-century skills will be powerful tools to convince policymakers that technologies must be incorporated in 21st-century curricula and assessments. If technologies are transforming learning, evidence of how new assessments document the transformations will be necessary. Consequently, just as technologies are fundamentally changing learning, they will also fundamentally transform our assessments of learning.

References

Adelman, N., Donnelly, M. B., Dove, T., Tiffany-Morales, J., Wayne, A., & Zucker, A. (2002). *The integrated studies of educational technology: Professional development and teachers' use of technology.* Washington, DC: SRI International.

American Association for the Advancement of Science. (1993). *Benchmarks for science literacy.* New York: Oxford University Press.

American Educational Research Association, American Psychological Association, & National Council on Measurement in Education. (1999). *Standards for educational and psychological testing.* Washington, DC: Author.

Bachelard, G. (1984). *The new scientific spirit.* Boston: Beacon.

Baxter, G. P., & Glaser, R. (1998). The cognitive complexity of science performance assessments. *Educational Measurement: Issues and Practice, 17*(3), 37–45.

Baxter, G., & Mislevy, R. J. (2005). *The case for an integrated design framework for assessing science inquiry* (PADI Technical Report No. 5). Menlo Park, CA: SRI International.

Becker, H. J. (1999). *Internet use by teachers* (Report No. 1). Irvine, CA: Center for Research on Information Technology and Organizations. Retrieved April 2, 2002, from http://www.crito.uci.edu/TLC/FINDINGS/internet-use/

Bennett, R. E., Jenkins, F., Persky, H., & Weiss, A. (2003). Assessing complex problem solving performances. *Assessment in Education, 10,* 347–373.

Bracewell, R., Breuleux, A., Laferriere, T., Benoit, J., & Abdous, M. (1998). *The emerging contribution of online resources and tools to classroom learning and teaching.* Vancouver, BC: TeleLearning Network Inc.

Bransford, J., Brown, A., & Cocking, R. (2000). *How people learn: Brain, mind, experience, and school.* Washington, DC: National Academy Press.

Burns, T. C., & Ungerleider, C. S. (2002). Information and communication technologies in elementary and secondary education. *International Journal of Educational Policy, Research, & Practice, 3*(4), 27–54.

Coley, R. J., Cradler, J., & Engel, P. K. (1999). *Computers and classrooms: The status of technology in U.S. schools.* Princeton, NJ: Educational Testing Service, Policy Information Center.

Collins, A., Brown, J. S., & Newman, S. E. (1989). Cognitive apprenticeship: Teaching the crafts of reading, writing, and mathematics. In L. B. Resnick (Ed.), *Knowing, learning and instruction: Essays in honor of Robert Glaser* (pp. 453–494). Hillsdale, NJ: Lawrence Erlbaum.

Crawford, V., & Toyama, Y. (2002). *Assessment of student technology proficiency and an analysis of the need for technology proficiency assessments: A review of state approaches.* Paper presented at the annual meeting of the American Educational Research Association, New Orleans, LA.

European Commission. (2000). *eEurope: An information society for all.* Brussels: Author.

Gobert, J., & Clement, J. (1999). Effect of student-generated diagrams versus student-generated summaries of conceptual understanding of causal and dynamic knowledge in plate tectonics. *Journal of Research in Science Teaching, 36*(1), 39–53.

Haertel, G. D., Lash, A., Javitz, H., & Quellmalz, E. (2006). *An instructional sensitivity study of science inquiry items from three large-scale science examinations.* Paper presented at the annual meeting of the American Educational Research Association, San Francisco, CA.

Holland, J. H. (1995). *Hidden order: How adaptation builds complexity.* New York: Addison-Wesley.

International Society for Technology in Education [ISTE]. (2000). *National educational technology standards for students: Connecting curriculum and technology.* Eugene, OR: Author.

Koomen, M. (2006). *The development and implementation of a computer-based assessment of science literacy in PISA 2006.* Paper presented at the annual meeting of the American Educational Research Association, San Francisco, CA.

Kozma, R. (2003). *Technology, innovation, and educational change: A global perspective.* Eugene, OR: International Society for Technology in Education.

Kozma, R., McGhee, R., Quellmalz, E., & Zalles, D. (2004). Closing the digital divide: Evaluation of world links. *International Journal of Educational Development, 24*(4), 361–381.

Lennon, M., Kirsch, I., Von Davier, M., Wagner, M., & Yamamoto, K. (2003). *Feasibility study for the PISA ICT literacy assessment.* Princeton, NJ: Educational Testing Service.

McFarlane, A. E., Harrison, C., Somekh, B., Scrimshaw, P., Harrison, A., & Lewin, C. (2000). *ImpacT2 project preliminary study 1: Establishing the relationship between networked technology and attainment.* Coventry, U.K.: British Educational Communications and Technology Agency.

Means, B., & Olson, K. (1995). *Technology's role in educational reform: Findings from a national study of innovating schools.* Menlo Park, CA: SRI International.

Means, B., Penuel, B., & Quellmalz, E. (2000). Developing assessments for tomorrow's classrooms. In W. Heineke & L. Blasi (Eds.), *Research methods for educational technology* (pp. 149–160). Greenwich, CT: Information Age Publishing.

Messick, S. (1994). The interplay of evidence and consequences in the validation of performance assessments. *Educational Researcher, 32,* 13–23.

Mislevy, R. J., Chudowsky, N., Draney, K., Fried, R., Gaffney, T., Haertel, G., et al. (2003). *Design patterns for assessing science inquiry* (PADI Technical Report 1). Menlo Park, CA: SRI International, Center for Technology in Learning.

National Council of Teachers of Mathematics. (2000). *Principles and standards for school mathematics.* Reston, VA: Author.

National Research Council. (1996). *National science education standards.* Washington DC: National Academy Press.

Organization for Economic Co-operation and Development. (2000a). *Measuring student knowledge and skills: The PISA 2000 assessment of reading, mathematical, and scientific literacy.* Paris: Author.

Organization for Economic Co-operation and Development. (2000b). *Survey of ICT concepts and skills* (Field version 1c). Paris: OECD Publications Service.

Partnership for 21st Century Skills. (2005). *Assessment of 21st century skills: The current landscape.* Tucson, AZ: Author.

Pea, R. D. (1993). Practices of distributed intelligence and designs for education. In G. S. Salomon (Ed.), *Distributed cognitions: Psychological and educational considerations* (pp. 47–87). Cambridge, U.K.: Cambridge University Press.

Pelgrum, W., & Anderson, R. (1999). *ICT and the emerging paradigm for life long learning: A worldwide educational assessment of infrastructure, goals, and practices.* Amsterdam: International Association for the Evaluation of Educational Achievement.

Pellegrino, J., Chudowsky, N., & Glaser, R. (2001). *Knowing what students know: The science and design of educational assessment.* Washington, DC: National Academy Press.

Quellmalz, E. S. (1987). Developing reasoning skills. In J. R. Baron & R. J. Sternberg (Eds.), *Teaching thinking skills: Theory and practice* (pp. 86–105). New York: W. H. Freeman.

Quellmalz, E. S., & Haertel, G. (2004, May). *Technology supports for state science assessment systems.* Paper commissioned by the National Research Council Committee on Test Design for K–12 Science Achievement. Washington, DC: National Research Council.

Quellmalz, E. S., & Haydel, A. M. (2002). *Using cognitive analysis to study the validities of science inquiry assessments.* Paper presented at the annual meeting of the American Educational Research Association, New Orleans, LA.

Quellmalz, E., & Hinojosa, T. (2000). *Technology supported assessment of technology proficiency—Assessment frameworks.* Paper presented at the annual meeting of the American Educational Research Association, New Orleans, LA.

Quellmalz, E. S., & Hoskyn, J. (1997). Classroom assessment of reasoning strategies. In G. D. Phye (Ed.), *Handbook of classroom assessment* (pp. 103–130). San Diego, CA: Academic Press.

Quellmalz, E. S., & Kozma, R. (2003). Designing assessments of learning with technology. *Assessment in Education, 10*(3), 389–407.

Quellmalz, E. S., & Kreikemeier, P. (2004). *Testing the alignment of items to the NSES inquiry standards.* Paper presented at the annual meeting of the American Educational Research Association, San Diego, CA.

Quellmalz, E. S., & Zalles, D. (1998). *World Links student assessment, 1998–1999 report.* Menlo Park, CA: SRI International.

Quellmalz, E. S., & Zalles, D. (2001). *World links for development: Student assessment Uganda field test, 2000.* Menlo Park, CA: SRI International.

Quellmalz, E. S., & Zalles, D. (2002). *Designing technology assessments: Cognitive-based modular design.* Paper presented at the annual meeting of the American Educational Research Association, New Orleans, LA.

Quellmalz, E. S., DeBarger, A. H., Haertel, G., Schank, P., Buckley, B. C., Gobert, J., et al. (in press). Exploring the role of technology-based simulations in science assessment: The Calipers project. In C. Stearns & J. Coffey (Eds.), *Science assessment: research and practical approaches for classroom teachers, school administrators, and school districts.* Washington, DC: National Science Teachers Association.

Riconscente, M., Mislevy, R. J., Hamel, L., & PADI Research Group. (2005). *An introduction to task templates.* (PADI Technical Report No. 5). Menlo Park, CA: SRI International.

Roschelle, J., Kaput, J., & Stroup, W. (2000). SimCalc: Accelerating students' engagement with the mathematics of change. In M. J. Jacobson & R. B. Kozma (Eds.), *Innovations in science and mathematics education: Advanced designs for technologies of learning* (pp. 47–75). Mahwah, NJ: Lawrence Erlbaum.

Shechtman, N., Roschelle, J., Haertel, G., Tatar, D., & Knudsen, J. (2005). *Measuring student gains in conceptual mathematics in scaling a technological intervention for middle school mathematics.* Paper presented at the annual meeting of the American Educational Research Association, Montreal, Canada.

U.S. Department of Education. (1996). *Getting America's students ready for the 21st century: Meeting the technology literacy challenge.* Washington, DC: U.S. Government Printing Office.

Venezky, R. L., & Davis, C. (2002). *Quo vademus? The transformation of schooling in a networked world.* Paris: Organization for Economic Co-operation and Development.

Wenglinski, H. (1998). *Does it compute? The relationship between educational technology and student achievement in mathematics.* Princeton, NJ: Educational Testing Service.

Zalles, D. R., & Vahey, P. (2005) *Assessing foundational data literacy.* Menlo Park, CA: SRI International.

Zalles, D., & Vahey, P. (2006, April). *Teaching and assessing foundational data literacy.* Paper delivered at annual meeting of the American Educational Research Association, San Franciso, CA.

Zalles, D., & Yarnall, L. (2000). *Using online tools to assess students' research and communication skills.* Paper presented at the Center for Innovative Learning Technologies Conference, Washington, DC.

Zalles, D. R., Quellmalz, E., & Gobert, J. (2006). *Inquiring with geoscience datasets: Instruction and assessment.* Paper presented at annual meeting of the American Geophysical Union, San Francisco, CA.

CHAPTER 33

Learning Management Systems and Virtual Learning Environments

A Higher-Education Focus

COLIN BASKIN
and NEIL ANDERSON
JAMES COOK UNIVERSITY, AUSTRALIA

Learning Management Systems and the Global Client Community

The e-mail arrived like all others, but came with the weight of expectation. Why would the presidents and CEOs of the world's two largest proprietary e-learning systems be issuing a joint e-mail? It began fairly innocuously: "We are writing you today directly to communicate some momentous news. Earlier today, WebCT and Blackboard signed a formal agreement expressing our intent to merge our companies" (Blackboard, 2005). It continued,

> This decision is one that has been made based on careful consideration by both entities. We believe that this union will have a positive impact on the global e-Learning community and on the individual clients of both companies. We want to communicate the rationale behind the merger and to provide some of the early details on what this news means for you. (Blackboard, 2005)

This proposed merger would leverage "the best of Blackboard and WebCT," to deliver an "improved online learning experience" in a single global company (read, community of practice) comprising "some of the brightest, most experienced talent in the e-Learning industry" (Blackboard, 2005). This would include redevelopment of both "Blackboard and WebCT products,

WebCT Vista and WebCT Campus Edition, and Blackboard Academic Suite and Blackboard Commerce Suite" with a "futures' orientation" (Blackboard, 2005). Expected to be finalized early in 2006, this in-principle agreement extols greater centralization and standardization within the proprietary e-learning community. It is also a useful point at which to commence this discussion on learning management systems and virtual learning environments in the higher education (HE) sector.

That higher education is facing the prospect of a single proprietary provider of learning management systems (LMS) and virtual learning environments (VLEs) with an express vision to "actively engage industry standards efforts" is a double-edged sword. The joint proprietors are sure the merger is a good thing. When this vision is underpinned by a mission to "develop common standards-based APIs, based on Building Blocks and PowerLinks" that enable "existing product lines to interoperate with one another" combining "the best features and usability characteristics from the two product lines into a new, standards-based product set" then benefits must surely accrue (Blackboard, 2005). Yet, we are compelled to ask, "Who benefits?" Downes (2005) raised the specter of the "digital native," that sometimes "n-gen" referent who not only approaches life, work, and play at "twitch speed," but who is busy changing the very nature of markets, in particular information and communication technology (ICT) markets (p. 2). These "smart markets" are more informed, more organized; people in these markets deliver far better information and support to each other than vendors can possibly provide. In the context of learning, Downes conceded, "[T]hese (emerging) trends are manifest in what is sometimes called 'learner-centered' or 'student-centered' design, which are essentially issues about the control of learning itself" (p. 2). Herein lays a compelling contest over the future of the LMS. John Hall (2003), from Oracle University, set the development of the LMS on a parallel track with other large-scale enterprise implementations—for example enterprise resource planning (ERP), customer relationship management (CRM), and supply chain management (SCM; p. 1). George Siemens (2004b) and Stephen Downes saw the LMS differently, spawned not by an emerging sense of management order, but conceived out of knowledge workers' shared sense of chaos, and the need for an end-user flexibility and control to move in paths driven by learning needs, and not by LMS design.

The material effects of a proprietary merger are compelling; bringing the e-learning community together "to broaden access to shared expertise, reusable technologies, faculty and developer networks" and for the promotion of "exemplary course programs" transforms a distributed network of e-learners into a "global client community" (Blackboard, 2005). This kind of digital rhetoric foregrounds the use of VLEs and locates learners, lecturers, and pedagogues as "users" of such technologies. The user label is an interesting one; it is an expression of a broader set of social relations, encompassing service-level relationships based on identified client needs. The good thing about being a client is that someone else works to meet your ICT needs for an agreed-upon fee. The problem with being a client is that clients are "done to" and "done for"; they are not expected to impose themselves on the technology but are much more expected to have the technology imposed on them. LMS technology is at risk here—at risk of becoming utilitarian, despite the fact that there may be more people than ever before accessing institutional learning through proprietary e-learning systems. The real challenge for e-learning systems is to deliver a VLE/LMS whose use will be inspired rather than patterned, proactive rather than reactive, and creative rather than reproductive. This chapter takes account of this challenge and points to areas within contemporary research that open productive intersections for a new social discourse on e-learning systems applications and development.

From the Global to the Local

E-learning has been around for approximately 10 years (Downes, 2005). It brackets ICT integration in education with contemporary changes in society, in which technology is the root cause of social evolution and the primary motivator for the digitization of education (Sasseville, 2004). ICTs are therefore considered powerful tools of social change, as they not only bring about changes in the way we deal with information, but also challenge how we think and how we view our world. The mere fact that new learning technologies enable greater access to information imbues this information with the joint qualities of being "technical" as well as "scientific." It is searchable, retrievable, and describable; it can be interrogated, amended, contested, disputed, and conscripted. It is "out there" in an objective sense—each piece a fractal, a potential learning object to be put together and organized for the purposes of learning delivery (Downes, 2005). The dominant platform for the delivery of e-learning is the World Wide Web, and the dominant mode of delivery the online course. The corollary of this is the need for a mechanism to manage such delivery; in its least structured form this would be a simple VLE or LMS, depending on which hemisphere and continent you come from. For some in education, a Web quest fits this definition of a learning organizer: for others, nothing but an enterprise solution would suffice. For the purposes of this discussion, both terms are used interchangeably, although this does not deny that some VLE/LMS solutions can be simple in composition, while others can be quite complex and elaborate (Baskin & Anderson, 2003a; Shaw & McCauley, 2003). The main "client" relationship featured in this kind of system is that of learner and learning provider, with a clear emphasis placed on core learning functions built around

- controlled access to curriculum that has been "chunked" for discrete assessment and reporting;
- tracking student activity and achievement against this curriculum through simple administration tools;

- a structured (learning) resource base and facilitated assessment suite;
- communication between the learner, provider, and learning technicians to support learner feedback;
- group communication suites to support collaborative learning; and
- links to parallel administrative systems, both in-house and external (Joint Information Systems Committee [JISC], 2003, p. 85–98).

An example of such a system, its core learning functions, and its "local" context of use is provided in the vignette that follows:

Melissa is a part-time student studying education at James Cook University in Cairns. One day each week she is required to travel 70 km from Mareeba on the Atherton tablelands to attend lectures for one of her subjects at the Cairns campus. Her second subject is conducted online in LearnJCU, the university-wide learning management system. She adopts a participation pattern of four entries to the site each week, and has identified this as the minimum amount of "hits" to stay abreast of course announcements, variations, updates, and just-in-time resources. This can sometimes be frustrating, as her work schedule on weekends is variable, and sometimes she just feels "too tired" to maintain the schedule. The concessions overall she believes are worth the effort; she has halved her petrol bill traveling to university each week, and her Internet costs are only $29.95 per month for broadband access ... 200 MB is plenty.

Her login ritual is straightforward; she uses a username and password to access her student gateway, enters the subject, reads all the announcements, and proceeds to the subject discussion board. Here, each week's material is laid out as an independent forum, and with 164 students in the course, there can be many threads to read through between each site visit. She has identified three fellow posters whom she thinks make more sense than the lecturer; she prioritizes their threads, and then looks for postings from her project group, which she groups chronologically, copies, and pastes to a running Microsoft Word log stored on her desktop as a record of group exchanges. She generally makes one posting or at best two, claiming that neither is particularly "earth shattering," but that each serves to let the learning community know that she is alive and participating. She then closes her Internet connection, and turns her attention to the word file on her desktop. She is working in a group project with three other students. This project involves examining the "culture" of a local school, and presenting findings in the form of a Web site for comments by other groups. Logging off the Internet she believes is a relic of times gone by, where her dial-up connection often meant the rest of the house was denied access to the telephone, while she connected to her learning materials. She understands that broadband now enables her to stay online and still take phone calls, but "old habits die hard." She opens the word file on her desktop, and completes responses to her group's requests and suggestions.

She later reconnects to the subject site, happy that connections to her broadband provider incur no dial-up costs. She notices another 15 messages have been posted to this week's discussion board, including a summary of this week's online lecture by the lecturer involved. She downloads the PDF file, saves it to her desktop, and proceeds to cut and paste her postings from her desktop document. She can always read the PDF document later.

The LMS Melissa used is essentially a piece of software that provides a standardized platform for delivering learning content in a supported and systematic way. Her local learning environment integrates with existing student and administration systems within her host university, what King (2002) described in total as a managed learning environment (MLE). She accesses learning content via the student portal, through which access to all component systems and services is provided. This includes

- built-in infrastructure and security-related features (single sign-on authentication and authorization to the portal and its component parts as separate subsystems);
- access to enterprise-wide information and services (directories, aliases, calendars, and news updates);
- group-level customization to discriminate separate services/information to defined subgroups; information "push" channels that form part of the subgroup customization; and
- individual customization facilities to support the sublevel customization efforts of users.

Learning materials manifest as folders, and folders constitute collections of files. A file is the smallest conception of a learning object, and learning objects by their very nature need to be grouped. Implicit in this modular structure of learning content is the sequencing and pacing of learning events, a form of curriculum design that contradicts Melissa's sporadic access and download patterns, and the 24/7 availability of all learning provider LMS content. Melissa defies this normalizing frame; she refuses to have the technology imposed upon her. She has determined her own login ritual and prioritizes subject announcements and discussion boards above all other VLE functionality. Within the discussion board, she identifies 3 out of a total of 163 fellow students for the collaborative value they offer her learning; none of her learning circle selections include the subject lecturer or subject tutors. Melissa's learning is strategic; she begins by building an association with her learning resources, determining the connections between LMS functionality and her perception of what needs to be learned. These associations are then integrated as a meaningful pattern of ideas, sourced by Melissa, with connections, in

benefits of generic content libraries as a first stage were obvious, primarily as just-in-time resources for the purposes of self-paced study and for cognitive apprenticeship into discourses of preference. Yet the production of generic resources for management training provided little competitive advantage to purchasing organizations; business was more interested in differentiation and the problem of being a client in the LMS supply chain was evident in early-generation libraries.

Robbins (2002) identified learning management systems as a second-generation response to organizational learning needs. With the advent of the Internet came the opportunity for interoperability; at the enterprise level this meant the LMS could be utilized to integrate functionality to enable the planning, tracking, measuring, and evaluation of employees, customers, and stakeholders. The LMS is a strategic infrastructure and essential architecture—it is a significant component of how every higher-education institution sees and positions itself in terms of its connections to local, national, and global higher-educational markets and agendas. Robbin's stage-three iteration of the LMS is the outsourced e-learning platform, a kind of e-learning intermediary popular among large textbook-publishing houses. Her culminating stage-four learning content management system was adopted by higher-education institutions, who saw this as an opportunity to consolidate and institutionalize ICTs as core practice at the enterprise level, embedded in a range of institutional practices including learning management, performance management, staff development, knowledge sourcing, knowledge sharing, knowledge dissemination, employee relations, capacity planning efforts, internal and external marketing, as well as administrative, accountability, and reporting compliance.

HE Organizations Consolidating and Institutionalizing ICTs

Like the wheel of retail, higher-education institutions have moved along the continuum from initiating ICTs in learning, to implementing ICTs for learning, toward institutionalizing ICTs as an enterprise-wide organizer for teaching and learning practices. Each of these phases can be seen, for example, in the evolution of Australian higher education, with most research (Baskin, Barker, & Woods, 2005; Bell, Bush, Nicholson, O'Brien, & Tran, 2002; McKnight et al., 2002) pointing to evidence that all institutions have moved from the implementation toward the institutionalization phase. This is no surprise, given that most ICT developments in higher education have stretched beyond experimentation, to include knowledge sharing among cohorts and groups of universities. ICTs are well and truly integrated into the mainstream operations of all 37 Australian universities. In an era of competition, this has lead to a focused and pragmatic use of ICTs to bring about consolidation and economies of scale within universities to take advantage of knowledge, dataset, and learning-object repositories. In turn, this is connected to research capacity, funding, quality, and policy imperatives—the very stuff of survival the universities in a competitive funding environment.

John Hall (2003), senior vice president of Oracle University, conceded that despite a shaky start in the 1990s, industry analysts are now bullish about enabling technologies buoyed by growing adoption rates and quick return on investment to organizations who adopt enterprise learning management system solutions. Not all drivers toward the consolidation of ICTs within higher-education institutions are demand pull; the need to professionally support and maintain a dispersed student body has largely been a demand push innovation. Innovative technology systems for student, staff, and financial support and administration form an important component of contemporary universities. These connect student to student, student to institution, and institution to institution. In some institutions, there is a visible integration of these support and administrative processes with the teaching and learning systems through the construction of member portals. Further focus on the development of university-wide knowledge/data object management systems to provide security (intellectual property and data protection), consistency, and economies (in that data/knowledge creation will not be needlessly duplicated) has seen many universities invest heavily in e-learning infrastructure and architecture. Although there is some attention to the pedagogies underlying e-learning, very often technology implementation or implementations of e-learning strategies primarily appear to be made with regard to cost and efficiency savings rather than to any commitment to improve teaching and learning from a pedagogical basis (Baskin & Anderson, 2003a).

LMSs, Teaching, and Learning

Daniel (1996) pointed to the fact that a new university would be required every week in order to sustain emerging participation rates in higher education. Given the implausibility of infrastructure growth of this kind and scope, higher-education providers have enlisted the potential of new information technologies to extend and support the administrative, research, teaching, and learning functions of the university. As universities grapple with identifying a future role for LMSs the level of practice by current academics, at large, has not delivered the "critical mass" (Rogers, 1995) of practitioners required to make adoption of new learning technologies self-sustaining. Academics are more likely to adapt LMSs for personal reasons, rather than to enhance teaching and learning (Macchiusi & Trinidad, 2000; Brennan, Miller, & Moniotte, 2001). As Macchiusi and Trinidad (2000) and Hagner and Schneebeck (2000) indicated, the perceived lack of leadership in growth-oriented learning opportunities within the global higher-education sector means many academic managers become bogged down with restructure behaviors at the expense of innovation uptake. This has lead to a learning system imbalance, wherein technology investment has outstripped investment in people, and "where information technology rather than 'pedagogy' is the driver of curriculum reform" (Celsi & Wolfinbarger, 2001, p. 308).

As a result, the limitations of "teacher bandwidth" have never been more acutely felt in an era where academic development involves the adaptation of an entirely new working identity. There is a sinking feeling that existing models for integrating LMSs into the higher-education curriculum fail to adequately address the learning, teaching, and research needs of the host communities. It is ambitious to assume any single medium is able to "resolve fundamental educational problems or alter the ways teachers understand teaching" (Ramsden, 1992, p. 161), but in the case of ICTs

- at the infrastructure level, Macchiusi and Trinidad (2000) pointed to a lack of uniformity in enterprise-wide computer hardware and software systems in universities, even where an institution has adapted a commercial LMS;
- there exists a diversity of "faculty" views on the role and value of ICTs at a time when "technological change has removed the spatial security of academic institutions by opening up and redefining the core concept of the delivery of learning" (Hagner & Schneebeck, 2000, p. 2);
- Vogel and Klassen (2001) suggested that with technology the role of the faculty member is not eliminated, but rather "their resource base gets larger and more varied as technology extends in a plurality of new directions" (p. 105);
- in terms of "job expansion," Dabbagh (2002) detailed that preparation time for face-to-face teaching requires 6 to 7 hours per week, compared to its LMS counterpart requiring 18 to 19 hours per week. Not only are teaching staff doing more, but they are required to do it differently and often in dual or multiple delivery modes;
- while the LMS is seen as an innovation in teaching and learning, teaching and learning success stories featuring LMSs often remain unsubstantiated (Baskin, Barker, & Woods, 2003; Tyner, 1998; Snyder, 1997; Ramsden, 1992). Evaluation studies, thus far, fail to reveal much of the anticipated improvement in learning outcomes (McNaught, 2002; Alexander, 1999; Alexander & McKenzie, 1998);
- a characteristic of institutions' initial choice of LMS products has been ease of use by staff as a main criterion for initial product selection (Morgan, 2003; Stiles, 2002). Staff think first in terms of delivery approaches (Tomes & Higgison, 1998) and later about how to convert traditional courses into electronic ones (Morgan, 2003; Phillips, 1998);
- in the use of LMSs in most institutions, there is evidence of effort spent on the conversion of existing lecture-based learning programs into modular materials which are distributed to learners along with traditional assignments and examinations as the sole means of assessment (Morgan, 2003; Littlejohn, 2002); and

- there is a growing criticism of mainstream commercial LMSs as content-centered, and their pedagogic bias such that they "fit" certain cohorts (and styles) of learners above others (Milligan, 1999).

To date, LMS uptake in higher education has focused primarily on trying to overlay new technologies on traditional forms of teaching, without making substantive changes to the character of teaching or to learner perceptions of the host institution. These conclusions led Shaw and McCauley (2003) to highlight the rarity of whole-institution strategies to the implementation of an LMS within the broader MLE, pointing more to their piecemeal and often accidental evolution. In particular, he stressed the need for institutions to find approaches to build on existing localized initiatives to better address issues of pedagogy, and to better manage the differences between MLEs (which are essentially processes) and LMSs (which are essentially software systems) to support enhanced learning (JISC, 2003; Shaw and McCauley, 2003; King, 2002). In essence, as a learning media, LMSs are seen not to sustain ongoing teaching and learning development in their current context of use, nor are they likely to deliver high organizational expectations of the digital campus.

Describing e-learning in the HE sector as a simplified cottage industry (see Figure 33.1.) McLean (2003) presented three converging institutional user platforms as (a) knowledge, (b) dataset, and (c) learning-object repositories.

McLean (2003) painted a compelling picture of the university, its cultures, and its practices, where digital assets are managed in discrete "faculty silos," and the duplication of faculty and central staff immersed in the process of Web-services development equates to little awareness of stewardship of these assets. Financial constraints on the upgrading and customization of proprietary business-critical server resources means little growth-oriented planning or agreement at the enterprise level on how to store and access digital learning content. The rapid take-up of content-management systems drives institutions deeper into a culture of "do it yourself" infrastructure management in which, until recently, there was a distinct lack of institutional metadata strategies. The net result is that systems' interoperability is limited, while organizational expectations for the digital campus remain high.

Where technical planning is a feature of strategic institutional planning in higher education, the discourse of Enterprise Resource Planning (ERP)

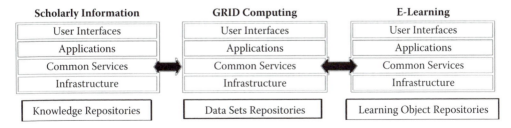

Figure 33.1 Converging ICT domains in higher education (McLean, 2003).

- the LMS interface is designer driven rather than end-user friendly. The learner is often and easily confused by the complexity and layers of the LMS interface;
- only recently have proprietary LMS providers begun to extend their basic platforms with toolsets beyond content sequencing and discussion forums. Many universities in Australia have carried a dual Blackboard and WebCT platform to maximize utility, with synchronous integration tools a recent innovation. These tools still comprise part of a "locked down" platform; and
- monocultural LMS tools limit learner options and opportunities. There is still an implicit assumption embedded within the LMS that functionality is the ultimate goal and teachers and learners need not go beyond what is currently possible to reconceptualize the curriculum itself.

Downes (2005) defined the knowledge-work of the "n-gen" as having moved well beyond the "gathering and accumulation of facts" and toward "the riding of waves on a dynamic environment," even posing the rhetorical question, "Do we need factory universities to learn" (p. 2)? In many ways, the attitudes of academics to widespread adoption of the LMS are understandable and predictable. If the university professor is to become a redundant intermediary, and the role of the LMS is to disintermediate teaching and learning processes, then academics are unlikely to contribute to their own demise through wholesale adoption. The LMS is much more likely to replicate existing higher-educational practices, than it is to challenge them (Morgan, 2003; Tomes & Higgison, 1998; Phillips, 1998). On the user side, major parts of the World Wide Web were replicating communications networks, in its transition from a read-only to a read-write environment. In narrating the shift from information transmitted to platform, Downes told an evolutionary tale spanning networks, blogs, Wikipedia, podcasting, and communities of practice. In his analysis, Downes, like Siemens (2004a), concluded that the emergence of a new model of learning is part of an impending revolution, but not of the technical kind. This kind of learning, and the purpose of new learning technologies, is socially constructed.

Attending to Learner Needs

Social presence theory (Short, Williams, & Christie, 1976) is based on the belief that "different media" convey different degrees of "perceived substance" to an interaction, with the quality of connection based on the amount of nonverbal communication made available to the receiver in a given exchange. In this regard, an LMS is a low-presence, and low-cue, media; the theory of social presence therefore suggests that LMSs will be "limited" in its attempts to facilitate the "cooperative interaction" of students in an e-learning environment. While no doubt an artifact of its time, social presence theory is elaborated and extended in related research by Sproull and Kiesler (1986), who suggested that social presence also extends to social context cues, which serve as indicators of appropriate "contextualized" behavior. Social context cues in a face-to-face setting govern the norms and practices of contact, social desirability, conversational turn taking, standards of disclosure, and a host of situational and context variables. However, social context cues are embedded in nonverbal communications. Given the absence of nonverbal cues in the LMS setting, it follows that where digital communication suites are involved we are less able to make subtle differentiations among communication stimuli, and therefore less able to exert control over ourselves in order to meet social expectations and to perform important social roles. As Sproull and Kiesler contended, this is more likely to lead to role ambiguity, increased anonymity, reduced self-regulation, and reduced self-awareness; a worst-case scenario could see LMSs as counterproductive to learning.

At risk in the LMS environment is the "fabric" of critical education, the very stuff of traditional higher education. The fear is that students will move away from active learner participation to browse through a "stockpile" of just-in-time information made available online (Blasi & Heinecke, 2000, p. 83). On top of this, as Lambier (2002) put it, LMSs seem to "feed of the limitations teachers often have to face" (p. 113) in the process of teaching. The emphases placed on time management, class management and efficiency, individualization and autonomy, information processing, and problem solving in an LMS environment promote a pedagogy that understates the value of deeper learning processes.

Three Pillars of Enquiry: Social Presence, Transactional Distance, and Social Affordance

Social Presence: An Interlocutory Space

Building on the theories of Short et al. (1976), Social Presence Theory argues that social presence is a critical component of learning. The theory of social presence presupposes that learning is best achieved in social environments and that any form of communication (virtual or real time) can be used to enhance or silence the social presence of others. Hence, both the face-to-face and the LMS have an intrinsic social presence value. The new social space we refer to as "cyberspace," is created according to in the areas of knowledge, new social relationships, new social roles, and a reconstructed (deconstructed) sense of self (Downes, 2005; Siemens, 2004a). The key feature of cyberspace (transcribed onto the LMS) is interaction, whereby a new sense of "self" and "community" can be mediated, negotiated, and, if required, continuously renegotiated. Wolfe (2000) suggested that within teaching and learning exchanges there have been three key changes in a shift away from a dominant cognitive view of learning, these being the concept of communication, the concept of interaction, and the conceptual model of context. The latter, the conceptual model of context, accounts for interaction, identity, and knowledge-construction processes within learners (Wolfe, 2000; Anderson, 1995). This model of context is not restricted to the coconstructed physical presence of others, but consists of what is known as the "interlocutory space" that provides each of us with access to socially recognizable meanings (Hymes, 1970).

With such a rich genealogy, social presence is something of a slippery concept. It is defined by its progenitors, Short et al. (1976), as the "degree of salience of the other person in the (mediated) interaction and the consequent salience of the interpersonal relationships" (p. 65). In other words, social presence refers to how real (Richardson & Swan, 2003) or three-dimensional (Stein & Wanstreet, 2003) a person or group is perceived to be despite the medium of communication; it is in essence an interlocutory space, a purely Vygotskian zone wherein one's ability to assemble and focus the presence of communicating subjects to the means of communication is determined (Short, Williams, & Christie, 1976). The LMS is the software expression of these relationships. Partee (2002) advocated social presence be enacted when a teacher e-mails notes to the students; this establishes an immediate and special contact, compared to the more traditional classroom in which there may be a large number of students and limited scope for definitive "social presence." Murray (2004), like Stiles (2002), found that while integrating an LMS into schools, most teachers simply applied the technologies over the top of traditional teaching practices, rather than reinventing new approaches to teaching and learning through innovative and divergent thinking. Schwitzer, Ancis, and Brown (2001) maintained that in order to encourage effective "e-learning," the facilitator must emphasize the "meaningfulness" of the learning material, rely upon learner-centered instructional approaches, provide positive interpersonal exchange, and attend to a host of student-diversity issues. Baskin and Anderson (2003b) found that women engaged in distance education embraced LMS communication tools, and were found to have a higher relative level of academic success, satisfaction, and sense of the social presence than their male counterparts did. Maor (2003) found that interaction and a corresponding perception of the social presence of others grew from the use of socially constructivist approaches to teaching and learning in an LMS setting. Taken together, these studies suggest that not only does the medium in part dictate the perception of social presence by its interactive limitations (such as the inability to convey nonverbal cues), but also that students tend to avoid certain interactions within certain media. This awareness of "social presence" as a structuring theory suggests that learning media can be facilitated in such a way that the perception of social presence is increased, which in turn greatly increases the ability to substitute ICT for face-to-face instances while achieving the same (or better), learning outcomes (Gunawardena & Zittle, 1997; Richardson & Swan, 2003; Stein & Wanstreet, 2003). In doing so, it shifts focus away from technological events (system components and capabilities), back onto critical teaching and learning events.

The relationship between interaction and social presence is a complex one. Picciano (2002) pointed out that students in traditional classrooms participate in social and communicative practices, from joining in discussions about a topic of study and sending and receiving nonverbal cues to interacting outside of the classroom. These kinds of interactions suggest social presence. The theory does not argue, however, that face-to-face classrooms by definition have high social presence; indeed, the reverse is particularly true if students or teachers feel alienated. Indeed, a common misconception is that social presence is a symptom of interaction (Picciano, 2002). In further attempts to quantify social presence, other researchers have measured a variety of indicators, including semantic differentials (Short et al., 1976) immediacy patterns (Gunawardena & Zittle, 1997), emotional expression (Garrison, Anderson, & Archer, 2000), and communication styles (Tu & McIsaac, 2002). To emphasize these connections, Tu and McIsaac (2002) redefined social presence as an outcome of intimacy and immediacy (which are themselves determined by the three dimensions of interactivity, social context, and online communication). They believe it unlikely that the LMS will replace face-to-face instruction. Nonetheless, they mention that with careful selection and attention to the three dimensions of interactivity, social context, and online communication, the LMS can enhance some less successful face-to-face teaching and learning situations (Tu & McIsaac, 2002).

Transactional Distance: Mapping Pedagogical Spaces

The pedagogical theory of transactional distance sits firmly within the learning theory of social constructivism. Dewey and Bentley (1949) derived the concept of a "learning transaction" to mean a transaction in which a person "shares learning" with the rest of his or her "group" in a way that is dialogic. The subsequent theory of transactional distance was originally formulated by Moore in the early 1970s and has since become a fundamental concept in distance and remote education (Faust, 2004). Indeed, Moore's concept of transactional distance replaced common understandings of what "distance education" is taken to mean. The latter emphasizes a geographical separation of learners and teachers rather than a pedagogical concept (Mueller, 1997). Moore and Kearsley (1996) suggested that while physical distance can lead to "a communications gap," transactional distance is the "psychological space of potential misunderstanding between the behaviours of instructors and those of the learners" (p. 200). As a result, transactional distance is not directly related to geographical distance (Faust, 2004) and even face-to-face environments can have some element of transactional distance (Mueller, 1997).

Faust (2004) argued that transactional distance is really a pedagogical distance determined by the balance of teaching and learning "structure and dialogue." In terms of transactional distance, "structure" relates to the rigidity/flexibility of the course of study, including its objectives, strategies, and its capacity to accommodate learner diversity. "Dialogue" refers to purposeful, constructive, and valued interaction. Moore's theory, at its simplest, posits that if the structure of the course is high and dialogue is low then there will be a larger transactional distance leading to psychological gaps, different teacher and learner behaviors, and increased likelihood for misunderstandings between participating parties. In this respect, it is much harder for learning to occur. On the other hand, if the dialogue is high and structure is low (e.g., more flexible) then the transactional distance will be much smaller (Faust, 2004). Transactional distance is therefore a subjective experience that varies according to learner autonomy and dependency (Moore, 1993; Mueller, 1997). "Learner autonomy" is a well-used concept within higher education and refers to the extent to which "in the teaching/learning relationship it is the learner rather than the teacher who determines the goals, the learning experiences, and evaluation decisions of the learning programme" (Mueller, 1997, p. 2). Moore's research indicates that as students progress toward autonomous learning, they are less likely to need dialogue and structure, and that for them the transactional distance in such courses will be much less than for learners with a higher degree of dependence (Moore, 1993). Conversely, learners with high dependency tend to favor courses with greater dialogue, relying on "a close relationship with an instructor" (Mueller, 1997, p. 5).

When applying theories of social presence and transactional distance to the use of LMSs in teaching and learning, we illuminate the possible explanation for the high value placed on face-to-face interactions (high dialogue) for large-group teaching, and the possible failure of the LMS (high structure, low dialogue) interactions for the same cohort of learners (Garrison, Anderson, & Archer, 2000; Richardson & Swan, 2003). Yet, the "social context" of education is affected by motivation and attitudes, as much as it is by teaching and learning (Foley, 2004; McInnis, 2003; Treleaven, 2004). Social presence within a face-to-face classroom can be associated with social cues; these same cues are now available and present in distance education through the LMS. The gestures, smiles, and praise that can be achieved though the face-to-face classrooms (Jordan & Le Metais, 2004) are also available within distance education via auditory video teleconferencing (Everett, 2001). Garrison and Anderson (2003) suggested that within the discourse of the classroom, the "success" of the learning event lies in the individual's ability to project him- or herself socially and emotionally as a person to the learning community. While the LMS is viewed as culturally neutral (Giovannetti, Kagame, & Tsui, 2003), it has its drawbacks insofar as media, materials, and services are often inappropriately transferred without attention being paid to the social setting or to the local recipient culture (Johns, Smith, & Strand, 2003). The literature on social presence and transactional distance points to the context of use as a critical determinant of learning through an LMS.

Social Affordance: Designing Pedagogical Space

Given the preceding discussion, "the LMS" is first and foremost a "pedagogical space" rather than a deliberate educational service-delivery strategy (Downes, 2005; Siemens, 2004b). The teacher and learner are geographically separated, but are connected via knowledge-construction processes, communicate via back channel and public discussion forums, and submit assignments via e-mail or digital drop-box, or by posting to a "designated" work area within the LMS (Howard, Schenk, & Discenza, 2004). Transactional distance within this concept of learning is defined by the psychological and communications space between teachers and learners. In their exploratory study of e-learning, Volet and Wosnitza (2004) concluded that engagement in asynchronous and synchronous learning activities reflects a substantial amount of "social interchange" and "meaningful learning"; however, only a limited social negotiation of meaning was found to exist. New learning media are essentially social, but not constructively so (Baskin & Henderson, 2005).

While the communication properties of the LMS may trigger social interactions, they do not necessarily sustain or direct learning engagement within that environment. Kreijns and Kirschner (2001) described this phenomenon as social affordance—namely, the amount of structure that exits in the design of the learning material (Bradner, 2001). Needless to say, this structure needs to be supported by the capabilities of the LMS. This is the precinct of e-moderating. A term made popular by Gilly Salmon (2004), *e-moderating* is the transitive term given to strategically tailoring educational experiences for the consumption of individuals—that is, using ICTs as a structuring resource for more effective teaching and learning. Kreijns and Kirschner (2001) would have suggested this meant designing for higher relative levels of social affordance. E-moderating draws on elements of both face-to-face teaching and traditional print-based distance teaching to construct new teaching and learning events, but also identifies the need for the introduction of a range of new understandings and techniques that are specific to e-learning delivery. The logic of linking social affordance with e-moderating is profound; if social presence is an attribute of the teaching and learning environment, and transactional distance frames teaching and learning events, then social affordance provides the means to "design" for better teaching and learning outcomes (Wenger, 1998). It is to this point we now wish to turn.

Social Presence, Transactional Distance, and Social Affordance as Learning Organizers

What follows is an illustration of how social presence, transactional distance, and social affordance conspire to create the conditions for teaching and learning, and how these might constructively align in an LMS. It is time for a return visit to Melissa.

Melissa is one member of the cohort cited here. The data captures and brackets the experience of 164 students over a 13-week period. The students involved had no previous experience of face-to-face university learning, nor had they any experience of learning through the agency of an LMS. The presumptions of the researchers were simple: if learners were exposed equally to face-to-face teaching and learning, as well as learning through an LMS, then we ought to be able to assign learning values to each learning event and be equally as able to make inferences based on a comparison of these values. So it was that students attended virtual and face-to-face lectures, tutorials, group projects, examinations, and study-skills workshops in equal degrees over a 13-week period. Students were subsequently asked to assign a learning index (rating 1 to 5) for each learning event, indicating the degree to which they either agreed or disagreed with each indicator statement using a 5-point Likert scale ("1 = strongly disagree" to "5 = strongly agree"). Across-group means were calculated, as were item average means for male (n = 61) and female (n = 103) students. Data presented here includes *Paired Sample t Tests* for differences between the ICT-enhanced and face-to-face experiences of male and female students.

In cross-sample comparisons, in all but one of the nine listed learning events (academic writing) female students assigned higher relative learning ratings to both LMS and face-to-face learning events than their male counterparts. (These differences in the perceptions are presented graphically in Figure 33.2.) The results indicate that in terms of LMS and face-to-face comparisons, female (M = 4.02) and male (M = 3.99) students are more likely to prefer face-to-face lectures, with male students assigning significantly less learning value to face-to-face ($t = -2.11$, df = 162, $p < 0.05$) as well as online ($t = -3.16$, df = 162, $p < 0.05$) lectures than female students. The same trend can be seen in patterns of interpersonal exchange; in the face-to-face ($t = -4.97$, df = 162, $p < 0.05$)

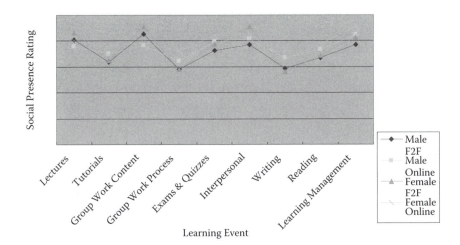

Figure 33.2 Learning events ratings face-to-face and online by gender (Baskin & Henderson, 2005).

and online ($t = -3.41$, df = 162, p < 0.05) settings, male students placed less learning value on interpersonal exchanges than their female counterparts.

Both male and female respondents rate group-work processes (skills) in face-to-face group work the same (M = 2.89), yet differ significantly in their perceptions of group-work processes in the online setting, with male students much more circumspect about the role of the LMS in facilitating group-work processes ($t = -2.47$, df = 162, p < 0.05). Male students present clear preferences for face-to-face group work tasks, but not in a tutorial setting in which applied learning exercises were the focus of tutorial tasks and activities. Males and females prefer LMS tutorials to face-to-face tutorials, but again male respondents assign a significantly lower learning weighting and preference ($t = -2.11$, df = 162, p < 0.05) for LMS tutorials than female students. Similarly, male students also reported significantly less preference for face-to-face exams and quizzes ($t = -2.20$, df = 162, p < 0.05). In regard to learning self-management, both male and female respondents assigned higher relative learning values to the LMS (sample mean, M = 4.43) as a learning manager, with female respondents reporting a significantly higher rating the males ($t = -2.26$, df = 162, p < 0.05; and $t = -2.59$, df = 162, p < 0.05). As an aside to this, male students also reported LMS group work (M = 4.27) as having a higher (but not significantly so) learning value than its face-to-face alternate (M = 3.85), while female respondents report a significant preference for face-to-face group work as the preferred environment for "doing group tasks" ($t = -3.60$, df = 162, p < 0.05).

New Questions for Tertiary Teachers

Effect differences reported here indicate that discernible differences in the "learning choices" and "patterns" of male and female LMS users do exist. But which constructs underlie student preferences in each case? How does this pattern of discrimination between face-to-face and LMS contexts capture the deeper split between the "public and private" knowledge-making processes of the learner? What kinds of knowledge are better supported by the face-to-face architecture of the classroom? In turn, what kinds of knowledge are better supported by the virtual architecture of the LMS? Is there a taxonomy of knowledge-construction processes that underlie (or should underlie) blended models of teaching and learning? This preference for differentiation and the capacity of the LMS to meet and extend this preference set beyond the face-to-face setting in the majority of learning events, points to a new application for LMSs at the university level. This preference goes beyond overlaying new technologies on traditional forms of teaching, toward the consideration of how social presence, transactional distance, and social affordance are expressed and enacted within teaching and learning environments.

- There does exist a real opportunity to improve the quality of teaching and learning through the adoption of new learning technologies.

Everett, G. (2001). Webpals: Linking students live across the world. *Principal Matters, 48,* 32–34.

Faust, R. (2004). *Transactional distance.* Retrieved March 30, 2004, from http://coe.sdsu.edu/eet/Articles/transactdist/index.htm

Foley, G. (Ed.). (2004). *Dimensions of adult learning: Adult education and training in a global era.* Crows Nest, New South Wales, Australia: Allen and Unwin.

Garrison, D., Anderson, T., & Archer, W. (2000). Critical inquiry in a text-based environment: Computer conferencing in higher education. *The Internet and Higher Education, 2*(2–3), 87–105.

Giovannetti, E., Kagamim, M., & Tsui, M. (Ed.). (2003). *The Internet revolution: A global perspective.* Cambridge, U.K.: Cambridge University Press.

Gunawardena, C. N., & Zittle, F. J. (1997). Social presence as a predictor of satisfaction within a computer-mediated conferencing environment. *The American Journal of Distance Education, 11*(3), 8–26.

Hagner, P., & Schneebeck, C. (2000). Engaging the faculty. In C. Barone & P. Hagner (Eds.), *Technology-enhanced teaching and learning: Leading and supporting the transformation on your campus* (pp. 1–12). San Francisco, CA: Jossey-Bass.

Hall, J. (2003). *Assessing learning management systems.* Retrieved November 15, 2005, from http://www.clomedia.com/content/templates/clo_feature.asp?articleid=91&zoneid=29

Howard, C., Schenk, K., & Discenza, R. (2004). Distance learning and University of Melbourne: Information science publishing. *Effectiveness: Changing Educational Paradigms for Online Learning.* London: Information Science Publishing.

Hymes, D. (1970). On Communicative Competence. In J. J. Gumperz and D. Hymes (Eds.), Directions in Sociolinguistics. New York: Holt, Rinehart and Winston.

Johns, S. K., Smith, L. M., & Strand, C. A. (2003). How cultures affect the use of information technology. *Accounting Forum (Adelaide), 27*(1), 84–109.

Joint Information Systems Committee (JISC). (2003). *Strategic activities: Managed learning environments.* Retrieved November 14, 2004 from http://www.jisc.ac.uk

Jordan, D. L., & LeMetais, J. (2004). Developing emotional intelligence in the classroom. *Education Horizons, 8*(1), 10–11, 36.

King, P. (2002). *The promise and performance of enterprise systems in higher education.* Retrieved March 14, 2004 from the Educause Center for Applied Research Web site: http://www.educause.edu/ecar/

Kreijns, K., & Kirschner, P. A. (2001). The social affordance of computer supported collaborative learning environments [Electronic version]. In D. Budny & G. Bjedov (Eds.), *Proceedings of the 31th ASEE/IEEE Frontiers in Education Conference* (session T1F). Piscataway, NJ: IEEE.

Lambeir, B. (2002). Comfortably numb in the digital era: Man's being as standing reserve or dwelling silently. In M. Peters (Ed.), *Heidegger, education and modernity* (pp. 109–117). New York: Rowman and Littlefield.

Lemke, J. (1996). Metamedia literacy: Transforming meanings and media. In D. Reinking (Ed.), *Literacy for the 21st century: Technological transformation in a post-typographical world* (pp. 289–309). New York: Erlbaum.

LittleJohn, A. (2002). New lessons from past experience: Recommendations for improving continuing professional development in the use of ICT. *Journal of Computer Assisted Learning, 18*(2), 166–174.

Macchiusi, L., & Trinidad, S. (2000, February 2–4). Implementing IT at an Australian university: Implications for university leaders. In A. Herrmann & M. M. Kulski (Eds.), *Flexible futures in tertiary teaching: Proceedings of the 9th Annual Teaching Learning Forum.* Perth, Australia: Curtin University of Technology. Retrieved November 5, 2003, from http://cea.curtin.edu.au/tlf/tlf2000/macchiusi.html

Maor, D. (2003). Teachers' and students' perspectives on on-line learning in a social constructivist learning environment. *Technology, Pedagogy and Education, 12*(2), 201–218.

McInnis, C. (2003). Emerging issues for teaching and learning in Australian universities. *BHERT News, 18,* 2–5.

McKnight, S., Halford, G., Coldwell, J., Corbitt, B., Mulready, P., & Smissen, I. (2002). *Evaluation of corporate applications for online teaching and learning*. Retrieved June 26, 2003, from Deakin University Web site: http://www.deakin.edu.au/lms_evaluation/old/

McLean, N. (2003). *E-learning and digital library trends*. Retrieved June 30, 2003, from Auckland University of Technology, National Library of New Zealand Forum Web site: http://www.natlib.govt.nz/files/e_learning/NMcLeanpresentation30june.ppt

McNaught, C. (2002). Views on staff development for networked learning. In C. Steeples & C. Jones (Eds.), *Networked learning: Perspectives and issues* (pp. 111–124). London: Springer-Verlag.

Mezirow, J. (1991). *Transformative dimensions of adult learning*. San Francisco: Jossey-Bass.

Milligan, C. (1999). *Delivering staff and professional development using virtual learning environments*. Edinburgh, U.K.: Herriot-Watt University. Retrieved March 14, 2004 from http://www.e-learningcentre.co.uk/eclipse/Resources/profdev.htm

Moore, M. (1993). Theory of transactional distance. In D. Keegan (Ed.), *Theoretical principles of distance education* (pp. 22–38). London: Routledge.

Moore, M., & Kearsley, G. (1996). *Distance education: A systems view*. Belmont, CA: Wadsworth Publishing Company.

Morgan, G. (2003). *Faculty use of course management systems*. Retrieved March 14, 2004 from the Educause Center for Applied Research Web site: http://www.educause.edu/ecar/

Mueller, C. (1997). *Transactional distance*. Retrieved March 30, 2004, from http://tecfa.unige.ch/staf/staf9698/mullerc/3/transact.html#210e

Murray, C. (2004). The avatars versus the fringe dwellers: Let the game begin. *Educare News, 144*, 56–57.

Partee, M. H. (2002). *Cyberteaching*. New York: University Press of America.

Phillips, R. (1998). What research says about the Internet. In C. McBeth, C. McLoughlin, & R. Atkinson (Eds.), *Planning for progress, partnership, & profit* (pp. 203–207). Perth, Australia: Australian Society for Educational Technology.

Picciano, A. G. (2002). Beyond student perceptions: Issues of interaction, presence and performance in an online course. *Journal of Asynchronous Learning Networks, 6*(1), 21–40.

Ramsden, P. (1992). *Learning to teach in higher education*. London: Routledge.

Richardson, J. C., & Swan, K. (2003). Examining social presence in online courses in relation to students' perceived learning and satisfaction. *Journal of Asynchronous Learning Networks, 7*(1), 68–87.

Robbins, S. (2002). The *evolution of the learning content management system*. Retrieved November 15, 2005, from http://www.elearnspace.org/Articles/lms.htm

Rogers, E. (1995). *Diffusion of innovations* (4th ed.). New York: The Free Press.

Salmon, G. (2004). E-moderating in higher education. In C. Howard, K. Schenk, & R. Discenza (Ed.), *Distance learning and university effectiveness: Changing educational paradigms for online learning* (pp. 56–78). London: Information Science Publishing.

Sasseville, B. (2004). Integrating information technology in the classroom: A comparative discourse analysis. *Canadian Journal of Learning and Technology, 30*(2), 5–27 [Electronic version]. Retrieved March 14, 2005, from http://www.cjlt.ca/content/vol30.2/cjlt30-2_art-1.html

Schwitzer, A. M., Ancis, J. R., & Brown, N. (2001). *Promoting student learning and student development at a distance*. Lanham, MD: American College Personnel Association.

Shaw, T., & McCauley, G. (2003). Infrastructure in education—time to learn lessons from elsewhere? *Conference Proceedings of the SSGRR-20025 International Conference*. Rome: Telecom Italia Learning Services.

Short, J., Williams, E., & Christie, B. (1976). *The social psychology of telecommunities*. London: John Wiley and Sons.

Siemens, G. (2004a). *Connectivism: A learning theory for the digital age*. Retrieved November 15, 2005, from www.elearnspace.org/Articles/connectivism.htm

Introduction to Part VI

The final section seeks to move us forward by demonstrating the potential of bringing multiple perspectives to bear on a single research study in the area of new literacies, analyzing it from several different lenses. Authors in each section of this volume nominated research studies for this final section, which they had found to be central to the work in their own area. We considered these nominations in our selections and reprint these studies here. In addition, we have invited commentary responses by central scholars who come from two different theoretical perspectives, disciplines, and/or methodological traditions. We believe it instructive to develop a better understanding of how differing perspectives can enrich our own understanding of a common work. Developing insights about how others might view a study will help us to peer into research with fresh lenses, enabling us to see greater complexity and richness in the work and, thus, coming to understand it better.

While each of us can benefit from this experience, we believe this final section may be especially instructive to new scholars who are just entering our research communities or who seek to do so. New scholars can benefit greatly by seeing how leaders in our fields think about essential questions of theory, research methodologies, standards for research publication, and the important next questions that require our attention. In short, we get to peer into some of the best minds in our field and consider how they think about issues of new literacies.

CHAPTER 34

Savannah

*Mobile Gaming and Learning?**

KERI FACER

NESTA FUTURELAB, ENGLAND

RICHARD JOINER and DANAE STANTON

UNIVERSITY OF BATH, ENGLAND

JO REID and RICHARD HULL

HEWLETT-PACKARD LABORATORIES, ENGLAND

DAVID KIRK

UNIVERSITY OF NOTTINGHAM, ENGLAND

Abstract

This paper reports a study that attempts to explore how using mobile technologies in direct physical interaction with space and with other players can be combined with principles of engagement and self-motivation to create a powerful and engaging learning experience. We developed a mobile gaming experience designed to encourage the development of children's conceptual understanding of animal behaviour. Ten children (five boys and five girls) aged between 11 and 12 years played and explored the game. The findings from this study offer interesting insights into the extent to which mobile gaming might be employed as a tool for supporting learning. It also highlights a number of major challenges that this format raises for the organisation of learning within schools and the design of such resources.

* Reprinted with permission of Blackwell Publishing Ltd., from Savannah: Mobile gaming and learning? K. Facer, R. Joiner, D. Stanton, J. Reid, R. Hull, & D. Kirk. *Journal of Computer Assisted Learning*, Vol. 20(6):399–409 (2004); permission conveyed through Copyright Clearance Center, Inc.

Introduction: Experiential Learning Through Mobile Gaming

Both mobile technologies and games technologies are increasingly seen as fertile ground for the development of resources to support learning. This interest is driven by a number of considerations: first, there is an increasing awareness that young people's digital cultures outside school are as likely to be shaped by interaction with mobile and games technologies as they are by desktop PC applications and that consequently, the school setting should at least begin to engage with these tools (see, for example, Facer et al., 2003; Holloway & Valentine, 2003); and second, educational theorists and researchers are beginning to identify these tools as potentially powerful resources in supporting the development of learning communities of offering experiential learning and in encouraging the development of meta-level thinking skills (see, for example, Roschelle & Pea, 2002; Andrews et al., 2003; Gee, 2003; Wegerif, 2003).

Mobile technologies, for example, enable children to interact simultaneously with both the physical world and with digital information. This shift in technical praxis promises new forms of educational experience away from the classroom (Roschelle & Pea, 2002). Coupling familiar actions (presence within the physical environment) with the unfamiliar (having a window onto digital resources), it is argued, promotes reflection and new ways of aiding children's learning (Rogers et al., 2002; Sharples et al., 2002; Price et al., 2003; Stanton et al., 2003).

Games technologies, by contrast, have for some time struggled to be taken seriously within the educational arena. Games, with their emphasis on fun and pleasure, and their often (to an adult eye) repetitive challenges, have until recently been seen as a distraction from the more serious business of computer-aided learning. Despite Malone's (1980) early research in this field, and Turkle's (1984) identification of the potential role of games in supporting 'learning how to learn', it is only relatively recently that sustained educational research has been carried out in this area. What research that does exist, however, is increasingly pointing towards the potential of computer games to offer children powerful opportunities not only to learn through experience, but to develop meta-level reflections on strategies for learning (for example, Gee, 2003; Kirriemuir & McFarlane, 2003; Squire, 2003).

Given recent technological developments, however, it seems to make sense to consider mobile learning and games-based learning not as distinct experiences, but as experiences that could fruitfully be combined. As developers explore ways in which they can become more than communication devices, mobile technology (whether phone or handheld PC) is now becoming seen as a potential games platform. As a result, a number of simple text-based multiplayer games are easily available on many mobile phones. At the same time, the new connectivity of handheld games devices is shifting the focus away from the individual player to the connected player able to find fellow gamers on any city street (Flintham et al., 2003).

This paper will report an innovative and exploratory project, which attempts to explore how the experience of using mobile technologies in direct physical interaction with space and with other players can be combined with the principles of engagement and self-motivated efforts to overcome challenges (Malone, 1980) characteristic of games play, in order to create a powerful and engaging learning experience. We wanted to explore, through this project, whether the combination of these different features of mobile and games technologies could encourage the development of children's conceptual understanding of, in this case, animal behaviour and interaction with the environment.

The Savannah Project

The game consists of two related areas of activity. In the first, children are able to play at 'being a pride of lions' outside in a playing field (100 m × 50 m), interacting with a virtual Savannah and exploring the opportunities and risks to lions in that space. Children are given global positioning systems (GPSs) linked to personal digital assistants (PDAs) through which they 'see', 'hear' and 'smell' the world of the Savannah as they navigate the real space outdoors. The second domain, the 'Den', is an indoors space where children can reflect on how well they have succeeded in the game, can access other resources to support their understanding and can develop strategies for surviving as lions in the virtual Savannah.

In order to 'sense' the Savannah, children use their handheld PDAs (with headphones), moving around the playing field outdoors acting as lions. They hear the sounds of the Savannah relating to the specific zones or wildlife there, they see still images of the environment and animals to be found in the zones and they 'smell' the scents to be found in those zones, through still pictures of animal paw prints. On these PDAs, the children can also 'mark' specific information and send it back to the Den for later analysis; in later levels they can also 'attack' specific features of the Savannah. They also have an energy bar that lets them know their specific energy levels at any time (see Fig. 34.1). The PDA also receives messages sent by facilitators in the Den—such as 'you are too hot', 'you are hungry' or on occasion 'You are dead—return to the Den'.

In the Den, there is an interactive whiteboard and flip chart. The whiteboard comprises a map of the Savannah, and a series of 'energy bars,' each of which relate to the relative energy of each individual lion. On returning to the Den, children can pull up on the whiteboard the trails that they have made in the Savannah, and recall the sounds and images that they encountered at specific points, 'marked' and sent back to the Den (see Fig. 34.2).

The virtual Savannah map comprises a number of zones including long grass, short grass, gully, kopje, spring and trees. These areas are also populated by

Figure 34.1 PDAs and headphones—with image, energy bar, and sight, send, and smell buttons.

the wildlife that one would find in those different parts of the Savannah. All these aspects of the gaming environment are based on research carried out as part of the BBC Natural History Unit's work in this area, and a specialist BBC 'lion expert' with over 10 year of experience working in African Savannahs was involved in designing the play space (see Fig. 34.3).

In the game, children are required to act as a pride of lions living in the Savannah. The main challenge for the children is to understand and survive in this territory. The environment contains a number of threats: for example, an

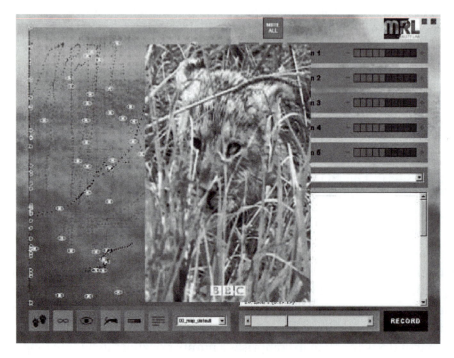

Figure 34.2 Interactive whiteboard screen level 1: Showing lion tracks, marks.

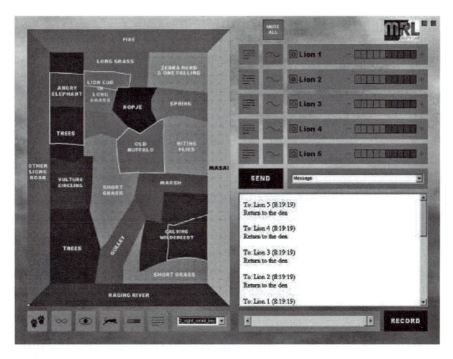

Figure 34.3 Level 2 Savannah "sound map" on Den interface.

angry elephant, an old water buffalo, bush fire and on the fringes of the territory, the Masai. All of these have to be avoided. Attacking them would lead to certain death. There is also another pride of lions and they have to kill any of this pride's cubs. A number of animals can be found in the Savannah that they could successfully kill and eat—essential for their survival. Some of these require one lion, and others require the whole pack to successfully kill them. There are also sources of water and shade. The children have to balance the costs and benefits of different types of activity—whether attacking, drinking, sleeping or running—in order to maintain their energy levels. They also have to negotiate with each other, in order to decide whether or how to collaborate in achieving the games objectives.

Technological Support

Savannah is a client/server system in which the handheld computers (iPAQ 5450) carried by the children/lions act as mobile clients to a PC-based game server. The mobile clients have integrated 802.11 b wireless networking capabilities, a full colour screen, a sound system, 256 Mb of file storage containing all the images and sounds used in the game and an attached GPS unit. These capabilities allow the mobile clients to:

- determine their locations in the outdoor game area;
- accept inputs from the users in the form of button events ('mark', 'attack');

- transmit location information and user interface events to the remote game server over the wireless network;
- accept responses from the game server that required individual clients to display a picture or a message, play a sound file or change the energy level shown on the client's screen.

The game server uses the information received from the mobile clients to determine what happens in the game and thus what the children/lions experience. For example, the server interprets incoming location information from the clients with respect to maps that relate the virtual Savannah to the physical game space. As a result, the server may instruct a client to render a sound, image or scent that represents something that a child/lion would encounter at that location in the virtual Savannah, such as an angry elephant.

The server also provides the data for the Den application and acts as a mediator between the Den and the client. During the game play, the Den application monitors and logs the movements, actions and consequences of the children/lions as reported to the server. At this point, the games server supporting the game was not fully automated; as a result, two members of the research team located in the Den were responsible for awarding and removing energy points from the children in the light of the children's actions in the field.

Study

We conducted an exploratory study to investigate children's use of Savannah and what they learnt about animal behaviour, research activities and collaboration after playing Savannah. It took place in a secondary school in Bristol (a city in the south-west of England). The children involved in the project were all from year 7 and were aged between 11 and 12 years. There were two groups: one group of five boys (day 1) and one group of five girls (day 2). The purpose of these first trials was both to test whether it was possible to overcome the technical challenges of building such a complex system combining games activities, media content and GPS, and to explore the underlying concepts concerning mobile game-based learning.

The days were organised into two challenges. In the first challenge, the children were told that they were a lion pride who had recently been displaced and had just arrived in a new area of the Savannah. The children had to get to know this area, understand what was in it and identify various threats and opportunities. The teacher introduced this challenge with a discussion about the types of habitat that might be found in a Savannah, and encouraged the children to consider what lions might need to survive there. During this phase, the children could NOT kill or be killed and so could freely explore the virtual Savannah. On each day, the group of children took two searches to fully explore the virtual Savannah outside. After each search the children went back to the Den and discussed with the teacher what they had found. The children used the flip chart paper to create a map of what they found and they used the interactive whiteboard to revisit their movements within the environment, examine where they had not searched and discuss how they could improve their search techniques.

In the second challenge, the children were told by the teacher that they had to learn to survive in the Savannah. In this challenge, the children could both die (if for example they attacked the wrong animal alone) and hunt, and their energy points would increase or decrease depending upon their actions. The group of boys had three games and the group of girls had four games and the games lasted approximately 15 min. After each phase the children went back in the Den and discussed with the teacher what had happened and what they could do differently in the next game. At the end of the day, the children had a discussion with the teacher about what they had learnt.

Observers of the trials were located both within the Den and outside in the play field. Within the Den two video cameras were set up to capture interactions and visual displays on the whiteboard, and two observers took field notes. Outside in the playing field, two observers watched each game and took field notes. A video camera with a radio microphone was trained on one child for each challenge—a different child for each challenge. At the end of each day, the children were interviewed in groups concerning their experience with Savannah. These interviews were videotaped. All the videotapes were transcribed.

Findings

As discussed in the introduction, the key challenges in designing the Savannah project have been to create an experience that encourages children's engagement and identification with their identity within the game, to encourage self-motivated attempts to overcome the obstacles in the game and thereby to achieve an understanding of the rule system on which it is based, namely, the rules of animal behaviour and interaction with the environment. We carried out an episodic analysis, where observers identified episodes in the game play and while the children were interviewed, which were concerned with either learning the rules of the game or engagement and identification. An independent observer classified these episodes and inter-observer reliability was adequate (80%).

Engagement and identification with games identity. Analysis of the video data provided some evidence to suggest that the students felt they were actually experiencing the Savannah, were identifying with their new roles 'as lions' and found it highly engaging. The students often talked in the game as if they were directly experiencing the simulation. During play, they exclaimed that 'I'm nearly dead', 'we're hot', 'we're attacking' and 'I'm dead'. Example 1 illustrates this point.

Example 1 (Game play)

G2   We need to get some water lets go
        Where's the water?
G3   We're too hot
        We're too hot are you?

Analysis of the post-interview also revealed evidence that students felt they were experiencing being on the savannah and found it engaging (see Examples 2–5).

Examples 2–5 (Interview)

2   B5   I actually thought that what was on the screen was actually what was real ...
3   G3   It felt like Africa
4   G4   The bit when it said it was getting too hot made it feel like Africa
5   B2   When there were flies I was like [turning head, to check where the flies were]'

This example also shows the importance of sound for making the children feel they were actually in the savannah. In the post-interview, two girls compared Savannah with horse-riding, saying that in both activities 'you could get killed'—suggesting that the perception of risk and identification with the role as lion was high.

The two most stimulating areas of the savannah were the fire and the Masai tribe; these zones triggered the most animation and physical response like dancing, singing, shouting or quickening of pace, some of which, such as the dancing, were repeated in the Den setting on hearing the sound again. Emotional responses to the play were also in evidence as the children responded visibly and audibly to the responses from the system. When they received a message that their attack was successful they cheered and punched the air; when they received a message that they were in danger they ran.

An interesting aspect of the game is its physical nature, which arguably contributes to the directness of the experience. When the children are running away from the elephant they are actually running and not moving an avatar in a desktop computer game and we would suggest that this aspect of Savannah supports children's learning. Furthermore, the physical nature of Savannah could contribute to children's enjoyment of the activity out in the field, because the physical exercise of running around a field and dancing can be an enjoyable experience in itself. These are characteristics of mobile gaming that are not shared with desktop gaming and we suggest that this could make mobile gaming more engaging and more direct than desktop gaming or simulations.

The engagement with the system was also evident when the children attributed significantly more intelligence to the system than it actually possessed, often assigning meaning to what was, in fact, little more than a vagary in the GPS. For example when the boys were all trying to group together to attack the elephant, one boy says 'Wait till I get it—damn the thing ran away man!' or when the GPS stopped transmitting and the image on their iPAQ froze, one boy shouted 'This lion is still chasing me!' On another occasion one boy said 'I've killed a bird and it's flown away'—when all that had happened was that he had seen a picture of a bird and then he moved into a new zone where a different image appeared.

At times, however, 'identification' with the role of lions broke down for a variety of technical reasons and because the design of the interaction within the game was not sufficiently sophisticated. On several early occasions, for example, the children had to come 'out of role' to allow difficulties with handsets or systems to be fixed. On others, the children expected a greater degree of sophistication in the system than was available. Example 6 shows that when the children were told they were too hot, the children moved into a watery area and began 'attacking' the water as they assumed that this would enable them to drink.

Example 6 (Game play)

G1	Do you attack it
G2	Attack the water
G1	You can't
	Do you attack
	It won't work
G2	I'm attacking the water
	You can't do it
G1	How do you get water [to observer]

All they needed to do was to stand in the water zone, but this was not clear and led to the only instance of a child directly addressing one of the observers during game play. At this point, the children were pulled out of the game experience to the reality of standing in a playing field working with very new and untested technology.

Post-interviews, particularly with the boys, also pointed out the extent to which this age group has grown up expecting rich and immersive media experiences when playing games. While observation of their game play suggested identification and immersion in the experience, these later reflections suggested that the children expected a much richer and interactive environment that, to date, this technology is unable to support (see Examples 7 and 8).

Example 7 (Interview)

B5   You couldn't like move around on the screen It was just like pictures

Example 8 (Interview)

B1   Also—the way that it worked
           That would actually do like a projection of where you are
           So you could see what is in front of you

What was also in evidence in post-interviews was the extent to which the children compared the experience with other perceived 'realities' of being in the Savannah. Most of the children, for example, were familiar with images of lion behaviours from television programmes, and explained how the games experience compared poorly with their perception of what they felt might happen in the 'real world' (see Example 9).

Example 9 (Interview)

G4   You couldn't like see all around the way around
G3   In reality you would like be able to move around and be able to see
           things a head of you
           So you could got away quicker
           If you were in danger
           You'd be able to see your other lions as well, not just other animals

This disjuncture between the reality of the games world and the reality of the actual Savannah is a problematic feature of the current game not only for the children in the study but also for the designers. There are a number of important technical challenges, for example, in achieving the responsiveness of the environment that the children would expect. More importantly, however, is the notion of different time scales in the 'real' Savannah as compared with the virtual Savannah. In the virtual Savannah, played out on a 100 m $\times$ 50 m playing field with no physical obstacles, for example, it is possible for children to traverse the area within 5 min. In a real Savannah, the same space would take lions several hours and would offer up numerous physical challenges— such as heat, other creatures and natural obstacles such as gullies, trees and marshes. The challenge of creating a 'real' experience of lions' day-to-day lives in a virtual environment mapped onto empty physical space remains on-going in terms of the prototype development.

Despite these caveats, however, identification with roles in games-play is not wholly reliant on 'realism', but on the perceived reality of the challenges within the game world. As one girl said during her post-interview 'when I watch the lion king, I'm kind of like watching, but now I know what it feels like to be a lion'. Children's identification with roles in the games illustrates the degree to which the children are directly experiencing the game in a way that can be qualitatively different from desktop gaming. However, the breakdowns in identification discussed above show that children's experience with the game was not always as direct as it could have been.

What have also emerged as of interest in the analysis of the video data are the numerous identities that children have to juggle in the games experience, which would lead us to look beyond simple 'identification with the role' as a feature of the learning experience. The children were required to act as 'lions acting as lions', as 'children acting as lions' and as 'children reflecting on their actions and the rules of the game' in order to play better. As Gee has noted, this is often a key feature of games play:

> Learning involves taking on and playing with identities in such a way that the learner has real choices (in developing the virtual identity) and ample opportunity to meditate on the relationship between new identities and old ones. There is a tripartite play of identities as learners relate, and reflect on, their multiple real-world identities, a virtual identity and a projective identity. (Gee, 2003, p. 208)

During the Savannah experience then, while children say 'I'm too hot' (as a lion), they are also saying 'Hey, look a lion cub—I'm going to kill it! Look I got points for that' when observing their energy points (child as lion), and also saying, on dying after deciding to attack the Masai, 'next time we wont do that!' (child as reflective games player).

The design of the day's experience, combining introduction to the game and reflection on play within the Den, with periods of play 'as lions', was intended to facilitate this interplay of identities as players and reflective learners. Children were encouraged, in the Den, to reflect on their success in mapping the Savannah play space and in achieving energy points. They were facilitated in this by being able to interrogate their actions, and 'relive' them by following the trials and actions they had made sequentially on the board. This process was facilitated by a teacher who had been asked to provide the children with the opportunity to reflect and to introduce them to relevant further information when it seemed useful. What was clearly observable from this process, however, was that another important aspect of children's identity as players of this game in a school setting was their identity as 'pupils'—when they were leading the reflection in the Den, interacting with the whiteboard and discussing their actions and strategies, they were highly engaged and motivated; when the locus of control in the Den rested with the teacher; however, they adopted a passive pupil identity that was resistant to engagement with the task. We will go on to explore this observation in more detail in the discussion.

Learning the 'Rules of the Game'. In principle, the interplay of different identities in a game should be an interplay between immersion and reflection, between the specifics of a particular challenge and coming to understand the rules of the game (Turkle 1984). If Savannah was designed successfully, then the children, through the games play, would begin to understand the rules that governed the game and, consequently, the rules that shape lion's behaviour in the wild.

In certain instances, we did see evidence that this was occurring. For example, a key feature of lion behaviour is quantification of risk—lions encountering lions from another pride will 'count' the numbers of their opponents before deciding whether to fight; they will calculate whether they have sufficient numbers to take on prey of different sizes. These features were all built into the game rules, with energy points awarded or deducted for children making the correct calculations. This sort of behaviour was encouraged by the game and in evidence in the children's play after their initial attempts (see Example 10).

Example 10 (Game play)

G3	What's this
G5	Wildebeest attack
G3	Attack a wildebeest
G5	Your not going to attack that all on your own
G5	Everyone attack it

Both groups became gradually aware that working in groups rather than isolation was likely to lead to greater success and also encouraged collaborative activities among the children. Example 11 shows the children coordinating their movements through the virtual space and worked together to perform attacks on prey.

Example 11 (Game play)

G4	A baby lion
	Do we attack it
G3	Yeah
G4	1, 2, 3 attack

These behaviours were reinforced by the facilitators' awarding of energy points, and were largely seen to be spontaneously developed behaviours. Indeed, it was one of the features that the boys in particular mentioned after playing (see Example 12).

Example 12 (Interview)

B1   Because we learnt to trust each other and know that if you attacked something, the others wouldn't leave you on your own to get killed

The game allowed the children to make and test hypotheses about the relative merits of working in groups to overcome prey of various sizes—for example, regardless of the number of children/lions attacking it, an angry elephant would always cause severe loss of energy points, and often death (as it would in the wild).

Similarly, the children were encouraged to become aware of the other threats that faced lions in the Savannah, such as human habitation, and to balance these with the opportunities these offered for energy in the form of food. Example 13 illustrates the children discussing these opportunities.

Example 13 (Game play)

G1   We have prey
G5   We have prey
         We have
G3   Yeah we have Goat
G5   River
G1   Grass
G3   Yeah but we have humans
G5   Okay
         Yeah but humans
G1   Prey
G3   They might make trouble

Other rules of the game environment were built into the geography of the Savannah itself, namely that there are features of the environment and threats in the environment that limit lion movements (fire, humans, other prides, features such as major rivers). Moreover, the game geography also served to highlight the richness and diversity of the Savannah; in other words, what kinds of animals there might be found sharing a lion's habitat, for example, other lions, zebra, wildebeest, elephants, vultures, biting flies and termites.

The children were, however, also coming to learn certain rules about the games environment that in fact conflicted with the generalised understanding of the Savannah that had been intended. For example, children had little understanding of the complexities of actual lion hunting strategies, which could be taught very effectively in this experiential manner. As can be seen from Example 14, they were happy to coordinate attacks and actively pursued this strategy but clearly there is far more to a lion hunt than collaborative timing of attack. No consideration was given to formation or strategy.

Example 13 (Game play)

G3	We got a lion
	Don't attack it
G1	Attack
G4	1, 2, 3 attack

Similarly, the children were not encouraged to develop an understanding of how lions actually use the territorial space of the Savannah. Due to the game design, they were being reinforced to think that lions spend equal amounts of time in all areas of the Savannah; this was because of a lack of accurate understanding about the structure of lion behaviour over a typical day, too much emphasis was placed on repeatedly killing prey (as the children found this to be the most rewarding aspect of the game), and the prey could be found all over the savannah. Thus the children were motivated to repeatedly search around the savannah, killing prey indiscriminately.

Part of this problem stems from a reinforced lack of differentiation in the game rules between the relative energy costs of going after some types of prey; the children began to think that it was beneficial to go after all types of prey and attack all types of threat without discrimination. The fact that the only digitally mediated interaction that the game afforded was of 'attacking' further privileged the strategy of coming together to attack, rather than reflecting on other actions a lion might use.

What was clear from this pilot study was that the children were very quickly coming to identify the rules and problems within the game, and as such, the main challenge to designers is to develop sufficiently sophisticated games rules, and sufficiently focused challenges in order to encourage the children to attempt different strategies to overcome these problems. For example, when specific challenges were presented to the children, such as the message 'you are too hot', then they were able to identify the need for water to cool themselves down (Example 3). Similarly, when they were low on energy, they understood that they needed to search for food. However, these types of challenges led only to fairly low-level strategic solutions (albeit solutions that were successful within the game as currently designed), namely, that certain animals required more than one lion to attack and that certain animals should not be attacked such as the Elephant and the Masai.

Discussion

The savannah prototype offers a number of interesting insights into the extent to which mobile gaming could be used as a tool for supporting learning, and a number of major challenges that this format raises for the organisation of learning within schools and the design of such resources.

One key aspect to emerge from the study was the importance of paying detailed attention to the question of how learners might 'manage' their identities as games players, as characters (lions) within a game, as strategic reflective thinkers about the game world and as pupils within a school setting. One of the least successful aspects of the trial was the attempt to combine a more formal 'schooled' experience with the games play. As many commentators are increasingly arguing in relation to computer games, in particular in relation to massively multiplayer online games, players are fully able to develop strategic and critical thinking in relation to computer games as part of a gaming community in which the dominant pedagogic approaches consist of just-in-time learning, trial and error and participation in activities with more knowledgeable others. Explicit teaching and injunctions to reflect on actions tend to occur only in response to specific requests rather than as a framing activity for the games play. From our observations, the greatest failure of the study to date was the failure to maximise the opportunity for the children to act as self-motivated learners in the Den setting, reflecting on and developing strategies for improved games play. Instead, perhaps out of our own concern about the limitations of the game structure, we offered children the opportunity to act as players outside, and then in the Den requested that they act 'as pupils' and listen to useful information. This failed to encourage children either to look for, or to use, the more complex theoretical information on lion behaviour that was available to them for use in the game.

What has become clear is that the use of games formats are unlikely to sit easily alongside traditional classroom power relations. Gamers are expert when they control their own learning alongside more knowledgeable peers. If these sorts of experiences are likely to be successful, we may need to build in the expectation that children as gamers are more likely to learn effectively by subsequently acting as mentors to novice learners (see Gee, 2003; Williamson, 2003). This will require some degree of courage, and, to be honest, some reorganisation of the school setting.

In order for this sort of model to be effective, it is clear that the challenges presented in the game require significant modification. In the Savannah game to date, we have two overarching challenges: 'map your new territory' and 'survive'. What emerged from the study was that children expect and respond effectively to significantly more focused challenges (for example, when told that they were hot and needed to do something about it). At the same time, the challenges were simply insufficiently 'challenging'—we had underestimated our players. For games to encourage the sorts of problem solving, hypothesis generation and testing that are in evidence in effective mainstream games and in the best learning environments, the challenges need to be real and complex and difficult to solve. They need to be, as Kirschner et al. (2002) call it, 'wicked-problems' that

Kirschner P., Buckingham Shum S., & Carr C. (2002). *Visualizing Argumentation, Software Tools for Collaborative and Educational Sense Making.* New York: Springer.

Malone T. (1980). *What makes things fun to learn? A study of intrinsically motivating computer games.* Palo Alto: Xerox.

Price S., Rogers Y., Scaife M., Stanton D., & Neale (2003). Using tangibles to promote novel forms of playful learning. *Interacting with Computers, 15,* 169–185.

Rogers Y., Scaife M., Gabrielli S., Smith H., & Harris E. (2002). A conceptual framework for mixed reality environments: designing novel learning activities for young children. *Presence, 11,* 677–686.

Roschelle J., & Pea R. D. (2002). A walk on the WILD side: how wireless handhelds may change computer-supported collaborative learning. In G. Stahl (Ed.), *Proceedings of the International Conference on Computer Support for Collaborative Learning 2002* (pp. 51–60). Mahwah, NJ: Lawrence Erlbaum Associates.

Sharples M., Corlett D., & Westmancott O. (2002). The design and implementation of a mobile learning resource. *Personal and Ubiquitous Computing, 6,* 220–234.

Squire K. (2003). *Gameplay in Context: Learning Through Participation in Communities of Civilization III Players.* Unpublished PhD Thesis. Instructional Systems Technology Department, Indiana University.

Stanton D., O'Malley C., Fraser M., Ng M., & Benford S. (2003). Situating historical events through mixed reality: adult–child interactions in the Storytent. In B. Wasson, S. Ludvigsen, & U. Hoppe (Eds.), *Proceedings of the International Conference on Computer Support for Collaborative Learning 2003* (pp. 293–303). Dordect: Kluwer.

Turkle S. (1984). *The second self: Computers and the human spirit.* Granada, London: Simon & Schuster, New York.

Wegerif R. (2003). *Thinking Skills, Technology and Learning: NESTA Futurelab Literature Review.* NESTA Futurelab, Bristol. Retrieved January 30, 2004, from http://www.nesta futurelab.org/research.

Williamson B. (2003). *The Participation of Children in the Design of New Technology: NESTA Futurelab Discussion Paper.* NESTA Futurelab, Bristol. Retrieved January 30, 2004, from http://www.nestafuturelab.org/research.

Commentary Responses

Being a Lion and Being a Soldier:
Learning and Games

JAMES PAUL GEE
ARIZONA STATE UNIVERSITY, USA

Learning in Popular Culture

In this chapter, we want to discuss the larger issue of the contribution modern video game technologies can make to learning by focusing on one paper: Facer et al.'s (2004) paper, "Savannah: Mobile Gaming and Learning?" (hereafter, "SMGL"). This paper is one of a number of recent educational studies that seek to draw on the power of modern popular culture to enhance school-based learning (McFarlane, Sparrowhawk, & Heald, 2002). In fact, SMGL (Facer et al., 2004) attempts to combine two popular technologies: wireless mobile devices and video games. Since both are used for powerful purposes outside school, SMGL argues that "the school setting should at least begin to engage with these tools" (p. 399).

Before we discuss SMGL (Facer et al., 2004) directly, we want to discuss the wider context in which the paper has appeared and the context in which it should be read. Then, we will turn to a direct discussion of the paper. Finally, we will place SMGL in the context of commercial video games that seek to teach "content," as does the project SMGL describes, though quite different content is involved in the two cases. Ultimately, what we are talking about is how modern "digital literacies" (in this case, video games) can deepen learning both inside and outside school as we know it, especially our current skill-and-drill sorting system. This project has a critical edge; however, we know too little as of yet to go right to critical politics in this area. We need to get a feeling for this new landscape before we can fully sort out the political responses we should have to our new media and their uses and abuses. Therefore, we leave deep critical responses—for example, claims that video games reflect cultural prejudices (e.g., *Grand Theft Auto: San Andreas Fault)* or commercial culture (e.g., *The Sims)*—aside for the time being.

Over the last few years, interest in the contrast between popular culture and school has risen (Gee, 2003, 2004; Johnson, 2005; Lankshear, 1997; Lankshear & Knobel, 2003; Prensky, 2006; Shaffer, Squire, Halverson, & Gee, 2005). Today, young people sometimes seem to engage in deeper learning in their popular culture than they do in school, especially schools devoted to skill-and-drill in the service of passing standardized tests.

SMGL (Facer et al., 2004) wants to draw on the power of gaming to recruit school-based learning, so we consider, for a moment, video games like *Rise of Nations*, *Age of Mythology*, *Deus Ex*, *The Elder Scrolls III: Morrowind*, and *Tony Hawk's Underground*. Modern commercial video games are long, complex, and difficult. If they could not be learned, they would not be played, and in fact, it has been argued that such games recruit learning as a form of pleasure (Gee, 2005). We survey a few of the learning features that good video games incorporate as a way to teach and to create active engagement (Games-to-Teach Team, 2003; Gee, 2003, 2004). The reader should contrast these features, as we discuss them, with how learning often works in schools today. It is learning features like these that the authors of SMGL wanted to recruit, and we can reflect, as well, on how well they did this when we more directly discuss SMGL (Facer et al., 2004). The following are some learning features that good video games often incorporate into their design.

Good video games offer players strong identities. Learning a new domain, whether physics or furniture making, requires learning to see and value work and the world in new ways, for example, the ways in which physicists or furniture makers do. In video games, players learn to view the virtual world through the eyes and values of a distinctive identity (e.g., Solid Snake in *Metal Gear Solid*) or one they themselves have built from the ground up (e.g., in *The Elder Scrolls III: Morrowind*).

Good video games make players think like scientists. Game play is built on a cycle typical of experimental science: hypothesize, probe the world, get a reaction, reflect on the results, re-probe to get better results.

Good video games let players be producers, not just consumers. An open-ended game like *The Elder Scrolls III: Morrowind* is, in the end, a different game for each player. Players codesign the game through their unique actions and decisions. At another level, many games come with software through which players can modify ("mod") them, producing new scenarios or whole new games (e.g., new skate parks in the *Tony Hawk* games).

Good games lower the consequences of failure. When players fail, they can start from their last saved game. Players are encouraged to take risks, explore, and try new things.

Good games allow players to customize the game to fit their learning and playing styles. Games often have different difficulty levels and many allow problems to be solved in multiple ways.

Thanks to all the preceding features, players feel a real sense of agency, ownership, and control; it is *their* game.

Learning, however, goes even deeper in good games. Research has shown that when learners are left free in problem spaces, they often hit on creative solutions to complex problems, but solutions that do not lead to good hypotheses for later, even easier problems (Gee, 2003). In good video games, problems are well ordered so that earlier ones lead to hypotheses that work well for later, harder problems.

Good games offer players a set of challenging problems and let them practice these problems until they have routinized their mastery. Then, the game throws a new class of problems at the players (this is sometimes called a "boss"), requiring them to rethink their taken-for-granted mastery. In turn, this new mastery is consolidated through repetition (with variation), only to be challenged again. This cycle of consolidation and challenge is the basis of the development of expertise in any domain (Bereiter & Scardamalia, 1993).

Good games stay within, but at the outer edge of, the player's "regime of competence" (diSessa, 2000); that is, they feel "doable," but challenging. This makes them pleasantly frustrating—a flow state for human beings (Csikszent-mihalyi, 1990).

Games encourage players to think about relationships—not isolated events—facts, and skills. In a game like *Rise of Nations*, players need to think about how each action they take might impact their future actions and the actions of the opposing players as they move their civilizations through the ages.

Games encourage a distinctive view of intelligence. Many baby boomers think that being smart is moving as fast and as efficiently as possible toward their goals. Games encourage players to thoroughly explore before moving on, to think laterally (not just linearly), and to use such exploration and lateral thinking to reconceive their goals from time to time. They encourage good ideas in a world full of high-risk, complex systems.

Games recruit smart tools. The virtual characters that players manipulate in games are "smart tools." They have skills and knowledge of their own, which they lend to the player. For example, the citizens in *Rise of Nations* know how to build cities, but the player needs to know where to build them. This means that the knowledge to play the game is distributed between the player and smart tools that themselves store knowledge.

Games often recruit cross-functional teams in which each person has a distinctive expertise (function) but can integrate well with the skills (functions) of the other team members (making the team cross-functional), just like modern, high-tech workplaces. In a multiplayer game like *World of Warcraft*, players play on teams in which each player has a different set of skills (functions).

Each player must master a specialty, since a Mage plays differently than a Warrior, but understand enough of each other's specializations to coordinate with them. Furthermore, on such teams, people are affiliated by their commitment to a common endeavor, not primarily by their race, class, ethnicity, or gender (Gee, 2004). The latter are available as resources for the whole group if or when players wish to use them. Thus, the core knowledge needed to play video games is distributed among a set of real people and, as we mentioned earlier, their smart tools, just as knowledge is distributed in a modern science lab or high-tech workplace.

Video games operate by a principle of performance before competence. Players can perform before they are competent because of the design of the game, the "smart tools" the game offers, and often, other, more advanced players (either in the game or in chat rooms) support them.

People are poor at dealing with lots of words out of context. Games usually give verbal information "just in time"—when players need and can use it—or "on demand" when players ask for it. Furthermore, research suggests that people really know what words mean only when they can hook them to the sorts of experiences to which they refer, that is, to the sorts of actions, images, or dialogues to which the words relate (Gee, 2004). This gives the words situated meanings, not just verbal ones. Games always situate ("show") the meanings of words and show how they vary across different actions, images, and dialogues. They do not just offer words for words ("definitions").

At this point, the reader should stop and ask himself or herself whether the features of video games we have just surveyed would or would not be good learning features to have in a school curriculum, even if no game were involved. We think most readers will say "yes" to this question. In fact, these learning features, which players see in good video games, are all well supported by research in the learning sciences (Gee, 2003, 2004, 2005). All of them could present in school, for example in learning science (diSessa, 2000), even if no game were present; however, today, they are often better represented in popular culture than in school. When we evaluate projects like SMGL (Facer et al., 2004), we can use these features—and others like them—as a checklist to see how "game-like" (versus traditional "school-like") the learning the project recruited was.

"Savannah: Mobile Gaming and Learning?"

Now, we turn to SMGL (Facer et al., 2004) and consider how it did or did not use these sorts of learning features connected to good games. SMGL reports on a project that explored the learning that occurred in a setting where 11- to 12-year-old children from Bristol, England, used mobile technologies in a game-like set of activities. These activities involved both moving around in real space (a field) and acting on the basis of virtual images seen and sounds heard via the mobile device.

The specific goal of the project was to develop children's conceptual understanding of animal behavior and interaction with the environment. The children played at "being a pride of lions" (Facer et al., 2004, p. 400) outside in a playing field. They had global positioning systems (GPSs) linked to personal digital assistants (PDAs) that allowed them to "see," "hear," and "smell" the world of the Savannah (via their PDAs with headphones) as they navigated the real playing field space outdoors (having to ignore, we suppose, the real sights and sounds of the field). The virtual Savannah map on the PDA comprised a number of zones including long grass, short grass, gully, kopje, spring, and trees. These areas were populated by various sorts of wildlife. Each zone was correlated with (and triggered by) a part of the real field through which the children moved. The children also had an energy bar that let them know their specific energy levels at any time.

In addition, the children engaged with an indoor space, called the "Den," where they worked with teachers to reflect on how well they had succeeded in the game, access other resources to support their understanding, and develop strategies for surviving as lions in the virtual Savannah. The "Den" operated less like a game and more like a classroom.

In this game, the children were required to act as a pride of lions. Their main challenge was to understand and survive in the Savannah. They had to balance the costs and benefits of different types of activity—whether attacking, drinking, sleeping, or running—in order to maintain their energy levels. They also had to negotiate with each other in order to decide whether or how to collaborate in achieving objectives.

The researchers reported that analyses of their data provided evidence to suggest that the students felt that they were actually experiencing the Savannah, that they were identifying with their new roles as lions, and that they found it highly engaging (Facer et al., 2004). The students often talked in the game as if they were directly experiencing the simulation. During play, they said things such as "I'm nearly dead," "We're hot," and "We're attacking" (p. 403).

The researchers remarked that an interesting aspect of the game is its physical nature, which they believed contributes to the "directness of the experience" (Facer et al., 2004, p. 403). They pointed out that when the children were, for example, running away from the elephant, they were actually running and not moving an avatar in a desktop computer game. This, they suggested, "supports children's learning" (p. 403), though it is not clear, to us at least, how.

While observation of game play suggested identification and immersion in the experience, the researchers nonetheless reported that the children, due to their experience with much more sophisticated commercial games and other media, expected a much richer and more interactive environment (Facer et al., 2004). A bigger problem, however, was the disjuncture between the reality of the game world and the reality of an actual Savannah. This was a problematic feature not only for the children in the study, but also for the researchers themselves.

One example of this disjuncture was the notion of different time scales in a real Savannah as compared to the virtual Savannah. In the virtual Savannah, played out on a playing field with no physical obstacles, for example, it is possible for children to traverse the area within five minutes. In a real Savannah, the same space would take lions several hours and would offer numerous physical challenges. The authors pointed out, then, that "[t]he challenge of creating a 'real' experience of lions' day-to-day lives in a virtual environment mapped onto empty physical space remains on-going in terms of the prototype development" (Facer et al, 2004, pp. 404–405). Despite these caveats, the researchers claimed,

> Identification with roles in games-play is not wholly reliant on "realism," but on the perceived reality of the challenges within the game world … Children's identification with roles in the games illustrates the degree to which the children are directly experiencing the game in a way that can be qualitatively different from desktop gaming. However, the breakdowns in identification discussed above show that children's experience with the game was not always as direct as it could have been. (p. 405)

One of the most interesting findings of the research was the numerous identities that the children had to juggle in the game's experience. This finding

> would lead us to look beyond simple "identification with the role" as a feature of the learning experience. The children were required to act as "lions acting as lions," as "children acting as lions" and as "children reflecting on their actions and the rules of the game" in order to play better. (Facer et al., 2004, p. 405)

During the Savannah experience, the children said things like "I'm too hot" (speaking as lion), but they also said things like "Hey, look a lion cub—I'm going to kill it! Look I got points for that" (child as lion) when observing their energy points. In addition, they said things like "Next time we won't do that!" (child as reflective game player) upon on their death after deciding to attack the Masai (Facer et al., 2004, p. 405).

The researchers hoped that the interplay of these different identities would lead to an interplay, as well, between immersion and reflection and between the specifics of a particular challenge and an understanding of the rules of the game (Facer et al., 2004). The researchers' intention was to design a game in which the rules that governed the game directly reflected the rules that shape lion behavior in the wild. This means that children could come to understand lion behavior (the academic goal) by understanding—through action and interaction—the rules of the video/mobile game. In certain instances, the researchers did see evidence that this was occurring:

For example, a key feature of lion behaviour is quantification of risk—lions encountering lions from another pride will "count" the numbers of their opponents before deciding whether to fight; they will calculate whether they have sufficient numbers to take on prey of different sizes. These features were all built into the game rules, with energy points awarded or deducted for children making the correct calculations. This sort of behaviour was encouraged by the game and in evidence in the children's play after their initial attempts. (pp. 405–406)

In addition, the children gradually became aware that working in groups, rather than in isolation, was likely to lead to greater success, and this encouraged collaborative activities among the children. At the same time, however, the children were also coming to learn certain rules about the game's environment that conflicted with the generalized understanding of the Savannah that the researchers had intended (Facer et al., 2004). For example, while the children did develop an understanding of how lions actually use the territorial space of the Savannah, due to the game design, they were being reinforced to think that lions spend equal amounts of time in all areas of the Savannah. This was due, it seems, to a lack of accurate understanding about the structure of lion behavior over a typical day. Too much emphasis was placed on repeatedly killing prey (as the children found this to be the most rewarding aspect of the game), and the prey could be found all over the Savannah. Thus, the children were motivated to repeatedly search around the Savannah, indiscriminately killing prey.

The researchers admitted that one of the least successful aspects of the project was the attempt to combine a more formal "school" experience with game play (Facer et al., 2004). Reflecting on the fact that, in popular culture, young people develop strategic and critical thinking in relation to video games as part of a gaming community, a community in which the dominant approach to learning is just-in-time learning, trial and error, and participation in activities with more knowledgeable peers, the researchers commented,

From our observations, the greatest failure of the study to date was the failure to maximise the opportunity for the children to act as self-motivated learners in the Den setting, reflecting on and developing strategies for improved games play. Instead, perhaps out of our own concern about the limitations of the game structure, we offered children the opportunity to act as players outside, and then in the Den requested that they act "as pupils" and listen to useful information. This failed to encourage children either to look for, or to use, the more complex theoretical information on lion behaviour that was available to them for use in the game. (p. 407)

In the end, the researchers said that it has become clear to them that the use of a games approach to learning is "unlikely to sit easily alongside traditional classroom power relations" (Facer et al., 2004, p. 407). Gamers in popular culture control their own learning with the help of more knowledgeable peers. If approaches like the one taken in SMGL are too successful, the researchers concluded that

> we may need to build in the expectation that children as gamers are more likely to learn effectively by subsequently acting as mentors to novice learners (see Gee, 2003; Williamson, 2003). This will require some degree of courage, and, to be honest, some reorganisation of the school setting. (p. 407)

Games and Learning

The Savannah project in SMGL (Facer et al., 2004) is a good project—both in terms of what worked and what did not—with which to think. To what extent does it draw on the power of video games—features of which we discussed in the first section—to create motivation and deep problem solving? The key to this issue lies in something directly stated in SMGL: The researchers' intention was to design a game in which the rules that governed the game directly reflected the rules that shape lion behavior in the wild. That is, what you do in the game—in terms of actions and goals—should directly correlate with and reflect what lions do in the wild. This match is the heart and soul of building a learning game. Where it was done well, the Savannah project worked well, and where it was not done well, the Savannah project did not work as well.

A video game is a rule system. Players seek to discover how these rules work in order to solve problems and accomplish goals. To do so, they control pieces of the in-game world (an avatar or a number of them). In SMGL (Facer et al., 2004), the children controlled their real bodies by moving around a real field, while watching images of lions and other things on a screen.

Many commercial games do not have "content" in the sense that algebra or chemistry has content (e.g., a body of facts, principles, and regularities that fall within a specific well-defined domain of knowledge). In this sense of "content," *Mario* has not got content. The Savannah project was, of course, intended to have content in the academic sense, though we will see soon that its actual content is not entirely clear.

Some commercial video games—oddly enough—do have content in the sense of a well-defined domain of knowledge. For example, the game *Full Spectrum Warrior* is about the knowledge needed to be a professional soldier, and *S.W.A.T.4* is about the knowledge needed to be a professional S.W.A.T. team member. Of course, being a soldier or a police officer is not like being a chemist or an historian, but they are all domains in which people act on the basis of special knowledge. It is around such domains that school and schooling are defined. Indeed, as we will see, what video games suggest to us learning theorists is that we should view things like being a chemist or an historian as roles people play, goals they have, and activities they do, rather than as a long list of facts outside any context of goals and action.

Oddly enough, it is not really clear what the content of the Savannah project in SMGL (Facer et al., 2004) is. It appears at first blush to be "acting and thinking like a lion." On reflection, however, it appears to be "acting and thinking like a human ecologist who studies lions." In reality, the game (outside in the field) is devoted mostly (but not entirely) to the first goal, and the nongame, school-like environment inside in the Den is devoted to the second goal. Two different rule sets occur here: a game-like one in role-playing a lion and a school-like one in learning about lion ecology. The children were not, however, encouraged to reflect on the differences between these roles—between the expertise of a lion and the expertise of a human ecologist and the relationships (and contrasts) between them.

To get a deeper view of how game rules and content can be married, we can look at one of the commercial games that consummates that marriage well: *Full Spectrum Warrior* (Gee, 2005). Such games reflect all the learning features we started with in the first section, so it is instructive to compare and contrast them with something like the Savannah project.

Full Spectrum Warrior teaches the player (yes, it is a teacher) how to be a professional soldier. It demands that the player thinks, values, and acts like one to win the game. In *Full Spectrum Warrior*, the player uses the buttons on the controller to give orders to the soldiers, as well as to consult a GPS device, radio for support, and communicate with command. The Instruction Manual that comes with the game makes it clear from the outset that players must think, act, and value like a professional soldier to play the game successfully: "Everything about your squad ... is the result of careful planning and years of experience on the battlefield. Respect that experience, soldier, since it's what will keep your soldiers alive." (Pandemic Studios, 2004, p. 2)

By the way, thinking and acting like a soldier is not the same thing as thinking and acting like a military historian or professional military strategist directing a whole war (actually, a quite different category of game devoted to the latter exists). Furthermore, simply reflecting on being and performing as a soldier will not, in and of itself, lead to the insights of the historian or the strategist (though they are relevant, of course). In addition, being and performing as a lion—even reflecting on being and performing as a lion—will not, in and of itself, lead to the insights of an ecologist. They are two different (though partially related) "games."

Beyond values, another important aspect of *Full Spectrum Warrior* is the fact that the virtual characters in the game (the soldiers in the squads) and the real-world player control different parts of the domain of military knowledge. We get the whole domain only when we put their knowledge together. The knowledge is *distributed* between them. A human (the player) shares knowledge with a virtual reality (the soldiers).

Full Spectrum Warrior is designed in such a way that certain knowledge and skills are built right into the virtual characters, both the soldiers and the enemies. Other knowledge must be learned and used by the player:

> The soldiers on your teams have been trained in movement formations, so your role is to select the best position for them on the field. They will automatically move to the formation selected and take up their scanning sectors, each man covering an arc of view. (Pandemic Studios, 2004, p. 15)

Thus, the virtual characters (the soldiers) have some knowledge (the various movement formations), and you, the player, have other knowledge (when and where to engage in such formations). This is true of every aspect of military knowledge in the game. Your soldiers know different things than you know and have mastered different bits of professional military practice than the bits you need to master to play the game. The game only works when the two different bits are put together—thought about and acted on—as a whole by the player who uses the virtual soldiers as smart tools or resources.

The player is immersed in activity, values, and ways of seeing. The player, however, is scaffolded by the knowledge built into the virtual characters and the weapons, equipment, and environments in the game. The player is also scaffolded by some quite explicit instruction given "just in time," when it can be understood in action and through experiences that make clear what the words really mean in context. The learner is not left to his or her own devices to rediscover the foundations of a professional practice that took hundreds of years to develop.

This distribution of knowledge allows for the operation of an important learning principle: "performance before competence" (Gee, 2005, p. 62). When players start the game, they have very little competence at being soldiers, but thanks to the fact that the virtual soldiers know a good deal, they can act right away and make at least some headway. They can start by performing, gain competence, and then, if they want, read those texts and actually understand them, thanks to the fact that they now have some images and experiences with which to comprehend them. In school, when students have little competence, they are expected to sit around and read a great deal of text before they get to do anything.

Many will object to *Full Spectrum Warrior* because of its ideology (values and worldview). What this type of game exemplifies, however, is that there is no real learning without some ideology. Adopting a certain set of values and a particular worldview is intimately connected to doing the activities and having the experiences that constitute any specific domain of knowledge. Physicists hold certain values and adopt a specific worldview because their knowledge making is based on seeing and valuing the world in certain ways. The values and worldview of astrologists comport badly with those of an astronomer; the values and world view of a creationist comport badly with those of an evolutionary biologist.

As one masters *Full Spectrum Warrior,* through scaffolded activity based on distributed knowledge, facts—many of them—come free. All sorts of arcane words and information that would be hard to retain through rote drill become part of one's arsenal (tools) through which activity is accomplished and experience is understood. For example, one player now knows what "bounding" means in military practice, how it is connected to military values, and its tactical role in achieving military goals. If another player knows only what it means in terms of a verbal definition, her or his understanding could not begin to compete with the first player.

All games involve content. They build a virtual world of a certain sort, but only some of them involve content in the same way school does—in terms of well-defined domains of knowledge. Players playing any game must reflectively become aware of how the game's content (world) is designed to facilitate or retard goals, choices, strategies, and actions. If that content were, however, a branch of science—for example, a certain type of biology—the player would have to consider the content of biology not as a set of passive facts, but as a domain of facts, information, values, and practices that enhance or retard certain goals, choices, strategies, and actions, namely those of a certain type of scientist. This, then, would be science not as inert content, but as a "way of life," as a way of being in the world that leads to certain sorts of values, goals, and actions rooted in a body of facts, information, and practices. That is, of course, what *Full Spectrum Warrior* does for soldiering and *S.W.A.T. 4* does for being a S.W.A.T. team member. It is too bad we have no *Full Spectrum Chemist, Historian,* or *Biologist* (though we do have a *Full Spectrum Urban Planner,* Will Wright's *SimCity*).

The theory of learning in many of our schools today is based on what we call the "content fetish" (Gee, 2004, pp. 117–118). The content fetish is the view that any academic area, whether it is physics, sociology, or history, is composed of a set of facts or a body of information, and the way learning should work is through teaching and testing such facts and information. Indeed, this is a view of schooling and knowledge that SMGL (Facer et al., 2004) is meant to combat, though, perhaps it did not combat it far enough, especially in the Den. *Know,* however, is a verb before it is a noun, as in *knowledge.* Any domain of knowledge, academic or not, is first and foremost a set of activities (special ways of acting and interacting to produce and use knowledge) and experiences (special ways of seeing, valuing, and being in the world). Physicists *do* physics, they *talk* physics, and when they are being physicists, they *see* and *value* the world in a different way than do nonphysicists. The same goes for good anthropologists, linguists, urban planners, army officers, doctors, artists, literary critics, historians, and so forth (diSessa, 2000; Lave, 1996; Ochs, Gonzales, & Jacoby, 1996; Shaffer, 2004).

SMGL (Facer et al., 2004) seeks, in some sense, to be a *Full Spectrum Lion*, but at times confounds and confuses this with trying to be a *Full Spectrum Lion Ecologist* (though this part is mostly played out in the Den outside of a gaming framework). Gaming was all right for playing a lion, but not for playing an ecologist, even though both are rule-governed (patterned) ways of being in the world and thus, open to being games. If we make them games, however, we need to be clear on which game we are playing (lion or ecologist, because each game has different rules and patterns), why we are playing it, and what the relationship is between the two games.

The Savannah project (SMGL), despite using wireless connections and handheld devices, does not have the sophisticated distribution of knowledge between computer characters and environments and real-world players of *Full Spectrum Warrior*. The virtual lions are not "smart" in the way that *Full Spectrum Warrior* soldiers are, and they do not scaffold the player's learning and growing skills like those soldiers do. Scaffolding is left, by and large, to teachers and texts outside the game. The match between the game rules (what players do to accomplish goals and win the game) and the knowledge and values of being a soldier is closer in *Full Spectrum Warrior* than it is between the game rules in the Savannah project and the knowledge and values of being either a lion or a lion ecologist.

In the end, SMGL (Facer et al., 2004) leaned too far toward school and not far enough toward solid gaming, and ironically, did not facilitate as deep a learning as it might have. In a good game, everything to be learned is tied tightly to the rules of the game and to the goals the player is trying to achieve by working within and understanding the full power of those rules. If the game has content in the academic sense, then the game rules need to be closely married to the content, so that in understanding one, the player understands the other. This is what *Full Spectrum Warrior* and *S.W.A.T.4* do so well. They achieve this over and above the learning features we discussed in the first section.

In SMGL (Facer et al., 2004), however, some elements float free of the game rules and goals. For example, running across a real field plays no integral role in the rules or goals of the lion game, and at times, contradicts those rules (e.g., five minutes across a field with no obstacles is not equal to hours of effort across a tough terrain). Going to the Den (the ecologist "game" played by school rules) is not well integrated with the rules and goals of the lion game. Indeed, even in the lion game, it would seem that confusion or confounding exists between thinking like a lion and thinking like a human ecologist. For example, lions do not meditate on their energy levels by looking at data. Rather, they get weaker, it gets harder to do things, and they have to deal with it or die—so, this is how it has to work in a game.

Nonetheless, the SMGL (Facer et al., 2004) was on to something important. A great power exists in the tri-part play of identities between "being a lion," "being a lion ecologist," and "being 'Susie,'" (an actual child with all her real world identities, desires, and interests). In the project, there is real potential for powerful interactions. If all three had consistently been "gamed" and their relationships and contrasts had been guided and reflected upon, things may have gotten even better. This would have been more like playing *Full Spectrum Warrior* (getting into the shoes of a soldier on the ground) than playing *Combat Mission 2: Barbarossa to Berlin* (getting into the shoes of a military strategist who looks at the big picture, mediates on the relationships between the two, and reflects, as well, on his or her own real-world identities, values, and desires and how they relate to being a soldier and a strategist). We could go further: playing war journalist, politician, and peace activist, comparing and contrasting all the way.

SMGL (Facer et al., 2004) is a good paper because it is honest and insightful about what worked and what did not. It is good design research—a type of research based on cycles of design, assess, critique, and try again—in that respect. What we have wanted to stress here is that this design research process could be aided by a deeper meditation on games and gaming. We are prepared to take schooling and school content seriously, but we are just learning to take games seriously.

One thing that SMGL (Facer et al., 2004) surely gets right is that game-like learning is not only about the game in the box, but also about a whole learning and social system built around the game. Wiring the learners together so they can collaborate and form a social system is a wonderful learning feature. SMGL is a good start at building a learning system around a game. In that respect, the authors are more in the position of the Army using *Full Spectrum Warrior* to train real troops than they are in the position of gamers playing a game for their own edification. Surely, we live in a world where we need to become as adept as—hopefully even better than—the Army at getting people to learn, especially to learn knowledge domains beyond fighting. In order to do that, we would have to make good games of our own.

In this chapter, we are trying to suggest a strategy for people who want to design games for content-based school-like learning—games like the Savannah project. The first part of the strategy is to reflect on the learning features incorporated into good commercial games, even if they do not involve academic content. The second part of the strategy is to reflect on good commercial games like *Full Spectrum Warrior* or *S.W.A.T. 4* or simulation games like *Zoo Tycoon*, *SimCity*, *Civilization*, or *Roller Coaster Tycoon* that do "teach" content, even if their content is politically "incorrect" or unappealing in some respects (as many people will find soldiering). This is another thing that we—educators—have to learn from popular culture.

References

Bereiter, C., & Scardamalia, M. (1993). *Surpassing ourselves: An inquiry into the nature and implications of expertise.* Chicago: Open Court.

Csikszentmihalyi, M. (1990). *Flow: The psychology of optimal experience.* New York: Harper Collins.

diSessa, A. A. (2000). *Changing minds: Computers, learning, and literacy.* Cambridge, MA: MIT Press.

Facer, K., Joiner, R., Stanton, D., Reid, J., Hull, R., & Kirk, D. (2005). Savannah: Mobile gaming and learning? *Journal of Computer Assisted Learning, 20,* 399–409.

Games-to-Teach Team. (2003). Design principles of next-generation digital gaming for education. *Educational Technology, 43,* 17–33.

Gee, J. P. (2003). *What video games have to teach us about learning and literacy.* New York: Palgrave/Macmillan.

Gee, J. P. (2004). *Situated language and learning: A critique of traditional schooling.* London: Routledge.

Gee, J. P. (2005). *Why video games are good for your soul: Pleasure and learning.* Melbourne, Australia: Common Ground.

Johnson, S. (2005). *Everything bad is good for you: How today's popular culture is actually making us smarter.* New York: Riverhead.

Lave, J. (1996). Teaching, as learning, in practice. *Mind, Culture, and Activity, 3,* 149–164.

Lankshear, C. (1997). *Changing literacies.* Buckingham, U.K.: Open University Press.

Lankshear, C., & Knobel, M. (2003). *New literacies: Changing knowledge and classroom learning.* Buckingham, U.K.: Open University Press.

McFarlane, A., Sparrowhawk, A., & Heald, Y. (2002). *Report on the educational use of games: An exploration by TEEM of the contribution which games can make to the education process.* St. Ives, Cambridgeshire, U.K.: TEEM.

Ochs, E., Gonzales, P., & Jacoby, S. (1996). "When I come down I'm in the domain state". In E. Ochs, E. Schegloff, & S. A. Thompson (Eds.), *Interaction and Grammar* (pp. 328–369). Cambridge, U.K.: Cambridge University Press.

Prensky, M. (2006). *Don't bother me Mom—I'm learning!* New York: Paragon.

Shaffer, D. W. (2004). Pedagogical praxis: The professions as models for post-industrial education. *Teachers College Record, 10,* 1401–1421.

Shaffer, D. W., Squire, K. D., Halverson, R., & Gee, J. P. (2005). Video games and the future of learning. *Phi Delta Kappan, 87*(2), 105–111.

Williamson, B. (2003) The participation of children in the design of new technology: Paper. Bristol, U.K.: NESTA Futurelab. Retrieved January 30, 2004 from http://www.nestafuturelab.org/research

Savannah: Mobile Gaming and Learning
A Review Commentary

SUSAN R. GOLDMAN
and JAMES W. PELLEGRINO
UNIVERSITY OF ILLINOIS AT CHICAGO, USA

Abstract

Over the course of our professorial lives, we have found ourselves adopting diverse professional roles that have allowed us to appreciate multiple perspectives on learning and the development of learning environments. Our commentary reflects these multiple perspectives. We first briefly describe these perspectives or lenses and then apply them in our comments on the Facer et al. (2004), article.

Multiple Perspectives

Despite differences in our specific areas of expertise, each of us was initially trained to study learning processes from the perspective of cognitive psychology in the 1970s. We were steeped in research designs and statistical techniques for examining trends in learning performances exhibited by groups of individuals. Because of a specialization in psycholinguistics, one of us (Goldman) also gained familiarity with theory and empirical methods in linguistics. Early in each of our careers, we found ourselves in a research context at the Learning Research and Development Center at the University of Pittsburgh, where the mission was to bring psychological research on learning to bear on educational issues. From the very beginning of our careers, we have been concerned not only with generating new knowledge, but also with asking, "What does this mean for real children and teachers in real schools?" As our interests and careers evolved and we had opportunities to work collaboratively with others, our journal articles, book chapters, presentations, and other scholarly artifacts reflected an increased concern with addressing the question and a host of successors. Among the latter are fundamental concerns about the very nature of learning itself, how it unfolds over time, what is learned including the cognitive, social, and situative aspects of developing competence and expertise in a content domain, and what are the conditions that support learning and teaching. Beyond issues of learning and what is to be learned, we have also come to appreciate the fact that any instructional intervention designed to impact students and teachers must be examined in terms of practicality, feasibility, scalability, and perceived relevance to various educational stakeholder communities. The interests of multiple communities determine whether new instructional materials or approaches will survive and prosper.

The burgeoning set of questions about learning and instructional innovations reflects what we have learned as we have attempted to bridge the worlds of university-based research and educational practice. These efforts have tremendously increased our understanding of the complexity of learning, teaching, schooling, and the impact of sophisticated and accessible technologies for supporting the enterprise. The potential of technology to impact educational practice remains enormous, but that potential has yet to be realized. Furthermore, the inability of technology to penetrate and/or transform educational practices and organizational structures and the lack of evidence of impact is now well documented (e.g., CTGV, 1996; Goldman, 2005; Haertel & Means, 2003; Pea, Wulf, Elliott, & Darling, 2003). The lack of penetration is a frequent source of frustration within the educational-technology community and of substantial skepticism by those outside it (e.g., Cuban, 2001). As part of our work in this multidisciplinary arena, we have also found that addressing the critical issues requires looking to disciplines beyond cognitive psychology, including sociolinguistics, psychometrics, anthropology, sociology, literacy studies, policy analysis, and learning in the disciplines. Indeed, we now identify strongly with the emerging field of learning sciences and its focus on individuals engaged singly or in groups in social, cognitive, and discourse practices that constitute learning. Along the way, we have been involved in a variety of activities beyond the typical laboratory-based empirical studies of learning. We have been active participants in a large, distributed group that developed instructional/educational technologies for learning and assessment (e.g., CTGV 1997, 2000). We have conducted both small, microethnographic and large evaluation studies of classrooms engaged in innovative instruction (e.g., CTGV, 1992; Goldman & Bloome, 2004) and have done analyses of assessments and assessment systems (e.g., Pellegrino & Goldman, 2007). We have also participated in the design and implementation of professional development for elementary- and middle-school teachers who were adopting innovative practices and reform curricula (e.g., Goldman, 2005; Raphael et al., 2006; Zech, Gause-Vega, Bray, Secules, & Goldman, 2000).

An additional set of experiences is relevant to understanding our commentary and includes the major editorial roles we have held over the course of our careers. Goldman is currently Associate Editor on three major journals in the field of learning and instruction: (a) *Cognition and Instruction,* (b) *Discourse Processes,* and (c) *Educational Research Review.* She is, or has been, on the Editorial Board of *Developmental Psychology, Learning and Instruction, Contemporary Psychology, Journal of Educational Psychology,* and *Reading Research Quarterly.* Pellegrino has served as Editor of the *Peabody Journal of Education,* Associate Editor of *The Review of Educational Research,* and is or has been on the Editorial Board of *Intelligence, Educational Evaluation and Policy Analysis, Cognition and Instruction,* and the *Journal of Technology, Learning, and Assessment,* as well as several other journals in the areas of cognition and instruction. We have been involved in editing several volumes including reports of the National Academy of Sciences (e.g., Donovan, Bransford, & Pellegrino, 1999; Pellegrino, Chudowsky, & Glaser, 2001) and both contributed to the work of a joint National Academy of Sciences and National Academy of Engineering Committee focused on *Improving Learning with Information Technology* (see Pea et al., 2003). Accordingly, we bring to this commentary substantial experience reviewing research on learning, instruction, and technology both prior to and subsequent to its ultimate publication. Our perspective on the editorial task, including the more explicit mentoring aspect of this task when working with graduate students, is that it is an ideal opportunity for learning—our own and that of the authors. We have spent a great deal of time thinking about the strength of a study's empirical findings, the argument, the presentation, and its implications. In the remainder of this commentary, we apply this perspective on the editorial task, as well as our perspective on the fields of learning, instruction, and technology, to structure our commentary on the Facer et al. (2004) piece.

Savannah: Mobile Gaming and Learning

The Savannah project is an interesting and exciting attempt to harness the engagement and enthusiasm that young people manifest in computer-based gaming environments for purposes of identifiable content learning. The effort reflects a continuation of the edutainment trend that emerged in the early to mid-90s and a more recent emphasis on informal learning including that which occurs in learning environments such as museums, after-school clubs, and other nontraditional learning settings (e.g., Nicolopolau & Cole, 1993; Gee, 2003; Halverson, 2005; Lemke, 2005; Nasir, 2005; Nasir & Saxe, 2003; Shaffer, Squire, Halverson, & Gee, 2005). *Savannah* capitalizes on the ease-of-use and mobility affordances of handheld technologies to create an educational gaming environment in which children immerse themselves in the game world by taking on the personae of the world's inhabitants. Since the publication of the Facer et al. (2004) article, other efforts have appeared such as *MUSHI* (Lyons, Lee, Quintana, & Soloway, 2006) and *Room Quake* (Moher, 2006) that similarly capitalize on technology's ability to create immersive contexts for learning. Thus, the work on *Savannah* is part of an emergent and important literature on the creation of learning environments that immerse learners in a virtual space that provides them with opportunities to learn concepts that pertain in real space. When game environments attempt to model real environments, especially ecosystems, there are, inevitably, transformations, and sometimes distortions, of time and space. There are important implications of such transformations for mapping between game worlds and real worlds, a point we return to later.

The Empirical Work

The Facer et al., (2004) paper reported a preliminary study of *Savannah*. The version of *Savannah* described in the article has two primary activity areas. The first is the experiential area. In this area, students assume the identity of lions living in the Savannah, move through areas of the larger space where different entities, including animal and human threats, are encountered, and attempt to survive various challenges. The physical space of the real African Savannah is mapped onto a game space of 100 m × 50 m for representation in the handheld device. The game space distance on the handheld can be covered within five minutes. This is a substantial reduction in the several hours that it would take lions to cover the same space in the Savannah. The handhelds act as mobile clients to the PC-based game server. A GPS system tracks movements, and the server reads all inputs from the clients and sends messages to the clients based on the information it receives from the clients. The second activity area is the Den. It contains a log of movements, actions, and consequences. The Den acts as a debriefing room that provides students with an opportunity to reflect on their activities in the Savannah and to prepare for further forays in the activity space. (For the work reported in the paper, the server Den communications had not been fully implemented in a technology platform.) The paper described the system and focused on information derived from 2 groups of 5 students (separate male and female groups) who each received three or four challenges over the course of a day to work through in the gaming environment. The challenges included initial exploration and familiarization with the affordances of the space followed by attempts at survival in the space. A control team monitored the students' activities while moving through the space, and a teacher mediated, especially when students returned from the experiential area to the Den. Students were observed and videotaped as they explored the Savannah using their handheld devices and in their interactions in the Den.

As a report on emerging uses of handheld technology for gaming environments that have the potential for use as learning contexts, the study is limited to an exploratory usability study. In so far as it describes the basics of the game and the technologies used, as well as student activities and reactions, it is a reasonable, albeit cursory, description of the game situation. Those interested in the specifics of the technology implementation will not find much detail. A major part of the article is devoted instead to reporting some of the initial findings regarding issues of student identity, role-playing, and learning the rules of the game. This material is largely descriptive and is candid in pointing out the strengths and limitations of the initial game design and activity structures; however, the report does little to inform us about the nature of the learning processes or certain key outcomes that might be of greatest interest to those concerned with issues of science content learning. It reports on what students (albeit only a very small, relatively homogeneous set of students) thought about the system and how they used it. As an initial usability study, it is adequate, but as a study of learning and instruction, the study design falls short on several dimensions and does not address a number of issues. Most importantly, as we discuss next, there is a lack of clarity about the learning goals, what would constitute evidence of learning, and ways to assess such learning. The data that are reported are not situated in the larger body of data that were collected. We elaborate on these points in the context of applying multiple evaluative criteria to the work.

Applying Multiple Evaluative Criteria

As a preface to our critical comments on Facer et al. (2004), we want to explicitly acknowledge that critiquing a published paper shares some properties with Monday-morning quarterbacking. Any game can always have been played differently. Any paper can always have included more information, taken into account additional related work, conducted additional analyses, or discussed other implications. This is especially true when multiple perspectives emanating from multiple communities of practice are applied to a published piece because the piece was written for a particular community of practice defined by the readership of the publication outlet. In other words, *any* piece of scholarly work can be evaluated from multiple perspectives and be found wanting with respect to one or more of those perspectives. This is a function of the nature of the work and its degree of match with what is typically valued by perspectives and audiences other than the one for which it was written. Different communities have different norms and expectations for publishing articles and even within a community such as instructional designers, different journal outlets serve the needs of different audiences. Thus, we faced a bit of a dilemma in providing a critique of the Facer et al. paper and admit at the outset that some of the questions we pose probably lie well beyond the scope of the expectations of the journal in which the paper appeared. We, however, pose such questions to provide our sense of the kinds of questions that design and development research must address if it is going to have widespread impact on children's learning, use of such technologies for content learning especially science, and learning in general.

First, we pose a series of questions relative to the stated intent of the work. This is admittedly an exploratory study in which the goals were to (a) establish whether the game environment captured the attention and interest of the students, (b) discover if the game provided an opportunity for them to learn something important about animal behavior in the wild, and (c) determine what aspects of the game environment were positive or negative features in accomplishing these broader goals. Pertinent to these goals is the question of whether the *Savannah* game environment is a legitimate rendition of the real-world environment that it represents. The answer to this question appears to be yes, given the descriptions of the elements of the real space depicted in the game world and how the space was constructed using the advice of Savannah experts. The animals, environmental features, and potential threats of the real Savannah are all represented in the game space, although there are no doubt liberties taken in the mapping and distribution.

At the same time, the *Savannah* game space is also supposed to be about the nature of animal behavior in the real Savannah; here is where major shortcomings in the mapping between the game world and the real world exist. First, as mentioned earlier, the real space is large and the capacity to traverse that space in a short time such as the 15-minute activity episodes used for game play are a potential source of major misconceptions about the behavior in question. Second, the activities of the animals in that space are also compressed in time, including the expenditure of energy, the hunting of prey, the avoidance of danger, and other elements of individual and group behavior that are the supposed targets of learning. Interview data from the youngsters indicate that the experience in the *Savannah* game did not align with their expectations of what might happen in the real world based on knowledge of lion behavior acquired previously from television and other sources. The authors were honest in concluding that these are serious issues and that the students experienced unrealistic activities that run counter to the science-learning objectives of game-based learning. For example, they stated the following about one of the game's major learning objectives. "The children were, however, also coming to learn certain rules about the game's environment that in fact conflicted with the generalized understanding of the Savannah that had been intended. For example, children had little understanding of the complexities of actual lion-hunting strategies, *strategies* [emphasis added] which could *have been* [emphasis added] taught very effectively in this experiential manner" (p. 406). They also noted, "Due to the game design, they were being reinforced to think that lions spend equal amounts of time in all areas of the Savannah; this was because of a lack of accurate understanding about the structure of animal behavior over a typical day, too much emphasis was placed on repeatedly killing prey" (pp. 406–407). Particularly troubling from the standpoint of learning the science of animal behavior is that the children acted in these ways despite their perception of the disparities between the gaming environment and the real world. In other words, their prior knowledge did not prevent them from acting in the gaming environment in ways that are not reflective of lions' behavior in the wild.

The problem we have pointed out about the match between the game world and the real world that is the focus of the learning is serious. Lack of correspondence between game worlds and real worlds with respect to the domain concepts and principles undermines the acceptance of gaming contexts for academic-learning purposes. Inaccuracies and the promotion of serious misconceptions need to be avoided in game environments. This is true for any technology-based platform dealing with scientific content including such contexts as simulations of events and processes operating on scales from the atomic and molecular level (see e.g., *Molecular Workbench* http://workbench. concord.org/; Tinker, 2000) to the global (see e.g., *MyWorld* http://www. worldwatcher.northwestern.edu/myworld/; Edelson & Gordin, 1998). Unless the science is correct, and the game rules maintain a close approximation to what is feasible in the real world, there is a genuine problem with games as educational environments. The authors noted this very clearly: "We are seeing a potential clash of realities. Whereas game designers creating the games children are used to playing outside school only have to create a compelling and exciting experience, designers of games for learning are required to create a compelling and exciting experience that is underpinned by the nature of the realities you are trying to enable children to understand" (p. 408). In other words, game environments have to meet content criteria that apply to other forms of instructional materials.

Apart from the content-learning issues, we raise a second question relative to the argument set forth in the paper. Did Facer et al. (2004) provide adequate evidence for the conclusions, positive and negative, about the outcomes of the students' activities and learning experiences? Here we have concerns about both the data that were collected and about data that should have been collected. Several issues exist with the data that were collected, analyzed, and reported. First, it appears that a wealth of information was obtained from the recordings and observations of the students as they moved through the game space as well as in the Den following each foray into the space. The data presented in the paper are excerpts from comments children made during game play and during interviews with the researchers following completion of their 1-day experience with the *Savannah* game. The authors provided us with only the barest glimpse of the full corpus of data, the method of coding and analyzing the data, and the basis of selecting the student remarks reported. The authors explained that observers watched and took field notes

2001). The personae that students take on are those of ethologists. Similarly, students act as geologists and seismologists in *Room Quake* (Moher, 2006). In *Room Quake*, the students' classroom becomes the world in which earthquakes occur, and their job is to be the seismologists attempting to use the data to locate the earthquake. Both *BGuILE* and *Room Quake* provide students with data rather than having them generate the data as *Savannah* does. The advantage of providing the data is that the text can help negotiate issues of time and space scales (*BGuILE*) or the tremors and aftershocks can be spaced in a real-world timescale (*Room Quake*).

Learning environments developed under this approach to gaming and immersive contexts must be explicit about (a) the intended learning objectives; (b) the supports external to the simulation, game, or immersive context necessary to enable students to reach these objectives; and (c) the kinds of evidence that indicate what affordances students have taken advantage of and the results of those experiences. As alluded to earlier, this approach must take very seriously the accuracy of the content and possibilities for students to develop misconceptions about important science (or other) content.

A second approach to the investigation of gaming contexts for learning is one adopted by Lemke, Gee, Halverson, Shaffer, Squire and others (see e.g., Lemke, 2004, 2005; Shaffer et al., 2005). These researchers have undertaken analyses of the kinds of learning in which students engage when they are playing commercially produced digital, multimedia games. Rather than design games, the goal of this approach is to understand what individuals learn when they play in these often-complex environments. These games require sophisticated skills for understanding verbal, visual, static, and dynamic information displays; synthesizing across multiple inputs; and systematically exploring the game space. This approach asks not how we can teach traditional classroom subject matter in game environments, but starts with the observation that youngsters are engaged in sophisticated learning strategies and are using complex, multiple literacy skills to negotiate the game world. The promise of this approach is in defining and better understanding productive ways in which to engage youngsters in approaching other areas of learning with the same engagement and interest they bring to gaming contexts.

Concluding Comments

Having designed technology-based instructional materials and having worked with teachers and students as they used these as well as other innovative materials, we recognize the complexities involved in creating learning environments—whether they are gaming environments or more traditional instructional materials. As well, it is often challenging to design research and assessment strategies that will provide evidence of the learning that occurs when youngsters engage with those environments. Thus, we applaud efforts such as those of Facer et al. (2004) and encourage them and other researcher/developers to continue this line of work. In so doing, the work needs to pay explicit attention to specifying the intended learning processes and outcomes and means for determining what learning is occurring, for whom, by what means, and how well. What are youngsters likely to know and be able to do if they spend time in any particular gaming environment? How will they be demonstrating what they know and are able to do? We are also eager to see if efforts to understand the knowledge and skills that gamers acquire reveal learning processes and habits of mind that prepare youngsters for learning outside of game contexts. That is, we may find that youngsters acquire very sophisticated multiple literacies within specific game contexts, but that the nature of the acquisition process does not support youngsters in being able to adapt what they have learned in gaming contexts for use in other situations. If this were the case, one direction we encourage is for researchers and designers to ask what could be done to enhance the learning experiences to increase the likelihood of youngsters acquiring knowledge that was usable in a broader set of contexts. A second, related direction is to examine the learning objectives and activities that occur outside of gaming contexts and question whether these are the most relevant for the 21st century.

References

Cognition and Technology Group at Vanderbilt. (1992). The Jasper series as an example of anchored instruction: Theory, program description, and assessment data. *Educational Psychologist, 27,* 291–315.

Cognition and Technology Group at Vanderbilt. (1996). Looking at technology in context: A framework for understanding technology and education. In D. C. Berliner & R. C. Calfee (Eds.), *The handbook of educational psychology* (pp. 807–840). New York: Macmillan Publishing.

Cognition and Technology Group at Vanderbilt. (1997). *The Jasper project: Lessons in curriculum, instruction, assessment, and professional development.* Mahwah, NJ: Erlbaum.

Cognition and Technology Group at Vanderbilt. (2000). Adventures in anchored instruction: Lessons from beyond the ivory tower. In R. Glaser (Ed.), *Advances in instructional psychology: Vol. 5. Educational design and cognitive science* (pp. 35–99). Mahwah, NJ: Erlbaum.

Cuban, L. (2001). *Oversold and underused: Computers in the classroom.* Cambridge, MA: Harvard University Press.

Donovan, M. S., Bransford, J., & Pellegrino, J. W. (1999). *How people learn: Bridging research and practice.* Washington, DC: National Academy Press.

Edelson, D. C., & Gordin, D. (1998). Visualization for learners: A framework for adapting scientists' tools. *Computers and Geosciences, 24*(7), 607–616.

Facer, K., Joiner, R., Stanton, D., Reidz, J., Hullz, R., & Kirk, D. (2004). Savannah: mobile gaming and learning? *Journal of Computer Assisted Learning, 20,* 399–409.

Gee, J. P. (2003). *What video games have to teach us about learning and literacy.* New York: Palgrave Macmillan.

Goldman, S. R. (2005). Designing for scalable educational improvement. In C. Dede, J. P. Honan, & L. C. Peters (Eds.), *Scaling up success: Lessons learned from technology-based educational improvement* (pp. 67–96). San Francisco: Josey Bass.

Goldman, S. R., & Bloome, D. M. (2004). Learning to construct and integrate. In A. F. Healy (Ed.), *Experimental cognitive psychology and its applications: Festshrift in honor of Lyle Bourne, Walter Kintsch, and Thomas Landauer* (pp. 169–182). Washington, DC: American Psychological Association.

Haertel, G., & Means, B. (Eds.). (2003). *Evaluating educational technology: Effective research designs for improving learning.* New York: Teachers College Press.

Halverson, R. (2005). What Can K–12 School Leaders Learn from Video Games and Gaming? *Innovate, 1(6).* Retrieved October 2, 2006, from http://www.innovateonline.info/index.php?view=article&id=81

Lemke, J. (2004). *Critical analysis across media: Games, franchises, and the new cultural order.* Paper presented at the First International Conference on Critical Discourse Analysis, Valencia, Spain.

Lemke, J. (2005). Multimedia genres and traversals. In E. Ventola, P. Muntigl, & H. Gruber (Eds.), *Approaches to genre* (Special issue of *Folia Linguistica*), 39(1-2), 45–56.

Lyons, L., Lee, J., Quintana, C., & Soloway, E. (2006). MUSHI: A multi-device framework for collaborative inquiry learning. In S. A. Barab, K. E. Hay, & D. T. Hickey (Eds.), *Proceedings of the international conference of the learning sciences* (pp. 453–459). Mahwah, NJ: Erlbaum.

Moher, T. (2006). Embedded phenomena: Supporting science learning with classroom-sized distributed simulations. *Proceedings of the ACM Conference on Human Factors in Computing Systems* (CHI '06, Montreal, Canada) 691–700.

Nasir, N. S. (2005). Individual cognitive structuring and the sociocultural context: Strategy shifts in the game of dominoes. *The Journal of the Learning Sciences, 14,* 5–34.

Nasir, N. S., & Saxe, G. B. (2003). Ethnic and academic identities: A cultural practice perspective on emerging tensions and their management in the lives of minority students. *Educational Researcher, 32*(5), 14–18.

Nicolopolou, A., & Cole, M. (1993). The fifth dimension, its playworld, and its institutional context: The generation and transmission of shared knowledge in the culture of collaborative learning. In E. A. Foreman, N. Minnick, & C. A. Stone (Eds.), *Contexts for learning sociocultural dynamics in children's development* (pp. 283–314) . New York: Oxford University Press.

Pea, R., Wulf, W., Elliott, S., & Darling, M. (Eds.). (2003). *Planning for two transformations in education and learning technology: Report of a workshop.* Washington, DC: National Academy Press.

Pellegrino, J. W., Chudowsky, N., & Glaser, R. (2001). *Knowing what students know: The science and design of educational assessment.* Washington, DC: National Academy Press.

Pellegrino, J. W., & Goldman, S. R. (2007). Beyond rhetoric: Realities and complexities of integrating assessment into teaching and learning. In C. Dwyer (Ed.), *The future of assessment: Shaping teaching and learning* (pp. 7–52). Mahwah, NJ: Erlbaum.

Raphael, T. E., Goldman, S. R., Au, K. H., Hirata, S., Weber, C. M., George, M., et al. (2006). *Toward second generation school reform models: A developmental model for literacy reform.*

Reiser, B. J., Tabak, I., Sandoval, W. A., Smith, B., Steinmuller, F., & Leone, T. J. (2001). BGuILE: Strategic and conceptual scaffolds for scientific inquiry in biology classrooms. In S. M. Carver & D. Klahr (Eds.), *Cognition and instruction: Twenty-five years of progress* (pp. 263–305). Mahwah, NJ: Erlbaum.

Shaffer, D. W., Squire, K. R., Halverson, R., & Gee, J. P. (2005). Video games and the future of learning. *Phi Delta Kappan, 87*(2), 104–111.

Tinker, R. (2000). Atomic-scale models: The key to science education reform. *Concord 4*(1), 4–5.

Zech, L., Gause-Vega, C., Bray, M. H., Secules, T., & Goldman, S. R. (2000). Content-based collaborative inquiry: Professional development for school reform. *Educational Psychologist, 35*(3), 207–217.

CHAPTER 35

The Nature of Middle School Learners' Science Content Understandings with the Use of Online Resources*

JOSEPH L. HOFFMAN,
HSIN-KAI WU,
JOSEPH S. KRAJCIK,
and ELLIOT SOLOWAY

UNIVERSITY OF MICHIGAN, USA

Abstract

Early research on using the World Wide Web indicated that middle school students did not explore much and used Web tools naively. In response to these challenges, an on-line research engine, Artemis, was designed to provide a permanent workspace and allow students access to preselective on-line resources. This study investigated the depth and accuracy of sixth-grade students' content understandings as well as their use of search and assess strategies when they used on-line resources via Artemis. Eight student pairs from two science classes experienced support from teachers and used scaffolded curriculum materials while completing four on-line inquiry units during 9 months. Multiple sources of data were collected, including video recordings of students' computer activities and conversations, students' artifacts and online postings, classroom and lab video recordings, and interview transcripts. Analyses of data showed that students constructed meaningful understandings through on-line inquiry, although the accuracy and depth of their understandings varied. The findings suggest that students might develop accurate and in-depth understandings if they use search and assess strategies appropriately, if resources are thoughtfully chosen, and if support from the learning environment is extensively provided. This research lends evidence to questions regarding the value of students engaging in on-line inquiry.

---

* Reprinted from Hoffman, J. L., Wu, H.-K., Krajcik, J. S., & Soloway, E. (2003). The nature of middle school learners' science content understandings with the use of online resources. *Journal of Research in Science Teaching*, 40(3), 323–346, Copyright © 2003. Reprinted with permission of Wiley-Liss, Inc., a subsidiary of John Wiley & Sons, Inc.

Educators in the 20th century have seen a number of technological innovations enter into science classrooms across the United States. The most recent innovation for classrooms, the use of the World Wide Web (WWW), offers yet another opportunity for enhancing the ways in which teachers teach and learners learn, although this claim has been left largely unexamined. The increased reliance on the World Wide Web for providing educational experiences to Grade K–12 learners requires the immediate attention of the research community. Advocates (Barrie & Presti, 1996; Kinzie, Larsen, Burch, & Boker, 1996; Ryder & Graves, 1997) speak to the potential of the WWW as an instructional tool for classrooms. The Internet and WWW could change the nature of learning by increasing access to instructional materials in a variety of media (Kinzie et al., 1996), promoting students' skills in information gathering and problem solving (Ryder & Graves, 1997), encouraging network collaborations (Tinker & Haavind, 1997), and having access to decentralized resources (Tinker & Haavind, 1997).

However, although a large collection of literature speaks to the positive nature of the use of WWW resources in science classrooms, other sources (Lookatch, 1995; Maddux, 1996; Winebrener, 1997; Stoll, 1998) remain pessimistic on its application as an instructional tool. Winebrener (1997) showed that students can become misled by viewing falsified information posted on the Web, frustrated owing to an inability to locate specific information easily, and confused with varying forms of navigation found on individual pages. Maddux (1996) supported these cautions and argued that the assumption that hypermedia and open-ended exploration of data are more consistent with the way children think has not been verified through research yet.

The complexity of these issues and messages provides uncertain guidance to policymakers and educators who continue to implement these tools in classrooms across the United States. Given the variety of literature for both positive aspects and challenges associated with using the WWW in Grade K–12 classrooms, it is critical to provide empirical evidence of its affect on schools.

This study was part of a series of design experiments within an intensive educational project and conducted based on principles delineated by Brown (1992) and Collins (1999). It was initiated in response to prior work on using the WWW (Hoffman, Kupperman, & Wallace, 1997; Lyons, Hoffman, Krajcik, & Soloway, 1997; Wallace, Kupperman, Krajcik, & Soloway, 2000) that showed a mismatch between the intended goals of the project and behaviors of students as they engaged in on-line investigations. Students did not explore much, did not evaluate sources, tended to seek answers rather than aim for understanding, and used Web tools naively. In response to this feedback, an information-seeking interface, Artemis,[1] was designed based on learner-centered design principles (Soloway, Guzdial, & Hay, 1994). This interface, including a research engine and a permanent workspace, allows students access to

---

[1] Artemis and its on-line learning activities are available at: http://www.webartemis.org

a digital library that contains preselective, preapproved, and age-appropriate on-line resources for middle school learners. It helps students focus on the content of the on-line resource, evaluate its usefulness, and synthesize information rather than spending the majority of time simply locating appropriate sites on the WWW.

In addition, Wallace et al. (2000) concluded that factors influencing student's actions during on-line sessions were the pedagogical approach employed by the teacher and corresponding degree of support received during the inquiry units, both on-and off-line. Therefore, this study developed on-line and off-line learning materials to provide scaffolding, which allowed students to accomplish tasks they could not do alone (Wood, Burner, & Ross, 1976; Palinscar & Brown, 1984), to support students' information-seeking activities as they asked question of interest, searched for information, assessed their findings, and created rich representations of their newly constructed understandings.

This yearlong study investigates the depth and accuracy of sixth-grade students' content understandings as well as their use of search and assess strategies as they used on-line resources via Artemis. This study focuses on the following questions:

1. What depth and accuracy of content understanding do learners demonstrate with the use of on-line resources? To what extent are these made visible in learners' products and conversations?
2. What insights can be suggested between learners' use of search and assess strategies and the depth and accuracy of content understandings that they demonstrate?
3. What insights can be suggested regarding the quality of on-line resources and the depth and accuracy of content understandings that they demonstrate?

This research lends evidence to questions regarding the value of the WWW as a viable medium for learning by providing an empirical perspective on students' emergent content understandings. Also, it follows learners throughout the entire school year, whereas previous studies did not measure changes that could have occurred through the year. Most importantly, this study provides support to theoretical claims made regarding the WWW and the impact it has on learning.

Theoretical Framework

The foundation of this study draws on interwoven contexts framing the environment in which learners participated. Students engaged in on-line information-seeking activities, partnered with technological tools designed to support inquiry, and received substantial scaffolding. As a result, students were expected to develop new science content understandings.

Information Seeking and Content Understandings

Numerous researchers described information seeking in electronic environments similar to the WWW. These descriptions suggest information seeking is a special case of problem solving (Marchionini, 1989) in which learners recognize and interpret an information problem, establish a plan of search, conduct the search, evaluate the results, and use information to solve a problem (Kuhlthau, 1993; Wallace, 1997). Whereas undirected searching leads to unexpected links or discrepant events related to their topic, highly directed searching is purposely used to find specific information (McNally & Kuhlthau, 1994). As learners engage in information-seeking activities, they move through predictable stages (i.e., initiation, selection, exploration, formulation, collection, presentation) and progress from ambiguity to clarity and from seeking general information to seeking specific information (McNally & Kuhlthau, 1994). Kuhlthau (1993) indicated that learners "construct their own points of view or understanding of a topic or problem" and increase their interest and confidence as they progress from initial conceptualizations of questions to the conclusion of the process.

In addition to information seeking, a variety of literature (Nickerson, 1995; Perkins, Crismond, Simmons, & Unger, 1995; Perkins & Simmons, 1988; Talsma, 1997) defined the nature of science content understandings. Content understanding is not only a recollection of facts and definitions associated with a particular subject area, but also the use of mapping schemes to associate concepts with referents and strategies for memorization and recall (Perkins & Simmons, 1988). Similarly, content understanding can be viewed as a matter of degree in which an individual understands concepts, principles, structures, or processes at a relatively deep level and is able to demonstrate certain behaviors (Nickerson, 1995). Therefore, understandings could be made evident to others in terms of overt behaviors as learners communicate or act in three ways (Perkins et al., 1995):

1. Offering explanations. Learners display this kind of understanding by giving examples, highlighting critical features, and responding to new situations. Learners who simply present facts and describe phenomena without the ability to explain concepts clearly lack understanding.
2. Articulating richly relational knowledge. Learners express this kind of understanding with explanations that link to related aspects of a concept or phenomena. Learners who use sparse knowledge involving one simple rule would display poor understanding.
3. Displaying a revisable and extensible web of explanation. Learners demonstrate this kind of understanding by revising and extending explanations beyond the original source of information (i.e., textbook, lecture, video, experiment) to new contexts or situations. Learners who simply

repeat back explanations and cannot extend them to new contexts lack robust understanding.

The notion of making depth of understanding public through explanation, articulation, and extension provides a concrete method of classifying learners' understandings. These newly constructed understandings are fragile and are subject to modification based on new information and additional learning experiences (Perkins et al., 1995).

Although the literature characterized the information-seeking process in electronic environments and provided definitions for science content understandings, the question of how the information-seeking process might interact with students' development of understanding is still unanswered. Using fine-grained data collection and analysis techniques, this study is designed to provide substantial insight into how learners construct understandings from using on-line resources.

Characteristics of the WWW

A large body of literature (e.g., Gordin, Gomez, Pea, Fishman, 1996; Lea & Scardamalia, 1997; Linn, 1996) showed that some characteristics of the WWW, such as providing a hypermedia-based environment and increasing access to primary resources via networks, are beneficial for learners.

Hypermedia can be defined as a method for organizing, structuring, and accessing information around a network of multimedia nodes connected together by links (Conclin, 1987). Browser software takes advantage of hypermedia design principles to make information easily accessible on the WWW. Users simply click on text (hypertext), graphical buttons (icons), or images (image maps) to navigate through various networks, sites, and pages within sites in a nonlinear manner. A hypermedia system permits the integration of text, graphics, audio, animation, and video into a "multidimensional learning environment" (Shepardson & Britsch, 1996), allows users to move easily among vast quantities of information allowing freedom from the linear, highly directed flow of printed text (Marchionini, 1988), and provides opportunities for the "exploration of alternatives" that can result in the understanding of relationships that were previously unrecognized (Heller, 1990). Thus, Salomon, Perkins, and Globerson (1991) suggested that learners can develop "intellectual partnerships" with hypermedia-based programs as the programs assume part of the burden of information processing as information is located, retrieved, and presented in a common format on the computer screen.

In addition to the affordances that hypermedia holds for learners, access to primary resources via networks provides unique opportunities for the construction of new understandings. The nature of Web-based resources is different from the resources normally available in Grade K–12 schools (Wallace,

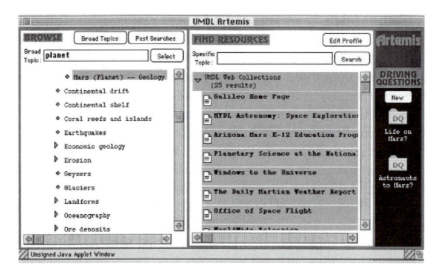

Figure 35.1 Artemis interface main screen.

can easily restore and retrieve resources for investigations. Broad Topics provide support by helping students generate keywords, recall prior knowledge, and view structures of a particular content area before initiating queries to the Digital Library. Collections also support students by providing useful resources pertinent to their driving question. Together, these features of Artemis scaffold students on-line inquiry by allowing them to focus on the contents of the resource, evaluate its usefulness, and synthesize information rather than spending the majority of time simply locating appropriate sites on the WWW.

MYDL: On-line Learning Materials

The MYDL provided printed and on-line learning materials to support middle school student inquiry on the WWW. MYDL included several Web pages to scaffold students' on-line inquiry. For example, a What to Do page gave a brief introduction to the science unit and the inquiry process. A Share page allowed students to click individual icons to reach on-line forms for sharing driving questions, sites pertinent to their questions, and comments or questions to other students.

Students used these materials as a tool to support their information-seeking activities as they asked question of interest, planned their inquiry, searched for information, assessed their findings, and created rich representations of their newly constructed understandings. The design goal of MYDL on-line learning materials was to provide a common framework for learners as they participated in information-seeking activities across a number of content areas.

Tactics and Strategies for Leading On-Line Investigations: Off-line Curriculum Materials

This study recognized the importance of communicating a comprehensive pedagogical model to teachers and students in an effort to promote a high degree of participation and thoughtfulness with inquiry-based learning. Thus, this study

Figure 35.2 MYDL investigation wheel.

developed a series of print-based scaffolding materials to support students and teachers during on-line units. *Tactics and Strategies for Leading On-line Investigations* (Hoffman & Eccleston, 1997) was a series of booklets providing guidance for teachers who were new to the Web or unfamiliar supporting student-led inquiry. It contained activity sheets for students to use and provided a process model, such as the Investigation Wheel (Figure 35.2), for scaffolding strategies for inquiry (i.e., asking, planning, searching, assessing, writing, creating).

Methods

Research Setting

This study was conducted in a public middle school located in a medium-size Midwestern city, serving approximately 830 students and employing 40 full-time equivalent teachers. The school drew students from a majority of middle-class and upper-middle-class families with a wide range of educational backgrounds. This middle school contained two computer-based classrooms (labs) located in the media center, with one dedicated to MYDL. Although the classroom was small, it accommodated 15 student pairs on computers. All computers were Power Macintosh 5260/100 with 13-in. color monitors, wired to the Internet via an ISDN line. A single low-capacity laser printer was available to students. Downloads and uploads between student computers and Internet Web sites were normally accomplished in a few seconds or less, except for peak usage periods during the day when transfer times could be extended to ≥ 15 seconds.

Participants

Two teachers participated in this study. Nanci,[2] the first teacher, had 10 years' experience teaching mathematics, science, geography, and foreign language

---

[2] Pseudonyms for teachers and students are used throughout this report, maintaining their gender and ethnicity.

Table 35.1 Coding Scheme for Depth of Content Understanding

Level	Code	Description
Recalling information (stating, repeating)	RF	Recall specific facts and isolated bits of information.
	RP	Recall processes, directions, and movements of phenomena with respect to time.
	RM	Recall methods, techniques, procedures utilized to support discovery and inquiry.
	RT	Recall theories, patterns, principles, and generalizations.
Offering explanations (telling, describing)	EF	Explain facts, information, and concepts.
	EP	Explain processes, directions, and movements of phenomena with respect to time.
	EM	Explain methods, techniques, procedures used to support discovery and inquiry.
	ET	Explain theories, patterns, principles, and generalizations.
Articulating relationships(expressing, relating)	AF	Articulate facts and concepts.
	AP	Articulate processes, directions, and movements of phenomena with respect to time.
	AM	Articulate methods, techniques, procedures used to support discovery and inquiry.
	AT	Articulate theories, patterns, principles, and generalizations.
Extending explanations (expand, revise)	XF	Extend facts and concepts.
	XP	Extend processes, directions, and movements of phenomena with respect to time.
	XM	Extend methods, techniques, procedures used to support discovery and inquiry.
	XT	Extend theories, patterns, principles, and generalizations.

major categories. When a response was considered incorrect or not accepted as factual in scientific terms or represented an alternately held conception, it was coded as Incorrect. A response was coded as None when the accuracy of understanding was demonstrated by a lack of response or the inability to extend a description or explanation to a higher level of understanding (i.e., "I do not know"). When a response was for the most part correct but contained some element of incorrect information or a hesitancy to respond, it was coded as Partial. When an accurate response was provided without incorrect or erroneous information, it was coded as Accurate.

Process video. Process videotapes were viewed, coded, and summarized. Episodes of student activity related to students' search strategies and assessment of resources were transcribed. Search strategies were coded when students developed possible search topics, queried the UMDL, and selected useful resources, such as navigating deep into sites, browsing the contents of pages, and pausing to read information related to their investigations. Assess strategies were coded when students assessed information obtained during the search process to determine whether it made sense, was interesting, and was trustworthy, and how it added to their understanding and inquiry. These episodes helped elaborate the analysis of how students who demonstrated deeper understandings search and assess on-line resources differently.

Process video was also used to evaluate the depth and accuracy of students' content understandings. Episodes related to understandings were transcribed and coded with a scheme similar to student interviews.

Artifacts. Student artifacts constructed at the conclusion of each inquiry unit also provided a fine-grained perspective on the development of understandings. The physical appearance of these artifacts was described, printed text and presentation dialogue transcribed, and coded using the scheme developed for student interviews. In addition to final artifacts, in-process artifacts such as MYDL activity sheets, on-line postings, and journal writings provided additional support for gaining insight on the sense-making process.

Classroom-lab video. Classroom-lab video recordings were collected to describe the implementation of scaffolded on-line and off-line materials and provided a perspective on how pedagogical supports might promote students' engagement with information-seeking activities. These data were not coded and analyzed in detail; rather, they were used to display the major events of the day and particular episodes related to on-line inquiry.

Data Synthesis

Content understandings. To answer the research questions, we combined the data for process videos, artifacts and interviews. Divisions for depth of understanding (specific facts, processes, methods, and theories) were consolidated into a single data point for each category to provide a graphic summary (see Figure 35.3 for an example). Determination of these summary points was based on the presence of any division of understanding in the category and the highest accuracy of understanding. However, incorrect understandings were also included in the summary along with partial or accurate understandings. This represented a student possessing an accurate depth of understanding for

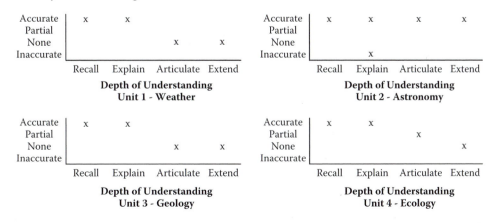

Figure 35.3 Content understanding summary for Angela and Jamie.

a single concept in a topic, but at the same time holding possible incorrect conceptions. These analyses provided the bulk of empirical evidence to make claims regarding students' depth and accuracy of understanding.

Search and assess strategies. In additional to content understandings, we identified inquiry strategies: Ask, Plan, Tools, Search, Assess, Write, Synthesize, and Create. In particular, we compared Search and Assess strategies for student pairs. This comparison allowed us to analyze how the use of strategies could possibly interact with students' development of content understandings and determined how students' strategies changed while engaging in multiple content units. A coding scheme (high, adequate, and low) was developed to rate students' engagement with each strategy (Table 35.2). Also, data from student artifacts helped inform the analysis and comparison of student pairs. Together, process video and artifact data were used to determine students' engagement in using Search and Assess strategies.

Quality of on-line resources. The design of Web sites students used during their on-line inquiry was evaluated. Process video and artifacts (including MYDL activity sheets, on-line postings, and final products) were reviewed to analyze the potential effect that Web page design had on the construction of student understandings. A coding scheme adapted from Hoffman, Kupperman, and Wallace (1997) was used to assess aspects (i.e., general design, context, navigation, content, interactivity) of Web site design for promoting the construction of understandings. This analysis focused on resources students spent time browsing, discussing, or writing about in MYDL activity sheets and journals. To investigate a possible connection between students' understandings and their use of on-line resources, comparisons were made between major sites students used during their inquiry and the depth and accuracy of understandings that could be possibly gained from those resources.

Emerging themes. Themes emerged as a result of coding, analyzing, and evaluating data. As data were coded and analyzed, notes, reflections, and examples were recorded with particular attention paid to students' development of understandings, engagement with Search and Assess strategies, and their use of on-line resources. These recordings provided the basis on which to add to ideas and explore reoccurring themes. Themes were then verified by confirming and disconfirming evidence from the data corpus (Erickson, 1986).

Results

Content Understandings: Depth

An analysis of process video, interviews, and artifacts shows that although students constructed meaningful understandings through on-line inquiry, the

Table 35.2 Engagement with Search-and-Assess Strategies

Engagement level	Search strategy	Assess strategy
High	Students carefully develop a number of possible broad and specific topics relating to their driving question, demonstrate thoughtfulness in the use of these terms for queries to the Digital Library, and are highly selective in their choice of resources. Students purposefully navigate deep into sites, browse the contents, and pause to read information related to their inquiry.	Students have a thoughtful discussion about the potential usefulness of a site before pursuing its contents in-depth. As students dig deep into the site, they judge whether the information is understandable, worthwhile, and trustworthy. Students also use multiple sources during their inquiry to compare and contrast the trustworthiness of information. When performing a formal critique of a site, students are able to provide a thoughtful assessment of both the appearance and content.
Adequate	Students develop a number of search topics related to their driving question and initiate queries to the Digital Library. Students are somewhat selective in their choice of resources but may not dig deep enough or commit adequate effort to locate information. Although students are eventually successful, some time is wasted in the search process.	Students judge whether information is relevant to their driving question before investing time in a site. Decisions are based on the site's content rather than appearance or title. The majority of time is spent with worthwhile and under-standable information; however, trust-worthiness of the source is based solely on the URL (.org, .edu, .com, .gov). Students are able to provide a limited critique of a site's appearance and content.
Low	Students exert little thought and planning in their acquisition of resources, do not dig deeply to locate useful information, and often needlessly repeat searches. The success of their query is often based on luck rather than the careful use of search strategies. Students often waste a significant amount of time surfing rather than browsing for information.	Students are quick to decide on the relevancy of sites, and this determination is often based on the site's title or first page. Information is often accepted although it does not relate directly to the driving question. Students do not discuss the trustworthiness of the site and consider all information good information. They are unable to critique a site's appearance and content effectively.

depth of their understandings varied. A majority of target students offered explanations, articulated relationships, and extended explanations during the interviews, but the explanations and relationships they provided were only partially accurate. Only few demonstrated the ability to expand accurate understandings to articulate and extend levels. In the following segment, Jamie could both articulate and extend their explanations.

Angela and Jamie (Pair 3): Astronomy Investigation (Unit 2).

Interviewer: Jamie, tell me what you learned about black holes.

Jamie: I learned that the black hole itself, the reason it is black and you can't see it is because it sucks in light and light cannot escape so you wouldn't see it and x-rays do detect them, but you don't see how big, you just see like the gravitational pulls and you can't see the particles . . . and, like, when they find one they know, they can track down how much gravitational pull it has, but they don't know how wide it is and they really don't know what size.

Interviewer: Why does it pull things into it?

Jamie: I know. The reason it pulls it in is because when the star, like, when the supernova occurs it blows up and, like, the dust particles and stuff gets, like, pulled together because of space and then after that they just sort of suck everything in because they are use to having a gravitational pull in a certain direction, so it continues to do it and it sort of makes, like, a funnel kind of shape . . . and everything sort of is just draining in it.

Interviewer: Anything else you learned about black holes?

Jamie: Well, ah, I wouldn't want to be sucked in one. It'd be, like, a painless way of committing suicide, though, because you'd only be alive for, like, a second.

Interviewer: Why would that be?

Jamie: Well, because it stretches you, it stretches you so much that you'd just be a strand of spaghetti and so because it's stretching you just collapse in on yourself.

Interviewer: Which would be a bad thing.

Jamie: Yeah [laughter].

This interview segment illustrates how some learners could reach beyond merely recalling information and express ideas with relating and linking concepts together, expanding concepts to new situations, and going beyond the original source of information.

On the other hand, some students were able to demonstrate accurate understandings in some units; however, the depths of these understandings were often limited to recalling information or offering simple explanations. The follow interview segment demonstrates how Edward and Kevin were confined to a simple restatement of facts (with sparse phrases) and could not provide additional explanation to specific questions.

Edward and Kevin (Pair 2): Weather Investigation (Unit 1).

Interviewer: What did you find out [about hurricanes]?

Edward: We found out that it needs seawater above 80° or 90° and that it is high pressure above the low pressure above the water and converging winds. That creates a hurricane and they go up like that.

Interviewer: So they go up ...

Edward:	It becomes like a cycle. They go up and it comes back down and it goes over and over again and it turns into a hurricane.
Interviewer:	Kevin, anything to add to that? What did you learn about hurricanes?
Kevin:	No, not much. Umm ... [long pause].

Although these students had some element of explanation in their responses, they had considerable difficulty moving beyond recalling discreet information. They were not able to explain that hurricanes require three conditions to form (and to strengthen): warm surface waters, high humidity, and the ability to concentrate heat vertically. This simple level of recall was typical of some learners participating in the study.

Students' understanding in terms of the four content units was also varied. Based on the analysis, a number of units had resulting understandings limited to recalling information (35%) or offering explanations (32%), and only a few demonstrated the ability to expand conceptualizations to articulate (22%) and extend (12%) levels. Some units (38%) did not produce content understandings beyond partial accuracy.

An interesting observation made during the analysis of data was the stark difference between the depth of understanding apparent in student artifacts (including presentations) and those articulated during student interviews. A review of final products and presentations revealed little about the true depth of learners' content understandings; these artifacts often communicated a simple recall of factual information. Student interviews permitted a fine-grained view of these understandings, and concepts were probed to determine depths of conceptualizations. This was true for all levels of student pairs, including those with the weakest understandings. The following example illustrates the contrast between artifact and interview.

Karley and Brooke (Pair 8) created a simple poster for their weather investigation ("What is El Niño?"). One section reads: "What is El Niño? El Niño is a disruption of the ocean's atmosphere. In other terms it is when the ocean water changes it [sic] temperature, sometimes it changes by 1 degree, 2 degrees, and even up to 5 degrees. This change really affects the weather sometimes in good ways and other times in bad ways. El Nino can cause severe tornadoes, hurricanes, floods, etc. In good ways it can make your winters milder and nicer and springs seem earlier."

Karley and Brooke (Pair 8): Weather Investigation (Unit 2).

Interviewer:	I noticed this winter we had a lot of warm days and we really didn't have as much rain or snow as we did normally. Why was that, if you said El Niño affected us? What caused us not to have as much cold or rain?

Karley: I think because, like, the cold weather we usually have was up more toward, like, Canada and the Upper Peninsula and we got what Tennessee and Kentucky usually have for their winters and that's usually just a little snow and warm days and stuff like that.

Interviewer: Oh, I see. So what you're saying is it just kind of pushed all the weather up. Do you think we are going to have to worry about this next year?

Karley: Probably not. Probably the ocean temperature won't change like it did this year. It will just stay at normal temperature.

Brooke: Yeah, it will probably just stay. It will probably go back to its normal temperature. It won't change.

Although the artifact listed only general facts related to the change in weather patterns, students were able to offer additional explanations during the interview to illustrate a deeper understanding of weather phenomena.

Content Understandings: Accuracy

An analysis of process video, interviews, and artifacts indicates that most understandings students developed during the units were at the partial level (44%), followed by the accurate level (39%). A number of students developed (or held to) inaccurate understandings. This implies students more frequently developed limited understandings of concepts and had difficulty obtaining accurate conceptualizations.

The root of their alternate conception may originate from a connection made from topics learned previously in science class. When asked about the source of information on comet motion, Robert replied:

Umm, they (the Web) don't have a lot of information about it but we found out about the energy in science and it didn't exactly say that the energy makes the comet move, but we just, like, after planning together what it says and all the things we read that the energy does make it move, but it's also the thing that they're orbiting around.

Although Robert had some knowledge of gravitational influences, he admitted the "energy inside" has a "bigger effect" on motion. A review of students' final artifact (newspaper article) shows similar incorrect conceptions.

Exciting news from NASA today. Two comets that are traveling fast are on track to collide in 5 days at 9:30 p.m. If you are outside watching you will be able to see it. Scientists believe you will see bright sparks of blue. Then there will be a bright flash of red then nothing. The energy in the middle of the [sic] is supposed to mix gases together and make another comet but nobody in [sic] sure. Comets, like meteors and asteroids, are powered by the energy within them.

An interesting insight is the presence of a larger percentage of accurate understandings in Heather's students (24% compared with 15%) and a higher frequency of inaccurate understandings (13% compared with 4%) in Nanci's students. These inaccurate understandings may have resulted from an incorrect construction of understandings, or evidence of previously held conceptions.

Strategies and Content Understandings

One theme emerging from this study suggests a connection between students' engagement with inquiry strategies (including Ask, Plan, Tools, Search, Assess, Write, Synthesize, and Create) and the depth of their content understandings. In an analysis of 32 inquiries (8 pairs of students working on four content units), 70% of students who demonstrated adequate overall engagement with inquiry strategies possessed some evidence of accurate understandings with no incorrect conceptions. In contrast, 83% of students who demonstrated low engagement possessed only partial understandings or understandings containing some form of inaccurate conceptions. When comparing inquiries for engagement level and highest depth of understanding (at accurate or partial levels), 35% of students who demonstrated adequate engagement overall with inquiry strategies could articulate relationships or extend explanations. In contrast, 14% of students who had low engagement communicated understandings at these levels. These results imply that students' level of engagement with inquiry strategies may be related to the development of their content understandings.

Search strategies. An analysis of process video and student artifacts may provide explanations for why students who highly or adequately engaged in on-line inquiry developed better content understandings. Students demonstrating accurate understandings and adequate and above engagement with Search strategies carefully developed a number of possible search topics relating to their driving question, demonstrated thoughtfulness in the use of these terms for queries to the UMDL, and were selective (high level) or somewhat selective (adequate level) in their choice of resources. Students purposefully (high level) navigated deep into sites, browsed the contents, and paused to read information related to their on-line inquiry. Evidence from process video (Tape 624B) and artifacts (MYDL Final Investigation Planning Sheet) depicts students' high engagement with Search strategies.

> Edward and Kevin (Pair 2) pause to develop search topics for their ecology on-line inquiry unit ("Why Are Zebra Mussels Bad for the Great Lakes and My Community?") before loading Artemis. They record "Zebra Mussels, Mussel, Great Lakes, Boats, Swimming, Community, Lakes, Great" on their activity sheet for use with queries to the Digital Library. Edward and Kevin enter "Great Lakes" as a broad topic search and browse the list of topics returned, noticing that only "Lakes" is highlighted. They add

"Zebra Mussels" as a specific topic, query the UMDL, and receive seven returns. Edward comments, "Look at all this information. Wow!"

Other evidence from artifacts (Student Journal entries) illustrates the thoughtfulness of students' topic selection and browsing during a geology unit.

We first went to our DQ folders to change their names. We then used geology for our broad topic. We looked in submarine geology and found volcanoes so we searched, we went into the UMDL collection of sites, and went into a volcanic hazard site. We then went to look at Fuego Volcano. The few graphics in the site were awesome, links, easy reading (about 8th-grade level). We explored about this volcanoes [sic] hazards, which were falling bombs, block, avalanches, and mud flows. We also explored its volcanic history. (Brad and Gabe, Pair 4)

Students demonstrating high engagement with Search strategies often invested more time than lower engaging pairs in the development of search topics. A review of process video activities for Brad and Gabe's (Pair 4) astronomy unit shows 2.3% of events devoted to commenting or discussing search topics. This contrasts with Grant and Robert (Pair 7), who had only 0.7% and demonstrated weaker content understandings.

Students who demonstrated low engagement exerted little thought and planning in their acquisition of resources, did not click deeply into sites to locate useful information, and often needlessly repeated searches. An episode from process video (Tape 578A) illustrates students' poor use of strategies.

Brooke and Karley (Pair 8) attempt to locate information on their driving question ("What are black holes?") during an astronomy unit. Students conduct a specific topic search on "black holes," receive 25 returns from the UMDL, and scroll through the list. Unfortunately, they do not see any returns with the words *black hole* in the title and assume the sites contain no information on their question. Brooke and Jamie continue to conduct a number of searches but invest little time in exploring the contents of returns or sites. Toward the end of the hour Karley comments, "This is, like, really pitiful. No one here knows what a black hole is. Everything on the Internet, nobody knows. Now to me that's pitiful ... . No one on the Internet knows what a black hole is, they just know all this other scientific crap."

The success of their efforts was often based on luck rather than careful use of Search strategies, and as a result they wasted a substantial amount of time surfing rather than browsing for information. The poor use of Search strategies might defer the development of content understandings.

Assess strategies. In addition to a high engagement in Search strategies demonstrated by students who demonstrated better content understandings, these students used more complicated strategies to assess on-line resources. They judged whether information was relevant to their driving question before investing time on a site. Decisions were based on a site's content rather than appearance or title. The majority of time was spent with worthwhile and understandable information; however, trustworthiness of the source was often based solely on the URL (e.g., .org, .com, .gov, .edu). They were able to provide a limited critique of a site's appearance and content. Evidence from process video (Tape 560A) and the MYDL Astronomy Cool Site Share Page illustrate students' engagement. The following episode demonstrates how students were thoughtful in their critique of resources and used content and appearance as measures of usefulness.

> Angela and Jamie (Pair 3) locate information on their astronomy question ("How do black holes form?") and pause to critique the site. Students discuss the ratings of various items on the MYDL Cool Site Share Page as they enter the information. "Black Holes and Neutron Stars, Description: This site had lots of interesting information. It was easy to find your way around and it had lots of interesting graphics. If you are studying black holes, this is a good site to look in. Critique: The appearance of Black Holes and Neutron stars is very interesting. The graphics were very interesting and informative. The content gave us most of our information that we needed to answer our driving question." Angela and Jamie rated this site a 10 for overall appearance and 9 for overall content.

Most students who developed relatively weak content understandings through on-line inquiry did not adequately engage with Assess strategies. These students were quick to decide on the relevancy of sites, and this determination was often based on the site's title or first page. Information was often accepted although it did not relate directly to the driving question. Students did not discuss the trustworthiness of sites and considered all information good information. They were unable to critique a site's appearance and content effectively. An episode from process video (Tape 593A) illustrates this poor use of strategies.

> Brett and Cedric (Pair 1) locate a site for their geology unit ("Why do some volcanoes blow off half a mountain and some only trickle out lava?"). The site (Mount St. Helens: Volcano Page) has an attractive graphic, clear hypertext links, and little text. Cedric comments, "It's cool already." Brett immediately records information without looking through the site and brags to other groups, "Yeesh, oh my God, we found the best site ... God, look at this site, we found everything about Mount St. Helens!" Brett and Cedric scroll through one page at the site looking at small thumbnail images and short two-sentence descriptions. Brett pauses to record the title, URL, and a few comments about the site.

In this study, although Assess and Search strategies were examined as separate categories of inquiry strategies, these two types of strategies were used seamlessly by highly engaged students. These students used Assess strategies to question the relevancy of a site before deciding on a board or specific topic for their next search. That is, how and what to search were determined by their evaluation of the sites, and the search results led to another assess–search cycle. Their decision was often based on the site's contents rather than the appearance. Student conversations and writings in this study provided a perspective in response to a need for developing student evaluation and critical thinking skills in information-seeking environments (Brouwer, 1997; Fitzgerald, 1997).

It is not surprising that as novice learners of on-line inquiry the sixth graders in this study did not use multiple sources to verify the accuracy of information found on-line. Their discussions often centered on an assessment of the site's URL rather than biographical information provided by the author. On the other hand, a review of classroom-lab video did not contain episodes where teachers explicitly directed students to compare resources during the content units other than one activity where students compared sites with opposing viewpoints. This may reflect that students require specific intervention to develop various components of individual strategies. To help middle school learners reach higher levels of engagement with assess strategies, more scaffolding for search and assess strategies could have been provided. This echoes the argument presented by Metz (1995), that with sufficient learning scaffolding, young learners are capable of performing science inquiry, even though their investigations are less sophisticated than those of adults and adolescents.

Pedagogical Practices and On-line Learning

This study found some differences between student pairs from the two classes, and these variations might be attributed to the efforts of the participating teachers. Although teachers were provided with a model for inquiry-based learning, their implementation of supports and scaffolds were considerably different. Whereas one teacher provided substantial scaffolding to assist students in developing strategies for asking questions, planning inquiry activities, using on-line tools, searching for resources, assessing sites, writing about information, and creating artifacts, the other teacher provided less support. It seems that students benefited from an instructional environment where teachers provided clear expectations for classroom activities, provided critique, elicited feedback from students, and focused on scaffolding individuals and also the group as a whole. These findings are supported by Wisnudel-Spitulnik (1999) in an assessment of teacher scaffolding practices with learners engaged in dynamic modeling. She extended the knowledge base previously established by Collins, Brown, and Newman (1989) and Perkins (1996) by observing that learners benefited from teachers articulating expectations, modeling desired activities, and carefully orchestrating feedback.

Mediating On-line Learning

Although conducting on-line investigations could be beneficial for students, an important issue for continued use of the WWW for content learning surfaced during the analysis of data. Eighteen percent of inquiries involved inaccurate understandings as students conducted inquiry with on-line resources. Although an information-rich environment such as the WWW provides ample access to a variety of resources, it does little to mediate student learning, challenge students' existing understandings, and promote opportunities for accommodation. This points to more design work needed in another iteration of the tools, complementary curriculum and teacher practices.

Some students posed questions not supported by the UMDL collections. More extensive collections (e.g., other content areas, broader content areas, fact-based resources) might affect student engagement and subsequent construction of understanding. In addition, scaffolds that sequence students' searching process and provide prompts to help them evaluate the quality of online resources could be designed for Artemis.

Based on the findings with sixth graders, the Investigation Wheel (e.g., ask, plan, search, assess, write, create) could be refined such as adding a synthesizing phase into it. In addition, according to sixth graders' performance on on-line inquiry, curriculum materials that support advanced search and assess strategies could be developed for seventh or eighth graders.

Teachers could provide more support to students as they attempt to make sense of information in an environment that does not foster the construction of understanding but merely provides information. Teachers should require students occasionally to suspend their on-line activities to have conversations about the information they are encountering. For example, teachers could encourage them to discuss questions such as what information is new to them, what information does not make sense, what they can do to know more, and what concepts they have learned would help them understand the new information. Through participation in these types of conversations, teachers can mediate student learning to enhance or correct in-process constructions of understanding.

Conclusions

This study expands on early attempts to describe how students interact and learn from on-line learning environments such as the WWW. Based on this work, it is clear that students can benefit from access to on-line resources when extensive support and scaffolding are provided by the teacher, but this is far from automatic. Expanded models for technology development, curriculum design, and pedagogical practices are required to instantiate on-line inquiry successfully through information seeking in content areas. Only through careful assessment of these models can the research community provide educators and policymakers with concrete guidance for using technological tools such as the WWW in today's schools.

Perkins, D. N., & Simmons, R. (1988). Patterns of misunderstanding: An integrative model for science, math, and programming. *Review of Educational Research, 58,* 303–326.

Rosenshine, B., & Meister, C. (1992). The use of scaffolds for teaching higher-level cognitive strategies. *Educational Leadership, 49,* 26–33.

Ryder, R. J., & Graves, M. F. (1997). Using the internet to enhance student's reading, writing, and information-gathering skills. *Journal of Adolescent & Adult Literacy, 40,* 244–254.

Salomon, G., Globerson, T., & Guterman, E. (1990). The computer as a zone of proximal development: Internalizing reading-related metacognitions from a Reading Partner. *Journal of Educational Psychology, 81,* 620–627.

Salomon, G., Perkins, D. N., & Globerson, T. (1991). Partners in cognition: Extending human intelligence with intelligent technologies. *Educational Researcher, 20,* 2–9.

Shepardson, D. P., & Britsch, S. J. (1996). When dinosaurs roamed: Hypermedia and the learning of mathematics and science. *Journal of Computers in Mathematics and Science Teaching, 15,* 7–18.

Soloway, E., Guzdial, M., & Hay, K. E. (1994). Learner-centered design: The challenge for human computer interaction in the 21st century. *Interactions, 1,* 36–48.

Stoll, C. (1998, August 12). Net pioneer calls computers mostly a waste. *The Dallas Morning News* [On-line]. (Available: http://spyglass1.sjmercury.com/breaking/docs/049448.htm?st.ne. fd.mnaw).

Talsma, V. L. (1997). *How can we measure student understandings in science?* Unpublished manuscript, University of Michigan, Ann Arbor.

Tinker, R. F. (1978). Microcomputers: Applications to physics teaching. *Physics Teacher, 16,* 436–445.

Tinker, R. F. (1996). Information technologies in science and mathematics education [On-line]. (Available: http://www.concord.org/pubs/pdf/enc-v7.pdf). Concord, MA: Concord Consortium.

Tinker, R. F. (1997). *The whole world in their hands* [On-line]. (Available: http://www.concord.org/pubs/pdf/future.pdf). Concord, MA: Concord Consortium.

Tinker, R. F., & Haavind, S. (1997). *Netcourses and netseminars: Current practice and new designs* [On-line]. (Available: http://www.concord.org/pubs/pdf/netcours.pdf). Concord, MA: Concord Consortium.

Tinker, R. F., & Papert, S. (1989). Tools for science education. *AETS Yearbook,* 5–27.

Wallace, R., Krajcik, J., & Soloway, E. (1996). *Digital libraries in the science classroom: An opportunity for inquiry* [On-line]. (Available: http://www.dlib.org/dlib/september96/umdl/09wallace.html). D-Lib Magazine.

Wallace, R. (1997). *On-line information seeking in a sixth grade classroom.* Unpublished manuscript. University of Michigan, Ann Arbor.

Wallace, R., Kupperman, J., Krajcik, J., & Soloway, E. (2000). Science on the Web: Students online in a sixth-grade classroom. *Journal of the Learning Sciences, 9,* 75–104.

Winebrener, J. (1997). Take the Internet with a grain (pound?) of salt. *Michigan Association for Computer-Related Technology Users in Learning, 17,* 19–21.

Wisnudel-Spitulnik, M. (1999, April). *Teaching for understanding: One teacher's use of instructional strategies to support model building.* Paper presented at the annual meeting of the National Association for Research in Science Teaching, Boston, MA.

Wood, D. J., Burner, J. S., & Ross, G. (1976). The role of tutoring in problem solving. *Journal of Child Psychology and Psychiatry, 17,* 89–100.

Commentary Responses

comprehension, or how learners integrate across accessed Web resources. Integration is important because it affords both quantitative and qualitative learning advantages (Hartman, 1995; Wolfe & Goldman, 2005); however, before turning to our twist on their study, it is worthwhile to first examine the study by Hoffman et al. and make note of what we can learn from this perspective.

Artemis and Use of Online Resources

Hoffman et al. (2003) began with the premise that the World Wide Web has the potential to support and improve student learning because it provides access to a wealth of information not available otherwise. This research team noted, however, that the research to date has been mixed. From their own previous work with sixth-grade students, Hoffman et al. concluded that there is a "mismatch between the intended goals of the project and behaviors of students as they engaged in on-line investigations" (p. 324). The project to which they referred is an inquiry science curriculum in which students search resources to learn the answers to provided questions. The purpose of the curriculum is to engage students in activities that lead to a deep understanding. Rather than working toward this deep understanding, however, students who participated in their previous studies did not search or evaluate resources extensively and tended to seek specific answers.

In response to these findings, the research team developed Artemis, a system interface designed to support students' Web-based learning. Artemis allowed access to a preselected library of resources, which could be searched using key terms. In addition, Artemis included a workspace for note taking and Driving Questions folders for organizing those notes. Offline materials, such as activity sheets and inquiry scaffolds were also included.

This study was conducted as a design experiment carried out in four 1-week periods over the course of the school year. During each study period, students received a question to pursue and used the World Wide Web, through Artemis, to learn the answer. In the study, 8 student pairs from two classrooms participated.

Multiple data sources were collected including (a) process videos, capturing online activities and dialogue; (b) artifacts, including activity sheets, posters, and journals and; (c) interviews, which probed for understandings 1 week after unit completion. The interview rubric coded student responses as: Recall of Information, Offering Explanations, Articulate Relationships, or Extend Explanations (Perkins, Crismond, Simmons, & Unger, 1995). Within these categories, responses were scored as either inaccurate, missing (none), partial, or accurate. Although artifacts were similarly coded, interviews were more revealing of student knowledge. Although the research team identified eight inquiry strategies, they chose only to evaluate online behaviors in regard to two of these: search and assess strategies. Thus, the results of this study do not speak to how students synthesized resources or created knowledge.

Online behaviors and knowledge outcomes were analyzed to address research questions regarding students' use of Artemis and learning. The relationship between online behaviors and learning outcomes were addressed by considering these data sources together. Findings show that the depth of knowledge that the students gained on each of the sections was generally shallow and limited mostly to direct recall of the online materials (35% recalled information, 12% extended explanations), and 44% of the understandings were only partially correct. Students who were more actively engaged in searching and used more complex assess strategies developed better content knowledge. Students who acquired weaker content knowledge took less time and used less sophisticated criteria to determine relevance.

From these results, the authors concluded that if students are appropriately supported, they can effectively use the World Wide Web to enhance learning. Unfortunately, however, we believe that Hoffman et al. (2003) overreached when they concluded that students in this study "partnered with technology to enhance their general capabilities and learning" (p. 340). Notwithstanding the issue of making causal claims from a study lacking a comparison group, these claims overlook both the overall poor learning outcomes and the variance across data sources. If Artemis so powerfully moved these students, more than 12% of the students should have performed at the level of explanation extension. Moreover, a higher percentage of students should have been actively engaged in search and used sophisticated assess strategies. Of course, had the research team included a comparison group, these questions may have been answered by lower performances in that control. Without that comparison group, we must settle for raising the issues and encouraging deeper consideration of the patterns in the results.

Setting aside these specific concerns on balance, the work by Hoffman et al. (2003) has much to offer. This research team demonstrated the utility of an interface system designed to support elementary-school students' Web-based inquiry. Consistent with our assignment in writing this chapter, however, we read the study by Hoffman and colleagues with an eye to the questions in which we are interested: (a) How did these students integrate across the various selected Web sites? and (b) To what degree did integration play a role in the construction of a deep understanding? Although, Hoffman and colleagues were largely silent on these questions, the data reported suggests that students did not integrate multiple Web sites to construct the most sophisticated understandings possible. Before we can support these assertions, we must first explain what we mean by integration, and we do so in the following section. Following this explanation, we critique Hoffman et al.'s work and suggest methodology that can accommodate questions of intertextuality.

Intertextuality and the Processes of Integration

As noted previously, we share Hoffman et al.'s (2003) belief that the range of resources available on the World Wide Web affords a unique learning opportunity. As we also noted, however, the evaluation of Artemis reported in Hoffman et al. focused on students' search and assess strategies. Our interests, by contrast, lie further up the learning stream. Specifically, we are interested in how students capitalize on the whole range of available materials—how they put the varied sites together to construct a more complete representation of the target concepts than any single resource can afford. These learning processes fall under the heading of intertextuality, which extends more common notions of readers' comprehension processes by encompassing not only within- but also between-text comprehension (e.g., Hayes-Roth & Thorndyke, 1979).

Kristeva (1969/1980) defined intertextuality as a "permutation of texts" (p. 36), a process in which a reader combines utterances from one text with utterances from an earlier read text. Because the reader combines between-text utterances, connections form so that the two texts remain together in long-term memory. Although much of the research that employs the intertextuality label has been done with traditional texts, the definition of text extends to include a variety of semiotic and representational systems (e.g., Hartman, 2000) including written, oral, signed, electronic, and pictorial texts (Bloome & Egan-Robertson, 1993).

When text is understood this broadly, one can see that the ideas of intertextuality are relevant to a wide range of research on student learning in complex environments. Learning from multiple external representations (e.g., Ainsworth, 1999), animations (Hegarty, Kriz, & Cate, 2003), and multimedia (Kozma & Russell, 1997) have all been studied through the lens of learners' cross-textual integration. In our own work, we have examined not only how readers integrate printed, traditional text (Van Meter, Kulikowich, Higley, & Litzinger, 2005), but also how drawing facilitates the integration of verbal and pictorial representations (Van Meter, 2001; Van Meter, Aleksic, Schwartz, & Garner, 2006), and how engineering students integrate symbol systems and domains of knowledge to solve problems (Litzinger, Van Meter, Wright, & Kulilowich, 2006). Each of these areas of work represents an interest in understanding how learners integrate across separate and separable information sources to acquire and apply combinatorial knowledge.

To read intertextually, or integrate two texts, a learner must generate inferences that connect the present text to the knowledge representation derived from previously read text(s). These inferences are generated when the correspondence between elements is recognized and used to map the two representations (Gernsbacher, 1990; Hayes-Roth & Thorndyke, 1977). Integration, the cognitive process by which mapping occurs, requires that both representations are held simultaneously in working memory (Cote & Goldman, 1999), which, of course, requires that the learner recognize the relevance of the prior knowledge representation. In addition, integration necessitates the alignment of the structural constraints given in each representation (Van Meter & Garner, 2005).

The value of integration lies in the constructed knowledge representation that results (e.g., Perfetti, Britt, & Georgi, 1995). An integrated representation differs from a nonintegrated representation both quantitatively and qualitatively. *Quantitative differences* are obtained because the integrated representation includes not only the concepts that overlapped in the two texts, but also those concepts that were unique to each. *Qualitative differences* refer to the structural properties of the integrated representation. When a learner connects the mental model under construction from one text with a previously stored knowledge representation, the resulting model is more complete and flexible (Van Meter & Garner, 2005). Hayes-Roth and Thorndyke (1979) described this advantage as an *intertextual loop,* a situation in which a learner's knowledge continues to evolve with each new textual encounter. Ainsworth (1999) described these benefits in a taxonomy of the purposes for multiple external representations. In this system, multiple representations promote deep understandings, constrain interpretations, and serve complimentary roles. Van Meter (2001) demonstrated the benefits of integration when she showed that elementary-school students who integrated verbal and pictorial representations generated higher quality problem solutions than students who did not integrate representations.

The research on intertextual integration reveals that the proverbial glass is both half full and half empty. The majority of studies examining readers' cross-text integration have found that, although evidence exists that readers generate these connections, intertextual reading does not happen to the degree that we would like. In a study we conducted with experts and knowledgeable readers (Van Meter et al., 2005), for example, we found that both groups of readers connected the text that they were reading with the text that had been read earlier. Unfortunately, however, these cross-text inferences happened only rarely and accounted for a small portion of all comprehension processes. Parallel results are found when considering the cross-modal integration required when readers learn from texts using different representational systems. College students in a study by Tabachneck-Schijf and Simon (1998), for instance, did not integrate text and graphic representations when learning economics principles in a hypertext environment. In our research on elementary-school students reading to learn science content (e.g., Van Meter, 2001), we found that readers who processed both verbal and pictorial representations did not fully integrate these unless they were directed to use a drawing strategy and that strategy was supported.

Other research has suggested that individual differences play a role in intertextual reading. In Hartman's (1995) study of eight proficient high-school readers reading five related texts, he found that five students could be classified as intertextual. The remaining three students were either intratextual or extratextual readers. Strømsø, Bråten, and Samuelstuen (2003) found similar individual differences in their study of college students reading to prepare for a high-stakes law exam. Reading materials in this study included the course textbook and two references. At three times, participants brought text materials to study sessions and thought aloud while preparing for the exam. Although Strømsø et al. found that readers did not integrate across texts to the extent that they could, there were individual differences. Some participants made multiple connections between the text resources and, importantly, the participants who generated the greatest number of intertextual inferences also obtained the highest scores on the law exam.

This brief review of the research on intertextuality leads to two conclusions. First, when readers integrate across textual representations, the knowledge acquired is of a higher quality than knowledge derived from a single source. This benefit is often understood through theoretical accounts of mental model construction including both Kintsch's (1998) Construction-Integration Theory and Paivio's (1990) Dual-Code Theory. Both theories converge on the tenet that readers must connect across representations of knowledge to construct internal representations that are supportive of deep understandings and problem solving. The second conclusion is that readers cannot be assumed to be reading intertextually. As the research reviewed demonstrated, integration is not a reliable comprehension process.

Taken together, these conclusions tell us that learners can benefit from efforts to integrate textual representations, but they are likely to need instructional direction and support to do so. Moreover, if intertextuality was an important concept when Kristeva first wrote about it in 1969 and 1980, it is even more so now. Students now operate in a world of new literacies, a world that contains a vast array of texts. If students are to fully exploit these learning opportunities, they must do more than search and locate single sites. From our perspective, they must also work to integrate sites. Unfortunately, emerging models of learning in new literacies have focused more on search and navigation and less on students' comprehension processes (see Kulikowich, this volume). The research by Hoffman et al. (2003) is an example of this focus. When we look at their data, we see reason to agree that systems like Artemis have a vital function in Web-based learning, but we are less optimistic about their findings with respect to learning outcomes and how students used the variety of Web sites to which they had access.

In the following section, we discuss our reasons for this conclusion. In doing so, our intent is to demonstrate how research such as the study reported by Hoffman et al. (2003) can be extended to address questions of within- and between-text comprehension. In doing so, the reader should understand that Hoffman et al.'s study serves as an illustration of how research on new literacies can address learning more completely. As such, the critique is offered as a means to move the field forward rather than an indictment of the research by this one particular team.

Hoffman and Colleagues: A Critique

We initiate our critique of Hoffman et al.'s (2003) study with concerns regarding the means by which this team assessed knowledge outcomes. In this study, all students completed the same artifacts and participated in interviews. The authors focused the analysis on interviews because this data was more informative with respect to understandings that were artifacts. Unfortunately, however, because the interviews were conducted inconsistently across participants, the artifacts are the only reliable means to compare students. As an illustration, consider the excerpts given on pages 335 to 336 in the Hoffman et al. paper. These excerpts, one from Jamie and one from the pair of Kevin and Edward, were included to illustrate differences in students' understandings. Instead, these excerpts illustrate differences in how students were interviewed. Both examples begin with the student providing some information about the topic. Jamie offers a fact about black holes and Edward provides a statement about the cause of hurricanes. The interviewer then responds in two very different ways. In the first example, Jamie is asked an initial "Why?" question (e.g., Why does it pull things into it?), which is then followed up with a second "Why?" question. By contrast, Edward is not asked any question at all. The interviewer only restates part of Edward's initial response before asking Kevin if he has anything to add. Not surprisingly, Jamie is credited with the ability to relate and expand concepts while Kevin and Edward are credited only with recall.

Although we agree with Hoffman et al.'s (2003) concern that the more piecemeal artifacts did not reveal the depth of student understandings (e.g., Wineburg & Martin, 2004), we are more concerned that the inconsistencies across interviews contributed to differences in the quality of knowledge that students expressed. It is unfortunate that these researchers did not use a measurement technique that would have yielded more reliable and valid knowledge indicators.

These inconsistencies are only part of the reason to be concerned about Hoffman et al.'s (2003) findings with respect to knowledge outcomes. Earlier, we mentioned that interview responses were coded according to a rubric that differentiated the quality of knowledge. Students who could offer extended explanations were credited with higher quality knowledge than those who recalled facts. In the example excerpt just given, Jamie's response was coded as an extended explanation, presumably because of her suggestion of jumping into a black hole to commit suicide. As we prepared to write this chapter, however, we wanted to know more about the Web resources these students used, so out of this curiosity, we did an Internet search. After typing "black holes"

& Higley, 2005) when the learner cannot be separated from the context (e.g., Collins, 1992). It is not our desire to revisit questions regarding the utility of design experiments, for that issue is addressed elsewhere (e.g., O'Donnell, 2004). Rather, we would like to consider this methodology from the perspective of the study of intertextuality.

In the review of research presented earlier, the point was made that readers tend to generate some connections between texts. Thus, the question is about the degree to which readers are intertextual. Answering this question requires a comparison between groups of readers or between readers at different times. In the study by Strømsø et al. (2003), for example, we learn that law students increase the degree of intertextuality over time and that those who perform best on outcome measures also generate the most between-text inferences. Moreover, it was the inclusion of comparisons that allowed Van Meter et al. (2005) to identify differences in the intertextuality of expert and knowledgeable readers. These comparisons provide a necessary window for evaluating the extent to which readers generate connections across representations. We cannot envision the possibility of evaluating the effectiveness of a tool, such as Artemis, for promoting intertextual reading without the inclusion of a comparison group. Accordingly, design experiments are unlikely to yield an understanding of how to promote intertextuality.

In summary, Hoffman et al. (2003) did not consider the role of intertextuality in their evaluation of Artemis. The coding rubrics for both online behaviors and learning outcomes were not sensitive to this dimension and were not applied in ways that would reveal students' integration across texts. Given the available data, it does not appear that students in this study read intertextually. Rather, students seemed intent on locating the single most helpful Web site. In part, this evaluation of students' performance is incomplete because Hoffman et al. did not include the comparison group that would allow us to evaluate Artemis on the basis of this criterion. It is one thing, however, to identify shortcomings in research and another to offer solutions regarding what can be done differently. In the space remaining, we share some recommendations on how methodology in the study of new literacies can be extended to address intertextuality.

Intertextuality and New Literacies: Research Recommendations

First and foremost, the study of intertextuality requires consideration of the knowledge sources that are studied. Sources must be known to the research team because only then is it possible to discern where participants obtained their knowledge. This fundamental point is relevant to both the development of appropriate outcome measures and the coding of online behaviors. This is no small point, however. When the study of new literacies is situated in an open environment, participants may not only encounter numerous sources, the specific sources studied may also differ between participants. In these cases, researchers need to track learners' behaviors and make a post hoc analysis of covered sources. With sources known, researchers can develop measures of learning as well as measures of online learning behaviors that capture integration across texts.

Although specific measurements for capturing integrated knowledge representations are not well established in the literature, it is possible to adapt more common techniques. One approach is to measure integration by assessing the degree to which participants express connected knowledge. With this approach, participants may respond to open-ended transfer or problem-solving questions. The scoring rubric is developed with consideration of how well the answer reflects multisourced knowledge.

The approach used by Guthrie and colleagues (Guthrie, Van Meter, McCann, & Wigfield, 1996; Guthrie, Van Meter, & Mitchell, 1994) in their evaluation of Concept-Oriented Reading Instruction illustrates this technique. Here, elementary-school students completed a performance assessment, which included a multichapter experimental text and knowledge questions. In one of these assessments, students learned about ponds and deserts. After reading to learn, students responded to a conceptual transfer question (e.g., Would a drained pond be like a desert? Why or why not?). Responses were coded according to a five-point rubric. To obtain the highest scores on this rubric, students had to express connected knowledge of ponds and deserts. Although an accurate response could be developed by providing information only about ponds or information from only one chapter, such a response would not receive a very high score.

The work of Guthrie and colleagues (Guthrie et al., 1994; Guthrie et al., 1996) not only illustrates the possibility of considering connected knowledge within the context of traditional learning and problem-solving measures, but also illustrates how the methods employed by Hoffman et al. (2003) could be adapted to consider this dimension. Along with development of sensitive scoring systems, such an accommodation requires two additional considerations. First, response prompts must require the expression of connected knowledge. In the context of the study by Hoffman et al., for example, students could have been asked to explain how black holes are similar to neutron stars. Second, as just stated, these questions must be developed in light of the texts that learners search. For instance, in Hoffman et al.'s unit on hurricanes, a transfer question requiring connected knowledge could be "How do hurricanes affect erosion patterns?" One cannot know, however, if this question requires connected knowledge unless one knows of the texts that students studied.

Because intertextuality is an online phenomenon, it can also be studied in the context of online behaviors. To do this, the research team must attend to learners' behaviors during study relative to the texts that the learner is using. In other words, it is not sufficient to simply code behaviors into categories of interest. These behaviors must also be coded with respect to the sources of knowledge to which they are applied.

Kozma, R. B., & Russell, J. (1997). Multimedia and understanding: Expert and novice responses to different representations of chemical phenomena. *Journal of Research in Science Teaching, 34*(9), 949–968.

Kristeva, J. (1969/1980) *Desire in language: A semiotic approach to literature and art.* New York: Columbia University Press.

Kulikowich, J. M., Edwards, M. N., Van Meter, P. N., & Higley, K. J. (2005). *Intervening to accelerate emergent expertise: A multiple method system for principled learning in mathematics.* Paper presented at the annual meeting of the American Psychological Association, Washington, DC.

Litzinger, T., Van Meter, P., Wright, M., & Kulikowich, J. A. (2006). *A cognitive study of modeling during problem solving.* Proceedings, American Society for Engineering Education Annual Conference and Exposition, Chicago, IL.

Neumann, S. B. (2000). What will be the influences of media on literacy in the next millennium? *Reading Research Quarterly, 35*(2), 276–277.

O'Donnell, A. (2004). A commentary on design research. *Educational Psychologist, 39*(4), 255–260.

Paivio, A. (1990). *Mental representations: A dual coding approach.* New York: Oxford University Press.

Perfetti, C. A., Britt, M. A., & Georgi, M. C. (1995) *Text-based learning and reasoning: Studies in history.* Hillsdale, NJ: Lawrence Erlbaum.

Perkins, D. N., Crismond, D., Simmons, R., & Unger, C. (1995). Inside understanding. In D. N. Perkins, J. L. Schwartz, M. M. West, & M. S. Wiske (Eds.), *Software goes to school: Teaching for understanding with new technologies* (pp. 70–87). New York: Oxford University Press.

Strømsø, H. I., Bråten, I., & Samuelstuen, M. S. (2003). Students' strategic use of multiple sources during expository text reading: A longitudinal think-aloud study. *Cognition and Instruction, 21*(2), 113–147.

Tabachneck-Schijf, H. J. M., & Simon, H. A. (1998). One person, multiple representations: An analysis of a simple, realistic multiple representation learning task. In M. W. van Someren, P. Reimann, H. P. A. Boshuizen, & T. deJong (Eds.), *Learning with multiple representations* (pp. 197–236). New York: Pergamon.

Van Meter, P. (2001). Drawing construction as a strategy for learning from text. *Journal of Educational Psychology, 69*, 129–140.

Van Meter, P., Aleksic, M., Schwartz, A., & Garner, J. (2006). Learner-generated drawing as a strategy for learning from content area text. *Contemporary Educational Psychology, 31*, 142–166.

Van Meter, P., & Garner, J. (2005). The promise and practice of learner-generated drawing: Literature review and synthesis. *Educational Psychology Review, 17*, 285–325.

Van Meter, P. N., Kulikowich, J. M., Higley, K., & Litzinger, T. (2005, April). *Integrating representational systems during comprehension of expository texts.* Paper presented at the annual meeting of the American Psychological Association, Montreal, Canada.

Wineburg, S., & Martin, D. (2004). Reading and rewriting history. *Educational Leadership, 62*(1), 42–45.

Wolfe, M., & Goldman, S. R. (2005). Relations between adolescents' text processing and reasoning. *Cognition and Instruction, 23*(4), 467.

Internet Pedagogy
Using the Internet to Achieve Student Learning Outcomes

ROBERT E. BLEICHER

CALIFORNIA STATE UNIVERSITY CHANNEL ISLANDS, USA

Introduction

This chapter is pitched at new educational researchers, particularly those interested in research on new literacies (Lankshear, 1997; Lankshear & Knobel, 2003). It will relate how I—a practicing educational researcher and teacher educator—interpret a specific research report in terms of my perspective on certain aspects of teaching and learning. The topic is a critical discussion about employing the Internet in pedagogical approaches to teaching children in our schools, which is becoming increasingly commonplace in elementary school as well as in high school and middle school (Heil, 2005). I will refer to the teaching strategy of employing the Internet to achieve student-learning outcomes as Internet pedagogy. To illustrate the pros and cons of this strategy, a typical research study in this area will be analyzed: Hoffman, Wu, Krajcik, and Soloway's (2003) , "The Nature of Learners' Science Content Understandings With the Use of Online Resources" (hereafter, "CUONR"), originally published in the *Journal of Research in Science Teaching*. A critical reading of a text is closely tied to the interpreter's beliefs and background, so I begin with a very short autobiographical sketch of me as author of this critique.

Rather, novices require extensive guidance from experts (teachers) to develop deep thought processing and conceptual understanding. This extensive guidance provides a scaffold to support learners as they proceed on an intellectual apprenticeship from their current state of understanding to a state that is progressively closer to experts' understanding. This idea of scaffolding moves the realm of conceptualizing how learning takes place from the private "inside-the-head of the individual" model to a more socially active learning model that takes cultural aspects of learning environments into account.

Moving in this direction, other researchers have developed the idea of building communities of learners viewing learning as taking place within what they define as a classroom culture (Crawford, Kelly, & Brown, 2000). This builds on earlier work by Lave and Wenger (1991), in which they compared school learning with apprenticeship learning models in which apprentices learn from experts through what they call legitimate peripheral participation. Toulmin (2000) added to this framework by further examining how knowledge building takes place as novices and experts participate in shared practices. In order to achieve these communities of shared practice, we need to understand the sociocommunicative nature of classroom discourse.

Sociocommunicative Discourse Theory

Cook-Gumperz and Gumperz (2002) regarded "discourse" as a sociocultural and political entity that subsumes ways of saying, writing, doing, being, valuing, and believing. A discourse facilitates communication and establishes social identity within a community. Teaching and learning of science are considered to occur in evolving communities of practice in which the discursive practices (e.g., talk, writing, cognition, argumentation, and representation) of participants are constantly changing. The catalysts for change are social interactions between participants and social structures such as conventions and norms (Anagnostopoulos, Basmadjian, & McCrory, 2005; Moje, Collazo, Carrillo, & Marx, 2001; Roth & Tobin, 2002).

Given the appropriate conditions in which particular interests in a group are supported, learning about a particular subject, such as science, can lead students to develop an increasingly science-like discourse. An important criterion for progressing in this direction is the extent to which students use their discursive resources to make sense of their experience and support claims with evidence (Townsend & Pace, 2005). According to Barton (1997), "[T]he experiences of everyone need to become part of the language of science if the experiences, beliefs, values and essence of all people are truly to be incorporated into science" (p. 155). Driver, Newton, and Osborne (2000) and Niaz, Aguilera, Maza, and Liendo (2002) expressed this as students learning better strategies to argue their points based on evidence collected during classroom activities/investigations. To examine how well students are learning through their developing argumentative skills, implies that the researcher needs to be able to analyze talk between students and students and the teacher using some system that allows argumentative strategies to be clearly delineated and tied back to earlier statements and claims of evidence.

The research suggests that in most classrooms students do not "talk science" in the sense that Lemke (2001) described science talk. Students do least well in school science when they are from social backgrounds where customarily used activity structures, preferred grammar, rhetorical patterns, and figures of speech are least like those used in science and the classroom (Wallace, 2004). When students can employ their own language resources, the language that they speak at home and in the streets, they are more likely to develop literacy skills that are the foundation for developing more canonical, mainstream discourses. There is a tendency for the primary discourses of children from homes of working class or unemployed not to connect well to a scientific discourse (Atwater, 1996). Accordingly, teachers enact the curriculum for such students to emphasize the learning of scientific facts and to de-emphasize conceptual learning, inquiry, and scientific habits of mind (Kang & Howren, 2004).

Classroom discourse supporting such a fact-orientated curriculum often follows a familiar three-part I-R-E (I for initiation, R for response, E for evaluation) pattern known to educational researchers since the early 1960s (e.g., Bellack, Kliebard, Hyman, & Smith, 1966). In general, this discourse pattern plays out when the teacher asks a question, the student responds, and the teacher evaluates the response. The same pattern was observed to be the dominant discourse structure in classroom discourse studies throughout the 1970s and 1980s, sometimes called I-R-F (F for feedback from the teacher; e.g., Edwards, & Mercer, 1987; Mercer, 1995; Stubbs & Robinson, 1979). Lemke (1990) renamed the IRE or IRF pattern "triadic dialogue." Use of the triadic dialogue tends to keep Lemke's thematic pattern of the science content implicit and effectively hidden from many students, despite the best efforts and intentions of a good teacher. Just like learning a foreign language, fluency in science requires practice at speaking, thinking, and writing (i.e., active use of language, grammar rules, and language games). Yet, in most science classrooms, students mainly listen to and read the language of science but they talk very little science, write less, and are seldom given adequate time to think about answers to challenging problems (Bleicher, Tobin, & McRobbie, 2003).

To avoid the methodological problems in discourse analysis identified by Klaasen and Lijnse (1996), it is crucial to adopt well-defined and trialed systems such as those used in interactional sociolinguistics (Bleicher, 1998; Gumperz, 1986), social semiotics (Halliday & Hasan, 1989), or discourse moves (Krussel, Springer, & Edwards, 2004). Gumperz's (1986) and Halliday's (1985) systems analyze the language used in social situations by breaking it down to basic units of communication that people use to make meaning through discourse in social interactions. Based on Halliday's (1985) methodology, Lemke (1990) conducted a field-based study, analyzing field notes and recordings from 60 classes, involving 20 different teachers at the junior and high school levels in biology, chemistry, physics, and earth science courses. Lemke described science dialogue in terms of two patterns: (a) organizational or activity structure in which people are interacting move by move and strategically playing within some particular set of expectations about what will happen next and (b) thematic pattern in which people construct complex meanings about a topic by combining words and other symbols. Using this theoretical framework, dialogue in a science classroom could be examined to ascertain the extent to which the organizational structure and thematic patterns were consistent with those evident in a field of science. This is the same problem area Shuell (1987) examined in an earlier study. Shuell differentiated between scientists' "science" and teachers and students' "science" that they studied at school. Hence, if organizational patterns being constructed in classroom dialogue were similar to those of professional scientists or even to science textbooks, then we could say that the students and teacher are engaged in "talking science." Science is more than an elaboration of concepts, ideas and theories because it is founded on an innate curiosity about the nature of the universe, which is only satisfied by active pursuit of understanding (Crawford, 2000). Science focuses on the solution of problems, on questions, and on unknowns (Knorr-Cetina, 1992), and therefore, it is important that teachers and students establish environments where useful information is generated and intertexuality of multiple data sources is considered (Varelas & Pappas, 2006). Science should be portrayed to students as a basic human enterprise characterized by local needs in concrete research situations (Roth, 1995). Such a dynamic view of science has been shown to have direct implications for learning by allowing students to develop more meaningful and integrated knowledge (Spier-Dance, Mayer-Smith, Dance, & Khan, 2005).

For the past 30 years, more than 400 national reports have called for fundamental changes in how we educate our children, particularly in mathematics and science (Hurd, 1994). These reports call for reforms aimed at developing scientific habits of mind by having students take a more active role in the learning of science content that has current relevance (Hawley, 2002). The warrant for these reforms is the recognition that it is not enough to learn facts about science, but that learning science must involve students in hands-on science activities that promote conceptual understanding.

Internet pedagogy, one of several new literacies now emerging in our schools and in society at large (Heil, 2005; Lankshear & Knobel, 2003; McFadden, 2001), has potential for pursuing these science-education reform goals. Keeping the aforementioned theoretical considerations about conceptual understanding and classroom discourse in mind, I now address a typical journal article (Hoffman et al., 2003) in the area in terms of its contribution to understanding how effective Internet pedagogy is in helping students achieve different levels of learning.

Synopsis

I begin with short synopsis of Hoffman et al.'s (2003) CUONR as background to the critique that follows.

The study rationale is that Internet pedagogy is hampered in its goals by students' lack of active Internet site exploration and knowledge of how to employ various search tools efficiently (Hoffman et al., 2003). In response to this problem, the researchers intervened with a specially designed "Internet research space" that provided user-friendly tools and preselected sites for specific science topic areas for middle school students. The study was designed to ascertain how much one group of sixth graders explored various science topic areas and the search strategies they employed to this end. The study examined how much students gained in content knowledge, the accuracy of that knowledge, and their depth of understanding—from mere factual recall to deeper conceptual explanations—of the content they were discovering through their online investigation.

The study focused on 16 students who worked in pairs on their science explorations in an Internet pedagogy environment (Hoffman et al., 2003). Data was collected from several sources. The most important of these were videotapes of the students working on the computer, including the sites they were exploring and the search strategies they employed, as well as the dyadic discourse going on between them as they engaged in these activities. The researchers also conducted in-depth oral interviews with the student pairs, probing for the accuracy and depth of their understandings of the science content that they hope is being learned through the Internet pedagogy. Short excerpts from some interview transcripts are included in the research report. The researchers adopted a theoretical framework from another researcher to analyze the data for the students' accuracy and depth of understanding of the science content being explored.

Analyses of data showed that students constructed meaningful understandings through Internet pedagogy, although the accuracy and depth of their understandings varied (Hoffman et al., 2003). Findings suggested that students could develop accurate and in-depth understandings if they could use higher efficiency search strategies appropriately. While the resources were preselected, the students still needed to evaluate them in terms of how far they provided good information for their investigations.

How Does CUONR Inform My Practice?

I will examine how CUONR (Hoffman et al., 2003) informs me as an educational researcher-teacher educator under several headings, and from the standpoint of my earlier discussion of conceptual understanding as the ideal outcome for learning and of the centrality of sociocommunicative classroom interactions to the learning process.

Theoretical Framework

Several aspects of the theory that framed CUONR resonate with my own theoretical framework for considering student learning (Hoffman et al., 2003). The overarching idea that the study "draws upon interwoven contexts framing the environment in which learners participated" aligns well with my beliefs (and those of many other researchers) about the intertexuality of classroom learning environments (Bleicher, 1998; Varelas & Pappas, 2006). This is a very important aspect of research reports. The underlying assumptions that researchers bring to their studies need to be stated explicitly early in the report so that other researchers can locate themselves theoretically and understand the conclusions that are subsequently drawn from analysis of the data collected. These assumptions need not match the reader's, although it makes for easier digestion of the report if they do. The greater the distance is between the reader and researcher's perspectives, the more need there is for explanation.

CUONR defines what is meant by "information seeking" on the Internet indicating stages for learner engagement including initiation, selection, exploration, formulation, collection, and presentation (Hoffman et al., 2003). While this seems, on its face, a good framework for describing what stages students may proceed through when they interface with the computer screen while searching for information, it tends to gloss questions raised by McFadden (2001) that explore how Internet surfers, particularly younger students, actually conceptualize the cyberspace that they are viewing. This has implications for the literature reviewed by COUNR's authors (Hoffman et al., 2003), which contends that Internet pedagogy has great promise but that students can be misled by viewing incorrect or even purposely falsified information on some Web sites. Heil (2005) found that while 71% of the junior high school students studied used the Internet for research, 85% of them either did not know how to critically evaluate the Internet sites or chose not to. These considerations aside, CUONR proceeds to the question about the depth of knowledge students can attain when they engage in Internet pedagogy (Hoffman et al., 2003).

Hoffman et al.'s (2003) study employs Perkins, Crismod, Simmons, and Unger's (1995) three-part framework for how students demonstrate their depth of understanding through explanation, articulation, and extension. This is an important theoretical argument, for it moves the focus of the study beyond merely demonstrating a list of facts and information that students might glean from Internet searches, which accords with the deeper understandings most educators hope their students will acquire (Jones & Read, 2005; Tytler, 2002). This framework provides an organizing theme for subsequent data analysis.

The researchers accepted that learning that is more complex, indicated by articulation and extension, is desired over mere explanation (Hoffman et al., 2003). Explanation is based on students recalling facts, principles, and theories accurately and clearly expressing them either in writing or verbally. Articulation involves a further step from explanation in which students demonstrate their awareness of connections between various facts, concepts, principles, and theories that they have explained. Extension is evident when students are able to explain the facts, concepts, principles, and theories that they have learned in new ways or for new situations. Such frameworks, while common in reports, are not always as well connected to the research questions as the one employed in this study is.

The authors argued for the salience of their study and why it contributes significantly to the literature (Hoffman et al., 2003). While prior research provides descriptions of what Internet pedagogy can add to student content understanding, this study goes further and examines how students construct such understandings. This caught my interest because I view learning and understanding as a socially constructed or socially mediated process that involves crucial interactions between an individual's internally held understanding and those of others with whom they interact (Bleicher, 1998; Cook-Gumperz & Gumperz, 2002). Hence, the study (Hoffman et al., 2003) has the potential to further inform and/or challenge my own views.

Research Methodology

Alongside the theoretical perspective of the researchers (Hoffman et al., 2003), the methods employed to collect data and make interpretations based on the analysis of those data are central to how far I trust a study's conclusions. The CUONR data was collected over a school year, in line with my view that understanding school learning environments requires taking time to get a sense of the cultural practices in the setting. I next look for multiple data sources, and this study collected numerous student work samples and student journals. Interview data, which are usually illuminating with respect to young learners, were also collected. The primary data source was strong: a videotaped collection of the actions and discourse of students engaged in Internet pedagogy. The analysis of work samples seemed to me appropriate and sound, although I found myself wanting more detail about how the interviews and the discourse recorded on videotapes were analyzed. In this area, the report failed to elucidate aspects of discourse in an Internet pedagogy setting that I want to know about given my perspective on how communication takes place through the words and actions of participants. The report provides only two short and, one assumes, verbatim transcripts of discourse between two different sets of students to illustrate two different levels of understanding being exhibited. Of course, many researchers do not undertake systematic discourse analysis of videotaped materials at all.

Notwithstanding my interest in more detail on this dimension, this study nonetheless afforded me many insights into the nature of student learning in Internet pedagogy settings.

Depth of Content Understanding

This was the key interest for me in reading this report (Hoffman et al., 2003). An interview transcript of one pair of students (Angela and Jamie) was presented to represent those few students who could articulate accurate understandings of concepts and extend that understanding in further explanation when probed by the interviewer. The discussion in the report supported my own experiences working with young learners and teaching those who were studying to become elementary school teachers. Most students can be taught facts and simple concepts, but relatively few can link concepts to one another in some recognizable map, a research finding well documented by Romance and Vitale (1999). Those who can map concepts often are able to extend their conceptual understanding into new areas considerably beyond the original facts and concept definitions introduced to them. This takes time and repeated activity settings. Even given the time and varied learning experiences, relatively few students can demonstrate this rare, but highly sought, outcome of transferring new conceptual understanding into new problem contexts. This accords with other researchers' findings. Kang and Howren (2004), for example, contended,

> One of the most difficult jobs of elementary school teachers is teaching science for conceptual understanding. Conceptual understanding requires students to organize facts and ideas into a meaningful concept in science. Facts and concepts form webs that can help students make connections between the concepts of science and their experiences. Moving beyond rote memorization of facts, conceptual understanding enables students to align intuitive ideas with scientific ones, making meaningful connections. Therefore, students can apply their understanding of concepts to multiple contexts. (p. 29)

CUONR (Hoffman et al., 2003) provides an example of a pair (Edward and Kevin) to represent the much more common situation in which students exhibit some understanding of facts and concepts but very limited ability to expand into new situations. Repeated efforts by the interviewer to elicit concept expansion, or even evidence that they were beginning to link one concept to another, resulted in the students restating only facts they knew. The authors reported that, over the four content units students studied, 35% of students were able to recall information, 32% were able to offer explanations, 22% were able to expand concepts, and only 12% were able to extend to deeper levels or new situations. Even at the level of recalling facts and stating simple concepts, only about one third were successful.

Methodology Matters

The authors noted that, whereas in their projects or presentations students might represent mere factual recall, when interviewed they were sometimes able to demonstrate the deeper conceptual understanding sought (Hoffman et al., 2003). This is important with respect to methodology: it matters how data pertinent to addressing research questions is collected. Cook-Gumperz and Gumperz (2002) explored related issues such as the interviewer-interviewee interactions that occur when collecting interview data. The face-to-face, real-time interviewing employed in the CUONR study meant that students could demonstrate deeper levels of knowledge that was not necessarily evident in their work samples or presentations by answering on-the-spot probes (Hoffman et al., 2003). Students are complex in how they learn and how they express that learning to make it visible to observers. In this respect, the CUONR reports met my interests as a research consumer in ways that reports that depend on only one or only a few data sources (e.g., a test result or a pre/post written survey) often do not.

Accuracy of Content Understanding

CUONR presents data and a discussion of the accuracy of student under-standing of facts and concepts (Hoffman et al., 2003). Although this is less of an interest to my own research agenda than considerations of surface versus deeper conceptual understanding, accuracy is an important concern for all educators. The study findings reflected a familiar pattern, with 44% of responses exhibiting partial understanding and 39% accurate understanding. These numbers illuminate why teachers often feel a need to spend much time at the level of helping learners gain accurate knowledge and find themselves pressed to work at attaining the goal of deeper conceptual understanding.

Teachers often are desperate to find new strategies for getting students to demonstrate that they can at least recall facts and concepts accurately. There is little sense in pursuing the next level of deeper conceptual understanding until there is a solid foundation of accurate knowledge to build upon. The research reported in CUONR supplies hard data that much time is spent at the first level of recall, with some time for explanation, but little time left for helping students reach the level of articulating and, finally, of expanding their explanations of their conceptual understanding (Hoffman et al., 2003).

Successful Search Strategies to Explain Differences in Accuracy and Depth of Learning

CUONR reports that two factors help explain the disparate student learning outcomes in this sample of middle school students: namely, (a) the search strategy employed and (b) the ability to evaluate the value of online resources (Hoffman et al., 2003). It is argued that those students who used more complicated search strategies and employed more effective decisions about whether a particular site would be worth the time spent consulting it for their investigation purposes ultimately demonstrate more accurate and deeper conceptual under-standing (i.e., the ability to articulate and expand). Since this was the most important question—what Internet searching strategies are most effective?—to examine, I was disappointed that the report does not provide more data in this section. The study's conclusion about search strategies, as stated here, is certainly plausible. Nonetheless, I did not go away from CUONR with as good a sense of what this looked like in the Internet pedagogy setting as I have from reading other reports. Despite ever-present limitations on space, research reports must help readers to come away with an adequate sense of what it was like for students and teachers in the learning environment. For example, McDonald's (2003) paper on the link between conversation and conceptual understanding leaves readers with a good idea of what the classroom environ-ment was like for students and how the interactions differed between the more successful learning groups and less successful. But I did not feel this way with CUONR (Hoffman et al., 2003).

Scaffolding

The concept of scaffolding first advanced by Vygotsky in the 1930s has reemerged as a key driver of current research and pedagogical approaches in school settings. In light of Gable's (2003) contention that novices require extensive guidance from experts to develop conceptual understanding, I found CUONR (Hoffman et al., 2003) very informative. The two teachers in this study employed Internet pedagogy differently. Enhanced student learning was exhibited in students with the teacher who provided a greater level of scaffolding. This involved stating clear expectations for students about what was required in their investigations, providing feedback to students on their work, requesting that students respond to that feedback and engage in stu-dent-teacher discourse, and modeling effective search strategies. This reso-nates strongly with my own teaching experience and theoretical perspective on expert-novice scaffolding as necessary for promoting deeper conceptual understanding in students.

Conclusions

Internet pedagogy might be viewed as a risky venture for achieving student learning outcomes unless teachers conduct regular checks to ascertain the accuracy of student learning. Gee's (2008) conclusion with respect to video games that the power for pedagogy lies in design resonates with the current study. CUONR (Hoffman et al., 2003) incorporates this idea by structuring the Internet environment for middle school students around providing access to the Middle Years Digital Library (MYDL) through Artemis—a specially designed interface that assists students develop their online information seek-ing skills. Artemis also provides a driving questions folder to help students develop metacognitive mental schemas for understanding why they are online gathering information. That is, Artemis helps students remember the question they are trying to answer by means of Internet research. In CUONR, students had the advantage of visiting only preselected Internet sites that would most likely yield productive information for their investigations. Even with this advantage, the data demonstrates that accuracy is a first concern followed closely by depth of understanding and the ability to demonstrate the deeper levels indicated by articulation and extension.

CUONR aims to delineate successful search strategies that might have supported those instances of deeper levels of understanding and greater accuracy in student learning outcomes evident in this study (Hoffman et al., 2003). This has potential to inform teachers and researchers about better ways to assist students toward these outcomes. From my own perspective on the importance of sociocommunication in classroom learning environments, however, I would have liked to see the report go further. A more in-depth discourse analysis of what students were saying to one another, to the teacher, and to researchers might have illuminated discourse elements supporting the more successful examples.

It is increasingly likely that on a given day visitors to classrooms will observe Internet pedagogy occurring somewhere and at some time. CUONR (Hoffman et al., 2003) adds to our knowledge base of best practices for getting the most out of time spent by students in online searches.

References

Anagnostopoulos, D., Basmadjian, K. G., & Mccrory, R. S. (2005). The decentered teacher and the construction of social space in the virtual classroom. *Teachers College Record, 107*, 1699–1729.

Atwater, M. (1996). Social constructivism: Infusion into the multicultural science education research agenda. *Journal of Research in Science Teaching, 33*, 821–838.

Barton, A. C. (1997). Liberatory science education: Weaving connections between feminist theory and science education. *Curriculum Inquiry, 27*, 141–163.

Bellack, A., Kliebard, H., Hyman, R., & Smith, F. (1966). *The language of the classroom.* New York: Teachers' College Press.

Bleicher, R. (1998). Classroom interactions: Using interactional sociolinguistics to make sense of recorded classroom talk. In J. Malone & B. Atweh (Eds.), *Aspects of postgraduate supervision and research in mathematics and science education* (pp. 85–104). Mahwah, NJ: Lawrence Erlbaum.

Bleicher, R., Tobin, K., & McRobbie, C. (2003). Opportunities to talk science in a high school chemistry classroom. *Research in Science Education, 33*, 319–339.

Chappell, K. K., & Killpatrick, K. (2003). Effects of concept-based instruction on students' conceptual understanding and procedural knowledge of calculus. *Primus, 13*, 17–37.

Cook-Gumperz, J., & Gumperz, J. J. (2002). Narrative accounts in gatekeeping interviews: Intercultural differences or common misunderstandings? *Language and Intercultural Communication, 2*, 25–36.

Crawford, B. A. (2000). Embracing the essence of inquiry: New roles for science teachers. *Journal of Research in Science Teaching, 37*, 916–937.

Crawford, T., Kelly, G., & Brown, C. (2000). Ways of knowing beyond facts and laws of science: An ethnographic investigation of student engagement in scientific practices. *Journal of Research in Science Teaching, 37*, 237–258.

Driver, R., Newton, P., & Osborne, J. (2000). Establishing the norms of scientific argumentation in classrooms. *Science Education, 84,* 287–312.

Edwards, D., & Mercer, N. (1987). *Common knowledge: The development of understanding in the classroom.* London: Routledge.

Gabel, D. (2003). Enhancing the conceptual understanding of science. *Educational Horizons, 81,* 70–76.

Gee, J. (2008). Being a lion and being a soldier: Learning and games. This volume, Ch. 34a.

Gibson, H. L., & Rea-Ramirez, M. A. (2002, January). Keeping the inquiry in curriculum designed to help students' conceptual understanding of cellular respiration. *Proceedings of the Annual International Conference of the Association for the Education of Teachers in Science,* Charlotte, NC: Asocociation for the Education of Teachers of Science. (Publication No. ED465634).

Grossen, B., Carnine, D., Romance, N., & Vitale, M. (1998). Effective strategies for teaching science. In E. Kameenui & D. Carnine (Eds.), *Effective teaching strategies that accommodate diverse learners* (pp.113–134). Upper Saddle River, NJ: Merrill.

Gumperz, J. J. (1986). Interactional sociolinguistics in the study of schooling. In J. Cook-Gumperz (Ed.), *The social construction of literacy* (pp. 45–68). Cambridge, U.K.: Cambridge University Press.

Halliday, M. (1985). *An introduction to functional grammar.* London: Edward Arnold.

Halliday, M., & Hasan, R. (1989). *Language, context, and text: Aspects of language in a social semiotic perspective.* Geelong, Australia: Deakin University.

Hawley, D. (2002). Building conceptual understanding in young scientists. *Journal of Geoscience Education, 50,* 363–371.

Heil, D. (2005). The Internet and student research: Teaching critical evaluation skills. *Teacher Librarian, 33,* 26–30.

Hoffman, J., Wu, H.-K., Krajcik, J. S., & Soloway, E. (2003). The nature of middle school learner's science content understandings with the use of on-line resources. *Journal of Research in Science Teaching, 40*(3), 323–346.

Hurd, P. (1994). New minds for a new age: Prologue to modernizing the science curriculum. *Science Education, 78,* 103–116.

Jones, D. K., & Read, S. J. (2005). Expert-novice differences in the understanding and explanation of complex political conflicts. *Discourse Processes: A Multidisciplinary Journal, 39,* 45–80.

Kang, N., & Howren, C. (2004). Teaching for conceptual understanding. *Science and Children, 42,* 28–32.

Kiraz, E. (2004). Unexpected impact of practicum: Experts learn from the novice. *Teacher Education and Practice, 17,* 71–88.

Knorr-Cetina, K. D. (1992). The couch, the cathedral, and the laboratory: On the relationship between experiment and laboratory in science. In A. Pickering (Ed.), *Science as practice and culture* (pp. 132–138). Chicago: University of Chicago Press.

Krussel, L., Springer, G. T., & Edwards, B. (2004). The teacher's discourse moves: A framework for analyzing discourse in mathematics classrooms. *School Science and Mathematics, 104,* 307.

Lankshear, C. (1997). *Changing literacies.* Buckingham, U.K.: Open University Press.

Lankshear, C., & Knobel, M. (2003). *New literacies: Changing knowledge and classroom learning.* Buckingham, U.K.: Open University Press.

Lave, J., & Wenger, E. (1991). *Situated learning: Legitimate peripheral participation.* Cambridge, U.K.: Cambridge University Press.

Lemke, J. L. (1990). *Talking science: Language, learning, and values.* Norwood, NJ: Ablex Publishing Co.

Lemke, J. L. (2001). Articulating community as sociocultural perspective on science education. *Journal of Research in Science Teaching, 32,* 373–385.

McDonald, J. T. (2003, March). *The connection between conversation and conceptual understanding.* Paper presented at the annual meeting of the National Association for Research in Science Teaching, Philadelphia, PA.

McFadden, T. G. (2001). Understanding the Internet: Model, metaphor, and analogy. *Library Trends, 50*, 87–109.

Mercer, N. (1995). *The guided construction of knowledge: Talk among teachers and learners.* Clevedon, UK: Multilingual Matters.

Moje, E. B., Callazo, T., Carrillo, R., & Marx, R. W. (2001). Maestro, what is quality?: Language literacy and discourse in project-based science. *Journal of Research in Science Teaching, 38*, 469–489.

Niaz, M., Aguilera, D., Maza, A., & Liendo, G. (2002). Arguments, contradictions, resistances, and conceptual change in students' understanding of atomic structure. *Science Education, 86*, 505–525.

Perkins, D. N., Crismond, D., Simmons, R., & Unger, C. (1995). Inside understanding. In D. N. Perkins, J. L. Schwartz, M. M. West, & M. S. Wiske (Eds.), *Software goes to school: Teaching for understanding with new technologies* (pp. 70–87). New York: Oxford University Press.

Romance, N., & Vitale, M. (1997). *Knowledge representation systems: Basis for the design of instruction for undergraduate course curriculum.* Paper presented at the eighth National Conference on Teaching and Learning, Jacksonville, FL.

Romance, N., & Vitale, M. (1999). Concept mapping as a tool for learning: Broadening the framework for student-centered instruction. *College Teaching, 47*, 74–79.

Roth, W. M. (1995). Knowing and interacting: A study of culture, practices, and resources in a grade 8 open-inquiry science classroom guided by a cognitive apprenticeship metaphor. *Cognition and Instruction, 13*, 73–128.

Roth, W. M., & Tobin, K. (2002). *At the elbow of another: Learning to teach by coteaching.* New York: Peter Lang.

Schmidt, W. H., McKnight, C., & Raizen, S. (1996). *A splintered vision: An investigation of US science and mathematics education.* Norwell, MA: Kluwer Academic Publishers.

Shuell, T. (1987). Cognitive psychology and conceptual change: Implications for teaching science. *Science Education, 71*, 239–250.

Spier-Dance, L., Mayer-Smith, J., Dance, N., & Khan, S. (2005). The role of student-generated analogies in promoting conceptual understanding for undergraduate chemistry students. *Research in Science & Technological Education, 23*, 163–178.

Stubbs, M., & Robinson, B. (1979). Analysing classroom language. In V. Lee (Ed.), *Language development: A reader.* London and Milton Keynes: Croom Helm and Open University Press.

Toulmin, S. (2000). Knowledge as shared procedures. In Y. Engeström, R. Miettinen, & R. L. Punamaki (Eds.), *Perspectives on activity theory* (pp. 53–64). New York: Cambridge University Press.

Townsend, J. S., & Pace, B. G. (2005). The many faces of Gertrude: Opening and closing possibilities in classroom talk. *Journal of Adolescent and Adult Literacy, 48*, 594–605.

Tytler, R. (2002). Teaching for understanding in science: Constructivist/conceptual change teaching approaches. *Australian Science Teachers' Journal, 48*(4), 30–35.

Varelas, M., & Pappas, C. C. (2006). Intertextuality in read-alouds of integrated science-literacy units in urban primary classrooms: Opportunities for the development of thought and language. *Cognition and Instruction, 24*, 211–259.

Wallace, K. R. (2004). Situating multiethnic identity: Contributions of discourse theory to the study of mixed heritage students. *Journal of Language Identity and Education, 3*, 195–213.

CHAPTER 36

Instant Messaging, Literacies, and Social Identities*

CYNTHIA LEWIS

UNIVERSITY OF IOWA, USA

BETTINA FABOS

UNIVERSITY OF NORTHERN IOWA, USA

Abstract

This study examined the functions of Instant Messaging (IM) among seven youths who regularly used this digital technology in their daily lives. Grounded in theories of literacy as a social and semiotic practice, this research asked what functions IM served in participants' lives and how their social identities shaped and were shaped by this form of digital literacy. To answer these questions, we conducted interviews and videotaped IM sessions, adapting a verbal reporting procedure to document the IM strategies used. Data analysis involved using qualitative coding procedures informed by grounded theory (Strauss, 1987; Strauss & Corbin, 1990), which led to three patterns related to the functions of IM: language use, social networks, and surveillance. On the level of language use, participants manipulated the tone, voice, word choice, and subject matter of their messages to fit their communication needs, negotiating multiple narratives in the process. On the level of social networks, they designed their practice to enhance social relationships and statuses across contexts. And on the level of surveillance, they circulated texts across buddies, combated unwanted messages, assumed alternative identities, and overcame restrictions to their online communication. These functions revealed that the technological and social affordances of IM, particularly related to patterns of circulation and the hybrid nature of textuality, give rise to a performative and multi-voiced social subject. Based on our findings, we discuss new conceptual directions for envisioning the teaching and learning of literacy in digitally mediated times.

* Reprinted from Lewis, C., & Fabos, B. (2005, October/November/December). Instant messaging, literacies, and social identities. *Reading Research Quaterly*, 40(4), 470–501. Reprinted with permission.

Everybody does it. It's like I've grown up on it. It's like how you felt about stuff when you were growing up.

—Sam

Sam, a 14-year-old girl, was one of seven participants in this study of young people's uses of Instant Messaging (IM). We want to take a moment to consider Sam's comment as a way of providing a conceptual framework for this study. To Sam, IM did not feel like *technology*, a term associated in many people's minds with objects that are complicated and difficult to understand or operate. When technology becomes "normal" in this way, it is no longer complicated, nor is it notable to its users. It is a fact of life, a way of being in the world, a producer of social subjects that find it unremarkable—so unremarkable that it seems "everybody does it."

The social subject that develops in relation to this invisible technology is one who expects access, expects to be connected to friends at the stroke of a key, and expects to read and write in particular ways that lead to fulfilling connections with those friends. As Bourdieu (1997) put it, "The experience of a world that is 'taken for granted' presupposes agreement between the dispositions of the agents and the expectations or demands immanent in the world into which they are inserted" (p. 147).

Sam's dispositions and the expectations placed upon her were in agreement. But it is important to note that these expectations did not emanate from her world at home. We suspect that because of Sam's assumption that "everybody does it," readers are imagining Sam to be middle class with economic resources that would locate her on the advantaged side of the digital divide. This was not the case. Sam happened to live in a community that had very inexpensive, municipally owned cable access, making home Internet access possible across class lines. Sam's parents were custodians who placed high value on their children's education and managed to purchase a computer to provide Sam with what they perceived to be a school advantage. Her mother found the computer to be mysterious and confusing—in other words, technological. Her father was an avid Internet user, but with concerns about Sam's interest in IM. Our point, for now, is that through the happenstance of living in a community with inexpensive cable access, through daily use, through peers who stayed connected, through generational and other social identities that we will discuss in this article, and through all the social codes and practices that come with these social identities, Sam was positioned as a social subject who took IM for granted—one who had ways of reading and writing that were natural to her as part of her daily practice with IM. These ways of reading and writing through a technology that she did not view as technological were different than ours, and, we suspect, different than most of her teachers.

The anxiety that results from this difference has been discussed by Luke and Luke (2004):

> The perception of crisis [over perceived loss of print literacy] is an artifact of a particular generational anxiety over new forms of adolescent and childhood identity and life pathways: fundamental ontological and teleological changes in childhood traceable to global economies, cultures, and technologies. (p. 105)

Here, they make clear that the crisis is not to be found in the child or adolescent as subject, but in the teacher, researcher, and policymaker as the adult subject whose anxieties about new adolescent identities lead to the valorization and reification of print culture.

We are interested in the kind of social subject constructed through IM—the social identities that shape and are shaped by the practice of IM. To this end, we examined the uses of IM among seven youth (four females and three males) who regularly used this technology in their daily lives. We wanted to know what functions IM served in their lives: For what purposes did they use this form of digital literacy? For what reasons and under what circumstances did they find it most compelling? These are the research questions that led us to understand more about our participants as social subjects who shape and are shaped by particular technologies. It is our hope that insights gleaned from this research will help us to make school literacy more engaging for students and more meaningful to their present and future lives in a digitally mediated world.

Instant messaging (IM) came of age in 2000. Although the interactive message tool dates back to the 1970s, when researchers began to send real-time text messages on Unix-based networks, the technology became instantly popular in the late 1990s, when America Online (AOL) engineers introduced the Buddy List (Guernsey, 2001). The list basically allows users to manage multiple simultaneous exchanges and also track their buddies' appearances and disappearances. Internet users, and young people especially, gravitated to the social and playful exchange tool, and IM became a communication phenomenon. Industry insiders called IM the latest "Killer App" (Weise, 2000), and technology trackers projected that IM would surpass e-mail as the primary online communication tool by 2005 (Latchford, 2003). By 2003, 70% of online teens ages 12–17 used instant messaging. One fourth of all online teens see IM as their main communication tool (Zucco, 2003). In the United States, IM use among youth has surpassed that of other forms of Information and Communication Technology (ICT), including chat rooms (Herring, 2004). Although users typically manage three or more ongoing exchanges at once (Lenhart, Rainie, & Lewis, 2001), each IM exchange is dyadic.

In light of its popularity among youth and the fact that reading and writing are central to its practice, IM seems an important form of literacy for researchers and educators to examine. IM motivates young people to engage in decoding, encoding, interpretation, and analysis, among other literacy processes, and yet very little empirical work has focused on this form of digital literacy. The published work that is available uses data clips from the findings of larger IM studies in order to make conceptual arguments (Lewis & Fabos, 2000; Lewis & Finders, 2002) or methodological ones (Jacobs, 2004). This research represents an empirical study meant to fill that gap.

Theoretical Framework

This study is grounded in theories of literacy as a social practice, especially as such literacies have been shaped by digital technologies (Kress, 2003; Lankshear & Knobel, 2003). Often referred to as the "New Literacy Studies" (Barton & Hamilton, 1998), "social literacies" (Gee, 1996; Street, 1995), or "situated literacies" (Barton, Hamilton, & Ivanic, 2000), theories of literacy as a social practice have shifted attention away from models based in psychology that emphasize individual cognition to models based in sociology, linguistics, literary theory, and anthropology that focus on the social, cultural, and political contexts of literacy.

Whereas New Literacy Studies informed our view of the dynamic, socially inscribed nature of IM activity, it did not provide a theory of identity to help us understand how our participants used IM to enact particular versions of self at particular times. Hall's (1996) take on identity as temporary attachments constructed within discursive practices has served this purpose. According to Hall, identities are positions we take up as though they are stable and cohesive. In a similar vein, Moje (2004) referred to identity positions as enactments of who we might be at a given time, in a given context, within a given set of social, economic, and historical relations. In this sense, at the same time that attachments or enactments of identity are generative and creative, they also instantiate economic and social structures.

Our identities shape and are shaped by what counts as knowledge, who gets to make it, who receives it, and so forth. As Kress, Jewitt, and Tsatsarelis (2000) pointed out in an article on the effects of new representational modes on educational practice, it is at the intersection of identity, knowledge, and pedagogy that social subjects are formed. The production of social subjects related to print literacies has been well established (see, for instance, Luke, 1992, 1994). Given the central role that identity plays in teaching and learning, we are interested in the kind of social subject constructed through IM practices and, moreover, how social identities shape the nature of IM practices.

This research is about a representational mode that blurs the boundaries of what many consider to be literacy. It is important that we define what we mean by the term. For the purposes of this article, we define *literacy* as the range of practices involved in the alphabetic coding of socially and culturally relevant signs and symbols (de Castell & Luke, 1986; Kress, 2003; Warshauer, 2002). Along with Kress (1997) and others, we view all signs, including all uses of print, as multimodal. The last two decades have brought important shifts in the meaning of literacy, underscoring its connection to orality (a position with a long history, of course) and ideology (Street, 1995). Yet those who have been most responsible for these shifts have continued to use literacy to refer to reading and writing in all of their social, cultural, political, and historical resonances (Heath, 1983; Street). We continue in that tradition of using the term as it relates specifically to reading and writing, in part because literacy when used to refer to all forms of knowledge (i.e., math literacy) or modes of communication (i.e., visual literacy) is too vague to be useful to educators and researchers. Our interest is quite specifically in how reading and writing (albeit in consort with other modes) are used within a specific computer-mediated communication (IM).

The term *literacy practices* has a special meaning among those who study the social nature of literacy within the framework of New Literacy Studies. These researchers are careful to distinguish between literacy events and literacy practices (Barton & Hamilton, 1998; Street, 1995). Literacy events are defined as any event involving a written text. Literacy practices, on the other hand, are what can be inferred from observable literacy events as embedded within broader social and cultural norms. Practices, the focus of our attention in this study, are more abstract, related to matters of codes and conventions, beliefs and attitudes, and legitimation and control. The next section reviews literature that points to changes in the nature of literacy practices as they relate to digital literacies.

Digital Literacies and Changing Practices

Although a number of studies include IM among discussions of other digital literacies or practices (Chandler-Olcott & Mahar, 2003; Holloway & Valentine, 2003; Snyder, Angus, & Sutherland-Smith, 2002; Young, Dillon, & Moje, 2002), there are very few studies as of yet that directly examine the social, textual, or pedagogical implications of IM (Jacobs, 2004; Lenhart et al., 2001; Lewis & Fabos, 2000; Lewis & Finders, 2002). Given the dearth of research directly related to IM, the following literature review will focus on two central features of digital literacies that informed our understanding of our participants' IM practices—social mediation and multimodality.

A caveat is necessary before we begin our review. Much of the scholarship having to do with digital literacies has focused on the differences between print and digital technologies, the resulting epistomogical shifts, and the

They describe these changing epistemologies as "more performance- and procedure-oriented than propositional, more collaborative than individualistic, and more concerned with making an impact on attention, imagination, curiosity, innovation, and so on, than with fostering truth, engendering rational belief, or demonstrating their justifiability" (p. 176).

This being the case, educators may want to promote flexible ways of knowing through literacy practices that work to foster such epistemologies. For instance, Lankshear and Knobel (2002) suggested "scenario planning" (pp. 25–27), a method of problem solving, decision making, and strategic planning for imagined futures. The emphasis in their work is on learning as an imaginative, divergent process that mixes modes, genres, roles, and environments. Other literacy scholars believe that what is needed in these times of multitasking and information overload is to slow down. Rather than worrying about covering works of literature, for instance, Sumara (2002) eloquently articulated the benefits of deliberative, reflective readings of literature in ways that invite readers to reinvent themselves as reading subjects. Burbules and Callister (2000) and Fabos (2004) argued for careful, critical readings of Internet sites and texts to uncover the politics of representation and commercial sponsorship. None of the work on digital literacies (or on new literacies, more generally) advocates for what anecdotally appears to be commonplace in many schools. That is, none of the scholarship argues for leaving new literacies outside the classroom door for fear that they might interfere with preparation for high-stakes tests, or that they are fraught with too many controversies, or simply that young people are doing quite well with these practices on their own time and the job of schools is to focus on more traditional forms of literacy.

This theoretical and empirical work on the socially mediated and multimodal nature of digital literacies informed our understanding of IM practices but also suggested avenues to us in need of research. Because so little empirical research on IM has been conducted, and few of the chat room studies (the closest cousin to IM) have focused on educational or literacy-related issues, we have much to learn about what compels many young people to spend a good chunk of time every day reading and writing IM messages.

Methods

Research Participants and Site

There were seven primary participants in this qualitative study (four girls and three boys), and they were all European American and between the ages of 14 and 17 (see Table 36.1). Sam (female), Karrie, Andy (male), Brian, and Abby were 14 during the time of our interviews; Carla was 15, and Jake was 17. (All names are pseudonyms.) Studies of computer-mediated communication often focus on middle class users. Our study includes two participants from working class families. Sam's and Abby's parents held blue-collar jobs. The families of

Table 36.1 Primary Research Participants

Name	Sex	Social class	Age	School type
Abby	F	working	14	Public high school, 9th grade
Andy	M	middle	14	Parochial junior high, 8th grade
Brian	M	middle	14	Parochial junior high, 8th grade
Carla	F	middle	15	Public high school, 10th grade
Jake	M	middle	17	Public high school, 12th grade
Karrie	F	middle	14	Public junior high, 8th grade (in another state)
Sam	F	working	14	Parochial junior high, 8th grade

the other participants were middle class, with parents working in the professional or business sectors.

Six participants—all but Carla—were from a midsize midwestern university town in the United States. Because the town was also adjacent to a larger city, the participants lived in a diverse metropolitan area of over 100,000 people. The town is unique from a technological standpoint because it boasts one of the few municipally owned cable systems in the country. In 1994, town residents approved the creation of a new fiber-optic cable network that would compete with cable conglomerate TCI and make both cable and high-speed Internet services a public utility. Residents, businesses, and public institutions in this town have thus enjoyed speedy Internet connections for over half a decade. Because of this low-cost cable connection, we were able to include participants at different socioeconomic levels who had cable access.

We identified our first three participants, Sam, Abby, and Carla, through purposive sampling. We wanted participants who were avid and dexterous IM users with Internet access in the home and some degree of rapport with one of us. Avid participation and home access seemed important, given the scarcity of empirical research on this topic. We wanted to be certain that we were studying young people who would have enough experience with IM to shed light on the practice. Bettina, coauthor of this article, knew Sam and Abby as occasional babysitters for her daughter. She was aware of their regular IM use and had an established rapport with both girls. We reasoned that an easy rapport would be essential to this study, given that the participants were being asked to share with an adult researcher an activity they often did not share with their own parents—one that sometimes included language and topics they would not want an adult to know about or in any way control. Our participants used IM to communicate with their peers, not with adults. It was important, therefore, that the interviewer be someone with whom the participants felt comfortable, someone whom they might view as not quite adult, a quasi-peer of sorts. Bettina, who had spent time chatting with Sam and Abby (not part of the same friendship circle) about school, boys, family, and other areas of their everyday lives, fit the bill. Carla was also an avid IM user with home Internet access. Although neither of us knew her before the study, her mother was a colleague of Cynthia (first author), thus making rapport easy to establish. The fact that Carla lived with her mother in a small town of 1,900 isolated from a metropolitan area also interested us in that it distinguished her from the other participants.

The four remaining participants, Andy, Brian, Jake, and Karrie, were selected through snowball sampling by way of Sam as our initial contact. Initial informal exchanges and frequent e-mail exchanges about IM between Sam and Bettina led us to Sam's best friend Karrie and their good friend Andy. Andy then led us to Brian. A year and a half later, when Sam had a boyfriend, Jake, we interviewed him as well. We wanted another male participant and hoped that having an older participant (Jake was 17) would provide a wider range of user interests and goals. All met the most important criteria of avid use of IM, home access, and the potential of easy rapport (due to Bettina's connection to Sam).

When we began the study in the spring of 1999, Sam attended eighth grade at a parochial junior high school. Karrie, her best friend, had just moved to another state but was visiting during the time of the interview with Sam. Sam was about to move to the public high school for ninth grade, the only public high school in this town of 35,000. Andy and Brian were eighth graders at the same parochial school. Abby was in ninth grade at the public high school. When we interviewed Jake over a year later, he was a twelfth grader at the public high school. Carla was enrolled as a tenth grader at the public high school in her small town. This study did not involve data related to participants' school experiences, but we know from self and parent reports that none of the participants had major difficulties at school. Abby's mother reported that Abby was an average student who was not especially interested in school, but all the other participants were viewed as good students. Sam and Karrie enjoyed writing and had in the past collaborated on a first chapter of an online book that was a spinoff of the TV series *Dawson's Creek*. Sam also mentioned that when she couldn't see Karrie on a regular basis, she would sometimes keep a notebook of her thoughts with the intention of sharing it with Karrie.

Data Sources and Procedures

We audiotaped semistructured interviews with our participants in participant homes. Because some of our participants were friends—Sam and Karrie; Andy and Brian—we interviewed them in teams, assuming that their collaborative responses might provide for richer data. This worked very well in the case of Sam and Karrie. In the case of Andy and Brian, however, the tandem interview was a bit thin, so we decided to follow up with an individual interview with Andy that proved to be more productive in addressing our research questions. Abby, Jake, and Carla were interviewed individually. All interviews lasted from 60 to 90 minutes. Our interview questions were divided into three categories (see Table 36.2) meant to elicit responses related to our research

Table 36.2 Protocol for Semistructured Interview

General questions

1. What are your reasons for using IM?
2. How did you learn about IM?
3. Who do you communicate with on IM. Why these people?
4. How much time each day do you typically IM?
5. Have you altered the amount of time spent on other activities because of your use of IM?
6. What kind of IM chats are the most satisfying to you and why?
7. What kind of IM chats are the least satisfying and why?
8. What are the IM topics you are most likely to focus on and why?
9. How many windows do you have open at a time?
10. Does IM require daily face-to-face contact?
11. Do you have access to your profile? If so, have you made any changes?
12. Do you see any problems with IM use? (If no answer, follow up by asking about marketing devices, cookies, and so on. Ask also about sexual harassment.)
13. What sort of computer facilities do you have at school? Any IM activity there? Why or why not?
14. What sort of computer facilities do you have at home? (Follow-up with questions about access and control.)

Peer and parent issues

15. How typical is it for students in your school to use IM?
16. How would you describe the kids who use IM?
17. How would you describe the kids who don't use IM?
18. Do kids talk about IM chats from the night before when at school?
19. For the kids who do not IM, does this have any affect on their lives in school or out of school? If so, please explain.
20. Are IM chats different than communicating by e-mail? By phone? By note? Face to face? By letter? If so, how? Which do you prefer?
21. How central is IM to your social life and friendships?
22. Does it affect your social life if you can't IM? How?
23. Who is it easiest and most satisfying for you to chat with on IM?
24. Is there anyone who is difficult to chat with on IM?
25. Do you ever pose as someone else in your IM chats? If so, how does this work? (Follow-up by asking if one gender does this more than another.)
26. How long do you wait before you respond to an IM message?
27. How many do you have on your buddy list?
28. Do you have more than one list meant to serve different purposes? If so, tell me about the purposes.
29. Have you ever received a message from someone you would rather not communicate with? Why would you rather not communicate with this person? What did you do?
30. What kind of parental guidelines support or restrict your IM use?
31. Are any of your friends barred from IM use by their parents?

Style

32. Do you think about your word choice during an IM session?
33. What makes a good IM writer? What makes a bad IM writer?
34. Do you use emoticons? Which are most important to you?
35. Do you do anything with your writing style to try to engage your reader?

foci on uses and compelling features of IM: (1) general appeal and procedural matters (such as time spent IMing), (2) peer and parent issues, and (3) style (such as word choice and tone). We used the same interview protocol across participants so that we could easily look for similarities and variations in their responses. However, as described in the methods section, during follow-up informal exchanges and during the videotaped sessions, we were able to ask specific questions geared to individual participants.

We also interviewed Sam's parents and younger sister as secondary participants. Her case was particularly interesting to us because we wanted more information about her family context given the family's modest income but major commitment to Sam's computer access. In addition to formal interviews, Bettina had many informal exchanges with Sam and Abby about their IM use. Although not audiotaped, these exchanges were recorded in reflective research memos shared with Cynthia throughout the study. We also followed up with one recent 30-minute interview with Abby and with Sam (separately), now both 18 years old, to ask them about any changes in IM technology in the last few years.

In addition to our audiotaped interviews, we conducted interviews on videotape with Sam, Abby, and Andy *as they engaged in IM*. Karrie was not videotaped because she had moved to another state, but she was an active IM buddy during Sam's videotaped session. By pointing the video camera at the computer screen rather than our participants, we recorded students' voices as they explained their actions and choices while simultaneously documenting the complex exchanges on the screen. These intensive, detailed sessions lasted from 60 to 90 minutes.

This procedure, sometimes known as protocol analysis—but also referred to as a think-aloud, a verbal report, or a verbal protocol—has been used as a means for understanding the process of cognition (e.g., Afflerbach, 1990; Haas & Flower, 1988). Researchers have typically given participants a certain text to read and asked them to verbalize their thoughts as they worked their way through a document. These verbal reports are audiotaped and used to understand how readers construct meaning from text. Unlike most researchers who have used the protocol analysis method, however, we were less interested in knowing what students' internal thinking processes were than we were in documenting their IM strategies.

Documenting our participants' IM strategies by watching them engage in these strategies at the same time that they tried to talk through them for our benefit came with advantages and disadvantages. The main advantage was that we were able to learn a great deal about the strategies employed by these IM users. Each think-aloud provided important illustrations that we could call upon when we analyzed our data. Because they involved actual IM exchanges and on-the-spot problem solving, these think-alouds also prompted our participants to explain aspects of IM that did not come up in our previous interview sessions. The main disadvantage was that the sessions sometimes felt more like interviews that involved demonstration than they did authentic IM sessions. For both Sam and Andy, the interviewer's questions sometimes became part of the IM exchanges with their buddies. Much of the data from the actual IM sessions told us more about our participants' strategies as IM users than it did the content of their messages. Thus, we learned both from the interviews and from talk surrounding the IM session that "meatier," more complex discussions were valued, but we did not witness any that we felt matched that description. As we discuss in the next section, Abby did not follow the pattern just described; she appeared to be completely immersed in her IM exchanges and less affected by the researcher's presence.

We did not videotape IM sessions with Brian, Carla, or Jake. We strongly felt that the only way that the videotaped think-aloud session would be useful would be if the rapport between researcher and participant were close and comfortable enough to allow for frank exchanges about topics that are not often shared with adults. Bettina had this kind of rapport with Sam and Abby. Her rapport with Andy was sufficiently comfortable to conduct the videotaped session, but not nearly as close as her relationship with Sam and Abby, and that difference revealed itself in ways that we explain in the next section on researchers' positions. We decided it would be best not to videotape Brian, who had become a participant through Andy rather than Sam and was a level more distant in terms of rapport. Cynthia attempted to videotape Carla at a time when Carla thought she would find buddies online, but, as it turned out, no buddies were online at that time. Because Carla used IM to chat with a smaller number of close friends, a time without online buddies was not entirely unusual. Scheduling problems kept us from trying again. We interviewed Jake to get an older, male perspective from someone who had once been an avid IM user but was now looking back on the experience. Videotaping an IM session with him would have detracted from the reflective, more distant stance he provided.

All interview and think-aloud sessions were fully transcribed. We transcribed the actual IM exchanges on the video screen, using bold font. We also transcribed the often simultaneous participant comments and explanations. Both kinds of data were essential to answer our research questions about these young people's uses of IM and the features of this communication technology that made it so compelling. In addition to the written IM exchanges and spoken explanations, we also transcribed nonverbal visual data and verbal data outside the think-aloud or IM parameters. This included gestures, postures, and actions such as laughing or eating as well as speech that included reading aloud parts of IM messages.

Researchers' Positions

Although we both share an interest in digital literacy practices in a digital age and use them extensively in our own professional and personal lives, neither

not wanting to limit our thinking about the transcripts, we decided to choose, at this point, a categorical rather than conceptual way of coding the transcripts after our first passes through all of the interview data. We did this by providing a context-specific category label for each episode. For example, one episode in the transcript with Carla was labeled "subjects" because all the speaker turns in that episode revolved around the kind of subjects one might talk about in an IM exchange.

Our next step was to read the interview episodes and the IM exchanges for their most prominent conceptual themes related to our research questions. The themes that were most salient throughout the transcripts again were the social and surveillance uses of IM. In addition, we decided to code for language play and other language features that our participants frequently shared with us. In the next section on findings, we include a subsection on language that highlights its foundational relationship to the social and surveillance functions. Through language use, the social networks were enhanced and the drama of surveillance unfolded.

Our final step in the process of analyzing interview and IM transcripts was to refine the three broad codes, which led us to examine the transcripts for distinctions among "social," "surveillance," and "language" functions for IM use. This selective coding procedure (Strauss & Corbin, 1990) resulted in distinctions within each category (e.g., social status, social connection, and gender relations within the "social" category) that are used to frame our findings section where we discuss them in terms of their thematic salience.

Due to the think-aloud nature of the IM sessions, the actual IM exchanges were frequently difficult to analyze separate from the think-aloud data in which they were embedded. Thus, the IM exchange was often coded in the same way as its surrounding turns. For example, during Andy's think-aloud, he received an IM that included loads of smiley faces in green, followed by a huge laughing face. When Bettina saw this, she exclaimed, "Oh my God. What did that person just do?" This led to the following exchange between Andy and his friend, whom we'll call "M."

Andy: What is that, M?
M: My friends
M: The Smilels
Andy: I think he spelled smileys wrong. He's not a very good speller.

In addition to this IM exchange, however, there were related comments and explanations between Andy and Bettina. For instance, after Andy's first turn above, he told Bettina "... and I guess he was getting bored and stuff and he just typed a whole bunch of letters." After M's first turn, Bettina noted, "Aren't they all a bunch of people? Look, they're all people," and Andy followed with "Oh, geez. He has time on his hands." This entire episode, including the IM message itself and the accompanying commentary, was coded as "language play."

In contrast, some IM exchanges were isolated from the think-aloud commentary. This was true of some exchanges for all three participants whose IM sessions we videotaped. However, Abby's IMs were entirely autonomous and needed to be coded separately. Abby negotiated the most windows of the IM sessions we observed—10 windows in all. Because the exchanges jumped quickly from one to the next and then back to an earlier one, with unrelated think-aloud explanations in between, it was very difficult to discern the thread of each conversation. In order to code this data, then, we produced one transcript of Abby's IM conversations in the order they occurred (chronologically jumping from one window to the next) and another transcript of her IM conversations organized by buddy (and, spatially, by window) as though each exchange were separated and without interruptions from other buddies. The contrast between the two transcripts reveals the challenge for IM users to keep track of the narrative thread of their exchanges with each buddy as they juggle multiple conversational threads. Even from a research perspective, it was far easier to code the second transcript, with Abby's exchanges with each of her buddies typed separately.

These procedures, which involved triangulating across interviews, video sessions, and both of our interpretations, led to the patterns discussed in the next section on findings.

Research Findings

In the following sections, we report our findings related to the language, social, and surveillance functions of Instant Messaging. Underlying these functions, however, are the distinctions participants made between the functions served by IM as compared to other forms of communication, such as e-mail, telephone, note passing, and online chat-rooms, and so we begin with these distinctions.

In general, these young people favored IM over all other kinds of communication. IM offered the excitement of successfully staying on top of the information flow. IM was convenient: Most friends were constantly online and available (no busy signals). If they weren't online, they would often identify through "away" messages where they were and when they would be back. Moreover, IM users could avoid long-distance phone bills when talking to friends who lived far away (as in the case of Sam and Karrie). IM also assuaged social relations, making all potentially threatening exchanges (such as face to face or telephone) less so. E-mail certainly had its value for telling longer stories and using, as Karrie said, "big words." In Jake's case, e-mail was useful in those situations when he needed more time to think about what he wanted to say. In this context, e-mail is a close relative to the passed note— one can be thoughtful, but the process of composing and delivering it takes more time. Overall, IM also trumped chat rooms. For our participants, chat may have been a fun diversion when life slowed down on the IM screen, but communicating with strangers was not nearly as engaging as communicating with one's peers.

We think it's important to introduce our findings section in this way because our participants' clear analyses of the differing functions of various technologies speak to their strategic and thoughtful approach to popular technology as it affected their lives. These young people were not duped by technology. Instead, they used it with a sense of purpose and informed participation that may be surprising to many adults concerned about the influence of computer-mediated communication on the lives and literacies of the younger generation.

This sense of purpose and agency is in keeping with what the New London Group (1996, 2000) meant when they argued that literacy involves the designing and redesigning of social futures. The core concept here is that in order to make meaning, one must have access to available resources for designs (semiotic systems), ways to engage in design (semiotic processes), and the means to transform designs (a combination of received meanings and the agency to redesign them). Design is a concept we find useful in understanding our participants' linguistic and social uses of IM. As the findings will show, the young people in our study accessed all the resources that IM afforded as well as those that they brought to the practice and used these resources to improvise and redesign their semiotic and social worlds.

Language as Design

As we analyzed our findings, it became clear that IM literacy was, in part, an extension of schooled literacy practices and, as such, reflected a level of literacy engagement that may be encouraging to educators. Our participants used language strategically and creatively in their IMs to initiate and sustain satisfying exchanges. As mentioned earlier, "talk" is a written performance in IM. The guiding tropes of the medium are "chat" and "conversation," indexing a sense of the spoken that must be achieved through writing. Participants used linguistic features to manipulate the written tone, voice, word choice, subject matter, and structure of messages in order to sustain interesting conversations and cut off those that were not of interest. However, beyond these uses of language within IMs, the young people we studied used language in complex ways in order to negotiate multiple messages and interweave these conversations into larger, overarching story lines.

Language Use within Messages
If the popular press suggests that all IM discourse is inane or incomprehensible, the participants in our study were clear that it was these kinds of exchanges that they wished to avoid. Unsatisfying conversations, to them, were ones that "don't go anywhere" or "just stop." These "boring" conversations, they said,

often had to do with a user maintaining a conversation (while juggling many others), but they also pointed to lack of creativity. Carla, for example, had no patience for IM conversations "where you end up talking to someone and they answer you in monosyllables. 'Uh.' 'Oh.' 'Cool.'" Satisfying IM chats, on the other hand, were ones where conversation flows—where creativity is apparent. "There are those people who I've talked to for over an hour," Abby reported. "A lot of people can come up with things that I never thought of."

Consequently, our participants consciously resorted to various narrative strategies to generate more interesting and flowing conversations with their peers. Andy appreciated the chance to converse with Sam over IM because he found her to be especially good at asking questions. "She's always ready for a question that she has for you," he said. "She doesn't sit there and ask you a question that she's already asked three times ... all her questions are like brand new." Sam also commented on her language techniques, admitting that she was purposeful in her use of metaphors. As she noted, IM "enhances my depth of thought, the way I think now, 'cause you can't explain things with your hands, you have to tell them, like using metaphors."

Our participants found other ways to experiment with language online as well. Jake recalled one IM discussion that was all word play:

> Sam and I last night, we just started out, she said "I want ..." and then I wrote "I want ..." and then we just went on for a whole exchange, for ten minutes all we started out with was "I want" and just anything that came to our heads.

Another exchange between Jake and a friend involved communicating solely through song titles.

Our participants also used nonlinguistic visual elements to supplement language in ways that served their needs. These elements either added to the drama of their individual exchanges or served as place holders so that buddies would wait to hear more rather than thinking the message was complete. For instance, we frequently saw our participants use ellipses to indicate that they were thinking rather than finished with the message. Sam withheld information to purposefully add tension to a conversation, noting that this was common practice in IM. In a similar vein, Sam and Karrie would often type "well" followed by an ellipses to function as a verbal pause.

Another important visual cue involved spelling, which, interestingly, mattered quite a lot to our participants. Afraid a buddy would infer that they weren't good spellers, Sam, Karrie, Carla, and Abby all used the code (*) to indicate that they spelled something wrong accidentally, demonstrating a skill for self-monitoring that teachers try to promote in students as they write for school purposes. ("A" in the following exchange is one of Abby's buddies.)

Abby: I'm here ☺
A: Your computer said u were away

A: about a month ago I IMed her just to say hey and stuff but she didn't talk so

B: talking on the phone [answering an earlier question from Abby]

B: u?

Abby: nothing much

Abby: just chattin'

Abby: yeah she does that to david too I think [written to Buddy A]

A: im surprised hed still talk to her, I haven't talked to her since

Abby: I don't think they talk much tho

This may not be the most stunning example of language use, but we include this chronological transcript of a small portion of Abby's IM session to show how challenging it can be to manage the continuing threads of these conversations as they occur in time. When arranged spatially, however, with each buddy (and corresponding window) in its place in the stack, as Abby had them, she was able to manage the conversational flow with each of her buddies, and juggle the story lines that shaped her social world. (See Appendix for an example of the same transcript organized spatially, with separate exchanges organized by buddy/window.)

As several of our participants reported, one storyline often takes precedence while others take on less importance. During this IM session, for instance, the constant thread from beginning to end was Buddy A's negative feelings toward Barb (pseudonym). This narrative tension began with the section we include here but surfaced throughout the session. Examining this IM transcript, we found out firsthand what scholars of digital literacies mean when they point to the skills needed to be a successful online reader and writer. Abby had to be able to scan across windows, spatially, to do the work of this kind of writing. She had to read and write quickly across surfaces, delving deeper only when a particular conversational thread kept surfacing, and thus demanding a more developed response. Thus she quickly said "hey" to several friends, told Buddy C she had been tanning, and dipped in and out of a more pressing exchange with Buddy A. Making on-the-spot decisions about where to focus one's attention is critical to managing the flow across messages. This is an act most of us are accustomed to performing in conversation, but one that the IM user must master in writing.

As we videotaped our three young IM writers, all were anxious, fearing that there would not be anyone online who would be interesting to talk to. In other words, they would not be able to demonstrate what a good session, with complex, interesting interactions, would look like. Indeed, we didn't witness the most successful sessions, according to our participants, in part because of the nature of the think-aloud (as described in the methods section). However, it was clear that interesting word choice, audience sensitivity, and a well-managed narrative that offered tension and excitement were what made IM worthwhile, and that some, like Sam (whose IM skills were revered by Andy), were better at this than others. It was also clear, however, that while Abby used these features to fluidly move through a range of social stances from sympathetic friend to casual acquaintance, she also was used by the discourses that were available to her. That is to say that the linguistic and semantic resources Abby draws upon are those typically associated with middle class white teens in the United States (and other Western countries). Tanning and e-mail, friendships and rivalries were the topics at hand, all in the talky, casual vernacular often expected of teens. Thus "teenhood" could be said to be inscribed in the text of Abby's IM talk. We had to look closer to understand how she managed the narrative flow of the conversation and attended to the demands of the rhetorical situation. As will become clear in the next section, the social context of IM is what drives the narrative and, at times, raises the language bar.

Social Networks as Design

Besides juggling language styles and message flow, we found that our participants were actively engaged in designing their social worlds through their IM use. Moreover, their social networks in turn enhanced their language use, providing the context for a richer and more satisfying writing session. In this section, we focus on two aspects of their social networks that repeatedly surfaced in the data: *social status* and *social connections*.

Social Status: Insider Knowledge and Audience Awareness

Most of the young people we talked to felt that IM enhanced their social status. Sam, Karrie, and Abbie, for example, believed that IM enabled them to establish a kind of social currency. According to Karrie, "I wouldn't be as cool to some friends if I didn't talk on the Internet." Indeed, not having Internet and IM access was the recipe, in our participants' minds, for social upheaval. Simply put, the online social world was contingent upon the offline social world at school. In fact, being "in the know" and knowing the inside jokes from the IM session the night before were seen as essential for social relations at school. Here, Abby vividly describes her social need for IM, given that, in her words "Everybody's always on!":

Abby:	I'll talk to my best friends, and me and my friends, it's like, "Oh it's 9 o'clock, I gotta get on the computer!" And it's like, if we can't, it's like, what am I going to do?! … I don't know. It's just part of my night.
Interviewer:	So what happens if you don't get on, if you miss a night. Do you feel/
Abby:	Well, I'll always feel that I don't know what's going on or I'm left out of something or, you know.
Interviewer:	So do you think you're kind of addicted to it?

world of IM, its textual nature (through written and visual modes), made it conducive to slipping in and out of new identities and storylines, but as this section reveals, IM identities and storylines very much intersect with lives offline. Social networks enhanced the IM experience, but various surveillance opportunities added a layer of drama to the online and offline worlds of IM.

Surveillance in the IM Landscape

Being both the agent and the object of surveillance played a central role in our participants' IM practices. These young people revealed their intricate understanding of how they could use the technology for their own surveillance purposes related to power and identity. They also understood the ways in which they were monitored by their parents and friends, and were often able to confound these monitoring attempts. In discussing this aspect of IM use, we focus on four mechanisms related to surveillance of or by others: IM features, circulation, posing, and parental regulation. As might be expected, most of our participants enjoyed being able to monitor the messages and locations of others but attempted not to be the object of surveillance.

IM Features

Surveillance features are built into the IM platform. Particular features enable users to monitor their buddies' online and offline activities and identities as well as to enable monitoring of their own. All of our participants understood how to use their profiles, buddy lists, user or screen names, and away messages to best serve their surveillance purposes. For instance, all the participants were adept at using the buddy list indicator to monitor their friends online and control the message flow. To combat excessive or unwanted messages, they would sometimes turn off their buddy list indicators so friends could no longer tell they were simultaneously online. Blocking particular people from the buddy list, so that these people would not know the user was online, served as another strong tactic. Other monitoring functions of the buddy list include a pop-up window that appears when the user clicks on a name. This pop-up provides information about the person on the buddy list such as the length of time in minutes that she or he has been online, a feature that several participants noted. All but one of our participants had divided their buddy lists into categories. Abby, for instance, divided hers so that she had a category for boys, girls, and "don't talk to's," allowing her to monitor who was online at a glance. Because gender relations were particularly central to Abby, these gender-inflected categories served her purposes.

Multiple user names were also employed by all of the participants, several of whom gave their very best friends access to all of their user names. As Carla explained,

Carla:	Well, I have different buddy lists ... . I have about 45 people on one list. Some of them are doubles, like I have three screen names for one person.
Interviewer:	Why would that be?
Carla:	Well, because [best friend's name] has three screen names and so I can tell when she's online and she can block other people but not me.
Interviewer:	Because you're good friends you gave them all of them.

In most cases, however, these multiple user names served the purpose of keeping IM buddies from recognizing when our participants were online. In other words, our participants would go online with a user name that they had not given to many people. This allowed them to remain online without being inundated with messages and instead be contacted only by good friends familiar with the user name. Later, if there were others whom they would like to IM, they would get online with a more widely distributed user name. Abby, for instance, had about 10 user names and often signed on with a user name that almost nobody knew just to see who got on before she switched to her usual user name.

The buddy list, always in view, carried the important information concerning who was active—at home and on or near a computer *and* receptive (being online but blocking their availability). As this list was constantly changing with the comings and goings of buddies, it contained a wealth of other information: when buddies got online, how long they'd been on, and whether they were "away"—online, but somewhere else in their house for a short period.

Away messages, frequently used to let others know where the IM user could be found, were especially useful in the summer when kids were rarely at home. As Jake explained,

> Like during the summer, you write "I'm down the street at such and such's house, stop by if you want to." Or some people say "call me." So you can find people that way. "I'm cleaning my room, stop by."

He added that those who did not have access to IM would not know where to find their friends as easily as those with IM access. Users clicked on these away icons and called up away messages. These messages were often succinct (e.g., "I am watching TV"). But the young people we talked to took great pleasure in reading them, not just to find out where that person was (hyperconnectivity being one of the reasons the technology is so attractive) but to find out how witty and clever their friends were in constructing them. During one session, for example, Abby enjoyed her friend's away message, "I'm being a good boy and helping my mom with the dishes, so leave a message." Although

Abby admitted she had boring away messages, she appreciated her friend's efforts to write longer, and quite clever, ones.

In a similar manner these young people used their profiles to list their cell phone numbers and to announce graduation parties, again to remain hyper-connected and, in a sense, monitored at all times. An interesting example of self-monitoring is evident in Carla's wish to keep her profile sparse. She realized that a singular profile, unless it was very sparse, would not attract all the different friends she had. When asked to talk about her concerns about writing a longer profile, she said, "It would worry me because I know different people in different ways. I feel like this person would think it was stupid, and this person would ... ." Carla had a sophisticated understanding of her multiple audiences in the IM landscape and carefully considered how best to address them all.

The categories that the participants listed in their IM profiles (e.g., student, female, midwest, likes horses) could be accessed by anyone and result in receiving IMs from people they did not know. Although this sometimes resulted in unpleasant instances of what Carla referred to as "cyber sex" messages, she did not want to block her profile because she enjoyed getting occasional messages from people she didn't know. In general, our participants did not seem overly concerned about the media hype they had heard about the dangers of the Internet. We had the sense that they did not see themselves as "innocent" and in need of protection, but were, instead, savvy about the cyber sex phenomenon and able to control what happens in this online geographic space. As Valentine et al. (2000) argued, based on their study of ICT use, young people did not assume "an artificial distinction between the corruption of on-line space and the sanctuary of the home" (p. 159) given that anything that might be available to them online was also available offline (e.g., sexually explicit images in magazines and on television). The buddy list, away messages, and profiles all added to the variety and drama of an IM session, while offering a means for these IM writers to define their online presence and mark their identities.

Circulation

Surveillance on IM is often achieved through the paths that messages travel as they are circulated. Leander and McKim (2003) suggested that examining how digital texts travel can lead to insights about the kinds of practices and relationships a particular technology affords. Our participants' IM connections and messages were often passed from one person to another in order to create a bond that depended on the surveillance of others.

One of the simplest methods of circulating participants' movements and messages online was through the commonly asked question, "Who else are you talking to?" resulting in IM buddies having indirect exchanges with a wider range of people through other buddies (e.g., "Tell her ..."). This simple question allowed the questioner to have some degree of knowledge about and control over the movements and conversations of buddies outside of the immediate dyad.

Far from being isolated units, conversations easily became part of other conversations within a given IM session. Participants routinely cut and pasted elements of one conversation and shared them with another buddy—often without disclosing their actions with the first buddy, who may have done the same with someone else. Some saw this kind of surveillance as representing a wish for community, a way of finding out who else is involved in their overlapping social worlds at the moment. However, others saw it as an entry into the landscape of gossip and deceit, with users lying to one another about their concurrent IM buddies. As Carla put it, "There are so many people going behind peoples' backs and lying to this person and this person knows something else, and you have to trust both of them not to talk to each other."

The sort of clandestine circulation that Carla would not want to be involved with was an intriguing part of the game for others. For instance, Andy knew that sometimes girls would pretend that their girlfriends who had a crush on him weren't with them when they asked him questions. Several of the girls also tried surreptitiously to discover who was currently talking to whom and what they happened to be talking about by IMing inquiries to friends and asking them to report back. Abby, for instance, would report to her girlfriends to tell them about her conversations with boys, sometimes cutting and pasting the most important parts for her girlfriends' pleasure. The way these texts circulated online, serving as a mechanism for surveillance, also reinforced our participants' IM landscape as a heteronormative space.

By circulating messages in this fashion, our participants cut and pasted, rearranged, and reconfigured elements of their lives to be offered up for scrutiny in the IM landscape. This kind of surveillance was expected—afforded through the technology and participants' relationships to the technology and to each other. IM produces identities that are accustomed to being both the agent and object of scrutiny and surveillance.

Posing

Posing involves the user in an attempt to take on the identity of someone else (another gender or another specific person in some of our examples). For instance, although related to chat room communication rather than IM, Karrie went so far as to track her boyfriend into a chat room, assume the male-sounding identity of snowboarder911, and try to find out what kind of exchanges he was having. Because the physical body is not present in Internet communication, these young people had more space for play, parody, and performance. They manipulated voice, tone, and subject matter to hide or transform their own identities and to monitor the interactions of others. Although our female participants were not using their IM experience to break down gendered frames of reference, they used these chats to claim some control over their position in the male/female binary. With their bodies out of view, they were able to alternately observe, monitor, and engage the words and minds of boys.

There were many examples throughout our data that revealed the pleasure most of these young people took in occasional posing. Sam's pleasure was evident in the following example:

Sam: This girl, she thinks I'm somebody else. She thinks I'm one of her friends, and she's like "Hey!" and I'm like "Hi!" and I start playing along with her. She thinks that I'm one of her school friends. She doesn't know it's me. She wrote to me twice now.

Interviewer: So she's this person that you're lying to, almost.

Sam: Yeah, you just play along. It's fun sometimes. It's comical. Because she'll say something like, "Oh [a boy] did this, and we're going to the ski house," or whatever, and I'm like "Oh God!," and like I'll just respond to her. I'll use the same exclamations where she uses them, and I'll try to talk like they do.

As mentioned in the section on language use, Sam strategically analyzed this girl's voice and tone in order to accomplish this parodic performance. What's most important to our theme in this section, however, is the way that posing can expand beyond individual exchanges as a complicated narrative emerges. When Sam saw the name Junelily24 appear as an "active" member of her buddy list, for example, she immediately IMed her best friend Karrie, saying "Junelily24 is online." When Abby asked her friends to "get on my name" when her computer broke down, she was hoping for playful and vicarious inclusion in the world from which she had been temporarily excluded. In this way posing and circulation are related mechanisms for surveillance in that the thrill of posing is often connected to the circulation of details about its effects.

The girls seemed generally to engage in more posing than did the boys, perhaps because they had more to gain by doing so. For example, Sam posed on occasion as someone who was "blond-haired, blue-eyed" because she believed having these particular media markers of beauty would extend exchanges with boys she didn't know. Given a social sphere that excludes the body, she inserted one that would work for her. However, the fact that she resorted to traditional markers of white feminine beauty in the rare social sphere where it need not be central shows that normative gender and race positions are not so easily erased, even in a space that is sometimes hailed as a new form of social existence (Jones, 1997) and multiple identities (Turkle, 1995).

Carla was one participant who was opposed to posing ("I have a big respect for the truth"). Nonetheless, she was aware of the function IM could serve in this regard. As she told us, "You can portray yourself any way you want to online. You can make yourself sound all smart and sophisticated, like whatever you want. And when you're face to face, people can see you, and you really can't hide very much."

In order to pose effectively, one must be able to perform an identity in writing that will sound "all smart and sophisticated" or some other set of attributes, and one must be able to shift into this mode with little forethought.

Parental Regulation

The IM practices of some of our participants were not heavily regulated by parents. Jake, at 17, had no restrictions whatsoever. Carla thought her dad might have worried a bit at first but no longer, because she rarely communicated with anyone she didn't know. Brian's parents restricted him from using chat rooms, and both Brian and Andy explained that their IM software restricted them from entering buddy chat rooms (group IM sessions). Brian occasionally worried about his parents looking over his shoulder as he IMed, mostly because he thought they might tease him if he was writing about a romantic interest or something else he wanted to keep private. Neither of them was supposed to stay online for more than half an hour or so and were expected to share the computer with siblings or parents. As the oldest child in the house, Brian had easier access than Andy, who had to contend with his older sister's extensive use of IM. Abby did not have restrictions placed on her IM activity. When she talked about her mother watching her IM, she did so in the context of her mother admiring her ability to juggle so many windows, referring to a time her mother asked her if she ever sent a message to the wrong person.

Of all of our participants, Sam's and Karrie's IM activities were most closely monitored by their parents. Because they were aware that their moves were also being watched and regulated by their parents, both girls became savvy in their ability to overcome restrictions on their online communication practices. Sam, whose father disallowed IM but allowed e-mails, had learned that she could block her buddy list every time her father was at home and never receive IM messages in his presence. She and Karrie also relied on a number code system. When Sam's father walked into the room, she typed a certain number (or the abbreviation POS for "Parents over Shoulder") and began to write about her homework so that he would not think she was wasting her time. This deception was part of the thrill of IM. As Sam put it, "It's kind of fun, 'cause your parents don't know what you mean, so if you wanted to tell them something you could make up anything you wanted to." Sam also continued to IM her friends when her father was at work, but covered her tracks by flooding the tracking device with educational sites and adding his name to her buddy list so she could track any time he was online during his workday. As Andy put it, Sam was sometimes "naughty" for clicking off her dad's privacy preference, which kept her from being able to IM, and then clicking it back on when he came home. However, her dad could access IM at work, which meant that

him, "casual acquaintance" with several other buddies, and "flirtatious friend" with Buddy G who wants her to put him in her info box. "Only if I can be in yours," she replied. Although face-to-face interaction is also performative (see, for instance, Bauman & Briggs, 1990; Conquergood, 1989; Goffman, 1959), the need to fluidly shift performances from audience to audience is unique to the dyadic yet nearly simultaneous nature of IM.

The enactment of these multiple identities calls into question what it means to have an authentic or personal voice as a writer. Envisioning voice as authentic or personal privileges stability across texts rather than the dynamic, fluid concept of voice exhibited by IM writers as they enact identities that depend upon a running analysis of complicated online and offline contexts. Identities are enacted as temporary attachments, as Hall would have it, in order to be recognized as a particular kind of person (Gee, 2000/2001) within particular histories of relationships and discursive formations. Sam uses a "softer, sweeter tone" with her friend Karrie one moment, before smoothly shifting to the voice of Junelily24 to pose as one of her crowd. In each case, the voice can be said to be authentic to the situation and audience at hand, but authenticity is not stable across these two texts.

We are not suggesting that there is no continuity of identity from one exchange to the next. Across Abby's conversations with her 10 buddies, for instance, her identity as a popular, socially adept teen who uses IM to focus primarily on her social life remains stable. She does not, by any means, seem like a different person with each exchange. And why would she want to? Her identity as a popular, social teen was a powerful one that was reiterated (Butler, 1990) with each exchange. In other words, Abby claims her identity as a popular, in-the-know teen across these conversations, thus performing a stable identity she values, one that serves her well. At the same time, however, each iteration of this identity rearticulates and fine-tunes it to the immediate needs of the particular conversational context (as already described).

One reason that Abby is able to manage these performances of self is that she is situated at once within the techno-social space of the Internet and the social-embodied space offline. In their article on the past and future of Internet research, Leander and McKim (2003) destabilized the offline/online binary that underlies much of this research and argued for methodologies that trace techno-social-embodied networks across contexts and bounded notions of time and space. Writers in the IM environment are constituted in voices, their own and others, that merge and overlap within and across contexts as the writing self is addressed by and answerable to others. Thus, it is always in process (Holland, Lachicotte, Skinner, & Cain, 2001).

The technological and social affordances of IM make visible a performative and multivoiced social subject. These affordances include patterns of circulation and textuality as described in our findings. Because IM technology affords easy circulation of texts, our participants' conversations were regularly shared across buddies, either cut and pasted or reported, and reconfigured along the way. Being an agentic participant in these patterns of circulation required quick, in-process thinking. It required that users swiftly assess the nature of the circulating text, the purpose or agenda that led to its circulation, the audiences involved, the allegiances it may foster or damage, and so forth. Participants performed selves—enacted identities—in relation to these circulating texts.

These patterns of circulation functioned to reinforce social connections, creating bonds between particular users, sometimes at the expense of others, adding the intrigue of surveillance to the IM experience, but also monitoring and reinforcing normative gender relations as discussed in our findings. Text messages circulated across class lines, with Abby and Sam, two working class participants, communicating regularly with middle class buddies. This may relate to the fact that digital technologies seem to foster affinity group connections related to common interests and shared norms over common class and race affiliations (Gee, 2002; Wellman, 2001). However, we believe that our participants' IM activity across class lines had more to do with other factors influencing friendship circles, such as attendance at parochial school and the geography of mixed-income neighborhoods, in addition to the very low cost of public utility cable access. We did not learn about any IM communication across lines of race or ethnicity in this predominately white town, reinforcing our finding that IM communication occurred primarily within friendship circles, loosely construed. The performative, multivoiced identities enacted through IM are constituted within existing discursive formations.

The hybrid nature of textuality in IM also contributes to performative and multivoiced enactments of identity. In their book on textual studies in post-modern times, Loizeaux and Fraistat (2002) had this to say about electronic textuality: "With its multimedia and networked capabilities, electronic textuality foregrounds the role played by the visual and aural elements of textuality, as well as the social and material ontologies of texts" (p. 5).

As discussed in our findings, the visual and aural elements of IM were prominent. Visually, this role was most often evident in the purposeful use of emoticons, color, and font types. The aural elements were most evident in the way that the textuality of writing was used to perform the textual qualities of speech. This blending of spoken and written textuality resulted in hybrid language forms to represent the casual, insider exchanges of informal speech through written textual features.

To achieve a speech-like quality, IM writers use syntax, vocabulary, and usage more common in speech as well as abbreviations to make for quick speech-like exchanges and to communicate paralinguistic features of face-to-face communication contexts. Using examples from Abby's extended IM exchange included in an earlier section, Abby's speech-like syntax included "I don't think they talk much tho" and her vocabulary included words with dropped endings, "just chattin'." Abby's abbreviations made for speedy responses, "Im" for "I am" and "u" for "you," as did her lack of punctuation. In other participants' IM exchanges, abbreviations such as LOL (laugh out loud) or POS (parents over shoulder) were used to communicate what interlocutors would have seen had they been communicating face to face. The textual shape that IM takes, then, is an innovative blending of speech and writing.

The textual shape of IM is significant as it relates to the kinds of social identities afforded through its use. Again, performativity and multivocality are central to this discussion. The identities our participants enacted in IM had to sound—and look, semiotically—like speech, but be accomplished through writing. Sam had to write her way into the textual worlds of the new group to which she wanted to belong, hearing the cadences of their inside jokes and trying to "sound" right in writing. She explicitly refers to her efforts to "talk like they do" when she poses as the friend of someone who accidentally got onto her buddy list. In this way, IM writers produce the sound of speech. However, according to Carla, this virtual speech takes on a life of its own with adept IM writers using the disembodied textuality of writing to "sound smart and sophisticated" in ways that go beyond face-to-face communication. The virtual, it seems, may idealize the real, becoming the way that real speech ought to sound, thus further interrupting any facile distinctions between the virtual and the real, between speech and writing. Enacting identities, then, involved performing multivocal textual repertoires with speed and flexibility, all within the boundaries of normative structures of gender and power. In spite of these boundaries, our participants were involved in the generative act of using texts in new ways, reconfiguring messages, cutting and pasting, parodying, and creating textual forms to fit their social needs.

IM Practices and the Schooling of Literacy

The social identities and subject positions that we have found to be central to IM are important to how we think about young people and their literacy learning in schools. As we have already argued, ways of knowing and ways of being are interrelated. Epistemologies and pedagogies intersect to produce available subject positions for students to take up. A discussion of all the ways that students may resist these subject positions are outside the scope of this article, but there is much evidence to suggest that students are produced as social subjects as they are initiated into particular academic, interpretive, and social ways of knowing and being.

IM draws on practices that shape users' relationships to knowledge and identities. IM practices demand that users adopt habits of mind that are flexible, adapting across genres and modes, performing enactments of self (or identity) that relate to changing discursive and social spaces. As stated earlier, however, the knowledge and identities that users bring to IM shape the technology and how it is used as well. Recall, for instance, that Carla's self-reported identity as someone who valued honesty in all her relationships kept her from capitalizing on the circulation or surveillance features of IM. Her IM repertoire did not include posing as someone she was not or circulating the texts of others without their knowledge. It is also important to note that all of the flexibility that IM affords is very much constrained by some quite inflexible norms related to gender and race. Indeed, in some cases, even agentic acts served to reproduce social structures, such as when Sam hacked into her profile only to include descriptors she thought would mark her as a desirable female. One might also view new conceptions of what it means to be an adolescent in changing times as somewhat inflexible in that normative notions of adolescent identity now include the desire for, if not facility with, digital and media technologies.

Kress et al. (2000) argued that the social politic outside of school—the global, fast-capital economy, the communicative webs, the multiple modes of representation—are all about multiplicity, performativity, flexibility, and adaptability, while the social politic in school remains centered on notions of stability, authenticity, and unity. It is obvious that typical ways of being in school leave out the compelling lives many young people live outside of school. Kress et al. argued further that for schools to meet the new demands of great economic and social change, educators need to begin to see learners as "remakers, constantly of the materials with which they engage" (p. 28).

Our participants were "remakers" of the textual and technological resources available to them through IM. It might be argued, however, that given their dexterity with this digitally mediated form of reading and writing, schools need not focus on such forms of literacy, but instead focus more on forms of literacy that students are less capable of mastering on their own but need to learn in order to be successful in school, at work, or as involved citizens. The logic of this argument lies in a perceived need to equip students with the skills and strategies they require to succeed in the current system and to teach them the deliberative reading and writing practices that are basic to certain kinds of analysis and critique. However, accomplishing these goals will not help prepare students for the kinds of epistemological shifts evident in our participants' practices and described in the work of scholars of new media and digital literacies.

Preparing for changing epistemologies, identities, and practices should not mean either appropriating young people's popular technologies for school use or disregarding the deep and deliberative reading and writing processes associated with analytic and critical understandings and interpretations. Although bringing IM or other forms of Internet communication into the classroom may be possible for particular projects and purposes, doing so should not be viewed as the lesson to learn from this research. In fact, such appropriation would change the objectives and motives of the activity, the roles of the young people engaging in the activity, and the group norms associated with the activity. One of the reasons that the youth we studied used IM literacy so productively is that they were very clear about these aspects of the activity.

textual forms as well as incorporate multimodal design in the service of complex topics that require careful examination and depth of analysis. Finally, through collaborative activity-based projects that cannot be accomplished without the use of multiple texts—print, media, and digital—students can use the full range of their reading and writing repertoires. Dramatic interpretations and other artistic modes of expression and response can contribute to the performative, multivoiced nature of the enterprise, thus developing flexible semiotic processes across social networks.

Our suggestions here are not meant to presume technological access and facility. Although we know that more students now have access to the Internet than did at the start of this study (see, for instance, U.S. Department of Commerce, 2002) there are still many students, particularly those from low-income families, who do not. These students frequently access the Internet through libraries and community centers, but the time and space for gaining access at these sites are limited. For this reason, we think it is important that educators focus on shifting dimensions of practice rather than on new technological tools (Lewis, Alvermann, & Leander, 2004). Most of our suggestions (other than the blog example, which depends on school rather than home access) relate to broader-based shifts—the kind that one experiences through many forms of popular culture that depend on interactivity, pastiche, intertextuality, and other qualities associated with the Internet (comics, videos, reality TV). (A critical appraisal of these forms of popular culture is beyond the scope of this article, but see Andrejevic, 2003, for an analysis of reality TV, which argues that the interactive elements of reality TV result in the commercial surveillance of viewers.) Focusing pedagogical reform on shifting dimensions of practice that apply to new forms of media and communication beyond those that depend on Internet access is one way to make sure that individuals without access can be full participants in the instruction.

Many scholars focus on the politics, economics, or social theories of digital technology (McChesney, 2000; Swiss, 2000), but only a few have conducted close analyses of particular forms of digital literacy and culture. This research contributes to that small body of work with the hope that learning more about the functions of IM and the epistemologies and social identities it fosters will move the field forward as we begin to reconceptualize the teaching and learning of literacy in digitally mediated times. A body of empirical research conducted in diverse geographical sites with participants who come from a range of ethnic and socioeconomic backgrounds and represent a wider range of IM interests and orientations toward social and sexual relationships is needed to move the study of literacy forward. Although we have pointed to implications related to social structures such as gender and social class, a more diverse set of participants and geographical sites may result in a study that has stronger implications for the material consequences of particular digital practices.

Finally, we want to refocus our lens to take in the forest as well as the trees. We have provided a detailed account of our participants' uses of IM and have described the changing epistemologies and attendant practices associated with IM use (multivocality, performativity, resourcefulness, hybrid textuality, and new forms of circulation and surveillance). As a community of literacy educators and researchers, if we let our "generational anxiety over new forms of adolescent and childhood identity and life pathways" (Luke & Luke, 2004, p. 105) get the best of us, if we mourn the loss of print literacy as we think we once knew it, then we may find ourselves schooling young people in literacy practices that disregard the vitality of their literate lives and the needs they will have for their literate and social futures at home, at work, and in their communities.

Lewis, C., Alvermann, D. E., & Leander, K. (2004, February). *Youth cultures, digital litera-cies, and intersecting methodologies*. Paper presented at the National Council of Teach-ers of English Assembly for Research, Berkeley, CA.

Lewis, C., & Fabos, B. (2000). But will it work in the heartland? A response to new multilit-eracies. *Journal of Adolescent & Adult Literacy, 43*, 462–469.

Lewis, C., & Finders, M. (2002). Implied adolescents and implied teachers: A generation gap for new times. In D.E. Alvermann (Ed.), *New literacies and digital technologies: A focus on adolescent learners* (pp. 101–113). New York: Peter Lang.

Loizeaux, E., & Fraistat, N. (2002). *Reimagining textuality: Textual studies in the late age of print*. Madison: University of Wisconsin Press.

Luke, A. (1992). The body literate: Discourse and inscription in early literacy training. *Lin-guistics and Education, 4*, 107–129.

Luke, A. (1994). On reading and the sexual division of literacy. *Journal of Curriculum Stud-ies, 26*, 361–381.

Luke, A., & Luke, C. (2004). Adolescence lost/childhood regained: On early intervention and the emergence of the techno-subject. *Journal of Early Childhood Literacy, 1*, 91–120.

Luke, C. (2003). Pedagogy, connectivity, multimodality, and interdisciplinarity. *Reading Research Quarterly, 38*, 397–403.

Manovich, L. (2001). *The language of new media*. Cambridge, MA: MIT Press.

Marshall, J. D., Smagorinsky, P., & Smith, M. W. (1995). *The language of interpretation: Patterns of discourse in discussions of literature*. Urbana, IL: National Council of Teachers of English.

McChesney, R. (2000). So much for the magic of technology and the free market: The World Wide Web and the corporate media system. In A. Herman & T. Swiss (Eds.), *The World Wide Web and contemporary cultural theory* (pp. 5–36). New York: Routledge.

Moje, E. B. (2004). Powerful spaces: Tracing the out-of-school literacy spaces of Latino/a youth. In K. Leander & M. Sheehy (Eds.), *Space matters: Assertions of space in literacy practice and research* (pp. 15–38). New York: Peter Lang.

Myers, J., Hammett, R., & McKillop, A. M. (1998). Opportunities for critical literacy and pedagogy in student-authored hypermedia. In D. Reinking, M. C. McKenna, L. D. Labbo, & R. D. Kieffer (Eds.), *Handbook of literacy and technology: Transformations in a post-typo-graphic world* (pp. 63–78). Mahwah, NJ: Erlbaum.

New London Group. (1996). A pedagogy of multiliteracies: Designing social futures. *Har-vard Educational Review, 66*, 60–92.

New London Group. (2000). A pedagogy of multiliteracies: Designing social futures. In B. Cope & M. Kalantzis (Eds.), *Multiliteracies: Literacy learning and the design of social futures* (pp. 9–37). New York: Routledge.

Reinking, D. (1998). Introduction: Synthesizing technological transformations of literacy in a post-typographic world. In D. Reinking, M. C. McKenna, L. D. Labbo, & R. D. Kieffer (Eds.), *Handbook of literacy and technology: Transformations in a post-typographic world* (pp. xi–xxx). Mahwah, NJ: Erlbaum.

Reinking, D., Labbo, L., & Mckenna, M.C. (2000). From assimilation to accommodation: A developmental framework for integrating digital technologies into literacy research and instruction. *Journal of Research in Reading, 23*, 110–122.

Snyder, I. (1997). *Page to screen: Taking literacy into the electronic era*. New York: Routledge.

Snyder, I., Angus, L., & Sutherland-Smith, W. (2002). Building equitable literate futures: Home and school computer-mediated literacy practices and disadvantage. *Cambridge Journal of Education, 32*, 367–383.

Strauss, A. L. (1987). *Qualitative analysis for social scientists*. Cambridge, England: Cam-bridge University Press.

Strauss, A. L., & Corbin, J. (1990). *Basics of qualitative research*. Newbury Park, CA: Sage.

Street, B. V. (1995). *Social literacies: Critical approaches to literacy in development, ethnog-raphy and education*. London: Longman.

Sumara, D. J. (2002). *Why reading literature in school still matters: Imagination, interpretation, insight*. Mahwah, NJ: Erlbaum.

Swiss, T. (2000). *Unspun: Key concepts for understanding the World Wide Web*. New York: New York University Press.

Turkle, S. (1995). *Life on the screen: Identity in the age of the Internet*. New York: Simon & Schuster.

U.S. Department of Commerce. (2002). *A nation online*. Washington, DC: Author.

Valentine, G., Holloway, S. L, & Bingham, N. (2000). Transforming cyberspace: Children's interventions in the new public sphere. In S. Holloway & G. Valentine (Eds.), *Children's geographies: Playing, living, learning* (pp. 156–173). London: Routledge.

von Sternberg, B. (2002, January 20). Where fingers do the talking. *Star Tribune*, p. 1A.

Warshauer, M. (2002). Languages.com: The Internet and linguistic pluralism. In I. Snyder (Ed.). *Silicon literacies* (pp. 62–74). New York: Routledge.

Weise, E. (2000, August 28). Instant messaging could change: Incompatibility draws ire, hackers. *USA Today*, p. 3D.

Wellman, B. (2001). Physical place and cyberplace: The rise of personalized networking. *International Journal of Urban and Regiona Research, 25*, 227–252.

Wellman, B. (2004). The three stages of Internet studies: Ten, five and zero years ago. *New Media and Society, 6*, 123–129.

Young, J. P., Dillon, D. R., & Moje, E. B. (2002). Shape-shifting portfolios: Millennial youth, literacies, and the game of life. In D. E. Alvermann (Ed.), *Adolescents and literacies in a digital world* (pp. 114–131). New York: Peter Lang.

Zucco, T. (2003, June 8). RU 2 OLD 4 THIS? Get used to it, it's how kids talk now. *St. Petersburg Times*, p. 1A.

APPENDIX

ABBY'S IM SEGMENT ORGANIZED SPATIALLY

Exchange with Buddy A

A:	so have u talked to barb?
Abby:	yeah but she didn't really say
Abby:	much
A:	ohh I see
Abby:	she said we could prolly do something
Abby:	but u guys should go ahead and make other plans
Abby:	b/c knowing her we probably won't be able to do anything
A:	ok then
A:	no offence but I can't stand people like her
Abby:	yeah I know....
A:	about a month ago I IMed her just to say hey and stuff but she didn't talk so
Abby:	yeah she does that to david too I think
A:	im surprised hed still talk to her, I haven't talked to her since
Abby:	I don't think they talk much tho

Exchange with Buddy C

C:	hey
Abby:	hey
C:	what's going on?
Abby:	nothing much.
Abby:	just got home from tanning

Exchange with Buddy D

D:	hey
Abby:	hey

Exchange with Buddy E

Abby:	I emailed u back
E:	yes!
Abby:	☺
Abby:	it was long

Exchange with Buddy F

F:	hey
Abby:	hey

Exchange with Buddy B

B:	talking on the phone [answering an earlier question from Abby]
B:	u?
Abby:	nothing much
Abby:	just chattin

Commentary Responses

In some respects, I reasoned, accepting the invitation to comment on the Lewis and Fabos (2005) article would afford an opportunity to engage in what Hellman (1973) had described as a way of examining, once the paint has aged (though admittedly in my case, by only a year or two), whether or not "what was there for [me] once … is there for [me] now" (p. 3). Of course, one might argue that aged paint is not the same as aged ink, or aged digits, for that matter; yet for my purposes, Hellman's words provided sufficient motivation to imagine a way that I might comment afresh on "Instant Messaging, Literacies, and Social Identities." In doing so, I abandoned the editor's role to take up a reviewer's stance. For me, the two are not the same. As editor, I relied heavily on reviewers' comments and recommendations; here, I report my own views, distanced in time and space from my earlier readings of the Lewis and Fabos (2005) manuscript.

What informs my views? This is not easily answered, and to say, "It depends" is in no way meant to convey a frivolous response. In fact, quite the opposite is intended. My work as a doctoral student at Syracuse University in the late 1970s was influenced to a large degree by cognitive psychologists and a postpositivist approach to research methodologies. Later, as I worked in an advisory capacity to doctoral students at the University of Georgia, I was exposed to a number of other fields of thought, including critical theory, cultural studies, media studies, feminism, and poststructuralism. More recently, I have tended to ask questions that require grounding in theories of literacy as a social practice informed by multimodal texts. It is here that my interests intersect with those of the authors of "Instant Messaging, Literacies, and Social Identities" (Lewis & Fabos, 2005).

Another point of intersection is our focus on youth. Although all three of us subscribe to a situated perspective on youth culture—one that argues for exploring how people (adolescents and adults alike) act provisionally at particular times given particular circumstances within various discourses—my own preference is to make relations of power the hub when inquiring into young people's digital literacy practices. Drawing from Michel Foucault (1975/1977), a French philosopher who wrote *Discipline and Punish*, among several other works, I tend to perceive of relations of power as mobile and capable of being modified or reversed. From this perspective, exercising power is not simply about dominating a relationship. Foucault maintained that there is no "fundamental, immutable gulf between those who exercise power and those who undergo it" (Rabinow, 1984, pp. 62–63). It is this notion that will frame, in part, my critique of the Lewis and Fabos article.

Overview of the Original Study

"Instant Messaging, Literacies, and Social Identities" (Lewis & Fabos, 2005) makes a substantial and unique contribution to the field of literacy education.

Although not the first to study instant messaging (IMing) practices among young people, Lewis and Fabos are among a handful of researchers to examine directly the pedagogical implications of IMing. Of equal note is the possibility that they may have been the first to have published a research paper in an archival journal that links the social and textual practices associated with IM to both the New Literacy Studies (NLS) and multimodality. (As of September 22, 2006, a search of the Internet offered no counter evidence to this possibility.)

The importance of this study, however, does not rest solely on its theoretical grounding. Its practical implications are every bit as strong. Drawing on a richly contextualized data set that included videotaped IM think-aloud sessions and audiotaped semistructured interviews with seven youths ranging in age from 14 to 17, Lewis and Fabos (2005) examined the everyday functions that IM served in their lives. Specifically, the researchers wanted to understand how young people's social identities shaped and were shaped by IM, an online literacy practice that their review of the literature showed to be inherently multimodal. Described as "talk" digitally written and performed, IM like other forms of chat is said to blur differences between writing and speaking as two distinctive modes of communication (C. Luke, 2003).

The verbal reporting procedure used in this study enabled the researchers to capture an array of participants' IM strategies. Relying on a substantial body of research on protocol analysis, Lewis and Fabos (2005) videotaped what they referred to as think-aloud sessions in which their participants tried to talk through their every move while online. As the researchers noted, this procedure came with both advantages and disadvantages. Although it prompted participants to engage with the researchers in ways that did not surface during some of the earlier semistructured interviews, the main disadvantage, as Lewis and Fabos noted, was that "the [think-aloud] sessions sometimes felt more like interviews that involved demonstration than they did authentic IM sessions" (p. 479). To their credit, the researchers fully transcribed all interview and think-aloud sessions. This included recording gestures, postures, and actions as well as speech (e.g., when participants read aloud portions of an IM message).

Qualitative data analysis procedures based in grounded theory involved open, axial, and selective coding techniques. Modifications were made to accommodate the fact that the actual IM exchanges frequently produced data that were difficult to analyze separately from the sessions in which they were embedded. Triangulation across interviews, videotaped think-aloud sessions, and the interpretations of both researchers resulted in the following findings:

1. Literacy practices involving IM are, in part, an extension of schooled literacy practices. For example, participants "used language in complex ways in order to negotiate multiple messages and interweave these con-

versations into larger, overarching story lines" (Lewis & Fabos, 2005, p. 482).

2. Social networks designed by the participants enhanced their social status, social connections, and language use. Using their insider knowledge of IM discourse, participants demonstrated audience awareness by strategically controlling IM interactions. This led Lewis and Fabos to speculate that "IM disrupts the virtual/real binary ... [in that] the disembodied world of IM, its textual nature (through written and visual modes), made it conducive to slipping in and out of new identities and storylines ... [that] intersect with lives offline" (p. 489).

3. Surveillance in the IM landscape consisted of circulating other people's messages, posing (e.g., attempting to take on the identity of someone else), and parental regulation. In Lewis and Fabos' view, "IM produces identities that are accustomed to being both the agent and object of scrutiny and surveillance" (p. 491). At the same time, they noted instances in which their participants were able to confound attempts at being monitored.

The implications drawn from these three major findings form the basis for the next section of the essay. In discussing them, my goal is to develop arguments informed by my concerns, perspective, and the work of others in the field of literacy education (or related fields) that may be taken up by researchers in the future. It is *not* my intent to argue persuasively—pro or con—for the study's implications, per se. Believing as I do that such implications will stand or fall on their individual merits, I simply want to use them here to suggest possible pathways for extending Lewis and Fabos' (2005) work in areas that I see as important for understanding and supporting young people and their literacy practices.

Key Implications of the Study: Groundwork for Future Research

Taking Lewis and Fabos (2005) at their word, "Instant Messaging, Literacies, and Social Identities" is a study that envisions the teaching and learning of literacy in digitally mediated times (see their abstract, p. 471). Arguably, it is that and more. For example, in their discussion of their findings, I infer a concern that readers (some, at least) may view multimodal digital technologies as having the potential to replace or negate more analytic or schooled forms of literacy. This worry connects to what I view as a more general worry in the field: namely, the in-school/out-of-school divide and the question of how to deal with it as researchers. A second concern that Lewis and Fabos put forth pertains to the material consequences of digital practices, such as IM, which evoke surveillance while simultaneously offering young people various escapes that may or may not be in their best interests. Issues of power and identity inherent in this concern cannot be ignored by researchers when designing studies that involve mechanisms of surveillance. Third, and last, is a concern that I sense in Lewis and Fabos' admonition to avoid letting anxiety over print literacy's so-called declining influence among youth discourage future research into this phenomenon. It is to each of these concerns that I now turn.

In-School/Out-of-School Divide

To restrict literacies to those that are either school-based or that take place outside of school would suggest that there are few if any relations between the two. Although strict classifications of spaces and practices have their roots in the physical, biological, and social sciences, and in the history of literacy—with written texts being privileged over texts passed on through oral practices (Collins & Blot, 2003)—it is also the case that multiple sign systems, especially those involving IM and art forms such as music, poetry, and drama, are readily available to, and used by, youth both in and out of school. Moreover, traditional forms of reading and writing instruction, including an awareness of audience and a concern for spelling correctly, are not located exclusively in schools, as Lewis and Fabos (2005) demonstrated in their study of seven young people engaged in IM sessions at home. Regardless of whether one's point of reference is in or out of school, most young people have at their disposal a wide range of texts and nonlinguistic resources from which to choose. Indeed, they are living in a time when multimodal forms of communication are increasingly the rule, and not the exception. Lewis and Fabos demonstrated an awareness of this trend when they wrote

> [M]any studies (too numerous to cite) point to the promise of computer technology as an instructional medium and learning tool. However, we are particularly interested in the conceptual direction our study provides. The question we believe should be asked is not how to actually use IM in the classroom but how to apply to school settings the literacy *practices* we observed young people take up with a great deal of engagement. (p. 496)

Yet, the tensions produced in maintaining what I view as a delicate balance between applying to school settings certain aspects of literacy *practices* associated with IM that youth find engaging and actually welcoming IM into the classroom are never far from the surface in Lewis and Fabos' (2005) discussion of their findings. For instance, while simultaneously theorizing how "regular IM activity [may offer] more experiences with the reading and writing processes and skills valued in school" (p. 475), they warn that "preparing for changing epistemologies, identities, and practices should not mean either appropriating young people's popular technologies for school use or disregarding the deep and deliberative reading and writing processes associated with analytic and critical understandings and interpretations" (p. 496).

It is this balance between theorizing and drawing implications for teaching and learning that makes "Instant Messaging, Literacies, and Social Identities"

(Lewis & Fabos, 2005) an important piece of research, one that others interested in studying young people's in- or out-of-school engagement with texts will no doubt find useful. While, from a Foucaultian perspective, I might wish for greater attention to issues surrounding relations of power, especially in research focusing on the spaces that IM practices inhabit and young people's identity enactments within those spaces, it is encouraging to read in Lewis and Fabos' extended discussion of the in-school/out-of-school divide an effort to avoid drawing overly simplistic distinctions between the two spaces. As I have written elsewhere (Alvermann & Eakle, 2006), to reify distinctions between in-school and out-of-school literacies mainly serves to separate these literacies from the very spaces that give them meaning and make them worth pursuing. It also limits what teachers and researchers can learn from students' literacy experiences, at least to the extent that students are willing to share their perceptions of those experiences. Listening to and observing youth as they communicate their familiarity with multiple texts across space, place, and time can provide valuable insights into how to approach both instruction and research—insights that might otherwise be lost or taken for granted in our rush to categorize literacy practices as either in-school or out-of-school and thus either worthy of our attention or not.

Surveillance and Issues of Power and Identity

In their discussion of how surveillance played a central role in their participants' IM practices, Lewis and Fabos (2005) wrote the following:

> Surveillance on IM is often achieved through the paths that messages travel as they are circulated. Leander and McKim (2003) suggested that examining how digital texts travel can lead to insights about the kinds of practices and relationships a particular technology affords. Our participants' IM connections and messages were often passed from one person to another in order to create a bond that depended on the surveillance of others … . Far from being isolated units, conversations easily became part of other conversations within a given IM session. Participants routinely cut and pasted elements of one conversation and shared them with another buddy—often without disclosing their actions with the first buddy, who may have done the same with someone else. Some saw this kind of surveillance as representing a wish for community, a way of finding out who else is involved in their overlapping social worlds at the moment. However, others saw it as an entry into the landscape of gossip and deceit, with users lying to one another about their concurrent IM buddies. (pp. 490–491)

As I read and reflected on this passage, I wanted to extend the discussion to include an analysis of how identities created in online spaces, such as IM, offer opportunities for studying the circulating relations of power inherent in those spaces. In particular, my attention was drawn to Davies' (2006) case study of Wiccan websites visited by teenaged girls. In this study, she used Foucault's (1986) article "Of Other Spaces" to explore the concept of online space. Drawing also from Sheehy and Leander's (2004) argument that "space is a product and process of social relations ... [rather than] static, as in metaphorical images of borders, centers, and margins" (p. 1), Davies (2006) treated space as an active, relational verb. Her 2-year, longitudinal analysis of thematically connected multimodal Web sites, the girls' literacy practices, and the identities they produced led her to conclude that

> The Internet allows youngsters to remain physically within the home yet reside with friends experimenting with a sense of independence. It is in this kind of arena where the young can challenge others' positioning of them as children; they can use the 'cloak' of the Internet to undermine age as a determining factor ... . [In effect, it is an arena that provides] a comfortable borderland which teenagers can escape to; a place joined to, but separate from the real world, with windows through which they can even see themselves. (p. 69)

Not unlike Gee's (2004) affinity spaces, in which participants take on different roles within social groups according to their expertise and experience within a particular group, Foucault's notion of "other spaces" provides an analytic tool for envisioning relations of power as mobile and capable of being modified or reversed. Having used such an analytic in my own study of online discussions that challenge the "not-yet adult" cultural model (Alvermann, 2006), I can see promise for troubling the notion of surveillance. Rather than focusing on young people's various escapes from surveillance that may or may not be in their best interests, future researchers might consider taking up Pahl and Rowsell's (2006) challenge to celebrate instances of practice that evoke power and agency within youth cultures while at the same time keeping "a close eye to the shifts of power across domains" (p. 13).

Print Literacy: A Declining Influence in Youth Culture?

Of all the implications discussed in Lewis and Fabos' (2005) article "Instant Messaging, Literacies, and Social Identities," it is the following one that piqued my interest the most. Contextually, this block quote should be read within the authors' concern about IM practices and the schooling of literacy:

> Finally, we want to refocus our lens to take in the forest as well as the trees. We have provided a detailed account of our participants' uses of IM and have described the changing epistemologies and attendant practices associated with IM use (multivocality, performativity, resourcefulness, hybrid textuality, and new forms of circulation and surveillance). As a community of literacy educators and researchers, if we let our "genera-

through research that takes into account the relations of power involved when studying young people's digital literacy and social practices in an increasingly multimodal environment.

References

Alvermann, D. E. (2006). Ned and Kevin: An online discussion that challenges the "not-yet adult" cultural model. In K. Pahl & J. Rowsell (Eds.), *Travel notes from the new literacy studies: Instances of practice* (pp. 39–56). Clevedon, U.K.: Multilingual Matters.

Alvermann, D. E., & Eakle, A. J. (2006). Dissolving learning boundaries: The doing, re-doing, and undoing of school. In D. Thiessen & A. Cook-Sather (Eds.), *International handbook of student experience in elementary and secondary school* (pp. 143–166). New York: Springer.

Collins, J., & Blot, R. K. (2003). *Literacy and literacies: Texts, power, and identity.* Cambridge, U.K.: Cambridge University Press.

Davies, J. (2006). Escaping to the borderlands: An exploration of the internet as a cultural space for teenaged Wiccan girls. In K. Pahl & J. Rowsell (Eds.), *Travel notes from the new literacy studies: Instances of practice* (pp. 57–71). Clevedon, U.K.: Multilingual Matters.

Foucault, M. (1977). *Discipline and punish* (A. M. Sheridan Smith, Trans.). New York: Vintage Books. (Original work published 1975.)

Foucault, M. (1986, Spring). Of other spaces (J. Miskowiec, Trans.). *Diacritics, 16*(1), 22–27.

Gee, J. P. (2004). *Situated language and learning: A critique of traditional schooling.* London: Routledge.

Hellman, L. (1973). *Pentimento: A book of portraits.* Boston: Little, Brown, and Co.

Hull, G. A., & Nelson, M. E. (2005). Locating the semiotic power of multimodality. *Written Communication, 22,* 224–261.

Kress, G., & Street, B. (2006). Foreword. In K. Pahl & J. Rowsell (Eds.), *Travel notes from the new literacy studies: Instances of practice* (pp. vii–x). Clevedon, U.K.: Multilingual Matters.

Kress, G., & van Leeuwen, T. (2001). *Multimodal discourse: The modes and media of contemporary communication.* London: Arnold.

Lankshear, C., & Knobel, M. (2003). *New literacies: Changing knowledge and classroom learning.* Philadelphia: Open University Press.

Leander, K. M., & McKim, K. (2003). Tracing the everyday "sitings" of adolescents on the Internet: A strategic adaptation of ethnography across online and offline spaces. *Education, Communication, & Information, 3,* 211–240.

Leu, D. J., Kinzer, C. K., Coiro, J. L., & Cammack, D. W. (2004). Toward a theory of new literacies emerging from the Internet and other information and communication technologies. In R. B. Ruddell & N. J. Unrau (Eds.), *Theoretical models and processes of reading* (5th ed., pp. 1570–1613). Newark, DE: International Reading Association.

Lewis, C., & Fabos, B. (2005). Instant messaging, literacies, and social identities. *Reading Research Quarterly, 40,* 470–501.

Luke, A., & Luke, C. (2004). Adolescence lost,childhood regained: On early intervention and the emergence of the techno-subject. *Journal of Early Childhood Literacy, 1,* 91–120.

Luke, C. (2003). Pedagogy, connectivity, multimodality, and interdisciplinarity. *Reading Research Quarterly, 38,* 397–403.

Mitchell, W. J. T. (2004, April). *Sounding the idols.* Paper presented at the conference on Visual Culture, University of California, Berkeley.

Moje, E. B. (2004). Powerful spaces: Tracing the out-of-school literacy spaces of Latino/a youth. In K. M. Leander & M. Sheehy (Eds.), *Spatializing literacy research and practice* (pp. 15–38). New York: Peter Lang.

New London Group. (1996). A pedagogy of multiliteracies: Designing social futures. *Harvard Educational Review, 66,* 60–92.

Pahl, K., & Rowsell, J. (2006). Introduction. In K. Pahl & J. Rowsell (Eds.), *Travel notes from the new literacy studies: Instances of practice* (pp. 1–15). Clevedon, U.K.: Multilingual Matters.

Rabinow, P. (Ed.). (1984). *The Foucault reader.* New York: Pantheon Books.

Reinking, D. (1998). Synthesizing technological transformations of literacy in a post-typographic world. In D. Reinking, M. C. McKenna, L. D. Labbo, & R. D. Kieffer (Eds.), *Handbook of literacy and technology: Transformations in a post-typographic world* (pp. xi–xxx). Mahwah, NJ: Erlbaum.

Sheehy, M., & Leander, K. M. (2004). Introduction. In K. M. Leander, & M. Sheehy (Eds.), *Spatializing literacy research and practice* (pp. 1–14). New York: Peter Lang.

CHAPTER 36b
Thoughts on the Lewis and Fabos
Article on Instant Messaging

DAVID REINKING

CLEMSON UNIVERSITY, USA

In this chapter, I respond to the editors' request that I share my thoughts and reactions to an article entitled "Instant Messaging, Literacies, and Identities," authored by Cynthia Lewis and Bettina Fabos (Lewis & Fabos, 2005) and published in *Reading Research Quarterly*. Following the editors' guidelines, my intent is to externalize my thoughts and reactions, not to stand in judgment of this piece in a way that is meant to inform the field about the appropriateness of the authors' theory, methods, findings, or interpretations. In fact, to do so would be presumptuous, given that this article has already passed muster within one of the most, if not the most, rigorous review processes in the field (more about that issue shortly).

Thus, this chapter is not a review or an essay critiquing the authors' work. Instead, it is an opportunity to reveal my own thinking as I read and reflected on this article based on my background, perspectives, and indeed, the inevitable biases that cloud all of our thinking to some extent. Put simply, but humbly, this chapter is more about me than about the authors or their article, because that is the stance the editors asked me to take. I agree with the editors that such an exercise could be edifying—certainly for me, and I hope for readers, and perhaps also to the authors. Rarely do authors have the opportunity to see what goes through the minds of a reader, other than the feedback received from a reviewer or an editor who must ultimately stand in judgment of their work, albeit hopefully toward constructive ends.

Another caveat is in order—one that starts the process of externalizing my thinking. This article has already entered my intellectual space on a much different plane. Because I was coeditor of *Reading Research Quarterly* (*RRQ*) when this article was reviewed, accepted, and published, I have already processed it in a much different way than I have been asked to do here. Wearing an editor's hat means absorbing oneself diligently and deeply in a constant, conscious, and often stressful quest to attain an appropriate and delicate balance between confidently exercising one's professional judgment without imposing one's personal views on authors—and ultimately, on the field. That balance is not easily achieved or maintained, and editors are human. The line is sometimes crossed; mistakes are made (and occasionally forgiven). After being involved in making editorial decisions about more than 1000 manuscripts across almost 12 years and two research journals, it is difficult to put that stance aside. It also feels particularly awkward to comment upon an article that I have dealt with previously in an editorial role. Further, for approximately 9 of those years, my responses to others' work in my role as editor has been a collaboration with Donna Alvermann, my good friend, colleague, and coeditor, who is writing her own separate reaction to the same article. To respond independently without her input and reactions seems odd, as if the world is a bit out of kilter.

That said, I hope it is clear why it would be impossible for me to return to this article without first reflecting on it as a product of our editorship. In that regard, I can say unequivocally that, although all *RRQ* articles are special, this one prompts some distinctly positive feelings about its appearance in *RRQ* under our editorship and good memories of its movement through the review process. Reading this article again under these new circumstances, however, inevitably brings back memories of a reviewer's concern or suggestion here and an editorial nudge there. Despite all of these caveats, or, more accurately, because of them, I welcome this unique opportunity to provide an unapologetically personal response to this article. In the sections that follow, I organize my reactions and reflections around each of the manuscript's major sections.

The Article's Introduction

What most caught my attention in the introductory section of Lewis and Fabos' (2005) article was the authors' presentation of their theoretical orientation, particularly, their careful attempts to define literacy and to position their work within that definition. I am little more than a dilettante in the theoretical fineries and intellectual subtleties of the substantial literature that characterizes literacy as social practice, but I have had many opportunities to read manuscripts that take such a perspective, including this one. Frankly, I think the obvious point that literacy has a social dimension is too often overtheorized and overintellectualized for my more pragmatic inclinations, particularly now, after that point has been made strongly and convincingly and no longer needs to confront any major resistance from a once-dominant cognitive perspective. There is a danger, I think, that dwelling too long on the theoretical and intellectual subtleties of literacy as social practice may prevent us from seeing, as the authors stated at the end of their article, the "forest as well as the trees" (Lewis & Fabos, 2005, p. 498). That is, consistent with the authors' purported goal, we need to get out there and see how literacy as social practice plays out in the world and in classrooms, and we need to figure out how those understandings can inform our efforts to help people become more literate and, presumably, to live more enriching and fulfilled lives. Debates and speculation about the epistemological implications to which the authors allude, which are perhaps intellectually interesting and obligatory to establishing a theoretical frame, often do not seem very consequential or pragmatically important (see Dillon, O'Brien, & Heilman, 2000). Such intellectualizing may also sometimes distract us from considering the more basic question of what we ultimately value in our efforts to instill literacy (e.g., skills for the work force; a critical, yet open-minded democratic point of view; self actualization) or from conducting research that explicitly guides our instruction toward instantiating those values through curriculum and instruction.

Lewis and Fabos (2005), however, nicely take what seem to me to be some of the old standbys and the current citations de rigueur in the literacy-as-social practice perspective and extend them cogently and convincingly into the digital realm, making a good case for the importance of studying instant messaging (IMing) from that perspective. An important point they make, which I think will not be lost on the readers who gravitate to this book and to this article, is that "the social aspects of IM are writ large" (p. 475). Indeed, they importantly extend that point by emphasizing that all digital literacies are inherently social, with IM being arguably quintessential in that regard.

This reminds me of discussions among members of our current research team on a federally funded grant aimed at investigating reading comprehension on the Internet among middle-grade students at risk of dropping out of school (see http://www.newliteracies.uconn.edu/iesproject/index.html). One of our goals is to develop and refine an Internet-comprehension framework that currently has the following major components: (a) generating good questions, (b) locating relevant information, (c) evaluating that information, (d) synthesizing the information, and (e) *communicating* the information to others (see Leu & Reinking, 2005). That is, communication, an inherently social act, must be included in any definition of comprehension on the Internet, and the immediacy of communication possible in digital environments amplifies the social dimension by closing the chasm of time and space between readers and writers.

That point, I believe, is critical and should figure into all of our research projects and agendas focusing on digital literacies. That is, any effort even remotely related to studying or developing digital literacies must attend to the influence of social factors to even a greater extent than for research limited to printed texts, the latter being arguably increasingly anachronistic, which is a point that this chapter punctuates. Thus, any study of digital literacies today without a consideration of social influences and effects is like studying fish on dry land. Further, if technology, as Latour (1991) argued, is society made durable, then even the existence of IM (and a host of other applications and genres of digital technologies in the realm of literacy such as e-mail, electronic journals, blogging, and even the Internet itself) powerfully instantiates our social lives and can only be understood in those terms. That view, I believe, is consistent with the authors' key distinction between *literacy events* and *literacy practices*. Online reading and writing, even more than printed forms, can never be understood entirely as simply literacy events. Instead, they instantiate literacy practice because they are more overtly and consistently social acts.

Further in that regard, I would extend the authors' point that "Literacy has always employed available technologies" (Lewis & Fabos, 2005, p. 475). I have argued elsewhere (Reinking, in press) that a unique aspect of the digital revolution is that it makes available open-ended possibilities for creating mechanisms for reading and writing. That is, the possibilities associated with the technology of print is relatively limited and constrained due to the relatively narrow range of forms and functions it provides. Digital technologies, on the other hand, are decidedly more malleable because they provide diverse tools that can be used to construct almost an infinite set of tools (after Ellis, 1974). Using some toys from my childhood, print technology is like a set of Lincoln logs that could be used to create a variety of log-cabin-type constructions, but digital technologies are like an erector set that might inspire a wide range of innovative Rube Goldberg constructions. Thus, to an infinitely greater extent than print technology, digital technology allows us to mold the acts of reading and writing to reflect what we value and need, which inevitably implicates our social lives. IM and blogging are good examples. Unlike print technology, digital technologies do not inexorably lead to the creation or promotion of these genres and forms; however, people do, using the capabilities that such an open-ended and dynamic technology affords them.

It is easier to argue, on the other hand, that the technology of print originated as a more pragmatic invention that created, as much as served, the social milieu (e.g., Eisenstein, 1983). For example, it might be argued that the concept of the printed book and the idea of an author being an authority isolated from readers are largely the byproducts of the more limited possibilities that print technology affords. In that case, the elevation of the social status of author was not a preexisting social condition; in fact, it was created by the technological contingencies of print. If it were easy to become a published author, we would not likely regard authors as authorities (e.g., see Kaufer & Carley, 1993; Hamilton, 2000). Likewise, digital technologies undermine that authority (Landow, 1997). These issues reflect the longstanding debates about the concept of technological determinism, which are issues that I find interesting, but not particularly relevant to my more pragmatic orientation, so I will not pursue them here (but see Slack & Wise, 2005, for a good discussion of ways to view technological determinism).

Nonetheless, I think Lewis and Fabos (2005) wisely recognize that we are living through a transitional period. They reject a point of view that focuses entirely on the new forms of digital literacy, and they acknowledge continuities and discontinuities between the print and the digital worlds. Specifically, they stated that they "were also interested in the ways that [participants'] online reading and writing practices may have been shaped by their print practices" (p. 475). This too, I believe, is an important perspective for researchers to take when investigating digital literacies. There are still likely to be many crossover influences between printed and electronic forms. For example, many literacy educators, consciously or unconsciously, continue to devalue digital forms of reading and writing, which may even serve to amplify the underground or new-wave feel to digital forms such as IM, blogs, and wikis. Likewise, the influence of digital forms on printed forms is most evident in the visual appearance of many printed texts that now have many of the characteristics of a Web site, although some Web sites also resemble printed forms such as newspapers. On the other hand, the authors also point out that for adolescents today, modes of reading and writing such as IM are becoming invisible, which may be somewhat contradictory to the previous point. Technologies that are so fully integrated into our daily routines that they are invisible are not likely to be influenced by earlier or related technologies (see Bruce & Hogan, 1998, for a possible way around this potential contradiction); however, the authors later provide evidence that the adolescents in their study still bring some conventional notions of literacy to IM.

The introductory vignette focusing on a 14-year-old girl who is adept at IM but comes from a working class family also suggests an important implication of this socially constructed dimension of IM and similar genres of digital communication. IM and other forms of digital literacy may embody a great equalizing force, undermining literacy's conventional societal role of creating and reinforcing hierarchical social distinctions (see Purves, 1998), although later in the article, Lewis and Fabos (2005) are cautious about drawing that conclusion. Social class, ascribed status, academic achievement, and professional accomplishment may all be left in the wake of the equality naturally fostered by digital technologies. Erudition in the world of Wikipedia is not limited to those with PhDs. Likewise, as the authors' work suggests, in academic environments, digital forms of communication are envoys of popular culture and may inspire more motivation to read and write for authentic, meaningful purposes unhampered by inauthentic evaluations of performance. For example, I have argued elsewhere (Reinking, 2001) that online multimedia texts are inherently more engaging than conventional printed texts. Of the several reasons I cite, one is particularly relevant to their article: Digital texts meet a wider range of social needs. That perspective corresponds well with the authors' section on digital literacy being engaging to adolescents in part because it is multimodal.

Other points in the introduction to the Lewis and Fabos (2005) article also caught my attention and prompted a reaction. For example, the authors do a good job, in my view, of sorting out the interrelated, but sometimes confusing, definitions of literacy, new literacies, and digital literacies, although I doubt that they intended to explicitly take on that task (see Lankshear & Knobel, 2003, who did). This panoply of terms has, in my view, been used loosely and interchangeably in the literature, which I find problematic. Specifically, I like their use of *the new literacies* as a broader term that encompasses, as opposed to being synonymous with, the term *digital literacies*. A pet peeve, and one that is awkward because close colleagues disagree with me on this issue (e.g., see Leu, Kinzer, Coiro, & Commack, 2004), is the use of the term *new literacies* to refer to reading and writing on the Internet or to online communication in general. In my view, such a usage unnecessarily conflates two different meanings of *new literacies* and has the added disadvantage of suggesting that reading and writing digitally continues to be new and not yet in the mainstream of literacy. What is new about new literacies is its new perspectives on literacy, not a new technology or new modes of reading and writing, although the digital technologies for reading and writing that have emerged during the previous 30 years have reinforced those new perspectives. Indeed, they have fundamentally shaped the reading and writing events that can now be viewed as a wider range of literacy practices thanks to the new literacies perspective.

The Article's Methods Section

While reading Lewis and Fabos' (2005) methods section, I was reminded, as I invariably am when I closely read the methods section of a research report, of the countless methodological decisions that researchers must make and how each decision typically entails trade offs and compromises, often influencing other decisions and potentially shaping findings and interpretations. Were these the best participants to address the authors' questions? Was familiarity with some of the participants an asset, as they argue, or a limitation because it may have inappropriate influenced participants' responses? Were their semi-structured interview questions the right ones? Were some of them too leading? Might they better have used a less intrusive, more efficient approach to collecting their verbal protocol data (e.g., software available to record students' actions on the screen as well as their comments)? These thoughts and questions extend beyond the obligatory discussion of a study's limitations, sometimes included in the discussion section of a research report. The best studies are not the ones that can make an airtight case for all such decisions and preempt any second-guessing after the fact, but are instead those suggesting that a researcher has carefully considered each methodological decision and could articulate reasons for those decisions, their implications, and the tradeoffs they entail. This study clearly has that feel, as one would expect of a study published in *RRQ*.

It is perhaps unfortunate that we do not communicate more clearly to our doctoral students the inherent messiness of our research and how all research reports are often idealized accounts that gloss over the messiness of conducting research with people in the world outside of a laboratory. Lewis and Fabos' (2005) report makes that messiness more explicit than most, which is refreshing. For example, they explain the difficulties they had in establishing an appropriate relationship with the participants in IM exchanges (and between themselves as professor and graduate student). They discuss the advantages and disadvantages of having students explain what they were doing while engaging in IM, including drawing the researcher into the IM conversation and having one participant quickly close a box that included language that might be offensive. I believe our research base would be enriched if we encouraged more honest revelations of such inevitable methodological difficulties, shortcomings, and failures, rather than to hide or gloss over them.

Lewis and Fabos (2005) conclude their methods section discussing their respective positions. In that section, they reveal that they "both share an interest in digital literacy practices in a digital age and use them extensively in [their] own professional and personal lives, [but] neither of [them] is an avid IM user, " preferring "e-mail and the phone" to IM, their overall preference for "deep reflective reading and writing," and they readily admit that their participants' "comfort level and expertise with IM technology far exceeded [their] own" (pp. 479–480). It is clear that, to some extent, they consider themselves interlopers within an unfamiliar culture, which raises some interesting methodological and conceptual issues that I, too, have experienced firsthand. Specifically, what are the advantages and disadvantages of researchers being competent, fully initiated, and indeed enthusiastic participants in a form of digital literacy that they are investigating? Are those qualities necessary for a researcher to design, plan, conduct, and report a research study aimed at understanding a particular form of digital literacy? On one hand, it would seem necessary to have some basic conceptual and technical understandings of a digital form such as IM to legitimately research it. On the other hand, if the technology is invisible (in the sense previously discussed here) for the researchers to the same extent as it is to participants, is it possible that they might miss certain dimensions of its use? Worse, is it possible that researchers may slip into biased advocacy within a research project based on their own experiences with and excitement about a digital form of communication? Perhaps that is no more a problem than in other objects of research for which a researcher has a personal stake, but it is an issue that should probably be addressed explicitly in research reports, as the authors have done here.

In that sense, studying digital literacies provides an option that studying print-based forms does not. No researchers who limit their work to printed texts are unschooled in those texts, nor are they disinclined to use them or like them. On the other hand, the outsider stance of the researchers in this study toward IM is likely to be more common among many researchers investigating digital literacies. Perhaps a desirable middle ground is to work collaboratively within a team of researchers who have a range skills and orientations pertaining to a particular type of online activity.

The Article's Research Findings

This section of the Lewis and Fabos (2005) article spoke to me most about the intrigue of IM in the lives of adolescents. The authors provide a detailed and enlightening glimpse into the adolescent psyche in relation to IM, not simply as a form of online communication, but as a form of social entertainment. In fact, that notion led me to consider that, to some extent, the entire report seems to be as much a sociological analysis of literacy as game-like entertainment as it is an analysis of literacy as purely a form of social communication. It would not surprise me, however, if the authors (and many readers invested in their theoretical orientation) objected to such a characterization. It occurs to me, though, that the distinction might be an important, if subtle, one. IM, at least in the adolescent world, may not be as much a means of communication as it is a game that one plays with friends, acquaintances, and sometimes some outsiders. The object of the game, however, is an interesting blend of language ability (e.g., spelling skill and how to deal with misspellings), technological savvy (e.g., knowing how to use the software and hardware to engage simultaneously in multiple conversations), and social gamesmanship including surveillance and manipulation (e.g., serving as interlocutor between parties with a romantic interest or purposefully delaying a response to assert one's control or dominance).

The game has added appeal because, for the most part, it can be played independent of adult supervision or interference. In fact, as the results of this study document, the rules and tools of this game enable participants to stymie adults' attempts to interfere with the game. This enticing mix is also seasoned with an element of risk, maybe even danger, from losing face or social status to the more serious risk of encountering a sexual predator, although the portraits of adolescents using IM in this study should be a bit reassuring to parents who worry about the latter. If one had to invent a game well suited to the adolescent world, I believe one would be hard pressed to create something as enticing and engaging as IM, and the results section documents why that is the case.

Thinking about IM as a game led me to an awareness that, to my knowledge, there has never been any systematic, scholarly consideration of reading and writing as a form of entertainment or amusement. Further, might IM specifically, and digital forms of reading and writing more generally, lead the way for the field to consider such a perspective? Reading and writing for entertainment or amusement is clearly a ubiquitous dimension of literacy from working crossword puzzles, to writing Haiku, to reading comic books (although I am ambivalent about whether reading an engaging novel might be considered entertainment or an amusement in the sense I am thinking about it here). Might we better understand digital literacies if we framed them not based on engaging mutations of more serious print-based forms, but as a venue for literacy that is essentially entertaining and game-like? To extend this thought beyond IM, might we conceptualize finding information on the Internet as a scavenger hunt with powerful and intriguing search tools and engaging multimedia displays to be in the realm of entertainment, at least much more so than locating information in printed books housed in a staid library and searched laboriously with relatively constrained search tools? Actually, Richard Lanham (1993) has touched on this point by characterizing print-based reading and writing as philosophical and serious (we look *through* texts for deeper meanings) and digital forms as rhetorical and less serious (we look *at* texts mindful of how their visual, and sometimes auditory, elements engage us and thus become part of textual meaning).

The fact that one of the participants in the Lewis and Fabos (2005) study commented that she watches much less television since she has engaged in IM seems to support my speculations here, and connects with the literature on television viewing and reading (e.g., Neumann, 1995). That is, watching television and reading—at least conventional reading of printed books—seem to meet different needs. Turning off the television does not automatically lead people to read a book, but may instead lead them to seek other activities that meet the same needs as television viewing, or simply to remain frustrated that certain needs are not being met. For the participants in this study, however, IM seemed to be more attractive than television as a form of entertainment, perhaps because of its decidedly social dimension. The fact that the entertainment was centered in social interaction also counters the often-expressed concern that digital technologies are inherently antisocial. They certainly have more social potential than television viewing.

There also seems to be an interestingly complex connection between technological characteristics and capabilities and how social, and perhaps other, needs might be met. For example, I can recall a time several years ago when my daughter, who was then an adolescent, got a phone call from a friend asking her to get online so they could chat there. Apparently, the technological features of IM had more appeal than the telephone, even though a telephone conversation would have been far more efficient. Similarly, I wonder if the participants in this study might reject the increasingly available capability to engage in online video interactions. Being able to see and to hear everyone involved in an online conversation would be far more efficient purely from the standpoint of communication, but it would likely undermine the social entertainment and game-like qualities of intrigue (particularly surveillance) that seem fundamental to IM and attractive to adolescents.

The Article's Discussion and Implications

Lewis and Fabos' (2005) discussion section revisited their dominant themes and theoretical concepts in light of their data and presented new food for thought, which is what I would expect to find in a good discussion section. I was also pleased that some of the ideas I encountered there seemed consistent with my own speculative reactions presented in the previous section of this chapter. For example, they characterized the essence of IM as "performative and multivoiced" (p. 493), which reinforces, I believe, the characterization of IM as primarily a form of social entertainment and amusement. This characterization also leads me further down my new path of considering whether that may indeed be an important and unexamined dimension of literacy, specifically in relation to digital forms of reading and writing. Lewis and Fabos' use of the term *performative* also gave me a new image or analogy. In light of that term, their description of participants' involvement in IM reminded me of improvisational theater, which is a form of entertainment and amusement for participants and for members of an audience, which are also, to some extent, the other performers. The performance analogy also leads the authors to speculate about how IM may connect to considering audience in the process of writing, which is one concrete example of how their work might inform instruction.

The authors concluded that participants "critically analyzed the language of IM in terms of the rhetorical context within which it was framed" (Lewis & Fabos, 2005, p. 495), which is consistent with Lanham's (1993) point, cited in the previous section. In the case of IM, however, there may be a more limited use of, and perhaps a resistance to, using the full range of multimedia tools to exercise all rhetorical options. I wish that I could question the participants along those lines. How would adding a live audio and video feed of each participant change the IM environment? Would it be IM any longer? Why not? Would it be as enjoyable? Such questions might reveal an interesting example of the tension between technological capabilities and the socially defined functions that they serve. It might also reveal how the technological capabilities of digital forms of reading and writing represent a toolbox for creating contingencies that serve whatever aspects of literacy we would like to develop or promote.

Along those lines, as the authors pointed out, IM "remediates" (see Bolter & Grusin, 2000) the patterns of oral communication. Nonetheless, that remediation plays out within the context of a distinctly different and pleasing pragmatics (in the linguistic sense) that permit socially motivated posing and posturing, all in a game-like atmosphere. As Lewis and Fabos (2005) stated,

"The knowledge and identities that users bring to IM shape the technology and how it is used" (p. 495). I wonder, however, about the extent to which participants' individual identities shaped how the technology was used and to what extent, on the other hand, the logistics of the technology and the unwritten rules and protocols of IM culture shaped individual user's identities. We express who we are when we write, but the contingencies and protocols of writing also change us (e.g., see Olson, 1994). I am always a little uncomfortable with, or maybe just confused by, the concept of *voice* as the authors and others have used it in our literature, presumably as a metaphor for our identities or inclinations for self-expression, although I realize this concept also has some sociopolitical overtones. The former is most certainly socially constructed and thus dynamic, and the latter perhaps a dimension of an individual's personality. Both are constructions open to outside influences. I wonder, therefore, if the authors' data presented any evidence of the technology shaping identity, rather than simply being a mechanism for expressing it.

Finally, in reading the discussion section, I focused on the Lewis and Fabos' (2005) implications for instruction. They raised what I think are some critical and largely unaddressed questions of major curricular import. For example, how should schools address the increasing divergence between conventional in-school literacies, which have been characteristically serious and abstract ("deep and deliberative" [p. 496], in the authors' words), and the more free-wheeling, informal, multimedia, identity-arousing (or identify-forming) literacies outside of school? Again, IM is a prime, although not the only, example. One response, which the authors seem to reject, is to define the school's role as being a site to foster (or perhaps preserve?) the currently more valued forms of literacy that are not as readily and intuitively mastered as are digital literacies. That logic might be supported by the fact that digital literacies such as IM are being mastered readily outside of school, and perhaps also by the reality that many educators tend not to be fully initiated or otherwise accepting of the digital literacies that are being acquired outside of school. The authors also argue, however, against the other extreme—importing IM wholesale into the classroom—because almost any way one might imagine doing so would distort and undermine the authenticity of IM.

Instead, Lewis and Fabos (2005) have taken what seems to be a reasonable middle ground. They have suggested that educators draw students into a discussion about IM as a form of out-of-school literacy and how it might inform in-school literacy. They have also suggested that educators might "apply some of the aptitudes fostered online to readings of more complex materials" (p. 497) and topics. They proposed that other online activities like blogs have many of the characteristics of IM, but these online activities lend themselves more readily to dealing with "complex topics that require careful examination and depth of analysis" (p. 497). Finally, they reiterated a common and important admonition related to integrating technology into literacy instruc-

CHAPTER 37

L2 Literacy and the Design of the Self*
A Case Study of a Teenager Writing on the Internet

WAN SHUN EVA LAM

UNIVERSITY OF CALIFORNIA, BERKELEY, USA

Abstract

This article presents a case study that uses ethnographic and discourse analytic methods to examine how electronic textual experiences in ESL figure in the identity formation and literacy development of the learner. First, the article reviews some recent work in literacy studies, L2 learning, and computer-mediated communication to provide a conceptual basis for studying discursive practices and identity formation in L2 learning. The results of a case study of a Chinese immigrant teenager's written correspondence with a transnational group of peers on the Internet then show how this correspondence relates to his developing identity in the use of English. This study develops the notion of textual identity for understanding how texts are composed and used to represent and reposition identity in the networked computer media. It also raises critical questions on literacy and cultural belonging in the present age of globalization and transborder relations.

* Reprinted with permission of Teachers of English to Speakers of Other Languages, from L2 literacy and the design of the self: Case study of a teenager writing on the Internet, Lam, W. S. E., TESOL Quarterly, 34(3), 457–482 (2000); permission conveyed through Copyright Clearance Center, Inc.

contradiction, or conflict with one another. As Weedon (1997) points out, identity is inherently unstable, and social identity, although constituted and governed by prevailing practices, is capable of resistance and innovations produced out of the clash between contradictory and competing practices. In this context of contradiction, learners somehow construct their identities through the selective appropriation of literacy resources.

Designing Identity through Voice

In studying L2 literacy development, researchers (e.g., McKay & Wong, 1996; Peirce, 1995) have shown how identity affects the ways in which learners develop and demonstrate their competence in the L2 and how they draw on diverse discourses and identities to assert and develop their voice in the L2. For example, Peirce (1995) has argued that learners' *investment*—a complex relationship of language learners to the target language contexts—influences their successes and failures in accomplishing their goals in the target language. Accordingly, when language learners speak, they are not only exchanging information with target language speakers but are constantly organizing and reorganizing a sense of who they are and how they relate to the social world. Zamel (1997) reveals the reflective and generative power of writing for learners in creating their own voices in an L2. Instead of viewing discourse practices as discrete sets of conventions or processes of enculturation that overdetermine the learners' identities, Zamel argues that students could appropriate elements from a diversity of discourses to create a new written voice.

Kramsch (2000a, in press) elaborates on this concept of voice, defining it as the process by which people create, maintain, or transform institutional roles and identities through the discursive choices they make. Whereas the notions of role and identity index the historical and social or collective formation of identity, the notion of voice reveals the inadequacy of historical and social categories to encompass all enunciable experiences. Kramsch (in press) describes voice as

> the act of meaning making itself (Bruner 1990: ch. 4), the choice of which role we will play, which identity we will put forth in our interaction with others. If identity and role stress the socially constructed nature of institutions, the concept of voice reminds us that institutions are created, maintained and changed by the individual utterance in discourse.

Kramsch (in press) notes that her notion of identity versus role versus voice shares an affinity with Goffman's (1981) three production formats in *discursive interaction:* principal, animator, and author. A *principal* is "someone whose position is established by the words that are spoken ... [who is active in] some special capacity as a member of a group, office, category, relationship, association, or whatever, some socially based source of self-identification" (p. 145). In other words, the principal is an identity that is established by social institutions (e.g., Chinese vs. Chinese American, immigrant, limited English proficient, masculine vs. feminine). An *animator* is "someone who openly speaks for someone else and in someone else's words, as we do, say, in reading a deposition or providing a simultaneous translation of a speech, without taking the position to which these words attest" (pp. 145–146). In other words, the animator is the actor type enacting existing social roles in society (e.g., a Chinese American youngster playing the role of model minority in the United States). Finally, an *author* is "someone who has selected the sentiments that are being expressed and the words in which they are encoded" (p. 144). The notion of voice captures this discursive process of consciously selecting, juxtaposing, or reworking existing social roles and identities in the representation of self and other.

This perspective of voice as a means of constructing one's identity is further elaborated by Kress's (2000) concept of *design*, which refers to the transformative use of available representational resources in the production of new meaning. Poststructuralist literacy scholars such as Kress (2000) and others in the New London Group (1996; Cope & Kalantzis, 2000) have suggested that design is an essential textual principle at a time when articulating one's voice can involve the complex orchestration of multiple modalities through electronic media within a growing diversity of linguistic and cultural affiliations. The concept of design is used to capture the transformative and innovative aspect of meaning making, in which language use is not only a matter of deploying existing representational resources according to conventions, but also a dynamic process of adopting and reshaping existing resources in different measures to create new meanings and ways of representing reality. As Kress (2000) remarks, "an adequate theory of semiosis will be founded on a recognition of the 'interested action' of socially located, culturally and historically formed individuals, as the remakers, the transformers, and the re-shapers of the representational resources available to them" (p. 155). Design involves the orchestration of existing resources—such as linguistic patterns, genres, and discourses—in potentially transformative ways to achieve the designer's communicative purpose, particularly when the designer's interest is at odds with existing representations of social reality. Through their collaboration in designing, people may alter and renegotiate their identities within their social communities. As a consequence, the communities in which they obtain representational resources are critical to the design of their identities and their literacy development.

Collective Identities in Computer-Mediated Communication

Computer-mediated communication (CMC) is a vehicle for the metaphorical construction of community, the crafting of multiple personae and collective identities, and the assumption of social roles in the temporal frame of on-line exchanges. The self-conscious and reflective nature of design in

CMC makes computer-mediated contexts an ideal site for observing Goffman's (1959; 1981, pp. 146–157) dramaturgical concept of discursive interaction in action. In Goffman's view, social life is akin to a staged drama in which individuals, as social actors, manage others' impressions of them and influence the context of interaction through their "personal front" (1959, p. 24)—their conduct and manner of self presentation. Discursively, this personal front appears in the social role and manner of speaking one adopts in interaction, the production format (as principal, animator, author) that signals the particular relation of the words to the speaker, or the use of an embedded first-person pronoun that serves as a narrative voice for the speaker. In Goffman's (1981) terms, the embedded voice is "figure in a statement who is present only in a world that is being told about, not in the world in which the current telling takes place" (p. 149). Like the poststructuralist conception of identity, Goffman's view of the self is "something of collaborative manufacture" (1959, p. 253) that must be produced and developed in specific interactions. Like stage actors, social actors enact roles, assume characters, and play through scenes when engaged in the everyday rituals of communication with one another. Research on CMC has provided some evidence of the significance of alternative social collectivities, role play, and stylistic innovation in CMC environments. Researchers in communication, linguistics, and cultural studies have pointed out the widespread use of *community* as a metaphor for CMC and examined the processes of its construction. For example, in her study of the asynchronous communication of newsgroup discussions,[2] Baym (1995) suggests that certain social dynamics in CMC, such as group-specific forms of expression, identity, social relationships, and behavioral norms, promote a sense of community. Tepper (1997) analyzes the use of *trolls*—insiders' jokes and peculiar forms of spelling—as a boundary mechanism for consolidating group culture and distinguishing insiders from outsiders.

The construction of community as a frame for interaction in the synchronous communication of Internet Relay Chat (IRC) is discussed by Bays (1998). By portraying in words the imagined physical setting of their conversation and the behaviors of the participants that form the context of their social encounter, the participants in the IRC group that Bays studied collectively constructed a sense of community as a notion associated with familiarity, sharing, and working together for the common good. For example, this group developed what Bays calls the *cookie convention*, in which members give cookies to each other as a sign of generosity and goodwill. Sanction is meted out to violators of the communal atmosphere, such as somebody who "acts aggressively" by using swear words. Aberrant behaviors as such are penalized by equally scath-

---

[2] In *asynchronous* communication, participants read and post messages to one another without having to be on-line simultaneously. Another form of CMC is *synchronous,* in which all participants are on-line at the same time and respond to one another immediately.

ing comments or the threat of being "kicked off" the channel. Bays notes that "physicality exists within the world of IRC as a frame in which the rules of interactive conduct and 'reality' within the CMC are based" (n.p.).

Some researchers suggest that one attraction of CMC is the variety of options it offers participants for designing their identities. Bays (1998) analyzes the crafting of nicknames as an aspect of the face that one adopts in negotiating one's identity in CMC. Composed of letters, numbers, punctuation, or other notations, the nickname is a sign of individuality and a carrier of sociological cues, such as age, gender, and interest. Hence, as some scholars (e.g., Turkle, 1995) argue, the donning of nicknames and other attributes in CMC makes it a social arena in which people may construct multiple roles and personae.

One reason for the many voices an individual might adopt through CMC is that the physical self is not presented through CMC's commonly used modes. CMC is believed by some to hold the potential for a "democratization of subject constitution" (Poster, 1997, p. 211; Turkle, 1995) because of the attenuation of highly conspicuous social cues (e.g., indicators of gender, ethnicity, or class) that come with face-to-face communication. Moreover, social norms and categories tend to be subverted in an arena that is more accepting of experimentation and in which the risks of social sanction are not as high. Yet, depending on the politics and social interests of the group and individuals, social norms can just as easily be intensified in the *bodyless pragmatics* (Hall, 1996) of CMC, in which communication relies heavily on the textual media. For example, Hall shows how participants in a feminist discussion list collectively construct particular linguistic practices that high-light what they believe to be the attributes of the female gender in order to promote feminist beliefs and protest the sexual harassment they experience elsewhere on the Internet.

Given its use for the expression of both community and individual identity, CMC has come to be seen as a *rhetorical device* (Lanham, 1993), in which a dramatic tension exists between unself-conscious verbal involvement and self-conscious textual design. Werry (1996) notes the interplay between involvement and detachment in the synchronous communication of IRC:

> When communicating on IRC there is a different sense of connection to the word; it does not belong to the speaker in the sense that a spoken word does … . Yet at the same time, words exist in a temporal frame-work which approximates oral discourse, which requires interactivity and involvement, and which invites the fabrication of the texture and signature of an individual speaker's voice. (p. 59)

Some analogues to oral discourse found in the written dialogues of IRC include using abbreviation, ellipsis, and a telegraphic style to simulate the speed and informality of oral conversation; signaling paralinguistic and prosodic cues by punctuation, capitalization, and spelling; and attempting to inscribe behaviors and gestures through words and emoticons. However, compared with face-to-face communication, this orate mode (a mode of language closer to everyday conversation; see, e.g., Kramsch, 1993), peculiar to IRC communication, is often characterized by a greater degree of reflectiveness and playful attention to form. Bays (1998) observes that the distinctive combination of textuality and temporality in IRC offers the opportunity to experiment with one's identity as an on-line presence.

L2 Identity through CMC

The many and varied opportunities for ESL learners to engage in literacy experiences on the Internet have not been investigated in depth. The aim of the present study, therefore, is to explore how literacy in an L2 is related to the discursive construction of identity as writing enters the electronic age and new forms of social networking emerge through World Wide Web-based communication. I draw on Goffman's (1959, 1981) dramaturgical view of interaction (the assumption of roles and characters in social interaction), Kramsch's (in press) notion of voice (the discursive construction of social and cultural affiliations), and Kress's (2000) semiotic notion of design (the transformative use of available discourses and norms of representation) to examine how a teenager constructs his textual identity in ESL in written correspondence with a transnational group of peers on the Internet via a home page on the World Wide Web and synchronous and asynchronous communication. In discussing the learner's literacy experiences, I use the term *textual identity* as an attempt to characterize the discursive strategies that he uses to articulate and position himself in written texts (and other semiotic media) as he negotiates diverse discourses on the Internet. Through this case study, I present an analysis of how texts are composed and used to represent and reposition identity in the cross-cultural milieu of Internet communication. By examining the relation between textuality and identity in the networked computer medium as it engenders literacy development in ESL, I draw implications for an expanded vision of literacy education in ESL in an age of global electronic communication.

Research Method

Context

The case study reported here forms part of an ongoing ethnographic research project that explores the cross-cultural literacy practices of adolescent immigrants in a city on the West Coast of the United States. In fall 1996, I began meeting students as a classroom observer in an urban high school where I had taught ESL and Chinese bilingual classes a few years before the study began. From the classroom and the school as a starting point, I interviewed the students about what they read and wrote, and observed some out-of-school settings where they practiced forms of literacy in their native and nonnative languages. The research takes an ethnographic approach to theory construction that is grounded in the everyday life of the people studied, their social activities in specific contexts, and the meanings these activities hold for them (Erickson, 1986; Glaser & Strauss, 1967; Ramanathan & Atkinson, 1999; Watson-Gegeo, 1988).

As a case study that emerged out of the larger ethnographic project, this investigation aims not to generalize from its findings but to expand and provide alternative visions of literacy development (see, e.g., Dyson, 1995). The indepth study of cases helps illuminate the situated nature of learning to read and write, and the complexity of individual persons and the practices of literacy. It holds the potential to destablize conceptual boundaries and contribute to new understandings of the concepts under study (Stake, 1995).

For this case study, I first interviewed the student in the fall of 1996 as part of the broader ethnographic project. I was away from the field site for the spring and summer of 1997 and, on my return in fall 1997, found that the student was actively involved in the Internet and that his ability to write in English had improved dramatically. Hence, I found it compelling to study how this student was learning English through the Internet.

Procedure

Over a 6-month period beginning in fall 1997, I used participant observation, in-depth interviews, and textual documentation to gather data on the student's computer experiences and activities, his personal background, and his schooling experiences. With his permission, over that period I collected 50 log files of his on-line chat (real-time conversation on the Internet) and e-mail and documents from his home page. Hence, I was able to observe the progression in his correspondences with some on-line chat mates and e-mail pen pals. I took field notes from direct observation of the student's computing activities while he showed me how he used different programs on the Web and from the files and documents that were stored on his computer. Field notes and documentation were also gathered from my own exploration of the Web sites and chat systems that the student used. I carried out four tape-recorded interviews that lasted approximately an hour each and conducted about seven brief exchanges (in person, on the phone, via e-mail, and via on-line chat) with the student to gather information on his personal background, history of computer use and Internet involvement, retrospective reflections on the texts that he produced on the Internet, and English learning experiences.

Besides using inductive thematic analysis to identify patterns in the field notes, interview transcripts, and Internet data, I also used Goffman's (1981) method of *interactional analysis* to examine the production format or speaking roles in the discursive exchanges of chat and e-mail. Through the research methods of critical discourse analysis (Fairclough, 1992b; Huckin, 1995; Kress, 1990), I examined how language as discourse—system(s) of beliefs and practices—was involved in the production, maintenance, and transformation of social relations and identities. In critical discourse analysis, discourse is viewed as a form of social action that has effects on social structures as well as being determined by them and so contributes to social continuity and social change. Specifically, I analyzed the use of metaphors, deictic pronouns, and modality in the discursive construction of social identities and relations in documents on the Web server and home page, in online chat, and in e-mail exchanges.

The Focal Student

Almon[3] emigrated from Hong Kong to the United States with his parents and younger brother in 1992, at the age of 12, and, once settled, the family rented a small apartment on the outer fringes of the Chinatown community. When I met Almon, a high school senior, at an after-school tutorial class in fall 1996, he expressed frustration over the fact that his English skills were still insufficient even though he had been in the country for 5 years. All of the friends he had made in and out of school were Chinese speakers. Most of his classes at school were ESL, bilingual, or remedial courses, which stigmatized him as a low-achieving student. For instance, he was enrolled in a remedial composition class designed for students who had failed the mandatory high school composition test that was required for graduation. All of the students in the class were immigrants and ESL learners, and the teacher put a great deal of emphasis on imparting the correct linguistic code to them through the use of grammar charts and corrections on their essays. On several occasions, Almon expressed worry about his future life and career, and considered his difficulty with English a crucial part of the problem:

> The Chinese are prospering quite okay here. The problem is mainly with discrimination. The Chinese have more problems with English, and so it's more difficult for them to find jobs. Even those who have been here for a long time don't speak like the native-born Americans . . . English is my biggest <u>problem</u> … . It's like this place isn't my world, I don't belong here. I guess it's going to be very hard for me to develop my career here. And I have a feeling that my English won't be that good even in 10 years.[4] (interview, October 15, 1996)

Here, Almon reveals a sense of his marginalized position in society and a perception that his inability to speak English like a native will hinder his prospects in life. English both signifies and constitutes his feeling of not belonging.

In fall 1997, when I returned to the field site after being away for 6 months and re-interviewed some of the students that I had first met a year before,

---

[3] The data presented here are also discussed in Kramsch, A'Ness, and Lam (in press). The names of the informant and his correspondents are pseudonyms.

[4] Quotations from recorded interviews are translations from Cantonese. Underlining represents Almon's code switching to English.

Almon described to me how he had become actively involved in learning about the Internet in the latter part of his senior year. After attending an introductory class on e-mail and browsing for information on the Web in the high school from which he would soon graduate, he continued to look up different Web sites for tutorials on how to make personal home pages and conduct on-line chat. By fall 1997, when he began his studies at a local junior college, he had almost completed a personal home page on a Japanese pop singer, had compiled a long list of names of on-line chat mates in several countries around the world, and was starting to write regularly to a few e-mail "pen pals" (Almon's term; interview, September 2, 1997). Almon pointed out to me that it was easier to express what he wanted to say by writing it out than by speaking in front of others. And in terms of his writing ability in English, he had made great strides and noted a "visible improvement" (interview, September 2, 1997). He could now write more fluently in school and was planning to take a public speaking class to improve his oral delivery skills. Commenting on the change in his writing, he said,

> [about learning to write English in school] I've always been poor in my English, writing in English. I couldn't write anything, and my mind just went blank all the time. Especially for the topics that I wasn't interested in, the writing topics, I couldn't write out anything ... I wasn't interested, like the way things are expressed in English is not that good, not as good as Chinese ... At first when I was using ICQ [pronounced "I seek you"; on-line instant messaging software], I don't know why, but my English is much better now than at that time. At that time when I typed, I was typing so slow, like typing space by space, and didn't really know how to type it. Later, after many times, I realized I could, even if it's still not very good, I can express myself much more easily now ... . It's not a matter of typing skill, it's the English ... . Now I've improved, it's because of ICQ or e-mail or other reasons ... . Now it's somewhat different, before I was the type who hated English, really, I didn't like English. Maybe it was a kind of escapism, knowing I wasn't doing well at it, and so I used hating it as a way to deal with the problem. But I think it's easier for me to write out something now ... [to] express better. (interview, October 5, 1997)

This qualitatively different relationship to English came with a newly discovered ability to express himself in writing via the electronic media, which also helped him overcome some of his fear and worry about the future:

> I've changed a lot in the last 2 months, actually. I have kind of changed my determination. I'm not as fearful, or afraid of the future, that I won't have a future. I'm not as afraid now ... . When I was feeling negative, I felt the world doesn't belong to me, and it's hard to survive here. And I felt not many people understand me, or would. I didn't feel like I belong to this world ... . But now I feel there's nothing much to be afraid of. It

really depends on how you go about it. It's not like the world always has power over you. It was [names of a few chat mates and e-mail pen pals] who helped me to change and encouraged me. If I hadn't known them, perhaps I wouldn't have changed so much … . Yeah, maybe the <u>Internet</u> has changed me. (interview, October 5, 1997)

Given the changes that Almon experienced through writing on the Internet-from a sense of alienation from the English language in his adopted country to a newfound sense of expressivity and solidarity when communicating in English with his Internet peers—what sorts of identities was he designing for himself as an English user on the Web, and what was the nature of the discourse community that supported his English learning?

Results: Designing a Textual Identity

Almon constructed a personal Web site through an international server, called *GeoCities*, advertised on the Web as follows:

Welcome to GeoCities, the largest and fastest growing community on the Internet … . At GeoCities, we provide members with free e-mail accounts, home pages and the best page building tools and online help resources to make personal publishing and community building as easy as writing a letter to a friend. More than 2 million people have already joined, and thousands more are signing up every day … . GeoCities is a thriving online community of people just like you. We call our members "homesteaders" because they've staked a claim on their own plot of "land" on the Internet … . There are 15 themed avenues (Entertainment, Arts & Literature, Sport & Recreation etc.) … . From the neighborhoods, you can peruse the best home pages, visit our exciting, interactive avenues, or just cruise the suburbs … . (*Geotour*, 1998, n.p.)

This ad shows that Web technology offers not only the virtual base for the construction, storage, and retrieval of electronic texts but also a full-fledged metaphor for the building of social and cultural communities. The fusion of the words "home" and "page" merges the two overlapping tropes "publishing" and "urban landscape" in an American lifestyle that is exported over the Internet. One can "peruse" the creative aspects of *texts* (or home pages) by "cruising" down the neighborhoods and suburbs of *contexts* (or themes). The names and themes of the more than 40 neighborhoods (with branches called *suburbs*) are characteristically empty symbols filled with stereotypical content. For example,

Paris is the neighborhood of: Romance, poetry, and the arts
Broadway: Theater, musical, show business
Athens: Education, literature, poetry, philosophy

Vienna: Classical music, opera, ballet
Madison Avenue: Advertising
Silicon Valley: Hardware, software, programming
Wellesley: A community of women
Tokyo: Anime and all things Asian (*Geotour*, 1998, n.p.)

Almon chose to settle his home page in "Tokyo," where a global community of Asians gathers around Japanese pop culture. Almon's online chat mates were located in such diverse sites as Canada, Hong Kong, Japan, Malaysia, and the United States.

Design

Almon designed his home page on a young Japanese popular J-pop) singer (or *idol*, in Japanese parlance) named Ryoko Hirosue out of his interest in J-pop music. He bought J-pop music and magazines in a Japantown district a few miles from his home. He followed the trends in J-pop culture closely by reading magazines, watching television programs imported from Japan on a local channel, and searching the growing number of Web sites on J-pop music and particular singers. He was able to understand some of the Japanese language used in these media because he had attended Japanese language classes in school. On why he chose Ryoko as the subject of his home page, Almon said, "Well, I am always into Japanese things ... and she was my idol at that time ... . If you are introducing some idols who are attractive, then people may read it." According to him, the intended audience of his home page are "those people who are interested in Japanese pop stars ... teenagers" (interview, November 10, 1997).

Almon designed his Ryoko page by using materials and sources from magazines and other Web sites on J-pop music and celebrities. He chose a pseudonym, Mr. Children (also the name of a J-pop music group), to designate himself; hence the home page is called *Mr. Children's Ryoko Page* (http://www.geocities.com/Tokyo/Garden/5088/frame.htm). It appears on the computer screen with a main page that presents a written introduction, an animated cartoon of Ryoko next to her name in Japanese *kanji* (Chinese characters in Japanese script), and a song of hers playing in the background. A side panel shows a list of buttons indicating the other parts of the home page that can be opened by clicking on them: a profile of Ryoko; a history page with her biographical information; a large selection of photos; a music section with songs that visitors can listen to on-line or download to their computers; several video clips; a section called "My Favorite Links" that provides, for example, links to other personal and institutional Web sites on J-pop music, particular singers like Ryoko, and Japanese animations; and a page with an Internet search engine. In a guest book, visitors may write comments or view other people's comments.

In the written text on the main page, Almon presents the topic of his home page, Ryoko Hirosue, and introduces himself as Mr. Children. Almon makes abundant use of the deictic pronouns *you* and *I* to address the audience of J-pop fans and himself throughout the text, and he refers to Ryoko as *she*. This usage creates an addresser-addressee relationship even as the discussion revolves around Ryoko. Almon highlights his ownership of the home page by the use of the first-person possessive in "my site" and "my homepage," and establishes himself as a knowledgeable and helpful member of the international J-pop community in statements like "No problem! ^_^ you'll find out anythings about her in my site."[5] In the second paragraph, Almon provides multiple channels of communication (e-mail and on-line chat using ICQ) through which Mr. Children and his readers/visitors can establish and maintain contact. Clearly, the home page introduces and represents not only the singer Ryoko but also Mr. Children, a participant in J-pop culture. Through his choice of linguistic features in the Web page (i.e., deictic pronouns to signal affiliations), Almon discursively constructs (Kramsch, in press) his new position as a member of the global J-pop community.

In the section "My Favorite Links," Almon forms associations with other home pages on Ryoko and various aspects of J-pop music, including animation (*anime,* as it is commonly abbreviated in Japan), and extends these associations to other interests of Internet users, friends' home pages, and computer games, a few of which contain the Chinese language. In regard to J-pop music, the section not only presents factual information but actively seeks to galvanize the J-pop fan community. This is exemplified in the use of imperatives (e.g., "Let join there ...", "Go check it now ...", "*Must Visit*") and the modal auxiliary verb *can* (e.g., "A lot of Ryoko's pictures you can get here," 'You can try to hear the brand-new songs ... ," "Here you can download a tons of mp3 files of song," "You can find all TK family official homepage here"). In statements like "If you think you are J-pop fan, but you have (n)ever visit this site and don't know what it's about, than I don't think you really are a J-pop fan," there is an active construction of who J-pop fans are and what they are supposed to do and know. Being a member of the J-pop fan community involves helping define one another's identity.

The rhetoric that runs through the page promotes both the music culture and industry and Almon himself in that culture, as can be seen in his adoption of the nickname Mr. Children. The descriptor for the link to the home page of the music group "Mr. Children innocent world" reads, "Please don't mistake this, this is not my home page. This is a regular Mr. Children page. *Check it out, and see why I like this group so much* [italics added]. They are so great!!!" Here Almon adopts an iconic figure in the music industry as an identification badge for a J-pop fan. The advertising discourse of the global music

---

[5] Almon uses both Western and Japanese versions of emoticons. The Japanese smiley ^_^ is more easily recognizable as a face than the Western version :-) because it is right-side up rather than sideways (rotated to the left), although the mouth does not curve upward as in the Western version (Pollack, 1996; Sugimoto & Levin, 2000).

and high-tech industry becomes a vehicle for Almon to introduce himself as a knowledgeable, valued member of the global J-pop community and participate in promoting its interests and resources. Almon actively acquires and deploys the promotional rhetoric of the Web as a discursive norm or design (Kress, 2000) that he uses not only to perpetuate the viability of the Web and music industries but to construct new social networks for himself with a transnational group of Asian peers.

Dramaturgical Interaction

Almon's dialogic exchanges with his on-line pen pals constructed gendered social roles that evidence Goffman's (1959; 1981, pp. 146–57) dramaturgical view of social interaction. The gendering aspect of their written exchanges is seen in Almon's preference for and closer relationship with his female pen pals:

> ... maybe I feel, I don't know, more comfortable with females. It doesn't have to be some kind of relationship, but with females, I like to, and can talk more easily ... . Boys ... they give you a different kind of encouragement. It's like encouraging you to talk. But the kind that the girls give is the encouragement to believe in yourself. (interview, December 12, 1997)

As opposed to the camaraderie between boys, Almon believes that girls are more able to foster self-knowledge and confidence. Female pen pals take on a nurturing, motherly, supportive role. Before writing the following posting to Ying, a Chinese female pen pal from Hong Kong, Almon had presented himself as a shy person in need of support, and Ying had responded accordingly:

> Hum ... you said you can share my happiness or sadness, that's great. It is a very important thing to be a good pal. So don't try to hide when I need to share things with you, okay. Also I would like to listen, if you have anything you want to share too. :-) (e-mail, August 25, 1997)

Seiko, a Japanese female living in the United States, gave him advice to which he responded:

> Seiko, arigatoo for your advice to me (>-0) [wink] I will try to more open myself, and be more talkative. But, it takes time to change. Hey, you know what, something can always control my sentiments. Can you guess it? ... Yeah, right. It's music. (e-mail, November 25, 1997)

Here is Almon's on-line exchange with Ada, a Hong Kong Chinese living in Canada:

Almon: I have some photo scans of my childhood and fellowship, I don't know if you are interesting to take look ...

Ada: oh ... i'm interested ... . I'm curious to see how you look when you're young.

Almon: Ok, I hope you don't feel sick by look at my pic. Hehe ^^
Ada: I'm sure I won't … .
Almon: the pic is very blur … .
Ada: You are very happy and cute when you're small : >
Almon: Yeah, I like my smile when I was a kid. But, I don't know will I smile like that again … hee hee.
Ada: … you'll have a smile like the one you had when you're a baby … if you can be as simple as a baby … I mean it in a nice way … . Remember Jesus told us that we have to be like a child if we want to go to heaven.
Almon: Yes, I'm 100% agreeing what you're saying. That's what I always thinking, so I very like the people childlike outside, but also mature inside … . (chat, October 22, 1997)

In this dialogue, Almon's hesitations about presenting and recovering the image in his childhood picture are exemplified in several negative statements ("I don't know if you are interesting"; "I hope you don't feel sick"; "I don't know will I smile"). These are reversed into the affirmative in Ada's replies ("i'm interested"; "I'm curious"; "I'm sure"; "you'll have a smile like the one you had"). Ada transforms the negative modality[6] of Almon's statements into a categorical and positive mode of declaration ("you *are* very happy and cute when you're small", "you*'ll* have a smile like the one you had when you're baby … if you *can be* as simple as a baby" [italics added]). By using the genre of electronic verbal exchange as a friendly counseling session, Ada fits squarely into the role of the nurturing female that Almon helps create through the way he presents himself textually in the dialogue.

Furthermore, these postings sound both very personal and very much like a role play. The hedges and qualifiers ("you know what?"; "Can you guess it?"; "hehe"; "oh"; "hum"; "okay") and the ellipses that signal pauses and hesitation, as well as the emoticons of the genre (>-0), establish a distance between Almon the author and Almon the narrator—between the world that is spoken about and the world in which the speaking occurs (Goffman, 1981, p. 147).

The distancing of the author (the composer of a text) and narrator (a role or character in the text) also allows them to adopt a mutually supportive, nurturing role across gender lines in the context of intentional friendship over the Internet. This is seen, for example, in an online circular posting between Almon and Ada, in which the first- and second-person pronouns serve as the deictics for narrative roles that can be associated at will with any speaker:

---

[6] As discussed in Simpson (1993), "*modality* refers broadly to a speaker's attitude towards, or opinion about, the truth of a proposition expressed by a sentence. It also extends to their attitude towards the situation or event described by a sentence" (p. 47).

You are my friend and I hope you know that's true.
No matter what happens I will stand by you.
I'll be there for you whenever you need.
To lend you a hand to do a good deed.
So just call on me when you need me my friend.
I will always be there even to the end.
Forward this promise to all your friends to show your friendship and see
who sends it back. (chat, December 5, 1997)

In the following exchange, Almon consoles Ying after she has expressed frustration over her relationship with her boyfriend:

Ying, I hope you don't mind, I don't know how to say things to cheer up
others. But I really hope you will feel better. Don't be troubled by those
people who are not true to you ... . You're so kind and understanding ...
You'll surely find somebody who truly loves you ... . I give you my blessing! ^_^ (e-mail, January 13, 1998)

Here Almon brackets his own authorial authority through the use of hedges
("I hope"; "I don't know"; "I really hope"). It is as though the utterances that
follow the initial qualifiers do not belong to the speaker in the normal sense
but are an animation of a gendered narrative voice that he has adopted in
this situation (Goffman, 1975, pp. 508–550). In fact, one has the feeling that
Almon is crossing gender lines and is taking on the nurturing, supportive voice
usually associated with the female identity.

As a form of communicative exchange that relies heavily on writing, the
genre of electronic dialogue constitutes a highly visible medium for the scripting of social roles (Goffman, 1959). This textual mode of role scripting may
variously fall within existing gender stereotypes or move beyond them. Almon's expectation and discursive construction of his interlocutors as "nurturing females," and his own partial adoption of this gendered role, show how
normative gender relations can be both reproduced and destablized in textual
communication within an electronic friendship network.

The gender roles adopted by the interlocutors reinforce the impression that
they are developing textual or rhetorical identities that are related to but different from their biographical identities. Almon tries to explain this to one of
his pen pals:

I believe most people has two different "I", one is in the realistic world,
one is in the imaginational world. There is no definition to define which
"I" is the original "I", though they might have difference. Because they
both are connect together. The reality "I" is develop by the environment
changing. The imaginative "I" is develop by the heart growing. But, sometime they will influence each other. For example me, "I" am very silent,
shy, straight, dummy, serious, outdate, etc. in the realistic world. But, "I"

in the imaginational world is talkative, playful, prankish, naughty, open, sentimental, clever, sometime easy to get angry, etc. ... I don't like the "I" of reality. I'm trying to change myself.

But, I think you usually would see "I" in imaginational world because I'm very open to writing e-mail to people. ^-^ How about you?? Do you have two different "I"?? hee hee. (e-mail, January 13, 1998)

Discussion: Identity and Literacy

What does all this have to do with English learning? One could argue, following Gee's (1996, 2000) theory of discourse, that Almon is actively acquiring, and also actively reproducing, the many discourses and narrative roles in the English networked electronic environment—Madison Avenue advertising (e.g., *GeoCities* promotional talk), adolescent Internet talk (e.g., emoticons, oral forms of language), popular psychology (e.g., the need to share and care, to change oneself), and religious discourse (e.g., references to Jesus). One may wish that Almon would acquire a more "proper" or "standard" written English. Yet it is precisely this worldliness of English and the discourses that adhere to its global spread (Pennycook, 1998) that have provided Almon with the linguistic tools to enter into a multicultural world of Japanese pop culture, where he finds a community that understands and supports him.

The adoption of a variety of discourses and the distancing of one's narrative and biographical selves could be characterized as the discursive strategies that Almon used to construct his identity and relations with a transborder network of peers on the Internet—an identity that is not available to him in the social environment and institutions of his adopted country. Although these discourses and narrative roles are often constrained by the dominant discourses in society (Fairclough, 1992b, 2000; Gee, 1996), they may be appropriated and rearticulated in one's own voice for one's own purposes in the process of meaning making and literacy development. For Almon, the imaginative *I*, or the textual self, has in some instances blurred the boundaries of stereotypical gender roles and destablized national borders as the defining characteristic of his minority social identity. Electronic networks may hold the potential to bring the textual and the social into creative tension with each other and serve the decentering function of what Lanham (1993) describes as the stylistic play on transparent reality.

The English that Almon acquired through his Internet involvement is the global English of adolescent pop culture rather than the standard English taught in ESL classes. Whereas classroom English appeared to contribute to Almon's sense of exclusion or marginalization (his inability to speak like a native), which paradoxically contradicts the school's mandate to prepare students for the workplace and civic involvement, the English he controlled on the Internet enabled him to develop a sense of belonging and connectedness to a global English-speaking community. Almon was learning not only more

English but also more relevant and appropriate English for the World Wide Web community he sought to become part of.

Conclusion and Implications for L2 Literacy Development

This case study describes how an immigrant teenager discursively constructed his identity in English with a transborder group of peers on the Internet. It compels us as TESOL practitioners and researchers to reconsider the significance of identity formation in the process of learning to read and write in an L2. The development of L2 literacy in networked electronic media is shown here to involve a generative process of self- and other fashioning in a particular communicative group. I have used Kress's (2000) semiotic notion of design and Kramsch's (in press) identity concept of voice to examine the discursive construction of textual self in Web-based communication, in which identity is understood not simply as a process of socialization into existing social groups and discourse communities, but also as a reflective and generative process for constructing alternative social networks and subject positions through the textual media.

Reinventing a Model of Communication

Indeed, networked electronic communication may have reinstated the significance of role play and drama (Goffman, 1959) in the understanding of language and literacy development in TESOL (see also Kramsch, A'Ness, & Lam, in press). In *Communication as Culture*, Carey (1988) has contrasted the transmission view of communication, which is by far the more common in most industrialized countries, with the ritual view of communication, which is less prominent but reaches far back in history and may provide an important but overlooked perspective. The transmission view of communication is signified by the conduit metaphor of "imparting," "sending," "transmitting," or "giving information to others" (p. 15) and leads to a view of language as transparent, objective, analytical, and a tool or instrument for action. A ritual view of communication, on the other hand, stresses the common roots of the terms *communion, community,* and *communication*. It sees communication as directed toward the formation of social relations and shared beliefs, and sees language as a symbolic process for creating, maintaining, or transforming social reality. Carey illustrates the ritual view in regard to newspaper reading:

> A ritual view of communication will focus on a different range of problems in examining a newspaper. It will, for example, view reading a newspaper less as sending or gaining information and more as attending a mass, a situation in which nothing new is learned but in which a particular view of the world is portrayed and confirmed. News reading, and writing, is a ritual act and moreover a dramatic one. What is arrayed before the reader is not pure information but a portrayal of the contending forces in the world. Moreover, as readers make their way through the

paper, they engage in a continual shift of roles or of dramatic focus ... . The model here is not that of information acquisition, though such acquisition occurs, but of dramatic action in which the reader joins a world of contending forces as an observer at a play. (pp. 20–21)

To understand the development of L2 literacy in the new networked computer media requires a model of communication that looks at how learners' identities are created through a ritual of role play and dramatic acts. As shown in this case study and the studies of CMC (see Murray, this issue), a prominent aspect of Internet-based communication is the use of textual and other semiotic tools to create communal affiliations and construct social roles and narrative representations of self. Within Almon's electronic peer-group network, some of the discourses that he adopted carry the dominant codes of commercial interests and gender relations, but Almon also appropriated them as a means to create an alternative self and social affiliations.

Hence, as computer technology becomes increasingly integral to the practice of TESOL in the 21st century, we as TESOL professionals need to reinvent an age-old model of communication to help students critically reflect on the social roles and relations they are constructing through their rituals of dramatic acts on the Internet. For example, we can guide students to become more critically conscious of the types of discourses they are adopting as the they develop facility with these discourses (Delpit, 1995; Fairclough, 1992a; Hammond & Macken-Horarik, 1999). Although the computer has often been portrayed as a pragmatic and informational technology, it can also be recognized and used as a creative forum for the construction of new forms of identity and solidarity that promote positive changes in society. (See Hawisher & Selfe, 2000, for a number of case studies that show how Web-based multimedia are used to promote social critique and social change.) For instance, with Almon, who is already quite conscious of the power of language to create a textual self, a teacher could reflect on and analyze the discursive choices he made in constructing his narrative voice (Kramsch, 2000b) and how those choices replicated or altered dominant discourses and gender relations. The use of computer technology in TESOL calls for both an imaginative and a critical approach to the production and reception of texts in the electronic media that allows the textual to produce a new design for the social (Kress, 2000). It underscores the importance of constructing *possible worlds* (Bruner, 1986) and transformative pedagogies (e.g., Pennycook, 1999a, 1999b) in the teaching and development of literacy in TESOL whereby students develop strategies of articulation that question dominant discourses and power relations and produce alternative visions of reality.

A Critical Conception of Language and Literacy

This study also raises critical issues for language and cultural identity in an age of globalization, transborder relations, and the popularization of Internet-based communication. The changes that Almon experienced in relation to the English language—from a sense of alienation relative to native-born Americans in U.S. society to a growing confidence in his expressive ability with a transnational group of peers—illustrate the variable nature of the use of varieties of English for exclusion or inclusion. Together with the current rethinking of the concept of culture in anthropology and cultural theory (see, e.g., Atkinson, 1999), this study calls into question the conjuncture of language with national culture, which often happens in the teaching of second or foreign languages, and argues for the recognition and valuing of multiple linguistic and cultural affiliations.

Facilitated by electronic media, the English language is becoming increasingly tied to the cultural expression of various groups of native and nonnative speakers around the world (see Warschauer, this issue). Rather than signifying Englishness, Americanness, or other exclusive cultural ideologies, the language may well be used to represent Japanese popular culture or diasporic Chinese relations. All this calls for a critical assessment of how students' chosen target language may diverge from the standard language in the English classroom and how their choice of target is simultaneously an act of investment and desire and a reaction to their marginal position in the English-speaking classroom and society (Ibrahim, 1999). TESOL in today's global, multicultural world needs a broad and critical conception of language and literacy that is responsive to students' relations to multiple target languages and cultural communities, and that actively creates opportunities for the students to use their positioning in other target languages to challenge and expand their notion of that standard as they are learning it. In this way, the development of literacy or multiple literacies in ESL may become not only an opportunity for gaining access to the standard language or dominant discourses but also a creative process of self-formation in light of diverse practices and ways of representing human experiences.

Acknowledgments

I thank Claire Kramsch for her insights and mentorship throughout the evolution of this article. I am grateful to Mark Warschauer and two anonymous reviewers for their very helpful comments on earlier drafts of this article, and to the editor of *TESOL Quarterly* for her continual support. My deep appreciation goes to Almon, who generously shared his work and experiences with me during this study and beyond.

The Author

Wan Shun Eva Lam is a PhD candidate in the language, literacy, and culture division of the Graduate School of Education at the University of California,

Berkeley. Her areas of specialization are literacy theory, language and culture, and the role of bilingual development in L2 learning.

References

Atkinson, D. (1999). TESOL and culture. *TESOL Quarterly, 33*, 625–654.

Auerbach, E. R., & Paxton, D. (1997). "It's not the English thing": Bringing reading research into the ESL classroom. *TESOL Quarterly, 31*, 237–261.

Barton, D., Hamilton, M., & Ivanic, R. (2000). *Situated literacies: Reading and witing in context*. London: Routledge.

Baym, N. K. (1995). The emergence of community in computer-mediated communication. In S. G. Jones (Ed.), *Cybersociety: Computer-mediated communication and community* (pp. 138–163). Thousand Oaks, CA: Sage.

Baynham, M. (1995). *Literacy practices: Investigating literacy in social contexts*. London: Longman.

Bays, H. (1998, January). Framing and face in Internet exchanges: A socio-cognitive approach. *Linguistic Online, 1*. Retrieved June 6, 2000, from the World Wide Web: http://viadrina .euv-frankfurt-o.de/~wjournal/bays.htm

Bruner, J. (1986). *Actual minds, possible worlds*. Cambridge, MA: Harvard University Press.

Bruner, J. (1990). *Acts of meaning*. Cambridge, MA: Harvard University Press.

Carey, J. W. (1988). *Communication as culture: Essays on media and society*. London: Unwin Hyman.

Christie, F. (1999). Genre theory and ESL teaching: A systemic functional perspective. *TESOL Quarterly 33*, 759–763.

Cope, B., & Kalantzis, M. (Eds.). (1993). *The powers of literacy: A genre approach to teaching writing*. Pittsburgh, PA: University of Pittsburgh Press.

Cope, B., & Kalantzis, M. (Eds.). (2000). *Multiliteracies: Literacy learning and the design of social futures*. London: Routledge.

Cushman, E. (1998). *The struggle and the tools: Oral and literate strategies in an inner city community*. Albany: State University of New York Press.

Delpit, L. (1995). *Other people's children: Cultural conflict in the classroom*. New York: New Press.

Dyson, A. H. (1995). *Children out of bounds: The power of case studies in expanding visions of literacy development* (Technical Report No. 73). Berkeley: University of California, Center for the Study of Writing.

Erickson, F. (1986). Qualitative methods in research on teaching. In M. C. Wittrock (Ed.), *Handbook of research on teaching* (pp. 119–1161). New York: Macmillan.

Fairclough, N. (Ed.). (1992a). *Critical language awareness*. London: Longman.

Fairclough, N. (1992b). *Discourse and social change*. Oxford: Blackwell.

Fairclough, N. (2000). Multiliteracies and language: Orders of discourse and intertextuality. In B. Cope & M. Kalantzis (Eds.), *Multiliteracies: Literacy learning and the design of social futures* (pp. 162–181). London: Routledge.

Gee, J. P. (1996). *Social linguistics and literacies: Ideology in discourses*. London: Falmer Press.

Gee, J. P. (2000, February). *Literacies, identities, and discourses*. Paper presented at the Acquisition of Advanced Literacy Conference, Davis, CA.

Geotour. (1998). GeoCities. Retrieved February 7, 1998, from the World Wide Web: http:// www.geocities.com/main/help/geotour

Glaser, B. G., & Strauss, A. (1967). *The discovery of grounded theory: Strategies for qualitative research*. Chicago: Aldine.

Goffman, E. (1959). *The presentation of self in everyday life*. Garden City, NY: Doubleday.

Goffman, E. (1975). *Frame analysis*. Harmondsworth, England: Penguin Books.

Goffman, E. (1981). *Forms of talk*. Philadelphia: University of Pennsylvania Press.

Grabe, W. (1991). Current developments in second language reading research. *TESOL Quarterly, 25*, 375–405.

Hall, K. (1996). Cyberfeminism. In S. C. Herring (Ed.), *Computer-mediated communication: Linguistic, social and cross-cultural perspectives* (pp. 147–170). Amsterdam: Benjamins.

Hammond, J., & Macken-Horarik, M. (1999). Critical literacy: Challenges and questions for ESL classrooms. *TESOL Quarterly, 33*, 528–544.

Hasan, R., & William, G. (Eds.). (1996). *Literacy in society*. New York: Longman.

Hawisher, G. E., & Selfe, C. L. (2000). *Global literacies and the World-Wide Web*. London: Routledge.

Heath, S. B. (1983). *Ways with words*. Cambridge: Cambridge University Press.

Huckin, T. N. (1995). Critical discourse analysis. In T. Miller (Ed.), Functional approaches to written text: Classroom applications. *TESOL-France Journal, 2*(2), 95–111.

Hyon, S. (1996). Genre in three traditions: Implications for ESL. *TESOL Quarterly, 30*, 693–722.

Ibrahim, A. (1999). Becoming Black: Rap and hip-hop, race, gender, identity, and the politics of ESL learning. *TESOL Quarterly, 33*, 349–369.

Ivanic, R. (1998). *Writing and identity: The discoursal construction of identity in academic writing*. Amsterdam: Benjamins.

Kern, R. (1995). Redefining the boundaries of foreign language literacy. In C. Kramsch (Ed.), *Redefining the boundaries of language study* (pp. 61–98). Boston: Heinle & Heinle.

Kramsch, C. (1993). *Culture and context in language teaching*. Oxford: Oxford University Press.

Kramsch, C. (2000a, March). *Linguistic identities at the boundaries*. Paper presented at the American Association of Applied Linguistics Conference, Vancouver, Canada.

Kramsch, C. (2000b). Social discursive constructions of self in L2 learning. In J. Lantolf (Ed.), *Sociocultural theory and second language learning* (pp. 133–154). Oxford: Oxford University Press.

Kramsch, C. (in press). Identity, role, and voice in interdiscursive (mis)communication. In J. House & G. Kasper (Eds.), *Misunderstandings in social life*. London: Longman.

Kramsch, C., A'Ness, F., & Lam, W. S. E. (in press). Authenticity and authorship in the computer-mediated acquisition of L2 literacy. *Language Learning & Technology, 4*(2).

Kress, G. (1990). Critical discourse analysis. *Annual Review of Applied Linguistics, 11*, 84–99.

Kress, G. (2000). Design and transformation: New theories of meaning. In B. Cope & M. Kalantzis (Eds.), *Multiliteracies: Literacy learning and the design of social futures* (pp. 153–161). London: Routledge.

Lanham, R. (1993). *The electronic word: Democracy, technology, and the arts*. Chicago: University of Chicago Press.

Lee, J. W., & Schallert, D. L. (1997). The relative contribution of L2 proficiency and L1 reading ability to L2 reading performance: A test of the threshold hypothesis in an EFL context. *TESOL Quarterly, 31*, 713–740.

Luke, A. (1996). Genres of power? Literacy education and the production of capital. In R. Hasan & G. Williams (Eds.), *Literacy in society* (pp. 308–338). New York: Longman.

McKay, S. (1993). Examining L2 composition ideology: A look at literacy education. *Journal of Second Language Writing, 2*, 65–81.

McKay, S. (1996). Literacy and literacies. In S. McKay & N. Hornberger (Eds.), *Sociolinguistics and language teaching* (pp. 421–445). New York: Cambridge University Press.

McKay, S., & Wong, S. L. (1996). Multiple discourses, multiple identities: Investment and agency in second-language learning among Chinese adolescent immigrant students. *Harvard Educational Review, 66*, 577–608.

New London Group. (1996). A pedagogy of multiliteracies: Designing social futures. *Harvard Educational Review, 66*, 60–92.

O'Malley, J. M., & Chamot, A. U. (1990). *Learning strategies in second language acquisition*. New York: Cambridge University Press.

Peirce, B. N. (1995). Social identity, investment, and language learning. *TESOL Quarterly, 29*, 9–32.

Pennycook, A. (1996). TESOL and critical literacies: Modern, post, or neo? *TESOL Quarterly, 30*, 163–171.

Pennycook, A. (1998). *English and the discourses of colonialism*. London: Routledge.

Pennycook, A. (Ed.). (1999a). Critical approaches to TESOL [Special-topic issue]. *TESOL Quarterly, 33*(3).

Pennycook, A. (1999b). Introduction: Critical approaches to TESOL. *TESOL Quarterly, 33*, 329–348.

Pollack, A. (1996, August 12). Happy in the East (^-^) or smiling :-) in the West. *New York Times*, p. D5.

Poster, M. (1997). Cyberdemocracy: Internet and the public sphere. In D. Porter (Ed.), *Internet culture* (pp. 201–218). New York: Routledge.

Raimes, A. (1991). Out of the woods: Emerging traditions in the teaching of writing. *TESOL Quarterly, 25*, 407–431.

Ramanathan, V., & Atkinson, D. (1999). Ethnographic approaches and methods in L2 writing research: A critical guide and review. *Applied Linguistics, 20*, 44–70.

Scollon, R., & Scollon, S. (1981). *Narrative, literacy, and face in interethnic communication*. Norwood, NJ: Ablex.

Scribner, S., & Cole, M. (1981). *The psychology of literacy*. Cambridge, MA: Harvard University Press.

Simpson, P. (1993). *Language, ideology and point of view*. London: Routledge.

Stake, R. E. (1995). *The art of case study research*. Thousand Oaks, CA: Sage.

Street, B. (Ed.). (1993). *Cross-cultural approaches to literacy*. Cambridge: Cambridge University Press.

Sugimoto, T., & Levin, J. A. (2000). Multiple literacies and multimedia: a comparison of Japanese and American uses of the Internet. In G. E. Hawisher & C. L. Selfe (Eds.), *Global literacies and the World-Wide Web* (pp. 133–153). NewYork: Routledge.

Swales, J. M. (1990). *Genre analysis: English in academic and research settings*. New York: Cambridge University Press.

Tepper, M. (1997). Usenet communities and the cultural politics of information. In D. Porter (Ed.), *Internet culture* (pp. 39–54). New York: Routledge.

Threadgold, T. (1997). *Feminist poetics: Poiesis, performance, histories*. London: Routledge.

Turkle, S. (1995). *Life on the screen: Identity in the age of the Internet*. New York: Simon & Schuster.

Watson-Gegeo, K. A. (1988). Ethnography in ESL: Defining the essentials. *TESOL Quarterly, 22*, 575–592.

Weedon, C. (1997). *Feminist practice and poststructuralist theory* (2nd ed.). Cambridge, MA. Blackwell.

Werry, C. C. (1996). Linguistic and interactional features of Internet Relay Chat. In S. C. Herring (Ed.), *Computer-mediated communication: Linguistic, social and cross-cultural perspectives* (pp. 47–63). Amsterdam: Benjamins.

Zamel, V. (1997). Toward a model of transculturation. *TESOL Quarterly, 31*, 341–352.

Commentary Responses

Critical Review

L2 Literacy and the Design of the Self:
A Case Study of a Teenager Writing on the Internet

CATHERINE BEAVIS

DEAKIN UNIVERSITY, AUSTRALIA

Research and practice in literacy education increasingly has come to recognize the pervasiveness and centrality of technology and digital culture in the social and textual lives of young people in much of the world, and the changes wrought by technology to print based conceptions of literacy. Correspondingly, there is growing recognition of the need for literacy education to take account of links between globalization, digital culture, and identity, as well as to reflect multimodal forms of meaning making epitomized in ICT-based texts and spaces of the kind described in Wan Shun Eva Lam's (2000) research.

Literacy, Digital Culture, and Identity

Studies of young people's engagement with online digital worlds and the kinds of literate and social practices, friendships and communities they engage in there, focus on a variety of textual forms or genres, but have a number of common foci. These include (a) an awareness of the global context of digital culture, including commercial and marketing forces; (b) the implications of young people's engagement in digital culture for constructions of identity and community; (c) an interest in the fluidity of and the overlaps between on- and offline literacies, identities and communities; (d) a focus on digital texts or sites themselves as social and textual entities and as an embodiment of multimodal forms of literacy or literacy as "design" (Kress, 2000); and (e) the belief that much might be learnt for schooling from the kinds of informal learning that goes on in these sites "out-of-school." While research into digital culture is an emerging field approached from a range of disciplines, most studies of interest to literacy educators have a common view of literacy as multimodal and as social practice. That is, they view literacy as purposeful, socially situated, and intimately connected to identity, and they view the learner as actively engaged in meaning making.

The spread of information and communications technologies (ICTs) has become so far reaching that for most young people these ICTs seem to have become a seamless, almost naturalized part of life. Numerical measures become a kind of shorthand for demonstrating the degree to which ICT and digital culture have become an everyday part of young people's lives. Usage statistics, for example, show that 86% of Australian children ages 5 to 14 used a computer at home in 2003, and 71% of children in this same age range played computer games (Australian Bureau of Statistics, 2003). Ownership figures provide a different way of envisaging the scale of this saturation. A Neilsen report for 2004, for example, shows that more than 84% of 7 to 17 year old Australians owned a computer game console in that year (Australian Film, Television, and Radio School, 2006). A third perspective comes from figures for participation in online-game-playing communities, with the multiplayer game *World of Warcraft*, for example, having more than six million players worldwide in 2006 (Australian Film, Television, and Radio School, 2006). Sales figures for computer games are frequently cited as exceeding those for Hollywood's box office; in 2003 "the videogame industry made a reported [US] \$9.3 billion—more than Hollywood box office movies (\$8.1 billion)" (Steinkuehler, 2004, p. 521). While unevenly distributed, this global media culture is not limited to the affluent nations of the West. The United Nations *World Youth Report 2005* contains reference to "a global media-driven youth culture" growing also in the developing world, created through the combination of modern-day media, ICT, and global connectedness, and which is "powerfully influencing the lives of young people on a global scale" (United Nations, 2005, p. 81).

The scale of this involvement, and the kinds of activities and immersion it implies, make it essential for literacy researchers and those concerned with the lives and education of young people to attend to what is happening in spaces such as these. As Nixon (2003) noted,

> Global popular media culture, including online culture, has become integrally bound up with children's and teenager's affiliations, identities and pleasures. Their participation in global media culture shapes the ways they communicate and the kinds of social identities they take on. It informs how they present themselves to others and their understandings about the social groups and communities to which they might conceivably belong. This kind of social participation is integrally bound up with the ways in

which symbolic meanings are made, negotiated, and contested, and is therefore of central interest to literacy research. (p. 407)

My own research has centered on computer games as emergent cultural forms and as exemplars of the changing nature of texts and literacy, on young people's engagement with them, and on what educators might learn from studying young people's games and game playing. My interest began with stand-alone, single player games and moved on to multiplayer and massively multiplayer games, as well as Local Area Network (LAN) game play in Internet cafés. I have also been interested in exploring the nature of games as text, the kinds of interactions and reading practices involved in playing games, the fascination of these textual worlds, and the kinds of experience and expectations about texts and reading that might be generated through playing games like these (Beavis, 1997, 2002; Beavis, Nixon, & Atkinson, 2005).

It quickly became apparent that game play was not just about literacy, text, and play, but was also situated, highly social, and linked to the negotiation and construction of identity. This is the case even with stand-alone games, but much more so with multiplayer, online games. Participation in game play and related sites involves the representation of self, interpretation of others, the formation and/or continuation of relationships on- and offline, participation in a community, negotiation around rules and ethics, and much more (Beavis, 2004; Beavis & Charles, 2005). Games are also seen as sites of learning, providing models of engagement from which educators can learn. As "networked semiotic domains" (Gee, 2003), games actively involve players in learning as they become increasingly expert, with principles of learning built into the games, which (should) also underline good teaching and educational resources (Gee, 2003; Shaffer, Squire, Halverson, & Gee, 2005). The notion of flow (Csikszentmihalyi, 2002) is often adduced to describe the sense of effortlessness brought about by deep immersion in the game, as epitomizing links between learning and pleasure when concentration is profound. As everyday "arenas of action" (Hutchby & Moran-Ellis, 2001, p. 2), games operate as a site for performativity, and the development and display of competence among one's peers. Like other forms of popular culture (cf. Dyson, 1997), computer games become a resource for the construction and negotiation of identity as well as for the achievement of a range of literacy and social practices (Steinkuehler, 2004; Gee, 2003; Thomas, 2005; Beavis & Charles, 2005, in press).

L2 Literacy and the Design of Self

Lam's (2000) research focuses on a different genre of global media culture: the fan home page or Web site. Her analysis, however, foregrounds similar concerns and qualities, and is framed by consistent theoretical positionings. Her study provides a detailed and closely textured account of the ways in which the construction and maintenance of a fan Web site devoted to the Japanese pop (J-pop) star Ryoko provides a context for its creator, Almon. The young Chinese American immigrant designs the site to create an authoritative and satisfying identity online where he is not handicapped by his lack of English-language fluency. On the contrary, he is able to use this site to present a version of himself as a knowledgeable insider, and to benefit from the friendship and advice of other Ryoko and J-pop fans who visit his home page. Lam's paper maps intimate links between identity, context, community, and literacy development—in a second language, in this instance—and shows how the opportunities and affordances offered by ICT and popular culture allow for the construction of a social space in which Almon can take risks, form relationships, strengthen his English, relocate himself as central rather than marginal, and take up a position of authority and expertise.

Published in 2000, Lam's study has become an important reference point for other research exploring the ways in which young people use online spaces to explore, play, interact, and construct versions of selves, and the greater richness and facility online spaces offer to young people in contrast with narrower, school-based versions of literacy and identity (e.g., Black, 2005). Studies such as Lam's (2000) provide insights into the often invisible literacy practices and expertise developed by young people in online and other informal learning situations (particularly, young people seen elsewhere as "failing"). Lam's studies also provide an opportunity for literacy educators to consider both characteristics of the context that seem to be facilitating this development (e.g., social context, community, purposefulness, intertextuality, multimodal literacies, and distributed learning) and the ways in which schools might learn from these.

The three questions at the heart of Lam's research remain central to studies concerned with literacy, young people, and digital media. While Lam's concern is with second language learners, her questions have broader ramifications for literacy and learning more generally:

- How do communities on the Internet act as contexts for L2 literacy use and development?
- What kinds of textual forms and cultural discourses are used and developed in these literacy practices?
- How are learners' identities in the L2 constructed through networked computer media? (p. 457)

Lam's (2000) paper begins with an outline of the theoretical framework for the research it reports. In calling on new literacy and poststructuralist perspectives to theorize links between literacy and identity in a second language context, Lam has broken away from more traditional L2 paradigms. The core concepts Lam identified are (a) *identity*, "as described in L2 literacy research," (b) *voice*, "the construction of roles and identities through discursive choices," (c) *design*, "the use of representational resources to construct meaning" and

(d) *self* "as a discursive formation" (p. 458). The section titled "Literacy in contexts" brings together New Literacy Studies perspectives on language as social practice, which underline "the contextual nature of reading and writing and the way literacy is intimately bound up with particular sociocultural contexts, institutions and social institutions (p. 458)" with two closely related views of discourse: sociolinguistic and poststructuralist. Gee's (2000) widely used account of (capital D) Discourse as "distinctive ways of 'being and doing' that allow people to enact and/or recognize a specific and socially situated identity" (p. 2, as cited in Lam, 2000, p. 459) is set against and contextualized within poststructuralist notions of discourse and identity as outlined by Weedon (1997) and others, to allow the exploration of interrelationships between discourse and identity, where identity is seen as social and the learner is situated within the midst of competing and conflicting discourses.

In such a context, Lam (2000) argued, "identity is inherently unstable, and social identity, though constituted and governed by prevailing practices, is capable of resistance and innovations produced out of the clash between contradictory and competing practices" (p. 459). This juxtaposition of new literacies studies and discourse theories is crucial in establishing the connections the research goes on to make between language and identity.

This section also introduced the concept of "voice," which is defined as "the process by which people create, maintain, or transform institutional roles and identities through the discursive choices they make" (Lam, 2000, p. 460). This contrasts with the essentialist version of "voice," which characterizes early "process writing" theory and pedagogy. A key concept in Lam's research is "design," which draws on Kress' (2000) social semiotic theory. Kress defined design as "the transformative use of available representational resources in the production of new meaning" (p. 460). The section closes with an account of the importance and characteristics of computer-mediated or online communication (CMC) as a research site for exploring literacy, community, and identity, and introduces identity as textually constructed in contexts such as these.

Design is a crucial concept in contemporary understandings of multimodal literacies, and in research that looks at the ways in which young people interact with and use the resources and opportunities offered by digital culture. It is central to expanded definitions of literacy that reflect the move from word to image, from page to screen, as the dominant media form. "Design" refers both to the "multiple modalities" and affordances of contemporary media and forms of literacy, and to the active use people make of the semiotic resources available to them in new ways, to create new meanings—including textual constructions and representations of self. As Lam (2000) described it, design is "transformative and innovative" (p. 461) and "not only a matter of deploying existing representational resources according to conventions, but also a dynamic process of adopting and reshaping existing resources in different measures to create new meanings and ways of representing reality" (p. 461).

The use of "design," in conjunction with sociolinguistic and poststructural notions of discourse, provides a powerful lens for exploring relations between language/semiotic resources and identity, and has continued to provide one of the most useful theoretical frameworks for researching young people's engagement with online media and digital literacies.

Although the use of ethnographic methodologies in literacy research has been controversial, due to accusations of relatively short time spent with those researched, a lack of ethnographic training and principles, and the collection of a limited range of data (cf. Tobin, 2005), in this instance, none of these criticisms hold. Lam (2000) has gathered a substantial and varied range of data over an extended period. Her data includes (mother tongue) interviews, participant observation, and textual documentation such as log files from online chat, e-mails, and field notes from direct observation of Almon on the computer as he showed Lam how to use various programs, and showed her files and documents he had stored. She introduced and described Almon, and noted the dramatic changes she encountered in his sense of self and written English fluency as a consequence of extended time spent online. To analyze the data, she used inductive thematic analysis, interactional analysis, and critical discourse analysis, respectively, to identify themes in the data, speaking roles and the ways "language as discourse ... was involved in the production, maintenance, and transformation of social relations and identities" (p. 466). Critical discourse analysis is specifically suited to this end, and enables a close-grained study of intersections between language, discourse, and identity.

Lam (2000) carefully described the intertextual and multilayered nature of Almon's home page, *Mr. Children's Ryoko Page*. To build his knowledge and expertise, Almon immersed himself in a wide range of popular genre: J-pop music and magazines, television programs and Web sites, drawing on knowledge of the language drawn from Japanese language classes and shopping in a nearby Japanese district. The site itself includes segmented screens, animations, sound, links, a guest book, and much more. Almon's online presence and identity has been established in dynamic ways within this complex mix. His use of language and the way he positions himself in relation to others who might visit his home page signals his authority, which is also supported by his evident deep knowledge of the J-pop phenomenon and exemplified by comprehensive hyperlinks and lists of related sites. The combination of this extensive familiarity with J-pop, invitations and directions issued to those who visit his site (other J-pop fans), and the opportunity for interaction built in through e-mail and ICQ exemplify the ways in which community and identity are both textually established and maintained. Through a detailed analysis of Almon's exchanges with sympathetic visitors to the site, Lam showed Almon's developing confidence and presentation of self. Already using language in ways that signal tentativeness and openness, Almon's exchanges (with supportive female visitors, particularly) build relationships and strengthen his written language through reciprocal exchange, at the same time as increasingly positioning him as agential and authoritative rather than marginal and alien to mainstream American community, as he had felt himself to be at the start of the study.

Lam (2000) has drawn a number of conclusions and implications from her study. Throughout it, language is seen as integrally involved in representation and the production of identity. She underlined the role of identity as "a reflective and generative process for constructing alternative social networks and subject positions through textual media" (p. 476) and argued for a view of communication that emphasizes "the formation of social relations and shared beliefs" (p. 477). Bringing together the focus on language, popular culture, identity and community, she pointed to the role of the Internet as a space which enables "the use of textual and other semiotic tools to create communal affiliations, construct social roles and narrative representations of self" (p. 477). She identified challenges presented to ways of thinking about constructions of English, language and cultural identity raised by globalization and technology, and by the kinds of English taught in schools that may be at odds with the kind of language ESL students desire. While her study is located within the area of Teaching English to Speakers of Other Languages (TESOL), it has implications well beyond this field with respect to studying literacy, identity, digital culture, education, and community.

The Contribution of Lam's Study to Researching Young People, Literacy, and New Media

Lam's (2000) three organizing questions—(a) how communities act as contexts for literacy use and development, (b) the kinds of textual forms and cultural discourses used and developed in these literacy practices, and (c) the ways in which identities are constructed through ICT—provide an ongoing frame of reference for researching young people's engagement with popular culture and the implications of this engagement for education and schools. While the genre at the center of Lam's study is the fan home page or Web site, her questions relate directly to other forms of digital culture and what educators can learn from them, including computer games. Indeed, computer games would seem to be sites par excellence for exploring links between text, identity, game play, literacy and community, for understanding more about the nature of multi-modal texts and literacies, about globalization and youth culture, and about flows and continuities between on- and offline worlds.

Information about matters such as these is crucial. The growth of the networked society and the spread of information and communications technology have brought significant challenges to schools and changes to traditional literacy. At a time when education departments and bureaucracies are struggling to respond to a globalized, networked society, and to imagine and implement curriculum that will prepare young people to be "tech savvy," literate, and informed citizens of present and future societies, the careful study of online some hypothetically comprehensive picture of the whole, issues concerning the extent of the researcher's knowledge of the site are well-bounded because her study is on Almon's usage primarily and not on fansite practices in general.

There remain one or two methodological issues that contemporary research on online postings and communities might address differently, and they center around ethics: (a) whether ethical approval from the "nonpresent" participants (Almon's "online pen pals") in circumstances such as these was sought or deemed necessary, and (b) the role and positioning of the person undertaking the research. Opinion is divided about whether online communications are already "published" and thus require no further ethical clearance because public disclosure has already occurred, or whether the citation of online exchanges violates expectations of privacy where at least one of the participants has not given permission for this to happen. Linked to this is the question of the visibility and positioning of the researcher in relation to the research. Poststructuralist conventions would normally suggest a more overt discussion of this relationship and positioning, and of the power dynamics likely to obtain between the researcher and those researched. In many respects, however, these questions arise from seeing the study through the lens of online rather than traditional ethnography, and are largely addressed by viewing Lam's (2000) work as primarily an ethnography in the physical world. Within this paradigm, her careful delineation of her role as an ethnographer, her descriptions of her interactions with Almon, and the ways in which her observations and analysis are based on specific textual exchanges largely address issues such as these.

Issues of Space and Place

A related area that has come to be of increasing interest and importance in research into literacy and cybercultures concerns the theorization of space and place, and a view of space as socially produced. Questions of place and space are particularly pertinent in research around cybercultures and online participation and interactions. In particular, researchers are seeking to understand the fluidity between on- and offline sites and literacies, and the uses people make of them (e.g., Bell, 2001; Steinkuehler, Black, & Clinton, 2005; Leander & Sheehy, 2005). Lam's study (2000) shows how, for Almon, the online space of the fansite provides the opportunity to build identity, relationships, and community that arise from and link back to his existence in the physical world. The resources he collates come from both physical and "virtual" worlds, and it is impossible to quarantine the online presence or identity he constructs from Almon in the offline world. She showed the socially constructed nature of *Mr. Children's Ryoko Page*, which is brought to life not just by the music, links, and animation Almon has provided, but also by Almon's words and presence there, as well as those of his "pen pals" and other visitors. It is significant that it is in the online spaces of his virtual world that Almon builds confidence and English fluency through written exchange. This has important ramifications for his "real"-world English literacy, identity, and social positioning. Recognition of the constructed nature of social space, and of the close and mutually informing interrelationships between "real" and "virtual" spaces are central features of research into young people's uses of digital culture and the Internet. They are also central to understanding the kinds of literacies and literacy communities that make up the contemporary world.

The Close-Grained Study of Actual Use

If schools and educators are to learn about the nature of young people's experiences of and with text, literacy, and identity in online contexts and communities, and learn from informal online learning environments such as the one Lam (2000) described, then close studies of actual use are essential. The attention paid to the possibilities and affordances of digital media contains much promise for education—particularly with respect to the kinds of learning online texts and sites facilitate—and the multimodal forms of meaning making they present. It is essential, however, that research focuses not just on the sites or the technology, but also on the practices, understandings, and identities they invite as well as the dynamic relationship between these. We need to attend to not only the texts and spaces of digital media, but also to the ways people use them. We must also focus on the interplay between these texts, technologies, and communities and the ways people live their lives. Almon's use of his fansite is purposeful and socially situated, arises directly out of his own interests, and is powerfully linked to his own agendas and production of identity.

Multimodality and Design

Lam's (2000) description of *Mr. Children's Ryoko Page* conveys a strong sense of the intertextual and multimodal nature of the site. As with studies of use, specific examples of the ways in which multiple texts and textual forms are constructed and interact in digital culture sites such as these provide much needed exemplars of the ways in which different elements combine, and with what effect and power. Such exemplars provide real-world information both about the ways in which multiple textual forms and references interlink in most popular culture and about the kinds of choices and expertise Almon has exercised in the creation of his page.

Concluding Comments

Lam's (2000) study has become a classic of its kind. I have not addressed its implications for second language learning, nor have I addressed the implications of the spread of ICT together with global population and commercial flows for the changing nature of English as an international language. I have also refrained from discussing the implications for the construction of gendered identities and the representation of self in online contexts, as well as

A Commentary on "L2 Literacy and the Design of Self": Electronic Representation and Social Networking

RICHARD P. DURÁN

UNIVERSITY OF CALIFORNIA, SANTA BARBARA, USA

Introduction

Research papers come to be in historical contexts that enrich their interpretation over time. Wan Lam's (2000) *TESOL Journal* paper "L2 Literacy and the Design of the Self: A Case Study of a Teenager Writing on the Internet" exemplifies this phenomenon. The paper is a rich theoretical and case study account of how new literacies approaches help us better frame and understand the way in which meaningful human communication creates social contexts for the projection of identity and support for second language (L2 language) development, by drawing on the representational possibilities and potential of electronic media and exchanges.

The year 2000 lies now a number of years behind us, and in hindsight, we can draw on this paper to advance some challenges that have emerged since that time that support the paper's insights regarding the projection of meaning via information communication technologies (ICT), but also to advance challenges regarding its early views on *what* new literacies are being acquired and *what consequences* these new literacies have for *what kinds* of L2 usage and literacy practices. While L2 learners are the focus of discussion, the issues cited can be generalized to Internet users at large, and to the new literacies enabled by the Internet. Developments in Internet use since 2000 via social networks relying on Internet portals such as MySpace, Facebook, and others make clear now that "sense of self" as constructed in personal Web pages, blogs, podcast forums, and other forms of social exchange systems in these networks has tremendous, seemingly unbounded possibilities. These personal Internet portals for individuals and groups become windows into cultural and social worlds that can become forums for communication and learning of any sort or end pursued by their makers and participants within, the policy and practical constraints of their host services (if they exist). With these thoughts as a prologue, I turn to Lam's (2000) paper.

Synopsis of the Paper and Further Elaborations

The key question investigated in the paper is how do communities on the Internet act as contexts for L2 literacy use and development? The paper appears in the *TESOL* journal, a prominent research journal for researchers and practitioners in the field of instruction of English to speakers of other languages. The *TESOL* organization itself has a long history and the organization and the *TESOL* flagship journal is widely respected for its leadership in coverage of current developments in the field of second language learning. Over the past 30 or so years, the organization and journal have increasingly come to serve as a medium for researchers and practitioners pursuing *communicative approaches* to second language learning (Savignon, 1997), and *TESOL's* publication of Lam's (2000) paper is significant in that it marks concern for the broader social dimensions of L2 learning that can be stimulated by Internet social communities.

Stepping back just a bit, it is helpful to mention some of the qualities of the communicative approaches to L2 learning. The approaches have as their basis that learning to use a second language proficiently is not well taught by focusing solely on the isolated learning of the grammatical and structural features of a language associated with control of the basic phonological, morphological, and sentence syntax features of a language. Beyond hearing and understanding words and connections among words in isolated contexts, learners need to experience and acquire competencies as participants in the social and pragmatic situations that accompany appropriate L2 language form and structure as norms for action and interaction. Included in this broader set of competencies are the ability to understand how utterances and sentences come to be connected in meaning making at the discourse level and to performing purposeful communicative acts in a setting and with participants with distinguishable social and cultural characteristics that affect how to communicate and how to interpret communications. Language learning and acquisition are social developmental processes as much or more than basic intrapsychological processes. Learning and acquiring L2 competencies requires becoming a person with identities that can exercise agency in real contexts with other cultural and social beings.

The Lam (2000) article presumes the foregoing sorts of views and introduces further concepts for theorizing communicative development in L2 drawing on classical sociolinguistic/ethnomethodogical and more recent *new literacies* approaches to explore how ICT enables opportunities for L2 learning. The former approach is prominent in the attention the paper gives to work by Erving Goffman (1959, 1974, 1981) and his views on the *presentation of self* and dramaturgical action. The basic ideas drawn from Goffman are that language users monitor how they interact and communicate with others so that users as social beings can evaluate whether their messages and identity are being understood as intended. Persons in everyday communication monitor the uptake of their utterances and actions in social and cultural settings and make adjustments in how they interact to pursue their intended goals in communication and collaboration with participants. Goffman viewed interaction as fundamentally a *drama* where participants seek to express and manage projection of their identity by modulating their appearance, gesture, and language *in situ* from moment-to-moment.

Citing Kramtsch (in press, as cited in Lam, 2000) and Kress (2000), Lam (2000) likewise appeals to the idea that language users (and language learners, in particular) *design* their intended self-identity through the *voices* instantiated by the roles they adopt in relation to other interlocutors, the discourse stances and language embodying these voices, and the social characteristics these voices seek to project from the perspective of a speaker/writer. Note that this theoretical perspective opens up questions about whether the projection of an intended self is the same as a self that is interpreted by other communicative participants. These questions become more complex when the intended self-projected by a language user draws on designs for self that emulate other selves who are projections of popular culture persona—more on this in the following section.

With the foregoing as background, Lam (2000) then argued that the emergence of the Internet as an interactive social medium creates opportunities for L2 learners to acquire and use new ICT literacies permitting expression of self-identity in multimedia rich ways in an instrumental manner supporting ever increasing L2 literacy acquisition. The author stated,

> Literacy learning is understood as a process by which the individual is socialized for group membership in specific literate communities and, in turn, participates in shaping the social practices of these communities. Accordingly, a central construct is the language user's *identity*, for in practicing any form of literacy, the user is at the same time enacting a particular social role and membership in a particular group. (p. 459)

This statement by Lam problemetizes the term literacy and invites further theoretical unpacking. What does literacy mean? While the term literacy or literacies is not explicitly defined by Lam, I will here presume for theoretical purposes that the term is not restricted to competence in reading and writing, but more generally refers to the full range of *semiotic capacities* of humans to represent and interpret cultural and social meanings in terms of symbolic actions, extending but not limited to use of natural language, gesture and motoric functioning, dress and appearance management, and creating and use of material artifacts associated with cultural and social experience. While this view of literacy is broad, and can indeed capture just about every facet and notion of human awareness and projection of identity, it resonates quite closely with a cultural-historical (or Vygotskian allied) perspective that holds that human mediation (or cognitive-social representation) and systems of mediation constitute what we mean by literacy and literacies (see, e.g., accounts of symbolic mediation by Vygotsky, 1978, and his interpreters, e.g., Cole, 1996; Wertsch, 1985). From this perspective, our very consciousness in the moment-to-moment (including how we project ourselves) derives from how we *read* our senses in the moment, interpret the social and physical surround, and how we interpret the goals and purposes of the moment read from the perspectives of ourselves and others in the surround.

Investigators such as Gee (2000, as cited by Lam, 2000), hold a similar perspective and also call attention to the notion of *Discourses* (with a capital *D*) to refer to the ways in which complex semiotic (or mediational systems) come to form systems of socially distributed practices and forms of representation that assert social and cultural group affiliation and expression of identity. The point here is that when persons assert affiliation, contrast, or disaffiliation with social and cultural groups and their stances, they afford their interlocutors the opportunity to take up their self-identities in particular ways based on the interpretation of these stances as they interact.

So what does all this have to do with learning of an L2 by participation in social spaces on the Internet? Lam's (2000) paper investigates how the medium of Internet chat communities provides important affordances for the development of L2 competencies by documenting a 6-month case study of Almon, a 17-year-old immigrant from Hong Kong newly residing in the United States and just completing high school there. Lam's initial interviews with Almon revealed that he had experienced considerable frustration in acquiring English and felt that he suffered social discrimination because of being stigmatized as an ESL student. Almon stated, "English is my biggest problem … It's like this place isn't my world, I don't belong here. Its going to be very hard for me to develop my career here" (Lam, 2000, p. 467). This quote from Almon reinforces Lam's point that it is essential to understand the relationship between L2 competence and identity. Specifically, it calls attention to the notion that being *someone* occurs in *someone's world* where thinking, acting, and using language allow participation and agency in that world. Almon does not want to be in a place where his agency and identity are not validated given his perceptions of his capacities. Further, he expresses concern that there are undesirable limitations on who he can become in the future.

Almon's response to his situation is to create a personal Web site hosted on the GeoCities Internet service in a cyberspace subcommunity region known as *Tokyo*. Tokyo is described on GeoCities as pertaining to *Anime and all things Asian* (Lam, 2000, p. 469). Lam overviewed how Almon went on to create a Web page centered on appreciation of a very well-known Japanese female singer *Ryoku Hirosue* who is affiliated with what is known as "J-pop," a popular culture movement/community based in Japan, but recognized internationally. Interestingly, while Almon's Web page became a medium for practicing and acquiring English, development of the page and its contents relied not just on English, but also on Almon's familiarity with kanji (Chinese characters used to represent Japanese), and Japanese popular cultural images and music as a medium for construction of his Internet identity. Almon titled his home page "Mr. Children's Ryoku Page" after a well-known J-pop music group known as Mr. Children. Almon, of course, is not Mr. Children in the usual way we think of how a name typically inscribes a unique physical person or a group.

Almon's fictive portrayal as the voice of the group Mr. Children has a nice fit with Goffman's (1974) notion of dramaturgical projection of self (Lam, 2000). When Mr. Children speaks in the words and images on Almon's Web site, who is speaking? Goffman proposed that in our everyday dramaturgical take up of communication we learn to interpret impersonation or animation as a fundamental format for communication of identity. Not only are we impersonating or animating ourselves as we interact, there are times and ways that we can simultaneously impersonate or animate others. Elaborating the dramaturgical analogy further, consider for example, how we can imagine the characters in a play as participants in the lived world of the play in another time and setting, while being copresent in the moment in a theater where participants are aware of their identities as audience and actors. Both kinds of worlds are coexisting in time and space, and both are dramas. Likewise, Almon has constructed a world where his voice is present as the author of the Web site and a communicator present in it, while it is also present as a communicator of the world as seen by the musical group Mr. Children.

Almon's Web site featured a written introduction, an animated cartoon of Ryoko next to her name in kanji, and a song of hers playing in the background (Lam, 2000). Other hot links on the left side of the home page connect to a biography of Ryoko, photos of her, and links to Ryoko musical clips. The Web site becomes not only a medium and window for communication with Mr. Children, and about Ryoko and J-pop culture, it also becomes a medium and window for communication with Almon and his possible selves.

Lam (2000) studied the exchanges in English Almon had with visitors to his Web site, with particular attention to how Almon began to use selected features of English. She paid particular attention to Almon's use of pronouns and idiomatic expressions to manifest his emerging, enhanced fluency in English, and identity as a competent English-speaking member of the J-pop community.

called attention to how Almon's usage of the term *you* advances his agency as an English speaker by voicing his authority as a communicator in English who has something of value to share regarding the J-pop community. This is a very good example to elaborate further, because in addition to what Lam noted, the expression's use of the term *here* is another deictic usage that builds on new literacies skills that rely on indexicality—the expectation that words and images can point to other words and images, and associated worldviews. What is the *here* pointing to in each of the foregoing utterances? At the level of having literacy on Internet usage, I believe that *here* is referring to a hot link (URL or pointer to a URL) to access targeted information and that this reference and usage make sense to persons who know how inscriptions on Web pages point to new information of value, and that there are ways to connect with a source Web site via appropriate cursor screen manipulations and a "select" action to activate an online connection. Almon's identity and those of his visitors have many voices and stances. We should not forget that Almon and his visitors also possess literacies tied to knowing how to use the Internet and these literacies are interacting deeply with other forms of identity and enablement of identity, and their related literacies.

The Lam (2000) paper ends with the suggestion that networked computer media represent a new and important tool to promote L2 acquisition in a global context and for the study of literacy acquisition among immigrants. The main point in her paper is that the Internet and Internet communities require building a better paradigm for understanding the semiotic possibilities of computer-based technology as a resource in identity development, and further, because of her study, that we need to formulate more adequately how the acquisition of L2 varieties might be affected. In particular, she noted that received views of what constitutes standard English in classrooms may not be consistent with the registers and varieties of English that L2 learners might develop fluency in through the medium of Internet social, cross-cultural communications.

It is valuable for readers to recognize that no one paper can capture the richness of an ongoing program of research, nor all the possible programs that might ensue from a seminal contributions. Lam's (2000) paper is seminal, and it emerged as she completed her PhD, and as such, while it is outside the bounds of this chapter, it is nonetheless useful to ask readers to seek out and understand where this work has gone (e.g., see Lam 2007). Some but not all of the concerns I will raise have been captured in Lam's more recent work and this work has gone far in recognizing and going beyond the changes in social uses of the Internet described at the start. That stated I wish to mention some of the practical issues that will prove problematic in realizing the idea that L2 learners use of the Internet for self-expression will easily lead to acquisition of certain kinds of competencies in L2 of the sort valued in schools as institutions, and perhaps in other institutions for employment. Finally, I will turn to some questions tied to the complexities of understanding how new literacies might interface with commodification of the Internet.

Academic Language Challenges Introduced by the Paper

Lam's (2000) paper is not intended to give an overview of how command of registers of English tied to in situ school communication might be systematically enhanced through Internet usage of the sort she describes. The real, everyday world of L2 learners in schools presents pragmatic, linguistic challenges that need characterization in their own right. Adamson (1993), among others, foresaw more than a decade ago the basic need to connect the identity development of L2 learners with their development of competence in the academic tasks they were asked to do in classrooms. His work is seminal in calling attention to how then current sociolinguistic studies of communicative competence and cognitive science needed to inform instructional practices for ESL students. He called attention to the importance of L2 students understanding the demands of academic task starting with appreciation of how tasks connected or did not connect with personal meaning making given students' unique cultural and linguistic backgrounds.

Researchers in the field of computer assisted language learning (see, e.g., papers published in *Language Learning and Technology*) have begun to explore the many ways that access to technology and use of technology can support L2 learners of specific L2 language structures and functions associated with academic registers of L2. Warschauer (2002), among the most prominent of these contributors, reminded us incessantly of the centrality of personal meaning making as the font for learning new language skills via technology. Yet it is fair to state that schools and teachers are reluctant to let go of their received views of literacies learned in the tradition of pen-and-paper, textbook instruction, particularly given the stranglehold of systems of curriculum standards and assessments geared to standards that have significant monetary and policy implications for schools. This stranglehold is particularly acute in the case of L2 learners, particularly immigrants from low-income and refugee backgrounds who, when classified as ELL, are a key target group for meeting *Adequate Yearly Progress* achievement test performance criteria in the United States, under the *No Child Left Behind* legislation. Following on Lam's (2000) paper, the closest rapprochement might appear to be for software developers and Internet portal designers to create social opportunities for Internet exchanges to embed use of activities resonating systematically with English language development standards and English language arts standards held by states and educational jurisdictions. But this may be for naught, given that most statements of English language arts standards are represented by rhetoric devoid of sense making in context for real communicative purposes as a central component. But also, surely, the results of research by Lam and others in the broader CALL community can find ways to make such a bridge. This ongoing area needs research attention.

The Internet Commodification Challenge

The allure of labeling new forms of representation and interaction cited by Lam (2000) as new literacies is unmistakable as a contemporary response to the rapid interconnection and sharing of information made possible by the Internet and ICT at large. The historical emergence of new forms of inscription via electronic means (Leu, Kinzer, Coiro, & Cammack, 2004) has amplified mutual awareness of peoples and identities on a global scale. This development has been characterized as multiplicative (op. cit.), as access to the Internet grows and as new electronic communities and social identities propagate and colonize hyperspace with real consequential impact on other forms of material and symbolic cultural, institutional, and social realities.

In proposing a dramaturgical view of literacy practices bound to expression and negotiation of self-identities, and agency, Lam's (2000) paper invites the deeper point that the dramaturgical projection of identity is central to all forms of literacy as meaning and sense making, and that these notions of identity projection and sense making are not just about communicating in language. They abound electronically in creating and navigating the images and media inscribed in Internet social Web sites. Lam's paper, closed with her stating the hope that development of multiple literacies by ESL learners via ICT will go beyond the values of purveyors of dominant discourses associated with reinforcing the notion of standard varieties of an L2 as the only varieties worth learning. One can sense, in addition, however, that there are other big D (Discourse) communities influencing the expression of self-identity and multiple literacies in a potentially hegemonic manner. The medium of social Web pages, supported by purveyors such as MySpace and Facebook, to name just two cyber-community outposts, is coming increasingly under the influence of their own and their inhabitant's commercial interests. Almon's social Web pages with their attention to popular culture connected to commercial interests alert researchers to these connections and how they might influence the expression of self-identity among some inhabitants of social Web pages.

Recently, MySpace began allowing its inhabitants to market and sell downloads of their music on social Web pages (Technology Review, 2006). The complication, of course, is that Internet sharing of sociocultural stances and identities on social Web pages can move from relatively cost-free casual exchanges of information to deeper cost intensive exchanges among social Web site participants. More needs to be understood about this potential and the extent to which social Internet participants will be attracted to buying and selling artifacts attesting to identities via purchases made of artifacts on the Internet. This is already happening of course, but the ways in which these dynamics will continue to evolve remains an unknown.

Yet, the foregoing comment rings somewhat off key if it is taken to mean that Internet users are totally unaware of the commodification of the Internet and some of its associated new literacies. Internet users have also increasing developed media literacy wiseness. They have become accustomed to the multivocality of media in popular culture and the new literacies properties of the Internet. I close with the transcript of a current video commercial that illustrates the awareness of this on the part of commercial interests who then structure their messages to consumers to play on their new literacies. The transcript humorously conveys the increasing multivocal analytic sophistication of both Internet users and those interested in its commodification of identity. The following segment resonates well with the discussion of indexicality and consciousness earlier in this review and the discussion of a person's need to establish and validate his or her identity. The example can also be read on multiple levels suggestive of additional ways in which new literacies are affecting our global sense of connectedness, quest for identity, and information consciousness.

Advertising Transcript—'Guru'

SEEKER: How did you become such a great master?

GURU: (Carradine) YellowBook.com.

SEEKER: YellowBook.com?

GURU: Everyone is searching for something.

SEEKER: Isn't YellowBook.com for buying stuff?

GURU: After all, it is a material world.

Let's say pizza makes you happy.

Just type in what and where.

SEEKER: But master, how do you show them the way?

GURU: YellowBook.com has a map feature . . . Infinite information.

GURU: YellowBook.Commmmm.

ANNCR: Quick. Local. Reliable.

References

Adamson, H. (1993). *Academic competence. Theory and classroom practice: Preparing ESL students for content courses.* White Plains, NY: Longman.

Bakhtin, M. M. (1986) *Speech genres and other late essays* (C. Emerson, & M. Holquist, Eds., V. W. McGee, Trans.). Austin: University of Texas Press.

Castek, J., Leu, D. J., Coiro, J., Gort, M., Henry, L., & Lima, C. O. (in press.). Developing new literacies among multilingual learners in the elementary grades. In L. Parker (Ed.), *Technology-based learning environments for young English learners: In and out of school connections.* Mahwah, NJ: Lawrence Erlbaum.

Cole, M. (1996). *Cultural psychology.* Cambridge, MA: Belknap, Harvard University Press.

Gee, J. P. (2000, February). *Literacies, identities, and discourses.* Paper presented at the Acquisition of Advanced Literacy Conference, Davis, CA.

Goffman, E. (1959). *The presentation of self in everyday life.* Garden City, NY: Doubleday.

Goffman, E. (1974). *Frame analysis: An essay on the organization of experience.* Cambridge, MA: Harvard University Press.

Goffman, E. (1981). *Forms of talk.* Philadelphia: University of Pennsylvania Press.

Halliday, M. A. K., & Hasan, R. (1976). *Cohesion in English.* London: Longman.

Kress, G. (2000). Design and transformation: New theories of meaning. In B. Cope & M. Kalantzis (Eds.), *Multiliteracies: Literacy, learning, and design of social futures* (pp. 153–161). London: Routledge.

Lam, W. S. E. (2000). L2 literacy and the design of the self: A case study of a teenager writing on the Internet. *TESOL Quarterly, 34*(3), 457–482.

Leu, D. J., Kinzer, C. K., Coiro, J. L., & Cammack, D. (2004). Toward a theory of new literacies emerging from the Internet and other information and communication technologies. In R. Ruddel, & N. Unrau (Eds.), *Theoretical models and processes of reading* (5th ed., pp. 1570–1613). Newark, DE: International Reading Association.

Savignon, S. (1997). *Communicative competence: Theory and classroom practice.* New York: McGraw-Hill.

Seely Brown, J., Collins, A. M., & Duguid, P. (1989). Situated learning and the culture of learning. *Educational Researcher, 18*(1), 32–42.

SIL International. (2006). *What is deixis?* Retrieved September 8, 2006, from http://www.sil.org/linguistics/glossaryoflinguisticterms/WhatIsDeixis.htm

Technology Review. (2006). *MySpace to enable members to sell their own music.* Retrieved September 5, 2006, from http://www.technologyreview.com/

Vygotsky, L. S. (1978). *Mind in society. The development of higher psychological processes* (M. Cole, V. J. Steiner, S. Scribner, & E. Souberman, Eds.). Cambridge, MA: Harvard University Press.

Warschauer, M. (2002). A developmental perspective on technology in language education. *TESOL Quarterly, 36*(3), 453–475.

Wertsch, J. V. (1985). *Vygotsky and the social formation of mind.* Cambridge, MA: Harvard University Press.

CHAPTER 38

The Journey Ahead*

Thirteen Teachers Report How the Internet Influences Literacy and Literacy Instruction in Their K–12 Classrooms

RACHEL A. KARCHMER

VIRGINIA COMMONWEALTH UNIVERSITY, USA

Abstract

The purpose of this study was to explore 13 K–12 teachers' reports of how the Internet influenced literacy and literacy instruction in their classrooms. The teachers, including ten women and three men, represented 11 different states in the U.S. and were considered exemplary at using technology by their colleagues. Labbo and Reinking's (1999) notion of multiple realities in relation to new technologies provided a framework for understanding the participants' perspectives of the Internet's relationship to literacy and literacy instruction. Constant-comparative analysis of data, including e-mail interviews, participants' reflective journals, Web pages, online articles, and lesson plans revealed three areas of focus: (a) the appropriateness of Internet material, (b) evaluating the accuracy of Internet material, and (c) publishing student work on the Internet. Findings indicated that the teachers viewed the Internet's influence on reading as an extension of traditional literacy skills. In addition, the elementary teachers noticed an increase in their students' motivation to write when their work was published on the Internet for a greater audience. However, the secondary teachers did not find this the case. Implications for teacher technology preparation and literacy research are discussed in light of the lessons learned from this study.

* Reprinted from Karchmer, R. A. (2001). The journey ahead: Thirteen teachers report how the Internet influences literacy and literacy instruction in their K-12 classrooms. *Reading Research Quarterly*, 36, 442–467. Reprinted with permission.

The purpose of this study was to explore 13 K–12 teachers' reports of how the Internet influenced literacy and literacy instruction in their classrooms. The teachers, all considered by their colleagues to be exemplary at using technology, shared stories describing if and how the Internet changed the way they viewed reading and writing in their classrooms.

Historically, there has always been a close relationship between literacy, technology, and literacy instruction. Consider, first, connections between literacy and technology; the nature of literacy has always been tightly entwined with the nature of the communication technology used in any historical period. As Leu and Kinzer (2000) pointed out, cuneiform technologies in Mesopotamia, papyrus technologies of Egypt and other civilizations, the technologies of the Middle Ages in Europe, and printing technologies developed initially by Gutenberg defined special aspects of literacy required to use them effectively (Boyarin, 1993; Diringer, 1968; Manguel, 1996).

Consider, second, the connections between the technologies of literacy and instruction; each technology of literacy, in conjunction with the cultural context in which it appeared, has defined important aspects of literacy instruction. One has only to notice the impact book technologies had on the widespread access to print material and the concomitant consequences for more universal literacy education to chart this relationship. Literacy, technology, and literacy instruction are closely linked.

Probably the most recent, and arguably the most powerful, example of this connection may be today's networked information and communication technologies (ICT), specifically the Internet. The Internet has changed the definition of literacy by introducing readers and writers to electronic texts that incorporate features not typically found in traditional written prose (Bolter, 1998; Reinking, 1998; Reinking, Labbo, & McKenna, 1997). Thus, the ability to communicate through animated graphics, video, digitized pronunciations, hyperlinks, and other information resources necessitates the development of new literacy skills and creates new opportunities for literacy instruction.

Although some may argue that the Internet has little to do with literacy or literacy instruction in schools, Leu and Kinzer (2000) strongly suggested that these constructs are quickly converging. They explained, "As the Internet enters our classrooms and as we envision the new literacies that Internet technologies permit, it is inevitable that literacy instruction and networked ICT … will also converge" (p. 111). Furthermore, they argued that global information economies will require students to be prepared to use Internet technologies to quickly gather and evaluate information, use that information to solve problems, and then quickly communicate their solutions to others. Inevitably, workplace demands in an information economy (Mikulecky & Kirkley, 1998) will require students to become proficient in using these new literacies of the Internet.

What does the convergence of literacy, literacy instruction, and Internet technologies mean for staff development and preservice teacher education? Statistics from the U.S. National Center for Education Statistics (2000a) indicated that 63% of instructional classrooms were connected to the Internet in the fall of 1999—more than double the number connected just 2 years earlier. Unfortunately, however, teachers are not generally prepared to use these new technologies of literacy or to teach children how to use them effectively. A recent U.S. national survey revealed that 80% of teachers do not feel well prepared to use educational technology in their teaching (National Center for Education Statistics, 1999a). It seems that teacher preparation for using new technologies with students has not yet caught up to the rapid rate of purchasing hardware and software. For example, during the 1998 to 1999 year schools in the United States spent more than 10 times the amount on Internet connections, hardware, and instructional software than was spent on teacher training (CEO Forum, 1999). It is crucial for teachers to be supported in how best to use these new technologies of literacy in their classrooms as much as they have been supported with the technology itself. This is especially important as the consequences of this convergence lead the field of literacy to view technology and literacy as integrated components of education rather than separate focal points (Labbo & Reinking, 1999).

Where is the information required to support classroom instruction in the new literacies of Internet technologies? One might initially look to the research literature. Unfortunately, few studies have been conducted in this area. In the third edition of the *Handbook of Reading Research*, Kamil, Intrator, and Kim (2000) discussed the limited amount of research related to literacy and technology, pointing out that a very small percentage of research articles in this area has been published in literacy journals. They provided a snapshot of the most common topics written about in the existing research, noting areas such as computers and writing, hypermedia, hypertext and literacy, multimedia effects on literacy, special populations, motivation, and computers and collaboration. No studies were reported on the new literacies of the Internet or on teacher preparation in this area; perhaps because these changes in the nature of literacy are so recent, very little information is available.

Another strategy would be to explore teachers' perceptions of how best to use the Internet with students. Previous research (Karchmer, 2000; Leu, Karchmer, & Leu, 1999; Wood, 1999) has suggested that educators who currently use the Internet to support teaching and learning provide important insights to how technology may effectively be used in the classroom. Their stories, including their successes and failures, provide the type of intricate information needed to understand the reality of technology use in the classroom. This was the approach taken in the investigation described in this article.

Because little previous work has been done in this area, it is important to recognize the exploratory nature of the work. Exploratory studies such as this are essential to begin to define instructional insights about the new literacies of Internet technologies, especially for the important preservice and inservice education that is needed.

Theoretical Orientation

Multiple Realities

Labbo and Reinking (1999) used the term *multiple realities* (p. 478) to explain that our interpretation of research and instruction depends upon our experiences in relation to environment, philosophical beliefs, and education. However, acknowledging that multiple realities exist forces us to suspend our own beliefs and attempt to understand how other perspectives may broaden our knowledge base.

The concept of multiple realities strongly pertains to researching the convergence of the Internet, literacy, and literacy instruction. Leu and Kinzer (2000) argued that as networked information and communication technologies become fundamental components of the education system, their influence on literacy and literacy instruction is inevitable. This makes it crucial that the research community begin to examine how these technologies influence teaching and instruction. However, the extent of Internet use in classrooms around the world varies depending upon factors such as finances, school policy, and teachers' interest in using the technology with their students. Clearly these factors will affect the extent of the convergence. Yet, as Labbo and Reinking (1999) argued, it is still imperative to study atypical environments:

> The perspective of multiple realities ... allows us to seek research-to-practice connections that are specific to particular instructional realities, that is, to focus on research findings that might be applied more confidently to particular situations rather than to seek principles so general as to be relatively meaningless in any particular context. (p. 480)

This notion of multiple realities enabled me to understand the participants' perspectives of the Internet's relationship to literacy and literacy instruction. It acted as a continual reminder that the teachers' views were based upon their experiences, including their environment, philosophical beliefs, and education.

Related Literature

In reviewing literature related to the convergence of literacy, literacy instruction, and the Internet, I looked at several pertinent areas. First, I explored why the Internet is important to classroom teaching and learning. With the skills needed to succeed in a global market, as well as evidence showing that students learn more effectively in the collaborative, active environment created by the Internet, schools are expected to teach students the essential literacy skills of today's workplace. Second, I reviewed research that argues electronic texts, the prevalent means by which communication takes place via the Internet, necessitate new literacy skills, thus redefining literacy. Third, I looked at research related to the challenges facing teacher education and staff development in light of the integration of new technologies in the classroom curriculum. Finally, I argued that much can be learned from those teachers already using the Internet regularly in their classrooms. This body of literature provides a framework for understanding how this study's findings provide an initial step toward understanding the Internet's influence on literacy and literacy instruction in K–12 classrooms.

Why the Internet is Important for Classroom Teaching and Learning

Internet technologies were not originally developed for public school use; however, they have quickly found their way into the classroom (CEO Forum, 1999). While schools in the United States are connecting to the Internet, other nations have similar plans. The United Kingdom, Finland, New Zealand, and Australia have all launched educational technology initiatives (Leu, 2000). Interest in preparing students to use technology effectively is permeating the globe.

The recent movement to connect schools around the world to the Internet is due to the perception that networked information resources will be central to children's futures (Bruce, 1997a; Drucker, 1994; Leu, 2000; Mikulecky & Kirkley, 1998; New London Group, 1996). Evidence exists that the global market is shifting its dependence from a manufacturing economy to an information economy that relies heavily upon quick and efficient communication (Leu & Kinzer, 2000; Mikulecky & Kirkley, 1998). The United States Department of Labor (2000) has highlighted the 10 fastest growing occupations projected for 1998 to 2008. The top 5 include computer engineers, computer support specialists, systems analysts, database administrators, and desktop publishing specialists. Each of these occupations relies heavily upon technological competencies. Moreover, these higher skilled jobs tend to demand higher pay than blue-collar occupations. Thus, in order to compete, employees need to know how to use new technologies, including the Internet, to work efficiently in the work environment (CEO Forum, 1999; White House Panel on Educational Technology, 1997). Schools are then left with the responsibility of preparing students to use these new technologies effectively.

Research (Bruce, 1997a; CEO Forum, 1999; Means et al., 1993; Mikulecky & Kirkley, 1998; White House Panel on Educational Technology, 1997) has suggested that schools must focus on four skill areas that have become important since the Internet's infusion into the global market. First, the ability to collaborate with others is crucial to the success of business today (Bruce, 1997a; Leu, 2000). Unlike manufacturing and agricultural industries that allowed work in isolation, present-day service requires employees to work collectively, often with distant colleagues. More emphasis is then put on collaborative work teams to gather information and make decisions that directly affect their job responsibilities. Mikulecky and Kirkley (1998) called this shift "Democratization of the Workplace" (p. 305). Many times the Internet is the vehicle that fosters the collaborative atmosphere necessary by making communication among workers more accessible.

To work together effectively, employees must be able to communicate (Bruce, 1997a; Leu & Kinzer, 2000). Corporations are increasingly using alternative means of communication, such as electronic mail and video conferences, to conduct business with clients around the world. Employees must be able not only to use these forms of communication, but also to present their thoughts clearly via these different methods if they expect to compete in the global job market.

According to the research, U.S. workers also need to know how to acquire and sift through information (Bruce, 1997a; Leu & Kinzer, 2000; Mikulecky & Kirkley, 1998; White House Panel on Educational Technology, 1997). Bruce (1997a) explained that today's workers need the skills to gather information from diverse resources, including both traditional and electronic means, and to merge that information to make common connections.

Finally, problem-solving skills are even more important. Individuals not only must be able to identify problematic issues, but also to create logical viable solutions. An example of one such problem is the question of information accuracy on the Internet. Workers must be prepared to evaluate material and decide its level of truthfulness. It is important to remember that anyone can publish on the Internet. This creates the critical challenge for educators to teach students how to evaluate information. Now, many would argue that this skill is already reinforced in K–12 education; however, the increased rate of Internet use necessitates possibly more thorough instruction.

In addition to the Internet's infusion into the global market, there is research indicating that the use of new technologies in teaching and learning may improve student achievement (Means et al., 1993; National Council for Accreditation of Teacher Education [NCATE], 1997). While some argue that technology use does not produce differences in student test scores (e.g., Clark, 1991; Oppenheimer, 1997), others suggest that the collaborative, student-centered environment the Internet creates leads to more active learning (CEO Forum, 1999; El-Hindi, 1998). For example, Nicaise and Barnes (1996) studied the relationship between technology, active learning, and teacher education when they created a mathematics methods course for new teachers. Like Perkins (1991), Nicaise and Barnes (1996) compared technology (in this case a combination of Internet resources and CDROM) to a tool that they used to promote a student-centered, active learning environment. They stated that the technology provided "crucial support" (p. 209) to the students in several ways, such as creating authentic tasks, opening communication and collaboration avenues with experienced teachers, and showcasing the students' work to a larger audience by posting assignments on a class Web page. While they acknowledged the lack of conclusive research supporting this type of teaching and learning, Nicaise and Barnes (1996) argued that teachers would begin to shift away from more traditional methods of teaching as they were exposed to ways to engage students in technology-supported active learning endeavors.

Although only limited research supports the claim that new technologies increase student learning, exploratory work has indicated that students are more receptive to the collaborative, inquiry-based learning that is quickly becoming a trademark of Internet use in the classroom (Baker, 2000; El-Hindi, 1998; Karchmer, 2000; Nicaise & Barnes, 1996).

Redefining Literacy

A crucial component of networked information resources, such as the Internet, is electronic text, the medium by which communication takes place. Several researchers (Bruce, 1997b; Leu, 2000; Reinking, 1995; Reinking et al., 1997) have argued that the characteristics of these texts redefine literacy by introducing new ways of reading and writing. As Reinking (1998) explained,

> Digital forms of expression are increasingly replacing printed forms and there is a widespread consensus, at least intuitively, that this shift has consequences for the way we communicate and disseminate information, how we approach the task of reading and writing, and how we think about helping people to become literate. (p. xv)

To begin with, print-based texts are fixed whereas electronic texts are interactive and malleable (Kaplan, 1991). The uses of electronic enhancements such as digitized pronunciations, graphics, and video are examples of how reading material can be manipulated and modified on the computer. Several researchers have explored how electronic texts differ from print-based texts (e.g., Leu & Reinking, 1996; Reinking & Rickman, 1990; Salomon, Globerson, & Guterman, 1989). For example, Reinking and Rickman (1990) examined sixth graders' vocabulary achievement when they read electronic texts that provided the meanings of difficult words. They found that those students using the computer-generated texts scored higher on follow-up vocabulary tests than their peers who read print-based texts and used print-based dictionaries and glossaries. Likewise, in their study of middle school students, Anderson-Inman and Horney (1993) found that at-risk readers who took advantage of the electronic resources available on electronic texts, such as digitized pronunciations and digital pictures, scored higher on comprehension measures than their peers who did not use the electronic textual aids.

The writing process, too, is interactive and malleable in digital environments. For example, Labbo (1996) studied kindergartners' electronic symbol making. The classroom was equipped with two computers loaded with KidPix 2, a word-processing program with artistic tools. Labbo reported that the students in her study interacted with the computer to create representations of play, art, and writing. They learned that by pressing different keys, they could manipulate the pictures on the screen. As Labbo and Kuhn (1998) later pointed out, "Children who discover tools that can aid in revision often form the concepts that print is malleable and that composing is a process involving manipulation of typographic symbols and ideas" (p. 86).

A second characteristic of electronic texts is the seamless incorporation of audiovisual features (Bolter, 1991; Reinking et al., 1997). Graphics are considered an integral part of the primary text within electronic environments, whereas they often are regarded as supplementary materials when combined with traditional written prose. For example, when reading print-based texts that are supplemented with pictures, the reader must decide when and how to interpret the graphics so the meaning of the primary text is clear. In electronic texts, the graphics are often part of the main body, and the reading process is usually more recursive in that the features are used in combination (Reinking & ChanLin, 1994).

This characteristic has implications not only for reading, but also for writing. In their study of a technology-rich fourth-grade classroom, Baker and Kinzer (1998) found that students who had difficulty creating illustrations by hand were able to construct pictures using technology enhancements. Computer-generated graphics were then used to supplement the meaning of their written prose. If students are expected to use hypermedia in the writing process, they must be taught how to combine audiovisuals and written prose effectively so their intended meaning is understood by the reader.

A third feature of electronic texts is the ability to access multiple resources connected to networked environments. When readers engage in print-based texts, they are confined to the limits of what is written on the paper in front of them. Reinking et al. (1997) argued that electronic texts eliminate such boundaries and provide readers and writers the opportunity to easily connect to relevant material.

However, Stahl, Hynd, Britton, McNish, and Bosquet (1996) found that merely making multiple resources available to students was not enough to benefit learning. In their research of high school students' use of multiple texts, Stahl et al. studied how the availability of numerous information resources affected 10th graders' understandings of the events related to the Vietnam War. After completing several measures to assess prior knowledge of the topic, students accessed multiple text documents compiled in hypercard stacks on school computers. The documents included excerpts from books, newspaper clippings, and historical documents. Using assignment sheets as guides, students chose the electronic texts on which to concentrate. Prior to the study, Stahl et al. suggested that providing students with multiple resources would "aid them in constructing a richer and more detailed mental model of that event, thus enhancing content knowledge" (p. 434). After looking at the data, they found that the 10th graders had a difficult time synthesizing and critiquing the information presented in the hypertext documents. They determined that students needed to be taught how to compare documents so they can think critically about the contents. Hence, providing students with the access to retrieve unlimited resources is not enough. Teachers must also prepare them to use the information effectively.

A fourth characteristic of electronic text is that it does not follow the same traditional linear organization as print-based text (Reinking et al., 1997).

Instead, hypertext allows readers to shift from one page to another through the use of electronic links. Hence, there is no fixed order that a hypertext must follow. Readers are afforded more active roles in the reading process when they navigate through hypertext. Some argue that readers become the author in that they decide which links to follow as they advance through the text. Therefore, they retrieve different understandings from the text depending upon the path they follow.

The nonlinear nature of electronic text also affects writing. It is fairly simple to connect prose to graphic aids and other electronic texts when composing on a computer. The author must consider not only the written prose, but also the meanings of the multimedia components added to the text. As Mitra and Cohen (1999) argued, "The role of the author is thus further altered because the author is not only the creator of new texts (and meanings) but also the facilitator of meanings by providing an index of specific WWW texts and images available in cyberspace" (p. 189). Thus, students must learn a new type of discourse grammar when composing electronic texts.

It is clear that electronic texts are different from print-based texts in a number of ways. They (a) are interactive and malleable, (b) incorporate audiovisual aids, (c) are easily connected to related texts, and (d) produce alternative text structures. With the increased use of digital texts, literacy now incorporates the ability to navigate through and make sense of a variety of features that set electronic texts apart from traditionally written prose. Literacy, then, no longer consists solely of interaction with the one-dimensional written page.

Challenges Faced by Teacher Education and Staff Development Programs

Obviously, teachers are a crucial component of the classroom environment. Most decide when they will cover a certain topic, how their lessons will be structured, and which materials they will use with their students. So, as the Internet becomes an important part of education, and as literacy is redefined by this new technology, it will be mandatory that teachers integrate this new resource with daily instruction so students can learn how to develop the new literacies this technology permits (Karchmer, 2000; National Council for Accreditation of Teacher Education [NCATE], 1997; White House Panel on Educational Technology, 1997). As mentioned earlier, 63% of U.S. classrooms were connected to the Internet in the fall of 1999, almost double the number connected 2 years earlier. However, small percentages of students in equipped classrooms spend significant instructional time per week on the computer (National Center for Education Statistics [NCES], 1999b). So, as Cuban (1993) pointed out, "Why is it that with all the talk of school reform and information technologies over the last decade, computers are used far less on a daily basis in classrooms than in other organizations?" (p. 185).

There could be several reasons that teachers who are privy to Internet connections do not use them in their classrooms as part of the curriculum. Balli,

a different way of looking at the teachers' perspectives leading to a focus on different aspects of the data.

There were times I had to step back from the data and remind myself of the biases I brought to the study. First, I have spent many hours navigating the Web, looking at classroom projects created by teachers. I am fascinated by the resources available to teachers and the Internet's potential for enhancing teaching and learning. Second, I composed the research and interview questions that were at the crux of this work. Therefore, the stories shared by the teachers were confined to how I chose to frame those queries. Third, I generated the analytic themes that became the basis of the research findings. Thus, in an effort to keep my assumptions in check, I wrote detailed analytic memos (Glaser & Strauss, 1967) that kept me aware of my preconceptions as I collected and analyzed the data.

Participants

Keeping in mind the extensive research reporting that most teachers are not prepared to use new technologies in their classrooms (e.g., CEO Forum, 1999; White House Panel on Educational Technology, 1997), I chose to explore the perspectives of teachers who were identified by other educators as exemplary at using the Internet with their students. Expert-novice literature (Angelo, 1996; Carter et al., 1987; Collinson, 1996; Livingston & Borko, 1989; Lowman, 1996) has suggested there is a great deal to be learned from exemplars in different fields. They tend to possess a combination of characteristics (Lowman, 1996) that sets them apart from their colleagues (Collinson, 1996). Thus, the stories of the exemplary teachers involved in this study can begin to inform the field of education about if and how new technologies affect literacy and literacy instruction.

It seems that groups of exemplary educators communicate regularly via the Internet (Karchmer, 2000; Leu et al., 1999). They subscribe to electronic mailing lists or listservs (e.g., RTeacher, Web66) where they ask questions pertaining to classroom practices and school policies, answer other teachers' questions about these issues, and share lesson plans and ideas for using the Internet with students. Several Web sites dedicated to highlighting outstanding classroom teachers' work with technology (e.g., Ed's Oasis, Global Schoolhouse) also exist. These are considered by many to be good places to locate innovative lesson plans.

To gather participants for this present study, I looked to educators who use the sources previously described (electronic mailing lists, Web sites). First, I sent out a call for nominations on four electronic mailing lists. The purpose of the call was to ask educators familiar with educational technology to nominate K–12 teachers they knew to be doing an exemplary job integrating the Internet and the classroom. In addition, the nominated teachers had to have used the technology in their classroom for at least 1 year. I received eight nominations from this solicitation.

Next, I contacted teachers directly who were highlighted on one of two Web sites devoted to exemplary Internet educators (Ed's Oasis and Global Schoolhouse). Those highlighted were described as exemplary because they "were developing successful, innovative, and advanced lessons using technology in their classrooms. In other words, they were leaders who by their being recognized ... can be an inspiration to other teachers who want to utilize technology in the classroom" (M. Hutchison, Ed's Oasis, personal communication, December 14, 1998). I sent e-mail messages to 10 highlighted classroom teachers who had at least 1 year of teaching experience using the Internet with their students; 9 were from Ed's Oasis and 1 was from Global Schoolhouse.

I also received nominations for participants through snowball sampling measures (Bogdan & Biklen, 1998). During the previous year, a colleague and I conducted an 8-month exploratory study on exemplary teachers' perspectives of Internet use in the classroom. Upon completion, I asked the 23 teachers involved to nominate colleagues who fit my participant criteria for this current study. I received 13 nominations from this method.

After receiving the names of prospective participants, I asked nominators to explain why they believed the teachers they highlighted were exemplary. Most of their responses correlated with Collinson's (1996) and Lowman's (1996) research. They stated that the nominated teachers were proficient with the Internet and facilitated its transition to the classroom curriculum. The nominees were also described as "innovative" because they tended to be among the few educators within the school system using the Internet to promote literacy and learning. In a few cases, the nominated teachers were recognized by their administration for their technology use and were then responsible for the technology preparation programs offered within their districts. As one nominator explained, "I feel that this teacher displays the drive, creativity, and leadership qualities of an exemplary teacher" (A. Keller, personal communication, January 11, 1999).

After receiving the nominators' explanations for highlighting certain teachers, it was difficult to create a blanket set of characteristics that reflected the meaning of the word *exemplary*. As Lowman (1996) advised, "The notion of the exemplary teacher shares much with any idealized concept ... it is difficult to achieve consensus on a general definition, but most people think they know a specific example when they see it" (p. 33). Although I recognized the possibility that other people might not consider these teachers exemplary, I reminded myself that the purpose of my work was not to define the meaning of an exemplary teacher. Hence, I was less concerned with the precision of the definition and more interested in having a label that assured me the teachers were successfully integrating the technology with their curriculum. Therefore, instead of restricting the nominators with my understanding of the term, I chose to let them define an exemplary teacher as they saw fit.

A total of 31 K–12 teachers were nominated as a result of my queries. After receiving the nominations, I sent each a letter explaining the nature of the study and an invitation to participate. Initially, 16 of the 31 teachers agreed to participate, but 3 discontinued correspondence within the first week of data collection, resulting in a total of 13 teachers.

Included in my work are the perspectives of 10 women and three men, all European American, representing 11 different states in the U.S. The schools in which these teachers taught included two rural, five suburban, and six urban districts as described by the participants. They taught grades ranging from kindergarten to 12th grade, including Title I reading services. Thus, there were eight elementary teachers (Title I and K–6) and five secondary teachers (7–12). The average number of years of teaching experience was 14.7. The number of years participating teachers had used the Internet in the classroom ranged from 1 to 6 years with an average of 3.3 years.

Computer availability varied among classrooms. Two teachers did not have Internet access in the classroom but did have access to a computer lab. A few teachers (3) had at least one Internet connection in the classroom and access to a computer lab. The remaining participants (8) had at least one online computer in the classroom. See Table 38.1 for a complete description of the participants' demographic information as well as a listing of pseudonyms used throughout this work.

Data Collection

Because the primary goal of this work was to gain a sense of teachers' perspectives, I collected various types of self-report data, such as semistructured interviews and participants' reflective journals. Many of the teachers shared other information with me, such as résumés, published articles, and Web pages. Collecting several forms of data immersed me in numerous versions of the teachers' stories, allowing me to consider each of their perspectives from different angles (Lincoln, 1997).

Using e-mail as data. The bulk of the data was compiled from individual interviews conducted via e-mail over 3 months. Tao and Reinking (1996) reviewed literature related to e-mail correspondence and found that this form of communication offered several benefits as a source of data. One was the disintegration of geographical boundaries. Because it has been reported (e.g., CEO Forum, 1999; Karchmer, 2000) that most teachers are not prepared to use Internet technologies in the classroom, I wanted to learn from a population of teachers who were considered technologically literate by their colleagues. Therefore, I chose to favor successful experience with the technology over location. In order to do that, I had to travel beyond my own geographical boundaries. The Internet provided me with the avenue to find expert teachers from a variety of settings who could inform my work.

A second benefit of collecting data by e-mail was the absence of timely pressures. Communication over the Internet could be synchronous (chat

Table 38.1 Demographic Information as Reported by Participants

Gender	Teacher (pseudonym)	Grade	State	Location	Years of teaching experience	Highest academic degree	Years of Internet use	Computer access	Classroom Web site
F	Bonnie	Title I	WV	Rural	21	M.S.	4	5 in class and lab access	
F	Leigh	K	OR	Urban	16	B.S.	2.5	4 in class	X
F	Emily	1	AL	Urban	6	M.S.	2	2 in class	X
F	Melanie	2	WI	Suburban	25	M.S.	5	6 in class 1 with Internet	X
F	Marcy	3	MD	Suburban	17	B.A.	5	1 in class and lab access	
M	Will	4	VA	Suburban	14	B.S.	4	1 in class	
M	David	4	AZ	Rural	8	B.S.	1.5	2 in class	X
F	Cindy	6	IL	Urban	19	M.S.	6	4 in class	
F	Terry	7-Math	VA	Suburban	10	B.A.	3	1 in class	X
F	Louise	7-Social studies	NC	Suburban	8	M.S.	1.5	Lab access only	
F	Julie	9-Health	IL	Urban	33	M.S.	2	1 in class	X
M	Adam	9/11-Social studies	MA	Urban	6	Ph.D.	5	1 in class and lab access	
F	Hannah	10/12-Language arts	IA	Urban	8	B.A.	3	Lab access only	

room, instant messenger) or asynchronous (e-mail). I chose to interview the participants in an asynchronous manner, which allowed them to think about their responses and reply at their convenience. All of the teachers had Internet access at work, but with the pressures and time constraints of the school day, a thoughtful response would not have always been possible. I felt their answers would be more reflective if I gave them the opportunity to respond to my queries at their leisure.

A third benefit of e-mail correspondence was the easy storage and manipulation of messages. Most of my data came via the Internet, therefore it was readily available in typed form and easily manipulated. My participants' insights and stories were then laid out in their words, with the punctuation and expression intact.

Although there were several positive aspects of e-mail correspondence, I felt it was necessary to examine the possible negative consequences of interviewing over the Internet. First, e-mail correspondence eliminated the richness of face-to-face discussions. In *Ambiguous Empowerment*, Chase (1995) argued that in order to really understand what her participants were telling her, she had to examine not only what they told her, but how they said it within an oral context. E-mail interviews did not allow for the same close examination of discourse.

Second, throughout my work, I continued to remind myself of how difficult it was to represent insights in writing alone. Although none of the participants voiced a dislike for written communication, it was always possible that some were not as effective writers as they were speakers (Hodder, 1994). The written correspondence also gave the participants the opportunity to think through their answers before sending them to me. This eliminated off-the-cuff remarks, which frequently occur in traditional interviews (Chase, 1995). Hence, I was privy to the information my participants chose to share with me only after careful reflection.

Conducting semistructured interviews. I began my semistructured e-mail interviews with my research question in mind: Do teachers report that the Internet influences literacy and literacy instruction in their classrooms? If so, how? Reminding myself that my participants had never met me, I took Bogdan and Biklen's (1998) advice and spent a few brief messages breaking the ice by filling the teachers in on my background and my interest in Internet use. Next I asked them questions that would provide me with background knowledge, such as demographic information, as well as details on the type of technology preparation they either received from their districts or obtained on their own.

After creating a more familiar correspondence environment, I began asking questions that pertained to literacy, literacy instruction, and the Internet: How do you use the Internet to support reading and writing? How do you feel the Internet has affected reading and writing in your classroom? and How is Internet reading and writing different than traditional reading and writing from a print-based book? After receiving the teachers' responses, I followed up with more individualized inquiries that were based on the information they shared about their personal experiences.

The correspondence was conducted asynchronously. Once a participant responded to my query, I read through the reply and made a list of questions that resulted from the response. I then e-mailed my new question(s), which usually asked the teacher to clarify the points made or to share stories that illustrated those points. I corresponded with each participant between 25 and 30 times throughout the course of data collection. Response length varied, but most replies to my queries were at least one full singles-paced page. It took approximately 3 months to collect enough data so that I felt immersed in their stories.

Reflective journals. I also explored the participants' perspectives through their reflective journal writing (Clandinin & Connelly, 1994). At the beginning of the study, the teachers were asked to keep weekly entries regarding their Internet-related experiences in or out of the classroom. The purpose was twofold. First, the journals informed the study by giving the participants an opportunity to consider topics not explored during the interview process. However, I probed them if it seemed the journal topics related to the research question and interview responses. This probing helped me connect the data.

The second reason for using journals was that they gave the teachers the opportunity to reflect upon their Internet use and convey its effects on teaching and learning in the classroom (Schön, 1983). I intentionally did not provide specific guidelines for the journals, because I perceived this writing exercise as an opportunity to share selfgenerated topics that might or might not directly relate to the purpose of the study, but might extend the participants' understanding of their own Internet use.

As the study began, I asked the teachers to send me at least one journal entry a week via e-mail. Although none of the teachers objected to the requirement, I received a varying number of entries throughout the 3 months of data collection. For the most part, the teachers wrote one of three types of reflections: (a) a step-by-step outline of the classroom technology use each week, (b) a general response to what lessons worked and what needed refinement, and (c) a combination of stories of specific technology-related experiences involving their students or colleagues.

Other data. Several additional forms of data were collected that helped achieve a better understanding of the participants' perspectives. Six of the teachers had classroom Web pages that posted student work, homework assignments, and projects their classes were involved in. All of the participants sporadically included Web addresses (either their own or someone else's they had referred to in class) in their responses to my queries when attempting to illustrate the stories they shared. A few (3) teachers sent me articles they had written for online journals that focused on their philosophy of teaching and learning. In addition, 2 teachers sent me digital pictures of their computer set-up so I could visualize how the technology was positioned in the classroom.

Data Analysis

Roughly 700 pages of interview transcripts (hard copies of e-mail correspondences), journal entries, and pages of ancillary materials were accumulated during the course of this study. To organize those data, I created individual folders in Microsoft 6.0 where I cut and pasted participants' interview responses and journal entries.

Analysis took place throughout data collection and writing as I used constant-comparative methodology (Bogdan & Biklen, 1998) in an attempt to create categories that captured the fundamental nature of my participants' stories. As in Ivey (1999), the analysis occurred in several phases. I began by highlighting key words and phrases during my initial readings of the transcripts. Afterwards, I wrote memos describing my preliminary impressions of the information shared. I reviewed the key words and phrases and compiled a list of the most frequently used, which led to my preliminary categories.

The memos also gave me an outlet to discuss my perceptions of how the data related to my research question, as well as time to reflect upon the biases I brought to the study. Next, I read the transcripts more closely, checking to see if my original thoughts were supported by the data. Those supported were organized into groups based upon similar components. Those that stood on their own were eliminated due to lack of data supporting them as emerging categories. This process was followed as new data were collected.

I narrowed down the categories to eight recurring themes including (a) appropriateness of Internet reading material, (b) reading level of Internet material, (c) textual aids used to support Internet material, (d) ensuring safe Internet use, (e) evaluating the accuracy of Internet material, (f) publishing student work on the Internet, (g) students' motivation to publish on the Internet, and (h) malleability of electronic writing. Near the end of data collection, I implemented a member-checking strategy (Lincoln & Guba, 1985) to be sure I was interpreting the participants' reports the way they understood them and to sift out connections between the eight themes. All 13 teachers received an e-mail message explaining that eight broad themes continued to surface as I analyzed the transcripts. I provided them with a list of the themes and asked for elaboration. For example, seven of the eight elementary teachers (Title I, K–6) found the theme focusing on publishing student work on the Internet to be highly important. However, with the exception of one, the secondary teachers (7–12) did not find this theme pertinent, mainly due to the absence of regular online publishing in these middle and high school classrooms. This distinction was extremely important to probe, and the member-checking strategy provided me with the opportunity to bring these differences in perspectives to light. In addition, this method helped consolidate the initial eight themes by highlighting overlaps, leading to a total of three major themes: (a) appropriateness of Internet material, (b) evaluating the accuracy of Internet material, and (c) publishing student work on the Internet, with subcategories relating to each. The following results section is structured around these themes and subcategories.

Results

The teachers reported that using the Internet with their students influenced certain aspects of literacy and literacy instruction in their classrooms, specifically related to reading and writing. Figure 38.1 illustrates the connections between the major themes and subcategories that emerged during data collection and analysis and how they piece together.

In addition, it is important to note that the subject and grade level the participants taught seemed to be a factor when discussing these changes in literacy and literacy instruction. The eight elementary level teachers (Title I, K–6) focused on the appropriateness of reading material found on the Internet, evaluating

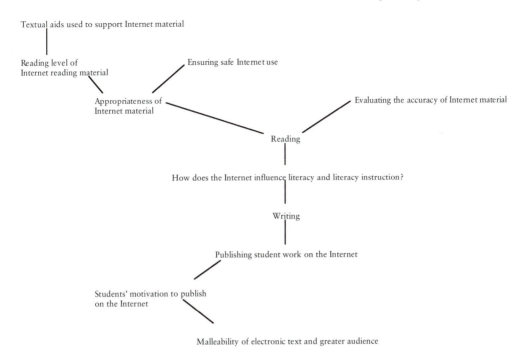

Figure 38.1 Graphic organizer of major themes and subcategories.

information accuracy, and publishing student work on the Internet. The five secondary school teachers (7–12) mainly concentrated on the appropriateness issue, specifically the precautions they took to ensure safe Internet use and the skills necessary to evaluate information found on the Internet, but they rarely discussed how writing was influenced. This information is illustrated in Table 38.2. The following results section is structured around the themes and subcategories, along with data demonstrating them in more depth.

Appropriateness of Internet Material

The teachers focused on two aspects of the appropriateness of reading material on the Internet: reading level and safe Internet use. The elementary-level teachers were mainly concerned with the reading level appropriate for their students, while the secondary-level teachers wrote about precautions to ensure safe Internet use.

Reading level. The elementary level teachers felt they needed to spend more time choosing reading material from the Internet than they had been when relying on graded texts. Unlike a textbook, which is often written for a specific grade level, the electronic text available on the Internet ranges from simple to difficult. Consequently, students can easily encounter reading material that is too challenging or too easy. The electronic text also encompasses different interactive text aids, such as audiovisuals and digitized speech (Reinking et al., 1997). Therefore, the teachers found that previewing the Web sites they

Table 38.2 Major Findings

Teacher (pseudonym)	Grade	Appropriateness of Internet material	Evaluating the accuracy of Internet material	Publishing student work on the Internet
Bonnie	Title I	Reading level	X	X
Leigh	K	Reading level	X	X
Emily	1	Reading level	X	X
Melanie	2	Reading level	X	X
Marcy	3	Reading level	X	X
Will	4	Reading level	X	X
David	4	Reading level and safe Internet use	X	X
Cindy	6	Reading level and safe Internet use	X	
Terry	7-Math	Safe Internet use	X	
Louise	7-Social studies	Safe Internet use	X	X
Julie	9-Health	Safe Internet use	X	
Adam	9/11-Social studies	Safe Internet use	X	
Hannah	10/12-Language arts	Safe Internet use	X	

planned to use in their lessons assured them that most of their students would be able to read the information presented.

When deciding on appropriate reading material for their students, the teachers looked at not only the text, but also the textual aids that accompanied it—a similar procedure to choosing print-based text. This way, if the text proved to be too challenging the students could use the textual aids for support. For example, Melanie (all teacher names are pseudonyms), the second-grade teacher, acknowledged that most of her students were "strong readers." However, she kept in mind her less able readers when choosing Internet Web sites. She stated the following in an interview response,

> I look for Web sites/pages which have a lot of white space and graphics. I also look for larger text on pages. Pages that have very little scrolling are good because students [in second grade] do not always have the patience to read all the text. For instance, I use the Weather Underground site instead of the Weather Channel site for work on weather in science because the W.U. site is organized in a clear easy-to-read manner with minimal text and lots of graphics.

Leigh, the kindergarten teacher, and Emily, the first-grade teacher, also relied on textual aids to help their students comprehend material found on the Internet. Both teachers had a difficult time finding material written for their students' reading level because most were emergent readers. Leigh "perused all sites before allowing the students to [look at them]," specifically looking for sites that included graphics. She wrote in an interview response, "The biggest problem are Web sites with too much text. I find sites with graphics. Pictures and any kind of animated graphics are very intriguing to my students." They also helped the kindergartners make sense of the material. Emily chose Web sites for her students that were created by other first-grade teachers and their classes. She explained in a journal entry that at these sites "I can usually find grade-level reading and projects that concern the same themes we are studying."

Sometimes it was not possible for the teachers to find appropriate Web sites for their students to use. Marcy, the third-grade teacher, encountered that difficulty when she prepared a lesson on Ghana. She explained that the sites she did find "included great pictures but text that was too hard for the students, or a page with no illustrations at all to help with context, a page with too many details or too much in-depth information." In this case the Internet was not the best source for information, and the students used library books and encyclopedias geared toward their reading level.

David, one of the fourth-grade teachers, also had a difficult time finding appropriate reading material, but it was usually for his weaker readers. However, he dealt with the issue differently than the other teachers in the study. Instead of investing time trying to find Web sites with easier reading levels and textual aids, he did not permit those students who had trouble reading to use the Internet in his classroom. He explained in a journal entry as follows:

> My weak readers, those in special ed, are not using the computers. What a statement to make, but it is correct. Their reading abilities make it so difficult to complete a task that they run out of time before completing whatever it is they must do.

Internet use was considered a supplemental activity in David's school because students were not required to exhibit technology-related competencies. He remarked, "As a teacher, I find myself supplementing and really teaching many things that are not part of the curriculum. At this time, computers and technology is one of those things." He explained that the only possible way to fit Internet use into the already busy day was to expect students to complete Internet activities independent of his guidance while he worked with others on the classroom curriculum. David wrote,

> The children need to be able to go to a computer and do what they have to without my assistance since I am teaching the class. I do not stop to answer their questions ... . The weaker readers are lost as their lack of reading skills hinders them.

It is important to point out that the teachers' interest in using Web sites with textual aids for literacy support was not so different than what they typically did with print-based reading material in the classroom. As Marcy explained in an interview response,

> We have spent a lot of time in our school this year putting emphasis on using textual aids when reading books, newspaper articles, magazines,

unsuitable Web sites. Adam explained in an interview response, "We have Net-Patrol on our network, which filters out many inappropriate sites." However, he had occasional problems with the monitoring system when it blocked sites that were actually acceptable in the classroom. This would interfere with some of his lessons as he was planning on using those sites with his students.

A third method of protecting students from inappropriate material was to completely prohibit online searches. The district that Cindy, the sixth-grade teacher, worked for chose to do this. Whenever Cindy wanted her students to use information on the Internet for research, she would have to conduct searches herself on the specified topics and bookmark the sites for her students to view during class. This controlled the students' Internet use and also put the burden of conducting student research on the teacher.

Finally, a fourth precaution was mentioned by Julie, the ninth-grade health teacher. In addition to the required permission slip, Julie talked to her students about the different types of information available on the Internet. She hoped that these discussions would help them make mature decisions about what they viewed on the Internet. She stated in an interview response,

> A couple of times my students have stumbled upon things I consider to be inappropriate, so I discuss that with them and have so far been able to use it as a learning tool to explain that in addition to lots of information, there is an abundance of misinformation and inappropriate information. I try to help them become intelligent and discriminant Internet users.

The issue of Internet safety affected teachers at varying grade levels. However, David and Cindy were the only elementary teachers to discuss it in depth. This may be due to the fact that they acted as the filter for inappropriate material by finding the appropriate Web sites and bookmarking them so students were never given the opportunity to view unsuitable locations.

Evaluating the Accuracy of Internet Material

Due to the ease in posting information on the Internet, it was important for the teachers to teach their students how to evaluate the accuracy of information found there. Although they taught their students to question information in print-based textbooks and encyclopedias, the elementary and secondary teachers felt the Internet made this issue much more prevalent. Will, a fourth-grade teacher, explained in a journal entry that "With the ease of publishing pages on the WWW, it is a dicey proposition to find authentic, well-documented, authoritative sources of information!" Furthermore, Hannah felt the vast amount of information on the Internet made it even more necessary for her to teach students how to evaluate reading material for information accuracy and reliability. She commented in an interview response that

> Technology has certainly changed the information around us, as well as the quality of it. I remember as a student thinking that if it was in

print, it must be true. Of course, this was pure naiveté, but at least the information in books was reviewed by someone and given some degree of credibility.

The teachers approached teaching and reinforcing the evaluation of Internet information in two ways: (a) They discussed with their students the importance of evaluating information and (b) they developed criteria so their students could evaluate information on their own.

Several teachers had not encountered many Web sites with inaccurate information, although they knew it was a possibility. When they did find discrepancies on Web sites, the teachers used the experience as an opportunity to discuss with their students the importance of evaluating reading material for accuracy. For example, if she questioned material, Emily remarked,

> I would explain to the students that this is not necessarily correct, and then we would talk about our sources that we learned the facts from. We would then write a note to the author of the Web page and explain why we may disagree with what is written.

Emily would turn the discrepancy into a learning experience—one in which her students had to think about and articulate why the information was incorrect.

Julie also reinforced the importance of evaluating information by speaking to her students about the types of materials found on the Internet. She wrote this in an interview response:

> I talk with students about being intelligent consumers throughout all of our class. I explain that there are a lot of sites that do not have a medical basis and that actually promote illegal activities. Although our school does not allow access to sites that are known trouble areas, I still want my students to know that as they search, there is a lot of junk out there.

When Leigh's students were confronted with inaccurate information, she talked to them about how to use multiple resources to find the correct information. Since the beginning of the school year, she taught her students to always use a variety of resources when researching a topic. She believed this would help them verify the information and highlight discrepancies. She remarked, "Because all information is not accurate, we check more than one source for appropriate information: books, [the Internet], interviews, encyclopedias."

In an effort to teach students how to evaluate online information on their own, several teachers developed Web page evaluation criteria, which provided students with substantial things to look for when deciding whether or not they should use a Web page as a source. For example, Will suggested that reputable Web sites include the following components:

1. An organization signature with address, telephone number, and e-mail contact.

I believe the students are being more careful with their language arts skills. Their errors are pretty easy to see, and they do not seem to have any problems with changing them. In paper and pencil writing, it is very difficult to get them to change what they have written.

Melanie also created a classroom Web page. At her site, she provided links to her students' published work, providing a "large audience" for her students, as well as a "real-life reason to practice proofreading skills." Melanie believed her class members were highly motivated by the prospect of other people reading their work. However, she pointed this out in an interview response:

In the primary grades, students who are good at writing do well if the assignment includes writing, students good at art do well if the assignment includes art, and so on. Technology levels the playing field somewhat. For example, writing and handwriting are easier, art applications/scanning/ photos make illustrations easier and so on.

Throughout our correspondence, Melanie wrote about publishing software and how it added an extra motivation for students who had difficulty with aspects of the writing process. They were more motivated to write for the Internet's audience when they were able to use software to increase the quality of their work. She explained, "I think the use of on-line publishing software is motivating for ALL students, but especially children who have difficulty with the physical act of writing and students who are not artistically inclined."

Some of the second graders in Melanie's class had trouble writing legibly due to immature motor skills. She stated that these students shied away from completing writing activities because of their laborious nature. She noted, "The students will avoid writing tasks, and even though they might have great ideas and much information to offer they do not demonstrate it in their writing." Publishing software such as KidsWord Deluxe and DreamWriter (word-processing programs) made writing more manageable for these students. Although it was time-consuming to type their work, it was still more efficient than trying to handwrite it. Melanie shared the following example in a journal entry:

A student in last year's class had handwriting that was generally illegible, and he would do nearly anything to avoid writing—sharpen pencils, count pages in his spiral notebook, watch his neighbors, etc. He became very anxious during writing time. When he was able to use a computer, he was able to create stories and reports. He was very proud of his work and began to enjoy it.

Once this student's work was readable, Melanie could post it on the Web page along with that of his classmates. This was very motivating for him.

Melanie also had students who were not very artistic, which made them uncomfortable with publishing their work. However, these students were able to use software such as ClipArt that provided them with ready-made pictures. They combined the clip art with their own designs to make better quality pieces. Melanie described it this way:

> Desktop publishing software often contains a draw/paint component with additional clip art, coloring book art, stamps, etc. Some students enjoy using the draw/paint component and are very confident in creating their own illustrations. However, some students feel more successful when mixing clip art or stamps to create their pictures.

Once again, the students were more motivated to complete writing assignments if they were able to create pieces they were proud to publish.

Bonnie, the Title I teacher, created a classroom Web page that showcased her students' work. She wrote in an interview response, "Our students are thrilled to have their writing published and many out-of-state relatives have the opportunity to read their work on-line." During the school year, some of Bonnie's students participated in the Mind's Eye Monster Exchange Project (www.monster exchange.org/index.htm), where classes exchanged written descriptions of an imaginary monster and the students had to draw pictures of what they thought the monster looked like. Bonnie's students were paired with a class in Australia. She wrote, "When writing for the Mind's Eye Monster Exchange Project, our third-grade students wrote more carefully when they considered that students in Australia would be reading their monster descriptions."

A few of the teachers did not post student work on classroom Web pages because they did not have the time or they had not developed a site yet. However, they did provide their students with opportunities to submit their work to Web sites designated to publishing student writing or they allowed students to create their own Web pages. For example, Will did not have a classroom Web page, but he felt online publishing opportunities were invaluable and greatly motivated most students to write and complete their best work. He often encouraged his students to submit their work to online children's journals for publication. He believed it empowered them by giving them "a voice" outside of the classroom. He stated in an interview response,

> More than any other thing, publishing on the WWW seems to be opening doors for giving children a voice where they have not had one with easy access up until now. Traditional children's periodicals (*Highlights*, *Cobblestone*) have been very limited in the amount of space they can offer and therefore the number of children they can publish. But online, there are endless possibilities to publish on commercial sites, as well as school Web pages and personal home pages.

At the time of this study, Louise's students were developing a Web site with a class in Thailand. She explained that her students exhibited much more motivation to complete this assignment than traditional handwritten projects that were only given to the teacher. Furthermore, the students took special care in making sure their work was accurate and polished. Louise reported this in an interview response:

> We are creating a Web page with the school in Thailand. The students are very good about proofreading both the text that is going on the page as well as proofing each other's e-mail messages they send [to the Thai students]. They very definitely do not want to give the impression that they are illiterate!

A few of Louise's students also created Web pages during the year to fulfill project requirements. Once again, the students were extremely motivated "when they knew an audience (other than the teacher) would be looking at it." Louise also stated that she "could see that they were more conscientious about the presentation of their information (including spelling, composition, and accuracy)." It seems that her students were aware of the ease with which electronic texts could be edited, making the revision process much more manageable. Louise shared the following story:

> One student, Jordan, created a Web page to publish the results of his independent study on the Suez Canal. He ran into some design problems and ended up entering his text but did not have time to spell check it. However, Jordan is an experienced computer user. He knew that he could quickly go back with some assistance (from me as a proofreader, the spell checker, or the dictionary) to make necessary corrections before the page goes on the Web. Jordan also knew that any changes/modifications that we agreed needed to be done when the project was evaluated can be easily incorporated without having to redo the entire project.

Thus, the malleability of electronic text may have contributed to the students' motivation to publish work on the Internet.

Although the teachers described most students as being motivated by online publishing, Will and Marcy pointed out that some students were not affected by it. Will commented in an interview response, "What I find is that children who have been reluctant writers previously continue to drag their feet on the computer. Yes, they are more engaged because of the interactivity. But they are not more fluent." Marcy supported this point. She wrote, "On-line publishing is highly motivational for students, provided the students feel comfortable keyboarding and the length of what they are writing is manageable." The teachers did not go into more detail about those students who were not motivated by online publishing. This is an area that needs to be further explored.

Discussion and Implications

As the number of Internet connections in schools increases, it is critical to understand how new technologies converge with classroom curriculum. The purpose of this study was to explore one such convergence, if and how the Internet influenced literacy and literacy instruction in K–12 classrooms. The work described in this study provides an initial step toward recognizing the Internet's presence in the classroom.

Limitations of the Study

The results of this research should be interpreted in relation to three limitations. First, the method of participant selection made it impossible to ensure a balance of gender, race, and ethnicity. Therefore, the work described in this article is limited to the perspectives of the 13 teachers involved. Although the participants' views may be similar to those of other teachers, it would be unfair to suggest they represent all teachers' views on the Internet's influence on literacy and literacy instruction.

Second, the method of data collection, done completely over the Internet, limited my interactions with the participants. The absence of face-to-face conversations and classroom site visits made it difficult to collect the rich descriptions typical of qualitative research. Furthermore, the data were based solely on self-reporting measures, and the participants' writing was the key to understanding their perspectives. Though none of them expressed a dislike for written communication, it is always possible that the teachers were unable to articulate the thoroughness of their responses through this medium.

Third, as the principal investigator, the theoretical and methodological choices I made inevitably affected this research (Labbo & Reinking, 1999). Thus, this is a study of both the teachers' perspectives and my work as a researcher.

Does the Internet Influence Literacy and Literacy Instruction in these Classrooms?

The teachers' realities of Internet use. Are the 13 teachers in this study at a point in their journey of Internet use where they notice new technologies redefining literacy and literacy instruction? Although previous research indicates that new technologies, such as the Internet, are redefining literacy (e.g., Leu, 2000; Reinking, 1998), the teachers in this study voiced different realities (Labbo & Reinking, 1999). As mentioned earlier, the teachers spoke of literacy in their classrooms in terms of reading and writing. It seemed that there were differences in how they viewed the Internet's influence on these two constructs. In terms of reading Internet material, the teachers reported that the skills required, such as effectively using electronic textual aids and evaluating online material, were extensions of what they taught students while reading print-based text. For example, the elementary teachers stated that they looked for electronic text that incorporated textual aids to help support their students' comprehension—much like they did with print-based text. While they did acknowledge the more interactive nature of the electronic textual aids, they did not voice concern over the complexities, in terms of instructing students on their use. Rather, they reported that teaching students to use electronic textual aids was neither easier nor more difficult than teaching print-based textual aids. Additionally, all of the teachers discussed the importance of teaching students to evaluate the accuracy of Internet material. Once again, the teachers reported that this was a skill they regularly taught for print-based text. The difference was that evaluating Internet material was more prevalent as the technology was used more frequently in the classroom. Therefore, it was necessary for all of the teachers to teach the skill in greater depth and also at an earlier age, as evaluation of information accuracy was not a skill usually spotlighted in early elementary grades.

In contrast, the elementary teachers and Louise, the seventh-grade social studies teacher, did recognize differences in their students' writing when they composed and published electronic texts. Recall, for example, Louise's report that her students were more likely to revise their work when it was composed on the computer and published online. Several other teachers echoed this view, including Melanie who reported that the malleability of electronic text made her nonartistic students more likely to include illustrations in their work. Although the teachers did not explicitly state that writing was being redefined by the technology, clearly there was a change as students' motivation to write increased when they published their work on the Internet.

The teachers' views of the Internet's influence on literacy and literacy instruction were not as extensive as some researchers have argued (Leu, 2000; Reinking et al., 1997). However, they provided important insights to these teachers' realities in relation to the extent of the convergence of the Internet, literacy, and literacy instruction in these 13 classrooms. Consider the differences between the elementary and secondary teachers' reports. One area the elementary teachers focused on was the reading level of Internet material. The secondary teachers, however, did not feel this was an issue. They stated that the abundant resources available on the Internet guaranteed that they or their students could find acceptable text. I suspect, though, there may be other reasons. For example, secondary teachers tended to define literacy in terms of content knowledge. What do students need to know? How and where do they find it? Secondary teachers do not usually provide reading assessment or instruction; therefore it would make sense that students' reading ability and text readability might not be major concerns for these teachers. In addition, it is possible that the students these teachers worked with did not have the types of reading difficulties apparent in other middle and high school classrooms. Therefore, it would not be difficult to find readable texts on the Internet. These differences in how the elementary and secondary teachers viewed reading may have affected the extent of the convergence of the Internet, literacy, and literacy instruction in their respective classrooms, leading to differing views.

Online publishing was a second area where the teachers' views differed by grade level. The elementary teachers noted an increase in their students' interest in writing when their work was published on the Internet. With the exception of one, Louise, the secondary teachers did not discuss this theme. This may be for several reasons. First, only two of the five secondary teachers maintained classroom Web pages. As stated previously, Louise did publish student work, but Julie's health class Web site was mainly a vehicle for her to communicate with students and parents outside of school by posting homework assignments and links to informative resources. Second, the secondary teachers in this study taught a variety of subjects including social studies, language arts, math, and health. It is possible that the teachers felt the subjects did not necessitate student publishing. Third, it is also possible that the Internet policies at the secondary teachers' schools did not permit student publishing. Like their views of reading, teachers' approaches to writing may have affected the extent of the convergence of the Internet, literacy, and literacy instruction in these classrooms.

Labbo and Reinking's (1999) notion of multiple realities reminds the research community that participants' perspectives are dependent upon their environment, philosophical beliefs, and education. Consequently, this study suggests that teachers' realities of reading and writing may greatly affect how the Internet influences literacy and literacy instruction.

Preparing students for today's literacy skills. There were commonalities in what researchers considered to be important literacy skills of the workplace and the skills the teachers reported they reinforced in the classroom. Recall the four skill areas highlighted as important since the Internet's infusion into the global market (Bruce, 1997a; CEO Forum, 1999; Means et al., 1993; Mikulecky & Kirkley, 1998; White House Panel on Educational Technology, 1997). These included the ability to (a) collaborate, (b) communicate, (c) acquire and sift through information, and (d) solve problems. The major themes that emerged in this study, along with the literacy activities teachers engaged their students in, supported these skill areas—for example, publishing student work on the Internet. Students in Bonnie's Title I class were involved in the Mind's Eye Monster Exchange Project where they exchanged written descriptions of monsters with an Australian class. The project encouraged them to be explicit in their descriptions so that children in another country could comprehend their writing and create an identical monster. This is one example of what Leu (2000) called an Internet Project—classes around the world coming together via the Internet to share a common activity and to learn from one another. Bonnie's elementary students had an authentic opportunity to work with others, thus strengthening both their collaboration and communication skills.

The elementary teachers' decision to publish student work also strengthened their students' ability to solve problems. As illustrated in the data, students were motivated to write well when they knew their work would be available to a wide audience. It was necessary then that the electronic texts the students created, including the words, graphics, and hyperlinks, were cohesive so that

*How Should the Literacy Community Keep Up with the
Changes Taking Place in K–12 Classrooms?*

A unique aspect of this study was the methodology employed to collect qualitative data. As literacy is influenced by the rapid development of new technologies, this approach provides the research community with an important
opportunity to experience the changes taking place in K–12 classrooms in
ways that keep up with the ever changing realities. Teacher and student Web
pages provide current windows into classrooms by posting student writing,
homework assignments, lecture notes, and collaborative projects. E-mail, listservs, and chat rooms provide the means for regularly communicating with
educators and students. Until recently, researchers had to physically visit a
classroom in order to interact with this rich information. Now, with the help
of the Internet, researchers are not confined to geographical boundaries and
can study classrooms around the world. While there is much to be learned
about this approach, this study provides an initial exploration of how it can be
used in the field of literacy.

Future Directions

Kamil et al. (2000) reviewed literacy journals and showed us that there is very
little research in the area of Internet technologies and literacy. However, new
work focusing on e-mail communications in elementary (McKeon, in press)
and postsecondary schools (Trathen & Moorman, in press) and studies of
how new technologies affect teachers' instructional practices (Baker, 2000)
are providing the research community with much needed insights. The work
presented in this article, I hope, will provide the literacy field with additional
future directions to explore.

First, because the design of this study was exploratory in nature, there were
several areas the teachers mentioned that need to be examined more thoroughly. To begin with, all of the teachers stated that it took a great deal of
time to view and choose appropriate Web sites for classroom use. This issue of
time is not unique to technology integration, but as schools begin to mandate
Internet use the issue will become more prevalent. It may help for the research
community to explore ways to ensure teachers have the time it takes to integrate the Internet effectively in their classrooms. Another area to explore is
Internet use with struggling readers. David, one of the fourth-grade teachers
in this study, stated that his special education students did not use the Internet because their reading skills were not high enough that they could use the
technology independently. While there is a body of literature focused on technology and struggling readers (e.g., Anderson-Inman & Horney, 1993, 1998),
it is important that we look at the dynamics of Internet-equipped classrooms
and suggest ways to support teachers with instructional strategies so that all
students are included in Internet use in the classroom. The findings from this

study also tell the research community the areas these 13 teachers were focused on in relation to the Internet's influence on literacy and literacy instruction. It seems they know *what* they need to teach (e.g., textual aids, evaluation of Internet text), but it may be helpful to further explore *how* best to teach these skills in light of new technologies (Leu, Mallette, & Karchmer, in press).

Second, this preliminary study highlights the importance of understanding how reading and writing on the Internet is different than reading and writing from a print-based book. We learned that teachers' and researchers' realities may be different as to the extent of the changes taking place; however, more in-depth explorations of this and the other issues mentioned may bring us closer to realizing how best to prepare our students for the literacy of today.

In conclusion, as the Internet becomes an even stronger presence in all facets of our lives, and as the technology converges with literacy and literacy instruction, educators must explore the possibilities it has to offer classrooms and the world of research. Lessons learned must be shared so that there are advances in knowledge of where new technologies will lead while proceeding through the next century. Consequently, like the teachers in this study, the literacy research community is navigating its journey of Internet use.

References

Anderson-Inman, L., & Horney, M. A. (1993, April). *Profiles of hypertext readers: Case studies from the ElectroText project*. Paper presented at the annual conference of the American Educational Research Association, Atlanta, GA.

Anderson-Inman, L., & Horney, M. A. (1998). Transforming text for at-risk readers. In D. Reinking, M. McKenna, L. D. Labbo, & R. Kieffer (Eds.), *Handbook of literacy and technology: Transformations in a pos-typographic world* (pp. 15–43). Mahwah, NJ: Erlbaum.

Angelo, T. A. (1996). Relating exemplary teaching to student learning. *New Directions for Teaching and Learning, 65*, 57–64.

Baker, E. A. (2000). Instructional approaches used to integrate literacy and technology. *Reading Online, 4*. Retrieved January 1, 2000 from the World Wide Web: www.readingonline.org/articles/baker/

Baker, E. A., & Kinzer, C. K. (1998). Effects of technology on process writing: Are they all good? In T. Shanahan & F. V. Rodriguez-Brown (Eds.), *47th yearbook of the National Reading Conference* (pp. 428–440). Chicago: National Reading Conference.

Balli, S. J., Wright, M. D., & Foster, P. N. (1997). Preservice teachers' field experiences with technology. *Educational Technology, 36*(5), 40–46.

Becker, H. J. (1991). When powerful tools meet conventional beliefs and institutional constraints. *The Computing Teacher, 18*(8), 6–9.

Bogdan, R. C., & Biklen, S. K. (1998). *Qualitative research in education: An introduction to theory and methods*. Boston: Allyn & Bacon.

Bolter, J. D. (1991). *Writing space: The computer, hypertext, and the history of writing*. Hillsdale, NJ: Erlbaum.

Bolter, J. D. (1998). Hypertext and the question of visual literacy. In D. Reinking, M. McKenna, L. D. Labbo, & R. Kieffer (Eds.), *Handbook of literacy and technology: Transformations in a post-typographic world* (pp. 3–13). Mahwah, NJ: Erlbaum.

Boyarin, J. (Ed.). (1993). *The ethnography of reading*. Berkeley, CA: University of California Press.

Perkins, D. N. (1991). Technology meets constructivism: Do they make a marriage? *Educational Technology, 5*, 18–23.

Reinking, D. (1995). Reading and writing with computers: Literacy research in a post-typographic world. In K. A. Hinchman, D. J. Leu, & C. K. Kinzer (Eds.), *Perspectives on literacy research and practice: 44th yearbook of the National Reading Conference* (pp. 17–33) Chicago: National Reading Conference.

Reinking, D. (1998). Synthesizing technological transformations of literacy in a post-typographical world. In D. Reinking, M. McKenna, L. D. Labbo, & R. Kieffer (Eds.), *Handbook of literacy and technology: Transformations in a post-typographic world* (pp. xi–xxx). Mahwah, NJ: Erlbaum.

Reinking, D., & Chanlin, L. J. (1994). Graphic aids in electronic texts. *Reading Research and Instruction, 33*, 207–232.

Reinking, D., Labbo, L., & McKenna, M. (1997). Navigating the changing landscape of literacy: Current theory and research in computer-based reading and writing. In J. Flood, S. B. Heath, & D. Lapp (Eds.), *Handbook of research on teaching literacy through the communicative and visual arts* (pp. 77–92). NY: Macmillan Library Reference.

Reinking, D., & Rickman, S. S. (1990). The effects of computer-mediated texts on the vocabulary learning and comprehension of intermediate-grade readers. *Journal of Reading Behavior, 22*, 395–411.

Report of the Webbased Education Commission to the President and Congress. (2000, December). *The power of the Internet for learning: Moving from promise to practice.* Retrieved January 2, 2001, from the World Wide Web: interact.hpcnet.org/webcommission/index.htm

Salomon, G., Globerson, T., & Guterman, E. (1989). The computer as a zone of proximal development: Internalizing reading-related metacognitions from a reading partner. *Journal of Educational Psychology, 81*, 620–627.

Schön, D. A. (1983). *The reflective practitioner.* New York: Basic Books.

Stahl, S. A., Hynd, C. R., Britton, B. K., McNish, M. M., & Bosquet, D. (1996). What happens when students read multiple source documents in history? *Reading Research Quarterly, 31*, 430–449.

Tao, L., & Reinking, D. (1996). *What research reveals about e-mail in education* (Report No. CS012853). Charleston, SC: Annual Meeting of the College Reading Association. (ERIC Document Reproduction Service No. ED 408 572).

Trathen, W., & Moorman, G. (in press). Using e-mail to create pedagogical dialogue in teacher education. *Reading Research and Instruction.*

United States Department of Labor. (2000). *Learning a living: A blueprint for highperformance. A SCANS report for America 2000.* Retrieved January 5, 2001, from the World Wide Web: www.ttrc.doleta.gov/SCANS/work.html

White House Panel on Educational Technology. (1997). *Report to the President on the use of technology to strengthen K 12 education in the United States.* Retrieved August 20, 1998 fromtheWorldWideWeb:www.whitehouse.gov/WH/EOP/OSTP/NSTC/PCAST/K–12ed.html#5.1

Wood, J. M. (1999). *Early literacy instruction and educational technologies: Three classroom-based models.* Unpublished doctoral dissertation, Harvard Graduate School of Education, Cambridge, MA.

Commentary Responses

Researching Technology and Literacy
Thirteen Ways of Looking at a Blackboard

COLIN HARRISON

UNIVERSITY OF NOTTINGHAM, ENGLAND

Introduction

Rachel Karchmer's (2001) landmark article on teachers' use of the Internet to support literacy instruction raises many issues that merit discussion. In offering a commentary on her article in a spirit of critical friendship, I shall make some comments on the methodology of the study, and I shall discuss in some detail the nature of literacy and the issue of whether using the Internet redefines literacy. Finally, I shall say something about truth. First, however, I will say a little about my own position.

My Research Background and Standpoint

Karchmer (2001) quoted, with approval, the essentially postmodern argument (p. 445) of Labbo and Reinking (1999), who used the concept of multiple realities to foreground the fact that one's interpretation of any set of events is constrained, framed, and filtered through a personal set of beliefs and philosophical and conceptual lenses. I share this view, and it is therefore appropriate for me to at least attempt to describe some of the beliefs, values, and preconceptions that I bring to this task.

Anyone who publishes a paper in the field of new technology should be aware that its shelf life may be brief, and that any valuable insights it contains at the time of publication may be outweighed by changes in the field that render its findings inaccurate or irrelevant even a few months later. I speak from experience here, since I am something of an expert in out-of-date research, having published my first paper on technology and literacy in 1981 (Harrison, 1981). That piece was partly philosophical, partly psephological, and partly based on research: It attempted to predict the future of the book, based on then current data on book publication and the purchase of new technology by schools. In many respects, the article was woefully ill-informed. At the time, the greatest threat to the book was not the Internet but schools' expenditure on hardware (the U.S. National Science Foundation did not launch the TCP/IP network, which grew to become the backbone of the Internet, until 1983). Even then, however, my research interests were close to those I have today: (a) the reading process and whether it is different in different contexts (Harrison, 2006); (b) the evaluation of how users, particularly children, learn from computers (Harrison, Lunzer, Tymms, Fitz-Gibbon, & Restorick, 2004); and (c) the implications for teachers of what we learn from research (Harrison, Pead, & Sheard, 2006).

Methodologically, I value many types of research: ethnographic approaches for the insights they provide into learning within multifaceted cultural contexts, case studies for their portrayal of the immediacy of learning in schools and other environments, and quantitative studies for the potential they offer of more widely generalizing from research, as well as their potential to influence those in power. As I indicated in my paper with Phil Gough (Harrison & Gough, 1996) on how we learn from research, however, while I have an eclectic and ecumenical disposition toward methodology, I take an essentially postmodern view of the concept of truth. I do not believe that research can get to the absolutes, but rather that truth is provisional and that the insights that research can offer are meaningful and indeed valuable only insofar as they are interpreted within communities of discourse that agree to adhere to a particular set of linguistic and cultural practices. I have been a research journal editor, and I have been involved in many multivariate statistical projects, but I am also a former high-school English teacher and failed blues guitarist. So my interpretation of Karchmer's paper (2001) is filtered not only through a lens that looks for methodological rigor and meta-analytical depth, but also through a belief that a single perspective on methodology is rarely enough. Karchmer's (2001) thirteen teachers sent me back to Wallace Stevens's (1963) 'Thirteen ways of looking at a blackbird', a wonderful poem that in its words and images offers many profound insights that are relevant to our understanding of the relationship between reality and representation, art and life, the real and the imagined, and the utterance and the echoing space after the utterance:

> I do not know which to prefer,
>
> The beauty of inflections
>
> Or the beauty of innuendoes,

The blackbird whistling

Or just after. (p. 44)

What Did Karchmer Have to Say?

In her article, Karchmer (2001) explored the reports of thirteen K–12 teachers on how the Internet was influencing literacy and literacy instruction in their classrooms. She argued (a) that changes in technology have always affected instruction, (b) that the Internet is prompting unprecedented change, and (c) that teachers lack models of good practice that they might draw upon to guide them through this period of change. Her theoretical orientation section follows Labbo and Reinking (1999) in arguing for a "multiple realities" approach to the problem, and her literature review embodies this stance, recognizing the importance of historical, economic, and utilitarian perspectives on technology and literacy, while at the same time emphasizing that researching the Internet brings us up against ontological and epistemological problems. Karchmer advanced the argument that the Internet redefines literacy and outlined the challenges this poses for the reader, for pedagogy, and for teacher development.

In her methodology section, Karchmer (2001) first identified her own stance, as an insider conducting research, then took some time describing the procedures that permitted her to identify the thirteen "exemplary educators" whose e-mail correspondence forms the basis of the data reported in the article. These asynchronously conducted interviews contained 25 to 30 exchanges and were supplemented by reflective e-journals that were kept on a weekly basis by the participants. The resulting transcripts were analyzed using a constant-comparative method, and the data were finally crystallized into eight themes, which were ultimately collapsed into three major themes: (a) the appropriateness of Internet material, (b) the evaluation of the accuracy of Internet material, and (c) the publication of student work on the Internet. The paper deals with each of these major themes in turn, drawing upon the comments of individual teachers as appropriate.

The discussion of this data is preceded by a comment on the limitations of the study, but then moves swiftly to the key question: Does the Internet influence literacy and literacy instruction in these teachers' classrooms? Karchmer's (2001) answer is interesting. Broadly speaking, and in contrast to much of the literature she cited, the teachers' reports did not suggest much in terms of their noticing any change in the processes of reading, nor was there much indication of a significant change in pedagogy. With writing, by contrast, the elementary teachers (plus one seventh-grade social-studies teacher) noted some differences in writing processes for students using the Internet compared with their writing on paper. Another primary-secondary contrast related to the teachers' use of the Internet for publishing: The primary teachers rated this as very important, but the secondary teachers did not see publishing as an important area. The teachers' reports provided evidence of an awareness of the potential of the Internet to widen students' knowledge of other cultures and of the importance of students developing a critical and, where necessary, skeptical stance toward Internet content. The issue of Internet safety was highlighted as important, as was the issue of how teachers might best learn how to integrate effective pedagogy using the Internet into their curriculum. Karchmer ended the paper with a look forward and a call for widespread consideration of the themes she has highlighted.

The Journey Ahead—Metaphor and Methodology

The title of Karchmer's (2001) article, "The Journey Ahead: Thirteen Teachers Report on How the Internet Influences Literacy and Literacy Instruction in Their K–12 Classrooms," is, when you think about it, quite surprising. The clause after the colon gives readers a sixteen-word abstract for the paper in the present tense, but the opening noun phrase seems, at first, to be somewhat out of place in a research journal. "The journey ahead" does not suggest an analytical review of research conducted in the past; it sounds poetic. It is a metaphor that steadfastly looks forward, almost celebrating the fact that the data in the paper may have a limited life span and looking beyond the data to lessons in the future. This sense of provisionality is pervasive and paradoxically may have contributed in important ways to the paper's robustness over time. In her methodology section (p. 450), Karchmer reminded herself and readers (a) of the biases she brought to the study, (b) that her questions circumscribed the data she would collect, and (c) that the categories within which she chose to collapse the data were her own and would necessarily have been filtered through her own preconceptions.

One could add to Karchmer's (2001) notes on the need for caution in interpreting this study some further methodological challenges. First, while Karchmer took care to obtain nominations from a variety of authoritative sources in order to identify her "exemplary educators," those reading her study have to deal with the possibility that her participants may not in fact have been wonderfully effective teachers. In a study of outstanding U.S. elementary school literacy teachers, Pressley, Allington, Wharton-MacDonald, Collins-Block, and Morrow (2001) reported that of the teachers nominated by their principals as exemplary, only half had students whose achievement was above average. Nearly all the nominated "exemplary" teachers were articulate, well-theorized curriculum innovators, but half turned out to be fluent apologists rather than highly effective teachers when their effectiveness was measured by its impact on student learning. To be fair, Karchmer judiciously avoided conflating nomination with effectiveness by saying that the teachers were "identified by other educators as exemplary" (p. 450). She also offered the reasonable argument that defining "exemplary" was not necessary; it was more important to go along with the internalized conceptions of members of the teachers' peer group.

Another methodological challenge relates to how the thirteen teachers used the Internet. Toward the end of the discussion section (p. 463), Karchmer reminded readers that the teachers had different ways of dealing with the issue of safe Internet use and that this included having one participant who worked in a school that totally prohibited online searching. When I read this, my reaction was surprise that a teacher ("Cindy" is cited as an example, but I had the feeling that there may have been others) in such a school was included in the study. How, I asked myself, could teachers who were unable to offer their students online access to the Internet be considered to be using the Internet to develop "literacy and literacy instruction in their K–12 classrooms"? Well, that reaction was harsh; rereading the paper reminded me that it was Cindy's district that had prohibited online searching (p. 457) and that Cindy was being creative in seeking to offer students an alternative route into Internet research. The substantive point remains, however, that what we call "Internet searching" massively varies in relation to how much filtering of content takes place.

It may be useful to think of Internet access as a continuum with different levels of access including (a) unfiltered; (b) software-filtered access that might, for example, block games and pornography; (c) system-level filters within which the student sees what might look like the whole Internet, but in reality has access only to a district-wide cache of sites that have been viewed earlier by teachers; (d) a much smaller school-level set of sites that can be viewed on its intranet; and (e) offline-only access to selected Internet material. I think that future studies of Internet use will need to be even more detailed and explicit than was Karchmer when they describe the nature of students' access to the Internet because factors such as navigation, readability, authenticity, and evaluation will all be significantly different for students who are at different points along the Internet access continuum.

Karchmer's (2001) methodology has many strong points, not the least of which is the care with which she describes her own decision making and the value positions that underpinned her decisions. She outlined some of these in the exemplary section on researcher stance (pp. 449–450); however, Karchmer also thoughtfully dealt with possible challenges to her methodology as they arose. One such area concerns her total reliance on e-mail as the basis for data collection. Given that the central theme of the study was how literacy impacts teachers and the pedagogy of literacy, it might be considered surprising that Karchmer did not visit any classrooms, nor did she ever meet with, phone, or chat to any of the teachers. Her defense of this decision, however, is compelling, in my view. As she pointed out (p. 450), the collection of e-data crosses geographical boundaries, thus making possible virtually instant contact with teachers from Oregon to North Carolina, and when it is asynchronous, it

ence difficulties within hypertext networks (Edwards & Hardman, 1989). The navigational challenges are different. Internet readers have three problems: (a) not knowing where to go next, (b) not knowing how to get there, and (c) not knowing where you are at a given time in relation to the whole (Edwards & Hardman, 1989).

Karchmer's (2001) teachers have less to say about the issue of navigation than one might have expected, but of course, navigation becomes important in direct relation to how much freedom a student has to search the whole Internet. In this study, the constraints of working with greatly filtered Web material will have reduced the challenge of navigation that many students face today when dealing with potential access to tens of billions of pages of the unfiltered Internet and the dozens of navigation tools that—if effectively used—constrain the dimensionality of the Internet.

Did Karchmer's Study "Redefine Literacy"?: A Social Practice View

It will be clear by now that, in my view, one of the most interesting and important aspects of Karchmer's (2001) work is her treatment of the issue of whether or not the Internet "redefines literacy." I am suggesting that if we focus on cognitive processes of reading, the answer is negative, or at least, that the article does not offer compelling evidence to the contrary. If we choose, however, to define literacy in terms of social practice, we arrive at a different answer. Karchmer has provided a good deal of evidence that both readers' and teachers' literacy practices on the Internet are very different from those in print environments. I have already suggested that issues of navigation and establishing one's current location on the Web are very different from print, and these strategic issues are certainly literacy practices. Just as important are the literacy practices associated with judging the veracity or authority of Internet material.

Karchmer quoted the words of one of her teachers to establish the point about information accuracy on the Internet: "Technology has certainly changed the information around us, as well as the quality of it" ("Hannah," p. 457). Perhaps the most change in literacy practice has taken place in this area. This theme binds together the two final parts of Karchmer's data: On the one hand, issues around the authority of text totally redefine how readers approach and evaluate information on the Internet; on the other, issues around students writing for the Web totally redefine and democratize the processes of publication. The biggest problem faced by the teachers in Karchmer's research is the extent to which the Internet has been exponentially developing to usher in a postmodern world in which truth is defined by counts of mouse clicks rather than by textbook or encyclopedia authors and the number of publishers matches the number of servers connected to the Internet.

What exactly has changed since 1999, when Karchmer (2001) collected her data, and do these changes suggest that the insights her teachers shared now seem irrelevant or plain wrong? Perhaps the biggest change has been in the much readier access of both teachers and students to the Internet. One feels that today, Karchmer would be unlikely to find a substantial number of teachers reporting that they had "not encountered web sites with inaccurate information" (p. 458). Similarly, a more recent U.K. survey of students' use of new technology reported that out-of-school computer use was far more influential on student learning than school-based use. In a one-week, time-sampled study, students spent up to 100 times longer on computers at home than they did at school, and at home, they were much more likely to have unfiltered access to the Internet (Becta, 2002).

In many ways, the Internet seems today to be more dangerous, with critical literacy skills even more important, as students have to deal not only with spoof information (such as the Web-based religion of Pastafarianism, created to challenge "Intelligent Design," which between June and September of 2005 went from 100 to 140,000 hits per day without publicity), but also with such insidious fare as Holocaust-denial sites that purport to be authoritative historical sources. In hindsight, Karchmer's (2001) teachers do not appear to have been naïve or overidealistic; they trusted their students to develop the skills that would be needed to manage this new learning environment, just as Karchmer trusted her teachers. She gave her teachers a voice, and attempted to let them speak for themselves, and they did so, often with vision as well as dignity. David, for example, argued the case that students were more careful over matters of editing and composing because in Web publication they had an authentic audience, and all the teachers agreed that working on the Internet was highly motivating.

Perhaps today we would be likely to turn a social-psychological or even social-justice lens toward the issue of why students found and still find the Internet so attractive. The dangers of the Internet, the lure of finding things that one is not supposed to see, and the possibility of discovering that the teacher might be wrong are understandably intriguing. So, too, is the possibility of finding a voice and of exploring the possibility of presenting or representing oneself to a billion others at a time when that identity is itself at melting point. Karchmer's (2001) teachers believed, for the most part, that publication using the Internet was full of exciting possibilities, not only for self-expression, but also for exploration of oneself in relation to others, including members of cultures very different to one's own. In this respect, Karchmer's article was prophetic: The winner of the International Reading Association's technology teacher of the year award in 2006 was Andrew Schofield, a teacher of teenagers in Vancouver, Canada, whose work on using presentation of self to change "biographies of despair" into "autobiographies of hope" impressively captured the ways in which technology can offer young people a route to self-expression and self-actualization that is as powerful as it is novel. Publication using new technologies is highly motivating and offers a chance to create and frame identity; it is a social practice capable of changing lives.

A Final Word

Karchmer's (2001) article is justly regarded as a landmark piece for many reasons. It is theoretically interesting in that it challenges and invites us to extend our conceptualizations of literacy. It is epistemologically interesting, in that it raises important issues around notions of verifiability, meaning, and the authority of knowledge in relation to both using and researching literacy on the Internet. It is methodologically interesting, in that it invites us to reconsider how we research literacy in new technological contexts. Finally, it is empirically interesting, in that it presents data that is wholly based on Web-collected accounts of literacy activity.

In many ways, Karchmer's (2001) article is about truth. Who is right in relation to the question of whether or not the Internet "redefines literacy"? How far can we trust assertions of the merits of one teacher from another? How trustworthy is Web content? I would suggest that Karchmer takes a postmodern position on these issues. Truth is provisional, methodology is problematic, and the Web changes the ground rules and often reverses the polarity of textual authority. The provisionality of a postmodern view, however, need not lead us to spiral downward into solipsism. Points of fixity and important values exist, though these are not absolutes. Like a GPS fix, the values and meanings that we agree upon are often more stable when they are based on multiple perspectives from a constellation of theories and methodologies.

Finally, therefore, I feel that we must trust Karchmer's view that a search for truth leads us to a deeper valuing of multiple perspectives, both in terms of our conceptualizations of reality and our conventions of representation. The process is reciprocal, too: A valuing of multiple perspectives leads us to a closer approximation to what is to be regarded as "true." As Wallace Stevens put it in "On the Road Home,"

It was when I said,

"There is no such thing as the truth,"

That the grapes seemed fatter.

The fox ran out of his hole. (p. 164)

References

Becta (2002). *ImpaCT2: The impact of information and communication technologies on pupil learning and attainment.* London: DfES. (DfES No. 0696/2002).

Eagleton, M. (2002, July/August). Making text come to life on the computer: Toward an understanding of hypermedia literacy. *Reading Online, 6*(1). Retrieved June 26, 2007 from http://www.readingonline.org/articles/art_index.asp?HREF=eagleton2/index.html

Edwards, D. M., & Hardman, L. (1989). Lost in hyperspace: Cognitive mapping and navigation in a hypertext environment. In R. McAleese (Ed.), *Hypertext: Theory and practice* (pp. 105–125). Oxford, U.K.: Intellect Books.

Harrison, C. (1981). The textbook as an endangered species: The implications of economic decline and technological advance on the place of reading in learning. *Oxford Review of Education*, 7(3), 231–240.

Harrison, C. (2006). Postmodern research and e-learning: Anatomy and representation. *European Educational Research Journal*, 5(2), 80–93.

Harrison, C., & Gough, P. B. (1996). Compellingness in reading research. *Reading Research Quarterly*, 31(3), 334–341.

Harrison, C., Lunzer, E. A., Tymms, P., Fitz-Gibbon, C. T., & Restorick, J. (2004). Use of ICT and its relationship with performance in examinations: A comparison of the ImpaCT2 project's research findings using pupil-level, school-level, and multilevel modelling data. *Journal of Computer Assisted Learning*, 20(5), 319–337.

Harrison, C., Pead, D., & Sheard, M. (2006). 'P, not-P, and possibly Q' literacy teachers learning from digital representations of the classroom. In D. Reinking, M. McKenna, L. D. Labbo, & R. Kieffer (Eds.), *Handbook of literacy and technology: Transformations in a post-typographic world* (2nd ed., pp. 310–330). Mahwah, NJ: Erlbaum.

Karchmer, R. A. (2001). The journey ahead: Thirteen teachers report how the internet influences literacy and literacy instruction in their K–12 classrooms. Reading Research Quarterly, 36(4), 442–466.

Labbo, L. D., & Reinking, D. (1999). Negotiating the multiple realities of technology in literacy research and instruction. *Reading Research Quarterly, 34(4), 478–492.*

Morkes, J., and Nielson, J. (1997). *Concise, scannable, and objective: How to write for the Web.* Retrieved on September 14, 2006, from http://www.useit.com/papers/webwriting/writing.html

Nielsen, J. (1997). *Be succinct! (Writing for the Web).* Retrieved September 14, 2006, from http://www.useit.com/alertbox/9703b.html

Pressley, M., Allington, R. L., Wharton-MacDonald, R., Collins-Block, C., & Morrow, L. (2001). *Learning to read: Lessons from exemplary first-grade classrooms.* New York: Guilford.

Reinking, D. (1998). Synthesizing technological transformations of literacy in a post-typographical world. In D. Reinking, M. McKenna, L. D. Labbo, & R. Kieffer (Eds.), *Handbook of literacy and technology: Transformations in a posttypographic world* (pp. xi–xxx). Mahwah, NJ: Erlbaum.

Stevens, W. (1963). *Selected poems* (pp. 43–46). London: Faber and Faber.

Stevens, W. (1971). *On the road home, palm at the end of the mind* (p. 164). New York: Alfred A. Knopf.

Wenger, M., & Payne, D. (1996). "Comprehension and retention of nonlinear text: Considerations of working memory and material-appropriate processing." *American Journal of Psychology*, 109, 93–130.

Synopsis

Karchmer's (2001) study explores the accounts of 13 teachers who reported on how the Internet influenced literacy curriculum and pedagogy in their classrooms. The 10 women and 3 men, all European American, taught kindergarten to grade 12 classes in 11 different states in the United States and were identified by colleagues as exemplary in their use of technology. Karchmer initially contacted educators who used electronic mailing lists and Web sites for teachers, in addition to teachers involved in a previous Internet-focused study, in order to solicit nominations. When asked to identify reasons why they had identified specific teachers, nominators stated that they were proficient in the use of the Internet in the curriculum and innovative in its use and, in some cases, were involved in providing professional development within their school districts. From 31 nominated teachers, 16 initially responded to Karchmer's invitation to participate but only 13 continued participating beyond the first few weeks.

The primary method of data collection was asynchronous e-mail correspondence conducted over 3 months. Semistructured interviews used this mode, with Karchmer making 25 to 30 communications with each participant. The teachers were also asked to keep weekly entries in a reflective journal in which they recorded their Internet-related experiences both in and out of the classroom. In addition, a range of other materials was collected, including class Web pages, lesson plans, work from school projects and articles three teachers had written for online journals. Data were analyzed using constant-comparative analysis and examined using an analytic framework drawn from Labbo and Reinking's (1999) notion of "multiple realities." This emphasises that research participants' attitudes and practices in relation to the use of new technologies are shaped by their education, philosophical beliefs, and environment.

Three key themes emerged from an analysis of the data: (a) the appropriateness of Internet material, (b) evaluating the accuracy of the material, and (c) publishing student work on the Internet. In relation to the first finding, elementary teachers were primarily concerned with the readability of the material children could access and the secondary teachers were worried about safety in relation to Internet use. Elementary teachers were apprehensive about needing to spend longer choosing appropriate reading material from the Web than print-based material, which was often graded. One teacher felt the challenges of Web-based material were such that he did not allow children with reading difficulties to access it. The secondary teachers were not concerned with the readability of the text in the Web, as the majority of children they taught were fluent readers. Like their primary colleagues, however, they worried that children could potentially access harmful material on the Internet. They addressed this by obtaining written parental permission for children to use the computers, employing firewalls or, in an extreme case, prohibiting pupils from conducting online searches at all.

Karchmer's (2001) discussion of the second theme to emerge from the analysis—evaluating the accuracy of Internet material—highlights the teachers' practice with regard to developing pupils' abilities to evaluate Web resources. Teachers reported talking with classes about identifying the sources of material, verifying information, and developing and using a set of criteria for the evaluation of sites. The final theme, publishing students' work on the Internet, addresses issues relating to motivation and audience. Several teachers reported that their pupils were more motivated to write for the Internet since they felt that having a global audience offered a purpose for writing. Students appeared to take a greater interest in the technical aspects and presentation of their work when it was written for the Web and enjoyed using facilities like clip-art offered by desktop publishing software. However, this work was conducted primarily in elementary schools; the secondary teachers did not discuss encouraging children to write for the Web.

In evaluating the findings, Karchmer (2001) addressed a number of key questions. First, she discussed how far the Internet influences literacy and literacy instruction in the classrooms of the teachers concerned. She suggested that the teachers did not feel that the Internet had changed the nature of literacy or literacy teaching in any fundamental way, despite indications otherwise. The teachers also felt that the Internet enabled them to reinforce specific skills in the classroom, skills that have been identified as key to the global market economy: collaboration, communication, and the abilities to acquire and evaluate information and to solve problems.

Karchmer (2001) concluded by discussing the implications of her work for teacher education and professional development. She suggested that preservice and in-service teacher programs should prepare educators for the use of the Internet in the curriculum and that teachers similar to those participating in the study should be used as exemplars. In addition, Karchmer advocated using the Internet as a professional development tool, suggesting that teachers should be encouraged to share ideas, projects and strategies on mailing lists and Web sites for educators. Finally, Karchmer reflected on how the literacy community should keep pace with the changes taking place due to the use of the Internet in schools. She proposed that the methodology employed in her own study, the analysis of Web-based materials, could be used to determine the changes taking place in curricula and pedagogy on a global scale.

Drawing on her findings, Karchmer (2001) identified future directions for research. In relation to issues raised by the teacher participants, she suggested that researchers need to investigate ways of ensuring that teachers have more time to integrate Internet use in their classroom practice. She identified the case of the teacher who reported not allowing children with special educational needs to use the Internet as raising an issue for further study. She also suggested that, while the teachers appeared to be confident about what to teach, they were less familiar with pedagogical strategies and this too could be a fruitful avenue for further study. Finally, Karchmer suggested that the differences between teachers' and researchers' perceptions of the changing nature of literacy invite further in-depth exploration. Given the increasing presence of the Internet in everyday lives, Karchmer argued that is important to share the lessons learned from studies such as this in order to inform future practice.

Positionality

I will examine the paper in the light of my own "multiple realities" (Labbo & Reinking, 1999) and draw from two specific theoretical paradigms within literacy research that have informed my own research agenda for some years. The first is the New Literacy Studies (NLS) tradition. This emphasises the situated nature of literacy practices, located as they are within specific social, cultural, historical, and economic contexts (Gee, 1996; Street, 1993). I refer particularly to work by Lankshear and Knobel (2003, 2004, 2006a, 2006b), who used lenses offered by NLS to view literacy as it is mediated and transformed through new technologies. Second, the review is informed by research that has highlighted the relationship between in- and out-of-school literacy practices, particularly in relation to popular culture and digital literacy practices (Carrington & Marsh, 2005; Davies, 2006; Dyson, 2002; Marsh & Millard, 2005; Merchant, 2004). Looking to the future, I weave together these two strands with sociological work undertaken in Australia on productive pedagogies for social justice (Hayes, Mills, Christie, & Lingard, 2006).

It is important to state at the outset that Karchmer (2001) presented a carefully conducted and well-documented study that offers valuable insights into teachers' practices with regard to Internet use. My analysis focuses not on the methodology employed, nor on the quality of the research report itself but, rather, on the issues raised by the teachers and the silences and gaps evident in their testimonies of classroom practice. It is inevitable that these gaps will have emerged during the years since the study was conducted, given the rapid changes that have taken place in relation to the use of the Internet in schools. I reinterpret some of the data presented in the light of the theoretical paradigms previously outlined and discuss how the teachers' practices relate to current concerns in the development of digital literacy curricula.

Dichotomous Mind-Sets

In the first instance, a significant question that needs to be raised is the validity of these teachers' status as exemplary practitioners in relation to the use of the Internet in classrooms. Karchmer (2001) did not narrow the nominating process by imposing strictly defined criteria, and she checked the validity of the claims made by examining the reasons given for the nomination of these particular teachers. However, there is very little evidence from the examples of practice offered by the teachers that this group would qualify as exemplary teachers in the current educational climate. Indeed, some of them demonstrate quite traditional attitudes toward the use of the Internet, what some might characterize as a traditional mind-set. Mind-sets are sets of attitudes, beliefs, and values about a specific issue that inform practice.

Lankshear and Knobel (2006a) suggested that there are two predominant mind-sets in relation to the use of new technologies in the literacy curriculum. The first mind-set is characterized by a set of assumptions relating to technology that suppose computers and other technologies enable us to undertake existing tasks in an improved manner. The world is very much as it has always been; what has changed is the way in which everyday practices are undertaken. The second mind-set, however, is predicated on the assumption that technologies have changed the way in which we live and that they have fundamentally transformed employment and leisure practices in the global flows and 'scapes of late modernity' (Appadurai, 1996). Lankshear and Knobel related these two mind-sets to degrees of familiarity with technologies. The newcomers to technological practices, those who grew up during an era when technology was less pervasive, are more likely to adhere to the first mind-set than are those who have been immersed in technology-rich worlds from a young age, the digital insiders. These insiders are, Lankshear and Knobel suggested, more likely to demonstrate the second mind-set. While dichotomies are always inevitably problematic because they fail to capture the complexities along any continuum, this characterization is helpful when trying to make sense of the way in which some educators respond to questions of technological innovation. In the case of the teachers in this study, there are distinct traces of the first mind-set.

In a number of the examples of practice given, it is primarily the teachers themselves who are in control of the learning. The elementary teachers in particular describe selecting the texts that children can access on screen in terms of their readability. Anxieties with regard to safe Internet use led one teacher to state, "I shy away from real online searches. I prefer to let the students search through the links I set up on my page" (Karchmer, 2001, p. 457). This approach is typical of the first mind-set in which, as Lankshear and Knobel (2006a) suggest education

> … operates on the presumption that the teacher is the ultimate authority on matters of knowledge and learning. Hence, whatever is addressed and done in the classroom must fall within the teacher's competence parameters, since he or she is to *direct learning*. (Lankshear and Knobel, 2006a, p. 55)

For some activities, teachers do need to guide beginning readers to appropriate sites but for others, an important part of the learning process for children would be to identify for themselves those sites that are appropriate for their needs. Children from very young ages are able to engage in such critical literacy practices (Comber & Simpson, 2001; Vasquez, 2004). In addition, there is a necessity for pupils to develop strategies for safe Internet use, and it is clear that this is often not addressed sufficiently well in schools (Valentine, Marsh, & Pattie, 2005), but such work needs to be undertaken with due recognition of the skills and strategies many children have already developed in relation to Internet use, rather than educators being overcautious about access and thus imposing limiting strategies.

The use of the concept of divergent mind-sets to review the practices of these teachers also explains an issue raised by Karchmer (2001) in her discussion of the findings. She pointed out, "The teachers' views of the Internet's influence on literacy and literacy instruction were not as extensive as some researchers have argued" (p. 462). This position is not surprising when considering that the teachers were approaching the use of the Internet within their curricula from a traditional mind-set. Indeed, the secondary teachers involved in the study did not allow pupils to publish work on the Internet, which further suggests that they would have little understanding of the differences between writing on- and offscreen. For practitioners to be mindful of the way in which literacy is being transformed by digital technologies, they would need to be engaged in practices that illustrated the changes in stark and challenging ways. This does not appear to be the case with the teachers in Karchmer's study at that point in time, although this cannot be simply attributed to the historical context for the study, as many teachers in more recent years also report limited practice with regard to the use of the Internet (Marsh, Brooks, Hughes, Ritchie, & Roberts, 2005; Valentine et al., 2005).

Narrow Curriculum

Not only were the teachers constrained by their attitudes toward the convergence of technology and literacy, they were also limited by their apparent lack of attention to children's out-of-school practices in the curriculum. Extensive work over the past decade attests to the need for educators to attend to these practices in order to ensure relevance and challenge (Alvermann, Moon, & Hagood, 1999; Dyson, 2002; Knobel, 2005; Marsh & Millard, 2005).

Apart from one activity described in the paper that involved children responding to pupils from schools in other countries in the "Mind's Eye Monster Exchange Project" (Karchmer, 2001, p. 460), the lessons outlined by the teachers were based on more conventional activities, such as using the Internet to search for information or posting stories about field trips and holidays on a class Web site. None of the activities described appeared to draw in any meaningful way on children's out-of-school experiences with technologies. This lack of attention to such experiences would have even more import in the current educational contexts, for there is now much evidence to suggest that children and young people have widespread experience of the use of the Internet and

Table 38b.1 0 to 6 Year-Olds' Use Of Media and New Technologies in the Home (Marsh et al., 2005)

Using TVs and DVDS	Using computers	Using console games	Using mobile phones	Other technologies
• Watching television • Watching films • Using the remote control to change channels • Rewinding and forwarding DVD/video players • Playing games on interactive TV using the red button	• Playing computer games • Using art packages • Using word processing packages • Using desktop publishing packages • Surfing the Internet • Playing games on the Internet • Printing off pages (e.g., pictures to color in) • Using chat rooms and MSN (with adult as scribe)	• Playing a range of console games, e.g., Rugrats, Sonic the Hedgehog • Using PlayStation2 EyeToy, which projects children's images on the screen	• Playing with toy or discarded mobile phones to conduct "pretend" conversations • Using real mobile phones to speak to relatives (with adult support) • Pretending to send text messages • Sending text messages with adults acting as scribes • Using the camera feature of mobile phones	• Using dance mats • Using karaoke machines • Using handheld computers to play games • Using electronic laptops • Using electronic keyboards • Reading electronic books • Playing with robot pets • Listening to radios and CD players • Using digital cameras—both still and video • Playing with electronic toys (e.g., PDAs, microwaves, bar scanners)

other new technologies outside classrooms. Many children enter elementary classrooms having already developed a variety of skills, knowledge, and experience in relation to digital literacy practices. For example, a study of 1,856 children, from birth to age 6 in England (Marsh et al., 2005), identified that they were engaged in a wide range of digital literacy practices in the home (see Table 38b.1).

Older children build on these early experiences and engage in practices such as texting, e-mailing, blogging, vlogging, using instant messaging systems and chat rooms, and downloading and uploading music and video files on a frequent basis (Burnett & Wilkinson, 2006). Schools need to rise to the challenge of meeting the needs of this generation of digital insiders by offering curricula and pedagogy that build on these experiences rather than ignore or marginalize them (Knobel, 2005).

It is important to remember that at the time of the data collection, the teachers in this study were operating within the Web 1.0 paradigm, rather than benefiting from the opportunities offered by Web 2.0, a development that has occurred over the last few years. *Web 2.0* is a term popularized in 2004 by Tim O'Reilly, the founder of the American media company O'Reilly Media. It refers to a second generation of products and services on the Web that facilitate collaboration and information sharing. Whereas the first generation of Internet products and services could be conceptualized as consisting of isolated blocks of information that could be accessed by users but not changed by them in any way, Web 2.0 applications are characterized by their abilities to enable users to contribute information, to upload texts and images, and to change Web pages—in other words, to become active users. To some extent, the term has been adopted without comprehensive agreement about what it means and there are other phrases used which refer to some of the same aspects of these Internet products and services, for example, "the semantic web" and "social software" (Owen, Grant, Sayers, & Facer, 2006). What these terms have in common is the intention to signal that these second-generation products and services facilitate communication between two or more people, and they promote interactivity and user-generated Web content (Lankshear & Knobel, 2006a).

A number of services and products offer rich opportunities for educators to use the Internet in classrooms in ways that further develop children's digital literacy skills and knowledge. In Marsh (2007), I outline the practice of one primary teacher in England, Peter, as he allows 7- and 8-year-old pupils to shape a blog on a dinosaur project in ways that meet their own interests and needs, rather than trying to address narrowly defined, teacher-driven objectives. This enabled the children to experiment with the affordances of blogging, for example, to upload films they created to social software sites in order to link them to their blog and to leave comments on each other's contributions. Blogging is one example of the way on which schools could use the Internet more productively in classrooms, but many others services facilitate collaboration and creativity, including Flickr (Davies, 2006) and wikis (Carrington, 2006). What these online spaces offer are opportunities for pupils to draw on their expertise, to forge affinity groups (Gee, 2004) with like-minded others, and to engage in the kinds of practices that are becoming increasingly important in a world in which navigation and manipulation of complex, online spaces and management of identities within such spaces are key skills.

This is not to suggest that Web 2.0 services and products cannot be used in ways that reflect a traditional mind-set; this is certainly possible (Lankshear & Knobel, 2006a). However, rather than simply use the applications in literacy practices that promote traditional, passive approaches to learning and teaching, Web 2.0 applications have the potential to transform classrooms into sites of active learning in which the students themselves become the experts. Burnett, Dickinson, Malden, Merchant, and Myers (2004) suggested that there are often two conceptions of curriculum and pedagogical change offered in relation to new media education: transformation, which entails a radical revisioning of the curriculum, or enrichment, which focuses on using technologies merely to add to current provision. Web 2.0, with its potential for engaging learners in digital communities of practice (Lave & Wenger, 1991) in which their multiple subjectivities can be explored, performed, and developed, calls for a transformation of classroom pedagogy such that the varied starting points of learners are recognized, they are able shape their own learning experience and develop agency in relation to curriculum content. This goes beyond current conceptualizations of "personalized learning," which often focus on differentiation within a relatively stable and standardized provision, to a dynamic account of pedagogy that challenges traditional notions of the teacher/learner/peer group relationships. There are now sufficient accounts of the kinds of subjectivities and practices needed for this to happen for it to begin to permeate practice (Lankshear & Knobel, 2004, 2006a, 2006b; Larson & Marsh, 2005; Pahl & Rowsell, 2005).

If the teachers in Karchmer's (2001) study were to be interviewed in the current climate, their experience of Web 2.0 resources and processes may well prove to have contributed to the further development of their understanding of the role and purposes of the Internet. Karchmer identified four skill areas that the teachers reinforced in their use of the Internet in the classroom: the abilities to (a) collaborate, (b) communicate, (c) acquire and sift through information, and (d) solve problems. However, in the examples of practice offered by the teachers, there is an emphasis on the abilities to (b) communicate and (c) acquire and sift through information. Much of the problem-solving appears to be down to the teachers—they are often the ones, for example, who decide on appropriate Web content—and apart from the example of the Monster Project, few details are offered of the way in which the teachers use the Internet to enable pupils to collaborate. While Karchmer reported that the elementary teachers were aware of the motivating influence of the use of the Web to post writing, there is little evidence that there was a concomitant awareness of the way in which a curriculum that reflects something of children's out-of-school lives and interests can motivate and engage learners (Dyson, 2002; Marsh & Millard, 2005).

Conclusion

Throughout this review, I have suggested that the limitations with regard to the practice of the teachers in Karchmer's (2001) study could be explained to some extent by considering the temporal context for the work. Teachers' use of technology within the literacy curriculum was even more limited 5 or 6 years ago than it is today, and the teachers in this study were clearly ahead of their colleagues in the development of their practices. Despite the changing context, which inevitably limits the lessons to be drawn from this study, there are a number of ways in which the paper nonetheless makes an important contribution to current considerations with regard to new literacy practices.

First, it highlights the importance of addressing these issues in preservice and in-service education. Karchmer (2001) argued that teachers should be made aware both of how to develop digital literacy practices and of why this is important, given a globalized knowledge economy. However, there is currently little evidence that this has been the case. Karchmer's call to action is as pertinent today as it was then and, given the varied experiences of preservice teachers themselves with regard to use of technologies (Robinson & Mackey, 2005), few assumptions can be made about the insider status of new recruits to the profession.

Second, Karchmer (2001) argued that further research needs to be undertaken with regard to teachers' conceptions of literacy, based on her identification of the way in which teachers did not feel that technology was transforming literacy in any fundamental manner. Karchmer thus rightly identified a significant disjuncture between theory and practice, but it is only by considering this in relation to Lankshear and Knobel's (2006a) work on mind-sets that we can begin to tease out the implications. Teachers need further opportunities to engage in the research process, to reflect on their curricula and pedagogy in the light of changing knowledge, and to take risks accordingly (Nixon & Comber, 2005). They need also, as Karchmer provided in this study, spaces and opportunities to have their experiences and concerns voiced and analyzed in order that policy and practice relate to teachers' "multiple realities" (Labbo & Reinking, 1999).

Third, Karchmer (2001) suggested that, although the teachers she worked with knew what they needed to teach (nonetheless, as I have suggested, this would not be sufficient for contemporary needs), there should be further exploration of *how* such skills and knowledge should be taught. I would endorse this call for an emphasis on pedagogies, but while Karchmer focused on the development of skills in relation to the use of the Internet, I would broaden this exploration to include knowledge and competences that will enable all learners to access, use, and create a range of digital texts. The inclusiveness of such a model is important for issues of social justice, particularly given the unequal distribution of access to technologies (which does not easily equate to aspects of identity such as socioeconomic status, ethnicity, or location). In the development of schooling that could provide such opportunities, the productive pedagogies model, developed in The Queensland School Reform Longitudinal Study (Hayes et al., 2006), offers a helpful framework. In this study, pedagogical practices in approximately 1,000 primary and secondary classrooms were mapped across four dimensions, dimensions that were derived from statistical analyses of observational data gathered in the classrooms. These four dimensions were (a) intellectual quality, (b) connectedness, (c) supportive classroom environment, and (d) engagement with, and valuing of, difference. Together, these dimensions constitute productive pedagogies that can facilitate social justice in schools in that they ensure learner agency, relevance, and challenge. Hayes et al. (2006) found that the most commonly observed features of practice were the pastoral care offered by teachers in a supportive classroom environment and, to a lesser extent, the intellectual challenge embedded within some of the lessons offered in classrooms. However, there was less extensive evidence of the connectedness and engagement with, and valuing of, difference dimensions in operation in schools. This was certainly the case, as I have argued, in relation to the teachers in Karchmer's study. I would suggest that the use of the Internet in classrooms can offer valuable opportunities to draw on these dimensions, given the connectedness with children's everyday lives it offers and the way in which meaningful engagement with the Internet can allow for and value differences between individuals and groups. This is an area for further research and one that addresses Karchmer's appeal to examine the how as well as the what.

Ultimately, Karchmer's (2001) study provides an opportunity for the educational community to reflect on how far along the "journey of Internet use" (p. 464) we have come in the years since the paper was published. In some ways, one might consider that the trajectory has been stilted, faltering, and prone to false leads and missed opportunities. In others ways, as many of the chapters in this *Handbook* attest, we have come so far along the path that we have reached an entirely new and different terrain, one that we have only just begun to map.

References

Alvermann, D., Moon, J. S., & Hagood, M. C. (1999). *Popular culture in the classroom: Teaching and researching critical media literacy.* Newark, DE: IRA/NRC.

Appadurai, A. J. (1996). *Modernity at large: Cultural dimensions of globalization.* Minneapolis: University of Minnesota Press.

Burnett, C., Dickinson, P., Malden, H., Merchant, G., & Myers, J. (2004). *Digital connections: Purposeful uses of email in the primary school.* Paper presented at United Kingdom Literacy Association's (UKLA) annual conference, Manchester.

Burnett, C., & Wilkinson, J. (2005). Holy lemons! Learning from children's use of the Internet in out-of-school contexts. *Literacy, 39,* 158–165.

Carrington, V. (2006). *Text, fugue, and digital technologies.* Paper presented at UKLA/Nara University Seminar on Digital Literacies, Nara University, Japan, May 2006.

Carrington, V., & Marsh, J. (2005). Editorial for special issue: Digital childhood and youth: New texts, new literacies. *Discourse: Studies in the Cultural Politics of Education, 26*(3), 277–286.

Comber, B., & Simpson (Eds.). (2001). *Negotiating critical literacies in classrooms.* Mahwah, NJ: Lawrence Erlbaum Associates.

Davies, J. (2006). Affinities and beyond!! Developing ways of seeing in online spaces. *E-learning, 3*(2), 217–234.

Dyson, A. H. (2002). *Brothers and sisters learn to write: Popular literacies in childhood and school cultures.* New York: Teachers College Press.

Gee, J. P. (2004). *Situated language and learning: A critique of traditional schooling.* London: Routledge.

Gee, J. P. (1996). *Sociolinguistics and literacies: Ideology in discourses* (2nd ed.). London: Taylor & Francis.

Hayes, D., Mills, M., Christie, P., & Lingard, B. (2006). *Teachers and schooling making a difference: Productive pedagogies, assessment and performance.* Sydney, Australia: Allen and Unwin.

Karchmer, R. A. (2001). The journey ahead: Thirteen teachers report how the Internet influences literacy and literacy instruction in their K–12 classrooms. *Reading Research Quarterly, 36,* 442–467.

Knobel, M. (2005). Technokids, Koala Trouble and *Pokémon*: Literacy, new technologies, and popular culture in children's everyday lives. In J. Marsh & E. Millard (Eds.), *Popular literacies: Childhood and schooling* (pp. 11–28). London: Routledge Falmer.

Labbo, L., & Reinking, D. (1999). Negotiating the multiple realities of technology in literacy research and instruction. *Reading Research Quarterly, 31,* 356–385.

Lankshear, C., & Knobel, M. (2006a). *New literacies: Everyday practices and classroom learning.* Maidenhead, Berkshire, U.K.: Open University Press.

Lankshear, C., & Knobel, M. (2006b, April). *Blogging as participation: The active sociality of a new literacy.* Paper presented at the American Educational Research Association's annual conference, San Francisco, CA.

Lankshear, C., & Knobel, M. (2004, April). *Planning pedagogy for i-Mode: Some principles for pedagogical decision-making.* Paper presented at the annual meeting of the American Education Research Association, San Diego, CA.

Lankshear, C., & Knobel, C. (2003). *New literacies: Changing knowledge and classroom learning.* Buckingham, U.K.: Open University Press.

Larson, J., & Marsh, J. (2005). *Making literacy real: Theories and practices for teaching and learning.* London: Sage.

Lave, J., & Wenger, E. (1991). *Situated learning.* Cambridge, U.K.: Cambridge University Press.

Marsh, J. (2007). New literacies and old pedagogies: Recontextualising rules and practices. *International Journal of Inclusive Education, 11*(3), 267–281.

Marsh, J., Brooks, G., Hughes, J., Ritchie, L., & Roberts, S. (2005). *Digital beginnings: Young children's use of popular culture, media and new technologies.* Sheffield, U.K.: University of Sheffield. Retrieved June 11, 2006, from http://www.digitalbeginings.shef .ac.uk/

Marsh, J., & Millard, E. (Eds.). (2005). *Popular literacies, childhood and schooling.* London: Routledge Falmer.

Merchant, G. (2004). Imagine all that stuff really happening: Narrative and identity in children's on-screen writing. *E-learning, 3*(1), 341–357.

Nixon, H., & Comber, B. (2005). Behind the scenes: Making movies in early years classrooms. In J. Marsh (Ed.), *Popular culture: New media and digital technology in early childhood* (pp. 219–236). London: Routledge Falmer.

Owen, M., Grant, L., Sayers, S., & Facer, K. (2006). *Social software and learning.* Bristol, U.K.: Nesta Futurelab. Retrieved August 28, 2006, from http://www.futurelab.org .uk/research/opening_education/social_software_01.htm

Pahl, K., & Rowsell, J. (Eds.). (2005). *Travel notes from the new literacy studies: Case studies in practice.* Clevedon, U.K.: Multilingual Matters.

Robinson, M., & Mackey, M. (2005). Assets in the classroom: Comfort and competence with media among teachers present and future. In J. Marsh & E. Millard (Eds.), *Popular literacies: Childhood and schooling* (pp. 200–220). London: Routledge Falmer.

Street, B. (Ed.). (1993). *Cross-cultural approaches to literacy.* London: Cambridge University Press.

Valentine, G., Marsh, J., & Pattie, C. (2005). *Children and young people's home use of ICT for educational purposes: The impact on attainment at key stages 1–4* (DfES No. RR672). London: HMSO.

Vasquez, V. (2004). *Negotiating critical literacies with young children.* Mahwah, NJ: Lawrence Erlbaum Associates.

About the Authors

Donna E. Alvermann is University of Georgia appointed Distinguished Research Professor of Language and Literacy Education. Presently, she is researching out-of-school-time learning to explore how Web-based multimodal texts and social networking foster motivation and a sense of self-efficacy among youth.

Neil Anderson is Professor and Deputy Head of the School of Education at James Cook University. His research focuses on gender and ICT use and social presence in e-learning environments.

Ronald E. Anderson is Professor Emeritus in the Department of Sociology at the University of Minnesota where he taught for 38 years. He is Co-Editor of the *Social Science Computer Review* and currently is working on the international SITES2006 survey on ICT in education.

Colin Baskin is a Senior Lecturer in the School of Education at James Cook University in Tropical North Queensland, Australia. His current research examines the role of cognitive objects and game-like playful learning in the lives of disengaged and marginalized school-aged learners, exploring possibilities for community development, empowerment, and self-sufficiency through the uptake of community technologies.

Richard Beach is Professor of English Education at the University of Minnesota. His research focuses on responses to literature and the media, identity construction, and digital writing.

Catherine Beavis is an Associate Professor in the School of Social and Cultural Studies in Education at Deakin University in Victoria, Australia. Her research focuses on young people and digital culture, with a particular focus on computer games, the changing nature of text, and their implications for English and literacy education.

Rebecca Ward Black is an Assistant Professor in the Department of Education, University of California, Irvine. Her research focuses on language acquisition and adolescents' literacy and social practices in online, popular culture-inspired spaces.

Ann Peterson Bishop is an Associate Professor in Library and Information Science at the University of Illinois at Urbana-Champaign. She studies the use and impact of computer-based information systems, social equity in access to information, and human-centered approaches to designing and evaluating information systems.

Robert E. Bleicher is an Associate Professor in Science Education at the California State University Channel Islands. His current research examines teacher confidence and classroom communciation.

Bertram (Chip) Bruce is a Professor in Library and Information Science at the University of Illinois at Urbana-Champaign. His research examines how ICT relates to the nature of knowledge, learning, democratic participation, community, and literacy.

Scott Bulfin is working on his PhD in the Faculty of Education, Monash University. His research focuses on literacies and cultural practices around digital technologies and new media across home, school, and community contexts.

Andrew Burn is Reader in Education and New Media, Institute of Education , University of London. His research draws on cultural studies and social semiotics and is particularly interested in the creation and analysis of multimodal media artifacts within popular culture.

Julie Coiro is an Assistant Professor of Reading in the School of Education at the University of Rhode Island. Her research focuses on online reading comprehension, new literacies of the Internet, and effective practices for technology integration and professional development.

Bridget Dalton is Assistant Professor of Learning, Literacy, and Culture at Vanderbilt University. Her research interests include technology and literacy, struggling readers, and universal design for learning.

Richard P. Durán is a Professor in the Gevirtz Graduate School of Education, University of California, Santa Barbara. His interests and research include cultural psychology and activity theory approaches to understanding literacy development and identity development of persons from immigrant and multicultural backgrounds.

John Elkins is Professor of Literacy Education at Griffith University and Emeritus Professor at The University of Queensland, Australia. His research interests include multimodal comprehension and how atypical learners engage with new literacies.

Bettina Fabos is an Assistant Professor in Visual Communication at the University of Northern Iowa. Her research focuses on critical literacy and internet commercialism.

Carla Firetto is a graduate student in the Educational Psychology program at The Pennsylvania State University. Her current work involves research on intertextuality and the processes of integration during problem solving.

James Paul Gee is Mary Lou Fulton Presidential Professor of Literacy Studies at Arizona State University. His research interests center on literacy, learning, identity and discourse, with a current emphasis on good video games, good learning, and the good of the soul.

Susan R. Goldman is Distinguished Professor of Psychology and Education and Co-Director of the Learning Sciences Research Institute at the University of Illinois at Chicago. Her research interests focus on learning and assessment in subject matter domains such as literacy, mathematics, history, and science and roles for technologies in supporting assessment, instruction, and learning. Her research involves collaborations with colleagues in other disciplines and with educational practitioners.

Geneva D. Haertel is Co-Director of the Assessment Research and Design in the Center for Technology in Learning at SRI International. Her research focuses on the application of evidence-centered design to assessments of student learning. Mostly recently, she has worked on the design and development of an online assessment design system.

Margaret C. Hagood is an Assistant Professor in the Department of Early Childhood, Elementary, and Middle Grades in the School of Education at the College of Charleston. Her research focuses on the ways that middle grades educators and students understand new literacies and utilize out-of-school literacies to improve their literacy performance in teaching and learning in in-school settings.

Colin Harrison is Professor of Literacy Studies in Education at the University of Nottingham. His work focuses on three areas: reading and reading comprehension processes, the impact of new technologies on literacy and pedagogy, and the impact of new technologies on teacher preparation and development.

Edys S. Quellmalz is Director of Technology Enhanced Assessments and Learning Systems at WestEd. Her work focuses on technology-enhanced performance assessments and the design of multi-level assessment systems.

David Reinking is the Eugene T. Moore Professor of Teacher Education, Clemson University. His research focuses on how digital forms of reading and writing affect literacy.

P.G. Schrader is an Assistant Professor of Educational Technology in the Department of Curriculum and Instruction at the University of Nevada, Las Vegas. His current research involves learning and cognition in dynamic, immersive environments such as hypertext, multimedia, and massively multiplayer online games.

Ilana Snyder is an Associate Professor in the Faculty of Education, Monash University, Australia. Her research focuses on changes to literacy, pedagogical, and cultural practices associated with the use of ICT in local and global contexts.

Kurt D. Squire is an Assistant Professor of Educational Communications and Technology in Curriculum and Instruction at the University of Wisconsin–Madison. He also is a Research Scientist at the Academic Advanced Distributed Learning (ADL) Co-Lab and currently serves as Director of the Games, Learning and Society Center.

Pippa Stein is an Associate Professor in Applied English Language Studies, Wits School of Education, University of Witwatersrand, Johannesburg. Her research interests are in multimodality, social semiotics and pedagogy within developing world contexts.

Constance A. Steinkuehler is an Assistant Professor in Curriculum and Instruction, University of Wisconsin–Madison. Her research is on cognition, learning and literacy in massively multiplayer online games (MMOs).

Angela Thomas is a Lecturer in English Education at the University of Sydney. Her research focuses on fan fiction, online role-playing, blogging, digital fiction, cyberculture, identity and learning in virtual worlds.

Steven L. Thorne is Assistant Professor in the Department of Linguistics and Applied Language Studies at Pennsylvania State University. His research examines second language development through the lenses of Internet mediation, contextual and usage-based approaches to language, and cultural-historical activity theory.

Nancy Thumim is researcher on an ESRC (Economic and Social Research Council)-funded project on Reality TV audiences and identities in the Sociology Department at Goldsmiths College. She is completing her Ph.D. on publicly funded user-generated content in the Media and Communications Department at the London School of Economics.

Len Unsworth is Professor in English and Literacies Education at the University of New England, Armidale, Australia. His research focuses on multiliteracies including the integration of visual and verbal literacies in using paper and electronic media in English and Literacy education and curriculum area learning and teaching.

Elizabeth Van Couvering is completing her doctorate at the London School of Economics on "The power of search: Strategies for gatekeeping the Internet." Her research investigates how search engines, some of the most important actors in new media landscape of the Internet, produce and display their results for users.

Peggy N. Van Meter is an Associate Professor in the Educational Psychology program at The Pennsylvania State University. In her current research, Dr. Van Meter is examining the cognitive processes underlying integration of knowledge representations during both learning and problem solving tasks.

Monique Volman is Professor of Education at the Centre for Educational Training, Assessment and Research (CETAR) of Vrije Universiteit Amsterdam and Associate Professor at the Department of Education of the same university. Her research focuses on learning environments for meaningful learning, diversity, and the use of ICT in education.

Paige Ware is Assistant Professor in the Department of Language, Literacy, and Learning at Southern Methodist University. Her research examines the use of technology for promoting second language writing for adolescents and the integration of telecollaboration into post-secondary language instruction.

Mark Warschauer is Professor of Education and Informatics at the University of California, Irvine. His research focuses on technology use and literacy development among culturally and linguistically diverse learners.

Dana J. Wilber is an Assistant Professor of Literacy at Montclair State University. Her research work focuses on remedial reading programs at the college level, the new literacies of adolescents and college-age students, and literacies associated with social networking sites.

Claire Wyatt-Smith is Professor and Dean in the Faculty of Education, Griffith University in Queensland, Australia. Her research focuses on literacy and new technologies, and assessment and of literacy achievement.

Patricia A. Young is an Assistant Professor in Literacy Education at the University of Maryland, Baltimore County. Her current research involves the development of the Culture Based Model, an intercultural instructional design framework, as well as the history of instructional design and technologies made by and for African Americans.

Author Index

Subject Index